# THE POWER OF
# FINE LITERATURE
## THE MASTERY OF
# LANGUAGE ARTS

PRENTICE HALL
LITERATURE

**Begin each selection with the Guide for Reading.**

Focus students on critical reading strategies.

Preview new vocabulary.

Activate prior knowledge through writing.

Focus their reading.

Present the literary term.

Introduce the author.

# The Power of Fine Literature,
# The Mastery of Critical Reading.

### Integrate the power of fine literature with critical reading to stimulate an active response.

**Begin each unit with Reading Actively.**

---

## READING ACTIVELY

### Nonfiction

Some people seem to gain more from their reading of nonfiction than others. Why? Most likely, they gain more because they read with an active mind. To read nonfiction successfully, you must interact with the information the author presents. Ask questions about this information and make predictions about where the information is leading. Pause to answer your predictions and to check your predictions. At appropriate points, stop to summarize the information you have received so far.

Use the following strategies to help you read actively.

**Question**

Ask questions about the information the author presents. What does the author reveal about the topic? Determine whether the author's conclusions seem based on the information given. In addition, question the author's purpose for writing.

**Predict**

Think about what you already know about the topic. Make predictions about the conclusions you think the author will reach based on this information. As you read, you will find out whether your predictions are accurate.

**Clarify**

As you read, try to find the answers to your questions and check the accuracy of your predictions. In this way, you will monitor, or guide, your own reading and so gain the fullest understanding of the information presented.

**Summarize**

Every now and then, pause to summarize, or review, the information the author has presented so far. What important points has the author made? How has the author supported this information?

**Pull It Together**

Determine the main idea of the entire selection. What did you find out about the topic? How do you feel about the topic?

On the facing page is a model showing how an active reader might read an essay.

310   Nonfiction

---

## MODEL

### *from* In Search of Our Mothers' Gardens

#### Alice Walker

**Questions:** What is the meaning of the title? What is the author's purpose for writing this essay?

My mother made all the clothes we wore, even my brothers' overalls. She made all the towels and sheets we used. She spent the summers canning vegetables and fruits. She spent the winter evenings making quilts enough to cover all our beds.

During the "working" day, she labored beside—not behind—my father in the fields. Her day began before sunup, and did not end until late at night. There was never a moment for her to sit down, undisturbed, to unravel her own private thoughts; never a time free from interruption—by work or the noisy inquiries of her many children. And yet, it is to my mother—and all our mothers who were not famous—that I went in search of the secret of what has fed that muzzled[1] and often mutilated,[2] but vibrant,[3] creative spirit that the black woman has inherited, and that pops out in wild and unlikely places to this day.

**Clarification:** The author's purpose is to uncover the secret of the black woman's creative spirit.

from *In Search of Our Mother's Gardens*   311

---

**Direct students to a model showing examples of active reading.**

3

**Up to 100 Grammar in Action lessons in each ATE . . . the teachable moment for skills mastery.**

Enrich your skills teaching with Grammar in Action lessons.

5 **Discussion** What sides of the narrator's character are revealed in this paragraph?

6 **Reading Strategy** Ask students to summarize Doodle's progress and to predict what further progress he might make.

7 **Discussion** Is Doodle a good name for William Armstrong? Why?

8 **Discussion** What character traits does the narrator's behavior reveal?

9 **Discussion** What kind of unspoken pact develops between the brothers?

tains billowed out in the afternoon sea breeze, rustling like palmetto fronds.[2]

It was bad enough having an invalid brother, but having one who possibly was not all there was unbearable, so I began to make plans to kill him by smothering him with a pillow. However, one afternoon as I watched him, my head poked between the irons posts of the foot of the bed, he looked straight at me and grinned. I skipped through the rooms, down the echoing halls, shouting, "Mama, he smiled. He's all there! He's all there!" and he was.

When he was two, if you laid him on his stomach, he began to try to move himself, straining terribly. The doctor said that with his weak heart this strain would probably kill him, but it didn't. Trembling, he'd push himself up, turning first red, then a soft purple, and finally collapse back onto the bed like an old worn-out doll. I can still see Mama watching him, her hand pressed tight across her mouth, her eyes wide and unblinking. But he learned to crawl (it was his third winter), and we brought him out of the front bedroom, putting him on the rug before the fireplace. For the first time he became one of us.

As long as he lay all the time in bed, we called him William Armstrong, even though it was formal and sounded as if we were referring to one of our ancestors, but with his creeping around on the deerskin rug and beginning to talk, something had to be done about his name. It was I who renamed him. When he crawled, he crawled backwards, as if he were in reverse and couldn't change gears. If you called him, he'd turn around as if he were going in the other direction, then he'd back right up to you to be picked up. Crawling backward made him look like a

doodle-bug, so I began to call him Doodle, and in time even Mama and Daddy thought it was a better name than William Armstrong. Only Aunt Nicey disagreed. She said caul babies should be treated with special respect since they might turn out to be saints. Renaming my brother was perhaps the kindest thing I ever did for him, because nobody expects much from someone called Doodle.

Although Doodle learned to crawl, he showed no signs of walking, but he wasn't idle. He talked so much that we all quit listening to what he said. It was about this time that Daddy built him a go-cart and I had to pull him around. At first I just paraded him up and down the piazza, but then he started crying to be taken out into the yard and it ended up by my having to lug him wherever I went. If I so much as picked up my cap, he'd start crying to go with me and Mama would call from wherever she was, "Take Doodle with you."

He was a burden in many ways. The doctor had said that he mustn't get too excited, too hot, too cold, or too tired and that he must always be treated gently. A long list of don'ts went with him, all of which I ignored once we got out of the house. To discourage his coming with me, I'd run with him across the ends of the cotton rows and careen him around corners on two wheels. Sometimes I accidentally turned him over, but he never told Mama. His skin was very sensitive, and he had to wear a big straw hat whenever he went out. When the going got rough and he had to cling to the sides of the go-cart, the hat slipped all the way down over his ears. He was a sight. Finally, I could see I was licked. Doodle was my brother and he was going to cling to me forever, no matter what I did, so I dragged him across the burning cotton field to share with him the only beauty I knew, Old Woman Swamp. I pulled the go-cart through the saw-tooth fern, down into the green dimness where the pal-

**2. palmetto fronds:** Palm leaves.

*190 Short Stories*

## Grammar in Action

When a writer uses **concrete details,** readers can see, hear, smell, taste, and feel what the writer is describing. For instance, if a writer merely says "dog," the reader will only have a vague or general idea of the type of animal the writer has in mind. If a writer specifies "German shepherd," however, readers will have a much more specific picture.

Notice how James Hurst uses concrete, specific details to enliven the following description:

*190*

. . . I dragged him across the *burning cotton field* to share with him the only beauty I knew, Old Woman Swamp. I pulled the go-cart through the *saw-tooth fern,* down into the *green dimness* where the *palmetto fronds* whispered by the stream, lifted him out and set him down in the *soft rubber grass* beside a *tall pine.* His eyes were round with wonder as he gazed about him, and his little hands began to stroke the *rubber grass.* Then he began to cry.

Without the concrete details, this passage would be much less effective:

# The Power of Fine Literature,
# The Mastery of Grammar and Usage Skills.

## Use fine literature as a springboard to teach grammar and usage skills.

**BOYS IN A PUNT**
*N. C. Wyeth*
*Courtesy of Dr. and Mrs. William A. Morton, Jr.*

### Humanities Note

Fine art, *Boys in a Punt*, by N.C. Wyeth. Newel Convers Wyeth (1882–1945), who was born in Needham, Massachusetts, lived during the time that is now known as the Golden Age of American Illustration—the time from the mid-1870's to approximately the 1920's. The age was so named because of the number of creative and well-known illustrators whose work was published during that period, including Winslow Homer, Howard Pyle, and N.C. Wyeth.

By the time he was a teenager, Wyeth knew he wanted to be an artist and enrolled in the Howard Pyle School of Illustration in Philadelphia, where he was taught by Howard Pyle.

While in school, Wyeth frequently took trips to Pyle's home at Chadds Ford, Pennsylvania, to roam the hills and woods of the Brandywine Valley. He later permanently moved to this area to raise his own family. Much of Wyeth's finest work, including *Boys in a Punt* was inspired by the rural life around him.

You might use the following questions for discussion.
1. The tone of a painting is the painter's attitude toward the subject. It may be established through the colors the artist chose or the composition. What is the tone of this painting? How does the tone of the painting complement the tone of the story?
2. Do you think Wyeth's illustration is appropriate for this story? Explain.

**Reinforce learning with blackline masters in the Teaching Portfolio.**

I pulled him across the field into a pretty swamp. It was dark and wet. I set him on the ground. He was startled and cried.

The many concrete details that Hurst includes enable readers to experience the swamp along with the two boys.

**Student Activity 1.** Identify the vague, general terms in the shorter passage above. Then locate the concrete details in Hurst's passage that bring the description to life.

**Student Activity 2.** Rewrite the vague shorter passage so that it is more concrete. However, make your description of Old Woman Swamp different from Hurst's.

**Guide learning with on-the-spot practice.**

191

5

# A writing program within a literature program.

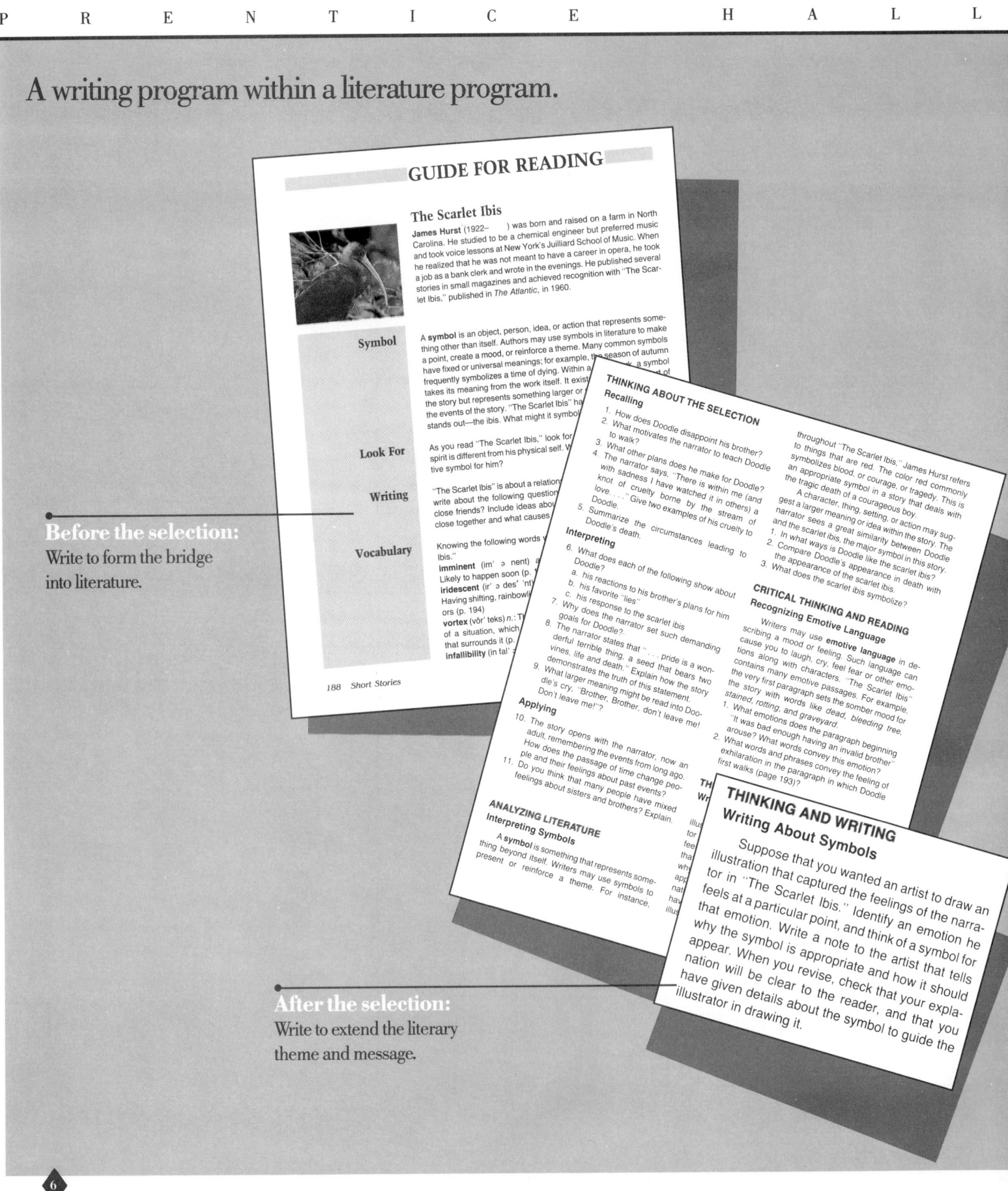

## GUIDE FOR READING

### The Scarlet Ibis

**James Hurst** (1922– ) was born and raised on a farm in North Carolina. He studied to be a chemical engineer but preferred music and took voice lessons at New York's Juilliard School of Music. When he realized that he was not meant to have a career in opera, he took a job as a bank clerk and wrote in the evenings. He published several stories in small magazines and achieved recognition with "The Scarlet Ibis," published in *The Atlantic*, in 1960.

**Symbol**

A **symbol** is an object, person, idea, or action that represents something other than itself. Authors may use symbols in literature to make a point, create a mood, or reinforce a theme. Many common symbols have fixed or universal meanings; for example, the season of autumn frequently symbolizes a time of dying. Within a ___ ___ ___ of takes its meaning from the work itself. It exist___ ___ the story but represents something larger or ___ the events of the story. "The Scarlet Ibis" ha___ stands out—the ibis. What might it symbol___

**Look For**

As you read "The Scarlet Ibis," look for ___ spirit is different from his physical self. W___ tive symbol for him?

**Writing**

"The Scarlet Ibis" is about a relation___ write about the following question___ close friends? Include ideas abou___ close together and what causes ___

**Vocabulary**

Knowing the following words ___ Ibis."

**imminent** (im' ə nent) a___
Likely to happen soon (p. ___
**iridescent** (ir' ə des' 'nt)___
Having shifting, rainbowli___
ors (p. 194)
**vortex** (vôr' teks) *n.*: T___
of a situation, which ___
that surrounds it (p. ___
**infallibility** (in fal' ___

188  Short Stories

---

## THINKING ABOUT THE SELECTION

### Recalling

1. How does Doodle disappoint his brother?
2. What motivates the narrator to teach Doodle to walk?
3. What other plans does he make for Doodle
4. The narrator says, "There is within me (and with sadness I have watched it in others) a knot of cruelty borne by the stream of love. . . ." Give two examples of his cruelty to Doodle.
5. Summarize the circumstances leading to Doodle's death.

### Interpreting

6. What does each of the following show about Doodle?
   a. his reactions to his brother's plans for him
   b. his favorite "lies"
   c. his response to the scarlet ibis
7. Why does the narrator set such demanding goals for Doodle?
8. The narrator states that ". . . pride is a wonderful terrible thing, a seed that bears two vines, life and death." Explain how the story demonstrates the truth of this statement.
9. What larger meaning might be read into Doodle's cry, "Brother, Brother, don't leave me! Don't leave me!"?

### Applying

10. The story opens with the narrator, now an adult, remembering the events from long ago. How does the passage of time change people and their feelings about past events?
11. Do you think that many people have mixed feelings about sisters and brothers? Explain.

## ANALYZING LITERATURE

### Interpreting Symbols

A **symbol** is something that represents something beyond itself. Writers may use symbols to present or reinforce a theme. For instance,

---

throughout "The Scarlet Ibis," James Hurst refers to things that are red. The color red commonly symbolizes blood, or courage, or tragedy. This is an appropriate symbol in a story that deals with the tragic death of a courageous boy.

A character, thing, setting, or action may suggest a larger meaning or idea within the story. The narrator sees a great similarity between Doodle and the scarlet ibis, the major symbol in this story.

1. In what ways is Doodle like the scarlet ibis?
2. Compare Doodle's appearance in death with the appearance of the scarlet ibis.
3. What does the scarlet ibis symbolize?

## CRITICAL THINKING AND READING

### Recognizing Emotive Language

Writers may use **emotive language** in describing a mood or feeling. Such language can cause you to laugh, cry, feel fear or other emotions along with characters. "The Scarlet Ibis" contains many emotive passages. For example, the very first paragraph sets the somber mood for the story, with words like *dead, bleeding tree, stained, rotting,* and *graveyard.*

1. What emotions does the paragraph beginning "It was bad enough having an invalid brother" arouse? What words convey this emotion?
2. What words and phrases convey the feeling of exhilaration in the paragraph in which Doodle first walks (page 193)?

## THINKING AND WRITING

### Writing About Symbols

Suppose that you wanted an artist to draw an illustration that captured the feelings of the narrator in "The Scarlet Ibis." Identify an emotion he feels at a particular point, and think of a symbol for that emotion. Write a note to the artist that tells why the symbol is appropriate and how it should appear. When you revise, check that your explanation will be clear to the reader, and that you have given details about the symbol to guide the illustrator in drawing it.

**Before the selection:**
Write to form the bridge
into literature.

**After the selection:**
Write to extend the literary
theme and message.

# The Power of Fine Literature,
# The Mastery of Writing.

## Choose from 5 writing activities for each selection.

**Extend the power and breadth of your writing program with these additional activities:**

- Fine Art Writing activities
- Selection Test essay questions
- Unit Test essay questions
- You the Writer Writing assignment
- You the Critic Writing assignment
- Writing Across the Curriculum activities
- Student writing models

**Plus — Writing About Literature Handbook**

A writing course right in the student book

**Three additional writing activities in the Teaching Portfolio meet the needs of all ability levels:**

- Less Challenging
- More Challenging
- The Student as Critic

---

### COMPOSITION

**Thinking and Writing**

Discuss the assignment with the students. Make sure they understand that the illustration should reveal emotion rather than story action.

**Prewriting:** Provide classroom time for students to identify the different feelings expressed by the narrator throughout the story. Have them write a list of the character's emotions. Have them suggest symbols that might represent each of the emotions on their list. Finally, have them discuss the purpose of an illustration—to enhance the text which it accompanies.

**Writing:** Allow time for students to write their first draft in class.

**Revising:** Provide time for students to revise their writing. Direct them to make sure that their explanation is clear and that they have included details about the symbol. Have them proofread their note and prepare a final draft. Finally, have students read each other's notes and select the ones they would give to artists.

### Guidelines for Evaluating Thinking and Writing

Keep the following questions in mind when evaluating students' papers.

1. Does the note describe a symbol that might be illustrated?
2. Does the note explain in what ways the symbol is appropriate to the emotions of the narrator during a particular part of the story?
3. Is the appearance of the symbol suggested with details?
4. Are the sentences grammatically correct? Are the words they punctuated correctly? Are the words spelled correctly?

### ALTERNATE COMPOSITION ASSIGNMENTS

Three writing assignments follow: Less Challenging, More Challenging, and The Student as Critic.

**Less Challenging**

Imagine that you are directing a television play of "The Scarlet Ibis." What stage settings will you need to convey the atmosphere and action

192   Short Stories

---

of the story? Write a report to your set designer listing the scenery you will need and describing the atmosphere each set should have. First make a list of settings that are important to the story. Freewrite about the atmosphere each setting should convey. Then write a first draft of your report. Revise the report, checking that your list is complete and is clearly stated. Finally, proofread your report and prepare a final draft.

**More Challenging**

Imagine that you are one of the parents in the story. What do you say to your son when you learn about Doodle's death? Are you angry that the older boy encouraged Doodle to exercise? Do you appreciate his guilt and shame? What thoughts do you have about the dead ibis? Keeping in character, freewrite to explore your feelings about the event. Then write a diary entry, that conveys your feelings. Revise your entry, making sure that you have discussed the ibis and ...

**The Student as Critic**

The following excerpt is the first sentence from "The Summer of Two Figs," another story by James Hurst.

> How like life that summer was—born of fulsome promise to fade into falling leaves unfulfilled, like the seven yards of white silk crepe which was bought to make Mama a party dress, but was requisitioned for a shroud.

Think about the meaning of this quotation. How does it apply to "The Scarlet Ibis"? Then write a short composition comparing the excerpt with the first paragraph of "The Scarlet Ibis." In your composition, discuss one of the following: (1) the author's use of symbols to create a mood; (2) the author's choice of words according to their sound as well as their meaning. First identify the similarities between the two passages. Make a list of details from each passage that support your ideas. Organize your ideas around a thesis statement. Then write a first draft of your composi-

## Teacher Backup
Selection background, check test, suggested readings, composition activities and evaluation guidelines, and answers to worksheets and tests.

## Vocabulary Check
Reinforce or test the words taught before the selection.

## Selection Test
Measure understanding of the literature through short answer questions and essay questions.

## Usage and Mechanic Worksheet
Integrate grammar and editing skills with literature.

## Grammar in Action Worksheet
Deepen the understanding of grammar and usage skills.

# The Teaching Portfolio – Redefining the Concept of Support for all the Language Arts.

## Everything you need to teach a selection is in one place.

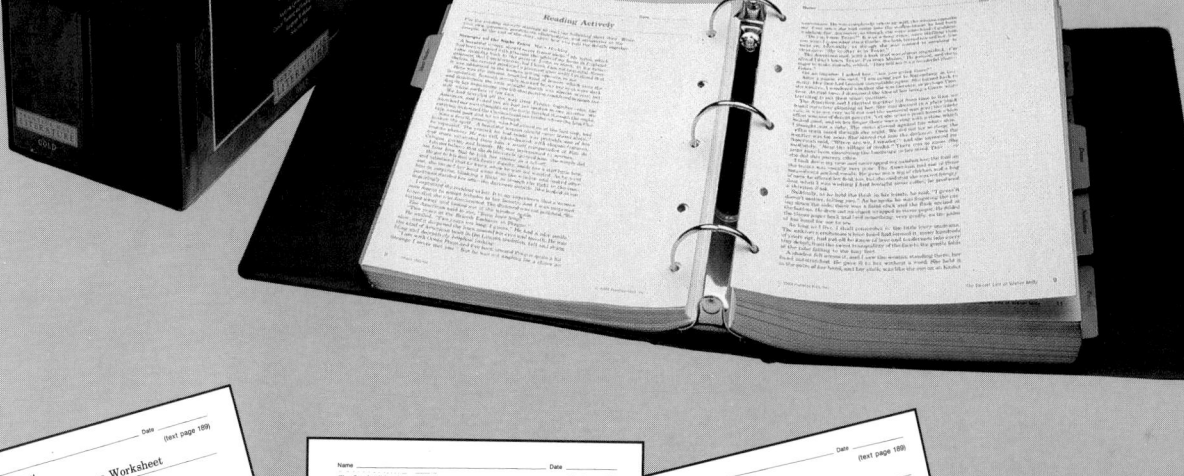

## Analyzing Literature Worksheet

Extends understanding of the literary element.

## Critical Thinking and Reading Worksheet

Promotes reading and reasoning.

## Language Worksheet

Beyond vocabulary to word origins, synonyms, dialects — and more.

# Fine Art Transparencies

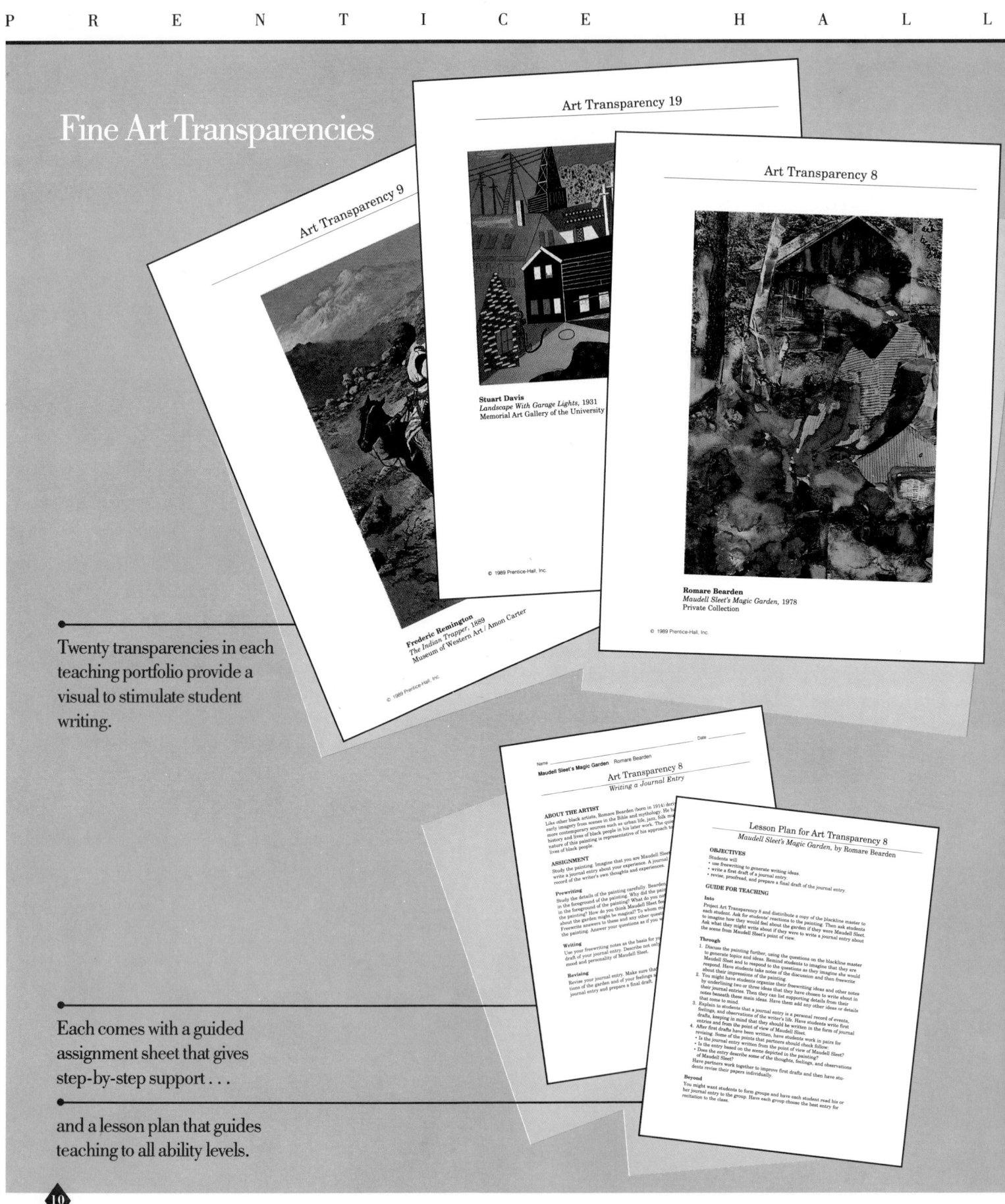

Twenty transparencies in each
teaching portfolio provide a
visual to stimulate student
writing.

Each comes with a guided
assignment sheet that gives
step-by-step support . . .

and a lesson plan that guides
teaching to all ability levels.

# Capture the Power of Integrating
# Fine Literature and the Humanities.

A fine arts program and classic cinema connected with literature.

## The Library of Video Classics

- Four feature length films per grade level, including the novel and the play.

- Viewing guides link the film with the literature to stimulate new ideas.

**Each Viewing Guide provides:**

- Previewing and After Viewing Questions – enhance critical thinking skills.

- Speaking and Listening activities – promote oral language skills through the impact of film.

- Writing activities – creative topics enhance students responsiveness.

- Ability level notes – ideas to challenge each student.

**Direct students to new discoveries with the dynamic combination of literature and cinema.**

## Study Guides

What if your favorite novel or play is not in Prentice Hall Literature? We still provide you with teaching support. Complete teaching guides for 40 novels and plays give you fresh insights to make the classic even more interesting and relevant. Each guide contains:

- Author Background
- Synopses of Plot, Setting, Theme and More
- Chapter-by-Chapter Teaching Plans
- Writing Assignments
- Guidelines for Dealing With Provocative Themes
- Blackline Master Handouts and Test

# Tailor the Literature Program to Your Own Classes.

## Library of Great Works

Now, the time-honored longer works of American, British, and world cultures available with Prentice Hall Literature

- Classic, unabridged editions
- Hardbound versions insure lasting value
- A Novel Study Guide for expert teaching support to bring the work to life

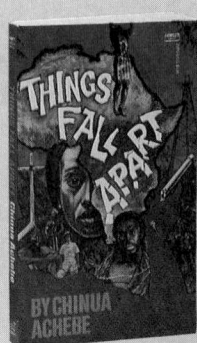

### Great Works

| | |
|---|---|
| Adventures of Huckleberry Finn | Nineteen Eighty Four |
| Brothers Karamazov | Our Town |
| Candide | Pride and Prejudice |
| Death of a Salesman | Red Badge of Courage |
| Don Quixote | Scarlet Letter |
| Great Gatsby | Siddartha |
| Hamlet | Tartuffe |
| Importance of Being Earnest | Things Fall Apart |
| Lord of the Flies | Wuthering Heights |

## Computer Test Bank

**Customize your literature testing program with instant tests on each selection**

For each selection choose from:
- Selection test
- Essay questions with evaluation guidelines
- Answer key

For each unit, choose from:
- Short answer test
- Essay tests

Powerful word processor for your made to order options.
- Write an unlimited number of new questions
- Delete questions

User friendly format for quick answers.
- Menus
- 800 customer service number

Annotated Teacher's Edition

# PRENTICE HALL
# LITERATURE

## GOLD

SECOND EDITION

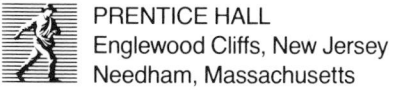 PRENTICE HALL
Englewood Cliffs, New Jersey
Needham, Massachusetts

ISBN 0-13-713314-6

10 9 8 7 6 5 4 3 2 1

**Cover and Title Page:** *The New Novel*, Winslow Homer, Fine Arts Museum, Springfield, Massachusetts

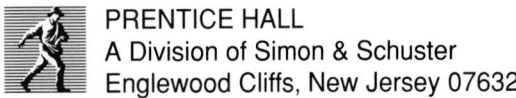
PRENTICE HALL
A Division of Simon & Schuster
Englewood Cliffs, New Jersey 07632

# CONTENTS

# The Prentice Hall Literature Program
## OVERVIEW

## THE STUDENT BOOK

The Prentice Hall Literature Program is a complete literature program, offering high-quality, appealing, traditional and contemporary literary selections, with study aids that will guide students into, through, and beyond the literature.

## Organization

The selections are organized by genre to encourage comprehensive study of the types of literature. The following list shows the units and the sections within each unit into which the selections are organized:

**The Short Story:** Plot, Character, Point of View, Setting, Theme

**Drama:** One-act Plays and Full-length Plays, including a Shakespearean Play

**Nonfiction:** Biographies and Personal Accounts, Types of Essays, Essays in the Arts and Sciences

**Poetry:** Narrative Poetry, Dramatic Poetry and the Speaker, Lyric Poetry, Word Choice and Tone, Imagery, Figurative Language and Tone, Musical Devices, Structure

**The Epic**

**The Novel:** A Complete Novel

The number and variety of selections offer choice and flexibility in meeting curriculum requirements as well as student needs and interests.

## Unique Features

Because the Prentice Hall Literature Program puts emphasis on the reading and appreciation of literature, it offers several unique features to help students become active readers.

**Reading Actively** Each unit begins with a feature called Reading Actively, which includes a set of strategies for effectively reading the literature in the unit. The strategies involve the reader in the text before reading and while reading. Such involvement and reaction are necessary if students are to learn. The active reading strategies include the following:

**For prose:** questioning, predicting, summarizing, clarifying

**For drama:** visualizing, questioning, predicting, clarifying, summarizing

**For poetry:** questioning, clarifying, listening, paraphrasing, summarizing

In the short story, nonfiction, and poetry units, this feature is followed by a Model for Reading Actively. This Model is annotated to demonstrate and explain to students how a good reader might use the active reading strategies to understand a selection. Students are encouraged to use these strategies as they read other selections in the unit. This feature provides a method of scaffolding—giving students help and support

while they acquire the skills to become successful readers of literature. To give students further practice with this process, there is an additional selection in the Teaching Portfolio which students can annotate themselves.

**Guide for Reading** All other selections begin with a Guide for Reading. This page, which precedes the selection, contains useful prereading information. The Guide for Reading prepares students for successful reading in five ways:
- A biography of the author provides insight into how the author came to write the selection.
- A literary focus section introduces the literary concept that is taught with the selection.
- The Look For provides a specific goal—thematic, stylistic, or meaning-oriented—to guide the students' reading of the selection.
- A motivational writing activity puts students in an appropriate frame of mind.
- A vocabulary list presents, in glossary format, words from the selection that might present difficulty in reading.

This Guide for Reading provides the necessary background to encourage comprehension, motivate students to read, and give them technical support to read successfully.

**Putting It Together** The short story, nonfiction, and poetry units also end with a feature called Putting It Together. This feature serves as a summary for reading and analyzing the particular types of literature and comprehending the literary elements and devices that are in them. For examples, the Putting It Together for short stories reviews plot, character, theme, and setting, and analyzes the application of these elements in a particular story. In the Teaching Portfolio, there is an additional selection that the students can annotate themselves.

Each selection is self-contained and complete so that you can use the selections in any order.

## After Reading

Features at the end of the selection are designed to foster comprehension and encourage constructive response, either personal or literary. They also encourage the growth of skills needed by students to become independent readers. These features comprise five areas:

**Thinking About the Selection:** These study questions are built upon three levels of comprehension: the literal, the interpretive, and the applied. The questions are grouped by three levels of increasing complexity: recalling (literal), interpreting (inference, analysis), and applying (generalization, extension, judgment). The different levels may be used as appropriate for different ability levels, or may be used to take all students through different levels of thinking.

**Analyzing Literature:** This section develops and reinforces the literary concept or skill introduced on the Guide for Reading page and applies it to the selection. It helps students to understand literary concepts and appreciate writers' techniques, thereby enabling them to respond appropriately to literature.

**Critical Thinking and Reading:** This section introduces students to those critical thinking and critical reading skills that are necessary for understanding literature. It gives them an opportunity to apply these skills to the literary selections.

**Understanding Language:** Knowledge and appreciation of language are developed in this section, which contains activities on language prompted by the selection. The activities may be geared toward helping students appreciate writers' use of language, master skills needed to increase their vocabulary, or prepare for SATs.

**Thinking and Writing:** This is a composition assignment arising from the selection. This assignment, which may be creative or analytical, is process-oriented, suggesting steps for prewriting, drafting, and revising.

## End of Unit

**Focus on Reading** At the end of each unit is a two-page lesson focusing on one reading skill appropriate to the type of literature students have read. For example, at the end of the short story unit, students take an in-depth look at relationships and see how patterns of relationships affect the stories they have read. At the end of the poetry unit, students review and practice making inferences about poetry. Each lesson is structured so that it provides an explanation of the skill, examples, and activities.

**You the Writer, You the Critic** At the end of each unit, there are six additional writing activities. Three of them, under You the Writer, are creative; three of them, under You the Critic, are analytical. Each activity is developed through the steps of the writing process.

## End of Book

Three handbooks are provided at the end of *Prentice Hall Literature:* Handbook of Writing About Literature, Handbook of Critical Thinking and Reading Terms, and Handbook of Literary Terms and Techniques.

**Handbook of Writing About Literature** The Handbook of Writing About Literature is divided into five sections. The first section introduces the process of writing. The second requires students to analyze and interpret literature and teaches them how to write about the specific elements of literary works. The third requires students to interpret and synthesize while teaching how to write about the work as a whole. The fourth provides instruction in evaluating literary works. The fifth guides the students in the creation of their own literary works.

This Handbook may be used for direct instruction or as support for the individual writing assignments in *Prentice Hall Literature*.

**Handbook of Critical Thinking and Reading Terms** The Handbook of Critical Thinking and Reading Terms provides an alphabetical arrangement of the terms taught in the Critical Thinking and Reading activities at the end of selections. Some entries expand upon the original definition and provide one or more examples. Other entries provide additional terms and definitions. This Handbook can be used to preteach terminology or to review information. It can also be used as an easy reference guide for students as they work on individual Critical Thinking and Reading assignments.

**Handbook of Literary Terms and Techniques** The Handbook of Literary Terms and Techniques provides an alphabetical guide to the literary terms introduced on the Guide for Reading page and taught in the Analyzing Literature activities at the end of selections. Each entry provides a full definition of the term or technique with one or more examples. The handbook can be used for preteaching, for review, or as a support for students as they work on individual Analyzing Literature activities.

# TEACHING SUPPORT

## THE ANNOTATED TEACHER'S EDITION

The annotated teacher's edition of *Prentice Hall Literature* is designed to be used both for planning and for actual in-class teaching. It offers planning aids and specific teaching suggestions for all selections. This planning and teaching material appears in the side columns next to the reduced student pages of each selection. These annotations, which correspond to the student material on that page, help you give your students positive and relevant experiences with literature by asking the right questions at the right time and by pointing out what is significant.

## Preparing the Lesson: Focus

The annotations on the opening pages of the selection help you plan your presentation of the material. Each selection begins with notes that suggest ways to introduce or enhance the prereading instruction or activities presented in the students' Guide for Reading. These notes help you present the material or adapt it for **less advanced** or **more advanced** students. In addition, an occasional **spelling tip** gives a hint for remembering the spelling of a troublesome word. Objectives for each selection are keyed to the end-of-selection material. This pages also includes a complete list of support material for this selection in the Teaching Portfolio and other program components. In the column next to the first page of the selection, you will find a **motivation/prior knowledge** suggestion and a **purpose-setting question** to prepare the students to read the selection. Frequently, **thematic ideas** are given. These suggest other selections in this book that treat themes similar to those under discussion. You may want to use these selections together to integrate and reinforce universal concepts and themes. **ESL strategies** suggest ways to make selections accessible to ESL students. All of these annotations help you effectively prepare your lesson.

## Teaching the Lesson: Presentation

You may use the notes throughout the pages of the selection to direct your discussion in class. As you and your students read the selection, you will find additional notes that enable you to customize the lesson for your class. They let you increase your students' involvement in the work and enrich their reading of it, while enabling them to deal with the particular genres. The following kinds of notes may direct your class discussions:

**Master Teacher Notes** These classroom tips from master teachers give an approach, a strategy, or a very special bit of information that enlivens the selection or increases appreciation.

**Humanities Notes** For each piece of fine art in the student book, there is a humanities note giving information on the work of art and the artist. These notes generally point out features of the piece of art that relate it to the work of literature with which it is presented. Additionally, the humanities note concludes with questions that you may use if you wish to discuss the art as part of your discussion of the work.

**Enrichment** Enrichment notes provide additional information on points of interest that arise in the selection. You may use this information to enrich your students' knowledge of the background of a selection and appreciation of it.

**Reading Strategies** Strategies to promote student comprehension of the literary text reinforce the emphasis on enabling students to read literature.

**Clarification** Words, phrases, or ideas that might be obstacles to student understanding are clarified to ensure comprehension.

**Discussion** Throughout the selection, you will find additional questions and points for discussion. These help you proceed through the selection with students, eliciting their understanding and appreciation of significant passages.

**Literary Focus** To promote understanding of the writer's techniques, literary focus annotations direct attention to those aspects of the selection that reflect the literary concept presented with it.

**Critical Thinking and Reading** These notes reinforce the critical thinking and reading skills developed throughout the program.

**Reader's Response** These notes ask a question designed to prompt students' personal response to the selection.

**Grammar in Action** Grammar in Action notes integrate language arts skills. These notes demonstrate the writer's use of particular grammatical or style points. They present a direct link between grammar and writing.

Occasional **commentary** and **primary source** notes add background or insight to the selection.

There are probably more notes than you need for presenting any given selection. We emphasize the importance of selecting those annotations that are best suited to your classes and course of instruction.

## Closure and Extension

Answers are provided for all questions in each feature following the selections. Where questions are open-ended, we present a suggested response or suggest points that students should note in their answers.

The annotations after the selection also include the following:

**Challenge** These questions take students beyond those given with the instruction.

**Publishing Student Writing** For many selections, additional notes suggest ways to publishing the writing students have done in the Thinking and Writing feature.

**Writing Across the Curriculum** Where appropriate, you will see suggestions for additional assignments or suggestions for relating the Thinking and Writing assignment to students' work in another discipline.

In addition, you will find teaching suggestions for the special features in the student book—Reading Actively, Putting It Together, Focus on Reading, and You the Writer, You the Critic.

## THE TEACHING PORTFOLIO

The Teaching Portfolio provides support for teaching and testing all of the selections and skills in *Prentice Hall Literature*.

## Fine Art Transparencies

Twenty fine art transparencies with blackline masters are provided in the Teaching Portfolio. These can be used to introduce selections and motivate students to read, or they may be used as additional writing assignments in response to art. The fine art is keyed into the selections through Master Teacher Notes in the Annotated Teacher's Edition. In the Portfolio, each transparency is accompanied by a writing assignment for students and a lesson plan for teaching that assignment.

## Beginning of Unit
Each unit begins with a list of objectives and a skills chart listing literary elements and skills covered in the unit. The chart also identifies all the blackline masters in the Teaching Portfolio that correlate to each selection.

## The Selections
Full teaching support is provided for each selection. This support material is organized by selection for your convenience. The support for each selection consists of the following: Teacher Backup, Grammar in Action Worksheet, Usage and Mechanics Worksheet, Vocabulary Check, Analyzing Literature Worksheet*, Critical Thinking and Reading Worksheet*, Language Worksheet* (there are always two of the starred three), and a Selection Test.

**Teacher Backup** Teacher Backup material is provided for each selection. This material consists of more information about the author, a critical quotation about the author, a summary of the selection, and a list of other works by the author. In addition, there is a Check Test that you can use to check if students have read the selection. Help in teaching and evaluating the writing assignment in the student text is provided as well as three alternative composition assignments for the students. One of these is less challenging than the assignment in the student text, one is more challenging, and one requires the student to write in response to literary criticism. Finally, answers to all worksheets and tests are provided.

**Grammar in Action Worksheets** These worksheets provide additional instruction and practice on the topic presented with a selection in the Annotated Teacher's Edition.

**Usage and Mechanics** The Usage and Mechanics Worksheet provides sentences dealing with the selection that contain errors in usage and mechanics. They provide additional practice with the skill presented in the Grammar in Action Worksheet. Such common problems as run-on sentences, sentence fragments, and subject–verb agreement are incorporated into these sentences as well as errors in spelling and punctuation. We suggest you have your students correct these sentences orally so that they can discuss each problem.

**Vocabulary Check** The Vocabulary Check tests mastery of the vocabulary words listed on the Guide for Reading page before each selection. This blackline master can be used as a test or as an in-class or at-home assignment.

**Worksheets** The Analyzing Literature Worksheet, Critical Thinking and Reading Worksheet, and Language Work-

sheet support and expand upon the skills taught at the end of the selection in the student book.

**Selections** Test A Selection Test is provided for each selection. This test requires students to demonstrate comprehension and interpretation of the selection and to apply the skills taught at the end of the selection. The test includes an essay question and a reader's response question.

**Annotated Models** For each selection that is annotated as a model in the student book (at the beginning of the short story, nonfiction, and poetry units), a selection is provided in the Teaching Portfolio for students to annotate themselves.

## End of Unit
Each unit ends with two unit tests: a short-answer test and an essay test, with guidelines for evaluating student responses to the essay test questions. In addition, a list of suggested projects, a bibliography, and list of audio-visual aids are included.

## End of Portfolio
At the end of the Teaching Portfolio are models of strong and weak student writing and a guide to evaluating student writing.

## STUDY GUIDES
Study Guides for major novels and plays are available with *Prentice Hall Literature*. These guides will help you teach many of the works of your choice as part of your total literature program. Each guide contains an overview of the novel or play, chapter-by-chapter lessons, assignments leading to essays and imaginative writing, guidelines for dealing with provocative themes, a bibliography, and blackline masters of skills and a test for the work.

## COMPUTER TEST BANK
The computer test bank provides the selection test and unit tests from the Teaching Portfolio on a computer disk. The program allows you to modify the selection tests by deleting items from the short-answer selection tests supplied, choosing a different essay question, and writing your own test questions. You can save your test for future use.

## LIBRARY OF VIDEO CLASSICS
The Library of Video Classics provides videotapes of films made of major works in this level. Each tape is accompanied by a Viewing Guide, which gives background on the film or director; a planning overview for the film; and previewing and after-viewing questions and activities.

# Composition Strand in Prentice Hall Literature

The following chart shows all composition activities and their location in the program. The activities are organized to take students into, through, and beyond the literature.

| Feature | In the Student Materials | In the Teacher Materials | Benefit |
|---|---|---|---|
| **Into the Literature** | | | |
| "Writing" activity *before* each selection | "Guide for Reading" page before each selection in student text | "Guide for Reading" teaching note in margin of Annotated Teacher's Edition | Writing before reading is an ideal technique for getting students into literature |
| **Through the Literature** | | | |
| "Thinking and Writing" composition activity after *each* selection | End of each selection in student text | In Teaching Portfolio: teaching notes for activity labeled with writing process steps; evaluation checklist for grading writing. In ATE: suggestions for publishing student writing | The writing activity that follows each selection provides an immediate opportunity to respond to the literary experience. The activity is in writing process format. |
| Three additional composition activities for *each* selection: Less Challenging, More Challenging, The Student as Critic | | Additional activities are in the Teaching Portfolio. These can be used as assignments, or as essay questions for tests. | Three additional activities for *each* selection let you meet the needs for lower ability levels, or provide enrichment. |
| "Handbook of Writing About Literature," made up of two-page writing lessons | Handbook section of at least 50 pages at the end of each student text | Notes and support for using the handbook in the Teaching Portfolio | Guided lessons lead students step-by-step through case studies and activities. |
| "Unit Test" essay questions that address several selections in a unit | | Tests in Teaching Portfolio comes with evaluation checklists | Sharpen thinking and writing skills with topics that compare and contrast thematic ideas, literary elements, and content. |
| **Beyond the Literature** | | | |
| "You the Writer" creative writing activity with each unit | End of each unit in student text | Guidelines for evaluating student writing are in Annotated Teacher's Edition | Students try their hand at expressive writing aided by imaginative prompts and step-by-step encouragement. |
| "You the Critic" literary criticism activity with each unit | End of each unit in student text | Teaching notes and guidelines for evaluating student writing in Annotated Teacher's Edition | Challenge analytical skills as your students respond to literary criticism. |
| "Writing Across the Curriculum" suggestions | | Suggestions in Annotated Teacher's Edition | Broaden writing opportunities to other subjects. Notes suggest assignments and inter-actions with other departments. |
| "Fine Art Writing Activity" (from full color art transparency) | Handout sheet | Twenty fine art color transparencies with accompanying blackline masters in Teaching Portfolio | Use the dynamic combination of literature and writing for a humanities-based writing activity. |
| "Student Writing Models" | | In the Teaching Portfolio: examples of strong and weak student compositions | Use the powerful motivator of peer learning to prompt better writing responses. |

# Skills Chart for Selections in Each Unit

The following chart shows the literary elements and integrated language arts skills covered with each selection. An asterisk (*) indicates that a worksheet appears in the Teaching Portfolio.

## SHORT STORIES

| Selection | Analyzing Literature | Critical Thinking and Reading | Understanding Language/ Speaking and Listening | Thinking and Writing | Grammar in Action |
|---|---|---|---|---|---|
| **Reading Actively** | | | | | |
| "The Secret Life of Walter Mitty," James Thurber, p. 3 | Understanding point of view* | Identifying wishful thinking | Finding Latin roots Understanding prefixes* | Continuing the story | Writing dialogue* |
| **Plot** | | | | | |
| "The Most Dangerous Game," Richard Connell, p. 13 | Understanding plot* | Analyzing sequence in a story* | | Writing about plot | Using dashes* Writing suspense* |
| "Sonata for Harp and Bicycle," Joan Aiken, p. 33 | Understanding suspense* | Recognizing relevant details | Understanding words from Greek myths* | Writing about suspense and foreshadowing | Using figurative language* |
| "The Interlopers," Saki, p. 43 | Understanding conflict* | Identifying causes and effects | Using context clues* | Writing about conflict | Using participles* |
| "The Lady or the Tiger?" Frank R. Stockton, p. 49 | Analyzing a dilemma | Analyzing solutions* | Using context clues* | Writing an ending | Varying sentence length* |
| **Character** | | | | | |
| "All the Years of Her Life," Morley Callaghan, p. 57 | Understanding characterization* | Recognizing stereotypes | Understanding phonetic spelling* | Writing about a person | Using active and passive voice* |
| **Point of View** | | | | | |
| "Uncle Marcos," Isabel Allende, p. 63 | Recognizing character traits | Understanding magical realism* | Recognizing hyperbole* | Writing about a memorable person | Recognizing adverb clauses* |
| "The Red-Headed League," Sir Arthur Conan Doyle, p. 71 | Understanding Motivation Recognizing character traits* | Contrasting characters' abilities* | Completing word analogies | Analyzing a detective's methods | Using single quotation marks* Examining deductive reasoning* |
| "Blues Ain't No Mockin Bird," Toni Cade Bambara, p. 91 | Understanding verisimilitude* | Noting relevant details* | Understanding dialect | Responding to meaning | |

# SHORT STORIES (continued)

| Selection | Analyzing Literature | Critical Thinking and Reading | Understanding Language/ Speaking and Listening | Thinking and Writing | Grammar in Action |
|---|---|---|---|---|---|
| "The Invalid's Story," Mark Twain, p. 99 | Understanding first-person narration | Identifying exaggeration* | Understanding idioms* | Writing a tall tale | Recognizing dialect* |
| "Before the End of Summer," Grant Moss, Jr., p. 107 | Recognizing limited point of view | Using narration to draw conclusions* | Choosing the meaning to fit the context* | Writing about characters | Writing dialogue* Using introductory adverb clauses* |
| "The Good Deed," Pearl S. Buck, p. 121 | Appreciating omniscient narration* | Making inferences about characters* | Using a pronunciation key | Reacting to a story | Recognizing compound-complex sentences* Using adverbs and adverb phrases* |
| **Setting** | | | | | |
| "The Cask of Amontillado," Edgar Allan Poe, p. 139 | Understanding setting | Analyzing the effect of setting* | Using word roots* | Creating a setting | Using action verbs* |
| "Beware of the Dog," Roald Dahl, p. 147 | Appreciating historical setting* | Making inferences* | Comparing British and American terms | Evaluating a story | Writing suspense* Using prepositional phrases* |
| "The Man to Send Rain Clouds," Leslie Marmon Silko, p. 159 | Recognizing the cultural setting* | Understanding cultural conflict* | Understanding words from Spanish | Writing about cultural practices | |
| "If I Forget Thee, Oh Earth,..." Arthur C. Clarke, p. 165 | Responding to setting in science fiction* | Understanding plausibility | Using vivid words* | Writing science fiction | Using adjective clauses* |
| **Theme** | | | | | |
| "A Very Old Man with Enormous Wings," Gabriel García Márquez, p. 173 | Understanding theme* | Identifying different interpretations | Using context to understand words* | Writing from a different perspective | Illustrating and giving examples* Using different sentence openers* |
| "The Gift of the Magi," O. Henry, p. 183 | Understanding key statements | Paraphrasing* | Tracing word histories* | Writing about theme | Determining author's tone* |
| "The Scarlet Ibis," James Hurst, p. 189 | Interpreting symbols* | Recognizing emotive language | Identifying simile and metaphor | Writing about symbols | Using concrete details* Understanding infinitives and infinitive phrases* |

## SHORT STORIES (continued)

| Selection | Analyzing Literature | Critical Thinking and Reading | Understanding Language/ Speaking and Listening | Thinking and Writing | Grammar in Action |
|---|---|---|---|---|---|
| "The Necklace," Guy de Maupassant, p. 201 | Understanding irony* | Making inferences about characters | Choosing the meaning that fits the context* | Responding to criticism | Varying sentences* |
| **Putting It Together** | | | | | |
| "Gwilan's Harp," Ursula K. Le Guin, p. 209 | Reviewing the short story | Comparing and contrasting* | Understanding synonyms and antonyms* | Writing about theme | Using imagery* |

## SKILLS CHART: DRAMA

| Selection | Analyzing Literature | Critical Thinking and Reading | Understanding Language/ Speaking and Listening | Thinking and Writing | Grammar in Action |
|---|---|---|---|---|---|
| *The Boor,* Anton Chekov, p. 227 | Understanding the one-act farce | Making inferences about characters* | Choosing the meaning that fits the context* | Writing about an unusual encounter | Using commas in a series* |
| *The Pen of my Aunt,* Gordon Daviot, p. 239 | Understanding staging* | Adapting a play for the movies* | Using the prefix *col-* | Writing about a play's meaning | Using brackets* |
| *The Miracle Worker,* Act I, William Gibson, p. 253 | Recognizing protagonist and antagonist | Comparing and contrasting characters* | Using specific words* | Writing about characters | Recognizing sentence fragments* |
| *The Miracle Worker,* Act II, p. 277 | Understanding conflict in drama | Recognizing causes and effects* | Recognizing and forming compound words* | Writing a scene | Using dashes* Writing directions* |
| *The Miracle Worker,* Act III, p. 301 | Understanding the theme of a play | Summarizing a play* | Recognizing the prefix *dis-* | Writing a review on a play | Using direct objects and subject complements |
| **The Shakespearean Play** | | | | | |
| *Romeo and Juliet,* Act I, William Shakespeare, p. 321 | Appreciating blank verse | Interpreting the effect of imagery* | Understanding words from Elizabethan times* | Writing a speech in blank verse | Using commas in poetry* |
| *Romeo and Juliet,* Act II, p. 347 | Understanding the dramatic foil* | | Interpreting personification* | Modernizing dialogue | Understanding antecedents* Determining author's tone* |

## DRAMA: (continued)

| Selection | Analyzing Literature | Critical Thinking and Reading | Understanding Language/ Speaking and Listening | Thinking and Writing | Grammar in Action |
|---|---|---|---|---|---|
| *Romeo and Juliet,* Act III, p. 369 | Understanding dramatic speeches | Inferring tone in a monologue* | Understanding allusions* | Writing a soliloquy | Using imagery* Using quotation marks with other punctuation* |
| *Romeo and Juliet,* Act IV, p. 395 | Understanding dramatic irony* | Predicting outcomes | Appreciating puns* | Writing an ending for the play | Using apostrophes* |
| *Romeo and Juliet,* Act V, p. 409 | Understanding tragedy and theme | Interpreting metaphorical language* | Using the context to find the meaning* | Responding to criticism | Using a noun of direct address* |

## SKILLS CHART: NONFICTION

| Selection | Analyzing Literature | Critical Thinking and Reading | Understanding Language/ Speaking and Listening | Thinking and Writing | Grammar in Action |
|---|---|---|---|---|---|
| Reading Actively | | | | | |
| "A Neighbor of Mine," Dorothy Canfield Fisher, p. 431 | Understanding anecdotes* | Recognizing generalizations* | Using sentence completion | Writing about a profession | |
| **Biographies and Personal Accounts** | | | | | |
| From *A Lincoln Preface,* Carl Sandburg, p. 439 | Understanding biography* | Evaluating the subject of a biography* | Completing verbal analogies | Writing a biographical sketch | Recognizing main idea and supporting detail* |
| "Of Dry Goods and Black Bow Ties," Yoshiko Uchida, p. 447 | Understanding characterization | Separating fact from opinion | Understanding synonyms* | Writing about characterization | Using transitions* |
| From *Dance to the Piper,* Agnes De Mille, p. 455 | Understanding autobiography | Separating details* | Fitting the context* | Writing an autobiographical sketch | Varying word order* |
| From *Kon Tiki,* Thor Heyerdahl, p. 465 | Understanding suspense | Understanding the sequence of events* | Learning seafaring terms | Writing about autobiography | Appreciating narrative writing* Using semicolons* |

# NONFICTION: (continued)

| Selection | Analyzing Literature | Critical Thinking and Reading | Understanding Language/ Speaking and Listening | Thinking and Writing | Grammar in Action |
|---|---|---|---|---|---|
| **Types of Essays** | | | | | |
| "Nameless, Tennessee," from *Blue Highways,* William Least Heat Moon, p. 477 | Understanding the narrative essay* | Summarizing an essay* | Understanding dialect | Writing a narrative essay | Recognizing supporting information* |
| "'Sayonara,'" Anne Morrow Lindbergh, p. 483 | Understanding the descriptive essay* | Comparing and contrasting words | Using dictionary entries* | Writing a descriptive essay | Using semicolons* |
| "The Loch Ness Monster," John McPhee, p. 489 | Understanding the expository essay* | Finding relevant evidence | Understanding words with the suffix *ity*\* | Writing an expository essay | Writing description* Varying sentence openers* |
| "'I Have a Dream,'" Martin Luther King, Jr., p. 499 | Understanding the persuasive essay* | Recognizing persuasive techniques | Delivering a speech Understanding synonyms and antonyms* | Writing about persuasion | Using parallel structure* |
| **Essays in the Arts and Sciences** | | | | | |
| "The Death of a Tree," Edwin Way Teale, p. 505 | Understanding transformation* | Creating a flow chart* | Understanding terms from biology | Writing about transformation | Using sensory impressions |
| "Georgia O'Keefe," Joan Didion, p. 511 | Character analysis* | Evaluating conclusions about art* | Understanding art terms | Writing about art | Using coordination* |
| "Single Room, Earth View," Sally Ride, p. 517 | Understanding scientific observation* | Finding the main idea of a paragraph* | Understanding scientific terms | Writing up an observation | Using *like* and *as*\* |
| "The Spreading 'You Know,'" James Thurber, p. 523 | Understanding illustration | Inferring a writer's purpose* | Understanding speech habits Understanding words with the prefix *over*\* | Writing about spoken language | |
| From *Shakespeare of London,* Marchette Chute, p. 527 | Understanding historical inference* | Evaluating historical inferences | Understanding theater terms* | Writing about inference | Understanding infinitives* |
| **Putting It Together** | | | | | |
| "Butch Cassidy," Bruce Chatwin, p. 533 | Understanding anecdotes* | Appreciating tone* | | Writing a travel narrative | Using the semicolon* |

# SKILLS CHART: POETRY

| Selection | Analyzing Literature | Critical Thinking and Reading | Understanding Language/ Speaking and Listening | Thinking and Writing | Grammar in Action |
|---|---|---|---|---|---|
| **Reading Actively** | | | | | |
| "Sympathy," Paul Laurence Dunbar, p. 547 | Understanding symbols* | | Understanding shades of difference* | Writing an extended definition | |
| **Narrative Poetry** | | | | | |
| "Casey at the Bat," Ernest Lawrence Thayer, p. 551 | Enjoying narrative poetry | Paraphrasing poetry* | Recognizing jargon* | Writing a narrative verse | |
| "The Ballad of William Sycamore," Stephen Vincent Benét, p. 557 | Understanding ballads* | Inferring the theme of a ballad | Discovering context clues* Completing word analogies | | Using capital letters* |
| "The Raven," Edgar Allan Poe, p. 563 | Understanding repetition and refrain* | Making inferences about the speaker* | | Responding to criticism | Using alliteration* |
| "The Charge of the Light Brigade," Alfred, Lord Tennyson, p. 569 | Understanding rhythm in poetry* | Understanding cause and effect | Using concise language for effect* Reading with expression | Writing a news report | |
| **Dramatic Poetry and the Speaker** | | | | | |
| "Incident in a Rose Garden," Donald Justice, p. 575 | Understanding dramatic poetry* | Interpreting personification | Effective word choices* | Continuing a poem | |
| "The Seven Ages of Man," William Shakespeare, p. 579 | Appreciating poems from plays* | | Understanding synonyms and antonyms* Appreciating vivid words | Imitating Shakespeare | |
| "The Runaway," Robert Frost, p. 584 "The Princess," Sara Henderson Hay, p. 587 "George Gray," Edgar Lee Masters, p. 588 | Understanding point of view Understanding a dramatic monologue* | Recognizing assertions | Reading aloud a dramatic monologue Language of contrast* | | Using colons* |
| **Lyric Poetry** | | | | | |
| "Winter," William Shakespeare, p. 592 | Understanding lyric poetry | | | Writing a lyric poem | |

# POETRY (continued)

| Selection | Analyzing Literature | Critical Thinking and Reading | Understanding Language/ Speaking and Listening | Thinking and Writing | Grammar in Action |
|---|---|---|---|---|---|
| "The Dark Hills," Edwin Arlington Robinson, p. 594 "The Funeral," Gordon Parks, p. 595 "Up-Hill," Christina Rossetti, p. 596 "I Hear an Army," James Joyce, p. 597 | | Interpreting connotative meaning<br><br>Interpreting symbols in lyric poetry*<br>Interpreting sensory words | Using general and specific words* | Writing about a lyric poem | |
| **Word Choice and Tone** | | | | | |
| "Meeting at Night," Robert Browning, p. 602 "Jabberwocky," Lewis Carroll, p. 604 | Understanding word choice* | | Understanding made-up words* | Writing a poem using made-up words | |
| "Macavity: The Mystery Cat," T. S. Eliot, p. 606 | | | Finding antonyms | Writing about tone | Using coordinating conjunctions* |
| "Solace," Dorothy Parker, p. 610 | Understanding an ironical tone | | | | |
| **Imagery** | | | | | |
| "Memory," Margaret Walker, p. 614 | Studying imagery* | | Appreciating vivid verbs* | Writing your own "memory" | Using commas with adjectives* |
| "The Meadow Mouse," Theodore Roethke, p. 615 | Understanding imagery | | | Writing about imagery | |
| "To be of use," Marge Piercy, p. 617 "The Space," Gary Soto, p. 618 "The Creation," James Weldon Johnson, p. 619 | | Appreciating the effects of imagery | | Writing a poem with imagery | |
| **Figurative Language** | | | | | |
| "The Eagle," Alfred, Lord Tennyson, p. 627 | Understanding similes | | | | Using punctuation in poetry* |

# POETRY (continued)

| Selection | Analyzing Literature | Critical Thinking and Reading | Understanding Language/ Speaking and Listening | Thinking and Writing | Grammar in Action |
|---|---|---|---|---|---|
| "I Wandered Lonely as a Cloud," William Wordsworth, p. 628 | | | | Writing a poem using a simile | |
| "A Dream Deferred," Langston Hughes, p. 630 | | | | Analyzing a poem | |
| "Dreams," Langston Hughes, p. 631 | Understanding metaphors | | | | |
| "The Sky is Low," Emily Dickinson, p. 632 | Understanding personification | | | Responding to criticism | |
| "Splinter," Carl Sandburg, p. 634 | Understanding figurative language* | | Using context clues* | Writing a poem | |
| **Musical Devices** | | | | | |
| "The Listeners," Walter de la Mare, p. 638 | Recognizing alliteration | | | | Using precise words* |
| "The Bells," Edgar Allan Poe, p. 640 | Recognizing forms of repetition | | Reading aloud "The Bells" | | Using denotation and connotation* |
| Ecclesiastes 3:1-8, King James Bible, p. 645 | Understanding parallelism | | | | |
| "I Hear America Singing," Walt Whitman, p. 647 | Understanding free verse Understanding musical devices and parallelism* | | Identifying synonyms* | Responding to criticism | |
| **Structure** | | | | | |
| "There Will Come Soft Rains," Sara Teasdale, p. 652 | Understanding structure | | | | |
| "maggie and milly and molly and may," E. E. Cummings, p. 653 | | | | Comparing structures | |
| "Sea-Fever," John Masefield, p. 654 | Understanding meter | | | | |
| "My Father's Song," Simon J. Ortiz, p. 656 | | | | | |
| "Cradle Song," Gabriela Mistral, p. 657 | Understanding structure* | | Recognizing related words* | Writing a critical evaluation | |

| Selection | Analyzing Literature | Critical Thinking and Reading | Understanding Language/ Speaking and Listening | Thinking and Writing | Grammar in Action |
|---|---|---|---|---|---|
| "The Sound of the Sea," Henry Wadsworth Longfellow, p. 660 Sonnet 30, William Shakespeare, p. 661 | Understanding a Petrarchan sonnet<br><br>Understanding the forms of the sonnet* Understanding a Shakespearean sonnet | | Exploring word origins* | | |
| Three Haiku, p. 664 Hokku Poems, Richard Wright, p. 665 "Pendulum," John Updike, p. 666 | Understanding haiku*<br><br>Understanding concrete poetry | | Appreciating concrete words* | Writing haiku<br><br>Writing a concrete poem | |
| **Putting It Together** | | | | | |
| "A Red, Red Rose," Robert Burns, p. 669 | Analyzing musical devices* | Analyzing the effect of musical devices | Interpreting dialect* | Writing a lyric | |

## SKILLS CHART: THE EPIC

| Selection | Analyzing Literature | Critical Thinking and Reading | Understanding Language/ Speaking and Listening | Thinking and Writing | Grammar in Action |
|---|---|---|---|---|---|
| The *Odyssey*, Part I, Homer, p. 681 | Understanding the epic hero* | Interpreting epithets | Recognizing allusions* | Writing about the epic hero | Using figurative language* Using appositives and appositive phrases* |
| The *Odyssey*, Part II, Homer, p. 717 | Understanding the plot of an epic | Inferring ways of life from epics Inferring customs and beliefs* | Interpreting Homeric similes* | Responding to criticism | Using parenthetical expressions* Using vivid verbs* |
| "Siren Song," Margaret Atwood, p. 744 "Ithaca," Constantine Cavafy, p. 746 | Understanding interpretations of the *Odyssey*￼* | | Recognizing modern allusions to the *Odyssey** | Interpreting the *Odyssey* creatively | |

## SKILLS CHART: THE NOVEL
## GREAT EXPECTATIONS, Charles Dickens

| Selection | Analyzing Literature | Critical Thinking and Reading | Understanding Language/ Speaking and Listening | Thinking and Writing | Grammar in Action |
|---|---|---|---|---|---|
| Chapters 1-8, p. 757 | Understanding point of view* | | Appreciating word histories* | Writing from another point of view | Using direct quotations* Using gerunds* |
| Chapters 9-15, p. 785 | Understanding characterization* | Drawing conclusions about characters | Understanding context clues* | Writing about art | Writing dialogue* Appreciating details of setting* |
| Chapters 16-23, p. 809 | Understanding plot and subplot | Predicting outcomes* | Understanding the Latin root *spect** | Extending the story | Using participial phrases* Using *who* and *whom** |
| Chapters 24-31, p. 835 | Understanding setting and atmosphere* | Identifying details that create setting | Exploring connotations* | Comparing and contrasting settings | Using prepositional phrases* Using parallelism* |
| Chapters 32-44, p. 857 | Understanding theme | Paraphrasing key statements* | Completing analogies* | Responding to the theme of a novel | Using subordination* Appreciating dialect* |
| Chapters 45-58, p. 899 | Understanding the novel as a whole | Using criteria to evaluate the novel* | Recognizing dialect* | Evaluating the novel | Using repetition* Understanding referent |

# PRENTICE HALL
# LITERATURE

COPPER

BRONZE

SILVER

GOLD

PLATINUM

THE AMERICAN EXPERIENCE

THE ENGLISH TRADITION

WORLD MASTERPIECES

*i*

# PRENTICE HALL
# LITERATURE

## GOLD

### SECOND EDITION

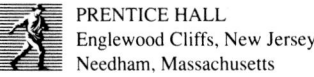
PRENTICE HALL
Englewood Cliffs, New Jersey
Needham, Massachusetts

## Humanities Note

Fine Art, *The New Novel* (detail), 1877, by Winslow Homer. Winslow Homer (1836–1910) was in many ways the quintessential American artist of the nineteenth century. Homer's style and subject matter were typical of the nation's interests and sensibilities. He was fascinated by light, shadow, and form and by the relationship between humans and nature. His subjects were all-American; he pictured ordinary people at work and play: school children, fishermen, farmers, people at rest or idly chatting.

Homer's experience as an illustrator for periodicals made him keenly aware of physical gesture and the story-telling possibilities in art. He captured—particularly in his watercolors, like this one—a sense of personality and naturalness unmatched by his contemporary artists.

This painting was done at the end of a period in his life when he had painted many delicate watercolors and oils of children and young women. They are mostly generalized, contemplative paintings. It was shortly after these delicate works were made that Homer turned toward more serious studies of men's struggles against the sea or the wilderness.

Many of his watercolor paintings, like this one, depict a young woman totally in tune with nature. Lying comfortably in a flowery field, the reader is bathed in warm sunlight and seems oblivious to her surroundings as she enjoys her new novel. Her head rests on her folded coat. Behind her is a thick bank of greenery, which contrasts both with her subtle coloring and the pale field of wildflowers before her.

Homer painted his watercolors outdoors. Particularly in his watercolors he allowed himself the freedom to picture momentary images that pleased him. Studies like this one that focused on nature's warm light and an appealing subject were among his most attractive works.

Art credits begin on page 1051.

COVER AND TITLE PAGE: *The New Novel* (detail), Winslow Homer, Fine Arts Museum, Springfield, Massachusetts

PRENTICE HALL
A Division of Simon & Schuster
Englewood Cliffs, New Jersey 07632

## STAFF CREDITS FOR PRENTICE HALL LITERATURE

**Editorial:** Eileen Thompson, Ellen Bowler, Philip Fried,
Daniel Jackson, Doug McCollum, Jane Standen,
Richard Hickox, Carol Schneider, Kelly Ackley

**Design:** Sue Walrath, Nancy Sharkey, Leslie Osher

**Photo Research:** Libby Forsyth

**Production:** Penny Hull, Suse Cioffi, Joan McCulley,
Marlys Lehmann, Lisa Meyerhoff, Cleasta Wilburn

**Editorial Systems:** Andrew Grey Bommarito,
Ralph O'Brien

**Marketing:** Carol Newman, Mollie Ledwith,
Tom Maksym

**Manufacturing:** Laura Sanderson,
Denise Herckenrath

**Permissions:** Doris Robinson

## ACKNOWLEDGMENTS

Grateful acknowledgment is made to the following for permission to reprint copyrighted material:

**Margarey Walker Alexander**
"Memory" from *For My People* by Margaret Walker, copyright 1942 Yale University Press. Reprinted by permission of Margaret Walker Alexander.

**Isabel Allende**
"Uncle Marcos" from *The House of the Spirits* by Isabel Allende, copyright 1982 by Isabel Allende. Published by Alfred A. Knopf, subsidiary of Random House, Inc., 1985. Reprinted by permission of the author.

(contiued on page 1049)

# CONTENTS

## SHORT STORIES

## DRAMA

## NONFICTION

## POETRY

*vii*

## THE EPIC

## THE NOVEL

*x*

# PRENTICE HALL
# LITERATURE
### GOLD

## Humanities Note

Fine art, *The Gulf Stream*, 1899, Winslow Homer. The painter and illustrator Winslow Homer (1836-1910), is known today for the marine, genre, and landscape paintings he produced in profusion.

In *The Gulf Stream* Homer explores the conflict of man against nature. This is a grim view of a man adrift in a disabled vessel surrounded by sharks. The ominous mood of the painting is emphasized by the inexplicable red splotches in the water. The hopelessness of the situation is emphasized by the ship passing out of sight in the upper left unseen by the man. This painting speaks of nature's impersonal power and man's weakness in the face of it. It leaves the viewer wondering what will become of the forlorn figure in the boat.

**THE GULF STREAM**
*Winslow Homer*
*The Metropolitan Museum of Art*

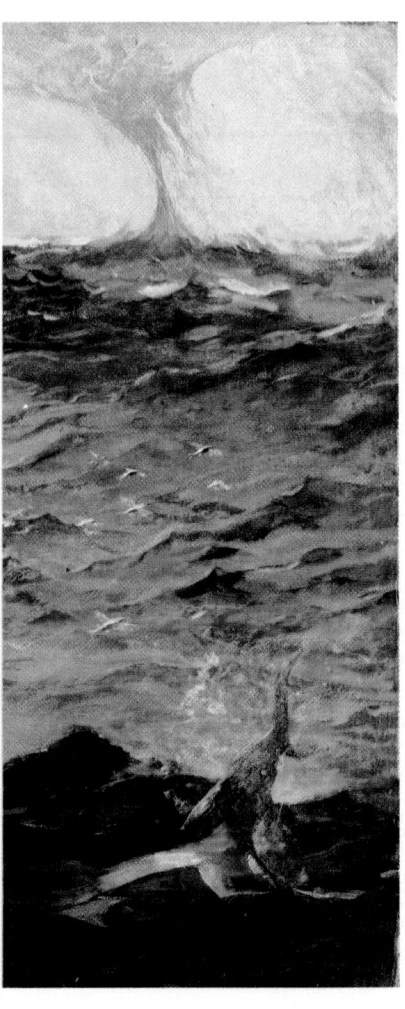

# SHORT STORIES

The writer Edgar Allan Poe defined the short story as a brief tale that can be read in one sitting. Poe believed that such a story could have a more powerful effect and give greater pleasure than a longer tale read at different sittings. The pleasure you will get from the short stories in this book is the special kind of pleasure that fiction offers.

Fiction is literature based on the writer's imagination and so contains made-up characters and events. However, although fiction is made up, it has its roots in life. Virginia Woolf has written,". . . fiction is like a spider's web, attached ever so lightly perhaps, but still attached to life at four corners."

The short stories in this unit are arranged according to the elements of plot, character, point of view, setting, and theme. Plot is the pattern of action in the story, while characters are the people who take part in the action. Point of view is the angle or perspective from which the story is told. Setting consists of where and when the action takes place, and theme is the insight into life revealed by the story.

Science fiction, action and adventure, mysteries—you will encounter these types of stories and others in this unit. You will also learn strategies that will help you read short stories with greater appreciation and understanding.

*1*

## The Short Story

**Reading Actively** The reading process outlined on this page is based on research into the ways that good readers construct meaning from fiction. This approach makes students aware of their reading habits, enabling them to monitor and improve their comprehension.

Although most good readers use these techniques unconsciously or intuitively, students can learn to become highly effective readers by making a conscious effort to follow this process until it becomes internalized.

Active reading means interacting with a text. Questioning not only keeps readers turning pages but, more important, forces them to explore the meaning of the text. By reflecting on what is happening within a story, what might happen as the story proceeds, and how the writer conveys this information, readers can become more sensitive and literate.

Introduce the strategies listed here and explain that they will help students become more effective readers. The model on the following pages contains the types of questions, predictions, clarifications, and summaries that an active reader might make while reading. It also shows the way an active reader might pull together these details after reading.

Ask students to pay attention to these annotations as they read. Also ask them to create their own questions, predictions, clarifications, and summaries, and, finally, to react to the story.

For further practice with the process, use "Stranger on the Night Train," by Mary Hocking—in the Teaching Portfolio, page 8, following the Teacher Backup for this selection—which students can annotate themselves. Encourage students to continue to use these strategies when reading other stories.

How should you read a short story? According to the philosopher John Locke: "Reading furnishes the mind only with materials of knowledge; it is thinking [that] makes what we read." In other words, gaining the most from reading depends on reading actively, or with a questioning mind.

Use the following strategies to help you read actively. They will help you interact with the short story and figure out what makes it effective.

**Question**      Become actively involved in the story by asking questions about what you are reading. For example, don't just accept the characters in a story at face value, but try to figure out what they are like and why they act as they do. Ask questions about why events occur and what will be the result of certain actions. Look at the setting and ask how it affects the characters and the plot. Then as you read, try to find the answers to your questions.

**Predict**      As you read, make predictions about what will happen next. Even when writing fiction, writers usually try to create a world that resembles real life. Therefore, bring your own experience to the short story and make predictions about what the characters will do and what will happen next based on your own knowledge and expectations of life.

**Clarify**      Find the answers to your questions and monitor your predictions, or check to see whether they turn out to be accurate. If there is something in the story you do not understand, stop to figure out the situation or find the meaning.

**Summarize**      At appropriate points in the story, pause to summarize or review what has happened so far. Then keep this summary in mind as you read the next segment of the short story.

**Pull It Together**      At the end of the story, pull all the details together. Determine the central point or insight of the story. In other words, what did it mean to you? React to it. Did you like it? Why or why not?

These strategies will help you recall details from the story, interpret what you have read, and apply the story to your life. On the facing page is a model showing how an active reader might read a story by interacting with it.

*2   Short Stories*

1 To learn how to read a short story actively
2 To understand point of view
3 To identify wishful thinking
4 To find Latin roots of English words
5 To write another daydream for Walter Mitty

**Support Material**

**Teaching Portfolio**
Teacher Backup, p. 5
Reading Actively, "Stranger on the Night Train," by Mary Hocking, p. 8
Grammar in Action Worksheet, *Writing Dialogue*, p. 12
Usage and Mechanics Worksheet, p. 14
Analyzing Literature Worksheet,

*Understanding Point of View*, p. 15
Language Worksheet, *Understanding Prefixes*, p. 16
Selection Test, p. 17

# The Secret Life of Walter Mitty

James Thurber

"We're going through!" The Commander's voice was like thin ice breaking. He wore his full-dress uniform, with the heavily braided white cap pulled down rakishly over one cold gray eye. "We can't make it, sir. It's spoiling for a hurricane, if you ask me." "I'm not asking you, Lieutenant Berg," said the Commander. "Throw on the power lights! Rev her up to 8,500! We're going through!" The pounding of the cylinders increased: ta-pocketa-pocketa-pocketa-*pocketa-pocketa*. The Commander stared at the ice forming on the pilot window. He walked over and twisted a row of complicated dials. "Switch on No. 8 auxiliary!" he shouted. "Switch on No. 8 auxiliary!" repeated Lieutenant Berg. "Full strength in No. 3 turret!" shouted the Commander. "Full strength in No. 3 turret!" The crew, bending to their various tasks in the huge, hurtling eight-engined Navy hydroplane,[1] looked at each other and grinned. "The Old Man'll get us through," they said to one another. "The Old Man ain't afraid of Hell!" . . .

"Not so fast! You're driving too fast!" said Mrs. Mitty. "What are you driving so fast for?"

"Hmm?" said Walter Mitty. He looked at his wife, in the seat beside him, with shocked astonishment. She seemed grossly unfamiliar, like a strange woman who had yelled at him in a crowd. "You were up to fifty-five," she said. "You know I don't like to go more than forty. You were up to fifty-five." Walter Mitty drove on toward Waterbury in silence, the roaring of the SN202 through the worst storm in twenty years of Navy flying fading in the remote, intimate airways of his mind. "You're tensed up again," said Mrs. Mitty. "It's one of your days. I wish you'd let Dr. Renshaw look you over."

---

1. **hydroplane** (hī′ drə plān) *n.*: A seaplane.

Walter Mitty stopped the car in front of the building where his wife went to have her hair done. "Remember to get those overshoes while I'm having my hair done," she said. "I don't need overshoes," said Mitty. She put her mirror back into her bag. "We've been all through that," she said, getting out of the car. "You're not a young man any longer." He raced the engine a little. "Why don't you wear your gloves? Have you lost your gloves?" Walter Mitty reached in a pocket and brought out the gloves. He put them on, but after she had turned and gone into the building and he had driven on to a red light, he took them off again. "Pick it up, brother!" snapped a cop as the light changed, and Mitty hastily pulled on his gloves and lurched ahead. He drove around the streets aimlessly for a time, and then he drove past the hospital on his way to the parking lot.

Clarification: Walter Mitty is having another daydream.

. . . "It's the millionaire banker, Wellington McMillan," said the pretty nurse. "Yes?" said Walter Mitty, removing his gloves slowly. "Who has the case?" "Dr. Renshaw and Dr. Benbow, but there are two specialists here, Dr. Remington from New York and Mr. Pritchard-Mitford from London. He flew over." A door opened down a long, cool corridor and Dr. Renshaw came out. He looked distraught and haggard. "Hello, Mitty," he said. "We're having the devil's own time with McMillan, the millionaire banker and close personal friend of Roosevelt. Obstreosis of the ductal tract.[2] Tertiary. Wish you'd take a look at him." "Glad to," said Mitty.

Question: How is the way people treat Mitty in the daydreams different from the way people treat Mitty in real life?

In the operating room there were whispered introductions: "Dr. Remington, Dr. Mitty. Mr. Pritchard-Mitford, Dr. Mitty." "I've read your book on streptothricosis," said Pritchard-Mitford, shaking hands. "A brilliant performance, sir." "Thank you," said Walter Mitty. "Didn't know you were in the States, Mitty," grumbled Remington. "Coals to Newcastle,[3] bringing Mitford and me up here for tertiary." "You are very kind," said Mitty. A huge, complicated machine, connected to the operating table, with many tubes and wires, began at this moment to go pocketa-pocketa-pocketa. "The new anesthetizer is giving way!" shouted an intern. "There is no one in the East who

---

**2. obstreosis of the ductal tract:** Thurber has invented this and other medical terms.
**3. coals to Newcastle:** The proverb, "bringing coals to Newcastle," means bringing things to a place unnecessarily—Newcastle, England, was a coal center and so did not need coal brought to it.

**Critical Thinking and Reading**
Have students look at the photographs included with this story. What scenes from the story do they illustrate? What can students infer about Walter Mitty from the details in the photographs and the expression on Walter Mitty's face?

**Critical Thinking and Reading**
Have students contrast Mitty's real personality with his imagined versions of himself. What connection might there be between them?

knows how to fix it!" "Quiet, man!" said Mitty, in a low, cool voice. He sprang to the machine, which was now going pocketa-pocketa-queep-pocketa-queep. He began fingering delicately a row of glistening dials. "Give me a fountain pen!" he snapped. Someone handed him a fountain pen. He pulled a faulty piston out of the machine and inserted the pen in its place. "That will hold for ten minutes," he said. "Get on with the operation." A nurse hurried over and whispered to Renshaw, and Mitty saw the man turn pale. "Coreopsis has set in," said Renshaw nervously. "If you would take over, Mitty?" Mitty looked at him and at the craven figure of Benbow, who drank, and at the grave, uncertain faces of the two great specialists. "If you wish," he said. They slipped a white gown on him; he adjusted a mask and drew on thin gloves; nurses handed him shining . . .

"Back it up, Mac! Look out for that Buick!" Walter Mitty jammed on the brakes. "Wrong lane, Mac," said the parking-lot attendant, looking at Mitty closely. "Gee. Yeh," muttered Mitty. He began cautiously to back out of the lane marked "Exit Only." "Leave her sit there," said the attendant. "I'll put her away." Mitty got out of the car. "Hey, better leave the key."

**Clarification:** Here Mitty returns to real life again. The parking-lot attendant treats Mitty as a foolish, bumbling man.

*The Secret Life of Walter Mitty* 5

"Oh," said Mitty, handing the man the ignition key. The attendant vaulted into the car, backed it up with insolent skill, and put it where it belonged.

They're so cocky, thought Walter Mitty, walking along Main Street; they think they know everything. Once he had tried to take his chains off, outside New Milford, and he had got them wound around the axles. A man had had to come out in a wrecking car and unwind them, a young, grinning garageman. Since then Mrs. Mitty always made him drive to a garage to have the chains taken off. The next time, he thought, I'll wear my right arm in a sling; they won't grin at me then. I'll have my right arm in a sling and they'll see I couldn't possibly take the chains off myself. He kicked at the slush on the sidewalk. "Overshoes," he said to himself, and he began looking for a shoe store.

When he came out into the street again, with the overshoes in a box under his arm, Walter Mitty began to wonder what the other thing was his wife had told him to get. She had told him, twice, before they set out from their house for Waterbury. In a way he hated these weekly trips to town—he was always getting something wrong. Kleenex, he thought, Squibb's, razor blades? No. Toothpaste, toothbrush, bicarbonate, carborundum, initiative and referendum?[4] He gave it up. But she would remember it. "Where's the what's-its-name?" she would ask. "Don't tell me you forgot the what's-its-name." A newsboy went by shouting something about the Waterbury trial.

**Prediction:** The newsboy's shout will trigger another daydream.

**Clarification:** The newsboy's shout about the trial triggers a daydream about the trial. How calm and competent Mitty is during the trial!

. . . "Perhaps this will refresh your memory." The District Attorney suddenly thrust a heavy automatic at the quiet figure on the witness stand. "Have you ever seen this before?" Walter Mitty took the gun and examined it expertly. "This is my Webley-Vickers 50.80," he said calmly. An excited buzz ran around the courtroom. The Judge rapped for order. "You are a crack shot with any sort of firearms, I believe?" said the District Attorney, insinuatingly. "Objection!" shouted Mitty's attorney. "We have shown that the defendant could not have

---

**4. carborundum** (kär′ bə run′ dəm), **initiative** (i nish′ē ə tiv) **and referendum** (ref′ ə ren′ dəm): Thurber is purposely making a nonsense list; carborundum is a hard substance used for scraping, initiative is the right of citizens to introduce ideas for laws, and referendum is the right of citizens to vote on laws.

## Grammar in Action

Writing **dialogue** can add an exciting element to your short stories. Dialogue, or conversation between characters in a work of literature, is usually punctuated like this:

"Back it up, Mac," the young parking attendant shouted.
"I'll do that." Mitty began to back up the exit ramp.

Notice that the exact words spoken are enclosed in quotation marks, and words or phrases that identify the speaker (*the young parking attendant shouted* and Mitty *began to back up the exit ramp*) are set off from the dialogue either with commas or end punctuation. To minimize confusion about who is speaking, most writers start a new paragraph for each change in speaker. Sometimes, however, a writer chooses a different style. Look at this passage from "The Secret Life of Walter Mitty."

". . . Perhaps this will refresh your memory." The District Attorney suddenly thrust a heavy automatic at the quiet figure on the witnesses stand. "Have you ever seen this before?" Walter Mitty took the gun and examined it expertly. "This is my Webley-Vickers 50.80," he said calmly. An excited buzz ran around the courtroom. The Judge rapped fired the shot. We have shown that he wore his right arm in a sling on the night of the fourteenth of July." Walter Mitty raised his hand briefly and the bickering attorneys were stilled. "With any known make of gun," he said evenly, "I could have killed Gregory Fitzhurst at three hundred feet *with my left hand.*" Pandemonium broke loose in the courtroom. A woman's scream rose above the bedlam and suddenly a lovely, dark-haired girl was in Walter Mitty's arms. The District Attorney struck at her savagely. Without rising from his chair, Mitty let the man have it on the point of the chin. "You miserable cur!" . . .

"Puppy biscuit," said Walter Mitty. He stopped walking and the buildings of Waterbury rose up out of the misty courtroom and surrounded him again. A woman who was passing laughed. "He said 'Puppy biscuit,'" she said to her companion. "That man said 'Puppy biscuit' to himself." Walter Mitty hurried on. He went into an A. & P., not the first one he came to but a smaller one farther up the street. "I want some biscuit for small, young dogs," he said to the clerk. "Any special brand, sir?" The greatest pistol shot in the world thought a moment. "It says 'Puppies Bark for It' on the box," said Walter Mitty.

**Summary:** A meek and mild man retreats into daydreams in which he is a cool, competent figure.

His wife would be through at the hairdresser's in fifteen minutes, Mitty saw in looking at his watch, unless they had trouble drying it; sometimes they had trouble drying it. She didn't like to get to the hotel first; she would want him to be there waiting for her as usual. He found a big leather chair in the lobby, facing a window, and he put the overshoes and the puppy biscuit on the floor beside it. He picked up an old copy of *Liberty* and sank down into the chair. "Can Germany Conquer the World Through the Air?" Walter Mitty looked at the pictures of bombing planes and of ruined streets.

**Prediction:** Here comes another daydream!

. . . "The cannonading has got the wind up in young Raleigh,[5] sir," said the sergeant. Captain Mitty looked up at him through tousled hair. "Get him to bed," he said wearily. "With the others. I'll fly alone." "But you can't, sir," said the sergeant anxiously. "It takes two men to handle that bomber and the

---

**5. has got the wind up in young Raleigh:** Has made young Raleigh nervous.

for order. "You are a crack shot with any sort of firearm, I believe?" said the District Attorney, insinuatingly. "Objection!" shouted Mitty's attorney. "We have shown that the defendant could not have fired the shot. . . ."

Notice how this passage departs from the conventional way of presenting dialogue. A new paragraph is not begun each time the speaker changes. Readers must rely on material outside the quotation marks to determine who says what.

**Student Activity 1.** Discuss with classmates the purpose and the effect of Thurber's way of presenting dialogue. In what way does the style suit the content of the story? Do you think the style is effective? Explain.

**Student Activity 2.** With a small group of classmates, brainstorm and list other situations in which a writer might choose an unconventional way of presenting dialogue. Then select one of these situations and write a passage of dialogue for it. Be prepared to discuss how the style you have chosen is related to the content of the passage.

Archies[6] are pounding hell out of the air. Von Richtman's circus[7] is between here and Saulier." "Somebody's got to get that ammunition dump," said Mitty. "I'm going over. Spot of brandy?" He poured a drink for the sergeant and one for himself. War thundered and whined around the dugout and battered at the door. There was a rending of wood and splinters flew through the room. "A bit of a near thing," said Captain Mitty carelessly. "The box barrage is closing in," said the sergeant. "We only live once, Sergeant," said Mitty, with his faint, fleeting smile. "Or do we?" He poured another brandy and tossed it off. "I never see a man could hold his brandy like you, sir," said the sergeant. "Begging your pardon, sir." Captain Mitty stood up and strapped on his huge Webley-Vickers automatic. "It's forty kilometers through hell, sir," said the sergeant. Mitty finished one last brandy. "After all," he said softly, "what isn't?" The pounding of the cannon increased; there was the rat-tat-tatting of machine guns, and from somewhere came the menacing pocketa-pocketa-pocketa of the new flame-throwers. Walter Mitty walked to the door of the dugout humming "Auprès de Ma Blonde."[8] He turned and waved to the sergeant. "Cheerio!" he said. . . .

Something struck his shoulder. "I've been looking all over this hotel for you," said Mrs. Mitty. "Why do you have to hide in this old chair? How did you expect me to find you?" "Things close in," said Walter Mitty vaguely. "What?" Mrs. Mitty said. "Did you get the what's-its-name? The puppy biscuit? What's in that box?" "Overshoes," said Mitty. "Couldn't you have put them on in the store?" "I was thinking," said Walter Mitty. "Does it ever occur to you that I am sometimes thinking?" She looked at him. "I'm going to take your temperature when I get you home," she said.

**Clarification:** The daydream ends, and Mrs. Mitty rudely brings Mr. Mitty back to reality.

They went out through the revolving doors that made a faintly derisive whistling sound when you pushed them. It was two blocks to the parking lot. At the drugstore on the corner she said, "Wait here for me. I forgot something. I won't be a minute." She was more than a minute. Walter Mitty lighted a cigarette. It began to rain, rain with sleet in it. He stood up

---

**6. Archies:** A slang term for antiaircraft guns.
**7. Von Richtman's circus:** A German airplane squadron.
**8. "Auprès de Ma Blonde"** (ō prɛ′ də mä blôn′ d): "Next to My Blonde," a popular French song.

against the wall of the drugstore, smoking. . . . He put his shoulders back and his heels together. "To hell with the handkerchief," said Walter Mitty scornfully. He took one last drag on his cigarette and snapped it away. Then, with that faint, fleeting smile playing about his lips, he faced the firing squad; erect and motionless, proud and disdainful, Walter Mitty the Undefeated, inscrutable to the last.

**Pulling It Together:** Mr. Mitty certainly is inscrutable to the last. The life he leads in his daydreams is very different from the life he leads in real life.

**James Grover Thurber** (1894–1961) was born and grew up in Columbus, Ohio. He began his writing career as a reporter for the *Columbus Evening Dispatch*. It was through his later work on *The New Yorker* magazine, however, that he became well known as a writer and a cartoonist. "The Secret Life of Walter Mitty," Thurber's most famous story, reveals his characteristic style of wit mixing sadness with humor.

*The Secret Life of Walter Mitty*   9

**More About the Author** James Thurber's fairy tales, completed after he became blind, share a common theme: "Love is the key which frees imagination. . . ." Ask students to discuss how an adult fairy tale may differ from children's fairy tales.

**Clarification** The word *inscrutable* comes from the Latin word parts *in,* meaning "not," and *scrutabilis,* meaning "searchable." Its current meaning is "mysterious" or "not easily understood."

**Reader's Response** Walter Mitty, like all of us at times, was afraid to take risks in his life. At what times in your life have you been afraid to do something new? How did you grapple with or overcome your fears?

## Closure and Extension

### ANSWERS TO THINKING ABOUT THE SELECTION
*Recalling*

1. Mitty's imagined characters include a hydroplane commander, a world-famous surgeon, a defendant in a murder trial, a fearless World War II flying ace, and a man facing a firing squad. All these characters are courageous and cool under pressure.
2. Mitty's second daydream is triggered when he passes a hospital and ends when a parking attendant yells at him. His third daydream is triggered by a newsboy shouting about a murder trial and ends when the words "You miserable cur" remind him that he needs to buy puppy biscuits. His fourth daydream is triggered by the title of a magazine article about World War II and ends when Mrs. Mitty hits him on the shoulder and speaks to him.

### Interpreting

3. Suggested Response: While Mitty is strong, brave, and capable in his daydreams, he is bumbling, absent-minded, and timid in real life.
4. Suggested Response: Mitty is treated as a respected hero in his daydreams and as an incompetent fool in real life.
5. Suggested Response: Mrs. Mitty's patronizing treatment of her husband is so demoralizing that the firing squad daydream may represent a final escape. Also, Mitty has stood up to her for the first time, and he may be anticipating what will happen to him when they get home.

### Applying

6. Answers will differ. Students may respond that often we laugh instead of cry.

(Answers begin on p. 9.)

## ANSWERS TO ANALYZING LITERATURE

1. Answers will differ, but most readers, remembering their own daydreams, will empathize with Mitty.
2. Suggested Response: Readers would have no insight into Mitty's secret life otherwise.
3. Suggested Response: It would be the story of an incompetent, bumbling, absent-minded fool. It would be difficult to empathize with Mitty because he would have no redeeming qualities.

## ANSWERS TO CRITICAL THINKING AND READING

1. Suggested Response: Mitty wishes he were a brilliant, respected doctor, scientist, researcher, and writer.
2. Suggested Response: Mitty wishes beautiful women were attracted to him.
3. Suggested Response: Mitty wishes he were a strong and able fighter so that people could not take advantage of him.

**Challenge** If Walter Mitty were living today, what might be the subjects of some of his daydreams?

## ANSWERS TO UNDERSTANDING LANGUAGE

1. Suggested Response: The Latin root of *derisive* is *deridere*, which means "to mock." *Derisive* means "ridiculing or mocking."
2. Suggested Response: The Latin root of *ignition* is *ignis*, which means "fire." Ignition is "a setting on fire."
3. Suggested Response: The Latin root of *insinuate* is *sinus*, which means "a bent or curved surface or hollow." In English *insinuate* means "to suggest something slyly or subtly, not straightforwardly."
4. Suggested Response: The Latin root of *revolving* is *volvere*, which means "to roll or turn around." In English *revolve* means "to turn on an axis, or to rotate."

## THINKING ABOUT THE SELECTION

### Recalling

1. Describe each of the five characters Mitty daydreams himself to be.
2. Explain what triggers Mitty's second, third, and fourth daydreams. How is he pulled out of each daydream?

### Interpreting

3. Compare and contrast Mitty in real life with Mitty in his daydreams.
4. Explain the significant difference between the way people treat Mitty in real life and the way they treat him in his daydreams.
5. Explain how Mrs. Mitty's personality triggers his last daydream. In what way is this daydream an apt comment upon Mitty's fate in real life?

### Applying

6. Mark Twain has written, "The secret source of humor is not joy but sorrow." Why do you think that humor and sorrow go hand-in-hand?

## ANALYZING LITERATURE

### Understanding Point of View

**Point of view** is the angle of vision from which a story is told. In "The Secret Life of Walter Mitty" the author takes you inside the mind of Walter Mitty and tells the story from his point of view. By telling a story from the point of view of one character, the author encourages you to sympathize with this character. You know what this character thinks or feels in a way you never can with people in real life. Because of this, you come to understand the character very well—often better than the other characters in the story do.

1. How do you come to feel about Walter Mitty as a result of his seeing the world through his eyes?
2. Why is it especially effective for this story to be told from the point of view of Walter Mitty?
3. How would the story have been different if Mrs. Mitty had told it?

*10    Short Stories*

## CRITICAL THINKING AND READING

### Identifying Wishful Thinking

**Wishful thinking** is a way of escaping from unpleasant situations into a more appealing world. The kinds of situations in which characters imagine themselves sometimes tell more about them than their words or actions do. If a character is meek and retiring like Walter Mitty is, his wishful thinking can reveal things about him that he otherwise tries to conceal.

Explain what wish or desire each of the following daydreams reveals.
1. " 'I've read your book on streptothricosis,' said Pritchard-Mitford, shaking hands. 'A brilliant performance, sir.' "
2. "A woman's scream rose above the bedlam and suddenly a lovely, dark-haired girl was in Walter Mitty's arms."
3. "Without rising from his chair, Mitty let the man have it on the point of the chin."

## UNDERSTANDING LANGUAGE

### Finding Latin Roots

Each of the following words from the story comes from Latin. Look up each word in the dictionary to see what its Latin root means. Explain how the meaning of the Latin root relates to the meaning of the English word.
1. derisive  2. ignition  3. insinuate  4. revolving

## THINKING AND WRITING

### Continuing the Story

Make up another daydream for Walter Mitty. First brainstorm to list possible situations in which Mitty might find himself. Remember that for Walter Mitty, at least in his daydreams, anything is possible! Then select one situation you would like to develop. Write the first draft of an episode relating this event. Whatever adventure you create, try to tell it in a humorous way, as Thurber does. When you revise your episode, make sure it is true to Mitty's personaiity. Proofread your episode.

**THINKING AND WRITING** For help with this assignment students can refer to Lesson 17, "Writing a Short Story," in the Handbook of Writing About Literature.

**Publishing Student Writing** You might divide the class into small groups and have students read their episodes to fellow group members. Then you can have each group select one episode to perform for the class as a radio play.

# Plot

**ANGST**
*Edvard Munch*
Three Lions

## Humanities Note

Fine Art, *Angst*, 1894, Edvard Munch. Edvard Munch (1863–1944), was a Norwegian painter and graphic artist who attended the School of Arts and Crafts in Oslo and studied in Paris. Munch's unique and complex psychological style is considered to be one of the first manifestations of Expressionism, the non-objective use of symbols, stylizations, and so on, to give objective expression to emotion and inner experience. The power of Munch's art was based on his obsession with depression, fear, and death. His exploration of these morbid subjects lent expressive weight to his art.

*Angst*, or "Anxiety," along with other paintings, was prepared by Munch as a motif for use in a series of large decorative murals entitled "The Frieze of Life." The frozen, haunted figures in this painting seem to be gripped with the overwhelming emotion of fear. The sky, caught by the forces of nature, swirls and twists above them, adding to the tension of the scene.

**More About the Author** Richard Connell started to earn money for his writing when he was ten years old, receiving ten cents for each baseball story he covered. He worked as city editor of a local newspaper when he was sixteen and in college he was editor of the school newspaper and magazine. Ask students how job experience gained when growing up is a good way to learn about a profession.

**Literary Focus** You might want to explain to students that the climax is usually the most dramatic point in the story. Tell students that when they reach this point, they will feel that the conflict is about to be resolved.

**Look For** Ask students to identify the main elements of the plot as they read—conflict, climax, and resolution.

**Writing/Prior Knowledge** Before students begin writing, have them discuss two meanings of the word *game* that might be relevant—"contest" and "quarry."

**Vocabulary** Have less advanced students work in pairs to learn the meanings and pronunciations of the vocabulary words.

**Spelling Tip** Students may have trouble spelling the /sk/ sound in *grotesque.* Point out that this sound is spelled by *sque* not only in *grotesque* but also in *brusquely* (page 56).

## The Most Dangerous Game

**Richard Connell** (1893–1949) was born in Dutchess County, New York. His love of writing began early: At ten, he was covering basketball games for his father's newspaper and at sixteen he was editing the paper. After serving in World War I, Connell lived in various cities in Europe and the United States, finally settling in Beverly Hills, California. The author of more than a hundred short stories, Connell drew upon his firsthand knowledge of life-and-death conflict when he wrote his gripping masterpiece—"The Most Dangerous Game."

**Plot**

The **plot** of a story is made up of a series of related events that include the conflict, the climax, and the resolution. The conflict is a struggle between opposing people or forces. The climax is the turning point in the story, the point at which the conflict comes to a head. The resolution shows how the situation turns out and ties up loose ends. At the beginning of the story, the author may provide background information, called exposition, which sets the scene for the conflict. As the story proceeds, this information may introduce complications that keep the plot from moving too smoothly toward its resolution.

**Look For**

In this action-packed story, a world-famous hunter falls off a ship near the coast of a mysterious island. As you read, look for what happens when the hunter becomes the hunted.

**Writing**

What do you think will turn out to be "the most dangerous game"? Freewrite, exploring your answer.

**Vocabulary**

Knowing the following words will help you as you read "The Most Dangerous Game."

**palpable** (pal′ pə b'l) *adj.*: Able to be touched or felt (p. 13)

**indolently** (in′ də lənt lē) *adv.*: Lazily, idly (p. 14)

**bizarre** (bi zär′) *adj.*: Odd in appearance (p. 17)

**naive** (nä ēv′) *adj.*: Unsophisticated (p. 22)

**scruples** (skrōō′ p'lz) *n.*: Misgivings about something one feels is wrong (p. 22)

**blandly** (bland′ lē) *adv.*: In a mild and soothing manner (p. 22)

**grotesque** (grō tesk′) *adj.*: Having a fantastic design (p. 24)

**futile** (fyōōt′ 'l) *adj.*: Useless; hopeless (p. 26)

12    Short Stories

---

1 To understand plot in a short story
2 To analyze the sequence of events in a short story
3 To write about plot

**Teaching Portfolio**
Teacher Backup, p. 19
Grammar in Action Worksheets, *Using Dashes,* p. 22; *Writing Suspense,* p. 24
Usage and Mechanics Worksheet, p. 26
Vocabulary Check, p. 27
Analyzing Literature Worksheet, *Understanding Plot,* p. 29

Critical Thinking and Reading Worksheet, *Analyzing Sequence in a Story,* p. 30
Selection Test, p. 31
Art Transparency 1: *Evening by the Sea,* by Karl Schmidt-Rottluff

# The Most Dangerous Game

### Richard Connell

"Off there to the right—somewhere—is a large island," said Whitney. "It's rather a mystery—"

"What island is it?" Rainsford asked.

"The old charts call it 'Ship-Trap Island,'" Whitney replied. "A suggestive name, isn't it? Sailors have a curious dread of the place. I don't know why. Some superstition—"

"Can't see it," remarked Rainsford, trying to peer through the dank tropical night that was palpable as it pressed its thick warm blackness in upon the yacht.

"You've good eyes," said Whitney, with a laugh, "and I've seen you pick off a moose moving in the brown fall bush at four hundred yards, but even you can't see four miles or so through a moonless Caribbean[1] night."

"Not four yards," admitted Rainsford. "Ugh! It's like moist black velvet."

"It will be light in Rio," promised Whitney. "We should make it in a few days. I hope the jaguar guns have come from Purdey's. We should have some good hunting up the Amazon.[2] Great sport, hunting."

"The best sport in the world," agreed Rainsford.

"For the hunter," amended Whitney. "Not for the jaguar."

"Don't talk rot, Whitney," said Rainsford. "You're a big-game hunter, not a philosopher. Who cares how a jaguar feels?"

"Perhaps the jaguar does," observed Whitney.

"Bah! They've no understanding."

"Even so, I rather think they understand one thing—fear. The fear of pain and the fear of death."

"Nonsense," laughed Rainsford. "This hot weather is making you soft, Whitney. Be a realist. The world is made up of two classes—the hunters and the huntees. Luckily, you and I are the hunters. Do you think we've passed that island yet?"

"I can't tell in the dark. I hope so."

"Why?" asked Rainsford.

"The place has a reputation—a bad one."

"Cannibals?" suggested Rainsford.

"Hardly. Even cannibals wouldn't live in such a God-forsaken place. But it's gotten into sailor lore, somehow. Didn't you notice that the crew's nerves seemed a bit jumpy today?"

"They were a bit strange, now you mention it. Even Captain Nielsen—"

"Yes, even that tough-minded old Swede, who'd go up to the devil himself and ask him for a light. Those fishy blue eyes held a look I never saw there before. All I could get out of him was: 'This place has an evil name among sea-faring men, sir.' Then he said to me, very gravely: 'Don't you feel anything?'— as if the air about us was actually poisonous.

---

**1. Caribbean** (kar′ ə bē′ ən): The Caribbean Sea, a part of the Atlantic Ocean bounded by South America, Central America, and the West Indies.

**2. Amazon** (am′ ə zän′): A large river in South America.

*The Most Dangerous Game* 13

## Presentation

**Motivation/Prior Knowledge** You might want to ask students to name the most dangerous sport they can imagine. Have them compare and contrast the dangers of the sports that are suggested. Then tell them that they will read about an even riskier activity.

**Master Teacher Note** Review with students the meaning of irony and an ironic situation. Tell them that there is a central irony in the plot of this story.

**Thematic Idea** Other selections that focus on a time for courage are "The Pen of My Aunt," page 239; "A Lincoln Preface," page 439; the excerpt from *Kon-Tiki*, page 465; and the excerpts from the *Odyssey*, page 681.

**Purpose-Setting Question** What is the meaning of the title?

1 **Enrichment** Discuss the fact that ships and planes have sometimes disappeared mysteriously. Cite the example of the Bermuda Triangle, whose vertices touch Bermuda, Miami, and Puerto Rico. What might account for increased dangers in that area?

2 **Discussion** Whitney claims animals understand fear—the fear of death and the fear of pain. Does Rainsford agree? Ask students with whom they agree or disagree.

**3 Discussion** Compare Whitney's feelings upon passing the island to Rainsford's statement about superstition.

**4 Discussion** Whitney believes that sailors possess an "extra sense" to detect danger. Do you think that this notion might be true?

**5 Reading Strategy** Up to this point, the descriptions of the island and the atmosphere should suggest a particular mood. Given that mood, predict what might happen next.

Now, you mustn't laugh when I tell you this—I did feel something like a sudden chill.

"There was no breeze. The sea was as flat as a plate-glass window. We were drawing near the island then. What I felt was a—a mental chill; a sort of sudden dread."

"Pure imagination," said Rainsford. "One superstitious sailor can taint the whole ship's company with his fear."

"Maybe. But sometimes I think sailors have an extra sense that tells them when they are in danger. Sometimes I think evil is a tangible thing—with wave lengths, just as sound and light have. An evil place can, so to speak, broadcast vibrations of evil. Anyhow, I'm glad we're getting out of this zone. Well, I think I'll turn in now, Rainsford."

"I'm not sleepy," said Rainsford. "I'm going to smoke another pipe on the after deck."

"Good night, then, Rainsford. See you at breakfast."

"Right. Good night, Whitney."

There was no sound in the night as Rainsford sat there, but the muffled throb of the engine that drove the yacht swiftly through the darkness, and the swish and ripple of the wash of the propeller.

Rainsford, reclining in a steamer chair, indolently puffed on his favorite brier. The sensuous drowsiness of the night was on him. "It's so dark," he thought, "that I could sleep without closing my eyes; the night would be my eyelids—"

An abrupt sound startled him. Off to the right he heard it, and his ears, expert in such matters, could not be mistaken. Again he heard the sound, and again. Somewhere, off in the blackness, someone had fired a gun three times.

Rainsford sprang up and moved quickly to the rail, mystified. He strained his eyes in the direction from which the reports had

*14   Short Stories*

come, but it was like trying to see through a blanket. He leaped upon the rail and balanced himself there, to get greater elevation; his pipe, striking a rope, was knocked from his mouth. He lunged for it; a short, hoarse cry came from his lips as he realized he had reached too far and had lost his balance. The cry was pinched off short as the blood-warm waters of the Caribbean Sea closed over his head.

## Grammar in Action

Skillful writers can use a single **dash** to emphasize a particular word or phrase, or to indicate a summary statement. A pair of dashes can set off a dramatic interrupting idea.

Notice how Richard Connell uses dashes in the following sentences:

Even so, I rather think they understand one thing—fear.
The world is made up of two classes—the hunters and the huntees.

Ten minutes of determined effort brought another sound to his ears—the most welcome he had ever heard—the muttering and growling of the sea breaking on a rocky shore.

In these examples, Connell takes full advantage of the possibilities of the dash. The slight pause that the dash introduces in the first two examples gives added emphasis to the following word or phrase. In the third example, the phrase set off by dashes is extremely dramatic.

**Student Activity 1.** Identify three additional sentences from "The Most Dangerous Game" in which Connell uses dashes. For each

He struggled up to the surface and tried to cry out, but the wash from the speeding yacht slapped him in the face and the salt water in his open mouth made him gag and strangle. Desperately he struck out with strong strokes after the receding lights of the yacht, but he stopped before he had swum fifty feet. A certain cool-headedness had come to him; it was not the first time he had been in a tight place. There was a chance that his cries could be heard by someone aboard the yacht, but that chance was slender, and grew more slender as the yacht raced on. He wrestled himself out of his clothes, and shouted with all his power. The lights of the yacht became faint and ever-vanishing fireflies; then they were blotted out entirely by the night.

6 **Discussion** How does Rainsford feel after falling overboard? What does he decide to do?

15

sentence, explain the purpose of the dash or dashes. Also, tell why this punctuation mark is or is not effective in each sentence.

**Student Activity 2.** Using Connell's sentences as models, write three original sentences in which dashes emphasize a word or phrase, indicate a summary, or set off a dramatic interruption.

**7 Discussion** This section describing Rainsford's struggle demonstrates his strength and will to survive. Which phrases illustrate these qualities?

**8 Discussion** Rainsford's examination of the area of crushed jungle leads him to several conclusions. What are they?

Rainsford remembered the shots. They had come from the right, and doggedly he swam in that direction, swimming with slow, deliberate strokes, conserving his strength. For a seemingly endless time he fought the sea. He began to count his strokes; he could do possibly a hundred more and then—

Rainsford heard a sound. It came out of the darkness, a high screaming sound, the sound of an animal in an extremity of anguish and terror.

He did not recognize the animal that made the sound; he did not try to; with fresh vitality he swam toward the sound. He heard it again; then it was cut short by another noise, crisp, staccato.

"Pistol shot," muttered Rainsford, swimming on.

Ten minutes of determined effort brought another sound to his ears—the most welcome he had ever heard—the muttering and growling of the sea breaking on a rocky shore. He was almost on the rocks before he saw them; on a night less calm he would have been shattered against them. With his remaining strength he dragged himself from the swirling waters. Jagged crags appeared to jut into the opaqueness, he forced himself upward, hand over hand. Gasping, his hands raw, he reached a flat place at the top. Dense jungle came down to the very edge of the cliffs. What perils that tangle of trees and underbrush might hold for him did not concern Rainsford just then. All he knew was that he was safe from his enemy, the sea, and that utter weariness was on him. He flung himself down at the jungle edge and tumbled headlong into the deepest sleep of his life.

When he opened his eyes he knew from the position of the sun that it was late in the afternoon. Sleep had given him new vigor; a sharp hunger was picking at him. He looked about him, almost cheerfully.

"Where there are pistol shots, there are men. Where there are men, there is food," he thought. But what kind of men, he wondered, in so forbidding a place? An unbroken front of snarled and ragged jungle fringed the shore.

He saw no sign of a trail through the closely knit web of weeds and trees; it was easier to go along the shore, and Rainsford floundered along by the water. Not far from where he had landed, he stopped.

Some wounded thing, by the evidence a large animal, had thrashed about in the underbrush; the jungle weeds were crushed down and the moss was lacerated; one patch of weeds was stained crimson. A small, glittering object not far away caught Rainsford's eye and he picked it up. It was an empty cartridge.

"A twenty-two," he remarked. "That's odd. It must have been a fairly large animal too. The hunter had his nerve with him to tackle it with a light gun. It's clear that the brute put up a fight. I suppose the first three shots I heard was when the hunter flushed his quarry[3] and wounded it. The last shot was when he trailed it here and finished it."

He examined the ground closely and found what he had hoped to find—the print of hunting boots. They pointed along the cliff in the direction he had been going. Eagerly he hurried along, now slipping on a rotten log or a loose stone, but making headway; night was beginning to settle down on the island.

Bleak darkness was blacking out the sea and jungle when Rainsford sighted the lights. He came upon them as he turned a

---

**3. flushed his quarry** (kwôr′ ē): Drove his prey into the open.

crook in the coast line, and his first thought was that he had come upon a village, for there were many lights. But as he forged along he saw to his great astonishment that all the lights were in one enormous building—a lofty structure with pointed towers plunging upward into the gloom. His eyes made out the shadowy outlines of a palatial château;[4] it was set on a high bluff, and on three sides of it cliffs dived down to where the sea licked greedy lips in the shadows.

"Mirage," thought Rainsford. But it was no mirage, he found, when he opened the tall spiked iron gate. The stone steps were real enough; the massive door with a leering gargoyle[5] for a knocker was real enough; yet about it all hung an air of unreality.

He lifted the knocker, and it creaked up stiffly, as if it had never before been used. He let it fall, and it startled him with its booming loudness. He thought he heard steps within; the door remained closed. Again Rainsford lifted the heavy knocker, and let it fall. The door opened then, opened as suddenly as if it were on a spring, and Rainsford stood blinking in the river of glaring gold light that poured out. The first thing Rainsford's eyes discerned was the largest man Rainsford had ever seen—a gigantic creature, solidly made and black-bearded to the waist. In his hand the man held a long-barreled revolver, and he was pointing it straight at Rainsford's heart.

Out of the snarl of beard two small eyes regarded Rainsford.

"Don't be alarmed," said Rainsford, with a smile which he hoped was disarming. "I'm no robber. I fell off a yacht. My name is Sanger Rainsford of New York City."

The menacing look in the eyes did not change. The revolver pointed as rigidly as if the giant were a statue. He gave no sign that he understood Rainsford's words, or that he had even heard them. He was dressed in uniform, a black uniform trimmed with gray astrakhan.[6]

"I'm Sanger Rainsford of New York," Rainsford began again. "I fell off a yacht. I am hungry."

The man's only answer was to raise with his thumb the hammer of his revolver. Then Rainsford saw the man's free hand go to his forehead in a military salute, and he saw him click his heels together and stand at attention. Another man was coming down the broad marble steps, an erect, slender man in evening clothes. He advanced to Rainsford and held out his hand.

In a cultivated voice marked by a slight accent that gave it added precision and deliberateness, he said: "It is a very great pleasure and honor to welcome Mr. Sanger Rainsford, the celebrated hunter, to my home."

Automatically Rainsford shook the man's hand.

"I've read your book about hunting snow leopards in Tibet, you see," explained the man. "I am General Zaroff."

Rainsford's first impression was that the man was singularly handsome; his second was that there was an original, almost bizarre quality about the general's face. He was a tall man past middle age, for his hair was a vivid white; but his thick eyebrows and pointed military mustache were as black as the night from which Rainsford had come. His eyes, too, were black and very bright. He had high cheek bones, a sharp-cut nose, a

---

**4. palatial château** (pə lā′ shəl s̸ha tō′): A mansion as luxurious as a palace.
**5. gargoyle** (gär′ goil) n.: A strange and distorted animal form projecting from a building.

**6. astrakhan** (as′ trə kan′) n.: Fur made from young lambs.

---

**9 Enrichment** The Gothic tradition in literature involves the supernatural, mystery, and horror. A well-known novel written in the tradition is *Frankenstein,* by Mary Shelley. Many of the stories are set in medieval castles or large, old, dark houses.

**10 Discussion** What does the writer mean by the phrase "an air of unreality"?

**11 Critical Thinking and Reading** The author creates a sense of drama in this section. Which words or phrases help do this?

**12 Reading Strategy** Predict who the man in the evening clothes might be. Is Rainsford safe with him?

**13 Discussion** Rainsford has two impressions of General Zaroff. How does the general's appearance influence Rainsford's opinion of him?

**14 Discussion** The general says that Ivan is ". . . like all his race, a bit of a savage." He adds that he and Ivan are of the same race. What does this indicate about the general?

**15 Critical Thinking and Reading** From the description of the dining room, what conclusions can you draw about the general's personality?

**16 Discussion** Why do you think the general is appraising Rainsford?

spare, dark face, the face of a man used to giving orders, the face of an aristocrat. Turning to the giant in uniform, the general made a sign. The giant put away his pistol, saluted, withdrew.

"Ivan is an incredibly strong fellow," remarked the general, "but he has the misfortune to be deaf and dumb. A simple fellow, but, I'm afraid, like all his race, a bit of a savage."

"Is he Russian?"

"He is a Cossack,"[7] said the general, and his smile showed red lips and pointed teeth. "So am I."

"Come," he said, "we shouldn't be chatting here. We can talk later. Now you want clothes, food, rest. You shall have them. This is a most restful spot."

Ivan had reappeared, and the general spoke to him with lips that moved but gave forth no sound.

"Follow Ivan, if you please, Mr. Rainsford," said the general. "I was about to have my dinner when you came. I'll wait for you. You'll find that my clothes will fit you, I think."

It was to a huge, beam-ceilinged bedroom with a canopied bed big enough for six men that Rainsford followed the silent giant. Ivan laid out an evening suit, and Rainsford, as he put it on, noticed that it came from a London tailor who ordinarily cut and sewed for none below the rank of duke.

The dining room to which Ivan conducted him was in many ways remarkable. There was a medieval magnificence about it; it suggested a baronial hall of feudal times with its oaken panels, its high ceiling, its vast refectory table where twoscore men

could sit down to eat. About the hall were the mounted heads of many animals—lions, tigers, elephants, moose, bears; larger or more perfect specimens Rainsford had never seen. At the great table the general was sitting, alone.

"You'll have a cocktail, Mr. Rainsford," he suggested. The cocktail was surpassingly good; and, Rainsford noted, the table appointments were of the finest—the linen, the crystal, the silver, the china.

They were eating *borsch*, the rich, red soup with whipped cream so dear to Russian palates. Half apologetically General Zaroff said: "We do our best to preserve the amenities of civilization here. Please forgive any lapses. We are well off the beaten track, you know. Do you think the champagne has suffered from its long ocean trip?"

"Not in the least," declared Rainsford. He was finding the general a most thoughtful and affable host, a true cosmopolite.[8] But there was one small trait of the general's that made Rainsford uncomfortable. Whenever he looked up from his plate he found the general studying him, appraising him narrowly.

"Perhaps," said General Zaroff, "you were surprised that I recognized your name. You see, I read all books on hunting published in English, French, and Russian. I have but one passion in my life, Mr. Rainsford, and it is the hunt."

"You have some wonderful heads here," said Rainsford as he ate a particularly well cooked filet mignon. "That Cape buffalo is the largest I ever saw."

"Oh, that fellow. Yes, he was a monster."

"Did he charge you?"

"Hurled me against a tree," said the gen-

---

**7. Cossack** (käs′ ak): A member of a people from southern Russia, famous for their fierceness.

**8. cosmopolite** (käz mäp′ ə līt′) *n.*: A person at home in all parts of the world.

eral. "Fractured my skull. But I got the brute."

"I've always thought," said Rainsford, "that the Cape buffalo is the most dangerous of all big game."

For a moment the general did not reply; he was smiling his curious red-lipped smile. Then he said slowly: "No. You are wrong, sir. The Cape buffalo is not the most dangerous big game." He sipped his wine. "Here in my preserve on this island," he said in the same slow tone, "I hunt more dangerous game."

Rainsford expressed his surprise. "Is there big game on this island?"

The general nodded. "The biggest."

"Really?"

"Oh, it isn't here naturally, of course. I have to stock the island."

"What have you imported, general?" Rainsford asked. "Tigers?"

The general smiled. "No," he said. "Hunting tigers ceased to interest me some years ago. I exhausted their possibilities, you see. No thrill left in tigers, no real danger. I live for danger, Mr. Rainsford."

The general took from his pocket a gold cigarette case and offered his guest a long black cigarette with a silver tip; it was perfumed and gave off a smell like incense.

"We will have some capital hunting, you and I," said the general. "I shall be most glad to have your society."

"But what game—" began Rainsford.

"I'll tell you," said the general. "You will be amused, I know. I think I may say, in all modesty, that I have done a rare thing. I have invented a new sensation. May I pour you another glass of port, Mr. Rainsford?"

"Thank you, general."

The general filled both glasses, and said: "God makes some men poets. Some He makes kings, some beggars. Me He made a hunter. My hand was made for the trigger, my father said. He was a very rich man with a quarter of a million acres in the Crimea,[9] and he was an ardent sportsman. When I was only five years old he gave me a little gun, specially made in Moscow for me, to shoot sparrows with. When I shot some of his prize turkeys with it, he did not punish me; he complimented me on my marksmanship. I killed my first bear in the Caucasus[10] when I was ten. My whole life has been one prolonged hunt. I went into the army—it was expected of noblemen's sons—and for a time commanded a division of Cossack cavalry, but my real interest was always the hunt. I have hunted every kind of game in every land. It would be impossible for me to tell you how many animals I have killed."

The general puffed at his cigarette.

"After the debacle[11] in Russia I left the country, for it was imprudent for an officer of the Czar to stay there. Many noble Russians lost everything. I, luckily, had invested heavily in American securities, so I shall never have to open a tea room in Monte Carlo or drive a taxi in Paris. Naturally, I continued to hunt—grizzlies in your Rockies, crocodiles in the Ganges, rhinoceroses in East Africa. It was in Africa that the Cape buffalo hit me and laid me up for six months. As soon as I recovered I started for the Amazon to hunt jaguars, for I had heard they were unusually cunning. They weren't." The Cossack sighed. "They were no match at all for a hunter with his wits about him, and a high-powered rifle. I was bitterly disappointed. I was lying in my tent with a split-

---

**9. Crimea** (krī mē′ ə): A region in southwestern Russia on the Black Sea.
**10. Caucasus** (kô′ kə səs): A mountain range in southern Russia.
**11. debacle** (di bäk′ 'l) n.: Bad defeat; Zaroff is referring to the Russian Revolution of 1917, a defeat for upper-class Russians like himself.

*The Most Dangerous Game* 19

**17 Discussion** How does Zaroff's reply create suspense?

**18 Reading Strategy** Have students summarize the important events to this point. Are there any clues that indicate what the "most dangerous game" might be?

**19 Discussion** How have the general's earlier experiences influenced his attitude toward hunting?

## Humanities Note

Illustration, *Hat, Knife and Gun in Woods,* by David Mann. Mann (1940-    ), who was born in Kansas City, Missouri, now lives in California. He has painted since he was a child under the guidance of his father, who was also an artist. *Hat, Knife and Gun in Woods* was done as an illustration for a book cover. In addition to being a book cover illustrator, Mann is an artist for *Easy Rider* magazine.

You might use the following questions for discussion:

1. What is the mood of the painting? How does the artist create the mood?
2. Explain why this is an effective and appropriate illustration for this story.

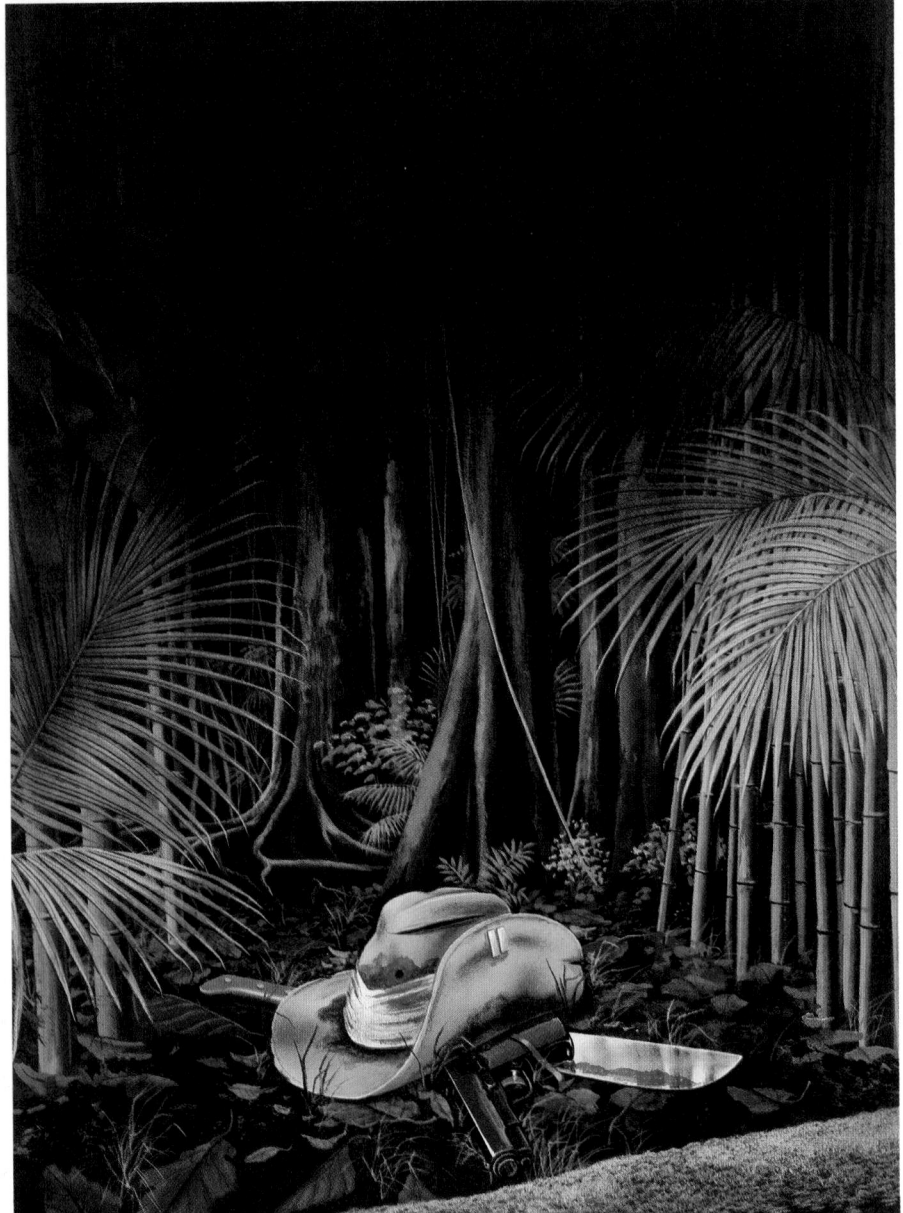

HAT, KNIFE, AND GUN IN WOODS
*David Mann*
*Sal Barracca & Associates*

ting headache one night when a terrible thought pushed its way into my mind. Hunting was beginning to bore me! And hunting, remember, had been my life. I have heard that in America business men often go to pieces when they give up the business that has been their life."

"Yes, that's so," said Rainsford.

The general smiled. "I had no wish to go to pieces," he said. "I must do something. Now, mine is an analytical mind, Mr. Rainsford. Doubtless that is why I enjoy the problems of the chase."

"No doubt, General Zaroff."

"So," continued the general, "I asked myself why the hunt no longer fascinated me. You are much younger than I am, Mr. Rainsford, and have not hunted as much, but you perhaps can guess the answer."

"What was it?"

"Simply this: hunting had ceased to be what you call 'a sporting proposition.' It had become too easy. I always got my quarry. Always. There is no greater bore than perfection."

The general lit a fresh cigarette.

"No animal had a chance with me any more. That is no boast; it is a mathematical certainty. The animal had nothing but his legs and his instinct. Instinct is no match for reason. When I thought of this it was a tragic moment for me, I can tell you."

Rainsford leaned across the table, absorbed in what his host was saying.

"It came to me as an inspiration what I must do," the general went on.

"And that was?"

The general smiled the quiet smile of one who has faced an obstacle and surmounted it with success. "I had to invent a new animal to hunt," he said.

"A new animal? You're joking."

"Not at all," said the general. "I never joke about hunting. I needed a new animal. I found one. So I bought this island, built this house, and here I do my hunting. The island is perfect for my purposes—there are jungles with a maze of trails in them, hills, swamps—"

"But the animal, General Zaroff?"

"Oh," said the general, "it supplies me with the most exciting hunting in the world. No other hunting compares with it for an instant. Every day I hunt, and I never grow bored now, for I have a quarry with which I can match my wits."

Rainsford's bewilderment showed in his face.

"I wanted the ideal animal to hunt," explained the general. "So I said: 'What are the attributes of an ideal quarry?' And the answer was, of course: 'It must have courage, cunning, and, above all, it must be able to reason.' "

"But no animal can reason," objected Rainsford.

"My dear fellow," said the general, "there is one that can."

"But you can't mean—" gasped Rainsford.

"And why not?"

"I can't believe you are serious, General Zaroff. This is a grisly joke."

"Why should I not be serious? I am speaking of hunting."

"Hunting? General Zaroff, what you speak of is murder."

The general laughed with entire good nature. He regarded Rainsford quizzically. "I refuse to believe that so modern and civilized a young man as you seem to be harbors romantic ideas about the value of human life. Surely your experiences in the war—"

"Did not make me condone cold-blooded murder," finished Rainsford stiffly.

Laughter shook the general. "How extraordinarily droll you are!" he said. "One

*The Most Dangerous Game* 21

20 **Discussion** Why did the general look for a more cunning animal to hunt? What does Zaroff fear?

21 **Discussion** How does the general's statement about the hunt add to the drama and suspense of the story?

22 **Discussion** What does the general mean by his assertion that "Instinct is no match for reason"? Why did that thought mark a tragic moment for him?

23 **Discussion** What does Rainsford think the general means by "a new animal"?

24 **Discussion** Has Rainsford guessed what the "new animal" is?

25 **Discussion** What animal is the general talking about?

26 **Critical Thinking and Reading** When the general refers to Rainsford's experiences in the war, what point is he making?

**27 Discussion** How does this im-age illustrate what the general means?

**28 Discussion** Compare the general's assertion that "Life is for the strong. . . ." with Rainsford's statement, at the beginning of the story, that "The world is made up of two classes—the hunters and the huntees." How are these two statements similar? Yet how do the two men differ?

**29 Discussion** What is ironic about General Zaroff's statement that he treats his "visitors with every consideration"?

does not expect nowadays to find a young man of the educated class, even in America, with such a naive, and, if I may say so, mid-Victorian point of view.[12] It's like finding a snuff-box in a limousine. Ah, well, doubtless you had Puritan ancestors. So many Americans appear to have had. I'll wager you'll forget your notions when you go hunting with me. You've a genuine new thrill in store for you, Mr. Rainsford."

"Thank you, I'm a hunter, not a murderer."

"Dear me," said the general, quite unruffled, "again that unpleasant word. But I think I can show you that your scruples are quite ill founded."

"Yes?"

"Life is for the strong, to be lived by the strong, and, if need be, taken by the strong. The weak of the world were put here to give the strong pleasure. I am strong. Why should I not use my gift? If I wish to hunt, why should I not? I hunt the scum of the earth—sailors from tramp ships—lascars,[13] blacks, Chinese, whites, mongrels—a thoroughbred horse or hound is worth more than a score of them."

"But they are men," said Rainsford hotly.

"Precisely," said the general. "That is why I use them. It gives me pleasure. They can reason, after a fashion. So they are dangerous."

"But where do you get them?"

The general's left eyelid fluttered down in a wink. "This island is called Ship-Trap," he answered. "Sometimes an angry god of the high seas sends them to me. Sometimes, when Providence is not so kind, I help Providence a bit. Come to the window with me."

12. **mid-Victorian point of view:** A point of view emphasizing proper behavior and associated with the time of Queen Victoria of England (1819–1901).
13. **lascars** (lăs′ kərz)*n.*: Oriental sailors, especially natives of India.

Rainsford went to the window and looked out toward the sea.

"Watch! Out there!" exclaimed the general, pointing into the night. Rainsford's eyes saw only blackness, and then, as the general pressed a button, far out to sea Rainsford saw the flash of lights.

The general chuckled. "They indicate a channel," he said, "where there's none: giant rocks with razor edges crouch like a sea monster with wide-open jaws. They can crush a ship as easily as I crush this nut." He dropped a walnut on the hardwood floor and brought his heel grinding down on it. "Oh, yes," he said, casually, as if in answer to a question, "I have electricity. We try to be civilized here."

"Civilized? And you shoot down men?"

A trace of anger was in the general's black eyes, but it was there for but a second, and he said, in his most pleasant manner: "Dear me, what a righteous young man you are! I assure you I do not do the thing you suggest. That would be barbarous. I treat these visitors with every consideration. They get plenty of good food and exercise. They get into splendid physical condition. You shall see for yourself tomorrow."

"What do you mean?"

"We'll visit my training school," smiled the general. "It's in the cellar. I have about a dozen pupils down there now. They're from the Spanish bark San Lucar that had the bad luck to go on the rocks out there. A very inferior lot, I regret to say. Poor specimens and more accustomed to the deck than to the jungle."

He raised his hand, and Ivan, who served as waiter, brought thick Turkish coffee. Rainsford, with an effort, held his tongue in check.

"It's a game, you see," pursued the general blandly. "I suggest to one of them that we go hunting. I give him a supply of food

**PEERING THROUGH THE JUNGLE**
Larry Noble

## Humanities Note

Illustration, *Peering Through the Jungle,* 1987, by Larry Noble. Noble (1948-    ), who was born in Tampa, Florida, now lives in Crestline, California. For many years Noble has been a free-lance artist for movie posters, advertising campaigns, book covers, and magazine covers, including *Forbes, World Tennis, Field and Stream,* and *Children's Digest.* He has done the cover illustration for and has been featured in *American Artists* magazine and *Step by Step* magazine. *Peeping Through the Jungle* was originally the book cover for *Life During Wartime.*

   You might use the following questions for discussion:
1. What emotions do you see in this soldier's gaze that might be the emotions of Sanger Rainsford in the story?
2. What similarities are there between Rainsford and a soldier of war? Why is this an appropriate illustration for the story? Explain.
3. Does this illustration reflect the setting of "The Most Dangerous Game"? Explain.

24

and an excellent hunting knife. I give him three hours' start. I am to follow, armed only with a pistol of the smallest caliber and range. If my quarry eludes me for three whole days, he wins the game. If I find him"—the general smiled—"he loses."

"Suppose he refuses to be hunted?"

"Oh," said the general, "I give him his option, of course. He need not play the game if he doesn't wish to. If he does not wish to hunt, I turn him over to Ivan. Ivan once had the honor of serving as official knouter[14] to the Great White Czar, and he has his own ideas of sport. Invariably, Mr. Rainsford, invariably they choose the hunt."

"And if they win?"

The smile on the general's face widened. "To date I have not lost," he said.

Then he added, hastily: "I don't wish you to think me a braggart, Mr. Rainsford. Many of them afford only the most elementary sort of problem. Occasionally I strike a tartar.[15] One almost did win. I eventually had to use the dogs."

"The dogs?"

"This way, please. I'll show you."

**30** The general steered Rainsford to a window. The lights from the windows sent a flickering illumination that made grotesque patterns on the courtyard below, and Rainsford could see moving about there a dozen or so huge black shapes; as they turned toward him, their eyes glittered greenly.

**31** "A rather good lot, I think," observed the general. "They are let out at seven every night. If anyone should try to get into my house—or out of it—something extremely re-

---

**14. knouter** (nout′ ər) *n*.: Someone who beats criminals with a leather whip, or knout.
**15. tartar** (tär′ tər) *n*.: A stubborn, violent person.

---

grettable would occur to him." He hummed a snatch of song from the Folies Bergère.[16]

"And now," said the general, "I want to show you my new collection of heads. Will you come with me to the library?"

"I hope," said Rainsford, "that you will excuse me tonight, General Zaroff. I'm really not feeling at all well."

"Ah, indeed?" the general inquired solicitously. "Well, I suppose that's only natural, after your long swim. You need a good, restful night's sleep. Tomorrow you'll feel like a new man, I'll wager. Then we'll hunt, eh? I've one rather promising prospect—"

Rainsford was hurrying from the room.

"Sorry you can't go with me tonight," called the general. "I expect rather fair sport—a big, strong black. He looks resourceful—Well, good night, Mr. Rainsford; I hope you have a good night's rest."

**32** The bed was good, and the pajamas of the softest silk, and he was tired in every fiber of his being, but nevertheless Rainsford could not quiet his brain with the opiate of sleep. He lay, eyes wide open. Once he thought he heard stealthy steps in the corridor outside his room. He sought to throw open the door; it would not open. He went to the window and looked out. His room was high up in one of the towers. The lights of the château were out now, and it was dark and silent, but there was a fragment of sallow moon, and by its wan light he could see, dimly, the courtyard; there, weaving in and out in the pattern of shadow, were black, noiseless forms; the hounds heard him at the window and looked up, expectantly, with their green eyes. Rainsford went back to the bed and lay down. By many methods he tried to put himself to sleep. He had achieved a

---

**16. Folies Bergère** (fô lē  ber zhär′): A musical theater in Paris.

---

## Grammar in Action

**Suspense** is that quality in a work of literature that makes us read on to see what will happen next. Writers create suspense with details that arouse curiosity in the reader and details that foreshadow, or hint at, what is to come. Richard Connell begins to build suspense in the first paragraphs of "The Most Dangerous Game":

"Off there to the right—somewhere—is a large island," said Whitney. "It's rather a mystery—"

"What island is it?" Rainsford asked.

"The old charts call it 'Ship-Trap Island,'" Whitney replied. A suggestive name, isn't it? Sailors have a curious dread of the place. I don't know why. Some superstition—"

Notice that in the passage, Whitney twice brings up the mystery that surrounds the island and both times lets his thoughts trail off before he says anything specific about this mystery. Additional suspense is created by the island's name.

Connell continues to use details to build suspense. What details can you find in this passage?

[Rainsford] sought to throw open the door; it would not open. He went to the window and looked out. His room was

---

**30 Discussion** Connell uses several descriptions in this paragraph. How do they add to the mood and tone of the story?

**31 Literary Focus** What is ironic about the general humming a tune from the Folies Bergère?

**32 Discussion** What mood does this passage call up? Which words and phrases contribute to this mood?

doze when, just as morning began to come, he heard, far off in the jungle, the faint report of a pistol.

General Zaroff did not appear until luncheon. He was dressed faultlessly in the tweeds of a country squire. He was solicitous about the state of Rainsford's health.

"As for me," sighed the general, "I do not feel so well. I am worried, Mr. Rainsford. Last night I detected traces of my old complaint."

To Rainsford's questioning glance the general said: "Ennui. Boredom."

Then, taking a second helping of crêpes suzette, the general explained: "The hunting was not good last night. The fellow lost his head. He made a straight trail that offered no problems at all. That's the trouble with these sailors; they have dull brains to begin with, and they do not know how to get about in the woods. They do excessively stupid and obvious things. It's most annoying. Will you have another glass of Chablis, Mr. Rainsford?"

"General," said Rainsford firmly, "I wish to leave this island at once."

The general raised his thickets of eyebrows; he seemed hurt. "But, my dear fellow," the general protested, "you've only just come. You've had no hunting—"

"I wish to go today," said Rainsford. He saw the dead black eyes of the general on him, studying him. General Zaroff's face suddenly brightened.

He filled Rainsford's glass with venerable Chablis from a dusty bottle.

"Tonight," said the general, "we will hunt—you and I."

Rainsford shook his head. "No, general," he said. "I will not hunt."

**33** The general shrugged his shoulders and delicately ate a hothouse grape. "As you wish, my friend," he said. "The choice rests entirely with you. But may I not venture to suggest that you will find my idea of sport more diverting than Ivan's?"

He nodded toward the corner to where the giant stood, scowling, his thick arms crossed on his hogshead of chest.

"You don't mean—" cried Rainsford.

"My dear fellow," said the general, "have I not told you I always mean what I say about hunting? This is really an inspiration. I drink to a foeman worthy of my steel—at last."

The general raised his glass, but Rainsford sat staring at him.

**34** "You'll find this game worth playing," the general said enthusiastically. "Your brain against mine. Your woodcraft against mine. Your strength and stamina against mine. Outdoor chess! And the stake is not without value, eh?"

"And if I win—" began Rainsford huskily.

"I'll cheerfully acknowledge myself defeated if I do not find you by midnight of the third day," said General Zaroff. "My sloop will place you on the mainland near a town."

The general read what Rainsford was thinking.

"Oh, you can trust me," said the Cossack. "I will give you my word as a gentleman and a sportsman. Of course you, in turn, must agree to say nothing of your visit here."

"I'll agree to nothing of the kind," said Rainsford.

**35** "Oh," said the general, "in that case—But why discuss that now? Three days hence we can discuss it over a bottle of Veuve Cliquot, unless—"

The general sipped his wine.

Then a businesslike air animated him. "Ivan," he said to Rainsford, "will supply you with hunting clothes, food, a knife. I suggest you wear moccasins; they leave a poorer trail. I suggest too that you avoid the big

*The Most Dangerous Game*  25

---

**33 Discussion** Why do you think the writer includes this detail?

**34 Discussion** How is this activity like "Outdoor chess"?

**35 Discussion** Why does General Zaroff believe Rainsford's refusal to keep silent about the island is not important enough to discuss now?

---

high up in one of the towers. The lights of the chateau were out now, and it was dark and silent, but there was a fragment of sallow moon, and by its wan light he could see, dimly, the courtyard; there, weaving in and out in the pattern of shadow, were black, noiseless forms; the hounds heard him at the window and looked up, expectantly, with their green eyes.

Note how details in the passage rule out each avenue of escape that Rainsford explores.

**Student Activity 1.** Find three other suspense-filled passages and copy these. Exchange papers with a partner and discuss why you choose the passages you did.

**Student Activity 2.** With a small group of classmates, decide on a plot and setting for a suspense-filled story. Then brainstorm a list of details that might be used to create suspense in that story. Use items from the list to help you draft the first paragraph of the story.

36 **Reading Strategy** Ask students to review Rainsford's remarks about hunting at the beginning of the story and to explain the irony of his present situation.

37 **Discussion** What does Rainsford mean when he says he is "in a picture with a frame of water"?

38 **Critical Thinking and Reading** What can you deduce about Rainsford from this passage?

swamp in the southeast corner of the island. We call it Death Swamp. There's quicksand there. One foolish fellow tried it. The deplorable part of it was that Lazarus followed him. You can imagine my feelings, Mr. Rainsford. I loved Lazarus; he was the finest hound in my pack. Well, I must beg you to excuse me now. I always take a siesta after lunch. You'll hardly have time for a nap, I fear. You'll want to start, no doubt. I shall not follow till dusk. Hunting at night is so much more exciting than by day, don't you think? Au revoir,[17] Mr. Rainsford, au revoir."

General Zaroff, with a deep, courtly bow, strolled from the room.

From another door came Ivan. Under one arm he carried khaki hunting clothes, a haversack of food, a leather sheath containing a long-bladed hunting knife; his right hand rested on a cocked revolver thrust in the crimson sash about his waist. . . .

Rainsford had fought his way through the bush for two hours. "I must keep my nerve. I must keep my nerve," he said through tight teeth.

He had not been entirely clear-headed when the château gates snapped shut behind him. His whole idea at first was to put distance between himself and General Zaroff, and, to this end, he had plunged along, spurred on by the sharp rowels of something very like panic. Now he had got a grip on himself, had stopped, and was taking stock of himself and the situation.

He saw that straight flight was futile; inevitably it would bring him face to face with the sea. He was in a picture with a frame of water, and his operations, clearly, must take place within that frame.

"I'll give him a trail to follow," muttered

17. **au revoir** (ō′ rə vwär′): French for "until we meet again."

*26 Short Stories*

Rainsford, and he struck off from the rude paths he had been following into the trackless wilderness. He executed a series of intricate loops; he doubled on his trail again and again, recalling all the lore of the fox hunt, and all the dodges of the fox. Night found him leg-weary, with his hands and face lashed by the branches, on a thickly wooded ridge. He knew it would be insane to blunder on through the dark, even if he had the strength. His need for rest was imperative and he thought: "I have played the fox, now I must play the cat of the fable." A big tree with a thick trunk and outspread branches was nearby, and, taking care to leave not the slightest mark, he climbed up into the crotch, and stretching out on one of the broad limbs, after a fashion, rested. Rest brought him new confidence and almost a feeling of security. Even so zealous a hunter as General Zaroff could not trace him there, he told himself; only the devil himself could follow that complicated trail through the jungle after dark. But, perhaps, the general was a devil—

An apprehensive night crawled slowly by like a wounded snake, and sleep did not visit Rainsford, although the silence of a dead world was on the jungle. Toward morning when a dingy gray was varnishing the sky, the cry of some startled bird focused Rainsford's attention in that direction. Something was coming through the bush, coming slowly, carefully, coming by the same winding way Rainsford had come. He flattened himself down on the limb, and through a screen of leaves almost as thick as tapestry, he watched. The thing that was approaching was a man.

It was General Zaroff. He made his way along with his eyes fixed in utmost concentration on the ground before him. He paused, almost beneath the tree, dropped to his knees and studied the ground. Rainsford's impulse was to hurl himself down like

**THE RED CEDAR**
*Emily Carr*
Vancouver Art Gallery

*The Most Dangerous Game*   27

**Humanities Note**

Fine art, *The Red Cedar,* by Emily Carr. Emily Carr (1871–1945), who was born in Victoria, British Columbia, is one of Canada's most gifted artists. Even as a child, Carr showed a strong desire to commit her life to art. Before she was twenty, Carr persuaded her parents to allow her to attend art school. She studied art in San Francisco, London, and Paris. Throughout her travels, Carr longed to return home. It was her homeland that provided the strongest influence in her artwork. Once home, Carr traveled to remote areas of British Columbia where she found the inspiration for some of her finest work. Here Carr painted native villages and dramatic images of the vast forests of the area, as illustrated in *The Red Cedar.*

You might use the following questions for discussion:
1. List the words that come to mind when you look at this painting.
2. Does this painting capture the mood of the story? Explain.

**39 Discussion** Considering General Zaroff's behavior, do you think he is aware of Rainsford's presence?

**40 Discussion** Why is Rainsford filled with terror?

**41 Discussion** How does the comparison of the two men to a cat and mouse suggest the barbarity of the hunt?

**42 Discussion** How do you think Rainsford feels as he hears these words?

a panther, but he saw the general's right hand held something metallic—a small automatic pistol.

The hunter shook his head several times, as if he were puzzled. Then he straightened up and took from his case one of his black cigarettes; its pungent incense-like smoke floated up to Rainsford's nostrils.

Rainsford held his breath. The general's eyes had left the ground and were traveling inch by inch up the tree. Rainsford froze there, every muscle tensed for a spring. But the sharp eyes of the hunter stopped before they reached the limb where Rainsford lay; a smile spread over his brown face. Very deliberately he blew a smoke ring into the air; then he turned his back on the tree and walked carelessly away, back along the trail he had come. The swish of the underbrush against his hunting boots grew fainter and fainter.

The pent-up air burst hotly from Rainsford's lungs. His first thought made him feel sick and numb. The general could follow a trail through the woods at night; he could follow an extremely difficult trail; he must have uncanny powers; only by the merest chance had the Cossack failed to see his quarry.

Rainsford's second thought was even more terrible. It sent a shudder of cold horror through his whole being. Why had the general smiled? Why had he turned back?

Rainsford did not want to believe what his reason told him was true, but the truth was as evident as the sun that had by now pushed through the morning mists. The general was playing with him! The general was saving him for another day's sport! The Cossack was the cat; he was the mouse. Then it was that Rainsford knew the full meaning of terror.

"I will not lose my nerve. I will not."

He slid down from the tree, and struck off again into the woods. His face was set and he forced the machinery of his mind to function. Three hundred yards from his hiding place he stopped where a huge dead tree leaned precariously on a smaller, living one. Throwing off his sack of food, Rainsford took his knife from its sheath and began to work with all his energy.

The job was finished at last, and he threw himself down behind a fallen log a hundred feet away. He did not have to wait long. The cat was coming again to play with the mouse.

Following the trail with the sureness of a bloodhound, came General Zaroff. Nothing escaped those searching black eyes, no crushed blade of grass, no bent twig, no mark, no matter how faint, in the moss. So intent was the Cossack on his stalking that he was upon the thing Rainsford had made before he saw it. His foot touched the protruding bough that was the trigger. Even as he touched it, the general sensed his danger and leaped back with the agility of an ape. But he was not quite quick enough; the dead tree, delicately adjusted to rest on the cut living one, crashed down and struck the general a glancing blow on the shoulder as it fell; but for his alertness, he must have been smashed beneath it. He staggered, but he did not fall; nor did he drop his revolver. He stood there, rubbing his injured shoulder, and Rainsford, with fear again gripping his heart, heard the general's mocking laugh ring through the jungle.

"Rainsford," called the general, "if you are within the sound of my voice, as I suppose you are, let me congratulate you. Not many men know how to make a Malay man-catcher. Luckily, for me, I too have hunted in Malacca. You are proving interesting, Mr. Rainsford. I am going now to have my wound dressed; it's only a slight one. But I shall be back. I shall be back."

When the general, nursing his bruised shoulder, had gone, Rainsford took up his flight again. It was flight now, a desperate, hopeless flight, that carried him on for some hours. Dusk came, then darkness, and still he pressed on. The ground grew softer under his moccasins; the vegetation grew ranker, denser; insects bit him savagely. Then, as he stepped forward, his foot sank into the ooze. He tried to wrench it back, but the muck sucked viciously at his foot as if it were a giant leech. With a violent effort, he tore his foot loose. He knew where he was now. Death Swamp and its quicksand.

His hands were tight closed as if his nerve were something tangible that some one in the darkness was trying to tear from his grip. The softness of the earth had given him an idea. He stepped back from the quicksand a dozen feet or so, and, like some huge prehistoric beaver, he began to dig.

Rainsford had dug himself in in France[18] when a second's delay meant death. That had been a placid pastime compared to his digging now. The pit grew deeper; when it was above his shoulders, he climbed out and from some hard saplings cut stakes and sharpened them to a fine point. These stakes he planted in the bottom of the pit with the points sticking up. With flying fingers he wove a rough carpet of weeds and branches and with it he covered the mouth of the pit. Then, wet with sweat and aching with tiredness, he crouched behind the stump of a lightning-charred tree.

He knew his pursuer was coming; he heard the padding sound of feet on the soft earth, and the night breeze brought him the perfume of the general's cigarette. It seemed to Rainsford that the general was coming with unusual swiftness; he was not feeling

his way along, foot by foot. Rainsford, crouching there, could not see the general, nor could he see the pit. He lived a year in a minute. Then he felt an impulse to cry aloud with joy, for he heard the sharp crackle of the breaking branches as the cover of the pit gave way; he heard the sharp scream of pain as the pointed stakes found their mark. He leaped up from his place of concealment. Then he cowered back. Three feet from the pit a man was standing, with an electric torch in his hand.

"You've done well, Rainsford," the voice of the general called. "Your Burmese tiger pit has claimed one of my best dogs. Again you score. I think, Mr. Rainsford, I'll see what you can do against my whole pack. I'm going home for a rest now. Thank you for a most amusing evening."

At daybreak Rainsford, lying near the swamp, was awakened by a sound that made him know that he had new things to learn about fear. It was a distant sound, faint and wavering, but he knew it. It was the baying of a pack of hounds.

Rainsford knew he could do one of two things. He could stay where he was and wait. That was suicide. He could flee. That was postponing the inevitable. For a moment he stood there, thinking. An idea that held a wild chance came to him, and, tightening his belt, he headed away from the swamp.

The baying of the hounds drew nearer, then still nearer, nearer, ever nearer. On a ridge Rainsford climbed a tree. Down a watercourse, not a quarter of a mile away, he could see the bush moving. Straining his eyes, he saw the lean figure of General Zaroff; just ahead of him Rainsford made out another figure whose wide shoulders surged through the tall jungle weeds; it was the giant Ivan, and he seemed pulled forward by some unseen force; Rainsford knew that Ivan must be holding the pack in leash.

---

**18. dug himself in in France:** Had dug a foxhole to protect himself during World War I.

43

**43 Discussion** What is Rainsford learning that he did not know when he first expressed his ideas about hunting?

**44 Critical Thinking and Reading** How does the author increase the suspense in the story at this point?

**45 Discussion** Why does Zaroff say that Rainsford "hadn't played the game"?

**46 Enrichment** Tell students that Marcus Aurelius believed that the world is governed by the benevolent force of Reason, and that each individual should be guided by reason and not by his or her passions. It is ironic for Zaroff to read Aurelius because the general is dominated by his passion for hunting, to the exclusion of reason. There is further irony in his admiration for Aurelius since the philosopher believed it was important for individuals to help one another.

**47 Literary Focus** How does the writer use the structure of the last sentence to maintain suspense until the end?

**Reader's Response** Would you have liked to be in Rainsford's position? Why or why not?

**Master Teacher Note** Use the overhead projector to show students Art Transparency 1, *Evening by the Sea,* by Karl Schmidt-Rottloff. Ask students to describe the setting. Have them speculate about the identity and purpose, if any, of the man in the foreground. Also, have them explain whether he is like Rainsford in any way. Does the mood of this painting correspond to that of the story?

They would be on him any minute now. His mind worked frantically. He thought of a native trick he had learned in Uganda. He slid down the tree. He caught hold of a springy young sapling and to it he fastened his hunting knife, with the blade pointing down the trail; with a bit of wild grapevine he tied back the sapling. Then he ran for his life. The hounds raised their voices as they hit the fresh scent. Rainsford knew now how an animal at bay feels.

He had to stop to get his breath. The baying of the hounds stopped abruptly, and Rainsford's heart stopped too. They must have reached the knife.

He shinnied excitedly up a tree and looked back. His pursuers had stopped. But the hope that was in Rainsford's brain when he climbed died, for he saw in the shallow valley that General Zaroff was still on his feet. But Ivan was not. The knife, driven by the recoil of the springing tree, had not wholly failed.

"Nerve, nerve, nerve!" he panted, as he dashed along. A blue gap showed between the trees dead ahead. Ever nearer drew the hounds. Rainsford forced himself on toward that gap. He reached it. It was the shore of the sea. Across a cove he could see the gloomy gray stone of the château. Twenty feet below him the sea rumbled and hissed. Rainsford hesitated. He heard the hounds. Then he leaped far out into the sea. . . .

When the general and his pack reached the place by the sea, the Cossack stopped. For some minutes he stood regarding the blue-green expanse of water. He shrugged his shoulders. Then he sat down, took a drink of brandy from a silver flask, lit a perfumed cigarette, and hummed a bit from *Madame Butterfly.*[19]

General Zaroff had an exceedingly good dinner in his great paneled dining hall that evening. With it he had a bottle of Pol Roger and half a bottle of Chambertin. Two slight annoyances kept him from perfect enjoyment. One was the thought that it would be difficult to replace Ivan; the other was that his quarry had escaped him; of course the American hadn't played the game—so thought the general as he tasted his after-dinner liqueur. In his library he read, to soothe himself, from the works of Marcus Aurelius.[20] At ten he went up to his bedroom. He was deliciously tired, he said to himself, as he locked himself in. There was a little moonlight, so, before turning on his light, he went to the window and looked down at the courtyard. He could see the great hounds, and he called: "Better luck another time," to them. Then he switched on the light.

A man, who had been hiding in the curtains of the bed, was standing there.

"Rainsford!" screamed the general. "How in God's name did you get here?"

"Swam," said Rainsford. "I found it quicker than walking through the jungle."

The general sucked in his breath and smiled. "I congratulate you," he said. "You have won the game."

Rainsford did not smile. "I am still a beast at bay," he said, in a low, hoarse voice. "Get ready, General Zaroff."

The general made one of his deepest bows. "I see," he said. "Splendid! One of us is to furnish a repast for the hounds. The other will sleep in this very excellent bed. On guard, Rainsford. . . ."

He had never slept in a better bed, Rainsford decided.

---

**19. *Madame Butterfly:*** An opera by Giacomo Puccini.

**20. *Marcus Aurelius*** (ô rē′ lē əs): A Roman emperor and philosopher (121–180 A.D.).

**Closure and Extension**
**ANSWERS TO THINKING ABOUT THE SELECTION**
*Recalling*

1. The island is called by that name because ships have mysteriously disappeared near it.
2. He falls overboard from a yacht while sailing near the island, and he swims to shore.
3. Zaroff treats Rainsford as a respected equal and guest at first.

## THINKING ABOUT THE SELECTION

### Recalling

1. Why is the island called Ship Trap Island?
2. How does Rainsford come to the island?
3. Explain how Zaroff's treatment of Rainsford changes during the story.
4. What three tricks does Rainsford use to elude Zaroff? What is the outcome of each trick?
5. Explain how Rainsford breaks the rules of the game at the end of the story.

### Interpreting

6. Why does Zaroff think of himself as "civilized"? In what ways might he be described as "uncivilized"?
7. Compare and contrast Rainsford's attitude toward hunting with Zaroff's.
8. Why does Rainsford call himself "a beast at bay"?
9. What are two possible meanings of the title?

### Applying

10. Do you think Rainsford will continue to hunt? Explain your answer.

## ANALYZING LITERATURE

### Understanding Plot

The **plot** of a story is a sequence of related events. It often begins with some **exposition** that provides important background information. It then presents a **conflict,** with the action rising to a **climax** and falling to a **resolution**.

Study the plot diagram below.

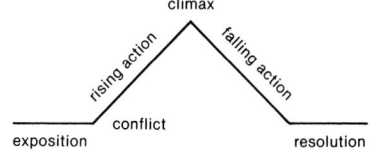

1. Identify the exposition and tell how it sets the scene for coming events.
2. Explain how the plot involves conflicts between two men; a person and nature; and two different views of life.
3. At what point is the climax reached?
4. How are the conflicts resolved?

## CRITICAL THINKING AND READING

### Analyzing Sequence in a Story

A writer **sequences,** or orders, events to create a certain effect. For example, by having Rainsford learn of the mystery surrounding Ship Trap Island at the beginning of the story, the writer creates suspense—the quality of a story that keeps you wondering and turning pages.

1. Why do you think the writer had Rainsford sit down to an elegant dinner with Zaroff before learning of the hunt?
2. Why do you think the writer had Zaroff relax and have dinner before discovering the surprise awaiting him in his room?

## THINKING AND WRITING

### Writing About Plot

Write a review of "The Most Dangerous Game" for a school literary magazine. Imagine that your readers have not read the story. First diagram the plot of the story. Make a list of the plot segments you particularly liked or disliked. Then write one or two paragraphs explaining why you liked or disliked the story, using the items on your list as examples. In revising, make sure you have included enough information to give your readers a sense of the story.

Later, he is put off by Rainsford's protests and makes him the quarry. During the hunt, he shows a kind of mocking respect and then disappointment as Rainsford refuses to play the game.
4. Rainsford creates a winding, difficult trail, but Zaroff finds him; Rainsford builds a Malay mancatcher trap, but the general is only slightly wounded; Rainsford digs a Burmese tiger pit, but one of Zaroff's dogs falls into it, not the general; and Rainsford uses a

hunting trick from Uganda which kills Ivan, not the general.
5. Instead of turning to fight or making further attempts to hide from or to kill the general, Rainsford appears to quit the "game" by leaping off a cliff into the sea.

### Interpreting

6. Suggested Response: He thinks he is civilized because he lives com-

fortably. He is uncivilized because he is a murderer.
7. Suggested Response: Both love hunting and, at first, Rainsford shares Zaroff's contempt for the hunted. Rainsford won't commit murder, however, while Zaroff will.
8. Suggested Response: A beast at bay is one which is cornered and has turned to defend itself, even if that means its death.
9. Suggested Response: The title refers to the general's human quarry and to the actual hunt itself.

### Applying

10. Answers will differ but most students will realize that Rainsford's experience will probably change his attitude towards hunting.

**Challenge** How do the shots that Rainsford hears while he is on the yacht foreshadow the later events in the story?

## ANSWERS TO ANALYZING LITERATURE

1. Suggested Response: The exposition includes the discussion between Whitney and Rainsford, the description of the island, Rainsford's fall from the boat, and his arrival on the island. It sets the scene by creating a suspenseful mood and stressing Rainsford's opinions and abilities.
2. Suggested Response: Rainsford and Zaroff fight a life-and-death battle. Also, they have different views about hunting humans. Finally, Rainsford must contend with the jungle and the sea to beat Zaroff.
3. Suggested Response: The climax is reached when Rainsford confronts Zaroff in the bedroom.
4. Suggested Response: The conflicts are resolved when Rainsford kills Zaroff.

## ANSWERS TO CRITICAL THINKING AND READING

1. Suggested Response: The elegant dinner prolongs the tension.
2. Suggested Response: This delay also heightens the suspense by making us wonder about Rainsford.

## THINKING AND WRITING

For help with this assignment, students can refer to Lesson 8, "Writing About Plot," in the Handbook of Writing About Literature.

**Publishing Student Writing**
Suggest that students submit their review for publication to the school newspaper or literary magazine.

## Focus

**More About the Author** Joan Aiken is known for writing humorous and imaginative stories. The titles of her books and stories are often memorable and witty. For example, her first collection of short stories was called *All You Ever Wanted,* which was followed by another collection called *More Than You Bargained For.* Ask students how a title can reflect not only the content but also the tone of a story.

**Literary Focus** Point out to students that two important ingredients of suspense are uncertainty and danger. Have them consider how each of these elements contributes to a suspenseful situation.

**Look For** Tell students that, as in this case, the title of a story can hint at a mystery.

**Writing/Prior Knowledge** You might want to divide the class into small groups and have students discuss these questions before they begin writing.

**Vocabulary** Have your less advanced students use the vocabulary words in a paragraph-length sketch of some eerie event.

### Sonata for Harp and Bicycle

**Joan Aiken** (1924–     ), daughter of Pulitzer Prize-winning American poet Conrad Aiken, was born in London. Her first short story was published when she was sixteen years old. Aiken worked as a librarian, editor, and advertising copywriter, but since 1961 she has devoted herself exclusively to writing. Aiken divides her time between New York City and London, where the story you are about to read takes place. "Sonata for Harp and Bicycle," like many of Aiken's works, is a tale of the supernatural.

**Suspense and Foreshadowing**

**Suspense** is the quality in a story that makes you keep reading in order to find out what will happen next. One way of creating suspense is through foreshadowing. **Foreshadowing** means giving the reader hints about events to come without actually saying what will happen. These hints are mysterious enough so that you cannot be certain where they will lead. When Jason asks Miss Golden for a hint about why employees are required to leave at five P.M., she mentions a fire escape, a bicycle, and a harp. These three words foreshadow the events of the story, but you need to read on to find out exactly how.

**Look For**

As you read "Sonata for Harp and Bicycle," look for clues to the mystery of why the Grimes Buildings must be avoided at night. What is the meaning of the fire escape, the bicycle, and the harp?

**Writing**

Why is it that people love a mystery? Why are they intrigued by the unknown? Freewrite, exploring your answer.

**Vocabulary**

Knowing the following words will help you as you read "Sonata for Harp and Bicycle."

**gaunt** (gônt) *adj.*: Looking grim, forbidding, or desolate (p. 33)

**encroaching** (in krōch′ iŋ) *adj.*: Intruding in a gradual or sneaking way (p. 33)

**multitudinous** (mul′ tə to͞od ′n əs) *adj.*: Very numerous (p. 33)

**tantalizingly** (tan′ tə līz′ iŋ lē) *adv.*: In a teasing or tormenting way (p. 34)

**furtive** (fur′ tiv) *adj.*: Preventing observation; sneaky (p. 36)

**reciprocate** (ri sip′ rə kāt′) *v.*: Give or feel in return (p. 38)

**nocturnal** (näk tur′ n'l) *adj.*: Done or happening at night (p. 38)

**gossamer** (gäs′ ə mər) *adj.*: Light, thin, and delicate (p. 39)

32   Short Stories

# Sonata for Harp and Bicycle

## Joan Aiken

"No one is allowed to remain in the building after five P.M.," Mr. Manaby told his new assistant, showing him into the little room that was like the inside of an egg carton.

"Why not?"

"Directorial policy," said Mr. Manaby. But that was not the real reason.

Gaunt and sooty, Grimes Buildings lurched up the side of a hill toward Clerkenwell.[1] Every little office within its dim and crumbling exterior owned one tiny crumb of light—such was the proud boast of the architect—but toward evening the crumbs were collected, absorbed and demolished as by an immense vacuum cleaner, and yielded to an uncontrollable mass of dark that came tumbling in through windows and doors to take their place. Darkness infested the building like a flight of bats returning willingly to roost.

"Wash hands, please. Wash hands, please," the intercom began to bawl in the passage at four-forty-five. Without much need of prompting the staff hustled like lemmings along the corridors to the green and blue-tiled washrooms that mocked the encroaching dusk with an illusion of cheerfulness.

"All papers into cases, please," the Tannoy[2] warned, five minutes later. "Look at your desks, ladies and gentlemen. Any documents left lying about? Kindly put them away. Desks must be left clear and tidy. Drawers must be shut."

A multitudinous shuffling, a rustling as of innumerable bluebottles[3] might have been heard by the attentive ear after this injunction, as the employees of Moreton Wold and Company thrust their papers into briefcases, clipped statistical abstracts together and slammed them into filing cabinets; dropped discarded copy into wastepaper baskets. Two minutes later, and not a desk throughout Grimes Buildings bore more than its customary coating of dust.

"Hats and coats on, please. Hats and coats on, please. Did you bring an umbrella? Have you left any shopping on the floor?"

At three minutes to five the home-going throng was in the lifts[4] and on the stairs; a clattering staccato-voiced flood momentarily darkened the great double doors of the building, and then as the first faint notes of St. Paul's[5] came echoing faintly on the frosty air, to be picked up near at hand by the louder chime of St. Biddulph's on the Wall, the entire premises of Moreton Wold stood empty.

"But why is it?" Jason Ashgrove, the new copywriter, asked his secretary. "Why are the staff herded out so fast in the eve-

---

1. **Clerkenwell:** A district of London.
2. **the Tannoy:** Loudspeaker.
3. **bluebottles** (blōō bät′ ′lz) *n.*: Flies.
4. **lifts** (lifts) *n.*: British for "elevators."
5. **St. Paul's:** A famous church in London.

*Sonata for Harp and Bicycle* 33

## Presentation

**Motivation/Prior Knowledge** Have students describe ghost stories they have heard or read. Ask them where these stories usually take place. Then tell them that the ghost story they are about to read takes place in a modern setting.

**Master Teacher Note** This ghost story involves a curse, and it challenges the reader to anticipate how the curse will be lifted. Students should concentrate on details that hint at ways in which the protagonist can overcome the curse.

**Purpose-Setting Question** Why is the title of this story an appropriate one?

1 **Enrichment** A sonata is a form of classical music in which particular musical themes are presented and developed. Bring in a recording like "Moonlight Sonata" by Ludwig van Beethoven, and play it for the class. Then ask the students what a sonata for a harp and bicycle might sound like. Discuss the humor of the title.

2 **Discussion** The writer tells us that Mr. Manaby's answer "was not the real reason." Do you think Mr. Manaby knows the real reason? Explain.

3 **Discussion** Discuss the writer's use of the word *infested*. Ask students what they know about bats that helps them understand the image the writer is trying to create in describing the darkness.

4 **Critical Thinking and Reading** The author uses similes in phrases such as "hustled like lemmings" and "a rustling as of innumerable bluebottles." What is the effect of such comparisons?

**Thematic Idea** Another selection that deals with fantasy and the unexplained is "The Loch Ness Monster" by John McPhee, page 489. You might have students compare the different attitudes toward unexplainable phenomena in these selections.

**5** **Literary Focus** What is it about Miss Golden's words and behavior that creates suspense?

**6** **Clarification** The terms *layout* and *copy* suggest that Jason and Miss Golden work for an advertising company.

**7** **Reading Strategy** The writer tells us what Miss Golden says is not true. Ask students why they might predict that Jason and Miss Golden may become romantically involved. Do they think Jason will realize how she feels about him?

**8** **Discussion** What do Jason's remarks and behavior reveal about his personality?

nings? Not that I'm against it, mind you, I think it's an admirable idea in many ways, but there is the liberty of the individual to be considered, don't you think?"

**5** "Hush!" Miss Golden, casting a glance towards the door, held up her felt-tip in warning or reproof." You mustn't ask that sort of question. When you are taken on to the Established Staff you'll be told. Not before."

"But I want to know now," said Jason in discontent. "Do you know?"

"Yes I do," Miss Golden answered tantalizingly. "Come on, or we shan't have done the Oat Crisp layout by a quarter to." And she stared firmly down at the copy in front of **6** her, lips folded, candyfloss hair falling over her face, lashes hiding eyes like peridots,[6] a girl with a secret.

Jason was annoyed. He rapped out a couple of rude and witty rhymes which Miss Golden let pass in a withering silence.

"What do you want for Christmas, Miss Golden? Sherry? Fudge? Bath cubes?"

"I want to go away with a clear conscience about Oat Crisps," Miss Golden re-**7** torted. It was not true; what she chiefly wanted was Mr. Jason Ashgrove, but he had not realized this yet.

"Come on, don't be a tease! I'm sure you haven't been on the Established Staff all that long," he coaxed her. "What happens when one is taken on, anyway? Does the Managing Director have us up for a confidential chat? Or are we given a little book called The Awful Secret of Grimes Buildings?"

**8** Miss Golden wasn't telling. She opened her desk drawer and took out a white towel and a cake of rosy soap.

"Wash hands, please! Wash hands, please!"

Jason was frustrated. "You'll be sorry," he said. "I shall do something desperate."

---

6. **peridots** (per′ ə däts′) *n.*: Yellowish-green gems.

"Oh no, you mustn't!" Her eyes were large with fright. She ran from the room and was back within a couple of minutes, still drying her hands.

"If I took you out to dinner, wouldn't you give me just a tiny hint?"

Side by side Miss Golden and Mr. Ashgrove ran along the green-floored corridors, battled down the white marble stairs, among the hundred other employees from the tenth

9 **Discussion** What mood does this description of London create? How is this mood appropriate to the story?

floor, and the nine hundred from the floors below.

He saw her lips move as she said something, but in the clatter of two thousand feet the words were lost.

" . . . f-f-fire escape," he heard, as they came into the momentary hush of the coir-carpeted entrance hall. And ". . . it's to do with a bicycle. A bicycle and a harp."

"I don't understand."

Now they were in the street, chilly with the winter-dusk smells of celery on barrows, of swept-up leaves heaped in faraway parks, and cold layers of dew sinking among the withered evening primroses in the building sites. London lay about them wreathed in twilit mystery and fading against the barred and smoky sky. Like a ninth wave the sound of traffic overtook and swallowed them.

9

"Please tell me!"

*Sonata for Harp and Bicycle*   35

But, shaking her head, she stepped onto a scarlet home-bound bus and was borne away from him.

Jason stood undecided on the pavement, with the crowds dividing round him as round the pier of a bridge. He scratched his head and looked about him for guidance.

**10** An ambulance clanged, a taxi screeched, a drill stuttered, a siren wailed on the river, a door slammed, a van hooted, and close beside his ear a bicycle bell tinkled its tiny warning.

A bicycle, she had said. A bicycle and a harp.

Jason turned and stared at Grimes Buildings.

Somewhere, he knew, there was a back way in, a service entrance. He walked slowly past the main doors, with their tubs of snowy chrysanthemums, and on up Glass Street. A tiny furtive wedge of darkness beckoned him, a snicket, a hacket, an alley carved into the thickness of the building. It was so narrow that at any moment, it seemed, the overtopping walls would come together and squeeze it out of existence.

Walking as softly as an Indian, Jason passed through it, slid by a file of dustbins,[7] and found the foot of the fire escape. Iron treads rose into the mist, like an illustration to a Gothic[8] fairytale.

He began to climb.

**11** When he had mounted to the ninth story he paused for breath. It was a lonely place. The lighting consisted of a dim bulb at the foot of every flight. A well of gloom sank beneath him. The cold fingers of the wind nagged and fluttered at the edges of his jacket, and he pulled the string of the fire-door and edged inside.

Grimes Buildings were triangular, with

the street forming the base of the triangle, and the fire escape the point. Jason could see two long passages coming toward him, meeting at an acute angle where he stood. He started down the left-hand one, tiptoeing in the cave-like silence. Nowhere was there any sound, except for the faraway drip of a tap. No night watchman would stay in the building; none was needed. No precautions **12** were taken. Burglars gave the place a wide berth.

Jason opened a door at random; then another. Offices lay everywhere about him, empty and forbidding. Some held lipstick-stained tissues, spilt powder, and orange-peel; others were still foggy with cigarette **13** smoke. Here was a director's suite of rooms—a desk like half an acre of frozen lake, inch-thick carpet, roses, and the smell of cigars. Here was a conference room with scattered squares of doodled blotting paper. All equally empty.

He was not sure when he first began to notice the bell. Telephone, he thought at first, and then he remembered that all the outside lines were disconnected at five. And this bell, anyway, had not the regularity of a telephone's double ring: there was a tinkle, **14** and then silence: a long ring, and then silence: a whole volley of rings together, and then silence.

Jason stood listening, and fear knocked against his ribs and shortened his breath. He knew that he must move or be paralyzed by it. He ran up a flight of stairs and found himself with two more endless green corridors beckoning him like a pair of dividers.

Another sound now: a waft of ice-thin notes, riffling up an arpeggio[9] like a flurry of sleet. Far away down the passage it echoed. Jason ran in pursuit, but as he ran the mu-

---

**7. dustbins:** British for "garbage cans."
**8. Gothic:** Mysterious.

**9. arpeggio** (är pej′ ō) n.: The notes of a chord played one after the other instead of together.

15 **Master Teacher Note** Make sure students are aware of the problem the writer faced in describing the ghost: to make something insubstantial seem real without sacrificing a sense of mystery. Ask the students if they think the description of the ghost is effective.

16 **Enrichment** Point out to the students that the name Daisy and the watchman's bicycle recall the song "A Bicycle Built for Two." Ask them how the lyrics of this song are appropriate to the story: "Daisy, Daisy, give me your answer do. I'm half crazy over the love of you…" This reference to a jaunty, old-fashioned song is a sign of the writer's sense of humor. Ask students to find other examples of humor in this story. Is humor appropriate in a ghost story?

sic receded. He circled the building, but it always outdistanced him, and when he came back to the stairs, he heard it fading away on to the story below.

He hesitated, and as he did so, heard once more the bell: the bicycle bell. It was approaching him fast, bearing down on him, urgent, menacing. He could hear the pedals, almost see the shimmer of an invisible wheel. Absurdly, he was reminded of the insistent clamor of an ice-cream vendor, summoning children on a sultry Sunday afternoon.

There was a little fireman's alcove beside him, with buckets and pumps. He hurled himself into it. The bell stopped beside him, and then there was a moment while his heart tried to shake itself loose in his chest. He was looking into two eyes carved out of expressionless air; he was held by two hands knotted together out of the width of dark.

"Daisy? Daisy?" came the whisper. "Is that you, Daisy? Have you come to give me your answer?"

Jason tried to speak, but no words came.

"It's *not* Daisy! Who are you?" The sibilants were full of threat. "You can't stay here! This is private property."

He was thrust along the corridor. It was like being pushed by a whirlwind—the fire door opened ahead of him without a touch, and he was on the openwork platform,

## 17 Critical Thinking and Reading
Jason thinks of Berenice Golden in his most desperate moment. What is important about this fact?

## 18 Enrichment
George Gordon, Lord Byron (1788–1824), was an adventurous nineteenth-century Romantic poet. Lord Byron enjoyed a reputation like that of certain rock musicians today. He traveled through Italy and other parts of Europe with an entourage of servants and a menagerie of wild animals. His scandalous behavior made him an outcast from the greater part of society, although he was a member of the English nobility. Someone who is *Byronic*, therefore, is dashing, handsome, and rebellious. Ask the students if they think Jason Ashgrove fits this description.

## 19 Discussion
In ghost stories an encounter with a spirit sometimes turns a character's hair white. Ask students why they think this might occur.

## 20 Literary Focus
Notice that the writer has held back the full story until this point. What is the effect of this delay? Would the story have been more enjoyable if we had known these facts from the start?

clutching the slender rail. Still the hands would not let him go.

"How about it?" the whisper mocked him. "How about jumping? It's an easy death compared with some."

Jason looked down into the smoky void. The darkness nodded to him like a familiar.[10]

**17**  "You wouldn't be much loss, would you? What have you got to live for?"

Miss Golden, Jason thought. She would miss me. And the syllables Berenice Golden lingered in the air like a chime. Drawing on some unknown deposit of courage he shook himself loose from the holding hands, and ran down the fire escape without looking back.

Next morning when Miss Golden, crisp, fragrant and punctual, shut the door of Room 92 behind her, she stopped short by the hat-pegs with a horrified gasp.

"Mr. *Ashgrove!* Your *hair!*"

"It makes me look very distinguished, don't you think?" he said.

**18**  It did indeed have this effect, for his Byronic[11] dark cut had changed to a stippled silver.

**19**  "How did it happen? You've not—" her voice sank to a whisper— *"You've not been in Grimes Buildings after dark?"*

"What if I have?"

"Have you?"

"Miss Golden—Berenice," he said earnestly. "Who was Daisy? I can see that you know. Tell me her story."

"Did you see him?" she asked faintly.

"Him?"

"William Heron—the Wailing Watchman. Oh," she exclaimed in terror. "I can see that

---

10. **a familiar:** A spirit.
11. **Byronic** (bī rän′ ik) *adj.*: Romantic, like the dashing British poet Lord Byron (1788-1824).

you must have. Then you are doomed— doomed!"

"If I'm doomed," said Jason, "let's have coffee and you tell me all about it."

"It all happened over fifty years ago," said Berenice, as she spooned out coffee powder with distracted extravagance. "Heron was the night watchman in this building, patrolling the corridors from dusk to dawn every night on his bicycle. He fell in love with a Miss Bell who taught the harp. She rented a room—this room—and gave lessons in it. She began to reciprocate his love, and they used to share a picnic supper every night at eleven, and she'd stay on a while to keep him company. It was an idyll,[12] among the fire buckets and the furnace pipes.

**20**

"On Christmas Eve he had summoned up the courage to propose to her. The day before he had told her that he was going to ask her a very important question. Next night he came to the Buildings with a huge bunch of roses and a bottle of wine. But Miss Bell never turned up.

"The explanation was simple. Miss Bell, of course, had been losing a lot of sleep through her nocturnal romance, as she gave lessons all day, and so she used to take a nap in her music room between seven and ten every evening, to save going home. In order to make sure that she would wake up, she persuaded her father, a distant relation of Graham Bell[13] who shared some of the more famous Bell's mechanical ingenuity, to install an alarm device, a kind of telephone, in her room, which called her every evening at ten. She was far too modest and shy to let Heron know that she spent those hours actually in the building, and to give him the chance of waking her himself.

---

12. **idyll** (ī′ d'l) *n.*: A romantic scene, usually in the country.
13. **Graham Bell:** Alexander Graham Bell (1847–1922), the inventor of the telephone.

## Grammar in Action

Writers incorporate **figurative language** into their writing to make it more interesting to read. Figurative language is writing or speech that is not meant to be interpreted literally. Figurative expressions often involve comparisons between two basically unlike things. Look at this figurative expression from the story.

Darkness infested the building *like a flight of bats* returning willingly to roost.

Notice that in the expression, the darkness is compared to a flight of bats returning home. In what ways are these two things alike?

Writers use figurative language to create for the reader vivid impressions of what they are describing. The expression in the example allows you to better imagine the speed as well as the smothering thickness of the coming darkness.

Now look at this expression. What two things are being compared?

. . . the electric typewriter, against which they were leaning, began chattering to itself in a frenzy of enthusiasm.

While the comparison in the first example is stated directly, the comparison in this one is implied, or suggested. Joan Aiken

**21** "Alas! On this important evening the gadget failed and she never woke up. Telephones were in their infancy at that time, you must remember.

"Heron waited and waited. At last, mad with grief and jealousy, having rung up her home and discovered that she was not there, he concluded that she had rejected him, ran to the fire escape, and cast himself off it, holding the roses and the bottle of wine. He jumped from the tenth floor.

"Daisy did not long survive him, but pined away soon after; since that day their ghosts have haunted Grimes Buildings, he vainly patrolling the corridors on his bicycle in search of her, she playing her harp in the small room she rented. *But they never meet.* And anyone who meets the ghost of William Heron will himself within five days leap down from the same fatal fire escape."

**22** She gazed at him with tragic eyes.

"In that case we mustn't lose a minute," said Jason and he enveloped her in an embrace as prolonged as it was ardent. Looking down at the gossamer hair sprayed across his shoulder, he added, "Just the same, it is a preposterous situation. Firstly, I have no intention of jumping off the fire escape—" here, however, he repressed a shudder as he remembered the cold, clutching hands of the evening before— "And secondly, I find it **23** quite nonsensical that those two inefficient ghosts have spent fifty years in this building without coming across each other. We must remedy the matter, Berenice. We must not begrudge our new-found happiness to others."

He gave her another kiss so impassioned that the electric typewriter against which they were leaning began chattering to itself in a frenzy of enthusiasm.

"This very evening," he went on, looking at his watch, "we will put matters right for that unhappy couple, and then, if I really have only five more days to live, which I don't for one moment believe, we will proceed to spend them together, my bewitching Berenice, in the most advantageous manner possible."

She nodded, spellbound.

"Can you work a switchboard?" She nodded again. "My love, you are perfection itself. Meet me in the switchboard room, then, at ten this evening. I would say, have dinner with me, but I shall need to make one or two purchases and see an old RAF[14] friend. You will be safe from Heron's curse in the switchboard room if he always keeps to the corridors."

"I would rather meet him and die with you," she murmured.

"My angel, I hope that won't be necessary. Now," he said sighing, "I suppose we should get down to our day's work." Strangely enough, the copy they wrote that **24** day, although engendered from such agitated minds, sold more packets of Oat Crisps than any other advertising matter before or since.

That evening when Jason entered Grimes Buildings he was carrying two bottles of wine, two bunches of red roses, and a large canvas-covered bundle. Miss Golden, **25** who had concealed herself in the telephone exchange before the offices closed for the night, gazed at these things with interest.

"Now," said Jason after he had greeted her, "I want you first of all to ring our own extension."

"No one will reply, surely?"

"I think *she* will reply."

Sure enough, when Berenice rang extension 170 a faint, sleepy voice, distant and yet clear, whispered, "Hullo?"

"Is that Miss Bell?"

---

**14. RAF:** Royal Air Force.

*Sonata for Harp and Bicycle* 39

---

**21 Clarification** Point out the irony and humor in the fact that Miss Bell was related to Alexander Graham Bell and that she failed to meet Heron because a telephone malfunctioned.

**22 Critical Thinking and Reading** How does Jason react to this information?

**23 Discussion** What is ironic about the ghosts' situation? Does Jason's description of the ghosts give any clue to his further actions?

**24 Discussion** Why did the advertising copy that Jason and Berenice wrote that day turn out so well?

**25 Reading Strategy** Ask students to predict what Jason will do with the things he has assembled.

---

indirectly compares the typewriter with a person when she says it is "chattering to itself in a frenzy of enthusiasm." The statement helps you imagine the scene, and it also suggests the author's lighthearted tone, or attitude toward the subject.

**Student Activity 1.** Find four other examples of figurative language in the story and write these on your paper. Read your choices to the class, discussing the comparison in each expression as well as the effect of that expression on the reader.

**Student Activity 2.** Work with a partner to write five original figurative expressions. Share your work with the rest of the class.

**Reader's Response** Would you have gone into the mysterious Grimes Buildings at night as Jason Ashgrove did? Why or why not?

". . . Yes."

Berenice went a little pale. Her eyes sought Jason's and, prompted by him, she said formally, "Switchboard here, Miss Bell, your ten o'clock call."

"Thank you," whispered the telephone.

"Excellent," Jason remarked, as Miss Golden replaced the receiver with a trembling hand. He unfastened his package and slipped its straps over his shoulders. "Now, plug in the intercom."

Berenice did so, and then announced, loudly and clearly, "Attention. Night watchman on duty, please. Night watchman on duty. You have an urgent summons to Room 92. You have an urgent summons to Room 92."

Her voice echoed and reverberated through the empty corridors, then the Tannoy coughed itself to silence.

"Now we must run. You take the roses, sweetheart, and I'll carry the bottles."

Together they raced up eight flights of stairs and along the green corridor to Room 92. As they neared the door a burst of music met them—harp music swelling out, sweet and triumphant. Jason took one of the bunches of roses from Berenice, opened the door a little way, and gently deposited the flowers, with the bottle, inside the door. As he closed it again Berenice said breathlessly, "Did you see anything?"

26 | "No," he said. "The room was too full of music."

His eyes were shining.

They stood hand in hand, reluctant to move away, waiting for they hardly knew what. Suddenly the door flew open again. Neither Berenice nor Jason, afterwards, cared to speak of what they saw then, but each was left with a memory, bright as the picture on a Salvador Dali[15] calendar, of a bicycle bearing on its saddle a harp, a bottle of wine, and a bouquet of red roses, sweeping improbably down the corridor and far, far away.

"We can go now," said Jason. He led Berenice to the fire door, tucking the other bottle of Mâcon into his jacket pocket. A black wind from the north whistled beneath, as they stood on the openwork iron platform, looking down.

"We don't want our evening to be spoiled by the thought of that curse hanging over us," he said, "so this is the practical thing to do. Hang on to the roses." And holding his love firmly, Jason pulled the ripcord of his RAF friend's parachute and leaped off the fire escape. | 27

A bridal shower of rose petals adorned the descent of Miss Golden, who was possibly the only girl to be kissed in mid-air in the district of Clerkenwell at ten minutes to midnight on Christmas Eve.

15. **Salvador Dali** (sal′ və dôr′ dä′ lē): A modern artist (1904– ) famous for his unusual pictures.

***ANSWERS TO THINKING ABOUT THE SELECTION***
*Recalling*

1. He wants to discover the mysterious secret which makes it necessary for all the employees to vacate the building by 5 P.M.
2. The Grimes Buildings are haunted by two ghosts who, when alive, were in love. The man, William Heron, was the building's night watchman. He used a bicycle to patrol the halls. The woman, Daisy Bell, gave harp lessons in Room 92. On the night that Heron had planned to propose to Daisy, she overslept and missed their usual nightly meeting. Heron, believing that Daisy's absence meant that she no longer loved him, jumped off the fire escape from the tenth floor.
3. Jason makes it possible for them to finally meet on Christmas Eve

by making sure that Daisy receives her wake-up call. The meeting that should have taken place fifty years earlier takes place now.
4. He borrows a parachute and jumps from the fire escape with Miss Golden in his arms, thereby safely fulfilling the curse.

*Interpreting*

5. Suggested Response: Neither thieves nor anyone else is brave

enough to go into the building after 5 P.M.
6. Suggested Response: She is in love with Jason.
7. Suggested Response: Attempting to solve the romantic problems of William and Daisy brings Jason and Berenice closer together.

*Applying*

8. Answers will differ but should include the fact that through their

## THINKING ABOUT THE SELECTION

### Recalling

1. Why does Jason Ashgrove first sneak into the Grimes Buildings after five P.M.?
2. How do the bicycle, the fire escape, and the harp relate to the building's secret?
3. What is Jason's plan for helping Daisy Bell and William Heron?
4. How does Jason avoid the fate that awaits anyone who sees Heron's ghost?

### Interpreting

5. Why don't the Grimes Buildings need a night watchman?
6. Why does Berenice Golden agree to meet Jason in the Grimes Buildings after dark?
7. In what way does love beget, or lead to, love in this story?

### Applying

8. How do the events in this story support the saying that "love conquers all"? Do you agree with this saying? Explain.

## ANALYZING LITERATURE

### Understanding Suspense

**Suspense** is the quality that makes you keep reading to find out what happens. Authors often use **foreshadowing,** or hints about what is to come, to create suspense. Suspense also comes from a sense of danger. For example, when Jason sneaks into the Grimes Buildings, you know that he is in danger, and the suspense builds as you wait to learn the nature of his peril.

1. What led you to suspect that the Grimes Buildings were haunted?
2. Explain how the following quotation is an example of foreshadowing: "Close beside his ear a bicycle bell tinkled its tiny warning."

## CRITICAL THINKING AND READING

### Recognizing Relevant Details

**Relevant details** move the plot forward or give insights into characters. Hints used in foreshadowing are relevant details; they relate directly to the outcome of the story. Jason's hair turning gray overnight is relevant because it shows how extreme his terror is and reveals to Berenice that he went into the building after dark.

Which of these details from "Sonata for Harp and Bicycle" are relevant because they help you predict what will happen next?
1. Jason was writing an Oat Crisp ad.
2. A tap was dripping in the empty building.
3. Daisy took a nap from 7 to 10 PM.

## UNDERSTANDING LANGUAGE

### Understanding Words from Greek Myths

Many English words come from the Greek language and mythology. For example, the word *tantalize* comes from the name *Tantalus,* a Greek king. He was punished in Hades by being able to see, but never reach, water and food.

Find the derivations of the following words in a dictionary. How do the derivations relate to the words' meanings?
1. echo
2. herculean
3. narcissism
4. lethe

## THINKING AND WRITING

### Writing About Suspense

Write a commercial for this story, giving examples of how the author uses foreshadowing to build suspense. Also mention any other techniques she uses to keep readers on the edge of their seats. Revise the commercial to be sure it conveys a sense of what the book is like without giving away the plot. Proofread your commercial and present it to your classmates.

*Sonata for Harp and Bicycle*  41

ogy. He was famous for his immense strength and for performing twelve nearly impossible tasks known as the Herculean Labors. *Herculean* has come to mean "a powerful person" or "a difficult job."
3. Suggested Response: *Narcissism* is derived from the name of a beautiful youth who in Greek mythology wasted away while admiring his own reflection. *Narcissism* has come to mean "an extreme love for one's self."
4. Suggested Response: *Lethe* is the Greek word for "forgetfulness." In Greek mythology, it is the name of the river in Hades that causes the dead to forget their lives on Earth when they drink from it. The modern meaning of the word is nearly the same —"forgetfulness or oblivion."

**Challenge** Is Jason Ashgrove a hero? What typical characteristics of a hero does Jason possess? Is there anything about his personality that is not traditionally heroic?

***THINKING AND WRITING***
For help with this assignment, students can refer to Lesson 12, "Writing About a Short Story," in the Handbook of Writing About Literature.

**Publishing Student Writing** Ask individual students to volunteer to present their commercials for "Sonata for Harp and Bicycle" in front of the class. Have the audience discuss the effectiveness of each performance.

own love, Jason and Berenice are able to work together to reunite William and Daisy and to end the haunting of the Grimes Buildings.

**Challenge** How does the humor of the story affect the suspenseful and fantastic aspects?

***ANSWERS TO ANALYZING LITERATURE***
1. Suggested Response: No one was allowed to remain in the building

after five P.M. and Miss Golden was frightened by the secret.
2. Suggested Response: This sentence is a foreshadowing of Jason's encounter with Heron's bicycle-riding ghost.

***ANSWERS TO CRITICAL THINKING AND READING***
Suggested Response: Only number three contains a relevant detail.

***ANSWERS TO UNDERSTANDING LANGUAGE***

1. Suggested Response: *Echo* is the Greek word for "sound." It is also the name of a nymph in Greek mythology who pined away for her lover until nothing was left of her but her voice. An echo is the repetition of a sound, especially a voice.
2. Suggested Response: *Herculean* is derived from the name of Hercules, a great hero of Greek mythol-

**Writing Across the Curriculum** Have students research and write a short report regarding the scientific perspective on ghosts or supernatural events. Inform the science department of this assignment, so that teachers can assist students.

## Focus

**More About the Author** H. H. Munro (Saki) had a strong interest in politics and often wrote about the public figures of his time. As Lewis Carroll did in *Alice in Wonderland,* he sometimes disguised these public figures as animals or other imaginative characters. Ask students why such disguise might have been necessary.

**Literary Focus** You may want to point out to students that the conflict is the focus of a story. The story usually moves toward a resolution of the conflict.

**Look For** Point out to students that a resolution can be ironical —different from what is expected. Ask them to look for the ironies in the resolution of this story. How do the ironies relate to the title?

**Writing/Prior Knowledge** Ask students whether conflict is always a negative thing. In what ways, if any, can conflict bring about positive results?

**Vocabulary** Have your less advanced students read these words, and when the words appear in the story, ask students to substitute a synonym for each.

**Spelling Tip** Point out the double c in *succor.* Some students may misspell this word *suckor.*

## The Interlopers

**Saki** (1870–1916) is the pen name of H. H. Munro, an English writer who was born in Burma, where his father was inspector general of the police force. In England, Saki worked as a journalist, writing political satire and serving as a correspondent to Russia and France. Saki served in the army during World War I and was killed in France. He wrote many short stories that, like "The Interlopers," end with some surprising twists.

**Conflict**

Most plots are built on **conflict,** or the struggle between opposing forces. An **external conflict** occurs between two or more characters or between a character and the forces of nature. An **internal conflict** occurs within a character who possesses opposing ideas or feelings. The two characters in "The Interlopers" inherited an external conflict from grandparents.

**Look For**

As you read "The Interlopers," look for the forces that oppose Ulrich von Gradwitz besides his old enemy, Georg Znaeym. How are the conflicts in this story resolved?

**Writing**

Everybody gets into conflicts from time to time. A conflict might appear trivial to the observer but seem tremendously serious to the participants. An example of such a conflict is when two customers in a store both think they should be the next one to receive service. Try to recall a similar conflict you have witnessed in a store or restaurant. Put yourself in the place of one of the parties. Freewrite, telling what has happened and why the conflict is important to you.

**Vocabulary**

Knowing the following words will help you as you read "The Interlopers."

**precipitous** (pri sip′ə təs) *adj.:* Steep; sheer (p. 43)

**marauders** (mə rôd′ ərz) *n.:* Raiders; people who take goods by force (p. 44)

**medley** (med′ lē) *n.:* A mixture of things not usually found together (p. 44)

**condolence** (kən dō′ ləns) *n.:* An expression of sympathy with a grieving person (p. 45)

**languor** (laŋ′ gər) *n.:* A lack of vigor, weakness (p. 45)

**succor** (suk′ər) *n.:* aid; help; relief (p. 46)

## Objectives

1  To understand conflict
2  To identify the causes and effects of conflict
3  To use context clues to identify word meanings
4  To write about conflict

## Support Material

**Teaching Portfolio**
Teacher Backup, p. 45
Grammar in Action Worksheet, *Using Participles,* p. 48
Usage and Mechanics Worksheet, p. 50
Vocabulary Check, p. 51
Analyzing Literature Worksheet, *Understanding Conflict,* p. 52

Language Worksheet, *Using Context Clues,* p. 53
Selection Test, p. 54

# The Interlopers

## Saki

In a forest of mixed growth somewhere on the eastern spurs of the Carpathians,[1] a man stood one winter night watching and listening, as though he waited for some beast of the woods to come within the range of his vision, and, later, of his rifle. But the game for whose presence he kept so keen an outlook was none that figured in the sportsman's calendar as lawful and proper for the chase; Ulrich von Gradwitz[2] patrolled the dark forest in quest of a human enemy.

The forest lands of Gradwitz were of wide extent and well stocked with game; the narrow strip of precipitous woodland that lay on its outskirt was not remarkable for the game it harbored or the shooting it afforded, but it was the most jealously guarded of all its owner's territorial possessions. A famous lawsuit, in the days of his grandfather, had wrested it from the illegal possession of a neighboring family of petty landowners; the dispossessed party had never acquiesced in the judgment of the Courts, and a long series of poaching affrays[3] and similar scandals had embittered the relationships between the families for three generations. The neighbor feud had grown into a personal one since Ulrich had come to be head of his family; if there was a man in the world whom he detested and wished ill to it was Georg Znaeym,[4] the inheritor of the quarrel and the tireless game-snatcher and raider of the disputed border-forest. The feud might, perhaps, have died down or been compromised if the personal ill will of the two men had not stood in the way; as boys they had thirsted for one another's blood, as men each prayed that misfortune might fall on the other, and this wind-scourged winter night Ulrich had banded together his foresters to watch the dark forest, not in quest of four-footed quarry, but to keep a lookout for the prowling thieves whom he suspected of being afoot from across the land boundary. The roebuck,[5] which usually kept in the sheltered hollows during a storm wind, were running like driven things tonight, and there was movement and unrest among the creatures that were wont to sleep through the dark hours. Assuredly there was a disturbing element in the forest, and Ulrich could guess the quarter from whence it came.

He strayed away by himself from the watchers whom he had placed in ambush on the crest of the hill, and wandered far down the steep slopes amid the wild tangle of undergrowth, peering through the tree trunks and listening through the whistling and skirling

---

1. **Carpathians** (kär pā' thē ənz): Mountains in central Europe.
2. **Ulrich von Gradwitz** (ool' rik fòn gräd' vitz)
3. **poaching affrays** (pōch' iŋ ə frāz'): Disputes about hunting on someone else's property.

---

4. **Georg Znaeym** (gā' ôrg znä' im)
5. **roebuck** (rō' buk') n.: Male deer.

---

**Presentation**

**Motivation/Prior Knowledge** Ask students if they know of the Hatfields and the McCoys. If they do not, explain that these two families from Kentucky and West Virginia, engaged in a bloody, long-standing feud. Tell them that such feuds often begin with an insult or injury, real or imagined, that must be avenged. The act of vengeance then prompts a response, resulting in a never-ending cycle. Feuds appear frequently in literature. For example, a feud is central to the plot of Shakespeare's *Romeo and Juliet*. Tell students that a feud plays an important part in this story as well.

**Master Teacher Note** Point out to students that the forest plays an important role in this story, almost as if it were a character itself. Ask students to look for evidence of this as they read.

**Purpose-Setting Question** Who are "the interlopers" in the title, and why do they deserve that name?

1 **Clarification** The word *interloper* is made of the prefix *inter-* (between or among) and the root word *lope* (to run or leap along). The original meaning of the word is "to interfere with another's trading rights or privileges." The word has developed a more general meaning as well—"to intrude in the affairs of others."

2 **Discussion** The disputed land was not particularly desirable. What does this fact reveal about the families who contested its ownership for so many years?

3 **Discussion** What do you learn about the depth of feeling between these two men?

**Thematic Idea** Another selection that deals with a long-standing feud is *Romeo and Juliet*, by Shakespeare, page 321. You might have students compare the resolution of each of these feuds.

**WINTER IN THE ROCKIES**
*Thomas Moran*
Three Lions

of the wind and the restless beating of the branches for sight or sound of the marauders. If only on this wild night, in this dark, lone spot, he might come across Georg Znaeym, man to man, with none to witness—that was the wish that was uppermost in his thoughts. And as he stepped round the trunk of a huge beech he came face to face with the man he sought.

The two enemies stood glaring at one another for a long silent moment. Each had a rifle in his hand, each had hate in his heart and murder uppermost in his mind. The chance had come to give full play to the passions of a lifetime. But a man who has been brought up under the code of a restraining

civilization cannot easily nerve himself to shoot down his neighbor in cold blood and without word spoken, except for an offense against his hearth and honor. And before the moment of hesitation had given way to action a deed of Nature's own violence overwhelmed them both. A fierce shriek of the storm had been answered by a splitting crash over their heads, and ere they could leap aside a mass of falling beech tree had thundered down on them. Ulrich von Gradwitz found himself stretched on the ground, one arm numb beneath him and the other held almost as helplessly in a tight tangle of forked branches, while both legs were pinned beneath the fallen mass. His heavy shooting-boots had saved his feet from being crushed to pieces, but if his fractures were not as serious as they might have been, at least it was evident that he could not move from his present position till some one came to release him. The descending twigs had slashed the skin of his face, and he had to wink away some drops of blood from his eyelashes before he could take in a general view of the disaster. At his side, so near that under ordinary circumstances he could almost have touched him, lay Georg Znaeym, alive and struggling, but obviously as helplessly pinioned down as himself. All round them lay a thick-strewn wreckage of splintered branches and broken twigs.

Relief at being alive and exasperation at his captive plight brought a strange medley of pious thank-offerings and sharp curses to Ulrich's lips. Georg, who was nearly blinded with the blood which trickled across his eyes, stopped his struggling for a moment to listen, and then gave a short, snarling laugh.

"So you're not killed, as you ought to be, but you're caught, anyway," he cried; "caught fast. Ho, what a jest, Ulrich von Gradwitz snared in his stolen forest. There's real justice for you!"

44    *Short Stories*

## Grammar in Action

A **participle** is a verb form that can function as an adjective to modify a noun or pronoun. Present participles end in *-ing* while regular past participles end in *-ed*. The participial endings of irregular verbs can vary:  *chosen*, for example, is the past participle of *choose*.

Since the same participle can serve as a verb or an adjective, you should not confuse these two functions. Here are some examples:

The wind was *whistling* through the trees. (present participle as verb)
The *whistling* wind shook the trees.  (present participle as adjective)
The news had *startled* her.  (past participle as verb)
*Startled*, she hardly knew how to react to the news.  (past participle as adjective)

Because it is a verb form, a participle used as an adjective seems to show action. Writers therefore use participles to make their

And he laughed again, mockingly and savagely.

"I'm caught in my own forest land," retorted Ulrich. "When my men come to release us you will wish, perhaps, that you were in a better plight than caught poaching on a neighbor's land, shame on you."

Georg was silent for a moment; then he answered quietly:

"Are you sure that your men will find much to release? I have men, too, in the forest tonight, close behind me, and *they* will be here first and do the releasing. When they drag me out from under these branches it won't need much clumsiness on their part to roll this mass of trunk right over on the top of you. Your men will find you dead under a fallen beech tree. For form's sake I shall send my condolences to your family."

"It is a useful hint," said Ulrich fiercely. "My men had orders to follow in ten minutes' time, seven of which must have gone by already, and when they get me out—I will remember the hint. Only as you will have met your death poaching on my lands I don't think I can decently send any message of condolence to your family."

"Good," snarled Georg, "good. We fight this quarrel out to the death, you and I and our foresters, with no cursed interlopers to come between us. Death and damnation to you, Ulrich von Gradwitz."

"The same to you, Georg Znaeym, forest-thief, game-snatcher."

Both men spoke with the bitterness of possible defeat before them, for each knew that it might be long before his men would seek him out or find him; it was a bare matter of chance which party would arrive first on the scene.

Both had now given up the useless struggle to free themselves from the mass of wood that held them down; Ulrich limited his endeavors to an effort to bring his one partially free arm near enough to his outer coat pocket to draw out his wine flask. Even when he had accomplished that operation it was long before he could manage the unscrewing of the stopper or get any of the liquid down his throat. But what a heaven-sent draft it seemed! It was an open winter, and little snow had fallen as yet, hence the captives suffered less from the cold than might have been the case at that season of the year; nevertheless, the wine was warming and reviving to the wounded man, and he looked across with something like a throb of pity to where his enemy lay, just keeping the groans of pain and weariness from crossing his lips.

"Could you reach this flask if I threw it over to you?" asked Ulrich suddenly; "there is good wine in it, and one may as well be as comfortable as one can. Let us drink, even if tonight one of us dies."

"No, I can scarcely see anything; there is so much blood caked round my eyes," said Georg, "and in any case I don't drink wine with an enemy."

Ulrich was silent for a few minutes, and lay listening to the weary screeching of the wind. An idea was slowly forming and growing in his brain, an idea that gained strength every time that he looked across at the man who was fighting so grimly against pain and exhaustion. In the pain and languor that Ulrich himself was feeling the old fierce hatred seemed to be dying down.

"Neighbor," he said presently, "do as you please if your men come first. It was a fair compact. But as for me, I've changed my mind. If my men are the first to come you shall be the first to be helped, as though you were my guest. We have quarreled like devils all our lives over this stupid strip of forest, where the trees can't even stand upright in a breath of wind. Lying here tonight, thinking, I've come to think we've been rather fools; there are better things in life than

*The Interlopers* 45

8 **Discussion** How does each man envision his rescue?

9 **Discussion** To whom is George referring when he says, ". . . with no cursed interlopers to come between us"?

10 **Discussion** How do Ulrich's remarks about the wine signal a change in his attitude and a possible end to the conflict?

11 **Literary Focus** What do you think motivates Ulrich's change of heart? Does this change reflect internal or external conflict?

descriptions more lively. The following participles, for instance, add to the drama of "The Interlopers":

A fierce shriek of the storm had been answered by a *splitting* crash over their heads, . . .
*The descending* twigs had slashed the skin of his face, . . .
Georg . . . then gave a short, *snarling* laugh.

**Student Activity 1.** Substitute an adjective for each of the participles from "The Interlopers." Explain whether the participle or the adjective creates the more vivid description.

**Student Activity 2.** Write five sentences of your own using participles as adjectives.

getting the better of a boundary dispute. Neighbor, if you will help me to bury the old quarrel I—I will ask you to be my friend."

Georg Znaeym was silent for so long that Ulrich thought, perhaps, he had fainted with the pain of his injuries. Then he spoke slowly and in jerks.

**12** "How the whole region would stare and gabble if we rode into the market square together. No one living can remember seeing a Znaeym and a von Gradwitz talking to one another in friendship. And what peace there would be among the forester folk if we ended our feud tonight. And if we choose to make peace among our people there is none other to interfere, no interlopers from outside. . . . You would come and keep the Sylvester night beneath my roof, and I would come and feast on some high day at your castle. . . . I would never fire a shot on your land, save when you invited me as a guest; and you should come and shoot with me down in the marshes where the wildfowl are. In all the countryside there are none that could hinder if we willed to make peace. I never thought to have wanted to do other than hate you all my life, but I think I have changed my mind about things too, this last half-hour. And you offered me your wine flask. . . . Ulrich von Gradwitz, I will be your friend."

For a space both men were silent, turning over in their minds the wonderful changes that this dramatic reconciliation would bring about. In the cold, gloomy forest, with the wind tearing in fitful gusts through the naked branches and whistling round the tree trunks, they lay and waited for the help that would now bring release and succor to both parties. And each prayed **13** a private prayer that his men might be the first to arrive, so that he might be the first to show honorable attention to the enemy that had become a friend.

Presently, as the wind dropped for a moment, Ulrich broke silence.

"Let's shout for help," he said; "in this lull our voices may carry a little way."

"They won't carry far through the trees and undergrowth," said Georg, "but we can try. Together, then."

The two raised their voices in a prolonged hunting call.

"Together again," said Ulrich a few minutes later, after listening in vain for an answering halloo.

"I heard something that time, I think," said Ulrich.

"I heard nothing but the pestilential wind," said Georg hoarsely.

There was silence again for some minutes, and then Ulrich gave a joyful cry.

"I can see figures coming through the wood. They are following in the way I came down the hillside."

Both men raised their voices in as loud a shout as they could muster.

"They hear us! They've stopped. Now they see us. They're running down the hill toward us," cried Ulrich. **14**

"How many of them are there?" asked Georg.

"I can't see distinctly," said Ulrich; "nine or ten."

"Then they are yours," said Georg; "I had only seven out with me."

"They are making all the speed they can, brave lads," said Ulrich gladly.

"Are they your men?" asked Georg. "Are they your men?" he repeated impatiently as Ulrich did not answer.

"No," said Ulrich with a laugh, the idiotic chattering laugh of a man unstrung with hideous fear.

"Who are they?" asked Georg quickly, **15** straining his eyes to see what the other would gladly not have seen. **16**

"*Wolves.*"

## THINKING ABOUT THE SELECTION

### Recalling

1. What is Ulrich doing in the forest?
2. What has kept the feud between the families going for three generations? How has the feud between Ulrich and Georg become personal?
3. How do Ulrich and Georg feel toward each other when they meet in the forest? Why can they not shoot each other?
4. How do they become trapped? Why does each hope that his men will come to the rescue?

### Interpreting

5. Why doesn't Georg consider himself a poacher when he hunts in the forest?
6. Why do you think Ulrich's and Georg's attitudes toward each other change?
7. Explain why what happens at the end is or is not different from what you expected.
8. Give two possible interpretations for the title of the story.

### Applying

9. If the two men had been saved, how would they have behaved toward each other years later?

## ANALYZING LITERATURE

### Understanding Conflict

A **conflict** is a struggle between opposing forces. An **external conflict** pits characters against each other or against the forces of nature. An **internal conflict** pits a character against himself or herself. For example, when Ulrich is trying to decide whether or not to share his wine with Georg, he is undergoing an internal conflict.

Find an example of each of the following types of conflict in "The Interlopers" and explain the nature of the conflict.

1. A character in conflict with another character
2. A character in conflict with nature
3. A character in conflict with himself

## CRITICAL THINKING AND READING

### Identifying Causes and Effects

Conflicts generally have causes. For example, the conflict between Ulrich's and Georg's grandfathers occurred because they both wanted the same piece of land. Conflicts also have effects. One effect of this conflict is that, generations later, Ulrich and Georg are enemies.

1. Identify one cause of the conflict between Ulrich and Georg and the tree.
2. Identify two effects of the conflict between Ulrich and Georg and the tree.

## UNDERSTANDING LANGUAGE

### Using Context Clues

When you come across words that have more than one meaning, you can use **context clues,** or the words and phrases around a word, to help you figure out which meaning the author intended. For example, Saki refers to "the shooting [the woodland] *afforded.*" The context shows that *afforded* means "supplied," not "had the means for."

Use context clues to identify the correct meaning of the italicized word.

1. "a neighboring family of *petty* landowners" (page 43)
2. "kept in the sheltered *hollows* during a storm wind" (page 43)
3. "caught *poaching* on a neighbor's land" (page 45)

## THINKING AND WRITING

### Writing About Conflict

Imagine that you were a friend of both Ulrich's and Georg's grandfathers when the feud began. Write a brief speech directed toward one of the two men trying to bring about a reconciliation. First describe the conflict in objective, or factual, terms. Then tell what effects it will have on the participants and on their friends and family. Finally, explain your ideas for a solution. Revise your draft to make the speech as convincing as possible. Deliver it to your classmates.

*The Interlopers* 47

(Answers begin on p. 46.)

Georg and Ulrich as best friends, or as having reverted to hating each other once they were rescued.

### ANSWERS TO ANALYZING LITERATURE

1. Suggested Response: An example is the conflict between Ulrich and Georg.
2. Suggested Response: Both Ulrich and Georg are victims of the fallen tree.
3. Suggested Response: Both Ulrich and Georg experience an internal conflict as they decide whether to become friends.

**Challenge** Would other endings to the story have been more satisfying? Explain.

### ANSWERS TO CRITICAL THINKING AND READING

1. Suggested Response: The wind is blowing violently.
2. Suggested Response: Ulrich and Georg become friends; they are unable to escape from the wolves.

### ANSWERS TO UNDERSTANDING LANGUAGE

1. In this context, *petty* means "small" or "unimportant."
2. In this context, *hollows* mean "small valleys."
3. In this context, *poaching* means "illegal hunting."

### THINKING AND WRITING

For help with this assignment, students can refer to Lesson 12, "Writing About a Short Story," in the Handbook of Writing About Literature.

### Publishing Student Writing

Have students create posters that advertise and briefly summarize their speeches. Display these posters around the classroom when students deliver their speeches to the class.

2. The feud continued because the new generations of both families were brought up to believe that the forest lands belonged to them. The feud has become personal because Ulrich and Georg have hated each other since they were young; they are no longer fighting because of the land dispute.
3. They hate each other. They will not shoot each other because they are both civilized men and cannot simply murder a person in cold blood.

4. They become trapped when a tree falls on them. Each man wants his own men to rescue him and kill his enemy.

### *Interpreting*

5. Suggested Response: Georg does not consider himself a poacher because he believes that he is hunting on land that belongs to him.
6. Answers may differ. Students may indicate that life-threatening situations tend to make people think

more seriously about the way they conduct their lives.

7. Answers will differ. The outcome was probably different from what most students expected because the conflict between the two men had been resolved.
8. Answers will differ but might include: Each of the men regards the other as an interloper; the wolves are interlopers.

### *Applying*

9. Answers will differ but might depict

## The Lady or the Tiger?

**Frank R. Stockton** (1834–1902) was born in Philadelphia, the third of nine children. An ancestor, Richard Stockton, was one of the signers of the Declaration of Independence. Stockton was an engraver by trade, but he spent much of his time writing stories. His earliest stories were for children, but later he began writing for adults. "The Lady or the Tiger?" is Stockton's best known work. When it was published in 1882, it caused much excitement as readers debated what the ending should be.

**Dilemma**

A **dilemma** is a situation in which a person must choose between two equal alternatives. There is no objective way to determine that one alternative is better than the other. Most often, the word *dilemma* is used in regard to situations in which both alternatives are equally unpleasant. You can learn something about the characters in stories by seeing how they react to dilemmas. For example, when the princess is faced with a dilemma in "The Lady or the Tiger?" the choice she makes depends upon the kind of person she is.

**Look For**

In this semibarbaric kingdom, justice is meted out impartially in the arena. As you read "The Lady or the Tiger?" look for what happens when the man the king's daughter loves is placed in the arena.

**Writing**

Ralph Waldo Emerson once wrote: "As a man thinketh so is he, and as a man chooseth so is he." Freewrite about what you think is the meaning of this quotation.

**Vocabulary**

Knowing the following words will help you as you read "The Lady or the Tiger?"

**exuberant** (ig zōō′ bər ənt) *adj.*: Very great; extreme (p. 49)
**bland** (bland) *adv.*: Pleasantly smooth; agreeable (p. 49)
**dire** (dīr) *adv.*: Dreadful; terrible (p. 50)
**retribution** (ret′ rə byōō′ shən) *n.*: Deserved punishment (p. 50)
**fervent** (fur′ vənt) *adj.*: Burning; passionate (p. 51)

**imperious** (im pir′ ē əs) *adj.*: Overbearing; arrogant, domineering (p. 51)
**ardor** (är′ dər) *n.*: Emotional warmth; passion (p. 51)
**aesthetic** (es thet′ ik) *adj.*: Sensitive to art and beauty (p. 51)

48 *Short Stories*

# The Lady or the Tiger?

## Frank R. Stockton

In the very olden time, there lived a semi-barbaric king, whose ideas, though somewhat polished, were still large, florid, and untrammeled,[1] as became the half of him which was barbaric. He was a man of exuberant fancy, and of an authority so irresistible that, at his will, he turned his varied fancies into facts. He was greatly given to self-communing, and when he and himself agreed upon anything, the thing was done. When every member of his domestic and political systems moved smoothly, his nature was bland and genial; but whenever there was a little hitch, he was blander and more genial still, for nothing pleased him so much as to make the crooked straight, and crush down uneven places.

Among the borrowed notions by which his barbarism had become modified was that of the public arena, in which, by exhibitions of manly and beastly valor, the minds of his subjects were refined and cultured.

But even here the exuberant and barbaric fancy asserted itself. The arena of the king was built to widen and develop the mental energies of the people. This vast amphitheater[2] with its encircling galleries, its mysterious vaults, and its unseen passages, was an agent of poetic justice, in which crime was punished, or virtue rewarded, by the decrees of an impartial and incorruptible chance.

When a subject was accused of a crime of sufficient importance to interest the king, public notice was given that on an appointed day the fate of the accused person would be decided in the king's arena. And this structure well deserved that name; for, although its form and plan were borrowed from afar, its purpose emanated[3] solely from the brain of this man.

When all the people had assembled in the galleries, and the king, surrounded by his court, sat high up on his throne of royal state on one side of the arena, he gave a signal, a door beneath him opened, and the accused subject stepped out into the amphitheater. Directly opposite him, on the other side of the enclosed space, were two doors, exactly alike and side by side. It was the duty and the privilege of the person on trial to walk directly to these doors and open one of them. He could open either door he pleased. He was subject to no guidance or influence but that of the aforementioned impartial and incorruptible chance. If he opened the one, there came out of it a hungry tiger, the fiercest and most cruel that could be procured, which immediately sprang upon him, and tore him to pieces, as a punishment for

---

**1. florid** (flôr′ id), **and untrammeled** (un tram′ ʼld): Showy and bold.
**2. amphitheater** (am′ fə thē′ ə tər) *n.*: An open space surrounded by rising rings of seats.

---

**3. emanated** (em′ ə nāt′ id) *v.*: Came.

## Presentation

**Motivation/Prior Knowledge** Ask students whether they know of anyone who has been punished unjustly. Why was the punishment unjust? Ask them to consider the problem of choosing a just punishment for any crime. Tell them that the selection deals with these issues.

**Thematic Idea** Another selection that deals with the consequences of forbidden love is *Romeo and Juliet,* page 321.

**Master Teacher Note** This story has achieved wide renown because of the clever ending, which does not provide readers with a resolution of the conflict. Tell students to be prepared to invent their own ending—and to back up their choice with details from the story.

**Purpose-Setting Question** What is the answer to the question in the title?

1 **Discussion** If students have read "The Most Dangerous Game," page 13, have them compare General Zaroff to the king. What is similar about the two characters?

2 **Clarification** The ancient Romans punished enemies or criminals by confining them in an arena with wild beasts.

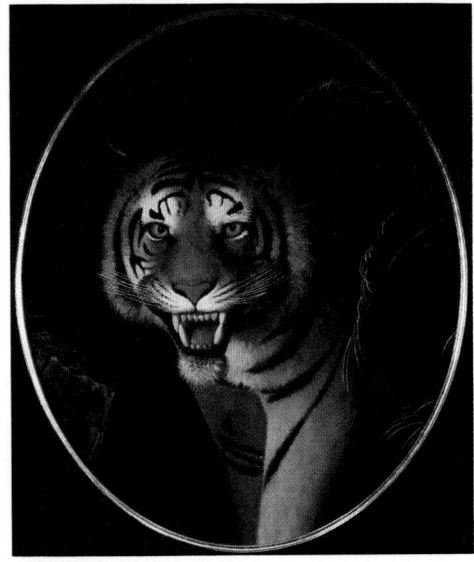

**TIGER**
*Samuel Marsden Brookes*
*The Oakland Museum*
*Kahn Collection*

3 his guilt. The moment that the case of the criminal was thus decided, doleful iron bells were clanged, great wails went up from the hired mourners posted on the outer rim of the arena, and the vast audience, with bowed heads and downcast hearts, wended slowly their homeward way, mourning greatly that one so young and fair, or so old and respected, should have merited so dire a fate.

But if the accused person opened the other door, there came forth from it a lady, the most suitable to his years and station that His Majesty could select among his fair subjects; and to this lady he was immediately married, as a reward of his innocence. It mattered not that he might already possess a wife and family, or that his affections might be engaged upon an object of his own selection. The king allowed no such subordinate arrangements to interfere with his great scheme of retribution and reward. The exercises, as in the other instance, took place immediately, and in the arena. Another door opened beneath the king, and a priest, followed by a band of choristers, and dancing maidens blowing joyous airs on golden horns and treading an epithalamic measure,[4] advanced to where the pair stood side by side, and the wedding was promptly and cheerily solemnized. Then the gay brass bells rang forth their merry peals, the people shouted glad hurrahs, and the innocent man, preceded by children strewing flowers on his path, led his bride to his home.

4 This was the king's semibarbaric method of administering justice. Its perfect fairness is obvious. The criminal could not know out of which door would come the lady. He opened either he pleased, without having the slightest idea whether, in the next instant, he was to be devoured or married. On some occasions the tiger came out of one door, and on some out of the other. The decisions of this tribunal[5] were not only fair, they were positively determinate.[6] The 5 accused person was instantly punished if he found himself guilty; and if innocent, he was rewarded on the spot, whether he liked it or not. There was no escape from the judgments of the king's arena.

6 The institution was a very popular one. When the people gathered together on one of the great trial days, they never knew whether they were to witness a bloody slaughter or a hilarious wedding. This element of uncertainty lent an interest to the occasion which it could not otherwise have attained. Thus, the masses were entertained and pleased, and the thinking part of the community

---

**4. epithalamic** (ep′ ə thə lā′ mik) **measure:** Marriage dance.
**5. tribunal** (trī byōo′ n'l) *n.:* Court.
**6. determinate** (di tʉr′ mi nit) *adj.:* Final.

could bring no charge of unfairness against this plan; for did not the accused person have the whole matter in his own hands?

This semibarbaric king had a daughter as blooming as his most florid fancies, and with a soul as fervent and imperious as his own. As is usual in such cases, she was the apple of his eye, and was loved by him above all humanity. Among his courtiers was a young man of that fineness of blood and lowness of station common to the conventional heroes of romance who love royal maidens. This royal maiden was well satisfied with her lover, for he was handsome and brave to a degree unsurpassed in all this kingdom, and she loved him with an ardor that had enough of barbarism in it to make it exceedingly warm and strong. This love affair moved on happily for many months, until, one day, the king happened to discover its existence. He did not hesitate nor waver in regard to his duty. The youth was immediately cast into prison, and a day was appointed for his trial in the king's arena. This, of course, was an especially important occasion, and His Majesty, as well as all the people, was greatly interested in the workings and development of this trial. Never before had such a case occurred—never before had a subject dared to love the daughter of a king. In after years such things became commonplace enough, but then they were, in no slight degree, novel and startling.

The tiger cages of the kingdom were searched for the most savage and relentless beasts, from which the fiercest monster might be selected for the arena, and the ranks of maiden youth and beauty throughout the land were carefully surveyed by competent judges, in order that the young man might have a fitting bride in case fate did not determine for him a different destiny. Of course, everybody knew that the deed with which the accused was charged had been done. He had loved the princess, and neither he, she, nor anyone else thought of denying the fact. But the king would not think of allowing any fact of this kind to interfere with the workings of the tribunal, in which he took such great delight and satisfaction. No matter how the affair turned out, the youth would be disposed of, and the king would take an aesthetic pleasure in watching the course of events, which would determine whether or not the young man had done wrong in allowing himself to love the princess.

The appointed day arrived. From far and near the people gathered, and thronged the great galleries of the arena, while crowds, unable to gain admittance, massed themselves against its outside walls. The king and his court were in their places, opposite the twin doors—those fateful portals, so terrible in their similarity!

All was ready. The signal was given. A door beneath the royal party opened, and the lover of the princess walked into the arena.

**Original illustration
from STORIES FROM THE ARABIAN NIGHTS**
*Edmund Dulac*

**10 Discussion** How does this youth's appearance add drama to the story?

**11 Reading Strategy** Have students read this section carefully for clues about the princess's decision. Ask them to predict what might happen to the prince.

10

Tall, beautiful, fair, his appearance was greeted with a low hum of admiration and anxiety. Half the audience had not known so grand a youth had lived among them. No wonder the princess loved him! What a terrible thing for him to be there!

As the youth advanced into the arena, he turned, as the custom was, to bow to the king. But he did not think at all of that royal personage; his eyes were fixed upon the princess, who sat to the right of her father. Had it not been for the portion of barbarism in her nature, it is probable that lady would not have been there. But her intense and fervid soul would not allow her to be absent on an occasion in which she was so terribly interested. From the moment that the decree had gone forth that her lover should decide his fate in the king's arena, she had thought of nothing, night or day, but this great event and the various subjects connected with it. Possessed of more power, influence, and force of character than anyone who had ever before been interested in such a case, she had done what no other person had done— she had possessed herself of the secret of the doors. She knew in which of the two rooms behind those doors stood the cage of the tiger, with its open front, and in which waited the lady. Through these thick doors, heavily curtained with skins on the inside, it was impossible that any noise or suggestion should come from within to the person who should approach to raise the latch of one of them. But gold, and the power of a woman's will, had brought the secret to the princess.

Not only did she know in which room stood the lady, ready to emerge, all blushing and radiant, should her door be opened, but she knew who the lady was. It was one of the fairest and loveliest of the damsels of the court who had been selected as the reward of the accused youth, should he be proved innocent of the crime of aspiring to one so far

above him; and the princess hated her. Often had she seen, or imagined that she had seen, this fair creature throwing glances of admiration upon the person of her lover, and sometimes she thought these glances were perceived and even returned. Now and then she had seen them talking together. It was but for a moment or two, but much can be said in a brief space. It may have been on unimportant topics, but how could she know that? The girl was lovely, but she had dared to raise her eyes to the loved one of the princess, and, with all the intensity of the savage blood transmitted to her through long lines of wholly barbaric ancestors, she hated the woman who blushed and trembled behind that silent door.

11

When her lover turned and looked at her, and his eye met hers as she sat there paler and whiter than anyone in the vast ocean of anxious faces about her, he saw, by that power of quick perception which is given to those whose souls are one, that she knew behind which door crouched the tiger, and behind which stood the lady. He had expected her to know it. He understood her nature, and his soul was assured that she would never rest until she had made plain to herself this thing, hidden to all other lookers-on, even to the king. The only hope for the youth in which there was any element of certainty was based upon the success of the princess in discovering this mystery, and the moment he looked upon her, he saw she had succeeded.

Then it was that his quick and anxious glance asked the question, "Which?" It was as plain to her as if he shouted it from where he stood. There was not an instant to be lost. The question was asked in a flash; it must be answered in another.

Her right arm lay on the cushioned parapet before her. She raised her hand, and made a slight, quick movement toward the

## Grammar in Action

Writers **vary their sentences** to maintain reader interest, eliminate choppy passages, and build suspense. The following paragraph by Frank R. Stockton illustrates this technique:

All was ready. The signal was given. A door beneath the royal party opened, and the lover of the princess walked into the arena. Tall, beautiful, fair, his appearance was greeted with a low hum of admiration and anxiety. Half the audience had not known so grand a youth had lived among them. No wonder the princess loved him! What a terrible thing for him to be there!

The paragraph opens with two short, almost staccato sentences. Following are three descriptive, smooth-flowing sentences of nearly equal length. The final two sentences are relatively short exclamations. Thus, the sentence length emphasizes the paragraph's three parts: the quick beginning signal, the audience's observation, and their emotional reaction.

right. No one but her lover saw her. Every eye but his was fixed on the man in the arena.

He turned, and with a firm and rapid step he walked across the empty space. Every heart stopped beating, every breath was held, every eye was fixed immovably upon that man. Without the slightest hesitation, he went to the door on the right, and opened it.

Now, the point of the story is this: Did the tiger come out of that door, or did the lady?

The more we reflect upon this question, the harder it is to answer. It involves a study of the human heart which leads us through devious mazes of passion, out of which it is difficult to find our way. Think of it, fair reader, not as if the decision of the question depended upon yourself, but upon that hot-blooded, semibarbaric princess, her soul at a white heat beneath the combined fires of despair and jealousy. She had lost him, but who should have him?

How often, in her waking hours and in her dreams, had she started in wild horror and covered her face with her hands as she thought of her lover opening the door on the other side of which waited the cruel fangs of the tiger!

But how much oftener had she seen him at the other door! How in her grievous reveries had she gnashed her teeth and torn her hair when she saw his start of rapturous delight as he opened the door of the lady! How her soul had burned in agony when she had seen him rush to meet that woman, with her flushing cheek and sparkling eye of triumph; when she had seen him lead her forth, his whole frame kindled with the joy of recovered life; when she had heard the glad shouts from the multitude, and the wild ringing of the happy bells; when she had seen the priest, with his joyous followers, advance to the couple, and make them man and wife before her very eyes; and when she had seen them walk away together upon their path of flowers, followed by the tremendous shouts of the hilarious multitude, in which her one despairing shriek was lost and drowned!

Would it not be better for him to die at once, and go to wait for her in the blessed regions of semibarbaric futurity?

And yet, that awful tiger, those shrieks, that blood!

Her decision had been indicated in an instant, but it had been made after days and nights of anguished deliberation. She had known she would be asked, she had decided what she would answer, and, without the slightest hesitation, she had moved her hand to the right.

The question of her decision is one not to be lightly considered, and it is not for me to presume to set up myself as the one person able to answer it. So I leave it with all of you: Which came out of the opened door—the lady or the tiger?

*The Lady or the Tiger?* 53

**Student Activity 1.** Read Stockton's paragraph again. Explain why Stockton might have returned to short sentences at the end of this passage.

**Student Activity 2.** Using Stockton's paragraph as a model, write a paragraph of your own. Vary your sentence length, as Stockton does, to build suspense and keep your readers interested in your description. Share your paragraph with your classmates when you are finished.

**Reader's Response** Which door would you choose?

(Answers begin on p. 53.)

5. Suggested Response: The king's justice is considered "perfectly fair" because it is based on chance. This form of justice is barbaric because it is unrelated to guilt or innocence. Because it has an aesthetic quality, however, the writer calls it and the king semi-barbaric.

6. Suggested Response: The princess has a fiery, passionate temperament, and this might have made her wish her lover dead, rather than see him in the arms of another lady.

## Applying

7. Answers may differ but should show students' awareness that such a system of punishment has no relationship to the crime, and is, therefore, not fair or just.

**Challenge** How would you have reacted if Stockton had written an ending in which either the tiger or the lady was behind the door?

## ANSWERS TO ANALYZING LITERATURE

1. Suggested Response: The princess's dilemma is a choice between losing the person she loves through death, or losing the person she loves through his marrying the maiden.

2. Suggested Response: The young man's dilemma is deciding which door he should choose. He must also decide whether the princess's advice is reliable.

## ANSWERS TO CRITICAL THINKING AND READING

Answers will differ but should include a direct yes or no answer to the first question and an explanation supported by details concerning the princess's character found in, or inferred from, the story.

## ANSWERS TO UNDERSTANDING LANGUAGE

1. Suggested Response: In this context, *impartial* means "incorrupt-

## THINKING ABOUT THE SELECTION

### Recalling

1. What is the king's method of trying accused criminals?
2. Of what crime is the young man accused?
3. How does the princess signal the young man when he is in the arena?

### Interpreting

4. Why are public trials in the arena so popular with the people of the kingdom?
5. In what way is the king's system of justice considered perfectly fair? Why does the author describe it and the king as semibarbaric?
6. How does the author describe the nature of the princess? How might this quality influence her decision?

### Applying

7. Imagine a modern equivalent of the king's arena—a lottery in which the accused picks a "to jail" ticket or a "go free" ticket. Would such a lottery be fair? Why or why not?

## ANALYZING LITERATURE

### Analyzing a Dilemma

A character who is confronted with a **dilemma** must choose between two equally balanced (and usually unpleasant) alternatives. In "The Lady or the Tiger?" each person sent into the arena was faced with a dilemma—either choice he made would have an unpleasant consequence.
1. Describe the dilemma the princess faces.
2. Describe the dilemma the young man faces.

## CRITICAL THINKING AND READING

### Analyzing Solutions

Characters in stories usually have problems to solve. The solutions involve making choices.

Because you are able to see the big picture, you are often in a better position to weigh the choices than the character is.

If you were the young man, would you follow the princess's direction? Explain your answer.

## UNDERSTANDING LANGUAGE

### Using Context Clues

**Context clues** are the words, phrases, and sentences around a word. You can use these clues to figure out the meaning of new words. In the sentence, "He did not hesitate nor waver in regard to his duty," the word *hesitate* helps you to know what *waver* means.

Use context clues to define the italicized words in the following phrases.
1. ". . . *impartial* and incorruptible chance." (paragraph 5, page 49)
2. ". . . *doleful* iron bells were clanged." (paragraph 1, page 50)
3. ". . . the twin doors—those fateful *portals* . . ." (paragraph 2, page 52)
4. "But her intense and *fervid* soul would not allow her to be absent . . . ." (paragraph 4, page 52)
5. ". . . which leads us through *devious* mazes of passion, out of which it is difficult to find our way." (paragraph 6, page 53)

## THINKING AND WRITING

### Writing an Ending

Write an ending for "The Lady or the Tiger?" Decide how you think the characters would behave. Think about which solution to "The Lady or the Tiger?" would be most satisfying to your readers and how you personally would like the story to turn out. When you revise your ending, be sure the suspense builds until the moment of revelation. Revise your ending and share it with your classmates.

able because working randomly."
2. Suggested Response: In this context, *doleful* means "mournful or sad."
3. Suggested Response: In this context, *portal* means "door."
4. Suggested Response: In this context, *fervid* means "intense or ardent."
5. Suggested Response: In this context, *devious* means "winding or not straightforward."

## THINKING AND WRITING
For help with this assignment, students can refer to Lesson 17, "Writing a Short Story," in the Handbook of Writing About Literature.

## Publishing Student Writing
Suggest to students that they create a book from the endings that they devise for "The Lady or the Tiger?" Have some students

volunteer to be writers, others illustrators, and others cover or page designers. Have them create a table of contents and an index. Side-staple the collection and make enough copies for the entire class. Suggest to students that they also include the original story. Ask one student to write a foreword explaining the purpose of the book and how it was created.

# Character

PASSING BY, 1924
*E. Martin Hennings*
*Museum of Fine Arts, Houston*

**Humanities Note**

Fine Art, *Passing By*, E. Martin Hennings. E. Martin Hennings (1886-1956), an American painter of Western scenes, was educated in academic art at the Art Institute of Chicago and the National Academy in Munich, Germany. He worked for a time as a commercial artist and muralist before moving to the artist's colony of Taos, New Mexico.

*Passing By* is a pleasant Western scene painted with technical proficiency. The dappled light coming through the trees creates a bright decorative pattern on the figures. The subject is obvious and is intended to appeal to a wide audience.

*Character* 55

# GUIDE FOR READING

## All the Years of Her Life

**Morley Callaghan** (1903–     ) was born in Toronto, Canada, and graduated from the University of Toronto. He worked as a reporter on the *Daily Star,* where he met the writer Ernest Hemingway, who helped him publish his stories in literary magazines. After some success as a writer, Callaghan gave up his earlier intention to become a lawyer and devoted all his time to writing stories and novels. His works often focus on questions involving personal loyalty and conscience, as in "All the Years of Her Life."

**Direct and Indirect Characterization**

**Characterization** refers to a character's personality or the method by which the writer reveals this personality. With **direct characterization** the writer tells you directly about the character. With **indirect characterization** the writer lets you learn about the characters through the dialogue and action. You might also learn about characters through their thoughts or through what other characters think about them. In "All the Years of Her Life" Callaghan allows the characters to reveal themselves through their thoughts and dialogue.

**Look For**

As you read "All the Years of Her Life," look for what the people say and how they act toward each other. What do their words and thoughts reveal about them? Would you like to know them? Why or why not?

**Writing**

The character Alfred in this story behaves in a way that disappoints others. Why do people sometimes disappoint others—even those they love? Freewrite, exploring your answer to this question.

**Vocabulary**

Knowing the following words will help you as you read "All the Years of Her Life."

**brusquely** (brusk′ lē) *adv.*: In an abrupt and curt manner (p. 57)
**blustered** (blus′ tərd) *v.*: Spoke in a noisy, swaggering manner (p. 57)
**indignation** (in′ dig nā′ shən) *n.*: Anger resulting from injustice (p. 57)

**contempt** (kən tempt′) *n.*: The feelings or attitude toward a person one considers unworthy (p. 58)
**humility** (hyo͞o mil′ ə tē) *n.*: Humbleness; lack of pride (p. 59)

# All the Years of Her Life

### Morley Callaghan

They were closing the drugstore, and Alfred Higgins, who had just taken off his white jacket, was putting on his coat and getting ready to go home. The little gray-haired man, Sam Carr, who owned the drugstore, was bending down behind the cash register, and when Alfred Higgins passed him, he looked up and said softly, "Just a moment, Alfred. One moment before you go."

The soft, confident, quiet way in which Sam Carr spoke made Alfred start to button his coat nervously. He felt sure his face was white. Sam Carr usually said, "Good night," brusquely, without looking up. In the six months he had been working in the drugstore Alfred had never heard his employer speak softly like that. His heart began to beat so loud it was hard for him to get his breath. "What is it, Mr. Carr?" he asked.

"Maybe you'd be good enough to take a few things out of your pocket and leave them here before you go," Sam Carr said.

"What things? What are you talking about?"

"You've got a compact and a lipstick and at least two tubes of toothpaste in your pockets, Alfred."

"What do you mean? Do you think I'm crazy?" Alfred blustered. His face got red and he knew he looked fierce with indignation. But Sam Carr, standing by the door with his blue eyes shining brightly behind his glasses and his lips moving underneath his gray moustache, only nodded his head a few times, and then Alfred grew very frightened and he didn't know what to say. Slowly he raised his hand and dipped it into his pocket, and with his eyes never meeting Sam Carr's eyes, he took out a blue compact and two tubes of toothpaste and a lipstick, and he laid them one by one on the counter.

"Petty thieving, eh, Alfred?" Sam Carr said. "And maybe you'd be good enough to tell me how long this has been going on."

"This is the first time I ever took anything."

"So now you think you'll tell me a lie, eh? What kind of a sap do I look like, huh? I don't know what goes on in my own store, eh? I tell you you've been doing this pretty steady," Sam Carr said as he went over and stood behind the cash register.

Ever since Alfred had left school he had been getting into trouble wherever he worked. He lived at home with his mother and his father, who was a printer. His two older brothers were married and his sister had got married last year, and it would have been all right for his parents now if Alfred had only been able to keep a job.

While Sam Carr smiled and stroked the side of his face very delicately with the tips of his fingers, Alfred began to feel that familiar terror growing in him that had been in him every time he had got into such trouble.

"I liked you," Sam Carr was saying. "I liked you and would have trusted you, and

*All the Years of Her Life*   57

## Presentation

**Motivation/Prior Knowledge** Tell students that *petty larceny* involves the theft of relatively inexpensive items. Ask them whether and how such criminals ought to be punished. Then tell them that, in this story, a young man commits petty larceny.

**Thematic Idea** Another selection that deals with passages and transformations is "Before the End of Summer" by Grant Moss, Jr., page 107.

**Purpose-Setting Question** What important change does Alfred experience in this story?

1 **Critical Thinking and Reading** How do Alfred's reactions to Mr. Carr's remarks indicate that Alfred knows something is wrong?

2 **Discussion** What does the word *blustered* reveal about Alfred's reaction?

3 **Discussion** Which character do you believe? Why?

4 **Discussion** Does this passage reveal any motives Alfred might have for stealing? Explain.

**5 Critical Thinking and Reading** What does Mr. Carr's uncertainty about what to do reveal about his feelings for Alfred?

**6 Literary Focus** What does the difference between what Alfred says and what he feels indicate about his character?

**7 Critical Thinking and Reading** Why do you think his expectations are so specific?

**8 Literary Focus** What is Alfred's greatest concern? What does this reveal about him?

**9 Critical Thinking and Reading** What do you think is going through the mind of each character?

**10 Discussion** Contrast Mrs. Higgins's manner with Alfred's expectations about the way she would behave.

**SELF-PORTRAIT 1944–5**
*Charley Toorop*
*Stedelijk Van Abbedmuseum, Eindhoven*

now look what I got to do." While Alfred watched with his alert, frightened blue eyes, Sam Carr drummed with his fingers on the counter. "I don't like to call a cop in point-blank,"[1] he was saying as he looked very worried. "You're a fool, and maybe I should call your father and tell him you're a fool. Maybe I should let them know I'm going to have you locked up."

"My father's not at home. He's a printer. He works nights," Alfred said.

"Who's at home?"

"My mother, I guess."

"Then we'll see what she says." Sam Carr went to the phone and dialed the number.

---

1. **point-blank:** Right away.

Alfred was not so much ashamed, but there was that deep fright growing in him, and he blurted out arrogantly, like a strong, full-grown man, "Just a minute. You don't need to draw anybody else in. You don't need to tell her." He wanted to sound like a swaggering, big guy who could look after himself, yet the old, childish hope was in him, the longing that someone at home would come and help him. "Yeah, that's right, he's in trouble," Mr. Carr was saying. "Yeah, your boy works for me. You'd better come down in a hurry." And when he was finished Mr. Carr went over to the door and looked out at the street and watched the people passing in the late summer night. "I'll keep my eye out for a cop," was all he said.

Alfred knew how his mother would come rushing in; she would rush in with her eyes blazing, or maybe she would be crying, and she would push him away when he tried to talk to her, and make him feel her dreadful contempt; yet he longed that she might come before Mr. Carr saw the cop on the beat passing the door.

While they waited—and it seemed a long time—they did not speak, and when at last they heard someone tapping on the closed door, Mr. Carr, turning the latch, said crisply, "Come in, Mrs. Higgins." He looked hard-faced and stern.

Mrs. Higgins must have been going to bed when he telephoned, for her hair was tucked in loosely under her hat, and her hand at her throat held her light coat tight across her chest so her dress would not show. She came in, large and plump, with a little smile on her friendly face. Most of the store lights had been turned out and at first she did not see Alfred, who was standing in the shadow at the end of the counter. Yet as soon as she saw him she did not look as Alfred thought she would look: she smiled, her blue eyes never wavered, and with a calmness and dignity that made them forget that her clothes seemed to have been thrown on her, she put out her hand to Mr. Carr and said politely, "I'm Mrs. Higgins. I'm Alfred's mother."

11 Mr. Carr was a bit embarrassed by her lack of terror and her simplicity, and he hardly knew what to say to her, so she asked, "Is Alfred in trouble?"

"He is. He's been taking things from the store. I caught him red-handed. Little things like compacts and toothpaste and lipsticks. Stuff he can sell easily," the proprietor said.

As she listened Mrs. Higgins looked at Alfred sometimes and nodded her head sadly, and when Sam Carr had finished she said gravely, "Is it so, Alfred?"

"Yes."

"Why have you been doing it?"

12 "I been spending money, I guess."

"On what?"

"Going around with the guys, I guess," Alfred said.

Mrs. Higgins put out her hand and touched Sam Carr's arm with an understanding gentleness, and speaking as though afraid of disturbing him, she said, "If you would only listen to me before doing anything." Her simple earnestness made her shy; her humility made her falter and look away, but in a moment she was smiling gravely again, and she said with a kind of patient dignity, "What did you intend to do, Mr. Carr?"

"I was going to get a cop. That's what I ought to do."

13 "Yes, I suppose so. It's not for me to say, because he's my son. Yet I sometimes think a little good advice is the best thing for a boy when he's at a certain period in his life," she said.

Alfred couldn't understand his mother's quiet composure, for if they had been at home and someone had suggested that he was going to be arrested, he knew she would be in a rage and would cry out against him. Yet now she was standing there with that gentle, pleading smile on her face, saying, "I wonder if you don't think it would be better just to let him come home with me. He looks a big fellow, doesn't he? It takes some of them a long time to get any sense," and they both stared at Alfred, who shifted away with a bit of light shining for a moment on his thin face and the tiny pimples over his cheekbone.

But even while he was turning away uneasily Alfred was realizing that Mr. Carr had become aware that his mother was really a fine woman; he knew that Sam Carr was puzzled by his mother, as if he had expected 14 her to come in and plead with him tearfully, and instead he was being made to feel a bit ashamed by her vast tolerance. While there was only the sound of the mother's soft, assured voice in the store, Mr. Carr began to nod his head encouragingly at her. Without being alarmed, while being just large and still and simple and hopeful, she was becoming dominant there in the dimly lit store. "Of course, I don't want to be harsh," Mr. Carr was saying. "I'll tell you what I'll do. I'll just fire him and let it go at that. How's that?" 15 and he got up and shook hands with Mrs. Higgins, bowing low to her in deep respect.

There was such warmth and gratitude in the way she said, "I'll never forget your kindness," that Mr. Carr began to feel warm and genial himself.

"Sorry we had to meet this way," he said. "But I'm glad I got in touch with you. Just wanted to do the right thing, that's all," he said.

"It's better to meet like this than never, isn't it?" she said. Suddenly they clasped hands as if they liked each other, as if they had known each other a long time. "Good night, sir," she said.

*All the Years of Her Life* 59

11 **Critical Thinking and Reading** How do you think Mr. Carr expected Mrs. Higgins to behave?

12 **Literary Focus** What can you infer about Alfred based on his responses?

13 **Discussion** Do you think that Mrs. Higgins is doing the right thing by convincing Mr. Carr not to call the police? Explain your answer.

14 **Reading Strategy** How do you think Alfred's awareness will affect him?

15 **Discussion** Why is Mrs. Higgins's patience and dignity more effective than anger or pleading would have been?

---

The following passage from "All the Years of Her Life" illustrates both active and passive voice:

Most of the store lights *had been turned out* and at first she *did* not *see* Alfred, who *was standing* in the shadow. . . . Yet as soon as she *saw* him she *did* not *look* as Alfred *thought* she *would look;* she *smiled,* her blue eyes never *wavered,* and . . . she *put out* her hand to Mr. Carr. . . .

The verb *turn* is in the passive voice; all the other verbs are active. Why? Good writers use the passive voice only when the doer is either unknown or unimportant. (It really does not matter who turned out the lights.) Otherwise, the active voice is preferable, because it makes writing more lively and direct.

**Student Activity.** Write four sentences of your own about Alfred, Mr. Carr, or Mrs. Higgins. Decide whether your verbs are in the active or passive voice. If you have used the passive voice, rewrite your sentence so that the verb is in the active voice.

16 **Critical Thinking and Reading**
Do Alfred's feelings indicate that he understands the seriousness of his crime or feels remorse for committing it? Explain.

17 **Literary Focus** Why do you think Mrs. Higgins responds angrily to Alfred's assurances that he will not misbehave again? What accounts for the difference between her apparent tolerance for Alfred in the store and her bitter anger at him now?

18 **Literary Focus** What do Alfred's thoughts at this moment reveal about him?

19 **Discussion** What accounts for the change in Mrs. Higgins?

20 **Critical Thinking and Writing** What does Alfred understand about his mother for the first time? Why does his new understanding signal the fact that his youth is over?

**Master Teacher Note** Place Art Transparency 2, *Tocito Waits for the Boarding School Bus,* by Grey Cohoe on the overhead projector. Ask students to comment on the relationship between the woman and the boy. Also have them comment on the mood of the picture. Then have them compare this mood with that of the story.

**Reader's Response** How would you have reacted if you were Alfred's mother? Explain.

"Good night, Mrs. Higgins. I'm truly sorry," he said.

The mother and son walked along the street together, and the mother was taking a long, firm stride as she looked ahead with her stern face full of worry. Alfred was afraid to speak to her, he was afraid of the silence that was between them, so he only looked ahead too, for the excitement and relief was still pretty strong in him; but in a little while, going along like that in silence made him terribly aware of the strength and the sternness in her: he began to wonder what she was thinking of as she stared ahead so grimly; she seemed to have forgotten that he walked beside her; so when they were passing under the Sixth Avenue elevated and the rumble of the train seemed to break the silence, he said in his old, blustering way, "Thank God it turned out like that. I certainly won't get in a jam like that again."

"Be quiet. Don't speak to me. You've disgraced me again and again," she said bitterly.

"That's the last time. That's all I'm saying."

"Have the decency to be quiet," she snapped. They kept on their way, looking straight ahead.

When they were at home and his mother took off her coat, Alfred saw that she was really only half-dressed, and she made him feel afraid again when she said, without even looking at him, "You're a bad lot. God forgive you. It's one thing after another and always has been. Why do you stand there stupidly? Go to bed, why don't you?" When he was going, she said, "I'm going to make myself a cup of tea. Mind, now, not a word about tonight to your father."

While Alfred was undressing in his bedroom, he heard his mother moving around the kitchen. She filled the kettle and put it on the stove. She moved a chair. And as he listened there was no shame in him, just wonder and a kind of admiration of her strength and repose. He could still see Sam Carr nodding his head encouragingly to her; he could hear her talking simply and earnestly, and as he sat on his bed he felt a pride in her strength. "She certainly was smooth," he thought. "Gee, I'd like to tell her she sounded swell."

And at last he got up and went along to the kitchen, and when he was at the door he saw his mother pouring herself a cup of tea. He watched and he didn't move. Her face, as she sat there, was a frightened, broken face utterly unlike the face of the woman who had been so assured a little while ago in the drugstore. When she reached out and lifted the kettle to pour hot water in her cup, her hand trembled and the water splashed on the stove. Leaning back in the chair, she sighed and lifted the cup to her lips, and her lips were groping loosely as if they would never reach the cup. She swallowed the hot tea eagerly, and then she straightened up in relief, though her hand holding the cup still trembled. She looked very old.

It seemed to Alfred that this was the way it had been every time he had been in trouble before, that this trembling had really been in her as she hurried out half-dressed to the drugstore. He understood why she had sat alone in the kitchen the night his young sister had kept repeating doggedly that she was getting married. Now he felt all that his mother had been thinking of as they walked along the street together a little while ago. He watched his mother, and he never spoke, but at that moment his youth seemed to be over; he knew all the years of her life by the way her hand trembled as she raised the cup to her lips. It seemed to him that this was the first time he had ever looked upon his mother.

**Closure and Extension**

**ANSWERS TO THINKING ABOUT THE SELECTION**
*Recalling*

1. Mr. Carr catches Alfred stealing items from the drug store.
2. Mr. Carr expects Mrs. Higgins to be upset and is prepared for an emotional reaction. Mrs. Higgins's quiet dignity in this situation both embarrasses and calms Mr. Carr.

## THINKING ABOUT THE SELECTION

### Recalling

1. Explain the situation that brings Alfred's mother to the store.
2. How does her manner surprise Sam Carr? Describe the effect of her manner on him.
3. How does Alfred's mother behave after she leaves the store?

### Interpreting

4. Sam says he liked Alfred before the incident. Do you think he really did? Cite passages that helped you decide.
5. Why does Alfred's mother refuse to talk to him on the walk home?
6. Near the end of the story, as Alfred watches his mother sip tea, the writer says, "at that moment his youth seemed to be over." What does Alfred see in his mother? What does this statement suggest?
7. What, if anything, does Alfred learn from this incident?

### Applying

8. How do you think Alfred will behave on the next job he gets?
9. If you were Alfred, what might you have done to resolve the situation with Sam?

## ANALYZING LITERATURE

### Understanding Characterization

With **direct characterization** writers state what the characters are like. With **indirect characterization** they show you indirectly what the characters are like through what the characters say and do. Very often, writers use both methods to reveal characters. In "All the Years of Her Life" most of the characterization occurs indirectly through the words, actions, and thoughts of the characters. For example, the writer states directly that Sam "usually said 'Good night,' brusquely."

Later, as the story develops, Sam behaves in a brusque manner, saying "I'll keep my eye out for a cop."

The following are direct statements about the characters in "All the Years of Her Life." Find an example in the story of the character's actions, thoughts, or words that shows the character trait indirectly. Explain your example.

1. Alfred's mother cares very much about him.
2. Sam is not as tough as he appears.
3. Alfred tends to be irresponsible.

## CRITICAL THINKING AND READING

### Recognizing Stereotypes

A **stereotype** is a fixed and oversimplified idea of what a type of person or group of people is like. A stereotyped image includes certain traits, characteristics, or behavior that are assumed to be typical. For example, one stereotype of women is that they are very emotional. However, Alfred's mother, who behaves in a very calm, reasoned manner, proves this stereotype false.

Show how the character named proves or disproves the following stereotypes.

1. Alfred: Bad kids don't care about anybody but themselves.
2. Sam: People in business think only about money.

## THINKING AND WRITING

### Writing About a Person

Think of someone you know and respect. Imagine that this person is about to hire a friend of yours. Write a letter to your friend telling what the prospective employer is like. Stress in your letter what kind of employer you think this person would be. When you revise your letter, try to add at least two strong adverbs to describe the person's behavior.

(Answers begin on p. 60.)

9. Answers will differ. Some students might respond that they would have asked for forgiveness.

**Challenge** How might the story have been different if Mrs. Higgins had allowed Mr. Carr to call the police? What might have happened if she had told Alfred's father what had happened?

### ANSWERS TO ANALYZING LITERATURE

1. Suggested Response: That she comes so quickly indicates that she cares about Alfred.
2. Suggested Response: Mr. Carr threatens to call the police, but calls Alfred's mother instead. Rather than firing Alfred immediately, he tells Alfred's mother, "I'll just fire him and let it go at that. How's that?"
3. Suggested Response: Alfred steals the items and then tries to bluster his way out of trouble.

### ANSWERS TO CRITICAL THINKING AND READING

1. Suggested Response: Alfred's awareness of his mother's pain at the end of this story disproves this stereotype.
2. Suggested Response: Mr. Carr never mentions the money Alfred's stealing cost him, nor does he ask Alfred to pay for the articles. Also he is concerned enough about the boy's future to call his mother instead of the police. These actions refute this stereotype.

### THINKING AND WRITING

For help with this assignment, students can refer to Lesson 2, "Drafting and Revising," in the Handbook of Writing About Literature.

**Publishing Student Writing** Ask for student volunteers to share their letters with the class. Have students decide for which employer they would most enjoy working.

3. Mrs. Higgins is so angry at Alfred that she cannot even speak to him.

### Interpreting

4. Answers will differ. Many students will respond that Mr. Carr probably did like Alfred, or he would have called the police instead of calling Mrs. Higgins
5. Suggested Response: Mrs. Higgins is very angry and disappointed in Alfred, and though she seemed calm at the store, she was

really very upset by Alfred's actions.
6. Suggested Response: Alfred sees his mother's strength disintegrate as she sits in the kitchen. He sees the disappointments she has experienced through the years. For the first time, he realizes that she has suffered because of his irresponsibility. The statement suggests that Alfred is now an aware adult rather than a thoughtless boy.
7. Suggested Response: Alfred realizes that his actions have an effect

on other people, specifically his mother. He realizes that she has suffered because of them.

### Applying

8. Answers will differ. Some students may believe that Alfred has learned a lesson from this experience. Others may believe that Alfred will forget the lesson and act irresponsibly again. Students should support their answers with examples from the story.

## Focus

**More About the Author** As a young girl, Isabel Allende lived with her grandmother. In an interview, Allende recalled that "I had a very lonely life when I was a child but very interesting—only adults around me, very extravagant people, a very extravagant family, really."

At 16, Allende left school and became a secretary in the Food and Agricultural Organization at the United Nations in Chile. She worked with journalists and soon became one herself. In a short period of time, she had her own television program, wrote for a radical women's magazine, and wrote plays and short stories for children. *The House of the Spirits* is her first novel, which captures and immortalizes the spirits of her extravagant family. Ask students how her uncle's death may have affected Allende's writing.

**Literary Focus** You might lead a discussion about eccentricity. Ask students to describe eccentric people they have known.

**Look For** Ask students to define the word *nonconformist*. Why do people become nonconformists? What role do they play in society? Tell the class to look for signs of nonconformity in Uncle Marcos, and for different characters' reactions to his behavior.

**Writing/Prior Knowledge** Discuss with students the following questions: "How much does a man live," and, "How long does a man spend dying?" Suggest to them that these questions might not be answered in terms of time. For example, one might say that some people do not live at all because they spend their whole lives dying.

## Uncle Marcos
## from *The House of the Spirits*

**Isabel Allende** (1942–    ), the niece of the former Chilean president Salvador Allende, was born in Lima, Peru. As a young girl she lived with her grandparents, who became the models for Esteban and Clara in her novel *The House of the Spirits*. In 1973, after General Pinochet overthrew her uncle's government, Allende fled to Venezuela with her husband and children where they now live in exile. Allende's novel is her memorial to "the house that I lost, the people that are dead, those that disappeared, the friends that were scattered all around the world."

**Character Traits**

**Character traits** are all of those qualities that make a person unique. Authors give their characters a number of different traits that together form their personalities.

**Look For**

In this story, Uncle Marcos is one of the many eccentric characters Allende brings to life in her novel. He is a highly unusual and endearing character. Clara describes him in a journal, from which her granddaughter narrates some fifty years after Clara's death. As you read this story, look for the traits that made Uncle Marcos a unique and special person to Clara when she was a young girl.

**Writing**

In her novel, Allende includes the following excerpt of a poem by Chilean poet Pablo Neruda:

> How much does a man live, after all?
> Does he live a thousand days, or one only?
> For a week, or for several centuries?
> How long does a man spend dying?
> What does it mean to say "for ever"?

Freewrite about your response to this poem. Based on your response, what kind of story do you think "Uncle Marcos" will be?

**Vocabulary**

Knowing the following words will help you as you read "Uncle Marcos."

**vanquished** (vaŋ′ kwish't) *adj.*: Defeated (p. 63)

**fetid** (fet′ id) *adj.*: Rancid; rank; smelly (p. 63)

**impassive** (im pas′ iv) *adj.*: Showing no emotion (p. 64)

**disconsolately** (dis kän′ sə lit lē) *adv.*: Unhappily (p. 66)

**Unrequited** (un ri kwīt′ id) *adj.*: Not returned; unreciprocated (p. 68)

## Objectives

1 To recognize character traits
2 To write about a memorable person

## Support Material

**Teaching Portfolio**
Teacher Backup, p. 83
Grammar in Action Worksheet, *Recognizing Adverb Clauses,* p. 86
Usage and Mechanics Worksheet, p. 88
Vocabulary Check, p. 89
Critical Thinking and Reading Worksheet, *Understanding Magical Realism,* p. 90

Language Worksheet, *Recognizing Hyperbole,* p. 91
Selection Test, p. 92

# Uncle Marcos

## from *The House of the Spirits*

### Isabelle Allende

. . . It had been two years since Clara had last seen her Uncle Marcos, but she remembered him very well. His was the only perfectly clear image she retained from her whole childhood, and in order to describe him she did not need to consult the daguerreotype[1] in the drawing room that showed him dressed as an explorer leaning on an old-fashioned double-barreled rifle with his right foot on the neck of a Malaysian tiger, the same triumphant position in which she had seen the Virgin standing between plaster clouds and pallid angels at the main altar, one foot on the vanquished devil. All Clara had to do to see her uncle was close her eyes and there he was, weather-beaten and thin, with a pirate's mustache through which his strange, sharklike smile peered out at her. It seemed impossible that he could be inside that long black box that was lying in the middle of the courtyard.

Each time Uncle Marcos had visited his sister Nívea's home, he had stayed for several months, to the immense joy of his nieces and nephews, particularly Clara, causing a storm in which the sharp lines of domestic order blurred. The house became a clutter of trunks, of animals in jars of formaldehyde,[2] of Indian lances and sailor's bundles. In every part of the house people kept tripping over his equipment, and all sorts of unfamiliar animals appeared that had traveled from remote lands only to meet their death beneath Nana's irate broom in the farthest corners of the house. Uncle Marcos's manners were those of a cannibal, as Severo put it. He spent the whole night making incomprehensible movements in the drawing room; later they turned out to be exercises designed to perfect the mind's control over the body and to improve digestion. He performed alchemy[3] experiments in the kitchen, filling the house with fetid smoke and ruining pots and pans with solid substances that stuck to their bottoms and were impossible to remove. While the rest of the household tried to sleep, he dragged his suitcases up and down the halls, practiced making strange, high-pitched sounds on savage instruments, and taught Spanish to a parrot whose native language was an Amazonic dialect. During the day, he slept in a hammock that he had strung between two columns in the hall, wearing only a loincloth that put Severo in a terrible mood but that Nívea forgave because Marcos had convinced her that it was the same costume in which Jesus of Nazareth had preached. Clara remembered perfectly, even though she had been only a tiny child, the first time her Uncle Marcos came to the house after one of his voyages. He settled in as if he planned to stay forever. After a short time, bored with having to appear at ladies' gatherings where the mistress of the house played the piano, with playing cards, and

---

1. **daguerreotype** (də ger′ ō tīp′) *n*.: An early type of photograph.
2. **formaldehyde** (fôr mal′ də hīd′) *n*.: A solution used as a preservative.
3. **alchemy** (al′ kə mē) *n*.: An early form of chemistry, with philosophic and magical associations.

*Uncle Marcos* 63

**Master Teacher Note** Tell students to notice that the excerpt they are about to read is divided into four anecdotes, each of which illustrates aspects of Uncle Marcos's personality. Suggest that, as they read, they note which character traits are illustrated by each anecdote. You might also suggest that students take note of how the author makes transitions from one anecdote to the next so that the piece holds together as a unit.

**Thematic Idea** You may wish to pair this selection with "A Very Old Man with Enormous Wings," page 173, another work by a South American author who incorporates fantastic details with realistic ones to create a magical effect.

## Presentation

**Motivation/Prior Knowledge** Ask students to think about people who have become legends in their own families. Invite the class to share family stories that may have become exaggerated or taken on elements of fantasy over the years. Tell students that the author shares such family legends in the selection they are about to read.

**Purpose-Setting Question** How does the author blend fantasy and reality to paint a vivid picture of a character?

1 **Literary Focus** From this introduction, try to predict some of Uncle Marcos's character traits.

2 **Clarification** The majority of this selection is a flashback in which Clara is remembering her Uncle Marcos.

3 **Discussion** What is meant by "the sharp lines of domestic order blurred"? What are some lines of domestic order in your home or classroom?

4 **Clarification** Nana is the housekeeper and takes care of Clara; Severo is Clara's father; Nivea is Clara's mother and the sister of Uncle Marcos.

5 **Clarification** Uncle Marcos is practicing some sort of meditation technique, such as yoga.

6 **Enrichment** The principal goal of alchemy was to turn "base" metals such as lead into gold. In Asian countries, alchemists sought to make an elixir that would give immortality to the one who drank it.

7 **Reading Strategy** Go back to the beginning of this paragraph and list all of Uncle Marcos's eccentric traits you have learned so far.

8 **Discussion** How might this feat be possible?

9 **Literary Focus** What character trait of Uncle Marcos does this belief reveal?

10 **Literary Focus** What does Antonieta's reaction to Uncle Marcos reveal about her character?

11 **Enrichment** The goosestep is an exaggerated style of marching practiced by Prussian soldiers, known for being the best drilled and disciplined in the German Army during World War I.

with dodging all his relatives' pressures to pull himself together and take a job as a clerk in Severo del Valle's law practice, he bought a barrel organ and took to the streets with the hope of seducing his Cousin Antonieta and entertaining the public in the bargain. The machine was just a rusty box with wheels, but he painted it with seafaring designs and gave it a fake ship's smokestack. It ended up looking like a coal stove. The organ played either a military march or a waltz, and in between turns of the handle the parrot, who had managed to learn Spanish although he had not lost his foreign accent, would draw a crowd with his piercing shrieks. He also plucked slips of paper from a box with his beak, by way of selling fortunes to the curious. The little pink, green, and blue papers were so clever that they always divulged the exact secret wishes of the customers. Besides fortunes there were little balls of sawdust to amuse the children. The idea of the organ was a last desperate attempt to win the hand of Cousin Antonieta after more conventional means of courting her had failed. Marcos thought no woman in her right mind could remain impassive before a barrel-organ serenade. He stood beneath her window one evening and played his military march and his waltz just as she was taking tea with a group of female friends. Antonieta did not realize the music was meant for her until the parrot called her by her full name, at which point she appeared in the window. Her reaction was not what her suitor had hoped for. Her friends offered to spread the news to every salon[4] in the city, and the next day people thronged the downtown streets hoping to see Severo del Valle's brother-in-law playing the organ and selling little sawdust balls with a moth-eaten parrot, for the sheer pleasure of proving that even in the best of families there could be good reason for embarrassment. In the face of this stain to the family reputation, Marcos was forced to give up organ grinding and resort to less conspicuous ways of winning over his Cousin Antonieta, but he did not renounce his goal. In any case, he did not succeed, because from one day to the next the young lady married a diplomat who was twenty years her senior; he took her to live in a tropical country whose name no one could recall, except that it suggested negritude,[5] bananas, and palm trees, where she managed to recover from the memory of that suitor who had ruined her seventeenth year with his military march and his waltz. Marcos sank into a deep depression that lasted two or three days, at the end of which he announced that he would never marry and that he was embarking on a trip around the world. He sold his organ to a blind man and left the parrot to Clara, but Nana secretly poisoned it with an overdose of cod-liver oil, because no one could stand its lusty glance, its fleas, and its harsh, tuneless hawking of paper fortunes and sawdust balls.

That was Marcos's longest trip. He returned with a shipment of enormous boxes that were piled in the far courtyard, between the chicken coop and the woodshed, until the winter was over. At the first signs of spring he had them transferred to the parade grounds, a huge park where people would gather to watch the soldiers file by on Independence Day, with the goosestep they had learned from the Prussians. When the crates were opened, they were found to contain loose bits of wood, metal, and painted cloth. Marcos spent two weeks assembling the contents according to an instruction manual written in English, which he was able to decipher thanks to his invincible imagination and a small dictionary. When the job was finished, it turned out to be a

---

**4. salon** (sə län′) *n.*: A regular gathering of distinguished guests that meets in a private home.

**5. negritude** (neg′ rə tōōd′) *n.*: Blacks and their cultural heritage.

*64 Short Stories*

## Grammar in Action

**Adverb clauses,** like adverbs, tell where, when, in what manner, to what extent, under what condition, or why. An adverb clause begins with a subordinating conjunction and includes a subject and verb. It may include complements and modifiers. In the sentence, *"When we finally reached home,* we were exhausted," the italicized words form an adverb clause telling when. The clause includes the subordinating conjunction *when,* the subject *we,* the verb *reached,* and the complement *home.* Because the clause precedes the verb, it is followed by a comma.

Writers use adverb clauses to vary their sentences, make their descriptions more specific, and clarify relationships between ideas. Note, for example, the following adverb clauses from "Uncle Marcos":

"Antonieta did not realize the music was meant for her *until the parrot called her by her full name . . ."*
*"When the job was finished,* it turned out to be a bird of prehistoric dimensions . . ."

Each clause begins with a subordinating conjunction; each has a subject; each includes a verb.

bird of prehistoric dimensions, with the face of a furious eagle, wings that moved, and a propeller on its back. It caused an uproar. The families of the oligarchy[6] forgot all about the barrel organ, and Marcos became the star attraction of the season. People took Sunday outings to see the bird; souvenir vendors and strolling photographers made a fortune. Nonetheless, the public's interest quickly waned. But then Marcos announced that as soon as the weather cleared he planned to take off in his bird and cross the mountain range. The news spread, making this the most talked-about event of the year. The contraption lay with its stomach on terra firma,[7] heavy and sluggish and looking more like a wounded duck than like one of those newfangled airplanes they were starting to produce in the United States. There was nothing in its appearance to suggest that it could move, much less take flight across the snowy peaks. Journalists and the curious flocked to see it. Marcos smiled his immutable[8] smile before the avalanche of questions and posed for photographers without offering the least technical or scientific explanation of how he hoped to carry out his plan. People came from the provinces to see the sight. Forty years later his great-nephew Nicolás, whom Marcos did not live to see, unearthed the desire to fly that had always existed in the men of his lineage. Nicolás was interested in doing it for commercial reasons, in a gigantic hot-air sausage on which would be printed an advertisement for carbonated drinks. But when Marcos announced his plane trip, no one believed that his contraption could be put to any practical use. The appointed day dawned full of clouds, but so many people had turned out

that Marcos did not want to disappoint them. He showed up punctually at the appointed spot and did not once look up at the sky, which was growing darker and darker with thick gray clouds. The astonished crowd filled all the nearby streets, perching on rooftops and the balconies of the nearest houses and squeezing into the park. No political gathering managed to attract so many people until half a century later, when the first Marxist candidate attempted, through strictly democratic channels, to become President. Clara would remember this holiday as long as she lived. People dressed in their spring best, thereby getting a step ahead of the official opening of the season, the men in white linen suits and the ladies in the Italian straw hats that were all the rage that year. Groups of elementary-school children paraded with their teachers, clutching flowers for the hero. Marcos accepted their bouquets and joked that they might as well hold on to them and wait for him to crash, so they could take them directly to his funeral. The bishop himself, accompanied by two incense bearers, appeared to bless the bird without having been asked, and the police band played happy, unpretentious music that pleased everyone. The police, on horseback and carrying lances, had trouble keeping the crowds far enough away from the center of the park, where Marcos waited dressed in mechanic's overalls, with huge racer's goggles and an explorer's helmet. He was also equipped with a compass, a telescope, and several strange maps that he had traced himself based on various theories of Leonardo da Vinci[9] and on the polar knowledge of the Incas. Against all logic, on the second try the bird lifted off without mishap and with a certain elegance, accompanied by

---

**6. oligarchy** (äl′ i gär′ kē) *n.*: Government ruled by a few.

**7. terra firma** (ter′ ə fʉ′ mə) *n.*: Firm earth, solid ground.

**8. immutable** (im myo͞ot′ ə bəl) *adj.*: Never changing.

---

**9. Leonardo da Vinci** (lē′ ə när′ dō də vin′ chē) . . . **Incas:** Leonardo da Vinci (1452–1519) was an Italian painter, sculptor, architect, and scientist. The Incas were native Americans who dominated ancient Peru until the Spanish conquest.

*Uncle Marcos* 65

---

**12 Reading Strategy** Describe the onlookers' reactions. Why did the public's interest wane so quickly? Tell students to take note of how the public's reactions change throughout Uncle Marcos's flight.

**13 Enrichment** The author is referring to the Andes Mountains. Stretching the entire west coast of South America, the Andes are the longest chain of mountains in the world, and second highest to the Himalayas of India and Tibet. It is about 500 miles across the widest part of the Andes.

**14 Discussion** Why is it typical of Marcos's character to withhold an explanation of how he is to carry out his plan?

**15 Enrichment** The author is referring to a blimp. Blimps are filled with helium, a lighter-than-air gas that keeps them aloft. They are still used for advertising purposes.

**16 Enrichment** The author is referring to her uncle, Salvador Allende, who was President of Chile from 1970 to 1973.

**17 Literary Focus** What character traits of Uncle Marcos does this sentence reveal?

**18 Reading Strategy** Try to visualize Uncle Marcos in detail as described by the narrator in this scene. What effect does the description achieve?

---

**Student Activity 1.** Locate the adverb clauses in the following sentences from the story. Identify the subordinating conjunction, the subject, the verb, and any complements or modifiers in each clause.
1. But when Marcos announced his plane trip, no one believed that his contraption could be put to any practical use.
2. Clara continued to stare at the sky long after her uncle had become invisible.

**Student Activity 2.** Write two original sentences using adverb clauses. In one sentence, place the adverb clause at the beginning of the sentence.

**19 Discussion** What comment on human nature in general is the author making? Do you agree that this is a typical public reaction to an important event? Can you think of any parallels in recent news reports?

**20 Reading Strategy** How does the word *ignorant* in this sentence achieve a humorous effect? Is it more ridiculous to suggest that Uncle Marcos reached the moon than to speculate that he disappeared into outer space?

**21 Discussion** Why is Severo sad? Why is he relieved?

**22 Discussion** Why doesn't Clara weep? Why is she watching the sky? What does it mean that she has "the patience of an astronomer"?

**23 Discussion** Does Uncle Marcos believe that he owes his survival to the prayers of the women and children? Why does he say that he believes this?

the creaking of its skeleton and the roar of its motor. It rose flapping its wings and disappeared into the clouds, to a send-off of applause, whistlings, handkerchiefs, drumrolls, and the sprinkling of holy water. All that remained on earth were the comments of the amazed crowd below and a multitude of experts, who attempted to provide a reasonable explanation of the miracle. Clara continued to stare at the sky long after her uncle had become invisible. She thought she saw him ten minutes later, but it was only a migrating sparrow. After three days the initial euphoria that had accompanied the first airplane flight in the country died down and no one gave the episode another thought, except for Clara, who continued to peer at the horizon.

After a week with no word from the flying uncle, people began to speculate that he had gone so high that he had disappeared into outer space, and the ignorant suggested he would reach the moon. With a mixture of sadness and relief, Severo decided that his brother-in-law and his machine must have fallen into some hidden crevice of the *cordillera*,[10] where they would never be found. Nívea wept disconsolately and lit candles to

San Antonio, patron of lost objects. Severo opposed the idea of having masses said, because he did not believe in them as a way of getting into heaven, much less of returning to earth, and he maintained that masses and religious vows, like the selling of indulgences, images, and scapulars,[11] were a dishonest business. Because of his attitude, Nívea and Nana had the children say the rosary[12] behind their father's back for nine days. Meanwhile, groups of volunteer explorers and mountain climbers tirelessly searched peaks and passes, combing every accessible stretch of land until they finally returned in triumph to hand the family the mortal remains of the deceased in a sealed black coffin. The intrepid traveler was laid to rest in a grandiose funeral. His death made him a hero and his name was on the front page of all the papers for several days. The same multitude that had gathered to see him off the day he flew away in his bird paraded past his coffin. The entire family wept as befit the occasion, except for Clara, who continued to watch the sky with the patience of an astronomer. One week after he had been buried, Uncle Marcos, a bright smile playing behind his pirate's mustache, appeared in person in the doorway of Nívea and Severo del Valle's house. Thanks to the surreptitious[13] prayers of the women and children, as he himself admitted, he was alive and well and in full possession of his faculties, including his sense of humor. Despite the noble lineage of his aerial maps, the flight had been a failure. He had lost his airplane and had to return on foot, but he had not broken any bones and his adventurous

---

**10. cordillera** (kôr′ dil yer′ə) *n.*: A system or chain of mountains.

**11. indulgences, images, and scapulars** (skap′ yə lərz): Indulgences are pardons for sins, images are pictures or sculptures of religious figures, and scapulars are garments worn by Roman Catholics as tokens of religious devotion.

**12. say the rosary:** Use a set of beads to say prayers, as Roman Catholics do.

**13. surreptitious** (sur′ əp tish′ əs) *adj.*: Secretive.

66   *Short Stories*

---

## Primary Source: The House of the Spirits

Allende's novel, *The House of the Spirits,* begins as Alba, the granddaughter of Clara, writes from exile to keep alive the memory of her past. It is not difficult to see that the character of Alba is based on the author herself. "When I left Chile," says Allende, "I didn't dare tell my grandfather. . . . I couldn't find the words." Years later when her grandfather, nearly a hundred years old, telephoned to tell her that he was dying, "I wanted to tell my grandfather that I was never going to forget him, he would never die, just as my grandmother had never died. . . . And I started writing a letter, telling him the same things he had told me when I was a child." The letter, never sent, evolved into *The House of the Spirits.*

spirit was intact. This confirmed the family's eternal devotion to San Antonio, but was not taken as a warning by future generations, who also tried to fly, although by different means. Legally, however, Marcos was a corpse. Severo del Valle was obliged to use all his legal ingenuity to bring his brother-in-law back to life and the full rights of citizenship. When the coffin was pried open in the presence of the appropriate authorities, it was found to contain a bag of sand. This discovery ruined the reputation, up till then untarnished, of the volunteer explorers and mountain climbers, who from that day on were considered little better than a pack of bandits.

Marcos's heroic resurrection made everyone forget about his barrel-organ phase. Once again he was a sought-after guest in all the city's salons and, at least for a while, his name was cleared. Marcos stayed in his sister's house for several months. One night he left without saying goodbye, leaving behind his trunks, his books, his weapons, his boots, and all his belongings. Severo, and even Nívea herself, breathed a sigh of relief. His visit had gone on too long. But Clara was so upset that she spent a week walking in her sleep and sucking her thumb. The little girl, who was only seven at the time, had learned to read from her uncle's storybooks and been closer to him than any other member of the family because of her prophesying powers. Marcos maintained that his niece's gift could be a source of income and a good opportunity for him to cultivate his own clairvoyance.[14] He believed that all human beings possessed this ability, particularly his own family, and that if it did not function well it was simply due to a lack of training. He bought a crystal ball in the Persian bazaar, insisting that it had magic powers and was from the East (although it was later

found to be part of a buoy from a fishing boat), set it down on a background of black velvet, and announced that he could tell people's fortunes, cure the evil eye, and improve the quality of dreams, all for the modest sum of five centavos.[15] His first customers were the maids from around the neighborhood. One of them had been accused of stealing, because her employer had misplaced a valuable ring. The crystal ball revealed the exact location of the object in question: it had rolled beneath a wardrobe. The next day there was a line outside the front door of the house. There were coachmen, storekeepers, and milkmen; later a few municipal employees and distinguished ladies made a discreet appearance, slinking along the side walls of the house to keep from being recognized. The customers were received by Nana, who ushered them into the waiting room and collected their fees. This task kept her busy throughout the day and demanded so much of her time that the family began to complain that all there ever was for dinner was old string beans and jellied quince.[16] Marcos decorated the carriage house with some frayed curtains that had once belonged in the drawing room but that neglect and age had turned to dusty rags. There he and Clara received the customers. The two divines wore tunics "color of the men of light," as Marcos called the color yellow. Nana had dyed them with saffron powder, boiling them in pots usually reserved for rice and pasta. In addition to his tunic, Marcos wore a turban around his head and an Egyptian amulet around his neck. He had grown a beard and let his hair grow long and he was thinner than ever before. Marcos and Clara were utterly convincing, especially because the child had no need to look into the crystal ball

---

**14. clairvoyance** (kler voi′ əns) *n.*: The ability to perceive things that are not in sight or can't be seen.

**15. centavos** (sen tä′ vōs) *n.*: Brazilian currency equal to ¹⁄₁₀₀ of a cruzeiro.

**16. quince** (kwins): A golden or greenish-yellow, hard, apple-shaped fruit.

*Uncle Marcos* 67

---

**24 Discussion** What might have motivated the explorers and mountain climbers to claim that they had found Uncle Marcos's body?

**25 Discussion** Why is Uncle Marcos's name cleared? What does this reaction reveal about human nature?

**26 Enrichment** This passage describes what the author herself had to do when she left Chile and fled to Venezuela after the overthrow of her uncle's government.

**27 Clarification** In the novel, *The House of the Spirits,* from which this selection is an excerpt, Clara is born with the supernatural abilities to move objects without touching them and to foretell the future.

**28 Discussion** Why do the municipal employees and distinguished ladies want to be unrecognized?

**29 Discussion** Why is it necessary for Uncle Marcos to look the part of a fortune teller? What does this detail reveal about his character?

**30 Reading Strategy** What words and phrases does the author use to suggest that Uncle Marcos and Clara are frauds? What does this fact reveal about Uncle Marcos's character? Tell students to look for more proof on the following page.

---

## Commentary: Chile

Chile is the southernmost country of South America, lying between the snow-capped peaks of the Andes Mountains and the Pacific Ocean. Chile has a long history of political upheaval, beginning in 1817 when it won its independence from the Spanish who had controlled the country since the sixteenth century. In 1970, Salvador Allende Gossens became president of Chile. Allende was the first Marxist to be democratically elected to head any country in the Western Hemisphere. In 1973, the military, led by General Augusto Pinochet Ugarte, forcibly took over Allende's government and arrested his supporters. Reports suggested that Allende had committed suicide during the coup, although many believe he was assassinated. Pinochet became the military dictator of the new government. In 1989, he allowed democratic elections to be held, but retained control of the military.

**31 Discussion** What is the reason for Clara's and Uncle Marcos's success as fortune tellers? Why do some people find comfort in visiting fortune tellers?

**32 Literary Focus** What character traits of Clara, Uncle Marcos, and Nana does this passage reveal?

**33 Clarification** Students may be unfamiliar with the word *macaws*. Tell them that macaws are a type of parrot that is indigenous to South and Central America.

**34 Enrichment** A lama is a high monk of Lamaism, a religion practiced in Tibet, Bhutan, Kashmir, Sikim, and Mongolia. Yak lard is a butter made from the milk of the yak, a stocky, long-haired wild ox.

**35 Enrichment** This passage describes a similar happening in the author's own life: Allende's grandmother kept journals of the family and daily life.

**36 Clarification** The author is referring to an event that occurs later in the novel.

**37 Reading Strategy** To what other trips in a coffin is the author referring?

to guess what her clients wanted to hear. She would whisper in her Uncle Marcos's ear, and he in turn would transmit the message to the client, along with any improvisations of his own that he thought pertinent. Thus their fame spread, because all those who arrived sad and bedraggled at the consulting room left filled with hope. Unrequited lovers were told how to win over indifferent hearts, and the poor left with foolproof tips on how to place their money at the dog tracks. Business grew so prosperous that the waiting room was always packed with people, and Nana began to suffer dizzy spells from being on her feet so many hours a day. This time Severo had no need to intervene to put a stop to his brother-in-law's venture, for both Marcos and Clara, realizing that their unerring guesses could alter the fate of their clients, who always followed their advice to the letter, became frightened and decided that this was a job for swindlers. They abandoned their carriage-house oracle and split the profits, even though the only one who had cared about the material side of things had been Nana.

Of all the del Valle children, Clara was the one with the greatest interest in and stamina for her uncle's stories. She could repeat each and every one of them. She knew by heart words from several dialects of the Indians, was acquainted with their customs, and could describe the exact way in which they pierced their lips and earlobes with wooden shafts, their initiation rites, the names of the most poisonous snakes, and the appropriate antidotes for each. Her uncle was so eloquent that the child could feel in her own skin the burning sting of snakebites, see reptiles slide across the carpet between the legs of the jacaranda[17] room divider, and hear the shrieks of macaws behind the drawing-room drapes. She did not

hesitate as she recalled Lope de Aguirre's search for El Dorado,[18] or the unpronounceable names of the flora and fauna her extraordinary uncle had seen; she knew about the lamas who take salt tea with yak lard and she could give detailed descriptions of the opulent women of Tahiti, the rice fields of China, or the white prairies of the North, where the eternal ice kills animals and men who lose their way, turning them to stone in seconds. Marcos had various travel journals in which he recorded his excursions and impressions, as well as a collection of maps and books of stories and fairy tales that he kept in the trunks he stored in the junk room at the far end of the third courtyard. From there they were hauled out to inhabit the dreams of his descendants, until they were mistakenly burned half a century later on an infamous pyre.

Now Marcos had returned from his last journey in a coffin. He had died of a mysterious African plague that had turned him as yellow and wrinkled as a piece of parchment. When he realized he was ill, he set out for home with the hope that his sister's ministrations and Dr. Cuevas's knowledge would restore his health and youth, but he was unable to withstand the sixty days on ship and died at the latitude of Guayaquil,[19] ravaged by fever and hallucinating about musky women and hidden treasure. The captain of the ship, an Englishman by the name of Longfellow, was about to throw him overboard wrapped in a flag, but Marcos, despite his savage appearance and his delirium, had made so many friends on board and seduced so many women that the passengers prevented him from doing so, and Longfellow

---

**17. jacaranda** (jak′ ə ran′ də): A type of tropical American tree.

**18. Lope de Aguirre's** (lō′ pā t͡hä ag ē′ rāz) . . . **El Dorado:** Lope de Aguirre was a Spanish adventurer (1510–1561) in colonial South America who searched for a lendendary country called El Dorado, which was supposedly rich in gold.

**19. Guayaquil** (gwī′ ä kēl′): A seaport in western Ecuador.

68 *Short Stories*

was obliged to store the body side by side with the vegetables of the Chinese cook, to preserve it from the heat and mosquitoes of the tropics until the ship's carpenter had time to improvise a coffin. At El Callao[20] they obtained a more appropriate container, and several days later the captain, furious at all the troubles this passenger had caused the shipping company and himself personally, unloaded him without a backward glance,

surprised that not a soul was there to receive the body or cover the expenses he had incurred. Later he learned that the post office in these latitudes was not as reliable as that of far-off England, and that all his telegrams had vaporized en route. Fortunately for Longfellow, a customs lawyer who was a friend of the del Valle family appeared and offered to take charge, placing Marcos and all his paraphernalia in a freight car, which he shipped to the capital to the only known address of the deceased: his sister's house. . . .

**38**

_____

**20. El Callao** (kə yä′ ō): A seaport in western Peru.

**39**

---

## THINKING ABOUT THE SELECTION
### Interpreting

1. What is each character's attitude toward Uncle Marcos? How do the other characters' attitudes differ from Clara's attitude?
2. Severo says, "Uncle Marcos's manners were those of a cannibal." What evidence from this story refutes Severo's claim?
3. What difference do you think Uncle Marcos made in Clara's life?

### Applying

4. Uncle Marcos is the embodiment of curiosity and imagination. He broadens Clara's view of the world, but he is often misunderstood by his family and the townspeople. How does a society value seemingly strange and innovative ideas? How does a society or culture benefit from such people and their innovations?
5. Allende immortalizes those who were dear to her by modeling her novel's characters after them. In what other ways might we immortalize those who are memorable?

## ANALYZING LITERATURE
### Recognizing Character Traits

Any quality that is part of a character's personality is a **character trait**. Some character traits are essential to the development of a story; others

are not but may help to make the character seem true to life. In Clara's journal she described the qualities of her uncle that captured her attention as a child—those qualities that seemed to her extravagant and enchanting.

1. List five of Uncle Marcos's character traits. What details in the story support your answer?
2. As a child, why might Clara have tended to focus on the extravagant aspects of her uncle's character?
3. Close your eyes and envision Uncle Marcos. What instructions would you give to an artist who was drawing a portrait of him? What actor would you cast to play him? Compare your vision with those of your classmates.

## THINKING AND WRITING
### Writing About a Memorable Person

Think about someone who is especially meaningful to you and whose spirit you would like to keep alive. Make a list of that person's character traits, including any extravagant or particularly unforgettable characteristics. Write about one memorable incident in which you and this person were involved. Weave into the story details that illustrate what this person means to you, in much the same way as Allende does in "Uncle Marcos." You may wish to add some fantastic details, but they should tell your readers something about the person's character.

*Uncle Marcos* 69

**38** **Literary Focus** Is this account of Uncle Marcos's death sad or humorous? How would Uncle Marcos have reacted to it?

**39** **Literary Focus** Why was Nivea's house Uncle Marcos's only known address? Which of Uncle Marcos's character traits does this final sentence emphasize?

**Reader's Response** Which character's response to Uncle Marcos is most like your own?

### ANSWERS TO ANALYZING LITERATURE

1. Answers may differ. Suggested Response: (1) adventurous—travel to exotic places all over the world
(2) romantic—tried to win Antonieta's hand by playing the barrel organ
(3) storyteller—told Clara captivating stories of his adventures
(4) daring—flew the airplane with his stories
(5) charming—was popular aboard ship.
2. Uncle Marcos brought Clara a taste of the exotic and romantic.
3. Students might refer to the photograph of Uncle Marcos at the beginning of the selection. They might choose actors who have played parts of eccentrics or adventurers in movies or television shows.

### THINKING AND WRITING
For help with this assignment, students can refer to Lesson 9, "Writing about Character."

**Publishing Student Writing** Compile students' work in a classroom book that students illustrate and name. Display it in the classroom or library for others to read and enjoy.

**Challenge** Ask students to define humor. Tell the class that the nineteenth-century French philosopher Henri Bergson thought of humor as the human spirit's weapon against social rigidities. Ask students how this definition of humor applies to Uncle Marcos.

_____

## Closure and Extension

### ANSWERS TO THINKING ABOUT THE SELECTION
#### Interpreting

1. Nana dislikes Uncle Marcos's untidy habits and his animals, but likes him enough to become his fortune-telling partner; Severo finds him irresponsible and uncivilized, but feels responsible for him; Nivea finds his eccentric

habits unsettling but loves him; Clara loves him and is enchanted by him.
2. The following evidence refutes Severo's claim: Uncle Marcos can make the airplane fly, has a keen sense of humor, owns many books, knows stories from all over the world, charms the passengers on the ship.
3. Suggested Response: He stimulated Clara's imagination and curiosity, broadening her world; his unorthodox behavior may have

led her to question conventional behavior and beliefs.

#### Applying

4. Answers may differ. Suggested Response: New ideas are usually met with suspicion; such people pave the way for change and progress.
5. Suggested Responses: We might commemorate them in other media, tell others about them, work for causes they supported, try to emulate them, erect memorials, or establish holidays in their honor.

**More About the Author** Sir Arthur Conan Doyle claimed that the character of Sherlock Holmes was based on his anatomy teacher, whose diagnostic skills he had greatly admired. Ask students whether they believe most fictional characters are based on real people.

**Literary Focus** You might have students reinforce their understanding of character traits by listing some that they think a detective should possess.

**Look For** Suggest that students write down Holmes's character traits as they read the selection.

**Writing/Prior Knowledge** You might divide the class into small groups and have students describe their imaginary friend to fellow group members.

**Vocabulary** Have your **less advanced** students study these words and use as many of them as possible in a single paragraph.

**Spelling Tip** Point out the two words that end in *x: hoax, vex.* Tell students that *x* can spell the sound /ks/ as in *box* and *coax.*

## The Red-headed League

**Sir Arthur Conan Doyle** (1859–1930) was born in Edinburgh, Scotland. He became a doctor, but he practiced medicine for only eight years. Three years after he wrote his first story about Sherlock Holmes, he gave up medicine to write full time. All of the Holmes stories are narrated by a medical man, the somewhat naive Doctor Watson. "The Red-headed League" was first published in *Strand* magazine in 1891. In it, as in other Holmes stories, Watson is amazed at Holmes's feats of deduction.

**Motivation**

**Motivation** is a character's reason or reasons for saying or doing something. What motivates a character to act may be a feeling or a goal. A character is likely to have many motives, both emotional and rational, for a particular action. When reading a detective story, motives are of particular interest because they reveal why the criminal committed the crime.

**Look For**

Imagine you are Sherlock Holmes setting out to solve the crime in "The Red-headed League." As Sherlock Holmes would, look for the clues that reveal who the criminals are and their reasons or motives for committing the crime.

**Writing**

Sherlock Holmes and Doctor Watson are two friends with similar interests but differing abilities. Suppose that you had a friend who was far more brilliant and talented than the average person. Freewrite about what your friendship with this person would be like. Discuss both the positive and the negative aspects.

**Vocabulary**

Knowing the following words will help you as you read "The Red-headed League."

**singular** (siŋ′ gyə lər) *adj.*: Extraordinary; rare (p. 71)

**avail** (ə vāl′) *v.*: Be of help (p. 78)

**hoax** (hōks) *n.*: A deceitful trick (p. 78)

**introspective** (in′ trə spek′ tiv) *adj.*: Causing one to look into one's own thoughts and feelings (p. 80)

**vex** (veks) *v.*: Annoy (p. 82)

**conundrums** (kə nun′ drəmz) *n.*: Puzzling questions or problems (p. 82)

**astuteness** (ə stōōt′ nis) *n.*: Shrewdness (p. 82)

**formidable** (fôr′mə də b'l) *adj.*: Awe-inspiring (p. 82)

### Objectives

1 To recognize character traits
2 To contrast characters' abilities
3 To complete word analogies
4 To analyze a detective's methods

## Support Material

**Teaching Portfolio**
Teacher Backup, p. 95
Grammar in Action Worksheets, *Using Single Quotation Marks,* p. 99; *Examining Deductive Reasoning,* p. 101
Usage and Mechanics Worksheet, p. 103
Vocabulary Check, p. 104
Analyzing Literature Worksheet, *Recognizing Character Traits,* p. 106

Critical Thinking and Reading Worksheet, *Contrasting Characters' Abilities,* p. 107
Selection Test, p. 108

# The Red-headed League

### Sir Arthur Conan Doyle

I had called upon my friend, Mr. Sherlock Holmes, one day in the autumn of last year and found him in deep conversation with a very stout, florid-faced, elderly gentleman with fiery red hair. With an apology for my intrusion, I was about to withdraw when Holmes pulled me abruptly into the room and closed the door behind me.

"You could not possibly have come at a better time, my dear Watson," he said cordially.

"I was afraid that you were engaged."

"So I am. Very much so."

"Then I can wait in the next room."

"Not at all. This gentleman, Mr. Wilson, has been my partner and helper in many of my most successful cases, and I have no doubt that he will be of the utmost use to me in yours also."

The stout gentleman half rose from his chair and gave a bob of greeting, with a quick little questioning glance from his small, fat-encircled eyes.

"Try the settee,"[1] said Holmes, relapsing into his armchair and putting his finger tips together, as was his custom when in judicial moods. "I know, my dear Watson, that you share my love of all that is bizarre and outside the conventions and humdrum routine of everyday life. You have shown your relish for it by the enthusiasm which has prompted you to chronicle, and, if you will

_____
**1. settee** (se tē′) *n.*: Small sofa.

excuse my saying so, somewhat to embellish so many of my own little adventures."

"Your cases have indeed been of the greatest interest to me," I observed.

"You will remember that I remarked the other day, just before we went into the very simple problem presented by Miss Mary Sutherland, that for strange effects and extraordinary combinations we must go to life itself, which is always far more daring than any effort of the imagination."

"A proposition which I took the liberty of doubting."

"You did, Doctor, but none the less you must come round to my view, for otherwise I shall keep on piling fact upon fact on you until your reason breaks down under them and acknowledges me to be right. Now, Mr. Jabez Wilson here has been good enough to call upon me this morning, and to begin a narrative which promises to be one of the most singular which I have listened to for some time. You have heard me remark that the strangest and most unique things are very often connected not with the larger but with the smaller crimes, and occasionally, indeed, where there is room for doubt whether any positive crime has been committed. As far as I have heard it is impossible for me to say whether the present case is an instance of crime or not, but the course of events is certainly among the most singular that I have ever listened to. Perhaps, Mr. Wilson, you would have the great kindness to

## Presentation

**Motivation/Prior Knowledge**
Write the heading, "World's Most Famous Detective," on the chalkboard and ask students to name characters they think might fit this title. Explain that many readers consider Sherlock Holmes the world's most famous detective because of his superior powers of deduction. Then ask students to consider whether his reputation is deserved as they read this story.

**Thematic Idea** Another selection in which the protagonist displays intelligence and courage is "The Most Dangerous Game," by Richard Connell, page 13.

**Purpose-Setting Question** How is Holmes able to make inferences from facts that seem puzzling or disconnected to others?

1 **Clarification** This is another way of saying that truth is stranger than fiction.

2 **Reading Strategy** Ask students to make predictions about the story based on this remark.

recommence your narrative. I ask you not merely because my friend Dr. Watson has not heard the opening part but also because the peculiar nature of the story makes me anxious to have every possible detail from your lips. As a rule, when I have heard some slight indication of the course of events, I am able to guide myself by the thousands of other similar cases which occur to my memory. In the present instance I am forced to admit that the facts are, to the best of my belief, unique."

The portly client puffed out his chest with an appearance of some little pride and pulled a dirty and wrinkled newspaper from the inside pocket of his great coat. As he glanced down the advertisement column, with his head thrust forward and the paper flattened out upon his knee, I took a good look at the man and endeavored, after the fashion of my companion, to read the indications which might be presented by his dress or appearance.

I did not gain very much, however, by my inspection. Our visitor bore every mark of being an average commonplace British tradesman, obese, pompous, and slow. He wore rather baggy gray shepherd's check trousers, a not over-clean black frock coat, unbuttoned in the front, and a drab waistcoat with a heavy brassy Albert chain, and a square pierced bit of metal dangling down as an ornament. A frayed top hat and a faded brown overcoat with a wrinkled velvet collar lay upon a chair beside him. Altogether, look as I would, there was nothing remarkable about the man save his blazing red head, and the expression of extreme chagrin and discontent upon his features.

Sherlock Holmes's quick eye took in my occupation, and he shook his head with a smile as he noticed my questioning glances. "Beyond the obvious facts that he has at some time done manual labor, that he takes snuff,[2] that he is a Freemason,[3] that he has been in China, and that he has done a considerable amount of writing lately, I can deduce nothing else."

Mr. Jabez Wilson started up in his chair, with his forefinger upon the paper, but his eyes upon my companion.

"How, in the name of good fortune, did you know all that, Mr. Holmes?" he asked. "How did you know, for example, that I did manual labor? It's as true as gospel, for I began as a ship's carpenter."

"Your hands, my dear sir. Your right hand is quite a size larger than your left. You have worked with it, and the muscles are more developed."

"Well, the snuff, then, and the Freemasonry?"

"I won't insult your intelligence by telling you how I read that, especially as, rather against the strict rules of your order, you use an arc-and-compass breastpin."

"Ah, of course, I forgot that. But the writing?"

"What else can be indicated by that right cuff so very shiny for five inches, and the left one with the smooth patch near the elbow where you rest it upon the desk?"

"Well, but China?"

"The fish that you have tattooed immediately above your right wrist could only have been done in China. I have made a small study of tattoo marks and have even contributed to the literature of the subject. That trick of staining the fishes' scales of a delicate pink is quite peculiar to China. When, in addition, I see a Chinese coin hanging from your watch-chain, the matter becomes even more simple."

Mr. Jabez Wilson laughed heavily. "Well, I never!" said he. "I thought at first that you had done something clever, but I see that there was nothing in it, after all."

"I begin to think, Watson," said Holmes, "that I make a mistake in explaining. '*Omne ignotum pro magnifico,*'[4] you know, and my poor little reputation, such as it is, will suffer shipwreck if I am so candid. Can you not find the advertisement, Mr. Wilson?"

"Yes, I have got it now," he answered with his thick red finger planted halfway down the column. "Here it is. This is what began it all. You just read it for yourself, sir."

---

2. **snuff:** Powdered tobacco.
3. **Freemason:** Member of a secret society.

---

4. **Omne ignotum pro magnifico** (äm' nä ig nō' t'm prō mag nē' fē kō): Latin for "Whatever is unknown is magnified."

*The Red-headed League*   73

4 **Discussion** What does this statement indicate about Sherlock Holmes's methods of deduction?

5 **Discussion** Compare and contrast Watson's deductions with those of Holmes.

6 **Discussion** Holmes's deduction about Mr. Wilson has nothing to do with the crime that will be committed. Why did the author include it?

7 **Clarification** After Holmes explains his methods of deduction, Mr. Wilson dismisses his talent saying, ". . .there was nothing in it, after all." Holmes then shares a joke with Watson in Latin, a language that Mr. Wilson would not understand; he explains that it would be better for his reputation not to explain his deductive methods to someone who cannot appreciate his ability.

**8** **Literary Focus** Why is Holmes in such high spirits? What does this indicate about his personality?

**9** **Reading Strategy** Ask students to listen to Mr. Wilson's story as Holmes would and try to predict which details will provide a clue to the mystery.

**10** **Critical Thinking and Reading** Why do you think Holmes makes this comment?

**11** **Discussion** Why do you think Spaulding is taking such an active part in getting Mr. Wilson this position?

I took the paper from him and read as follows:

To the Red-headed League:

On account of the bequest of the late Ezekiah Hopkins, of Lebanon, Pennsylvania, U.S.A., there is now another vacancy open which entitles a member of the League to a salary of £4[5] a week for purely nominal services. All red-headed men who are sound in body and mind, and above the age of twenty-one years, are eligible. Apply in person on Monday, at eleven o'clock, to Duncan Ross, at the offices of the League, 7 Pope's Court, Fleet Street.

"What on earth does this mean?" I ejaculated after I had twice read over the extraordinary announcement.

Holmes chuckled and wriggled in his chair, as was his habit when in high spirits. "It is a little off the beaten track, isn't it?" said he. "And now, Mr. Wilson, off you go at scratch and tell us all about yourself, your household, and the effect which this advertisement had upon your fortunes. You will first make a note, Doctor, of the paper and the date."

"It is *The Morning Chronicle* of April 27, 1890. Just two months ago."

"Very good. Now, Mr. Wilson?"

"Well, it is just as I have been telling you, Mr. Sherlock Holmes," said Jabez Wilson, mopping his forehead; "I have a small pawnbroker's business at Coburg Square, near the City. It's not a very large affair, and of late years it has not done more than just give me a living. I used to be able to keep two assistants, but now I only keep one; and I would have a job to pay him but that he is

5. **£4:** Four pounds in British money—a large amount at the time in which the story is set.

willing to come for half wages so as to learn the business."

"What is the name of this obliging youth?" asked Sherlock Holmes.

"His name is Vincent Spaulding, and he's not such a youth, either. It's hard to say his age. I should not wish a smarter assistant, Mr. Holmes; and I know very well that he could better himself and earn twice what I am able to give him. But, after all, if he is satisfied, why should I put ideas in his head?"

"Why, indeed? You seem most fortunate in having an employee who comes under the full market price. It is not a common experience among employers in this age. I don't know that your assistant is not as remarkable as your advertisement."

"Oh, he has his faults, too," said Mr. Wilson. "Never was such a fellow for photography. Snapping away with a camera when he ought to be improving his mind, and then diving down into the cellar like a rabbit into its hole to develop his pictures. That is his main fault, but on the whole he's a good worker. There's no vice in him."

"He is still with you, I presume?"

"Yes, sir. He and a girl of fourteen, who does a bit of simple cooking and keeps the place clean—that's all I have in the house, for I am a widower and never had any family. We live very quietly, sir, the three of us; and we keep a roof over our heads and pay our debts, if we do nothing more.

"The first thing that put us out was that advertisement. Spaulding, he came down into the office just this day eight weeks, with this very paper in his hand, and he says:

" 'I wish to the Lord, Mr. Wilson, that I was a red-headed man.'

" 'Why that?' I asks.

" 'Why,' says he, 'here's another vacancy on the League of the Red-headed Men. It's worth quite a little fortune to any man who gets it, and I understand that there are more vacancies than there are men, so that the trustees are at their wits' end what to do with the money. If my hair would only change color, here's a nice little crib all ready for me to step into.'

" 'Why, what is it, then?' I asked. You see, Mr. Holmes, I am a very stay-at-home man, and as my business came to me instead of my having to go to it, I was often weeks on end without putting my foot over the doormat. In that way I didn't know much of what was going on outside, and I was always glad of a bit of news.

" 'Have you never heard of the League of the Red-headed Men?' he asked with his eyes open.

" 'Never.'

" 'Why, I wonder at that, for you are eligible yourself for one of the vacancies.'

" 'And what are they worth?' I asked.

" 'Oh, merely a couple of hundred a year, but the work is slight, and it need not interfere very much with one's other occupations.'

"Well, you can easily think that that made me prick up my ears, for the business has not been over-good for some years, and an extra couple of hundred would have been very handy.

" 'Tell me all about it,' said I.

" 'Well,' said he, showing me the advertisement, 'you can see for yourself that the League has a vacancy, and there is the address where you should apply for particulars. As far as I can make out, the League was founded by an American millionaire, Ezekiah Hopkins, who was very peculiar in his ways. He was himself red-headed, and he had a great sympathy for all red-headed men; so when he died it was found that he had left his enormous fortune in the hands of trustees, with instructions to apply the interest to the providing of easy berths to men whose hair is of that color. From all I hear it is splendid pay and very little to do.'

" 'But,' said I, 'there would be millions of red-headed men who would apply.'

" 'Not so many as you might think,' he answered. 'You see it is really confined to Londoners, and to grown men. This American had started from London when he was young, and he wanted to do the old town a good turn. Then, again, I have heard it is no use your applying if your hair is light red, or dark red, or anything but real bright, blazing, fiery red. Now, if you cared to apply, Mr. Wilson, you would just walk in; but perhaps it would hardly be worth your while to put yourself out of the way for the sake of a few hundred pounds.'

"Now, it is a fact, gentlemen, as you may see for yourselves, that my hair is of a very full and rich tint, so that it seemed to me that if there was to be any competition in the matter I stood as good a chance as any man that I had ever met. Vincent Spaulding seemed to know so much about it that I thought he might prove useful so I just ordered him to put up the shutters for the day and to come right away with me. He was very willing to have a holiday,[6] so we shut the business up and started off for the address that was given us in the advertisement.

"I never hope to see such a sight as that again, Mr. Holmes. From north, south, east, and west every man who had a shade of red in his hair had tramped into the city to answer the advertisement. Fleet Street was choked with red-headed folk, and Pope's Court looked like a coster's orange barrow.[7] I should not have thought there were so many in the whole country as were brought together by that single advertisement. Every

---

**6. holiday:** A day off from work; a vacation.
**7. coster's orange barrow:** Pushcart of a seller of oranges.

**12** **Reading Strategy** Summarize Mr. Wilson's description of the Red-headed League. Make special note of the facts that seem suspicious.

**13** **Discussion** Why does Mr. Wilson take Spaulding with him when he applies for the job?

**12**

**13**

**14 Critical Thinking and Reading**
Do you think Mr. Spaulding's interest in getting Mr. Wilson to the office is unusual? Support your answer.

shade of color they were—straw, lemon, orange, brick, Irish-setter, liver, clay; but, as Spaulding said, there were not many who had the real vivid flame-colored tint. When I saw how many were waiting, I would have given it up in despair; but Spaulding would

not hear of it. How he did it I could not imagine, but he pushed and pulled and butted until he got me through the crowd, and right up to the steps which led to the office. There was a double stream upon the stair, some going up in hope, and some coming back dejected; but we wedged in as well as we could and soon found ourselves in the office."

"Your experience has been a most entertaining one," remarked Holmes as his client paused and refreshed his memory with a huge pinch of snuff. "Pray continue your very interesting statement."

"There was nothing in the office but a couple of wooden chairs and a deal table, behind which sat a small man with a head that was even redder than mine. He said a few words to each candidate as he came up, and then he always managed to find some fault in them which would disqualify them. Getting a vacancy did not seem to be such a very easy matter, after all. However, when our turn came the little man was much more favorable to me than to any of the others, and he closed the door as we entered, so that he might have a private word with us.

" 'This is Mr. Jabez Wilson,' said my assistant, 'and he is willing to fill a vacancy in the League.'

" 'And he is admirably suited for it,' the other answered. 'He has every requirement. I cannot recall when I have seen anything so fine.' He took a step backward, cocked his head on one side, and gazed at my hair until I felt quite bashful. Then suddenly he plunged forward, wrung my hand, and congratulated me warmly on my success.

" 'It would be injustice to hesitate,' said he. 'You will, however, I am sure, excuse me for taking an obvious precaution.' With that he seized my hair in both his hands, and tugged until I yelled with the pain. 'There is water in your eyes,' said he as he released me. 'I perceive that all is as it should be. But we have to be careful, for we have twice been deceived by wigs and once by paint. I could tell you tales of cobbler's wax which would disgust you with human nature.' He stepped over to the window and shouted through it at the top of his voice that the vacancy was filled. A groan of disappointment came up from below, and the folk all trooped away in different directions until there was not a red head to be seen except my own and that of the manager.

" 'My name,' said he, 'is Mr. Duncan Ross, and I am myself one of the pensioners upon the fund left by our noble benefactor. Are you a married man, Mr. Wilson? Have you a family?'

"I answered that I had not.

"His face fell immediately.

" 'Dear me!' he said gravely, 'that is very serious indeed! I am sorry to hear you say that. The fund was, of course, for the propogation and spread of the red-heads as well as for their maintenance. It is exceedingly unfortunate that you should be a bachelor.

"My face lengthened at this, Mr. Holmes, for I thought that I was not to have the vacancy after all; but after thinking it over for a few minutes he said that it would be all right.

" 'In the case of another,' said he, 'the objection might be fatal, but we must stretch a point in favor of a man with such a head of hair as yours. When shall you be able to enter upon your new duties?'

" 'Well, it is a little awkward, for I have a business already,' said I.

" 'Oh, never mind about that, Mr. Wilson!' said Vincent Spaulding. 'I should be able to look after that for you.'

" 'What would be the hours?' I asked.

" 'Ten to two.'

"Now a pawnbroker's business is mostly done of an evening, Mr. Holmes, especially Thursday and Friday evening, which is just before pay-day: so it would suit me very well to earn a little in the mornings. Besides, I knew that my assistant was a good man, and that he would see to anything that turned up.

" 'That would suit me very well,' said I. 'And the pay?'

" 'Is £4 a week.'

" 'And the work?'

" 'Is purely nominal.'

" 'What do you call purely nominal?'

" 'Well, you have to be in the office, or at least in the building, the whole time. If you leave, you forfeit your whole position forever. The will is very clear upon that point. You don't comply with the conditions if you budge from the office during that time.'

" 'It's only four hours a day, and I should not think of leaving,' said I.

---

**15 Critical Thinking and Reading** What is unusual about the manner in which Mr. Wilson is treated by the head of the league?

**16 Discussion** What qualifications does Mr. Wilson have for the job at the league?

**17 Discussion** Do you think that Mr. Spaulding might be motivated by something other than kindness?

**18 Discussion** Why do you think the man stresses these conditions?

**19 Critical Thinking and Reading** What inferences can you make about the Red-headed League based on what you have read about it so far?

**20 Reading Strategy** Summarize Mr. Wilson's experience at the Red-headed League, stressing the points you think most significant.

" 'No excuse will avail,' said Mr. Duncan Ross; 'neither sickness nor business nor anything else. There you must stay, or you lose your billet.'⁸

" 'And the work?'

" 'Is to copy out the Encyclopedia Britannica. There is the first volume of it in that press. You must find your own ink, pens, and blotting-paper, but we provide this table and chair. Will you be ready tomorrow?'

" 'Certainly,' I answered.

" 'Then, good-bye, Mr. Jabez Wilson, and let me congratulate you once more on the important position which you have been fortunate enough to gain.' He bowed me out of the room, and I went home with my assistant, hardly knowing what to say or do, I was so pleased at my own good fortune.

"Well, I thought over the matter all day, and by evening I was in low spirits again; for I had quite persuaded myself that the whole affair must be some great hoax or fraud, though what its object might be I could not imagine. It seemed altogether past belief that anyone could make such a will, or that they would pay such a sum for doing anything so simple as copying out the Encyclopedia Britannica. Vincent Spaulding did what he could to cheer me up, but by bedtime I had reasoned myself out of the whole thing. However, in the morning I determined to have a look at it anyhow, so I bought a penny bottle of ink, and with a quill-pen, and seven sheets of foolscap paper,⁹ I started off for Pope's Court.

"Well, to my surprise and delight, everything was as right as possible. The table was set out ready for me, and Mr. Duncan Ross was there to see that I got fairly to work. He started me off upon the letter A, and then he left me; but he would drop in from time to time to see that all was right with me. At two o'clock he bade me good-day, complimented me upon the amount that I had written, and locked the door of the office after me.

"This went on day after day, Mr. Holmes, and on Saturday the manager came in and planked down four golden sovereigns for my week's work. It was the same next week, and the same the week after. Every morning I was there at ten, and every afternoon I left at two. By degrees Mr. Duncan Ross took to coming in only once of a morning, and then, after a time, he did not come in at all. Still, of course, I never dared to leave the room for an instant, for I was not sure when he might come, and the billet was such a good one, and suited me so well, that I would not risk the loss of it.

"Eight weeks passed away like this, and I had written about Abbots and Archery and Armor and Architecture and Attica, and hoped with diligence that I might get on to the B's before very long. It cost me something in foolscap, and I had pretty nearly filled a shelf with my writings. And then suddenly the whole business came to an end."

"To an end?"

"Yes, sir. And no later than this morning. I went to my work as usual at ten o'clock, but the door was shut and locked, with a little square of cardboard hammered on to the middle of the panel with a tack. Here it is, and you can read for yourself."

He held up a piece of white cardboard about the size of a sheet of notepaper. It read in this fashion:

THE RED-HEADED LEAGUE

IS

DISSOLVED.

October 9, 1890.

---

8. **billet** (bil′ it) *n.*: Position, job.
9. **foolscap paper:** Writing paper.

## Grammar in Action

**Single quotation marks** show a quotation within a quotation and never appear without being accompanied by double quotation marks. Dialogue sometimes requires single quotation marks when a speaker is repeating the exact words of another speaker. Note the following example from "The Red-headed League":

" 'Oh,' said he, 'his name was William Morris . . . He moved out yesterday.'

" 'Where could I find him?'

" 'Oh, at his new offices. He did tell me the address. Yes. 17 King Edward Street, near St. Paul's.'

"I started off, Mr. Holmes, but when I got to that address. . . no one in it had ever heard of either Mr. William Morris or Mr. Duncan Ross."

"And what did you do then?" asked Holmes.

In the above passage, Jabez Wilson is reporting to Sherlock

Sherlock Holmes and I surveyed this curt announcement and the rueful face behind it, until the comical side of the affair so completely overtopped every other consideration that we both burst out into a roar of laughter.

"I cannot see that there is anything very funny," cried our client, flushing up to the roots of his flaming head. "If you can do nothing better than laugh at me, I can go elsewhere."

"No, no," cried Holmes, shoving him back into the chair from which he had half risen. "I really wouldn't miss your case for the world. It is most refreshingly unusual. But there is, if you will excuse my saying so, something just a little funny about it. Pray what steps did you take when you found the card upon the door?"

21

"I was staggered, sir. I did not know what to do. Then I called at the offices round, but none of them seemed to know anything about it. Finally, I went to the landlord, who is an accountant living on the ground floor, and I asked him if he could tell me what had become of the Red-headed League. He said that he had never heard of any such body. Then I asked him who Mr. Duncan Ross was. He answered that the name was new to him.

" 'Well,' said I, 'the gentleman at No. 4.'

" 'What, the red-headed man?'

" 'Yes.'

" 'Oh,' said he, 'his name was William Morris. He was a solicitor[10] and was using my room as a temporary convenience until his new premises were ready. He moved out yesterday.'

" 'Where could I find him?'

" 'Oh, at his new offices. He did tell me

---

10. **solicitor:** A member of the legal profession.

the address. Yes, 17 King Edward Street, near St. Paul's.'

"I started off, Mr. Holmes, but when I got to that address it was a manufactory of artificial kneecaps, and no one in it had ever heard of either Mr. William Morris or Mr. Duncan Ross."

"And what did you do then?" asked Holmes.

"I went home to Saxe-Coburg Square, and I took the advice of my assistant. But he could not help me in any way. He could only say that if I waited I should hear by post. But that was not quite good enough, Mr. Holmes. I did not wish to lose such a place without a struggle, so, as I had heard that you were good enough to give advice to poor folk who were in need of it, I came right away to you."

"And you did very wisely," said Holmes. "Your case is an exceedingly remarkable one, and I shall be happy to look into it. From what you have told me I think that it is possible that graver issues hang from it than might at first sight appear."

"Grave enough!" said Mr. Jabez Wilson. "Why, I have lost four pound a week."

"As far as you are personally concerned," remarked Holmes, "I do not see that you have any grievance against this extraordinary league. On the contrary, you are, as I understand, richer by some £30, to say nothing of the minute knowledge which you have gained on every subject which comes under the letter A. You have lost nothing by them."

22

"No, sir. But I want to find out about them, and who they are, and what their object was in playing this prank—if it was a prank—upon me. It was a pretty expensive joke for them, for it cost them two and thirty pounds."

"We shall endeavor to clear up these

*The Red-headed League* 79

---

21 **Discussion** After the league is dissolved, what circumstances lead Mr. Wilson to question its validity?

22 **Literary Focus** What attitude does Holmes take about this case? What is his attitude toward Mr. Wilson? What does this indicate about Holmes's character?

---

Holmes a conversation that he, Wilson, had with the landlord. Single quotation marks are used to set off the exact words of that earlier conversation. The double quotation marks indicate the conversation in the present with Holmes. Note that double quotation marks begin each new paragraph but end only in the fourth and fifth paragraphs, marking a change of speaker.

**Student Activity 1.** Read paragraphs 6-10 in the second column of page 74. Note each set of quotation marks. Decide who is speaking. How did you recognize that the speaker changed?

**Student Activity 2.** Write a brief dialogue between two speakers in which one speaker repeats the exact words of a third speaker. Use single quotation marks to show the quotation within the quotation.

**23 Discussion** Why do you think Holmes is interested in the assistant?

**24 Critical Thinking and Reading** Why do you think Holmes is so excited when he hears this description of Spaulding?

**25 Discussion** Why does Holmes say that more bizarre crimes are easier to figure out than "commonplace, featureless crimes"?

**26 Master Teacher Note** Notice the techniques that Holmes uses to help him concentrate. In other stories, he plays a violin. Tell students that people use many different devices to help them concentrate. Some take a walk or pace a room, while others prefer to sit still like Holmes. Have students describe the techniques that they use to focus their attention on a problem. Ask them why such devices are helpful.

**27 Critical Thinking and Reading** What does "introspective" mean? How do you think that going to a concert will help Holmes solve this case?

points for you. And, first, one or two questions, Mr. Wilson. This assistant of yours who first called your attention to the advertisement—how long had he been with you?"

"About a month then."

"How did he come?"

"In answer to an advertisement."

"Was he the only applicant?"

"No, I had a dozen."

"Why did you pick him?"

"Because he was handy and would come cheap."

"At half-wages, in fact."

"Yes."

"What is he like, this Vincent Spaulding?"

"Small, stout-built, very quick in his ways, no hair on his face, though he's not short of thirty. Has a white splash of acid upon his forehead."

Holmes sat up in his chair in considerable excitement. "I thought as much," said he. "Have you ever observed that his ears are pierced for earrings?"

"Yes, sir. He told me that a gypsy had done it for him when he was a lad."

"Hum!" said Holmes, sinking back in deep thought. "He is still with you?"

"Oh, yes, sir; I have only just left him."

"And has your business been attended to in your absence?"

"Nothing to complain of, sir. There's never very much to do of a morning."

"That will do, Mr. Wilson. I shall be happy to give you an opinion upon the subject in the course of a day or two. Today is Saturday, and I hope that by Monday we may come to a conclusion."

"Well, Watson," said Holmes when our visitor had left us, "what do you make of it all?"

"I make nothing of it," I answered frankly. "It is a most mysterious business."

"As a rule," said Holmes, "the more bizarre a thing is the less mysterious it proves to be. It is your commonplace, featureless crimes which are really puzzling, just as a commonplace face is the most difficult to identify. But I must be prompt over this matter."

"What are you going to do, then?" I asked.

"To smoke," he answered. "It is quite a three pipe problem, and I beg that you won't speak to me for fifty minutes." He curled himself up in his chair, with his thin knees drawn up to his hawk-like nose, and there he sat with his eyes closed and his black clay pipe thrusting out like the bill of some strange bird. I had come to the conclusion that he had dropped asleep, and indeed was nodding myself, when he suddenly sprang out of his chair with the gesture of a man who has made up his mind and put his pipe down upon the mantelpiece.

"Sarasate[11] plays at the St. James's Hall this afternoon," he remarked. "What do you think, Watson? Could your patients spare you for a few hours?"

"I have nothing to do today. My practice is never very absorbing."

"Then put on your hat and come. I am going through the City first, and we can have some lunch on the way. I observe that there is a good deal of German music on the program, which is rather more to my taste than Italian or French. It is introspective, and I want to introspect. Come along!"

We traveled by the Underground as far as Aldersgate; and a short walk took us to Saxe-Coburg Square, the scene of the singular story which we had listened to in the morning. It was a poky, little, shabby-genteel place, where four lines of dingy two-storied brick houses looked out into a small railed-

---

**11. Sarasate** (sä rä sä′ tä): Spanish violinist and composer.

in enclosure, where a lawn of weedy grass and a few clumps of faded laurel bushes made a hard fight against a smoke-laden and uncongenial atmosphere. Three gilt balls and a brown board with "JABEZ WILSON" in white letters, upon a corner house, announced the place where our red-headed client carried on his business. Sherlock Holmes stopped in front of it with his head on one side and looked it all over, with his eyes shining brightly between puckered lids. Then he walked slowly up the street, and then down again to the corner, still looking keenly at the houses. Finally he returned to the pawnbroker's, and, having thumped vigorously upon the pavement with his stick two or three times, he went up to the door and knocked. It was instantly opened by a bright-looking, clean-shaven young fellow, who asked him to step in.

"Thank you," said Holmes, "I only wished to ask you how you would go from here to the Strand."

"Third right, fourth left," answered the assistant promptly, closing the door.

"Smart fellow, that," observed Holmes as we walked away. "He is, in my judgment, the fourth smartest man in London, and for daring I am not sure that he has not a claim to be third. I have known something of him before."

"Evidently," said I, "Mr. Wilson's assistant counts for a good deal in this mystery of the Red-headed League. I am sure that you inquired your way merely in order that you might see him."

"Not him."

"What then?"

"The knees of his trousers."

"And what did you see?"

"What I expected to see."

"Why did you beat the pavement?"

"My dear doctor, this is a time for observation, not for talk. We are spies in an en-

emy's country. We know something of Saxe-Coburg Square. Let us now explore the parts which lie behind it."

The road in which we found ourselves as we turned round the corner from the retired Saxe-Coburg Square presented as great a contrast to it as the front of a picture does to the back. It was one of the main arteries which conveyed the traffic of the City to the north and west. The roadway was blocked with the immense stream of commerce flowing in a double tide inward and outward, while the footpaths were black with the hurrying swarm of pedestrians. It was difficult to realize as we looked at the line of fine

*The Red-headed League* 81

28 **Critical Thinking and Reading** Why does Holmes thump his walking stick on the pavement outside Mr. Wilson's house?

29 **Discussion** Discuss what possible clues might be found by examining the knees of Mr. Spaulding's trousers.

30 **Reading Strategy** Summarize the observations Holmes has made since he arrived at Saxe-Coburg Square.

31 **Discussion** Which building do you think will be significant for this case?

32 **Enrichment** *Conundrum* originally meant "a riddle whose answer is a pun, or play on words." However, the meaning of this word has expanded to include "any puzzling question or problem." The assumption, however, is that a conundrum always has a clear solution. This is not always the case with a mystery.

33 **Master Teacher Note** Holmes's violin, like his pipe, is one of his trademarks. What are some of Holmes's other trademarks? Ask students why writers sometimes give their characters certain trademarks. Have them recall trademarks of other characters in fiction or film. If students were to create a detective of their own, what trademarks would they give him or her?

34 **Reading Strategy** Summarize what Watson says about Holmes's "dual nature."

35 **Critical Thinking and Reading** Why might the fact that it is Saturday complicate matters?

36 **Discussion** How has the lighter mood of the story changed?

shops and stately business premises that they really abutted on the other side upon the faded and stagnant square which we had just quitted.

"Let me see," said Holmes, standing at the corner and glancing along the line, "I should like just to remember the order of the houses here. It is a hobby of mine to have an exact knowledge of London. There is Mortimer's, the tobacconist, the little newspaper shop, the Coburg branch of the City and Suburban Bank, the Vegetarian Restaurant, and McFarlane's carriage-building depot. That carries us right on to the other block. And now, Doctor, we've done our work, so it's time we had some play. A sandwich and a cup of coffee, and then off to violin land, where all is sweetness and delicacy and harmony, and there are no red-headed clients to vex us with their conundrums."

My friend was an enthusiastic musician, being himself not only a very capable performer but a composer of no ordinary merit. All the afternoon he sat in the stalls wrapped in the most perfect happiness, gently waving his long, thin fingers in time to the music, while his gently smiling face and his languid, dreamy eyes were as unlike those of Holmes, the sleuthhound, Holmes the relentless, keen-witted, ready-handed criminal agent, as it was possible to conceive. In his singular character the dual nature alternately asserted itself, and his extreme exactness and astuteness represented, as I have often thought, the reaction against the poetic and contemplative mood which occasionally predominated in him. The swing of his nature took him from extreme languor to devouring energy; and, as I knew well, he was never so truly formidable as when, for days on end, he had been lounging in his armchair amid his improvisations and his black-letter editions. Then it was that the lust of the chase would suddenly come upon him, and that his brilliant reasoning power would rise to the level of intuition, until those who were unacquainted with his methods would look askance at him as on a man whose knowledge was not that of other mortals. When I saw him that afternoon so enwrapped in the music at St. James's Hall I felt that an evil time might be coming upon those whom he had set himself to hunt down.

"You want to go home, no doubt, Doctor," he remarked as we emerged.

"Yes, it would be as well."

"And I have some business to do which will take some hours. This business at Coburg Square is serious."

"Why serious?"

"A considerable crime is in contemplation. I have every reason to believe that we shall be in time to stop it. But today being Saturday rather complicates matters. I shall want your help tonight."

"At what time?"

"Ten will be early enough."

"I shall be at Baker Street at ten."

"Very well. And, I say, Doctor, there may be some little danger, so kindly put your army revolver in your pocket." He waved his hand, turned on his heel, and disappeared in an instant among the crowd.

I trust that I am not more dense than my neighbors, but I was always oppressed with a sense of my own stupidity in my dealings with Sherlock Holmes. Here I had heard what he had heard, I had seen what he had seen, and yet from his words it was evident that he saw clearly not only what had happened but what was about to happen, while to me the whole business was still confused and grotesque. As I drove home to my house in Kensington I thought over it all, from the extraordinary story of the red-headed copier of the Encyclopedia down to the visit to Saxe-Coburg Square, and the ominous words with which he had parted from me. What was this nocturnal expedition, and why should I go armed? Where were we going, and what were we to do? I had the hint from Holmes that this smooth-faced pawnbroker's assistant was a formidable man—a man who might play a deep game. I tried to puzzle it out, but gave it up in despair and set the matter aside until night should bring an explanation.

It was a quarter past nine when I started from home and made my way across the Park, and so through Oxford Street to Baker Street. Two hansoms[12] were standing at the door, and as I entered the passage I heard the sound of voices from above. On entering his room I found Holmes in animated conversation with two men, one of whom I recognized as Peter Jones, the official police agent, while the other was a long, thin, sad-faced man, with a very shiny hat and oppressively respectable frock coat.

"Ha! our party is complete," said Holmes, buttoning up his pea-jacket and taking his heavy hunting crop from the rack. "Watson, I think you know Mr. Jones, of Scotland Yard? Let me introduce you to Mr. Merryweather, who is to be our companion in tonight's adventure."

"We're hunting in couples again, Doctor, you see," said Jones in his consequential way. "Our friend here is a wonderful man for starting a chase. All he wants is an old dog to help him to do the running down."

"I hope a wild goose may not prove to be the end of our chase," observed Mr. Merryweather gloomily.

"You may place considerable confidence in Mr. Holmes, sir," said the police agent loftily. "He has his own little methods, which are, if he won't mind my saying so, just a little too theoretical and fantastic, but he has the makings of a detective in him. It is not too much to say that once or twice, as in that business of the Sholto murder and the Agra treasure, he has been more nearly correct than the official force."

"Oh, if you say so, Mr. Jones, it is all right," said the stranger with deference. "Still, I confess that I miss my rubber.[13] It is the first Saturday night for seven-and-twenty years that I have not had my rubber."

"I think you will find," said Sherlock Holmes, "that you will play for a higher stake tonight than you have ever done yet, and that the play will be more exciting. For you, Mr. Merryweather, the stake will be some £30,000; and for you, Jones, it will be the man upon whom you wish to lay your hands."

"John Clay, the murderer, thief, smasher, and forger. He's a young man, Mr. Merryweather, but he is at the head of his profession, and I would rather have my bracelets on him than on any criminal in London. He's a remarkable man, is young John Clay. His grandfather was a royal duke, and he himself has been to Eton[14] and Oxford.[15] His brain is as cunning as his fingers, and though we meet signs of him at every turn, we never know where to find the man himself. He'll crack a crib[16] in Scotland one week, and be raising money to build an orphanage in Cornwall the next. I've been on his track for years and have never set eyes on him yet."

"I hope that I may have the pleasure of introducing you tonight. I've had one or two

_____
12. **hansoms:** Two-wheeled covered carriages for two passengers.

_____
13. **rubber:** Card games.
14. **Eton:** A famous British secondary school for boys.
15. **Oxford:** The oldest university in Great Britain.
16. **crack a crib:** Break into and rob a house.

*The Red-headed League* 83

37 **Critical Thinking and Reading** You might review some of the questions raised by Holmes in the course of the investigation. Can you answer any of the questions that Dr. Watson poses?

38 **Reading Strategy** Does the fact that 30,000 pounds are at stake help you to predict the crime that will be committed?

39 **Discussion** What character already introduced might fit this brief description of John Clay?

**40 Discussion** Why do you think that Mr. Merryweather, a bank director, has been invited to go along?

**41 Critical Thinking and Reading** Contrast what Holmes says about Jones's talents with what Jones has said about Holmes's ability.

**42 Reading Strategy** Predict where Holmes and the others are going, basing your answer on the buildings listed by Holmes on page 82.

**43 Discussion** How has Conan Doyle prepared us for Merryweather's discovery of the hollow sound?

little turns also with Mr. John Clay, and I agree with you that he is at the head of his profession. It is past ten, however, and quite time that we started. If you two will take the first hansom, Watson and I will follow in the second."

Sherlock Holmes was not very communicative during the long drive and lay back in the cab humming the tunes which he had heard in the afternoon. We rattled through an endless labyrinth of gas-lit streets until we emerged into Farrington Street.

40 "We are close there now," my friend remarked. "This fellow Merryweather is a bank director, and personally interested in the matter. I thought it as well to have Jones

41 with us also. He is not a bad fellow, though an absolute imbecile in his profession. He has one positive virtue. He is as brave as a bulldog and as tenacious as a lobster if he gets his claws upon anyone. Here we are, and they are waiting for us."

We had reached the same crowded thoroughfare in which we had found ourselves in the morning. Our cabs were dismissed, and, following the guidance of Mr. Merryweather, we passed down a narrow passage and through a side door, which he opened for us. Within there was a small corridor, which

42 ended in a very massive iron gate. This also was opened, and led down a flight of winding stone steps, which terminated at another formidable gate. Mr. Merryweather stopped to light a lantern, and then conducted us down a dark, earth-smelling passage, and so, after opening a third door, into a huge vault or cellar, which was piled all round with crates and massive boxes.

"You are not very vulnerable from above," Holmes remarked as he held up the lantern and gazed about him.

43 "Nor from below," said Mr. Merryweather, striking his stick upon the flags which lined the floor. "Why, dear me, it sounds quite hollow!" he remarked, looking up in surprise.

"I must really ask you to be a little more quiet!" said Holmes severely. "You have already imperiled the whole success of our expedition. Might I beg that you would have the goodness to sit down upon one of those boxes, and not to interfere?"

The solemn Mr. Merryweather perched himself upon a crate, with a very injured expression upon his face, while Holmes fell upon his knees upon the floor and, with the lantern and a magnifying lens, began to examine minutely the cracks between the stones. A few seconds sufficed to satisfy him, for he sprang to his feet again and put his glass in his pocket.

"We have at least an hour before us," he remarked, "for they can hardly take any steps until the good pawnbroker is safely in bed. Then they will not lose a minute, for the sooner they do their work the longer time they will have for their escape. We are at present, Doctor—as no doubt you have divined—in the cellar of the City branch of one of the principal London banks. Mr. Merryweather is the chairman of directors, and he will explain to you that there are reasons why the more daring criminals of London should take a considerable interest in this cellar at present."

"It is our French gold," whispered the director. "We have had several warnings that an attempt might be made upon it."

"Your French gold?"

"Yes. We had occasion some months ago to strengthen our resources and borrowed for that purpose 30,000 napoleons from the Bank of France. It has become known that we have never had occasion to unpack the money, and that it is still lying in our cellar. The crate upon which I sit contains 2,000

## Grammar in Action

Sherlock Holmes's success as a detective lies in his skill at **deduction,** or arriving at a conclusion based on a set of observable facts. Holmes is a skilled observer, noting details that those around him—especially Watson—often overlook. He is then able to see in these details, each based on reliable observation, an overall pattern. The pattern—how all the details fit together, how they are related—provides him with the solution to the mystery.

Note the details that Holmes has so far learned about this case.
Spaulding, Mr. Wilson's assistant, works for half the current wage.
Spaulding spends a great deal of time developing photographs in the basement of the shop.
Spaulding sends Wilson to the League of Red-headed Men.
Wilson spends four hours in the middle of the day at the League.
Without warning, the League is dissolved.
When Holmes and Watson call on Spaulding, Holmes checks the knees of that man's trousers.

napoleons packed between layers of lead foil. Our reserve of bullion is much larger at present than is usually kept in a single branch office, and the directors have had misgivings upon the subject."

"Which were very well justified," observed Holmes. "And now it is time that we arranged our little plans. I expect that within an hour matters will come to a head. In the meantime, Mr. Merryweather, we must put the screen over that dark lantern."

"And sit in the dark?"

"I am afraid so. I had brought a pack of cards in my pocket, and I thought that, as we were a *partie carrée*,[17] you might have your rubber after all. But I see that the enemy's preparations have gone so far that we cannot risk the presence of a light. And, first of all, we must choose our positions. These are daring men, and though we shall take them at a disadvantage, they may do us some harm unless we are careful. I shall stand behind this crate, and do you conceal yourselves behind those. Then, when I flash a light upon them, close in swiftly. If they fire, Watson, have no compunction about shooting them down."

I placed my revolver, cocked, upon the top of the wooden case behind which I crouched. Holmes shot the slide across the front of his lantern and left us in pitch darkness—such an absolute darkness as I have never before experienced. The smell of hot metal remained to assure us that the light was still there, ready to flash out at a moment's notice. To me, with my nerves worked up to a pitch of expectancy, there was something depressing and subduing in the sudden gloom, and in the cold dank air of the vault.

---

**17. partie carrée** (pär tē′ cä rā′): French for "group of four."

"They have but one retreat," whispered Holmes. "That is back through the house into Saxe-Coburg Square. I hope that you have done what I asked you, Jones?"

"I have an inspector and two officers waiting at the front door."

"Then we have stopped all the holes. And now we must be silent and wait."

What a time it seemed! From comparing notes afterwards it was but an hour and a quarter, yet it appeared to me that the night must have almost gone, and the dawn be breaking above us. My limbs were weary and stiff, for I feared to change my position; yet my nerves were worked up to the highest pitch of tension, and my hearing was so acute that I could not only hear the gentle breathing of my companions, but I could distinguish the deeper, heavier in-breath of the bulky Jones from the thin, sighing note of the bank director. From my position I could look over the case in the direction of the floor. Suddenly my eyes caught the glint of a light.

At first it was but a lurid spark upon the stone pavement. Then it lengthened out until it became a yellow line, and then, without any warning or sound, a gash seemed to open and a hand appeared; a white, almost womanly hand, which felt about in the center of the little area of light. For a minute or more the hand, with its writhing fingers, protruded out of the floor. Then it was withdrawn as suddenly as it appeared, and all was dark again save the single lurid spark which marked a chink between the stones.

Its disappearance, however, was but momentary. With a rending, tearing sound, one of the broad, white stones turned over upon its side and left a square, gaping hole, through which streamed the light of a lantern. Over the edge there peeped a clean-cut, boyish face, which looked keenly about it,

*The Red-headed League*  85

**44 Critical Thinking and Reading** How does the description of their preparations heighten the suspense?

**45 Discussion** How does Watson's description of what he was feeling and hearing add to the suspense?

**46 Discussion** Why do you think that it is so effective to describe the criminal's hand as it first appears from the tunnel?

Holmes taps with his cane on the street outside the pawnshop.
Holmes visits the busy commercial street that lies behind the pawnshop.
Holmes learns that the Coburg branch of the City and Suburban Bank has a great deal of gold in its vaults.

**Student Activity 1.** With a small group of classmates, briefly review the story, and add any additional information to the list of observations. Then discuss each item on the list. Can you see a pattern? What conclusion might be drawn from these facts?

**Student Activity 2.** Report your conclusion to the rest of the class, comparing and contrasting it with those arrived at by other groups.

47 **Critical Thinking and Reading**
Can you identify the two men who
climb out of the tunnel?

47 and then, with a hand on either side of the aperture, drew itself shoulder-high and waist-high, until one knee rested upon the edge. In another instant he stood at the side of the hole and was hauling after him a companion, lithe and small like himself, with a pale face and a shock of very red hair.

"It's all clear," he whispered. "Have you the chisel and the bags? Great Scott! Jump, Archie, jump, and I'll swing for it."

Sherlock Holmes had sprung out and seized the intruder by the collar. The other dived down the hole, and I heard the sound of rending cloth as Jones clutched at his skirts. The light flashed upon the barrel of a revolver, but Holmes's hunting crop came down on the man's wrist, and the pistol clinked upon the stone floor.

"It's no use, John Clay," said Holmes blandly. "You have no chance at all."

"So I see," the other answered with the utmost coolness. "I fancy that my pal is all right, though I see you have got his coat-tails."

"There are three men waiting for him at the door," said Holmes.

"Oh, indeed! You seem to have done the thing very completely. I must compliment you."

"And I you," Holmes answered. "Your red-headed idea was very new and effective."

"You'll see your pal again presently," said Jones. "He's quicker at climbing down holes than I am. Just hold out while I fix the derbies."[18]

48

"I beg that you will not touch me with your filthy hands," remarked our prisoner as the handcuffs clattered upon his wrists. "You may not be aware that I have royal blood in my veins. Have the goodness, also, when you address me always to say 'sir' and 'please.'"

"All right," said Jones with a stare and a snigger. "Well, would you please, sir, march upstairs, where we can get a cab to carry your Highness to the police station?"

"That is better," said John Clay serenely. He made a sweeping bow to the three of us and walked quietly off in the custody of the detective.

"Really, Mr. Holmes," said Mr. Merryweather as we followed them from the cellar, "I do not know how the bank can thank you or repay you. There is no doubt that you have detected and defeated in the most complete manner one of the most determined attempts at bank robbery that have ever come within my experience."

"I have had one or two little scores of my own to settle with Mr. John Clay," said

---

18. **derbies:** Handcuffs.

---

Holmes. "I have been at some small expense over this matter, which I shall expect the bank to refund, but beyond that I am amply repaid by having had an experience which is in many ways unique, and by hearing the very remarkable narrative of the Red-headed League."

"You see, Watson," he explained in the early hours of the morning as we sat over a glass of whisky and soda in Baker Street, "it was perfectly obvious from the first that the only possible object of this rather fantastic business of the advertisement of the League, and the copying of the Encyclopedia, must be to get this not over-bright pawnbroker out of the way for a number of hours every day. It was a curious way of managing it, but, really, it would be difficult to suggest a better. The method was no doubt suggested to Clay's ingenious mind by the color of his accomplice's hair. The £4 a week was a lure which must draw him, and what was it to them, who were playing for thousands? They put in the advertisement, one rogue has the temporary office, the other rogue incites the man to apply for it, and together they manage to secure his absence every morning in the week. From the time that I heard of the assistant having come for half wages, it was obvious to me that he had some strong motive for securing the situation."

"But how could you guess what the motive was?"

"Had there been women in the house, I should have suspected a mere vulgar intrigue. That, however, was out of the question. The man's business was a small one, and there was nothing in his house which could account for such elaborate preparations, and such an expenditure as they were at. It must, then, be something out of the house. What could it be? I thought of the assistant's fondness for photography, and his

49

---

48 **Critical Thinking and Reading** What do John Clay's remarks reveal about his personality?

49 **Discussion** How does Holmes reveal his opinion of John Clay's intelligence?

**50 Discussion** Are you satisfied by Holmes's explanation of the case? Were you able to predict some of the developments?

**51 Literary Focus** *Ennui* means "boredom." What do Holmes's remarks about ennui reveal about his personality?

**52 Master Teacher Note** One critic has written that, in a good detective story, the reader should always have the same information as the detective. Otherwise, the detective has an unfair advantage. Have students evaluate "The Red-headed League" according to this criterion. Then have them discuss whether it is a fair standard by which to measure a detective story.

**Reader's Response** With whom do you more easily identify, Sherlock Holmes or Doctor Watson? Explain.

---

trick of vanishing into the cellar. The cellar! There was the end of this tangled clue. Then I made inquiries as to this mysterious assistant and found that I had to deal with one of the coolest and most daring criminals in London. He was doing something in the cellar—something which took many hours a day for months on end. What could it be, once more? I could think of nothing save that he was running a tunnel to some other building.

"So far I had got when we went to visit the scene of action. I surprised you by beating upon the pavement with my stick. I was ascertaining whether the cellar stretched out in front or behind. It was not in front. Then I rang the bell, and, as I hoped, the assistant answered it. We have had some skirmishes, but we had never set eyes upon each other before. I hardly looked at his face. His knees were what I wished to see. You must yourself have remarked how worn, wrinkled, and stained they were. They spoke of those hours of burrowing. The only remaining point was what they were burrowing for. I walked round the corner, saw that the City and Suburban Bank abutted on our friend's premises, and felt that I had solved my problem. When you drove home after the concert I called upon Scotland Yard and upon the chairman of the bank directors, with the result that you have seen."

"And how could you tell that they would make their attempt tonight?" I asked.

**50**

"Well, when they closed their League offices that was a sign that they cared no longer about Mr. Jabez Wilson's presence—in other words, that they had completed their tunnel. But it was essential that they should use it soon, as it might be discovered, or the bullion might be removed. Saturday would suit them better than any other day, as it would give them two days for their escape. For all these reasons I expected them to come tonight."

"You reasoned it out beautifully," I exclaimed in unfeigned admiration. "It is so long a chain, and yet every link rings true."

"It saved me from ennui,"[19] he answered, yawning. "Alas! I already feel it closing in upon me. My life is spent in one long effort to escape from the commonplaces of existence. These little problems help me to do so."

**51**

"And you are a benefactor of the race," said I.

He shrugged his shoulders. "Well, perhaps, after all, it is of some little use," he remarked. " '*L'homme c'est rien—l'oeuvre c'est tout*,'[20] as Gustave Flaubert wrote to George Sand."[21]

**52**

---

19. **ennui** (än' wē): Boredom.
20. *L'homme c'est rien—l'oeuvre c'est tout* (lum sä rē''n lʉvr sä tū): French for "Man is nothing—the work is everything."
21. **Gustave Flaubert** (gūs täv' flō bär') **. . . George Sand:** Notable French novelists of the nineteenth century.

---

## Closure and Extension

### ANSWERS TO THINKING ABOUT THE SELECTION
*Recalling*

1. Wilson wants Holmes to find out what happened to the Red-headed League.
2. He thumps the pavement in front of Wilson's house to hear if it is hollow; he knocks on Wilson's door in order to check the assistant's appearance for clues; and he checks the back of Wilson's house to see what buildings it faces.
3. The true purpose of the Red-headed League was to remove Mr. Wilson from his house so that a tunnel could be dug from the house to the bank's vault.
4. Holmes, Watson, Jones, and Merryweather hide in the dark, waiting for the appearance of John Clay and his accomplice. When Clay comes up from the tunnel, Holmes grabs him by the collar and knocks Clay's pistol out of his hand with a hunting crop. Jones tears the coat of Clay's accomplice as he makes a temporary getaway.

## THINKING ABOUT THE SELECTION

### Recalling

1. Explain the mystery that Jabez Wilson wants Sherlock Holmes to solve.
2. What three actions does Holmes take when he first visits Saxe-Coburg Square? What is the reason behind each of these actions?
3. Explain the true purpose of the Red-headed League.
4. Describe what happens in the bank's cellar on Saturday night.

### Interpreting

5. From what clues does Holmes know the real identity of Spaulding?
6. Find three deductions Holmes makes from what he learns at Saxe-Coburg Square. Explain the reasoning behind each.

### Applying

7. Would a real detective be able to solve a crime using Holmes's methods? Explain.

## ANALYZING LITERATURE

### Understanding Motivation

**Motivation** is a character's reasons for behaving in a certain way. In a detective story, when you understand a character's motives, you better understand the character and his or her reasons for committing the crime. At the end of this story, Holmes directly reveals the criminals' motives for committing the crime.

Explain the criminals' motives for the following actions:

1. Establishing the Red-headed League
2. Digging a tunnel between the pawn shop and the bank
3. Working for Mr. Wilson for half wages

## CRITICAL THINKING AND READING

### Contrasting Characters' Abilities

Both Sherlock Holmes and Dr. Watson examine Mr. Wilson's appearance. From their observa-

tions, only Holmes reasons correctly to conclusions about Wilson's past activities.

1. What is the difference between their powers of observation?
2. What observations does Holmes make in Saxe-Coburg Square that Watson does not?
3. Give two examples to show that Holmes is a better observer than Watson.
4. Give an example of Holmes's logical reasoning that Watson is unable to perform.

## UNDERSTANDING LANGUAGE

### Completing Word Analogies

A **word analogy** shows a relationship that two sets of words share. The words may be related as synonyms, antonyms, cause and effect, and so on. For example, in the analogy *autumn* is to *fall* as *narrative* is to *story,* the relationship in both pairs is that of synonyms. On standardized tests, analogy problems are set up this way:

autumn:fall :: narrative:story

To complete word analogy problems, first determine the relationship in the given pair of words. Then complete the second pair of words to show the same relationship.

Think of a word to complete the following analogies.

1. stout:portly :: dingy:
2. bizarre:humdrum :: pompous:
3. rueful:grave :: vacancy:

## THINKING AND WRITING

### Analyzing a Detective's Methods

Write instructions for someone who wants to become a detective like Holmes. Analyze the steps that Holmes takes to solve the mystery of the Red-headed League. Then tell how the steps can be applied to other mysteries. Revise your instructions so they will be clear to someone who has not read the story.

*The Red-headed League* 89

(Answers begin on p. 88.)

## ANSWERS TO CRITICAL THINKING AND READING

1. Suggested Response: Watson pays attention to the general appearance of Mr. Wilson, looking at his clothes and watch chain. Holmes pays much more attention to detail, noticing which part of his attire shows wear, what is attached to his watch chain, and even the difference in the sizes of Mr. Wilson's hands.
2. Suggested Response: He observes that the pavement in front of the house is not hollow, that Spaulding's trousers are worn and dirty at the knees, and that a bank adjoins Mr. Wilson's property.
3. Answers will differ. Students may respond, for instance, that Holmes observes the Freemason breast-pin that Wilson is wearing and also observes that the knees of Spaulding's trousers are dirty.
4. Answers will differ. Students may mention that Holmes was able to reason that the robbers would strike on Saturday so that they would have more time for their escape.

## ANSWERS TO UNDERSTANDING LANGUAGE

Answers will differ. Possible choices are:

1. grimy, muddy, soiled
2. meek, modest
3. emptiness, hollowness

**Challenge** Do you think Holmes really agrees with the quote from Flaubert he uses? Explain.

## THINKING AND WRITING

For help with this assignment, students can refer to Lesson 2, "Drafting and Revising," in the Handbook of Writing About Literature.

**Publishing Student Writing** You might have students share their guidelines with the class.

### Interpreting

5. Suggested Response: He knows the assistant is Spaulding when he is described as small and stoutly built, with a hairless face, a white mark on his forehead, and pierced ears.
6. Suggested Response: He deduces that Mr. Wilson's cellar extends behind the house, because the pavement in front does not sound hollow when he strikes it. He de-

duces that Clay has been digging a tunnel, because the knees of his trousers are worn and stained. He deduces that the prospective crime is robbery, because a bank is right next to Mr. Wilson's property.

### Applying

7. Answers will differ, depending upon whether students believe that Holmes's methods are sound or whether the stories are overly contrived by the author.

## ANSWERS TO ANALYZING LITERATURE

Suggested Responses:

1. He establishes the Red-headed League to get the pawnbroker out of the way for a few hours every day.
2. The tunnel is a secret passageway into the bank.
3. By asking for half the wages, he is sure of securing the position above the other applicants.

## Blues Ain't No Mockin Bird

**More About the Author** After graduating from Queens College in 1959, Toni Cade Bambara attended universities in Florence, Paris, and New York. She studied dance and film making, and worked as a social investigator for the New York State Department of Welfare. Her writing centers on the emerging identity of the black woman. How might Bambara's background have influenced her writing?

**Literary Focus** You might ask students to think of characteristic gestures, expressions, or speech habits of people they know. Lead a discussion about how a writer might use one or more such mannerisms to make a character more realistic.

**Look For** Tell students that the story they are about to read can be considered from two points of view—the family's, or the film makers'. Suggest that, as they read, they watch for details that make the reader identify with the family's point of view.

**Writing/Prior Knowledge** You might play one or two blues recordings by artists such as Bessie Smith, Muddy Waters, or B. B. King. Ask students to share their responses to the music. Have them identify the subjects of the lyrics, and suggest other subjects that could be expressed by blues music.

**Verisimilitude**

**Toni Cade Bambara** (1939–    ) was born and raised in New York City. She grew up reading the stories of black heroes. Her interest in her Afro-American heritage is shown by her last name—a name she assumed after finding it on a sketchbook in her great-grandmother's trunk. Bambara is the name of an African tribe known for its intricate wood carvings. She has published two collections of short stories—*Gorilla, My Love,* from which "Blues Ain't No Mockin Bird" was taken, and *The Sea Birds Are Still Alive*—and a novel, *The Salt Eaters.*

When reading a work of fiction, often we expect the characters to be true to life or realistic. **Verisimilitude,** which literally means "similar to the truth," is the appearance of truth or reality in a work of fiction. A writer creates verisimilitude by giving characters the mannerisms, speech, and character traits of real people. In "Blues Ain't No Mockin Bird," Bambara creates characters who have the qualities, characteristics, and actions of people who are believable and true to life. Because they are true to life, we respond to them as we do toward people we know.

**Look For**

While reading "Blues Ain't No Mockin Bird," look for the details the author uses to create realistic characters and situations. For example, the narrator's recollections of the past, as she watches her grandmother, make her a realistic character. Also be aware of the way you respond to the characters. Do you like some of them? Dislike others? Share the family's anger? Why?

**Writing**

The blues is a type of music that arouses strong feelings in both the listener and the musician or singer. Freewrite about the types of experiences that might lead someone to sing the blues. Share your response with your classmates.

**Vocabulary**

Knowing the following words will help you as you read "Blues Ain't No Mockin Bird."
**lassoed** (las′ ōd) *v.:* Wrapped around (p. 91)
**formality** (fôr mal′ ə tē) *n.:* Established rules or customs (p. 94)

### Objectives

1 To understand verisimilitude
2 To note relevant details
3 To understand dialect
4 To respond to meaning

### Support Material

**Teaching Portfolio**
Teacher Backup, p. 111
Usage and Mechanics Worksheet, p. 114
Vocabulary Check, p. 115
Analyzing Literature Worksheet, *Understanding Verisimilitude,* p. 116
Critical Thinking and Reading Worksheet, *Noting Relevant Details,* p. 117
Selection Test, p. 118

# Blues Ain't No Mockin Bird

## Toni Cade Bambara

1 The puddle had frozen over, and me and Cathy went stompin in it. The twins from next door, Tyrone and Terry, were swingin so high out of sight we forgot we were waitin our turn on the tire. Cathy jumped up and came down hard on her heels and started tap-dancin. And the frozen patch splinterin every which way underneath kinda spooky.

2 "Looks like a plastic spider web," she said. "A sort of weird spider, I guess, with many mental problems." But really it looked like the crystal paperweight Granny kept in the parlor. She was on the back porch, Granny was, making the cakes drunk. The old ladle dripping rum into the Christmas tins, like it used to drip maple syrup into the pails when we lived in the Judson's woods, like it poured cider into the vats when we were on the Cooper place, like it used to scoop buttermilk and soft cheese when we lived at the dairy.

3 "Go tell that man we ain't a bunch of trees."

"Ma'am?"

"I said to tell that man to get away from here with that camera." Me and Cathy look over toward the meadow where the men with the station wagon'd been roamin around all mornin. The tall man with a huge camera lassoed to his shoulder was buzzin our way.

4 "They're makin movie pictures," yelled Tyrone, stiffenin his legs and twistin so the tire'd come down slow so they could see.

"They're makin movie pictures," sang out Terry.

5 "That boy don't never have anything original to say," say Cathy grown-up.

By the time the man with the camera had cut across our neighbor's yard, the twins were out of the trees swingin low and Granny was onto the steps, the screen door bammin soft and scratchy against her palms. "We thought we'd get a shot or two of the house and everything and then—"

6 "Good mornin," Granny cut him off. And smiled that smile.

"Good mornin," he said, head all down the way Bingo does when you yell at him about the bones on the kitchen floor. "Nice place you got here, aunty. We thought we'd take a—"

"Did you?" said Granny with her eyebrows. Cathy pulled up her socks and giggled.

7 "Nice things here," said the man, buzzin his camera over the yard. The pecan barrels, the sled, me and Cathy, the flowers, the printed stones along the driveway, the trees, the twins, the toolshed.

8 "I don't know about the thing, the it, and the stuff," said Granny, still talkin with her eyebrows. "Just people here is what I tend to consider."

Camera man stopped buzzin. Cathy giggled into her collar.

"Mornin, ladies," a new man said. He

**Master Teacher Note** Explain to students that blues music was developed from the work songs that black slaves improvised as a form of communication. Many blues lyrics express loneliness or sorrow, while others reflect a humorous or defiant attitude to life's troubles.

The mockingbird is able to imitate the songs of other birds. In American folklore, it sings to mourn for a lost love.

**Thematic Idea** You might group this selection with "Uncle Marcos," page 63, and "Before the End of Summer," page 107, two stories in which strong family relationships and vivid characterization are central.

## Presentation

**Motivation/Prior Knowledge** Have students imagine that a camera crew was sent to film their school for a documentary. What reasons might they have for not wanting their school to be filmed?

**Purpose-Setting Question** Why doesn't Granny want her family and house filmed?

1 **Literary Focus** Why did the author choose first person narration for this story? Why does she write in dialect?

2 **Critical Thinking and Reading** What do these details reveal about the two characters in this dialogue?

3 **Discussion** What does Granny mean by this statement?

4 **Critical Thinking and Reading** What does this dialogue reveal about each twin?

5 **Reading Strategy** Why does the narrator describe Cathy as a grown up? Watch for other descriptions of Cathy in the story.

6 **Discussion** How would you describe Granny's expression?

7 **Discussion** By enumerating the "things" in the yard, what does the narrator reveal about the cameraman's attitude toward the family?

8 **Discussion** What does Granny's statement imply about her attitude toward the cameramen?

9 **Discussion** How has the twins' attitude toward the men changed? Why has it changed?

10 **Reading Strategy** What might Cathy's giggling and smiling foreshadow?

11 **Discussion** How does Granny feel about being called "aunty"? Why?

12 **Clarification** Food stamps are given by the government to people who cannot afford to buy sufficient food for themselves and their families. The stamps can be exchanged for food at grocery stores.

13 **Reading Strategy** What might Smilin man hope Granny will say? How might he have finished his sentence? What does this show about his attitude?

14 **Clarification** According to certain religious doctrines, a mortal sin is a sin of the most severe type.

15 **Critical Thinking and Reading** What do you learn about Granny from this anecdote?

16 **Discussion** For what purpose was the person in the story saving the end of the film?

17 **Discussion** Why has the author waited to reveal Cathy's relationship to the family? Why do you think she had to be "picked up"? How does this change or add to your feelings about the Cain family?

18 **Critical Thinking and Reading** Who are Mr. Judson and Mrs. Cooper? Why do they make Granny angry? How does this reinforce what you have already learned about Granny?

19 **Literary Focus** How would you describe Grandaddy Cain's facial expression when he has "rocks all in his jaw"?

---

had come up behind us when we weren't lookin. "And gents," discoverin the twins givin him a nasty look. "We're filmin for the county," he said with a smile. "Mind if we shoot a bit around here?"

"I do indeed," said Granny with no smile. Smilin man was smiling up a storm. So was Cathy. But he didn't seem to have another word to say, so he and the camera man backed on out the yard, but you could hear the camera buzzin still. "Suppose you just shut that machine off," said Granny real low through her teeth, and took a step down off the porch and then another.

"Now, aunty," Camera said, pointin the thing straight at her.

"Your mama and I are not related."

Smilin man got his notebook out and a chewed-up pencil. "Listen," he said movin back into our yard, "we'd like to have a statement from you . . . for the film. We're filmin for the county, see. Part of the food stamp campaign. You know about the food stamps?"

Granny said nuthin.

"Maybe there's somethin you want to say for the film. I see you grow your own vegetables," he smiled real nice. "If more folks did that, see, there'd be no need—"

Granny wasn't sayin nuthin. So they backed on out, buzzin at our clothesline and the twins' bicycles, then back on down to the meadow. The twins were danglin in the tire, lookin at Granny. Me and Cathy were waitin, too, cause Granny always got somethin to say. She teaches steady with no let-up. "I was on this bridge one time," she started off. "Was a crowd cause this man was goin to jump, you understand. And a minister was there and the police and some other folks. His woman was there, too."

"What was they doin?" asked Tyrone.

"Tryin to talk him out of it was what they was doin. The minister talkin about how it was a mortal sin, suicide. His woman takin bites out of her own hand and not even knowin it, so nervous and cryin and talkin fast."

"So what happened?" asked Tyrone.

"So here comes . . . this person . . . with a camera, takin pictures of the man and the minister and the woman. Takin pictures of the man in his misery about to jump, cause life so bad and people been messin with him so bad. This person takin up the whole roll of film practically. But savin a few, of course."

"Of course," said Cathy, hatin the person. Me standin there wonderin how Cathy knew it was "of course" when I didn't and it was *my* grandmother.

After a while Tyrone say, "Did he jump?"

"Yeh, did he jump?" say Terry all eager.

And Granny just stared at the twins till their faces swallow up the eager and they don't even care any more about the man jumpin. Then she goes back onto the porch and lets the screen door go for itself. I'm lookin to Cathy to finish the story cause she knows Granny's whole story before me even. Like she knew how come we move so much and Cathy ain't but a third cousin we picked up on the way last Thanksgivin visitin. But she knew it was on account of people drivin Granny crazy till she'd get up in the night and start packin. Mumblin and packin and wakin everybody up sayin, "Let's get on away from here before I kill me somebody." Like people wouldn't pay her for things like they said they would. Or Mr. Judson bringin us boxes of old clothes and raggedy magazines. Or Mrs. Cooper comin in our kitchen and touchin everything and sayin how clean it all was. Granny goin crazy, and Granddaddy Cain pullin her off the people, sayin, "Now, now, Cora." But next day loadin up the truck, with rocks all in his jaw, madder than Granny in the first place.

92    *Short Stories*

---

**ESL Teaching Strategy** In addition to dialect, Bambara uses colloquial expressions to make the dialogue more real and the language more colorful. Students who speak English as a second language may find the numerous colloquial expressions in the story difficult to understand. They may need help with expressions such as *aunty*, as a familiar form of address for an older woman; *with no let-up,* meaning "constantly"; *all eager,* meaning "eagerly"; and *so their faces swallow up the eager,* meaning "the eagerness fades from their faces."

You might wish to pair your ESL students with another student from the class. As students read the story, the partners can help ESL students understand the colloquial expressions.

**SHARECROPPER**
*Elizabeth Catlett*
Courtesy Evan Tibbs Collection

## Humanities Note

Fine art, *Sharecropper*, 1966, by Elizabeth Catlett. Elizabeth Catlett (1919–), who was born in Washington, D.C., is a sculptor and printmaker. Her typical subject matter is the struggle and achievements of black people.

Catlett's work has been strongly influenced by the American artist Grant Wood (1892–1942), who is best known for American Gothic, a rather stark painting of an American farm couple. "Grant Wood," Catlett said, "insisted that we work with the subject matter that we know best. What I know best is black people, especially black women."

*Sharecropper* is a linocut—a print made from a design cut into the surface of a linoleum block. Because this medium allows for little shading, transitions from black to white are abrupt, with little subtlety of line or tone. It is particularly well-suited to simple, direct expression in which lines and areas are strong and bold.

1. How does *Sharecropper* reflect the struggles and achievements of black people?
2. How does Toni Cade Bambara in "Blues Ain't No Mockin Bird" achieve this same goal?
3. Describe the woman in Catlett's print. How is she similar to Granny Cain?

**20** "I read a story once," said Cathy soundin like Granny teacher. "About this lady Goldilocks who barged into a house that wasn't even hers. And not invited, you understand. Messed over the people's groceries and broke up the people's furniture. Had the nerve to sleep in the folks' bed."

"Then what happened?" asked Tyrone. "What they do, the folks, when they come in to all this mess?"

"Did they make her pay for it?" asked Terry, makin a fist. "I'd've made her pay me."

I didn't even ask. I could see Cathy actress was very likely to just walk away and leave us in mystery about this story which I heard was about some bears. **21**

"Did they throw her out?" asked Tyrone, like his father sounds when he's bein extra nasty-plus to the washin-machine man.

"Woulda," said Terry. "I woulda gone upside her head with my fist and—"

"You woulda done whatcha always do— go cry to Mama, you big baby," said Tyrone. So naturally Terry starts hittin on Tyrone, **22**

*Blues Ain't No Mockin Bird*   93

**20 Discussion** How does Cathy's rendition of the story of the three bears differ from the traditional telling of the tale?

**21 Discussion** If Cathy walked away without finishing the story, whom would she be imitating? Why does the narrator call her "Cathy actress"?

**22 Literary Focus** Does this piece of dialogue advance the plot? Why does the author include it?

**Cooperative Learning** A group of students may enjoy visiting a museum to look for other prints, drawings, and paintings that depict people who remind them of the characters in this story. As an alternative to visiting a museum, you might consider having students look through art books. Suggest that students choose a piece of art they particularly like and write a research report on the artist and his or her work.

**23 Critical Thinking and Reading**
What do we learn about Granny from this passage?

**24 Critical Thinking and Reading**
What is your first impression of Granddaddy Cain? How do the colors in this scene contribute to your impression of the character?

**25 Discussion** What does the narrator think Smilin and Camera are going to do?

**26 Discussion** What does Cathy mean by this? Do you believe that her explanation is correct? How has the author prepared you to trust her judgment?

**27 Literary Focus** What word would you use to describe this scene? What might be the author's purpose in making it so strong?

**28 Critical Thinking and Reading**
What do Granny's words and tone tell the reader about the relationship between her and Granddaddy Cain?

**29 Literary Focus** What specific details in this paragraph make the scene seem real to the reader?

**30 Critical Thinking and Reading**
How does this passage characterize Camera and Smilin? How does it show the contrast between the two men and Grandaddy Cain?

**31 Literary Focus** What is making the "low groaning music"? Why is this detail important to the story?

and next thing you know they tumblin out the tire and rollin on the ground. But Granny didn't say a thing or send the twins home or step out on the steps to tell us about how we can't afford to be fightin amongst ourselves. She didn't say nuthin. So I get into the tire to take my turn. And I could see her leanin up against the pantry table, starin at the cakes she was puttin up for the Christmas sale, mumblin real low and grumpy and holdin her forehead like it wanted to fall off and mess up the rum cakes.

Behind me I hear before I can see Granddaddy Cain comin through the woods in his field boots. Then I twist around to see the shiny black oilskin cuttin through what little left there was of yellows, reds, and oranges. His great white head not quite round cause of this bloody thing high on his shoulder, like he was wearin a cap on sideways. He takes the shortcut through the pecan grove, and the sound of twigs snapping overhead and underfoot travels clear and cold all the way up to us. And here comes Smilin and Camera up behind him like they was goin to do somethin. Folks like to go for him sometimes. Cathy say it's because he's so tall and quiet and like a king. And people just can't stand it. But Smilin and Camera don't hit him in the head or nuthin. They just buzz on him as he stalks by with the chicken hawk slung over his shoulder, squawkin, drippin red down the back of the oilskin. He passes the porch and stops a second for Granny to see he's caught the hawk at last, but she's just starin and mumblin, and not at the hawk. So he nails the bird to the toolshed door, the hammerin crackin through the eardrums. And the bird flappin himself to death and droolin down the door to paint the gravel in the driveway red, then brown, then black. And the two men movin up on tiptoe like they was invisible or we were blind, one.

"Get them persons out of my flower bed, Mister Cain," say Granny moanin real low like at a funeral.

"How come your grandmother calls her husband 'Mister Cain' all the time?" Tyrone whispers all loud and noisy and from the city and don't know no better. Like his mama, Miss Myrtle, tell us never mind the formality as if we had no better breeding than to call her Myrtle, plain. And then this awful thing—a giant hawk—come wailin up over the meadow, flyin low and tilted and screamin, zigzaggin through the pecan grove, breakin branches and hollerin, snappin past the clothesline, flyin every which way, flyin into things reckless with crazy.

"He's come to claim his mate," say Cathy fast, and ducks down. We all fall quick and flat into the gravel driveway, stones scrapin my face. I squinch my eyes open again at the hawk on the door, tryin to fly up out of her death like it was just a sack flown into by mistake. Her body holdin her there on that nail, though. The mate beatin the air overhead and clutchin for hair, for heads, for landin space.

The camera man duckin and bendin and runnin and fallin, jigglin the camera and scared. And Smilin jumpin up and down swipin at the huge bird, tryin to bring the hawk down with just his raggedy ole cap. Granddaddy Cain straight up and silent, watchin the circles of the hawk, then aimin the hammer off his wrist. The giant bird fallin, silent and slow. Then here comes Camera and Smilin all big and bad now that the awful screechin thing is on its back and broken, here they come. And Graddaddy Cain looks up at them like it was the first time noticin, but not payin them too much mind cause he's listenin, we all listen, to that low groanin music comin from the porch. And we figure any minute, somethin in my back tells me any minute now, Granny gonna bust through that screen with somethin in her hand and murder on her mind. So Granddaddy say above the buzzin, but quiet, "Good day, gentlemen." Just like that. Like he'd invited them in to play cards and they'd stayed too long and all the sandwiches were gone and Reverend Webb was droppin by and it was time to go.

They didn't know what to do. But like Cathy say, folks can't stand Granddaddy tall and silent and like a king. They can't neither. The smile the men smilin is pullin the mouth back and showin the teeth. Lookin like the wolf man, both of them. Then Granddaddy holds his hand out—this huge hand I used to sit in when I was a baby and he'd carry me through the house to my mother like I was a gift on a tray. Like he used to on the trains. They called the other men just waiters. But they spoke of Granddaddy separate and said, The Waiter. And said he had engines in his feet and motors in his hands and couldn't no train throw him off and couldn't nobody turn him round. They were big enough for motors, his hands were. He held that one hand out all still and it gettin to be not at all a hand but a person in itself.

"He wants you to hand him the camera," Smilin whispers to Camera, tiltin his head to talk secret like they was in the jungle or somethin and come upon a native that don't speak the language. The men start untyin the straps, and they put the camera into that great hand speckled with the hawk's blood all black and crackly now. And the hand don't even drop with the weight, just the fingers move, curl up around the machine. But Granddaddy lookin straight at the men. They lookin at each other and everywhere but at Granddaddy's face.

"We filmin for the county, see," say Smilin. "We puttin together a movie for the food stamp program . . . filmin all around these parts. Uhh, filmin for the county."

"Can I have my camera back?" say the tall man with no machine on his shoulder, but still keepin it high like the camera was still there or needed to be. "Please, sir."

Then Granddaddy's other hand flies up like a sudden and gentle bird, slaps down fast on top of the camera and lifts off half like it was a calabash[1] cut for sharing.

"Hey," Camera jumps forward. He gathers up the parts into his chest and everything unrollin and fallin all over. "Whatcha tryin to do? You'll ruin the film." He looks down into his chest of metal reels and things like he's protectin a kitten from the cold.

"You standin in the misses' flower bed," say Granddaddy. "This is our own place."

The two men look at him, then at each other, then back at the mess in the camera man's chest, and they just back off. One sayin over and over all the way down to the meadow, "Watch it, Bruno. Keep ya fingers off the film." Then Granddaddy picks up the hammer and jams it into the oilskin pocket, scrapes his boots, and goes into the house. And you can hear the squish of his boots headin through the house. And you can see the funny shadow he throws from the parlor window onto the ground by the string-bean patch. The hammer draggin the pocket of the oilskin out so Granddaddy looked even wider. Granny was hummin now—high, not low and grumbly. And she was doin the cakes again, you could smell the molasses from the rum.

"There's this story I'm goin to write one day," say Cathy dreamer. "About the proper use of the hammer."

"Can I be in it?" Tyrone say with his hand up like it was a matter of first come, first served.

"Perhaps," say Cathy, climbin onto the tire to pump us up. "If you there and ready."

---

**1. calabash** (kal′ ə bash′) n.: A large gourdlike fruit.

32 **Literary Focus** Why did the author include this anecdote? How do they change your feelings about Granddaddy Cain?

33 **Discussion** How do you interpret the men's words and actions? How would you describe their feelings right now?

34 **Discussion** Why does Smilin repeat that they are filming "for the county"?

35 **Discussion** Why has Camera's tone changed?

36 **Discussion** Why does Granddaddy Cain say, "This is our own place"?

37 **Discussion** How do you think the two men would describe this experience?

38 **Discussion** Does the narrator believe that Cathy will write a story? What might Cathy mean by, "the proper use of the hammer"?

39 **Critical Thinking and Reading** How does Tyrone's question and gesture reinforce the author's previous characterization of him?

40 **Discussion** What will Tyrone have to do in order to be in Cathy's story?

**Reader's Response** How did you react when you read the scene involving Granddaddy Cain and the two hawks?

---

**Enrichment** For a different perspective on photographers and the media, you might present to the class the following quotations from interviews with two war photographers. Then lead a discussion about responsible journalism.

W. Eugene Smith: "My camera, my intentions stopped no man from falling. Photographs could cause compassionate horror within the viewer, they might also prod the conscience of that viewer into taking action."

Don McCullin: "Someone may have been killed . . . and I'm going to photograph it.

. . . People think that because a person has been killed he's no longer useful. Of course he's useful. He's useful to say, 'Look what's happened to that young man.'

. . . We need something very quick to understand that we as human beings are not permitted to allow this."

## ANSWERS TO THINKING ABOUT THE SELECTION

### Recalling

1. They are making a documentary film about people who use food stamps.
2. He destroys their film by exposing it to light.

### Interpreting

3. They see the family as types, not as individuals.
4. The cameramen are like the photographer: they see people only as news items.
5. Like Goldilocks, the two men are intruders. She invades the privacy of the bears' home.
6. Granddaddy's killing of the mate reveals that he will take strong, even harsh, measures to accomplish his ends.
7. The male hawk tries to defend its mate; Granddaddy Cain defends Granny.
8. The Cains have suffered sorrow and hardships; thus they are "singing the blues." Their song, however, is one of life and survival.

### Applying

9. Some may feel that individual privacy is sacred; others, that an informed public is more important; some, that it depends on how sensitively media people handle such situations.

## ANSWERS TO ANALYZING LITERATURE

1. Students will admire Granny's resilience, courage, assertiveness, pride, sensitivity, generosity, and love for her family.
2. Students will admire Granddaddy Cain's courage, strength, pride, loyalty, gentleness, and love for his family. Some may find his treatment of the hawk inhumane.
3. Most will share the narrator's response that the reporters are insensitive, ignorant, and cowardly. Students who see the story from the reporters' point of view may respond more sympathetically.

## ANSWERS TO CRITICAL THINKING AND READING

1. The children are swinging on a tire, (they are country people who

---

## THINKING ABOUT THE SELECTION

### Recalling

1. Why are the two men filming the Cain family and their home?
2. How does Granddaddy Cain get rid of the cameramen?

### Interpreting

3. What is the cameramen's attitude toward the Cain family?
4. What is the main point of Granny's story about the man who attempted suicide?
5. How is the story of Goldilocks similar to the Cain's predicament?
6. What does killing the hawk's mate reveal about Granddaddy Cain's character?
7. How do the two hawks resemble Granny and Granddaddy Cain?
8. The title of the story indicates that the sound of the blues is not similar to the bitter-sweet music of a mocking bird, that according to legend sings of death. How is the blues different? Why is this an appropriate title for this story?

### Applying

9. In part, this story examines the ethics (standards of conduct and moral judgment) of the news media. Do you believe the media have a right to intrude in others' lives to achieve their goals? Why?

## ANALYZING LITERATURE

### Understanding Verisimilitude

Verisimilitude means creating characters that are believable and realistic—characters of flesh and blood that make us respond to them as real people.

1. Describe Granny's chief qualities. How do you respond to her?
2. Describe Granddaddy's chief qualities. How do you respond to him?
3. Describe the reporters' chief qualities. How do you respond to them?

---

## CRITICAL THINKING AND READING

### Noting Relevant Details

Authors often fill their stories with details that give readers a feeling for the world in which the story takes place. Some details move the plot forward or provide insight into the characters. In "Blues Ain't No Mockin Bird," Bambara provides a wealth of details that, taken together, reveal significant information about the characters and their way of life.

1. What details of the first paragraph provide insight into Granny and the family?
2. What about the family is revealed in Smilin man's simple comment, "I see you grow your own vegetables"?

## UNDERSTANDING LANGUAGE

### Understanding Dialect

Dialect is the way of speaking that is common to people in a particular region or group. Pronunciation, vocabulary, and sentence structure are affected by dialect. For example, consider this sentence from the story: "That boy don't never have anything original to say." In standard English, this sentence would appear as: That boy doesn't ever have anything original to say.

Find five examples of dialect in the story and rewrite them in standard English. Share your examples with your classmates. Then explain how the use of dialect makes the story more effective.

## THINKING AND WRITING

### Responding to Meaning

Like Granny, Cathy is able to tell stories that are entertaining yet also prove a point. At the end of the story, Cathy says she is going to write a story about the proper use of a hammer. Imagine you are Cathy and write this story. What is the "proper use of the hammer" and how was it improperly or properly used in "Blues Ain't No Mockin Bird"? Let a classmate read and respond to your story before you write a final draft.

---

do not have swings in their yard); Cathy compares the cracks in the ice with a plastic spider web, (she has an active imagination); Granny made maple syrup when they lived in the Judson's woods, cider on the Cooper place, and buttermilk and cheese at the dairy, (the family has moved around a lot; Granny is resourceful).
2. They are resourceful, hardworking, proud, and independent.

## ANSWERS TO UNDERSTANDING LANGUAGE

Students may choose examples such as, "She teaches steady with no let-up," on p. 92. (She is always teaching.)

## THINKING AND WRITING

For help with this assignment, students can refer to Lesson 17,

"Writing a Short Story," in the Handbook of Writing About Literature.

**Publishing Student Writing** Have volunteers read their stories aloud. Then display students' work on a bulletin board or classroom wall for others to read and enjoy.

**Challenge** Ask students to write their stories in dialect.

# Point of View

OPEN DOORWAY ON THE BEACH
*K. Rodko*
*Three Lions*

**Humanities Note**

Fine Art, *Open Doorway on the Beach*, Karl Rodko. Karl Rodko is an American artist. This charming view of sunlight and sea is given added interest by the perspective through a doorway. The contrast between the inside and outside world makes the viewer yearn to step through the doorway into the sunlit air, filled with the sound of gulls and the surf and the smells of the sea. The cheerful colors and simplified forms of this painting add to its pleasing effect.

## Focus

**More About the Author** Mark Twain was the best known and most successful author of his generation. He took pride in his ability to publish books that appealed to the public. Ask students to discuss what subjects a contemporary author might choose to capture the attention of readers.

**Literary Focus** Point out to students that, although this is a first-person narration, the narrator tells the story long after the incident occurred. This enables him to share with the reader the joke that events played on him.

**Look For** Tell students that one method of understanding the character of the narrator is to pay attention to the way he describes the other characters in the story. Another clue to the narrator's personality is the way in which he describes himself and his motivations.

**Writing/Prior Knowledge** Have students list adjectives that describe smells. The list should include adjectives that describe both pleasant and unpleasant odors. Students can then use this list in their freewriting assignment.

**Vocabulary** Have your less advanced students read these words aloud so that they can be sure of the pronunciation.

**Spelling Tip** Point out the four words ending in *ous: prodigious, deleterious, ominous, judicious.*

---

## The Invalid's Story

**Mark Twain** (1835–1910) was born Samuel Langhorne Clemens in Florida, Missouri, and grew up in the river town of Hannibal. He worked as a steamboat pilot on the Mississippi River, and he took his pen name from a sounding cry used on Mississippi steamboats—*by the mark, twain* means "two fathoms deep." Twain also worked as a printer, prospector, reporter, editor, and lecturer. Writing, however, was his true calling. A talented humorist, Twain's special brand of wit is clearly seen in "The Invalid's Story."

**First-Person Narration**

Authors may write stories from a number of **points of view,** or perspectives. With **first-person narration,** the story is told by one of the characters in it, with the character referring to himself or herself as "I." The character who tells the story in this way is called the narrator.

By using the first-person point of view, the author makes the story seem immediate. However, first person point of view has some limitations. Since the author can reveal only what the narrator would know or observe, you get only one side of the story. You have to make inferences based on what other characters say and do to get a wider picture.

**Look For**

As you read "The Invalid's Story," ask, What kind of person is the narrator? How does the way he tells the story add to the humor?

**Writing**

People spend more time thinking and talking about what they see, hear, and taste than about what they smell. However, some researchers feel that it is the power of smell that has the greatest ability to call forth memories. Freewrite about this underrated sense, describing the effect of a pleasant or unpleasant odor.

**Vocabulary**

Knowing the following words will help you as you read "The Invalid's Story."

**prodigious** (prə dij′ əs) *adj.:* Enormous (p. 99)

**deleterious** (del′ ə tir′ ē əs) *adj.:* Injurious; harmful to health or well-being (p. 100)

**ominous** (äm′ ə nəs) *adj.:* Threatening (p. 100)

**judicious** (jōō dish′ əs) *adj.:* Showing good judgment (p. 102)

**placidly** (plac′ id lē) *adv.:* Calmly; quietly (p. 102)

**desultory** (des′ l tôr′ ē) *adj.:* Random (p. 103)

**stifling** (sti′ fliŋ) *adj.:* Suffocating (p. 104)

---

### Objectives

1 To understand first-person narration
2 To identify exaggeration
3 To understand idioms
4 To write a tall tale

### Support Material

**Teaching Portfolio**
Teacher Backup, p. 121
Grammar in Action Worksheet, *Recognizing Dialect,* p. 125
Usage and Mechanics Worksheet, p. 127
Vocabulary Check, p. 128
Critical Thinking and Reading Worksheet, *Identifying Exaggeration,* p. 129

Language Worksheet, *Understanding Idioms,* p. 130
Selection Test, p. 131

# The Invalid's Story

### Mark Twain

I seem sixty and married, but these effects are due to my condition and sufferings, for I am a bachelor, and only forty-one. It will be hard for you to believe that I, who am now but a shadow, was a hale, hearty man two short years ago—a man of iron, a very athlete!—yet such is the simple truth. But stranger still than this fact is the way in which I lost my health. I lost it through helping to take care of a box of guns on a two-hundred-mile railway journey one winter's night. It is the actual truth, and I will tell you about it.

I belong in Cleveland, Ohio. One winter's night, two years ago, I reached home just after dark, in a driving snowstorm, and the first thing I heard when I entered the house was that my dearest boyhood friend and schoolmate, John B. Hackett, had died the day before, and that his last utterance had been a desire that I would take his remains home to his poor old father and mother in Wisconsin. I was greatly shocked and grieved, but there was no time to waste in emotions; I must start at once. I took the card, marked "Deacon Levi Hackett, Bethlehem, Wisconsin," and hurried off through the whistling storm to the railway station. Arrived there I found the long white-pine box which had been described to me; I fastened the card to it with some tacks, saw it put safely aboard the express car, and then ran into the eating room to provide myself with a sandwich and some cigars. When I returned, presently, there was my coffin-box *back again*, apparently, and a young fellow examining around it, with a card in his hands, and some tacks and a hammer! I was astonished and puzzled. He began to nail on his card, and I rushed out to the express car, in a good deal of a state of mind, to ask for an explanation. But no—there was my box, all right, in the express car; it hadn't been disturbed. [The fact is that without my suspecting it a prodigious mistake had been made. I was carrying off a box of *guns* which that young fellow had come to the station to ship to a rifle company in Peoria, Illinois, and *he* had got my corpse!] Just then the conductor sang out "All aboard," and I jumped into the express car and got a comfortable seat on a bale of buckets. The expressman was there, hard at work—a plain man of fifty, with a simple, honest, good-natured face, and a breezy, practical heartiness in his general style. As the train moved off a stranger skipped into the car and set a package of peculiarly mature and capable Limburger cheese[1] on one end of my coffin-box—I mean my box of guns. That is to say, I know *now* that it was Limburger cheese, but at that time I never had heard of the article in my life, and of course was wholly ignorant of its character. Well, we sped through the wild night, the bitter storm raged on, a cheerless

------

1. **Limburger cheese:** A cheese with a strong odor.

**3 Critical Thinking and Reading**
Why do you think Twain includes these details?

**4 Discussion** How might your response to this detail be different if you did not know about the cheese?

**5 Discussion** Why might a warm fire affect the smell coming from the cheese? How does this description heighten the humor of the story?

misery stole over me, my heart went down, down, down! The old expressman made a brisk remark or two about the tempest and the arctic weather, slammed his sliding doors to, and bolted them, closed his window down tight, and then went bustling around, here and there and yonder, setting things to rights, and all the time contentedly humming "Sweet By and By," in a low tone, and flatting a good deal. Presently I began to detect a most evil and searching odor stealing about on the frozen air. This depressed my spirits still more, because of course I attributed it to my poor departed friend. There was something infinitely saddening about his calling himself to my remembrance in this dumb, pathetic way, so it was hard to keep the tears back. Moreover, it distressed me on account of the old expressman, who, I was afraid, might notice it. However, he went humming tranquilly on, and gave no sign; and for this I was grateful. Grateful, yes, but still uneasy; and soon I began to feel more and more uneasy every minute, for every minute that went by that odor thickened up the more, and got to be more and more gamy and hard to stand. Presently, having got things arranged to his satisfaction, the expressman got some wood and made up a tremendous fire in his stove. This distressed me more than I can tell, for I could not but feel that
it was a mistake.
I was sure that the effect would be deleterious upon my poor departed friend. Thompson—the expressman's name was Thompson, as I found out in the course of the night—now went poking around his car, stopping up whatever stray cracks he could find, remarking that it didn't make any difference what kind of a night it was outside, he calculated to make *us* comfortable, anyway. I said nothing, but I believed he was not choosing the right way. Meantime he was humming to himself just as before; and meantime, too, the stove was getting hotter and hotter, and the place closer and closer. I felt myself growing pale and qualmish,[2] but grieved in silence and said nothing. Soon I noticed that the "Sweet By and By" was gradually fading out; next it ceased altogether, and there was an ominous stillness. After a few moments Thompson said—

"Pfew! I reckon it ain't no cinnamon 't I've loaded up thish-year stove with!"

He gasped once or twice, then moved toward the cof—gun-box, stood over that Limburger cheese part of a moment, then

---

**2. qualmish** (kwäm' ish) *adj.*: Slightly ill.

## Grammar in Action

To present a realistic portrait of a character, writers have the character speak in **dialect**. This type of speech is characterized by words, pronunciations, and sentence structure not common in standard English. To capture the flavor of dialect, writers may purposely misspell words to show unusual pronunciations, use contractions and poor grammar, and insert colorful language. The following passage from "The Invalid's Story" shows how Twain uses dialect:

" . . . One day you're hearty and strong . . . and next day he's *cut down like the grass*, and the *places which knowed him* then knows him no more forever, as *Scriptur'* says. *Yes'ndeedy,* it's awful solemn and *cur'us*; but we've all got to go, one time or another; *they ain't no getting around it.*"

6 **Discussion** Why is Thompson so sure that this particular corpse is really dead?

7 **Critical Thinking and Reading** How does Thompson's way of speaking contribute to the humor of the story?

8 **Discussion** What is humorous about this apparently serious remark?

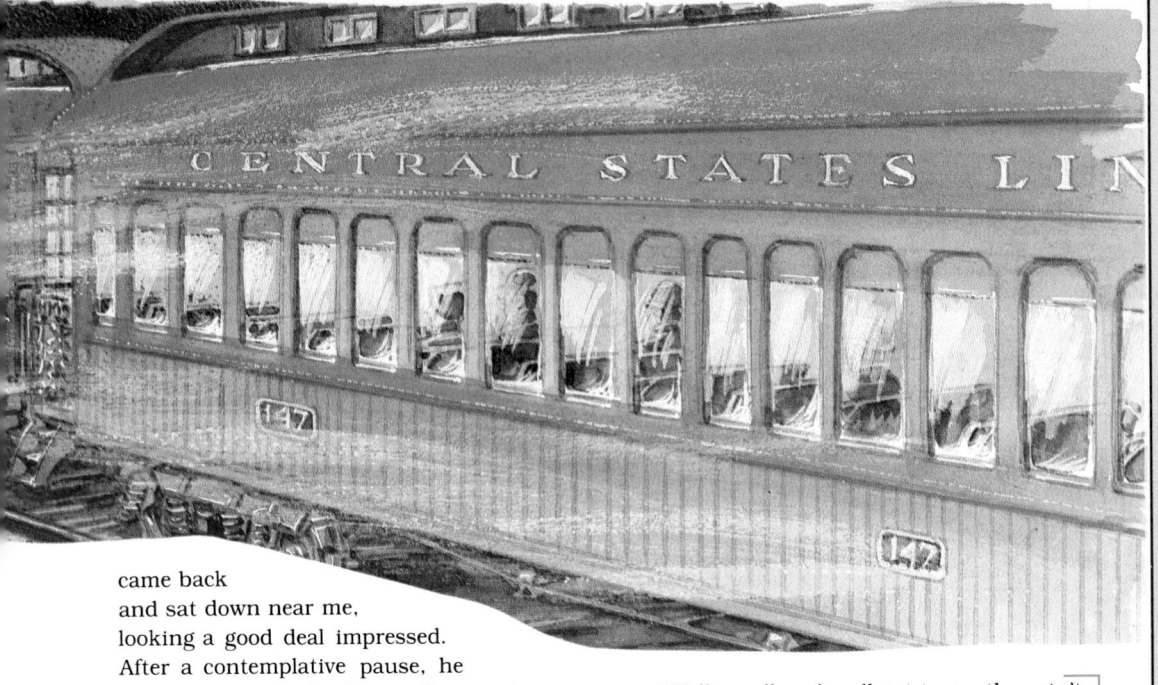

came back
and sat down near me,
looking a good deal impressed.
After a contemplative pause, he said, indicating the box with a gesture—

"Friend of yourn?"

"Yes," I said with a sigh.

"He's pretty ripe, *ain't* he!"

Nothing further was said for perhaps a couple of minutes, each being busy with his own thoughts; then Thompson said, in a low, awed voice—

"Sometimes it's uncertain whether they're really gone or not—*seem* gone, you know—body warm, joints limber—and so, although you *think* they're gone, you don't really know. I've had cases in my car. It's perfectly awful, becuz *you* don't know what minute they'll rise up and look at you!" Then, after a pause, and slightly lifting his elbow toward the box,—"But *he* ain't in no trance! No, sir, I go bail for *him!*"

We sat some time, in meditative silence, listening to the wind and the roar of the train; then Thompson said, with a good deal of feeling:

"Well-a-well, we've all got to go, they ain't no getting around it. Man that is born of woman is of few days and far between, as Scriptur'[3] says. Yes, you look at it any way you want to, it's awful solemn and cur'us: they ain't *nobody* can get around it; *all's* got to go—just *everybody*, as you may say. One day you're hearty and strong"—here he scrambled to his feet and broke a pane and stretched his nose out at it a moment or two, then sat down again while I struggled up and thrust my nose out at the same place, and this we kept on doing every now and then—"and next day he's cut down like the grass, and the places which knowed him then knows him no more forever, as Scriptur' says. Yes'ndeedy, it's awful solemn and cur'us: but we've all got to go, one time or another: they ain't no getting around it."

There was another long pause; then—

_____

**3. Scriptur':** Scripture, the Bible.

*The Invalid's Story* 101

---

Twain indicates unusual pronunciations with words like "Yes'ndeedy" and "cur'us"; he purposely uses incorrect grammar in phrases like "places which knowed him" and "they ain't no getting around it"; and he inserts colorful figures of speech based on the Bible, such as "cut down like the grass." By accurately reproducing Thompson's dialect, Twain makes his story both humorous and realistic.

**Student Activity 1.** Identify a similar passage from the story. Point out each technique Twain uses to write dialect. Note any misspellings, unusual contractions, examples of poor grammar, and colorful figures of speech.

**Student Activity 2.** Rewrite a dialect passage from "The Invalid's Story" in standard English, omitting all dialect. Read the original passage and the revised passage aloud. Discuss the differences between the two. Which is more effective? Why?

9 **Discussion** What does this statement mean?

10 **Master Teacher Note** Twain's
tone in this story is chatty and
conversational. Ask students to
give some examples of the way
Twain achieves this effect.

11 **Discussion** How would you paraphrase this passage without using dialect?

12 **Critical Thinking and Reading**
Whenever Thompson mentions
the odor, he talks as though the
corpse is deliberately causing the
situation. How does this add to the
humor of the story?

"What did he die of?"
I said I didn't know.
"How long has he ben dead?"
It seemed judicious to enlarge the facts to fit the probabilities; so I said:
"Two or three days."
But it did no good; for Thompson received it with an injured look which plainly said, "Two or three *years*, you mean." Then he went right along, placidly ignoring my statement, and gave his views at considerable length upon the unwisdom of putting off burials too long. Then he lounged off toward the box, stood a moment, then came back on a sharp trot and visited the broken pane, observing:
" 'Twould 'a' ben a dum sight better, all around, if they'd started him along last summer."

Thompson sat down and buried his face in his red silk handkerchief, and began to slowly sway and rock his body like one who is doing his best to endure the almost unendurable. By this time the fragrance—if you may call it fragrance—was just about suffocating, as near as you can come at it. Thompson's face was turning gray; I knew mine hadn't any color left in it. By and by Thompson rested his forehead in his left hand, with his elbow on his knee, and sort of waved his red handkerchief toward the box with his other hand, and said:
"I've carried a many a one of 'em—some of 'em considerable overdue, too—but, lordy, he just lays over 'em all!—and does it *easy*. Cap, they was heliotrope[4] to *him!*"

This recognition of my poor friend gratified me, in spite of the sad circumstances, because it had so much the sound of a compliment.
Pretty soon it was plain that something

---

**4. heliotrope** (hē′ lē ə trōp′) *n.*: A sweet-smelling plant.

had got
to be done.
I suggested cigars. Thompson
thought it was a good idea. He said:
"Likely it'll modify him some."
We puffed gingerly along for a while, and tried hard to imagine that things were improved. But it wasn't any use. Before very long, and without any consultation, both cigars were quietly dropped from our nerveless fingers at the same moment. Thompson said, with a sigh:
"No, Cap, it don't modify him worth a cent. Fact is, it makes him worse, becuz it appears to stir up his ambition. What do you reckon we better do, now?"
I was not able to suggest anything; indeed, I had to be swallowing and swallowing all the time, and did not like to trust myself

to speak.

Thompson fell to maundering,[5] in a desultory and low-spirited way, about the miserable experiences of this night; and he got to referring to my poor friend by various titles—sometimes military ones, sometimes civil ones; and I noticed that as fast as my poor friend's effectiveness grew, Thompson promoted him accordingly—gave him a bigger title. Finally he said:

"I've got an idea. Suppos'n' we buckle down to it and give the Colonel a bit of a shove toward t'other end of the car?—about ten foot, say. He wouldn't have so much influence, then, don't you reckon?"

I said it was a good scheme. So we took

in a good fresh breath at the broken pane, calculating to hold it till we got through; then we went there and bent over that deadly cheese and took a grip on the box. Thompson nodded "All ready," and then we threw ourselves forward with all our might; but Thompson slipped, and slumped down with his nose on the cheese, and his breath got loose. He gagged and gasped, and floundered up and made a break for the door, pawing the air and saying hoarsely, "Don't hender me!—gimme the road! I'm a-dying; gimme the road!" Out on the cold platform I sat down and held his head awhile, and he revived. Presently he said:

"Do you reckon we started the Gen'rul any?"

I said no; we hadn't budged him.

"Well, then, *that* idea's up the flume. We got to think up something else. He's suited wher' he is, I reckon; and if that's the way he feels about it, and has made up his mind that he don't wish to be disturbed, you bet he's a-going to have his own way in the business. Yes, better leave him right wher' he is, long as he wants it so; becuz he holds all the trumps, don't you know, and so it stands to reason that the man that lays out to alter his plans for him is going to get left."

But we couldn't stay out there in that mad storm; we should have frozen to death. So we went in again and shut the door, and began to suffer once more and take turns at the break in the window. By and by, as we were starting away from a station where we had stopped a moment Thompson pranced in cheerily, and exclaimed:

"We're all right, now! I reckon we've got the Commodore this time. I judge I've got the stuff here that'll take the tuck out of him."

It was carbolic acid. He had a carboy[6] of

---

**5. maundering** (môn' dər iŋ) *v.*: Talking in an unconnected way.

**6. carboy** (kär' boi) *n.*: A large glass bottle enclosed in basketwork to prevent it from breaking.

*The Invalid's Story*　103

13 **Discussion** Why does Thompson change the titles he gives to the corpse?

14 **Discussion** What is the irony in the use of the adverb "deadly" to describe the cheese?

15 **Discussion** How does the increasing strength of the odor correlate with the powers that Thompson attributes to the corpse?

16 **Reading Strategy** Recall the titles that Thompson has given the dead man.

**17 Critical Thinking and Reading**
How is this statement ironical?

**18 Critical Thinking and Reading**
What "work" is Thompson referring to when he says, "I never did see one of 'em warm up to his work so . . ."?

**19 Discussion** How is this description ironical?

**20 Clarification** Mr. Thompson believes that he has contracted typhoid fever because of his exposure to the stench of the corpse. Typhoid fever is a general infection which includes a high fever and rose-colored spots on the chest and abdomen. It can lead to serious complications and can be fatal.

**21 Discussion** Why does the author refer to "imagination" as the cause of his ruined health?

**Reader's Response** Has there ever been a time when you let your imagination run away with you? Explain.

---

it. He sprinkled it all around everywhere: in fact he drenched everything with it, rifle-box, cheese and all. Then we sat down, feeling pretty hopeful. But it wasn't for long.

**17** You see the two perfumes began to mix, and then—well, pretty soon we made a break for the door: and out there Thompson swabbed his face with his bandanna and said in a kind of disheartened way:

**18** "It ain't no use. We can't buck agin *him*. He just utilizes everything we put up to modify him with, and gives it his own flavor and plays it back on us. Why, Cap, don't you know, it's as much as a hundred times worse in there now than it was when he first got a-going. I never *did* see one of 'em warm up to his work so, and take such a dumnation interest in it. No, sir, I never did, as long as I've ben on the road: and I've carried a many a one of 'em, as I was telling you."

We went in again after we were frozen pretty stiff: but my, we couldn't *stay* in, now. So we just waltzed back and forth, freezing, and thawing, and stifling, by turns. In about an hour we stopped at another station: and as we left it Thompson came in with a bag, and said—

"Cap, I'm a-going to chance him once more—just this once: and if we don't fetch him this time, the thing for us to do, is to just throw up the sponge and withdraw from the canvass.[7] That's the way *I* put it up."

He had brought a lot of chicken feathers, and dried apples, and leaf tobacco, and rags, and old shoes, and sulphur, and asafetida,[8]

---

**7. withdraw from the canvass** (kan' vəs): Give up the attempt.
**8. asafetida** (as' ə fet' ə də) *n.*: A bad-smelling substance from certain plants, used as medicine.

---

and one thing or another: and he piled them on a breadth of sheet iron in the middle of the floor, and set fire to them.

When they got well started, I couldn't see, myself, how even the corpse could stand it. All that went before was just simply poetry **19** to that smell—but mind you, the original smell stood up out of it just as sublime as ever—fact is, these other smells just seemed to give it a better hold: and my, how rich it was! I didn't make these reflections there—there wasn't time—made them on the platform. And breaking for the platform, Thompson got suffocated and fell: and before I got him dragged out, which I did by the collar, I was mighty near gone myself. When we revived, Thompson said dejectedly:

"We got to stay out here, Cap. We got to do it. They ain't no other way. The Governor wants to travel alone, and he's fixed so he can outvote us."

And presently he added:

"And don't you know, we're *pisoned*. It's **20** *our* last trip, you can make up your mind to it. Typhoid fever is what's going to come of this. I feel it a-coming right now. Yes, sir, we're elected, just as sure as you're born."

We were taken from the platform an hour later, frozen and insensible, at the next station, and I went straight off into a virulent fever, and never knew anything again for three weeks. I found out, then, that I had **21** spent that awful night with a harmless box of rifles and a lot of innocent cheese: but the news was too late to save *me*: imagination had done its work, and my health was permanently shattered: neither Bermuda nor any other land can ever bring it back to me. This is my last trip: I am on my way home to die.

**Closure and Extension**

**ANSWERS TO THINKING ABOUT THE SELECTION**
*Recalling*

1. The purpose of his journey is to take his friend's corpse to his parents in Wisconsin.
2 The narrator confuses the coffin box with an identical box of rifles. He takes the box of rifles by mistake. A stranger enters the car and

## THINKING ABOUT THE SELECTION

### Recalling

1. What is the purpose of the narrator's journey?
2. Describe the mistake the narrator makes at the train station. How does the stranger complicate the mistake?
3. How do weather conditions make the narrator's journey particularly uncomfortable? Why do Thompson's efforts to make the car comfortable have the opposite effect?
4. According to the narrator, what long-term effect does the journey have on him?

### Interpreting

5. Explain the difference between what the narrator and Thompson believe to be true and what is really true.
6. How would the experience have differed if they had known the source of the odor?

### Applying

7. Think of a joke you have heard or a funny situation in a book or movie whose humor depends on the difference between appearance and reality. Share it with your classmates.

## ANALYZING LITERATURE

### Understanding First-Person Narration

With **first-person narration,** one of the characters in the story relates the events. This character, who uses the pronoun *I* or *we,* tells the story from his or her **point of view,** or perspective. In "The Invalid's Story" the narrator tells about events long after they happened, and he knows more than he did when the events occurred.

1. What two facts does the narrator learn after the events of the story took place?
2. How does the fact that the narrator takes the events so seriously add to the humor?
3. Retell the part of the story in which the odor first surfaces (end of paragraph 1, page 100) from Thompson's point of view.

## CRITICAL THINKING AND READING

### Identifying Exaggeration

An **exaggeration** is an overstatement. It is often used for humor. For example, in this story the narrator exaggerates the effects of the trip when he says, "I seem sixty and married, but these effects are due to my condition and sufferings, for I am a bachelor, and only forty-one."

1. Why does the narrator exaggerate the length of time his friend has been dead? How does Thompson respond to this exaggeration?
2. Find the military terms Thompson uses to refer to the corpse. Why does he promote the corpse as the story goes on?
3. Explain how the narrator's statement at the end brings the story to a humorous conclusion.

## UNDERSTANDING LANGUAGE

### Understanding Idioms

An **idiom** is a phrase that has a meaning that is not necessarily clear from the meanings of the words in it. The idiom *buckle down,* for example, means "set to work energetically." What does each of the following idioms from "The Invalid's Story" mean?

1. go bail for (page 101)
2. cut down (page 101)
3. up the flume (page 103)
4. holds all the trumps (page 103)

## THINKING AND WRITING

### Writing a Tall Tale

Write a tall tale of your own. The plot should hinge on an absurd exaggeration, such as having the main character climb Mount Everest in one hour. Brainstorm to form a list of possible exaggerated events for your tall tale. Select a character and have this character narrate the events in the first person. When you revise the tale, be sure the events follow logically from your exaggeration. Proofread your tall tale and share it with your classmates.

*The Invalid's Story* 105

(Answers begin on p. 104.)

night with a "harmless box of rifles and a lot of innocent cheese."
2. Suggested Response: The narrator's solemnity would have been appropriate if the box contained a corpse. Because we know that the box contains rifles and the smell is caused by cheese, the narrator's seriousness seems ridiculous.
3. Answers will differ. Students may indicate that Thompson would begin to wonder about the odor and then realize it was coming from the corpse.

### ANSWERS TO CRITICAL THINKING AND READING

1. Suggested Response: The narrator exaggerates the length of time the corpse has been dead because of the strength of the odor. Thompson responds in disbelief because he thinks the odor is strong enough for the corpse to have been dead for a much longer period.
2. Suggested Response: The military terms Thompson uses to refer to the corpse are Colonel, Gen'rul, and Commodore. The corpse gets promoted as the odor grows stronger.
3. Suggested Response: The narrator humorously exaggerates the harmful effects of the trip.

### ANSWERS TO UNDERSTANDING LANGUAGE

1. to guarantee
2. dies
3. worthless
4. has power, or the upper hand

### THINKING AND WRITING

For help with this assignment, students can refer to Lesson 17, "Writing a Short Story," in the Handbook of Writing About Literature.

### Publishing Student Writing

Collect all the tall tales in a booklet. Have students design the cover and the table of contents, and include illustrations with each tale. You might have several copies made and ask the school librarian to display one.

---

leaves a package of Limburger cheese on top of the coffin.
3. It is a gloomy, bitterly cold, and stormy night. By lighting the stove, the expressman heats the car and the cheese, making the odor stronger.
4. Because of the journey, his health was permanently ruined.

*Interpreting*

5. Suggested Response: The narrator and the expressman both believe that the odor is coming from the decaying corpse. The true source of the odor is the Limburger cheese.
6. Answers will differ. Students may respond that if the men had known that the cheese was the source of the odor, they could have thrown it away and spent the journey comfortably warm in the train.

*Applying*

7. Answers will differ. Students should share examples that depend on the difference between appearance and reality.

**Challenge** The phrase "grisly humor" refers to humor based on topics that are usually considered unpleasant or repellent. How is this story an example of grisly humor?

### ANSWERS TO ANALYZING LITERATURE

1. Suggested Response: The narrator learns that he had spent the

**More About the Author** Grant Moss, Jr., is presently teaching at Grambling College in Louisiana. Ask students why they think college teaching is a good profession for a writer.

**Literary Focus** Discuss with students the various points of view from which a story may be told. Have students give examples of other stories written from the third-person point of view. Explain to students that the author's use of limited third-person narration helps readers see how difficult Bennie's problem is for him and how much he grows in the course of the story.

**Look For** You might have students look for the author's use of description and dialogue to show how Bennie grows and learns to accept the imminent death of his grandmother.

**Writing/Prior Knowledge** Have students discuss how they think it might feel to live in a remote area far away from other people. Then have students complete the freewriting assignment.

**Vocabulary** Have your less advanced students use each word in a sentence that reflects its meaning.

## Before the End of Summer

**Grant Moss, Jr.** has written short stories that appeared in such magazines as *The New Yorker, Essence,* and *Opportunity* during the 1960's. "Before the End of Summer" was first published in the October 15, 1960, issue of *The New Yorker,* and it has since appeared in many anthologies. The story offers a vivid depiction of life among blacks in the rural South as well as a touching portrayal of a close-knit and loving family.

**Third-Person Narration**

When authors use **third-person narration,** the narrator is a voice outside the story who refers to all the characters as *he, she,* or *they.* Sometimes the narrator relates the events from the **point of view,** or perspective, of one of the characters. This method is referred to as **limited third-person narration**. With limited third-person narration, the reader sees events through the eyes of one character and knows only what that character knows. In "Before the End of Summer" the narrator relates the events as Bennie, the ten-year-old hero, learns them. The child's limited experience and understanding give the story its special slant.

**Look For**

Stewart Alsop has written: "A dying man needs to die, as a sleepy man needs to sleep." One of the hardest lessons children and adults have to learn is acceptance of death. As you read "Before the End of Summer," look for ways in which Bennie changes as he comes to accept the fact that his grandmother is dying.

**Writing**

Bennie lives in a remote area, far from other houses. He must often spend his summer days without any companions his own age. Imagine yourself living in these circumstances. Freewrite about how you would pass the time.

**Vocabulary**

Knowing the following words will help you as you read "Before the End of Summer."

**rawboned** (rô' bōnd') *adj.:* Having little flesh or fat covering the bones; lean (p. 111)

**plaits** (plăts) *n.:* Braids (p. 112)

**glistened** (glis' 'nd) *v.:* Shone or sparkled with reflected light (p. 117)

## Objectives

1 To recognize limited point of view
2 To use narration to draw conclusions
3 To choose the meaning of a word to fit the context
4 To write an essay about characters in a story

## Support Material

**Teaching Portfolio**
Teacher Backup, p. 133
Grammar in Action Worksheets, *Writing Dialogue,* p. 137; *Recognizing Introductory Adverb Clauses,* p. 139
Usage and Mechanics Worksheet, p. 141
Vocabulary Check, p. 142
Critical Thinking and Reading Worksheet, *Using Narration to*

*Draw Conclusions,* p. 143
Language Worksheet, *Choosing the Meaning to Fit the Context,* p. 144
Selection Test, p. 145

# Before the End of Summer

## Grant Moss, Jr.

When Dr. Frazier came, Bennie's grandmother told him to run down to the spring and wade in the stream that flowed from it across the pasture field to Mr. Charley Miller's pond, or play under the big oak tree that stood between her field and Mr. Charley Miller's. He started along the path, but when he was about midway to the spring he stopped. He had waded in the stream and caught minnows all that morning. He had played under the oak tree all yesterday afternoon. He had asked his grandmother to let him walk the mile and a half down the road to James and Robert Lee Stewart's to play, but she had not let him go. There was nothing he wanted to do alone. He wanted someone to play with. He turned and went back and crept under the window of his grandmother's room. Their voices floated low and quiet out into the cool shade that lay over the house.

"How long will it be?" he heard his grandmother say.

"Before the end of summer."

"Are you sure?"

"Yes. You should have sent for me long ago."

"I've passed my threescore and ten years. I'm eighty-four."

What did they mean? Perhaps he ought not to be listening.

"How will it come? Tell me, Doctor. I can stand it."

"There will be sharp, quick pains like the ones you've been having. Your heart cannot stand many more attacks. It grows weaker with each one, even though you're able to go about your work as you did before the attack came. I'm going to leave you a prescription for some pills that will kill the pain almost instantly. But that's about all they will do. When an attack comes, take two with a glass of water. They'll make you drop off to sleep. One time you won't wake up."

Now Bennie understood. But he could not turn and run away.

There was a brief silence. Then his grandmother said, "Don't tell Birdie nor anybody else."

"But you can't stay here alone with the child all day long. Why, he's only ten years old."

"I know. . . . Doctor, there ain't anyone to come stay with me. Birdie must go to the Fieldses' to work. You know it's just Birdie, the boy, and me. I got no close kin. My husband, my three sons, and my other daughter's been dead for years now. You see, I know death, Doctor. I know it well. I'm just not use to it."

"No one is," Dr. Frazier said.

"Here's what I want to do. I'll go on just like before. There ain't nothin' else for me to do. When an attack comes, I'll take the two pills and I'll send Bennie runnin' down the road for May Mathis. She'll come. May will come. I know nobody I'd rather have set beside me than May. I knowed her all my life.

## Presentation

**Motivation/Prior Knowledge** Have students discuss how people react when they find out someone they care for is moving away or dying. Tell them that this story deals with such a situation.

**Thematic Idea** Another selection that deals with passages and transformations is "The Ballad of William Sycamore" by Stephen Vincent Benét, page 557.

**Master Teacher Note** The focus of the story is the way that the boy confronts and deals with his grandmother's imminent death. Have students look for details that show the boy trying to understand death.

**Purpose-Setting Question** What character traits does Bennie reveal as he lives with the secret of his grandmother's approaching death?

1 **Critical Thinking and Reading** Most of this story is told from the point of view of a child. How does this paragraph reveal a young boy's perceptions?

2 **Reading Strategy** Have students predict what they think might happen as a result of Bennie's eavesdropping.

3 **Discussion** What does Bennie finally understand? Why is he unable to move?

4 **Discussion** What does Bennie's grandmother mean when she says she knows death but is not used to it?

**5 Discussion** Did you realize before this point in the story that the narrator and his family were black? If so, what made you realize it?

**6 Discussion** How does Bennie react to his secret knowledge?

**7 Discussion** Why does Bennie want to be by himself?

**8 Discussion** Why do you think Bennie stays outdoors most of the day? How might these actions reflect Bennie's thoughts about his grandmother's death?

Me and her done talked about this thing many times. It's July now. July the seventh. Then August—then September. But here I go runnin' on and on. Let me get your money. You've got to be paid. You've got to live."

"Please," Dr. Frazier said.

"No harm meant."

In a moment, Bennie heard them walking out onto the porch through the door of her room. Then he could see them as they crossed the yard to the gate, where Dr. Frazier's horse and buggy stood. He was a little man, with a skin that was almost black. He climbed into his buggy and started up the road toward the town, which was three miles away, and she stood and looked after him. Her back was to the house. People said that Bennie's grandmother had Indian blood in her veins, for she had high cheekbones and her nose was long and straight, but her mouth was big. Her eyes seemed as though they were buried way back in her head, in a mass of wrinkles. They danced and twinkled whenever they looked at him. She was a big woman, and she wore long full skirts that came all the way to the ground.

She closed the gate and started back to the house, and it came to Bennie that he was alone with her, and that she was going to die soon. He turned and ran noiselessly across the back yard, through the back gate, and down the path to the spring.

When he reached the spring, he kept running. He ran across the pasture field and up the hill to the barbed-wire fence that divided his grandmother's land from Mr. Charley Miller's. He threw himself to the ground and rolled under the fence, picked himself up on the other side, and ran through Mr. Charley Miller's field of alfalfa and into the woods, until at last he fell exhausted in the cool damp grass of a shaded clearing.

His grandmother was going to die. She might even be dead now. She was going to lie cold and still, in a long black casket that would be put into a hearse that would take her to church in town. The Reverend Isaiah Jones would preach her funeral. People would cry, because people liked his grandmother. His mother would cry. He would cry. And now he was crying, and he could not stop crying.

But at last he did, and he sat up and took from his pocket the clean white rag that his grandmother had given him to use as a handkerchief and dried his eyes. He must get up and go back to the house. He would have to be alone with his grandmother until his mother came home from the Fieldses' after she had cooked their supper. And he must tell no one what he had heard Dr. Frazier say to his grandmother.

He found her sitting in her big rocking chair, her hands clasped in her lap. "You been gone a long time," she said. "The water bucket's empty. Take it and go fill it at the spring. Time for me to be gettin' up from here and cookin' supper."

When he got back from the spring, he found her laying a fire in the kitchen stove.

It was nearly dark when he saw his mother coming, and he ran to meet her. She looked at him closely and said, "Bennie, why on earth did you run so fast?"

He could only say breathlessly, "I don't know," He added quickly, "What did you bring me?" Sometimes she brought him a piece of cake or pie, or the leg of a chicken from the Fieldses'. Today she did not have anything.

It was a long time before he went to sleep that night.

The next day, he stayed outdoors and only went into the house when his grandmother called him to do something for her. She did not notice.

On Sunday, his mother did not go to the Fieldses'. In the morning, they went to church. That afternoon, Mr. Joe Bailey drove

**NEGRO BOY**
*Eastman Johnson*
*National Academy of Design*

**Humanities Note**

Fine Art, *Negro Boy*, 1860, by Eastman Johnson. Eastman Johnson (1824-1906), an American artist, studied art in Europe and was strongly influenced by the style of the Dutch artists, especially Rembrandt. When he returned to the United States, he developed his style further, painting the American rural and frontier subjects he loved.

Johnson painted striking character studies, as well as scenes of American life. He used dramatic light and broad, fluid strokes of paint to dramatize his subjects. There is a freshness and immediacy in his work. *Negro Boy* is the diploma picture he painted for the National Academy of Design in New York when he became a full member.

Have students look at the setting of this painting and its central figure, the black child. You might then use these questions for discussion.

1. Do you think that this portrait is an accurate portrayal of the young boy in the story? Explain.
2. What appears to be this child's mood?
3. How is that mood reflected in the setting?

**9 Reading Strategy** Have students summarize how Bennie's eavesdropping has affected him so far.

up to the house in his horse and buggy to take Bennie's mother for a buggy ride. She had put on her pretty blue-flowered dress and her big wide-brimmed black straw hat with the red roses around its crown and the black ribbon that fell over the brim and down her back. She looked very pretty and as pleased as she could be. Bennie wanted to go riding with them. Once, he had asked Mr. Joe if he could go along, and Mr. Joe had grinned and said yes, but Bennie's mother had not been pleased at all, for some reason. This Sunday, after they had gone, his grandmother let him walk the mile and a half down the road to play with James and Robert Lee Stewart.

He knew that his grandmother was preparing to die. He came upon her kneeling in prayer beside her bed with its high headboard that almost touched the ceiling. As she sat in her rocking chair, she said the Twenty-third Psalm. He knew only the first verse: "The Lord is my shepherd; I shall not want."

Now he felt toward his grandmother the way he felt toward certain people, only more

*Before the End of Summer* 109

10 **Discussion** What do you think Bennie means when he says that his grandmother made him stand away from her?

11 **Clarification** In the world of this story, whites are distant figures.

12 **Discussion** What do you think Bennie means?

so. There was a feeling that made people seem strange—a feeling that came from them to you—that made you stand away from them. There was Miss Sally Cannon, his teacher. You did not go close to Miss Sally. She made you sit still and always keep your reader or your spelling book open on your desk, or do your arithmetic problems. If she caught you whispering or talking, she called you up to the front of the room and gave you several stinging lashes on your legs or across your back with one of the long switches that always lay across her desk. You did not go close to Miss Sally unless you had to. You did not go close to Dr. Frazier or the Reverend Isaiah Jones. Teachers, doctors, and preachers were special people.

You did not go close to white people, either. Sometimes when he and his grandmother went to town, they would stop at the Fieldses'. They would walk up the long green yard and go around the big red brick house, with its tall white columns, to the kitchen, where his mother was: it always seemed a nice place to be, even on a hot summer day. His mother and his grandmother would chuckle over something that Miss Marion Fields or Mr. Ridley Fields had done. They would stop smiling the minute Miss Marion came into the room, and they would become like people waiting in the vestibule of a church for the prayer to be finished so they could go in. He knew that he acted the same way.

Miss Marion had light-brown hair and light-brown eyes. His grandmother said that she was like a sparrow, for she was a tiny woman. She always wore a dress that was pretty enough to wear to church. The last time he was at the Fieldses', Miss Marion came into the kitchen. After she had spoken to his grandmother, she turned to him. He was sitting in a chair near the window, and he felt himself stiffen both inside and out-

side. She said, "I declare, Birdie, Bennie's the prettiest colored child I ever did see. Lashes long as a girl's. Is he a good boy, Hannah?"

"He's a quiet child," his grandmother said. "Sometimes I think he's too quiet, but he's a good child—at least when I got my eyes on him." They all laughed.

"I'm sure Bennie's good," Miss Marion said. "Be a good boy, Bennie. Eat plenty and grow strong, and when you're big enough to work, Mr. Ridley will be glad to give you work here on his place. We're so glad to have your mother here with us. Now, be good, won't you?"

"Yes, Ma'am," he answered.

"Birdie, give him a piece of that lemon pie you baked for supper. Well, Hannah, it's been nice talking with you again. Always stop on your way to town."

Two weeks to the day after Dr. Frazier's visit, Miss May Mathis came to see his grandmother. She was much shorter than his grandmother—a plump woman, who always wore long black-and-white checked gingham[1] dresses that fell straight down from her high full breasts to her knees and then flared outward. Her chin was sharp, with folds of flesh around it. Her nose was wide and flat. She had small, snapping black eyes. Her skin was like cream that had been kept too long and into which hundreds of tiny black specks had fallen.

As she came into the yard, she asked Bennie if his grandmother was at home. She said she would sit on the porch, where it was cool. He ran into the house to tell his grandmother that she was there.

His grandmother put away her sewing

---

1. **gingham** (giŋ′ əm) *adj.*: A cotton cloth, usually woven in stripes, checks, or plaids (most often, a noun).

## Grammar in Action

Knowing how to write **dialogue** will make your own short stories fun to write and interesting to read. Dialogue, or conversation between characters in a work of literature, is enclosed in quotation marks. A new paragraph is started each time the speaker changes. Read these lines of dialogue from the story:

His grandmother put away her sewing and went out on the porch. "May, I'm glad you come. I've been lookin' for you," she said.

"I'd been here sooner, but my stomach's been givin' me trouble lately. Sometimes I think my time ain't long."
"Hush—hush! You'll live to see me put under the ground."
"Well, the day before yesterday I spent half the day in bed. I thought I'd have to send John for you." Miss May answered, and she went into a long account of the illness that troubled her.

Notice that in this excerpt the two middle paragraphs are made up entirely of quoted material, with no words or phrases that identify the speaker. How can you tell who is speaking?

The context of the work helps you keep track of the speaker in dialogue such as this: In the first paragraph, readers are told and went out on the porch. "May, I'm glad you come. I've been lookin' for you," she said.

"I'd been here sooner, but my stomach's been givin' me trouble lately. Sometimes I think my time ain't long."

"Hush—hush! You'll live to see me put under the ground."

"Well, the day before yesterday I spent half the day in bed. I thought I'd have to send John for you," Miss May answered, and she went into a long account of the illness that troubled her.

Bennie got up from the edge of the porch and ran around the house. The two old women paid no attention to his going. He knew what his grandmother would say to Miss May. She would tell Miss May how she wanted to be dressed for burial. She would name the song she wanted to be sung over her. He had heard the same conversation many times. Now it was different. What they were talking about would soon "come to pass," as his grandmother would say. Miss May did not know, but he knew.

He went out of the back gate and down the path to the spring. He waded in the stream awhile, catching minnows in his hands and then letting them go. He went across the pasture field. He broke off a persimmon bush to use as a switch, and he chased his grandmother's cow about the pasture a bit. But the cow was old and soon grew tired of moving when he hit her with the switch. Then he went to the big oak tree that stood between the fields and sat down. He stayed there until he saw Miss May Mathis going out of the front gate.

The July days went slowly by, one much like another. It grew hotter and hotter.

One day when he walked into the house after playing a long time in the stream and the pasture field, he found his grandmother quietly sleeping in her big rocking chair. He saw a bottle full of big white pills on the dresser. It had not been there when he left the house. An empty glass stood beside the pills. He felt too frightened to move. Her breast was rising and falling evenly. She stirred and then opened her eyes.

She seemed dazed and not to see him for a moment. Then her lips curved into a queer smile, and a twinkle came into her eyes. "Must have dropped off to sleep like a baby," she said. "Run outdoors and play. I'll set here awhile and then I'll get up and start supper."

Later on, she called him and asked if he could make out with milk and cold food from dinner. She left the milking for his mother to do when she came home from the Fieldses'. But the next morning his grandmother was all right, and he thought that she was not going to die that summer, after all.

One morning, a little after his mother had gone to the Fieldses', Mr. John Mathis drove up. He turned his horse and buggy around to face the way he had come. Then he walked up the path to the house. He was a tall, rawboned man with a bullet-shaped head, and he looked exactly like what he was—a deacon[2] in a church.

"What is it, John?" Bennie's grandmother asked.

"It's May. She was sick all day yesterday. Last night I had to get the doctor for her. Jennie Stewart's there now."

"I'll be ready to go in a minute," his grandmother said.

On the way to the Mathises', Bennie sat on the back of the buggy. His grandmother and Mr. John said only a few words. When they reached the house, his grandmother told him to keep very quiet and to be good,

---

**2. deacon** (dēk''n) n.: A church officer who helps the minister.

13

14

*Before the End of Summer*   111

13 **Discussion** Why is he frightened?

14 **Discussion** Why does Bennie's grandmother smile strangely?

that Grandmother is talking. In the next, context makes it clear that Miss May answers her. Grandmother then responds, and Miss May answers by telling about her illness.

**Student Activity 1.** In the story, find another passage of dialogue in which the speaker is not always identified. Share this passage with a partner, discussing who is speaking each line.

**Student Activity 2.** Choose one of the passages and practice reading the speech of the characters aloud with your partner. Present your reading to the class.

**Student Activity 3.** Write a brief conversation between two people. Use punctuation and paragraphs to help you indicate who is speaking.

**15 Discussion** What does his grandmother mean?

**16 Discussion** How do you think she feels?

**17 Discussion** Do you think this passage indicates a change in Bennie's attitude toward his grandmother's death? Explain.

and she went inside at once. There were people on the porch, and people continued to come and go. It was midafternoon, and still his grandmother had not come from within the house. A Ford car drove up to the gate. In it were Philomena Jones and her mother. Philomena was a year younger than Bennie. She had a sharp little yellow face, big black eyes that went everywhere, and she wore her hair in two long plaits. "Come on," she said, "and let's play something." When they were out of hearing of the grown-up people, she said, "Miss May going to die."

"How do you know?"

"I heard my mama say she was. She's old. When you're old you have to die."

Next, Philomena said, "Your mama's tryin' to catch Mr. Joe Bailey for a husband. Mama said it's time she's getting another husband if she's ever going to get one."

"You stop talkin'!" Bennie told her.

"She said your pa's been dead nine years now and if your mama don't hurry and take Mr. Joe Bailey—that is, if she can get him—she may never get a chance to marry again."

"If you don't stop talking', I'll hit you!"

"No, you won't. I'm not scared of you, even if you are a boy, and I'll say what I want to. Mama said, 'Birdie Wilson's in her forties, if she a day, and if a woman lets herself get into her forties without marryin', her chance are mighty slim after that.' I'm goin' to marry when I'm twenty."

"Nobody'd want you. You talk too much."

"I don't, neither."

"I won't play with you. I'm goin' back to the porch," he said.

Philomena stayed in the yard a little longer. She carried on an imaginary conversation with a person who seemed as eager to talk as she. After a while, she ran back to the porch and sat down and gave her attention to what the grown-up people were saying, now and then putting in a word herself.

Then his grandmother came out from the house. People stopped talking at the sight of her face. "May's gone," she said.

The people on the porch bowed their heads, and their faces became as though they were already at Miss May Mathis's funeral.

His grandmother looked very tired. After a moment, she said, "The Lord giveth and the Lord taketh. Blessed be the name of the Lord." There was a silence. Then she spoke again. "I thought May would do for me what I have to do for her now." She turned and went back into the house. Some of the women rose and followed her.

The people who remained on the porch spoke in low voices. Someone wondered when the funeral would be. Someone wondered if Miss May's sister Ethel, who lived in St. Louis, would come. Someone hoped that it would not rain the day of the funeral.

Then Mr. John Mathis and Bennie's grandmother came out on the porch. Mr. John said, "Hannah, you done all you could do. May couldn't have had a better friend. You're tired now. I'll send you home."

At home, his grandmother seemed not to notice him. Her eyes seemed to be taking a great sad rest. She sent him to the spring to get water to cook supper.

As he walked down the path, he thought about his grandmother. He felt more sorry for her than he felt fear of her. Miss May Mathis was dead; he could not run and get her now.

On Sunday afternoon at two o'clock at the Baptist Church, Miss May Mathis's funeral service was held. There was a procession of buggies, surreys,[3] and even a few automobiles from the house to the church. Mr. Joe Bailey came and took Bennie's

---

**3. surreys** (sur′ ēz) *n.pl.*: Light, horse-drawn carriages.

mother, his grandmother, and him to church. The funeral was a long one. He sat beside his grandmother and listened to the prayers, the songs, and the sermon, all the time dreading the moment when the flowers would be taken from the gray casket, the casket would be opened, and the people would file by to see the body for the last time.

The Reverend Isaiah Jones described Heaven as a land flowing with milk and honey, a place where people ate fruit from the tree of life, wore golden slippers, long white robes, and starry crowns, and rested forever. The Reverend Isaiah Jones was certain that Miss May Mathis was there, resting in the arms of Jesus, done with the sins and sorrows of this world. Bennie wondered why Mr. John covered his face with his hands, and why Miss May's sister Ethel, who had come all the way from St. Louis, cried out, and why people cried, if Miss May was so happy in this land. It seemed that they should be glad for her, so glad they would not cry. Or did they cry because they were glad? He could not understand. The Reverend Jones said that they would see Miss May on the Resurrection morning.[4] Bennie could not understand this, either.

At last the gray casket was opened, and people began to file by it. And at last he was close. His mother went by, and then Mr. Joe. Now his grandmother. The line of people stopped, waiting expectantly. His grandmother stood and looked down on Miss May for a long time. She did not cry out. She simply stood there and looked down, and finally she moved on. Now he was next. Miss May Mathis looked as though she had simply combed her hair and piled it on top of her head, put on her best black silk dress, pinned her big old pearl brooch to its lace

4. **the Resurrection** (rez′ ə rek′ shən) **morning:** In Christian teaching, the time when the dead come back to life.

collar, picked up a white handkerchief with one hand, and then decided that instead of going to church she would sleep a little while. As he looked down on her, he was not as afraid as he'd thought he would be.

Outside the church, as the procession was forming to go to the graveyard, Dr. Frazier came up to his grandmother and asked how she was.

"As well as could be expected, Doctor," his grandmother said. And then, in a low voice, "I've had only one."

"You got through it all right."

"Yes."

"And this?"

"I've managed to get through it."

"You will be careful."

"Yes."

"Now?"

"He'll have to go to the Stewarts'."

They did not know that he understood what they were talking about, even if none of the other people around them did. He heard two women whispering. One said to the other, "It's wonderful the way Aunt Hannah took it." He felt very proud of his grandmother.

Now his grandmother's footsteps were slower as she moved about the house and yard. He kept the garden and the flower beds along the yard fences weeded, the stove box full of wood, the water bucket full all the time, without her having to ask him to do these things for her. He overheard her say to his mother, "Child does everything without being told. It ain't natural."

"Reckon he's not well?" his mother asked anxiously.

"Don't think so. He eats well. Maybe the trouble is the child don't have nobody to play with every day. He'll be all right when fall comes and school starts."

18 **Discussion** Why is Bennie confused? How is his confusion typical of young people who tend to interpret everything literally?

19 **Discussion** What do you think Bennie's grandmother is thinking as she stands and looks down at Miss May?

20 **Discussion** How might the death of Miss May have affected Bennie's feelings about his grandmother's death?

21 **Critical Thinking and Reading** What do you know about Bennie from the fact that he keeps the garden and flower beds weeded and the water bucket full without being told?

**ANNA WASHINGTON DERRY, 1927**
*Laura Wheeler Waring*
National Museum of American Art
The Smithsonian Institution

22 August came, and it grew hotter. The sun climbed up the sky in the morning and down the sky in the evening like a tired old man with a great load on his back going up and down a hill. Then one hot mid-August day dawned far hotter and sultrier than the one just past. It grew still hotter during the early part of the morning, but by midday there was a change, for there was a breeze, and in the west a few dark clouds gathered in the sky. His grandmother said, "I believe the rain will come at last."

About three o'clock, the wind rose suddenly. It bent the top of the big oak tree that stood in the yard. There were low rumbles of thunder.

"Bennie, Bennie, come! Let's get the chickens up!" his grandmother called to him.

By the time all the chickens were safe in the henhouse and chicken coops, it was time to go into the house and put the windows down. The wind lifted the curtains almost to the ceiling. They got the windows down. His grandmother went into the kitchen. He went out on the porch. He wanted to watch the

*114   Short Stories*

clouds, for he had never seen any bigger or blacker or quite so low to the earth—he was sure they must be touching the ground somewhere. He wanted to see what the wind did to the trees, the corn, and the grass.

At last the rain fell, first in great drops that were blown onto the edge of the porch by the wind and felt cool and good as they touched his face. They made him want to run out into the yard. Then the rain came so quickly and so heavily, and with it so much wind, that it came up on the porch and almost pushed him back into the house. The thunder roared and there were flashes of lightning.

"Bennie, Bennie, where are you?" his grandmother called, and when he went inside she said, "Set down—set down in the big chair there or come into my room if you want to. I'm goin' to just set in my rocker."

"I'll stay here," he said, and he went to the big chair near the fireplace and sat down.

"There—there—just set there. I'll leave the door open."

He tried to keep from thinking what might happen if his grandmother had one of her spells, but he could not. He went to the fireplace. The back of the fireplace was wet; water stood on it in drops that looked like tears on a face. He stood and looked at it awhile, then he sat down in the big chair. There was nothing else to do but to sit there.

He heard her cry out. The cry was sharp and quick. Then it was cut off.

She called him. "Bennie! Bennie!" Her voice was thick.

He could not move.

"Bennie!"

He went into the room where she was.

She sat on the side of her bed. She was breathing hard, and in one hand she had the bottle of white pills. "Get me a glass of water. One of my spells done come over me."

He went into the kitchen and got a glass from the kitchen safe and filled it with water from the bucket that sat on the side table. Then he went back to her and gave her the water.

She took it and put two pills in her mouth and gulped them down with the water. She was breathing hard. "Pull off my shoes," she said.

As he was unlacing the high-top shoes she always wore, she gave a little cry. He felt her body tremble. "Just a bit of pain. Don't worry. I'm all right," she said. "It's gone," she added a moment later.

When he got her shoes off, he lifted her legs onto the bed, and she lay back and closed her eyes. "Go into the front room," she said, "and close the door behind you and stay there until the storm is past. I'm goin' to drop off to sleep—and if I'm still asleep when the storm is over, just let me sleep until your mama comes. Don't come in here. Don't try to wake me. 'Twon't do me no harm to take me a long good sleep."

He could not move. He could only stand there and stare at her.

"Hear me? Go on, I tell you. Go on—don't, I'll get up from here and skin you alive."

He crept from the room, closing the door after him.

He went to the big chair and sat down. He must not cry. Crying could not help him. There was nothing to do but to sit there until the storm was past.

The rain and the wind came steadily now. He sat back in the big chair. He wondered about his mother. Was she safe at the Fieldses'? He wondered if the water had flowed into the henhouse and under the chicken coops, where the little chickens were. If it had, some of the little chickens might get drowned. The storm lasted so long that it began to seem to him that it had always been there.

At last he became aware that the room

**23** **Discussion** Why is this an effective simile?

**24** **Discussion** Why does she tell him not to disturb her?

**25** **Discussion** Why is Bennie unable to move?

23

24

25

**26 Discussion** How does the felling of the oak relate to the grand-mother's imminent death?

**27 Discussion** Why do you think she cannot continue?

**28 Discussion** What does Bennie's grandmother mean?

was growing lighter and the rain was not so hard. The thunder and lightning were gone. Then, almost as suddenly as it had begun, the storm was over.

He got up and went out on the porch. Everything was clean. Everything looked new. There were little pools of water everywhere, and it was cool. There were a few clouds in the sky, but they were white and light gray. He looked across the field toward Mr. Charley Miller's, and he opened his eyes wide when he saw that the storm had blown down the big oak tree. He started to run back into the house to tell his grandmother that the storm had blown the tree down, and then he stopped. After a minute, he stepped down from the porch. The wet grass felt good on his bare feet.

He felt his grandmother in the doorway even before he heard her call. He turned and looked at her. She had put on her shoes and the long apron she always wore. She came out on the porch, and he decided that she looked as though her sleep had done her good.

**26** He remembered the tree, and he cried, "Look—look, Grannie! The storm blowed down the tree between your field and Mr. Charley Miller's."

**27** "That tree was there when me and your grandpa came here years and years ago," she said. "The Lord saw fit to let it be blowed down in this storm. I— I—" She broke off and went back into the house.

He ran into the house and said to her, "I'm goin' down to the spring. I bet the stream's deep as a creek."

"Don't you get drowned like old Pharaoh's army,"[5] she said.

___

5. **drowned like old Pharaoh's** (fer′ ōz) **army:** Pharaoh was the title of the kings of Egypt; the Biblical story (Exodus 14:28) tells that the Egyptian army was drowned while chasing the Israelites across the Red Sea.

*116 Short Stories*

The storm drove away the heat, for the days were now filled with cool winds that came and rattled the cornstalks and the leaves on the oak tree in the yard. There were showers. The nights were long and cool; the wind came into the rooms, gently pushing aside the neat white curtains to do so.

One morning when he went into the kitchen to get hot water and soap to take to the back porch to wash his face and hands, he found his mother and grandmother busy talking. They stopped the moment they saw him. His mother's face seemed flushed and uncomfortable, but her eyes were very bright.

"Done forgot how to say good mornin' to a body?" his grandmother said.

"Good mornin', Grannie. Good mornin', Mama."

"That's more like it."

"Good mornin', Bennie," his mother said. She looked at him, and he had a feeling that she was going to come to him and take him in her arms the way she used to do when he was a little boy. But she did not.

**28** His grandmother laughed. "Well, son, Mr. Joe Bailey went and popped the question to your mama last night."

His mother blushed. He did not know what to say to either of them. He just stood and looked at them.

"What you goin' to say to that?" his mother said.

All he could think to say was "It's all right."

His grandmother laughed again, and his mother smiled at him the way she did when he ran down the road to meet her and asked her to let him carry the packages that she had.

"When will they be married?" he asked.

"Soon," his mother said.

"Where will they live—here?"

"That ain't been settled yet," his grandmother said. "Nothin' been settled. They just

## Grammar in Action

Adverb clauses modify verbs, adjectives, adverbs, or verbals by telling where, when, in what manner, to what extent, under what condition, or why. An **introductory adverb clause** appears at the beginning of a sentence. Like other adverb clauses, this one begins with a subordinating conjunction and includes a subject and verb. It may also include complements and modifiers.

Read the following passage from the story. Notice how the writer begins each of the first four sentences with a subject. Then,

to vary his sentences, he begins the last one with an adverb clause:

> His mother was going to marry Mr. Joe Bailey. He did mind a little. He knew that was what she wanted. He liked Mr. Joe. *When Mr. Joe smiled at him,* he always had to smile back at him; something seemed to make him do so.

By inserting an introductory adverb clause, he varies the rhythm and length of his sentences.

**Student Activity 1.** Identify the introductory adverb clauses in the following sentences. Indicate the word that each clause modifies.

got engaged last night while they were settin' in the front room and you was sleepin' in your bed. Things can be settled later." She gave a sigh that his mother did not hear. But he heard it.

He poured water from the teakettle into the wash pan and took the pan out on the back porch and washed and dried his hands. He looked across the fields and hills. The sun had not come up yet, but the morning lay clear and soft and quiet as far as his eyes could see.

His mother was going to marry Mr. Joe Bailey. He did mind a little. He knew that was what she wanted. He liked Mr. Joe. When Mr. Joe smiled at him, he always had to smile back at him; something seemed to make him do so.

After his mother had gone to the Fieldses', he and his grandmother sat down to breakfast at the table in the kitchen. His grandmother never ate a meal without saying grace. Usually she gave thanks just for the food that they were about to eat. This morning she asked the Lord to bless his mama, Mr. Joe, and him, and she thanked the Lord for answering all her prayers.

As they ate, she talked to him. She spoke as though she were talking to herself, expecting no answer from him, but he knew that she meant for him to listen to her words, and he knew why she was talking to him. "Joe Bailey will make your mama a good husband and you a good father to take the place of your father who you never knew. The Lord took your father when your father was still young, but that was the Lord's will. Joe Bailey will be good to you, for he is a good man. Mind him. Don't make trouble between him and your mama. Hear me?"

"Yes, Ma'am."

"Don't you worry about where you'll stay. You'll be with your mama. Hear me?"

"Yes'm."

She sat silent for a moment, and then she added, "Well, no matter if your mama is going to marry Mr. Joe Bailey. We got to work today just like we always has. No matter what comes, we have to do the little things that our hands find to do. Soon as you finish eatin', go to the spring and get water and fill the pot and the tubs."

August drew toward its close, but the soft cool days stayed on, and they were calm and peaceful. His grandmother cooked the meals, and washed and ironed their own clothes and those that his mother brought home from the Fieldses' and Mr. Charley Miller's. Sometimes Bennie wondered if she had put from her mind the things that Dr. Frazier had said to her that day he listened under the window. Sometimes it seemed to him that he had never crept close to the window and listened to her and Dr. Frazier. The summer seemed just like last summer and the summer before that.

One day near the end of the month, Mr. John Mathis stopped by the house on his way to town. He was on horseback, riding a big black horse whose sides glistened. He hailed Bennie's grandmother, and she came out on the porch to pass the time of day with him.

"Ever see such a fine summer day, John?" she said.

"It's not a summer day, Hannah. It's a fall day. It's going to be an early fall this year."

"Think so?" his grandmother asked. Her face changed, but Mr. John did not notice.

"I can feel it. I can feel it in the air. The smell of fall is here already." Then they fell to talking about the church and people they knew.

She stood on the porch and watched Mr. John ride up the road on his big black horse. Often that day, she came out on the porch and stood and looked across the fields and hills.

**29 Discussion** What do you think bothers Bennie about his mother marrying Joe Bailey?

**30 Discussion** Why does Bennie doubt that he eavesdropped?

**31 Discussion** Why do you think Bennie's grandmother's face changes?

1. Although the sleet and wind tore at his shattered leg, Rob continued the struggle to get help.
2. While Amanda waited anxiously in the next room, the doctor studied the test results.
3. If we hurry, we can catch the last bus.

**Student Activity 2.** Write a paragraph modeled on the one by Grant Moss, Jr. Use four sentences with the same structure and length. Then add a longer fifth sentence that begins with an adverb clause.

**32 Discussion** Why do you think Bennie is no longer afraid? What events in the story may have helped him to change? How do you think he feels?

**33 Discussion** What makes Bennie start to run as fast as he can?

**Reader's Response** If you were Bennie, would you have acted as he did? Why or why not?

When Bennie went outside for the first time the next morning and looked around him, he did not see a single cloud in the sky. The quiet that lay about him felt like a nice clean sheet you pull over your head before you go to sleep at night that shuts out everything to make a space both warm and cool just for you. The day grew warm. A little after midday, clouds began to float across the sky, but for the most part it remained clear and very blue. He played in the yard under the oak tree, and then he went down to the spring and played. In the afternoon, he rolled his hoop up and down the road in front of the house. He grew tired of this and went and sat under the tree.

He was still sitting under the tree when his grandmother cried out. She gave a sharp sudden cry, like the cry people make when they've been stung by a bee or a wasp. He got to his feet. Then he heard her call. "Bennie! Bennie!"

He ran into the house and into her room. She sat in her big rocking chair, leaning forward a little, her hands clutching the arms of the chair. She was breathing hard. He had never seen her eyes as they were now. "Water—the pills—in the dresser."

He ran into the kitchen and got a glass of water and ran back to the room and gave it to her and then went to the dresser and got the bottle of pills. He unscrewed the top and took out two of them and gave them to her.

She put the pills in her mouth and gulped them down with water. Then she leaned back and closed her eyes. At last she breathed easier, and in a few moments she opened her eyes. "Run and get—get Miss— No, go get your mama. Hurry! Your grandmother is very sick."

It was a long way to the Fieldses'—even longer than to the Stewarts'! He stood still and looked at her. She was a big woman, and the chair was a big chair. Now she seemed smaller—lost in the chair.

"Hurry—hurry, child."

"Grannie, I'll stay with you until you go to sleep, if you want me to," he heard himself say.

"No! No! Hurry!"

"I heard you and Dr. Frazier talking that day."

"Child! Child! You knew all the time?"

"Yes, Grannie."

"When I drop off to sleep, I won't wake up. Your grandmother won't wake up here."

"I know."

"You're not afraid?"

He shook his head.

She seemed to be thinking hard, and at last she said, "Set down, child. Set down beside me."

He pulled up the straight chair and sat down facing her.

"Seems like I don't know what to say to you, Bennie. Be a good boy. Seems like I can't think any more. Everything leavin' me—leavin' me."

"I'll set here until you go to sleep, and then I'll go and get mama."

"That's a good boy," she said, and she closed her eyes.

He sat still and quiet until her breath came softly and he knew that she was asleep. It was not long. Then he got up and walked from the room and out of the house.

He did not look back, and he did not run until he was a good way down the road. Then suddenly he began to run, and he ran as fast as he could.

32

33

118 *Short Stories*

**Closure and Extension**

**ANSWERS TO THINKING ABOUT THE SELECTION**
*Recalling*

1. The doctor tells Bennie's grandmother that she will die before the end of summer. Bennie eavesdrops and finds this out.
2. At first he is very frightened by the seizures. After Miss May's funeral, he seems to accept them better.

118

## THINKING ABOUT THE SELECTION

### Recalling

1. What does Dr. Frazier tell Bennie's grandmother? How does Bennie learn what is said?
2. How does Bennie react to his grandmother's seizures?
3. In what two ways does Bennie's life change by the end of the story?

### Interpreting

4. Why doesn't Bennie's grandmother share the doctor's conclusions with Bennie's mother?
5. Why doesn't Bennie discuss what he has learned with his mother or his grandmother?
6. How does May Mathis's funeral help Bennie prepare for his grandmother's death?
7. Compare Bennie's reactions to death at the beginning and at the end of the selection.

### Applying

8. Explain what a person can gain from the experience of losing someone close.

## ANALYZING LITERATURE

### Recognizing Limited Point of View

In **third-person narration,** the narrator uses the pronouns *he, she,* and *they* to identify the characters. With **limited third-person narration,** the narrator tells the story from the **point of view** of one of the characters, and the reader learns only what that character knows or sees. For example, if the narrator told about the summer in "Before the End of Summer" from the mother's point of view, you would not learn that the grandmother is going to die or that Bennie is aware of the grandmother's condition.

1. Explain what Bennie does not understand about Miss May's funeral.
2. How might the story change if it were told from the grandmother's point of view?
3. Do you think the story is more effective for being told from Bennie's point of view? Explain your answer.

## CRITICAL THINKING AND READING

### Using Narration to Draw Conclusions

When authors use limited third-person narration, they do not give you an objective picture of a character from the outside. You must draw conclusions about the character from his or her thoughts and feelings. You know that Bennie is considered to be a "good boy," for example, because he hears the adults say he is.

What evidence in the story supports or refutes each of the following conclusions?
1. Bennie is a loving grandson.
2. Bennie does not have many friends.

## UNDERSTANDING LANGUAGE

### Choosing the Meaning to Fit the Context

When you read a word with more than one meaning, you use the context, or the words and sentences around it, to determine the correct meaning. For example, in this sentence, "She stirred and opened her eyes," the context shows that *stirred* means "roused from sleep."

Give the meaning of *lashes* in each of the following quotations from the story:
1. ". . . she . . . gave you several stinging lashes on your legs or across your back. . . ."
2. "Lashes long as a girl's."

## THINKING AND WRITING

### Writing About Characters

In "Before the End of Summer" Bennie acts as your eyes and ears: You observe his world through him. Bennie is also deeply affected by the events. List all the details you learn about Bennie. Then write an essay explaining what you think of Bennie and how he behaves. When you revise, think about how well you have shown that you understand Bennie's point of view.

(Answers begin on p. 118.)

### ANSWERS TO ANALYZING LITERATURE

1. Suggested Respone: Bennie cannot understand why people cry when they know that she is happy wherever she is.
2. Answers will differ. Students may respond that Bennie's growth would not be as clear to the reader.
3. Answers will differ. Students could support either side of this question. They should use examples from the story and sound arguments to back up their answers.

### ANSWERS TO CRITICAL THINKING AND READING

1. Suggested Response: Evidence to support this conclusion includes: He cries when he hears that his grandmother is going to die. He is proud of his grandmother for the way she handles herself at Miss May's funeral. He does his chores before his grandmother has to ask him to.
2. Suggested Response: Evidence to support this conclusion includes the fact that Bennie plays by himself throughout the story. He is also referred to as a quiet boy. His only friends seem to be two boys who live down the road.

### ANSWERS TO UNDERSTANDING LANGUAGE

1. In this sentence, the word refers to a blow with a whip or other object.
2. In this sentence, the word refers to eyelashes.

### THINKING AND WRITING

For help with this assignment, students can refer to Lesson 9, "Writing About Character," in the Handbook of Writing About Literature.

### Publishing Student Writing

Call on volunteers to read aloud one or two main points from their reports. List the most frequently made points on the chalkboard.

3. He learns to accept death and takes more responsibility for his actions.

### Interpreting

4. Suggested Response: Grandmother feels that Bennie's mother has enough to worry about.
5. Suggested Response: He probably does not know exactly what to say, or he does not want them to know that he had been eavesdropping.
6. Suggested Response: Her death enables Bennie to experience the death of someone he has known but whom he is not as close to. He comes to realize that the experience is not necessarily frightening and terrible. He thinks that Miss May looks as if she had dressed for church and then had decided to lie down a while. He is not as afraid as he had expected to be.
7. Suggested Response: When Bennie first hears that his grandmother is going to die, he runs until he is exhausted, throws himself on the ground, and cries. At the end of the story, he refuses to leave his grandmother's side, talks with her, and sits with her until he knows that she is asleep. He is no longer afraid and is able to accept her death.

### Applying

8. Answers will differ. Students may respond that a person can discover resources of strength in himself or herself.

# Focus

**More About the Author** Pearl Buck received the Nobel Prize for Literature "for rich and genuine portrayals of Chinese life and masterpieces of biography." Her most famous book, *The Good Earth,* overshadowed her many other writings. Ask students to consider how an author might feel about having one book that receives more attention than anything else he or she has written.

**Literary Focus** Write the term *omniscient point of view* on the chalkboard. Explain that the word *omniscient* means "all knowing." Ask students to discuss the advantages and disadvantages of using a narrator who stands outside the story and looks into the minds of all its characters.

**Look For** Your less advanced students may have difficulty understanding omniscient narration. You might review first-person narration with them and then contrast it with omniscient narration.

**Writing/Prior Knowledge** Discuss with students how we sometimes take for granted what we see and know about the country in which we live. Then have students complete the writing assignment.

**Vocabulary** Have your less advanced students use each word in a sentence. Then have them substitute a synonym for the word.

**Spelling Tip** Point out the double *l* in *compelled.* Without the suffix *-ed,* the word is spelled *compel.* However, the *l* is doubled when adding any suffix beginning with a vowel: *compelling, compeller.*

# GUIDE FOR READING

## The Good Deed

**Pearl S. Buck** (1892–1973) was born in Hillsboro, West Virginia, but grew up in China, where her parents were missionaries. She went to college in the United States, then returned to China as a missionary. Buck, who wrote more than eighty-five books, received the Nobel Prize for Literature in 1938. Like her most widely read novel, *The Good Earth,* the story you are about to read is set within a Chinese community. In the case of "The Good Deed," however, the community is located in the United States.

### Omniscient Narration

A story told by a **third-person narrator** is told by a voice outside the story. With **omniscient narration** this voice is all-seeing and all-knowing. The omniscient narrator can tell you things that the characters in the story do not know. The narrator can also enter the minds of all characaters and tell you what they think and feel and how they view events. In "The Good Deed," the narrator tells parts of the story from the *point of view,* or perspective, of old Mrs. Pan and other parts from other points of view.

### Look For

As you read "The Good Deed," look for the places at which the narrator stops telling the story from one character's point of view and starts telling it from another's. How does this shift in perspective affect your understanding?

### Writing

Imagine that you just arrived from a foreign country. Look out your window with a stranger's eyes. Freewrite about what you see. Describe the view as if you had never seen it before.

### Vocabulary

Knowing the following words will help you as you read "The Good Deed."

**abashed** (ə basht′) *adj.*: Ill-at-ease; ashamed (p. 125)
**profoundly** (prə found′ lē) *adv.*: Deeply; intensely (p. 125)
**compelled** (kəm peld′) *v.*: Forced (p. 125)
**repressed** (ri prest′) *v.*: Kept down; held back (p. 127)
**indignation** (in′ dig nā′ shən)

*n.*: Anger resulting from injustice (p. 127)
**surfeited** (sur fit id) *adj.*: Supplied to excess (p. 128)
**pertly** (purt′ lē) *adv.*: In a saucy manner (p. 129)
**tentative** (ten′ tə tiv lē) *adj.*: Done with hesitation (p. 134)

## Objectives

1 To appreciate omniscient narration
2 To make inferences about characters
3 To use a pronunciation key
4 To write a letter reacting to "The Good Deed"

## Support Material

**Teaching Portfolio**
Teacher Backup, p. 147
Grammar in Action Worksheet, *Recognizing Compound-Complex Sentences,* p. 151; *Using Adverbs and Adverb Phrases,* p. 153
Usage and Mechanics Worksheet, p. 155
Vocabulary Check, p. 156
Analyzing Literature Worksheet,

*Appreciating Omniscient Narration,* p. 158
Critical Thinking and Reading Worksheet, *Making Inferences About Characters,* p. 159
Selection Test, p. 160

# The Good Deed

## Pearl S. Buck

Mr. Pan was worried about his mother. He had been worried about her when she was in China, and now he was worried about her in New York, although he had thought that once he got her out of his ancestral village in the province of Szechuen[1] and safely away from the local bullies, who took over when the distant government fell, his anxieties would be ended. To this end he had risked his own life and paid out large sums of sound American money, and he felt that day when he saw her on the wharf, a tiny, dazed little old woman, in a lavender silk coat and black skirt, that now they would live happily together, he and his wife, their four small children and his beloved mother, in the huge safety of the American city.

It soon became clear, however, that safety was not enough for old Mrs. Pan. She did not even appreciate the fact, which he repeated again and again, that had she remained in the village, she would now have been dead, because she was the widow of the large landowner who had been his father and therefore deserved death in the eyes of the rowdies in power.

Old Mrs. Pan listened to this without reply, but her eyes, looking very large in her small withered face, were haunted with homesickness.

"There are many things worse than

---

1. **Szechuen** (se′ chwän): A province of south central China.

---

death, especially at my age," she replied at last, when again her son reminded her of her good fortune in being where she was.

He became impassioned when she said this. He struck his breast with his clenched fists and he shouted, "Could I have forgiven myself if I had allowed you to die? Would the ghost of my father have given me rest?"

"I doubt his ghost would have traveled over such a wide sea," she replied. "That man was always afraid of the water."

Yet there was nothing that Mr. Pan and his wife did not try to do for his mother in order to make her happy. They prepared the food that she had once enjoyed, but she was now beyond the age of pleasure in food, and she had no appetite. She touched one dish and another with the ends of her ivory chopsticks, which she had brought with her from her home, and she thanked them prettily. "It is all good," she said, "but the water is not the same as our village water; it tastes of metal and not of earth, and so the flavor is not the same. Please allow the children to eat it."

She was afraid of the children. They went to an American school and they spoke English very well and Chinese very badly, and since she could speak no English, it distressed her to hear her own language maltreated by their careless tongues. For a time she tried to coax them to a few lessons, or she told them stories, to which they were too busy to listen. Instead they preferred to look

---

### Presentation

**Motivation/Prior Knowledge** Ask students to imagine that they have just been offered the opportunity to live for a year in another country. Let volunteers discuss which country they would choose. Then ask them what difficulties they might face in adjusting to another country. Tell them that the protagonist of this story faces such difficulties.

**Thematic Idea** Another selection that deals with new Americans and the immigration experience is "Of Dry Goods and Black Bow Ties," page 447.

**Master Teacher Note** Old Mrs. Pan upholds the values of traditional Chinese culture, while many of the younger people have adapted these values to American life. You might want to have students note this contrast as they read. Also, ask students to consider the particular aspect or aspects of Chinese culture that each character chooses to retain. Have them speculate about why the character made such a choice.

**Purpose-Setting Question** What kinds of problems does Mrs. Pan encounter in adjusting to American life?

1 **Literary Focus** This story is told from the omniscient, or all-knowing, point of view. How is this point of view reflected in the opening paragraph?

2 **Critical Thinking and Reading** What does the writer suggest about Mrs. Pan in this paragraph?

3 **Discussion** What does Mrs. Pan's retort reveal about her character?

4 **Discussion** Why is Mrs. Pan afraid of her grandchildren?

5 **Discussion** Why does Sophia not hear the noise?

6 **Discussion** What do you think Mr. Pan meant when he said that the children were not taught as he was in China? Why is this difficult for Mrs. Pan to accept?

7 **Critical Thinking and Reading** Why is being of no use the most difficult thing for Mrs. Pan?

at the moving pictures in the box that stood on a table in the living room. She gave them up finally and merely watched them contemplatively when they were in the same room with her and was glad when they were gone. She liked her son's wife. She did not understand how there could be a Chinese woman who had never been in China, but such her son's wife was. When her son was away, she could not say to her daughter-in-law, "Do you remember how the willows grew over the gate?" For her son's wife had no such memories. She had grown up here in the city and she did not even hear its noise. At the same time, though she was so foreign, she was very kind to the old lady, and she spoke to her always in a gentle voice, however she might shout at the children, who were often disobedient.

The disobedience of the children was another grief to old Mrs. Pan. She did not understand how it was that four children could all be disobedient, for this meant that they had never been taught to obey their parents and revere their elders, which are the first lessons a child should learn.

"How is it," she once asked her son, "that the children do not know how to obey?"

Mr. Pan had laughed, though uncomfortably. "Here in America the children are not taught as we were in China," he explained.

"But my grandchildren are Chinese nevertheless," old Mrs. Pan said in some astonishment.

"They are always with Americans," Mr. Pan explained. "It is very difficult to teach them."

Old Mrs. Pan did not understand, for Chinese and Americans are different beings, one on the west side of the sea and one on the east, and the sea is always between. Therefore, why should they not continue to live apart even in the same city? She felt in her heart that the children should be kept at home and taught those things which must be learned, but she said nothing. She felt lonely and there was no one who understood the things she felt and she was quite useless. That was the most difficult thing: She was of no use here. She could not even remember which spout the hot water came from and which brought the cold. Sometimes she turned on one and then the other, until her son's wife came in briskly and said, "Let me, Mother."

So she gave up and sat uselessly all day, not by the window, because the machines and the many people frightened her. She sat where she could not see out; she looked at a few books, and day by day she grew thinner and thinner until Mr. Pan was concerned beyond endurance.

One day he said to his wife, "Sophia, we must do something for my mother. There is no use in saving her from death in our village if she dies here in the city. Do you see how thin her hands are?"

"I have seen," his good young wife said. "But what can we do?"

"Is there no woman you know who can speak Chinese with her?" Mr. Pan asked. "She needs to have someone to whom she can talk about the village and all the things she knows. She cannot talk to you because you can only speak English, and I am too busy making our living to sit and listen to her."

Young Mrs. Pan considered. "I have a friend," she said at last, "a schoolmate whose family compelled her to speak Chinese. Now she is a social worker here in the city. She visits families in Chinatown and this is her work. I will call her up and ask her to spend some time here so that our old mother can be happy enough to eat again."

"Do so," Mr. Pan said.

That very morning, when Mr. Pan was

## Grammar in Action

Like many professional writers, Pearl S. Buck uses a number of different sentences structures to add variety to her work. Among these are **compound-complex sentences.** A compound-complex sentence is made up of two or more independent clauses and one or more dependent clauses. Look at this sentence from the selection:

At the same time, though she was so foreign, she was always very kind to the old lady, and she spoke to her always in a gentle voice, however she might shout at the children, who were often disobedient.

This sentence contains three independent clauses: *she was very kind to the old lady, she spoke to her always in a gentle voice,* and *she might shout at the children.* The two dependent, or subordinate, clauses are *though she was so foreign* and *who were often disobedient.*

Look at this sentence from "The Good Deed." How many independent clauses does it contain? How many dependent clauses?

Lili Yang promised, and within a few days she came to the apartment and young Mrs. Pan led her into the inner room, which was old Mrs. Pan's room and where she always sat, gone, young Mrs. Pan made the call and found her friend, Lili Yang, and she explained everything to her.

"We are really in very much trouble," she said finally. "His mother is thinner every day, and she is so afraid she will die here. She has made us promise that we will not bury her in foreign soil but will send her coffin back to the ancestral village. We have promised, but can we keep this promise, Lili? Yet I am so afraid, because I think she will die, and Billy will think he must keep his promise and he will try to take the coffin back and then he will be killed. Please help us, Lili."

Lili Yang promised and within a few days she came to the apartment and young Mrs. Pan led her into the inner room, which was old Mrs. Pan's room and where she always sat, wrapped in her satin coat and holding a magazine at whose pictures she did not care to look. She took up that magazine when her daughter-in-law came in, because she did not want to hurt her feelings, but the pictures frightened her. The women looked bold and evil, and sometimes they wore only a little silk stuff over their legs and this shocked her. She wondered that her son's wife would put such a magazine into her hands, but she did not ask questions. There would have **8** been no end to them had she once begun, and the ways of foreigners did not interest her. Most of the time she sat silent and still, her head sunk on her breast, dreaming of the village, the big house there where she and her husband had lived together with his parents and where their children were born. She knew that the village had fallen into the hands of their enemies and that strangers lived in the house, but she hoped even so that the land was tilled. All that she remembered was the way it had been when she was a young woman and before the evil had come to pass.

She heard now her daughter-in-law's voice, "Mother, this is a friend. She is Miss Lili Yang. She has come to see you."

Old Mrs. Pan remembered her manners. She tried to rise but Lili took her hands and begged her to keep seated.

"You must not rise to one so much younger," she exclaimed. **9**

Old Mrs. Pan lifted her head. "You speak such good Chinese!"

"I was taught by my parents," Lili said. She sat down on a chair near the old lady.

Mrs. Pan leaned forward and put her hand on Lili's knee. "Have you been in our own country? she asked eagerly.

Lili shook her head. "That is my sorrow. I have not and I want to know about it. I have come here to listen to you tell me."

"Excuse me," young Mrs. Pan said, "I must prepare the dinner for the family."

She slipped away so that the two could be alone and old Mrs. Pan looked after her sadly. "She never wishes to hear; she is always busy."

"You must remember in this country we have no servants," Lili reminded her gently.

"Yes," old Mrs. Pan said, "and why not? I have told my son it is not fitting to have my daughter-in-law cooking and washing in the kitchen. We should have at least three servants: one for me, one for the children and one to clean and cook. At home we had many more but here we have only a few rooms."

Lili did not try to explain. "Everything is different here and let us not talk about it," she said. "Let us talk about your home and the village. I want to know how it looks and what goes on there." **10**

Old Mrs. Pan was delighted. She smoothed the gray satin of her coat as it lay on her knees and she began.

"You must know that our village lies in a wide valley from which the mountains rise as sharply as tiger's teeth."

*The Good Deed* 123

**8** **Discussion** What does her lack of interest in foreigners tell you about her character?

**9** **Master Teacher Note** You might point out that dialogue is very important in this story because characters discuss cultural differences.

**10** **Discussion** Why do you think Lili tells Mrs. Pan that she does not want to talk about America? Why is this pleasing to Mrs. Pan?

wrapped in her satin coat and holding a magazine at whose pictures she did not care to look.

The sentence contains three independent clauses: *Lili Yang promised, within a few days she came to the apartment,* and *Mrs. Pan led her into the inner room.* It also contains the following three dependent clauses: *which was old Mrs. Pang's room, where she always sat,* and, *at whose pictures she did not care to look.*

**Student Activity 1.** Find three more compound-complex sentences in the story. Identify the independent and dependent clauses in each sentence.

**Student Activity 2.** Write a short essay about a good deed you've performed. Use at least two compound-complex sentences in your essay.

11 **Critical Thinking and Reading** What does this description reveal about Mrs. Pan and her life in China? How does it help you to understand her character?

12 **Discussion** Why is Mrs. Pan shocked when she finds out that Lili is twenty-seven and still referred to as "Miss"?

13 **Reading Strategy** Have students give three examples so far of Mrs. Pan's dissatisfaction with customs in this country.

"Is it so?" Lili said, making a voice of wonder.

"It is, and the village is not a small one. On the contrary, the walls encircle more than one thousand souls, all of whom are relatives of our family."

"A large family," Lili said.

"It is," old Mrs. Pan said, "and my son's father was the head of it. We lived in a house with seventy rooms. It was in the midst of the village. We had gardens in the courtyards. My own garden contained also a pool wherein are aged goldfish, very fat. I fed them millet and they knew me."

"How amusing." Lili saw with pleasure that the old lady's cheeks were faintly pink and that her large beautiful eyes were beginning to shine and glow. "And how many years did you live there, Ancient One?"

"I went there as a bride. I was seventeen." She looked at Lili, questioning, "How old are you?"

Lili smiled, somewhat ashamed, "I am twenty-seven."

Mrs. Pan was shocked. "Twenty-seven? But my son's wife called you Miss."

"I am not married," Lili confessed.

Mrs. Pan was instantly concerned. "How is this?" she asked. "Are your parents dead?"

"They are dead," Lili said, "but it is not their fault that I am not married."

Old Mrs. Pan would not agree to this. She shook her head with decision. "It is the duty of the parents to arrange the marriage of the children. When death approached, they should have attended to this for you. Now who is left to perform the task? Have you brothers?"

"No," Lili said, "I am an only child. But please don't worry yourself, Madame Pan. I am earning my own living and there are many young women like me in this country."

Old Mrs. Pan was dignified about this. "I

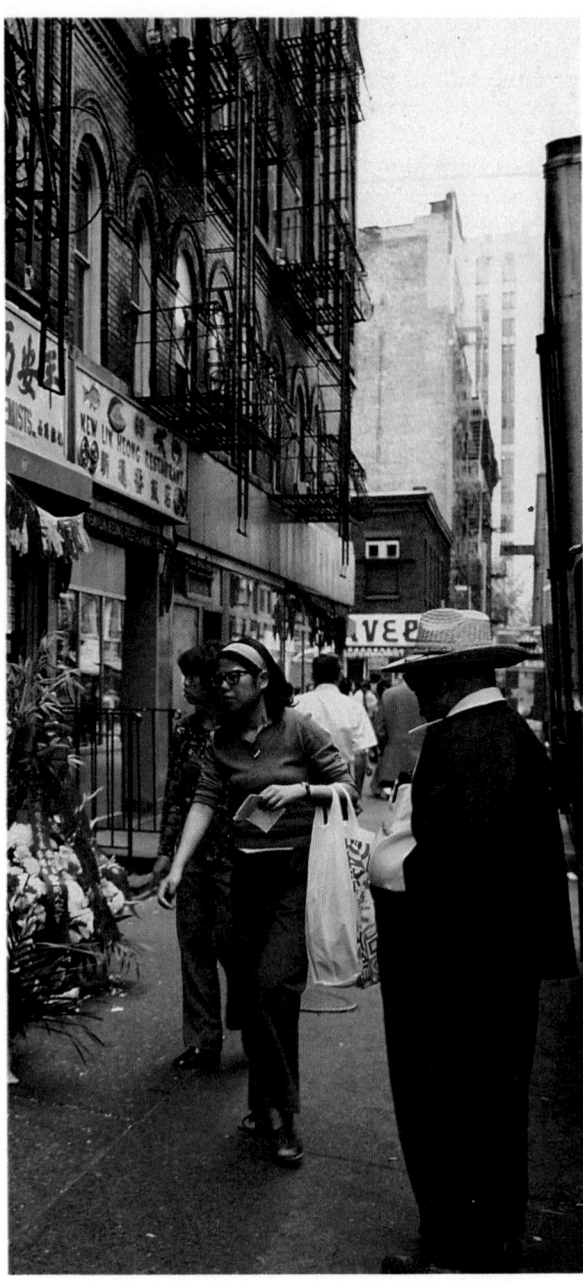

cannot be responsible for what other persons do, but I must be responsible for my own kind," she declared. "Allow me to know the names of the suitable persons who can arrange your marriage. I will stand in the place of your mother. We are all in a foreign country now and we must keep together and the old must help the young in these important matters."

Lili was kind and she knew that Mrs. Pan meant kindness. "Dear Madame Pan," she said. "Marriage in America is very different from marriage in China. Here the young people choose their own mates."

"Why do you not choose, then?" Mrs. Pan said with some spirit.

Lili Yang looked abashed. "Perhaps it would be better for me to say that only the young men choose. It is they who must ask the young women."

"What do the young women do?" Mrs. Pan inquired.

"They wait," Lili confessed.

"And if they are not asked?"

"They continue to wait," Lili said gently.

"How long?" Mrs. Pan demanded.

"As long as they live."

Old Mrs. Pan was profoundly shocked. "Do you tell me that there is no person who arranges such matters when it is necessary?"

"Such an arrangement is not thought of here," Lili told her.

"And they allow their women to remain unmarried?" Mrs. Pan exclaimed. "Are there also sons who do not marry?"

"Here men do not marry unless they wish to do so."

Mrs. Pan was even more shocked. "How can this be?" she asked. "Of course, men will not marry unless they are compelled to do so to provide grandchildren for the family. It is necessary to make laws and create customs so that a man who will not marry is de-

**14 Discussion** What are the benefits or disadvantages of an arranged marriage?

**15 Discussion** What does Lili mean? What does her reluctance to say this reveal about her?

**16 Discussion** Why does Mrs. Pan say this?

**17 Critical Thinking and Reading** Do you think this is an accurate prediction? Why or why not?

**18 Reading Strategy** How does Lili's visit help Mrs. Pan forget herself? Have students predict what Mrs. Pan has in mind for Lili.

nounced as an unfilial son and one who does not fulfill his duty to his ancestors."

15 "Here the ancestors are forgotten and parents are not important," Lili said unwillingly.

16 "What a country is this," Mrs. Pan exclaimed. "How can such a country endure?"

Lili did not reply. Old Mrs. Pan had unknowingly touched upon a wound in her heart. No man had ever asked her to marry him. Yet above all else she would like to be married and to have children. She was a good social worker, and the head of the Children's Bureau sometimes told her that he would not know what to do without her and she must never leave them, for then there would be no one to serve the people in Chinatown. She did not wish to leave except to be married, but how could she find a husband? She looked down at her hands, clasped in her lap, and thought that if she had been in her own country, if her father had not come here as a young man and married here, she would have been in China and by now the mother of many children. Instead what would become of her? She would grow older and older, and twenty-seven was already old, and at last hope must die. She knew several American girls quite well; they liked her, and she knew that they faced the same fate. They, too, were waiting. They tried very hard; they went in summer to hotels and in winter to ski lodges, where men gathered and were at leisure enough to think about them, and in confidence they told one another of their efforts. They compared their experiences and they asked anxious questions. "Do you think men like talkative women or quiet ones?" "Do you think men like lipstick or none?" Such questions they asked of one another and who could answer them? If a girl succeeded in winning a proposal from a man, then all the other girls envied her and asked her special questions and immediately she became someone above

them all, a successful woman. The job which had once been so valuable then became worthless and it was given away easily and gladly. But how could she explain this to old Mrs. Pan?

Meanwhile Mrs. Pan had been studying Lili's face carefully and with thought. This was not a pretty girl. Her face was too flat, and her mouth was large. She looked like a girl from Canton and not from Hangchow or Soochow.[2] But she had nice skin, and her eyes, though small, were kind. She was the sort of girl, Mrs. Pan could see, who would make an excellent wife and a good mother, but certainly she was one for whom a marriage must be arranged. She was a decent, plain, good girl and, left to herself, Mrs. Pan could predict, nothing at all would happen. She would wither away like a dying flower.

17

Old Mrs. Pan forgot herself and for the first time since she had been hurried away from the village without even being allowed to stop and see that the salted cabbage, drying on ropes across the big courtyard, was brought in for the winter. She had been compelled to leave it there and she had often thought of it with regret. She could have brought some with her had she known it was not to be had here. But there it was and it was only one thing among others that she had left undone. Many people depended upon her and she had left them, because her son compelled her, and she was not used to this idleness that was killing her day by day.

18

Now as she looked at Lili's kind, ugly face it occurred to her that here there was something she could do. She could find a husband for this good girl, and it would be counted for merit when she went to heaven. A good deed is a good deed, whether one is

---

**2. Canton** (kan tän´) **... Hangchow** (haŋ´ c/hou´) **... Soochow** (soo´ chou´): Cities in China: Canton is in the southeast, and Hangchow and Soochow are in the east.

in China or in America, for the same heaven stretches above all.

She patted Lili's clasped hands. "Do not grieve anymore," she said tenderly. "I will arrange everything."

"I am not grieving," Lili said.

"Of course, you are," Mrs. Pan retorted. "I see you are a true woman, and women grieve when they are not wed so that they can have children. You are grieving for your children."

Lili could not deny it. She would have been ashamed to confess to any other person except this old Chinese lady who might have been her grandmother. She bent her head and bit her lip; she let a tear or two fall upon her hands. Then she nodded. Yes, she grieved in the secret places of her heart, in the darkness of the lonely nights, when she thought of the empty future of her life.

"Do not grieve," old Mrs. Pan was saying, "I will arrange it; I will do it."

It was so comforting a murmur that Lili could not bear it. She said, "I came to comfort you, but it is you who comfort me." Then she got up and went out of the room quickly because she did not want to sob aloud. She was unseen, for young Mrs. Pan had gone to market and the children were at school, and Lili went away telling herself that it was all absurd, that an old woman from the middle of China who could not speak a word of English would not be able to change this American world, even for her.

Old Mrs. Pan could scarcely wait for her son to come home at noon. She declined to join the family at the table, saying that she must speak to her son first.

When he came in, he saw at once that she was changed. She held up her head and she spoke to him sharply when he came into the room, as though it was her house and not his in which they now were.

"Let the children eat first," she commanded, "I shall need time to talk with you and I am not hungry."

He repressed his inclination to tell her that he was hungry and that he must get back to the office. Something in her look made it impossible for him to be disobedient to her. He went away and gave the children direction and then returned.

"Yes, my mother," he said, seating himself on a small and uncomfortable chair.

Then she related to him with much detail and repetition what had happened that morning; she declared with indignation that she had never before heard of a country where no marriages were arranged for the young, leaving to them the most important event of their lives and that at a time when their judgment was still unripe, and a mistake could bring disaster upon the whole family.

"Your own marriage," she reminded him, "was arranged by your father with great care, our two families knowing each other well. Even though you and my daughter-in-law were distant in this country, yet we met her parents through a suitable go-between, and her uncle here stood in her father's place, and your father's friend in place of your father, and so it was all done according to custom though so far away."

Mr. Pan did not have the heart to tell his mother that he and his wife Sophia had fallen in love first, and then, out of kindness to their elders, had allowed the marriage to be arranged for them as though they were not in love, and as though, indeed, they did not know each other. They were both young people of heart, and although it would have been much easier to be married in the American fashion, they considered their elders.

"What has all this to do with us now, my mother?" he asked.

"This is what is to do," she replied with spirit. "A nice, ugly girl of our own people came here today to see me. She is twenty-

19 **Literary Focus** What does the omniscient narrator reveal about Lili's thoughts and feelings?

20 **Discussion** How does Mrs. Pan comfort Lili?

21 **Discussion** What does the fact that Mr. Pan and Sophia fell in love but then allowed their marriage to be arranged indicate about them and their attitude toward traditional Chinese culture?

seven years old and she is not married. What will become of her?"

"Do you mean Lili Yang?" her son asked.

"I do," she replied. "When I heard that she has no way of being married because, according to the custom of this country, she must wait for a man to ask her—"

Old Mrs. Pan broke off and gazed at her son with horrified eyes.

"What now?" he asked.

"Suppose the only man who asks is one who is not at all suitable?"

"It is quite possible that it often happens thus," her son said, trying not to laugh.

"Then she has no choice," old Mrs. Pan said indignantly. "She can only remain unmarried or accept one who is unsuitable."

"Here she has no choice," Mr. Pan agreed, "unless she is very pretty, my mother, when several men may ask and then she has choice." It was on the tip of his tongue to tell how at least six young men had proposed to his Sophia, thereby distressing him continually until he was finally chosen, but he thought better of it. Would it not be very hard to explain so much to his old mother, and could she understand? He doubted it. Nevertheless, he felt it necessary at least to make one point.

"Something must be said for the man also, my mother. Sometimes he asks a girl who will not have him, because she chooses another, and then his sufferings are intense. Unless he wishes to remain unmarried he must ask a second girl, who is not the first one. Here also is some injustice."

Old Mrs. Pan listened to this attentively and then declared, "It is all barbarous. Certainly it is very embarrassing to be compelled to speak of these matters, man and woman, face to face. They should be spared; others should speak for them."

She considered for a few seconds and then she said with fresh indignation, "And what woman can change the appearance her

ancestors have given her? Because she is not pretty is she less a woman? Are not her feelings like any woman's: is it not her right to have husband and home and children? It is well-known that men have no wisdom in such matters; they believe that a woman's face is all she has, forgetting that everything else is the same. They gather about the pretty woman, who is surfeited with them, and leave alone the good woman. And I do not know why heaven has created ugly women always good but so it is, whether here or in our own country, but what man is wise enough to know that? Therefore his wife should be chosen for him, so that the family is not burdened with his follies."

Mr. Pan allowed all this to be said and then he inquired, "What is on your mind, my mother?"

Old Mrs. Pan leaned toward him and lifted her forefinger. "This is what I command you to do for me, my son. I myself will find a husband for this good girl of our people. She is helpless and alone. But I know no one; I am a stranger, and I must depend upon you. In your business there must be young men. Inquire of them and see who stands for them, so that we can arrange a meeting between them and me; I will stand for the girl's mother. I promised it."

Now Mr. Pan laughed heartily. "Oh, my mother!" he cried. "You are too kind, but it cannot be done. They would laugh at me, and do you believe that Lili Yang herself would like such an arrangement? I think she would not. She has been an American too long."

Old Mrs. Pan would not yield, however, and in the end he was compelled to promise that he would see what he could do. Upon this promise she consented to eat her meal, and he led her out, her right hand resting upon his left wrist. The children were gone and they had a quiet meal together, and after it she said she felt that she would sleep.

## Grammar in Action

Using **adverbs** in your own writing will make it more vivid and exciting for your audience. Adverbs modify verbs, adjectives, or other adverbs. The italicized words in the sentences below are adverbs. The arrow points from the adverb to the word modified.

In the middle of his explanation, he coughed *loudly*.

It is *very* bad for women.

She spoke *quite* softly.

When a prepositional phrase (into the pool, on the antique hall table) functions as an adverb, it is an **adverb phrase.** The italicized items in these sentences from the story are adverb phrases. The arrows point to the words modified.

She considered this *for a few seconds* and then she said *with fresh indignation,* "And what woman can change the appearance her ancestors have given her?"

She got up and tidied her hair and tottered *on her small feet over to the window*.

**Student Activity 1.** Find at least five examples of sentences containing adverbs or adverb phrases in the selection. Copy these on your paper.

This was good news, for she had not slept well since she came, and young Mrs. Pan led her into the bedroom and helped her to lie down and placed a thin quilt over her.

When young Mrs. Pan went back to the small dining room where her husband waited to tell her what his mother had said, she listened thoughtfully.

"It is absurd," her husband said, "but what shall we do to satisfy my mother? She sees it as a good deed if she can find a husband for Lili Yang."

Here his wife surprised him. "I can see some good in it myself," she declared. "I have often felt for Lili. It is a problem, and our mother is right to see it as such. It is not only Lili—it is a problem here for all young women, especially if they are not pretty." She looked quizzically at her husband for a moment and then said, "I too used to worry when I was very young, lest I should not find a husband for myself. It is a great burden for a young woman. It would be nice to have someone else arrange the matter."

"Remember," he told her, "how often in the old country the wrong men are arranged for and how often the young men leave home because they do not like the wives their parents choose for them."

"Well, so do they here," she said pertly. "Divorce, divorce, divorce!"

"Come, come," he told her. "It is not so bad."

"It is very bad for women," she insisted. "When there is divorce here, then she is thrown out of the family. The ties are broken. But in the old country, it is the man who leaves home and the woman stays on, for she is still the daughter-in-law and her children will belong to the family, and however far away the man wants to go, she has her place and she is safe."

Mr. Pan looked at his watch. "It is late and I must go to the office."

"Oh, your office," young Mrs. Pan said in an uppish voice,[3] "what would you do without it?"

They did not know it but their voices roused old Mrs. Pan in the bedroom, and she opened her eyes. She could not understand what they said for they spoke in English, but she understood that there was an argument. She sat up on the bed to listen, then she heard the door slam and she knew her son was gone. She was about to lie down again when it occurred to her that it would be interesting to look out of the window to the street and see what young men there were coming to and fro. One did not choose men from the street, of course, but still she could see what their looks were.

She got up and tidied her hair and tottered on her small feet over to the window and opening the curtains a little she gazed into the street really for the first time since she came. She was pleased to see many Chinese men, some of them young. It was still not late, and they loitered in the sunshine before going back to work, talking and laughing and looking happy. It was interesting to her to watch them, keeping in mind Lili Yang and thinking to herself that it might be this one or that one, although still one did not choose men from the street. She stood so long that at last she became tired and she pulled a small chair to the window and kept looking through the parted curtain.

Here her daughter-in-law saw her a little later, when she opened the door to see if her mother-in-law was awake, but she did not speak. She looked at the little satin-clad figure, and went away again, wondering why it was that the old lady found it pleasant today to look out of the window when every other day she had refused the same pleasure.

It became a pastime for old Mrs. Pan to look out of the window every day from then

---

**3. in an uppish voice:** Scornfully.

25 **Literary Focus** Why do you think Mr. Pan is surprised by his wife's attitude?

26 **Reading Strategy** Have students predict what Mr. Pan and his wife will do.

27 **Discussion** Why is looking out of the window with interest an important change for Mrs. Pan?

**Student Activity 2.** Exchange papers with a classmate and discuss the sentences, pointing out the words modified by each adverb or adverb phrase.

28 **Discussion** How does her wish to have the window open indicate an important change in her?

29 **Discussion** Why is the thought of going downstairs and out into the street so terrifying to Mrs. Pan?

30 **Reading Strategy** Have students summarize some of the reasons Mrs. Pan has for calling this country "barbarous."

on. Gradually she came to know some of the young men, not by name but by their faces and by the way they walked by her window, never, of course looking up at her, until one day a certain young man did look up and smile. It was a warm day, and she had asked that the window be opened, which until now she had not allowed, for fear she might be assailed by the foreign winds and made ill. Today, however, was near to summer, she felt the room airless and she longed for freshness.

After this the young man habitually smiled when he passed or nodded his head. She was too old to have it mean anything but courtesy and so bit by bit she allowed herself to make a gesture of her hand in return. It was evident that he belonged in a china shop across the narrow street. She watched him go in and come out; she watched him stand at the door in his shirt sleeves on a fine day and talk and laugh, showing, as she observed, strong white teeth set off by two gold ones. Evidently he made money. She did not believe he was married, for she saw an old man who must be his father, who smoked a water pipe,[4] and now and then an elderly woman, perhaps his mother, and a younger brother, but there was no young woman.

She began after some weeks of watching to fix upon this young man as a husband for Lili. But who could be the go-between except her own son?

She confided her plans one night to him, and, as always, he listened to her with courtesy and concealed amusement. "But the young man, my mother, is the son of Mr. Lim, who is the richest man on our street."

"That is nothing against him," she declared.

"No, but he will not submit to an ar-

---

**4. water pipe:** A pipe with a long tube passing through an urn of water.

rangement, my mother. He is a college graduate. He is only spending the summer at home in the shop to help his father."

"Lili Yang has also been to school."

"I know, my mother, but, you see, the young man will want to choose his own wife, and it will not be someone who looks like Lili Yang. It will be someone who—"

He broke off and made a gesture which suggested curled hair, a fine figure and an air. Mrs. Pan watched him with disgust. "You are like all these other men, though you are my son," she said and dismissed him sternly.

Nevertheless, she thought over what he had said when she went back to the window. The young man was standing on the street picking his fine teeth and laughing at friends who passed, the sun shining on his glistening black hair. It was true he did not look at all obedient; it was perhaps true that he was no more wise than other men and so saw only what a girl's face was. She wished that she could speak to him, but that, of course, was impossible. Unless—

She drew in a long breath. Unless she went downstairs and out into that street and crossed it and entered the shop, pretending that she came to buy something! If she did this, she could speak to him. But what would she say, and who would help her cross the street? She did not want to tell her son or her son's wife, for they would suspect her and laugh. They teased her often even now about her purpose, and Lili was so embarrassed by their laughter that she did not want to come anymore.

Old Mrs. Pan reflected on the difficulty of her position as a lady in a barbarous and strange country. Then she thought of her eldest grandson, Johnnie. On Saturday, when her son was at his office and her son's wife was at the market, she would coax Johnnie to lead her across the street to the china shop; she would pay him some money, and in the shop she would say he was looking for two bowls to match some that had been broken. It would be an expedition, but she might speak to the young man and tell him—what should she tell him? That must first be planned.

This was only Thursday and she had only two days to prepare. She was very restless during those two days, and she could not eat. Mr. Pan spoke of a doctor whom she indignantly refused to see, because he was a man and also because she was not ill. But Saturday came at last and everything came about as she planned. Her son went away, and then her son's wife, and she crept downstairs with much effort to the sidewalk where her grandson was playing marbles and beckoned him to her. The child was terrified to see her there and came at once, and she pressed a coin into his palm and pointed across the street with her cane.

"Lead me there," she commanded and, shutting her eyes tightly, she put her hand on his shoulder and allowed him to lead her to the shop. Then to her dismay he left her and ran back to play and she stood wavering on the threshold, feeling dizzy, and the young man saw her and came hurrying toward her. To her joy he spoke good Chinese, and the words fell sweetly upon her old ears.

"Ancient One, Ancient One," he chided her kindly. "Come in and sit down. It is too much for you."

He led her inside the cool, dark shop and she sat down on a bamboo chair.

"I came to look for two bowls," she said faintly.

"Tell me the pattern and I will get them for you," he said. "Are they blue willow pattern or the thousand flowers?"

"Thousand flowers," she said in the same faint voice, "but I do not wish to disturb you."

"I am here to be disturbed," he replied with the utmost courtesy.

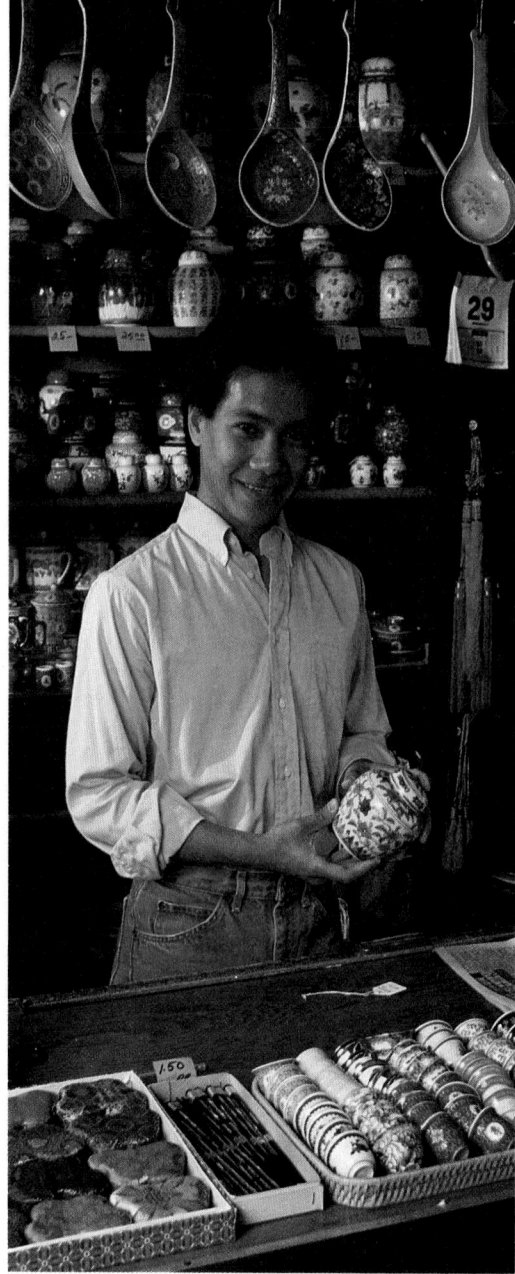

*The Good Deed    131*

31 **Discussion** Why do you think Mrs. Pan's grandson is terrified?

32 **Discussion** Why does Mrs. Pan shut her eyes?

33 **Discussion** How do you think Mrs. Pan feels about talking to this man? Why?

34 **Discussion** What do you think Mrs. Pan means when she says, "What is beautiful to one is not so to another"?

He brought out some bowls and set them on a small table before her and she fell to talking with him. He was very pleasant; his rather large face was shining with kindness and he laughed easily. Now that she saw him close, she was glad to notice that he was not too handsome; his nose and mouth were big, and he had big hands and feet.

"You look like a countryman," she said. "Where is your ancestral home?"

"It is in the province of Shantung,"[5] he replied, "and there are not many of us here."

"That explains why you are so tall," she said. "These people from Canton are small. We of Szechuen are also big and our language is yours. I cannot understand the people of Canton."

From this they fell to talking of their own country, which he had never seen, and she told him about the village and how her son's father had left it many years ago to do business here in this foreign country and how he had sent for their son and then how she had been compelled to flee because the country was in fragments and torn between many leaders. When she had told this much, she found herself telling him how difficult it was to live here and how strange the city was to her and how she would never have looked out of the window had it not been for the sake of Lili Yang.

"Who is Lili Yang?" he asked.

Old Mrs. Pan did not answer him directly. That would not have been suitable. One does not speak of a reputable young woman to any man, not even one as good as this one. Instead she began a long speech about the virtues of young women who were not pretty, and how beauty in a woman made virtue unlikely, and how a woman not beautiful was always grateful to her husband

---

5. **Shantung** (shan′ tuŋ′): A province of northeastern China.

and did not consider that she had done him a favor by the marriage, but rather that it was he who conferred the favor, so that she served him far better than she could have done were she beautiful.

To all this the young man listened, his small eyes twinkling with laughter.

"I take it that this Lili Yang is not beautiful," he said.

Old Mrs. Pan looked astonished. "I did not say so," she replied with spirit. "I will not say she is beautiful and I will not say she is ugly. What is beautiful to one is not so to another. Suppose you see her sometime for yourself, and then we will discuss it."

"Discuss what?" he demanded.

"Whether she is beautiful."

Suddenly she felt that she had come to a point and that she had better go home. It was enough for the first visit. She chose two bowls and paid for them and while he wrapped them up she waited in silence, for to say too much is worse than to say too little.

When the bowls were wrapped, the young man said courteously. "Let me lead you across the street, Ancient One."

So, putting her right hand on his left wrist, she let him lead her across and this time she did not shut her eyes, and she came home again feeling that she had been a long way and had accomplished much. When her daughter-in-law came home she said quite easily, "I went across the street and bought these two bowls."

Young Mrs. Pan opened her eyes wide. "My mother, how could you go alone?"

"I did not go alone," old Mrs. Pan said tranquilly. "My grandson led me across and young Mr. Lim brought me back."

Each had spoken in her own language with helpful gestures.

Young Mrs. Pan was astonished and she said no more until her husband came home, when she told him. He laughed a great deal and said, "Do not interfere with our old one. She is enjoying herself. It is good for her."

But all the time he knew what his mother was doing and he joined in it without her knowledge. That is to say, he telephoned the same afternoon from his office to Miss Lili Yang, and when she answered, he said, "Please come and see my old mother again. She asks after you every day. Your visit did her much good."

Lili Yang promised, not for today but for a week hence, and when Mr. Pan went home he told his mother carelessly, as though it were nothing, that Lili Yang had called him up to say she was coming again next week.

Old Mrs. Pan heard this with secret excitement. She had not gone out again, but every day young Mr. Lim nodded to her and smiled, and once he sent her a small gift of fresh ginger root. She made up her mind slowly but she made it up well. When Lili Yang came again, she would ask her to take her to the china shop, pretending that she wanted to buy something, and she would introduce the two to each other; that much she would do. It was too much, but, after all, these were modern times, and this was a barbarous country, where it did not matter greatly whether the old customs were kept or not. The important thing was to find a husband for Lili, who was already twenty-seven years old.

So it all came about, and when Lili walked into her room the next week, while the fine weather still held, old Mrs. Pan greeted her with smiles. She seized Lili's small hand and noticed that the hand was very soft and pretty, as the hands of most plain-faced girls are, the gods being kind to such women and giving them pretty bodies when they see that ancestors have not bestowed pretty faces.

"Do not take off your foreign hat," she told Lili. "I wish to go across the street to that shop and buy some dishes as a gift for my son's wife. She is very kind to me."

Lili Yang was pleased to see the old lady so changed and cheerful and in all innocence she agreed and they went across the street and into the shop. Today there were customers, and old Mr. Lim was there too, as well as his son. He was a tall, withered man, and he wore a small beard under his chin. When he saw old Mrs. Pan he stopped what he was doing and brought her a chair to sit upon while she waited. As soon as his customer was gone, he introduced himself, saying that he knew her son.

"My son has told me of your honored visit last week," he said. "Please come inside and have some tea. I will have my son bring the dishes, and you can look at them in quiet. It is too noisy here."

She accepted his courtesy, and in a few minutes young Mr. Lim came back to the inner room with the dishes while a servant brought tea.

Old Mrs. Pan did not introduce Lili Yang, for it was not well to embarrass a woman, but young Mr. Lim boldly introduced himself, in English.

"Are you Miss Lili Yang?" he asked. "I am James Lim."

"How did you know my name?" Lili asked, astonished.

"I have met you before, not face to face, but through Mrs. Pan," he said, his small eyes twinkling. "She has told me more about you than she knows."

Lili blushed. "Mrs. Pan is so old-fashioned," she murmured. "You must not believe her."

"I shall only believe what I see for myself," he said gallantly. He looked at her frankly and Lili kept blushing. Old Mrs. Pan had not done her justice, he thought. The young woman had a nice, round face, the

35 **Discussion** What is his reason for assisting his mother with her plan?

36 **Discussion** What is ironic about this passage?

37 **Discussion** Why does Lili blush?

38 **Discussion** Why do you think Mrs. Pan is so cautious when talking about marriage?

39 **Clarification** It was customary in Chinese culture for the woman not to be too talkative but rather to encourage a man to talk about himself.

sort of face he liked. She was shy, and he liked that also. It was something new.

Meanwhile old Mrs. Pan watched all this with amazement. So this was the way it was: The young man began speaking immediately, and the young woman blushed. She wished that she knew what they were saying but perhaps it was better that she did not know.

She turned to old Mr. Lim, who was sitting across the square table sipping tea. At least here she could do her duty. "I hear your son is not married," she said in a tentative way.

"Not yet," Mr. Lim said. "He wants first to finish learning how to be a Western doctor."

"How old is he?" Mrs. Pan inquired.

"He is twenty-eight. It is very old but he did not make up his mind for some years, and the learning is long."

"Miss Lili Yang is twenty-seven," Mrs. Pan said in the same tentative voice.

The young people were still talking in English and not listening to them. Lili was telling James Lim about her work and about old Mrs. Pan. She was not blushing anymore; she had forgotten, it seemed, that he was a young man and she a young woman. Suddenly she stopped and blushed again. A woman was supposed to let a man talk about himself, not about her.

"Tell me about your work," she said. "I wanted to be a doctor, too, but it cost too much."

"I can't tell you here," he said. "There are customers waiting in the shop and it will take a long time. Let me come to see you, may I? I could come on Sunday when the shop is closed. Or we could take a ride on one of the riverboats. Will you? The weather is so fine."

"I have never been on a riverboat," she said. "It would be delightful."

She forgot her work and remembered that he was a young man and that she was a young woman. She liked his big face and the way his black hair fell back from his forehead and she knew that a day on the river could be a day in heaven.

The customers were getting impatient. They began to call out and he got up. "Next Sunday," he said in a low voice. "Let's start early. I'll be at the wharf at nine o'clock."

"We do not know each other," she said, reluctant and yet eager. Would he think she was too eager?

He laughed. "You see my respectable father, and I know old Mrs. Pan very well. Let them guarantee us."

He hurried away, and old Mrs. Pan said immediately to Lili, "I have chosen these four dishes. Please take them and have them wrapped. Then we will go home."

Lili obeyed, and when she was gone, old Mrs. Pan leaned toward old Mr. Lim.

"I wanted to get her out of the way," she said in a low and important voice. "Now, while she is gone, what do you say? Shall we arrange a match? We do not need a go-between. I stand as her mother, let us say, and you are his father. We must have their horoscopes read, of course, but just between us, it looks as though it is suitable, does it not?"

Mr. Lim wagged his head, "If you recommend her, Honorable Old Lady, why not?"

Why not, indeed? After all, things were not so different here, after all.

"What day is convenient for you?" she asked.

"Shall we say Sunday?" old Mr. Lim suggested.

"Why not?" she replied. "All days are good, when one performs a good deed, and what is better than to arrange a marriage?"

"Nothing is better," old Mr. Lim agreed. "Of all good deeds under heaven, it is the best."

They fell silent, both pleased with themselves, while they waited.

*The Good Deed* 135

**40 Discussion** Why does Mrs. Pan think that things are suitable between Lili and James?

**41 Reading Strategy** Have students summarize what good deeds performed by others helped to bring about this good deed.

**Reader's Response** Would you like to have your marriage arranged by someone else? Why or why not?

**Closure and Extension**

**ANSWERS TO THINKING ABOUT THE SELECTION**
*Recalling*

1. Mrs. Pan's son brought her to New York because she would be in danger if she continued to live in her village in China. She had a hard time adapting to customs in the United States.

2. Lili Yang visits because Mr. Pan and Sophia asked her to come and speak with their mother, who needs someone to speak with about China.
3. Mrs. Pan wants to arrange a marriage for Lili because Lili is 27 and still unmarried. Also, her parents, who would normally be responsible for arranging a marriage, are dead.
4. She achieves happiness for herself and Lili.

### Interpreting

5. Suggested Response: She tells him this because she is thinking about how unhappy she is in a new and bewildering environment.
6. Suggested Response: Old Mrs. Pan's attitudes toward marriage and other matters are different from those of her family. The story also points up the human need for love and acceptance that underlies cultural attitudes.
7. Suggested Response: Any day is suitable for performing a good deed.

### Applying

8. Answers will differ. Students may respond that the best solution is a combination of the old and new, reflecting the best qualities of each.

**Challenge** What do you think old Mrs. Pan's grandchildren thought of her?

## ANSWERS TO ANALYZING LITERATURE

1. Suggested Response: This passage is told from Lili's perspective.
2. Suggested Response: This passage is told from Mrs. Pan's perspective.

## ANSWERS TO CRITICAL THINKING AND READING

1. Suggested Response: Mrs. Pan needs to be active to have a sense of worth in her life. She is also feeling sorry for herself and resisting accepting a different lifestyle.
2. Suggested Response: Lili is very sensitive and very sad.

## THINKING ABOUT THE SELECTION
### Recalling

1. Why did old Mrs. Pan come to New York? Why is she dissatisfied with life in New York?
2. Why does Lili Yang visit old Mrs. Pan?
3. Explain why old Mrs. Pan wants to arrange a marriage for Lili. What is her reaction to the fact that marriages are not generally arranged in the United States?
4. What does old Mrs. Pan achieve both for herself and for Lili?

### Interpreting

5. Why does old Mrs. Pan tell her son, "There are many things worse than death, especially at my age"? Of what things might she be thinking?
6. In what way does this story reveal a clash of cultures? In what way does it also point out the similarities between cultures?
7. Explain old Mrs. Pan's statement near the end of the story: "All days are good, when one performs a good deed."

### Applying

8. Do you think it important for people to hold on to the old as well as accept the new? Use details from life to support your answer.

## ANALYZING LITERATURE
### Appreciating Omniscient Narration

In **omniscient narration,** the narrator can reveal anything a character knows, thinks, and feels and can tell parts of the story from different perspectives. The narrator in "The Good Deed" can tell what both Mrs. Pan and Lili are feeling at the same moment. Reread the following paragraphs to decide from whose perspective each is told.

1. Paragraph 4, column 1, page 126, beginning, "Lili did not reply."
2. Paragraph 3, column 2, page 129, beginning, "She got up and tidied her hair . . ."

## CRITICAL THINKING AND READING
### Making Inferences About Characters

Omniscient narrators tell what characters think and feel. You can use this information to make **inferences** about the characters. For example, when old Mrs. Pan thinks, "it would be interesting to look out of the window to the street and see what young men there were coming to and fro," you can infer that she is beginning to take an interest in the world around her.

Make at least one inference about a character based on each of these statements.

1. "That was the most difficult thing: She [old Mrs. Pan] was of no use here" (page 122).
2. "It was so comforting a murmur that Lili could not bear it" (page 127).

## UNDERSTANDING LANGUAGE
### Using a Pronunciation Key

You can find out how to pronounce a word from a dictionary. First look at the respelling following the entry word. Then check the pronunciation key to see how each letter and symbol in the respelling is pronounced. Use the pronunciation key in the Glossary to pronounce the Chinese place names in the footnotes. Then answer these questions: For example, the respelling of *Canton* in the footnote on page 126 is (kan tän′). The pronunciation key in the Glossary shows that the *a* (a) is pronounced like the *a* in *fat* and the *o* (ä) is pronounced like the *a* in *car*.

1. Is the *oo* in *Soochow* pronounced like the *oo* in *fool* or the *oo* in *foot*?
2. Is the *ow* in *Hangchow* pronounced like the *ew* in *drew* or the *ou* in *cloud*?

## THINKING AND WRITING
### Reacting to a Story

Pick one character from "The Good Deed." Write him or her a letter telling how the story made you feel. When you revise the letter, try to find concrete images and examples to help your reader understand your thoughts.

## ANSWERS TO UNDERSTANDING LANGUAGE

1. The *oo* is pronounced like the *oo* in *fool.*
2. The *ow* is pronounced like the *ou* in *cloud.*

## THINKING AND WRITING

For help with this assignment, students may refer to Lesson 12, "Writing About a Short Story," in the Handbook of Writing About Literature.

### Publishing Student Writing

Have students divide into groups according to the character to whom they wrote a letter. Have students in each group compile notes from all the letters into one composite letter to be read aloud to the rest of the class.

### Writing Across the Curriculum

You might have students research and report on some aspect of Chinese culture. Consider informing the social studies department of this assignment, so that teachers can provide guidance.

# Setting

**SUMMERTIME**
*Mary Cassatt*
Three Lions

## Humanities Note

Fine Art, *Summertime*, Mary Cassatt. Mary Cassatt (1844-1926), was an American Impressionist. She met with strong opposition from her prominent Philadelphia family when she expressed a desire to go abroad to study painting. Undeterred, she established herself in Paris and began to paint. Her work attracted the attention of Edgar Degas, the famous French Impressionist painter. At his invitation she joined the Parisian circle of Impressionists. Her work with them won her acclaim throughout Europe.

Marry Cassatt is well known for paintings of her favorite subject, women and children. *Summertime* is this subject at its sentimental best. Filled with the essence of summer, this sunny canvas is pleasant and cheerful. The masterly composition and harmonious colors celebrate the setting and the simple pleasures of rowing on a pond and feeding ducks.

## Focus

**More About the Author** Edgar Allan Poe is considered one of the originators of both the modern short story itself and the detective story. Ask students why they think the short story has been such a successful literary form in the modern world.

**Literary Focus** You might have students suggest possible settings for a horror story. Have them specify the most suitable place, time, and historical era.

**Look For** Have students consider how the setting affects the mood of the story.

**Writing/Prior Knowledge** You might divide the class into small groups and have them discuss the question before they begin writing.

**Vocabulary** Have less advanced students learn the words before they begin reading. Ask more advanced students to look up the etymologies of the words.

**Spelling Tip** Students may find the spelling of the word *niche* easier to remember if they think of a word that almost rhymes with it, *quiche*. Both words are of French origin.

## The Cask of Amontillado

**Edgar Allan Poe** (1809–1849) was born in Boston to a family of traveling actors. After losing both parents before he was three, Poe was raised by John Allan of Richmond, Virginia. He attended the University of Virginia and the United States Military Academy at West Point. Despite his recognized talent for writing, he was unable to succeed in his jobs or his personal life. Poe is perhaps best known for his horror stories, which have the eerie atmosphere of nightmares. "The Cask of Amontillado" is one of these stories.

**Setting**

**Setting** is the place and time of a story's action. The setting of "The Cask of Amontillado," for example, is Italy sometime during an earlier century. Some stories contain detailed descriptions of the setting if the setting is important to the story. Poe tells you the specific house in which the action occurs, the season, the time of day, and the exact time span the plot covers. More important, by giving very specific details, he creates a mood that is appropriate for the action.

**Look For**

Part of the inspiration for "The Cask of Amontillado" came from the catacombs in Paris. These extensive underground vaults and chambers served as the burial grounds for the early Christians. As you will see, the setting of "The Cask of Amontillado" is an important part of the story. As you read the story, pay attention to the descriptions of the setting. What effect is created by these chambers of darkness? What specific details increase the horror?

**Writing**

The desire for revenge motivates the main character. Crimes of revenge are often in the news. Why is revenge such a powerful motivator? Brainstorm with your classmates and write possible reasons.

**Vocabulary**

Knowing the following words will help you as you read "The Cask of Amontillado."

**precluded** (pri klōōd′ id) *v.*: Made impossible in advance (p. 139)
**impunity** (im pyōō′ nə tē) *n.*: Freedom from punishment (p. 139)
**unredressed** (un ri drest′) *adj.*: Not set right (p. 139)
**retribution** (ret′ rə byōō′ s/hən)

*n.*: Deserved punishment (p. 139)
**catacombs** (kat′ ə kōmz′) *n.*: Vaults or passages in an underground burial place (p. 140)
**niche** (nich) *n.*: A recess in a wall (p. 143)
**fettered** (fet′ ərd) *v.*: Encircled with metal fasteners (p. 143)

### Objectives

1 To understand setting
2 To analyze the effect of setting
3 To create a setting

### Support Material

**Teaching Portfolio**
Teacher Backup, p. 163
Grammar in Action Worksheet, *Using Action Verbs*, p. 167
Usage and Mechanics Worksheet, p. 169
Vocabulary Check, p. 170
Critical Thinking and Reading Worksheet, *Analyzing the Effect of Setting*, p. 171

Language Worksheet, *Using Word Roots*, p. 172
Selection Test, p. 173
**Library of Video Classics**: The Cask of Amontillado and the Necklace

# The Cask of Amontillado[1]

### Edgar Allan Poe

The thousand injuries of Fortunato I had borne as I best could, but when he ventured upon insult I vowed revenge. You, who so well know the nature of my soul, will not suppose, however, that I gave utterance to a threat. *At length* I would be avenged; this was a point definitely settled—but the very definitiveness with which it was resolved precluded the idea of risk. I must not only punish but punish with impunity. A wrong is unredressed when retribution overtakes its redresser. It is equally unredressed when the avenger fails to make himself felt as such to him who has done the wrong.

It must be understood that neither by word nor deed had I given Fortunato cause to doubt my good will. I continued, as was my wont, to smile in his face, and he did not perceive that my smile *now* was at the thought of his immolation.[2]

He had a weak point—this Fortunato—although in other regards he was a man to be respected and even feared. He prided himself on his connoisseurship[3] in wine. Few Italians have the true virtuoso spirit.[4] For the most part their enthusiasm is adopted to suit the time and opportunity, to practice imposture[5] upon the British and Austrian millionaires. In painting and gemmary,[6] Fortunato, like his countrymen, was a quack, but in the matter of old wines he was sincere. In this respect I did not differ from him materially; I was skillful in the Italian vintages myself, and bought largely whenever I could.

It was about dusk, one evening during the supreme madness of the carnival season,[7] that I encountered my friend. He accosted me with excessive warmth, for he had been drinking much. The man wore motley.[8] He had on a tight-fitting parti-striped dress, and his head was surmounted by the conical cap and bells. I was so pleased to see him that I thought I should never have done wringing his hand.

I said to him, "My dear Fortunato, you are luckily met. How remarkably well you are looking today. But I have received a pipe[9] of what passes for Amontillado, and I have my doubts."

"How?" said he. "Amontillado? A pipe? Impossible! And in the middle of the carnival!"

"I have my doubts," I replied; "and I was

---

**1. Amontillado** (ə män′ tə lä′ dō) *n.*: A pale, dry sherry.
**2. immolation** (im′ ə lā shən) *n.*: Sacrifice.
**3. connoisseurship** (kän′ ə sur′ ship) *n.*: Expert judgment.
**4. virtuoso** (vʉr′ choo wō′ sō) **spirit:** Knowledge of the arts.
**5. practice imposture** (im päs′ chər): Deceive.
**6. gemmary** (jem′ ə rē′) *n.*: Knowledge of precious stones.
**7. carnival season:** A time of celebration before Lent.
**8. motley** (mät′ lē) *n.*: A clown's multicolored costume.
**9. pipe** (pīp) *n.*: A large barrel.

*The Cask of Amontillado* 139

## Presentation

**Motivation/Prior Knowledge** Ask students what qualities make a person a good actor. Then tell them that the narrator of this story uses his acting ability to gain revenge.

**Thematic Idea** Other selections in which revenge is an important motivation are *Romeo and Juliet,* page 321, and the *Odyssey,* page 681.

**Purpose-Setting Question** Do you think that the narrator is sane?

**1 Discussion** What kind of insult could have motivated thoughts of revenge?

**2 Discussion** What does the narrator's pretense at good will reveal about his character?

**3 Discussion** What do you think Fortunato's name means? What might be ironic about this meaning?

**4 Discussion** Why does the narrator use a cask of wine to lure Fortunato?

5 **Critical Thinking and Reading**
Why do you think the narrator praises Fortunato's expertise as a wine-taster?

6 **Discussion** If the narrator really wants to revenge himself on Fortunato, why is he so nice to him at this point?

7 **Discussion** Do you think it is an accident that the servants happen to be away at this time? Explain.

silly enough to pay the full Amontillado price without consulting you in the matter. You were not to be found, and I was fearful of losing a bargain."

"Amontillado!"

"I have my doubts."

"Amontillado!"

"And I must satisfy them."

"Amontillado!"

"As you are engaged, I am on my way to Luchresi. If any one has a critical turn it is he. He will tell me——"

"Luchresi cannot tell Amontillado from sherry."

"And yet some fools will have it that his taste is a match for your own."

"Come, let us go."

"Whither?"

"To your vaults."

"My friend, no; I will not impose upon your good nature. I perceive you have an engagement. Luchresi——"

"I have no engagement—come."

"My friend, no. It is not the engagement, but the severe cold with which I perceive you are afflicted. The vaults are insufferably damp. They are encrusted with niter."[10]

"Let us go, nevertheless. The cold is merely nothing. Amontillado! You have been imposed upon. And as for Luchresi, he cannot distinguish sherry from Amontillado."

Thus speaking, Fortunato possessed himself of my arm; and putting on a mask of black silk and drawing a *roquelaure*[11] closely about my person, I suffered him to hurry me to my palazzo.[12]

There were no attendants at home; they had absconded to make merry in honor of the time. I had told them that I should not return until the morning, and had given them explicit orders not to stir from the house. These orders were sufficient, I well knew, to insure their immediate disappearance, one and all, as soon as my back was turned.

I took from their sconces two flambeaux,[13] and giving one to Fortunato, bowed him through several suites of rooms to the archway that led into the vaults. I passed down a long and winding staircase, requesting him to be cautious as he followed. We came at length to the foot of the descent, and stood together upon the damp ground of the catacombs of the Montresors.

The gait of my friend was unsteady, and

---

13. **flambeaux** (flam' bōz) *n.*: Lighted torches.

---

10. **niter** (nīt' ər) *n.*: White or gray mineral.
11. **roquelaure** (räk' ə lôr') *n.*: Knee-length cloak.
12. **palazzo** (pä lät' sö) *n.*: Palace.

the bells upon his cap jingled as he strode.

"The pipe," he said.

"It is farther on," said I; "but observe the white webwork which gleams from these cavern walls."

He turned towards me, and looked into my eyes with two filmy orbs that distilled the rheum of intoxication.

"Niter?" he asked, at length.

"Niter," I replied. "How long have you had that cough?"

"Ugh! ugh! ugh!—ugh! ugh! ugh!—ugh! ugh! ugh!—ugh! ugh! ugh!—ugh! ugh! ugh!"

My poor friend found it impossible to reply for many minutes.

"It is nothing," he said, at last.

"Come," I said, with decision, "we will go back; your health is precious. You are rich, respected, admired, beloved; you are happy, as once I was. You are a man to be missed. For me it is no matter. We will go back; you will be ill, and I cannot be responsible. Besides, there is Luchresi——"

"Enough," he said; "the cough is a mere nothing; it will not kill me. I shall not die of a cough."

"True—true," I replied; "and, indeed, I had no intention of alarming you unnecessarily—but you should use all proper caution. A draft of this Medoc will defend us from the damps."

Here I knocked off the neck of a bottle which I drew from a long row of its fellows that lay upon the mold.

"Drink," I said, presenting him the wine.

He raised it to his lips with a leer. He paused and nodded to me familiarly, while his bells jingled.

"I drink," he said, "to the buried that repose around us."

"And I to your long life."

He again took my arm, and we proceeded.

*The Cask of Amontillado* 141

8 **Discussion** Why do you think the narrator continually throws the name of Luchresi at Fortunato? How does this affect Fortunato?

9 **Master Teacher Note** Point out to students the irony of Fortunato's statement, "I shall not die of a cough," and the narrator's reply, "True—true." Have students look for other similar examples of irony.

**Critical Thinking and Reading**
How are the Montresor coat of arms and its motto significant to the story?

**11 Discussion** Why does Fortunato lean "heavily" on Montresor's arm? Why is this a significant detail?

**12 Literary Focus** Why is the description of the setting in the crypt so important to the plot? What mood does the description evoke?

"These vaults," he said, "are extensive."

"The Montresors," I replied, "were a great and numerous family."

"I forget your arms."[14]

"A huge human foot d'or, in a field azure; the foot crushes a serpent rampant whose fangs are imbedded in the heel."[15]

"And the motto?"

"*Nemo me impune lacessit.*"[16]

"Good!" he said.

The wine sparkled in his eyes and the bells jingled. My own fancy grew warm with the Medoc. We had passed through long walls of piled skeletons, with casks and puncheons[17] intermingling, into the inmost recesses of the catacombs. I paused again, and this time I made bold to seize Fortunato by an arm above the elbow.

"The niter!" I said; "see, it increases. It hangs like moss upon the vaults. We are below the river's bed. The drops of moisture trickle among the bones. Come, we will go back ere it is too late. Your cough——"

"It is nothing," he said; "let us go on. But first, another draft of the Medoc."

I broke and reached him a flagon of De Grâve. He emptied it at a breath. His eyes flashed with a fierce light. He laughed and threw the bottle upwards with a gesticulation I did not understand.

I looked at him in surprise. He repeated the movement—a grotesque one.

"You do not comprehend?" he said.

"Not I," I replied.

"Then you are not of the brotherhood."

"How?"

"You are not of the masons."[18]

"Yes, yes," I said; "yes, yes."

"You? Impossible! A mason?"

"A mason," I replied.

"A sign," he said, "a sign."

"It is this," I answered, producing from beneath the folds of my *roquelaure* a trowel.

"You jest," he exclaimed, recoiling a few paces. "But let us proceed to the Amontillado."

"Be it so," I said, replacing the tool beneath the cloak and again offering him my arm. He leaned upon it heavily. We continued our route in search of the Amontillado. We passed through a range of low arches, descended, passed on, and descending again, arrived at a deep crypt, in which the foulness of the air caused our flambeaux rather to glow than flame.

At the most remote end of the crypt there appeared another less spacious. Its walls had been lined with human remains, piled to the vault overhead, in the fashion of the great catacombs of Paris. Three sides of this interior crypt were still ornamented in this manner. From the fourth side the bones had been thrown down, and lay promiscuously upon the earth, forming at one point a mound of some size. Within the wall thus exposed by the displacing of the bones, we perceived a still interior crypt or recess, in depth about four feet, in width three, in height six or seven. It seemed to have been constructed for no especial use within itself, but formed merely the interval between two of the colossal supports of the roof of the catacombs, and was backed by one of their circumscribing walls of solid granite.

It was in vain that Fortunato, uplifting his dull torch, endeavored to pry into the

---

**14. arms:** Coat of arms, a design and motto used by a family.
**15. A huge . . . in the heel:** A large golden foot crushing a snake, shown against a blue background.
**16. *Nemo me impune lacessit:*** Latin for "No one attacks me with impunity."
**17. puncheons** (pun′ chənz) *n.:* Large barrels.

---

**18. masons:** The Freemasons, an international secret society.

## Grammar in Action

There are two main kinds of verbs: action verbs and linking verbs. An **action verb** is a verb that tells what action someone or something is performing. The action may be mental as well as physical:

The kites *soared* in the March wind. (physical action)
Dad *remembered* newspaper kites. (mental action)

Careful use of action verbs can make writing seem lively. The following sentences show how Edgar Allan Poe uses action verbs:

I *broke* and *reached* him a flagon of De Grâve. He *emptied* it at a breath. His eyes *flashed* with a fierce light. He *laughed* and *threw* the bottle upwards with a gesticulation I did not *understand*.

The action verbs, appearing one right after another, add power-depth of the recess. Its termination the feeble light did not enable us to see.

"Proceed," I said; "herein is the Amontillado. As for Luchresi——"

"He is an ignoramus," interrupted my friend, as he stepped unsteadily forward, while I followed immediately at his heels. In an instant he had reached the extremity of the niche, and finding his progress arrested by the rock, stood stupidly bewildered. A moment more and I had fettered him to the granite. In its surface were two iron staples, distant from each other about two feet, horizontally. From one of these depended a short chain, from the other a padlock. Throwing the links about his waist, it was but the work of a few seconds to secure it. He was too much astounded to resist. Withdrawing the key I stepped back from the recess.

"Pass your hand," I said, "over the wall; you cannot help feeling the niter. Indeed, it is *very* damp. Once more let me *implore* you to return. No? Then I must positively leave you. But I must first render you all the little attentions in my power."

13

"The Amontillado!" ejaculated my friend, not yet recovered from his astonishment.

"True," I replied; "the Amontillado."

**13 Discussion** In what tone of voice does the narrator make this comment? Explain.

*The Cask of Amontillado* 143

fully to the sense of menace and horror. Note, too, that almost all of the actions described by these verbs are physical.

**Student Activity 1.** Indicate which of the following verbs are action verbs:

1. We *continued*, our route in search of the Amontillado.
2. We *passed* through a range of low arches, *descended*, *passed* on, and descending again, *arrived* at a deep crypt. . . .

3. At the most remote end of the crypt there *appeared* another less spacious.
4. we *perceived* a still interior crypt or recess. . . .

**Student Activity 2.** Using vivid action verbs, write four sentences about revenge.

14 **Discussion** Does the narrator discover these building materials by accident? Why or why not?

15 **Discussion** Why does Montresor begin to yell?

16 **Discussion** What else might be making the narrator ill?

**Reader's Response** What did you think was most horrifying about this story? Why?

14  As I said these words I busied myself among the pile of bones of which I have before spoken. Throwing them aside, I soon uncovered a quantity of building stone and mortar. With these materials and with the aid of my trowel, I began vigorously to wall up the entrance of the niche.

I had scarcely laid the first tier of the masonry when I discovered that the intoxication of Fortunato had in a great measure worn off. The earliest indication I had of this was a low moaning cry from the depth of the recess. It was *not* the cry of a drunken man. There was then a long and obstinate silence. I laid the second tier, and the third, and the fourth; and then I heard the furious vibrations of the chain. The noise lasted for several minutes, during which, that I might hearken to it with the more satisfaction, I ceased my labors and sat down upon the bones. When at last the clanking subsided, I resumed the trowel, and finished without interruption the fifth, the sixth, and the seventh tier. The wall was now nearly upon a level with my breast. I again paused, and holding the flambeaux over the masonwork, threw a few feeble rays upon the figure within.

A succession of loud and shrill screams, bursting suddenly from the throat of the chained form, seemed to thrust me violently back. For a brief moment I hesitated, I trembled. Unsheathing my rapier,[19] I began to grope with it about the recess; but the thought of an instant reassured me. I placed my hand upon the solid fabric of the catacombs, and felt satisfied. I reapproached the wall; I replied to the yells of him who clamored. I reechoed, I aided, I surpassed them in volume and in strength. I did this, and the clamorer grew still.

15

---

19. **rapier** (rā′ pē ər) *n*.: A slender, two-edged sword.

It was now midnight, and my task was drawing to a close. I had completed the eighth, the ninth, and the tenth tier. I had finished a portion of the last and the eleventh; there remained but a single stone to be fitted and plastered in. I struggled with its weight; I placed it partially in its destined position. But now there came from out the niche a low laugh that erected the hairs upon my head. It was succeeded by a sad voice, which I had difficulty in recognizing as that of the noble Fortunato. The voice said—

"Ha! ha! ha!—he! he! he!—a very good joke, indeed—an excellent jest. We will have many a rich laugh about it at the palazzo—he! he! he!—over our wine—he! he! he!"

"The Amontillado!" I said.

"He! he! he!—he! he! he!—yes, the Amontillado. But is it not getting late? Will not they be awaiting us at the palazzo, the Lady Fortunato and the rest? Let us be gone."

"Yes," I said, "let us be gone."

*"For the love of God, Montresor!"*

"Yes," I said, "for the love of God!"

But to these words I hearkened in vain for a reply. I grew impatient. I called aloud—

"Fortunato!"

No answer. I called again—

"Fortunato!"

No answer still. I thrust a torch through the remaining aperture and let it fall within. There came forth in return only a jingling of the bells. My heart grew sick; it was the dampness of the catacombs that made it so. I hastened to make an end of my labor. I forced the last stone into its position; I plastered it up. Against the new masonry I reerected the old rampart of bones. For the half of a century no mortal has disturbed them. *In pace requiescat!*[20]

16

---

20. *In pace requiescat!*: Latin for "May he rest in peace!"

**Closure and Extension**

**ANSWERS TO THINKING ABOUT THE SELECTION**
*Recalling*

1. Montresor flatters Fortunato by asking his help in identifying a fine wine, and he tempts him with the prospect of sampling it.

## THINKING ABOUT THE SELECTION

### Recalling

1. Explain how Montresor persuades Fortunato to come to his house.
2. Find three hints that Montresor gives to Fortunato of what he intends to do. How does Montresor interpret each hint?
3. What happens to Fortunato at the end of the story?

### Interpreting

4. The nature of the insult Fortunato offered Montresor is never clear. Do you think it really happened or occurred only in Montresor's mind? Explain your answer. How does not knowing make the horror even greater?
5. Explain how the Montresors' family motto and coat of arms are appropriate.
6. What character traits make Fortunato such an easy prey for Montresor?
7. Why does Montresor keep urging Fortunato to turn back?
8. How long ago did the crime Montresor relates occur? What does this fact tell you about the effect of the crime on Montresor?

### Applying

9. Suppose you were a police detective in Italy when this story took place and you suspected that Montresor had killed Fortunato. How might you get proof of the crime?

## ANALYZING LITERATURE

### Understanding Setting

The **setting** of a story is the place and the time of the action. Often a setting, such as that in "The Cask of Amontillado," is central to the story, as important as the characters and events.

1. Describe the setting at the beginning of the story, when Montresor meets Fortunato.
2. Where does Montresor take Fortunato? Describe this setting, contrasting it with the first.

## CRITICAL THINKING AND READING

### Analyzing the Effect of Setting

In "The Cask of Amontillado" Poe has created every detail of setting to contribute to his intended effect. When you examine the details carefully, you can see how each detail fits with his plan.

1. Give two reasons why the carnival setting is appropriate for Montresor's plan and therefore for the plot.
2. Suppose that Montresor's wine cellar were not in the catacombs. How would the plot change?
3. Could the story have taken place during the day? Why or why not?
4. What details of the setting contribute to the horror of the story?

## THINKING AND WRITING

### Creating a Setting

You are planning to write a horror story in the style of Edgar Allan Poe. You want to set the scene so that your reader gets a physical sense of it. Since it is dark, you cannot use visual details; you must use only details of hearing and touch. Brainstorm for ideas. Then write a paragraph describing your setting. Revise it, adding words that suggest sounds and feelings.

*The Cask of Amontillado* 145

### ANSWERS TO ANALYZING LITERATURE

1. Suggested Response: They are in the street at dusk during carnival time.
2. Montresor takes Fortunato to the crypt under his house. It is dark, damp, dreary, and oppressive. This setting contrasts with the revelry, excitement, and "madness" of the carnival.

**Challenge** What challenges and opportunities would a director face in adapting this story for the screen?

### ANSWERS TO CRITICAL THINKING AND READING

1. Suggested Response: At the carnival, he can pretend to meet Fortunato casually. Also, he can count on the fact that Fortunato will be drunk and distracted.
2. Suggested Response: If Montresor's wine cellar had not been in the catacombs, he would have had to lure Fortunato by some other means, or he would have had to devise some other method of disposing of him.
3. Answers will differ. Most students will realize that the daytime is less suited to the mood of the story. Also, night provides a cover for Montresor's plan.
4. Suggested Response: The crypt, which is a tomb, and the presence of bones contribute to the horror.

### THINKING AND WRITING

For help with this assignment, students can refer to Lesson 7, "Writing About Setting," in the Handbook of Writing About Literature.

**Publishing Student Writing**
You might ask volunteers to share their paragraphs with the class.

**Writing Across the Curriculum**
You might have students illustrate their writing assignments. If you do, consider informing the art department so that art teachers can provide assistance and materials.

2. He points out the niter which is used as a preservative. He tells Fortunato that he is a man to be missed. He shows Fortunato a trowel when asked if he is a mason. Montresor fails to understand these hints.
3. Fortunato is chained and then walled up in the vaults.

### Interpreting

4. Answers will differ. Students may respond that Montresor is so strange that he might have imagined the insult. The possibility that there was no insult makes the "punishment," and Montresor's careful planning of it, even more horrible.
5. Suggested Response: The coat of arms and motto are appropriate because they reflect the same spirit of unforgiving revenge that Montresor displays.
6. Suggested Response: He is an easy prey because he is vain and somewhat foolish.

7. Suggested Response: Montresor's urging Fortunato to turn back is reverse psychology. The more he encourages him to turn back, the more it makes Fortunato want to go on.
8. Suggested Response: Fifty years have passed since the crime occurred. He still feels the effect of the horror that he experienced.
9. Answers will differ. Students might respond that they would interview Montresor extensively, hoping that he would make a slip.

## Focus

**More About the Author** Roald Dahl is married to the American actress Patricia McNeil. Ask students to compare and contrast the art of writing with the art of acting.

**Literary Focus** You may want to review with students the history of World War II. Pay special attention to the role that Britain played in the war.

**Look For** Tell students that they may have to read between the lines to spot some of these clues.

**Writing/Prior Knowledge** You might have students discuss real or imagined situations before they begin writing.

**Vocabulary** Have your **more advanced** students write a synonym and an antonym for each word that is listed.

## Beware of the Dog

**Roald Dahl** (1916–     ) was born and raised in Wales. During World War II, he served as a fighter pilot in the British Royal Air Force and was shot down over the Libyan Desert. As a result, he spent sixteen weeks in a German hospital. Many of Dahl's short stories are based in part on his wartime experiences. One of his best, "Beware of the Dog," is notable also for the manner in which Dahl relates the suspense-filled events in a matter-of-fact tone.

**Historical Setting**

A story that takes place in the past may have a **historical setting;** that is, its time and place are those of a significant event in history. "Beware of the Dog" has a historical setting; it takes place in Europe during World War II. To understand "Beware of the Dog," you must know that at the time the story takes place England is at war with Germany and German forces occupy France. English fighter planes fly bombing missions over France, hoping to destroy German bases. This is a story in which the events depend on this setting.

**Look For**

The main character in "Beware of the Dog" is a fighter pilot who has to bail out over the English Channel. As you read the story, find the details that give the pilot clues about where he has landed.

**Writing**

How do you think people generally react in situations where they suspect that information is being withheld from them? Do they panic? Do they think clearly? Freewrite, exploring your answers to these questions.

**Vocabulary**

Knowing the following words will help you as you read "Beware of the Dog."

**undulating** (un' joo lat iŋ) *adj.:* Moving in waves (p. 147)
**delirious** (di lir' ē əs) *adj.* In a state of temporary mental confusion, characterized by delu-

sions and incoherence (p. 152)
**obsession** (əb sesh' ən) *n.:* Compulsive preoccupation with an idea (p. 153)

## Objectives

1  To appreciate the use of a historical setting
2  To make inferences
3  To compare British and American terms
4  To evaluate a story

## Support Material

**Teaching Portfolio**
Teacher Backup, p. 175
Grammar in Action Worksheets, *Writing Suspense*, p. 179; *Using Prepositional Phrases*, p. 181
Usage and Mechanics Worksheet, p. 183
Vocabulary Check, p. 184
Analyzing Literature Worksheet, *Appreciating Historical Setting*, p. 185

Critical Thinking and Reading Worksheet, *Making Inferences*, p. 186
Selection Test, p. 187

# Beware of the Dog

## Roald Dahl

Down below there was only a vast white undulating sea of cloud. Above there was the sun, and the sun was white like the clouds, because it is never yellow when one looks at it from high in the air.

He was still flying the Spitfire.[1] His right hand was on the stick and he was working the rudder-bar with his left leg alone. It was quite easy. The machine was flying well. He knew what he was doing.

Everything is fine, he thought. I'm doing all right. I'm doing nicely. I know my way home. I'll be there in half an hour. When I land I shall taxi in and switch off my engine and I shall say, help me to get out, will you.

1. **Spitfire:** A fighter plane used by the British during World War II.

3 **Master Teacher Note** You may want to tell students that the writer uses the limited third-person point of view in telling this story. In other words, the writer narrates events from the perspective of a particular character and refers to that character as "he."

4 **Critical Thinking and Reading** How do you think the pilot was shot?

## Great Britain and Europe World War II

IRELAND

GREAT BRITAIN

NORTH SEA

DENMARK

NETHERLANDS

GERMANY

Brighton

STRAIT OF DOVER

ENGLISH CHANNEL

BELGIUM

LUX.

NORTH ATLANTIC OCEAN

FRANCE

SWITZERLAND

AUSTRIA

0        100 Miles
0        100 Kilometers

☐ Neutral country
☐ Greatest extent of German control during WW II

I shall make my voice sound ordinary and natural and none of them will take any notice. Then I shall say, someone help me to get out. I can't do it alone because I've lost one of my legs. They'll all laugh and think that I'm joking.

3  He glanced down again at his right leg. There was not much of it left. The cannon-shell had taken him on the thigh, just above the knee, and now there was nothing but a great mess and a lot of blood. But there was no pain. When he looked down, he felt as though he were seeing something that did not belong to him. It had nothing to do with

him. It was just a mess which happened to be there in the cockpit; something strange and unusual and rather interesting. It was like finding a dead cat on the sofa.

He really felt fine, and because he still felt fine, he felt excited and unafraid.

I won't even bother to call up on the radio for the blood-wagon, he thought. It isn't necessary. And when I land I'll sit there quite normally and say, some of you fellows come and help me out, will you, because I've lost one of my legs. That will be funny. I'll laugh a little while I'm saying it; I'll say it calmly and slowly, and they'll think I'm joking. When Yorky comes up onto the wing, I'll say, Yorky have you fixed my car yet. Then when I get out I'll make my report.

Then he saw the sun shining on the engine cowling[2] of his machine. He saw the sun shining on the rivets in the metal, and he remembered the airplane and he remembered where he was. He realized that he was no longer feeling good; that he was sick and giddy. His head kept falling forward onto his chest because his neck seemed no longer to have any strength. But he knew that he was flying the Spitfire. He could feel the handle of the stick[3] between the fingers of his right hand.

I'm going to pass out, he thought. Any moment now I'm going to pass out.

He looked at his altimeter.[4] Twenty-one thousand. To test himself he tried to read the hundreds as well as the thousands. Twenty-one thousand and what? As he looked the dial became blurred and he could

not even see the needle. He knew then that he must bail out; that there was not a second to lose, otherwise he would become unconscious. Quickly, frantically, he tried to slide back the hood with his left hand, but he had not the strength. For a second he took his right hand off the stick and with both hands he managed to push the hood back. The rush of cold air on his face seemed to help. He had a moment of great clearness. His actions became orderly and precise. That is what happens with a good pilot. He took some quick deep breaths from his oxygen mask, and as he did so, he looked out over the side of the cockpit. Down below there was only a vast white sea of cloud and he realized that he did not know where he was.

It'll be the Channel,[5] he thought. I'm sure to fall in the drink.

He throttled back, pulled off his helmet, undid his straps, and pushed the stick hard over to the left. The Spitfire dripped its port wing and turned smoothly over onto its back. The pilot fell out.

As he fell, he opened his eyes, because he knew that he must not pass out before he had pulled the cord. On one side he saw the sun; on the other he saw the whiteness of the clouds, and as he fell, as he somersaulted in the air, the white clouds chased the sun and the sun chased the clouds. They chased each other in a small circle; they ran faster and faster and there was the sun and the clouds and the clouds and the sun, and the clouds came nearer until suddenly there was no longer any sun but only a great whiteness. The whole world was white and

---

**2. cowling** (kou′ liŋ) *n.*: A detachable metal cover for an airplane engine.
**3. the stick:** Short for "control stick," which controls the vertical and horizontal flight of an airplane.
**4. altimeter** (al tim′ ə tər) *n.*: An instrument for measuring the height of the aircraft above the surface of the earth or the sea.

---

**5. the Channel:** The English Channel, a body of water separating Britain from France; during much of World War II, the Germans occupied France, and British and German airplanes fought over the Channel.

5 **Discussion** Why do you think he still feels fine?

6 **Discussion** What is happening to the pilot?

*Beware of the Dog* 149

8 **Discussion** Why does the writer not explain how the pilot got to this room?

9 **Discussion** What do you think happened?

10 **Discussion** Where do you think the pilot is?

11 **Discussion** Why do you think the nurse downplays his injury?

7 there was nothing in it. It was so white that sometimes it looked black, and after a time it was either white or black, but mostly it was white. He watched it as it turned from white to black, then back to white again, and the white stayed for a long time, but the black lasted only for a few seconds. He got into the habit of going to sleep during the white periods, of waking up just in time to see the world when it was black. The black was very quick. Sometimes it was only a flash, a flash of black lightning. The white was slow and in the slowness of it, he always dozed off.

8 One day, when it was white, he put out a hand and he touched something. He took it between his fingers and crumpled it. For a time he lay there, idly letting the tips of his fingers play with the thing which they had touched. Then slowly he opened his eyes, looked down at his hand and saw that he was holding something which was white. It was the edge of a sheet. He knew it was a sheet because he could see the texture of the material and the stitchings on the hem. He screwed up his eyes and opened them again quickly. This time he saw the room. He saw the bed in which he was lying; he saw the gray walls and the door and the green curtains over the window. There were some roses on the table by his bed.

Then he saw the basin on the table near the roses. It was a white enamel basin and beside it there was a small medicine glass.

9 This is a hospital, he thought. I am in a hospital. But he could remember nothing. He lay back on his pillow, looking at the ceiling and wondering what had happened. He was gazing at the smooth grayness of the ceiling which was so clean and gray, and then suddenly he saw a fly walking upon it. The sight of this fly, the suddenness of seeing this small black speck on a sea of gray, brushed the surface of his brain, and

quickly, in that second, he remembered everything. He remembered the Spitfire and he remembered the altimeter showing twenty-one thousand feet. He remembered the pushing back of the hood with both hands and he remembered the bailing out. He remembered his leg.

It seemed all right now. He looked down at the end of the bed, but he could not tell. He put one hand underneath the bedclothes and felt for his knees. He found one of them, but when he felt for the other, his hand touched something which was soft and covered in bandages.

Just then the door opened and a nurse came in.

"Hello," she said. "So you've waked up at last."

She was not good-looking, but she was large and clean. She was between thirty and forty and she had fair hair. More than that he did not notice.

"Where am I?"

10 "You're a lucky fellow. You landed in a wood near the beach. You're in Brighton.[6] They brought you in two days ago, and now you're all fixed up. You look fine."

"I've lost a leg," he said.

11 "That's nothing. We'll get you another one. Now you must go to sleep. The doctor will be coming to see you in about an hour." She picked up the basin and the medicine glass and went out.

But he did not sleep. He wanted to keep his eyes open because he was frightened that if he shut them again everything would go away. He lay looking at the ceiling. The fly was still there. It was very energetic. It would run forward very fast for a few inches, then it would stop. Then it would run forward

--------

6. **Brighton** (brīt′ 'n): A city in southern England, on the English Channel.

150   *Short Stories*

## Grammar in Action

**Suspense** is that quality in a work of literature that makes us read on to see what will happen next. Writers create suspense with details that arouse curiousity in the reader, who then reads on to find out what will happen next. For example, early in this story we learn that the main character is still flying his plane although his leg has been shot away. As he imagines what will happen when he returns to England from his bombing run, he thinks:

. . . Then I shall say, someone help me to get out. I can't do it alone because I've lost one of my legs.

We read on to see what will happen next, and we learn that the flier, realizing he is about to pass out, rolls his plane over so that he can fall out of it. Again, we read on to see what's going to happen.

The airman awakens in a hospital room; the nurse tells him he's in Brighton, England. However, he soon hears a sound that makes him wonder:

Suddenly he jerked his head sharply to one side. Anyone who has been bombed can tell the noise of a Junkers 88. They can tell most other German bombers for that matter . . .

again, stop, run forward, stop, and every now and then it would take off and buzz around viciously in small circles. It always landed back in the same place on the ceiling and started running and stopping all over again. He watched it for so long that after a while it was no longer a fly, but only a black speck upon a sea of gray, and he was still watching it when the nurse opened the door, and stood aside while the doctor came in. He was an Army doctor, a major, and he had some last war ribbons on his chest. He was bald and small, but he had a cheerful face and kind eyes.

"Well, well," he said. "So you've decided to wake up at last. How are you feeling?"

"I feel all right."

"That's the stuff. You'll be up and about in no time."

The doctor took his wrist to feel his pulse.

"By the way," he said, "some of the lads from your squadron were ringing up and asking about you. They wanted to come along and see you, but I said that they'd better wait a day or two. Told them you were all right and that they could come and see you a little later on. Just lie quiet and take it easy for a bit. Got something to read?" He glanced at the table with the roses. "No. Well, nurse will look after you. She'll get you anything you want." With that he waved his hand and went out, followed by the large clean nurse.

When they had gone, he lay back and looked at the ceiling again. The fly was still there and as he lay watching it he heard the noise of an airplane in the distance. He lay listening to the sound of its engines. It was a long way away. I wonder what it is, he thought. Let me see if I can place it. Suddenly he jerked his head sharply to one side. Anyone who has been bombed can tell the noise of a Junkers 88. They can tell most other German bombers for that matter, but especially a Junkers 88. The engines seem to sing a duet. There is a deep vibrating bass voice and with it there is a high pitched tenor. It is the singing of the tenor which makes the sound of a JU-88 something which one cannot mistake.

He lay listening to the noise and he felt quite certain about what it was. But where were the sirens and where the guns? That German pilot certainly had a nerve coming near Brighton alone in daylight.

The aircraft was always far away and soon the noise faded away into the distance. Later on there was another. This one, too, was far away, but there was the same deep undulating bass and the high singing tenor and there was no mistaking it. He had heard that noise every day during the Battle.[7]

He was puzzled. There was a bell on the table by the bed. He reached out his hand and rang it. He heard the noise of footsteps down the corridor. The nurse came in.

"Nurse, what were those airplanes?"

"I'm sure I don't know. I didn't hear them. Probably fighters or bombers. I expect they were returning from France. Why, what's the matter?"

"They were JU-88's. I'm sure they were JU-88's. I know the sound of the engines. There were two of them. What were they doing over here?"

The nurse came up to the side of his bed and began to straighten out the sheets and tuck them in under the mattress.

"Gracious me, what things you imagine. You mustn't worry about a thing like that.

---

**7. the Battle:** The Battle of Britain, a fight between the British and German air forces from August to October, 1940, for control of British airspace; the Germans lost this battle.

12 **Discussion** Why does the presence of the planes confuse and frighten the pilot?

13 **Discussion** Why does the nurse dismiss his concerns?

Suspense continues to build as the nurse assures him he is mistaken.

**Student Activity 1.** Find another suspense-filled passage and discuss it with a partner, explaining why you choose the passage you did.

**Student Activity 2.** With a small group of classmates, decide on a plot and setting for a suspense-filled story. Then brainstorm a list of details that might be used to create suspense in that story. Use items from the list to help you draft the first paragraph of the story.

14 **Critical Thinking and Reading**
Do you think the pilot is delirious or imagining things?

15 **Discussion** What is the significance of this memory?

Would you like me to get you something to read?"

"No, thank you."

She patted his pillow and brushed back the hair from his forehead with her hand.

"They never come over in daylight any longer. You know that. They were probably Lancasters[8] or Flying Fortresses."[9]

"Nurse."

"Yes."

"Could I have a cigarette?"

"Why certainly you can."

She went out and came back almost at once with a packet of Players and some matches. She handed one to him and when he had put it in his mouth, she struck a match and lit it.

"If you want me again," she said, "just ring the bell," and she went out.

Once toward evening he heard the noise of another aircraft. It was far away, but even so he knew that it was a single-engined machine. It was going fast; he could tell that. He could not place it. It wasn't a Spit, and it wasn't a Hurricane.[10] It did not sound like an American engine either. They make more noise. He did not know what it was, and it worried him greatly. Perhaps I am very ill, he thought. Perhaps I am imagining things. Perhaps I am a little delirious. I simply do not know what to think.

That evening the nurse came in with a basin of hot water and began to wash him.

"Well," she said, "I hope you don't still think that we're being bombed."

She had taken off his pajama top and was soaping his right arm with a flannel. He did not answer.

She rinsed the flannel in the water,

---

8. **Lancasters:** British bombers.
9. **Flying Fortresses:** American bombers.
10. **Hurricane:** A British fighter plane.

rubbed more soap on it, and began to wash his chest.

"You're looking fine this evening," she said. "They operated on you as soon as you came in. They did a marvelous job. You'll be all right. I've got a brother in the R.A.F.,"[11] she added. "Flying bombers."

He said, "I went to school in Brighton."

She looked up quickly. "Well, that's fine," she said. "I expect you'll know some people in the town."

"Yes," he said, "I know quite a few."

She had finished washing his chest and arms. Now she turned back the bedclothes so that his left leg was uncovered. She did it in such a way that his bandaged stump remained under the sheets. She undid the cord of his pajama trousers and took them off. There was no trouble because they had cut off the right trouser leg so that it could not interfere with the bandages. She began to wash his left leg and the rest of his body. This was the first time he had had a bed-bath and he was embarrassed. She laid a towel under his leg and began washing his foot with the flannel. She said, "This wretched soap won't lather at all. It's the water. It's as hard as nails."

He said, "None of the soap is very good now and, of course, with hard water it's hopeless." As he said it he remembered something. He remembered the baths which he used to take at school in Brighton, in the long stone-floored bathroom which had four baths in a room. He remembered how the water was so soft that you had to take a shower afterwards to get all the soap off your body, and he remembered how the foam used to float on the surface of the water, so that you could not see your legs underneath. He remembered that sometimes they were

---

11. **R.A.F.:** The Royal Air Force of Great Britain.

given calcium tablets because the school doctor used to say that soft water was bad for the teeth.

"In Brighton," he said, "the water isn't . . ."

He did not finish the sentence. Something had occurred to him; something so fantastic and absurd that for a moment he felt like telling the nurse about it and having a good laugh.

She looked up. "The water isn't what?" she said.

"Nothing," he answered. "I was dreaming."

She rinsed the flannel in the basin, wiped the soap off his leg and dried him with a towel.

"It's nice to be washed," he said. "I feel better." He was feeling his face with his hand. "I need a shave."

"We'll do that tomorrow," she said. "Perhaps you can do it yourself then."

That night he could not sleep. He lay awake thinking of the Junkers 88's and of the hardness of the water. He could think of nothing else. They *were* JU-88's, he said to himself. I know they were. And yet it is not possible, because they would not be flying around so low over here in broad daylight. I know that it is true and yet I know that it is impossible. Perhaps I am ill. Perhaps I am behaving like a fool and do not know what I am doing or saying. Perhaps I am delirious. For a long time he lay awake thinking these things, and once he sat up in bed and said aloud, "I will prove that I am not crazy. I will make a little speech about something complicated and intellectual. I will talk about what to do with Germany after the war." But before he had time to begin, he was asleep.

He woke just as the first light of day was showing through the slit in the curtains over the window. The room was still dark, but he could tell that it was already beginning to get light outside. He lay looking at the gray light which was showing through the slit in the curtain and as he lay there he remembered the day before. He remembered the Junkers 88's and the hardness of the water; he remembered the large pleasant nurse and the kind doctor, and now a small grain of doubt took root in his mind and it began to grow.

He looked around the room. The nurse had taken the roses out the night before. There was nothing except the table with a packet of cigarettes, a box of matches and an ashtray. The room was bare. It was no longer warm or friendly. It was not even comfortable. It was cold and empty and very quiet.

Slowly the grain of doubt grew, and with it came fear, a light, dancing fear that warned but did not frighten; the kind of fear that one gets not because one is afraid, but because one feels that there is something wrong. Quickly the doubt and the fear grew so that he became restless and angry, and when he touched his forehead with his hand, he found that it was damp with sweat. He knew then that he must do something; that he must find some way of proving to himself that he was either right or wrong, and he looked up and saw again the window and the green curtains. From where he lay, that window was right in front of him, but it was fully ten yards away. Somehow he must reach it and look out. The idea became an obsession with him and soon he could think of nothing except the window. But what about his leg? He put his hand underneath the bedclothes and felt the thick bandaged stump which was all that was left on the right hand side. It seemed all right. It didn't hurt. But it would not be easy.

He sat up. Then he pushed the bedclothes aside and put his left leg on the floor. Slowly, carefully, he swung his body over un-

**16 Discussion** Why does he not complete his sentence?

**17 Discussion** What do you think the pilot suspects?

**18 Discussion** Why has the feeling in the room changed?

**19 Discussion** Explain the distinction that the writer is making.

20 **Discussion** What does the pilot's determination to get to the window reveal about his character?

21 **Discussion** Why is the description of this setting important to the rest of the story?

22 **Discussion** In what language is the sign written? What do you think it means?

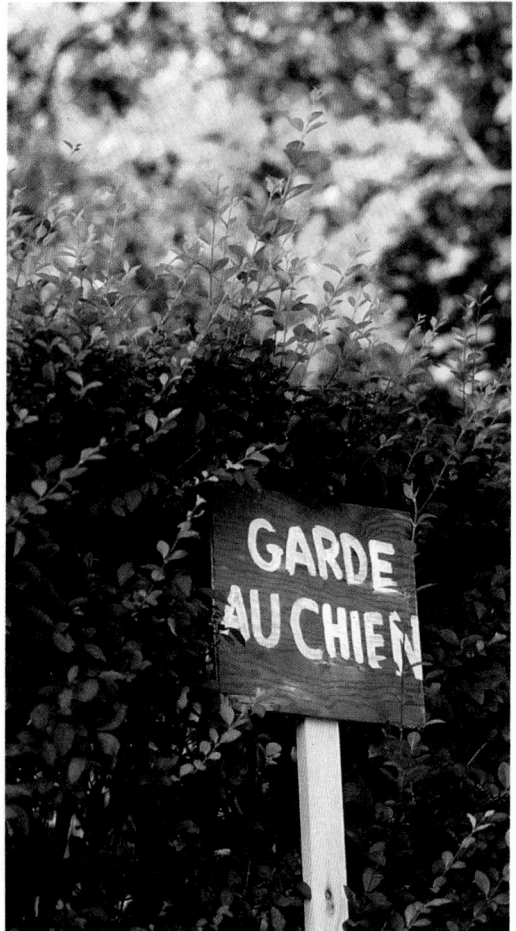

over toward the window. He would reach forward as far as he could with his arms, then he would give a little jump and slide his left leg along after them. Each time he did it, it jarred his wound so that he gave a soft grunt of pain, but he continued to crawl across the floor on two hands and one knee. When he got to the window he reached up, and one at a time he placed both hands on the sill. Slowly he raised himself up until he was standing on his left leg. Then quickly he pushed aside the curtains and looked out.

He saw a small house with a gray tiled roof standing alone beside a narrow lane, and immediately behind it there was a plowed field. In front of the house there was an untidy garden, and there was a green hedge separating the garden from the lane. He was looking at the hedge when he saw the sign. It was just a piece of board nailed to the top of a short pole, and because the hedge had not been trimmed for a long time, the branches had grown out around the sign so that it seemed almost as though it had been placed in the middle of the hedge. There was something written on the board with white paint. He pressed his head against the glass of the window, trying to read what it said. The first letter was a G, he could see that. The second was an A, and the third was an R. One after another he managed to see what the letters were. There were three words, and slowly he spelled the letters out aloud to himself as he managed to read them. G-A-R-D-E A-U C-H-I-E-N. *Garde au chien.*[12] That is what it said.

He stood there balancing on one leg and holding tightly to the edges of the window sill with his hands, staring at the sign and at the whitewashed lettering of the words.

til he had both hands on the floor as well; then he was out of bed, kneeling on the carpet. He looked at the stump. It was very short and thick, covered with bandages. It was beginning to hurt and he could feel it throbbing. He wanted to collapse, lie down on the carpet and do nothing, but he knew that he must go on.

With two arms and one leg, he crawled

---

12. ***Garde au chien*** (gärd ō shē ən): French for "Beware of the dog."

## Grammar in Action

A **prepositional phrase** is a group of words made up of a preposition and a noun or pronoun, called the object of the preposition. The phrase may also include modifiers. Since prepositional phrases function as adjectives or adverbs, writers use such phrases to add important descriptive details to sentences. (A prepositional phrase functioning as an adjective is called an adjective phrase; one functioning as an adverb is called an adverb phrase.)

*After a hearty breakfast*, the men headed to the wharf.
  (adverb phrase, modifying the verb *headed*)
The box *in the corner closet* is full of old shoes.
  (adjective phrase, modifying the noun *box*)

The following passage from "Beware of the Dog" shows how Roald Dahl uses prepositional phrases to make his descriptions more concrete and suspenseful:

*With two arms and one leg*, he crawled over *toward the window*. He would reach . . . *with his arms*, then . . . give a little

For a moment he could think of nothing at all. He stood there looking at the sign, repeating the words over and over to himself. Slowly he began to realize the full meaning of the thing. He looked up at the cottage and at the plowed field. He looked at the small orchard on the left of the cottage and he looked at the green countryside beyond. "So this is France," he said. "I am in France."

Now the throbbing in his right thigh was very great. It felt as though someone was pounding the end of his stump with a hammer and suddenly the pain became so intense that it affected his head. For a moment he thought he was going to fall. Quickly he knelt down again, crawled back to the bed and hoisted himself in. He pulled the bedclothes over himself and lay back on the pillow, exhausted. He could still think of nothing at all except the small sign by the hedge and the plowed field and the orchard. It was the words on the sign that he could not forget.

It was some time before the nurse came in. She came carrying a basin of hot water and she said, "Good morning, how are you today?"

He said, "Good morning, nurse."

The pain was still great under the bandages, but he did not wish to tell this woman anything. He looked at her as she busied herself with getting the washing things ready. He looked at her more carefully now. Her hair was very fair. She was tall and big-boned and her face seemed pleasant. But there was something a little uneasy about her eyes. They were never still. They never looked at anything for more than a moment and they moved too quickly from one place to another in the room. There was something about her movements also. They were too

sharp and nervous to go well with the casual manner in which she spoke.

She set down the basin, took off his pajama top and began to wash him.

"Did you sleep well?"

"Yes."

"Good," she said. She was washing his arms and his chest.

"I believe there's someone coming down to see you from the Air Ministry after breakfast," she went on. "They want a report or something. I expect you know all about it. How you got shot down and all that. I won't let him stay long, so don't worry."

He did not answer. She finished washing him and gave him a toothbrush and some toothpowder. He brushed his teeth, rinsed his mouth and spat the water out into the basin.

Later she brought him his breakfast on a tray, but he did not want to eat. He was still feeling weak and sick and he wished only to lie still and think about what had happened. And there was a sentence running through his head. It was a sentence which Johnny, the Intelligence Officer of his squadron, always repeated to the pilots every day before they went out. He could see Johnny now, leaning against the wall of the dispersal hut with his pipe in his hand, saying, "And if they get you, don't forget, just your name, rank, and number. Nothing else. For God's sake, say nothing else."

"There you are," she said as she put the tray on his lap. "I've got you an egg. Can you manage all right?"

"Yes."

She stood beside the bed. "Are you feeling all right?"

"Yes."

"Good. If you want another egg I might be able to get you one."

"This is all right."

23 **Literary Focus** What does the fact that the pilot is in France signify?

24 **Discussion** Why does the pilot look more closely at the nurse? What does his inspection reveal?

25 **Critical Thinking and Reading** Why does the pilot remain silent?

jump and slide his left leg along *after them.* Each time . . . , it jarred his wound so that he gave a soft grunt of *pain,* but he continued to crawl *across the floor on two hands and one knee.* When he got *to the window* he reached up, and one *at a time,* he placed both hands *on the sill.*

By using prepositional phrases to describe the hero's actions in detail, Dahl keeps the reader wondering what the man will discover.

**Student Activity 1.** Identify the prepositional phrases in the paragraph from "Beware of the Dog," that begins "He saw a small house . . . "

**Student Activity 2.** Write a paragraph describing someone about to make an important discovery and use prepositional phrases to make the action concrete and suspenseful.

26 **Clarification** If the officer were really British, he would know the pilot's squadron.

27 **Discussion** Why does Peter answer the question in this way?

28 **Reading Strategy** Have students predict what they think will happen to Peter Williamson.

**Reader's Response** At what point did you realize that the pilot was in trouble? What details led you to your suspicions?

"Well, just ring the bell if you want any more." And she went out.

He had just finished eating, when the nurse came in again.

She said, "Wing Commander Roberts is here. I've told him that he can only stay for a few minutes."

She beckoned with her hand and the Wing Commander came in.

"Sorry to bother you like this," he said.

He was an ordinary R.A.F. officer, dressed in a uniform which was a little shabby. He wore wings and a D.F.C.[13] He was fairly tall and thin with plenty of black hair. His teeth, which were irregular and widely spaced, stuck out a little even when

---

**13. D.F.C.:** The initials of a medal, the Distinguished Flying Cross.

he closed his mouth. As he spoke he took a printed form and a pencil from his pocket and he pulled up a chair and sat down.

"How are you feeling?"

There was no answer.

"Tough luck about your leg. I know how you feel. I hear you put up a fine show before they got you."

The man in the bed was lying quite still, watching the man in the chair.

The man in the chair said, "Well, let's get this stuff over. I'm afraid you'll have to answer a few questions so that I can fill in this combat report. Let me see now, first of all, what was your squadron?" | 26

The man in the bed did not move. He looked straight at the Wing Commander and he said, "My name is Peter Williamson. My rank is Squadron Leader and my number is nine seven two four five seven." | 27 28

---

## THINKING ABOUT THE SELECTION

### Recalling

1. What has happened to the pilot at the beginning of the story?
2. When he wakes up, how does he learn he is in Brighton?
3. How does he finally learn where he really is?

### Interpreting

4. When the human body experiences a great physical injury, it often goes into shock, a state in which the mind or emotions do not function properly. Find three details that indicate that the pilot is suffering from shock at the beginning of the story.
5. In what way does the pilot's bailing out over the English Channel complicate his situation?
6. What two details make the pilot begin to suspect that something is not right in his situation?
7. What physical sensations does the pilot experience whenever he becomes suspicious?
8. At the end of the story, why does the pilot give the Wing Commander only his name, rank, and serial number?
9. What is the significance of the title?

### Applying

10. Sometimes, because of shock, people become unnaturally calm in the face of the worst disasters. Do you think that the matter-of-fact

*156   Short Stories*

**Closure and Extension**

**ANSWERS TO THINKING ABOUT THE SELECTION**
*Recalling*

1. The pilot has been wounded and is flying back to England. When he realizes he is not going to be able to make it back, he bails out of his aircraft.

tone by which the author mirrors the pilot's calmness adds to the tension in the story? Why or why not?

## ANALYZING LITERATURE

### Appreciating Historical Setting

A **historical setting** is one in which significant events in history have occurred. Although most of "Beware of the Dog" takes place in a hospital room, the historical background is crucial to your appreciation and understanding of the story.

1. What is the first clue in the story that the pilot is not in Brighton, England, as he has been informed?
2. What detail of the setting makes clear to the pilot that he is in France?
3. What does this information mean to the pilot?

## CRITICAL THINKING AND READING

### Making Inferences

An **inference** is a reasonable conclusion you make based on evidence in a story. For example, in this story you are never told directly that the nurse is lying to the pilot. However, you probably made this inference on the basis of her reactions to the pilot's questions.

Use evidence from the story to answer the following questions.

1. Who do you think the nurse, the doctor, and the Wing Commander really are?
2. What do you think is their reason for lying to the pilot?

## UNDERSTANDING LANGUAGE

### Comparing British and American Terms

Although the British and the Americans speak the same language, there are many differences in the vocabulary. For example, in this story the doctor, speaking in British English, says to the pilot, "some of the lads from your squadron were ringing up and asking about you." An American would probably say something like, "some of the fellows (or guys) were calling and asking about you."

Perhaps you've become aware of some British terms from films or from your reading. Can you match each of the following British terms with its American counterpart?

1. lift
2. lorry
3. petrol
4. macintosh

a. truck
b. raincoat
c. elevator
d. fuel

## THINKING AND WRITING

### Evaluating a Story

Imagine that you work for a company that produces a weekly television series called *On The Edge: Tales of Mystery and Suspense*. Your job is to find short stories that can be effectively turned into one-hour television shows. You have just finished reading "Beware of the Dog." List the reasons that would or would not make this story a good show for your series. Then write a memorandum to the producer recommending whether or not to use this story. Support your recommendation with details from the story. Revise your memo, presenting your reasons in order from the least to the most important. Then prepare your final draft.

Beware of the Dog 157

(Answers begin on p. 156.)

**Challenge** Extend the story by adding one or two more paragraphs that tell what happens to Peter Williamson.

## ANSWERS TO ANALYZING LITERATURE

1. Suggested Response: He does not hear sirens and guns when German fighter planes fly overhead.
2. Suggested Response: The sign "Beware of the Dog" is written in French.
3. Suggested Response: It means he is in enemy territory.

## ANSWERS TO CRITICAL THINKING AND READING

1. Suggested Response: They are Germans. When Peter looks closely at the nurse, he notices that she is light-haired. He also notices that the doctor and nurse do not look directly at him for any length of time.
2. Suggested Response: They want to deceive him so that he will provide them with information. The nurse says that the leader wants a report about how he was shot down.

## ANSWERS TO UNDERSTANDING LANGUAGE

Suggested Responses:
1. lift: c. elevator
2. lorry: a. truck
3. petrol: d. fuel
4. macintosh: b. raincoat

## THINKING AND WRITING

For help with this assignment, students can refer to Lesson 15, "Evaluating a Literary Work," in the Handbook of Writing About Literature.

### Publishing Student Writing

Have students exchange memos. Then have them assume the role of the producer and write comments.

---

2. He asks the nurse.
3. His suspicions are aroused by the sound of enemy aircraft and the fact that the water is hard, not soft as he remembered it to be. Finally, he crawls over to the window and reads a sign that is written in French. He knows then that he is in France.

### Interpreting

4. Suggested Response: He talks to himself as if he is not badly injured; he feels as though his injured leg

does not belong to him; and he feels excited and unafraid.
5. Suggested Response: He cannot be sure whether he will drown or which side will rescue him.
6. Suggested Response: He hears planes which he believes to be German fighters. The nurse indicates that the water is hard, but the pilot recalls that when he lived in Brighton, the water was soft.
7. Suggested Response: Just before he looks at the sign, his forehead is damp with sweat.

8. Suggested Response: He knows that he is a prisoner, and therefore should not give any more information.
9. The title refers to the sign in French that the pilot sees when he crawls to the window. It confirms his suspicions that he is not in Britain.

### Applying

10. Answers will differ. Students may respond that the discordance between the tone and the seriousness of the situation creates suspense.

## The Man to Send Rain Clouds

**Leslie Marmon Silko** (1948–    ) was born in Albuquerque, New Mexico, and raised on the Laguna Pueblo reservation. In works such as *Ceremony* and *Storyteller,* she explores the power of the myths and traditional ritual she learned as a child. Silko has been described as "a child of more than one culture" because she is a descendant of English- and Spanish-speaking settlers as well as of Pueblo Indians. The conflicting demands of different cultures dominate "The Man to Send Rain Clouds."

**Setting and Culture**

The **setting** of a story is not only the place and time in which the events occur, but it is also the cultural background against which the action takes place. The customs, ideas, values, and beliefs of the society in which the story occurs provide what might be called the cultural setting. In "The Man to Send Rain Clouds," these aspects of setting form an even more important background than the physical background.

**Look For**

To accept another person's culture is to see the world through another person's eyes. As you read "The Man to Send Rain Clouds," look for details that relate to the customs and beliefs of the Pueblo Indians. How do their customs and rituals conflict with those of another culture in the region?

**Writing**

How can you learn about a group of people? Structures, spaces, and objects all reveal something about the people who make and use them. On your next trip to or from school, play the anthropologist, that is, a scientist who studies the origin and cultural development of a people. List the places you pass and make notes about the role they play in the culture of your area.

**Vocabulary**

Knowing the following words will help you as you read "The Man to Send Rain Clouds."

**arroyo** (ə rōi′ ō) *n.*: A dry gully (p. 159)

**cloister** (klois′ tər) *n.*: A place devoted to religious seclusion (p. 161)

**pagans** (pā′ gənz) *n.*: People who are not Christians, Moslems, or Jews (p. 162)

**perverse** (pər vʉrs′) *adj.*: Persisting in error (p. 162)

# The Man to Send Rain Clouds

### Leslie Marmon Silko

They found him under a big cottonwood tree. His Levi jacket and pants were faded light blue so that he had been easy to find. The big cottonwood tree stood apart from a small grove of winterbare cottonwoods which grew in the wide, sandy arroyo. He had been dead for a day or more, and the sheep had wandered and scattered up and down the arroyo. Leon and his brother-in-law, Ken, gathered the sheep and left them in the pen at the sheep camp before they returned to the cottonwood tree. Leon waited under the tree while Ken drove the truck through the deep sand to the edge of the arroyo. He squinted up at the sun and unzipped his jacket—it sure was hot for this time of year. But high and northwest the blue mountains were still in snow. Ken came sliding down the low, crumbling bank about fifty yards down, and he was bringing the red blanket.

Before they wrapped the old man, Leon took a piece of string out of his pocket and tied a small gray feather in the old man's long white hair. Ken gave him the paint. Across the brown wrinkled forehead he drew a streak of white and along the high cheekbones he drew a strip of blue paint. He paused and watched Ken throw pinches of corn meal and pollen into the wind that fluttered the small gray feather. Then Leon painted with yellow under the old man's broad nose, and finally, when he had painted green across the chin, he smiled.

"Send us rain clouds, Grandfather." They laid the bundle in the back of the pickup and covered it with a heavy tarp before they started back to the pueblo.

They turned off the highway onto the sandy pueblo road. Not long after they passed the store and post office they saw Father Paul's car coming toward them. When he recognized their faces he slowed his car and waved for them to stop. The young priest rolled down the car window.

"Did you find old Teofilo?" he asked loudly.

Leon stopped the truck. "Good morning, Father. We were just out to the sheep camp. Everything is O.K. now."

"Thank God for that. Teofilo is a very old man. You really shouldn't allow him to stay at the sheep camp alone."

"No, he won't do that any more now."

"Well, I'm glad you understand. I hope I'll be seeing you at Mass[1] this week—we missed you last Sunday. See if you can get old Teo-

---

1. **mass** (mas): A church service celebrated by Roman Catholics.

*The Man to Send Rain Clouds*   159

**Thematic Idea** Other selections that deal with differences among cultures are "The Good Deed," page 121, and "'Sayonara,'" page 483.

## Presentation

**Motivation/Prior Knowledge** Tell students that Silko once said that she wrote, "because I love the stories, the feelings, the words." Point out to them that the story they are about to read reflects Silko's deep feeling for Native American culture.

**Master Teacher Note** Use an overhead projector to show students Art Transparency 3, *Arizona Corral,* by Millard Sheets. Have students discuss the feelings that this landscape calls up. Then tell them that the story takes place in a similar environment.

You might also want to point out that the Pueblo Indians, whose beliefs and customs are described in the story, have lived in this region for many hundreds of years. Pueblo Indians have the oldest civilization north of Mexico. When the Spanish first came to America during the sixteenth century, for example, they found Pueblo villages that were already old. With the arrival of the Spanish, many Pueblos converted to Christianity. Tell students that in this story they will see how Native Americans and Christian beliefs coexist.

**Purpose-Setting Question** How does this story show the clash of Native American and Christian beliefs?

1 **Discussion** Why do the men take care of the sheep first?

2 **Literary Focus** What Native American customs are revealed in this passage?

3 **Enrichment** Tell students that the term *pueblo* refers to a village of Pueblo Indians.

4 **Discussion** Why does Leon not tell the young priest that Teofilo is dead?

**5** **Literary Focus** Do you think their lack of outward grief may reveal cultural differences? Explain.

**6** **Literary Focus** What native American customs does this passage describe?

**7** **Literary Focus** Why do you think Louise sprinkled corn meal around the body? Can you think of any customs observed by other groups of people that are similar?

**8** **Literary Focus** How does this request reflect the coexistence of two cultures?

filo to come with you." The priest smiled and waved at them as they drove away.

Louise and Teresa were waiting. The table was set for lunch, and the coffee was boiling on the black iron stove. Leon looked at Louise and then at Teresa.

"We found him under a cottonwood tree in the big arroyo near sheep camp. I guess he sat down to rest in the shade and never got up again." Leon walked toward the old man's bed. The red plaid shawl had been shaken and spread carefully over the bed, and a new brown flannel shirt and pair of stiff new Levi's were arranged neatly beside the pillow. Louise held the screen door open while Leon and Ken carried in the red blanket. He looked small and shriveled, and after they dressed him in the new shirt and pants he seemed more shrunken.

**5** It was noontime now because the church bells rang the Angelus.[2] They ate the beans with hot bread, and nobody said anything until after Teresa poured the coffee.

Ken stood up and put on his jacket. "I'll see about the gravediggers. Only the top layer of soil is frozen. I think it can be ready before dark."

**6** Leon nodded his head and finished his coffee. After Ken had been gone for a while, the neighbors and clanspeople came quietly to embrace Teofilo's family and to leave food on the table because the gravediggers would come to eat when they were finished.

The sky in the west was full of pale yellow light. Louise stood outside with her hands in the pockets of Leon's green army jacket that was too big for her. The funeral was over, and the old men had taken their candles and

medicine bags[3] and were gone. She waited until the body was laid into the pickup before she said anything to Leon. She touched his arm, and he noticed that her hands were still dusty from the corn meal that she had **7** sprinkled around the old man. When she spoke, Leon could not hear her.

"What did you say? I didn't hear you."

"I said that I had been thinking about something."

"About what?"

"About the priest sprinkling holy water **8** for Grandpa. So he won't be thirsty."

Leon stared at the new moccasins that Teofilo had made for the ceremonial dances in the summer. They were nearly hidden by the red blanket. It was getting colder, and the wind pushed gray dust down the narrow pueblo road. The sun was approaching the long mesa where it disappeared during the winter. Louise stood there shivering and watching his face. Then he zipped up his jacket and opened the truck door. "I'll see if he's there."

Ken stopped the pickup at the church, and Leon got out; and then Ken drove down the hill to the graveyard where people were waiting. Leon knocked at the old carved door with its symbols of the Lamb.[4] While he waited he looked up at the twin bells from the king of Spain with the last sunlight pouring around them in their tower.

The priest opened the door and smiled when he saw who it was. "Come in! What brings you here this evening?"

The priest walked toward the kitchen, and Leon stood with his cap in his hand, playing with the earflaps and examining the

---

**2. Angelus** (an' ja ləs): A bell rung at morning, noon, and evening to announce a prayer.

**3. medicine bags:** Bags containing objects that were thought to have special powers.

**4. the Lamb:** Jesus Christ, as the sacrificial Lamb of God.

FEAST DAY, SAN JUAN PUEBLO, 1921
*William Penhallow Henderson*
National Museum of American Art
Smithsonian Institution

Humanities Note

Fine Art, *Feast Day: San Juan Pueblo*, 1921, by William Henderson. After Henderson (1877-1943), who was an easterner, settled in Santa Fe, he quickly adapted to the dramatic landscape and was fascinated by the Spanish and Indian cultures. He traveled to Indian Pueblos by horseback, carefully memorizing the color and movement of the rituals and dances and sketching them when he returned home. Whether painting with soft pastels or bold oils, he caught the spirit and air of his adopted home. Discuss with the students the texture and feeling of this work. Have them identify the people that are gathered, their expressions, the church, and the hills in the background.

1. What seems to be the mood of the setting?
2. Do you believe that this picture is an appropriate accompaniment to the story? Why or why not?

**9 Discussion** How does Leon seem to feel about making his request? Do you think he would have made this request on his own? Why or why not?

**10 Reading Strategy** How do you think Father Paul will respond to Leon's request?

living room—the brown sofa, the green armchair, and the brass lamp that hung down from the ceiling by links of chain. The priest dragged a chair out of the kitchen and offered it to Leon.

9    "No thank you, Father. I only came to ask you if you would bring your holy water to the graveyard."

The priest turned away from Leon and looked out the window at the patio full of shadows and the dining-room windows of the nuns' cloister across the patio. The curtains were heavy, and the light from within faintly penetrated; it was impossible to see the nuns inside eating supper. "Why didn't you tell me he was dead? I could have brought the Last Rites[5] anyway."    10

---

**5. the Last Rites:** A religious ceremony for a dying person or for someone who has just died.

*The Man to Send Rain Clouds*   161

11 **Discussion** Why does Leon believe that last rites were not necessary?

**12** **Literary Focus** Have students compare Leon's reasons for wanting the father to sprinkle holy water and Father Paul's reasons for doing so. What does this indicate about the conflict between Christian and Native American traditions?

**13** **Discussion** Why do you think the priest has decided to sprinkle holy water on the grave?

**14** **Literary Focus** The headlights on the highway emphasize that this story takes place in relatively modern times. Why is this detail important?

**Reader's Response** What did you find most interesting about Native American beliefs in this story? most surprising? Explain.

**11** Leon smiled. "It wasn't necessary, Father."

The priest stared down at his scuffed brown loafers and the worn hem of his cassock. "For a Christian burial it was necessary."

His voice was distant, and Leon thought that his blue eyes looked tired.

"It's O.K. Father, we just want him to have plenty of water."

The priest sank down into the green chair and picked up a glossy missionary magazine. He turned the colored pages full of lepers and pagans without looking at them.

"You know I can't do that, Leon. There should have been the Last Rites and a funeral Mass at the very least."

Leon put on his green cap and pulled the flaps down over his ears. "It's getting late, Father. I've got to go."

When Leon opened the door Father Paul stood up and said, "Wait." He left the room and came back wearing a long brown overcoat. He followed Leon out the door and across the dim churchyard to the adobe steps in front of the church. They both stooped to fit through the low adobe entrance. And when they started down the hill to the graveyard only half of the sun was visible above the mesa.

The priest approached the grave slowly, wondering how they had managed to dig into the frozen ground; and then he remembered that this was New Mexico, and saw the pile of cold loose sand beside the hole. The people stood close to each other with little clouds of steam puffing from their faces. The priest looked at them and saw a pile of jackets, gloves, and scarves in the yellow, dry tumbleweeds that grew in the graveyard. He looked at the red blanket, not sure that Teofilo was so small, wondering if it wasn't some perverse Indian trick—something they did in March to ensure a good harvest—wondering

if maybe old Teofilo was actually at sheep camp corraling the sheep for the night. But there he was, facing into a cold dry wind and squinting at the last sunlight, ready to bury a red wool blanket while the faces of his parishioners were in shadow with the last warmth of the sun on their backs.

His fingers were stiff, and it took him a long time to twist the lid off the holy water. Drops of water fell on the red blanket and soaked into dark icy spots. He sprinkled the grave and the water disappeared almost before it touched the dim, cold sand; it reminded him of something—he tried to remember what it was, because he thought if he could remember he might understand this. He sprinkled more water; he shook the container until it was empty, and the water fell through the light from sundown like August rain that fell while the sun was still shining, almost evaporating before it touched the wilted squash flowers.

The wind pulled at the priest's brown Franciscan robe[6] and swirled away the corn meal and pollen that had been sprinkled on the blanket. They lowered the bundle into the ground, and they didn't bother to untie the stiff pieces of new rope that were tied around the ends of the blanket. The sun was gone, and over on the highway the eastbound lane was full of headlights. The priest walked away slowly. Leon watched him climb the hill, and when he had disappeared within the tall, thick walls, Leon turned to look up at the high blue mountains in the deep snow that reflected a faint red light from the west. He felt good because it was finished, and he was happy about the sprinkling of the holy water; now the old man could send them big thunderclouds for sure.

---

**6. Franciscan** (fran sis′ kən) **robe:** The robe worn by a member of the Franciscan religious order, founded in 1209 by Saint Francis of Assisi.

**Closure and Extension**

**ANSWERS TO THINKING ABOUT THE SELECTION**
*Recalling*

1. They find the body of the old man.
2. Father Paul asks them if they found Teofilo and they say yes, but do not tell him that Teofilo is dead.
3. Louise asks Leon to have Father Paul come and sprinkle holy water on the body.

## THINKING ABOUT THE SELECTION

### Recalling

1. What do Leon and Ken find at the opening of the story?
2. Explain what happens when Leon and Ken meet Father Paul on the highway.
3. Why does Leon ask Father Paul for holy water?
4. How does Father Paul respond to the request?

### Interpreting

5. Why doesn't Leon tell Father Paul about Teofilo's death?
6. Why is Father Paul upset about the burial ceremony?
7. What insight into the Pueblo people does Father Paul gain during the ceremony?

### Applying

8. If you were Father Paul, what would you have done in response to Leon's request?

## ANALYZING LITERATURE

### Recognizing the Cultural Setting

The customs and cultural attitudes of the society in which a story takes place form a part of its setting. There are two cultures at play in "The Man to Send Rain Clouds," both of whose customs and beliefs affect the story. For example, the rituals related to death are important aspects of the story's cultural setting.

1. Point out two details that illustrate the Pueblo Indian customs or beliefs.
2. Point out three details that give evidence of the Christian rituals or beliefs.

## CRITICAL THINKING AND READING

### Understanding Cultural Conflict

When two cultures meet, the different customs and values of the groups can lead to conflict.

For example, the Pueblo Indians in "The Man to Send Rain Clouds" have become members of Father Paul's church but cling to their Indian beliefs and customs.

Describe a situation you have read about or know about personally in which two cultures have clashed. What customs, values, or ways of behaving were involved in the clash? How did the conflict conclude?

## UNDERSTANDING LANGUAGE

### Understanding Words from Spanish

Many English words come from the Spanish language. For example, the word *pueblo* comes from a Spanish word meaning "people" or "population." The words that follow are of Spanish origin. Look up each word, give its meaning, and give the Spanish word and meaning from which it comes.

1. patio      3. corral
2. mesa       4. mustang

## THINKING AND WRITING

### Writing About Cultural Practices

Choose a festival, holiday, or other celebration that people in your community observe. You might select an annual street fair, Independence Day, or a wedding, for example. Describe this event in an article for publication in a foreign magazine from a country you choose. Include details to help your readers understand your customs and culture. When you revise your article, make clear the significance of the details you have described.

You might like to try to revise your article for a magazine in another country as unlike the first as possible.

*The Man to Send Rain Clouds*   163

(Answers begin on p. 162.)

paint on the old man's face, and Louise sprinkles corn meal around the body.
2. Three details illustrating Christian beliefs are: The last rites, the sprinkling of holy water, and Mass.

### ANSWERS TO CRITICAL THINKING AND READING

Answers will differ. Some students may refer to the story "The Good Deed," which describes such a conflict.

### ANSWERS TO UNDERSTANDING LANGUAGE

Suggested Responses:
1. The word *patio*, which means "courtyard," comes from the Spanish word *patio*, which has the same meaning.
2. The word *mesa*, which means "a high plateau," comes from the Spanish word for table—*mesa*.
3. The word *corral*, which means "an enclosure for horses," comes from the Spanish *corro*, which means "ring."
4. The word *mustang*, which means "a wild horse," comes from the Spanish word *mestengo*—"wild."

### THINKING AND WRITING

Before they begin writing, students can refer to Lesson 2, "Drafting and Revising," in the Handbook of Writing About Literature.

### Publishing Student Writing

You might want to ask volunteers to share their articles with the class.

### Writing Across the Curriculum

You might have students choose another culture and research some of its customs, beliefs, and practices. Then have them make a chart comparing and contrasting that culture to their own. Consider informing the social studies department of this assignment so that social studies teachers can provide guidance to students.

4. He is upset that they did not ask him to administer the last rites to the old man, but he agrees.

### Interpreting

5. Answers will differ. Students may respond that Leon did not tell Father Paul about Teofilo's death because he wanted to bury Teofilo according to traditional Pueblo customs. He did not want Father Paul to interfere by using Christian ceremonies.
6. Suggested Response: Father Paul realizes that the Native Americans are not observing Christian rituals.
7. Answers will differ. Students may respond that he learns that the Pueblos retain traditional beliefs.

### Applying

8. Answers will differ. Students may respond that they might have done the same thing as Father Paul in order to stay in touch with the people. Others may respond that they would have denied Leon's request in order to emphasize the sanctity of Catholic ceremonies. Students should support any answer they give.

**Challenge** Ask students to write two diary entries—one in which Leon describes his feelings about the burial and one in which the priest describes his feelings.

### ANSWERS TO ANALYZING LITERATURE

1. Suggested Response: Leon puts

## Focus

**More About the Author** You might tell students that Arthur C. Clarke writes articles about science as well. A number of years ago, he wrote an article predicting the development of communication satellites. Ask students what breakthroughs in technology they think will occur in the next ten years.

**Literary Focus** Point out to students that even though writers like Clarke often set their stories in the future, they include details that will seem realistic to readers.

**Look For** Ask students to consider how the title reflects the story's theme.

**Writing/Prior Knowledge** In preparation for this assignment, have students meet in small groups and brainstorm about the things that they like to do best. Then have them consider which of those things they might not be able to do if they lived in a far-away land or world.

**Vocabulary** Have less advanced students write a sentence for each word. Then have students read each of their sentences to a partner, leaving a blank for the word. The partner should try to identify the missing word by referring to the vocabulary list.

**Spelling Tip** Write the word *phosphorescence* on the board. Remind students that the sound /f/ can be spelled by the letters *ph*.

## "If I Forget Thee, Oh Earth . . ."

**Arthur C. Clarke** (1917–    ), born in Somerset, England, has been fascinated with science and science fiction since childhood. While in the Air Force during World War II, he wrote and published his first science-fiction stories. Since then, he has written many stories. His most famous work is a collaboration with Stanley Kubrick on the screenplay for *2001: A Space Odyssey,* a film based on his story "The Sentinel." " 'If I Forget Thee, Oh Earth . . . ,' " like much science fiction, deals with the future consequences of today's technology.

### Setting in Science Fiction

The **setting** of science-fiction stories is usually the future. Using ideas of science or space travel, science-fiction writers may take you to places that do not now exist or that are currently beyond reach. For example, " 'If I Forget Thee, Oh Earth . . .' " opens in a space colony. When a setting like this one is part of a story, you might ask yourself what bearing the setting has on the plot.

### Look For

Although set in the future, science-fiction stories often reveal truths about contemporary life. As you read " 'If I Forget Thee, O Earth . . . ,' " look for the insights the story reveals about life on Earth today. What is it about our imperfect world that we should treasure?

### Writing

The characters in this story live far from the place they consider home. Imagine that you are an exile, living far from home. Freewrite about the things that you would miss most.

### Vocabulary

Knowing the following words will help you as you read " 'If I Forget Thee, Oh Earth . . .' "

**crepitation** (krep′ ətā sһən) *n.*: A crackling sound (p. 167)

**benison** (ben′ əz′n) *n.*: A blessing (p. 168)

**exile** (eg′ zīl) *n.*: Enforced removal from one's native land (p. 168)

**phosphorescence** (fäs′ fə res′ ′ns) *n.*: Emission of light resulting from exposure to radiation (p. 168)

**pyre** (pīr) *n.*: A pile of wood on which a body is burned at a funeral (p. 168)

**perennial** (pə ren′ ē əl) *adj.*: Lasting through the year or for a long time (p. 168)

**pilgrimage** (pil′ grəm ij) *n.*: A journey to a sacred place or shrine; a special trip to a place of personal significance (p. 168)

---

### Objectives

1. To respond to setting in science fiction
2. To understand plausibility
3. To write a science fiction story

### Support Material

**Teaching Portfolio**
Teacher Backup, p. 199
Grammar in Action Worksheet, *Using Adjective Clauses*, p. 203
Usage and Mechanics Worksheet, p. 205
Vocabulary Check, p. 206
Analyzing Literature Worksheet, *Responding to Setting in Science Fiction*, p. 208

Language Worksheet, *Using Vivid Words*, p. 209
Selection Test, p. 210

# "If I Forget Thee, Oh Earth . . ."

### Arthur C. Clarke

When Marvin was ten years old, his father took him through the long, echoing corridors that led up through Administration and Power, until at last they came to the uppermost levels of all and were among the swiftly growing vegetation of the Farmlands. Marvin liked it here: it was fun watching the great, slender plants creeping with almost visible eagerness toward the sunlight as it filtered down through the plastic domes to meet them. The smell of life was everywhere, awakening inexpressible longings in his heart: no longer was he breathing the dry, cool air of the residential levels, purged of all smells but the faint tang of ozone.[1] He wished he could stay here for a little while, but Father would not let him. They went onward until they had reached the entrance to the Observatory, which he had never visited: but they did not stop, and Marvin knew with a sense of rising excitement that there could be only one goal left. For the first time in his life, he was going Outside.

There were a dozen of the surface vehicles, with their wide balloon tires and pressurized cabins, in the great servicing chamber. His father must have been expected, for they were led at once to the little scout car waiting by the huge circular door of the airlock. Tense with expectancy, Marvin settled himself down in the cramped cabin while his father started the motor and checked the controls. The inner door of the lock slid open and then closed behind them: he heard the roar of the great air pumps fade slowly away as the pressure dropped to zero. Then the "Vacuum" sign flashed on, the outer door parted, and before Marvin lay the land which he had never yet entered.

He had seen it in photographs, of course: he had watched it imaged on television screens a hundred times. But now it was lying all around him, burning beneath the fierce sun that crawled so slowly across the jet-black sky. He stared into the west, away from the blinding splendor of the sun—and there were the stars, as he had been told but had never quite believed. He gazed at them for a long time, marveling that anything could be so bright and yet so tiny. They were intense unscintillating points, and suddenly he remembered a rhyme he had once read in one of his father's books:

> *Twinkle, twinkle, little star,*
> *How I wonder what you are.*

Well, *he* knew what the stars were. Whoever asked that question must have been very stupid. And what did they mean by

---

**1. ozone** (ō′ zōn) *n.*: A form of oxygen with a sharp odor.

"twinkle"? You could see at a glance that all the stars shone with the same steady, unwavering light. He abandoned the puzzle and turned his attention to the landscape around him.

**4** They were racing across a level plain at almost a hundred miles an hour, the great balloon tires sending up little spurts of dust

behind them. There was no sign of the Colony: in the few minutes while he had been gazing at the stars, its domes and radio towers had fallen below the horizon. Yet there were other indications of man's presence, for about a mile ahead Marvin could see the curiously shaped structures clustering round the head of a mine. Now and then a puff of

## Grammar in Action

An **adjective clause** is a subordinate clause that modifies a noun or pronoun by telling what kind or which one. It begins with a relative pronoun or relative adverb, includes a subject and verb, and may have complements and modifiers:

The book *that is bound in red leather* belongs to me.

Notice that the clause is next to the noun it modifies, *book*. The relative pronoun *that* introduces the clause and is its subject. The

verb, *is bound*, is modified by *in red leather*, a prepositional phrase.

Writers use adjective clauses to add detail to their descriptions. In the following sentences, Arthur Clarke uses adjective clauses for this purpose:

The ground fell sharply away beneath them in a dizzying slope *whose lower stretches were lost in shadow.*
For hours they drove through valleys and past the foot of mountains *whose peaks seemed to comb the stars* . . . .

vapor would emerge from a squat smokestack and would instantly disperse.

They were past the mine in a moment: Father was driving with a reckless and exhilarating skill as if—it was a strange thought to come into a child's mind—he were trying to escape from something. In a few minutes they had reached the edge of the plateau on which the Colony had been built. The ground fell sharply away beneath them in a dizzying slope whose lower stretches were lost in shadow. Ahead, as far as the eye could reach, was a jumbled wasteland of craters, mountain ranges, and ravines. The crests of the mountains, catching the low sun, burned like islands of fire in a sea of darkness: and above them the stars still shone as steadfastly as ever.

There could be no way forward—yet there was. Marvin clenched his fists as the car edged over the slope and started the long descent. Then he saw the barely visible track leading down the mountainside, and relaxed a little. Other men, it seemed, had gone this way before.

Night fell with a shocking abruptness as they crossed the shadow line and the sun dropped below the crest of the plateau. The twin searchlights sprang into life, casting blue-white bands on the rocks ahead, so that there was scarcely need to check their speed. For hours they drove through valleys and past the foot of mountains whose peaks seemed to comb the stars, and sometimes they emerged for a moment into the sunlight as they climbed over higher ground.

And now on the right was a wrinkled, dusty plain, and on the left, its ramparts and terraces rising mile after mile into the sky, was a wall of mountains that marched into the distance until its peaks sank from sight below the rim of the world. There was no sign that men had ever explored this land, but once they passed the skeleton of a crashed rocket, and beside it a stone cairn[2] surmounted by a metal cross.

It seemed to Marvin that the mountains stretched on forever: but at last, many hours later, the range ended in a towering, precipitous headland[3] that rose steeply from a cluster of little hills. They drove down into a shallow valley that curved in a great arc toward the far side of the mountains: and as they did so, Marvin slowly realized that something very strange was happening in the land ahead.

The sun was now low behind the hills on the right: the valley before them should be in total darkness. Yet it was awash with a cold white radiance that came spilling over the crags beneath which they were driving. Then, suddenly, they were out in the open plain, and the source of the light lay before them in all its glory.

It was very quiet in the little cabin now that the motors had stopped. The only sound was the faint whisper of the oxygen feed and an occasional metallic crepitation as the outer walls of the vehicle radiated away their heat. For no warmth at all came from the great silver crescent that floated low above the far horizon and flooded all this land with pearly light. It was so brilliant that minutes passed before Marvin could accept its challenge and look steadfastly into its glare, but at last he could discern the outlines of continents, the hazy border of the atmosphere, and the white islands of cloud. And even at this distance, he could see the glitter of sunlight on the polar ice.

It was beautiful, and it called to his heart across the abyss of space. There in that shining crescent were all the wonders that

---

**2. cairn** (kern) *n*.: A pile of stones left as a monument.
**3. precipitous headland:** Steep cliff.

5 **Critical Thinking and Reading**
On what planet or satellite are they?

6 **Discussion** How does this description heighten the suspense?

5

6

---

. . . the range ended in a towering, precipitous headland *that rose steeply from a cluster of little hills.*
They drove down into a shallow valley *that curved in a great arc toward the far side of the mountains.* . . .

**Student Activity 1.** Analyze the four adjective clauses in Clarke's description of the lunar landscape. Find the relative pronoun or relative adverb, the subject and verb, and any modifiers or complements in each. Then decide which noun or pronoun each adjective clause modifies.

**Student Activity 2.** Using Clarke's sentences as models, write your own description of an unusual landscape. You may use other relative pronouns (*which, who, whom*), or relative adverbs (*before, since, when, where, why*) to introduce your adjective clauses.

7 **Discussion** At what planet are they looking?

8 **Reading Strategy** Ask students to summarize the story that Marvin's father tells him.

9 **Discussion** Why will Marvin someday bring his son to the same place and tell him the same story that his father told him?

**Reader's Response** What do you think the future will be like?

7 he had never known—the hues of sunset skies, the moaning of the sea on pebbled shores, the patter of falling rain, the unhurried benison of snow. These and a thousand others should have been his rightful heritage, but he knew them only from the books and ancient records, and the thought filled him with the anguish of exile.

Why could they not return? It seemed so peaceful beneath those lines of marching cloud. Then Marvin, his eyes no longer blinded by the glare, saw that the portion of the disk that should have been in darkness was gleaming faintly with an evil phosphorescence: and he remembered. He was looking upon the funeral pyre of a world—upon the radioactive aftermath of Armageddon.[4] Across a quarter of a million miles of space, the glow of dying atoms was still visible, a perennial reminder of the ruinous past. It would be centuries yet before that deadly glow died from the rocks and life could return again to fill that silent, empty world.

8 And now Father began to speak, telling Marvin the story which until this moment had meant no more to him than the fairy tales he had once been told. There were many things he could not understand: it was impossible for him to picture the glowing, multicolored pattern of life on the planet he had never seen. Nor could he comprehend the forces that had destroyed it in the end, leaving the Colony, preserved by its isolation, as the sole survivor. Yet he could share the agony of those final days, when the Colony had learned at last that never again would the supply ships come flaming down through the stars with gifts from home. One

---

**4. Armageddon** (är′ mə ged′ 'n): In the Bible, the place where the final battle between good and evil was to be fought.

by one the radio stations had ceased to call: on the shadowed globe the lights of the cities had dimmed and died, and they were alone at last, as no men had ever been alone before, carrying in their hands the future of the race.

Then had followed the years of despair, and the long-drawn battle for survival in their fierce and hostile world. That battle had been won, though barely: this little oasis of life was safe against the worst that Nature could do. But unless there was a goal, a future toward which it could work, the Colony would lose the will to live, and neither machines nor skill nor science could save it then.

So, at last, Marvin understood the purpose of this pilgrimage. He would never walk beside the rivers of that lost and legendary world, or listen to the thunder raging above its softly rounded hills. Yet one day—how far ahead?—his children's children would return to claim their heritage. The winds and the rains would scour the poisons from the burning lands and carry them to the sea, and in the depths of the sea they would waste their venom until they could harm no living things. Then the great ships that were still waiting here on the silent, dusty plains could lift once more into space, along the road that led to home.

9 That was the dream: and one day, Marvin knew with a sudden flash of insight, he would pass it on to his own son, here at this same spot with the mountains behind him and the silver light from the sky streaming into his face.

He did not look back as they began the homeward journey. He could not bear to see the cold glory of the crescent Earth fade from the rocks around him, as he went to rejoin his people in their long exile.

*"If I Forget Thee, Oh Earth . . ."* 169

### ANSWERS TO THINKING ABOUT THE SELECTION
*Recalling*

1. Marvin's father takes him from the moon colony and across the lunar landscape in a surface vehicle. After many hours they reach a place where they can view Earth from the moon. There Marvin's father tells him about the end of life on Earth.
2. The source of the radiance is the sun reflecting off the face of Earth —earthlight.
3. Marvin discovers that his homeland, Earth, has been made uninhabitable by nuclear pollution.
4. They share a dream that one day Marvin's children's children will return to a cleansed Earth to reclaim their heritage.

### *Interpreting*

5. Suggested Response: Marvin's father had waited to take him Outside until Marvin was old enough to fully understand and share his dream of humans returning to Earth.
6. Suggested Response: The people of the colony cannot return to Earth because no one can live in the atmosphere poisoned by radioactivity.
7. Suggested Response: His father seems to regard the journey almost as a sacred rite. He wants to pass on to his son a love of Earth and a wish to have their descendants live there again.
8. Suggested Response: The "anguish of exile" refers to the pain of not being able to return to one's home.
9. Suggested Response: A pilgrimage is a journey to a holy place. Marvin and his father travel to a place where they can view their homeland. The goal of returning there seems almost sacred to Marvin's father.

(Answers begin on p. 169.)

*Applying*

10. Suggested Response: Marvin's father thinks that this goal gives life in the Colony a meaning and higher purpose.
11. Answers will differ. Most students will respond that they would pass on the story and sense of mission to their child.

**Challenge** Ask students to imagine that they live hundreds of years after this story and that the people from the Colony have returned to Earth. Have them discuss the problems and solutions of beginning life again on this planet. How would they organize life on Earth differently so that the planet would never again be uninhabitable?

## ANSWERS TO ANALYZING LITERATURE

1. Suggested Response: The colony is located on the moon. They drive through a lunar landscape. The author also states that Earth is a quarter of a million miles away—the distance from Earth to the moon.
2. Suggested Response: Marvin sees that the valley ahead, which should have been dark, is "awash with a cold white radiance." Then he sees a "great silver crescent that floated low above the far horizon."
3. Answers will differ. Most students will respond that people in the colony do not venture out very much. Earth is seen and remembered as a place of wonder where people can experience the miracles of nature.

## ANSWERS TO CRITICAL THINKING AND READING

1. Suggested Response: Men have already been to the moon, and it is possible for them to land there and return to earth. Lunar craft have been developed to travel over the moon's landscape. Colonies may be established on the moon in the next century.
2. Suggested Response: Current knowledge of growing food in protected environments could lead to the type of agriculture described in the moon colony. Current nuclear technology makes it possible to destroy life on Earth.

## THINKING ABOUT THE SELECTION
### Recalling

1. Describe the journey Marvin's father takes him on when he is ten years old.
2. What is the source of the "cold white radiance" that lights the landscape in front of Marvin and his father's vehicle?
3. What does Marvin discover on the journey?
4. What is the dream that Marvin and his father share?

### Interpreting

5. Why had Marvin never been Outside before?
6. Why are the people of the Colony unable to return to Earth?
7. How does Marvin's father feel about the journey?
8. What is meant by the phrase "the anguish of exile" (page 168)?
9. Why does the author use the word *pilgrimage* to describe Marvin's journey?

### Applying

10. How do you think the dream of returning to Earth affects everyday life in the Colony?
11. Imagine that you are Marvin. You are now grown up and have a ten-year-old child. What will you tell your child?

## ANALYZING LITERATURE
### Responding to Setting in Science Fiction

The **setting** of science-fiction stories is usually the future, a future affected by developments in science and technology. Scientific knowledge and developments make the setting of " 'If I Forget Thee, Oh Earth . . .' " both possible and necessary.

1. Where is the Colony located? Give clues from the story to support your answer.
2. "Marvin slowly realized that something very strange was happening in the land ahead." Identify two descriptions that contribute to Marvin's awareness that there is something strange about the land ahead.
3. Contrast life in the Colony with the vision and memory of life on Earth.

## CRITICAL THINKING AND READING
### Understanding Plausibility

Although the setting of " 'If I Forget Thee, Oh Earth . . .' " does not exist in reality, Clarke describes it with enough familiar details to make it seem plausible, that is, true or likely while you are reading about it, and perhaps at some actual time in the future. Such details make this imagined setting of the future real to readers.

1. What aspects of the setting of " 'If I Forget Thee, Oh Earth . . .' " are based on real or possible scientific developments?
2. What current scientific knowledge could lead to the future Clarke imagines?
3. What aspects of the setting would be entirely familiar to somebody living today?
4. Despite realistic details, why is the story still outside the realm of reality?
5. If Arthur C. Clarke had lived one hundred years ago and written " 'If I Forget Thee, Oh Earth . . .' " then, would the details of the story's setting be considered largely realistic or largely fantastic? Explain.

## THINKING AND WRITING
### Writing Science Fiction

Write your own science-fiction story. Brainstorm with your classmates about what some recent scientific developments you have read or heard about might lead to. Build the plot of your story around these consequences. Revise your story, adding realistic details of setting that your readers will be able to relate to.

3. Answers will differ. Students may respond that those who have seen films of the moon landings would recognize the lunar landscape. Also, astronauts have taken pictures of the Earth from outer space.
4. Suggested Response: The story remains outside the realm of reality because we do not have the technology to establish a permanent colony on the moon.
5. Suggested Response: One hundred years ago this story would have seemed fantastic because no one had escaped Earth's gravitational pull and journeyed in space. Also, the destruction of life on earth would have been almost inconceivable.

### THINKING AND WRITING
Have students refer to Lesson 17, "Writing a Short Story," in the Handbook of Writing About Literature.

**Publishing Student Writing**
You might want to collect students' stories in a book.

**Writing Across the Curriculum**
You might want students to research and report on space exploration. Consider informing the science department of this assignment so that teachers can assist students.

# Theme

**SUMMERTIME**
*Raoul Dufy*
Three Lions

## Humanities Note

Fine Art, *Summertime*, Raoul Dufy. Raoul Dufy (1877-1953), a French painter, studied art at the Ecole des Beaux-Arts in Paris. Rejecting the old masters at the Louvre as "terrifying," Dufy drew inspiration from Van Gogh, Matisse, and the Impressionists. His style evolved into one uniquely his own in which he joyfully depicts what he sees around him in a stylized way that does not sacrifice realism.

*Summertime* captures the symbols and the essence of summer. He does this within the limited format of the painting through the division of the picture plane into geometric shapes. Grouped around a central image, a tree, vignettes of many of Dufy's favorite things: field work, farms, streams, fishermen, cows. These images are unified by the consistent color of the canvas. This highly decorative quality of this salute to summer is similar in feeling to a tapestry or quilt.

## Focus

**More About the Author** After studying law briefly at the National University of Colombia, Gabriel García Márquez worked in several Colombia cities as a journalist, in Europe as a correspondent for a Colombian newspaper, and in New York City for a Cuban news agency. Before publishing his fiction, he supplemented his income by writing film scripts.

Ask students how they think that García Márquez's legal and journalistic training might have contributed to his way of seeing and describing his world.

**Literary Focus** To help students understand the concept of theme, ask them to consider what larger meaning lies beyond the simple events of a well-known fairy tale or myth. Explain that writers often use events in the lives of characters to represent a truth about the larger world.

**Look For** "What gives literary value is mystery," says García Márquez. Ask students why we need mysteries, both in our lives and in the fiction we read.

**Teaching to the Ability Levels** Point out to less advanced students that theme is not what happens in the story, although theme may be revealed by the action. Emphasize that what happens to the characters in a short story has significance that results in the theme.

**Writing/Prior Knowledge** Before students begin the writing activity, have them briefly describe their vision of what an angel is. Then have them describe their reactions.

**Vocabulary** Because these are difficult words, you may wish to put these words and others in the selection on flash cards. Have pairs of students periodically test each other on the words.

*172*

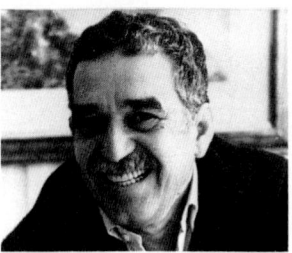

## A Very Old Man with Enormous Wings

**Gabriel García Márquez** (1928–    ) was born in Aracataca, Colombia, and now lives in Mexico City. Growing up in a land of sharp contrasts, he saw hunger exist side-by-side with great wealth, and everyday people cohabit a land of strange and unusual creatures. He was awarded the Nobel Prize for Literature in 1982 for his novel *One Hundred Years of Solitude*. "A Very Old Man with Enormous Wings," from his short story collection *Leaf Storm,* shows a deep understanding of the magical reality of the people of his native land.

**Theme**

The **theme** of a story is the general idea or insight into life that the story presents. To understand the theme of a story, it is sometimes necessary to understand the literary style in which the piece was written. Magical realism—popular among Latin American writers—reveals the mysterious and miraculous elements that are hidden in everyday life. In this story, the theme, or the realization about life, stems from the fusion of a fantastic event—in this case, an angel's appearance—with the reality of the characters' everyday lives.

**Look For**

Peter Prescott, a literary critic for *Newsweek,* wrote the following about this story: "For García Márquez the world contains mysteries that we need and can easily live with, but also miracles that we cannot understand, that speak for forces unknown to men." As you read, look for the mysteries in this story.

**Write**

In this story, Pelayo and Elisenda, the story's central characters, are visited by a man who they think is an angel. Imagine that a similar event happened to you. Write about your reactions.

**Vocabulary**

Knowing the following words will help you as you read "A Very Old Man with Enormous Wings."

**celestial** (sə les′ chəl) *adj.*: Of heaven; divine (p. 173)

**magnanimous** (mag nan′ ə məs) *adj.*: Noble in mind; high-souled, especially in overlooking injury or insult (p. 175)

**impertinences** (im pʉrt′ 'n əns əs) *n.*: Examples of insolence or lack of respect (p. 176)

**terrestrial** (tə res′ trē əl) *adj.*: Of this world; earthly (p. 176)

**prudence** (prood′ 'ns) *n.*: Practical, sound judgment (p. 176)

**proliferated** (prō lif′ ər āt′ id) *v.*: Grew rapidly (p. 177)

**providential** (präv′ ə den′ shəl) *adj.*: As if decreed by God (p. 177)

*172   Short Stories*

## Objectives

1 To recognize possible themes in a short story
2 To identify multiple interpretations of an event
3 To use context to understand words
4 To write a story from a different perspective

## Support Material

**Teaching Portfolio**
Teacher Backup, p. 213
Grammar in Action Worksheets, *Illustrating and Giving Examples,* p. 219; *Using Different Sentence Openers,* p. 217
Usage and Mechanics Worksheet, p. 221
Vocabulary Check, p. 222
Analyzing Literature Worksheet, *Understanding Theme,* p. 223

Language Worksheet, *Using Context Clues,* p. 224
Selection Test, p. 225

# A Very Old Man with Enormous Wings

## A Tale for Children

### Gabriel García Márquez

On the third day of rain they had killed so many crabs inside the house that Pelayo had to cross his drenched courtyard and throw them into the sea, because the newborn child had a temperature all night and they thought it was due to the stench. The world had been sad since Tuesday. Sea and sky were a single ash-gray thing and the sands of the beach, which on March nights glimmered like powdered light, had become a stew of mud and rotten shellfish. The light was so weak at noon that when Pelayo was coming back to the house after throwing away the crabs, it was hard for him to see what it was that was moving and groaning in the rear of the courtyard. He had to go very close to see that it was an old man, a very old man, lying face down in the mud, who, in spite of his tremendous efforts, couldn't get up, impeded by his enormous wings.

Frightened by that nightmare, Pelayo ran to get Elisenda, his wife, who was putting compresses on the sick child, and he took her to the rear of the courtyard. They both looked at the fallen body with mute stupor. He was dressed like a ragpicker. There were only a few faded hairs left on his bald skull and very few teeth in his mouth, and his pitiful condition of a drenched great-grandfather had taken away any sense of grandeur he might have had. His huge buzzard wings, dirty and half-plucked, were forever entangled in the mud. They looked at him so long and so closely that Pelayo and Elisenda very soon overcame their surprise and in the end found him familiar. Then they dared speak to him, and he answered in an incomprehensible dialect with a strong sailor's voice. That was how they skipped over the inconvenience of the wings and quite intelligently concluded that he was a lonely castaway from some foreign ship wrecked by the storm. And yet, they called in a neighbor woman who knew everything about life and death to see him, and all she needed was one look to show them their mistake.

"He's an angel," she told them. "He must have been coming for the child, but the poor fellow is so old that the rain knocked him down."

On the following day everyone knew that a flesh-and-blood angel was held captive in Pelayo's house. Against the judgment of the wise neighbor woman, for whom angels in those times were the fugitive survivors of a celestial conspiracy, they did not have the heart to club him to death. Pelayo watched over him all afternoon from the kitchen, armed with his bailiff's club, and before going to bed he dragged him out of the mud

*A Very Old Man with Enormous Wings*  173

**Thematic Idea** Magical realism, in which the imaginary often outweighs the laws of logic, is popular among South American writers. You might consider pairing this story with "Uncle Marcos" by Isabel Allende, page 63. Ask students to compare and contrast the authors' purposes in using fantastic details and the effects of the details on the stories.

## Presentation

**Motivation/Prior Knowledge** Put the following statement on the chalkboard: "Seeing is believing." Ask students if, from their experience, this is an accurate statement. Have their perceptions ever misled them? How do people react to the unknown, the mysterious, or the bizarre? What in human nature makes these reactions necessary?

Tell students that the characters in "A Very Old Man with Enormous Wings" have a variety of reactions to the sudden appearance of an old man. Have students note how these reactions change during the course of the story.

**Purpose-Setting Question** How are the lives of Pelayo and Elisenda changed by the old man with enormous wings?

**1 Reading Strategy** Ask students to make inferences about the story based on its subtitle.

**2 Enrichment** Students may be interested to know that the author based many of the settings of his short stories and novels on the Atlantic seacoast town where he was born.

**3 Discussion** How does the physical description of the old man with wings contradict the typical image of an angel?

**4 Critical Thinking and Reading** Why and how does Pelayo and Elisenda's initial reaction of nightmare and mute stupor change to one of familiarity?

**5 Discussion** Why is the neighbor woman sure that the old man is an angel who has come for the child?

**6 Discussion** Describe the way in which Pelayo treats the old man. Why does he treat someone who is supposed to be an angel in this manner?

174    *Short Stories*

## Primary Source

In the following quotation from *Harper's* magazine, Earl Shorris illustrates the way in which history and the social and cultural climates at the time influence the fiction that writers produce.

It is also necessary to consider García Márquez as a moralist, a political man; for myth, though it negates history by making circles of time and events, relates to the way we live; it is not made in a vacuum, but in the depths of experience. García Márquez writes of exploitation, coloni-alism, and revolution from the point of view of a man who was influenced in his childhood by a grandfather who lived out his days as one of the leavings of a revolution in a town called Aracataca, which was exploited and then abandoned by banana barons from the United States.

You might discuss with students how "A Very Old Man with Enormous Wings" supports Shorris' claim.

and locked him up with the hens in the wire chicken coop. In the middle of the night, when the rain stopped, Pelayo and Elisenda were still killing crabs. A short time afterward the child woke up without a fever and with a desire to eat. Then they felt magnanimous and decided to put the angel on a raft with fresh water and provisions for three days and leave him to his fate on the high seas. But when they went out into the courtyard with the first light of dawn, they found the whole neighborhood in front of the chicken coop having fun with the angel, without the slightest reverence, tossing him things to eat through the openings in the wire as if he weren't a supernatural creature but a circus animal.

Father Gonzaga arrived before seven o'clock, alarmed at the strange news. By that time onlookers less frivolous than those at dawn had already arrived and they were making all kinds of conjectures concerning the captive's future. The simplest among them thought that he should be named mayor of the world. Others of sterner mind felt that he should be promoted to the rank of five-star general in order to win all wars. Some visionaries[1] hoped that he could be put to stud in order to implant on earth a race of winged wise men who could take charge of the universe. But Father Gonzaga, before becoming a priest, had been a robust woodcutter. Standing by the wire, he reviewed his catechism[2] in an instant and asked them to open the door so that he could take a close look at that pitiful man who looked more like a huge decrepit hen among the fascinated chickens. He was lying in a corner drying his open wings in the sunlight

---

1. **visionaries** (vizh′ ən er′ ēz) *n.*: People whose ideas, plans, and so on, are impractical, too idealistic, or fantastic; dreamers.
2. **catechism** (kat′ ə kiz′ əm) *n.*: A handbook of questions and answers for teaching the principles of a religion.

*A Very Old Man with Enormous Wings*   175

## Commentary: Interpreting "A Very Old Man with Enormous Wings"

"A Very Old Man with Enormous Wings" is particularly intriguing because it can be read on several levels. It is a delightful fantasy for children, filled with strange and fantastic situations, humorous details, and a distinctive blend of surrealism and innocence.

On a more complex level, however, the story presents some interesting themes that appear frequently in the work of South American writers. The angel's decrepitude and his fall from his former home suggest physical decay and loss of innocence while his uncommunicative nature and isolation suggest alienation. The weakness of the church is conveyed in the preposterous ecclesiastical investigation of the angel. The absurd attempts to explain the angel's appearance logically and to discover his reasons for being there demonstrate the limits of human reason. The respected authorities of the village—the doctor and the priest—can reach no agreement on what is real and what is fantastic. Finally, the angel's reduction to being a sideshow freak for the monetary gain of Pelayo and Elisenda implies a condemnation of capitalistic exploitation.

Using their observations about the various themes in the short story, students might comment on the picture of South American society that the author portrays in "A Very Old Man with Enormous Wings."

among the fruit peels and breakfast leftovers that the early risers had thrown him. Alien to the impertinences of the world, he only lifted his antiquarian[3] eyes and murmured something in his dialect when Father Gonzaga went into the chicken coop and said good morning to him in Latin. The parish priest had his first suspicion of an imposter when he saw that he did not understand the language of God or know how to greet His ministers. Then he noticed that seen close up he was much too human: he had an unbearable smell of the outdoors, the back side of his wings was strewn with parasites and his main feathers had been mistreated by terrestrial winds, and nothing about him measured up to the proud dignity of angels. Then he came out of the chicken coop and in a brief sermon warned the curious against the risks of being ingenuous. He reminded them that the devil had the bad habit of making use of carnival tricks in order to confuse the unwary. He argued that if wings were not the essential element in determining the difference between a hawk and an airplane, they were even less so in the recognition of angels. Nevertheless, he promised to write a letter to his Bishop so that the latter would write to his primate so that the latter would write to the Supreme Pontiff in order to get the final verdict from the highest courts.

His prudence fell on sterile hearts. The news of the captive angel spread with such rapidity that after a few hours the courtyard had the bustle of a marketplace and they had to call in troops with fixed bayonets to disperse the mob that was about to knock the house down. Elisenda, her spine all twisted from sweeping up so much marketplace trash, then got the idea of fencing in the yard and charging five cents admission to see the angel.

_____
3. **antiquarian** (an′ ti kwer′ ē ən) _adj._: Old-fashioned; outdated.

*176   Short Stories*

The curious came from far away. A traveling carnival arrived with a flying acrobat who buzzed over the crowd several times, but no one paid any attention to him because his wings were not those of an angel but, rather, those of a sidereal bat. The most unfortunate invalids on earth came in search of health: a poor woman who since childhood had been counting her heartbeats and had run out of numbers; a Portuguese man who couldn't sleep because the noise of the stars disturbed him; a sleepwalker who got up at night to undo the things he had done while awake; and many others with less serious ailments. In the midst of that shipwreck disorder that made the earth tremble, Pelayo and Elisenda were happy with fatigue, for in less than a week they had crammed their rooms with money and the line of pilgrims waiting their turn to enter still reached beyond the horizon.

The angel was the only one who took no part in his own act. He spent his time trying to get comfortable in his borrowed nest, befuddled by the hellish heat of the oil lamps and sacramental candles that had been placed along the wire. At first they tried to make him eat some mothballs, which, according to the wisdom of the wise neighbor woman, were the food prescribed for angels. But he turned them down, just as he turned down the papal[4] lunches that the penitents[5] brought him, and they never found out whether it was because he was an angel or because he was an old man that in the end he ate nothing but eggplant mush. His only supernatural virtue seemed to be patience. Especially during the first days, when the hens pecked at him, searching for the stellar

_____
4. **papal** (pā′ pəl) _adj._: Appropriate for the pope or the papacy.
5. **penitents** (pen′ i tənts) _n._: People receiving or intending to receive the sacrament of penance, which involves the confession and repentance of sin or wrongdoing.

## Grammar in Action

Skillful writers **illustrate and give examples** in addition to making statements. In "A Very Old Man with Enormous Wings," for example, García Márquez sets the scene and tone of the story by making a statement about the sad world in which the characters live and backs it up with examples that create an image in the reader's mind:

The world had been sad since Tuesday. Sea and sky were a single ash-gray thing and the sands of the beach, which

on March nights glimmered like powdered light, had become a stew of mud and rotten shellfish. The light was so weak at noon that when Pelayo was coming back to the house after throwing away the crabs, it was hard for him to see what it was that was moving and groaning in the rear of the courtyard.

Similarly, when García Márquez describes Father Gonzaga's observations about how human and how unlike an angel the old man looks, he supports his claim with examples:

Then he noticed that seen close up he was much too human: he had an unbearable smell of the outdoors, the back side of his wings was strewn with parasites and his main feathers had been mistreated by terrestrial winds, parasites that proliferated in his wings, and the cripples pulled out feathers to touch their defective parts with, and even the most merciful threw stones at him, trying to get him to rise so they could see him standing. The only time they succeeded in arousing him was when they burned his side with an iron for branding steers, for he had been motionless for so many hours that they thought he was dead. He awoke with a start, ranting in his hermetic[6] language and with tears in his eyes, and he flapped his wings a couple of times, which brought on a whirlwind of chicken dung and lunar dust and a gale of panic that did not seem to be of this world. Although many thought that his reaction had been one not of rage but of pain, from then on they were careful not to annoy him, because the majority understood that his passivity was not that of a hero taking his ease but that of a cataclysm[7] in repose.

Father Gonzaga held back the crowd's frivolity with formulas of maidservant inspiration while awaiting the arrival of a final judgment on the nature of the captive. But the mail from Rome showed no sense of urgency. They spent their time finding out if the prisoner had a navel, if his dialect had any connection with Aramaic,[8] how many times he could fit on the head of a pin, or whether he wasn't just a Norwegian with wings. Those meager letters might have come and gone until the end of time if a providential event had not put an end to the priest's tribulations.

It so happened that during those days, among so many other carnival attractions, there arrived in town the traveling show of the woman who had been changed into a spider for having disobeyed her parents. The admission to see her was not only less than the admission to see the angel, but people were permitted to ask her all manner of questions about her absurd state and to examine her up and down so that no one would ever doubt the truth of her horror. She was a frightful tarantula the size of a ram and with the head of a sad maiden. What was most heartrending, however, was not her outlandish shape but the sincere affliction with which she recounted the details of her misfortune. While still practically a child she had sneaked out of her parents' house to go to a dance, and while she was coming back through the woods after having danced all night without permission, a fearful thunderclap rent the sky in two and through the crack came the lightning bolt of brimstone that changed her into a spider. Her only nourishment came from the meatballs that charitable souls chose to toss into her mouth. A spectacle like that, full of so much human truth and with such a fearful lesson, was bound to defeat without even trying that of a haughty angel who scarcely deigned to look at mortals. Besides, the few miracles attributed to the angel showed a certain mental disorder, like the blind man who didn't recover his sight but grew three new teeth, or the paralytic[9] who didn't get to walk but almost won the lottery, and the leper whose sores sprouted sunflowers. Those consolation miracles, which were more like mocking fun, had already ruined the angel's reputation when the woman who had been changed into a spider finally crushed him completely. That was how Father Gonzaga was cured forever of his insomnia[10] and Pelayo's courtyard went back

---

**6. hermetic** (hər met′ ik) *adj.*: Obscure; hard to understand.
**7. cataclysm** (kat′ ə kliz′ əm) *n.*: A violent upheaval.
**8. Aramaic** (ar′ ə mā′ ik) *n.*: A Semitic language that was the common language throughout the Near East from *c.* 300 B.C. to *c.* A.D. 650; one of its dialects was spoken by Jesus and his disciples.

---

**9. paralytic** (par′ ə lit′ ik) *n.*: A person having paralysis.
**10. insomnia** (in säm′ nē ə) *n.*: Chronic inablility to sleep.

*A Very Old Man with Enormous Wings* 177

---

**14 Discussion** Have students describe the angel's responses during his captivity. Are his responses those that one might expect from an angel? Explain.

**15 Discussion** What is significant about the way in which Rome reacts to the appearance of an angel?

**16 Discussion** Why does the author include the story about the woman who had been changed into a tarantula? Contrast the townspeople's reactions to her with their reaction to the angel.

**17 Discussion** Why is the angel a disappointment to the townspeople?

---

and nothing about him measured up to the proud dignity of angels.

**Student Activity 1.** Find two more passages in "A Very Old Man with Enormous Wings" in which García Márquez illustrates character traits, setting and tone, or ideas. Identify the words which seem most vivid.

**Student Activity 2.** Write a brief passage of your own in which you illustrate someone's youth, inexperience, physical dexterity, musical ability, comic behavior, or some other personality trait. Do not mention the specific trait. When you finish, read the passage aloud and ask your listeners to identify the trait you are highlighting.

18 **Discussion** What does this statement reveal about human nature?

19 **Discussion** Have students discuss the meaning of the sentence. What does this detail reveal about the old man? Does it further affirm or disprove that he is an angel? Why?

20 **Clarification** Point out to students that the angel, portrayed as a lonely, proud individual, asserts a sense of dignity in spite of his treatment by a brutal society.

21 **Reading Strategy** Compare and contrast the doctor's reaction to the angel with that of the priest. Which reaction seems more accurate? Why?

22 **Discussion** How have Pelayo and Elisenda's reactions and behavior changed since they discovered the angel?

to being as empty as during the time it had rained for three days and crabs walked through the bedrooms.

The owners of the house had no reason to lament. With the money they saved they built a two-story mansion with balconies and gardens and high netting so that crabs wouldn't get in during the winter, and with iron bars on the windows so that angels wouldn't get in. Pelayo also set up a rabbit warren close to town and gave up his job as bailiff for good, and Elisenda bought some satin pumps with high heels and many dresses of iridescent silk, the kind worn on Sunday by the most desirable women in those times. The chicken coop was the only thing that didn't receive any attention. If they washed it down with creolin[11] and burned tears of myrrh[12] inside it every so often, it was not in homage[13] to the angel but to drive away the dungheap stench that still hung everywhere like a ghost and was turning the new house into an old one. At first, when the child learned to walk, they were careful that he not get too close to the chicken coop. But then they began to lose their fears and got used to the smell, and before the child got his second teeth he'd gone inside the chicken coop to play, where the wires were falling apart. The angel was no less standoffish with him than with other mortals, but he tolerated the most ingenious infamies with the patience of a dog who had no illusions. They both came down with chicken pox at the same time. The doctor who took care of the child couldn't resist the temptation to listen to the angel's heart, and he found so much whistling in the heart and so many sounds in his kidneys that it

seemed impossible for him to be alive. What surprised him most, however, was the logic of his wings. They seemed so natural on that completely human organism that he couldn't understand why other men didn't have them too.

When the child began school it had been some time since the sun and rain had caused the collapse of the chicken coop. The angel went dragging himself about here and there like a stray dying man. They would drive him out of the bedroom with a broom and a moment later find him in the kitchen. He seemed to be in so many places at the same time that they grew to think that he'd been duplicated, that he was reproducing himself all through the house, and the exasperated and unhinged Elisenda shouted that it was awful living in that hell full of angels. He could scarcely eat and his antiquarian eyes had also become so foggy that he went about bumping into posts. All he had left were the bare cannulae[14] of his last feathers. Pelayo threw a blanket over him and

---

**11. creolin** (krē′ ə lin) *n*.: Possibly an antiseptic.
**12. myrrh** (mur) *n*.: A fragrant, bitter-tasting perfume.
**13. homage** (häm′ ij) *n*.: Anything done to show reverence, honor, or respect.

**14. cannulae** (kan′ yoō lē′) *n*.: Tubes that are inserted into the body.

178    *Short Stories*

---

## Grammar in Action

Authors avoid monotony in their writing by varying their sentence patterns. One way to vary a sentence is to use different **sentence openers.**

In addition to its subject, a sentence can begin with one-word modifiers, phrases, clauses, or a combination of these openers.

García Márquez uses a variety of sentence openers in "A Very Old Man with Enormous Wings." Examine the following sentences and notice the type of sentence openers García Márquez used:

In the middle of the night, when the rain stopped, Pelayo and Elisenda were still killing crabs.

Standing by the wire, he reviewed his catechism in an instant and asked them to open the door so that he could take a close look at that pitiful man who looked more like a decrepit hen among the fascinated chickens.

Alien to the impertinences of the world, he only lifted his antiquarian eyes and murmured something in his dialect when Father Gonzaga went into the chicken coop and said good morning to him in Latin.

A Very Old Man with Enormous Wings 179

In the first sentence García Márquez uses both a prepositional phrase and an adverbial clause; in the second he uses a participal phrase; and in the third he uses an adjective with its modifiers.

**Student Activity 1.** Find three other sentences with differing sentence openers from the story. Name the type of opener each sentence uses.

**Student Activity 2.** Write a paragraph about your impressions of this story. Use at least four different sentence openers. Exchange papers with a partner and name the sentence openers in your partner's paper.

extended him the charity of letting him sleep in the shed, and only then did they notice that he had a temperature at night, and was delirious with the tongue twisters of an old Norwegian. That was one of the few times they became alarmed, for they thought he was going to die and not even the wise neighbor woman had been able to tell them what to do with dead angels.

And yet he not only survived his worst winter, but seemed improved with the first sunny days. He remained motionless for several days in the farthest corner of the courtyard, where no one would see him, and at the beginning of December some large, stiff feathers began to grow on his wings, the feathers of a scarecrow, which looked more like another misfortune of decrepitude. But he must have known the reason for those changes, for he was quite careful that no one should notice them, that no one should hear the sea chanteys that he sometimes sang under the stars. One morning Elisenda was cutting some bunches of onions for lunch when a wind that seemed to come from the high seas blew into the kitchen. Then she went to the window and caught the angel in his first attempt at flight. They were so clumsy that his fingernails opened a furrow in the vegetable patch and he was on the point of knocking the shed down with the ungainly flapping that slipped on the light and couldn't get a grip on the air. But he did manage to gain altitude. Elisenda let out a sigh of relief, for herself and for him, when she saw him pass over the last houses, holding himself up in some way with the risky flapping of a senile vulture. She kept watching him even when she was through cutting the onions and she kept on watching until it was no longer possible for her to see him, because then he was no longer an annoyance in her life but an imaginary dot on the horizon of the sea.

## THINKING ABOUT THE SELECTION

### Recalling

1. Describe the old man.
2. According to the wise neighbor woman, why has the old man come to Pelayo and Elisenda's house?
3. For what two reasons does Father Gonzaga suspect the old man is not an angel?

### Interpreting

4. What inferences do you make about the people who come to see the old man?
5. Why do the villagers' attitudes toward the angel change? For example, why do the villagers treat the old man first "without the slightest reverence" and then want to name him the "mayor of the world" or promote him "to the rank of a five-star general in order to win all wars"?

6. In what way is the woman who was turned into a tarantula "full of so much human truth and with such a fearful lesson"?
7. Explain Elisenda's reaction at the end of the story.
8. How do you interpret the character of the old man? Support your answer.

### Applying

9. Throughout the course of human history, people have tried to make meaning out of their world. For example, long ago people interpreted thunder as an angry god hurling thunder bolts. Even today, when a terrible disaster occurs, some people say, "There must be a reason why this occurred." Why do you think it is so important to humans to find meaning in even amazing occurrences? In what way has this drive led to the development of science?

---

**23 Discussion** For what reasons might the angel be getting better? Why should he be careful that no one notice the changes?

**24 Reading Strategy** In what ways was the old man an annoyance to Elisenda? What does this reaction to the old man reveal about her?

**Reader's Response** Would you have held the angel captive and treated him as unkindly as Pelayo and Elisenda did? Why or why not?

**Speaking and Listening** Divide students into pairs and have them develop questions that they might use to interview an angel who suddenly appeared in their neighborhood. Give each student the opportunity to play the roles of angel and interviewer. Students might then present their results to the class in the format of a news report or a talk-show interview.

**Challenge** The author gives us no indication that Pelayo, Elisenda, or the villagers have learned anything from the angel. What "human truth" or "fearful lesson" might the old man with wings have taught them? How might their lives differ after his departure?

## Closure and Extension

### ANSWERS TO THINKING ABOUT THE SELECTION
*Recalling*

1. The old man is bald and practically toothless. Dressed like a ragpicker, he has dirty, half-plucked wings that are covered with mud. He has a strong sailor's voice but speaks an incomprehensible dialect.
2. The wise neighbor believes that the angel has come for Pelayo and Elisenda's sick child. She says that the angel is so old that he was knocked down by the rain.
3. Father Gonzaga suspects that the old man is an imposter because he does not know the language of God (Latin) and because he looks too human, lacking the dignity of angels.

*Interpreting*

4. Answers will differ. Suggested response: The people who come to see the old man are sensation seekers or those pursuing their own gain, such as cures for their ailments or forgiveness for their sins.
5. Answers will differ. Suggested response: At first they treat the angel harshly like a curiosity or a caged animal there for their amusement. They then regard him as a major, general, or stud—just in case he truly is a messenger from God.
6. Answers will differ. Suggested response: The tarantula story is much easier for the villagers to understand. Her punishment for disobeying her parents was straightforward and readily apparent. There are understandable reasons for her state and for her appearance—there are no such reasons for the angel's appearance.

## ANALYZING LITERATURE

### Understanding Theme

The **theme** of a story is an insight into life, or the point the story is making. In the context of magical realism, the theme lies in what happens when the magical or fantastic enters the ordinary, everyday lives of the characters.

1. What important insight does this story convey to you about life?
2. Imagine that you were telling friends what this story meant to you. One of your friends says, "I didn't see that." How would you respond? What details would you point out?
3. The subtitle of the story is "A Tale for Children." Why?

## CRITICAL THINKING AND READING

### Identifying Different Interpretations

When you make an **interpretation**, you explain the meaning of something, make something understandable, or express your perception of something. In "A Very Old Man with Enormous Wings," for example, each character has his or her own interpretation or perception of who the old man is. Pelayo and Elisenda believe he is "a castaway from some foreign ship"; the neighbor woman claims he is an angel; and Father Gonzaga thinks he is an imposter.

1. What other interpretations of who the old man is do the villagers propose?
2. García Márquez wrote this story in response to critics' interpretations of his novel *One Hundred Years of Solitude*. In what way does this tale send a cautionary note to critics who interpret the symbols used in literature?

## UNDERSTANDING LANGUAGE

### Using Context to Understand Words

When you read an unfamiliar word, you can often figure out its meaning from **context**—that is, from the words, phrases, and sentences that surround it. After reading that a very old man with enormous wings is lying face down in the mud in Pelayo and Elisenda's courtyard, you can guess that their reaction—that of *mute stupor*—means that they were shocked senseless and speechless.

Use the context of the following sentences to help you define the italicized words. Then use each word in a sentence that demonstrates its meaning.

1. "There were only a few faded hairs left on his bald skull and very few teeth in his mouth, and his pitiful condition of a drenched great-grandfather had taken away any sense of *grandeur* he might have had." (p. 173)
2. "Against the judgment of the wise neighbor woman, for whom angels in those times were the *fugitive* survivors of a celestial conspiracy, they did not have the heart to club him to death." (p. 173)
3. "The angel was no less standoffish with him than with other mortals, but he tolerated the most ingenious *infamies* with the patience of a dog who had no illusions." (p. 178)
4. He could scarcely eat and his *antiquarian* eyes had also become so foggy that he went on bumping into posts.

## THINKING AND WRITING

### Writing from a Different Perspective

In "A Very Old Man with Enormous Wings," García Márquez describes the old man's appearance and the villagers' reaction to him, but we learn very little about what the old man thinks and feels. Imagine that you were the old man in García Márquez's story and rewrite the story from your perspective as the old man. Try to penetrate the old man's personality, thoughts, and feelings. Review your work with a peer, asking your partner if you adequately and accurately portray the old man. Does your partner get a real sense of who the old man is? Write a final draft.

*A Very Old Man with Enormous Wings* 181

---

2. Answers will differ. Students should cite numerous examples to support their interpretation.
3. Answers will differ. Suggested Response: The subtitle implies that his short story resembles a fairy tale in its simplicity, its humor, its mixture of the real the supernatural, its universality, and its theme.

### ANSWERS TO CRITICAL THINKING AND READING

1. Answers will differ. Other interpretations of the old man's identity include a healer, a side-show freak, a prisoner, and a human.
2. Answers will differ. Suggested Response: The author may have been trying to indicate that one interpretation of a symbol or a circumstance is just that—one perception. García Márquez may have been cautioning critics that to hold up one interpretation as valid is to do a disservice both to readers and authors.

### ANSWERS TO UNDERSTANDING LANGUAGE

Answers may vary. Suggested Responses:

1. *grandeur:* impressiveness. The old hotel still retained a sense of grandeur.
2. *fugitive:* running away. Harriet Tubman helped fugitive slaves reach the North.
3. *infamies:* evil acts. Jesse James was notorious for his many infamies.
4. *antiquarian:* old; no longer useful. His attitude was antiquarian and no longer appreciated.

### THINKING AND WRITING

For help with this assignment, students can refer to Lesson 2, "Drafting and Revising," in the Handbook of Writing About Literature.

**Publishing Student Writing** You might want to have volunteers read their accounts to the class or publish them in the school newspaper.

---

7. Elisenda seems to lack any gratefulness for the angel's part in bringing her money and an easier life. She is annoyed and even infuriated by the angel's intrusion into her home. She greets his departure with relief.
8. Answers will differ. Suggested response: The old man serves as a symbol rather than as a fully developed character. Uncommunicative, coldly indifferent, he seems to represent a loss of innocence and a fall from grace into an unhappy earthly existence.

### Applying

9. Answers will differ. Most students will understand the human need for comprehending and mastering the unknown. The desire to know what lies beyond Earth has led to space travel. The desire to cure and control disease has led to advances in medicine, and so forth.

### ANSWERS TO ANALYZING LITERATURE

1. Answers will differ. Some students will interpret the story pessimistically: that although people want to understand the unknown or the mysterious, they have predominantly selfish motives. Other students may note that there are certain things that no one can explain and that it is absurd to try. Still others may note how people respond indifferently to the miraculous.

## Focus

**More About the Author** O. Henry had little formal education. He drew his themes and plots from his experiences as a pharmacist, cowboy, draftsman, bank teller, and convicted embezzler. Ask students whether they think a fiction writer must have a wide experience of life.

**Literary Focus** Have students work in small groups and brainstorm for ideas that might be used as the theme of a story. Ask them to select the idea they find the most interesting and consider the kind of story in which that theme could be developed. What kind of characters would the story have and what would be the situation? Have each group report to the class the problem that the characters would resolve in its story and see if other students can predict what the theme might be.

**Look For** O. Henry at times removes himself from the narrator's role of advancing the plot and makes comments to the reader. Ask students to consider the purpose of these comments and to decide whether they relate to the theme.

**Writing/Prior Knowledge** It has been said that the best gift is the one you would most like yourself. Ask students to consider this idea as they do the assignment.

**Vocabulary** Ask your **less advanced** students how *ravages* might *depreciate* something, how someone could *instigate* something in a *discreet* way, how *chaste* and *meretricious* might be used as antonyms, and how *cascade* might be used to describe a person's hair.

**Spelling Tip** Point out the second *e* in *meretricious*. Some students may misspell this word *meritricious*.

### The Gift of the Magi

**O. Henry** (1862–1910) was born William Sydney Porter in Greensboro, North Carolina. As a young man, he moved to Texas where he worked as a bank teller. Because he was convicted of embezzling funds from the bank, he served time in prison. It was while in prison that he began writing short stories. After his release O. Henry moved to New York, which is the setting for many of his stories. He is most famous for his use of surprise or twist endings. "The Gift of the Magi," one of his most popular works, has an unexpected twist at the end.

**Key Statements as a Clue to Theme**

The **theme** of a story is an insight into life that the author presents through characters and action. This insight may be about problems, conditions, or situations in human life. Often an author will include key statements that point to the theme, as O. Henry does in "The Gift of the Magi."

**Look For**

As you read "The Gift of the Magi," look for statements that have meanings beyond the specific events of the story. Use these statements to lead you to the theme.

**Writing**

In this story two people exchange special gifts. Think of a special person, a friend, or a famous person you admire. Supposing that you had unlimited money to spend on a gift for that person, list some gifts you might buy. Pick the one you think would be the best and freewrite about why you chose that one.

**Vocabulary**

Knowing the following words will help you as you read "The Gift of the Magi."

**instigates** (in′ stə gāts′) *v.*: Urges on; stirs up (p. 183)
**depreciate** (di prē′ s̸hē āt′) *v.*: Reduce in value (p. 184)
**cascade** (kas kād′) *n.*: A waterfall (p. 184)
**chaste** (c̸hāst) *adj.*: Pure or clean in style; not ornate (p. 184)

**meretricious** (mer′ ə trish′ əs) *adj.*: Attractive in a cheap, flashy way (p. 184)
**ravages** (rav′ ij iz) *n.*: Ruins; devastating damages (p. 184)
**discreet** (dis krēt′) *adj.*: Tactful; respectful (p. 185)

### Objectives

1 To understand key statements
2 To understand how to paraphrase
3 To trace word histories
4 To write about theme

### Support Material

**Teaching Portfolio**
Teacher Backup, p. 227
Grammar in Action Worksheet, *Determining Author's Tone*, p. 231
Usage and Mechanics Worksheet, p. 233
Vocabulary Check, p. 234
Critical Thinking and Reading Worksheet, *Paraphrasing*, p. 235

Language Worksheet, *Tracing Word Histories*, p. 236
Selection Test, p. 237
Art Transparency 4: *Fleurs sur Fond Rouge*, by Marc Chagall

# The Gift of the Magi

## O. Henry

One dollar and eighty-seven cents. That was all. And sixty cents of it was in pennies. Pennies saved one and two at a time by bulldozing the grocer and the vegetable man and the butcher until one's cheeks burned with the silent imputation of parsimony[1] that such close dealing implied. Three times Della counted it. One dollar and eighty-seven cents. And the next day would be Christmas.

There was clearly nothing to do but flop down on the shabby little couch and howl. So Della did it. Which instigates the moral reflection that life is made up of sobs, sniffles, and smiles, with sniffles predominating.

While the mistress of the home is gradually subsiding from the first stage to the second, take a look at the home. A furnished flat[2] at $8 per week. It did not exactly beggar description,[3] but it certainly had that word on the lookout for the mendicancy squad.[4]

In the vestibule below was a letter-box into which no letter would go, and an electric button from which no mortal finger could coax a ring. Also appertaining thereunto was a card bearing the name "Mr. James Dillingham Young."

The "Dillingham" had been flung to the breeze during a former period of prosperity when its possessor was being paid $30 per week. Now, when the income was shrunk to $20, the letters of "Dillingham" looked blurred, as though they were thinking seriously of contracting to a modest and unassuming D. But whenever Mr. James Dillingham Young came home and reached his flat above he was called "Jim" and greatly hugged by Mrs. James Dillingham Young, already introduced to you as Della. Which is all very good.

Della finished her cry and attended to her cheeks with the powder rag. She stood by the window and looked out dully at a gray cat walking a gray fence in a gray backyard. Tomorrow would be Christmas Day, and she had only $1.87 with which to buy Jim a present. She had been saving every penny she could for months, with this result. Twenty dollars a week doesn't go far. Expenses had been greater than she had calculated. They always are. Only $1.87 to buy a present for Jim. Her Jim. Many a happy hour she had spent planning for something nice for him. Something fine and rare and sterling—something just a little bit near to being worthy of the honor of being owned by Jim.

There was a pier glass[5] between the windows of the room. Perhaps you have seen a pier glass in an $8 flat. A very thin and very agile person may, by observing his reflection

---

1. **silent imputation** (im pyōō tā′ shən) **of parsimony** (pär′ sə mō′ nē): Silent accusation of stinginess.
2. **flat** (flat) *n.*: Apartment.
3. **beggar description:** Resist description.
4. **mendicancy** (men′ di ken′ sē) **squad:** Police who arrested beggars.

5. **pier** (pir) **glass:** A tall mirror.

*The Gift of the Magi*  183

4 **Critical Thinking and Reading**
Ask students to infer what two emotions these descriptive details might suggest. What clue do they see to a possible solution to Della's problem?

5 **Discussion** Ask students to discuss the possible importance of this descriptive paragraph to the telling of the story. What does O. Henry establish here?

6 **Discussion** How does the writer hint at what is going on in Della's mind?

7 **Discussion** What further clue to Della's intentions does the writer give?

8 **Clarification** Point out to students that at the time this story is set, women used heated metal rods called *curling irons* to curl their hair.

in a rapid sequence of longitudinal strips, obtain a fairly accurate conception of his looks. Della, being slender, had mastered the art.

4 Suddenly she whirled from the window and stood before the glass. Her eyes were shining brilliantly, but her face had lost its color within twenty seconds. Rapidly she pulled down her hair and let it fall to its full length.

5 Now, there were two possessions of the James Dillingham Youngs in which they both took a mighty pride. One was Jim's gold watch that had been his father's and his grandfather's. The other was Della's hair. Had the Queen of Sheba[6] lived in the flat across the airshaft, Della would have let her hair hang out the window some day to dry just to depreciate Her Majesty's jewels and gifts. Had King Solomon been the janitor, with all his treasures piled up in the basement, Jim would have pulled out his watch every time he passed, just to see him pluck at his beard from envy.

6 So now Della's beautiful hair fell about her rippling and shining like a cascade of brown waters. It reached below her knee and made itself almost a garment for her. And then she did it up again nervously and quickly. Once she faltered for a minute and stood still while a tear or two splashed on the worn red carpet.

On went her old brown jacket; on went her old brown hat. With a whirl of skirts and with the brilliant sparkle still in her eyes, she fluttered out the door and down the stairs to the street.

7 Where she stopped the sign read: "Mme. Sofronie. Hair Goods of All Kinds." One flight up Della ran, and collected herself, panting. Madame, large, too white, chilly, hardly looked the "Sofronie."

"Will you buy my hair?" asked Della.

"I buy hair," said Madame. "Take yer hat off and let's have a sight at the looks of it."

Down rippled the brown cascade.

"Twenty dollars," said Madame, lifting the mass with a practiced hand.

"Give it to me quick," said Della.

Oh, and the next two hours tripped by on rosy wings. Forget the hashed metaphor. She was ransacking the stores for Jim's present.

She found it at last. It surely had been made for Jim and no one else. There was no other like it in any of the stores, and she had turned all of them inside out. It was a platinum fob chain[7] simple and chaste in design, properly proclaiming its value by substance alone and not by meretricious ornamentation—as all good things should do. It was even worthy of The Watch. As soon as she saw it she knew that it must be Jim's. It was like him. Quietness and value—the description applied to both. Twenty-one dollars they took from her for it, and she hurried home with the 87 cents. With that chain on his watch Jim might be properly anxious about the time in any company. Grand as the watch was he sometimes looked at it on the sly on account of the old leather strap that he used in place of a chain.

8 When Della reached home her intoxication gave way a little to prudence and reason. She got out her curling irons and lighted the gas and went to work repairing the ravages made by generosity added to love. Which is always a tremendous task, dear friends—a mammoth task.

Within forty minutes her head was covered with tiny, close-lying curls that made her look wonderfully like a truant schoolboy. She looked at her reflection in the mirror long, carefully, and critically.

---

**6. Queen of Sheba:** In the Bible, the beautiful queen who visited King Solomon to test his wisdom.

**7. fob** (fäb) **chain:** A small chain connecting a watch to its pocket.

## Grammar in Action

**Tone** refers to the author's attitude toward his or her subject. Readers determine tone from the way a subject is presented and described. The tone of a work of literature can often be stated in one or two words, such as *admiring, very sarcastic, highly respectful, angry,* and so forth. What is O. Henry's attitude toward the characters and situation in this story? Read this passage:

Now there were two possessions of the James Dillingham Youngs in which they both took a great and mighty pride. One was Jim's gold watch that had been his father's and his grandfather's. The other was Della's hair. Had the queen of Sheba lived in the flat across the airshaft, Della would have let her hair hang out the window some day to dry just to depreciate Her Majesty's jewels and gifts. Had King Solomon been the janitor, with all his treasures piled up in the basement, Jim would have pulled out his watch every time he passed, just to see him pluck at his beard with envy.

The author's amused fondness for the young couple is shown in a description in which even their vanity is treated with affection.

"If Jim doesn't kill me," she said to herself, "before he takes a second look at me, he'll say I look like a Coney Island[8] chorus girl. But what could I do—oh! what could I do with a dollar and eighty-seven cents?"

At 7 o'clock the coffee was made and the frying-pan was on the back of the stove hot and ready to cook the chops.

Jim was never late. Della doubled the fob chain in her hand and sat on the corner of the table near the door that he always entered. Then she heard his step on the stair away down on the first flight, and she turned white for just a moment. She had a habit of saying little silent prayers about the simplest everyday things, and now she whispered: "Please God, make him think I am still pretty."

The door opened and Jim stepped in and closed it. He looked thin and very serious. Poor fellow, he was only twenty-two—and to be burdened with a family! He needed a new overcoat and he was without gloves.

Jim stopped inside the door, as immovable as a setter at the scent of quail. His eyes were fixed upon Della, and there was an expression in them that she could not read, and it terrified her. It was not anger, nor surprise, nor disapproval, nor horror, nor any of the sentiments that she had been prepared for. He simply stared at her fixedly with that peculiar expression on his face.

Della wriggled off the table and went for him.

"Jim, darling," she cried, "don't look at me that way. I had my hair cut off and sold it because I couldn't have lived through Christmas without giving you a present. It'll grow out again—you won't mind, will you? I just had to do it. My hair grows awfully fast. Say 'Merry Christmas!' Jim, and let's be happy. You don't know what a nice—what a

_____
**8. Coney Island:** A beach and amusement park in Brooklyn, New York.

beautiful, nice gift I've got for you."

"You've cut off your hair?" asked Jim, laboriously, as if he had not arrived at that patent fact yet even after the hardest mental labor.

"Cut it off and sold it," said Della. "Don't you like me just as well, anyhow? I'm me without my hair, ain't I?"

Jim looked about the room curiously.

"You say your hair is gone?" he said, with an air almost of idiocy.

"You needn't look for it," said Della. "It's sold, I tell you—sold and gone, too. It's Christmas Eve, boy. Be good to me, for it went for you. Maybe the hairs of my head were numbered," she went on with a sudden serious sweetness, "but nobody could ever count my love for you. Shall I put the chops on, Jim?"

Out of his trance Jim seemed quickly to wake. He enfolded his Della. For ten seconds let us regard with discreet scrutiny some inconsequential object in the other direction. Eight dollars a week or a million a year—what is the difference? A mathematician or a wit would give you the wrong answer. The Magi brought valuable gifts, but that was not among them. This dark assertion will be illuminated later on.

Jim drew a package from his overcoat pocket and threw it upon the table.

"Don't make any mistake, Dell," he said, "about me. I don't think there's anything in the way of a haircut or a shave or a shampoo that could make me like my girl any less. But if you'll unwrap that package you may see why you had me going a while at first."

White fingers and nimble tore at the string and paper. And then an ecstatic scream of joy; and then, alas! a quick feminine change to hysterical tears and wails, necessitating the immediate employment of all the comforting powers of the lord of the flat.

For there lay The Combs—the set of

9

10

11

---

9 **Discussion** What more practical gift might Della have purchased for Jim? Do you agree or disagree with Della's choice? Why?

10 **Reading Strategy** Ask students to predict what Jim might have purchased for her.

11 **Master Teacher Note** Authors at times use allusions to characters and situations from other stories or from history. Through the use of an allusion an author can bring to the reader's mind ideas and emotions from another situation. Ask students to consider what the allusion to the Magi might contribute to this story.

---

**Student Activity 1.** Find two other passages in the story that convey the author's tone and discuss these with your classmates.

**Student Activity 2.** Discuss with a partner your own attitude about a particular subject, and then write a paragraph about it. Exchange drafts and discuss ways to improve compositions.

**12 Literary Focus** How can the couple be both "foolish" and "wisest"? How does this apparent contradiction suggest the theme?

**Reader's Response** What is the most precious gift you have ever received? What made it so special?

combs, side and back, that Della had worshipped for long in a Broadway window. Beautiful combs, pure tortoise shell, with jeweled rims—just the shade to wear in the beautiful vanished hair. They were expensive combs, she knew, and her heart had simply craved and yearned over them without the least hope of possession. And now, they were hers, but the tresses that should have adorned the coveted adornments were gone.

But she hugged them to her bosom, and at length she was able to look up with dim eyes and a smile and say: "My hair grows so fast, Jim!"

And then Della leaped up like a little singed cat and cried, "Oh, oh!"

Jim had not yet seen his beautiful present. She held it out to him eagerly upon her open palm. The dull precious metal seemed to flash with a reflection of her bright and ardent spirit.

"Isn't it a dandy, Jim? I hunted all over town to find it. You'll have to look at the time a hundred times a day now. Give me your

watch. I want to see how it looks on it."

Instead of obeying, Jim tumbled down on the couch and put his hands under the back of his head and smiled.

"Dell," said he, "let's put our Christmas presents away and keep 'em a while. They're too nice to use just at present. I sold the watch to get the money to buy your combs. And now suppose you put the chops on."

The Magi, as you know, were wise men—wonderfully wise men—who brought gifts to the Babe in the manger. They invented the art of giving Christmas presents. Being wise, their gifts were no doubt wise ones, possibly bearing the privilege of exchange in case of duplication. And here I have lamely related to you the uneventful chronicle of two foolish children in a flat who most unwisely sacrificed for each other the greatest treasures of their house. But in a last word to the wise of these days let it be said that of all who give gifts these two were the wisest. Of all who give and receive gifts, such as they are wisest. Everywhere they are wisest. They are the magi.

12

*186   Short Stories*

**Closure and Extension**

**ANSWERS TO THINKING ABOUT THE SELECTION**
*Recalling*

1. They prize Jim's watch and Della's long hair.
2. Della sells her hair to buy Jim a watch fob.

## THINKING ABOUT THE SELECTION

### Recalling

1. At the beginning of the story, what possessions do Jim and Della prize the most?
2. How does Della manage to buy Jim a gift that she thinks is worthy of him?
3. Why is Jim particularly sorry that Della has cut her hair?
4. Why is Jim dismayed when he opens Della's gift to him?

### Interpreting

5. How do Della and Jim feel toward each other? Give evidence from the story that shows their feelings.
6. An ironic situation is one in which actions lead to an unexpected outcome. Explain how the ending of this story is an ironic situation.
7. Why does the author compare Della and Jim to the Magi?

### Applying

8. If you were either Jim or Della, How would you feel about the gift you received?

## ANALYZING LITERATURE

### Understanding Key Statements

The **theme** of a story is a general statement about life. Usually a theme is implied through the characters and action of the story. You can often find key statements in a story that serve as clues to the theme. For example, the statement, "I'm me without my hair, ain't I?" makes the point that people's characters are more important than their superficial appearance.

1. What point does each of the following key statements make?
   a. ". . . two foolish children in a flat who most unwisely sacrificed for each other the greatest treasures of their house."
   b. "Of all who give and receive gifts, such as they are wisest."
2. In your own words, state the theme of "The Gift of the Magi."

## CRITICAL THINKING AND READING

### Paraphrasing

When you paraphrase a statement or a passage in a text, you restate it in your own words. For example, you might paraphrase the sentence, "Quietness and value—the description applied to both [the watch chain and Jim]," as follows: "Both Jim and the watch chain showed quality in an inconspicuous way."

Paraphrase each of these statements.

1. ". . . repairing the ravages made by generosity added to love . . . is always a tremendous task."
2. "I don't think there's anything in the way of a haircut or a shave or a shampoo that could make me like my girl any less."

## UNDERSTANDING LANGUAGE

### Tracing Word Histories

Many words have interesting histories, which you can find in the etymologies in your dictionary. For example, the word *flat*, meaning an apartment, is an alteration of the Old English word *flet*, referring to a floor of a dwelling. Use a dictionary to trace the histories of these words.

1. Magi     3. comb
2. fob        4. ransack

## THINKING AND WRITING

### Writing About Theme

Write an essay about the theme of "The Gift of the Magi." First, state the theme in your own words. Then make notes about how the characters, the setting, and the events contribute to it. Organize your notes into an outline and draft your essay, showing how O. Henry has used the story elements to illustrate the theme. Finally, revise your essay, checking that each of your points supports your statement of the theme.

*The Gift of the Magi*   187

has not sold his watch and cannot afford to buy her a gift. What might their feelings be in each of these situations? Would they be more happy or less happy than they were at the end of this story? Why?

### ANSWERS TO ANALYZING LITERATURE

1. Suggested Response:
   a. They were foolish in giving up the one possession that gave them the most satisfaction in life.
   b. They were wise in allowing their love to motivate their giving.
2. Suggested Response: Giving in a spirit of love is more valuable than any material gift.

### ANSWERS TO CRITICAL THINKING AND READING

1. Suggested Response: It is hard to fix the damage that people inflict on themselves when acting out of love and a spirit of self-sacrifice.
2. Suggested Response: No matter how much you changed your appearance, I would love you just as much.

### ANSWERS TO UNDERSTANDING LANGUAGE

1. Magi: from the Old Persian *magus* referring to a priestly class; *magic* comes from the same source
2. fob: from German *fuppe* referring to a small pocket like the one used to hold a watch
3. comb: from Old High German word for comb—*kamb*
4. ransack: from the Old Norse word for the search of a house—*rannsaka*.

---

3. Jim loved Della's long hair and bought her expensive combs to wear in her hair.
4. Jim is dismayed at receiving the gift of a watch fob because he has sold his watch to buy the combs for Della.

### Interpreting

5. Suggested Response: They love each other very much. Each was willing to sacrifice his or her most precious possession to buy a gift for the other.

6. Suggested Response: The fact that Della cannot use her combs because she sold her hair and Jim cannot use his watch fob because he has sold his watch, makes the end of the story ironic.

7. Suggested Response: The Magi were wise men who gave precious gifts to the infant Christ. Della and Jim were wise in sacrificing their most precious possessions to give each other gifts—their giving demonstrated their love.

### Applying

8. Answers will differ. Most students will realize that they would feel some disappointment at their loss but greater satisfaction in the knowledge of someone's love.

**Challenge** Imagine that Jim has sold his watch to buy Della the combs, but she has not cut off her hair and has no gift to give him. Or imagine that Della cut off her hair to buy Jim the watch fob, but he

### THINKING AND WRITING

For help with this assignment, students can refer to Lesson 11, "Writing About Theme," in the Handbook of Writing About Literature.

### Publishing Student Writing

Ask students to share their essays with the class.

## Focus

**More About the Author** James Hurst himself wrote, "The ancient Egyptians worshiped the ibis because they believed it destroyed the crocodiles. In their liturgy, it took second place only to the phoenix. So I chose as my symbol a scarlet ibis, the most beautiful and rare member of the ibis family . . . I wanted a bird to represent Doodle—not Doodle's physical self, but his spirit. Certainly, Doodle inside had much more to admire than his outside . . . This bird must be destined to die as Doodle was to die." Ask students why writers use symbols in their stories.

**Literary Focus** Symbols are often visible representations of something invisible, such as a concept, idea, or hidden truth. Although the ibis is a symbol for Doodle and both are visible, the bird represents a quality within Doodle that is not evident from his appearance.

**Look For** Have students consider what an unusual bird like a scarlet ibis might symbolize.

**Writing/Prior Knowledge** Divide the class into small groups and have students discuss these questions before writing.

**Vocabulary** You might have your students organize a vocabulary baseball game. They should divide into two teams with one student serving as umpire. The pitcher of one team throws out a vocabulary word to a batter from the other team and asks that student to define the word or to use the word in a sentence. The student can advance to first base by responding correctly. Any member of the pitcher's team can challenge the answer, and the umpire must rule if the student is safe or out.

## The Scarlet Ibis

**James Hurst** (1922–     ) was born and raised on a farm in North Carolina. He studied to be a chemical engineer but preferred music and took voice lessons at New York's Juilliard School of Music. When he realized that he was not meant to have a career in opera, he took a job as a bank clerk and wrote in the evenings. He published several stories in small magazines and achieved recognition with "The Scarlet Ibis," published in *The Atlantic,* in 1960.

**Symbol**

A **symbol** is an object, person, idea, or action that represents something other than itself. Authors may use symbols in literature to make a point, create a mood, or reinforce a theme. Many common symbols have fixed or universal meanings; for example, the season of autumn frequently symbolizes a time of dying. Within a given work, a symbol takes its meaning from the work itself. It exists as an integral part of the story but represents something larger or more significant beyond the events of the story. "The Scarlet Ibis" has many symbols, but one stands out—the ibis. What might it symbolize?

**Look For**

As you read "The Scarlet Ibis," look for the ways in which Doodle's spirit is different from his physical self. Why is the scarlet ibis an effective symbol for him?

**Writing**

"The Scarlet Ibis" is about a relationship between two brothers. Free-write about the following question: Can two brothers or sisters be close friends? Include ideas about what brings brothers and sisters close together and what causes conflict between them.

**Vocabulary**

Knowing the following words will help you as you read "The Scarlet Ibis."

**imminent** (im′ ə nent) *adj.*: Likely to happen soon (p. 192)

**iridescent** (ir′ ə des′ 'nt) *adj.*: Having shifting, rainbowlike colors (p. 194)

**vortex** (vôr′ teks) *n.*: The center of a situation, which draws all that surrounds it (p. 194)

**infallibility** (in fal′ ə bil′ ə tē) *n.*: The condition of being unable to fail (p. 194)

**entrails** (en′ trālz) *n.*: Internal organs, specifically intestines (p. 194)

**precariously** (pri′ ker′ ē əs lē) *adv.*: Insecurely (p. 195)

**evanesced** (ev ə nest′) *v.*: Faded away (p. 198)

## Objectives

1  To interpret symbols
2  To recognize emotive language
3  To write about symbols

## Support Material

**Teaching Portfolio**
Teacher Backup, p. 239
Grammar in Action Worksheet, *Using Concrete Details,* p. 243; *Using Infinitive Phrases,* p. 245
Usage and Mechanics Worksheet, p. 247
Vocabulary Check, p. 248
Analyzing Literature Worksheet, Interpreting Symbols, p. 249
Language Worksheet, Identifying Simile and Metaphor, p. 250
Selection Test, p. 251

# The Scarlet Ibis

James Hurst

It was in the clove of seasons, summer was dead but autumn had not yet been born, that the ibis lit in the bleeding tree. The flower garden was stained with rotting brown magnolia petals and ironweeds grew rank amid the purple phlox. The five o'clocks by the chimney still marked time, but the oriole nest in the elm was untenanted and rocked back and forth like an empty cradle. The last graveyard flowers were blooming, and their smell drifted across the cotton field and through every room of our house, speaking softly the names of our dead.

It's strange that all this is still so clear to me, now that the summer has long since fled and time has had its way. A grindstone stands where the bleeding tree stood, just outside the kitchen door, and now if an oriole sings in the elm, its song seems to die up in the leaves, a silvery dust. The flower garden is prim, the house a gleaming white, and the pale fence across the yard stands straight and spruce. But sometimes (like right now), as I sit in the cool, green-draped parlor, the grindstone begins to turn, and time with all its changes is ground away—and I remember Doodle.

Doodle was just about the craziest brother a boy ever had. Of course, he wasn't a crazy crazy like old Miss Leedie, who was in love with President Wilson and wrote him a letter every day, but was a nice crazy, like someone you meet in your dreams. He was born when I was six and was, from the out-set, a disappointment. He seemed all head, with a tiny body which was red and shriveled like an old man's. Everybody thought he was going to die—everybody except Aunt Nicey, who had delivered him. She said he would live because he was born in a caul[1] and cauls were made from Jesus' nightgown. Daddy had Mr. Heath, the carpenter, build a little mahogany coffin for him. But he didn't die, and when he was three months old Mama and Daddy decided they might as well name him. They named him William Armstrong, which was like tying a big tail on a small kite. Such a name sounds good only on a tombstone.

I thought myself pretty smart at many things, like holding my breath, running, jumping, or climbing the vines in Old Woman Swamp, and I wanted more than anything else someone to race to Horsehead Landing, someone to box with, and someone to perch with in the top fork of the great pine behind the barn, where across the fields and swamps you could see the sea. I wanted a brother. But Mama, crying, told me that even if William Armstrong lived, he would never do these things with me. He might not, she sobbed, even be "all there." He might, as long as he lived, lie on the rubber sheet in the center of the bed in the front bedroom where the white marquisette cur-

1. **caul** (kôl) *n*.: The membrane enclosing a baby at birth.

*The Scarlet Ibis*   189

**5 Discussion** What sides of the narrator's character are revealed in this paragraph?

**6 Reading Strategy** Ask students to summarize Doodle's progress and to predict what further progress he might make.

**7 Discussion** Is Doodle a good name for William Armstrong? Why?

**8 Discussion** What character traits does the narrator's behavior reveal?

**9 Discussion** What kind of unspoken pact develops between the brothers?

tains billowed out in the afternoon sea breeze, rustling like palmetto fronds.[2]

It was bad enough having an invalid brother, but having one who possibly was not all there was unbearable, so I began to make plans to kill him by smothering him with a pillow. However, one afternoon as I watched him, my head poked between the irons posts of the foot of the bed, he looked straight at me and grinned. I skipped through the rooms, down the echoing halls, shouting, "Mama, he smiled. He's all there! He's all there!" and he was.

When he was two, if you laid him on his stomach, he began to try to move himself, straining terribly. The doctor said that with his weak heart this strain would probably kill him, but it didn't. Trembling, he'd push himself up, turning first red, then a soft purple, and finally collapse back onto the bed like an old worn-out doll. I can still see Mama watching him, her hand pressed tight across her mouth, her eyes wide and unblinking. But he learned to crawl (it was his third winter), and we brought him out of the front bedroom, putting him on the rug before the fireplace. For the first time he became one of us.

As long as he lay all the time in bed, we called him William Armstrong, even though it was formal and sounded as if we were referring to one of our ancestors, but with his creeping around on the deerskin rug and beginning to talk, something had to be done about his name. It was I who renamed him. When he crawled, he crawled backwards, as if he were in reverse and couldn't change gears. If you called him, he'd turn around as if he were going in the other direction, then he'd back right up to you to be picked up. Crawling backward made him look like a

doodle-bug, so I began to call him Doodle, and in time even Mama and Daddy thought it was a better name than William Armstrong. Only Aunt Nicey disagreed. She said caul babies should be treated with special respect since they might turn out to be saints. Renaming my brother was perhaps the kindest thing I ever did for him, because nobody expects much from someone called Doodle.

Although Doodle learned to crawl, he showed no signs of walking, but he wasn't idle. He talked so much that we all quit listening to what he said. It was about this time that Daddy built him a go-cart and I had to pull him around. At first I just paraded him up and down the piazza, but then he started crying to be taken out into the yard and it ended up by my having to lug him wherever I went. If I so much as picked up my cap, he'd start crying to go with me and Mama would call from wherever she was, "Take Doodle with you."

He was a burden in many ways. The doctor had said that he mustn't get too excited, too hot, too cold, or too tired and that he must always be treated gently. A long list of don'ts went with him, all of which I ignored once we got out of the house. To discourage his coming with me, I'd run with him across the ends of the cotton rows and careen him around corners on two wheels. Sometimes I accidentally turned him over, but he never told Mama. His skin was very sensitive, and he had to wear a big straw hat whenever he went out. When the going got rough and he had to cling to the sides of the go-cart, the hat slipped all the way down over his ears. He was a sight. Finally, I could see I was licked. Doodle was my brother and he was going to cling to me forever, no matter what I did, so I dragged him across the burning cotton field to share with him the only beauty I knew, Old Woman Swamp. I pulled the go-cart through the saw-tooth fern, down into the green dimness where the pal-

**2. palmetto fronds:** Palm leaves.

## Grammar in Action

When a writer uses **concrete details,** readers can see, hear, smell, taste, and feel what the writer is describing. For instance, if a writer merely says "dog," the reader will only have a vague or general idea of the type of animal the writer has in mind. If a writer specifies "German shepherd," however, readers will have a much more specific picture.

Notice how James Hurst uses concrete, specific details to enliven the following description:

. . . I dragged him across the *burning cotton field* to share with him the only beauty I knew, Old Woman Swamp. I pulled the go-cart through the *saw-tooth fern,* down into the *green dimness* where the *palmetto fronds* whispered by the stream, lifted him out and set him down in the *soft rubber grass* beside a *tall pine.* His eyes were round with wonder as he gazed about him, and his little hands began to stroke the *rubber grass.* Then he began to cry.

Without the concrete details, this passage would be much less effective:

metto fronds whispered by the stream. I lifted him out and set him down in the soft rubber grass beside a tall pine. His eyes were round with wonder as he gazed about him, and his little hands began to stroke the rubber grass. Then he began to cry.

"For heaven's sake, what's the matter?" I asked, annoyed.

"It's so pretty," he said. "So pretty, pretty, pretty."

After that day Doodle and I often went down into Old Woman Swamp. I would gather wildflowers, wild violets, honeysuckle, yellow jasmine, snakeflowers, and water lilies, and with wire grass we'd weave them into necklaces and crowns. We'd bedeck ourselves with our handiwork and loll about thus beautified, beyond the touch of the everyday world. Then when the slanted rays of the sun burned orange in the tops of the pines, we'd drop our jewels into the stream and watch them float away toward the sea.

There is within me (and with sadness I have watched it in others) a knot of cruelty borne by the stream of love, much as our blood sometimes bears the seed of our destruction, and at times I was mean to Doodle. One day I took him up to the barn loft and showed him his casket, telling him how we all had believed he would die. It was covered with a film of Paris green[3] sprinkled to kill the rats, and screech owls had built a nest inside it.

Doodle studied the mahogany box for a long time, then said, "It's not mine."

"It is," I said. "And before I'll help you down from the loft, you're going to have to touch it."

"I won't touch it," he said sullenly.

"Then I'll leave you here by yourself," I threatened, and made as if I were going down.

Doodle was frightened of being left.

---

3. **Paris green:** A poisonous green powder.

"Don't go leave me, Brother," he cried, and he leaned toward the coffin. His hand, trembling, reached out, and when he touched the casket he screamed. A screech owl flapped out of the box into our faces, scaring us and covering us with Paris green. Doodle was paralyzed, so I put him on my shoulder and carried him down the ladder, and even when we were outside in the bright sunshine, he clung to me, crying, "Don't leave me. Don't leave me."

When Doodle was five years old, I was embarrassed at having a brother of that age who couldn't walk, so I set out to teach him. We were down in Old Woman Swamp and it was spring and the sick-sweet smell of bay flowers hung everywhere like a mournful song. "I'm going to teach you to walk, Doodle," I said.

He was sitting comfortably on the soft grass, leaning back against the pine. "Why?" he asked.

I hadn't expected such an answer. "So I won't have to haul you around all the time."

"I can't walk, Brother," he said.

"Who says so?" I demanded.

"Mama, the doctor—everybody."

"Oh, you can walk," I said, and I took him by the arms and stood him up. He collapsed onto the grass like a half-empty flour sack. It was as if he had no bones in his little legs.

"Don't hurt me, Brother," he warned.

"Shut up. I'm not going to hurt you. I'm going to teach you to walk." I heaved him up again, and again he collapsed.

This time he did not lift his face up out of the rubber grass. "I just can't do it. Let's make honeysuckle wreaths."

"Oh yes you can, Doodle," I said. "All you got to do is try. Now come on," and I hauled him up once more.

It seemed so hopeless from the beginning that it's a miracle I didn't give up. But

*The Scarlet Ibis* 191

10 **Discussion** Why do you think the beauty of the swamp caused Doodle to cry?

11 **Discussion** What was Doodle learning from his brother during their visits to the swamp?

12 **Enrichment** Discuss with students the concept of ambivalence. How is it possible to have two opposite and conflicting feelings toward someone at the same time?

13 **Discussion** Is the narrator's behavior cruel? Explain.

14 **Discussion** Why does the narrator want to teach Doodle to walk?

I pulled him across the field into a pretty swamp. It was dark and wet. I set him on the ground. He was startled and cried.

The many concrete details that Hurst includes enable readers to experience the swamp along with the two boys.

**Student Activity 1.** Identify the vague, general terms in the shorter passage above. Then locate the concrete details in Hurst's passage that bring the description to life.

**Student Activity 2.** Rewrite the vague shorter passage so that it is more concrete. However, make your description of Old Woman Swamp different from Hurst's.

15 **Discussion** Why is this an important moment in the story?

16 **Discussion** Why does the narrator feel this was his accomplishment as well as Doodle's? Does he have a right to share in Doodle's glory?

17 **Discussion** Do you agree that the narrator was a slave to pride? Why? How does this statement relate to his earlier confession about having "a knot of cruelty"?

18 **Reading Strategy** Ask students to summarize all the progress Doodle has made since birth. Ask them to predict what might happen to him in the future.

19 **Discussion** What do you think the narrator means by "lies"?

all of us must have something or someone to be proud of, and Doodle had become mine. I did not know then that pride is a wonderful, terrible thing, a seed that bears two vines, life and death. Every day that summer we went to the pine beside the stream of Old Woman Swamp, and I put him on his feet at least a hundred times each afternoon. Occasionally I too became discouraged because it didn't seem as if he was trying, and I would say, "Doodle, don't you *want* to learn to walk?"

He'd nod his head, and I'd say, "Well, if you don't keep trying, you'll never learn." Then I'd paint for him a picture of us as old men, white-haired, him with a long white beard and me still pulling him around in the go-cart. This never failed to make him try again.

Finally one day, after many weeks of practicing, he stood alone for a few seconds. When he fell, I grabbed him in my arms and hugged him, our laughter pealing through the swamp like a ringing bell. Now we knew it could be done. Hope no longer hid in the dark palmetto thicket but perched like a cardinal in the lacy toothbrush tree, brilliantly visible. "Yes, yes," I cried, and he cried it too, and the grass beneath us was soft and the smell of the swamp was sweet.

With success so imminent, we decided not to tell anyone until he could actually walk. Each day, barring rain, we sneaked into Old Woman Swamp, and by cotton-picking time Doodle was ready to show what he could do. He still wasn't able to walk far, but we could wait no longer. Keeping a nice secret is very hard to do, like holding your breath. We chose to reveal all on October eighth, Doodle's sixth birthday, and for weeks ahead we mooned around the house, promising everybody a most spectacular surprise. Aunt Nicey said that, after so much talk, if we produced anything less tremen-

dous than the Resurrection,[4] she was going to be disappointed.

At breakfast on our chosen day, when Mama, Daddy, and Aunt Nicey were in the dining room, I brought Doodle to the door in the go-cart just as usual and had them turn their backs, making them cross their hearts and hope to die if they peeked. I helped Doodle up, and when he was standing alone I let them look. There wasn't a sound as Doodle walked slowly across the room and sat down at his place at the table. Then Mama began to cry and ran over to him, hugging him and kissing him. Daddy hugged him too, so I went to Aunt Nicey, who was thanks praying in the doorway, and began to waltz her around. We danced together quite well until she came down on my big toe with her brogans, hurting me so badly I thought I was crippled for life.

Doodle told them it was I who had taught him to walk, so everyone wanted to hug me, and I began to cry.

"What are you crying for?" asked Daddy, but I couldn't answer. They did not know that I did it for myself; that pride, whose slave I was, spoke to me louder than all their voices, and that Doodle walked only because I was ashamed of having a crippled brother.

Within a few months Doodle had learned to walk well and his go-cart was put up in the barn loft (it's still there) beside his little mahogany coffin. Now, when we roamed off together, resting often, we never turned back until our destination had been reached, and to help pass the time, we took up lying. From the beginning Doodle was a terrible liar and he got me in the habit. Had anyone stopped to listen to us, we would have been sent off to Dix Hill.

My lies were scary, involved, and usually

---

4. **the Resurrection** (rez′ ə rek′ shən): The rising of Jesus Christ from the dead after his death and burial.

**BOYS IN A PUNT**
*N. C. Wyeth*
Courtesy of Dr. and Mrs. William A. Morton, Jr.

*The Scarlet Ibis* 193

20 **Critical Thinking and Reading**
Discuss this story with students. What emotions does it evoke? What does it indicate about Doodle?

21 **Discussion** Are the narrator's goals sensible? Explain

22 **Discussion** What mood does this passage call up?

23 **Clarification** World War I ended in November of 1918. During the summer, major battles were being fought in France.

24 **Discussion** Why does the author include this passage? How does it relate to the story?

pointless, but Doodle's were twice as crazy. People in his stories all had wings and flew wherever they wanted to go. His favorite lie was about a boy named Peter who had a pet peacock with a ten-foot tail. Peter wore a golden robe that glittered so brightly that when he walked through the sunflowers they turned away from the sun to face him. When Peter was ready to go to sleep, the peacock spread his magnificent tail, enfolding the boy gently like a closing go-to-sleep flower, burying him in the gloriously iridescent, rustling vortex. Yes, I must admit it. Doodle could beat me lying.

Doodle and I spent lots of time thinking about our future. We decided that when we were grown we'd live in Old Woman Swamp and pick dog-tongue for a living. Beside the stream, he planned, we'd build us a house of whispering leaves and the swamp birds would be our chickens. All day long (when we weren't gathering dog-tongue) we'd swing through the cypresses on the rope vines, and if it rained we'd huddle beneath an umbrella tree and play stickfrog. Mama and Daddy could come and live with us if they wanted to. He even came up with the idea that he could marry Mama and I could marry Daddy. Of course, I was old enough to know this wouldn't work out, but the picture he painted was so beautiful and serene that all I could do was whisper Yes, yes.

Once I had succeeded in teaching Doodle to walk, I began to believe in my own infallibility and I prepared a terrific development program for him, unknown to Mama and Daddy, of course. I would teach him to run, to swim, to climb trees, and to fight. He, too, now believed in my infallibility, so we set the deadline for these accomplishments less than a year away, when, it had been decided, Doodle could start to school.

That winter we didn't make much progress, for I was in school and Doodle suffered

from one bad cold after another. But when spring came, rich and warm, we raised our sights again. Success lay at the end of summer like a pot of gold, and our campaign got off to a good start. On hot days, Doodle and I went down to Horsehead Landing and I gave him swimming lessons or showed him how to row a boat. Sometimes we descended into the cool greenness of Old Woman Swamp and climbed the rope vines or boxed scientifically beneath the pine where he had learned to walk. Promise hung about us like the leaves, and wherever we looked, ferns unfurled and birds broke into song.

That summer, the summer of 1918, was blighted. In May and June there was no rain and the crops withered, curled up, then died under the thirsty sun. One morning in July a hurricane came out of the east, tipping over the oaks in the yard and splitting the limbs of the elm trees. That afternoon it roared back out of the west, blew the fallen oaks around, snapping their roots and tearing them out of the earth like a hawk at the entrails of a chicken. Cotton bolls were wrenched from the stalks and lay like green walnuts in the valleys between the rows, while the cornfield leaned over uniformly so that the tassels touched the ground. Doodle and I followed Daddy out into the cotton field, where he stood, shoulders sagging, surveying the ruin. When his chin sank down onto his chest, we were frightened, and Doodle slipped his hand into mine. Suddenly Daddy straightened his shoulders, raised a giant knuckly fist, and with a voice that seemed to rumble out of the earth itself began cursing heaven, hell, the weather, and the Republican Party. Doodle and I, prodding each other and giggling, went back to the house, knowing that everything would be all right.

And during that summer, strange names were heard through the house: Château Thierry, Amiens, Soissons, and in her bless-

*194 Short Stories*

---

## Grammar in Action

Knowing how to use infinitives correctly will avoid confusion and will make your writing clear and accurate. An **infinitive** is the form of a verb that comes after the word *to* and acts as a noun, adjective, or adverb. When an infinitive has modifiers or a complement, it is called an **infinitive phrase.** Read the following sentences in which James Hurst uses infinitives and infinitive phrases.

"Of course, I was old enough *to know this wouldn't work out.*"

"I would teach him *to run, to swim, to climb trees,* and *to fight.*"

Notice that the first sentence contains an infinitive phrase, whereas the second contains infinitives.

It is important not to confuse infinitives and infinitive phrases with prepositional phrases that can also begin with the word *to.*

Writers need to be aware of several rules governing the use of infinitives. First, when using several infinitives in a series, the same form of the verb must be used each time. Sometimes writers are careless and combine infinitives with the *ing* form of ing at the supper table, Mama once said, "And bless the Pearsons, whose boy Joe was lost at Belleau Wood."[5]

So we came to that clove of seasons. School was only a few weeks away, and Doodle was far behind schedule. He could barely clear the ground when climbing up the rope vines and his swimming was certainly not passable. We decided to double our efforts, to make that last drive and reach our pot of gold. I made him swim until he turned blue and row until he couldn't lift an oar. Wherever we went, I purposely walked fast, and although he kept up, his face turned red and his eyes became glazed. Once, he could go no further, so he collapsed on the ground and began to cry.

"Aw, come on, Doodle," I urged. "You can do it. Do you want to be different from everybody else when you start school?"

"Does it make any difference?"

"It certainly does," I said. "Now, come on," and I helped him up.

As we slipped through dog days, Doodle began to look feverish, and Mama felt his forehead, asking him if he felt ill. At night he didn't sleep well, and sometimes he had nightmares, crying out until I touched him and said, "Wake up, Doodle. Wake up."

It was Saturday noon, just a few days before school was to start. I should have already admitted defeat, but my pride wouldn't let me. The excitement of our program had now been gone for weeks, but still we kept on with a tired doggedness. It was too late to turn back, for we had both wandered too far into a net of expectations and had left no crumbs behind.

Daddy, Mama, Doodle, and I were seated at the dining-room table having lunch. It

was a hot day, with all the windows and doors open in case a breeze should come. In the kitchen Aunt Nicey was humming softly. After a long silence, Daddy spoke. "It's so calm, I wouldn't be surprised if we had a storm this afternoon."

"I haven't heard a rain frog," said Mama, who believed in signs, as she served the bread around the table.

"I did," declared Doodle. "Down in the swamp."

"He didn't," I said contrarily.

"You did, eh?" said Daddy, ignoring my denial.

"I certainly did," Doodle reiterated, scowling at me over the top of his iced-tea glass, and we were quiet again.

Suddenly, from out in the yard, came a strange croaking noise. Doodle stopped eating, with a piece of bread poised ready for his mouth, his eyes popped round like two blue buttons. "What's that?" he whispered.

I jumped up, knocking over my chair, and had reached the door when Mama called, "Pick up the chair, sit down again, and say excuse me."

By the time I had done this, Doodle had excused himself and had slipped out into the yard. He was looking up into the bleeding tree. "It's a great big red bird!" he called.

The bird croaked loudly again, and Mama and Daddy came out into the yard. We shaded our eyes with our hands against the hazy glare of the sun and peered up through the still leaves. On the topmost branch a bird the size of a chicken, with scarlet feathers and long legs, was perched precariously. Its wings hung down loosely, and as we watched, a feather dropped away and floated slowly down through the green leaves.

"It's not even frightened of us," Mama said.

"It looks tired," Daddy added. "Or maybe sick."

Doodle's hands were clasped at his

---

5. **Château Thierry** (shả tō tye rē'), **Amiens** (a myan'), **Soissons** (swä sôn'), . . . **Belleau** (be lō') **Wood:** Places in France where battles were fought during World War I.

*The Scarlet Ibis* 195

25 **Reading Strategy** Ask students to note the connection between this sentence and the first sentence of the story. Help students to understand that they are now at the same point of time as indicated in the first paragraph of the story.

26 **Discussion** Is the narrator pushing his brother too hard to achieve their goals? Why?

27 **Discussion** What does Doodle's question reveal about his changing mood?

28 **Discussion** How is Doodle's failing health related to his changed mood?

29 **Discussion** What keeps the narrator so determined to push ahead with their plans?

30 **Literary Focus** What qualities of the ibis does the author stress?

the verb. Note in the following sentence the confusion that can arise when the wrong verb form is used:

I would teach him to run, to swim, to climb trees, and fighting.

Secondly, writers should never split an infinitive by inserting an adverb between the word *to* and the verb. For example, never write:

I would teach him to quickly run.

The sentence should read:

I would teach him to run quickly.

**Student Activity 1.** Identify the infinitives and infinitive phrases in the following sentences. Revise any sentences that use the wrong form of the verb.
1. "He began to move himself, straining terribly."
2. "Doodle, don't you want to learn walking?"
3. "Black clouds began to gather in the southwest."

**Student Activity 2.** Write three original sentences in which you use infinitives or infinitive phrases.

## Humanities Note

Fine art, *Scarlet Ibis,* by John James Audubon. Audubon (1785–1851) was born in Santo Domingo (Haiti). Throughout Audubon's childhood on the island, his interest in birds and drawing birds developed. When he was an adult this interest was insatiable and he thought of little else.

Audubon is recognized as one of the first to study and paint the birds of America. His paintings are most noted for their life-size depiction of birds in their natural habitat. For example, in the original painting of the scarlet ibis, this South American bird is depicted in its natural habitat: wading along a tropical beach where the water is shallow and close to a swampy area. It is here the scarlet ibis will hunt for its food and build its nest.

You might use the following questions for discussion.

1. Why do you think it was important to Audubon to paint birds in their natural surrounding?

2. Why might Hurst in this story have displaced the scarlet ibis from its natural surroundings?

3. The scarlet ibis dies in an unfamiliar place. Why is this an important detail in the story?

31 **Literary Focus** How does the fact that the bird is out of place relate to Doodle?

**SCARLET IBIS**
*John James Audubon*
*New York Historical Society*

over the eyes and the long white beak unhinged. Its legs were crossed and its clawlike feet were delicately curved at rest. Even death did not mar its grace, for it lay on the earth like a broken vase of red flowers, and we stood around it, awed by its exotic beauty.

"It's dead," Mama said.

"What is it?" Doodle repeated.

"Go bring me the bird book," said Daddy.

I ran into the house and brought back the bird book. As we watched, Daddy thumbed through its pages. "It's a scarlet ibis," he said, pointing to a picture. "It lives in the tropics—South America to Florida. A storm must have brought it here."

Sadly, we all looked back at the bird. A scarlet ibis! How many miles it had traveled to die like this, in *our* yard, beneath the bleeding tree.

"Let's finish lunch," Mama said, nudging us back toward the dining room.

"I'm not hungry," said Doodle, and he knelt down beside the ibis.

"We've got peach cobbler for dessert," Mama tempted from the doorway.

Doodle remained kneeling. "I'm going to bury him."

"Don't you dare touch him," Mama warned. "There's no telling what disease he might have had."

"All right," said Doodle. "I won't."

Daddy, Mama, and I went back to the dining-room table, but we watched Doodle through the open door. He took out a piece of string from his pocket and, without

31

throat, and I had never seen him stand still so long. "What is it?" he asked.

Daddy shook his head. "I don't know, maybe it's—"

At that moment the bird began to flutter, but the wings were uncoordinated, and amid much flapping and a spray of flying feathers, it tumbled down, bumping through the limbs of the bleeding tree and landing at our feet with a thud. Its long, graceful neck jerked twice into an S, then straightened out, and the bird was still. A white veil came touching the ibis, looped one end around its neck. Slowly, while singing softly *Shall We Gather at the River,* he carried the bird around to the front yard and dug a hole in the flower garden, next to the petunia bed. Now we were watching him through the front window, but he didn't know it. His awkwardness at digging the hole with a shovel whose handle was twice as long as he was made us laugh, and we covered our mouths with our hands so he wouldn't hear.

When Doodle came into the dining room, he found us seriously eating our cobbler. He was pale and lingered just inside the screen door. "Did you get the scarlet ibis buried?" asked Daddy.

Doodle didn't speak but nodded his head.

"Go wash your hands, and then you can have some peach cobbler," said Mama.

"I'm not hungry," he said.

"Dead birds is bad luck," said Aunt Nicey, poking her head from the kitchen door. "Specially *red* dead birds!"

As soon as I had finished eating, Doodle and I hurried off to Horsehead Landing. Time was short, and Doodle still had a long way to go if he was going to keep up with the other boys when he started school. The sun, gilded with the yellow cast of autumn, still burned fiercely, but the dark green woods through which we passed were shady and cool. When we reached the landing, Doodle said he was too tired to swim, so we got into a skiff and floated down the creek with the tide. Far off in the marsh a rail was scolding, and over on the beach locusts were singing in the myrtle trees. Doodle did not speak and kept his head turned away, letting one hand trail limply in the water.

After we had drifted a long way, I put the oars in place and made Doodle row back against the tide. Black clouds began to gather in the southwest, and he kept watching them, trying to pull the oars a little faster. When we reached Horsehead Landing, lightning was playing across half the sky and thunder roared out, hiding even the sound of the sea. The sun disappeared and darkness descended, almost like night. Flocks of marsh crows flew by, heading inland to their roosting trees, and two egrets, squawking, arose from the oyster-rock shallows and careened away.

Doodle was both tired and frightened, and when he stepped from the skiff he collapsed onto the mud, sending an armada of fiddler crabs rustling off into the marsh grass. I helped him up, and as he wiped the mud off his trousers, he smiled at me ashamedly. He had failed and we both knew it, so we started back home, racing the storm. We never spoke (What are the words that can solder cracked pride?), but I knew he was watching me, watching for a sign of mercy. The lightning was near now, and from fear he walked so close behind me he kept stepping on my heels. The faster I walked, the faster he walked, so I began to run. The rain was coming, roaring through the pines, and then, like a bursting Roman candle, a gum tree ahead of us was shattered by a bolt of lightning. When the deafening peal of thunder had died, and in the moment before the rain arrived, I heard Doodle, who had fallen behind, cry out, "Brother, Brother, don't leave me! Don't leave me!"

The knowledge that Doodle's and my plans had come to naught was bitter, and that streak of cruelty within me awakened. I ran as fast as I could, leaving him far behind with a wall of rain dividing us. The drops stung my face like nettles, and the wind flared the wet glistening leaves of the bordering trees. Soon I could hear his voice no more.

I hadn't run too far before I became tired, and the flood of childish spite evanesced as

*The Scarlet Ibis*   197

32 **Discussion** Why is Doodle's reaction to the bird's death different from that of the rest of the family?

33 **Discussion** How might Aunt Nicey's remark foreshadow what will happen in the story?

34 **Discussion** Why do the narrator and Doodle seem to be in different worlds?

35 **Discussion** What is the meaning of the phrase in parentheses?

36 **Reading Strategy** When has Doodle said this before? How are the situations similar?

37 **Discussion** Why does the narrator's cruelty emerge at this moment?

**Literary Focus** Compare the description of Doodle to that of the ibis after it had fallen from the tree. How does that incident foreshadow the end of the story?

**Reader's Response** How did your feelings change as you read this story?

---

well. I stopped and waited for Doodle. The sound of rain was everywhere, but the wind had died and it fell straight down in parallel paths like ropes hanging from the sky. As I waited, I peered through the downpour, but no one came. Finally I went back and found him huddled beneath a red nightshade bush beside the road. He was sitting on the ground, his face buried in his arms, which were resting on his drawn-up knees. "Let's go, Doodle," I said.

He didn't answer, so I placed my hand on his forehead and lifted his head. Limply, he fell backwards onto the earth. He had been bleeding from the mouth, and his neck and the front of his shirt were stained a brilliant red.

"Doodle! Doodle!" I cried, shaking him, but there was no answer but the ropy rain. He lay very awkwardly, with his head thrown far back, making his vermilion neck appear unusually long and slim. His little legs, bent sharply at the knees, had never before seemed so fragile, so thin.

I began to weep, and the tear-blurred vision in red before me looked very familiar. "Doodle!" I screamed above the pounding storm and threw my body to the earth above his. For a long long time, it seemed forever, I lay there crying, sheltering my fallen scarlet ibis from the heresy[6] of rain.

---

6. **heresy** (her′ ə sē): An idea opposed to the beliefs of a religion or philosophy.

---

## Closure and Extension

### ANSWERS TO THINKING ABOUT THE SELECTION
*Recalling*

1. The narrator wanted someone to race, box, and climb trees with, but Doodle could do none of these.

2. The narrator said he was embarrassed to have a brother who could not walk.

3. The narrator also planned to teach Doodle to run, swim, climb trees, and fight.

4. The narrator demonstrated his cruelty when he forced Doodle to touch the coffin and when he left him behind during the rainstorm.

5. After the ibis had died, the narrator made a final attempt to get Doodle to achieve the physical goals set for him. Doodle was too tired to try. As they ran home during a rainstorm, Doodle got left behind, collapsed, and died.

*Interpreting*

6. Suggested Response:
   a. Doodle was not enthusiastic about the plans, but to please his brother he demonstrated courage and tried his best.
   b. Doodle had a vivid imagination.
   c. Doodle felt a kinship with this exotic outsider.

7. Suggested Response: His pride caused him to want a brother who could accomplish these goals.

8. Suggested Response: Because of the narrator's pride in achieving a goal, he worked tenaciously to teach Doodle to walk. Because of this same pride, he forced Doodle to overtax himself in achieving new goals, and Doodle died.

9. Answers will differ. Doodle may have realized that he would soon die.

## THINKING ABOUT THE SELECTION

### Recalling

1. How does Doodle disappoint his brother?
2. What motivates the narrator to teach Doodle to walk?
3. What other plans does he make for Doodle?
4. The narrator says, "There is within me (and with sadness I have watched it in others) a knot of cruelty borne by the stream of love. . . ." Give two examples of his cruelty to Doodle.
5. Summarize the circumstances leading to Doodle's death.

### Interpreting

6. What does each of the following show about Doodle?
   a. his reactions to his brother's plans for him
   b. his favorite "lies"
   c. his response to the scarlet ibis
7. Why does the narrator set such demanding goals for Doodle?
8. The narrator states that " . . . pride is a wonderful terrible thing, a seed that bears two vines, life and death." Explain how the story demonstrates the truth of this statement.
9. What larger meaning might be read into Doodle's cry, "Brother, Brother, don't leave me! Don't leave me!"?

### Applying

10. The story opens with the narrator, now an adult, remembering the events from long ago. How does the passage of time change people and their feelings about past events?
11. Do you think that many people have mixed feelings about sisters and brothers? Explain.

## ANALYZING LITERATURE

### Interpreting Symbols

A **symbol** is something that represents something beyond itself. Writers may use symbols to present or reinforce a theme. For instance, throughout "The Scarlet Ibis," James Hurst refers to things that are red. The color red commonly symbolizes blood, or courage, or tragedy. This is an appropriate symbol in a story that deals with the tragic death of a courageous boy.

A character, thing, setting, or action may suggest a larger meaning or idea within the story. The narrator sees a great similarity between Doodle and the scarlet ibis, the major symbol in this story.

1. In what ways is Doodle like the scarlet ibis?
2. Compare Doodle's appearance in death with the appearance of the scarlet ibis.
3. What does the scarlet ibis symbolize?

## CRITICAL THINKING AND READING

### Recognizing Emotive Language

Writers may use **emotive language** in describing a mood or feeling. Such language can cause you to laugh, cry, feel fear or other emotions along with characters. "The Scarlet Ibis" contains many emotive passages. For example, the very first paragraph sets the somber mood for the story with words like *dead, bleeding tree, stained, rotting,* and *graveyard*.

1. What emotions does the paragraph beginning "It was bad enough having an invalid brother" arouse? What words convey this emotion?
2. What words and phrases convey the feeling of exhilaration in the paragraph in which Doodle first walks (page 193)?

## THINKING AND WRITING

### Writing About Symbols

Suppose that you wanted an artist to draw an illustration that captured the feelings of the narrator in "The Scarlet Ibis." Identify an emotion he feels at a particular point, and think of a symbol for that emotion. Write a note to the artist that tells why the symbol is appropriate and how it should appear. When you revise, check that your explanation will be clear to the reader, and that you have given details about the symbol to guide the illustrator in drawing it.

*The Scarlet Ibis* 199

(Answers begin on p. 198.)

2. Suggested Response: Doodle's neck was stained red; his head thrown back made his neck appear long and slim; his little legs were bent sharply at the knees. These descriptions all suggest the ibis's appearance at the foot of the tree.
3. Suggested Response: The scarlet ibis was a beautiful, delicate, and wounded bird that symbolized the inner beauty, delicate nature, and imminent death of Doodle. They were both unusual and lovely, but out of place in their worlds.

## ANSWERS TO CRITICAL THINKING AND READING

1. Suggested Response: This paragraph conveys the emotions of depression and anger through the words "invalid," "not all there," "unbearable," "kill," and "smothering." The paragraph also conveys exhilaration, hope, and anticipation through the words "grinned," "skipped," "shouting," "smiled," and "he's all there."
2. Suggested Response: The words and phrases that convey a feeling of exhilaration are "hugged," "laughter pealing," "ringing bell," "perched like a cardinal," "brilliantly visible," "soft," and "sweet."

## THINKING AND WRITING

You might suggest that, before they begin writing, students refer to Lesson 12, "Writing About a Short Story," in the Handbook of Writing About Literature.

### Publishing Student Writing

Have students exchange notes and actually try to draw a symbol based on a fellow student's instructions.

### Writing Across the Curriculum

You might want students to create their own illustrations, based on their notes. If you do, perhaps inform the art department. Art teachers might provide assistance and materials.

---

### Applying

10. Answers will differ. Students may respond that, although adults have memories of how they felt as children, they can view childhood from an adult's perspective. Also, certain events stand out more clearly, while others fade as time passes.
11. Answers will differ. Students may respond that, although siblings often feel a family kinship and enjoy a close relationship, they can also feel competitive at times.

**Challenge** Ask students to imagine that they have a brother like Doodle. What could they do to make themselves and their brother feel good about themselves? What things did the narrator do that they would avoid?

### ANSWERS TO ANALYZING LITERATURE

1. Suggested Response: Doodle was as beautiful inside as the ibis was in appearance. The ibis was crippled and could not fly; Doodle was crippled and could not do many things. The ibis struggled against a great storm until its strength gave out and it died. Doodle also struggled with all his strength until he died.

**More About the Author** Guy de Maupassant (gē də mō pə sänt) is more highly regarded outside his own country than in France. For some critics, his popular success is reason enough to devalue his work. Ask students to discuss the relationship between popular success and literary merit. In what way can popular success be a drawback for a serious writer?

**Literary Focus** Irony can be shown in many ways. In this story it is shown through dramatic contrasts and a surprise ending. Point out that irony is quite common in everyday speech. Nicknames often have an ironic intent.

**Look For** Your less advanced students may find irony a difficult concept to grasp. It may be helpful to preview the Analyzing Literature questions on page 207 so that these questions can guide their reading.

**Writing/Prior Knowledge** Before they begin the freewriting activity, have students discuss this quotation from Shakespeare's *Julius Caesar,* "The fault, dear Brutus, is not in our stars, / But in ourselves, that we are underlings." Encourage students to consider the roles that luck and self-determination play in a person's life.

**Vocabulary** Have your less advanced students read these words aloud so that you can be sure they know them.

**Spelling Tip** Write the words *resplendent* and *exorbitant* on the board. Tell students that the suffixes *-ent* and *-ant* are both used to form adjectives. There is no satisfactory rule for determining which to use.

# GUIDE FOR READING

## The Necklace

**Guy de Maupassant** (gē də mō pə sänt) (1850–1893) was born and grew up in the province of Normandy, France. After serving in the Franco-Prussian War, he worked in a poorly paid job as a government clerk. During this period, though, he practiced writing and became the literary apprentice of the renowned nineteenth-century writer, Gustave Flaubert. Maupassant is considered the best-known short story writer in the world. ''The Necklace'' reflects his first-hand knowledge of the world of civil servants and the bourgeoisie, or middle class.

**Irony**

**Irony** is a contrast between an expected outcome and the actual outcome or between appearance and reality. For example, a man may court rich and famous people as a way of furthering his career. However, he may find that the friend he abandoned on his climb to the top becomes a wealthy industrialist who holds the key to his success in her hands. We call this turn of events *ironic.* By using irony, a writer may suggest that life is more complicated than it may at first appear.

**Look For**

In his stories, Maupassant often tried to get below the surface of things, to reveal what was hidden from view. As you read ''The Necklace,'' try to separate the appearance of things from reality.

**Writing**

Do you think that people's lives are determined by destiny, or can people take control of the direction of their lives? Freewrite about the roles of destiny and choice in people's lives.

**Vocabulary**

Knowing the following words will help you as you read ''The Necklace.''

**déclassée** (dā′ klä sā′) *adj.*: lowered in social status (p. 201)
**rueful** (ro̅o̅′ fəl) *adj.*: causing sorrow or pity (p. 201)
**anguish** (an′ gwish) *n.*: great suffering (p. 204)
**resplendent** (ri splen′ dənt) *adj.*: shining brightly (p. 204)
**dejection** (di jek′ shən) *n.*: lowness of spirits (p. 205)

**exorbitant** (ig zôr′ bə tənt) *adj.*: exceeding the appropriate limits (p. 205)
**coarse** (kôrs) *adj.*: rough, crude, unrefined (p. 206)
**disheveled** (di shev′ 'ld) *adj.*: disarranged and untidy (p. 206)
**profoundly** (prə found′ lē) *adv.*: deeply and intensely (p. 206)

1 To understand irony
2 To make inferences about characters
3 To respond to criticism

### Support Material

**Teaching Portfolio**
Teacher Backup, p. 253
Grammar in Action Worksheet, *Varying Sentences*, p. 257
Usage and Mechanics Worksheet, p. 259
Vocabulary Check, p. 260
Analyzing Literature Worksheet, *Understanding Irony*, p. 261
Language Worksheet, *Choosing the Meaning That Fits the Context*, p. 262

Selection Test, p. 263
Art Transparency 5: *Sunday Afternoon on the Island of La Grande Jatte*, by Georges Seurat
**Library of Video Classics:** The Cask of Amontillado and The Necklace

# The Necklace

## Guy de Maupassant

She was one of those pretty, charming young women who are born, as if by an error of Fate, into a petty official's family. She had no dowry,[1] no hopes, not the slightest chance of being appreciated, understood, loved, and married by a rich and distinguished man; so she slipped into marriage with a minor civil servant at the Ministry of Education.

Unable to afford jewelry, she dressed simply; but she was as wretched as a *déclassée*, for women have neither caste nor breeding—in them beauty, grace, and charm replace pride of birth. Innate refinement, instinctive elegance, and suppleness of wit give them their place on the only scale that counts, and these qualities make humble girls the peers of the grandest ladies.

She suffered constantly, feeling that all the attributes of a gracious life, every luxury, should rightly have been hers. The poverty of her rooms—the shabby walls, the worn furniture, the ugly upholstery—caused her pain. All these things that another woman of her class would not even have noticed, tormented her and made her angry. The very sight of the little Breton girl who cleaned for her awoke rueful thoughts and the wildest dreams in her mind. She dreamt of thick-carpeted reception rooms with Oriental hangings, lighted by tall, bronze torches, and with two huge footmen in knee breeches, made drowsy by the heat from the stove, asleep in the wide armchairs. She dreamt of great drawing rooms upholstered in old silks, with fragile little tables holding priceless knickknacks, and of enchanting little sitting rooms redolent of perfume, designed for tea-time chats with intimate friends—famous, sought-after men whose attentions all women longed for.

When she sat down to dinner at her round table with its three-day-old cloth, and watched her husband opposite her lift the lid of the soup tureen and exclaim, delighted: "Ah, a good homemade beef stew! There's nothing better . . ." she would visualize elegant dinners with gleaming silver amid tapestried walls peopled by knights and ladies and exotic birds in a fairy forest; she would think of exquisite dishes served on gorgeous china, and of gallantries whispered and received with sphinx-like smiles[2] while eating the pink flesh of trout or wings of grouse.

She had no proper wardrobe, no jewels, nothing. And those were the only things that she loved—she felt she was made for them. She would have so loved to charm, to be envied, to be admired and sought after.

She had a rich friend, a schoolmate from the convent she had attended, but she didn't like to visit her because it always made her so miserable when she got home again. She would weep for whole days at a time from sorrow, regret, despair, and distress.

---

**1. dowry** (dou′ rē) *n.*: The property that a woman brought to her husband at marriage.

**2. gallantries whispered and received with sphinx** (sfiŋks)-**like smiles:** Flirtatious compliments whispered and received with mysterious smiles.

Then one evening her husband arrived home looking triumphant and waving a large envelope.

"There," he said, "there's something for you."

She tore it open eagerly and took out a printed card which said:

"The Minister of Education and Madame Georges Ramponneau[3] request the pleasure of the company of M. and Mme. Loisel[4] at an evening reception at the Ministry on Monday, January 18th."

Instead of being delighted, as her husband had hoped, she tossed the invitation on the table and muttered, annoyed:

"What do you expect me to do with that?"

"Why, I thought you'd be pleased, dear. You never go out and this would be an occasion for you, a great one! I had a lot of trouble getting it. Everyone wants an invitation; they're in great demand and there are only a few reserved for the employees. All the officials will be there."

She looked at him, irritated, and said impatiently:

"I haven't a thing to wear. How could I go?"

It had never even occurred to him. He stammered:

"But what about the dress you wear to the theater? I think it's lovely. . . ."

He fell silent, amazed and bewildered to see that his wife was crying. Two big tears escaped from the corners of her eyes and rolled slowly toward the corners of her mouth. He mumbled:

"What is it? What is it?"

But, with great effort, she had overcome her misery; and now she answered him calmly, wiping her tear-damp cheeks:

"It's nothing. It's just that I have no evening dress and so I can't go to the party. Give the invitation to one of your colleagues whose wife will be better dressed than I would be."

He was overcome. He said:

"Listen, Mathilde,[5] how much would an evening dress cost—a suitable one that you could wear again on other occasions, something very simple?"

She thought for several seconds, making her calculations and at the same time estimating how much she could ask for without eliciting an immediate refusal and an exclamation of horror from this economical government clerk.

At last, not too sure of herself, she said:

"It's hard to say exactly but I think I could manage with four hundred francs."

He went a little pale, for that was exactly the amount he had put aside to buy a rifle so that he could go hunting the following summer near Nanterre, with a few friends who went shooting larks around there on Sundays.

However, he said:

"Well, all right, then. I'll give you four hundred francs. But try to get something really nice."

As the day of the ball drew closer, Madame Loisel seemed depressed, disturbed, worried—despite the fact that her dress was ready. One evening her husband said:

"What's the matter? You've really been very strange these last few days."

And she answered:

"I hate not having a single jewel, not one stone, to wear. I shall look so dowdy.[6] I'd almost rather not go to the party."

He suggested:

"You can wear some fresh flowers. It's

---

**3. Madame Georges Ramponneau** (ma dam′ zhôrzh ram pə nō′)
**4. Loisel** (lwa zel′)

---

**5. Mathilde** (ma tēld′)
**6. dowdy** (dou′ dē) *adj.*: Shabby.

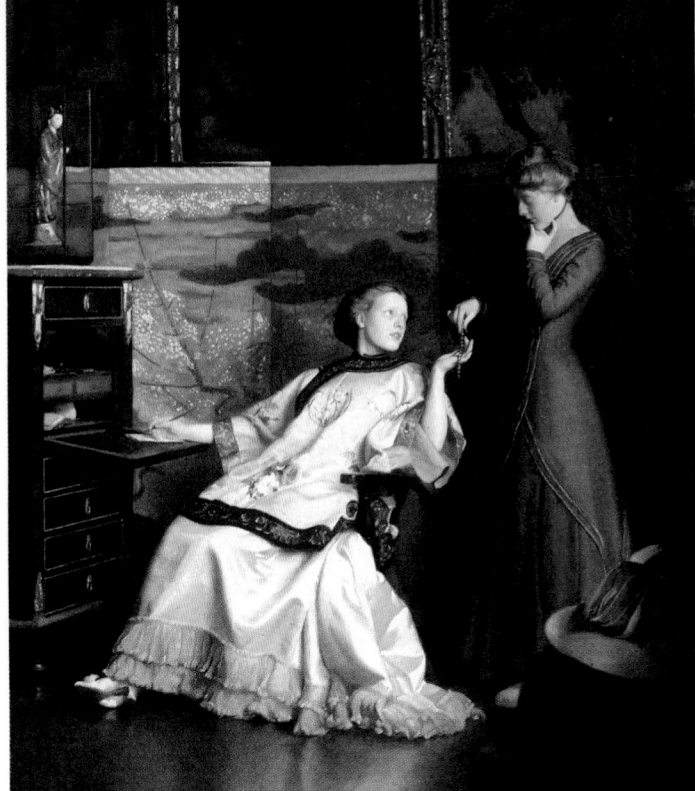

THE NEW NECKLACE, 1910
William McGregor Paxton
Museum of Fine Arts, Boston

## Humanities Note

Fine Art, *The New Necklace*, 1910, by William McGregor Paxton. William McGregor Paxton (1869–1941), an American, studied in Boston and in Paris. He is best known for works like *The New Necklace*, which depict the leisure class. Attention to details of texture characterize his work.

Point out to students the ease of the posture of the seated woman. The ruffle of the white dress, with its ample folds, the rich embroidery of the blouse, the insouciant angle of the arm—all mark her as someone of wealth. By contrast, the plainly cut black dress of the other woman, whose hand to the throat and straight carriage bespeak a reserve and a distance from wealth and necklaces, clearly informs us that she is not the owner of the necklace. Have the students note all the fine details in the painting. How do these details of elegant tapestries, fine furniture, and richly tailored gowns suggest Madame Loisel's dream world? Point out that although the necklace is small in comparison to the other objects in the room, it is the focal point of the ladies' attention.

1. How does the central importance of the necklace suggest the symbolic role the necklace plays in the story?
2. What seems to be the mood in this painting?
3. Is this work of art appropriate to illustrate this story? As you answer, think of the characters, the feeling, and the details in both the art and the story.

considered very chic[7] at this time of year. For ten francs you can get two or three beautiful roses."

That didn't satisfy her at all.

**10** "No . . . there's nothing more humiliating than to look poverty-stricken among a lot of rich women."

Then her husband exclaimed:

"Wait—you silly thing! Why don't you go and see Madame Forestier[8] and ask her to lend you some jewelry. You certainly know her well enough for that, don't you think?"

She let out a joyful cry.

"You're right. It never occurred to me."

The next day she went to see her friend and related her tale of woe.

7. **chic** (shēk) *n.*: Fashionable.
8. **Forestier** (fô rə styā')

Madame Forestier went to her mirrored wardrobe, took out a big jewel case, brought it to Madame Loisel, opened it, and said:

"Take your pick, my dear."

Her eyes wandered from some bracelets to a pearl necklace, then to a gold Venetian cross set with stones, of very fine workmanship. She tried on the jewelry before the mirror, hesitating, unable to bring herself to take them off, to give them back. And she kept asking:

"Do you have anything else, by chance?"

"Why yes. Here, look for yourself. I don't know which ones you'll like."

**12** All at once, in a box lined with black satin, she came upon a superb diamond necklace, and her heart started beating with overwhelming desire. Her hands trembled as

*The Necklace* 203

**10 Discussion** Ask students to discuss whether they think Mathilde would really have looked poverty-stricken. Was it just in her mind? Was it a ploy to get her husband to buy her jewelry? What does her statement suggest about her?

**11 Literary Focus** Mme. Loisel hesitates before making the fateful decision of choosing the necklace. Her hesitation at this point increases the irony of what happens to her because of the necklace.

**12 Reading Strategy** Considering the title of the story, students should understand that the decision Mathilde is about to make is a very important one. What can they predict about the choice she will make and its effect on her life?

13 **Reading Strategy** Have students summarize the story to this point, emphasizing what they have learned about Mme. Loisel.

14 **Reading Strategy** Have students predict what might happen to Mme. Loisel as a result of the ball.

15 **Literary Focus** Her triumph at the ball contrasts with her life to come.

16 **Discussion** Contrast Mme. Loisel's beauty and splendor with her husband's dullness.

17 **Literary Focus** Point out the irony in the naming of their street (Street of Martyrs). How does the name hint at their life to come?

she picked it up. She fastened it around her neck over her high-necked dress and stood there gazing at herself ecstatically.

Hesitantly, filled with terrible anguish, she asked:

"Could you lend me this one—just this and nothing else?"

"Yes, of course."

She threw her arms around her friend's neck, kissed her ardently, and fled with her treasure.

The day of the party arrived. Madame Loisel was a great success. She was the prettiest woman there—resplendent, graceful, beaming, and deliriously happy. All the men looked at her, asked who she was, tried to get themselves introduced to her. All the minister's aides wanted to waltz with her. The minister himself noticed her.

She danced enraptured—carried away, intoxicated with pleasure, forgetting everything in this triumph of her beauty and the glory of her success, floating in a cloud of happiness formed by all this homage, all this admiration, all the desires she had stirred up—by this victory so complete and so sweet to the heart of a woman.

When she left the party, it was almost four in the morning. Her husband had been sleeping since midnight in a small, deserted sitting room, with three other gentlemen whose wives were having a wonderful time.

He brought her wraps so that they could leave and put them around her shoulders—the plain wraps from her everyday life whose shabbiness jarred with the elegance of her evening dress. She felt this and wanted to escape quickly so that the other women, who were enveloping themselves in their rich furs, wouldn't see her.

Loisel held her back.

"Wait a minute. You'll catch cold out there. I'm going to call a cab."

But she wouldn't listen to him and went hastily downstairs. Outside in the street, there was no cab to be found; they set out to look for one, calling to the drivers they saw passing in the distance.

They walked toward the Seine,[9] shivering and miserable. Finally, on the embankment, they found one of those ancient nocturnal broughams[10] which are only to be seen in Paris at night, as if they were ashamed to show their shabbiness in daylight.

It took them to their door in the Rue des Martyrs, and they went sadly upstairs to their apartment. For her, it was all over. And he was thinking that he had to be at the Ministry by ten.

She took off her wraps before the mirror so that she could see herself in all her glory once more. Then she cried out. The necklace was gone; there was nothing around her neck.

Her husband, already half undressed, asked:

"What's the matter?"

She turned toward him in a frenzy:

"The . . . the . . . necklace—it's gone."

He got up, thunderstruck.

"What did you say? . . . What! . . . Impossible!"

And they searched the folds of her dress, the folds of her wrap, the pockets, everywhere. They didn't find it.

He asked:

"Are you sure you still had it when we left the ball?"

"Yes. I remember touching it in the hallway of the Ministry."

"But if you had lost it in the street, we would have heard it fall. It must be in the cab."

"Yes, most likely. Do you remember the number?"

"No. What about you—did you notice it?"

"No."

---

**9. Seine** (sān): A river flowing through Paris.
**10. broughams** (brōōms) *n.*: Horse-drawn carriages.

## Grammar in Action

Authors **vary sentence structure** to keep readers' interest and add drama to their writing. The three basic sentence types are *simple*—a single, independent clause; *compound*—two or more independent clauses; and *complex*—an independent clause and one or more subordinate clauses. By using a mixture of simple, compound, and complex sentences, authors make their writing lively and clear.

In the following passage from "The Necklace," for example, Guy de Maupassant uses a variety of sentence types:

They walked toward the Seine, shivering and miserable. Finally, on the embankment, they found one of those ancient nocturnal broughams which are only to be seen in Paris at night, as if they were ashamed to show their shabbiness in daylight.

It took them to their door in the Rue des Martyrs, and they

They looked at each other in utter dejection. Finally Loisel got dressed again.

"I'm going to retrace the whole distance we covered on foot," he said, "and see if I can't find it."

And he left the house. She remained in her evening dress, too weak to go to bed, sitting crushed on a chair, lifeless and blank.

Her husband returned at about seven o'clock. He had found nothing.

He went to the police station, to the newspapers to offer a reward, to the offices of the cab companies—in a word, wherever there seemed to be the slightest hope of tracing it.

She spent the whole day waiting, in a state of utter hopelessness before such an appalling catastrophe.

Loisel returned in the evening, his face lined and pale; he had learned nothing.

"You must write to your friend," he said, "and tell her that you've broken the clasp of the necklace and that you're getting it mended. That'll give us time to decide what to do."

She wrote the letter at his dictation.

By the end of the week, they had lost all hope.

Loisel, who had aged five years, declared: "We'll have to replace the necklace."

The next day they took the case in which it had been kept and went to the jeweler whose name appeared inside it. He looked through his ledgers:

"I didn't sell this necklace, madame. I only supplied the case."

Then they went from one jeweler to the next, trying to find a necklace like the other, racking their memories, both of them sick with worry and distress.

In a fashionable shop near the Palais Royal, they found a diamond necklace which they decided was exactly like the other. It was worth 40,000 francs. They could have it for 36,000 francs.

They asked the jeweler to hold it for them for three days, and they stipulated that he should take it back for 34,000 francs if the other necklace was found before the end of February.

Loisel possessed 18,000 francs left him by his father. He would borrow the rest.

He borrowed, asking a thousand francs from one man, five hundred from another, a hundred here, fifty there. He signed promissory notes,[11] borrowed at exorbitant rates, dealt with usurers and the entire race of moneylenders. He compromised his whole career, gave his signature even when he wasn't sure he would be able to honor it, and horrified by the anxieties with which his future would be filled, by the black misery about to descend upon him, by the prospect of physical privation and moral suffering, went to get the new necklace, placing on the jeweler's counter 36,000 francs.

When Madame Loisel went to return the necklace, Madame Forestier said in a faintly waspish tone:

"You could have brought it back a little sooner! I might have needed it."

She didn't open the case as her friend had feared she might. If she had noticed the substitution, what would she have thought? What would she have said? Mightn't she have taken Madame Loisel for a thief?

Madame Loisel came to know the awful life of the poverty-stricken. However, she resigned herself to it with unexpected fortitude. The crushing debt had to be paid. She would pay it. They dismissed the maid; they moved into an attic under the roof.

She came to know all the heavy household chores, the loathsome work of the kitchen. She washed the dishes, wearing down her pink nails on greasy casseroles and the bottoms of saucepans. She did the

---

11. **promissory** (präm′ i sôr′ ē) **notes:** Written promises to pay back borrowed money.

*The Necklace* 205

18 **Discussion** Have students evaluate Loisel's plan. What complications could arise from it?

19 **Discussion** What will replacing the necklace mean to them?

20 **Reading Strategy** The author raises a doubt in the reader's mind about the necklace. Why would someone buy a very expensive necklace from one jeweler and a case from another? Ask students if this provides them with any indication of what might happen. What is their prediction?

21 **Master Teacher Note** Many of the most exclusive shops in Paris are near the Palais Royal. Ask students to name equivalent shopping areas in the United States, for example New York's Fifth Ave., Chicago's Michigan Ave., Los Angeles' Rodeo Dr., Dallas' Galleria.

22 **Clarification** At the time of this story 36,000 francs was worth about $7,200. The effects of inflation since then would increase the value of the necklace tremendously.

23 **Discussion** Have students discuss the degree of sacrifice Loisel was willing to make to follow his plan. What labels would they put on his actions—wise, honorable, foolish, stubborn, short-sighted, practical?

24 **Discussion** Contrast Mathilde's way of life now with a kind of life she thought she deserved. What is surprising about her behavior?

went sadly upstairs to their apartment. For her, it was all over. And he was thinking that he had to be at the Ministry by ten.

Notice that the first sentence is simple; the second, complex; the third, compound; the fourth, simple; and the fifth, complex. This variety of sentence structures produces an interesting rhythm and keeps the passage from being choppy.

**Student Activity 1.** Choose another passage of at least ten lines from "The Necklace" and analyze the structure of the sentences.

**Student Activity 2.** Using de Maupassant's passage as a model, write about an experience you had as you left a friend's house. Vary the structure of your sentences as de Maupassant does.

25 **Reading Strategy** Have students summarize what the lost necklace has cost the Loisels, not in money but in their way of life, in their expectations and hopes for the future. Ask them to predict what lies ahead for the couple.

26 **Discussion** Ask students to discuss the truth of this statement. To what degree was it fate and to what degree the Loisels' own actions that created the situation? Is this the theme of the story? Support your answer.

27 **Discussion** Contrast this Mme. Loisel with the one who went to the ball. Did she deserve what happened to her? Why or why not?

28 **Literary Focus** Have students contrast the way the situation appeared to the Loisels with the facts. In what way is this contrast ironic? Ask students to discuss whether or not they were surprised at the end of the story. How does this add to the story's irony?

29 **Discussion** Ask students to discuss how Mathilde's choice of the imitation necklace is symbolic of her character. What might the necklace symbolize?

**Reader's Response** Describe a situation in which you learned a lesson similar to the one Mathilde Loisel learned in this story.

laundry, washing shirts and dishcloths which she hung on a line to dry; she took the garbage down to the street every morning, and carried water upstairs, stopping at every floor to get her breath. Dressed like a working-class woman, she went to the fruit store, the grocer, and the butcher with her basket on her arm, bargaining, outraged, contesting each sou[12] of her pitiful funds.

Every month some notes had to be honored and more time requested on others.

Her husband worked in the evenings, putting a shopkeeper's ledgers in order, and often at night as well, doing copying at twenty-five centimes a page.

And it went on like that for ten years.

After ten years, they had made good on everything, including the usurious rates and the compound interest.

Madame Loisel looked old now. She had become the sort of strong woman, hard and coarse, that one finds in poor families. Disheveled, her skirts askew, with reddened hands, she spoke in a loud voice, slopping water over the floors as she washed them. But sometimes, when her husband was at the office, she would sit down by the window and muse over that party long ago when she had been so beautiful, the belle of the ball.

How would things have turned out if she hadn't lost that necklace? Who could tell? How strange and fickle life is! How little it takes to make or break you!

Then one Sunday when she was strolling along the Champs Elysées[13] to forget the week's chores for a while, she suddenly caught sight of a woman taking a child for a walk. It was Madame Forestier, still young, still beautiful, still charming.

---

**12. sou** (soo) *n.*: A former French coin, worth very little; the centime (sän´ tēm), mentioned later, was also of little value.
**13. Champs Elysées** (shän zā lē zā´): A fashionable street in Paris.

Madame Loisel started to tremble. Should she speak to her? Yes, certainly she should. And now that she had paid everything back, why shouldn't she tell her the whole story?

She went up to her.

"Hello, Jeanne."

The other didn't recognize her and was surprised that this plainly dressed woman should speak to her so familiarly. She murmured:

"But . . . madame! . . . I'm sure . . . You must be mistaken."

"No, I'm not. I am Mathilde Loisel."

Her friend gave a little cry.

"Oh! Oh, my poor Mathilde, how you've changed!"

"Yes, I've been through some pretty hard times since I last saw you and I've had plenty of trouble—and all because of you!"

"Because of me? What do you mean?"

"You remember the diamond necklace you lent me to wear to the party at the Ministry?"

"Yes. What about it?"

"Well, I lost it."

"What are you talking about? You returned it to me."

"What I gave back to you was another one just like it. And it took us ten years to pay for it. You can imagine it wasn't easy for us, since we were quite poor. . . . Anyway, I'm glad it's over and done with."

Madame Forestier stopped short.

"You say you bought a diamond necklace to replace that other one?"

"Yes. You didn't even notice then? They really were exactly alike."

And she smiled, full of a proud, simple joy.

Madame Forestier, profoundly moved, took Mathilde's hands in her own.

"Oh, my poor, poor Mathilde! Mine was false. It was worth five hundred francs at the most!"

---

no dress as beautiful as those the other women will wear so she cannot go to the ball.

2. She borrows the necklace because she feels she must wear jewelry with her new dress. Her husband suggests she borrow something from her rich friend.

3. Although dissatisfied, Mathilde had a comfortable bourgeois life. Now the Loisels have to live in poverty, working night and day to pay their debt.

4. The necklace she lost was not an expensive one, but a cheap imitation.

*Interpreting*

5. Suggested Response: She is dissatisfied because she feels she should have a gracious, luxurious life rather than only an ordinary middle-class existence.

6. Suggested Response: Both are glittering and both are not what they seem to be.

7. Suggested Response: She goes

**Closure and Extension**

**ANSWERS TO THINKING ABOUT THE SELECTION**
*Recalling*

1. The invitation displeases her because she believes that she has

# THINKING ABOUT THE SELECTION

## Recalling

1. Why does the invitation her husband brings home displease Madame Loisel?
2. Why does Madame Loisel borrow a necklace from her friend, Madame Forestier?
3. How do the lives of the Loisels change after the necklace is lost?
4. What does Madame Loisel eventually discover about the necklace?

## Interpreting

5. At the beginning of the story, why is Madame Loisel dissatisfied with her life?
6. In what way are the borrowed necklace and Madame Loisel's dreams of life in high society the same?
7. How does Madame Loisel change during the course of the story?

## Applying

8. If you had been in Madame Loisel's situation, how would you have solved the problem of the lost necklace? Explain.

# ANALYZING LITERATURE

## Understanding Irony

**Irony** is the contrast between the expected outcome and the actual outcome or between appearance or reality. For example, in "The Necklace," Madame Loisel is a pretty, proud young woman who feels that the attributes of a gracious life should rightly be hers. It is ironic that because of her pride, she comes to know not splendor and wealth, but "the awful life of the poverty stricken."

1. After her great success at the ball, Madame Loisel creeps slowly upstairs, because for her, she thinks, all is over. How does this thought turn out to be truer than she expected?
2. The street the Loisels live on is the Rue des Martyrs, or Avenue of the Martyrs. Why is the name of this street ironic?

3. In what way is the ending of the story ironic?
4. Madame Loisel thinks, "How strange and fickle life is! How little it takes to make or break you!" What do this statement and the ironic tone of the story suggest about the complexity of life?

# CRITICAL THINKING AND READING

## Making Inferences About Characters

When you make inferences about characters, you decide what they are like based on evidence in the story. For example, when you read the beginning of "The Necklace," you probably inferred that Monsieur Loisel is content with his station in life. You based your inference on evidence: his pleasure in the homemade beef stew, his feeling of triumph in receiving the invitation, and his bewilderment at his wife's dissatisfaction.

1. Which of the following adjectives fits Madame Loisel: *self-centered, generous, warm, envious*? Support your answer.
2. How are the things Madame Loisel values different from the things her husband values?
3. In what essential way are Madame and Monsieur Loisel alike? Support your answer.

# THINKING AND WRITING

## Responding to Criticism

The critic Theophil Spoerri has written that Maupassant's stories are "the perfected expression of an age which had lost itself amid things." Discuss the meaning of this statement with your classmates. Do you think the Loisels are or are not representative of a materialistic age? Jot down reasons that support your answer. Next, imagine you are writing for a high-school literary magazine. Using "The Necklace" as your example, write an essay supporting or reputing Spoerri's comment. Revise your essay, making sure that your argument is clear and that you have provided adequate support. Finally, proofread your essay and prepare a final draft.

*The Necklace* 207

(Answers begin on p. 206.)

## ANSWERS TO CRITICAL THINKING AND READING

1. Suggested Response: She is self-centered and envious. Her reactions to her living conditions and to the invitation to the ball show that she thinks only of herself. Her reactions to her friend and to the other women at the ball reveal that she is envious.
2. Suggested Response: She values the life of the rich. Her husband is content with his own station in life. Madame Loisel places her own happiness above all things. Her husband is willing to deny himself in order to make his wife happy.
3. Suggested Response: Both are proud. They do not tell Madame Forestier about the lost necklace but instead replace it and slave for ten years to repay the debts incurred

**Challenge** Think of all you have learned about the character traits of the Loisels. How would you expect them to react to the news that they had replaced an imitation necklace with a real one? What would each of them do as a result? What would their life be like after the discovery?

## THINKING AND WRITING

For help with this assignment, students can refer to Lesson 11, "Writing About Theme," in the Handbook of Writing About Literature.

### Publishing Student Writing

Ask for student volunteers to read their essays aloud. Have students in the audience record at least one noteworthy feature of each essay.

### Writing Across the Curriculum

You might want students to research and report about the middle class in France during the 1880's. If you do, perhaps inform the social studies department. Social studies teachers might provide guidance for students in conducting research.

---

from being a vain and dissatisfied middle-class young woman to becoming a hard-working drudge. She loses her looks and becomes coarse and old before her time. She still lapses into unreality, however, and dreams about the ball. She blames her friend for her troubles.

### Applying

8. Answers will differ. Students may respond that telling her friend about losing the necklace and of-

fering to pay for it would be one solution.

**Challenge** How do you think Maupassant wants you to feel toward Madame Loisel? Find evidence that supports your answer.

## ANSWERS TO ANALYZING LITERATURE

1. Suggested Response: Her former middle-class life of comfort and security is also over because she has lost the necklace.

2. Suggested Response: The name of the street mirrors the Loisels' fate— they must endure great suffering.
3. Suggested Response: The Loisels endure poverty and hard work for ten years to replace a diamond necklace that turns out to be a cheap imitation.
4. Suggested Response: Conditions in life continually change and you cannot be sure what the future will hold. No matter how carefully you may plan, fate can move your life in an entirely different direction.

**Putting It Together** After students have read a number of short stories and learned about various literary elements, they should realize how all these elements work together. The information on this page is a review of the major elements of the short story. Students can then apply their knowledge to "Gwilan's Harp" by Ursula K. Le Guin. As you discuss this story with them, point out that the notes in the side column are examples of observations an active reader might make in "putting it together." Advise them, however, that their own comments and observations might be different.

If you wish to give your students further practice with this process, use "You Need to Go Upstairs," by Rumer Godden, Teaching Portfolio, page 269, following the Teacher Backup for this selection, which students can annotate themselves.

# PUTTING IT TOGETHER

## The Short Story

An active reader reads not only for meaning but also to appreciate the way the author has put together the elements of the short story to create an effective work. The best way to gain this appreciation is by asking and answering questions about the elements as you read. Below are some of the types of questions you might ask yourself as you go through a short story.

**Plot**

**Plot** is the sequence of events in a short story. Do you know the order in which the events occur? Do you understand how they are related to each other? Why has the author chosen to unfold the story in this way?

**Characters**

**Characters** are the people, and sometimes the animals, who take part in the story. Who are the main characters? Who are the minor characters? How has the author presented these characters? How do you think the author expects you to feel about them?

**Point of View**

**Point of view** is the vantage point from which a story is told. Does the author stand outside the story and have one character tell it? Does the author step into the story and comment on characters and events? Are you taken inside the minds of only one character, a few, or even all of them? Why has the author chosen to relate the story in this way?

**Setting**

**Setting** is the place and time of the events of the story. Where and when does the story take place? How much detail does the author give you about the setting? What kind of atmosphere or mood does the author create in describing the setting?

**Theme**

**Theme** is the general idea about life that the author wants to communicate. How has the author constructed the story so that the theme is revealed to the reader? Does the main character change in a significant way that reveals the theme? Does the main character learn something about life? Is the theme stated or implied?

The questions in the margin of the following story are meant to give you practice in becoming an active reader. Many can be answered right away, while others will require you to read further in the story.

208    Short Stories

## Support Material

**Teaching Portfolio**
Teacher Backup, p. 265
Putting It Together, "You Need to Go Upstairs," by Rumer Godden, p. 269
Grammar in Action Worksheet, *Using Imagery*, p. 273
Usage and Mechanics Worksheet, p. 275
Critical Thinking and Reading Worksheet, *Comparing and Contrasting*, p. 276

Language Worksheet, *Understanding Synonyms and Antonyms*, p. 277
Selection Test, p. 278

# Gwilan's Harp

## Ursula K. Le Guin

The harp had come to Gwilan from her mother, and so had her mastery of it, people said. "Ah," they said when Gwilan played, "you can tell, that's Diera's touch," just as their parents had said when Diera played, "Ah, that's the true Penlin touch!" Gwilan's mother had had the harp from Penlin, a musician's dying gift to the worthiest of pupils. From a musician's hands Penlin too had received it; never had it been sold or bartered for, nor any value put upon it that can be said in numbers. A princely and most incredible instrument it was for a poor harper to own. The shape of it was perfection, and every part was strong and fine: the wood as hard and smooth as bronze, the fittings of ivory and silver. The grand curves of the frame bore silver mountings chased with long intertwining lines that became waves and the waves became leaves, and the eyes of gods and stags looked out from among the leaves that became waves and the waves became lines again. It was the work of great craftsmen, you could see that at a glance, and the longer you looked the clearer you saw it. But all this beauty was practical, obedient, shaped to the service of sound. The sound of Gwilan's harp was water running and rain and sunlight on the water, waves breaking and the foam on the brown sands, forests, the leaves and branches of the forest and the shining eyes of gods and stags among the leaves when the wind blows in the valleys. It was all that and none of that. When Gwilan played, the harp made music; and what is music but a little wrinkling of the air?

Play she did, wherever they wanted her. Her singing voice was true but had no sweetness, so when it was songs and ballads she accompanied the singers. Weak voices were borne up by her playing, fine voices gained a glory from it; the loudest, proudest singers might keep still a verse to hear her play alone. She played with flute and reed-flute and tambour[1], and

---

1. **tambour** (tam′ boor) *n.*: A drum.

**Title:** Why has the author called this story "Gwilan's Harp"?

**Character:** Who is Gwilan? Is she the main character?

**Theme:** Why has the author described the harp in such detail?

**Setting:** Where and when is this story taking place? Is it occurring in a real place at a real time or does the author mean the story to have an almost mythic quality?

*Gwilan's Harp*   209

## Presentation

**Motivation/Prior Knowledge** Have students think about a valuable and irreplaceable possession. What gives this possession its value to them? Does it have a practical use? How might their lives be different if they no longer had it? Then tell students that the main character in this story must deal with the loss of an irreplaceable possession.

**Master Teacher Note** The action in "Gwilan's Harp" is internal rather than external. This may pose a difficulty for students who look for external events in a plot. It may help students to know before reading the story that the "action" occurs mainly in the character's mind as she reacts to the major events in her life.

**Thematic Idea** Another selection that deals with personal transformations and acceptance of life's trials and tribulations is "The Miracle Worker," by William Gibson, page 253. You might also have students compare Gwilan's journey toward self-knowledge with Pip's in *Great Expectations*, page 757.

**Purpose-Setting Question** The model question asked with the title sets a purpose for reading this story.

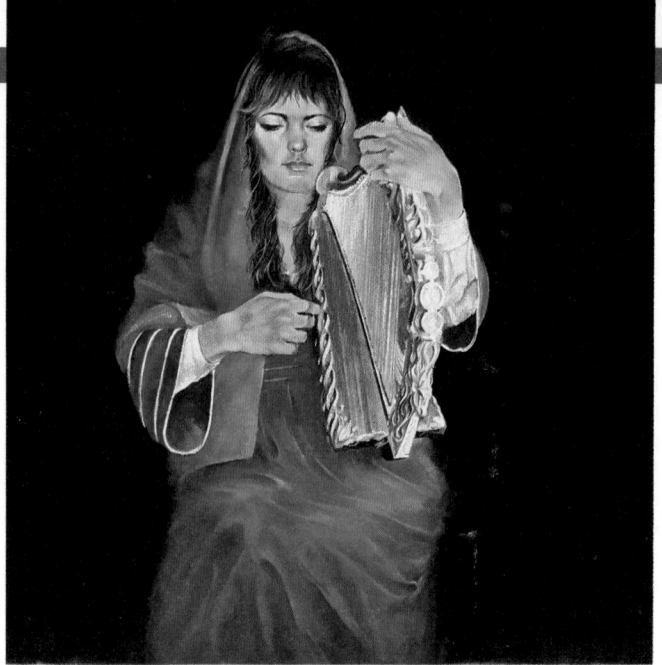

**Point of View:** Why has the author chosen to tell this story in the third person? What effect does this point of view have on the story?

the music made for the harp to play alone, and the music that sprang up of itself when her fingers touched the strings. At weddings and festivals it was, "Gwilan will be here to play," and at music-day competitions, "When will Gwilan play?"

She was young; her hands were iron and her touch was silk; she could play all night and the next day too. She travelled from valley to valley, from town to town, stopping here and staying there and moving on again with other musicians on their wanderings. They walked, or a wagon was sent for them, or they got a lift on a farmer's cart. However they went, Gwilan carried her harp in its silk and leather case at her back or in her hands. When she rode she rode with the harp and when she walked she walked with the harp, and when she slept, no, she didn't sleep with the harp, but it was there where she could reach out and touch it. She was not jealous of it, and would change instruments with another harper gladly; it was a great pleasure to her when at last they gave her back her own, saying with sober envy, "I never played so fine an instrument." She kept it clean, the mountings polished, and strung it with the harpstrings made by old Uliad, which cost as much apiece as a whole set of common harpstrings. In the heat of summer she carried it in the shade of her body, in the bitter winter it shared her cloak. In a firelit hall she did not sit with it very near the fire, nor yet too far away, for changes of heat and cold would change the voice of it, and perhaps harm the frame. She did not look after herself with half the care. Indeed she saw no need to. She knew there were other harpers, and would be other harpers; most not as good, some better. But the harp was the best. There had not been and there would not be a better. Delight and service were due and fitting to it. She was not its owner but its player. It was her music, her joy, her life, the noble instrument.

> **Theme:** Does the harp have symbolic value? Is it a key to the theme of the story?

She was young; she travelled from town to town; she played *A Fine Long Life* at weddings, and *The Green Leaves* at festivals. There were funerals, with the burial feast, the singing of elegies,[2] and Gwilan to play *The Lament*[3] *of Orioth*, the music that crashes and cries out like the sea and the sea-birds, bringing relief and a burst of tears to the grief-dried heart. There were music-days, with a rivalry[4] of harpers and a shrilling of fiddlers and a mighty outshouting of tenors.[5] She went from town to town in sun and rain, the harp on her back or in her hands. So she was going one day to the yearly music-day at Comin, and the landowner of Torm Vale was giving her a lift, a man who so loved music that he had traded a good cow for a bad horse, since the cow would not take him where he could hear music played. It was he and Gwilan in a rickety cart, and the lean-necked roan[6] stepping out down the steep, sunlit road from Torm.

A bear in the forest by the road, or a bear's ghost, or the shadow of a hawk: the horse shied half across the road. Torm had been discussing music deeply with Gwilan, waving his hands to conduct a choir of voices, and the reins went flipping out of those startled hands. The horse jumped like a cat, and ran. At the sharp curve of the road the cart swung round and smashed against the rocky cutting. A wheel leapt free and rolled, rocking like a top, for a few yards. The roan went

---

**2. elegies** (el' ə jēz) *m.*: Songs of mourning.
**3. lament** (lə ment') *n.*: Song of mourning.
**4. rivalry** (rī' v'l rē) *n.*: Competition.
**5. tenors** (ten' ərs) *n.*: Singers with voices ranging about an octave, or eight full notes, above and below middle C.
**6. roan** (rōn) *n.*: A horse of a solid color such as reddish brown or black but with a thick sprinkling of white hair.

*Gwilan's Harp*   211

**Reading Strategy** Have students note the additional separating space on this page. Ask why there might be more space before this paragraph.

plunging and sliding down
the road with half the wrecked cart dragging
behind, and was gone, and the road lay silent in the
sunlight between the forest trees.

Torm had been thrown from the cart, and lay stunned for a minute or two.

**Plot:** What effect will the breaking of the harp have on the plot? What will happen to Gwilan and Torm?

Gwilan had clutched the harp to her when the horse shied, but had lost hold of it in the smash. The cart had tipped over and dragged on it. It was in its case of leather and embroidered silk, but when, one-handed, she got the case out from under the wheel and opened it, she did not take out a harp, but a piece of wood, and another piece, and a tangle of strings, and a sliver of ivory, and a twisted shell of silver chased with lines and leaves and eyes, held by a silver nail to a fragment of the frame.

It was six months without playing after that, since her arm had broken at the wrist. The wrist healed well enough, but there was no mending the harp; and by then the land-owner of Torm had asked her if she would marry him, and she had said yes. Sometimes she wondered why she had said yes, having never thought much of marriage before, but if she looked steadily into her own mind she saw the reason why.

She saw Torm on the road in
the sunlight kneeling by the broken harp,
his face all blood and dust, and he was weeping.
When she looked at that she saw that the time for rambling
and roving was over and gone. One day is the day for moving
on, and overnight, the next day, there is no more good in moving on, because you have come where you were going to.

Gwilan brought to the marriage a gold piece, which had
been the prize last year at Four Valleys music-day; she had
sewn it to her bodice[7] as a brooch, because where on earth
could you spend a gold piece. She also had two silver pieces,
five coppers, and a good winter cloak. Torm contributed house
and household, fields and forests, four tenant farmers even
poorer than himself, twenty hens, five cows, and forty sheep.

They married in the old way, by themselves, over the
spring where the stream began, and came back and told the
household. Torm had never suggested a wedding, with singing and harp-playing, never a word of all that. He was a man
you could trust, Torm was.

What began in pain, in tears, was never free from the fear
of pain. The two of them were gentle to each other. Not that

**Theme:** Is this statement significant? Is it a key to theme? What does it mean?

---

**7. bodice** (bäd′ is) *n.*: Upper part of a woman's dress.

**Point of View:** The author's voice is very clear. What effect does this have on the story?

they lived together thirty years without some quarreling. Two rocks sitting side by side would get sick of each other in thirty years, and who knows what they say now and then when nobody is listening. But if people trust each other they can grumble, and a good bit of grumbling takes the fuel from wrath. Their quarrels went up and burnt out like bits of paper, leaving nothing but a feather of ash, a laugh in bed in the dark. Torm's land never gave more than enough, and there was no money saved. But it was a good house, and the sunlight was sweet on those high stony fields. There were two sons, who grew up into cheerful sensible men. One had a taste for roving, and the other was a farmer born; but neither had any gift of music.

Gwilan never spoke of wanting another harp. But about the time her wrist was healed, old Uliad had a traveling musician bring her one on loan; when he had an offer to buy it at its worth he sent for it back again. At that time Torm would have it that there was money from selling three good heifers[8] to the landowner of Comin High Farm, and the money should buy a harp, which it did. A year or two later an old friend, a flute player still on his travels and rambles, brought her a harp from the south as a present. The three-heifers harp was a common instrument, plain and heavy; the Southern harp was delicately carved and gilt, but cranky to tune and thin of voice. Gwilan could draw sweetness from the one and strength from the other. When she picked up a harp, or spoke to a child, it obeyed her.

**Character:** What effect does the author's use of direct characterization have on the story? Does it make the story seem more distant and removed?

She played at all festivities and funerals in the neighborhood, and with the musician's fees she bought good strings; not Uliad's strings, though, for Uliad was in his grave before her second child was born. If there was a music-day nearby she went to it with Torm. She would not play in the competitions, not for fear of losing but because she was not a harper now, and if they did not know it, she did. So they had her judge the competitions, which she did well and mercilessly. Often in the early years musicians would stop by on their travels, and stay two or three nights at Torm; with them she would play the Hunts of Orioth, the Dances of Cail, the difficult and learned music of the North, and learn from them the

---

8. **heifers** (hef′ ərz) *n.*: Young cows.

## Grammar in Action

An **image** is a word or phrase that appeals to one of the five senses—sight, hearing, touch, taste, smell. By appealing to the reader's senses, use of image, or **imagery,** allows that reader to experience what is being described. Look at this passage from the story:

Even in winter evenings there was music in the house of Torm: she played the harp—usually the three heifers one,

sometimes the fretful Southerner—and Torm's good tenor voice, and the boys singing, first a sweet treble, later on a husky unreliable baritone; and one of the farm's men was a lively fiddler; and the shepherd Keth, when he was there, played on the pipes, though he never could tune them to anyone else's note.

To what sense does the passage appeal? "Winter evenings" appeals to the sense of touch; "there was music in the house," "Torm's good tenor voice . . . was a lively fiddler," and "played on the pipes, though he never could tune them to anyone else's note" all appeal to our sense of hearing.

To what sense does this sentence appeal?

new songs. Even in winter evenings there was music in the house of Torm: she played the harp—usually the three-heifers one, sometimes the fretful Southerner—and Torm's good tenor voice, and the boys singing, first a sweet treble, later on in husky unreliable baritone;[9] and one of the farm's men was a lively fiddler; and the shepherd Keth, when he was there, played on the pipes, though he never could tune them to anyone else's note. "It's our own music-day tonight," Gwilan would say. "Put another log on the fire, Torm, and sing *The Green Leaves* with me, and the boys will take the descant."[10]

Her wrist that had been broken grew a little stiff as the years went on; then the arthritis came into her hands. The work she did in house and farm was not easy work. But then who, looking at a hand, would say it was made to do easy work? You can see from the look of it that it is meant to do difficult things, that it is the noble, willing servant of the heart and mind. But the best servants get clumsy as the years go on. Gwilan could still play the harp, but not as well as she had played, and she did not much like half-measures. So the two harps hung on the wall, though she kept them tuned. About that time the younger son went wandering off to see what things looked like in the north, and the elder married and brought his bride to Torm. Old Keth was found dead up on the mountain in the spring rain, his dog crouched silent by him and the sheep nearby. And the drouth came, and the good year, and the poor year, and there was food to eat and to be cooked and clothes to wear and to be washed, poor year or good year. In the depth of a winter Torm took ill. He went from a cough to a high fever to quietness, and died while Gwilan sat beside him.

> Theme: Is the author speaking just of the hand here, or does this statement have a deeper significance?

Thirty years, how can you say how long that is, and yet no longer than the saying of it: thirty years. How can you say how heavy the weight of thirty years is, and yet you can hold all of them together in your hand lighter than a bit of ash, briefer than a laugh in the dark. The thirty years began in pain; they passed in peace, contentment. But they did not end there. They ended where they began.

---

**9. baritone** (bar′ ə tōn′) *n.*: A deep-toned male voice between a bass and a tenor.
**10. descant** (des′ kant) *n.*: In two-part singing, the added melody sung above the main theme.

*Gwilan's Harp* 215

---

Old Keth was found dead up on the mountain in the spring rain, his dog crouched silent by him and the sheep nearby.

The image of the shepherd with his animals, the dog loyally beside him, appeals to the sense of sight. To what senses do *silent, up on the mountain,* and *in the spring rain* appeal?

**Student Activity 1.** Find three more passages that contain imagery in the story and copy these, noting the senses appealed to in each passage. Share these passages with a small group of classmates, discussing the imagery in each one.

**Student Activity 2.** Write a short passage that contains imagery. Read your first draft to a partner or small group and discuss ways to make the images more effective.

**Discussion** Have students look for evidence to prove that Gwilan has been stifling anger for thirty years. Why has her anger surfaced at this time? Why is it appropriate for her to sing a lament?

**More About the Author** Ursula Le Guin's father was an anthropologist, and her mother was a writer. Ask students to discuss how the professions of a writer's parents might influence his or her writing style and choice of subjects.

**Reader's Response** What talent do you have that was "passed down" to you?

**Character:** What is Gwilan's motivation? Why does she want to smash the harps?

**Theme:** How does what Gwilan learns reveal the theme?

**Putting It Together:** Gwilan learns to see herself as part of the cycle of life.

Gwilan got up from her chair and went into the hearth-room. The rest of the household were asleep. In the light of her candle she saw the two harps hung against the wall, the three-heifers harp and the gilded Southern harp, the dull music and the false music. She thought, "I'll take them down at last and smash them on the hearthstone, crush them till they're only bits of wood and tangles of wire, like my harp." But she did not. She could not play them at all any more, her hands were far too stiff. It is silly to smash an instrument you cannot even play.

"There is no instrument left that I can play," Gwilan thought, and the thought hung in her mind for a while like a long chord, until she knew the notes that made it. "I thought my harp was myself. But it was not. It was destroyed, I was not. I thought Torm's wife was myself, but she was not. He is dead, I am not. I have nothing left at all now but myself. The wind blows from the valley, and there's a voice on the wind, a bit of a tune. Then the wind falls, or changes. The work has to be done, and we did the work. It's their turn now for that, the children. There's nothing left for me to do but sing. I never could sing. But you play the instrument you have." So she stood by the cold hearth and sang the melody of Orioth's Lament. The people of the household wakened in their beds and heard her singing, all but Torm; but he knew that tune already. The untuned strings of the harps hung on the wall wakened and answered softly, voice to voice, like eyes that shine among the leaves when the wind is blowing.

**Ursula K. Le Guin** (1929–    ) was born in Berkeley, California. This highly imaginative writer is best known for her works of science fiction and fantasy. Among her award-winning works are *The Left-Hand of Darkness* and *The Earthsea Trilogy*. Although "Gwilan's Harp" does not contain dragons and wizards, it does have an almost magical quality about it.

216   Short Stories

**Closure and Extension**

### ANSWERS TO THINKING ABOUT THE SELECTION
*Recalling*

1. Gwilan plays the harp she inherited from her mother.
2. The horse bolts and the cart in which Gwilan and Torm are riding is wrecked. Her harp is smashed in the accident.
3. From one she gains sweetness; from the other she gains strength.
4. The thirty years begin with the pain of the accident and loss of the harp and end with the pain of Torm's death.
5. Gwilan plays the instrument of her own voice as she sings.

*Interpreting*

6. Suggested Response: Gwilan sees the compassion Torm has for her when her harp is destroyed.
7. Suggested Response: When the harp is destroyed, Gwilan senses that it is time for her to move on with her life. She is practical in marrying Torm, she works hard in her marriage, and she shapes her life to serve her family. She also has been obedient to the craft of music.
8. Suggested Response: A person must do many difficult things in order to lead a successful and productive life.
9. Suggested Response: Gwilan

## THINKING ABOUT THE SELECTION
### Recalling

1. What instrument does Gwilan play at the beginning of the story?
2. What happens on the ride to the music festival at Comin that causes Gwilan's life to change?
3. What does Gwilan gain from the two instruments she plays during her marriage?
4. How do the thirty years with Torm end where they began?
5. What instrument does Gwilan learn to play at the end of the story?

### Interpreting

6. What does Gwilan see in Torm that makes her agree to marry him?
7. The author describes the beauty of the harp as "practical, obedient, shaped to the service of sound." In what way does Gwilan's life also fit this description?
8. The author writes, "But then who, looking at a hand, would say it was made to do easy work? You can see from the look of it that it is meant to do difficult things. . . ." What else does this story suggest is meant to do difficult things?
9. What does Gwilan learn at the end of the story?

### Applying

10. Gwilan received as a legacy from her mother not only the harp but also her mother's love and respect for music. What legacies do we receive from others?

## ANALYZING LITERATURE
### Reviewing the Short Story

The elements of *plot, character, point of view, setting,* and *theme* work together in a story to create a total effect. Sometimes, though, one element dominates, or is more important than the others. Think of all these elements in regard to "Gwilan's Harp."

1. Give a brief summary of the plot.
2. Do the characters seem like people you know or more like types? Why?
3. What method does the author use to tell the story?
4. What role does setting play in the story?
5. What is the theme?
6. Which element do you think dominates this story?

## CRITICAL THINKING AND READING
### Comparing and Contrasting

A **comparison** shows the similarities between things. A **contrast** shows the differences. Often an author will use comparison and contrast to highlight the theme of a story.

1. How are Gwilan and Torm alike?
2. How are Gwilan's children different from her?
3. Compare and contrast the three-heifers harp and the Southern harp.
4. Compare and contrast these two harps and Gwilan's harp.

## THINKING AND WRITING
### Writing About Theme

Ecclesiastes 3:1 reads: "To everything there is a season, and a time for everything under heaven." Discuss this quotation with your classmates. Then write a composition explaining how this quotation applies to "Gwilan's Harp." Show how Gwilan learns to play a different instrument at each stage of her life. Be sure to support your explanation with evidence from the story. Revise your composition. Then prepare a final draft and share it with your classmates.

*Gwilan's Harp* 217

(Answers begin on p. 216.)

2. Suggested Response: The characters are more like types than real people because their actions over the thirty years are summarized rather than described in detail.
3. The story is told from the limited third-person point of view.
4. Suggested Response: The setting, never clearly defined, seems to be a distant place and time, almost like a place in a fairy tale. The musical instruments are also part of the setting.
5. Suggested Response: The theme of the story is that a person can overcome loss, which is inevitable in life, by calling on his or her deepest resources.
6. Answers will differ. Some students might suggest that the character of Gwilan dominates; others might suggest that the theme of loss and the overcoming of loss dominates.

### ANSWERS TO CRITICAL THINKING AND READING

1. Suggested Response: Both Gwilan and Torm love music, they are both gentle and affectionate, and they both share a love of family.
2. Suggested Response: Gwilan's children did not inherit her gift for music.
3. Suggested Response: The three-heifers harp is plain and heavy and its music is strong. The Southern harp is delicately carved and gilded; its music is sweet, but it is cranky to tune and thin of voice.
4. Suggested Response: Neither of the harps given to Gwilan during her marriage has the magical qualities of sound and the beauty of the harp she had inherited from her mother.

### THINKING AND WRITING

For help with this assignment, students can consult Lesson 11, "Writing About Theme," in the Handbook of Writing About Literature.

**Writing Across the Curriculum**
You might have students research and report on the craft of making musical instruments. Consider informing the music department of this assignment, so that teachers can assist students.

learns that she, like all others, must learn to make the best of what she has in life, to "play the instrument you have."

### Applying
10. Answers will differ. Students may respond that we receive the legacy of freedom from those who founded and those who have defended our country. We receive the legacy of love from those who have raised us. We receive the legacy of education from those who have taught us.

**Challenge** This story develops its theme from Gwilan's experiences in life. What do you think Torm learned about life? What might the theme be if the story were written about him?

### ANSWERS TO ANALYZING LITERATURE

1. Suggested Response: Gwilan is recognized for the beautiful music she creates on the priceless harp she inherited from her mother. When the harp is destroyed, she marries and raises her sons. When her husband dies thirty years later, she suffers a second great loss. She realizes, however, that she must draw on her own inner strength and continue to live.

**FOCUS ON READING**
**Understanding Relationships**

Emphasize that meaning in sentences is often dependent on the relationships between ideas. It is important for students to be able to recognize such relationships when reading and to be able to express them clearly when writing.

### Answers to the Activity

1. *cause:* the water was hard
   *effect:* the pilot knew he wasn't in Brighton
2. *cause:* Zaroff was bored with hunting
   *effect:* he developed a new game
3. *cause:* the criminal wanted Wilson out of the way
   *effect:* he set up the Red-headed League.
4. *cause:* the accused choose their own punishment
   *effect:* the king considered his system of government fair
5. *cause:* Alfred had been getting into trouble ever since he left school
   *effect:* his mother was not surprised when she received a call from Sam Carr

---

# FOCUS ON READING

# Understanding Relationships

**Relationships** are connections. Ideas, characters, and events may be connected in a variety of ways. Three important relationship patterns are cause and effect, comparison and contrast, and order of importance.

## Cause and Effect

A **cause** is what makes something happen. An **effect** is the result.

For example, read the following sentence:

Gwilan began to sing because her voice was the only instrument she had left.

The cause is her voice being the only instrument she has left. The effect is her beginning to sing.

The following words often signal a cause-and-effect relationship.

| as | so | therefore | accordingly | consequently | so that |
|----|----|-----------|-------------|--------------|---------|
| for | thus | as a result | in order to | because | since |

## Activity

Identify the cause and the effect in each sentence below.
1. The pilot knew he wasn't in Brighton because the water was hard.
2. Zaroff was bored with hunting; as a result, he developed a new game.
3. The criminal mastermind set up the Red Headed League in order to get Wilson out of the way.
4. The king considered his system of government fair, since the accused chose his or her own punishment.
5. Alfred had been getting into trouble ever since he left school; consequently, his mother was not surprised when she received the call from Sam Carr.

## Comparison and Contrast

When you **compare** items, you show how they are alike. When you **contrast,** you show how they are different. For example, you could compare the three-heifers harp and the Southern harp from "Gwilan's Harp" by showing how they are both stringed instruments. You can contrast them by showing how the first is plain and heavy, while the second is delicately carved and light.

218   *Short Stories*

The following words often signal a comparison.

| like | similarly | both | alike | same |
|------|-----------|------|-------|------|

These words often signal a contrast.

| but | although | in contrast |
|-----|----------|-------------|
| in spite of | on the contrary | whereas |
| yet | nevertheless | instead |
| on the other hand | while | |

**Activity**

Select two characters from two different selections in this unit. Write a paragraph showing how they are similar. Then write another paragraph showing how they are different. Use signal words to show the relationship between ideas.

## Order of Importance

In literature, as in life, some ideas are more important than others. When you arrange ideas according to order of importance, you start with the most important idea and build to the less important one. By ordering details this way, you create a climatic effect.

**Activity**

In "The Cask of Amontillado," Montressor never names the thousand injuries he suffered from Fortunato. Keeping in character, and remembering that Fortunato was sensitive to the merest slight, list ten injuries he might have suffered. Then arrange your list according to order of importance.

Now pretend to be Montressor. Write a narrative in which you confess your crime to a police officer. Tell the motive for your crime by relating the injuries you suffered. Save the greatest injury for last.

*Focus on Reading* 219

The writing assignments on page 220 have student write creatively, while those on page 221 have them think about the short stories and write critically.

## Short Stories

### YOU THE WRITER
Guidelines for Evaluating Assignment 1

1. Does the description of the setting create a dominant impression?
2. Does the description establish and state the place and time?
3. Is the dominant impression supported by concrete, clearly-stated details?
4. Is the description organized chronologically and free from grammar, usage, and mechanics errors?

### Guidelines for Evaluating Assignment 2

1. Does the character sketch focus on an interesting anecdote?
2. Does it include dialogue?
3. Does the sketch emphasize personality and actions, but include some physical characteristics?
4. Has the student included specific and colorful details?
5. Is the character sketch free from grammar, usage, and mechanics errors?

### Guidelines for Evaluating Assignment 3

1. Has the student rewritten the beginning of the story from the first-person viewpoint of one of its characters?
2. Has the student patterned the beginning after the original but given it the slant of the character's viewpoint?
3. Has the student included details that accurately present the narrator's point of view?
4. Is the new beginning free from grammar, usage, and mechanics errors?

# YOU THE WRITER

**Assignment**

**1.** The *setting* of a story is the place and time in which that story happens. Imagine a setting for a short story and write a complete description of it.

**Prewriting.** Choose one setting. Then divide a piece of paper into two columns. In the first one, under the heading "Place," list words that describe that specific place. In the second column, under "Time," jot down details of the time.

**Writing.** Establish and state the place and time. Arrange your description according to time. (What do you see first, second, etc.?) Select concrete details to describe what you see.

**Revising.** When you revise, make sure your dominant impression is clearly stated and supported by specific details.

**Assignment**

**2.** Writers create the characters in a story by carefully choosing the character traits they wish to include. Write a character sketch of an imaginary person that makes that character believable.

**Prewriting.** Jot down character traits that reveal the following: (1) physical descriptions, (2) typical dialogue of the person, (3) details that show how the character treats others and how other people relate to him/her, (4) details that express the character in action, (5) specific adjectives that describe the character's personality.

**Writing.** Focus on an interesting anecdote about your character. Include details that show your character in action, for it is through actions that we learn what people are like. Include some dialogue. Have your sketch emphasize personality and actions, but include some physical characteristics.

**Revising.** As you revise your character sketch, make sure you have included specific and colorful details.

**Assignment**

**3.** The *point of view* of a story is the vantage point from which it is told. Choose a story that you have read and rewrite the beginning of it from the point of view of one of the minor characters in the story.

**Prewriting.** List the characters in the short story you have selected and choose a minor character to be the narrator. Make a list of the details in the story that this character would know about.

**Writing.** Rewrite the story you have chosen from the first-person viewpoint of one of its minor characters. Pattern the story after the original, but it will take on the slant of the character's viewpoint.

**Revising.** Revise your version of the story to include details that accurately present the narrator's point of view.

# ◼️ YOU THE CRITIC ◼️

**Assignment**

**1.** The *theme* of a story is its insight into life. Choose one of the stories you have read in this section and discuss its theme.

**Prewriting.** Before you write, look for the ways in which the author presents the theme and list them. Write down passages that seem to best state, directly or indirectly, the theme of the story.

**Writing.** Now write an essay. In the first paragraph, state what you feel is the theme of the story. Support this statement in the body of your essay. Write a concluding paragraph that sums up your main points.

**Revising.** When you revise, add, if needed, supportive details for your thesis.

**Assignment**

**2.** Henry James, a writer and critic, said "Nothing, of course, will ever take the place of the good old fashion 'liking' a work of art or not liking it." Write a review of your favorite short story.

**Prewriting.** Outline the plot and characters in the short story. Next to these points, jot down why you feel the plot works.

**Writing.** In your essay, begin by stating your opinion of the story. Then briefly describe the plot and characters. Emphasize the elements of the short story you thought were well done. Conclude by summing up your main points as to why this story "worked" or appealed to you.

**Revising.** When you revise, check that your review would persuade someone else to read this story.

**Assignment**

**3.** Write an essay that carefully analyzes and evaluates the plot of one of the short stories you read in this unit. Include the elements of conflict, suspense, climax, and resolution.

**Prewriting.** Create a map outlining the plot of the short story you have selected.

**Writing.** Begin writing by briefly describing the plot. Then describe the major conflicts in the plot and the problem to be solved by the main character. Next evaluate how the suspense is created as it builds toward the climax. Describe the climax of the story. Then analyze the conclusion. Are all the conflicts resolved? Is the main problem overcome? Is the ending a satisfying one? Did it leave any open ends or strands to the story? Finally, use your last paragraph to summarize whether or not you felt this plot was a good one.

**Revising.** Check your writing to see whether or not you provided specific details for each element of the plot. Could passages from the story be used to support your points?

*You the Critic* 221

---

*Guidelines for Evaluating Assignment 1*

1. Does the student state the theme of the story in the first paragraph of the essay?
2. Has the student supported the statement in the body of the essay with sufficient, specific detail from the story?
3. Does the concluding paragraph sum up the student's main points?
4. Is the essay free from grammar, usage, and mechanics errors?

*Guidelines for Evaluating Assignment 2*

1. Does the student begin the review by stating his or her opinion of the story?
2. Does the body of the review briefly describe the plot and characters, emphasizing the elements the student thought were well done?
3. Does the review end with a summary of the main points about why this story appealed to the student?
4. Does the review persuade the reader to read the story?
5. Is the review free from grammar, usage, and mechanics errors?

*Guidelines for Evaluating Assignment 3*

1. Does the student begin the evaluation by briefly describing the plot?
2. Has the student described the major conflict and the problems to be solved by the main characters?
3. Has the student analyzed how the suspense is created as it builds toward the climax and then described the climax itself?
4. Does the student analyze the conclusion?
5. Has the student supported his or her points with specific details and passages from the story?
6. Is the essay free from grammar, usage, and mechanics errors?

## Humanities Note

Fine Art, *The Sheridan Theatre,* 1937, Edward Hopper. Edward Hopper (1882-1967), an American painter, studied painting in New York City with Robert Henri and on his own in Paris. Hopper, a realist, painted rural, urban, and suburban American scenes. He portrayed with simple honesty the beauty and the ugliness of everyday surroundings. He took the mundane and the ordinary and turned them into something unforgettable.

*The Sheridan Theatre* is painted with the objective observation that is Hopper's hallmark. Hopper was fascinated with the interiors of theaters and painted them many times. This scene, a theater in darkness half lit at the rear, is a challenge that he met successfully. The mood of mystery and loneliness may result from the artist's detachment and the stark, direct, architectural rendering of the forms of a darkened theater.

THE SHERIDAN THEATRE, 1937
*Edward Hopper*
*Collection of the Newark Museum*

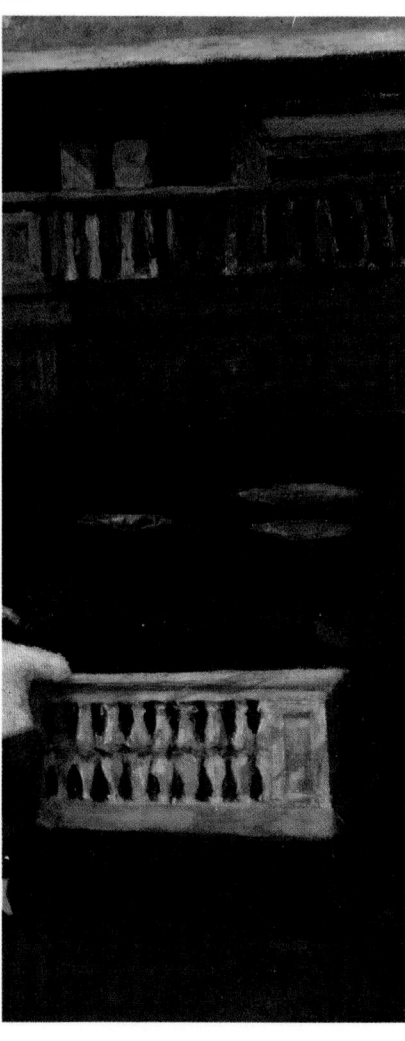

# DRAMA

Drama is literature that is meant to be performed before an audience. Like a short story, it may contain the elements of plot, character, setting, and theme. In drama, actors take the parts of the characters. The story is unfolded through their words, which we call dialogue, and their actions. Usually the playwright includes stage directions that tell the actors how to behave upon the stage. Drama has other elements, too—lighting, sets, props, costumes—that bring the play alive on the stage.

Some of the earliest forms of drama were parts of religious rituals and festivals in ancient times. They were performed out-of-doors in huge amphitheaters. Today you may see drama performed in a theater, or you may see a play produced as a movie. You may see plays performed on television, or you may have drama come into your home through radio or even audio cassettes.

One type of dramatic work is tragedy. The word *tragedy* comes from a Greek word meaning "goat song." Although scholars do not agree on the explanations for the name, most agree that its origin has some connection to a religious rite. A tragedy is a dramatic work in which a person of noble birth is brought down by a single weakness or fatal flaw. Another type of dramatic composition is comedy. The word *comedy* is based on an ancient Greek word that means "a merrymaker; a singer." Obviously, comedy is very different from tragedy. In comedy, the protagonist usually triumphs over his or her limitations so that the play has a happy ending. Today, the dividing line between comedy and tragedy has become blurred, with most plays having elements of each.

In this unit you will read a variety of plays, two of them contemporary and two of them older.

223

# Drama

Drama, as a form of literature, contains one-act plays and full-length plays. As a story, a play shows a character in conflict—facing a problem that gets progressively worse until it reaches a crisis. At this crisis the character acts decisively to solve the problem. His or her action speedily brings about the end of the story.

A play is told mostly through dialogue, the speech of the characters. This convention does not allow the audience to look directly into the minds of the characters to see from the inside what they are thinking and feeling. The audience must infer a character's thoughts and feelings from the dialogue. A second way in which the audience infers thoughts and feelings is from physical movements and gestures. A character who slams the door is angry. One who cries is upset.

Plays are meant to be performed. When you read a play, you are reading a script. The stage directions, printed in italics and in brackets, are intended to show the actors when and how to move and to suggest to the director what kinds of sound effects and lighting are needed and what the stage should look like. Stage directions use a particular vocabulary. *Right, left, up, down,* and *center* refer to areas of the stage as the actors see it. Picture the stage like this:

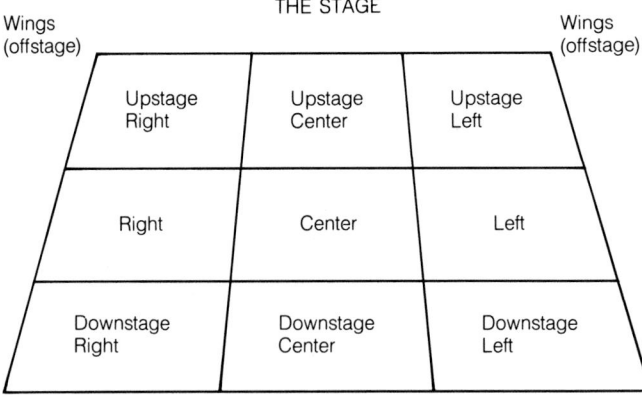

THE STAGE

| Wings (offstage) | | | Wings (offstage) |
|---|---|---|---|
| Upstage Right | Upstage Center | Upstage Left | |
| Right | Center | Left | |
| Downstage Right | Downstage Center | Downstage Left | |

Curtain

Just as you read stories actively, you should also read drama actively. Reading actively involves seeing the play in your mind while you continually question the meaning of what the actors are saying and doing.

The following strategies will help you read drama actively. Reading actively will help you to enjoy and appreciate the plays in this unit.

**Visualize**

Picture the stage and the characters in action. Use the directions and information supplied by the playwright to create the scene in your mind. Hear the characters speak; listen to their tone of voice. Let them show you what is happening.

**Question**

What is each character like? What situation does each character face? What is the conflict? What motives and traits does each character reveal by his or her words and actions?

**Predict**

Building on the play's conflict and the characters' motives, predict what you think will happen. How will the conflict be resolved? What will become of each character?

**Clarify**

Be sure that you can make sense of the characters' words or actions. If something is not clear to you, perhaps you need to review to find a clue in earlier words or actions. Look for answers to your questions, and check your predictions.

**Summarize**

Occasionally pause to review what has happened. What is the conflict? What is happening toward its resolution? Put the characters' actions and words together to form your summary.

**Pull It Together**

Finally pull together all the elements of the play. What does the play mean? What has it revealed about life? What does it say to you?

You will be a more effective reader if you use these strategies when you read drama. You will be better able to understand the conflict and resolution of a play and apply your understanding to your world.

**Reading Actively** Point out that a play requires a different kind of reading from a story in prose. Reading a play involves learning to interpret stage directions and to visualize scenes. The creative reader also practices what Coleridge called "the willing suspension of disbelief"; that is, the reader accepts the conventions of the drama and judges the play on its own terms.

**Master Teacher Note** Close reading of a play helps students to understand the author's intentions. While the class is reading any of the plays in this unit, you might use part of a class period to have students look through a play and find lines that were written to achieve any of the following purposes:
(1) to reveal a character trait of the speaker
(2) to advance the action of the plot
(3) to create mood
(4) to show the speaker's attempt to persuade by appealing to another's needs or wishes

## Focus

**More About the Author** Sometimes Chekhov thought his medical training hurt his writing because this training destroyed any illusions he might have had. Other times he believed his study of medicine gave him a better knowledge of people. Ask students to consider the advantages and disadvantages of medical training for a writer.

**Literary Focus** Point out that some situation comedies on television are farces. In such comedies, an already ridiculous situation is made even more so by the antics of the actors. Farce is particularly effective for television shows, which require fast-paced action.

**Look For** Tell students that the stage directions, which are italicized and appear in brackets, are a clue to the exaggerated behavior.

**Writing/Prior Knowledge** Consider dividing the class into small groups and having students first recount to their group the situation about which they will write.

**Vocabulary** You might ask **less advanced** students to work in pairs to create a paragraph containing four of the six vocabulary words.

**Spelling Tip** Point out that *creditors* ends in *ors*, not *ers*.

## The Boor

**Anton Chekhov** (1860–1904) was born in Taganrog, a small town in Russia. As a young medical student, he wrote comic sketches to support himself. Later, when licensed to practice medicine, he devoted himself more and more to writing and less and less to medicine. His best stories and plays are humorous, realistic portrayals that capture the weaknesses of human nature. Through the use of exaggerated comedy, or farce, *The Boor* reveals how unpredictable human nature can be.

### The One-Act Farce

A **one-act play** is a short play whose performance time is normally less than an hour. Relatively few characters are presented, and the setting often remains the same from start to finish. The plot of a one-act play will generally be much simpler than that of a full-length play, rising rapidly and directly to the climax, and then coming to the end. A one-act play, therefore, is the dramatic equivalent of a short story.

*The Boor* is a **one-act farce**—a comedy whose humor is especially wild, exaggerated, and fast-paced. The laughter that comes as a result of farce is often due to the outrageous situations and preposterous behavior of the characters.

### Look For

As you read *The Boor,* look for how the exaggerated behavior of Madame Popova and Smirnov creates farcical humor. How do remarks and actions reveal how odd and changeable human nature can be?

### Writing

You probably have heard the saying that there is a fine line between love and hate. Can the line be so fine that two people who claim to hate each other are really in love? Freewrite about a situation you have encountered in real life, in literature, or in movies that illustrates your answer to this question.

### Vocabulary

Knowing the following words will help you as you read *The Boor.*

**comply** (kəm plī′) *v.*: Act as requested (p. 229)

**creditors** (kred′ it ərz) *n.*: Persons to whom money is owed (p. 230)

**row** (rou) *n.*: Noisy quarrel (p. 230)

**bamboozle** (bam bōō′ z'l) *v.*: Trick (p. 232)

**impudence** (im′ pyōō dəns) *n.*: Disrespect (p. 233)

**impunity** (im pyōō′ nə tē) *n.*: Freedom from punishment (p. 234)

# The Boor

## Anton Chekhov

## A Jest In One Act

---

### CHARACTERS

**Yelena Ivanovna Popova** (yil yēn′ ə ē vän′ uv na pä paw′ və), a little widow with dimpled cheeks, a landowner.

**Grigory Stepanovich Smirnov** (gri gôr′ ē ste pän′ ə vich smir′ nôf), a middle-aged gentleman farmer.

**Luka** (loo′ kə), Mme. Popova's footman, an old man.

---

[*The drawing room in Mme. Popova's manor house. Mme. Popova, in deep mourning, her eyes fixed on a photograph, and Luka.*]

**LUKA.** It isn't right, madam. You're just killing yourself. The maid and the cook have gone berrying, every living thing rejoices, even the cat knows how to enjoy life and wanders through the courtyard catching birds, but you stay in the house as if it were a convent and take no pleasure at all. Yes, really! It's a whole year now, I figure, that you haven't left the house!

**MME. POPOVA.** And I never will leave it . . . What for? My life is over. He lies in his grave, and I have buried myself within these four walls. We are both dead.

**LUKA.** There you go again! I oughtn't to listen to you, really. Nikolay Mihailovich is dead, well, there is nothing to do about it, it's the will of God; may the kingdom of Heaven be his. You have grieved over it, and that's enough; there's a limit to everything. One can't cry and wear mourning forever. The time came when my old woman, too, died. Well? I grieved over it, I cried for a month, and that was enough for her, but to go on wailing all my life, why, the old woman isn't worth it. [*Sighs.*] You've forgotten all your neighbors. You don't go out and you won't receive anyone. We live, excuse me, like spiders—we never see the light of day. The mice have eaten the livery.[1] And it isn't as if there were no nice people around—the county is full of gentlemen. A regiment is quartered at Ryblov and every officer is a good-looker, you can't take your eyes off them. And every Friday there's a ball at the camp, and 'most every day the military band is playing. Eh, my dear lady, you're young and pretty, just peaches and cream, and you could lead a life of pleasure. Beauty doesn't

---

1. **livery** (liv′ ər ē) *n*.: Servants' uniforms.

*The Boor*  227

**Motivation/Prior Knowledge** You might ask students if they have ever seen a person's feelings for someone else change very rapidly. Have them briefly describe the situation they remember—which may come from everyday life, television, or the movies. Then tell them that the main characters in *The Boor* experience very rapid changes of emotion.

**Master Teacher Note** You might want to tell students that farce originally referred to clowning and horseplay that actors added to a drama on the spur of the moment. Even today, antic movement is an important aspect of farce. Have students consider how the play would be different if the characters did not move in this fashion.

**Purpose-Setting Question** Why might this play be less humorous if it consisted of five acts rather than one?

1 **Clarification** Yelena's middle name is her patronymic name—derived from her father's name. The suffix *-ovna* means "daughter of" and so her middle name literally means "daughter of Ivan." Grigory's patronymic name—his middle name—means "son of Stepan" because *-ovich* means "son of" in Russian.

2 **Discussion** What do the terms *drawing room* and *manor* tell you about Mme. Popova's social status?

3 **Enrichment** You might want to tell students that in the exposition or introduction to a play, the playwright sets the scene by giving important details from the past. Ask students to consider, as they continue to read, why Mme. Popova's mourning for her husband is important to the action of the play.

**Thematic Idea** Another selection that deals with transformations and the human need for acceptance is "The Scarlet Ibis," by James Hurst, page 189.

4 **Discussion** How does Luka indicate that his place in the house is different from that of a mere hired helper?

5 **Discussion** Why do you think Mme. Popova wants to be true to her husband, at all costs?

6 **Clarification** *Shafts* are the two long poles by which a horse is harnessed to a vehicle.

7 **Discussion** Why does Mme. Popova insist that Toby be given an extra measure of oats?

8 **Reading Strategy** Ask students to predict what sort of person Smirnov is.

9 **Enrichment** Russian officers were often given tracts of land as a pension when they retired.

4 last forever, you know. In ten years' time you'll find yourself wanting to strut like a pea-hen and dazzle the officers, but it will be too late.

**MME. POPOVA.** [*Resolutely*] I beg you never to mention this to me again! You know that since Nikolay Mihailovich died, life has been worth nothing to me. You think that I am alive, but it only seems so to you! I vowed to myself that never to the day of my death would I take off my mourning or see the light. Do you hear me? Let his shade see how I love him! Yes, I know, it is no secret to you that he was often unjust to me, cruel, and . . . even unfaithful, but I shall be true to the end, and prove to him how I can love. There, in the other world, he will find me just the same as I was before he died . . .

5 

**LUKA.** Instead of talking like that, you ought to go and take a walk in the garden, or have Toby or Giant put in the shafts and drive out to pay calls on the neighbors.

6 

**MME. POPOVA.** Oh! [*Weeps*]

**LUKA.** Madam! Dear madam! What's wrong? Bless you!

**MME. POPOVA.** He was so fond of Toby! When he drove out to the Korchagins and the Vlasovs it was always with Toby. What a wonderful driver he was! How graceful he was, when he pulled at the reins with all his might! Do you remember? Toby, Toby! Tell them to give him an extra measure of oats today.

7 

**LUKA.** Very well, madam. [*The doorbell rings sharply.*]

**MME. POPOVA.** [*Startled*] Who is it? Say that I am at home to no one.

**LUKA.** Very good, madam. [*Exits*]

**MME. POPOVA.** [*Looking at the photograph*] You shall see, *Nicolas*, how I can love and forgive. My love will die only with me, when my poor heart stops beating. [*Laughs through her tears*] And aren't you ashamed? I am a good, faithful little wife, I've locked myself in and shall remain true to you to the grave, and you . . . aren't you ashamed, you naughty boy? You were unfaithful to me, you made scenes, you left me alone for weeks . . .

[LUKA *enters.*]

**LUKA.** [*Disturbed*] Madam, someone is asking for you, wants to see you . . .

**MME. POPOVA.** But you told him, didn't you, that since my husband's death I receive no one?

**LUKA.** Yes, I did, but he wouldn't listen to me, he says it's a very urgent matter.

**MME. POPOVA.** I do not receive anyone!

8 

**LUKA.** I told him, but . . . he's a perfect devil . . . he curses and barges right in . . . he's in the dining-room now.

**MME. POPOVA.** [*Annoyed*] Very well, ask him in . . . What rude people! [*Exit* LUKA.] How irritating! What do they want of me? Why do they have to intrude on my solitude? [*Sighs*] No, I see I shall really have to enter a convent. [*Pensively*] Yes, a convent . . .

[*Enter* SMIRNOV *and* LUKA]

**SMIRNOV.** [*To* LUKA] Blockhead, you talk too much. You jackass! [*Seeing* MME. POPOVA, *with dignity*] Madam, I have the honor to introduce myself: Landowner Grigory Stepanovich Smirnov, lieutenant of the artillery, retired. I am compelled to disturb you in connection with a very weighty matter.

9 

**MME. POPOVA.** [*Without offering her hand*] What do you wish?

**SMIRNOV.** At his death your late husband, with whom I had the honor of being acquainted, was in my debt to the amount of

1200 rubles,[2] for which I hold two notes. As I have to pay interest on a loan to the Land Bank tomorrow, I must request you, madam, to pay me the money today.

**MME. POPOVA.** Twelve hundred. . . . And for what did my husband owe you the money?

**SMIRNOV.** He used to buy oats from me.

**MME. POPOVA.** [*Sighing, to* LUKA] So don't forget, Luka, to tell them to give Toby an extra measure of oats.

[*Exit* LUKA. *To* SMIRNOV]

If Nikolay Mihailovich owed you money, I shall pay you, of course; but you must excuse me, I haven't any ready cash today. The day after tomorrow my steward[3] will be back from town and I will see that he pays you what is owing to you, but just now I cannot comply with your request. Besides, today is exactly seven months since my husband's death and I am in no mood to occupy myself with money matters.

**2. rubles** (rōō' b'lz) *n.*: Money used in Russia.
**3. steward** (stōō' ərd) *n.*: The manager of an estate.

**SMIRNOV.** And I am in the mood to be carried out feet foremost if I don't pay the interest tomorrow. They'll seize my estate!

**MME. POPOVA.** The day after tomorrow you will receive your money.

**SMIRNOV.** I need the money today, not the day after tomorrow.

**MME. POPOVA.** I am sorry, but I cannot pay you today.

**SMIRNOV.** And I can't wait till the day after tomorrow.

**MME. POPOVA.** But what can I do if I don't have the money now!

**SMIRNOV.** So you can't pay me?

**MME. POPOVA.** No, I can't.

**SMIRNOV.** H'm . . . So that's your last word?

**MME. POPOVA.** My last word.

**SMIRNOV.** Your last word? Positively?

**MME. POPOVA.** Positively.

10 **Literary Focus** Farce is a dramatic form that is based upon exaggeration. Is there anything exaggerated about Mme. Popova's devotion to her husband?

11 **Discussion** How does the play seem to be shaping up as a conflict between an immovable object and an irresistible force? Explain which character is the object and which is the force.

12 **Critical Thinking and Reading** How do these brief exchanges affect the pace of the play?

**13 Enrichment** You might point out to students that Chekhov includes this bit of exposition to help explain Smirnov's state of mind.

**14 Discussion** Why do you think Smirnov focuses on this particular reason that Mme. Popova gave for not paying him?

**15 Clarification** A *milksop* is a weak, soft, unmanly person.

**16 Discussion** What biased idea about women does Smirnov have?

**17 Clarification** *Outriders* are "attendants on horseback who ride out ahead of or beside a coach."

**SMIRNOV.** Many thanks. I'll make a note of it. [*Shrugs his shoulders*] And they want me to keep cool! I meet the tax commissioner on the road, and he asks me: "Why are you always in a bad humor, Grigory Stepanovich?" But in heaven's name, how can I help being in a bad humor? I'm in desperate need of money. I left home yesterday morning at dawn and called on all my debtors and not one of them paid up! I wore myself out, slept the devil knows where. . . . Finally I come here, fifty miles from home, hoping to get something, and I'm confronted with a "mood." How can I help getting in a temper?

**MME. POPOVA.** I thought I made it clear to you that you will get your money as soon as my steward returns from town.

**SMIRNOV.** I didn't come to your steward, but to you! What the devil—pardon the expression—do I care for your steward!

**MME. POPOVA.** Excuse me, sir, I am not accustomed to such language or to such a tone. I won't listen to you any more. [*Exits rapidly*]

**SMIRNOV.** That's a nice thing! Not in the mood . . . husband died seven months ago! What about me? Do I have to pay the interest or don't I? I'm asking you: do I have to pay the interest or don't I? Well, your husband died, you're not in the mood, and all that . . . and your steward, devil take him, has gone off somewhere, but what do you want me to do? I to escape my creditors in a balloon, eh? Or take a running start and dash my head against a wall? I call on Gruzdev, he's not at home, Yaroshevich is hiding, I had an awful row with Kuritzyn and nearly threw him out of the window; Mazutov has an upset stomach, and this one isn't in the mood! Not one scoundrel will pay up! And it's all because I've spoiled them, because I'm a milksop, a softy, a weak sister. I'm too gentle with them altogether! But wait! You'll find out what I'm like! I won't let you make a fool of me, devil take it! I'll stay right here till she pays up! Ugh! I'm in a perfect rage today, in a rage! Every one of my nerves is trembling with fury, I can hardly breathe. Ouf! I even feel sick! [*Shouts*] You there! [*Enter* LUKA]

**LUKA.** What do you wish?

**SMIRNOV.** Give me some *kvass*[4] or a drink of water! [*Exit* LUKA] No, but the logic of it! A fellow is in desperate need of cash, is on the point of hanging himself, but she won't pay up, because, you see, she isn't in the mood to occupy herself with money matters! Real petticoat logic! That's why I've never liked to talk to women, and I don't now. I'd rather sit on a powder-keg than talk to a woman. Brr! I'm getting gooseflesh—that skirt made me so furious! I just have to see one of these poetic creatures from a distance and my very calves begin to twitch with rage. It's enough to make me yell for help. [*Enter* LUKA]

**LUKA.** [*Handing* SMIRNOV *a glass of water*] Madam is ill and will see no one.

**SMIRNOV.** Get out!

[*Exit* LUKA]

Ill and will see no one! All right, don't see me. I'll sit here until you pay up. If you're sick for a week, I'll stay a week; if you're sick a year, I'll stay a year. I'll get my own back, my good woman. You won't get round me with your widow's weeds[5] and your dimples . . . We know those dimples! [*Shouts through the window*] Semyon, take out the horses! We're not leaving so soon! I'm staying on! Tell them at the stables to give the horses oats. You blockhead, you've let the left outrider's leg get caught in the reins again! [*Mimicking*

---

**4. kvass** (kväs) *n.*: A Russian drink made from rye or barley.
**5. widow's weeds:** Black mourning clothes.

*the coachman*] "It don't matter" . . . I'll show you "don't matter." [*Walks away from the window*] It's horrible . . . the heat is terrific, nobody has paid up, I slept badly, and here's this skirt in mourning, with her moods! I have a headache. Shall I have more water? Yes, I think I will. [*Shouts*] You there!

[*Enter* LUKA]

**LUKA.** What do you wish?

**SMIRNOV.** Give me a glass of water.

[*Exit* LUKA]

Ouf! [*Sits down and looks himself over*] I cut a fine figure, I must say! All dusty, boots dirty, unwashed, uncombed, straw on my vest. The little lady must have taken me for a highwayman. [*Yawns*] It's a bit uncivil to barge into a drawing-room in such shape, but never mind . . . I'm no caller, just a creditor, and there are no rules as to what the creditor should wear.

[*Enter* LUKA]

**LUKA.** [*Handing* SMIRNOV *the water*] You allow yourself too many liberties, sir . . .

**SMIRNOV.** [*Crossly*] What?

**LUKA.** I . . . nothing . . . I just meant . . .

**SMIRNOV.** To whom do you think you're talking? Shut up!

**LUKA.** [*Aside*] There's a demon in the house . . . The Evil Spirit must have brought him . . .

[*Exit* LUKA]

**SMIRNOV.** Oh, what a rage I'm in! I'm mad enough to grind the whole world to powder. I feel sick. [*Shouts*] You there!

[*Enter* MME. POPOVA]

**MME. POPOVA.** [*With downcast eyes*] Sir, in my solitude I've long since grown unaccustomed to the human voice, and I cannot bear shouting. I beg you not to disturb my peace!

**SMIRNOV.** Pay me my money and I'll drive off.

**MME. POPOVA.** I told you in plain language, I have no ready cash now. Wait till the day after tomorrow.

**SMIRNOV.** And I had the honor of telling you in plain language that I need the money today, not the day after tomorrow. If you don't pay me today, I'll have to hang myself tomorrow.

**MME. POPOVA.** But what shall I do if I have no money? How odd!

**SMIRNOV.** So you won't pay me now, eh?

**MME. POPOVA.** I can't.

**SMIRNOV.** In that case I stay and I'll sit here till I get the money. [*Sits down*] You'll pay me the day after tomorrow? Excellent. I'll sit here till the day after tomorrow. [*Jumps up*] I ask you: Do I have to pay the interest tomorrow or don't I? Or do you think I'm joking?

**MME. POPOVA.** Sir, I beg you not to shout. This is no stable.

**SMIRNOV.** Never mind the stable, I'm asking you: Do I have to pay the interest tomorrow or not?

**MME. POPOVA.** You don't know how to behave in the presence of ladies!

**SMIRNOV.** No, madam, I do know how to behave in the presence of ladies!

**MME. POPOVA.** No, you do not! You are a rude, ill-bred man! Decent people don't talk to women that way!

**SMIRNOV.** Admirable! How would you like me to talk to you? In French, eh? [*Rages, and lisps*] *Madame, je vous prie,*[6] I am delighted

---

**6. *Madame, je vous prie*** (ma dam′ jə voo prē′): French for "Madam, I beg you."

**18 Critical Thinking and Reading**
What inferences can you draw about Smirnov from his speech and actions?

**19 Critical Thinking and Reading**
You might want to point out to students that an audience watching the play would know quite well what Smirnov looked like. Ask them why Chekhov chose to have Smirnov become aware of his disheveled appearance and then dismiss it as not important.

**20 Clarification** Tell students that in Russia at this time, the ability to speak French was considered a sign of good breeding and upper class status. By speaking a few French phrases to Mme. Popova, Smirnov is showing that he could speak French if he wanted to and is also making fun of Mme. Popova's notions of what is proper.

**21** **Discussion** How do you think Smirnov's present attitude toward women results from his past experiences with them?

**22** **Critical Thinking and Reading** How are Mme. Popova and Smirnov similar in their experience with the opposite sex?

that you do not pay me my money . . . Ah, *pardonnez-moi* if I have discommoded you![7] It's such delightful weather today! And how your mourning becomes you! [*Scrapes his foot*]

**MME. POPOVA.** That's rude and silly.

**SMIRNOV.** [*Mimicking her*] Rude and silly! I don't know how to behave in the presence of ladies! Madam, I've seen more ladies than you've seen sparrows! I've fought three duels on account of women, I've jilted twelve women and been jilted by nine! Yes, madam! Time was when I played the fool, sentimentalized, used honeyed words, went out of my way to please, bowed and scraped . . . I used to love, pine, sigh at the moon, feel blue, melt, freeze . . . I loved passionately, madly, all sorts of ways, devil take me; I chattered like a magpie about the emancipation of women,[8] I wasted half my fortune on affairs of the heart, but now, please excuse me! Now you won't bamboozle me! Enough! Dark eyes, burning eyes, ruby lips, dimpled cheeks, the moon, whispers, timid breathing . . . I wouldn't give a brass farthing for all this now, madam. Present company excepted, all women, young or old, put on airs, pose, gossip, are liars to the marrow of their bones, are malicious, vain, petty, cruel, revoltingly unreasonable, and as for this [*Taps his forehead*], pardon my frankness, a sparrow can give ten points to any philosopher in skirts! You look at one of these poetic creatures: She's all muslin and fluff, an airy demi-goddess, a million transports,[9] but look into her soul and what do you see but a common crocodile! [*Grips the back of his chair so that it cracks and breaks*] But what is most revolting, this crocodile for some reason imagines that the tender feelings are her special province, her privilege, her monopoly! Why, devil take it, hang me by my feet on that nail, but can a woman love anything except a lap-dog? When she's in love all she can do is whimper and turn on the waterworks! While a man suffers and makes sacrifices, her love finds expression only in swishing her train and trying to get a firmer grip on your nose. You, madam, have the misfortune of being a woman, so you know the nature of women down to the ground. Tell me honestly, then, did you ever see a woman who was sincere, faithful, and constant? You never did! Only old women and frights are faithful and constant. You'll sooner come across a horned cat or a white woodcock than a constant woman!

**MME. POPOVA.** Allow me to ask, then, who, in your opinion, is faithful and constant in love? Not man?

**SMIRNOV.** Yes, madam, man!

**MME. POPOVA.** Man! [*With bitter laughter*] Man is faithful and constant in love! That's news! [*Hotly*] What earthly right do you have to say that? Men faithful and constant! If such is the case, let me tell you that of all the men I have ever known my late husband was the best. I loved him passionately, with my whole soul, as only a young, deep-natured woman can love. I gave him my youth, my happiness, my life, my fortune; I lived and breathed by him; I worshiped him like a heathen, and . . . and what happened? This best of men deceived me shamelessly at every step! After his death I found a whole drawerful of love letters in his desk, and while he was alive—I can't bear to recall it!—he would leave me alone for weeks on end; he flirted with other women before my very eyes; he

---

**7. pardonnez-moi** (pär dən′ ā mwä′) **if I have discommoded** (dis′ kə mōd′ id) **you:** Pardon me if I have bothered you.
**8. emancipation of women:** The freeing of women to do many of the things that men do.
**9. transports** (trans′ pôrts) *n.*: Strong emotions of joy or delight.

## Grammar in Action

A **series** is a list of items, usually separated by commas. The items in a series can be nouns, verbs, single-word modifiers, or phrases:

We played checkers, chess, and bridge. (nouns)
We ate, conversed, and laughed. (verbs)
Lively, sensitive, and intelligent, the host was the star of the evening. (adjectives)

We proposed toasts to our hostess, to our good health, and to our friendship. (prepositional phrases)

Dramatists use series to create distinctive speech rhythms and give insights into their characters. In *The Boor,* for example, Chekhov has Smirnov speak in series to illustrate his impatience, ill humor, and impulsive manner of talking:

Time was when I played the fool, sentimentalized, used honeyed words, went out of my way to please, bowed and squandered my money and mocked my feelings. And in spite of it all, I loved him and was faithful to him. More than that, he died, and I am still faithful to him, still constant. I have buried myself forever within these four walls, and I will not take off my mourning till I go to my grave.

**SMIRNOV.** [*Laughing scornfully*] Mourning! I wonder who you take me for! As if I didn't know why you are masquerading in black like this and why you've buried yourself within four walls! Of course I do! It's so mysterious, so poetic! Some cadet or some puny versifier will ride past the house, glance at the windows, and say to himself: "Here lives the mysterious Tamara who, for love of her husband, has buried herself within four walls." We know those tricks!

**MME. POPOVA.** [*Flaring up*] What! How dare you say this to me!

**SMIRNOV.** You've buried yourself alive, but you haven't forgotten to powder your nose.

**MME. POPOVA.** How dare you talk to me like that!

**SMIRNOV.** Please don't scream. I'm not your steward! Allow me to call a spade a spade. I'm no woman and I'm used to talking straight from the shoulder! So please don't shout!

**MME. POPOVA.** I'm not shouting, you are shouting! Please leave me alone!

**SMIRNOV.** Pay me my money, and I'll go.

**MME. POPOVA.** I won't give you any money.

**SMIRNOV.** No, madam, you will!

**MME. POPOVA.** Just to spite you, I won't give you a penny. Only leave me alone!

**SMIRNOV.** I haven't the pleasure of being either your husband or your fiancé, so kindly, no scenes. [*Sits down*] I don't like them.

**MME. POPOVA.** [*Choking with rage*] You've sat down?

**SMIRNOV.** I've sat down.

**MME. POPOVA.** I ask you to leave.

**SMIRNOV.** Give me my money . . . [*Aside*] Oh, what a rage I'm in, what a rage!

**MME. POPOVA.** Such impudence! I don't want to talk to you. Please get out. [*Pause*] Are you going? No?

**SMIRNOV.** No.

**MME. POPOVA.** No?

**SMIRNOV.** No!

**MME. POPOVA.** Very well then,

[*Enter* LUKA]

Luka, show this gentleman out!

**LUKA.** [*Approaching* SMIRNOV] Sir, be good enough to leave when you are asked to. Don't be—

**SMIRNOV.** [*Jumping to his feet*] Shut up! Who do you think you're talking to! I'll make hash of you!

**LUKA.** [*Clutching at his heart*] Mercy on us! Holy saints! [*Drops into an armchair*] Oh, I'm sick, I'm sick! I can't get my breath!

**MME. POPOVA.** But where is Dasha? Dasha? [*Shouts*] Dasha! Pelageya! Dasha! [*Rings*]

**LUKA.** Oh, they've all gone berrying . . . There's no one here . . . I'm sick, water!

**MME. POPOVA.** [*To* SMIRNOV] Please, get out!

**SMIRNOV.** Can't you be a little more civil?

**MME. POPOVA.** [*Clenching her fists and stamping her feet*] You're a boor! A brute, a bully, a monster!

**SMIRNOV.** What! What did you say?

*The Boor*  233

23 **Discussion** What evidence is there that Mme. Popova likes to think of herself as suffering and noble?

24 **Clarification** A *puny versifier* is an inferior poet.

25 **Discussion** What point is Smirnov trying to make?

26 **Discussion** What is humorous about Mme. Popova's fury?

scraped . . . I used to love, pine, sight at the moon, feel blue, melt, freeze. . . . Present company excepted, all women . . . put on airs, pose, gossip . . . are malicious, vain, petty, cruel, revoltingly unreasonable. . . .

**Student Activity 1.** Reread the example passage from *The Boor*. Identify the grammatical form of the items in each of the series that Smirnov uses.

**Student Activity 2.** Write a speech for Mme. Popova in which she answers the attack that Smirnov makes on women. Have her use at least three series.

**27** **Literary Focus** Remind students that a farce is based on ridiculous and preposterous situations. What is ridiculous about the proposed duel? Even though the duel is ridiculous, how does Chekhov convince you that Smirnov is capable of challenging Mme. Popova to "shoot it out"?

**28** **Reading Strategy** Ask students to predict whether Mme. Popova and Smirnov will fight the duel.

**29** **Discussion** How has Mme. Popova's behavior surprised Smirnov?

**30** **Reading Strategy** You might ask students to predict again what will happen. If their prediction has changed, have them explain what led to this change of thought.

**31** **Discussion** How is the tone of these speeches different from that of their previous exchanges? How does this changed tone make the situation seem even more ridiculous?

**MME. POPOVA.** I said that you were a brute, a monster.

**SMIRNOV.** [*Advancing upon her*] Excuse me, but what right have you to insult me?

**MME. POPOVA.** Yes, I insulted you. What of it? Do you think I'm afraid of you?

**SMIRNOV.** And you think, just because you're a poetic creature, you can insult people with impunity, eh? I challenge you!

**LUKA.** Mercy on us! Holy saints! Water!

**SMIRNOV.** We'll shoot it out!

**MME. POPOVA.** Just because you have big fists and bellow like a bull, you think I'm afraid of you, eh? Bully!

**SMIRNOV.** I challenge you! I won't allow anybody to insult me, and it makes no difference to me that you're a woman, a member of the weaker sex.

**MME. POPOVA.** [*Trying to outshout him*] Brute, brute, brute!

**SMIRNOV.** It's high time to abandon the prejudice that men alone must pay for insults. Equal rights are equal rights, devil take it! I challenge you!

**MME. POPOVA.** You want to shoot it out? Well and good.

**SMIRNOV.** This very minute.

**MME. POPOVA.** This very minute. I have my husband's pistols. I'll bring them directly. [*Walks rapidly away and turns back*] What pleasure it will give me to put a bullet into your brazen head! Devil take you! [*Exits*]

**SMIRNOV.** I'll bring her down like a duck. I'm no boy, no sentimental puppy. There's no weaker sex as far as I'm concerned.

**LUKA.** [*To* SMIRNOV] Master, kind sir! [*Going down on his knees*] Have pity on an old man, do me a favor—go away from here!

You've frightened me to death, and now you want to fight a duel!

**SMIRNOV.** [*Not listening to him*] A duel! That's equal rights, that's emancipation! That's equality of the sexes for you! I'll bring her down as a matter of principle. But what a woman! [*Mimics her*] "Devil take you . . . I'll put a bullet into your brazen head." What a woman! She flushed and her eyes shone! She accepted the challenge! Word of honor, it's the first time in my life that I've seen one of that stripe.

**LUKA.** Kind master, please go away, and I will pray for you always.

**SMIRNOV.** That's a woman! That's the kind I understand! A real woman! Not a sour-faced, spineless crybaby, but a creature all fire and gunpowder, a cannonball! It's a pity I have to kill her!

**LUKA.** [*Crying*] Sir, kind sir, please go away!

**SMIRNOV.** I positively like her! Positively! Even though she has dimples in her cheeks, I like her! I am even ready to forgive her the debt . . . And I'm not angry any more. A remarkable woman!

[*Enter* MME. POPOVA *with the pistols*]

**MME. POPOVA.** Here are the pistols. But before we fight, please show me how to shoot. I never held a pistol in my hands before.

**LUKA.** Lord, have mercy on us! I'll go and look for the gardener and the coachman. Why has this calamity befallen us? [*Exits*]

**SMIRNOV.** [*Examining the pistols*] You see, there are several makes of pistols. There are Mortimers, specially made for duelling, they are fired with the percussion cap. What you have here are Smith and Wesson triple-action, central-fire revolvers with extractors. Excellent pistols! Worth ninety rubles a pair at least. You hold the revolver like this . . .

[*Aside*] The eyes, the eyes! A woman to set you on fire!

**MME. POPOVA.** Like this?

**SMIRNOV.** Yes, like this. Then you cock the trigger . . . and you take aim like this . . . throw your head back a little! Stretch your arm out properly . . . Like this . . . Then you press this gadget with this finger, and that's all there is to it . . . The main thing is: Keep cool and take aim slowly. . . . And try not to jerk your arm.

**MME. POPOVA.** Very well. It's inconvenient to shoot indoors, let's go into the garden.

**SMIRNOV.** All right. Only I warn you, I'll fire into the air.

**MME. POPOVA.** That's all that was wanting. Why?

**SMIRNOV.** Because . . . because . . . It's my business why.

**MME. POPOVA.** You're scared, eh? Ah, ah, ah! No, sir, don't try to get out of it! Be so good as to follow me. I shan't rest until I've drilled a hole in your forehead . . . this forehead that I hate so! Scared?

**SMIRNOV.** Yes, I am scared.

**MME. POPOVA.** You're lying! Why do you refuse to fight?

**SMIRNOV.** Because . . . because I . . . like you.

**MME. POPOVA.** [*Laughing bitterly*] He likes me! He dares to say that he likes me! [*Shows him the door*] You may go.

**SMIRNOV.** [*Silently puts down the revolver, takes his cap and walks to the door; there he stops and for half a minute the pair look at each other without a word; then he says, hesitatingly approaching* MME. POPOVA] Listen . . . Are you still angry? I'm in a devil of a temper myself, but you see . . . how shall I put it? . . . the thing is . . . you see . . . it's

this way . . . in fact . . . [*Shouts*] Well, am I to blame if I like you? [*Clutches the back of his chair; it cracks and breaks*] The devil! What fragile furniture you have! I like you. You understand. I've almost fallen in love.

**MME. POPOVA.** Go away from me. I hate you.

**SMIRNOV.** God, what a woman! Never in my life have I seen anything like her! I'm lost. I'm done for. I'm trapped like a mouse.

**MME. POPOVA.** Go away, or I'll shoot.

**SMIRNOV.** Shoot! You can't understand what happiness it would be to die before those enchanting eyes . . . to die of a revolver shot fired by this little velvet hand! I've lost my mind. Think a moment and decide right now, because if I leave this house, we'll never see each other again. Decide. I'm a landed gentleman, a decent fellow, with an income of ten thousand a year; I can put a bullet through a penny thrown into the air; I have a good stable. Will you be my wife?

**MME. POPOVA.** [*Indignant, brandishing the revolver*] We'll shoot it out! Come along! Get your pistol.

**SMIRNOV.** I've lost my mind. I don't understand anything. [*Shouts*] You there! Some water!

**MME. POPOVA.** [*Shouts*] Come! Let's shoot it out!

**SMIRNOV.** I've lost my mind. I've fallen in love like a boy, like a fool. [*Seizes her by the hand; she cries out with pain*] I love you. [*Goes down on his knees*] I love you as I've never loved before. I jilted twelve women and was jilted by nine. But I didn't love one of them as I do you. I've gotten sentimental. I'm melting. I'm weak as water. Here I am on my knees like a fool, and I offer you my hand. It's a shame, a disgrace! For five years I've not been in love. I took a vow. And suddenly

*The Boor*  235

**32** **Discussion** In what way have the roles of the main characters reversed?

**33** **Discussion** How does Chekhov make this confession of love seem ridiculous?

**34** **Critical Thinking and Reading** What is humorous about this proposal of marriage?

35 **Discussion** How do you know that Mme. Popova is beginning to change her mind about Smirnov?

36 **Discussion** How does the sudden appearance of the armed servants contribute to the humor of this scene?

**Reader's Response** Even though this play is a farce, do you think such situations can happen in real life? Explain.

I'm bowled
over, swept off my feet.
I offer you my hand—yes
or no? You won't? Then don't!
[*Rises and walks rapidly to the door*]

**MME. POPOVA.** Wait a minute.

**SMIRNOV.** [*Stops*] Well?

35 **MME. POPOVA.** Never mind. Go . . . But no, wait a minute . . . No, go go! I detest you! Or no . . . don't go! Oh, if you knew how furious I am, how furious! [*Throws the revolver on the table*] My fingers are cramped from holding this vile thing. [*Tears her handkerchief in a fit of temper*] What are you standing there for? Get out!

**SMIRNOV.** Good-by.

**MME. POPOVA.** Yes, yes, go! [*Shouts*] Where are you going? Wait a minute . . . But no, go away . . . Oh, how furious I am! Don't come near me, don't come near me!

**SMIRNOV.** [*Approaching her*] I'm disgusted with myself! Falling in love like a moon-calf,[10] going down on my knees. It gives me gooseflesh. [*Rudely*] I love you. What on earth made me fall in love with you? Tomorrow I have to pay the interest. And we've started mowing. And here are you! . . .
[*Puts his arm around her waist*]
I shall never forgive myself
for this.

**MME. POPOVA.** Get away from me! Hands off! I hate you! Let's shoot it out!

[*A prolonged kiss. Enter* LUKA *with an ax, the gardener with a rake, the coachman with a pitchfork, and hired men with sticks.*]

36

**LUKA.** [*Catching sight of the pair kissing*] Mercy on us! Holy saints! [*Pauses*]

**MME. POPOVA.** [*Dropping her eyes*] Luka, tell them at the stables that Toby isn't to have any oats at all today.

_____

**10. moon-calf** (mōōn′ kaf′) *n.*: A foolish young man.

*236   Drama*

**ANSWERS TO THINKING ABOUT THE SELECTION**
*Recalling*

1. Mme. Popova is in mourning for her husband and lives the life of a recluse—she neither leaves the house nor receives guests.

2. He is angry because Mme. Po-pova cannot pay him immediately and because she is in no mood to occupy herself with money matters. He has not gotten along well with women in the past. He has jilted many, and many have jilted him.

3. Her husband died seven months ago. He was unfaithful to her and left her alone for weeks. Also, he was an excellent driver and bought oats from Smirnov.

4. Smirnov and Mme. Popova fall in love with each other.

*Interpreting*

5. Suggested Response: Mme. Po-pova stands up to him when he challenges her to a duel. His admiration for her courage changes his anger to love.

6. Suggested Response: Toby is associated in her mind with her former husband. Now that she is in love with Smirnov, she does not want to honor her former husband's memory by giving Toby extra oats.

7. Suggested Response: Mme. Po-pova did not really love her husband, who was cruel and unfaithful. Her exaggerated mourning is a way of pointing up her husband's wickedness. She is therefore ready to fall in love with someone else.

*Applying*

8. Students' answers will differ. Students may respond that love is unexplainable—there is no reason

## THINKING ABOUT THE SELECTION

### Recalling

1. Describe Mme. Popova's way of life as it is revealed early in the play.
2. Give two reasons why Smirnov is so angry and upset with Mme. Popova. Describe his past relations with women.
3. What do you learn about Mme. Popova's husband?
4. Why does the duel between Mme. Popova and Smirnov never take place?

### Interpreting

5. Why do Smirnov's feelings for Mme. Popova change from anger to love?
6. What is the meaning of Mme. Popova's final remark that Toby not be given oats?
7. From what you learned earlier in the play about Mme. Popova and her husband, why is her sudden change of heart at the end not surprising?

### Applying

8. An old French proverb says: "Try to reason about love, and you will lose your reason." First discuss the meaning of this proverb. Then explain how it relates to The Boor.

## ANALYZING LITERATURE

### Understanding the One-Act Farce

A **one-act play** is a brief drama with few characters, usually one setting, and a simple plot. The action of a one-act play usually begins at a point that is already close to the climax and ending. One type of play is the farce.

Like comedy in general, a **farce** often centers on an absurd situation. Unlike most comedies, however, a farce greatly exaggerates the characters and their behavior, presenting outrageous situations and preposterous reactions. In a farce, the fast pace and the ridiculousness of the action are intended to make you laugh.

1. Smirnov enters and an angry conflict between him and Mme. Popova develops. Soon the two of them are embracing. Explain why this situation is outrageous and the behavior of the two characters preposterous.
2. Point out at least three examples of farcical exaggeration in The Boor.
3. Find three examples of physical actions that give the play a wild, farcical quality. Explain why each is or is not effective.

## CRITICAL THINKING AND READING

### Making Inferences About Characters

Since a play consists primarily of dialogue, the inferences you make about characters are based largely on what the characters say and how they say it. In a farce, characters are drawn with a broad stroke—one or two traits stand out, and their behavior emphasizes these characteristics.

1. Describe Mme. Popova's personality. What is her most important trait? How does her behavior emphasize this characteristic?
2. A boor is a rude, bad-mannered person. Tell why the word boor does or does not fully describe the personality of Smirnov. Use his behavior in the play to support your answer.

## THINKING AND WRITING

### Writing About an Unusual Encounter

Imagine that you are Luka. Write about the confrontation between Mme. Popova and Smirnov from your point of view. Imagine that your account will be read by a fellow servant who lives and works on another Russian estate. First think about the personality traits of Mme. Popova and Smirnov. Then select details from the confrontation that will make the two people come alive. When you revise, try to make your account entertaining as well as accurate. Proofread your account and share it with your classmates.

*The Boor 237*

action and his words of love makes him seem like a clown.

## ANSWERS TO CRITICAL THINKING AND READING

1. Suggested Response: Mme. Popova is a very dramatic person. She nearly weeps at the mention of her former husband's horse, talks to her husband's photograph as if he can hear her, leaves the room abruptly when Smirnov talks roughly, and agrees to fight a duel with him.
2. Students' answers will vary. Students may respond that Smirnov does seem like a boor because he barges into Mme. Popova's house, rudely refuses to leave, breaks her furniture, threatens her servants, and even challenges her to a duel. Also, he is dressed very sloppily. Insightful students will realize, however, that Smirnov hides his more tender feelings under this rough exterior—these feelings emerge at the end of the play.

**Challenge** How do you think Smirnov and Mme. Popova would get along once they married? Would their relationship be calm or stormy? Write some dialogue for a scene that takes place after the events of the play and shows how they interact.

## THINKING AND WRITING

You might want to have students refer to Lesson 14, "Writing About Drama," in the Handbook of Writing About Literature.

**Publishing Student Writing**
Consider having students read their letters aloud to the class.

**Writing Across the Curriculum**
You might ask students to research and report on daily life on a Russian estate during the late nineteenth century. Consider informing the social studies department of this assignment, so that social studies teachers can help students to find appropriate resource materials.

for it. If you try to make sense of it, you will drive yourself crazy. In The Boor, two people who seem to hate each other, and who have opposing points of view, fall in love. It would be impossible for them to understand why or to explain how this happened.

## ANSWERS TO ANALYZING LITERATURE

1. Suggested Response: In everyday life, the relationship between two

people does not usually change so quickly and dramatically.

2. Suggested Response: Three examples of exaggeration are: the lengths to which Mme. Popova goes in order to "honor" the memory of her cruel husband; Smirnov's extreme rage and refusal to leave when he finds that Mme. Popova cannot pay him that day; and Smirnov's challenging Mme. Popova to a duel.

3. Suggested Response: Luka acts

as if he is having a heart seizure when Smirnov threatens him—Luka's action makes him seem ridiculous because he is so overcome by Smirnov's words. Smirnov breaks the chair just as he tells Mme. Popova that a woman is ". . . a common crocodile." The exaggerated action effectively points up the exaggerated and ridiculous attack on women. Finally, Smirnov seizes and hurts Mme. Popova's hand while proclaiming his love for her. The contrast between his rough

## The Pen of My Aunt

**Gordon Daviot** (1897–1952), whose real name was Elizabeth Mackintosh, was born in Inverness, Scotland. She taught physical education for several years in England but gave up teaching to care for her invalid father in her home. There she began writing and for the rest of her life devoted herself to little else, publishing under the pseudonyms Gordon Daviot and Josephine Tey. *The Pen of My Aunt* uses the stage to bring to life a dangerous period of history, the World War II years when Nazi Germany controlled France.

**Staging**

**Staging** is the art of bringing a play to life on stage. It includes everything needed to transform a play from a written work to a theatrical production. Acting, costumes, scenery, props, lighting, and sound effects are some of the main aspects of staging. To read a play properly, you need to stage it in your imagination.

**Look For**

As you read *The Pen of My Aunt,* hold in mind a picture of a well-furnished room in a country house. Also visualize the characters: The lady of the house is an elegant, refined mature woman; her maid, Simone, is no more than twenty years old; the stranger is a young man; the corporal, also young, is German. Keep in mind that the play is set in France when it was controlled by the Nazis during World War II.

**Writing**

What kinds of bravery and patriotic effort are possible away from the combat zones of a war? Freewrite about some of the ways that civilians can display heroism during war.

**Vocabulary**

Knowing the following words will help you as you read *The Pen of My Aunt.*

**combatant** (käm′ bə tənt) *adj.*: Prepared for fighting (p. 240)
**flouting** (flout′iŋ) *v.*: Showing scorn or contempt for (p. 241)
**anathema** (ə nath′ə mə) *n.*: Something greatly detested (p. 241)
**hypothetical** (hī′ pə thet′ i k'l) *adj.*: Assumed, supposed (p. 241)
**speculation** (spek′ yə lā′ shən)

*n.*: Consideration of some subject or idea (p. 241)
**credentials** (kri den′ shəlz) *n.*: Papers that show a person's credits and qualifications (p. 242)
**noncommissioned** (nän′ kə mish′ ənd) *adj.*: Referring to enlisted soldiers of a rank no higher than sergeant major (p. 245)

# The Pen of My Aunt

## Gordon Daviot

---

### CHARACTERS

**Madame**　　　　　　　　**Stranger**
**Simone** (sē mōn')　　**Corporal**

---

[*The scene is a French country house during the Occupation.*[1] *The lady of the house is seated in her drawing-room.*]

**SIMONE.** [*Approaching*] Madame! Oh, madame! Madame, have you——

**MADAME.** Simone.

**SIMONE.** Madame, have you seen what——

---

1. **Occupation:** Period from 1940 to 1944 when France was controlled by the Nazis.

**MADAME.** Simone!

**SIMONE.** But madame——

**MADAME.** Simone, this may be an age of barbarism, but I will have none of it inside the walls of this house.

**SIMONE.** But madame, there is a—there is a——

**MADAME.** [*Silencing her*] Simone. France may be an occupied country, a ruined na-

**Thematic Idea** Other selections that focus on experiences with war are "Beware of the Dog," page 147, and "The Charge of the Light Brigade," page 569. You might also want to use with this play the following selections dealing with courage: "The Most Dangerous Game," page 13; the excerpt from *Kon-Tiki,* page 465; and the excerpt from the *Odyssey,* page 681.

**4 Discussion** Why do you think that Madame insists so strongly that good manners be observed?

**5 Reading Strategy** Ask students to summarize what the opening dialogue between Madame and Simone has revealed about Madame's attitude toward the Nazis.

**6 Clarification** Servants would be expected to observe such formalities in a wealthy French home of this time.

**7 Discussion** How do you know that German soldiers have already been billeted with Madame?

**8 Clarification** The Combatant branch was made up of soldiers engaged in fighting. The "beasts of Administration" were those who performed such activities as checking papers, questioning people, making arrests, and so on.

**9 Discussion** What does Madame's comment reveal about Simone?

**10 Literary Focus** If this were a movie, the camera would probably focus on the outside door and foyer. Why would this speech probably be eliminated?

tion, and a conquered race, but we will keep, if you please, the usages of civilization.

**SIMONE.** Yes, madame.

**MADAME.** One thing we still possess, thank God; and that is good manners. The enemy never had it; and it is not something they can take from *us*.

**SIMONE.** No, madame.

**MADAME.** Go out of the room again. Open the door——

**SIMONE.** Oh, *madame*! I wanted to tell you——

**MADAME.** —open the door, shut it behind you—quietly—take two paces into the room, and say what you came to say. [SIMONE *goes hastily out, shutting the door. She reappears, shuts the door behind her, takes two paces into the room, and waits.*] Yes, Simone?

**SIMONE.** I expect it is too late now; they will be here.

**MADAME.** Who will?

**SIMONE.** The soldiers who were coming up the avenue.

**MADAME.** After the last few months I should not have thought that soldiers coming up the avenue was a remarkable fact. It is no doubt a party with a billeting order.[2]

**SIMONE.** [*Crossing to the window*] No, madame, it is two soldiers in one of their little cars, with a civilian between them.

**MADAME.** Which civilian?

**SIMONE.** A stranger, madame.

**MADAME.** A stranger? Are the soldiers from the Combatant branch?

———————
**2. billeting order:** Written order to provide lodging for soldiers.

**SIMONE.** No, they are those beasts of Administration. Look, they have stopped. They are getting out.

**MADAME.** [*At the window*] Yes, it is a stranger. Do you know him, Simone?

**SIMONE.** I have never set eyes on him before, madame.

**MADAME.** You would know if he belonged to the district?

**SIMONE.** Oh, madame, I know every man between here and St. Estèphe.

**MADAME.** [*Dryly*] No doubt.

**SIMONE.** Oh, merciful God, they are coming up the steps.

**MADAME.** My good Simone, that is what the steps were put there for.

**SIMONE.** But they will ring the bell and I shall have to——

**MADAME.** And you will answer it and behave as if you had been trained by a butler and ten upper servants instead of being the charcoal-burner's daughter from over at Les Chênes. [*This is said encouragingly, not in unkindness.*] You will be very calm and correct——

**SIMONE.** Calm! Madame! With my inside turning over and over like a wheel at a fair!

**MADAME.** A good servant does not have an inside, merely an exterior. [*Comforting*] Be assured, my child. You have your place here; that is more than those creatures on our doorstep have. Let that hearten you——

**SIMONE.** Madame! They are not going to ring. They are coming straight in.

**MADAME.** [*Bitterly*] Yes. They have forgotten long ago what bells are for.

[*Door opens*]

**STRANGER.** [*In a bright, confident, casual tone*] Ah, there you are, my dear aunt. I am so glad. Come in, my friend, come in. My dear aunt, this gentleman wants you to identify me.

**MADAME.** Identify you?

**CORPORAL.** We found this man wandering in the woods——

**STRANGER.** The corporal found it inexplicable that anyone should wander in a wood.

**CORPORAL.** And he had no papers on him——

**STRANGER.** And I rightly pointed out that if I carry all the papers one is supposed to these days, I am no good to God or man. If I put them in a hip pocket, I can't bend forward; if I put them in a front pocket, I can't bend at all.

**CORPORAL.** He said that he was your nephew, madame, but that did not seem to us very likely, so we brought him here.

[*There is the slightest pause; just one moment of silence.*]

**MADAME.** But of course this is my nephew.

**CORPORAL.** He is?

**MADAME.** Certainly.

**CORPORAL.** He lives here?

**MADAME.** [*Assenting*] My nephew lives here.

**CORPORAL.** So! [*Recovering*] My apologies, madame. But you will admit that appearances were against the young gentleman.

**MADAME.** Alas, Corporal, my nephew belongs to a generation who delight in flouting appearances. It is what they call "expressing their personality," I understand.

**CORPORAL.** [*With contempt*] No doubt, madame.

**MADAME.** Convention is anathema to them, and there is no sin like conformity. Even a collar is an offense against their liberty, and a discipline not to be borne by free necks.

**CORPORAL.** Ah yes, madame. A little more discipline among your nephew's generation, and we might not be occupying your country today.

**STRANGER.** You think it was that collar of yours that conquered my country? You flatter yourself, Corporal. The only result of wearing a collar like that is varicose veins in the head.

**MADAME.** [*Repressive*] Please! My dear boy. Let us not descend to personalities.

**STRANGER.** The matter is not personal, my good aunt, but scientific. Wearing a collar like that retards the flow of fresh blood to the head, with the most disastrous consequences to the gray matter of the brain. The hypothetical gray matter. In fact, I have a theory——

**CORPORAL.** Monsieur,[3] your theories do not interest me.

**STRANGER.** No? You do not find speculation interesting?

**CORPORAL.** In this world one judges by results.

**STRANGER.** [*After a slight pause of reflection*] I see. The collared conqueror sits in the high places, while the collarless conquered lies about in the woods. And who comes best out of that, would you say? Tell me, Corporal, as man to man, do you never have a mad, secret desire to lie unbuttoned in a wood?

**CORPORAL.** I have only one desire, monsieur, and that is to see your papers.

_____

3. **monsieur** (mə syö′): French for Mr. or sir.

*The Pen of My Aunt*    241

11 **Discussion** How do you know that Madame has never met the stranger?

12 **Literary Focus** Have students explain the importance of this stage direction.

13 **Discussion** Why does Madame say, "My nephew lives here," rather than "He lives here"?

14 **Clarification** *Varicose veins* are "veins that are abnormally swollen."

15 **Discussion** Why do you think the stranger places so much emphasis on the pleasure he feels in going out into the woods?

16 **Critical Thinking and Reading** What inference can you make about the Corporal's personality?

**17** **Reading Strategy** Have students predict what will happen next.

**18** **Discussion** How does Simone give the stranger clues for answering her questions? Do you think that this exchange could really fool someone? Explain.

**19** **Critical Thinking and Reading** Why do you think the stranger recites a list of every document he has?

**STRANGER.** [*Taken off-guard and filling in time*] My papers?

**MADAME.** But is that necessary, Corporal? I have already told you that——

**CORPORAL.** I know that madame is a very good collaborator[4] and in good standing——

**MADAME.** In that case——

**CORPORAL.** But when we begin an affair we like to finish it. I have asked to see monsieur's papers, and the matter will not be finished until I have seen them.

**MADAME.** You acknowledge that I am in "good standing," Corporal?

**CORPORAL.** So I have heard, madame.

**MADAME.** Then I must consider it a discourtesy on your part to demand my nephew's credentials.

**CORPORAL.** It is no reflection on madame. It is a matter of routine, nothing more.

**STRANGER.** [*Murmuring*] The great god Routine.

**MADAME.** To ask for his papers was routine; to insist on their production is discourtesy. I shall say so to your Commanding Officer.

**CORPORAL.** Very good, madame. In the meantime, I shall inspect your nephew's papers.

**MADAME.** And what if I——

**STRANGER.** [*Quietly*] You may as well give it up, my dear. You could as easily turn a steamroller. They have only one idea at a time. If the Corporal's heart is set on seeing my papers, he shall see them. [*Moving toward the door*] I left them in the pocket of my coat.

**SIMONE.** [*Unexpectedly, from the background*] Not in your *linen* coat?

---

**4. collaborator** (kə lab′ ə rāt′ ər): Person who helps an enemy invader of his or her country.

**STRANGER.** [*Pausing*] Yes. Why?

**SIMONE.** [*With apparently growing anxiety*] Your *cream* linen coat? The one you were wearing yesterday?

**STRANGER.** Certainly.

**SIMONE.** Merciful Heaven! I sent it to the laundry!

**STRANGER.** To the laundry!

**SIMONE.** Yes, monsieur; this morning; in the basket.

**STRANGER.** [*In incredulous anger*] You sent my coat, *with my papers in the pocket*, to the laundry!

**SIMONE.** [*Defensive and combatant*] I didn't know monsieur's papers were in the pocket.

**STRANGER.** You didn't know! You didn't know that a packet of documents weighing half a ton were in the pocket. An identity card, a *laisser passer*,[5] a food card, a drink card, an army discharge, a permission to wear civilian clothes, a permission to go farther than ten miles to the east, a permission to go more than ten miles to the west, a permission to——

**SIMONE.** [*Breaking in with spirit*] How was I to know the coat was heavy! I picked it up with the rest of the bundle that was lying on the floor.

**STRANGER.** [*Snapping her head off*] My coat was on the back of the chair.

**SIMONE.** It was on the floor.

**STRANGER.** On the back of the chair!

**SIMONE.** It was on the floor with your dirty shirt and your pajamas, and a towel and what not. I put my arms round the whole

---

**5. *laisser passer*** (le sā pä sā′): French for a pass allowing a person to travel.

thing and then—woof! into the basket with them.

**STRANGER.** I tell you that coat was on the back of the chair. It was quite clean and was not going to the laundry for two weeks yet—if then. I hung it there myself, and ——

**MADAME.** My dear boy, what does it matter? The damage is done now. In any case, they will find the papers when they unpack the basket, and return them tomorrow.

**STRANGER.** If someone doesn't steal them. There are a lot of people who would like to lay hold of a complete set of papers, believe me.

**MADAME.** [*Reassuring*] Oh, no. Old Fleureau (flŏ′ rō) is the soul of honesty. You have no need to worry about them. They will be back first thing tomorrow, you shall see; and then we shall have much pleasure in sending them to the Administration Office for the Corporal's inspection. Unless, of course, the Corporal insists on your personal appearance at the office.

**CORPORAL.** [*Cold and indignant*] I have seen monsieur. All that I want now is to see his papers.

**STRANGER.** You shall see them, Corporal, you shall see them. The whole half-ton of them. You may inspect them at your leisure. Provided, that is, that they come back from the laundry to which this idiot has consigned them.

**MADAME.** [*Again reassuring*] They will come back, never fear. And you must not blame Simone. She is a good child, and does her best.

**SIMONE.** [*With an air of belated virtue*] I am not one to pry into pockets.

**MADAME.** Simone, show the Corporal out, if you please.

**SIMONE.** [*Natural feeling overcoming her for a moment*] He knows the way out. [*Recovering*] Yes, madame.

**MADAME.** And Corporal, try to take your duties a little less literally in future. My countrymen appreciate the spirit rather than the letter.

**CORPORAL.** I have my instructions, madame, and I obey them. Good day, madame. Monsieur.

[*He goes, followed by* SIMONE—*door closes. There is a moment of silence.*]

**STRANGER.** For a good collaborator, that was a remarkably quick adoption.

**MADAME.** Sit down, young man. I will give you something to drink. I expect your knees are none too well.

**STRANGER.** My knees, madame, are pure gelatin. As for my stomach, it seems to have disappeared.

**MADAME.** [*Offering him the drink she has poured out*] This will recall it, I hope.

**STRANGER.** You are not drinking, madame?

**MADAME.** Thank you, no.

**STRANGER.** Not with strangers. It is certainly no time to drink with strangers. Nevertheless, I drink the health of a collaborator. [*He drinks*] Tell me, madame, what will happen tomorrow when they find that you have no nephew?

**MADAME.** [*Surprised*] But of course I have a nephew. I tell lies, my friend; but not *silly* lies. My charming nephew has gone to Bonneval (bun văl′) for the day. He finds country life dull.

**STRANGER.** Dull? This—this heaven?

**MADAME.** [*Dryly*] He likes to talk and here there is no audience. At Headquarters in Bonneval he finds the audience sympathetic.

*The Pen of My Aunt   243*

**20 Discussion** Why do you think Madame is certain that the papers will come back from the laundry, while the stranger says that they may come back?

**21 Clarification** Madame is asking the Corporal not to be so strict in applying the law.

**22 Discussion** What does Madame mean by the phrase "not *silly* lies"?

**23** **Clarification** The Balkans include Albania, continental Greece, Bulgaria, most of Yugoslavia, and parts of Turkey and Romania. The Levant includes those countries on the eastern shore of the Mediterranean, from Egypt to Turkey.

**24** **Discussion** How will Madame persuade her nephew to cooperate?

**25** **Literary Focus** Another reason for staging the play in the drawing room is that this is where Madame would be most likely to keep her notebook and pen.

**26** **Clarification** A quill pen is made from the hollow, horny part of a large goose feather.

**27** **Reading Strategy** Ask students to recall television programs, films, or books in which a character destroys or attempts to destroy incriminating evidence.

STRANGER. [*Understanding the implication*] Ah.

MADAME. He believes in the Brotherhood of Man—if you can credit it.

STRANGER. After the last six months?

**23** MADAME. His mother was American, so he has half the Balkans in his blood. To say nothing of Italy, Russia, and the Levant.

STRANGER. [*Half-amused*] I see.

MADAME. A silly and worthless creature, but useful.

STRANGER. Useful?

MADAME. I—borrow his cloak.

STRANGER. I see.

MADAME. Tonight I shall borrow his identity papers, and tomorrow they will go to the office in St. Estèphe.

STRANGER. But—he will have to know.

MADAME. [*Placidly*] Oh, yes, he will know, of course.

STRANGER. And how will you persuade such an enthusiastic collaborator to deceive his friends?

**24** MADAME. Oh, that is easy. He is my heir.

STRANGER. [*Amused*] Ah.

MADAME. He is, also, by the Mercy of God, not too unlike you, so that his photograph will not startle the Corporal too much tomorrow. Now tell me what you were doing in my wood.

STRANGER. Resting my feet—I am practically walking on my bones. And waiting for tonight.

MADAME. Where are you making for? [*As he does not answer immediately*] The coast? [*He nods*] That is four days away—five if your feet are bad.

STRANGER. I know it.

MADAME. Have you friends on the way?

STRANGER. I have friends at the coast, who will get me a boat. But no one between here and the sea.

MADAME. [*Rising*] I must consult my list of addresses. [*Pausing*] What was your service?

STRANGER. Army.

MADAME. Which Regiment?

STRANGER. The 79th.

MADAME. [*After the faintest pause*] And your Colonel's name?

STRANGER. Delavault was killed in the first week, and Martin took over.

**25** MADAME. [*Going to her desk*] A "good collaborator" cannot be too careful. Now I can consult my notebook. A charming color, is it not? A lovely shade of red.

**26** STRANGER. Yes—but what has a red quill pen to do with your notebook?—Ah, you write with it of course—stupid of me.

MADAME. Certainly I write with it—but it is also my notebook—look—I only need a hairpin—and then—so—out of my quill pen comes my notebook—a tiny piece of paper—but enough for a list of names.

STRANGER. You mean that you keep that list on your desk? [*He sounds disapproving.*]

MADAME. Where did you expect me to keep it, young man? In my corset? Did you ever try to get something out of your corset in a hurry? What would you advise as the ideal quality in a hiding-place for a list of names?

STRANGER. That the thing should be difficult to find, of course.

**27** MADAME. Not at all. That it should be easily destroyed in emergency. It is too big for me to swallow—I suspect they do that only in

*244 Drama*

books—and we have no fires to consume it, so I had to think of some other way. I did try to memorize the list, but what I could not be sure of remembering were those that—that had to be scored off. It would be fatal to send someone to an address that—that was no longer available. So I had to keep a written record.

**STRANGER.** And if you neither eat it nor burn it when the moment comes, how do you get rid of it?

**MADAME.** I could, of course, put a match to it, but scraps of freshly-burned paper on a desk take a great deal of explaining. If I ceased to be looked on with approval my usefulness would end. It is important therefore that there should be no sign of anxiety on my part: no burned paper, no excuses to leave the room, no nods and becks and winks. I just sit here at my desk and go on with my letters. I tilt my nice big inkwell sideways for a moment and dip the pen into the deep ink at the side. The ink flows into the hollow of the quill, and all is blotted out. [*Consulting the list*] Let me see. It would be good if you could rest your feet for a day or so.

**STRANGER.** [*Ruefully*] It would.

**MADAME.** There is a farm just beyond the Marnay crossroads on the way to St. Estèphe——[*She pauses to consider.*]

**STRANGER.** St. Estèphe is the home of the single-minded Corporal. I don't want to run into him again.

**MADAME.** No, that might be awkward; but that farm of the Cherfils would be ideal. A good hiding-place, and food to spare, and fine people——

**STRANGER.** If your nephew is so friendly with the invader, how is it that the Corporal doesn't know him by sight?

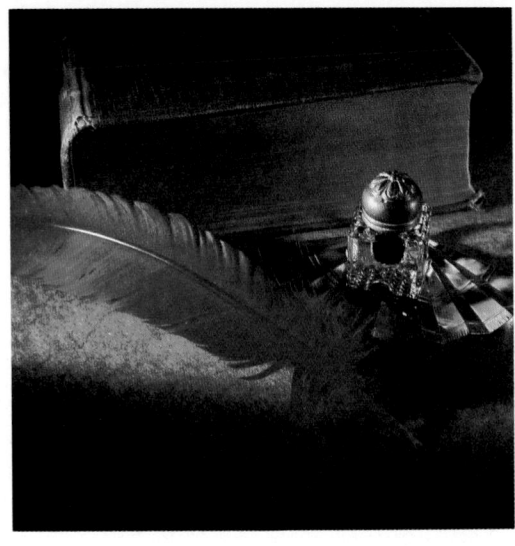

**MADAME.** [*Absently*] The unit at St. Estèphe is a noncommissioned one.

**STRANGER.** Does the Brotherhood of Man exclude sergeants, then?

**MADAME.** Oh, definitely. Brotherhood does not really begin under field rank, I understand.

**STRANGER.** But the Corporal may still meet your nephew somewhere.

**MADAME.** That is a risk one must take. It is not a very grave one. They change the personnel every few weeks, to prevent them becoming too acclimatized. And even if he met my nephew, he is unlikely to ask for the papers of so obviously well-to-do a citizen. If you could bear to go *back* a little——

**STRANGER.** Not a step! It would be like—like denying God. I have got so far, against all the odds, and I am not going a yard back. Not even to rest my feet!

**MADAME.** I understand; but it is a pity. It is

*The Pen of My Aunt 245*

28 **Discussion** How do you know that the stranger is not the only person she has helped?

29 **Discussion** Why would Madame's usefulness end if she ceased to be "looked on with approval"?

30 **Discussion** Explain how Madame can destroy her list easily.

31 **Discussion** Compare the two Nazi units. Why is Madame sure that her nephew and the Corporal will not meet?

32 **Discussion** Why is the stranger so insistent that he not go backwards?

**33 Discussion** Why would it be dangerous for the stranger to stay at her home?

**34 Enrichment** Consider telling students that, during World War II, resistance fighters in France and other occupied countries developed a network of places to shelter those fleeing from the Germans. Tell students that this network resembled the Underground Railroad by means of which black slaves escaped to freedom in pre–Civil War America.

**35 Discussion** What does the Corporal's response to Madame's order reveal about him?

**36 Reading Strategy** Have students predict the outcome of this incident.

**37 Literary Focus** Consider pointing out to students that if this were a movie, the scene with Simone and the gardener might have been included.

a long way to the Cherfils (sher fēs') farm—two miles east of the Marnay crossroads it is, on a little hill.

**STRANGER.** I'll get there; don't worry. If not tonight then tomorrow night. I am used to sleeping in the open by now.

**MADAME.** I wish we could have you here, but it is too dangerous. We are liable to be billeted on at any moment, without notice. However, we can give you a good meal, and a bath. We have no coal, so it will be one of those flat-tin-saucer baths. And if you want to be very kind to Simone you might have it somewhere in the kitchen regions and so save her carrying water upstairs.

**STRANGER.** But of course.

**MADAME.** Before the war I had a staff of twelve. Now I have Simone. I dust and Simone sweeps, and between us we keep the dirt at bay. She has no manners but a great heart, the child.

**STRANGER.** The heart of a lion.

**MADAME.** Before I put this back you might memorize these: Forty Avenue Foch (fōsh), in Crest, the back entrance.

**STRANGER.** Forty Avenue Foch, the back entrance.

**MADAME.** You may find it difficult to get into Crest, by the way. It is a closed area. The pot boy[6] at the Red Lion in Mans (màn).

**STRANGER.** The pot boy.

**MADAME.** Denis (də nē') the blacksmith at Laloupe. And the next night should take you to the sea and your friends. Are they safely in your mind?

**STRANGER.** Forty Avenue Foch in Crest: the pot boy at the Red Lion in Mans: and Denis

---

**6. pot boy:** Dishwasher.

*246 Drama*

the blacksmith at Laloupe (lä lōōp'). And to be careful getting into Crest.

**MADAME.** Good. Then I can close my notebook—or roll it up, I should say—then—it fits neatly, does it not? Now let us see about some food for you. Perhaps I could find you other clothes. Are these all you——

[*The* CORPORAL's *voice is heard mingled in fury with the still more furious tones of* SIMONE. *She is yelling: "Nothing of the sort, I tell you, nothing of the sort," but no words are clearly distinguishable in the angry row.*

*The door is flung open, and the* CORPORAL *bursts in dragging a struggling* SIMONE *by the arm.*]

**SIMONE.** [*Screaming with rage and terror*] Let me go, you foul fiend, you murdering foreign creature, let me go. [*She tries to kick him.*]

**CORPORAL.** [*At the same time*] Stop struggling, you lying deceitful little bit of no-good.

**MADAME.** Will someone explain this extraordinary——

**CORPORAL.** This creature——

**MADAME.** Take your hand from my servant's arm, Corporal. She is not going to run away.

**CORPORAL.** [*Reacting to the voice of authority and automatically complying*] Your precious servant was overheard telling the gardener that she had never set eyes on this man.

**SIMONE.** I did not! Why should I say anything like that?

**CORPORAL.** With my own ears I heard her, my own two ears. Will you kindly explain that to me if you can.

**MADAME.** You speak our language very well, Corporal, but perhaps you are not so quick to understand.

## Grammar in Action

Dramatists use **brackets** to enclose information that is not part of the dialogue. Brackets resemble parentheses, but their purpose differs. Generally, brackets enclose explanatory words or other information added within a quotation. In a play, brackets enclose stage directions, instructions for interpreting dialogue, and other information. Bracketed material may be in the form of paragraphs, a sentence, a phrase, or only a single word. The following excerpts from *The Pen of My Aunt* illustrate:

[The Corporal's voice is heard mingled in fury with the still more furious tones of Simone . . . . No words are clearly distinguishable in the angry row.
The door is flung open, and the Corporal bursts in dragging a struggling Simone by the arm.]
[Screaming with rage and terror]
[She tries to kick him.]
[At the same time]
[Reacting to the voice of authority and automatically complying]

**CORPORAL.** I understand perfectly.

**MADAME.** What Simone was saying to the gardener was no doubt what she was announcing to all and sundry at the pitch of her voice this morning.

**CORPORAL.** [*Unbelieving*] And what was that?

**MADAME.** That she *wished* she had never set eyes on my nephew.

**CORPORAL.** And why should she say that?

**MADAME.** My nephew, Corporal, has many charms, but tidiness is not one of them. As you may have deduced from the episode of the coat. He is apt to leave his room——

**SIMONE.** [*On her cue, in a burst of scornful rage*] Cigarette ends, pajamas, towels, bedclothes, books, papers—all over the floor like a *flood*. Every morning I tidy up, and in two hours it is as if a bomb had burst in the room.

**STRANGER.** [*Testily*] I told you already that I was sor——

**SIMONE.** [*Interrupting*] As if I had nothing else to do in this enormous house but wait on you.

**STRANGER.** Haven't I said that I——

**SIMONE.** And when I have climbed all the way up from the kitchen with your shaving water, you let it get cold; but will you shave in cold? Oh no! I have to bring up another——

**STRANGER.** I didn't ask you to climb the stairs, did I?

**SIMONE.** And do I get a word of thanks for bringing it? Do I indeed? You say; "*Must* you bring it in that hideous jug; it offends my eyes."

**STRANGER.** So it does offend my eyes!

**MADAME.** Enough, enough! We had enough of that this morning. You see, Corporal?

**CORPORAL.** I could have sworn——

**MADAME.** A natural mistake, perhaps. But I think you might have used a little more common sense in the matter. [*Coldly*] And a great deal more dignity. I don't like having my servants manhandled.

**CORPORAL.** She refused to come.

**SIMONE.** Accusing me of things I never said!

**MADAME.** However, now that you are here again you can make yourself useful. My nephew wants to go into Crest the day after tomorrow, and that requires a special pass. Perhaps you would make one out for him.

**CORPORAL.** But I——

**MADAME.** You have a little book of permits in your pocket, haven't you?

**CORPORAL.** Yes. I——

**MADAME.** Very well. Better make it valid for two days. He is always changing his mind.

**CORPORAL.** But it is not for me to grant a pass.

**MADAME.** You sign them, don't you?

**CORPORAL.** Yes, but only when someone tells me to.

**MADAME.** Very well, if it will help you, I tell you to.

**CORPORAL.** I mean, permission must be granted before a pass is issued.

**MADAME.** And have you any doubt that a permission will be granted to my nephew?

**CORPORAL.** No, of course not, madame.

**MADAME.** Then don't be absurd, Corporal. To be absurd twice in five minutes is too often. You may use my desk—and my own special pen. Isn't it a beautiful quill, Corporal?

*The Pen of My Aunt* 247

38
39
40
41

**38 Critical Thinking and Reading** You might have students recall the previous argument between the stranger and Simone and compare it with this one. How does this second argument make it seem even more likely that the stranger is Madame's nephew?

**39 Discussion** Why is it good psychology to scold the Corporal and then ask him to do something for the stranger?

**40 Discussion** How does the author inject humor into this serious situation?

**41 Discussion** What is ironic about Madame's offering the Corporal her pen?

---

The bracketed explanations tell what is happening offstage, give stage directions, and suggest interpretations of dialogue.

**Student Activity 1.** Find five more bracketed passages in *The Pen of My Aunt*. Tell what purpose each serves for the reader and for the actor or actress.

**Student Activity 2.** Write a short dramatic scene showing what happens to the stranger after he leaves Madame's house at the end of the play. Use brackets to provide the reader or actors with essential information.

**42** **Discussion** How does the Corporal feel about his country, as compared to France?

**43** **Clarification** A *miscreant* is "an evildoer or villain."

**44** **Discussion** How does Madame put the Corporal on the defensive?

**45** **Discussion** Explain the meaning of this sentence.

**CORPORAL.** Thank you, madame, no. *We* Germans have come a long way from the geese.

**MADAME.** Yes?

**CORPORAL.** I prefer my fountain-pen. It is a more efficient implement. [*He writes*] For the 15th and the 16th. "Holder of identity card number"——What is the number of your identity, monsieur?

**STRANGER.** I have not the faintest idea.

**CORPORAL.** You do not know?

**STRANGER.** No. The only numbers I take an interest in are lottery numbers.

**SIMONE.** I know the number of monsieur's card.

**MADAME.** [*Afraid that she is going to invent one*] I don't think that likely, Simone.

**SIMONE.** [*Aware of what is in her mistress's mind, and reassuring her*] But I really *do* know, madame. It is the year I was born, with two "ones" after it. Many a time I have seen it on the outside of the card.

**CORPORAL.** It is good that someone knows.

**SIMONE.** It is—192411.

**CORPORAL.** 192411. [*He fills in the dates.*]

**MADAME.** [*As he nears the end*] Are you going back to St. Estèphe (sant ə stəf') now, Corporal?

**CORPORAL.** Yes, madame.

**MADAME.** Then perhaps you will give my nephew a lift as far as the Marnay crossroads.

**CORPORAL.** It is not permitted to take civilians as passengers.

**STRANGER.** But you took me here as a passenger.

**CORPORAL.** That was different.

*248 Drama*

**MADAME.** You mean that when you thought he was a miscreant you took him in your car, but now that you know he is my nephew you refuse?

**CORPORAL.** When I brought him here it was on service business.

**MADAME.** [*Gently reasonable*] Corporal, I think you owe me something for your general lack of tact this afternoon. Would it be too much to ask you to consider my nephew a miscreant for the next hour while you drive him as far as the Marnay crossroads?

**CORPORAL.** But——

**MADAME.** Take him to the crossroads with you and I shall agree to forget your—your lack of efficiency. I am sure you are actually a very efficient person, and likely to be a sergeant any day now. We won't let a blunder or two stand in your way.

**CORPORAL.** If I am caught giving a lift to a civilian, I shall *never* be a sergeant.

**MADAME.** [*Still gentle*] If I report on your conduct this afternoon, tomorrow you will be a private.

**CORPORAL.** [*After a long pause*] Is monsieur ready to come now?

**STRANGER.** Quite ready.

**CORPORAL.** You will need a coat.

**MADAME.** Simone, get monsieur's coat from the cupboard in the hall. And when you have seen him off, come back here.

**SIMONE.** Yes, madame.

[*Exit* SIMONE]

**CORPORAL.** Madame.

**MADAME.** Good day to you, Corporal.

[*Exit* CORPORAL]

**STRANGER.** Your talent for blackmail is remarkable.

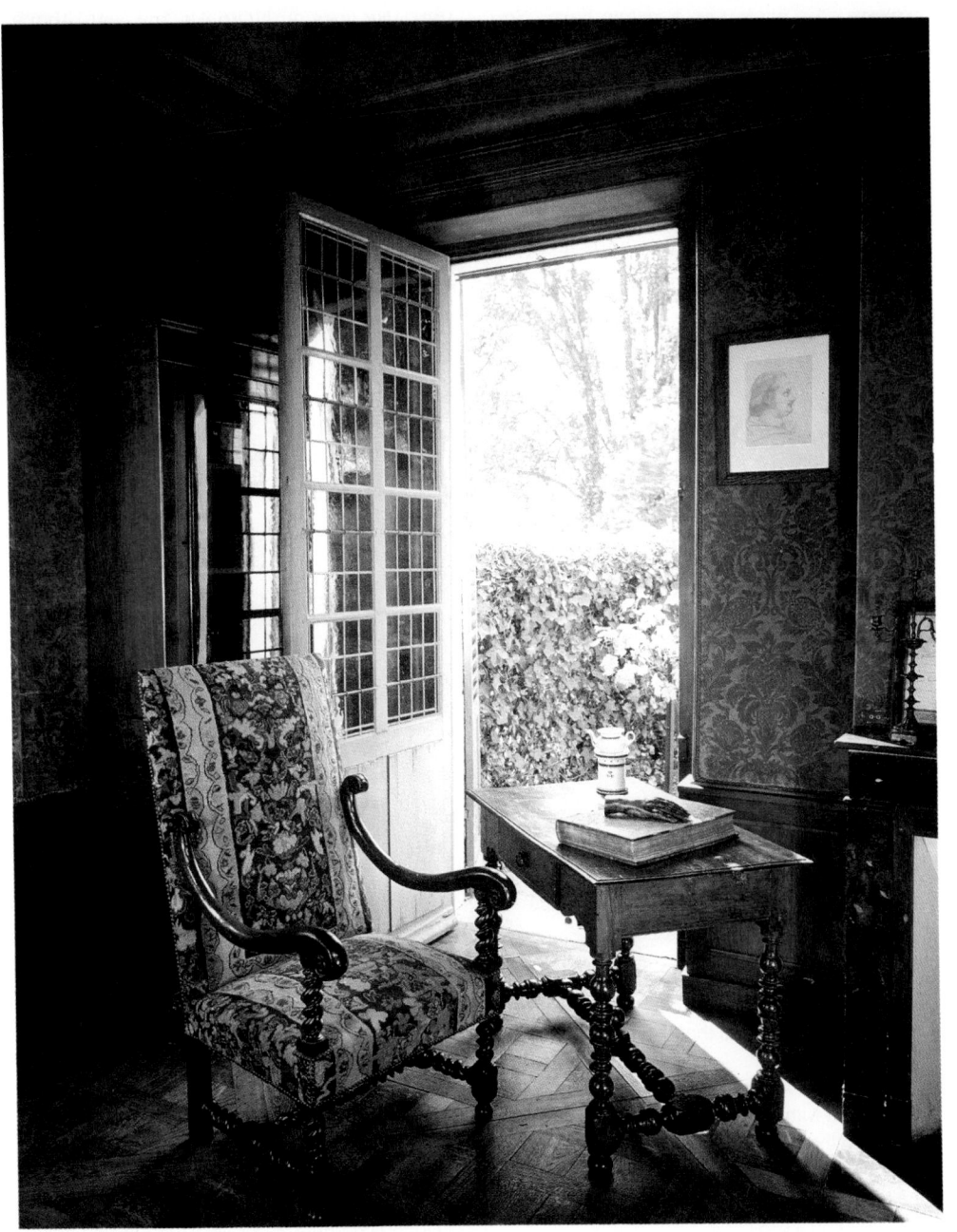

**MADAME.** The place has a yellow barn. You had better wait somewhere till evening, when the dogs are chained up.

46 ⌐**STRANGER.** I wish I had an aunt of your caliber. All mine are authorities on crochet.[7]

  **MADAME.** I could wish you were my nephew. Good luck, and be careful. Perhaps one day you will come back, and dine with me, and ⌐tell me the rest of the tale.

[*The sound of a running engine comes from outside.*]

**STRANGER.** Two years today, perhaps?

**MADAME.** One year today.

**STRANGER.** [*Softly*] Who knows? [*He lifts her hand to his lips.*] Thank you, and *au revoir*.[8] [*Turning at the door*] Being sped on my way by the enemy is a happiness I had not anticipated. I shall never be able to repay you for

---

7. **crochet** (krō shā′) *n.*: Kind of needlework.
8. *au revoir* (ō′ rə vwär′): French for "goodbye."

that. [*He goes out*] [*Off*] Ah, my coat—thank you, Simone.

[*Sound of car driving off.*]

MADAME *pours out two glasses. As she finishes,* SIMONE *comes in, shutting the door* ⌐*correctly behind her and taking two paces* 47 *into the room.*]

**SIMONE.** You wanted me, madame?

**MADAME.** You will drink a glass of wine with me, Simone.

**SIMONE.** With you, madame!

**MADAME.** You are a good daughter of France and a good servant to me. We shall drink a 48 toast together.

**SIMONE.** Yes, madame.

**MADAME.** [*Quietly*] To Freedom.

**SIMONE.** [*Repeating*] To Freedom. May I add ⌐a bit of my own, madame?

**MADAME.** Certainly.

**SIMONE.** [*With immense satisfaction*] And a very bad end to that Corporal!

---

**THINKING ABOUT THE SELECTION**

**Recalling**

1. Describe the deceptions that Madame, Simone, and the stranger resort to in order to convince the Corporal that the stranger is Madame's nephew.

2. Why can the stranger use the nephew's identity papers without fear of the nephew's turning him in to the authorities?

3. Explain the special use to which Madame puts her red quill pen. Why is the pen especially effective for this use?

250   *Drama*

4. How does Madame explain Simone's comments to the gardener that she had never before set eyes on the stranger?

5. How does Madame persuade the Corporal to help the stranger escape?

**Interpreting**

6. Compare and contrast the strengths of Madame and Simone.

7. As soon as the Corporal enters with the stranger, Madame, Simone, and the stranger act in perfect harmony to fool the Corporal. Does such sudden perfect role-playing seem

believable to you? Give reasons for your opinion.

8. During the Nazi occupation of France, many French people performed acts of great courage. Discuss the role of courage in this play.

### Applying

9. Although Madame acts courageously against the Germans, people believe her to be a collaborator. Do you think it takes more courage to act courageously without people knowing it than to behave courageously in the spotlight? Explain your answer.

## ANALYZING LITERATURE

### Understanding Staging

**Staging** a play means producing it on stage, using actors, costumes, scenery, props, lighting, sound effects, and other methods to make the play come alive.

1. If you were directing *The Pen of My Aunt,* how would you costume each of the characters?
2. How would you furnish Madame's drawing room?
3. Choose one of the characters, and describe in general how an actor playing that character should approach his or her role.

## CRITICAL THINKING AND READING

### Adapting a Play for the Movies

Many plays written for the stage are later made into movies. When they are, the staging usually changes. A movie director can "open up" a stage play by setting some of the action outdoors. Different interior locations may be used. There will probably be more physical action, and therefore less dialogue. Such staging changes are necessary because moviegoers expect to see outdoor scenes, changes of setting, and physical action.

1. If you were going to turn *The Pen of My Aunt* into a movie, what outdoor scenes based on material in the stage play would you include? Briefly describe two or three.
2. How might you indicate the Nazi presence in France? What other background information, or exposition, might you provide?

## UNDERSTANDING LANGUAGE

### Using the Prefix *Col*

Many English words contain the prefix *col,* which means "with" or "together." For example, in *The Pen of My Aunt* you encountered the word *collaborator,* meaning "a person who works with an enemy invader." The following words also contain this prefix. Using a dictionary if necessary, tell what each word means, and explain how it contains the idea "with" or "together."

1. collapse          3. collide
2. collect           4. collusion

## THINKING AND WRITING

### Writing About a Play's Meaning

Write an essay about the meaning of *The Pen of My Aunt.* First answer these questions: What is the chief reason that the events turn out as they do? What qualities of the characters matter the most? What other important causes seem to contribute to the situation at the very end? Then answer this fundamental question: What does this play reveal to me about life? The answer to this question may be considered a statement about the meaning of the play. Once you can state what the play reveals to you about life, select specific details to support your basic statement. When you revise your essay, concentrate on making this statement as clear and exact as possible. Then be sure that you have supported it well enough to convince readers to accept your view. Share your essay with your classmates.

*The Pen of My Aunt   251*

(Answers begin on p. 250.)

**Challenge** Imagine that you will be presenting this drama as a radio play. What special sound effects would make the performance more realistic? Also, what type of voice should each character have? Explain.

### ANSWERS TO CRITICAL THINKING AND READING

1. Students' answers will vary. Some outdoor scenes might include the Corporal arresting the stranger, the Corporal and the stranger appearing at Madame's front door, Simone talking to the gardener, and the Corporal driving the stranger away from Madame's country house.
2. Students' answers will differ. Some devices might include roadblocks with German soldiers, Nazi flags, and scenes of soldiers stopping civilians to ask them for their papers. Exposition could include a brief introductory section, with a map, showing how much of Europe the Nazi troops had occupied.

### ANSWERS TO UNDERSTANDING LANGUAGE

1. collapse—fall down or fall to pieces (the Latin prefix and root mean "fall together")
2. collect—gather (the Latin prefix and root mean "gather together")
3. collide—crash (the Latin prefix and root mean "strike together")
4. collusion—conspiracy (the Latin prefix and root mean "play with")

### THINKING AND WRITING

Before beginning this assignment, students might refer to Lesson 14, "Writing About Drama," in the Handbook of Writing About Literature.

**Publishing Student Writing** You might want to display students' work on the class bulletin board.

**Writing Across the Curriculum** Consider having students research and report on the German conquest of France in World War II. You might want to inform the social studies department of this assignment, so that teachers can guide students' research.

the courage of Simone, who is probably risking her life to confirm the stranger's story.

### Applying

9. Students' answers will vary. Many students will probably realize that it is even more difficult to act courageously when people are unaware of your heroism and you do not have an audience.

### ANSWERS TO ANALYZING LITERATURE

1. Answers will differ. Most students

will realize that the Corporal should wear a German military uniform, the stranger should be dressed casually and look as though he has been walking in the woods, Simone might be wearing a maid's uniform, and Madame should be dressed like a well-to-do older woman.
2. Answers will differ. Many students will probably take a cue from the accompanying picture and will suggest that the room be furnished with substantial, expensive-looking, old-fashioned furniture. Most

important, the room should include a desk with a pen and a notebook on it.
3. Students' answers will differ. Most students will realize that they must take into account the following traits—Madame is cool, and aristocratic, and always keeps control of herself; Simone is more fiery and impatient; the stranger should convey, very subtly, that he is bluffing; and the Corporal is unimaginative, someone who always follows rules and takes orders.

### The Miracle Worker, Act I

**William Gibson** (1914–    ) was born in New York City. In his first successful play, *Two for the Seesaw,* a character says, "... after the verb to love, to help is the sweetest in the tongue." These words express a major theme in Gibson's work, one that is clearly seen in his most famous play, *The Miracle Worker,* which is based on the real-life story of the teacher Annie Sullivan and her student Helen Keller, a seven-year-old girl who is unable to see, hear, or speak. The original title of this play was *After the Verb to Love.*

**Protagonist and Antagonist**

The **protagonist** is the central character of a play. He or she will be engaged in a struggle or conflict with another character or group of characters. This other character, or group of characters, is the **antagonist**. In traditional drama, the conflict between the protagonist and the antagonist develops and intensifies until it reaches a climax, the high point of the play. At that point the conflict is settled by the victory of one of the characters.

**Look For**

In order to help a person, you sometimes have to make this person do things he or she may not want to do. As you read Act I of *The Miracle Worker,* look for the ways that Annie Sullivan treats Helen harshly in order to help her.

**Writing**

*The Miracle Worker* is about the efforts of a young woman to help a girl unable to see, hear, or speak. What if you had to take complete responsibility for the life of such a child? Imagine the many challenges you would have! One of the most basic would be the challenge of communication. Freewrite about some of the methods you would try in order to communicate with the child.

**Vocabulary**

Knowing the following words will help you as you read Act I of *The Miracle Worker.*

**vigil** (vij′ əl) *n.*: A watchful staying awake (p. 253)
**vivacious** (vi vā′ shəs) *adj.*: Lively (p. 254)
**pantomime** (pan′ tə mīm′) *n.*: Wordless actions or gestures as a means of expression (p. 255)

**obstinate** (äb′ stə nit) *adj.*: Stubborn (p. 259)
**bristling** (bris′liŋ) *v.*: Becoming tense with fear or anger (p. 260)

252   Drama

# The Miracle Worker

### William Gibson

```
CHARACTERS

A Doctor      Helen       James                     Blind Girls
Kate          Martha      Anagnos (an ag' nŏs)      A Servant
Keller        Percy       Annie Sullivan            Offstage Voices
              Aunt Ev     Viney
```

TIME. *The 1880's*
PLACE. *In and around the Keller homestead in Tuscumbia, Alabama; also, briefly, the Perkins Institution for the Blind, in Boston.*

## ACT I

*[It is night over the Keller homestead. Inside, three adults in the bedroom are grouped around a crib, in lamplight. They have been through a long vigil, and it shows in their tired bearing and disarranged clothing. One is a young gentlewoman with a sweet girlish face,* KATE KELLER; *the second is an elderly* DOCTOR, *stethoscope at neck, thermometer in fingers; the third is a hearty gentleman in his forties with chin whiskers,* CAPTAIN ARTHUR KELLER.]

**DOCTOR.** She'll live.

**KATE.** Thank God.

*[The* DOCTOR *leaves them together over the crib, packs his bag.]*

**DOCTOR.** You're a pair of lucky parents. I can tell you now, I thought she wouldn't.

**KELLER.** Nonsense, the child's a Keller, she has the constitution of a goat. She'll outlive us all.

**DOCTOR.** [*Amiably*] Yes, especially if some of you Kellers don't get a night's sleep. I mean you, Mrs. Keller.

**KELLER.** You hear, Katie?

**KATE.** I hear.

**KELLER.** [*Indulgent*] I've brought up two of them, but this is my wife's first, she isn't battle-scarred yet.

**KATE.** Doctor, don't be merely considerate, will my girl be all right?

**DOCTOR.** Oh, by morning she'll be knocking down Captain Keller's fences again.

**KATE.** And isn't there anything we should do?

**KELLER.** [*Jovial*] Put up stronger fencing, ha?

**DOCTOR.** Just let her get well, she knows how to do it better than we do.

*[He is packed, ready to leave.]*

*The Miracle Worker* 253

---

6 **Critical Thinking and Reading** Ask students to contrast these two reactions.

7 **Reading Strategy** You might ask students to predict how these two parents will deal with their physically challenged daughter.

8 **Clarification** Curtains do not close to show changes in scenes. Lighting and the sound of distant belfry chimes indicate the passage of time at this point. Have students watch for similar changes of scene throughout the play.

Main thing is the fever's gone, these things come and go in infants, never know why. Call it acute congestion of the stomach and brain.

**KELLER.** I'll see you to your buggy, Doctor.

**DOCTOR.** I've never seen a baby, more vitality, that's the truth.

[*He beams a good night at the baby and* KATE, *and* KELLER *leads him downstairs with a lamp. They go down the porch steps, and across the yard, where the* DOCTOR *goes off left;* KELLER *stands with the lamp aloft.* KATE *meanwhile is bent lovingly over the crib, which emits a bleat; her finger is playful with the baby's face.*]

**KATE:** Hush. Don't you cry now, you've been trouble enough. Call it acute congestion, indeed, I don't see what's so cute about a congestion, just because it's yours. We'll have your father run an editorial in his paper, the wonders of modern medicine, they don't know what they're curing even when they cure it. Men, men and their battle scars, we women will have to—

[*But she breaks off, puzzled, moves her finger before the baby's eyes.*]

Will have to—Helen?

[*Now she moves her hand, quickly.*]

Helen.

[*She snaps her fingers at the baby's eyes twice, and her hand falters; after a moment she calls out, loudly.*]

Captain, Captain, will you come—

[*But she stares at the baby, and her next call is directly at her ears.*]

Captain!

[*And now, still staring,* KATE *screams.* KELLER *in the yard hears it, and runs with the lamp back to the house.* KATE *screams*

again, *her look intent on the baby and terrible.* KELLER *hurries in and up.*]

**KELLER.** Katie? What's wrong?

**KATE.** Look.

[*She makes a pass with her hand in the crib, at the baby's eyes.*]

**KELLER.** What, Katie? She's well, she needs only time to—

**KATE.** She can't see. Look at her eyes.

[*She takes the lamp from him, moves it before the child's face.*]

She can't see!

**KELLER.** [*Hoarsely*] Helen.

**KATE.** Or hear. When I screamed she didn't blink. Not an eyelash—

**KELLER.** Helen. Helen!

**KATE.** She can't *hear* you!

**KELLER.** *Helen!*

[*His face has something like fury in it, crying the child's name;* KATE *almost fainting presses her knuckles to her mouth, to stop her own cry.*

*The room dims out quickly.*

*Time, in the form of a slow tune of distant belfry chimes which approaches in a crescendo and then fades, passes; the light comes up again on a day five years later, on three kneeling children and an old dog outside around the pump.*

*The dog is a setter named* BELLE, *and she is sleeping. Two of the children are Negroes,* MARTHA *and* PERCY. *The third child is* HELEN, *six and a half years old, quite unkempt, in body a vivacious little person with a fine head, attractive, but noticeably blind, one eye larger and protruding; her gestures are abrupt, insistent, lacking in human restraint, and her face never smiles. She is flanked by the other two, in a litter of paper-doll cutouts, and while* [9] *they speak* HELEN's *hands thrust at their faces in turn, feeling baffledly at the movements of their lips.*]

**MARTHA.** [*Snipping*] First I'm gonna cut off this doctor's legs, one, two, now then—

**PERCY.** Why you cuttin' off that doctor's legs?

**MARTHA.** I'm gonna give him a operation. Now I'm gonna cut off his arms, one, two. Now I'm gonna fix up—

[*She pushes* HELEN's *hand away from her mouth.*]

You stop that.

**PERCY.** Cut off his stomach, that's a good operation.

**MARTHA.** No, I'm gonna cut off his head first, he got a bad cold.

**PERCY.** Ain't gonna be much of that doctor left to fix up, time you finish all them opera—

[*But* HELEN *is poking her fingers inside his mouth, to feel his tongue; he bites at them, annoyed, and she jerks them away.* HELEN *now fingers her own lips, moving them in imitation, but soundlessly.*]

**MARTHA.** What you do, bite her hand?

**PERCY.** That's how I do, she keep pokin' her fingers in my mouth, I just bite 'em off.

**MARTHA.** What she tryin' do now?

**PERCY.** She tryin' talk. She gonna get mad. Looka her tryin' talk.

[HELEN *is scowling, the lips under her fingertips moving in ghostly silence, growing more and more frantic, until in a bizarre rage she bites at her own fingers. This*

*sends* PERCY *off into laughter, but alarms* MARTHA.]

**MARTHA.** Hey, you stop now.

[*She pulls* HELEN's *hand down.*]

You just sit quiet and—

[*But at once* HELEN *topples* MARTHA *on her back, knees pinning her shoulders down, and grabs the scissors.* MARTHA *screams.* PERCY *darts to the bell string on the porch, yanks it, and the bell rings.*

*Inside, the lights have been gradually coming up on the main room, where we see the family informally gathered, talking, but in pantomime:* KATE *sits darning socks near a cradle, occasionally rocking it;* CAPTAIN KELLER *in spectacles is working over newspaper pages at a table; a benign visitor in a hat,* AUNT EV, *is sharing the sewing basket, putting the finishing touches on a big shapeless doll made out of towels; an indolent young man,* JAMES KELLER, *is at the window watching the children.*   [10]

*With the ring of the bell,* KATE *is instantly on her feet and out the door onto the porch, to take in the scene; now we see what these five years have done to her, the girlish playfulness is gone, she is a woman steeled in grief.*]   [11]

**KATE.** [*For the thousandth time*] Helen.

[*She is down the steps at once to them, seizing* HELEN's *wrists and lifting her off* MARTHA; MARTHA *runs off in tears and screams for momma, with* PERCY *after her.*]

Let me have those scissors.

[*Meanwhile the family inside is alerted,* AUNT EV *joining* JAMES *at the window;* CAPTAIN KELLER *resumes work.*]

**JAMES.** [*Blandly*] She only dug Martha's eyes out. Almost dug. It's always almost, no point worrying till it happens, is there?   [12]

*The Miracle Worker* 255

9 **Discussion** What does Helen seem to sense about the importance of lips and mouths?

10 **Discussion** Why do you think the playwright has the lights gradually come up on this scene while Helen fights with Martha?

11 **Discussion** What do you think has changed Kate over the past five years?

12 **Discussion** How do you know this incident has occurred before?

13 **Discussion** What is Kate trying to tell Helen? Does Helen understand?

14 **Discussion** Why is it important to know this background information about the Kellers' attempts to have Helen treated?

15 **Discussion** What does Helen suddenly realize about the doll?

**KELLER.** A refreshing suggestion. What?

[KATE *entering turns* HELEN *to* AUNT EV, *who gives her the towel doll.*]

**AUNT EV.** Why, this very famous oculist[1] in Baltimore I wrote you about, what was his name?

**KATE.** Dr. Chisholm.

**AUNT EV.** Yes, I heard lots of cases of blindness people thought couldn't be cured he's cured, he just does wonders. Why don't you write to him?

**KELLER.** I've stopped believing in wonders.

**KATE.** [*Rocks the cradle*] I think the Captain will write to him soon. Won't you, Captain?

**KELLER.** No.

**JAMES.** [*Lightly*] Good money after bad, or bad after good. Or bad after bad—

**AUNT EV.** Well, if it's just a question of money, Arthur, now you're marshal you have this Yankee money. Might as well—

**KELLER.** Not money. The child's been to specialists all over Alabama and Tennessee, if I thought it would do good I'd have her to every fool doctor in the country.

**KATE.** I think the Captain will write to him soon.

**KELLER.** Katie. How many times can you let them break your heart?

**KATE.** Any number of times.

[HELEN *meanwhile sits on the floor to explore the doll with her fingers, and her hand pauses over the face: this is no face, a blank area of towel, and it troubles her. Her hand searches for features, and taps questioningly for eyes, but no one notices.*]

---

1. **oculist** (ăk′ yə list)*n.*: An old-fashioned term for an eye specialist.

[*They gaze out, while* KATE *reaches for the scissors in* HELEN's *hand. But* HELEN *pulls the scissors back, they struggle for them a moment, then* KATE *gives up, lets* HELEN *keep them. She tries to draw* HELEN *into the house.* HELEN *jerks away.* KATE *next goes down on her knees, takes* HELEN's *hands gently, and using the scissors like a doll, makes* HELEN *caress and cradle them; she points* HELEN's *finger housewards.* HELEN's *whole body now becomes eager; she surrenders the scissors,* KATE *turns her toward the door and gives her a little push,* HELEN *scrambles up and toward the house, and* KATE *rising follows her.*]

**AUNT EV.** How does she stand it? Why haven't you seen this Baltimore man? It's not a thing you can let go on and on, like the weather.

**JAMES.** The weather here doesn't ask permission of me, Aunt Ev. Speak to my father.

**AUNT EV.** Arthur. Something ought to be done for that child.

256 *Drama*

## Grammar in Action

A **fragment** is a group of words that does not express a complete thought. It is usually advisable to avoid fragments in writing; however, dramatists and fiction writers often use fragments in dialogue to make conversation seem realistic. These fragments are usually understandable from the context:

"What made you leave the scene of the accident?" (Sentence)

"Fear." (Fragment)
"Of what?" (Fragment)
"I don't know. I was just scared." (Sentences)

Notice the mixture of complete sentences and fragments in the following passage from *The Miracle Worker*.

**KATE.** As long as there's the least chance. For her to see. Or hear, or—

**KELLER.** There isn't. Now I must finish here.

*She then yanks at her* AUNT'S *dress, and taps again vigorously for eyes.*]

**AUNT EV.** What, child?

[*Obviously not hearing,* HELEN *commences to go around, from person to person, tapping for eyes, but no one attends or understands.*]

**KATE.** [*No break*] As long as there's the least chance. For her to see. Or hear, or—

**KELLER.** There isn't. Now I must finish here.

**KATE.** I think, with your permission, Captain, I'd like to write.

**KELLER.** I said no, Katie.

**AUNT EV.** Why, writing does no harm, Arthur, only a little bitty letter. To see if he can help her.

**KELLER.** He can't.

**KATE.** We won't know that to be a fact, Captain, until after you write.

**KELLER.** [*Rising, emphatic*] Katie, he can't.

[*He collects his papers.*]

**JAMES.** [*Facetiously*] Father stands up, that makes it a fact.

**KELLER.** You be quiet! I'm badgered enough here by females without your impudence.

[JAMES *shuts up, makes himself scarce.* HELEN *now is groping among things on* KELLER'S *desk, and paws his papers to the floor.* KELLER *is exasperated.*]

Katie.

[KATE *quickly turns* HELEN *away, and retrieves the papers.*]

I might as well try to work in a henyard as in this house—

**JAMES.** [*Placating*] You really ought to put her away, Father.

**KATE.** [*Staring up*] What?

**JAMES.** Some asylum. It's the kindest thing.

**AUNT EV.** Why, she's your sister, James, not a nobody—

**JAMES.** Half sister, and half—mentally defective, she can't even keep herself clean. It's not pleasant to see her about all the time.

**KATE.** Do you dare? Complain of what you *can* see?

**KELLER.** [*Very annoyed*] This discussion is at an end! I'll thank you not to broach it again, Ev.

[*Silence descends at once.* HELEN *gropes her way with the doll, and* KELLER *turns back for a final word, explosive.*]

I've done as much as I can bear, I can't give my whole life to it! The house is at sixes and sevens from morning till night over the child, it's time some attention was paid to Mildred here instead!

**KATE.** [*Gently dry*] You'll wake her up, Captain.

**KELLER.** I want some peace in the house, I don't care how, but one way we won't have it is by rushing up and down the country every time someone hears of a new quack. I'm as sensible to this affliction as anyone else, it hurts me to look at the girl.

**KATE.** It was not our affliction I meant you to write about, Captain.

[HELEN *is back at* AUNT EV, *fingering her dress, and yanks two buttons from it.*]

**AUNT EV.** Helen! My buttons.

[HELEN *pushes the buttons into the doll's face.* KATE *now sees, comes swiftly to kneel, lifts* HELEN'S *hand to her own eyes in question.*]

**KATE.** Eyes?

*The Miracle Worker* 257

16 **Critical Thinking and Reading** What can you infer about James and his relationship with his father?

17 **Critical Thinking and Reading** Why does Helen rip off Aunt Ev's buttons and push them into the doll's face?

**KATE.** I think, with your permission, Captain, I'd like to write.

**KELLER.** I said no, Katie.

**AUNT EV.** Why, writing does no harm, Arthur, only a little bitty letter. To see if he can help her.

**Student Activity 1.** Identify the fragments in this passage. Explain how each manages to express a complete thought.

**Student Activity 2.** Rewrite the passage from *The Miracle Worker* eliminating all the fragments. Then explain which passage sounds most like normal speech.

**18 Critical Thinking and Reading**
How does this remark conflict with his earlier statement that "the least she can have are the little things she wants"? What are Keller's divided feelings about his daughter?

**19 Discussion** What evidence is there that Helen is intelligent even though she cannot understand what is going on?

[HELEN *nods energetically.*]

She wants the doll to have eyes.

[*Another kind of silence now, while* KATE *takes pins and buttons from the sewing basket and attaches them to the doll as eyes.* KELLER *stands, caught, and watches morosely.* AUNT EV *blinks, and conceals her emotion by inspecting her dress.*]

**AUNT EV.** My goodness me, I'm not decent.

**KATE.** She doesn't know better, Aunt Ev. I'll sew them on again.

**JAMES.** Never learn with everyone letting her do anything she takes it into her mind to—

**KELLER.** You be quiet!

**JAMES.** What did I say now?

**KELLER.** You talk too much.

**JAMES.** I was agreeing with you!

**KELLER.** Whatever it was. Deprived child, the least she can have are the little things she wants.

[JAMES, *very wounded, stalks out of the room onto the porch; he remains here, sulking.*]

**AUNT EV.** [*Indulgently*] It's worth a couple of buttons, Kate, look.

[HELEN *now has the doll with eyes, and cannot contain herself for joy; she rocks the doll, pats it vigorously, kisses it.*]

This child has more sense than all these men Kellers, if there's ever any way to reach that mind of hers.

[*But* HELEN *suddenly has come upon the cradle, and unhesitatingly overturns it; the swaddled baby tumbles out, and* CAPTAIN KELLER *barely manages to dive and catch it in time.*]

**KELLER.** Helen!

[*All are in commotion, the baby screams, but* HELEN *unperturbed is laying her doll in its place.* KATE *on her knees pulls her hands off the cradle, wringing them;* HELEN *is bewildered.*]

**KATE.** Helen, Helen, you're not to do such things, how can I make you understand—

**KELLER.** [*Hoarsely*] Katie.

**KATE.** How can I get it into your head, my darling, my poor—

**KELLER.** Katie, some way of teaching her an iota of discipline has to be— 18

**KATE.** [*Flaring*] How can you discipline an afflicted child? Is it her fault?

[HELEN'S *fingers have fluttered to her* MOTHER'S *lips, vainly trying to comprehend their movements.*] 19

**KELLER.** I didn't say it was her fault.

**KATE.** Then whose? I don't know what to do! How can I teach her, beat her—until she's black and blue?

**KELLER.** It's not safe to let her run around loose. Now there must be a way of confining her, somehow, so she can't—

**KATE.** Where, in a cage? She's a growing child, she has to use her limbs!

**KELLER.** Answer me one thing, is it fair to Mildred here?

**KATE.** [*Inexorably*] Are you willing to put her away?

[*Now* HELEN'S *face darkens in the same rage as at herself earlier, and her hand strikes at* KATE'S *lips.* KATE *catches her hand again, and* HELEN *begins to kick, struggle, twist.*]

**KELLER.** Now what?

**KATE.** She wants to talk, like—*be* like you and me.

[*She holds* HELEN *struggling until we hear from the child her first sound so far, an inarticulate weird noise in her throat such as an animal in a trap might make; and* KATE *releases her. The second she is free* HELEN *blunders away, collides violently with a chair, falls, and sits weeping.* KATE *comes to her, embraces, caresses, soothes her, and buries her own face in her hair, until she can control her voice.*]

20 Every day she slips further away. And I don't know how to call her back.

**AUNT EV.** Oh, I've a mind to take her up to Baltimore myself. If that doctor can't help her, maybe he'll know who can.

**KELLER.** [*Presently, heavily*] I'll write the man, Katie.

[*He stands with the baby in his clasp, staring at* HELEN's *head, hanging down on* KATE's *arm.*]

[*The lights dim out, except the one on* KATE *and* HELEN. *In the twilight,* JAMES, AUNT EV, *and* KELLER *move off slowly, formally, in separate directions;* KATE *with* HELEN *in her arms remains, motionless, in an image which overlaps into the next scene and fades only when it is well under way.*]

Without pause, from the dark down left we hear a man's voice with a Greek accent speaking.]

**ANAGNOS.** —who could do nothing for the girl, of course. It was Dr. Bell who thought she might somehow be taught. I have written the family only that a suitable governess, Miss Annie Sullivan, has been found here in Boston—

[*The lights begin to come up, down left, on a long table and chair. The table contains equipment for teaching the blind by touch— a small replica of the human skeleton,* stuffed animals, models of flowers and plants, piles of books. The chair contains a girl of 20, ANNIE SULLIVAN, *with a face which in repose is grave and rather obstinate, and when active is impudent, combative, twinkling with all the life that is lacking in* HELEN's, *and handsome; there is a crude vitality to her. Her suitcase is at her knee.* ANAGNOS, *a stocky bearded man, comes into the light only toward the end of his speech.*]

**ANAGNOS.** —and will come. It will no doubt be difficult for you there, Annie. But it has been difficult for you at our school too, hm? Gratifying, yes, when you came to us and could not spell your name, to accomplish so much here in a few years, but always an Irish battle. For independence.

[*He studies* ANNIE, *humorously; she does not open her eyes.*]

This is my last time to counsel you, Annie, and you do lack some—by some I mean *all*—what, tact or talent to bend. To others. And what has saved you on more than one occasion here at Perkins is that there was nowhere to expel you to. Your eyes hurt?

**ANNIE.** My ears, Mr. Anagnos.

[*And now she has opened her eyes; they are inflamed, vague, slightly crossed, clouded by the granular growth of trachoma,[2] and she often keeps them closed to shut out the pain of light.*]

**ANAGNOS.** [*Severely*] Nowhere but back to Tewksbury,[3] where children learn to be saucy. Annie, I know how dreadful it was there, but that battle is dead and done with, why not let it stay buried?

---

**2. trachoma** (trə kō′ mə)*n.*: A disease of the eyelid and eyeball.
**3. Tewksbury:** A town in Massachusetts, the location of an institution for the poor.

**20 Discussion** Why do you think Helen is becoming more of a problem?

**21 Discussion** Why do you think the playwright has the characters exit in this manner, leaving Kate and Helen behind? What mood does he create by ending the scene like this?

**22 Critical Thinking and Reading** What can you infer about Annie from the stage directions and from Anagnos's words?

**23 Reading Strategy** You might want to ask students to look for references to this phase of Annie's life as the play unfolds.

24 **Discussion** Why does Anagnos compare Helen to a safe? What does Annie's question mean?

25 **Literary Focus** How does the playwright prepare us for the struggle between the protagonist and the main antagonist?

26 **Discussion** Why does Anagnos suggest that Annie tell the family about her background?

27 **Critical Thinking and Reading** What do you think Annie is feeling?

**ANNIE.** [*Cheerily*] I think God must owe me a resurrection.

**ANAGNOS.** [*A bit shocked*] What?

**ANNIE.** [*Taps her brow*] Well, He keeps digging up that battle!

**ANAGNOS.** That is not a proper thing to say, Annie. It is what I mean.

**ANNIE.** [*Meekly*] Yes. But I know what I'm like, what's this child like?

**ANAGNOS.** Like?

**ANNIE.** Well—Bright or dull, to start off.

**ANAGNOS.** No one knows. And if she is dull, you have no patience with this?

**ANNIE.** Oh, in grownups you have to, Mr. Anagnos. I mean in children it just seems a little—precocious, can I use that word?

**ANAGNOS.** Only if you can spell it.

**ANNIE.** Premature. So I hope at least she's a bright one.

**ANAGNOS.** Deaf, blind, mute—who knows? She is like a little safe, locked, that no one can open. Perhaps there is a treasure inside.

**ANNIE.** Maybe it's empty, too?

**ANAGNOS.** Possible. I should warn you, she is much given to tantrums.

**ANNIE.** Means something is inside. Well, so am I, if I believe all I hear. Maybe you should warn *them*.

**ANAGNOS.** [*Frowns*] Annie. I wrote them no word of your history. You will find yourself among strangers now, who know nothing of it.

**ANNIE.** Well, we'll keep them in a state of blessed ignorance.

**ANAGNOS.** Perhaps *you* should tell it?

**ANNIE.** [*Bristling*] Why? I have enough trouble with people who don't know.

*260 Drama*

**ANAGNOS.** So they will understand. When you have trouble.

**ANNIE.** The only time I have trouble is when I'm right.

[*But she is amused at herself, as is* ANAGNOS.]

Is it my fault it's so often? I won't give them trouble, Mr. Anagnos, I'll be so ladylike they won't notice I've come.

**ANAGNOS.** Annie, be—humble. It is not as if you have so many offers to pick and choose. You will need their affection, working with this child.

**ANNIE.** [*Humorously*] I hope I won't need their pity.

**ANAGNOS.** Oh, we can all use some pity.

[*Crisply*]

So. You are no longer our pupil, we throw you into the world, a teacher. *If* the child can be taught. No one expects you to work miracles, even for twenty-five dollars a month. Now, in this envelope a loan, for the railroad, which you will repay me when you have a bank account. But in this box, a gift. With our love.

[ANNIE *opens the small box he extends, and sees a garnet ring. She looks up, blinking, and down.*]

I think other friends are ready to say goodbye.

[*He moves as though to open doors.*]

**ANNIE.** Mr. Anagnos.

[*Her voice is trembling.*]

Dear Mr. Anagnos, I—

[*But she swallows over getting the ring on her finger, and cannot continue until she finds a woebegone joke.*]

Well, what should I say, I'm an ignorant

opinionated girl, and everything I am I owe to you?

**ANAGNOS.** [*Smiles*] That is only half true, Annie.

**ANNIE.** Which half? I crawled in here like a drowned rat, I thought I died when Jimmie died, that I'd never again—come alive. Well, you say with love so easy, and I haven't *loved* a soul since and I never will, I suppose, but this place gave me more than my eyes back. Or taught me how to spell, which I'll never learn anyway, but with all the fights and the trouble I've been here it taught me what help is, and how to live again, and I don't want to say goodbye. Don't open the door, I'm crying.

**ANAGNOS.** [*Gently*] They will not see.

[*He moves again as though opening doors, and in comes a group of girls, 8-year-olds to 17-year-olds; as they walk we see they are blind.* ANAGNOS *shepherds them in with a hand.*]

**A CHILD.** Annie?

**ANNIE:** [*Her voice cheerful.*] Here, Beatrice.

[*As soon as they locate her voice they throng joyfully to her, speaking all at once;* ANNIE *is down on her knees to the smallest, and the following are the more intelligible fragments in the general hubbub.*]

**CHILDREN.** There'a a present. We brought you a going-away present, Annie!

**ANNIE.** Oh, now you shouldn't have—

**CHILDREN.** We did, we did, where's the present?

**SMALLEST CHILD.** [*Mournfully*] Don't go, Annie, away.

**CHILDREN.** Alice has it. Alice! Where's Alice? Here I am! Where? Here!

[*An arm is aloft out of the group, waving a present;* ANNIE *reaches for it.*]

**ANNIE.** I have it. I have it, everybody, should I open it?

**CHIDREN.** Open it! Everyone be quiet! Do, Annie! She's opening it. Ssh!

[*A settling of silence while* ANNIE *unwraps it. The present is a pair of smoked glasses, and she stands still.*]

Is it open, Annie?

**ANNIE.** It's open.

**CHILDREN.** It's for your eyes, Annie. Put them on, Annie! 'Cause Mrs. Hopkins said your eyes hurt since the operation. And she said you're going where the sun is *fierce.*

**ANNIE.** I'm putting them on now.

**SMALLEST CHILD.** [*Mournfully*] Don't go, Annie, where the sun is fierce.

**CHILDREN.** Do they fit all right?

**ANNIE.** Oh, they fit just fine.

**CHILDREN.** Did you put them on? Are they pretty, Annie?

**ANNIE.** Oh, my eyes feel hundreds of per cent better already, and pretty, why, do you know how I look in them? Splendiloquent. Like a race horse!

**CHILDREN.** [*Delighted*] There's another present! Beatrice! We have a present for Helen, too! Give it to her, Beatrice. Here, Annie!

[*This present is an elegant doll, with movable eyelids and a momma sound.*]

It's for Helen. And we took up a collection to buy it. And Laura dressed it.

**ANNIE.** It's beautiful!

**CHILDREN.** So, don't forget, you be sure to give it to Helen from us, Annie!

**ANNIE.** I promise it will be the first thing I give her. If I don't keep it for myself, that is, you know I can't be trusted with dolls!

*The Miracle Worker* 261

**28** **Reading Strategy** Have students summarize what they know about Annie up to this point.

**29** **Discussion** How do the girls feel about Annie?

**30** **Discussion** What does this scene reveal about Annie?

**31** **Clarification** This change in the color of the light signals a scene from the past. Such a scene is usually called a flashback.

**32** **Literary Focus** Consider pointing out to students the effective staging here. Three scenes—one from the past and two in the present—are tied together with the three words, "Annie! Annie?" and "Coming!"

**SMALLEST CHILD.** [*Mournfully*] Don't go, Annie, to her.

**ANNIE.** [*Her arm around her.*] Sarah, dear, I don't *want* to go.

**SMALLEST CHILD.** Then why are you going?

**ANNIE.** [*Gently*] Because I'm a big girl now, and big girls have to earn a living. It's the only way I can. But if you don't smile for me first, what I'll just have to do is—

[*She pauses, inviting it.*]

**SMALLEST CHILD.** What?

**ANNIE.** Put *you* in my suitcase, instead of this doll. And take *you* to Helen in Alabama!

[*This strikes the children as very funny, and they begin to laugh and tease the smallest child, who after a moment does smile for* ANNIE.]

**ANAGNOS.** [*Then*] Come, children. We must get the trunk into the carriage and Annie into her train, or no one will go to Alabama. Come, come.

[*He shepherds them out and* ANNIE *is left alone on her knees with the doll in her lap. She reaches for her suitcase, and by a subtle change in the color of the light, we go with her thoughts into another time. We hear a boy's voice whispering; perhaps we see shadowy intimations of these speakers in the background.*]

**BOY'S VOICE.** Where we goin', Annie?

**ANNIE.** [*In dread*] Jimmie.

**BOY'S VOICE.** Where we goin'?

**ANNIE.** I said—I'm takin' care of you—

**BOY'S VOICE.** Forever and ever?

**MAN'S VOICE.** [*Impersonal*] Annie Sullivan, aged nine, virtually blind. James Sullivan, aged seven—What's the matter with your leg, Sonny?

262 *Drama*

**ANNIE.** Forever and ever.

**MAN'S VOICE.** Can't he walk without that crutch?

[ANNIE *shakes her head, and does not stop shaking it.*]

Girl goes to the women's ward. Boy to the men's.

**BOY'S VOICE.** [*In terror*] Annie! Annie, don't let them take me—Annie!

**ANAGNOS.** [*Offstage*] Annie! Annie?

[*But this voice is real, in the present, and* ANNIE *comes up out of her horror, clearing her head with a final shake; the lights begin to pick out* KATE *in the* KELLER *house, as* ANNIE *in a bright tone calls back.*]

**ANNIE.** Coming!

[*This word catches* KATE, *who stands half turned and attentive to it, almost as though hearing it. Meanwhile* ANNIE *turns and hurries out, lugging the suitcase.*]

The room dims out; the sound of railroad wheels begins from off left, and maintains itself in a constant rhythm underneath the following scene; the remaining lights have come up on the KELLER homestead. JAMES is lounging on the porch, waiting. In the upper bedroom which is to be ANNIE'S, HELEN is alone, puzzledly exploring, fingering and smelling things, the curtains, empty drawers in the bureau, water in the pitcher by the washbasin, fresh towels on the bedstead. Downstairs in the family room KATE turning to a mirror hastily adjusts her bonnet, watched by a Negro servant in an apron, VINEY.]

**VINEY.** Let Mr. Jimmy go by hisself, you been pokin' that garden all day, you ought to rest your feet.

**KATE.** I can't wait to see her, Viney.

**VINEY.** Maybe she ain't gone be on this train neither.

**KATE.** Maybe she is.

**VINEY.** And maybe she ain't.

**KATE.** And maybe she is. Where's Helen?

**VINEY.** She upstairs, smellin' around. She know somethin' funny's goin' on.

**KATE.** Let her have her supper as soon as Mildred's in bed, and tell Captain Keller when he comes that we'll be delayed tonight.

**VINEY.** Again.

**KATE.** I don't think we need say *again*. Simply delayed will do.

[*She runs upstairs to* ANNIE'S *room,* VINEY *speaking after her.*]

**VINEY.** I mean that's what he gone say. "What, again?"

[VINEY *works at setting the table. Upstairs* KATE *stands in the doorway, watching* HELEN'S *groping explorations.*]

**KATE.** Yes, we're expecting someone. Someone for my Helen.

[HELEN *happens upon her skirt, clutches her leg;* KATE *in a tired dismay kneels to tidy her hair and soiled pinafore.*]

Oh, dear, this was clean not an hour ago.

[HELEN *feels her bonnet, shakes her head darkly, and tugs to get it off.* KATE *retains it with one hand, diverts* HELEN *by opening her other hand under her nose.*]

Here. For while I'm gone.

[HELEN *sniffs, reaches, and pops something into her mouth, while* KATE *speaks a bit guiltily.*]

I don't think one peppermint drop will spoil your supper.

[*She gives* HELEN *a quick kiss, evades her*

hands, and hurries downstairs again. Meanwhile CAPTAIN KELLER *has entered the yard from around the rear of the house, newspaper under arm, cleaning off and munching on some radishes; he sees* JAMES *lounging at the porch post.*]

**KELLER.** Jimmie?

**JAMES.** [*Unmoving*] Sir?

**KELLER.** [*Eyes him*] You don't look dressed for anything useful, boy.

**JAMES.** I'm not. It's for Miss Sullivan.

**KELLER.** Needn't keep holding up that porch, we have wooden posts for that. I asked you to see that those strawberry plants were moved this evening.

**JAMES.** I'm moving your—Mrs. Keller, instead. To the station.

**KELLER.** [*Heavily*] Mrs. Keller. Must you always speak of her as though you haven't met the lady?

[KATE *comes out on the porch, and* JAMES *inclines his head.*]

**JAMES.** [*Ironic*] Mother.

[*He starts off the porch, but sidesteps* KELLER'S *glare like a blow.*]

I said mother!

**KATE.** Captain.

**KELLER.** Evening, my dear.

**KATE.** We're off to meet the train, Captain. Supper will be a trifle delayed tonight.

**KELLER.** What, again?

**KATE.** [*Backing out*] With your permission, Captain?

[*And they are gone.* KELLER *watches them offstage, morosely.*]

[*Upstairs* HELEN *meanwhile has groped for her mother, touched her cheek in a mean-*

*The Miracle Worker* 263

**33 Discussion** How do you think Helen knows that something unusual is happening?

**34 Discussion** Why does Helen want to take off Kate's bonnet? What does she realize?

**35 Critical Thinking and Reading** Compare and contrast James with Keller. Why do you think there is so much tension between them?

36 **Discussion** How has Helen worked out a language of her own?

37 **Discussion** What does this speech reveal about Keller?

38 **Discussion** Why do you think that people constantly give Helen snacks? What does this practice suggest about their attitude toward her?

39 **Discussion** How does James seem to feel about Annie? Why do you think he feels this way?

36 *ingful gesture, waited, touched her cheek, waited, then found the open door, and made her way down. Now she comes into the family room, touches her cheek again;* VINEY *regards her.*]

**VINEY.** What you want, honey, your momma?

[HELEN *touches her cheek again.* VINEY *goes to the sideboard, gets a tea-cake, gives it into* HELEN's *hand;* HELEN *pops it into her mouth.*]

Guess one little tea-cake ain't gone ruin your appetite.

[*She turns* HELEN *toward the door.* HELEN *wanders out onto the porch, as* KELLER *comes up the steps. Her hands encounter him, and she touches her cheek again, waits.*]

**KELLER.** She's gone.

[*He is awkward with her; when he puts his hand on her head, she pulls away.* KELLER *stands regarding her, heavily.*]

37 She's gone, my son and I don't get along, you don't know I'm your father, no one likes me, and supper's delayed.

[HELEN *touches her cheek, waits.* KELLER *fishes in his pocket.*]

38 Here. I brought you some stick candy, one nibble of sweets can't do any harm.

[*He gives her a large stick candy;* HELEN *falls to it.* VINEY *peers out the window.*]

**VINEY.** [*Reproachfully*] Cap'n Keller, now how'm I gone get her to eat her supper you fill her up with that trash?

**KELLER.** [*Roars*] Tend to your work!

[VINEY *beats a rapid retreat.* KELLER *thinks better of it, and tries to get the candy away from* HELEN, *but* HELEN *hangs on to it; and when* KELLER *pulls, she gives his leg a kick.* KELLER *hops about,* HELEN *takes ref-*

*264 Drama*

*uge with the candy down behind the pump, and* KELLER *then irately flings his newspaper on the porch floor, stamps into the house past* VINEY *and disappears.*

*The lights half dim on the homestead, where* VINEY *and* HELEN *going about their business soon find their way off. Meanwhile, the railroad sounds off left have mounted in a crescendo to a climax typical of a depot at arrival time, the lights come up on stage left, and we see a suggestion of a station. Here* ANNIE *in her smoked glasses and disarrayed by travel is waiting with her suitcase, while* JAMES *walks to meet her; she has a battered paper-bound book, which is a Perkins report,[4] under her arm.*]

**JAMES.** [*Coolly*] Miss Sullivan?

**ANNIE.** [*cheerily*] Here! At last, I've been on trains so many days I thought they must be backing up every time I dozed off—

**JAMES.** I'm James Keller.

**ANNIE.** James?

[*The name stops her.*]

I had a brother Jimmie. Are you Helen's?

**JAMES.** I'm only half a brother. You're to be her governess?

39 **ANNIE.** [*Lightly*] Well. Try!

**JAMES.** [*Eying her*] You look like half a governess.

[KATE *enters.* ANNIE *stands moveless, while* JAMES *takes her suitcase.* KATE's *gaze on her is doubtful, troubled.*]

Mrs. Keller, Miss Sullivan.

[KATE *takes her hand.*]

---

**4. Perkins report:** One of the annual reports by Dr. Samuel G. Howe, founder of the Perkins Institution, describing his methods for teaching blind and deaf children.

**KATE.** [*Simply*] We've met every train for two days.

[ANNIE *looks at* KATE'S *face, and her good humor comes back.*]

**ANNIE.** I changed trains every time they stopped, the man who sold me that ticket ought to be tied to the tracks—

**JAMES.** You have a trunk, Miss Sullivan?

**ANNIE.** Yes.

[*She passes* JAMES *a claim check, and he bears the suitcase out behind them.* ANNIE *holds the battered book.* KATE *is studying her face, and* ANNIE *returns the gaze; this is a mutual appraisal, southern gentlewoman and working-class Irish girl, and* ANNIE *is not quite comfortable under it.*]

You didn't bring Helen, I was hoping you would.

**KATE.** No, she's home.

[*A pause.* ANNIE *tries to make ladylike small talk, though her energy now and then erupts; she catches herself up whenever she hears it.*]

**ANNIE.** You—live far from town, Mrs. Keller?

**KATE.** Only a mile.

**ANNIE.** Well. I suppose I can wait one more mile. But don't be surprised if I get out to push the horse!

**KATE.** Helen's waiting for you, too. There's been such a bustle in the house, she expects something, heaven knows what.

[*Now she voices part of her doubt, not as such, but* ANNIE *understands it.*]

I expected—a desiccated[5] spinster. You're very young.

**ANNIE.** [*Resolutely*] Oh, you should have

---

5. **desiccated** (des′ i kāt′ id): Dried up.

seen me when I left Boston. I got much older on this trip.

**KATE.** I mean, to teach anyone as difficult as Helen.

**ANNIE.** I mean to try. They can't put you in jail for trying!

**KATE.** Is it possible, even? To teach a deaf-blind child *half* of what an ordinary child learns—has that ever been done?

**ANNIE.** Half?

**KATE.** A tenth.

**ANNIE.** [*Reluctantly*] No.

[KATE'S *face loses its remaining hope, still appraising her youth.*]

Dr. Howe did wonders, but—an ordinary child? No, never. But then I thought when I was going over his reports—

[*She indicates the one in her hand.*]

—he never treated them like ordinary children. More like—eggs everyone was afraid would break.

**KATE.** [*A pause*] May I ask how old you are?

**ANNIE.** Well, I'm not in my teens, you know! I'm twenty.

**KATE.** All of twenty.

[ANNIE *takes the bull by the horns, valiantly.*]

**ANNIE.** Mrs. Keller, don't lose heart just because I'm not on my last legs. I have three big advantages over Dr. Howe that money couldn't buy for you. One is his work behind me, I've read every word he wrote about it and he wasn't exactly what you'd call a man of few words. Another is to *be* young, why, I've got energy to do anything. The third is, I've been blind.

[*But it costs her something to say this.*]

**40 Discussion** Is Annie eager to meet Helen? How do you know?

**41 Discussion** Why is it hard for Annie to tell Kate that she has been blind?

40

41

**Discussion** Why do you think Kate is surprised by Annie's answer?

**Literary Focus** Consider telling students that the main conflict in this drama occurs between the protagonist and the antagonist; however, conflicts also occur *within* Annie Sullivan, the protagonist. Ask them what these lines reveal about Annie's divided feelings.

**Literary Focus** You might want to tell students that playwrights sometimes use props—movable articles that are part of the setting—to reveal a relationship between characters. Since Helen cannot speak, this device is especially important in *The Miracle Worker*. Ask students to follow the action involving the suitcase and consider what this action suggests about the developing relationship between Annie and Helen.

**KATE.** [*Quietly*] Advantages.

**ANNIE.** [*Wry*] Well, some have the luck of the Irish, some do not.

[KATE *smiles; she likes her.*]

**KATE.** What will you try to teach her first?

**ANNIE.** First, last, and—in between, language.

**KATE.** Language.

**ANNIE.** Language is to the mind more than light is to the eye. Dr. Howe said that.

**KATE.** Language.

[*She shakes her head.*]

We can't get through to teach her to sit still. You *are* young, despite your years, to have such—confidence. Do you, inside?

[ANNIE *studies her face; she likes her, too.*]

**ANNIE.** No, to tell you the truth I'm as shaky inside as a baby's rattle!

[*They smile at each other, and* KATE *pats her hand.*]

**KATE.** Don't be.

[JAMES *returns to usher them off.*]

We'll do all we can to help, and to make you feel at home. Don't think of us as strangers, Miss Annie.

**ANNIE.** [*Cheerily*] Oh, strangers aren't so strange to me. I've known them all my life!

[KATE *smiles again,* ANNIE *smiles back, and they precede* JAMES *offstage.*

The lights dim on them, having simultaneously risen full on the house; VINEY *has already entered the family room, taken a water pitcher, and come out and down to the pump. She pumps real water. As she looks offstage, we hear the clop of hoofs, a carriage stopping, and voices.*]

**VINEY.** Cap'n Keller! Cap'n Keller, they comin'!

[*She goes back into the house, as* KELLER *comes out on the porch to gaze.*]

She sure 'nuff came, Cap'n.

[KELLER *descends, and crosses toward the carriage; this conversation begins offstage and moves on.*]

**KELLER.** [*Very courtly*] Welcome to Ivy Green, Miss Sullivan. I take it you are Miss Sullivan—

**KATE.** My husband, Miss Annie, Captain Keller.

**ANNIE.** [*Her best behavior*] Captain, how do you do.

**KELLER.** A pleasure to see you, at last. I trust you had an agreeable journey?

**ANNIE.** Oh, I had several! When did this country get so big?

**JAMES.** Where would you like the trunk, father?

**KELLER.** Where Miss Sullivan can get at it, I imagine.

**ANNIE.** Yes, please. Where's Helen?

**KELLER.** In the hall, Jimmie—

**KATE.** We've put you in the upstairs corner room, Miss Annie, if there's any breeze at all this summer, you'll feel it—

[*In the house the setter* BELLE *flees into the family room, pursued by* HELEN *with groping hands; the dog doubles back out the same door, and* HELEN *still groping for her makes her way out to the porch; she is messy, her hair tumbled, her pinafore now ripped, her shoelaces untied.* KELLER *acquires the suitcase, and* ANNIE *gets her hands on it too, though still endeavoring to*] *live up to the general air of propertied manners.[6]*]

**KELLER.** *And* the suitcase—

**ANNIE.** [*Pleasantly*] I'll take the suitcase, thanks.

**KELLER.** Not at all, I have it, Miss Sullivan.

**ANNIE.** I'd like it.

**KELLER.** [*Gallantly*] I couldn't think of it, Miss Sullivan. You'll find in the south we—

**ANNIE.** Let me.

**KELLER.** —view women as the flowers of civiliza—

**ANNIE.** [*Impatiently*] I've got something in it for Helen!

[*She tugs it free;* KELLER *stares.*]

Thank you. When do I see her?

**KATE.** There. There is Helen.

[ANNIE *turns, and sees* HELEN *on the porch. A moment of silence. Then* ANNIE *begins across the yard to her, lugging her suitcase.*]

**KELLER.** [*Sotto voce[7]*] Katie—

[KATE *silences him with a hand on his arm. When* ANNIE *finally reaches the porch steps she stops, contemplating* HELEN *for a last moment before entering her world. Then she drops the suitcase on the porch with intentional heaviness,* HELEN *starts with the jar, and comes to grope over it.* ANNIE *puts forth her hand, and touches* HELEN'S. HELEN *at once grasps it, and commences to explore it, like reading a face. She moves her hand on to* ANNIE'S *forearm, and dress; and* ANNIE *brings her face within reach of* HELEN'S

---

**6. the general air of propertied manners:** Atmosphere of refinement and wealth.

**7. sotto voce** (sät′ ō vō′ chē): In a low voice.

*fingers, which travel over it, quite without timidity, until they encounter and push aside the smoked glasses.* ANNIE'S *gaze is grave, unpitying, very attentive. She puts her hands on* HELEN'S *arms, but* HELEN *at once pulls away, and they confront each other with a distance between. Then* HELEN *returns to the suitcase, tries to open it, cannot.* ANNIE *points* HELEN'S *hand overhead.* HELEN *pulls away, tries to open the suitcase again;* ANNIE *points her hand overhead again.* HELEN *points overhead, a question, and* ANNIE, *drawing* HELEN'S *hand to her own face, nods.* HELEN *now begins tugging the suitcase toward the door; when* ANNIE *tries to take it from her, she fights her off and backs through the doorway with it.* ANNIE *stands a moment, then follows her in, and together they get the suitcase up the steps into* ANNIE'S *room.*]

**KATE.** Well?

**KELLER.** She's very rough, Katie.

**KATE.** I like her, Captain.

**KELLER.** Certainly rear a peculiar kind of young woman in the north. How old is she?

**KATE.** [*Vaguely*] Ohh— Well, she's not in her teens, you know.

**KELLER.** She's only a child. What's her family like, shipping her off alone this far?

**KATE.** I couldn't learn. She's very close-mouthed about some things.

**KELLER.** Why does she wear those glasses? I like to see a person's eyes when I talk to—

**KATE.** For the sun. She was blind.

**KELLER.** Blind.

**KATE.** She's had nine operations on her eyes. One just before she left.

**KELLER.** Blind, good heavens, do they expect one blind child to teach another? Has she

**45 Discussion** How do Keller's notions about women differ from Annie's? To what extent do their viewpoints reflect regional differences between the North and South?

45

*The Miracle Worker* 267

46 **Discussion** If you were audition-ing young actresses for Helen's part, what qualities would you look for?

47 **Enrichment** You might want to explain to students that the finger alphabet is a system in which each letter is represented by a different position of the fingers. To communicate, a person forms the letters in another person's palm.

Deaf people who are sighted can also communicate by sign-ing—making hand signals that stand for letters and ideas. Ask students if they have seen speeches on television being translated into sign language.

Students may also be inter-ested to learn that scientists have tried to teach chimpanzees the sign language of the deaf, with some success.

experience at least, how long did she teach there?

**KATE.** She was a pupil.

**KELLER.** [*Heavily*] Katie, Katie. This is her first position?

**KATE.** [*Bright voice*] She was valedictorian—

**KELLER.** Here's a houseful of grownups can't cope with the child, how can an inexperi-enced half-blind Yankee schoolgirl manage her?

[JAMES *moves in with the trunk on his shoulder.*]

**JAMES.** [*Easily*] Great improvement. Now we have two of them to look after.

**KELLER.** You look after those strawberry plants!

[JAMES *stops with the trunk.* KELLER *turns from him without another word, and mar-ches off.*]

**JAMES.** Nothing I say is right.

**KATE.** Why say anything?

[*She calls.*]

Don't be long, Captain, we'll have supper right away—

[*She goes into the house, and through the rear door of the family room.* JAMES *trudges in with the trunk, takes it up the steps to* ANNIE'S *room, and sets it down outside the door. The lights elsewhere dim somewhat.*

Meanwhile, inside, ANNIE *has given* HELEN *a key; while* ANNIE *removes her bonnet,* HELEN *unlocks and opens the suitcase. The first thing she pulls out is a voluminous shawl. She fingers it until she perceives what it is; then she wraps it around her, and acquiring* ANNIE'S *bonnet and smoked glasses as well, dons the lot: the shawl swamps her, and the bonnet settles down*

upon the glasses, but she stands before a mirror cocking her head to one side, then to the other, in a mockery of adult action. AN-NIE *is amused, and talks to her as one might to a kitten, with no trace of company manners.*]

**ANNIE.** All the trouble I went to and that's how I look?

[HELEN *then comes back to the suitcase, gropes for more, lifts out a pair of female drawers.*]

Oh, no. Not the drawers!

[*But* HELEN *discarding them comes to the elegant doll. Her fingers explore its fea-tures, and when she raises it and finds its eyes open and close, she is at first startled, then delighted. She picks it up, taps its head vigorously, taps her own chest, and nods questioningly.* ANNIE *takes her finger, points it to the doll, points it to* HELEN, *and touching it to her own face, also nods.* HELEN *sits back on her heels, clasps the doll to herself, and rocks it.* ANNIE *studies her, still in bonnet and smoked glasses like a caricature of herself, and addresses her humorously.*]

All right, Miss O'Sullivan. Let's begin with doll.

[*She takes* HELEN'S *hand; in her palm* AN-NIE'S *forefinger points, thumb holding her other fingers clenched.*]

D.

[*Her thumb next holds all her fingers clenched, touching* HELEN'S *palm.*]

O.

[*Her thumb and forefinger extend.*]

L.

[*Same contact repeated.*]

L.

48 **Discussion** What is James's opinion of the plan to teach Helen?

49 **Discussion** How does Annie view Helen differently from the Keller family?

[*She puts* HELEN's *hand to the doll.*]

Doll.

**JAMES.** You spell pretty well.

[ANNIE *in one hurried move gets the drawers swiftly back into the suitcase, the lid banged shut, and her head turned, to see* JAMES *leaning in the doorway.*]

Finding out if she's ticklish? She is.

[ANNIE *regards him stonily, but* HELEN *after a scowling moment tugs at her hand again, imperious.* ANNIE *repeats the letters, and* HELEN *interrupts her fingers in the middle, feeling each of them, puzzled.* ANNIE *touches* HELEN's *hand to the doll, and begins spelling into it again.*]

**JAMES.** What is it, a game?

**ANNIE.** [*Curtly*] An alphabet.

**JAMES.** Alphabet?

**ANNIE.** For the deaf.

[HELEN *now repeats the finger movements in air, exactly, her head cocked to her own hand, and* ANNIE's *eyes suddenly gleam.*]

Ho. How *bright* she is!

**JAMES.** You think she knows what she's doing?

[*He takes* HELEN's *hand, to throw a meaningless gesture into it; she repeats this one too.*]

*The Miracle Worker* 269

**50** **Literary Focus** How do James's comments add to the drama of the encounter between Annie and Helen?

**51** **Clarification** It is thought that Spanish monks invented the finger alphabet so they could communicate without speaking, thereby keeping their vows of silence.

**52** **Discussion** Why does Annie remove the cake?

She imitates everything, she's a monkey.

**ANNIE.** [*Very pleased*] Yes, she's a bright little monkey, all right.

[*She takes the doll from* HELEN, *and reaches for her hand;* HELEN *instantly grabs the doll back.* ANNIE *takes it again, and* HELEN's *hand next, but* HELEN *is incensed now; when* ANNIE *draws her hand to her face to shake her head no, then tries to spell to her,* HELEN *slaps at* ANNIE's *face.* ANNIE *grasps* HELEN *by both arms, and swings her into a chair, holding her pinned there, kicking, while glasses, doll, bonnet fly in various directions.* JAMES *laughs.*]

**JAMES.** She wants her doll back.

**ANNIE.** When she spells it.

**JAMES.** Spell, she doesn't know the thing has a name, even.

**ANNIE.** Of course not, who expects her to, now? All I want is her fingers to learn the letters.

**JAMES.** Won't mean anything to her.

[ANNIE *gives him a look. She then tries to form* HELEN's *fingers into the letters, but* HELEN *swings a haymaker instead, which* ANNIE *barely ducks, at once pinning her down again.*]

Doesn't like that alphabet, Miss Sullivan. You invent it yourself?

[HELEN *is now in a rage, fighting tooth and nail to get out of the chair, and* ANNIE *answers while struggling and dodging her kicks.*]

**ANNIE.** Spanish monks under a—vow of silence. Which I wish *you'd* take!

[*And suddenly releasing* HELEN's *hands, she comes and shuts the door in* JAMES's *face.* HELEN *drops to the floor, groping around for the doll.* ANNIE *looks around*

desperately, sees her purse on the bed, rummages in it, and comes up with a battered piece of cake wrapped in newspaper; with her foot she moves the doll deftly out of the way of* HELEN's *groping, and going on her knee she lets* HELEN *smell the cake. When* HELEN *grabs for it,* ANNIE *removes the cake and spells quickly into the reaching hand.*]

Cake. From Washington up north, it's the best I can do.

[HELEN's *hand waits, baffled.* ANNIE *repeats it.*]

C, a, k, e. Do what my fingers do, never mind what it means.

[*She touches the cake briefly to* HELEN's *nose, pats her hand, presents her own hand.* HELEN *spells the letters rapidly back.* ANNIE *pats her hand enthusiastically, and gives her the cake;* HELEN *crams it into her mouth with both hands.* ANNIE *watches her, with humor.*]

Get it down fast, maybe I'll steal that back too. Now.

[*She takes the doll, touches it to* HELEN's *nose, and spells again into her hand.*]

D, o, l, l. Think it over.

[HELEN *thinks it over, while* ANNIE *presents her own hand. Then* HELEN *spells three letters.* ANNIE *waits a second, then completes the word for* HELEN *in her palm.*]

L.

[*She hands over the doll, and* HELEN *gets a good grip on its leg.*]

Imitate now, understand later. End of the first les—

[*She never finishes, because* HELEN *swings the doll with a furious energy, it hits* ANNIE *squarely in the face, and she falls back*

270    Drama

*with a cry of pain, her knuckles up to her mouth.* HELEN *waits, tensed for further combat. When* ANNIE *lowers her knuckles she looks at blood on them; she works her lips, gets to her feet, finds the mirror, and bares her teeth at herself. Now she is furious herself.*]

You little wretch, no one's taught you any manners? I'll—

[*But rounding from the mirror she sees the door slam,* HELEN *and the doll are on the outside, and* HELEN *is turning the key in the lock.* ANNIE *darts over, to pull the knob; the door is locked fast. She yanks it again.*]

Helen! Helen, let me out of—

[*She bats her brow at the folly of speaking, but* JAMES, *now downstairs, hears her and turns to see* HELEN *with the key and doll groping her way down the steps;* JAMES *takes in the whole situation, makes a move to intercept* HELEN, *but then changes his mind, lets her pass, and amusedly follows her out onto the porch. Upstairs* ANNIE *meanwhile rattles the knob, kneels, peers through the keyhole, gets up. She goes to the window, looks down, frowns.* JAMES *from the yard sings gaily up to her:*]

**JAMES.**
  Buffalo girl, are you coming out tonight,
  Coming out tonight,
  Coming out—

[*He drifts back into the house.* ANNIE *takes a handkerchief, nurses her mouth, stands in the middle of the room, staring at door and window in turn, and so catches sight of herself in the mirror, her cheek scratched, her hair disheveled, her handkerchief bloody, her face disgusted with herself. She addresses the mirror, with some irony.*]

**ANNIE.** Don't worry. They'll find you, you're not lost. Only out of place.

[*But she coughs, spits something into her palm, and stares at it, outraged.*]

And toothless.

[*She winces.*]

Oo! It hurts.

[*She pours some water into the basin, dips the handkerchief, and presses it to her mouth. Standing there, bent over the basin in pain—with the rest of the set dim and unreal, and the lights upon her taking on the subtle color of the past—she hears again, as do we, the faraway voices, and slowly she lifts her head to them; the boy's voice is the same, the others are cracked old crones in a nightmare, and perhaps we see their shadows.*]

**BOY'S VOICE.** It hurts. Annie, it hurts.

**FIRST CRONE'S VOICE.** Keep that brat shut up, can't you, girlie, how's a body to get any sleep in this damn ward?

**BOY'S VOICE.** It hurts. It hurts.

**SECOND CRONE'S VOICE.** Shut up, you!

**BOY'S VOICE.** Annie, when are we goin' home? You promised!

**ANNIE.** Jimmie—

**BOY'S VOICE.** Forever and ever, you said forever—

[ANNIE *drops the handkerchief, averts to the window, and is arrested there by the next cry.*]

Annie? Annie, you there? Annie! It *hurts!*

**THIRD CRONE'S VOICE.** Grab him, he's fallin'!

**BOY'S VOICE.** *Annie!*

**DOCTOR'S VOICE.** [*A pause, slowly*] Little girl.

53 **Literary Focus** How does James's action, or lack of action, heighten conflict?

54 **Discussion** Why do you think Annie remembers the past at this particular moment?

Little girl, I must tell you your brother will be going on a—

[But ANNIE *claps her hands to her ears, to shut this out; there is instant silence.*

*As the lights bring the other areas in again,* JAMES *goes to the steps to listen for any sound from upstairs.* KELLER *re-entering from left crosses toward the house; he passes* HELEN *on route to her retreat under the pump.* KATE *re-enters the rear door of the family room, with flowers for the table.*]

**KATE.** Supper is ready, Jimmie, will you call your father?

**JAMES.** Certainly.

[*But he calls up the stairs, for* ANNIE'S *benefit.*]

Father! Supper!

**KELLER.** [*At the door*] No need to shout. I've been cooling my heels for an hour. Sit down.

**JAMES.** Certainly.

**KELLER.** Viney!

[VINEY *backs in with a roast, while they get settled around the table.*]

**VINEY.** Yes, Cap'n, right here.

**KATE.** Mildred went directly to sleep, Viney?

**VINEY.** Oh yes, that babe's a angel.

**KATE.** And Helen had a good supper?

**VINEY.** [*Vaguely*] I dunno, Miss Kate, somehow she didn't have much of a appetite tonight—

55 **KATE.** [*A bit guilty*] Oh. Dear.

**KELLER.** [*Hastily*] Well, now. Couldn't say the same for my part, I'm famished. Katie, your plate.

**KATE.** [*Looking*] But where is Miss Annie?

[*A silence*]

**JAMES.** [*Pleasantly*] In her room.

**KELLER.** In her room? Doesn't she know hot food must be eaten hot? Go bring her down at once, Jimmie.

**JAMES.** [*Rises*] Certainly. I'll get a ladder.

**KELLER.** [*Stares*] What?

**JAMES.** I'll need a ladder. Shouldn't take me long.

**KATE.** [*Stares*] What shouldn't take you—

**KELLER.** Jimmie, do as I say! Go upstairs at once and tell Miss Sullivan supper is getting cold—

**JAMES.** She's locked in her room.

**KELLER.** Locked in her—

**KATE.** What on earth are you—

**JAMES.** Helen locked her in and made off with the key.

**KATE.** [*Rising*] And you sit here and say nothing?

**JAMES.** Well, everyone's been telling me not to say anything.

[*He goes serenely out and across the yard, whistling.* KELLER *thrusting up from his chair makes for the stairs.*]

**KATE.** Viney, look out in back for Helen. See if she has that key.

**VINEY.** Yes, Miss Kate.

[VINEY *goes out the rear door.*]

**KELLER.** [*Calling down*] She's out by the pump!

[KATE *goes out on the porch after* HELEN, *while* KELLER *knocks on* ANNIE'S *door, then rattles the knob, imperiously.*]

Miss Sullivan! Are you in there?

**ANNIE.** Oh, I'm in here, all right.

**KELLER.** Is there no key on your side?

**ANNIE.** [*With some asperity*] Well, if there was a key in here, *I* wouldn't be in here. Helen took it, the only thing on my side is me.

**KELLER.** Miss Sullivan, I—

[*He tries, but cannot hold it back.*]

Not in the house ten minutes, I don't see *how* you managed it!

[*He stomps downstairs again, while* ANNIE *mutters to herself.*]

56 **ANNIE.** And even I'm not on my side.

**KELLER.** [*Roaring*] Viney!

**VINEY.** [*Reappearing*] Yes, Cap'n?

**KELLER.** Put that meat back in the oven!

[VINEY *bears the roast off again, while* KELLER *strides out onto the porch.* KATE *is with* HELEN *at the pump, opening her hands.*]

**KATE.** She has no key.

**KELLER.** Nonsense, she must have the key. Have you searched in her pockets?

**KATE.** Yes. She doesn't have it.

**KELLER.** Katie, she must have the key.

**KATE.** Would you prefer to search her yourself, Captain?

**KELLER.** No, I would not prefer to search her! She almost took my kneecap off this evening, when I tried merely to—

[JAMES *reappears carrying a long ladder, with* PERCY *running after him to be in on things.*]

Take that ladder back!

**JAMES.** Certainly.

[*He turns around with it.* MARTHA *comes skipping around the upstage corner of the house to be in on things, accompanied by the setter* BELLE.]

**KATE.** She could have hidden the key.

**KELLER.** Where?

**KATE.** Anywhere. Under a stone. In the flower beds. In the grass—

**KELLER.** Well, I can't plow up the entire grounds to find a missing key! Jimmie!

**JAMES.** Sir?

**KELLER.** Bring me a ladder!

**JAMES.** Certainly.

[VINEY *comes around the downstage side of the house to be in on things; she has* MILDRED *over her shoulder, bleating.* KELLER *places the ladder against* ANNIE'S *window and mounts.* ANNIE *meanwhile is running about making herself presentable, washing the blood off her mouth, straightening her clothes, tidying her hair. Another Negro servant enters to gaze in wonder, increasing the gathering ring of spectators.*]

**KATE.** [*Sharply*] What is Mildred doing up?

**VINEY.** Cap'n woke her, ma'am, all that hollerin'.

**KELLER.** Miss Sullivan!

[ANNIE *comes to the window, with as much air of gracious normality as she can manage;* KELLER *is at the window.*]

**ANNIE.** [*Brightly*] Yes, Captain Keller?

**KELLER.** Come out!

**ANNIE.** I don't see how I can. There isn't room.

**KELLER.** I intend to carry you. Climb onto my shoulder and hold tight.

**ANNIE.** Oh, no. It's—very chivalrous of you, but I'd really prefer to—

56 **Discussion** What does Annie mean?

*The Miracle Worker* 273

**57** **Discussion** What might Helen be thinking as she does these things?

**58** **Literary Focus** You might want to tell students that the two characters left on stage are the protagonist and the main antagonist. Ask students why the playwright would want to focus on these two as the first act ends. Then ask them which character seems to have the upper hand at this point.

**59** **Reading Strategy** Ask students to predict whether Annie will be able to teach Helen.

**Reader's Response** If you were Annie, how would you have handled Helen's tantrums and seeming unwillingness to learn? Explain.

## Closure and Extension

### ANSWERS TO THINKING ABOUT THE SELECTION
*Recalling*

1. She is like a wild, untrained animal—violent, seemingly unteachable, and undisciplined.
2. As she gropes around, her hands seem to be very sensitive and able to recognize individuals or things. She has also developed a kind of sign language in which touching her cheek means "mother."
3. Mrs. Keller is willing to continue her search for help for Helen, regardless of how often the news is heartbreaking. Captain Keller

---

274

---

**KELLER.** Miss Sullivan, follow instructions! I will not have you also tumbling out of our windows.

[ANNIE *obeys, with some misgivings.*]

I hope this is not a sample of what we may expect from you. In the way of simplifying the work of looking after Helen.

**ANNIE.** Captain Keller, I'm perfectly able to go down a ladder under my own—

**KELLER.** I doubt it, Miss Sullivan. Simply hold onto my neck.

[*He begins down with her, while the spectators stand in a wide and somewhat awe-stricken circle, watching.* KELLER *half-misses a rung, and* ANNIE *grabs at his whiskers.*]

My *neck*, Miss Sullivan!

**ANNIE.** I'm sorry to inconvenience you this way—

**KELLER.** No inconvenience, other than having that door taken down and the lock replaced, if we fail to find that key.

**ANNIE.** Oh, I'll look everywhere for it.

**KELLER.** Thank you. Do not look in any rooms that can be locked. There.

[*He stands her on the ground.* JAMES *applauds.*]

**ANNIE.** Thank you very much.

[*She smooths her skirt, looking as composed and ladylike as possible.* KELLER *stares around at the spectators.*]

**KELLER.** Go, go, back to your work. What are you looking at here? There's nothing here to look at.

[*They break up, move off.*]

Now would it be possible for us to have supper, like other people?

*274   Drama*

---

[*He marches into the house.*]

**KATE.** Viney, serve supper. I'll put Mildred to sleep.

[*They all go in.* JAMES *is the last to leave, murmuring to* ANNIE *with a gesture.*]

**JAMES.** Might as well leave the l, a, d, d, e, r, hm?

[ANNIE *ignores him, looking at* HELEN; JAMES *goes in too. Imperceptibly the lights commence to narrow down.* ANNIE *and* HELEN *are now alone in the yard,* HELEN *seated at the pump, where she has been oblivious to it all, a battered little savage, playing with the doll in a picture of innocent contentment.* ANNIE *comes near, leans against the house, and taking off her smoked glasses, studies her, not without awe. Presently* HELEN *rises, gropes around to see if anyone is present;* ANNIE *evades her hand, and when* HELEN *is satisfied she is alone, the key suddenly protrudes out of her mouth. She takes it in her fingers, stands thinking, gropes to the pump, lifts a loose board, drops the key into the well, and hugs herself gleefully.* ANNIE *stares. But after a moment she shakes her head to herself, she cannot keep the smile from her lips.*]     57

**ANNIE.** You *devil.*

[*Her tone is one of great respect, humor, and acceptance of challenge.*]     58

You think I'm so easily gotten rid of? You have a thing or two to learn, first. I have nothing else to do.

[*She goes up the steps to the porch, but turns for a final word, almost of warning.*]     59

And nowhere to go.

[*And presently she moves into the house to the others, as the lights dim down and out, except for the small circle upon* HELEN *solitary at the pump, which ends the act.*]

---

feels that they have exhausted every resource and that there is no point in being disappointed again.
4. Annie Sullivan was a young orphan, nearly blind, who grew up in a poorhouse. After her brother died, she went to the Perkins School for the Blind. Several operations restored some of her sight. She is a strong person, obstinate, not willing to give up. But she is also haunted by her past and feels guilty because she feels she let her brother down.

5. She feels Helen must learn language. There is no limit to what a person can learn if he or she has a knowledge of language. She wants to teach Helen to associate words with things through the use of finger language.

*Interpreting*

6. Suggested Response: Annie's persistence, strength, obstinacy, and willingness to accept a challenge will be important. Annie has

been blind herself so she can sympathize with some of Helen's problems.
7. Suggested Response: Annie felt responsible for her brother, but she could not save him. She might feel that she is getting a second chance to save someone.
8. Suggested Response: The family is continually disrupted by Helen and her unruly behavior. No meal is ever peaceful, and there is always the danger of violence, as when Helen attacks Martha with the scissors.

## THINKING ABOUT THE SELECTION

### Recalling

1. What is Helen like at age six when Annie comes to teach her?
2. Explain how Helen uses her hands in an effort to establish connections with others.
3. How do Captain and Mrs. Keller differ in their views of what to do for Helen?
4. Describe Annie Sullivan's background, personality, and physical condition.
5. What does Annie consider the most important thing to teach Helen? How does she plan to teach this to Helen?

### Interpreting

6. Which of Annie's qualities are likely to play an important role in her relationship with Helen? What advantages does Annie have?
7. What is the link between Annie's memories of her brother and her present situation?
8. What effect has Helen had on the life of her family?

### Applying

9. Annie says, "Language is to the mind more than light is to the eye." What does her remark imply about the importance of language?

## ANALYZING LITERATURE

### Recognizing Protagonist and Antagonist

The **protagonist** is the central character of a play. The **antagonist** is the character or characters in conflict with him or her. As you read a play, you will probably be wondering how events will turn out for the protagonist. Will he or she meet with success or failure?

1. Is Annie or Helen the protagonist of the play? Give reasons for your opinion.
2. What problems do you expect the protagonist to encounter?

## CRITICAL THINKING AND READING

### Comparing and Contrasting Characters

**Comparing** and **contrasting** characters means noting the similarities and differences between them. Noticing these similarities and differences will increase your understanding of the characters and of what the playwright may be suggesting about life.

Compare and contrast the characters in each of the following pairs.
1. Kate and Captain Keller
2. Annie and Helen
3. Annie and Captain Keller

## UNDERSTANDING LANGUAGE

### Using Specific Words

**Specific words** are more concrete, definite, and precise than general words. For example, the physician attending Helen is described as "an elderly DOCTOR, stethoscope at neck, thermometer in fingers. . . ." Gibson could have described him as "an elderly doctor with his instruments." However, the specific words "stethoscope at neck, thermometer in fingers" give a clearer picture.

Rewrite each of the following sentences, replacing general words with more specific ones.
1. The police are pursuing an adult person driving a large vehicle.
2. After finishing school, a relative of mine became an employee of a well-known company.

## THINKING AND WRITING

### Writing About Characters

Imagine that you have been visiting the Kellers. Write a letter to a friend in which you give specific descriptions of the Keller family—Captain Keller, Mrs. Keller, James, and Helen—as you have observed them. First decide what words or actions of the characters illustrate their traits. Then write a short paragraph about each person. When you revise your letter, ask "How can I make this description more clear, vivid, and exact?"

*The Miracle Worker*  275

about Helen's ability to learn. Both are unwilling to discipline Helen.
2. Suggested Response: Annie and Helen are much alike. Both are strong, obstinate, and intelligent. Also, both have been physically challenged. However, Annie has overcome her handicap, while Helen is still frustrated by her inability to communicate. Annie is disciplined, but Helen is wild.
3. Both Annie and Keller are strong, stubborn characters. She is a woman used to taking care of herself, while he is a southern gentleman used to taking care of women. They disagree about the best way to handle Helen.

### ANSWERS TO UNDERSTANDING LANGUAGE

1. Answers will differ. Suggested Response: The police are pursuing a tall, thin man driving a blue Cadillac.
2. Students' answers will differ. Suggested Response: After finishing school, my older brother became a computer programmer for IBM.

### THINKING AND WRITING

For help with this assignment students may refer to Lesson 9, "Writing About Character," in the Handbook of Writing About Literature.

### Publishing Student Writing

Collect the letters in a notebook. At the close of the play, have students read and reconsider these opinions.

---

*Applying*

9. Students' answers will differ. Students may respond that without language we cannot know the world or make sense of it—we are not fully human. That is why language is more important for the mind than light is for the eye.

**Challenge** Helen was born over one hundred years ago. If she were a child today, what opportunities might she have for training and education?

### ANSWERS TO ANALYZING LITERATURE

1. Suggested Response: Annie is the protagonist. The title indicates that she is the most important character. Also, she has to struggle against Helen and other members of the Keller family to accomplish her goal.
2. Students' answers will differ. They may respond that Helen will resist her efforts. Also, Keller and James do not seem to have a high opinion of her and may hinder her work. In

general, the family seems unable or unwilling to discipline Helen.

### ANSWERS TO CRITICAL THINKING AND READING

1. Suggested Response: Kate is rather young. Keller is older. It is his second marriage, her first. He makes the decisions and is protective of his wife. Kate seems to have more sympathy for others, while Keller is colder. She is supportive of Annie, while he is not optimistic

### Writing Across the Curriculum

You might have students research and report on various types of sign language. Consider informing the science and social studies departments of this assignment, so that teachers can guide students to appropriate resource materials.

**Literary Focus** You might re-mind students that the charac-ters in a play can experience internal conflicts. However, the playwright must find the means to communicate these internal conflicts to the audience. Ask students how Gibson dramatizes Annie's internal conflict.

**Look For** Call attention to the fact that the date of this play is only about twenty years after the Civil War. Aristocratic southern-ers such as Captain Keller would still have had strong feelings about the war. These feelings seem to influence his attitude to-ward Annie, a northerner.

**Writing/Prior Knowledge** Have students compare this proverb with Annie's statement that "Lan-guage is to the mind more than light is to the eye." How are their meanings alike? How do they re-late to Helen?

**Vocabulary** Have more ad-vanced students create ques-tions that elicit the meaning of these words; for example, "What word would you use to say that a person could not speak well?" "How could you describe some-one who did not show any emo-tion?" Then have students ex-change papers and answer each other's questions with the correct word.

## The Miracle Worker, Act II

**Conflict in Drama**

**Conflict** is so basic to drama that drama may be defined as the story of a conflict told primarily in dialogue and presented before an audi-ence. Conflict may be classified as external or internal. External con-flicts include those between one individual and another, between an individual and society, and between an individual and a force such as destiny or fate. An internal conflict is between an individual and him-self or herself. The character is torn by conflicting feelings or wants.

**Look For**

In Act II of *The Miracle Worker,* a number of different conflicts will be presented. Look for both external and internal ones. In particular no-tice the different conflicts that Annie Sullivan experiences. Which indi-viduals is she in conflict with? Also notice the references to the Civil War and to Civil War generals. How are these references relevant to the action of the play?

**Writing**

According to one Chinese proverb: "Give a man a fish, and you will feed him for a day. Teach a man to fish, and you will feed him for a lifetime." Freewrite about the meaning of this proverb. How does it relate to education in general?

**Vocabulary**

Knowing the following words will help you as you read Act II of *The Miracle Worker.*

**impassively** (im pas′ iv lē) *adv.*: In an unfeeling or unemo-tional manner (p. 277)

**inarticulate** (in′ är tik′ yə lit) *adj.*: Not able to speak well (p. 277)

**deferential** (def′ ə ren′ shəl) *adj.*: Very respectful (p. 279)

**wrath** (rath) *n.*: Intense anger (p. 282)

**ire** (īr) *n.*: Anger (p. 282)

**sullen** (sul′ ən) *adj.*: Showing resentment (p. 284)

---

### Objectives

1  To understand conflict in drama
2  To recognize causes and effects when reading a drama
3  To write a scene extend-ing Act II of *The Miracle Worker.*

### Support Material

**Teaching Portfolio**
Teacher Backup, p. 337
Grammar in Action Worksheets, *Using Dashes,* p. 340; *Writing Directions,* p. 342
Usage and Mechanics Work-sheet, p. 344
Vocabulary Check, p. 345
Critical Thinking and Reading Worksheet, *Recognizing Caus-es and Effects,* p. 346

Language Worksheet, *Recogniz-ing and Forming Compound Words,* p. 347
Selection Test, p. 348

## ACT II

[*It is evening.*

*The only room visible in the* KELLER *house is* ANNIE'S, *where by lamplight* ANNIE *in a shawl is at a desk writing a letter; at her bureau* HELEN *in her customary unkempt state is tucking her doll in the bottom drawer as a cradle, the contents of which she has dumped out, creating as usual a fine disorder.*

ANNIE *mutters each word as she writes her letter, slowly, her eyes close to and almost touching the page, to follow with difficulty her penwork.*]

ANNIE. "... and, nobody, here, has, attempted, to, control, her. The, greatest, problem, I, have, is, how, to, discipline, her, without, breaking, her, spirit."

[*Resolute voice*]

"But, I, shall, insist, on, reasonable, obedience, from, the, start—"

[*At which point* HELEN, *groping about on the desk, knocks over the inkwell.* ANNIE *jumps up, rescues her letter, rights the inkwell, grabs a towel to stem the spillage, and then wipes at* HELEN'S *hands;* HELEN *as always pulls free, but not until* ANNIE *first gets three letters into her palm.*]

Ink.

[HELEN *is enough interested in and puzzled by this spelling that she proffers her hand again; so* ANNIE *spells and impassively dunks it back in the spillage.*]

Ink. It has a name.

[*She wipes the hand clean, and leads* HELEN *to her bureau, where she looks for something to engage her. She finds a sewing card, with needle and thread, and going to her knees, shows* HELEN'S *hand how to connect one row of holes.*]

Down. Under. Up. And be careful of the needle—

[HELEN *gets it, and* ANNIE *rises.*]

Fine. You keep out of the ink and perhaps I can keep out of—the soup.

[*She returns to the desk, tidies it, and resumes writing her letter, bent close to the page.*]

"These, blots, are, her, handiwork. I—"

[*She is interrupted by a gasp:* HELEN *has stuck her finger, and sits sucking at it, darkly. Then with vengeful resolve she seizes her doll, and is about to dash its brains out on the floor when* ANNIE *diving catches it in one hand, which she at once shakes with hopping pain but otherwise ignores, patiently.*]

All right, let's try temperance.

[*Taking the doll, she kneels, goes through the motion of knocking its head on the floor, spells into* HELEN'S *hand:*]

Bad, girl.

[*She lets* HELEN *feel the grieved expression on her face.* HELEN *imitates it. Next she makes* HELEN *caress the doll and kiss the hurt spot and hold it gently in her arms, then spells into her hand:*]

Good, girl.

[*She lets* HELEN *feel the smile on her face.* HELEN *sits with a scowl, which suddenly clears; she pats the doll, kisses it, wreathes her face in a large artificial smile, and bears the doll to the washstand, where she carefully sits it.* ANNIE *watches, pleased.*]

Very good girl—

[*Whereupon* HELEN *elevates the pitcher and dashes it on the floor instead.* ANNIE *leaps to her feet, and stands inarticulate;* HELEN

*The Miracle Worker* 277

### Presentation

**Motivation/Prior Knowledge**
Ask students to imagine that they are Annie Sullivan. How would they teach Helen Keller? What would they stress? What rewards or punishments would they use?

**Master Teacher Note** You might remind students that Act I ends with Helen throwing a key to a bedroom door into the well. Keys are important symbols in this play. While they are used to lock someone in or out, they are also symbols of unlocking the human mind. Helen's ability to learn is locked inside her, and so far no one has found the key.

**Purpose-Setting Question**
What external conflicts does Annie face in this act? What internal conflicts does she experience?

1 **Discussion** If these descriptive scenes were removed, how would the play be different?

2 **Discussion** Is Helen usually able to find her way around without causing accidents? Why or why not?

3 **Discussion** What does Annie mean about keeping out of "the soup"?

4 **Discussion** Why does Annie continue spelling to Helen?

5 **Discussion** Why does Annie compare Helen's head to a mousetrap?

6 **Discussion** Do you think Annie is being cruel? Explain.

*calmly gropes back to sit to the sewing card and needle.*

ANNIE *manages to achieve self-control. She picks up a fragment or two of the pitcher, sees* HELEN *is puzzling over the card, and resolutely kneels to demonstrate it again. She spells into* HELEN'S *hand.*

KATE *meanwhile coming around the corner with folded sheets on her arm, halts at the doorway and watches them for a moment in silence: she is moved, but level:*]

**KATE.** [*Presently*] What are you saying to her?

[ANNIE *glancing up is a bit embarrassed, and rises from the spelling, to find her company manners.*]

**ANNIE.** Oh, I was just making conversation. Saying it was a sewing card.

**KATIE.** But does that—

[*She imitates with her fingers.*]

—mean that to her?

**ANNIE.** No. No, she won't know what spelling is till she knows what a word is.

**KATE.** Yet you keep spelling to her. Why?

**ANNIE.** [*Cheerily*] I like to hear myself talk!

**KATE.** The Captain says it's like spelling to the fence post.

**ANNIE.** [*A pause*] Does he, now.

**KATE.** Is it?

**ANNIE.** No, it's how I watch you talk to Mildred.

**KATE.** Mildred.

**ANNIE.** Any baby. Gibberish, grown-up gibberish, babytalk gibberish, do they understand one word of it to start? Somehow they begin to. If they hear it, I'm letting Helen hear it.

**KATE.** Other children are not—impaired.

**ANNIE.** Ho, there's nothing impaired in that head, it works like a mousetrap!

**KATE.** [*Smiles*] But after a child hears how many words, Miss Annie, a million?

**ANNIE.** I guess no mother's ever minded enough to count.

[*She drops her eyes to spell into* HELEN'S *hand, again indicating the card;* HELEN *spells back, and* ANNIE *is amused.*]

**KATE.** [*Too quickly*] What did she spell?

**ANNIE.** I spelt card. She spelt cake!

[*She takes in* KATE'S *quickness, and shakes her head, gently.*]

No, it's only a finger-game to her, Mrs. Keller. What she has to learn first is that things have names.

**KATE.** And when will she learn?

**ANNIE.** Maybe after a million and one words.

[*They hold each other's gaze;* KATE *then speaks quietly.*]

**KATE.** I should like to learn those letters, Miss Annie.

**ANNIE.** [*Pleased*] I'll teach you tomorrow morning. That makes only half a million each!

**KATE.** [*Then*] It's her bedtime.

[ANNIE *reaches for the sewing card,* HELEN *objects,* ANNIE *insists, and* HELEN *gets rid of* ANNIE'S *hand by jabbing it with the needle.* ANNIE *gasps, and moves to grip* HELEN'S *wrist; but* KATE *intervenes with a proffered sweet, and* HELEN *drops the card, crams the sweet into her mouth, and scrambles up to search her mother's hands for more.* ANNIE *nurses her wound, staring after the sweet.*]

I'm sorry, Miss Annie.

**ANNIE.** [*Indignantly*] Why does she get a reward? For stabbing me?

**KATE.** Well—

[*Then, tiredly*]

We catch our flies with honey, I'm afraid. We haven't the heart for much else, and so many times she simply cannot be compelled.

**ANNIE.** [*Ominous*] Yes. I'm the same way myself.

[KATE *smiles, and leads* HELEN *off around the corner.* ANNIE *alone in her room picks up things and in the act of removing* HELEN's *doll gives way to unmannerly temptation: she throttles it. She drops it on her bed, and stands pondering. Then she turns back, sits decisively, and writes again, as the lights dim on her.*]

[*Grimly*] "The, more, I, think, the, more, certain, I, am, that, obedience, is, the, gateway, through, which, knowledge, enters, the, mind, of, the, child—"

[*On the word "obedience" a shaft of sunlight hits the water pump outside, while* ANNIE's *voice ends in the dark, followed by a distant cockcrow; daylight comes up over another corner of the sky, with* VINEY's *voice heard at once.*]

**VINEY.** Breakfast ready!

[VINEY *comes down into the sunlight beam, and pumps a pitcherful of water. While the pitcher is brimming we hear conversation from the dark; the light grows to the family room of the house where all are either entering or already seated at breakfast, with* KELLER *and* JAMES *arguing the war.[1]* HELEN *is wandering around the table to explore the contents of the other plates. When* ANNIE *is in her chair, she watches* HELEN.

---

1. **the war:** The Civil War (1861–1865) between the North (Union) and the South (Confederacy).

---

VINEY *re-enters, sets the pitcher on the table;* KATE *lifts the almost empty biscuit plate with an inquiring look,* VINEY *nods and bears it off back, neither of them interrupting the men.* ANNIE *meanwhile sits with fork quiet, watching* HELEN, *who at her mother's plate pokes her hand among some scrambled eggs.* KATE *catches* ANNIE's *eyes on her, smiles with a wry gesture.* HELEN *moves on to* JAMES's *plate, the male talk continuing,* JAMES *deferential and* KELLER *overriding.*]

**JAMES.** —no, but shouldn't we give the devil his due, father? The fact is we lost the South two years earlier when he outthought us behind Vicksburg.[2]

**KELLER.** Outthought is a peculiar word for a butcher.

**JAMES.** Harness maker, wasn't he?

**KELLER.** I said butcher. his only virtue as a soldier was numbers and he led them to slaughter with no more regard than for so many sheep.

**JAMES.** But even if in that sense he was a butcher, the fact is he—

**KELLER.** And a drunken one, half the war.

**JAMES.** Agreed, father. If his own people said he was I can't argue he—

**KELLER.** Well, what is it you find to admire in such a man, Jimmie, the butchery or the drunkenness?

**JAMES.** Neither, father, only the fact that he beat us.

**KELLER.** He didn't.

**JAMES.** Is it your contention we won the war, sir?

---

2. **Vicksburg:** A Mississippi city attacked during the Civil War by Ulysses S. Grant (1822–1885), the Union general to whom James is referring.

---

*The Miracle Worker* 279

**7 Critical Thinking and Reading** Contrast Annie's and Kate's views of the "reward." Why do their views differ?

**8 Reading Strategy** What do you think Annie's ominous tone implies?

**9 Literary Focus** Why do you think Gibson includes a scene with the whole family after a scene with only a few characters?

**10 Clarification** In numerous places two or even three actions may be taking place at once. Notice Helen's activities as Keller and James have been speaking. No one, except Annie, seems to be aware of them.

**11 Reading Strategy** As students read this discussion between James and Keller, have them notice the unspoken parallels between Annie and General Grant. Both invaded the South, were obstinate, and so forth. Ask students to look for other references to the Civil War as they read.

**KELLER.** He didn't beat us at Vicksburg. We lost Vicksburg because Pemberton gave Bragg five thousand of his cavalry and Loring, whom I knew personally for a nincompoop before you were born, marched away from Champion's Hill with enough men to have held them, we lost Vicksburg by stupidity verging on treason.

**JAMES.** I would have said we lost Vicksburg because Grant was one thing no Yankee general was before him—

**KELLER.** Drunk? I doubt it.

**JAMES.** Obstinate.

**KELLER.** Obstinate. Could any of them compare even in that with old Stonewall?[3] If he'd been there we would still have Vicksburg.

**JAMES.** Well, the butcher simply wouldn't give up, he tried four ways of getting around Vicksburg and on the fifth try he got around. Anyone else would have pulled north and—

**KELLER.** He wouldn't have got around if we'd had a Southerner in command, instead of a half-breed Yankee traitor like Pemberton—

[*While this background talk is in progress,* HELEN *is working around the table, ultimately toward* ANNIE'S *plate. She messes with her hands in* JAMES'S *plate, then in* KELLER'S, *both men taking it so for granted they hardly notice. Then* HELEN *comes groping with soiled hands past her own plate, to* ANNIE'S; *her hand goes to it, and* ANNIE, *who has been waiting, deliberately lifts and removes her hand.* HELEN *gropes again,* ANNIE *firmly pins her by the wrist, and removes her hand from the table.* HELEN *thrusts her hands again,* ANNIE *catches them, and* HELEN *begins to flail and make noises; the interruption brings* KELLER'S *gaze upon them.*]

12

---

**3. old Stonewall:** The nickname of Thomas J. Jackson (1824–1863), a Confederate general.

280 *Drama*

What's the matter there?

**KATE.** Miss Annie. You see, she's accustomed to helping herself from our plates to anything she—

**ANNIE.** [*Evenly*] Yes, but *I'm* not accustomed to it.

**KELLER.** No, of course not. Viney!

**KATE.** Give her something, Jimmie, to quiet her.

**JAMES.** [*Blandly*] But her table manners are the best she has. Well.

[*He pokes across with a chunk of bacon at* HELEN'S *hand, which* ANNIE *releases; but* HELEN *knocks the bacon away and stubbornly thrusts at* ANNIE'S *plate,* ANNIE *grips her wrists again, the struggle mounts.*]

**KELLER.** Let her this time, Miss Sullivan, it's the only way we get any adult conversation. If my son's half merits that description.

[*He rises.*]

I'll get you another plate.

**ANNIE.** [*Gripping Helen*] I have a plate, thank you.

**KATE.** [*Calling*] Viney! I'm afraid what Captain Keller says is only too true, she'll persist in this until she gets her own way.

**KELLER.** [*At the door*] Viney, bring Miss Sullivan another plate—

**ANNIE.** [*Stonily*] I have a plate, nothing's wrong with the *plate*, I intend to keep it.

[*Silence for a moment, except for* HELEN'S *noises as she struggles to get loose; the* KELLERS *are a bit nonplussed, and* ANNIE *is too darkly intent on* HELEN'S *manners to have any thoughts now of her own.*]

**JAMES.** Ha. You see why they took Vicksburg?

**KELLER.** [*Uncertainly*] Miss Sullivan. One

plate or another is hardly a matter to struggle with a deprived child about.

**ANNIE.** Oh, I'd sooner have a more—

[HELEN *begins to kick,* ANNIE *moves her ankles to the opposite side of the chair.*]

—heroic issue myself, I—

**KELLER.** No, I really must insist you—

[HELEN *bangs her toe on the chair and sinks to the floor, crying with rage and feigned injury;* ANNIE *keeps hold of her wrists, gazing down, while* KATE *rises.*]

Now she's hurt herself.

**ANNIE.** [*Grimly*] No, she hasn't.

**KELLER.** Will you please let her hands go?

**KATE.** Miss Annie, you don't know the child well enough yet, she'll keep—

**ANNIE.** I know an ordinary tantrum well enough, when I see one, and a badly spoiled child—

**JAMES.** Hear, hear.

**KELLER.** [*Very annoyed*] Miss Sullivan! You would have more understanding of your pupil if you had some pity in you. Now kindly do as I—

**ANNIE.** Pity?

[*She releases* HELEN *to turn equally annoyed on* KELLER *across the table; instantly*

13

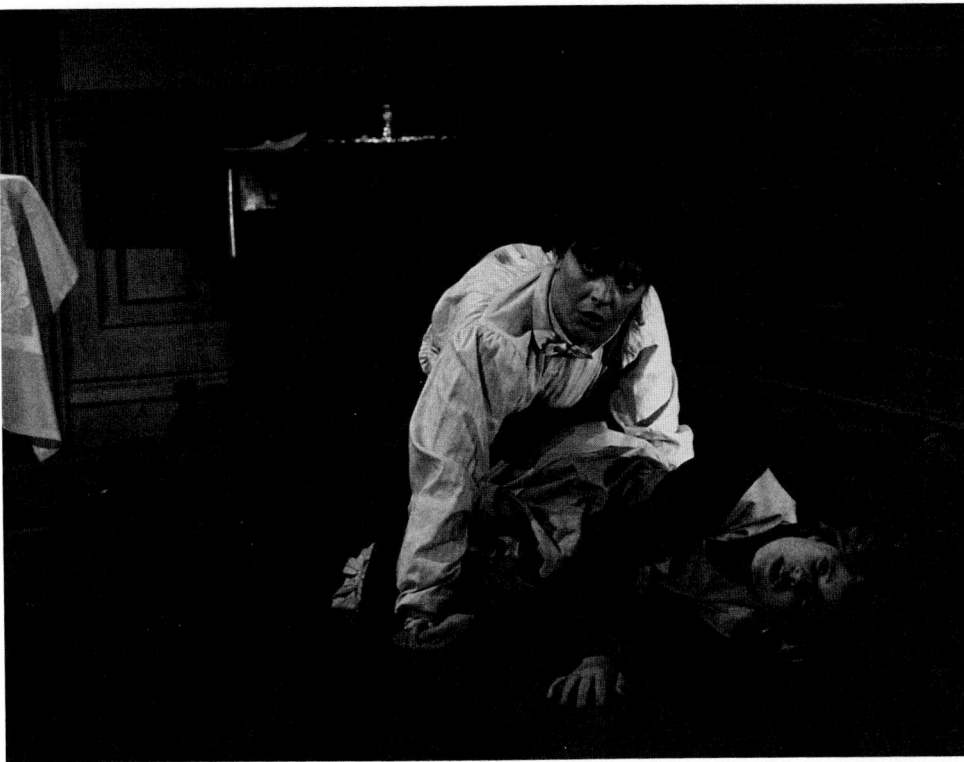

**13 Discussion** Compare and contrast Keller's and Annie's views.

**14 Discussion** What does Annie mean by this statement?

**15 Discussion** Is James beginning to change his mind about what Annie is trying to do? Explain.

**13**

[HELEN *scrambles up and dives at* ANNIE's *plate. This time* ANNIE *intercepts her by pouncing on her wrists like a hawk, and her temper boils.*]

For this *tyrant*? The whole house turns on her whims, is there anything she wants she doesn't get? I'll tell you what I pity, that the sun won't rise and set for her all her life, and every day you're telling her it will, what good will your pity do her when you're under the strawberries, Captain Keller?

**KELLER.** [*Outraged*] Kate, for the love of heaven will you—

**KATE.** Miss Annie, please, I don't think it serves to lose our—

**14**

**ANNIE.** It does you good, that's all. It's less trouble to feel sorry for her than to teach her anything better, isn't it?

**KELLER.** I fail to see where you have taught her anything yet, Miss Sullivan!

**ANNIE.** I'll begin this minute, if you'll leave the room, Captain Keller!

**KELLER.** [*Astonished*] Leave the—

**ANNIE.** Everyone, please.

[*She struggles with* HELEN, *while* KELLER *endeavors to control his voice.*]

**KELLER.** Miss Sullivan, you are here only as a paid teacher. Nothing more, and not to lecture—

**ANNIE.** I can't *unteach* her six years of pity if you can't stand up to one tantrum! Old Stonewall, indeed. Mrs. Keller, you promised me help.

**KATE.** Indeed I did, we truly want to—

**ANNIE.** Then leave me alone with her. Now!

**KELLER.** [*In a wrath*] Katie, will you come outside with me? At once, please.

[*He marches to the front door.* KATE *and*

*282 Drama*

JAMES *follow him. Simultaneously* ANNIE *releases* HELEN's *wrists, and the child again sinks to the floor, kicking and crying her weird noises;* ANNIE *steps over her to meet* VINEY *coming in the rear doorway with biscuits and a clean plate, surprised at the general commotion.*]

**VINEY.** Heaven sakes—

**ANNIE.** Out, please.

[*She backs* VINEY *out with one hand, closes the door on her astonished mouth, locks it, and removes the key.* KELLER *meanwhile snatches his hat from a rack, and* KATE *follows him down the porch steps.* JAMES *lingers in the doorway to address* ANNIE *across the room with a bow.*]

**15**

**JAMES.** If it takes all summer, general.

[ANNIE *comes over to his door in turn, removing her glasses grimly; as* KELLER *outside begins speaking,* ANNIE *closes the door on* JAMES, *locks it, removes the key, and turns with her back against the door to stare ominously at* HELEN, *kicking on the floor.*]

JAMES *takes his hat from the rack, and going down the porch steps joins* KATE *and* KELLER *talking in the yard,* KELLER *in a sputter of ire.*]

**KELLER.** This girl, this—cub of a girl—*presumes!* I tell you, I'm of half a mind to ship her back to Boston before the week is out. You can inform her so from me!

**KATE.** [*Eyebrows up*] I, Captain?

**KELLER.** She's a *hireling!* Now I want it clear, unless there's an apology and complete change of manner she goes back on the next train! Will you make that quite clear?

**KATE.** Where will you be, Captain, while I am making it quite—

**KELLER.** At the office!

## Grammar in Action

When characters are engaged in a conflict, their strong emotions may cause them to interrupt one another's speech. Playwrights indicate such interruptions with **dashes**. The following lines from *The Miracle Worker* illustrate this technique:

**KELLER.** [*Outraged*] Kate for the love of heaven will you—

**KATE.** Miss Annie, please. I don't think it serves to lose our—

**ANNIE.** It does you good, that's all. It's less trouble to feel sorry for her than to teach her anything better, isn't it?

**KELLER.** I fail to see where you have taught her anything yet, Miss Sullivan!

**ANNIE.** I'll begin this minute, if you'll leave the room, Captain Keller!

**KELLER.** [*Astonished*] Leave the—

**ANNIE.** Everyone, please.

[*He begins off left, finds his napkin still in his irate hand, is uncertain with it, dabs his lips with dignity, gets rid of it in a toss to* JAMES, *and marches off.* JAMES *turns to eye* KATE.]

**JAMES.** Will you?

[KATE'S *mouth is set, and* JAMES *studies it lightly.*]

I thought what she said was exceptionally intelligent. I've been saying it for years.

**KATE.** [*Not without scorn*] To his face?

[*She comes to relieve him of the white napkin, but reverts again with it.*]

16 Or will you take it, Jimmie? As a flag?

[JAMES *stalks out, much offended, and* KATE *turning stares across the yard at the house; the lights narrowing down to the following pantomime in the family room leave her motionless in the dark.*

17 ANNIE *meanwhile has begun by slapping both keys down on a shelf out of* HELEN'S *reach; she returns to the table, upstage,* HELEN'S *kicking has subsided, and when from the floor her hand finds* ANNIE'S *chair empty she pauses.* ANNIE *clears the table of* KATE'S, JAMES'S, *and* KELLER'S *plates; she gets back to her own across the table just in time to slide it deftly away from* HELEN'S *pouncing hand. She lifts the hand and moves it to* HELEN'S *plate, and after an instant's exploration,* HELEN *sits again on the floor and drums her heels.* ANNIE *comes around the table and resumes her chair.*
18 *When* HELEN *feels her skirt again, she ceases kicking, waits for whatever is to come, renews some kicking, waits again.* ANNIE *retrieving her plate takes up a forkful of food, stops it halfway to her mouth, gazes at it devoid of appetite, and half-lowers it; but after a look at* HELEN *she*

*sighs, dips the forkful toward* HELEN *in a for-your-sake toast, and puts it in her own mouth to chew, not without an effort.*

HELEN *now gets hold of the chair leg, and half-succeeds in pulling the chair out from under her.* ANNIE *bangs it down with her rear, heavily, and sits with all her weight.* HELEN'S *next attempt to topple it is unavailing, so her fingers dive in a pinch at* AN-NIE'S *flank.* ANNIE *in the middle of her mouthful almost loses it with startle, and* 19 *she slaps down her fork to round on* HELEN. *The child comes up with curiosity to feel what* ANNIE *is doing, so* ANNIE *resumes eating, letting* HELEN'S *hand follow the movement of her fork to her mouth; whereupon* HELEN *at once reaches into* ANNIE'S *plate.* ANNIE *firmly removes her hand to her own plate.* HELEN *in reply pinches* ANNIE'S *thigh, a good mean pinchful that makes* ANNIE *jump.* ANNIE *sets the fork down, and sits with her mouth tight.* HELEN *digs another pinch into her thigh, and this time* ANNIE *slaps her hand smartly away;* HELEN *retaliates with a roundhouse fist that catches* AN-NIE *on the ear, and* ANNIE'S *hand leaps at once in a forceful slap across* HELEN'S 20 *cheek;* HELEN *is the startled one now.* AN-NIE'S *hand in compunction falters to her own face, but when* HELEN *hits at her again,* ANNIE *deliberately slaps her again.* HELEN *lifts her fist irresolute for another roundhouse,* ANNIE *lifts her hand resolute for another slap, and they freeze in this posture, while* HELEN *mulls it over. She thinks better of it, drops her fist, and giving* ANNIE *a wide berth, gropes around to her* MOTHER'S *chair, to find it empty; she blunders her way along the table upstage, and encountering the empty chairs and missing plates, she looks bewildered; she gropes back to her* 21 MOTHER'S *chair, again touches her cheek and indicates the chair, and waits for the world to answer.*

*The Miracle Worker*  283

The dashes help set the fast pace for the speeches and keep the audience interested in the building argument. Actors and actresses delivering these lines must make the interruptions seem as lifelike as possible.

**Student Activity 1.** Reread the passage from *The Miracle Worker*. Decide which words have been omitted from the sentences interrupted by dashes. Explain how you reached your conclusions.

**Student Activity 2.** Write a brief dialogue between two people engaged in a conflict. Use dashes to show dramatic interruptions. Ask your classmates to read the dialogue and guess which words are missing.

22 **Discussion** Do you think Annie is being unnecessarily cruel?

23 **Discussion** What does Annie want Helen to do? Why?

24 **Reading Strategy** Ask students to predict what will happen.

ANNIE *now reaches over to spell into her hand, but* HELEN *yanks it away; she gropes to the front door, tries the knob, and finds the door locked, with no key. She gropes to the rear door, and finds it locked, with no key. She commences to bang on it.* ANNIE *rises, crosses, takes her wrists, draws her resisting back to the table, seats her, and releases her hands upon her plate; as* AN-NIE *herself begins to sit,* HELEN *writhes out of her chair, runs to the front door, and tugs and kicks at it.* ANNIE *rises again, crosses, draws her by one wrist back to the table, seats her, and sits;* HELEN *escapes back to the door, knocking over her* MOTHER'S *chair en route.* ANNIE *rises again in pursuit, and this time lifts* HELEN *bodily from behind and bears her kicking to her chair. She deposits her, and once more turns to sit.* HELEN *scrambles out, but as she passes* ANNIE *catches her up again from behind and deposits her in the chair;* HELEN *scrambles out on the other side, for the rear door, but* ANNIE *at her heels catches her up and deposits her again in the chair. She stands behind it.* HELEN *scrambles out to her right, and the instant her feet hit the floor* ANNIE *lifts and deposits her back; she scrambles out to her left, and is at once lifted and deposited back. She tries right again and is deposited back, and tries left again and is deposited back, and now feints* ANNIE *to the right but is off to her left, and is promptly deposited back. She sits a moment, and then starts straight over the tabletop, dishware not-withstanding;* ANNIE *hauls her in and deposits her back, with her plate spilling in her lap, and she melts to the floor and crawls under the table, laborious among its legs and chairs; but* ANNIE *is swift around the table and waiting on the other side when she surfaces, immediately bearing her aloft;* HELEN *clutches at* JAMES'S *chair for anchorage, but it comes with her, and halfway back she abandons it to the floor.*

ANNIE *deposits her in her chair, and waits.* HELEN *sits tensed motionless. Then she tentatively puts out her left foot and hand,* AN-NIE *interposes her own hand, and at the contact* HELEN *jerks hers in. She tries her right foot,* ANNIE *blocks it with her own, and* HELEN *jerks hers in. Finally, leaning back, she slumps down in her chair, in a sullen biding.*

ANNIE *backs off a step, and watches;* HELEN *offers no move.* ANNIE *takes a deep breath. Both of them and the room are in considerable disorder, two chairs down and the table a mess, but* ANNIE *makes no effort to tidy it; she only sits on her own chair, and lets her energy refill. Then she takes up knife and fork, and resolutely addresses her food.* HELEN'S *hand comes out to explore, and seeing it* ANNIE *sits without moving; the child's hand goes over her hand and fork, pauses—*ANNIE *still does not move—and withdraws. Presently it moves for her own plate, slaps about for it, and stops, thwarted. At this,* ANNIE *again rises, recovers* HELEN'S *plate from the floor and a handful of scattered food from the deranged tablecloth, drops it on the plate, and pushes the plate into contact with* HELEN'S *fist. Neither of them now moves for a pregnant moment—until* HELEN *suddenly takes a grab of food and wolfs it down.* AN-NIE *permits herself the humor of a minor bow and warming of her hands together; she wanders off a step or two, watching.* HELEN *cleans up the plate.*

*After a glower of indecision, she holds the empty plate out for more.* ANNIE *accepts it, and crossing to the removed plates, spoons food from them onto it; she stands debating the spoon, tapping it a few times on* HELEN'S *plate; and when she returns with the plate she brings the spoon, too. She puts the spoon first into* HELEN'S *hand, then sets the plate down.* HELEN *discarding the spoon* reaches with her hand, and ANNIE stops it by the wrist; she replaces the spoon in it. HELEN impatiently discards it again, and again ANNIE stops her hand, to replace the spoon in it. This time HELEN throws the spoon on the floor. ANNIE after considering it lifts HELEN bodily out of the chair, and in a wrestling match on the floor closes her fingers upon the spoon, and returns her with it to the chair. HELEN again throws the spoon on the floor. ANNIE lifts her out of the chair again; but in the struggle over the spoon HELEN with ANNIE on her back sends her sliding over her head; HELEN flees back to her chair and scrambles into it. When AN-NIE comes after her she clutches it for dear

life; ANNIE pries one hand loose, then the other, then the first again, then the other again, and then lifts HELEN by the waist, chair and all, and shakes the chair loose. HELEN wrestles to get free, but ANNIE pins her to the floor, closes her fingers upon the spoon, and lifts her kicking under one arm; with her other hand she gets the chair in place again, and plunks HELEN back on it. When she releases her hand, HELEN throws the spoon at her.

ANNIE now removes the plate of food. HELEN grabbing finds it missing, and commences to bang with her fists on the table. ANNIE collects a fistful of spoons and descends with them and the plate on HELEN; she lets her smell the plate, at which HELEN ceases banging, and ANNIE puts the plate down and a spoon in HELEN's hand. HELEN throws it on the floor. ANNIE puts another spoon in her hand. HELEN throws it on the floor. ANNIE puts another spoon in her hand. HELEN throws it on the floor. When ANNIE comes to her last spoon she sits next to HELEN, and gripping the spoon in HELEN's hand compels her to take food in it up to her mouth. HELEN sits with lips shut. ANNIE waits a stolid moment, then lowers HELEN's hand. She tries again; HELEN's lips remain shut. ANNIE waits, lowers HELEN's hand. She tries again; this time HELEN suddenly opens her mouth and accepts the food. ANNIE lowers the spoon with a sigh of relief, and HELEN spews the mouthful out at her face. ANNIE sits a moment with eyes closed, then takes the pitcher and dashes its water into HELEN's face, who gasps astonished. ANNIE with HELEN's hand takes up another spoonful, and shoves it into her open mouth. HELEN swallows involuntarily, and while she is catching her breath ANNIE forces her palm open, throws four swift letters into it, then another four, and bows toward her with devastating pleasantness.]

**ANNIE.** Good girl.

[ANNIE lifts HELEN's hand to feel her face nodding; HELEN grabs a fistful of her hair, and yanks. The pain brings ANNIE to her knees, and HELEN pummels her; they roll under the table, and the lights commence to dim out on them.

Simultaneously the light at left has been rising, slowly, so slowly that it seems at first we only imagine what is intimated in the yard: a few ghostlike figures, in silence, motionless, waiting. Now the distant belfry chimes commence to toll the hour, also very slowly, almost—it is twelve—interminably; the sense is that of a long time passing. We

25

286  Drama

can identify the figures before the twelfth stroke, all facing the house in a kind of watch: KATE is standing exactly as before, but now with the baby MILDRED sleeping in her arms, and placed here and there, unmoving, are AUNT EV in her hat with a hanky to her nose, and the two Negro children, PERCY and MARTHA with necks outstretched eagerly, and VINEY with a knotted kerchief on her head and a feather duster in her hand.

The chimes cease, and there is silence. For a long moment none of the group moves.]

**VINEY.** [Presently] What am I gone do, Miss Kate? It's noontime, dinner's comin', I didn't get them breakfast dishes out of there yet.

[KATE says nothing, stares at the house. MARTHA shifts HELEN's doll in her clutch, and it plaintively says momma.]

**KATE.** [Presently] You run along, Martha.

[AUNT EV blows her nose.]

**AUNT EV.** [Wretchedly] I can't wait out here a minute longer, Kate, why, this could go on all afternoon, too.

**KATE.** I'll tell the captain you called.

**VINEY.** [To the children] You hear what Miss Kate say? Never you mind what's going on here.

[Still no one moves.]

You run along tend your own bizness.

[Finally VINEY turns on the children with the feather duster.]

Shoo!

[The two children divide before her. She chases them off. AUNT EV comes to KATE, on her dignity.]

**AUNT EV.** Say what you like, Kate, but that child is a *Keller*.

## Grammar in Action

One of the most basic forms of descriptive writing is **writing directions.** Playwrights, such as William Gibson, rely on writing accurate instructions to tell directors and actors what actions they are to take. Writing directions involves telling how to do something in a series of logical steps. Writers of everything from cookbooks to plays are required to write directions, and the success of their work depends to a great extent on how easy it is to follow the directions they write. Look at these stage directions from *The Miracle Worker.*

. . . ANNIE lowers the spoon with a sigh of relief, and HELEN spews the mouthful out at her face. ANNIE sits for a moment with eyes closed, then takes the pitcher and dashes its water into HELEN's face, who gasps astonished. ANNIE with HELEN's hand takes up another spoonful, and shoves it into her open mouth. HELEN swallows involuntarily, and while she is catching her breath ANNIE forces her palm open, throws four swift letters into it, then another four, and bows toward her with devastating pleasantness.

[*She opens her parasol, preparatory to leaving.*]

I needn't remind you that all the Kellers are cousins to General Robert E. Lee.[4] I don't know *who* that girl is.

[*She waits; but* KATE *staring at the house is without response.*]

The only Sullivan I've heard of—from Boston too, and I'd think twice before locking her up with that kind—is that man John L.[5]

[*And* AUNT EV *departs, with head high. Presently* VINEY *comes to* KATE, *her arms out for the baby.*]

**VINEY.** You give me her, Miss Kate, I'll sneak her in back, to her crib.

[*But* KATE *is moveless, until* VINEY *starts to take the baby;* KATE *looks down at her before relinquishing her.*]

**KATE.** [*Slowly*] This child never gives me a minute's worry.

**VINEY.** Oh yes, this one's the angel of the family, no question bout *that.*

[*She begins off rear with the baby, heading around the house; and* KATE *now turns her back on it, her hand to her eyes. At this moment there is the slamming of a door, and when* KATE *wheels* HELEN *is blundering down the porch steps into the light, like a ruined bat out of hell.* VINEY *halts, and* KATE *runs in;* HELEN *collides with her mother's knees, and reels off and back to clutch them as her savior.* ANNIE *with smoked glasses in hand stands on the porch, also much undone, looking as though she had indeed just taken Vicksburg.* KATE *taking in* HELEN's *ravaged state becomes steely in her gaze up at* ANNIE.]

---

**4. General Robert E. Lee:** (1807–1870), leader of the Confederate forces in the Civil War.
**5. John L.:** John L. Sullivan (1858–1918), a champion boxer.

**KATE.** What happened?

[ANNIE *meets* KATE's *gaze, and gives a factual report, too exhausted for anything but a flat voice.*]

**ANNIE.** She ate from her own plate.

[*She thinks a moment.*]

She ate with a spoon. Herself.

[KATE *frowns, uncertain with thought, and glances down at* HELEN.]

And she folded her napkin.

[KATE's *gaze now wavers, from* HELEN *to* ANNIE, *and back.*]

**KATE.** [*Softly*] Folded—her napkin?

**ANNIE.** The room's a wreck, but her napkin is folded.

[*She pauses, then:*]

I'll be in my room, Mrs. Keller.

[*She moves to re-enter the house; but she stops at* VINEY's *voice.*]

**VINEY.** [*Cheery*] Don't be long, Miss Annie. Dinner be ready right away!

[VINEY *carries* MILDRED *around the back of the house.* ANNIE *stands unmoving, takes a deep breath, stares over her shoulder at* KATE *and* HELEN, *then inclines her head graciously, and goes with a slight stagger into the house. The lights in her room above steal up in readiness for her.*

KATE *remains alone with* HELEN *in the yard, standing protectively over her, in a kind of wonder.*]

**KATE.** [*Slowly*] Folded her napkin.

[*She contemplates the wild head in her thighs, and moves her fingertips over it, with such a tenderness, and something like a fear of its strangeness, that her own eyes close; she whispers, bending to it.*]

*The Miracle Worker* 287

26 **Discussion** How do differences between the North and South surface again?

27 **Discussion** Why does Kate's gaze become "steely"?

28 **Critical Thinking and Reading** Why do you think Annie does not go into all the details of the battle?

29 **Discussion** Why does this particular detail seem to mean so much to Kate?

---

Notice that these, like most, directions are given in chronological, or time, order. The steps to be taken are organized according to which is to be done first, second, third, and so on, to the completion of the task. The test of how well directions are written is how well those directions can be followed.

**Student Activity 1.** With a small group of classmates, select another passage of stage directions from the play. Discuss these, noting which directions apply to the actors themselves and which refer to how the stage set itself is to look. Then take parts and practice reading the scene according to the stage directions. Review the directions and try again. Are the directions easy to follow? What makes you feel as you do?

**Student Activity 2.** Write directions on how to do something. Choose an activity that has at least four or five steps. Exchange papers with a classmate and discuss whether the directions are easy to understand and to follow. Revise your directions based on this conference.

**30** **Literary Focus** Kate's inner conflict of hope and fear has finally surfaced. Ask students to explain why she is crying?

**31** **Discussion** Why has Annie gone to her suitcase?

**32** **Reading Strategy** Ask students to predict how these memories will influence Annie.

My Helen—folded her napkin—

**30** [*And still erect, with only her head in surrender,* KATE *for the first time that we see loses her protracted war with grief; but she will not let a sound escape her, only the grimace of tears comes, and sobs that shake her in a grip of silence. But* HELEN *feels them, and her hand comes up in its own wondering, to interrogate her mother's face, until* KATE *buries her lips in the child's palm.*

*Upstairs,* ANNIE *enters her room, closes the door, and stands back against it; the lights, growing on her with their special color, commence to fade on* KATE *and* HELEN. *Then*

**31** ANNIE *goes wearily to her suitcase, and lifts it to take it toward the bed. But it knocks an object to the floor, and she turns back to regard it. A new voice comes in a cultured murmur, hesitant as with the effort of remembering a text:*]

**32** **MAN'S VOICE.** This—soul—

[ANNIE *puts the suitcase down, and kneels to the object; it is the battered Perkins report, and she stands with it in her hand, letting memory try to speak:*]

This—blind, deaf, mute—woman—

[ANNIE *sits on her bed, opens the book, and finding the passage, brings it up an inch from her eyes to read, her face and lips following the overheard words, the voice quite factual now.*]

Can nothing be done to disinter this human soul? The whole neighborhood would rush to save this woman if she were buried alive by the caving in of a pit, and labor with zeal until she were dug out. Now if there were one who had as much patience as zeal, he might awaken her to a consciousness of her immortal—

[*When the boy's voice comes,* ANNIE *closes her eyes, in pain.*]

**288** *Drama*

**BOY'S VOICE.** Annie? Annie, you there?

**ANNIE.** Hush.

**BOY'S VOICE.** Annie, what's that noise?

[ANNIE *tries not to answer; her own voice is drawn out of her, unwilling.*]

**ANNIE.** Just a cot, Jimmie.

**BOY'S VOICE.** Where they pushin' it?

**ANNIE.** To the deadhouse.

**BOY'S VOICE.** Annie. Does it hurt to be dead?

[ANNIE *escapes by opening her eyes, her hand works restlessly over her cheek; she retreats into the book again, but the cracked old crones interrupt, whispering,* ANNIE *slowly lowers the book.*]

**FIRST CRONE'S VOICE.** There is schools.

**SECOND CRONE'S VOICE.** There is schools outside—

**THIRD CRONE'S VOICE.** —schools where they teach blind ones, worse'n you—

**FIRST CRONE'S VOICE.** To read—

**SECOND CRONE'S VOICE.** To read and write—

**THIRD CRONE'S VOICE.** There is schools outside where they—

**FIRST CRONE'S VOICE.** There is schools—

[*Silence.* ANNIE *sits with her eyes shining, her hand almost in a caress over the book. Then:*]

**BOY'S VOICE.** You ain't goin' to school, are you, Annie?

**ANNIE.** [*Whispering*] When I grow up.

**BOY'S VOICE.** You ain't either, Annie. You're goin' to stay here take care of me.

**ANNIE.** I'm goin' to school when I grow up.

**BOY'S VOICE.** You said we'll be together, forever and ever and ever—

**ANNIE.** [*Fierce*] I'm goin' to school when I grow up!

**DOCTOR'S VOICE.** [*Slowly*] Little girl. Little girl, I must tell you. Your brother will be going on a journey, soon.

[ANNIE *sits rigid, in silence. Then the boy's voice pierces it, a shriek of terror.*]

**BOY'S VOICE:** *Annie!*

[*It goes into* ANNIE *like a sword, she doubles onto it; the book falls to the floor. It takes her a racked moment to find herself and what she was engaged in here; when she sees the suitcase she remembers, and lifts it once again toward the bed. But the voices are with her, as she halts with suitcase in hand.*]

**FIRST CRONE'S VOICE.** Goodbye, Annie.

**DOCTOR'S VOICE.** Write me when you learn how.

**SECOND CRONE'S VOICE.** Don't tell anyone you came from here. Don't tell anyone—

**THIRD CRONE'S VOICE.** Yeah, don't tell anyone you came from—

**FIRST CRONE'S VOICE.** Yeah, don't tell anyone—

**SECOND CRONE'S VOICE.** Don't tell any—

[*The echoing voices fade. After a moment* ANNIE *lays the suitcase on the bed; and the last voice comes faintly, from far away.*]

**BOY'S VOICE.** Annie. It hurts, to be dead. Forever.

[ANNIE *falls to her knees by the bed, stifling her mouth in it. When at last she rolls blindly away from it, her palm comes down on the open report; she opens her eyes, regards it dully, and then, still on her knees, takes in the print.*]

**MAN'S VOICE.** [*Factual*] —might awaken her to a consciousness of her immortal nature.

The chance is small indeed; but with a smaller chance they would have dug desperately for her in the pit; and is the life of the soul of less import than that of the body?

[ANNIE *gets to her feet. She drops the book on the bed, and pauses over her suitcase; after a moment she unclasps and opens it. Standing before it, she comes to her decision; she at once turns to the bureau, and taking her things out of its drawers, commences to throw them into the open suitcase.*

*In the darkness down left a hand strikes a match, and lights a hanging oil lamp. It is* KELLER'S *hand, and his voice accompanies it, very angry; the lights rising here before they fade on* ANNIE *show* KELLER *and* KATE *inside a suggestion of a garden house, with a bay-window seat toward center and a door at back.*]

**KELLER.** Katie, I will not *have* it! Now you did not see when that girl after supper tonight went to look for Helen in her room—

**KATE.** No.

**KELLER.** The child practically climbed out of her window to escape from her! What kind of teacher *is* she? I thought I had seen her at her worst this morning, shouting at me, but I come home to find the entire house disorganized by her—Helen won't stay one second in the same room, won't come to the table with her, won't let herself be bathed or undressed or put to bed by her, or even by Viney now, and the end result is that *you* have to do more for the child than before we hired this girl's services! From the moment she stepped off the train she's been nothing but a burden, incompetent, impertinent, ineffectual, immodest—

**KATE.** She folded her napkin, Captain.

**KELLER.** What?

*The Miracle Worker* 289

**33 Discussion** What has Annie decided to do?

**34 Discussion** How would you answer Keller's arguments?

33

34

35

36

**35 Discussion** What has Helen's folded napkin come to symbolize to Kate?

**36 Literary Focus** As Annie knocks on the door, she is faced with external conflicts—opposition from Keller—as well as internal ones—fears about her ability to help Helen.

**37 Critical Thinking and Reading** Why do you think Keller is nervous?

**38 Clarification** *Vexedly* means "in an irritated or annoyed manner."

**39 Discussion** Why do you think Keller changes his mind about firing Annie?

**40 Discussion** Why is Annie cheerful?

---

**KATE.** Not ineffectual. Helen did fold her napkin.

**KELLER.** What in heaven's name is so extraordinary about folding a napkin?

**KATE.** [*With some humor*] Well. It's more than you did, Captain.

**KELLER.** Katie. I did not bring you all the way out here to the garden house to be frivolous. Now, how does Miss Sullivan propose to teach a deaf-blind pupil who won't let her even touch her?

**KATE.** [*A pause*] I don't know.

**KELLER.** The fact is, today she scuttled any chance she ever had of getting along with the child. If you can see any point or purpose to her staying on here longer, it's more than—

**KATE.** What do you wish me to do?

**KELLER.** I want you to give her notice.

**KATE.** I can't.

**KELLER.** Then if you won't, I must. I simply will not—

[*He is interrupted by a knock at the back door. KELLER after a glance at KATE moves to open the door; ANNIE in her smoked glasses is standing outside. KELLER contemplates her, heavily.*]

Miss Sullivan.

**ANNIE.** Captain Keller.

[*She is nervous, keyed up to seizing the bull by the horns again, and she assumes a cheeriness which is not unshaky.*]

Viney said I'd find you both over here in the garden house. I thought we should—have a talk?

**KELLER.** [*Reluctantly*] Yes, I— Well, come in.

[*ANNIE enters, and is interested in this room; she rounds on her heel, anxiously,*

*studying it. KELLER turns the matter over to* KATE, *sotto voce.*]

Katie.

**KATE.** [*Turning it back, courteously*] Captain.

[KELLER *clears his throat, makes ready.*]

**KELLER.** I, ah—wanted first to make my position clear to Mrs. Keller, in private. I have decided I—am not satisfied—in fact, am deeply dissatisfied—with the manner in which—

**ANNIE.** [*Intent*] Excuse me, is this little house ever in use?

**KELLER.** [*With patience*] In the hunting season. If you will give me your attention, Miss Sullivan.

[ANNIE *turns her smoked glasses upon him; they hold his unwilling stare.*]

I have tried to make allowances for you because you come from a part of the country where people are—women, I should say—come from who—well, for whom—

[*It begins to elude him.*]

—allowances must—be made. I have decided, nevertheless, to—that is, decided I—

[*Vexedly*]

Miss Sullivan, I find it difficult to talk through those glasses.

**ANNIE.** [*Eagerly, removing them*] Oh, of course.

**KELLER.** [*Dourly*] Why do you wear them, the sun has been down for an hour.

**ANNIE.** [*Pleasantly, at the lamp*] Any kind of light hurts my eyes.

[*A silence;* KELLER *ponders her, heavily.*]

**KELLER.** Put them on. Miss Sullivan, I have decided to—give you another chance.

**ANNIE.** [*Cheerfully*] To do what?

37

38

39

40

**KELLER.** To—remain in our employ.

[ANNIE'S *eyes widen.*]

But on two conditions. I am not accustomed to rudeness in servants or women, and that is the first. If you are to stay, there must be a radical change of manner.

**ANNIE.** [*A pause*] Whose?

**KELLER.** [*Exploding*] Yours, young lady, isn't it obvious? And the second is that you persuade me there's the slightest hope of your teaching a child who flees from you now like the plague, to anyone else she can find in this house.

**ANNIE.** [*A pause*] There isn't.

[KATE *stops sewing, and fixes her eyes upon* ANNIE.]

**KATE.** What, Miss Annie?

**ANNIE.** It's hopeless here. I can't teach a child who runs away.

41 **KELLER.** [*Nonplussed*] Then—do I understand you—propose—

**ANNIE.** Well, if we all agree it's hopeless, the next question is what—

**KATE.** Miss Annie.

[*She is leaning toward* ANNIE, *in deadly earnest; it commands both* ANNIE *and* KELLER.]

I am not agreed. I think perhaps you—underestimated Helen.

**ANNIE.** I think everybody else here does.

**KATE.** She did fold her napkin. She learns, she learns, do you know she began talking when she was six months old? She could say "water." Not really—"wahwah." "Wahwah," but she meant water, she knew what it meant, and only six months old, I never saw a child so—bright, or outgoing—

[*Her voice is unsteady, but she gets it level.*]

It's still in her, somewhere, isn't it? You should have seen her before her illness, such a good-tempered child—

**ANNIE.** [*Agreeably*] She's changed.

[*A pause,* KATE *not letting her eyes go; her appeal at last is unconditional, and very quiet.*]

**KATE.** Miss Annie, put up with it. And with us.

**KELLER.** Us!

**KATE.** Please? Like the lost lamb in the parable, I love her all the more.

**ANNIE.** Mrs. Keller, I don't think Helen's worst handicap is deafness or blindness. I think it's your love. And pity. **42**

**KELLER.** Now what does that mean?

**ANNIE.** All of you here are so sorry for her you've kept her—like a pet, why, even a dog you housebreak. No wonder she won't let me come near her. It's useless for me to try to teach her language or anything else here. I might as well—

**KATE.** [*Cuts in*] Miss Annie, before you came we spoke of putting her in an asylum.

[ANNIE *turns back to regard her. A pause*]

**ANNIE.** What kind of asylum?

**KELLER.** For mental defectives.

**KATE.** I visited there. I can't tell you what I saw, people like—animals, with—*rats*, in the halls, and—

[*She shakes her head on her vision.*]

What else are we to do, if you give up?

**ANNIE.** Give up?

**KATE.** You said it was hopeless.

**ANNIE.** Here. Give up, why, I only today saw what has to be done, to begin!

*The Miracle Worker* 291

**41 Clarification** *Nonplussed* means "perplexed and unable to speak or act."

**42 Discussion** Why does Annie think Helen's worst handicap is her parents' love and pity?

43 **Discussion** Evaluate Annie's idea.

44 **Discussion** Why do you think Annie chooses this moment to tell the Kellers about her past?

[*She glances from* KATE *to* KELLER, *who stare, waiting; and she makes it as plain and simple as her nervousness permits.*]

I—want complete charge of her.

**KELLER.** You already have that. It has resulted in—

**ANNIE.** No, I mean day and night. She has to be dependent on me.

**KATE.** For what?

**ANNIE.** Everything. The food she eats, the clothes she wears, fresh—

[*She is amused at herself, though very serious.*]

—air, yes, the air she breathes, whatever her body needs is a—primer, to teach her out of. It's the only way, the one who lets her have it should be her teacher.

[*She considers them in turn; they digest it,* KELLER *frowning,* KATE *perplexed.*]

Not anyone who *loves* her, you have so many feelings they fall over each other like feet, you won't use your chances and you won't let me.

**KATE.** But if she runs from you—*to* us—

**ANNIE.** Yes, that's the point. I'll have to live with her somewhere else.

**KELLER.** What!

**ANNIE.** Till she learns to depend on and listen to me.

**KATE.** [*Not without alarm*] For how long?

**ANNIE.** As long as it takes.

[*A pause. She takes a breath.*]

I packed half my things already.

**KELLER.** Miss—Sullivan!

[*But when* ANNIE *attends upon him he is speechless, and she is merely earnest.*]

292   *Drama*

**ANNIE.** Captain Keller, it meets both your conditions. It's the one way I can get back in touch with Helen, and I don't see how I can be rude to you again if you're not around to interfere with me.

**KELLER.** [*Red-faced*] And what is your intention if I say no? Pack the other half, for home, and abandon your charge to—to—

**ANNIE.** The asylum?

[*She waits, appraises* KELLER's *glare and* KATE's *uncertainty, and decides to use her weapons.*]

I grew up in such an asylum. The state almshouse.

[KATE's *head comes up on this, and* KELLER *stares hard;* ANNIE's *tone is cheerful enough, albeit level as gunfire.*]

Rats—why, my brother Jimmie and I used to play with the rats because we didn't have toys. Maybe you'd like to know what Helen will find there, not on visiting days? One ward was full of the—old women, crippled, blind, most of them dying, but even if what they had was catching there was nowhere else to move them, and that's where they put us. There were younger ones across the hall, with T.B., and epileptic fits, and some insane. The room Jimmie and I played in was the deadhouse, where they kept the bodies till they could dig—

**KATE.** [*Closes her eyes*] Oh, my dear—

**ANNIE.** —the graves.

[*She is immune to* KATE's *compassion.*]

No, it made me strong. But I don't think you need send Helen there. She's strong enough.

[*She waits again; but when neither offers her a word, she simply concludes.*]

No, I have no conditions, Captain Keller.

**KATE.** [*Not looking up*] Miss Annie.

**ANNIE.** Yes.

**KATE.** [*A pause*] Where would you—take Helen?

**ANNIE.** Ohh—

[*Brightly*]

Italy?

**KELLER.** [*Wheeling*] What?

**ANNIE.** Can't have everything, how would this garden house do? Furnish it, bring Helen here after a long ride so she won't recognize it, and you can see her every day. If she doesn't know. Well?

**KATE.** [*A sigh of relief*] Is that all?

**ANNIE.** That's all.

**KATE.** Captain.

[KELLER *turns his head; and* KATE'S *request is quiet but firm.*]

With your permission?

**KELLER.** [*Teeth in cigar*] Why must she depend on you for the food she eats?

**ANNIE.** [*A pause*] I want control of it.

**KELLER.** Why?

**ANNIE.** It's a way to reach her.

**KELLER.** [*Stares*] You intend to *starve* her into letting you touch her?

**ANNIE.** She won't starve, she'll learn. All's fair in love and war, Captain Keller, you never cut supplies?

**KELLER.** This is hardly a war!

**ANNIE.** Well, it's not love. A siege is a siege.

45 **KELLER.** [*Heavily*] Miss Sullivan. Do you *like* the child?

**ANNIE.** [*Straight in his eyes*] Do you?

[*A long pause*]

**KATE.** You could have a servant here—

**ANNIE.** [*Amused*] I'll have enough work without looking after a servant! But that boy Percy could sleep here, run errands—

**KATE.** [*Also amused*] We can let Percy sleep here, I think, Captain?

**ANNIE.** [*Eagerly*] And some old furniture, all our own—

**KATE.** [*Also eager*] Captain? Do you think that walnut bedstead in the barn would be too—

**KELLER.** I have not yet consented to Percy! Or to the house, or to the proposal! Or to Miss Sullivan's—staying on when I—

[*But he erupts in an irate surrender.*]

Very well, I consent to everything!

[*He shakes the cigar at* ANNIE.]

46 For two weeks. I'll give you two weeks in this place, and it will be a miracle if you get the child to tolerate you.

**KATE.** Two weeks? Miss Annie, can you accomplish anything in two weeks?

**KELLER.** Anything or not, two weeks, then the child comes back to us. Make up your mind, Miss Sullivan, yes or no?

**ANNIE.** Two weeks. For only one miracle?

[*She nods at him, nervously.*]

I'll get her to tolerate me.

[KELLER *marches out, and slams the door.* KATE *on her feet regards* ANNIE, *who is facing the door.*]

47 **KATE.** [*Then*] You can't think as little of love as you said.

[ANNIE *glances questioning.*]

Or you wouldn't stay.

**ANNIE.** [*A pause*] I didn't come here for love. I came for money!

45 **Literary Focus** The conflict between Annie and Keller reaches its high point here, as they trade questions about liking Helen. Why is the question important?

46 **Discussion** How is Keller's use of the word *miracle* an example of foreshadowing?

47 **Discussion** What may Kate know about Annie's feelings that Annie has not yet realized?

*The Miracle Worker* 293

**48 Discussion** Explain Annie's gesture.

**49 Literary Focus** We know James's external conflict with his father. What inner conflict does he reveal to Annie here?

48 [KATE *shakes her head to this, with a smile; after a moment she extends her open hand.* ANNIE *looks at it, but when she puts hers out it is not to shake hands, it is to set her fist in* KATE's *palm.*]

**KATE.** [*Puzzled*] Hm?

**ANNIE.** A. It's the first of many. Twenty-six!

[KATE *squeezes her fist, squeezes it hard, and hastens out after* KELLER. ANNIE *stands as the door closes behind her, her manner so apprehensive that finally she slaps her brow, holds it, sighs, and, with her eyes closed, crosses herself for luck.*

*The lights dim into a cool silhouette scene around her, the lamp paling out, and now, in formal entrances, persons appear around* ANNIE *with furniture for the room:* PERCY *crosses the stage with a rocking chair and waits;* MARTHA *from another direction bears in a stool,* VINEY *bears in a small table, and the other Negro servant rolls in a bed partway from left; and* ANNIE, *opening her eyes to put her glasses back on, sees them. She turns around in the room once, and goes into action, pointing out locations for each article; the servants place them and leave, and* ANNIE *then darts around, interchanging them. In the midst of this—while* PERCY *and* MARTHA *reappear with a tray of food and a chair, respectively—*JAMES *comes down from the house with* ANNIE's *suitcase, and stands viewing the room and her quizzically;* AN-NIE *halts abruptly under his eyes, embarrassed, then seizes the suitcase from his hand, explaining herself brightly.*]

**ANNIE.** I always wanted to live in a doll's house!

[*She sets the suitcase out of the way, and continues;* VINEY *at left appears to position a rod with drapes for a doorway, and the other servant at center pushes in a wheel-*barrow *loaded with a couple of boxes of* HELEN's *toys and clothes.* ANNIE *helps lift them into the room, and the servant pushes the wheelbarrow off. In none of this is any heed taken of the imaginary walls of the garden house, the furniture is moved in from every side and itself defines the walls.*

ANNIE *now drags the box of toys into center, props up the doll conspicuously on top; with the people melted away, except for* JAMES, *all is again still. The lights turn again without pause, rising warmer.*]

**JAMES.** You don't let go of things easily, do you? How will you—win her hand now, in this place?

**ANNIE.** [*Curtly*] Do I know? I lost my temper, and here we are!

**JAMES.** [*Lightly*] No touching, no teaching. Of course, you *are* bigger—

**ANNIE.** I'm not counting on force, I'm counting on her. That little imp is dying to know.

**JAMES.** Know what?

**ANNIE.** Anything. Any and every crumb in God's creation. I'll have to use that appetite too.

[*She gives the room a final survey, straightens the bed, arranges the curtains.*]

**JAMES.** [*A pause*] Maybe she'll teach you.

**ANNIE.** Of course.

49 **JAMES.** That she isn't. That there's such a thing as—dullness of heart. Acceptance. And letting go. Sooner or later we all give up, don't we?

**ANNIE.** Maybe you all do. It's my idea of the original sin.

**JAMES.** What is?

**ANNIE.** [*Witheringly*] Giving up.

**JAMES.** [*Nettled*] You won't open her. Why

can't you let her be? Have some—pity on her, for being what she is—

**ANNIE.** If I'd ever once thought like that, I'd be dead!

**JAMES.** [*Pleasantly*] You will be. Why trouble?

[ANNIE *turns to glare at him; he is mocking.*]

Or will you teach me?

[*And with a bow, he drifts off.*

Now in the distance there comes the clopping of hoofs, drawing near, and nearer, up to the door; and they halt. ANNIE *wheels to face the door. When it opens this time, the* KELLERS—KATE *in traveling bonnet,* KELLER *also hatted—are standing there with* HELEN *between them; she is in a cloak.* KATE *gently cues her into the room.* HELEN *comes in groping, baffled, but interested in the new surroundings;* ANNIE *evades her exploring hand, her gaze not leaving the child.*]

**ANNIE.** Does she know where she is?

**KATE.** [*Shakes her head*] We rode her out in the country for two hours.

**KELLER.** For all she knows, she could be in another town—

[HELEN *stumbles over the box on the floor and in it discovers her doll and other battered toys, is pleased, sits to them, then becomes puzzled and suddenly very wary. She scrambles up and back to her mother's thighs, but* ANNIE *steps in, and it is hers that* HELEN *embraces.* HELEN *recoils, gropes, and touches her cheek instantly.*]

**KATE.** That's her sign for me.

**ANNIE.** I know.

[HELEN *waits, then recommences her groping, more urgently.* KATE *stands indecisive,*

and takes an abrupt step toward her, but ANNIE'S *hand is a barrier.*]

In two weeks.

**KATE.** Miss Annie, I— Please be good to her. These two weeks, try to be very good to her—

**ANNIE.** I will.

[KATE, *turning then, hurries out. The* KELLERS *cross back of the main house.*

ANNIE *closes the door.* HELEN *starts at the door jar, and rushes it.* ANNIE *holds her off.* HELEN *kicks her, breaks free, and careens around the room like an imprisoned bird, colliding with furniture, groping wildly, repeatedly touching her cheek in a growing panic. When she has covered the room, she commences her weird screaming.* ANNIE *moves to comfort her, but her touch sends* HELEN *into a paroxysm of rage: she tears away, falls over her box of toys, flings its contents in handfuls in* ANNIE'S *direction, flings the box too, reels to her feet, rips curtains from the window, bangs and kicks at the door, sweeps objects off the mantelpiece and shelf, a little tornado incarnate, all destruction, until she comes upon her doll and, in the act of hurling it, freezes. Then she clutches it to herself, and in exhaustion sinks sobbing to the floor.* ANNIE *stands contemplating her, in some awe.*]

Two weeks.

[*She shakes her head, not without a touch of disgusted bewilderment.*]

What did I get into now?

[*The lights have been dimming throughout, and the garden house is lit only by moonlight now, with* ANNIE *lost in the patches of dark.*

KATE, *now hatless and coatless, enters the family room by the rear door, carrying a lamp.* KELLER, *also hatless, wanders si-*

*The Miracle Worker  295*

50

51 **Discussion** Why does Keller react so violently?

52 **Discussion** What does James mean?

53 **Critical Thinking and Reading** Earlier Keller asked Annie if she *liked* Helen; here Kate asks the same question. Why do you think she asks?

54 **Literary Focus** How is this moment a turning point in Annie's internal conflict?

multaneously around the back of the main house to where JAMES has been waiting, in the rising moonlight, on the porch.]

**KELLER.** I can't understand it. I had every intention of dismissing that girl, not setting her up like an empress.

**JAMES.** Yes, what's her secret, sir?

**KELLER.** Secret?

**JAMES.** [Pleasantly] That enables her to get anything she wants out of you? When I can't.

[JAMES turns to go into the house, but KELLER grasps his wrist, twisting him half to his knees. KATE comes from the porch.]

**KELLER.** [Angrily] She does *not* get anything she—

**JAMES.** [In pain] Don't—don't—

**KATE.** Captain.

**KELLER.** He's afraid.

[He throws JAMES away from him, with contempt.]

What *does* he want out of me?

**JAMES.** [An outcry] My God, don't you know?

[He gazes from KELLER to KATE.]

Everything you forgot, when you forgot my mother.

**KELLER.** What!

[JAMES wheels into the house. KELLER takes a stride to the porch, to roar after him.]

One thing that girl's secret is not, she doesn't fire one shot and disappear!

[KATE stands rigid, and KELLER comes back to her.]

Katie. Don't mind what he—

**KATE.** Captain, I am proud of you.

**KELLER.** For what?

*296    Drama*

**KATE.** For letting this girl have what she needs.

**KELLER.** Why can't my son be? He can't bear me, you'd think I treat him as hard as this girl does Helen—

[He breaks off, as it dawns in him.]

**KATE.** [Gently] Perhaps you do.

**KELLER.** But he has to learn some respect!

**KATE.** [A pause, wryly] Do you like the child?

[She turns again to the porch, but pauses, reluctant.]

How empty the house is, tonight.

[After a moment she continues on in. KELLER stands moveless, as the moonlight dies on him.

The distant belfry chimes toll, two o'clock, and with them, a moment later, comes the boy's voice on the wind, in a whisper.]

**BOY'S VOICE.** Annie. Annie.

[In her patch of dark ANNIE, now in her nightgown, hurls a cup into a corner as though it were her grief, getting rid of its taste through her teeth.]

**ANNIE.** No! No pity, I won't have it.

[She comes to HELEN, prone on the floor.]

On either of us.

[She goes to her knees, but when she touches HELEN's hand the child starts up awake, recoils, and scrambles away from her under the bed. ANNIE stares after her. She strikes her palm on the floor, with passion.]

I *will* touch you!

[She gets to her feet, and paces in a kind of anger around the bed, her hand in her hair, and confronting HELEN at each turn.]

How, how? How do I—

[ANNIE *stops. Then she calls out urgently, loudly.*]

Percy! Percy!

[*She moves swiftly to the drapes, at left.*]

Percy, wake up!

[PERCY's *voice comes in a thick sleepy mumble, unintelligible.*]

Get out of bed and come in here, I need you.

[ANNIE *darts away, finds and strikes a match, and touches it to the hanging lamp; the lights come up dimly in the room, and* PERCY *stands bare to the waist in torn overalls between the drapes, with eyes closed, swaying.* ANNIE *goes to him, pats his cheeks vigorously.*]

Percy. You awake?

**PERCY.** No'm.

**ANNIE.** How would you like to play a nice game?

**PERCY.** Whah?

**ANNIE.** With Helen. She's under the bed. Touch her hand.

[*She kneels* PERCY *down at the bed, thrusting his hand under it to contact* HELEN's; HELEN *emits an animal sound and crawls to the opposite side, but commences sniffing.* ANNIE *rounds the bed with* PERCY *and thrusts his hand again at* HELEN; *this time* HELEN *clutches it, sniffs in recognition, and comes scrambling out after* PERCY, *to hug him with delight.* PERCY *alarmed struggles, and* HELEN's *fingers go to his mouth.*]

**PERCY.** Lemme go. Lemme go—

[HELEN *fingers her own lips, as before, moving them in dumb imitation.*]

She tryin' talk. She gonna hit me—

**ANNIE.** [*Grimly*] She *can* talk. If she only knew, I'll show you how. She makes letters.

[*She opens* PERCY's *other hand, and spells into it.*]

This one is C. C.

[*She hits his palm with it a couple of times, her eyes upon* HELEN *across him;* HELEN *gropes to feel what* PERCY's *hand is doing, and when she encounters* ANNIE's *she falls back from them.*]

She's mad at me now, though, she won't play. But she knows lots of letters. Here's another, A. C, a. C, a.

[*But she is watching* HELEN, *who comes groping, consumed with curiosity;* ANNIE *makes the letters in* PERCY's *hand, and* HELEN *pokes to question what they are up to. Then* HELEN *snatches* PERCY's *other hand, and quickly spells four letters into it.* ANNIE *follows them aloud.*]

C, a, k, e! She spells cake, she gets cake.

[*She is swiftly over to the tray of food, to fetch cake and a jug of milk.*]

She doesn't know yet it means this. Isn't it funny she knows how to spell it and doesn't *know* she knows?

[*She breaks the cake in two pieces, and extends one to each;* HELEN *rolls away from her offer.*]

Well, if she won't play it with me, I'll play it with you. Would you like to learn one she doesn't know?

**PERCY.** No'm.

[*But* ANNIE *seizes his wrist, and spells to him.*]

**ANNIE.** M, i, l, k. M is this. I, that's an easy one, just the little finger. L is this—

[*And* HELEN *comes back with her hand, to*

*The Miracle Worker* 297

**55 Critical Thinking and Reading**
Why do you think Annie starts playing with Percy? What strategy might she have in mind?

55

**56 Discussion** Why has Annie's strategy succeeded?

**57 Discussion** What does Annie mean by this statement?

**58 Discussion** Do you think Annie has a new understanding of love? Explain.

**Reader's Response** Try to imagine what life would be like if you were Helen. What do you think you would miss most? Why?

## Closure and Extension

### ANSWERS TO THINKING ABOUT THE SELECTION
*Recalling*

1. Her chief problem is how to discipline Helen without breaking her spirit. She will insist on reasonable obedience.
2. Annie hopes that by spelling the names of things into Helen's hand, she can teach Helen to connect the object with the name.
3. In her battle, Annie succeeds in making Helen eat from her own plate, with a spoon, and then fold her napkin.
4. Annie is convinced she cannot teach Helen if she does not have complete control over her actions. She feels she cannot be successful in a place where Helen can go to family members for love and pity when things do not go her way.

*Interpreting*

5. Suggested Response: While Annie and Kate are friends, they dis-

---

*feel the new word.* ANNIE *brushes her away, and continues spelling aloud to* PERCY. HELEN'S *hand comes back again, and tries to get in;* ANNIE *brushes it away again.* HELEN'S *hand insists, and* ANNIE *puts it away rudely.*]

No, why should I talk to you? I'm teaching Percy a new word. L. K is this—

[HELEN *now yanks their hands apart; she butts* PERCY *away, and thrusts her palm out insistently.* ANNIE'S *eyes are bright, with glee.*]

Ho, you're *jealous*, are you!

[HELEN'S *hand waits, intractably waits.*]

All *right*.

[ANNIE *spells into it,* milk; *and* HELEN *after a moment spells it back to* ANNIE. ANNIE *takes her hand, with her whole face shining. She gives a great sigh.*]

Good! So I'm finally back to where I can touch you, hm? Touch and go! No love lost, but here we go.

[*She puts the jug of milk into* HELEN'S *hand and squeezes* PERCY'S *shoulder.*]

You can go to bed now, you've earned your sleep. Thank you.

[PERCY *stumbling up weaves his way out through the drapes.* HELEN *finishes drinking, and holds the jug out, for* ANNIE; *when* ANNIE *takes it,* HELEN *crawls onto the bed, and makes for sleep.* ANNIE *stands, looks down at her.*]

Now all I have to teach you is—one word. Everything.

[*She sets the jug down. On the floor now* ANNIE *spies the doll, stoops to pick it up, and with it dangling in her hand, turns off the lamp. A shaft of moonlight is left on* HELEN *in the bed, and a second shaft on the rocking chair; and* ANNIE, *after putting off her*

*298 Drama*

---

*smoked glasses, sits in the rocker with the doll. She is rather happy, and dangles the doll on her knee, and it makes its momma sound.* ANNIE *whispers to it in mock solicitude.*]

Hush, little baby. Don't—say a word—

[*She lays it against her shoulder, and begins rocking with it, patting its diminutive behind; she talks the lullaby to it, humorously at first.*]

Momma's gonna buy you—a mockingbird: If that—mockingbird don't sing—

[*The rhythm of the rocking takes her into the tune, softly, and more tenderly.*]

Momma's gonna buy you a diamond ring: If that diamond ring turns to brass—

[*A third shaft of moonlight outside now rises to pick out* JAMES *at the main house, with one foot on the porch step; he turns his body, as if hearing the song.*]

Momma's gonna buy you a looking-glass: If that looking-glass gets broke—

[*In the family room a fourth shaft picks out* KELLER *seated at the table, in thought; and he, too, lifts his head, as if hearing.*]

Momma's gonna buy you a billy goat: If that billy goat won't pull—

[*The fifth shaft is upstairs in* ANNIE'S *room, and picks out* KATE, *pacing there; and she halts, turning her head, too, as if hearing.*]

Momma's gonna buy you a cart and bull: If that cart and bull turns over, Momma's gonna buy you a dog named Rover; If that dog named Rover won't bark—

[*With the shafts of moonlight on* HELEN, *and* JAMES, *and* KELLER, *and* KATE, *all moveless, and* ANNIE *rocking the doll, the curtain ends the act.*]

---

agree about the treatment of Helen. Annie also has a conflict with James, who feels that her efforts will not be successful. Finally, Annie has a conflict with Keller, who finds it difficult to give up his role as decision-maker. Also, he feels that Annie is too harsh with Helen.

6. Suggested Response: Annie believes that Helen should be taught to sit quietly and eat from her own

plate with her own utensils. Her parents have allowed her to help herself with her hands from anyone's plate. Keller says that giving Helen this freedom is the only way they can have any adult conversation at mealtime.

7. Suggested Response: The events of the play take place not very long after the Civil War. Also, the Kellers are cousins of Robert E. Lee, the leader of the Southern

forces during the war. Annie, as a Northerner seems like an outsider and James humorously compares her to General Grant. Annie's struggle to teach Helen is therefore associated with the Civil War.

8. Suggested Response: Annie's brother did not want her to go to school. He wanted her to take care of him "forever." When he died,

298

# THINKING ABOUT THE SELECTION

## Recalling

1. According to the letter she is writing at the start of Act II, what is Annie's chief problem with Helen, and what will Annie insist on from the start?
2. What is the idea behind the hand-spelling Annie uses with Helen?
3. Explain what Annie achieves in her battle with Helen in the breakfast room.
4. Why does Annie want to live alone with Helen in the garden house?

## Interpreting

5. Describe Annie's conflicts with other individuals.
6. Contrast the views of Annie and Helen's parents regarding Helen's behavior at meals.
7. Explain the connection between the references to Civil War battles and generals and the action of the play.
8. Summarize Annie's past as it is revealed in Act II and explain how it affects her work with Helen.
9. In her letter, Annie writes, ". . . obedience, is, the, gateway, through, which, knowledge, enters, the, mind, of, the, child—." Explain how the events of the play illustrate the truth of this statement?

## Applying

10. What is the difference between authority and self-control? Why is each necessary for education?

## ANALYZING LITERATURE

### Understanding Conflict in Drama

**Conflict,** whether external or internal, is the essence or heart of drama. If you understand the basic conflict of a play and why it concludes as it does, you understand the play.

1. Describe the basic conflict of *The Miracle Worker*.
2. At this point in your reading, how do you think that the conflict will conclude? Give reasons for your opinion.
3. An underlying conflict in this play is that between James and Captain Keller. Describe this conflict.

## CRITICAL THINKING AND READING

### Recognizing Causes and Effects

A **cause** is an action, event, or situation that produces a result. An **effect** is the result produced by a cause. One way to understand a play or other kind of story is to analyze the chain of causes and effects that advance the plot. This means noticing how one event causes another event, which is the effect, and how that effect becomes the cause of yet another event, and so on to the end.

1. According to Annie, what is the cause of Helen's terrible table manners and generally awful behavior?
2. Early in Act II, Annie alone in her room picks up Helen's doll and throttles it. What is the cause of her anger?
3. By the end of the first two acts, what effect have Annie's efforts had on Helen?

## THINKING AND WRITING

### Writing a Scene

Extend Act II by writing a brief scene in which Annie, at the end of her lullaby, falls asleep and dreams. In this dream scene, characters from either her past or her present life would appear to her. The scene would end with Annie waking up.

Before you write, imagine the kind of dream Annie might have. Think of how it might express her activities, fears, or hopes. What characters would appear? What would they say or do?

When you have answered such questions as these, write the scene as it might appear in the printed version of the play, with dialogue and stage directions. When you revise, concentrate on improving the scene as an expression of Annie's hidden thoughts and feelings. Share the scene with your classmates.

*The Miracle Worker* 299

(Answers begin on p. 298.)

once Annie has complete control over Helen, she may be able to teach her. Some may feel, however, that Annie will not be able to accomplish her goal in two weeks.

3. Suggested Response: James is angry at his father because he has remarried. James feels ignored and unloved. Keller resents James's attitude, feels he is weak, and treats him as if he were a child.

## ANSWERS TO CRITICAL THINKING AND READING

1. Suggested Response: Annie feels that the family encourages Helen's bad table manners by giving in to any and all of her actions. She says, about this situation—"It's less trouble to feel sorry for her than to teach her anything better. . .".
2. Suggested Response: Annie is angry because Kate, rather than letting Annie discipline Helen, has given her a piece of candy, almost as a reward for her actions.
3. Suggested Response: By the end of this act, Helen will let Annie touch her again. Also, Helen has learned to spell words with finger language, but still does not connect the word to the thing. Finally, Helen has—once at least—eaten from her own plate and folded her napkin.

## THINKING AND WRITING

For help with this assignment, students can refer to Lesson 19, "Writing a Short Dramatic Sketch," in the Handbook of Writing About Literature.

## Publishing Student Writing

You might want to have a group of students act out some of these scenes for the rest of the class.

## Writing Across the Curriculum

Ask students to research and report on some of the Civil War references in the play—the battle of Vicksburg, Ulysses S. Grant, Stonewall Jackson, and Robert E. Lee. Consider informing the social studies department of this assignment, so that social studies teachers can provide guidance for students.

Annie felt as if she let him down by telling him that she wanted to go to school. Her guilt about not being able to save her brother increases her determination to help Helen.

9. Suggested Response: Only when Annie makes Helen obey her at the breakfast table, can she begin to teach her to eat with a spoon and fold her napkin.

gested Response: Authority is the right of someone in charge to determine goals and set limits. Self-control is a person's ability to perform these same functions for himself or herself. Without discipline and authority, no learning could take place at all. However, students who do not have inner discipline cannot learn on their own.

**Challenge** Have students prepare a brief summary of Annie's

life up to the time she leaves for Alabama.

## ANSWERS TO ANALYZING LITERATURE

1. Suggested Response: The basic conflict is Annie's struggle to reach and unlock the mind of Helen. To achieve this goal, Annie must battle against Helen herself and other members of her family.
2. Students' answers will differ. Most students will probably feel that

## Applying

10. Students' answers will differ. Sug-

## Focus

**Literary Focus** Sometimes themes are presented as direct and thoughtful statements. Sometimes they must be inferred. In this play, Annie's statement at the beginning of the act suggests the theme: "There's only one way out, for you, and it's language."

**Look For** It may be helpful for students to summarize what they know about Annie so far. Help them realize that only a strong, persistent person with a good sense of humor would be able to perservere in the face of such difficulties.

**Writing/Prior Knowledge** Have students discuss the old saying, "If at first you don't succeed, try, try again." Is persistence at the top of their list of suggestions? What other qualities might also be helpful?

**Vocabulary** Have your less advanced students read the words and their meanings several times. Then have them write a short paragraph about a real incident. They must write at least four sentences and use all the words in the list.

**Spelling Tip** Point out the silent *b* in *subtle*.

## The Miracle Worker, Act III

**Theme in Drama**

The **theme** of a play is the central idea, or insight into life, that the play expresses. Since conflict is the heart of drama, understanding why the basic conflict of a play develops and concludes as it does brings you very close to an understanding of the play's theme. Imagine, for example, a young woman who wants to succeed as a dancer. She is told that she lacks talent or physical ability. She does poorly at auditions and fails to get parts. She suffers injuries in training. However, she continues to fight against these discouragements, keeps practicing, and eventually is invited to join a dance company. You could say that the triumph of persistence, discipline, and effort over failure and discouragement is the theme of this story. Such a statement explains why the conflict is resolved as it is.

**Look For**

As you read Act III of *The Miracle Worker,* look for the character traits in Annie that have the greatest effect on the outcome of the action. What are these traits? What other conditions are important? How would you state the play's central idea or insight into life?

**Writing**

Think of a situation in which someone overcame opposition or discouragement and succeeded in achieving a goal. What personal qualities were needed? What else may have been important? List three or four suggestions you would make to someone in a similar situation.

**Vocabulary**

Knowing the following words will help you as you read Act III of *The Miracle Worker.*

**interminable** (in tʉr′ mi nə b'l) *adj.*: Lasting or seeming to last forever (p. 301)

**haggard** (hag′ ərd) *adj.*: Worn, as from lack of sleep (p. 302)

**painstakingly** (pānz′ tā′ kiŋ lē)

*adv.*: Acting very carefully (p. 305)

**subtly** (sut′lē) *adv.*: In a delicately suggestive way (p. 308)

**aversion** (ə vʉr′ zhən) *n.*: Intense dislike (p. 312)

## Objectives

1 To understand the theme of a play
2 To summarize a play
3 To write a review of a play

## Support Material

**Teaching Portfolio**
Teacher Backup, p. 351
Grammar in Action Worksheet, *Using Direct Objects and Subject Complements,* p. 354
Usage and Mechanics Worksheet, p. 356
Vocabulary Check, p. 357
Critical Thinking and Reading Worksheet, *Summarizing a Play,* p. 358

Language Worksheet, *Recognizing the Prefix -dis,* p. 359
Selection Test, p. 360

## ACT III

[*The stage is totally dark, until we see* AN-NIE *and* HELEN *silhouetted on the bed in the garden house.* ANNIE'S *voice is audible, very patient, and worn; it has been saying this for a long time.*]

**ANNIE.** Water, Helen. This is water. W, a, t, e, r. It has a *name.*

[*A silence. Then:*]

Egg, e, g, g. It has a *name,* the name stands for the thing. Oh, it's so simple, simple as birth, to explain.

[*The lights have commenced to rise, not on the garden house but on the homestead. Then:*]

Helen, Helen, the chick *has* to come out of its shell, sometime. You come out, too.

[*In the bedroom upstairs, we see* VINEY *un-hurriedly washing the window, dusting, turning the mattress, readying the room for use again; then in the family room a dimin-ished group at one end of the table—*KATE, KELLER, JAMES*—finishing up a quiet break-fast; then outside, down right, the other Negro servant on his knees, assisted by* MARTHA, *working with a trowel around a new trellis and wheelbarrow. The scene is one of everyday calm, and all are oblivious to* ANNIE'S *voice.*]

There's only one way out, for you, and it's language. To learn that your fingers can talk. And say anything, anything you can name. This is mug. Mug, m, u, g. Helen, it has a *name.* It—has—a—*name*—

[KATE *rises from the table.*]

**KELLER.** [*Gently*] You haven't eaten, Katie.

**KATE.** [*Smiles, shakes her head*] I haven't the appetite. I'm too—restless, I can't sit to it.

**KELLER.** You should eat, my dear. It will be a long day, waiting.

**JAMES.** [*Lightly*] But it's been a short two weeks. I never thought life could be so—noiseless, went much too quickly for me.

[KATE *and* KELLER *gaze at him, in silence.* JAMES *becomes uncomfortable.*]

**ANNIE.** C, a, r, d. Card. C, a—

**JAMES.** Well, the house has been practically normal, hasn't it?

**KELLER.** [*Harshly*] Jimmie.

**JAMES.** Is it wrong to enjoy a quiet breakfast, after five years? And you two even seem to enjoy each other—

**KELLER.** It could be even more noiseless, Jimmie, without your tongue running every minute. Haven't you enough feeling to imag-ine what Katie has been undergoing, ever since—

[KATE *stops him, with her hand on his arm.*]

**KATE.** Captain.

[*To* JAMES]

It's true. The two weeks have been normal, quiet, all you say. But not short. Intermin-able.

[*She rises, and wanders out; she pauses on the porch steps, gazing toward the garden house.*]

**ANNIE.** [*Fading*] W, a, t, e, r. But it means *this.* W, a, t, e, r. *This.* W, a, t—

**JAMES.** I only meant that Miss Sullivan is a boon. Of contention, though, it seems.[1]

**KELLER.** [*Heavily*] If and when you're a par-ent, Jimmie, you will understand what sepa-ration means. A mother loses a—protector.

---

**1. a boon. Of contention:** A boon, or gift, but also a bone of contention—the subject of a dispute.

*The Miracle Worker* **301**

## Presentation

**Motivation/Prior Knowledge**
Have students recall a time when they learned something new. Have them discuss the difficul-ties of such an experience. Then tell them that Helen's difficulties in learning language were almost overwhelming.

**Master Teacher Note** You might want to point out to students that while Helen is isolated by blind-ness and deafness, characters who are not handicapped are isolated as well. James and Kel-ler, for example, are isolated from each other because they are un-able to communicate and share feelings. Have students look for the ways that Helen's progress affects the isolation of other fami-ly members.

**Purpose-Setting Question**
What effect does Helen's return to her family have on her?

**1 Clarification** The first part of this scene includes actions that are taking place simultaneously.

**2 Discussion** Contrast what the two weeks have meant to James and to Kate.

3  **Discussion** What does Keller mean? About whom is he talking?

4  **Discussion** What conflict seems to be ending?

**JAMES.** [*Baffled*] Hm?

**KELLER.** You'll learn, we don't just keep our children safe. They keep us safe.

[*He rises, with his empty coffee cup and saucer.*]

There are of course all kinds of separation, Katie has lived with one kind for five years. And another is disappointment. In a child.

[*He goes with the cup out the rear door.* JAMES *sits for a long moment of stillness. In the garden house the lights commence to come up;* ANNIE, *haggard at the table, is writing a letter, her face again almost in contact with the stationery;* HELEN, *apart on the stool, and for the first time as clean and neat as a button, is quietly crocheting an endless chain of wool, which snakes all around the room.*]

**ANNIE.** "I, feel, every, day, more, and, more, in—"

[*She pauses, and turns the pages of a dictionary open before her; her finger descends the words to a full stop. She elevates her eyebrows, then copies the word.*]

"—adequate."

[*In the main house* JAMES *pushes up, and goes to the front doorway, after* KATE.]

**JAMES.** Kate?

[KATE *turns her glance.* JAMES *is rather weary.*]

I'm sorry. Open my mouth, like that fairy tale, frogs jump out.

**KATE.** No. It has been better. For everyone.

[*She starts away, up center.*]

**ANNIE.** [*Writing*] "If, only, there, were, some-one, to, help, me, I, need, a, teacher, as, much, as, Helen—

**JAMES.** Kate.

302    *Drama*

[KATE *halts, waits.*]

What does he want from me?

**KATE.** That's not the question. Stand up to the world, Jimmie, that comes first.

**JAMES.** [*A pause, wryly*] But the world is him.

**KATE.** Yes. And no one can do it for you.

**JAMES.** Kate.

[*His voice is humble.*]

At least we— Could you—be my friend?

**KATE.** I am.

[KATE *turns to wander, up back of the garden house.* ANNIE'S *murmur comes at once; the lights begin to die on the main house.*]

**ANNIE.** "—my, mind, is, undisiplined, full, of, skips, and, jumps, and—"

[*She halts, rereads, frowns.*]

Hm.

[ANNIE *puts her nose again in the dictionary, flips back to an earlier page, and fingers down the words;* KATE *presently comes down toward the bay window with a trayful of food.*]

Disinter—disinterested—disjoin—dis—

[*She backtracks, indignant.*]

Disinterested, disjoin— Where's disipline?

[*She goes a page or two back, searching with her finger, muttering.*]

What a dictionary, have to know how to spell it before you can look up how to spell it, dis-ciple, *discipline!* Diskipline.

[*She corrects the word in her letter.*]

Undisciplined.

[*But her eyes are bothering her, she closes them in exhaustion and gently fingers the eyelids.* KATE *watches her through the window.*]

**KATE.** What are you doing to your eyes?

[ANNIE *glances around; she puts her smoked glasses on, and gets up to come over, assuming a cheerful energy.*]

**ANNIE.** It's worse on my vanity! I'm learning to spell. It's like a surprise party, the most unexpected characters turn up.

**KATE.** You're not to overwork your eyes, Miss Annie.

**ANNIE.** Well.

[*She takes the tray, sets it on her chair, and carries chair and tray to* HELEN.]

Whatever I spell to Helen I'd better spell right.

**KATE.** [*Almost wistful*] How—serene she is.

**ANNIE.** She learned this stitch yesterday. Now I can't get her to stop!

[*She disentangles one foot from the wool chain, and sets the chair before* HELEN. HELEN, *at its contact with her knee feels the plate, promptly sets her crocheting down, and tucks the napkin in at her neck, but* ANNIE *withholds the spoon; when* HELEN *finds it missing, she folds her hands in her lap, and quietly waits.* ANNIE *twinkles at* KATE *with mock devoutness.*]

Such a little lady, she'd sooner starve than eat with her fingers.

[*She gives* HELEN *the spoon, and* HELEN *begins to eat, neatly.*]

**KATE.** You've taught her so much, these two weeks. I would never have—

**ANNIE.** Not enough.

[*She is suddenly gloomy, shakes her head.*]

Obedience isn't enough. Well, she learned

two nouns this morning, key and water, brings her up to eighteen nouns and three verbs.

**KATE.** [*Hesitant*] But—not—

**ANNIE.** No. Not that they mean things. It's still a finger-game, no meaning.

[*She turns to* KATE, *abruptly.*]

Mrs. Keller—

[*But she defers it; she comes back, to sit in the bay and lift her hand.*]

Shall we play our finger-game?

**KATE.** How will she learn it?

**ANNIE.** It will come.

[*She spells a word:* KATE *does not respond.*]

**KATE.** How?

**ANNIE.** [*A pause*] How does a bird learn to fly?

[*She spells again.*]

We're born to use words, like wings, it has to come.

**KATE.** How?

**ANNIE.** [*Another pause, wearily*] All right. I don't know how.

[*She pushes up her glasses, to rub her eyes.*]

I've done everything I could think of. Whatever she's learned here—keeping herself clean, knitting, stringing beads, meals, setting-up exercises each morning, we climb trees, hunt eggs, yesterday a chick was born in her hands—all of it I spell, everything we do, we never stop spelling. I go to bed with—writer's cramp from talking so much!

**KATE.** I worry about you, Miss Annie. You must rest.

**ANNIE.** Now? She spells back in her *sleep,*

**5 Discussion** On what other occasions has Annie displayed humor? How has her sense of humor helped her?

**6 Critical Thinking and Reading** Paraphrase Annie's reason for believing Helen will learn language.

**7 Critical Thinking and Reading** Why do you think Annie keeps spelling to Helen?

her fingers make letters when she doesn't know! In her bones those five fingers know, that hand aches to—speak out, and something in her mind is asleep, how do I—nudge that awake? That's the one question.

**KATE.** With no answer.

**ANNIE.** [*Long pause*] Except keep at it. Like this.

[*She again begins spelling—I, need—and* KATE'S *brows gather, following the words.*]

**KATE.** More—time?

[*She glances at* ANNIE, *who looks her in the eyes, silent.*]

Here?

**ANNIE.** Spell it.

[KATE *spells a word—no—shaking her head;* ANNIE *spells two words—why, not—back, with an impatient question in her eyes; and* KATE *moves her head in pain to answer it.*]

**KATE.** Because I can't— ⌐ 8

304  *Drama*

**ANNIE.** Spell it! If she ever learns, you'll have a lot to tell each other, start now.

[KATE *painstakingly spells in air. In the midst of this the rear door opens, and KELLER enters with the setter* BELLE *in tow.*]

**KELLER.** Miss Sullivan? On my way to the office, I brought Helen a playmate—

**ANNIE.** Outside please, Captain Keller.

**KELLER.** My dear child, the two weeks are up today, surely you don't object to—

**ANNIE.** [*Rising*] They're not up till six o'clock.

**KELLER.** [*Indulgent*] Oh, now. What difference can a fraction of one day—

**ANNIE.** An agreement is an agreement. Now you've been very good, I'm sure you can keep it up for a few more hours.

[*She escorts* KELLER *by the arm over the threshold; he obeys, leaving* BELLE.]

**KELLER.** Miss Sullivan, you are a tyrant.

**ANNIE.** Likewise, I'm sure. You can stand there, and close the door if she comes.

**KATE.** I don't think you know how eager we are to have her back in our arms—

**ANNIE.** I do know, it's my main worry.

**KELLER.** It's like expecting a new child in the house. Well, she *is*, so—composed, so—

[*Gently*]

Attractive. You've done wonders for her, Miss Sullivan.

**ANNIE.** [*Not a question*] Have I.

**KELLER.** If there's anything you want from us in repayment tell us, it will be a privilege to—

**ANNIE.** I just told Mrs. Keller. I want more time.

**KATE.** Miss Annie—

**ANNIE.** Another week.

[HELEN *lifts her head, and begins to sniff.*]

**KELLER.** We miss the child. *I* miss her, I'm glad to say, that's a different debt I owe you—

**ANNIE.** Pay it to Helen. Give *her* another week.

**KATE.** [*Gently*] Doesn't she miss us?

**KELLER.** Of course she does. What a wrench this unexplainable—exile must be to her, can you say it's not?

**ANNIE.** No. But I—

[HELEN *is off the stool, to grope about the room; when she encounters* BELLE, *she throws her arms around the dog's neck in delight.*]

**KATE.** Doesn't she need affection too, Miss Annie?

**ANNIE.** [*Wavering*] She—never shows me she needs it, she won't have any—caressing or—

**KATE.** But you're not her mother.

**KELLER.** And what would another week accomplish? We are more than satisfied, you've done more than we ever thought possible, taught her constructive—

**ANNIE.** I can't promise anything. All I can—

**KELLER.** [*No break*] —things to do, to behave like—even look like—a human child, so manageable, contented, cleaner, more—

**ANNIE.** [*Withering*] Cleaner.

**KELLER.** Well. We say cleanliness is next to godliness, Miss—

**ANNIE.** Cleanliness is next to nothing, she has to learn that everything has its name! That words can be her *eyes*, to everything in the world outside her, and inside too, what is she without words? With them she can

---

9 **Discussion** Why does Annie insist Kate do finger spelling?

10 **Discussion** Why is this a worry to Annie?

11 **Discussion** Why do you think that Helen does not show physical affection for Annie?

12 **Discussion** Compare Annie's and Keller's feelings about what has been accomplished in two weeks. Which one is satisfied?

13 **Reading Strategy** Ask students to predict whether Annie's fears will be borne out.

14 **Discussion** How does Keller feel about Annie's hopes for Helen?

15 **Discussion** What does Keller imply when he asks, "Is the opposite true, for you?"

16 **Discussion** Why does Annie, who is normally so combative, surrender in this case?

think, have ideas, be reached, there's not a thought or fact in the world that can't be hers. You publish a newspaper, Captain Keller, do I have to tell you what words are? And she has them already—

**KELLER.** Miss Sullivan.

**ANNIE.** —eighteen nouns and three verbs, they're in her fingers now, I need only time to push *one* of them into her mind! One, and everything under the sun will follow. Don't you see what she's learned here is only clearing the way for that? I can't risk her unlearning it, give me more time alone with her, another week to—

**KELLER.** Look.

[*He points, and* ANNIE *turns.* HELEN *is playing with* BELLE'S *claws; she makes letters with her fingers, shows them to* BELLE, *waits with her palm, then manipulates the dog's claws.*]

What is she spelling?

[*A silence.*]

**KATE.** Water?

[ANNIE *nods.*]

**KELLER.** Teaching a dog to spell.

[*A pause*]

The dog doesn't know what she means, any more than she knows what you mean, Miss Sullivan. I think you ask too much, of her and yourself. God may not have meant Helen to have the—eyes you speak of.

**ANNIE.** [*Toneless*] I mean her to.

**KELLER.** [*Curiously*] What is it to you?

[ANNIE'S *head comes slowly up.*]

You make us see how we indulge her for our sake. Is the opposite true, for you?

**ANNIE.** [*Then*] Half a week?

**KELLER.** An agreement is an agreement.

**ANNIE.** Mrs. Keller?

**KATE.** [*Simply*] I want her back.

[*A wait;* ANNIE *then lets her hands drop in surrender, and nods.*]

**KELLER.** I'll send Viney over to help you pack.

**ANNIE.** Not until six o'clock. I have her till six o'clock.

**KELLER.** [*Consenting*] Six o'clock. Come, Katie.

[KATE *leaving the window joins him around back, while* KELLER *closes the door; they are shut out.*

*Only the garden house is daylit now, and the light on it is narrowing down.* ANNIE *stands watching* HELEN *work* BELLE'S *claws. Then she settles beside them on her knees, and stops* HELEN'S *hand.*]

**ANNIE.** [*Gently*] No.

[*She shakes her head, with* HELEN'S *hand to her face, then spells.*]

Dog, D, o, g. Dog.

[*She touches* HELEN'S *hand to* BELLE. HELEN *dutifully pats the dog's head, and resumes spelling to its paw.*]

Not water.

[ANNIE *rolls to her feet, brings a tumbler of water back from the tray, and kneels with it, to seize* HELEN'S *hand and spell.*]

Here. Water. *Water.*

[*She thrusts* HELEN'S *hand into the tumbler.* HELEN *lifts her hand out dripping, wipes it daintily on* BELLE'S *hide, and taking the tumbler from* ANNIE, *endeavors to thrust* BELLE'S *paw into it.* ANNIE *sits watching, wearily.*]

I don't know how to tell you. Not a soul in the world knows how to tell you. Helen, Helen.

[*She bends in compassion to touch her lips to* HELEN'S *temple, and instantly* HELEN *pauses, her hands off the dog, her head slightly averted. The lights are still narrowing, and* BELLE *slinks off. After a moment* ANNIE *sits back.*]

Yes, what's it to me? They're satisfied. Give them back their child and dog, both housebroken, everyone's satisfied. But me, and you.

[HELEN'S *hand comes out into the light, groping.*]

Reach. *Reach!*

[ANNIE *extending her own hand grips* HELEN'S; *the two hands are clasped, tense in the light, the rest of the room changing in shadow.*]

I wanted to teach you—oh, everything the earth is full of, Helen, everything on it that's ours for a wink and it's gone, and what we are on it, the—light we bring to it and leave behind in—words, why, you can see five thousand years back in a light of words, everything we feel, think, know—and share, in words, so not a soul is in darkness, or done with, even in the grave. And I know, I *know*, one word and I can—put the world in your hand—and whatever it is to me, I won't take less! How, how, how do I tell you that *this*—

[*She spells.*]

—means a *word*, and the word means this *thing*, wool?

[*She thrusts the wool at* HELEN'S *hand;* HELEN *sits, puzzled.* ANNIE *puts the crocheting aside.*]

Or this—s, t, o, o, l—means this *thing*, stool?

17

[*She claps* HELEN'S *palm to the stool.* HELEN *waits, uncomprehending.* ANNIE *snatches up her napkin, spells:*]

Napkin!

[*She forces it on* HELEN'S *hand, waits, discards it, lifts a fold of the child's dress, spells.*]

Dress!

[*She lets it drop, spells.*]

F, a, c, e, face!

[*She draws* HELEN'S *hand to her cheek, and pressing it there, staring into the child's responseless eyes, hears the distant belfry begin to toll, slowly: one, two, three, four, five, six.*

*On the third stroke the lights stealing in around the garden house show us figures waiting:* VINEY, *the other servant,* MARTHA, PERCY *at the drapes, and* JAMES *on the dim porch.* ANNIE *and* HELEN *remain, frozen. The chimes die away. Silently* PERCY *moves the drape-rod back out of sight;* VINEY *steps into the room—not using the door—and unmakes the bed; the other servant brings the wheelbarrow over, leaves it handy, rolls the bed off;* VINEY *puts the bed linens on top of a waiting boxful of* HELEN'S *toys, and loads the box on the wheelbarrow;* MARTHA *and* PERCY *take out the chairs, with the trayful, then the table; and* JAMES, *coming down and into the room, lifts* ANNIE'S *suitcase from its corner.* VINEY *and the other servant load the remaining odds and ends on the wheelbarrow, and the servant wheels it off.* VINEY *and the children departing leave only* JAMES *in the room with* ANNIE *and* HELEN. JAMES *studies the two of them, without mockery, and then, quietly going to the door and opening it, bears the suitcase out, and housewards. He leaves the door open.*]

18

17 **Literary Focus** How does this speech relate to the play's theme?

18 **Discussion** Compare this action with the move into the garden house. What feelings does the move back to the main house call up?

**19 Discussion** Compare Helen's display of affection for her mother with Annie's statement about Helen's need on page 305.

**20 Discussion** How do these voices from the past sum up Annie's inner conflict?

**21 Discussion** Why is Keller pleased while Annie is not?

KATE *steps into the doorway, and stands.* ANNIE *lifting her gaze from* HELEN *sees her; she takes* HELEN'S *hand from her cheek, and returns it to the child's own, stroking it there twice, in her mother-sign, before spelling slowly into it:*]

M, o, t, h, e, r. Mother.

[HELEN *with her hand free strokes her cheek, suddenly forlorn.* ANNIE *takes her hand again.*]

M, o, t, h—

[*But* KATE *is trembling with such impatience that her voice breaks from her, harsh.*]

**KATE.** Let her *come!*

[ANNIE *lifts* HELEN *to her feet, with a turn, and gives her a little push. Now* HELEN *begins groping, sensing something, trembling herself; and* KATE *falling one step in onto her knees clasps her, kissing her.* HELEN *clutches her, tight as she can.* KATE *is inarticulate, choked, repeating* HELEN'S *name again and again. She wheels with her in her arms, to stumble away out the doorway;* ANNIE *stands unmoving, while* KATE *in a blind walk carries* HELEN *like a baby behind the main house, out of view.*

ANNIE *is now alone on the stage. She turns, gazing around at the stripped room, bidding it silently farewell, impassively, like a defeated general on the deserted battlefield. All that remains is a stand with a basin of water; and here* ANNIE *takes up an eyecup, bathes each of her eyes, empties the eyecup, drops it in her purse, and tiredly locates her smoked glasses on the floor. The lights alter subtly; in the act of putting on her glasses* ANNIE *hears something that stops her, with head lifted. We hear it too, the voices out of the past, including her own now, in a whisper:*]

*308 Drama*

**BOY'S VOICE.** You said we'd be together, forever— You promised, forever and—*Annie!*

**ANAGNOS' VOICE.** But that battle is dead and done with, why not let it stay buried?

**ANNIE'S VOICE.** [*Whispering*] I think God must owe me a resurrection.

**ANAGNOS' VOICE.** What?

[*A pause, and* ANNIE *answers it herself, heavily.*]

**ANNIE.** And I owe God one.

**BOY'S VOICE.** Forever and ever—

[ANNIE *shakes her head.*]

—forever, and ever, and—

[ANNIE *covers her ears.*]

—forever, and ever, and ever—

[*It pursues* ANNIE; *she flees to snatch up her purse, wheels to the doorway, and* KELLER *is standing in it. The lights have lost their special color.*]

**KELLER.** Miss—Annie.

[*He has an envelope in his fingers.*]

I've been waiting to give you this.

**ANNIE.** [*After a breath*] What?

**KELLER.** Your first month's salary.

[*He puts it in her hand.*]

With many more to come, I trust. It doesn't express what we feel, it doesn't pay our debt. For what you've done.

**ANNIE.** What have I done?

**KELLER.** Taken a wild thing, and given us back a child.

**ANNIE.** [*Presently*] I taught her one thing, no. Don't do this, don't do that—

## Grammar in Action

A **complement** is word or a group of words that completes the meaning of the predicate of a sentence. There are two broad kinds of complements. Direct objects complete the meaning of sentences with action verbs. Predicate nominatives or predicate adjectives complete the meaning of sentences with linking verbs.

The driver raced his *engine.* (direct object of the action verb *raced*)

Our team was the *winner.* (predicate nominative after the linking verb *was*)
The speech team has usually been *victorious.* (predicate adjective after the linking verb *has been*)

Writers use many different complements to complete basic sentence patterns. The following sentences from *The Miracle Worker* illustrate a variety of complements:

**KELLER.** It's more than all of us could, in all the years we—

**ANNIE.** I wanted to teach her what language is. I wanted to teach her yes.

**KELLER.** You will have time.

**ANNIE.** I don't know how. I know without it to do nothing but obey is—no gift, obedience without understanding is a—blindness, too. Is that all I've wished on her?

**KELLER.** [*Gently*] No, no—

**ANNIE.** Maybe. I don't know what else to do. Simply go on, keep doing what I've done, and have—faith that inside she's— That inside it's waiting. Like water, underground. All I can do is keep on.

**KELLER.** It's enough. For us.

**ANNIE.** You can help, Captain Keller.

**KELLER.** How?

**ANNIE.** Even learning no has been at a cost. Of much trouble and pain. Don't undo it.

**KELLER.** Why should we wish to—

**ANNIE.** [*Abruptly*] The world isn't an easy place for anyone, I don't want her just to obey but to let her have her way in everything is a lie, to *her*, I can't—

[*Her eyes fill, it takes her by surprise, and she laughs through it.*]

And I don't even love her, she's not my child! Well. You've got to stand between that lie and her.

**KELLER.** We'll try.

**ANNIE.** Because *I* will. As long as you let me stay, that's one promise I'll keep.

**KELLER.** Agreed. We've learned something too, I hope.

[*A pause*]

Won't you come now, to supper?

**ANNIE.** Yes.

[*She wags the envelope, ruefully.*]

Why doesn't God pay His debts each month?

**KELLER.** I beg your pardon?

**ANNIE.** Nothing. I used to wonder how I could—

[*The lights are fading on them, simultaneously rising on the family room of the main house, where* VINEY *is polishing glassware at the table set for dinner.*]

—earn a living.

**KELLER.** Oh, you do.

**ANNIE.** I really do. Now the question is, can I survive it!

[KELLER *smiles, offers his arm.*]

**KELLER.** May I?

[ANNIE *takes it, and the lights lose them as he escorts her out.*

*Now in the family room the rear door opens, and* HELEN *steps in. She stands a moment, then sniffs in one deep grateful breath, and her hands go out vigorously to familiar things, over the door panels, and to the chairs around the table, and over the silverware on the table, until she mets* VINEY; *she pats her flank approvingly.*]

**VINEY.** Oh, we glad to have you back too, prob'ly.

[HELEN *hurries groping to the front door, opens and closes it, removes its key, opens and closes it again to be sure it is unlocked, gropes back to the rear door and repeats the procedure, removing its key and hugging herself gleefully.*

AUNT EV *is next in by the rear door, with a relish tray; she bends to kiss* HELEN's *cheek.*]

*The Miracle Worker* 309

**22 Discussion** What does Annie think is "waiting" inside Helen?

**23 Reading Strategy** Have students predict whether Keller will keep his promise.

**24 Discussion** At what other time has a key been an important prop? How is the key also a symbol?

Annie is now *alone* on the stage. She turns, gazing around at the stripped room. . . . All that remains is a *stand* with a basin of water; and here Annie takes up an *eyecup*, bathes *each* of her eyes, empties the *eyecup*, drops *it* in her purse, and tiredly locates her smoked *glasses* on the floor.

*Alone* is a predicate adjective; *stand* is a predicate nominative; and the other italicized words are direct objects. Notice that each complement answers the question *what*? after the verb.

**Student Activity 1.** Find the verb to which each complement in the passage belongs. Identify it as an action verb or a linking verb.

**Student Activity 2.** Write six sentences describing an important scene in a real or imaginary play. Use different types of complements in your sentences.

**25** **Discussion** What do James' action and words signify?

**26** **Discussion** Why does James mention this particular story from the Bible when saying grace?

[HELEN *finds* KATE *behind her, and thrusts the keys at her.*]

**KATE.** What? Oh.

[*To* EV]

Keys.

[*She pockets them, lets* HELEN *feel them.*]

Yes, *I'll* keep the keys. I think we've had enough of locked doors, too.

[JAMES, *having earlier put* ANNIE'S *suitcase inside her door upstairs and taken himself out of view around the corner, now reappears and comes down the stairs as* ANNIE *and* KELLER *mount the porch steps. Following them into the family room, he pats* ANNIE'S *hair in passing, rather to her surprise.*]

**JAMES.** Evening, general.

[*He takes his own chair opposite.*

VINEY *bears the empty water pitcher out to the porch. The remaining suggestion of garden house is gone now, and the water pump is unobstructed;* VINEY *pumps water into the pitcher.*

KATE *surveying the table breaks the silence.*]

**KATE.** Will you say grace, Jimmie?

[*They bow their heads, except for* HELEN, *who palms her empty plate and then reaches to be sure her mother is there.* JAMES *considers a moment, glances across at* ANNIE, *lowers his head again, and obliges.*]

**JAMES.** [*Lightly*] And Jacob was left alone, and wrestled with an angel until the breaking of the day; and the hollow of Jacob's thigh was out of joint, as he wrestled with him; and the angel said, Let me go, for the day breaketh. And Jacob said, I will not let thee go, except thou bless me. Amen.

310 *Drama*

[ANNIE *has lifted her eyes suspiciously at* JAMES, *who winks expressionlessly and inclines his head to* HELEN.]

Oh, you angel.

[*The others lift their faces;* VINEY *returns with the pitcher, setting it down near* KATE, *then goes out the rear door; and* ANNIE *puts a napkin around* HELEN.]

**AUNT EV.** That's a very strange grace, James.

**KELLER.** Will you start the muffins, Ev?

**JAMES.** It's from the Good Book, isn't it?

**AUNT EV.** [*Passing a plate*] Well, of course it is. Didn't you know?

**JAMES.** Yes, I knew.

**KELLER.** [*Serving*] Ham, Miss Annie?

**ANNIE.** Please.

**AUNT EV.** Then why ask?

**JAMES.** I meant it *is* from the Good Book, and therefore a fitting grace.

**AUNT EV.** Well. I don't know about *that.*

**KATE.** [*With the pitcher*] Miss Annie?

**ANNIE.** Thank you.

**AUNT EV.** There's an awful *lot* of things in the Good Book that I wouldn't care to hear just before eating.

[*When* ANNIE *reaches for the pitcher,* HELEN *removes her napkin and drops it to the floor.* ANNIE *is filling* HELEN'S *glass when she notices it; she considers* HELEN'S *bland expression a moment, then bends, retrieves it, and tucks it around* HELEN'S *neck again.*]

**JAMES.** Well, fitting in the sense that Jacob's thigh was out of joint, and so is this piggie's.

**AUNT EV.** I declare, James—

**KATE.** Pickles, Aunt Ev?

**AUNT EV.** Oh, I should say so, you know my opinion of your pickles—

**KATE.** This is the end of them, I'm afraid. I didn't put up nearly enough last summer, this year I intend to—

[*She interrupts herself, seeing* HELEN *deliberately lift off her napkin and drop it again to the floor. She bends to retrieve it, but* ANNIE *stops her arm.*]

**KELLER.** [*Not noticing*] Reverend looked in at the office today to complain his hens have stopped laying. Poor fellow, *he* was out of joint, all he could—

[*He stops too, to frown down the table at* KATE, HELEN, *and* ANNIE *in turn, all suspended in midmotion.*]

**JAMES.** [*Not noticing*] I've always suspected those hens.

**AUNT EV.** Of what?

**JAMES.** I think they're Papist. Has he tried—

[*He stops, too, following* KELLER'S *eyes.* ANNIE *now stops to pick the napkin up.*]

**AUNT EV.** James, now you're pulling my—lower extremity, the first thing you know we'll be—

[*She stops, too, hearing herself in the silence.* ANNIE, *with everyone now watching, for the third time puts the napkin on* HELEN. HELEN *yanks it off, and throws it down.* ANNIE *rises, lifts* HELEN'S *plate, and bears it away.* HELEN, *feeling it gone, slides down and commences to kick up under the table; the dishes jump.* ANNIE *contemplates this for a moment, then coming back takes* HELEN'S *wrists firmly and swings her off the chair.* HELEN *struggling gets one hand free, and catches at her mother's skirt; when* KATE *takes her by the shoulders,* HELEN *hangs quiet.*]

**KATE.** Miss Annie.

**ANNIE.** No.

**KATE.** [*A pause*] It's a very special day.

**ANNIE.** [*Grimly*] It will be, when I give in to that.

[*She tries to disengage* HELEN'S *hand;* KATE *lays hers on* ANNIE'S.]

**KATE.** Please. I've hardly had a chance to welcome her home—

**ANNIE.** Captain Keller.

**KELLER.** [*Embarrassed*] Oh. Katie, we—had a little talk, Miss Annie feels that if we indulge Helen in these—

**AUNT EV.** But what's the child done?

**ANNIE.** She's learned not to throw things on the floor and kick. It took us the best part of two weeks and—

**AUNT EV.** But only a napkin, it's not as if it were breakable!

**ANNIE.** And everything she's learned *is?* Mrs. Keller, I don't think we should—play tug-of-war for her, either give her to me or you keep her from kicking.

**KATE.** What do you wish to do?

**ANNIE.** Let me take her from the table.

**AUNT EV.** Oh, let her stay, my goodness, she's only a child, she doesn't have to wear a napkin if she doesn't want to her first evening—

**ANNIE.** [*Level*] And ask outsiders not to interfere.

**AUNT EV.** [*Astonished*] Out—outsi— I'm the child's *aunt!*

**KATE.** [*Distressed*] Will once hurt so much, Miss Annie? I've—made all Helen's favorite foods, tonight.

[*A pause*]

**KELLER.** [*Gently*] It's a homecoming party, Miss Annie.

27 **Discussion** What does each person slowly realize is happening?

28 **Literary Focus** How does the old conflict resurface?

**29 Discussion** What does James mean as he repeats his statement?

**30 Discussion** Have students infer what Kate must be thinking as she tells Annie to take Helen.

[ANNIE *after a moment releases* HELEN. *But she cannot accept it, at her own chair she shakes her head and turns back, intent on* KATE.]

**ANNIE.** She's testing you. You realize?

**JAMES.** [*To Annie*] She's testing you.

**KELLER.** Jimmie, be quiet.

[JAMES *sits, tense.*]

Now she's home, naturally she—

**ANNIE.** And wants to see what will happen. At your hands. I said it was my main worry, is this what you promised me not half an hour ago?

**KELLER.** [*Reasonably*] But she's *not* kicking, now—

**ANNIE.** And not learning not to. Mrs. Keller, teaching her is bound to be painful, to everyone. I know it hurts to watch, but she'll live up to just what you demand of her, and no more.

**JAMES.** [*Palely*] She's testing *you.*

**KELLER.** [*Testily*] Jimmie.

**JAMES.** I have an opinion, I think I should—

**KELLER.** No one's interested in hearing your opinion.

**ANNIE.** *I'm* interested, of course she's testing me. Let me keep her to what she's learned and she'll go on learning from me. Take her out of my hands and it all comes apart.

[KATE *closes her eyes, digesting it;* ANNIE *sits again, with a brief comment for her.*]

Be bountiful, it's at her expense.

[*She turns to* JAMES, *flatly.*]

Please pass me more of—her favorite foods.

[*Then* KATE *lifts* HELEN'S *hand, and turning*

312 Drama

her toward ANNIE, *surrenders her;* HELEN *makes for her own chair.*]

**KATE.** [*Low*] Take her, Miss Annie.

**ANNIE.** [*Then*] Thank you.

[*But the moment* ANNIE *rising reaches for her hand,* HELEN *begins to fight and kick, clutching to the tablecloth, and uttering laments.* ANNIE *again tries to loosen her hand, and* KELLER *rises.*]

**KELLER.** [*Tolerant*] I'm afraid you're the difficulty, Miss Annie. Now I'll keep her to what she's learned, you're quite right there—

[*He takes* HELEN'S *hands from* ANNIE, *pats them;* HELEN *quiets down.*]

—but I don't see that we need send her from the table, after all, she's the guest of honor. Bring her plate back.

**ANNIE.** If she was a seeing child, none of you would tolerate one—

**KELLER.** Well, she's not, I think some compromise is called for. Bring her plate, please.

[ANNIE'S *jaw sets, but she restores the plate, while* KELLER *fastens the napkin around* HELEN'S *neck; she permits it.*]

There. It's not unnatural, most of us take some aversion to our teachers, and occasionally another hand can smooth things out.

[*He puts a fork in* HELEN'S *hand;* HELEN *takes it. Genially*]

Now. Shall we start all over?

[*He goes back around the table, and sits.* ANNIE *stands watching.* HELEN *is motionless, thinking things through, until with a wicked glee she deliberately flings the fork on the floor. After another moment she plunges her hand into her food, and crams a fistful into her mouth.*]

**31 JAMES.** [*Wearily*] I think we've started all over—

[KELLER *shoots a glare at him, as* HELEN *plunges her other hand into* ANNIE'S *plate.* ANNIE *at once moves in, to grasp her wrist, and* HELEN *flinging out a hand encounters the pitcher; she swings with it at* ANNIE; AN-NIE *falling back blocks it with an elbow, but the water flies over her dress.* ANNIE *gets her breath, then snatches the pitcher away in one hand, hoists* HELEN *up bodily under the other arm, and starts to carry her out, kicking.* KELLER *stands.*]

**ANNIE.** [*Savagely polite*] Don't get up!

**KELLER.** Where are you going?

**ANNIE.** Don't smooth anything else out for me, don't interfere in any way! I treat her like a seeing child because I *ask* her to see, I *expect* her to see, don't undo what I do!

**KELLER.** Where are you taking her?

**ANNIE.** To make her fill this pitcher again!

[*She thrusts out with* HELEN *under her arm, but* HELEN *escapes up the stairs and* ANNIE *runs after her.* KELLER *stands rigid.* AUNT EV *is astounded.*]

**32 AUNT EV.** You let her speak to you like that, Arthur? A creature who *works* for you?

**KELLER.** [*Angrily*] No. I don't.

[*He is starting after* ANNIE *when* JAMES, *on his feet with shaky resolve, interposes his chair between them in* KELLER'S *path.*]

**JAMES.** Let her go.

**KELLER.** What!

**JAMES.** [*A swallow*] I said—let her go. She's right.

(KELLER *glares at the chair and him.* JAMES *takes a deep breath, then headlong:*)

She's right, Kate's right, I'm right, and you're wrong. If you drive her away from here it will be over my dead—chair, has it never occurred to you that on one occasion you might be consummately wrong?

[KELLER'S *stare is unbelieving, even a little fascinated.* KATE *rises in trepidation, to mediate.*]

**KATE.** Captain.

[KELLER *stops her with his raised hand; his eyes stay on* JAMES'S *pale face, for a long hold. When he finally finds his voice, it is gruff.*]

**KELLER.** Sit down, everyone.

[*He sits.* KATE *sits.* JAMES *holds onto his chair.* KELLER *speaks mildly.*]

Please sit down, Jimmie.

[JAMES *sits, and a moveless silence prevails;* KELLER'S *eyes do not leave him.*]

ANNIE *has pulled* HELEN *downstairs again by one hand, the pitcher in her other hand, down the porch steps, and across the yard to the pump. She puts* HELEN'S *hand on the pump handle, grimly.*]

**ANNIE.** All right. Pump.

[HELEN *touches her cheek, waits uncertainly.*]

No, she's not here. Pump!

[*She forces* HELEN'S *hand to work the handle, then lets go. And* HELEN *obeys. She pumps till the water comes, then* ANNIE *puts the pitcher in her other hand and guides it under the spout, and the water tumbling half into and half around the pitcher douses* HELEN'S *hand.* ANNIE *takes over the handle to keep water coming, and does automatically what she has done so many times before, spells into* HELEN'S *free palm:*]

*The Miracle Worker* 313

**31 Discussion** Both Keller and James have used the term *start all over*. Does each mean the same thing? Explain.

**32 Discussion** Why is Aunt Ev shocked?

33 **Discussion** As students read the following paragraphs of stage directions, have them try to describe what must be happening in Helen's mind.

Water. W, a, t, e, r. *Water.* It has a—*name*—

33 [*And now the miracle happens.* HELEN *drops the pitcher on the slab under the spout, it shatters. She stands transfixed.* ANNIE *freezes on the pump handle: there is a change in the sundown light, and with it a change in* HELEN's *face, some light coming into it we have never seen there, some struggle in the depths behind it; and her lips tremble, trying to remember something the muscles around them once knew, till at last it finds its way out, painfully, a baby sound buried under the debris of years of dumbness.*]

**HELEN.** Wah. Wah.

[*And again, with great effort*]

Wah. Wah.

[HELEN *plunges her hand into the dwindling water, spells into her own palm. Then she gropes frantically,* ANNIE *reaches for her hand, and* HELEN *spells into* ANNIE's *hand.*]

**ANNIE.** [*Whispering*] Yes.

[HELEN *spells into it again.*]

Yes!

[HELEN *grabs at the handle, pumps for more water, plunges her hand into its spurt and grabs* ANNIE's *to spell it again.*]

Yes! Oh, my dear—

[*She falls to her knees to clasp* HELEN's *hand, but* HELEN *pulls it free, stands almost bewildered, then drops to the ground, pats it swiftly, holds up her palm, imperious.* ANNIE *spells into it:*]

314 *Drama*

Ground.

[HELEN *spells it back.*]

Yes!

[HELEN *whirls to the pump, pats it, holds up her palm, and* ANNIE *spells into it.*]

Pump.

[HELEN *spells it back.*]

Yes! Yes!

[*Now* HELEN *is in such an excitement she is possessed, wild, trembling, cannot be still, turns, runs, falls on the porch steps, claps it, reaches out her palm, and* ANNIE *is at it instantly to spell:*]

Step.

[HELEN *has no time to spell back now, she whirls groping, to touch anything, encounters the trellis, shakes it, thrusts out her palm, and* ANNIE *while spelling to her cries wildly at the house.*]

Trellis. Mrs. Keller! *Mrs. Keller!*

[*Inside,* KATE *starts to her feet.* HELEN *scrambles back onto the porch, groping, and finds the bell string, tugs it; the bell rings, the distant chimes begin tolling the hour, all the bells in town seem to break into speech while* HELEN *reaches out and* ANNIE *spells feverishly into her hand.* KATE *hurries out, with* KELLER *after her;* AUNT EV *is on her feet, to peer out the window; only* JAMES *remains at the table, and with a napkin wipes his damp brow. From up right and left the servants—*VINEY, *the two Negro children, the other servant—run in, and stand watching from a distance as* HELEN, *ringing the bell, with her other hand encounters her mother's skirt; when she throws a hand out,* ANNIE *spells into it:*]

Mother.

[KELLER *now seizes* HELEN'S *hand, she touches him, gestures a hand, and* ANNIE *again spells:*]

Papa—She *knows!*

[KATE *and* KELLER *go to their knees, stammering, clutching* HELEN *to them, and* ANNIE *steps unsteadily back to watch the threesome,* HELEN *spelling wildly into* KATE'S *hand, then into* KELLER'S, KATE *spelling back into* HELEN'S; *they cannot keep their hands off her, and rock her in their clasp.*]

34 **Enrichment** Most of us might find it hard to imagine Helen's excitement. But ask students to think back to a time in their lives when they found the key to understanding a math process or a science experiment—when suddenly it was all so clear.

35 **Clarification** Helen cannot hear the bell, but its clamor proclaims her understanding.

36 **Discussion** What do you think Kate and Keller are feeling as Helen uses language for the first time?

**37 Discussion** How does this scene signal a resolution of the main conflict?

**38 Discussion** The symbolism of the keys has become apparent. Why does Helen give the keys to Annie? How are the keys related to a theme of the play?

**39 Discussion** How does the silence relate to the resolution of Annie's inner conflict?

**40 Discussion** How does the action here summarize the end of the conflicts within the family? How is everyone now able to see more clearly?

**Reader's Response** How did you feel after reading this play? Explain.

---

*Then* HELEN *gropes, feels nothing, turns all around, pulls free, and comes with both hands groping, to find* ANNIE. *She encounters* ANNIE'S *thighs,* ANNIE *kneels to her,* HELEN'S *hand pats* ANNIE'S *cheek impatiently, points a finger, and waits; and* ANNIE *spells into it:*]

37  Teacher.

[HELEN *spells it back, slowly;* ANNIE *nods.*]

Teacher.

[*She holds* HELEN'S *hand to her cheek. Presently* HELEN *withdraws it, not jerkily, only with reserve, and retreats a step. She stands thinking it over, then turns again and stumbles back to her parents. They try to embrace her, but she has something else in mind, it is to get the keys, and she hits* KATE'S *pocket until* KATE *digs them out for her.*

ANNIE *with her own load of emotion has retreated, her back turned, toward the pump, to sit;* KATE *moves to* HELEN, *touches her hand questioningly, and* HELEN *spells a word to her.* KATE *comprehends it, their first act of verbal communication, and she can hardly utter the word aloud, in wonder, gratitude, and deprivation; it is a moment in which she simultaneously finds and loses a child.*]

**KATE.** Teacher?

[ANNIE *turns; and* KATE, *facing* HELEN *in her direction by the shoulders, holds her back, holds her back, and then relinquishes her.* HELEN *feels her way across the yard, rather shyly, and when her moving hands touch* ANNIE'S *skirt she stops. Then she holds out the keys and places them in* ANNIE'S *hand. For a moment neither of them moves. Then* HELEN *slides into* ANNIE'S *arms, and lifting away her smoked glasses, kisses her on the cheek.* ANNIE *gathers her in.*

38

KATE *torn both ways turns from this, gestures the servants off, and makes her way into the house, on* KELLER'S *arm. The servants go, in separate directions.*

*The lights are half down now, except over the pump.* ANNIE *and* HELEN *are here, alone in the yard.* ANNIE *has found* HELEN'S *hand, almost without knowing it, and she spells slowly into it, her voice unsteady, whispering:*]

**ANNIE.** I, love, Helen.

[*She clutches the child to her, tight this time, not spelling, whispering into her hair.*]

Forever, and—

[*She stops. The lights over the pump are taking on the color of the past, and it brings* ANNIE'S *head up, her eyes opening, in fear; and as slowly as though drawn she rises, to listen, with her hand on* HELEN'S *shoulders. She waits, waits, listening with ears and eyes both, slowly here, slowly there: and hears only silence. There are no voices. The color passes on, and when her eyes come back to* HELEN *she can breathe the end of her phrase without fear:*]

39

—ever.

[*In the family room* KATE *has stood over the table, staring at* HELEN'S *plate, with* KELLER *at her shoulder; now* JAMES *takes a step to move her chair in, and* KATE *sits, with head erect, and* KELLER *inclines his head to* JAMES; *so it is* AUNT EV, *hesitant, and rather humble, who moves to the door.*

40

*Outside* HELEN *tugs at* ANNIE'S *hand, and* ANNIE *comes with it.* HELEN *pulls her toward the house; and hand in hand, they cross the yard, and ascend the porch steps, in the rising lights, to where* AUNT EV *is holding the door open for them.*

*The curtain ends the play.*]

316   Drama

---

## Closure and Extension

### ANSWERS TO THINKING ABOUT THE SELECTION
*Recalling*

1. Helen now keeps herself clean, eats neatly, knits and strings beads, exercises, and knows eighteen nouns and three verbs.
2. The Kellers miss her, and they feel she needs their affection.

3. She makes them promise that they will uphold her behavior standards. She is afraid their love and pity will undo all she has achieved.
4. Helen realizes that the word Annie is spelling in her palm stands for the water she feels on her fingers. Annie prepared for this "miracle" by constantly spelling out words for Helen.

*Interpreting*

5. Suggested Response: She means that through words you can learn about the world and its history.
6. Suggested Response: Helen is challenging Annie and the family to see if they will make her obey the rules Annie has established.
7. Suggested Response: As a baby, Helen had said "wah-wah," meaning "water." This memory enables her to connect that spoken word with the water flowing over her hands and the word Annie has spelled.
8. Suggested Response: Kate feels wonder at her child's understand =

## THINKING ABOUT THE SELECTION
### Recalling

1. Describe the progress Helen has made after two weeks with Annie in the garden house.
2. Give two reasons for the Kellers' insistence that Helen be returned to them when the two weeks have ended.
3. What does Annie make the Kellers promise when she and Helen return? Explain the reason for her request.
4. What is the "miracle" that occurs at last? How is it the result of hard work?

### Interpreting

5. At one point Annie says, "—words, why, you can see five thousand years back in a light of words. . . ." What does she mean?
6. Why does Helen's behavior change when she returns to her home?
7. Explain why Helen can connect the feel of water with the baby sound *wah-wah*.
8. At the end of the play, why does Kate feel "wonder, gratitude, and deprivation"? How does she simultaneously find and lose her child?

### Applying

9. If you had to work with a seriously handicapped or disabled person, what lesson could you draw from the example of Annie Sullivan?

## ANALYZING LITERATURE
### Understanding the Theme of a Play

The **theme** of a play is its central idea or insight into life. A statement of the theme should reflect why the conflict concludes as it does. Another way to approach the theme is to ask, "What accounts for the way the characters' lives have changed by the end of the play?" An accurate answer to this question would also touch upon the play's central idea or insight.

1. Annie's attempt to teach Helen might have ended in failure. Why did it succeed?

2. Tell how and why each of the following characters has changed by the end of the play: Annie, Captain Keller, Mrs. Keller, and James.
3. State in a sentence the theme of *The Miracle Worker*. You might try expressing it in this form: "The theme of the play is that _____ can triumph over _____."

## CRITICAL THINKING AND READING
### Summarizing a Play

**Summarizing** a play means retelling briefly its plot, or story. Summarizing can help you understand a play, novel, or complex short story. Moreover, a summary that tells not only what happened but also why it happened shows how well you have understood motives, cause-and-effect relationships, and other elements that propel the story from its beginning to its end.

1. Without explaining why they occur, list the main events of each of the three acts.
2. For each event you listed, tell what caused it and what it led to.
3. Now retell the story of the play in a clear, complete summary that makes clear why the events occurred as they did.

## THINKING AND WRITING
### Writing a Review of a Play

A **review** of a play gives the reader a clear idea of what the play is about. It also tells why the reviewer liked or did not like it. Ultimately a review should help the reader to answer the question, "Shall I go see this play?"

Write a review of *The Miracle Worker* as if it were going to appear in your school newspaper. Base the first part of your review on the summary you wrote for Critical Thinking and Reading, but do not tell how the play ends or give away too much of the plot. In evaluating the play, try to be objective. Tell what is good or bad about it.

When you revise your review, make sure that it is fair to the play and would be useful to someone who was trying to decide whether to see it.

*The Miracle Worker* 317

(Answers begin on p. 316.)

### ANSWERS TO CRITICAL THINKING AND READING

1. Suggested Response:
(Act I)
a. Helen becomes blind and deaf.
b. Annie Sullivan comes to teach Helen.
c. Helen locks Annie in her room.
(Act II)
a. Helen hurts Annie with a needle.
b. Annie has a confrontation with Helen at the table.
c. Annie is given charge of Helen and they move into the garden house.
(Act III)
a. Annie and Helen return.
b. Helen misbehaves at the table.
c. Helen learns to connect the word *water* with what it stands for.
2. If students cannot recall each cause and result of the above events, suggest they reread parts of the act to find answers.
3. Answers will differ but students should give the events and their causes in a concise and chronological order.

**Challenge** Finger spelling is not as easy as it looks. Challenge students to learn and use the finger alphabet. They can find it illustrated in many encyclopedias or in reference books about the deaf. Divide the class into pairs to practice spelling words into each other's hands.

### THINKING AND WRITING
For help with this assignment, students can refer to Lesson 15, "Evaluating a Literary Work," in the Handbook of Writing About Literature.

**Publishing Student Writing**
Ask for volunteers to present their reviews orally.

**Writing Across the Curriculum**
You might have students work with the school librarian to create a bibliography of books by and about Helen Keller as well as those about other persons who have overcome great odds to achieve success.

ing of language. She is grateful for this breakthrough, but she also feels deprived because now Annie—the teacher—will be the most important person in Helen's life. Kate finds a child who can communicate with her and at the same time loses her to Annie.

### Applying
9. Answers will differ. Most students will realize that Annie Sullivan's example teaches the importance of

knowledge, firmness, persistence, and love.

### ANSWERS TO ANALYZING LITERATURE
1. Suggested Response: It succeeded because Annie Sullivan had studied teaching techniques, was firm and persistent, and genuinely cared for her pupil.
2. Suggested Response: Annie has more confidence in her teaching

ability, has overcome her guilt about her brother, and has come to love Helen. Captain Keller learns that he can be wrong and develops a new respect for his son. Kate learns that giving in to Helen can harm her. Finally, James learns how to stand up for himself and develops a new sense of self-respect.
3. Suggested Response: The theme of this play is that knowledge, persistence, and love can overcome the harmful effects of a handicap.

# Romeo and Juliet

Of all the love stories ever written, that of Romeo and Juliet is the most famous. To many people Shakespeare's tragic lovers represent the essence of romantic love. When Shakespeare wrote *The Tragedy of Romeo and Juliet,* he was a young man, and the play is a young man's play about young love.

### The Theater in Shakespeare's Day

*Romeo and Juliet,* like most of Shakespeare's plays, was produced in a public theater. Public theaters were built around roofless courtyards without artificial light. Performances, therefore, were given only during daylight hours. Surrounding the courtyard were three levels of galleries with benches where wealthier playgoers sat. Poorer spectators, called groundlings, stood and watched a play from the courtyard, which was called the pit.

The stage was a platform that extended into the pit. Actors entered and left the stage from doors located behind the platform. The portion of the galleries behind and above the stage was used primarily as dressing and storage rooms. The second-level gallery right above the stage, however, was used as an upper stage. It would have been here that the famous balcony scene in *Romeo and Juliet* was enacted.

There was no scenery in the theaters of Shakespeare's day. Settings were indicated by references in the dialogue. As a result, one scene could follow another in rapid succession. There were, however, elaborate costumes and plenty of props. Thus, the plays produced in Shakespeare's day were fast-paced, colorful productions. Usually a play lasted two hours.

One other difference between Shakespeare's theater and today's is that acting companies of the sixteenth century were made up only of men and boys. Women did not perform on the stage. Young boys performed female roles.

Although Shakespeare did not have the advantages of the modern theater to draw on, the theaters of his day must be considered highly sophisticated. The greatest dramas in our language were produced on the sixteenth-century English stage. This fact alone suggests how advanced the theater arts were when Shakespeare was writing his masterpieces.

*Johannes De Witt's drawing of the Swan
Theater, London, c. 1596*
The Granger Collection

## Some Common Elizabethan Words

As you read *Romeo and Juliet,* most of the unfamiliar words and phrases you will encounter are explained in footnotes. The following, however, appear so frequently that learning them now will make your reading of the play easier.

against: For, in preparation for
alack: Alas (an exclamation of sorrow)
an, and: If
anon: Soon      hie: Hurry
aye: Yes      hither: Here
but: Only, except for      marry: Indeed
e'en: Even      whence: Where
e'er: Ever      wilt: Will, will you
haply: Perhaps      withal: In addition, notwithstanding
happy: Fortunate      would: Wish
hence: Away, from here

Johannes De Witt's drawing of the Swan Theatre, London, c. 1596. Johannes De Witt, a priest from Utrecht, was visiting London in 1596. In addition to making notes, he made this unique sketch of the interior of a theater. His notes, translated from Latin, include the following description: "Of all the theatres, however, the largest and most magnificent is that one of which the sign is a swan, called in the vernacular the Swan Theatre; for it accommodates in its seats three thousand persons, and it is built of a mass of flint stones (of which there is a prodigious supply in London), and supported by wooden columns painted in such excellent imitation of marble that it is able to deceive even the most cunning. Since its form resembles that of a Roman work, I have made a sketch of it above."

The Swan, which had opened its doors to the public by the summer of 1596, had the features of a typical threater of the Elizabethan period, where Shakespeare and his company would have played.

## The Tragedy of Romeo and Juliet, Act I

**William Shakespeare** (1564–1616) was born in Stratford-on-Avon, in England. As a young man he went to London, where he wrote and acted in plays. Considered the greatest playwright in the English language, before he retired to Stratford, in 1610, he wrote thirty-seven plays, 154 sonnets, and several longer poems. *Romeo and Juliet* is based on a story that first appeared in Italy many years before. Shakespeare's genius, however, transformed this story of star-crossed lovers into the most famous love story the world has ever known.

### Focus

**More About The Author** You might want to tell students that Shakespeare worked very closely with a successful troupe of actors in London. In addition to writing plays for them he acted in their productions and was a shareholder in their earnings. Ask students why such a close association with a theater company might be advantageous for a playwright.

**Literary Focus** To help students understand the rhythm of blank verse, suggest they intone an iambic foot as de-DUMM. An iamb is an unstressed syllable followed by a stressed one. Have them read aloud the first four lines of the prologue to feel the meter.

**Look For** You might point out to students that prose is considered less elevated than blank verse and therefore suitable for the lower-class characters. But when upper-class characters are engaged in humorous situations or light conversation with word plays and puns, they often use prose also.

**Writing/Prior Knowledge** Discuss with students what laws and methods of enforcement would be necessary in this situation.

**Vocabulary** Have your **less advanced** students read the words and their meanings several times. Then have them write sentences, using one of the words in each sentence.

**Blank Verse**

**Blank verse** is unrhymed verse written in iambic pentameter, or ten-syllable lines in which every second syllable is stressed. For example, when Romeo sees Juliet appear at her window, he exclaims,

> But soft! What light through yonder window breaks?
> It is the east, and Juliet is the sun!

Much of *Romeo and Juliet* is written in blank verse. This meter is well suited to serious subjects and has been used in many of the greatest poems and verse dramas of British and American literature.

**Look For**

Lord Chesterfield wrote: "In nature, the most violent passions are silent; in tragedy they must speak, and speak with dignity too." As you read *Romeo and Juliet,* look for how the blank verse lends dignity to the passions expressed by the main characters. Why do the characters lower in the social order speak in prose?

**Writing**

Imagine that you are the ruler of a town in which two families have been feuding. Fights have taken place several times. If you were to meet with the heads of the families, what would you say to restore peace? Make notes for a short speech designed to end the feud.

**Vocabulary**

Knowing the following words will help you as you read Act I of *Romeo and Juliet.*

**pernicious** (pər nish′ əs) *adj.*: Causing great injury or ruin (p. 325)

**augmenting** (ôg ment′ iŋ) *v.*: Increasing, enlarging (p. 326)

**grievance** (grē′ vəns) *n.*: Injustice; complaint (p. 327)

**transgression** (trans gresh′ ən) *n.*: Wrongdoing, sin (p. 328)

**heretics** (her′ ə tiks) *n.*: Those who hold to a belief opposed to the established teachings of a church (p. 332)

### Objectives

1 To appreciate blank verse

2 To interpret the effect of imagery

3 To write a speech in blank verse

### Support Material

**Teaching Portfolio**
Teacher Backup, p. 363
Grammar in Action Worksheet, *Using Commas in Poetry,* p. 367
Usage and Mechanics Worksheet, p. 370
Vocabulary Check, p. 371
Critical Thinking and Reading Worksheet, *Interpreting the Effect of Imagery,* p. 372

Language Worksheet, *Understanding Words from Elizabethan Times,* p. 373
Selection Test, p. 374
Library of Video Classics: *Romeo and Juliet*

# The Tragedy of Romeo and Juliet

## William Shakespeare

### CHARACTERS

**Chorus**

**Escalus,** Prince of Verona

**Paris,** a young count, kinsman to the Prince

**Montague**

**Capulet**

**An old Man,** of the Capulet family

**Romeo,** son to Montague

**Mercutio,** kinsman to the Prince and friend to Romeo

**Benvolio,** nephew to Montague and friend to Romeo

**Tybalt,** nephew to Lady Capulet

**Friar Lawrence**  } Franciscans
**Friar John**

**Balthasar,** servant to Romeo

**Sampson**  } servants to Capulet
**Gregory**

**Peter,** servant to Juliet's nurse

**Abram,** servant to Montague

**An Apothecary**

**Three Musicians**

**An Officer**

**Lady Montague,** wife to Montague

**Lady Capulet,** wife to Capulet

**Juliet,** daughter to Capulet

**Nurse to Juliet**

**Citizens of Verona,** Gentlemen and Gentlewomen of both houses, Maskers, Torchbearers, Pages, Guards, Watchmen, Servants, and Attendants

Scene: Verona; Mantua

## THE PROLOGUE

[*Enter* CHORUS]

**CHORUS**. Two households, both alike in dignity,[1]
    In fair Verona, where we lay our scene,
    From ancient grudge break to new mutiny,[2]
       Where civil blood makes civil hands unclean.[3]
5 From forth the fatal loins of these two foes
    A pair of star-crossed[4] lovers take their life;
    Whose misadventured piteous overthrows[5]
       Doth with their death bury their parents' strife.
    The fearful passage of their death-marked love,

1. **dignity:** High social rank.
2. **mutiny:** Violence.
3. **Where . . . unclean:** In which the blood of citizens stains citizens' hands.
4. **star-crossed:** Ill-fated by the unfavorable positions of the stars.
5. **Whose . . . overthrows:** Whose unfortunate sorrowful destruction.

*The Tragedy of Romeo and Juliet, Prologue* 321

322　*Drama*

10    And the continuance of their parents' rage,
      Which, but[6] their children's end, naught could remove,
      Is now the two hours' traffic[7] of our stage;
      The which if you with patient ears attend,
      What here shall miss, our toil shall strive to mend.[8]

                                                    [Exit.]

## Act I

**Scene i.** *Verona. A public place.*

[*Enter* SAMPSON *and* GREGORY, *with swords and bucklers,*[1] *of the house of Capulet.*]

**SAMPSON.** Gregory, on my word, we'll not carry coals.[2]

**GREGORY.** No, for then we should be colliers.[3]

**SAMPSON.** I mean, and we be in choler, we'll draw.[4]

**GREGORY.** Ay, while you live, draw your neck out of collar.[5]

5  **SAMPSON.** I strike quickly, being moved.

**GREGORY.** But thou art not quickly moved to strike.

**SAMPSON.** A dog of the house of Montague moves me.

**GREGORY.** To move is to stir, and to be valiant is to stand. Therefore, if thou art moved, thou run'st away.

10  **SAMPSON.** A dog of that house shall move me to stand. I will take the wall[6] of any man or maid of Montague's.

**GREGORY.** That shows thee a weak slave; for the weakest goes to the wall.

**SAMPSON.** 'Tis true; and therefore women, being the
15  weaker vessels, are ever thrust to the wall. Therefore I will push Montague's men from the wall and thrust his maids to the wall.

**GREGORY.** The quarrel is between our masters and us their men.

20  **SAMPSON.** 'Tis all one. I will show myself a tyrant. When I have fought with the men, I will be civil with the maids—I will cut off their heads.

**GREGORY.** The heads of the maids?

**SAMPSON.** Ay, the heads of the maids or their maiden-
25  heads. Take it in what sense thou wilt.

*The Tragedy of Romeo and Juliet, Act I, Scene i*   323

**6. but:** Except.
**7. two hours' traffic:** Two hours' business.
**8. What . . . mend:** What is not clear in this prologue we actors shall try to clarify in the course of the play.

**1. bucklers:** Small shields.

**2. carry coals:** Endure insults.
**3. colliers:** Sellers of coal.
**4. and . . . draw:** If we are angered, we'll draw our swords.
**5. collar:** The hangman's noose.

**6. take the wall:** Assert superiority by walking nearest the houses and therefore farthest from the gutter.

4 **Reading Strategy** Summarize what this play is about.

5 **Clarification** These plays had no scenery to speak of but costumes indicated whether an actor was playing a noble or a servant. Servants wore the coats of arms of the families for whom they worked so the audience would not be confused.

6 **Clarification** The first scene of every Shakespearean tragedy was planned to get the attention of the groundlings, people of the lower classes who stood in the pit to watch the plays. Shakespeare used comedy, the supernatural, or violence to get their interest. Why might this scene have appealed to the groundlings?

**GREGORY.** They must take it in sense that feel it.

**SAMPSON.** Me they shall feel while I am able to stand; and
'tis known I am a pretty piece of flesh.

**GREGORY.** 'Tis well thou art not fish; if thou hadst, thou
30   hadst been Poor John. Draw thy tool![7] Here comes two
of the house of Montagues.

[*Enter two other Servingmen,* ABRAM *and* BALTHASAR.]

**SAMPSON.** My naked weapon is out. Quarrel! I will back
thee.

**GREGORY.** How? Turn thy back and run?

35   **SAMPSON.** Fear me not.

**GREGORY.** No, marry. I fear thee!

**SAMPSON.** Let us take the law of our sides;[8] let them begin.

**GREGORY.** I will frown as I pass by, and let them take it as
they list.[9]

40   **SAMPSON.** Nay, as they dare. I will bite my thumb[10] at
them, which is disgrace to them if they bear it.

**ABRAM.** Do you bite your thumb at us, sir?

**SAMPSON.** I do bite my thumb, sir.

**ABRAM.** Do you bite your thumb at us, sir?

45   **SAMPSON.** [*Aside to* GREGORY] Is the law of our side if I say
ay?

**GREGORY.** [*Aside to* SAMPSON] No.

**SAMPSON.** No, sir, I do not bite my thumb at you, sir; but
I bite my thumb, sir.

50   **GREGORY.** Do you quarrel, sir?

**ABRAM.** Quarrel, sir? No, sir.

**SAMPSON.** But if you do, sir, I am for you. I serve as good
a man as you.

**ABRAM.** No better.

55   **SAMPSON.** Well, sir.

[*Enter* BENVOLIO.]

**GREGORY.** Say "better." Here comes one of my master's
kinsmen.

**7. tool:** Weapon.

**8. take . . . sides:** Make
sure the law is on our side.

**9. list:** Please.

**10. bite . . . thumb:** Make
an insulting gesture.

324   *Drama*

**SAMPSON.** Yes, better, sir.

**ABRAM.** You lie.

60  **SAMPSON.** Draw, if you be men. Gregory, remember thy
swashing[11] blow.                                   [*They fight.*]

> **11. swashing:** Hard
> downward swordstroke.

**BENVOLIO.** Part, fools!
Put up your swords. You know not what you do.

[*Enter* TYBALT.]

**TYBALT.** What, art thou drawn among these heartless
hinds?[12]

65  Turn thee, Benvolio; look upon thy death.

> **12. heartless hinds:** Cow-
> ardly servants. **Hind** also
> meant "a female deer."

**BENVOLIO.** I do but keep the peace. Put up thy sword,
Or manage it to part these men with me.

**TYBALT.** What, drawn, and talk of peace? I hate the word
As I hate hell, all Montagues, and thee.

70  Have at thee, coward!                            [*They fight.*]

[*Enter an* OFFICER, *and three or four Citizens with clubs or
partisans.*[13]]

**OFFICER.** Clubs, bills,[14] and partisans! Strike! Beat them
down!
Down with the Capulets! Down with the Montagues!

> **13. partisans:** Spearlike
> weapons with broad blades.
> **14. bills:** Weapons con-
> sisting of hook-shaped
> blades with long handles.

[*Enter old* CAPULET *in his gown, and his* WIFE.]

**CAPULET.** What noise is this? Give me my long sword, ho!

**LADY CAPULET.** A crutch, a crutch! Why call you for a
sword?

75  **CAPULET.** My sword, I say! Old Montague is come
And flourishes his blade in spite[15] of me.

> **15. spite:** Defiance.

[*Enter old* MONTAGUE *and his* WIFE.]

**MONTAGUE.** Thou villain Capulet!— Hold me not; let me go.

**LADY MONTAGUE.** Thou shalt not stir one foot to seek a foe.

[*Enter* PRINCE ESCALUS, *with his Train.*[16]]

> **16. Train:** Attendants.

**PRINCE.** Rebellious subjects, enemies to peace,
80  Profaners[17] of this neighbor-stainèd steel—
Will they not hear? What, ho! You men, you beasts,
That quench the fire of your pernicious rage
With purple fountains issuing from your veins!

> **17. Profaners:** Those who
> show disrespect or
> contempt.

*The Tragedy of Romeo and Juliet, Act I, Scene i*   325

**8 Enrichment** Tybalt's name comes from a word that means "bold." Benvolio is from Latin words that mean "I wish" and "well." From what you know about them so far, how appropriate are their names?

**9 Discussion** What makes this scene humorous and serious at the same time?

On pain of torture, from those bloody hands
85  Throw your mistempered[18] weapons to the ground
And hear the sentence of your movèd prince.
Three civil brawls, bred of an airy word
By thee, old Capulet, and Montague,
Have thrice disturbed the quiet of our streets
90  And made Verona's ancient citizens
Cast by their grave beseeming ornaments[19]
To wield old partisans, in hands as old,
Cank'red with peace, to part your cank'red hate.[20]
If ever you disturb our streets again,
95  Your lives shall pay the forfeit of the peace.
For this time all the rest depart away.
You, Capulet, shall go along with me;
And, Montague, come you this afternoon,
To know our farther pleasure in this case,
100 To old Freetown, our common judgment place.
Once more, on pain of death, all men depart.

[*Exit all but* MONTAGUE, *his* WIFE, *and* BENVOLIO.]

**MONTAGUE.** Who set this ancient quarrel new abroach?[21]
Speak, nephew, were you by when it began?

**BENVOLIO.** Here were the servants of your adversary
105 And yours, close fighting ere I did approach.
I drew to part them. In the instant came
The fiery Tybalt, with his sword prepared;
Which, as he breathed defiance to my ears,
He swung about his head and cut the winds,
110 Who, nothing hurt withal, hissed him in scorn.
While we were interchanging thrusts and blows,
Came more and more, and fought on part and part,[22]
Till the Prince came, who parted either part.

**LADY MONTAGUE.** O, where is Romeo? Saw you him today?
115 Right glad I am he was not at this fray.

**BENVOLIO.** Madam, an hour before the worshiped sun
Peered forth the golden window of the East,
A troubled mind drave me to walk abroad;
Where, underneath the grove of sycamore
120 That westward rooteth from this city side,
So early walking did I see your son.
Towards him I made, but he was ware[23] of me
And stole into the covert[24] of the wood.
I, measuring his affections[25] by my own,

**18. mistempered:** Hardened for a wrong purpose; bad-tempered.

**19. Cast . . . ornaments:** Put aside their dignified and appropriate clothing.
**20. Cank'red . . . hate:** Rusted from lack of use, to put an end to your malignant feuding.

**21. Who . . . abroach?:** Who reopened this old fight?

**22. on . . . part:** On one side and the other.

**23. ware:** Aware; wary.
**24. covert:** Hidden place.
**25. measuring . . . affections:** Judging his feelings.

*326  Drama*

## Grammar in Action

Poetry is one of the most concentrated and difficult forms of literature. It is therefore especially important for poets to use **commas** to set apart modifiers, signify series, and clarify which groups of words should be read together.

Notice how Shakespeare uses commas to clarify meaning in the following passage from *Romeo and Juliet:*

1 **Montague.** Many a morning hath he there been seen,
2 With tears augmenting the fresh morning's dew.
3 Adding to clouds more clouds with his deep sighs;
4 But all so soon as the all-cheering sun
5 Should in the farthest East begin to draw
6 The shady curtains from Aurora's bed
7 Away from light steals home my heavy son
8 And private in his chamber pens himself,
9 Shuts up his windows, locks fair daylight out,
10 And makes himself an artificial night.

Which then most sought where most might not be
125     found,[26]
Being one too many by my weary self,
Pursued my humor not pursuing his,[27]
And gladly shunned who gladly fled from me.

**MONTAGUE.** Many a morning hath he there been seen,
130   With tears augmenting the fresh morning's dew,
Adding to clouds more clouds with his deep sighs;
But all so soon as the all-cheering sun
Should in the farthest East begin to draw
The shady curtains from Aurora's[28] bed,
135   Away from light steals home my heavy[29] son
And private in his chamber pens himself,
Shuts up his windows, locks fair daylight out,
And makes himself an artificial night.
Black and portentous[30] must this humor prove
140   Unless good counsel may the cause remove.

**BENVOLIO.** My noble uncle, do you know the cause?

**MONTAGUE.** I neither know it nor can learn of him.

**BENVOLIO.** Have you importuned[31] him by any means?

**MONTAGUE.** Both by myself and many other friends;
145   But he, his own affections' counselor,
Is to himself—I will not say how true—
But to himself so secret and so close,
So far from sounding[32] and discovery,
As is the bud bit with an envious worm
150   Ere he can spread his sweet leaves to the air
Or dedicate his beauty to the sun.
Could we but learn from whence his sorrows grow,
We would as willingly give cure as know.

[*Enter* ROMEO.]

**BENVOLIO.** See, where he comes. So please you step aside;
155   I'll know his grievance, or be much denied.

**MONTAGUE.** I would thou wert so happy by thy stay
To hear true shrift.[33] Come, madam, let's away.

               [*Exit* MONTAGUE *and* WIFE.]

**BENVOLIO.** Good morrow, cousin.

**ROMEO.**               Is the day so young?

**BENVOLIO.** But new struck nine.

---

*The Tragedy of Romeo and Juliet, Act I, Scene i*    327

**26. Which . . . found:** Which wanted to be where there was no one else.
**27. Pursued . . . his:** Followed my own mind by not following after Romeo.

**28. Aurora:** Goddess of the dawn.
**29. heavy:** Sad, moody.

**30. portentous:** Promising bad fortune.

**31. importuned:** Questioned deeply.

**32. sounding:** Understanding.

**33. I . . . shrift:** I hope you are lucky enough to hear him confess the truth.

The commas at the end of line 1 and 2 help show that lines 2 and 3 contain participial phrases to describe Romeo, the subject in line 1. (In line 2, Shakespeare has inverted the natural word order, which should read: Augmenting with tears. . . . ) The absence of commas at the end of lines 4 and 5 tells the reader to connect the thoughts from line to line. Indeed, the subject *sun* in line 4 has its verb in line 5 and its direct object in line 6. The series of four verbs in lines 8, 9, and 10 is clearly separated by commas.

**Student Activity 1.** Select another passage of similar length from *Romeo and Juliet* and study the use of commas in it. What do the commas tell you about how to read the passage with meaning?

**Student Activity 2.** Work in pairs, each of you selecting a speech of at least eight lines. Copy the passage, omitting commas. Then read the passage your partner copied. Explain whether or not the lack of commas affected your ability to understand the speech.

**14 Discussion** What does Romeo mean by this statement?

**15 Discussion** Explain the reason for Romeo's strange actions.

**16 Critical Thinking and Reading** What images does Romeo use to describe love? How do these images reflect his agitated state of mind?

**ROMEO.**                                    Ay me! Sad hours seem long.
160   Was that my father that went hence so fast?

**BENVOLIO.** It was. What sadness lengthens Romeo's
      hours?

**ROMEO.** Not having that which having makes them short.

**BENVOLIO.** In love?

**ROMEO.** Out—

165 **BENVOLIO.** Of love?

**ROMEO.** Out of her favor where I am in love.

**BENVOLIO.** Alas that love, so gentle in his view,[34]
      Should be so tyrannous and rough in proof![35]

**ROMEO.** Alas that love, whose view is muffled still,[36]
170   Should without eyes see pathways to his will!
      Where shall we dine? O me! What fray was here?
      Yet tell me not, for I have heard it all.
      Here's much to do with hate, but more with love.[37]
      Why then, O brawling love, O loving hate,
175   O anything, of nothing first created!
      O heavy lightness, serious vanity,
      Misshapen chaos of well-seeming forms,
      Feather of lead, bright smoke, cold fire, sick health,
      Still-waking sleep, that is not what it is!
180   This love feel I, that feel no love in this.
      Dost thou not laugh?

**BENVOLIO.**                    No, coz,[38] I rather weep.

**ROMEO.** Good heart, at what?

**BENVOLIO.**                    At thy good heart's oppression.

**ROMEO.** Why, such is love's transgression.
      Griefs of mine own lie heavy in my breast,
185   Which thou wilt propagate, to have it prest
      With more of thine.[39] This love that thou hast shown
      Doth add more grief to too much of mine own.
      Love is a smoke made with the fume of sighs;
      Being purged, a fire sparkling in lovers' eyes;
190   Being vexed, a sea nourished with loving tears.
      What is it else? A madness most discreet,[40]
      A choking gall,[41] and a preserving sweet.
      Farewell, my coz.

**BENVOLIO.**                    Soft![42] I will go along.

**34. view:** Appearance.
**35. in proof:** When experienced.

**36. whose . . . still:** Cupid is traditionally represented as blindfolded.

**37. but . . . love:** Loyalty to family and love of fighting. In the following lines Romeo speaks of love as a series of contradictions—a union of opposites.

**38. coz:** Cousin.

**39. Which . . . thine:** Which griefs you will increase by adding your own sorrow to them.

**40. discreet:** Intelligently sensitive.
**41. gall:** A bitter liquid.

**42. Soft!:** Hold on a minute.

And if you leave me so, you do me wrong.

195 **ROMEO.** Tut! I have lost myself; I am not here;
This is not Romeo, he's some other where.

**BENVOLIO.** Tell me in sadness,[43] who is that you love?

            **43. in sadness:** Seriously.

**ROMEO.** What, shall I groan and tell thee?

**BENVOLIO.**        Groan? Why, no;
But sadly tell me who.

200 **ROMEO.** Bid a sick man in sadness make his will.
Ah, word ill urged to one that is so ill!
In sadness, cousin, I do love a woman.

**BENVOLIO.** I aimed so near when I supposed you loved.

**ROMEO.** A right good markman. And she's fair I love.

205 **BENVOLIO.** A right fair mark, fair coz, is soonest hit.

**ROMEO.** Well, in that hit you miss. She'll not be hit
With Cupid's arrow. She hath Dian's wit,[44]
And, in strong proof[45] of chastity well armed,
From Love's weak childish bow she lives uncharmed.

            **44. Dian's wit:** The mind of Diana, goddess of chastity.
            **45. proof:** Armor.
            **46. stay:** Endure, put up with.

210 She will not stay[46] the siege of loving terms,
Nor bide th' encounter of assailing eyes,
Nor ope her lap to saint-seducing gold.
O, she is rich in beauty; only poor
That, when she dies, with beauty dies her store.[47]

            **47. That . . . store:** In that her beauty will die with her if she does not marry and have children.

**BENVOLIO.** Then she hath sworn that she will still live
215 chaste?

**ROMEO.** She hath, and in that sparing make huge waste;
For beauty, starved with her severity,

17

**18 Discussion** What has Romeo's love sworn not to do?

**19 Critical Thinking and Reading** Compare and contrast Romeo and Benvolio.

**20 Enrichment** Tell students that scenery was not used very much in Elizabethan plays. Changes of scene were not usually indicated by changes in scenery.

**21 Discussion** What does Capulet think the chances are for keeping the peace?

**22 Clarification** Girls married at a younger age because the average life span was shorter.

18 220
Cuts beauty off from all posterity.[48]
She is too fair, too wise, wisely too fair
To merit bliss by making me despair.[49]
She hath forsworn to[50] love, and in that vow
Do I live dead that live to tell it now.

**BENVOLIO.** Be ruled by me; forget to think of her.

**ROMEO.** O, teach me how I should forget to think!

225 **BENVOLIO.** By giving liberty unto thine eyes.
Examine other beauties.

19 **ROMEO.**                              'Tis the way
To call hers, exquisite, in question more.[51]
These happy masks that kiss fair ladies' brows,
Being black puts us in mind they hide the fair.
230 He that is strucken blind cannot forget
The precious treasure of his eyesight lost.
Show me a mistress that is passing fair:
What doth her beauty serve but as a note
Where I may read who passed that passing fair?[52]
235 Farewell. Thou canst not teach me to forget.

**BENVOLIO.** I'll pay that doctrine, or else die in debt.[53]

[*Exit.*]

20 **Scene ii.** *A street.*

[*Enter* CAPULET, COUNTY PARIS, *and the* CLOWN, *his Servant.*]

21 **CAPULET.** But Montague is bound as well as I,
In penalty alike; and 'tis not hard, I think,
For men so old as we to keep the peace.

**PARIS.** Of honorable reckoning[1] are you both,
5 And pity 'tis you lived at odds so long.
But now, my lord, what say you to my suit?

22 **CAPULET.** But saying o'er what I have said before:
My child is yet a stranger in the world,
She hath not seen the change of fourteen years;
10 Let two more summers wither in their pride
Ere we may think her ripe to be a bride.

**PARIS.** Younger than she are happy mothers made.

**CAPULET.** And too soon marred are those so early made.
Earth hath swallowed all my hopes[2] but she;
15 She is the hopeful lady of my earth.[3]
But woo her, gentle Paris, get her heart;

**48. in . . . posterity:** By denying herself love and marriage, she wastes her beauty, which will not live on in future generations.
**49. She . . . despair:** She is being too good—she'll earn happiness in heaven by dooming me to live without her love.
**50. forsworn to:** Sworn not to.

**51. 'Tis . . . more:** That way will only make her beauty more strongly present in my mind.

**52. who . . . fair:** Who surpassed in beauty that very beautiful woman.
**53. I'll . . . debt:** I'll teach you to forget, or else die trying.

**1. reckoning:** Reputation.

**2. hopes:** Children.
**3. She . . . earth:** My hopes for the future rest in her; she will inherit all that is mine.

*330   Drama*

330

My will to her consent is but a part.
And she agreed, within her scope of choice
Lies my consent and fair according voice,[4]
20   This night I hold an old accustomed feast,
Whereto I have invited many a guest,
Such as I love; and you among the store,
One more, most welcome, makes my number more.
At my poor house look to behold this night
25   Earth-treading stars[5] that make dark heaven light.
Such comfort as do lusty young men feel
When well-appareled April on the heel
Of limping Winter treads, even such delight
Among fresh fennel buds shall you this night
30   Inherit at my house. Hear all, all see,
And like her most whose merit most shall be;
Which, on more view of many, mine, being one,
May stand in number, though in reck'ning none.[6]
Come, go with me. [*To* SERVANT, *giving him a paper*]
Go, sirrah, trudge about
35   Through fair Verona; find those persons out
Whose names are written there, and to them say
My house and welcome on their pleasure stay.[7]

[*Exit with* PARIS.]

**SERVANT.** Find them out whose names are written here?
It is written that the shoemaker should meddle with his
40   yard and the tailor with his last, the fisher with his pencil and the painter with his nets;[8] but I am sent to find
those persons whose names are here writ, and can
never find what names the writing person hath here
writ. I must to the learned. In good time![9]

[*Enter* BENVOLIO *and* ROMEO.]

45   **BENVOLIO.** Tut, man, one fire burns out another's
burning;
    One pain is less'ned by another's anguish;
Turn giddy, and be holp by backward turning;[10]
    One desperate grief cures with another's languish.
Take thou some new infection to thy eye,
50   And the rank poison of the old will die.

**ROMEO.** Your plantain leaf[11] is excellent for that.

**BENVOLIO.** For what, I pray thee?

**ROMEO.**                              For your broken shin.

**BENVOLIO.** Why, Romeo, art thou mad?

*The Tragedy of Romeo and Juliet, Act I, Scene ii*   331

**4. and . . . voice:** If she
agrees, I will consent to and
agree with her choice.

**5. Earth-treading
stars:** Young ladies.

**6. Which . . . none:** If
you look at all the young
girls, you may see her as
merely one among many,
and not worth special admiration.

**7. stay:** Await.

**8. shoemaker . . . nets:**
The servant is confusing
workers and their tools. He
intends to say that people
should stick with what they
know.

**9. In good time!** Just in
time! The servant has seen
Benvolio and Romeo, who
can read.

**10. Turn . . . turning:** If
you're dizzy from turning
one way, turn the other
way.

**11. plantain leaf:** A leaf
used to stop bleeding.

23 **Discussion** How does this
speech represent a continuation
of the previous discussion between Benvolio and Romeo?

**24 Discussion** Who is welcome to come to Capulet's traditional party?

**25 Discussion** Chance plays an important part in the events of the play. How do you think this chance meeting will advance the plot?

**ROMEO.** Not mad, but bound more than a madman is;
55  Shut up in prison, kept without my food,
Whipped and tormented and—God-den,[12] good fellow.

**12. God-den:** Good afternoon; good evening.

**SERVANT.** God gi' go-den. I pray, sir, can you read?

**ROMEO.** Ay, mine own fortune in my misery.

**SERVANT.** Perhaps you have learned it without book.
60  But, I pray, can you read anything you see?

**ROMEO.** Ay, if I know the letters and the language.

**SERVANT.** Ye say honestly. Rest you merry.[13]

**13. Rest you merry:** May God keep you happy—a way of saying farewell.

**ROMEO.** Stay, fellow; I can read.  [*He reads the letter.*]
"Signior Martino and his wife and daughters;
65  County Anselm and his beauteous sisters;
The lady widow of Vitruvio;
Signior Placentio and his lovely nieces;
Mercutio and his brother Valentine;
Mine uncle Capulet, his wife and daughters;
70  My fair niece Rosaline; Livia;
Signior Valentio and his cousin Tybalt;
Lucio and the lively Helena."
A fair assembly. Whither should they come?

**SERVANT.** Up.

75  **ROMEO.** Whither? To supper?

**SERVANT.** To our house.

**ROMEO.** Whose house?

**SERVANT.** My master's.

**ROMEO.** Indeed I should have asked you that before.

80  **SERVANT.** Now I'll tell you without asking. My master is the
great rich Capulet; and if you be not of the house of
Montagues, I pray come and crush a cup of wine. Rest
you merry.  [*Exit*]

**24**

**BENVOLIO.** At this same ancient[14] feast of Capulet's
85  Sups the fair Rosaline whom thou so loves;
With all the admirèd beauties of Verona.
Go thither, and with unattainted[15] eye
Compare her face with some that I shall show,
And I will make thee think thy swan a crow.

**25**

**14. ancient:** Long-established, traditional.

**15. unattainted:** Unprejudiced.

90  **ROMEO.** When the devout religion of mine eye
Maintains such falsehood, then turn tears to fires:

*332  Drama*

And these, who, often drowned, could never die,
Transparent heretics, be burnt for liars![16]
One fairer than my love? The all-seeing sun
95   Ne'er saw her match since first the world begun.

**BENVOLIO.** Tut! you saw her fair, none else being by,
Herself poised with herself in either eye;[17]
But in that crystal scales[18] let there be weighed
Your lady's love against some other maid
100   That I will show you shining at this feast,
And she shall scant show well that now seems best.

**ROMEO.** I'll go along, no such sight to be shown,
But to rejoice in splendor of mine own.[19]            [*Exit.*]

**Scene iii.** *A room in* CAPULET'S *house.*

[*Enter* CAPULET'S WIFE, *and* NURSE.]

**LADY CAPULET.** Nurse, where's my daughter? Call her
forth to me.

**NURSE.** Now, by my maidenhead at twelve year old,
I bade her come. What, lamb! What, ladybird!
5   God forbid, where's this girl? What, Juliet!

[*Enter* JULIET.]

**JULIET.** How now? Who calls?

**NURSE.**                              Your mother.

**JULIET.**                                    Madam, I am here.
What is your will?

**LADY CAPULET.** This is the matter—Nurse, give leave[1]
awhile;
We must talk in secret. Nurse, come back again.
10   I have rememb'red me; thou's hear our counsel.[2]
Thou knowest my daughter's of a pretty age.

**NURSE.** Faith, I can tell her age unto an hour.

**LADY CAPULET.** She's not fourteen.

**NURSE.**                              I'll lay fourteen of my teeth—
And yet, to my teen[3] be it spoken, I have but four—
15   She's not fourteen. How long is it now
To Lammastide?[4]

**LADY CAPULET.**      A fortnight and odd days.[5]

**NURSE.** Even or odd, of all days in the year,

*The Tragedy of Romeo and Juliet, Act I, Scene iii*   333

---

**16. When . . . liars!:**
When I see Rosaline as just
a plain-looking girl, may my
tears turn to fire and burn
my eyes out!

**17. Herself . . . eye:** Rosaline compared with no
one else.

**18. crystal scales:** Your
eyes.

**19. mine own:** My own
love, Rosaline.

**1. give leave:** Leave us
alone.

**2. thou's . . . counsel:**
You shall hear our conference.

**3. teen:** Sorrow.

**4. Lammastide:** August
1, a holiday celebrating the
summer harvest.

**5. A fortnight and odd
days:** Two weeks plus a few
days.

---

**26**

**26 Discussion** Contrast the reasons that Benvolio and Romeo offer for attending the party.

**Enrichment** Tell students that *The Tragedy of Romeo and Juliet* first appeared in print in 1597. The play was popular among critics and the general public even though it was a pirated version, put together from actors' memories as a way of cashing in on the play's success. The second edition, which was published in 1599 and considered a superior version to the first, was apparently printed from Shakespeare's working papers.

Come Lammas Eve at night shall she be fourteen.
Susan and she (God rest all Christian souls!)
20   Were of an age.[6] Well, Susan is with God;
She was too good for me. But, as I said,
On Lammas Eve at night shall she be fourteen;
That shall she, marry; I remember it well.
'Tis since the earthquake now eleven years.
25   And she was weaned (I never shall forget it),
Of all the days of the year, upon that day;
For I had then laid wormwood to my dug,
Sitting in the sun under the dovehouse wall.
My lord and you were then at Mantua.
30   Nay, I do bear a brain. But, as I said,
When it did taste the wormwood on the nipple
Of my dug and felt it bitter, pretty fool,
To see it tetchy and fall out with the dug!
Shake, quoth the dovehouse! 'Twas no need, I
     trow,
35   To bid me trudge.
And since that time it is eleven years,
For then she could stand high-lone; nay, by th'
     rood,
She could have run and waddled all about;
For even the day before, she broke her brow;
40   And then my husband (God be with his soul!
'A was a merry man) took up the child.
"Yea," quoth he, "dost thou fall upon thy face?
Thou wilt fall backward when thou hast more wit;
Wilt thou not, Jule?" and, by my holidam,
45   The pretty wretch left crying and said, "Ay."
To see now how a jest shall come about!
I warrant, and I should live a thousand years,
I never should forget it. "Wilt thou not, Jule?"
     quoth he,
And, pretty fool, it stinted and said, "Ay."

**LADY CAPULET.** Enough of this. I pray thee hold thy
50     peace.

**NURSE.** Yes, madam. Yet I cannot choose but laugh
To think it should leave crying and say, "Ay."
And yet, I warrant, it had upon it brow
55   A bump as big as a young cock'rel's stone;
A perilous knock; and it cried bitterly.
"Yea," quoth my husband, "fall'st upon thy face?
Thou wilt fall backward when thou comest to age,

**6. Susan . . . age:** Susan, the Nurse's child, and Juliet were the same age.

334   *Drama*

## Commentary: Lammas Day

Juliet's birthday, which is on Lammas Eve, marked a time of great celebration for Elizabethans. Lammas (loaf mass) Day, an annual August celebration of the summer harvest, was honored with a day of feasting and game playing. The day usually began by thanking God for a good harvest and blessing the grains and breads and was followed by a glorious feast.

The Lammas feast featured breads and pastries of all types that were paraded through the feast hall or prominently displayed. The highlight of the day was the bread making. Bakers baked bread in all shapes and sizes, including geometric, animal, and celestial shapes. They also sculptured bread into castles and multi-decked warships. The meal was served on bread, or the courses themselves consisted of types of bread, such as currant buns, shortbread, gingerbread, and cucumber bread.

After the meal, feasters participated in a playlet called "Bringing Home the Bacon," that reminded them that true love is hard work. Traditionally, since the fourteenth century, a prize— half a pig—was given to any couple who, after a year and a day

Wilt thou not, Jule?" It stinted and said, "Ay."

**JULIET.** And stint thou too, I pray thee, nurse, say I.

60 **NURSE.** Peace, I have done. God mark thee to His grace!
Thou wast the prettiest babe that e'er I nursed.
And I might live to see thee married once,
I have my wish.

**LADY CAPULET.** Marry, that "marry" is the very theme
65 I came to talk of. Tell me, daughter Juliet,
How stands your dispositions to be married?

**JULIET.** It is an honor that I dream not of.

**NURSE.** An honor? Were not I thine only nurse,
I would say thou hadst sucked wisdom from thy
teat.

**LADY CAPULET.** Well, think of marriage now. Younger than
70 you,
Here in Verona, ladies of esteem,
Are made already mothers. By my count,
I was your mother much upon these years
That you are now a maid.[7] Thus then in brief:
75 The valiant Paris seeks you for his love.

**NURSE.** A man, young lady! Lady, such a man
As all the world—Why, he's a man of wax.[8]

**LADY CAPULET.** Verona's summer hath not such a flower.

**NURSE.** Nay, he's a flower, in faith—a very flower.

**LADY CAPULET.** What say you? Can you love the
80 gentleman?
This night you shall behold him at our feast.
Read o'er the volume of young Paris' face,
And find delight writ there with beauty's pen;
Examine every married lineament,
85 And see how one another lends content;[9]
And what obscured in this fair volume lies
Find written in the margent[10] of his eyes.
This precious book of love, this unbound lover,
To beautify him only lacks a cover.[11]
90 The fish lives in the sea, and 'tis much pride
For fair without the fair within to hide.
That book in many's eyes doth share the glory,
That in gold clasps locks in the golden story;
So shall you share all that he doth possess,
95 By having him making yourself no less.

**7. I . . . maid:** I was your mother when I was as old as you are now.

**8. he's . . . wax:** He's a model of a man.

**9. Examine . . . content:** Examine every harmonious feature of his face, and see how each one enhances every other. Throughout this speech, Lady Capulet compares Paris to a book.
**10. margent:** margin. Paris's eyes are compared to the margin of a book, where whatever is not clear in the text (the rest of his face) can be explained by notes.
**11. cover:** A metaphor for wife.

*The Tragedy of Romeo and Juliet, Act I, Scene iv* 335

28 **Clarification** In Shakespeare's time, the word *marry* was also used as an exclamation. Shakespeare is playing on both meanings in this passage.

29 **Discussion** How does Juliet feel about marriage?

30 **Critical Thinking and Reading** Is this extended metaphor effective? Explain.

of marriage, could swear that they did not have any regrets about being married. Couples—real or pretend—who asserted they had no regrets were placed on trial, at which they had to prove their claim. Twelve guests (the jury) and a judge questioned the couples to try to disprove their claim. The result was usually a humorous dialogue of "What if . . ." questions and ingenious responses. For example, the judge might ask the wife: "What if your husband chased the dog into the banquet hall, which spooked the cat, which leapt into the bowl of cream, which splashed the guest of honor?" The wife then had to give an immediate response to prove her gladness that her husband caused these unfortunate events. After the couples were ques-

tioned, the jury would then decide the verdict and name the couple that would "bring home the bacon."

The last event of the day was a candlelight procession around the feast hall. Everyone carried a small loaf of bread in which a candle was placed. Afterward, they would set aside three quarters of the bread to be eaten the following day. They preserved the remaining quarter for the next year's celebration, at which time the bread would be made into crumbs and fed to the birds to indicate the beginning of the new festival.

31 **Discussion** How can Romeo and his friends go to the party and not be recognized?

**NURSE.** No less? Nay, bigger! Women grow by men.

**LADY CAPULET.** Speak briefly, can you like of Paris' love?

**JULIET.** I'll look to like, if looking liking move;[12]
But no more deep will I endart mine eye
100    Than your consent gives strength to make it fly.[13]

[*Enter* SERVINGMAN.]

**SERVINGMAN.** Madam, the guests are come, supper served up, you called, my young lady asked for, the nurse cursed in the pantry, and everything in extremity. I must hence to wait. I beseech you follow straight.    [*Exit.*]

105 **LADY CAPULET.** We follow thee. Juliet, the County stays.[14]

**NURSE.** Go, girl, seek happy nights to happy days. [*Exit.*]

**Scene iv.** *A street*

[*Enter* ROMEO, MERCUTIO, BENVOLIO, *with five or six other* MASKERS; TORCHBEARERS.]

31

**ROMEO.** What, shall this speech[1] be spoke for our excuse?
Or shall we on without apology?

**BENVOLIO.** The date is out of such prolixity.[2]
We'll have no Cupid hoodwinked with a scarf,
5    Bearing a Tartar's painted bow of lath,

*336 Drama*

12. **I'll . . . move:** If looking favorably at someone leads to liking him, I'll look at Paris in a way that will lead to liking him.

13. **But . . . fly:** But I won't look harder than you want me to.

14. **the County stays:** The Count, Paris, is waiting.

1. **this speech:** Romeo asks whether he and his companions, being uninvited guests, should follow custom by announcing their arrival in a speech.

2. **The . . . prolixity:** Such wordiness is outdated. In the following lines, Benvolio says, in sum: "Let's forget about announcing our entrance with a show. The other guests can look us over as they see fit. We'll dance a while, then leave."

Scaring the ladies like a crowkeeper,
Nor no without-book prologue, faintly spoke
After the prompter, for our entrance;
But, let them measure us by what they will,
10 We'll measure them a measure and be gone.

**ROMEO.** Give me a torch. I am not for this ambling.
Being but heavy,[3] I will bear the light.

**3. heavy:** Weighed down with sadness.

**MERCUTIO.** Nay, gentle Romeo, we must have you dance.

**ROMEO.** Not I, believe me. You have dancing shoes
15 With nimble soles; I have a soul of lead
So stakes me to the ground I cannot move.

**MERCUTIO.** You are a lover. Borrow Cupid's wings
And soar with them above a common bound.

**ROMEO.** I am too sore enpiercèd with his shaft
20 To soar with his light feathers; and so bound
I cannot bound a pitch above dull woe.
Under love's heavy burden do I sink.

**MERCUTIO.** And, to sink in it, should you burden love—
Too great oppression for a tender thing.

25 **ROMEO.** Is love a tender thing? It is too rough,
Too rude, too boist'rous, and it pricks like thorn.

**MERCUTIO.** If love be rough with you, be rough with love.
Prick love for pricking, and you beat love down.
Give me a case to put my visage[4] in.
30 A visor for a visor![5] What care I
What curious eye doth quote deformities?[6]
Here are the beetle brows shall blush for me.

**4. visage:** Mask.

**5. A visor . . . visor!:** A mask for a mask—which is what my real face is like!
**6. quote deformities:** Notice my ugly features.

**BENVOLIO.** Come, knock and enter; and no sooner in
But every man betake him to his legs.[7]

35 **ROMEO.** A torch for me! Let wantons light of heart
Tickle the senseless rushes[8] with their heels;
For I am proverbed with a grandsire phrase,[9]
I'll be a candleholder and look on;
The game was ne'er so fair, and I am done.[10]

**7. betake . . . legs:** Start dancing.
**8. Let . . . rushes:** Let fun-loving people dance on the floor coverings.
**9. proverbed . . . phrase:** Directed by an old saying.
**10. The game . . . done:** No matter how much enjoyment may be had, I won't have any.
**11. Dun's . . . word!:** Lie low like a mouse—that's what a constable waiting to make an arrest might say.
**12. Dun:** Proverbial name for a horse.

**MERCUTIO.** Tut! Dun's the mouse, the constable's own
40    word![11]
If thou art Dun,[12] we'll draw thee from the mire
Of this sir-reverence love, wherein thou stickest
Up to the ears. Come, we burn daylight, ho!

**ROMEO.** Nay, that's not so.

*The Tragedy of Romeo and Juliet, Act I, Scene iv* 337

32 **Discussion** What does Benvolio's plan suggest about his personality?

33 **Discussion** Why do you think Mercutio teases Romeo?

34 **Enrichment** Mercutio's name comes from that of the Roman god Mercury, who was known for eloquence, cleverness, and thievery.

35 **Discussion** What does this speech reveal about Mercutio? To what extent does he resemble the god after whom he was named?

**36 Discussion** How would you describe the relationship between Romeo and Mercutio?

**37 Enrichment** You might point out to students that Elizabethans enjoyed long, lyrical speeches like this one.

**Cooperative Learning** Mercutio's Queen Mab speech contains images that reflect his personality. Have groups of students make a collage or sculpture of what they believe are the images that reflect Mercutio's personality. Each student should be responsible for one aspect of the project. For example, one student might gather all the materials, one or two might put the project together, and another might present the project. When students are finished, have them present their projects to the class, explaining why they chose the images they did and what their artwork says about Mercutio.

**MERCUTIO.**                    I mean, sir, in delay
45    We waste our lights in vain, like lights by day.
      Take our good meaning, for our judgment sits
      Five times in that ere once in our five wits.[13]

**ROMEO.** And we mean well in going to this masque,
      But 'tis no wit to go.

**MERCUTIO.**                    Why, may one ask?

**ROMEO.** I dreamt a dream tonight.

50    **MERCUTIO.**                    And so did I.

**ROMEO.** Well, what was yours?

**MERCUTIO.**                    That dreamers often lie.

**ROMEO.** In bed asleep, while they do dream things true.

**MERCUTIO.** O, then I see Queen Mab[14] hath been with you.
      She is the fairies' midwife, and she comes
55    In shape no bigger than an agate stone
      On the forefinger of an alderman,
      Drawn with a team of little atomies[15]
      Over men's noses as they lie asleep;
      Her wagon spokes made of long spinners'[16] legs,
60    The cover, of the wings of grasshoppers;
      Her traces, of the smallest spider web;
      Her collars, of the moonshine's wat'ry beams;
      Her whip, of cricket's bone; the lash, of film;[17]
      Her wagoner, a small gray-coated gnat,
65    Not half so big as a round little worm
      Pricked from the lazy finger of a maid;
      Her chariot is an empty hazelnut,
      Made by the joiner squirrel or old grub,[18]

**13. Take . . . wits:** Understand my intended meaning. That shows more intelligence than merely following what your senses perceive.

**14. Queen Mab:** The queen of fairyland.

**15. atomies:** Creatures.

**16. spinners:** Spiders.

**17. film:** Spider's thread.

**18. old grub:** An insect that bores holes in nuts.

## Commentary: The Power of the Stars and Planets

Reread Romeo's statement at the end of Act I, Scene iv, ll. 106, in which he says he is fearful that his life will be cut short as determined by the stars. Point out to students that belief in the stars' influence on humankind and in astrology were common in the sixteenth century.

Many Elizabethans believed in astrology—the notion that the positions of the moon, sun, and planets—were responsible for their general dispositions. For example, they believed that the zodiac sign under which a person was born and the position of the planets at that time determined his or her general character.

Elizabethans also believed that the planetary influences that determined a person's character were apart from the control the stars had on humankind. They believed the stars determined a person's fate. For example, it was the stars that determined if a person would live a long and happy life or a short life wrought with unhappiness. It is this belief that causes Romeo to be fearful that his life will be cut short as the stars have fated.

Time out o' mind the fairies' coachmakers.
70  And in this state she gallops night by night
Through lovers' brains, and then they dream of love;
On courtiers' knees, that dream on curtsies straight;
O'er lawyers' fingers, who straight dream on fees;
O'er ladies' lips, who straight on kisses dream,
75  Which oft the angry Mab with blisters plagues,
Because their breath with sweetmeats[19] tainted are.
Sometimes she gallops o'er a courtier's nose,
And then dreams he of smelling out a suit;[20]
And sometime comes she with a tithe pig's[21] tail
80  Tickling a parson's nose as 'a lies asleep,
Then he dreams of another benefice.[22]
Sometime she driveth o'er a soldier's neck,
And then dream he of cutting foreign throats,
Of breaches, ambuscadoes,[23] Spanish blades,
85  Of healths[24] five fathom deep; and then anon
Drums in his ear, at which he starts and wakes,
And being thus frighted, swears a prayer or two
And sleeps again. This is that very Mab
That plats[25] the manes of horses in the night
90  And bakes the elflocks[26] in foul sluttish hairs,
Which once untangled much misfortune bodes.
This is the hag, when maids lie on their backs,
That presses them and learns them first to bear,
Making them women of good carriage.[27]
This is she—

95  **ROMEO.**          Peace, peace, Mercutio, peace!
Thou talk'st of nothing.

**MERCUTIO.**                    True, I talk of dreams;
Which are the children of an idle brain,
Begot of nothing but vain fantasy;
Which is as thin of substance as the air,
100  And more inconstant than the wind, who woos
Even now the frozen bosom of the North
And, being angered, puffs away from thence,
Turning his side to the dew-dropping South.

**BENVOLIO.** This wind you talk of blows us from ourselves.
105  Supper is done, and we shall come too late.

**ROMEO.** I fear, too early; for my mind misgives
Some consequence yet hanging in the stars
Shall bitterly begin his fearful date
With this night's revels and expire the term

*The Tragedy of Romeo and Juliet, Act I, Scene v*  339

**19. sweetmeats:** Candy.
**20. smelling . . . suit:** Finding someone who has a petition (suit) for the king and who will pay the courtier to gain the king's favor for the petition.
**21. tithe pig:** A pig donated to a parson.
**22. benefice:** A church appointment that included a guaranteed income.
**23. ambuscadoes:** Ambushes.
**24. healths:** Toasts ("To your health!").

**25. plats:** Tangles.
**26. elflocks:** Tangled hair.

**27. carriage:** Posture.

38 **Critical Thinking and Reading** How does Mercutio's imagery reflect his personality?

39 **Reading Strategy** Have students identify where else in this act "the stars" and fate have been mentioned.

Because many Elizabethans feared the stars determined their fate, they sought astrologers to tell them their horoscopes. To determine the horoscopes, astrologers would track the stars and the movements of the sun, moon, and planets and predict the effect these would have on humankind. Elizabethan astrologers, it seems, were unaware of Copernicus' theory of planetary order, which was published in 1543, fifty-two years before *Romeo and Juliet* was written. Astrologers believed that the Earth was at the center of the universe and that the sun, moon, and planets revolved around it.

Ask students why Romeo and Juliet might have been referred to as "star-crossed lovers" and their love said to be "death-mark'd" in the play's prologue (p. 347).

40 **Discussion** Why do you think Shakespeare included this exchange?

41 **Discussion** What is Capulet's mood?

42 **Discussion** What is the atmosphere of the party?

110 Of a despisèd life, closed in my breast,
By some vile forfeit of untimely death.[28]
But he that hath the steerage of my course
Direct my sail! On, lusty gentlemen!

**BENVOLIO.** Strike, drum.

[*They march about the stage, and retire to one side.*]

**Scene v.** *A hall in* CAPULET's *house.*

[SERVINGMEN *come forth with napkins.*]

**FIRST SERVINGMAN.** Where's Potpan, that he helps not to take away? He shift a trencher![1] He scrape a trencher!

**SECOND SERVINGMAN.** When good manners shall lie all in one or two men's hands, and they unwashed too, 'tis a
5   foul thing.

**FIRST SERVINGMAN.** Away with the join-stools, remove the court cupboard, look to the plate. Good thou, save me a piece of marchpane,[2] and, as thou loves me, let the porter let in Susan Grindstone and Nell. Anthony, and
10   Potpan!

**SECOND SERVINGMAN.** Ay, boy, ready.

**FIRST SERVINGMAN.** You are looked for and called for, asked for and sought for, in the great chamber.

**THIRD SERVINGMAN.** We cannot be here and there too.
15   Cheerly, boys! Be brisk awhile, and the longer liver take all.                                                    [*Exit.*]

[*Enter* CAPULET, *his* WIFE, JULIET, TYBALT, NURSE, *and all the* GUESTS *and* GENTLEWOMEN *to the* MASKERS.]

**CAPULET.** Welcome, gentlemen! Ladies that have their toes
Unplagued with corns will walk a bout[3] with you.
Ah, my mistresses, which of you all
20   Will now deny to dance? She that makes dainty,[4]
She I'll swear hath corns. Am I come near ye now?
Welcome, gentlemen! I have seen the day
That I have worn a visor and could tell
A whispering tale in a fair lady's ear,
25   Such as would please. 'Tis gone, 'tis gone, 'tis gone.
You are welcome, gentlemen! Come, musicians, play.
                    [*Music plays, and they dance.*]
A hall,[5] a hall! Give room! And foot it, girls.
More light, you knaves, and turn the tables up,

**28. my mind . . . death:** My mind is fearful that some future event, fated by the stars, shall start to run its course tonight and cut my life short.

**1. trencher:** Wooden platter.

**2. marchpane:** Marzipan, a confection made of sugar and almonds.

**3. walk a bout:** Dance a turn.

**4. makes dainty:** Hesitates, acts shy.

**5. A hall:** Clear the floor, make room for dancing.

## Literary Element: Imagery

Images are words and phrases that appeal to the senses—sight, sound, smell, touch, and taste. Imagery is the use of images throughout any given work to form an overall picture, tone, or impression.

In *Romeo and Juliet,* a dominate image is light. Have students read Romeo's description of Juliet in Act I, Scene v.

Then ask them to read aloud the lines that contain images of light, for example, "O, she doth teach the torches to burn bright!"

Afterward, read the quotation that follows by Caroline Spurgeon, from *Shakespeare's Imagery and What it Tells Us,* in which she comments on the light imagery in *Romeo and Juliet:*

> To Juliet, Romeo is 'day in night'; to Romeo, Juliet is the sun rising from the east, and when they soar to love's ecstasy, each alike pictures the other as stars in heaven, shedding such brightness as puts to shame the heavenly bodies themselves. (p. 310).

Ask students what tone or impression the light imagery elicits.

In contrast to his light imagery, Shakespeare also uses

And quench the fire; the room is grown too hot.
30 Ah, sirrah, this unlooked-for sport comes well.
Nay, sit; nay, sit, good cousin Capulet;
For you and I are past our dancing days.
How long is't now since last yourself and I
Were in a mask?

**SECOND CAPULET.** By'r Lady, thirty years.

35 **CAPULET.** What, man? 'Tis not so much, 'tis not so much;
'Tis since the nuptial of Lucentio,
Come Pentecost as quickly as it will,
Some five-and-twenty years, and then we masked.

**SECOND CAPULET.** 'Tis more, 'tis more. His son is elder, sir;
His son is thirty.

40 **CAPULET.**            Will you tell me that?
His son was but a ward[6] two years ago.

**6. ward:** A minor.

**ROMEO.** [*To a* SERVINGMAN] What lady's that which doth
enrich the hand
Of yonder knight?

**SERVINGMAN.**            I know not, sir.

45 **ROMEO.** O, she doth teach the torches to burn bright!
It seems she hangs upon the cheek of night
As a rich jewel in an Ethiop's ear—
Beauty too rich for use, for earth too dear!
So shows a snowy dove trooping with crows
50 As yonder lady o'er her fellows shows.
The measure done, I'll watch her place of stand
And, touching hers, make blessèd my rude hand.
Did my heart love till now? Forswear[7] it, sight!
For I ne'er saw true beauty till this night.

**7. Forswear:** Deny.
**8. antic face:** Strange, fantastic mask.
**9. fleer:** Mock.

55 **TYBALT.** This, by his voice, should be a Montague.
Fetch me my rapier, boy. What! Dares the slave
Come hither, covered with an antic face,[8]
To fleer[9] and scorn at our solemnity?
Now, by the stock and honor of my kin,
60 To strike him dead I hold it not a sin.

**CAPULET.** Why, how now, kinsman? Wherefore storm you
so?

**TYBALT.** Uncle, this is a Montague, our foe,
A villain, that is hither come in spite
To scorn at our solemnity this night.

*The Tragedy of Romeo and Juliet, Act I, Scene v* 341

43 **Discussion** How does this good-natured argument reflect the advanced age of the participants?

44 **Literary Focus** Romeo's description of Juliet is written in iambic pentameter couplets rather than blank verse. This change of form makes the speech stand out.

45 **Critical Thinking and Reading** What can you infer about Tybalt from this speech?

**Master Teacher Note** Because much of Act I, Scene v, takes place during the Capulet's party, you might want to give students a taste of Elizabethan music and food. For example, you might play *Robin is to the Greenwood Gone,* performed by Paul O'Dette (Book of the Month Club recording number 67-6553); *The Scholars: The Silver Swan and Other Elizabethan and Jacobean Madrigals* (Book of the Month Club recording number 97-6556); or any similar recordings. You might also look for recordings of Elizabethan music performed by Julian Bream or composed by John Dowland.

For a taste of Elizabethan food, you or your students might prepare some Elizabethan dishes from *To the Queen's Taste* by Lorna Sass, published by The Metropolitan Museum of Art, 1976.

images of darkness, which generate a different tone or impression. Have students compare the images of darkness in the following passages from *Romeo and Juliet* with the light imagery in the preceding quotation. For example, what tone or impression do the following lines from Act III, Scene v, containing imagery of darkness and rain present the reader?

When the sun sets, the air doth drizzle dew;
But for the sunset of my brother's son
It rains downright. (Act III, Sc. v, 11. 127-129)
More light and light: more dark and dark our woes!
(Act III, Sc. v, 11. 36)

**Student Activity.** In addition to images of light and dark, Shakespeare also includes images of poison, graves, dreams, and color, each of which create its own tone and impression for the reader. In a notebook, trace one of these recurring images through the play as follows: Divide a sheet of paper into four columns. In one column copy the lines; in the second, indicate the location of the lines; in the third, state who said them; and in the fourth, note what impression or tone the lines convey. Then as a class discuss the role of these images and their importance to the play.

**46 Discussion** Give two reasons why Capulet restrains Tybalt.

**47 Discussion** Why is Capulet so angry at Tybalt?

**48 Reading Strategy** Have students predict what Tybalt will do.

**CAPULET.** Young Romeo is it?

65 **TYBALT.**                     'Tis he, that villain Romeo.

**46**

**CAPULET.** Content thee, gentle coz,[10] let him alone.
'A bears him like a portly gentleman,[11]
And, to say truth, Verona brags of him
To be a virtuous and well-governed youth.
70 I would not for the wealth of all this town
Here in my house do him disparagement.[12]
Therefore be patient; take no note of him.
It is my will, the which if thou respect,
Show a fair presence and put off these frowns,
75 An ill-beseeming semblance[13] for a feast.

**TYBALT.** It fits when such a villain is a guest.
I'll not endure him.

**47**

**CAPULET.**               He shall be endured.
What, goodman[14] boy! I say he shall. Go to![15]
Am I the master here, or you? Go to!
80 You'll not endure him, God shall mend my soul![16]
You'll make a mutiny among my guests!
You will set cock-a-hoop.[17] You'll be the man!

**TYBALT.** Why, uncle, 'tis a shame.

**CAPULET.**                     Go to, go to!
You are a saucy boy. Is't so, indeed?
85 This trick may chance to scathe you.[18] I know what.
You must contrary me! Marry, 'tis time—
Well said, my hearts!—You are a princox[19]—go!
Be quiet, or—More light, more light!—For shame!
I'll make you quiet. What!—Cheerly, my hearts!

**48**

90 **TYBALT.** Patience perforce with willful choler meeting[20]
Makes my flesh tremble in their different greeting.
I will withdraw; but this intrusion shall,
Now seeming sweet, convert to bitt'rest gall.     [*Exit.*]

**ROMEO.** If I profane with my unworthiest hand
95 This holy shrine,[21] the gentle sin is this:
My lips, two blushing pilgrims, ready stand
To smooth that rough touch with a tender kiss.

**JULIET.** Good pilgrim, you do wrong your hand too much,
Which mannerly devotion shows in this;
100 For saints have hands that pilgrims' hands do touch,
And palm to palm is holy palmers'[22] kiss.

**ROMEO.** Have not saints lips, and holy palmers too?

342   *Drama*

**10. coz:** Here *coz* is used as a term of address for any relative.
**11. 'A . . . gentleman:** He behaves like a dignified gentleman.

**12. disparagement:** Insult.

**13. ill-beseeming semblance:** Inappropriate appearance.

**14. goodman:** A term of address for someone below the rank of gentleman.
**15. Go to!:** An expression of angry impatience.
**16. God . . . soul!:** An expression of impatience, equivalent to *God save me!*
**17. You will set cock-a-hoop:** You want to swagger like a barnyard rooster.

**18. This . . . you:** This trait of yours may turn out to hurt you.
**19. princox:** Rude youngster, wise guy.

**20. Patience . . . meeting:** Enforced self-control mixing with strong anger.

**21. shrine:** Juliet's hand.

**22. palmers:** Pilgrims, who at one time carried palm branches from the Holy Land.

**JULIET.** Ay, pilgrim, lips that they must use in prayer.

**ROMEO.** O, then, dear saint, let lips do what hands do!
105    They pray; grant thou, lest faith turn to despair.

**JULIET.** Saints do not move,[23] though grant for prayers'
    sake.

**ROMEO.** Then move not while my prayer's effect I take.
    Thus from my lips, by thine my sin is purged.

                                                    *[Kisses her.]*

**JULIET.** Then have my lips the sin that they have took.

110 **ROMEO.** Sin from my lips? O trespass sweetly urged![24]
    Give me my sin again.                    *[Kisses her.]*

**JULIET.**                You kiss by th' book.[25]

**NURSE.** Madam, your mother craves a word with you.

**ROMEO.** What is her mother?

**NURSE.**                Marry, bachelor,
    Her mother is the lady of the house,
115    And a good lady, and a wise and virtuous.
    I nursed her daughter that you talked withal.
    I tell you, he that can lay hold of her
    Shall have the chinks.[26]

**ROMEO.**              Is she a Capulet?
    O dear account! My life is my foe's debt.[27]

120 **BENVOLIO.** Away, be gone; the sport is at the best.

23. **move:** Initiate involvement in earthly affairs.

24. **O . . . urged!:** Romeo is saying, in substance, that he is happy. Juliet calls his kiss a sin, for now he can take it back—by another kiss.
25. **by th' book:** As if you were following a manual of courtly love.

26. **chinks:** Cash.
27. **My life . . . debt:** Since Juliet is a Capulet, Romeo's life is at the mercy of the enemies of his family.

**Reader's Response** If you were Juliet's or Romeo's best friend, what advice would you give to the "star-crossed lover" at the end of Act I? For example, would you discourage or encourage him or her from falling in love? Why?

**ROMEO.** Ay, so I fear; the more is my unrest.

**CAPULET.** Nay, gentlemen, prepare not to be gone;
We have a trifling foolish banquet towards.[28]
Is it e'en so?[29] Why then, I thank you all.
125   I thank you, honest gentlemen. Good night.
More torches here! Come on then; let's to bed.
Ah, sirrah, by my fay,[30] it waxes late;
I'll to my rest.     [*Exit all but* JULIET *and* NURSE.]

**JULIET.** Come hither, nurse. What is yond gentleman?

130  **NURSE.** The son and heir of old Tiberio.

**JULIET.** What's he that now is going out of door?

**NURSE.** Marry, that, I think, be young Petruchio.

**JULIET.** What's he that follows here, that would not dance?

**NURSE.** I know not.

135  **JULIET.** Go ask his name—If he is marrièd,
My grave is like to be my wedding bed.

**NURSE.** His name is Romeo, and a Montague,
The only son of your great enemy.

140  **JULIET.** My only love, sprung from my only hate!
Too early seen unknown, and known too late!
Prodigious[31] birth of love it is to me
That I must love a loathèd enemy.

**NURSE.** What's this? What's this?

**JULIET.**                    A rhyme I learnt even now.
Of one I danced withal.   [*One calls within,* "Juliet."]

145  **NURSE.**              Anon, anon!
Come, let's away; the strangers all are gone.   [*Exit.*]

**28. towards:** Being prepared.
**29. Is . . . so?:** Is it the case that you really must leave?

**30. fay:** Faith.

**31. Prodigious:** Monstrous; foretelling misfortune.

## THINKING ABOUT THE SELECTION
### Recalling

1. Explain what you learn from the Prologue about the fate of Romeo and Juliet and the feud between the two families.
2. Why does the Prince want to settle the feud? With what penalty does he threaten the Montagues and Capulets for fighting?
3. Why is Romeo filled with melancholy in the first scene? How does Benvolio react to his mood?
4. What similar advice does Capulet give Paris and Benvolio give Romeo? What is the effect of the advice on Romeo?
5. Describe Juliet's response to her mother's announcement that Paris wishes to marry her.

344  *Drama*

6. Describe Romeo's reaction when he first sees Juliet.
7. Describe Romeo's and Juliet's reactions upon learning each other's identity.

## Interpreting

8. Compare and contrast the personalities of Romeo and Juliet in Act I. Explain what is unusual about the way they speak to each other when they first meet.
9. Explain the possible threats to their love that are already present in Act I.
10. How does Juliet's comment when she asks her nurse to find out Romeo's name echo back to the Prologue? Find lines Romeo spoke earlier in the scene that have the same effect.

## Applying

11. Romeo and Juliet fall in love at first sight. Do you believe love at first sight is possible? Explain your answer.

## ANALYZING LITERATURE

### Appreciating Blank Verse

**Blank verse** is unrhymed iambic pentameter. Normally, a line of such verse will consist of ten syllables with every second syllable stressed. However, poets and playwrights like Shakespeare often depart from the normal pattern for a number of reasons: to avoid monotony, to imitate the rhythms of real speech, to vary the "music" of the verse, and so on.

On a separate piece of paper, indicate the pattern of unaccented and accented syllables in lines 52–57 of Mercutio's Queen Mab speech (Scene iv). Use the mark ˘ for an unaccented syl-

lable and the mark ´ for an accented one. This is how the first line should look:

Ŏ, thén Ĭ seé Queĕn Máb hăth beén wĭth you.

## CRITICAL THINKING AND READING

### Interpreting the Effect of Imagery

Throughout the play, imagery creates mood, reveals character, suggests ideas, and otherwise affects your response. In Scene v reread lines 94–111, which Romeo and Juliet speak when they first meet. Then answer the following questions about them.

1. What kind of imagery is introduced by the words "shrine," "sin," and "saints"?
2. How does this imagery affect your view of Romeo and Juliet?
3. Explain what the imagery suggests about Romeo and Juliet's love.

## THINKING AND WRITING

### Writing a Speech in Blank Verse

Using the notes you made before you started reading Act I, write a speech to stop the fighting between two feuding families. Use Escalus's speech as a model for content and organization. Then rewrite your speech in blank verse. You can do so by changing individual words and phrases to fit the thought content into the blank-verse pattern.

When you revise your speech, read it aloud to hear how it sounds. See if you can increase its force and persuasiveness. Deliver your speech to a group of your classmates, and ask their opinion of its effectiveness.

She ĭs thĕ faíriĕs' mídwife, ănd shĕ comes
Ĭn shápe nŏ bíggĕr thăn ăn ágăte stóne
Ŏn thĕ fórefíngĕr ŏf ăn áldĕrmăn,
Dráwn wĭth ă teám ŏf líttlĕ átomĭes
Óvĕr mén's nósĕs ăs thĕy lie ăsleép;

**Challenge** Have students compare the meter of this play with the meter of *The Song of Hiawatha* by Longfellow.

### ANSWERS TO CRITICAL THINKING AND READING

1. Suggested Response: These words portray images associated with religious worship.
2. Answers will differ. Many students will respond that this imagery makes them take more seriously the love between Romeo and Juliet.
3. Suggested Response: This imagery suggests that their love is in some way holy and pure.

### THINKING AND WRITING

For help with this assignment, students can refer to Lesson 18, "Writing a Poem," in the Handbook of Writing About Literature.

**Publishing Student Writing**
Have students mark the unaccented and accented syllables on a copy of their speech and then have a classmate use these marked copies to read the speech aloud.

**Writing Across the Curriculum**
You might have students research and report on some aspect of life in Elizabethan times. Consider informing the social studies department of this assignment, so that teachers can guide students to appropriate resources.

7. He feels his life is at the mercy of his enemy. She thinks it is a cruel twist of fate to love an enemy.

### Interpreting
8. Answers will differ. Most students will realize that Romeo is moody, impulsive, and romantic. Also, his wayward behavoir is a source of concern to his parents. Juliet, by contrast, is a dutiful young girl who, before meeting Romeo, does not seem to have given much thought to love.

When they meet, they are so in tune with each other that their words create a sonnet. Also, they use religious imagery.
9. Suggested Response: Tybalt threatens retaliation against Romeo. Juliet's family is considering her marriage to someone else.
10. Suggested Response: She says her only love has sprung from her only hate, an echo of the prologue's line, "From forth the fatal loins of these two foes." Romeo says, "My life is my foe's debt."

### Applying
11. Answers will differ. Some students will agree; most will probably feel that true love comes after two people have come to know and enjoy being with each other.

### ANSWERS TO ANALYZING LITERATURE

Ŏ, thén, Ĭ seé Queĕn Máb hăth beén wĭth you.

## Focus

**Literary Focus** Suggest to students that the "straight man" in a comedy team is a kind of dramatic foil for the comic. Have students think of comedy teams that function in this way.

**Look For** You might want to tell students that many of the complications arise from the need to keep this love secret.

**Writing/Prior Knowledge** Before students begin to write, clarify for them the meaning of the word *infatuation*.

**Vocabulary** Have less advanced students read the words and their definitions several times.

## The Tragedy of Romeo and Juliet, Act II

**The Dramatic Foil**

**A dramatic foil** is a character who highlights or brings out the personality traits of another character in a play. Usually the foil contrasts with the other character, and the contrast serves to emphasize the other character's traits. For example, in Act I of *Romeo and Juliet,* Benvolio, who tries to quiet the brawling servants, is a dramatic foil to the fiery Tybalt. More important, by his calm and sensible disposition, he is a dramatic foil to the moody, emotional Romeo.

**Look For**

Near the end of Act I, Juliet says:

> My only love, sprung from my only hate!
> Too early seen unknown, and known too late!
> Prodigious birth of love it is to me
> That I must love a loathèd enemy.

As you read Act II, look for the complications that arise from this love between enemies.

**Writing**

Divide a piece of paper into two columns. Head one column "Love" and the other "Infatuation." Under the appropriate heading, write down some of the signs and characteristics that indicate love and some of the ones that indicate infatuation.

**Vocabulary**

Knowing the following words will help you as you read Act II of *Romeo and Juliet*.

**kinsmen** (kinz′ mən) *n.*: Relatives (p. 350)

**cunning** (kun′ iŋ) *n.*: Cleverness, slyness (p. 351)

**variable** (ver′ ē ə b'l) *adj.*: Changeable, inconstant (p. 352)

**procure** (prō kyoor′) *v.*: Get, obtain (p. 353)

**vile** (vīl) *adj.*: Worthless, cheap, low (p. 354)

**sallow** (sal′ ō) *adj.*: Of a sickly pale-yellowish complexion (p. 356)

**waverer** (wā′ vər ər) *n.*: One who changes or is unsteady (p. 356)

**lamentable** (lam′ ən tə b'l) *adj.*: Distressing, sad (p. 357)

**unwieldy** (un wēl′ dē) *adj.*: Awkward, clumsy (p. 363)

346 Drama

---

### Objectives

1 To understand the dramatic foil
2 To interpret personification
3 To modernize dialogue

### Support Material

**Teaching Portfolio**
Teacher Backup, p. 377
Grammar in Action Worksheets, *Understanding Antecedents,* p. 380; *Determining Author's Tone,* p. 382
Usage and Mechanics Worksheet, p. 384
Vocabulary Check, p. 385

Analyzing Literature, *Understanding the Dramatic Foil,* p. 387
Language Worksheet, *Interpreting Personification,* p. 388
Selection Test, p. 389

# Act II

## PROLOGUE

[*Enter* CHORUS.]

**CHORUS.** Now old desire[1] doth in his deathbed lie,
  And young affection gapes to be his heir;[2]
That fair[3] for which love groaned for and would die,
  With tender Juliet matched, is now not fair.
5 Now Romeo is beloved and loves again,
  Alike bewitchèd[4] by the charm of looks;
But to his foe supposed he must complain,[5]
  And she steal love's sweet bait from fearful hooks.
Being held a foe, he may not have access
10  To breathe such vows as lovers use to swear,
And she as much in love, her means much less
  To meet her new belovèd anywhere;
But passion lends them power, time means to meet,
Temp'ring extremities with extreme sweet.[6]      [*Exit.*]

**Scene i.** *Near* CAPULET's *orchard.*

[*Enter* ROMEO *alone.*]

**ROMEO.** Can I go forward when my heart is here?
  Turn back, dull earth,[1] and find thy center[2] out.

[*Enter* BENVOLIO *with* MERCUTIO. ROMEO *retires.*]

**BENVOLIO.** Romeo! My cousin Romeo! Romeo!

**MERCUTIO.**                                              He is wise
  And, on my life, hath stol'n him home to bed.

5 **BENVOLIO.** He ran this way and leapt this orchard wall.
  Call, good Mercutio.

**MERCUTIO.**                   Nay, I'll conjure[3] too.
  Romeo! Humors! Madman! Passion! Lover!
  Appear thou in the likeness of a sigh;
  Speak but one rhyme, and I am satisfied!
10 Cry but "Ay me!" pronounce but "love" and "dove";
  Speak to my gossip[4] Venus one fair word,
  One nickname for her purblind son and heir,
  Young Abraham Cupid, he that shot so true
  When King Cophetua loved the beggar maid!
15 He heareth not, he stirreth not, he moveth not;
  The ape is dead,[5] and I must conjure him.
  I conjure thee by Rosaline's bright eyes,

**1. old desire:** Romeo's love for Rosaline.
**2. young . . . heir:** Romeo's new love for Juliet is eager to replace his love for Rosaline.
**3. fair:** Beautiful woman (Rosaline).
**4. Alike bewitchèd:** Both Romeo and Juliet are enchanted.
**5. complain:** Address his words of love.

**6. Temp'ring . . . sweet:** Easing their difficulties with great delights.

**1. dull earth:** Lifeless body.
**2. center:** Heart, or possibly soul (Juliet).

**3. conjure:** Recite a spell to make Romeo appear.

**4. gossip:** Merry old lady.

**5. The ape is dead:** Romeo, like a trained monkey, seems to be playing dead.

*The Tragedy of Romeo and Juliet, Act II, Scene i*   347

**5 Discussion** Why is it ironic that Mercutio teases Romeo about Rosaline?

**6 Discussion** Explain the metaphor that Romeo uses to describe Juliet. How does this figure of speech reveal Romeo's feelings about her?

5

By her high forehead and her scarlet lip,
By her fine foot, straight leg, and quivering thigh,
20  And the demesnes that there adjacent lie,
That in thy likeness thou appear to us!

**BENVOLIO.** And if he hear thee, thou wilt anger him.

**MERCUTIO.** This cannot anger him. 'Twould anger him
To raise a spirit in his mistress' circle
25  Of some strange nature, letting it there stand
Till she had laid it and conjured it down.
That were some spite; my invocation
Is fair and honest; in his mistress' name,
I conjure only but to raise up him.

30  **BENVOLIO.** Come, he hath hid himself among these trees
To be consorted⁶ with the humorous⁷ night.
Blind is his love and best befits the dark.

**MERCUTIO.** If love be blind, love cannot hit the mark.
Now will he sit under a medlar tree
35  And wish his mistress were that kind of fruit
As maids call medlars⁸ when they laugh alone.
O, Romeo, that she were, O that she were
An open *et cetera*, thou a pop'rin pear!
Romeo, good night. I'll to my truckle bed;⁹
40  This field bed is too cold for me to sleep.
Come, shall we go?

**BENVOLIO.**             Go then, for 'tis in vain
To seek him here that means not to be found.

[*Exit with others.*]

***Scene ii.*** CAPULET'S *orchard.*

**ROMEO.** [*Coming forward*] He jests at scars that never felt
a wound.

[*Enter* JULIET *at a window.*]

6

But soft! What light through yonder window breaks?
It is the East, and Juliet is the sun!
5  Arise, fair sun, and kill the envious moon,
Who is already sick and pale with grief
That thou her maid art far more fair than she.
Be not her maid, since she is envious.
Her vestal livery¹ is but sick and green,
10  And none but fools do wear it. Cast it off.
It is my lady! O, it is my love!

**6. consorted:** Associated.
**7. humorous:** Humid; moody, like a lover.

**8. medlars:** An applelike fruits.

**9. truckle bed:** A trundle-bed, placed under a larger bed when not in use.

**1. livery:** Clothing or costume worn by a servant.

348 *Drama*

## Grammar in Action

Pronouns get their meaning from the words they stand for. These words are called **antecedents.** Personal pronouns agree with their antecedents in number, person, and gender, as follows:

Jerri paid for *her* mother's new ring. (*Her* refers to *Jerri,* both the pronoun and its antecedent are singular, third person, feminine.)
Holmes and *his* client ate *their* meal in silence. (*His* refers to *Holmes;* both are singular, third person, masculine. *Their* refers to *Holmes . . . and client,* both the antecedent and the pronoun are plural, third person.)

Since poetry is such a concentrated literary form, poets must be especially careful in their use of pronouns and antecedents. Note the following examples from *Romeo and Juliet:*

1. But soft! What light through yonder window breaks?
2. *It* is the East, and Juliet is the sun!
3. Arise, fair sun, and kill the envious moon,
4. *Who* is already sick and pale with grief
5. That *thou her* maid art far more fair than *she.*
6. Be not *her* maid, since *she* is envious.

O, that she knew she were!
She speaks, yet she says nothing. What of that?
Her eye discourses; I will answer it.
15 I am too bold; 'tis not to me she speaks.
Two of the fairest stars in all the heaven,
Having some business, do entreat her eyes
To twinkle in their spheres[2] till they return.
What if her eyes were there, they in her head?
20 The brightness of her cheek would shame those stars
As daylight doth a lamp; her eyes in heaven
Would through the airy region stream so bright
That birds would sing and think it were not night.
See how she leans her cheek upon that hand,
25 O, that I were a glove upon that hand,
That I might touch that cheek!

**JULIET.**                              Ay me!

**ROMEO.**                                    She speaks.
O, speak again, bright angel, for thou art
As glorious to this night, being o'er my head,
As is a wingèd messenger of heaven
30 Unto the white-upturnèd wond'ring eyes
Of mortals that fall back to gaze on him
When he bestrides the lazy puffing clouds
And sails upon the bosom of the air.

**JULIET.** O Romeo, Romeo! Wherefore art thou Romeo?[3]
35 Deny thy father and refuse thy name;
Or, if thou wilt not, be but sworn my love,
And I'll no longer be a Capulet.

**ROMEO.** [*Aside*] Shall I hear more, or shall I speak at this?

**JULIET.** 'Tis but thy name that is my enemy.
40 Thou art thyself, though not[4] a Montague.
What's Montague? It is nor hand, nor foot,
Nor arm, nor face. O, be some other name
Belonging to a man.
What's in a name? That which we call a rose
45 By any other name would smell as sweet.
So Romeo would, were he not Romeo called,
Retain that dear perfection which he owes[5]
Without that title. Romeo, doff[6] thy name;
And for thy name, which is no part of thee,
Take all myself.

50 **ROMEO.**                    I take thee at thy word.

2. **spheres:** Orbits.

3. **Wherefore . . . Romeo?**
Why are you Romeo—a
Montague?

4. **though not:** Even if you
were not.

5. **owes:** Owns, possesses.
6. **doff:** Remove.

*The Tragedy of Romeo and Juliet, Act II, Scene ii*   349

7

8

**7 Discussion** What solutions does Juliet suggest to deal with the problem of their families' enmity?

**8 Enrichment** Point out to students that this scene contains many lines that have become well-known quotations. Have students write some of these famous lines in their notebooks and consider why they have had such an appeal.

In line 2, the pronoun *it* refers to *window*. *Who* in line 4 refers to *moon*. *Thou* in line 5 refers to *sun* (or Juliet). *Her* and *she* in lines 5 and 6 both refer to *moon*. If Shakespeare had not used pronouns and antecedents correctly, readers would have been unable to unravel the meaning.

**Student Activity 1.** Identify the antecedents of the italicized pronouns in the following passage:

**Juliet** (to Romeo). Well, do not swear. Although I joy in *thee*,
*I* have no joy of this contract tonight.
*It* is too rash, too unadvised, too sudden;
Too like the lightning, which doth cease to be
Ere one can say *it* lightens . . .

**Student Activity 2.** Write a brief description of your reaction to Romeo or Juliet. Underline each pronoun and circle its antecedent.

Call me but love, and I'll be new baptized;
Henceforth I never will be Romeo.

**JULIET.** What man art thou, thus bescreened in night,
So stumblest on my counsel?[7]

7. **counsel:** Secret thoughts.

**ROMEO.**                                        By a name
55    I know not how to tell thee who I am.
My name, dear saint, is hateful to myself
Because it is an enemy to thee.
Had I it written, I would tear the word.

**JULIET.** My ears have yet not drunk a hundred words
60    Of thy tongue's uttering, yet I know the sound.
Art thou not Romeo, and a Montague?

**ROMEO.** Neither, fair maid, if either thee dislike.

**JULIET.** How camest thou hither, tell me, and wherefore?
The orchard walls are high and hard to climb,
65    And the place death, considering who thou art,
If any of my kinsmen find thee here.

**ROMEO.** With love's light wings did I o'erperch[8] these walls;
For stony limits cannot hold love out,
And what love can do, that dares love attempt.
70    Therefore thy kinsmen are no stop to me.

8. **o'erperch:** Fly over.

9 **Reading Strategy** Have students compare and contrast Romeo and Juliet as they confess their love. Who is more impulsive? Who is more realistic?

10 **Discussion** How do Romeo's first words echo a previous speech of Juliet's?

11 **Critical Thinking and Reading** Why do you think Romeo and Juliet fall in love so quickly?

**JULIET.** If they do see thee, they will murder thee.

**ROMEO.** Alack, there lies more peril in thine eye
    Than twenty of their swords! Look thou but sweet,
    And I am proof[9] against their enmity.

75 **JULIET.** I would not for the world they saw thee here.

**ROMEO.** I have night's cloak to hide me from their eyes;
    And but[10] thou love me, let them find me here.
    My life were better ended by their hate
    Than death proroguèd,[11] wanting of thy love.

80 **JULIET.** By whose direction found'st thou out this place?

**ROMEO.** By love, that first did prompt me to inquire.
    He lent me counsel, and I lent him eyes.
    I am no pilot; yet, wert thou as far
    As that vast shore washed with the farthest sea,
85     I should adventure[12] for such merchandise.

**JULIET.** Thou knowest the mask of night is on my face;
    Else would a maiden blush bepaint my cheek
    For that which thou hast heard me speak tonight.
    Fain would I dwell on form[13]—fain, fain deny
90     What I have spoke; but farewell compliment![14]
    Dost thou love me? I know thou wilt say "Ay";
    And I will take thy word. Yet, if thou swear'st,
    Thou mayst prove false. At lovers' perjuries,
    They say Jove laughs. O gentle Romeo,
95     If thou dost love, pronounce it faithfully.
    Or if thou thinkest I am too quickly won,
    I'll frown and be perverse[15] and say thee nay,
    So thou wilt woo; but else, not for the world.
    In truth, fair Montague, I am too fond,[16]
100     And therefore thou mayst think my havior light;[17]
    But trust me, gentleman, I'll prove more true
    Than those that have more cunning to be strange.[18]
    I should have been more strange, I must confess,
    But that thou overheard'st, ere I was ware,
105     My truelove passion. Therefore pardon me,
    And not impute this yielding to light love,
    Which the dark night hath so discoverèd.[19]

**ROMEO.** Lady, by yonder blessèd moon I vow,
    That tips with silver all these fruit-tree tops—

110 **JULIET.** O, swear not by the moon, th' inconstant moon,
    That monthly changes in her circle orb,

9. **proof:** Protected, as by armor.

10. **And but:** Unless.

11. **proroguèd:** Postponed.

12. **adventure:** Risk a long journey, like a sea adventurer.

13. **Fain . . . form:** Eagerly would I follow convention (by acting reserved).
14. **compliment:** Conventional behavior.

15. **be perverse:** Act contrary to my true feelings.
16. **fond:** Affectionate.
17. **my havior light:** My behavior immodest or unserious.

18. **strange:** Distant and cold.

19. **discoverèd:** Revealed.

12 **Enrichment** Point out to students the "t" alliteration in this line. Then have them make the "t" sound, noticing the position of their tongue. How does this alliteration contribute to the meaning of the line?

13 **Discussion** Why does Juliet call the moon inconstant?

*The Tragedy of Romeo and Juliet, Act II, Scene ii*   351

14 **Discussion** Why is Juliet concerned about this love? How does the imagery she uses reflect her concern?

15 **Discussion** How has Juliet changed as a result of her love?

Lest that thy love prove likewise variable.

**ROMEO.** What shall I swear by?

**JULIET.**                              Do not swear at all;
115     Or if thou wilt, swear by thy gracious self,
        Which is the god of my idolatry,
        And I'll believe thee.

**ROMEO.**                    If my heart's dear love—

**JULIET.** Well, do not swear. Although I joy in thee,
        I have no joy of this contract[20] tonight.        **20. contract:** Betrothal.
        It is too rash, too unadvised, too sudden;
120     Too like the lightning, which doth cease to be
        Ere one can say it lightens. Sweet, good night!
        This bud of love, by summer's ripening breath,
        May prove a beauteous flow'r when next we meet.
        Good night, good night! As sweet repose and rest
125     Come to thy heart as that within my breast!

**ROMEO.** O, wilt thou leave me so unsatisfied?

**JULIET.** What satisfaction canst thou have tonight?

**ROMEO.** Th' exchange of thy love's faithful vow for mine.

**JULIET.** I gave thee mine before thou didst request it;
130     And yet I would it were to give again.

**ROMEO.** Wouldst thou withdraw it? For what purpose, love?

**JULIET.** But to be frank[21] and give it thee again.         **21. frank:** Generous.
        And yet I wish but for the thing I have.
        My bounty[22] is as boundless as the sea,               **22. bounty:** What I have
135     My love as deep; the more I give to thee,               to give.
        The more I have, for both are infinite.
        I hear some noise within. Dear love, adieu!

                        [NURSE *calls within.*]

        Anon, good nurse! Sweet Montague, be true.
        Stay but a little, I will come again.          [*Exit.*]

140 **ROMEO.** O blessèd, blessèd night! I am afeard,
        Being in night, all this is but a dream,
        Too flattering-sweet to be substantial.[23]            **23. substantial:** Real.

                    [*Enter* JULIET *again.*]

**JULIET.** Three words, dear Romeo, and good night indeed.
        If that thy bent[24] of love be honorable,             **24. bent:** Purpose, in-
145     Thy purpose marriage, send me word tomorrow,           tention.

*352    Drama*

## Grammar in Action

**Tone** refers to the author's attitude toward his or her subject. Readers determine tone from the way a subject is presented and described. Within a work of literature, writers may show different attitudes toward the various characters. These attitudes are indicated in the same way that attitude toward the subject is.

In drama, tone is conveyed by what characters say and do and by what other characters say about them. At this point in the play, readers know that Juliet is a dutiful daughter who has not yet considered the possibility of love or marriage. We have learned that Romeo—until he saw Juliet—has been in love with Rosaline. Romeo's friends seem not to take this love for Rosaline seriously, suggesting that it is an infatuation that will last only until Romeo sees a more beautiful woman.

What do these lines suggest about Shakespeare's attitude toward Juliet?:

**JULIET**: Well do not swear. Although I joy in thee,
I have no joy of this contract tonight.
It is too rash, too unadvised, too sudden . . .
**JULIET**: My bounty is as boundless as the sea,

By one that I'll procure to come to thee,
Where and what time thou wilt perform the rite;
And all my fortunes at thy foot I'll lay
And follow thee my lord throughout the world.

150 **NURSE.** [*Within*] Madam!

**JULIET.** I come anon.—But if thou meanest not well,
I do beseech thee—

**NURSE.** [*Within*] Madam!

**JULIET.**                    By and by²⁵ I come.—
To cease thy strife²⁶ and leave me to my grief.
Tomorrow will I send.

**ROMEO.**                    So thrive my soul—

155 **JULIET.** A thousand times good night!          [*Exit.*]

**ROMEO.** A thousand times the worse, to want thy light!
Love goes toward love as schoolboys from their books;
But love from love, toward school with heavy looks.

[*Enter* JULIET *again.*]

160 **JULIET.** Hist! Romeo, hist! O for a falc'ner's voice
To lure this tassel gentle²⁷ back again!
Bondage is hoarse²⁸ and may not speak aloud,
Else would I tear the cave where Echo²⁹ lies
And make her airy tongue more hoarse than mine
With repetition of "My Romeo!"

165 **ROMEO.** It is my soul that calls upon my name.
How silver-sweet sound lovers' tongues by night,
Like softest music to attending ears!

**JULIET.** Romeo!

**ROMEO.**          My sweet?

**JULIET.**                    What o'clock tomorrow
Shall I send to thee?

**ROMEO.**                    By the hour of nine.

170 **JULIET.** I will not fail. 'Tis twenty year till then.
I have forgot why I did call thee back.

**ROMEO.** Let me stand here till thou remember it.

**JULIET.** I shall forget, to have thee still stand there,
Rememb'ring how I love thy company.

175 **ROMEO.** And I'll stay, to have thee still forget,

25. **By and by:** At once.
26. **strife:** Efforts.

27. **tassel gentle:** Male falcon.
28. **Bondage is hoarse:** Being bound in by my family restricts my speech.
29. **Echo:** In classical mythology the nymph Echo, unable to win the love of Narcissus, wasted away in a cave until nothing was left of her but her voice.

*The Tragedy of Romeo and Juliet, Act II, Scene ii*   353

16 **Clarification** Explain to students that falconry, or the art of training falcons to hunt, was familiar to Elizabethans. Falconers would call out commands to their birds.

17 **Enrichment** Point out to students that there are many references to names in this scene. Why is this subject so important for these lovers?

My love as deep; the more I give to thee,
The more I have; for both are infinite. . . .
If that thy bent of love be honorable,
Thy purpose marriage, send me word tomorrow . . .

These passages suggest that Juliet is fickle. In the first passage, although Juliet uses the word *joy* twice, she is not joyful; she is, in fact, confused and despondent. In the second passage, Juliet's tone is more cheerful as she is reveling in her love of Romeo.

**Student Activity 1.** Find two passages that suggest Shakespeare's attitude toward Juliet. Discuss these with your classmates and teacher.

**Student Activity 2.** Work with a partner to find passages that show Shakespeare's attitude toward Romeo. Compare and contrast these with the attitude toward Juliet.

**18 Master Teacher Note** Point out to students that this entire scene is written in rhymed couplets, rather than in blank verse. Have students discuss Shakespeare's possible motivations for this change.

**19 Critical Thinking and Reading** Find and describe examples of personification in the first six lines of Friar Lawrence's speech.

**20 Discussion** Have students consider why Shakespeare bothered to describe Friar Lawrence's special talent with herbs.

Forgetting any other home but this.

**JULIET.** 'Tis almost morning. I would have thee gone—
And yet no farther than a wanton's[30] bird,
That lets it hop a little from his hand,
180 Like a poor prisoner in his twisted gyves,[31]
And with a silken thread plucks it back again,
So loving-jealous of his liberty.

**ROMEO.** I would I were thy bird.

**JULIET.**                                    Sweet, so would I.
Yet I should kill thee with much cherishing.
185 Good night, good night! Parting is such sweet sorrow
That I shall say good night till it be morrow.    [*Exit.*]

**ROMEO.** Sleep dwell upon thine eyes, peace in thy breast!
Would I were sleep and peace, so sweet to rest!
Hence will I to my ghostly friar's[32] close cell,[33]
190 His help to crave and my dear hap[34] to tell.    [*Exit.*]

30. **wanton's:** Spoiled, playful child's.
31. **gyves** (jīvz): Chains.

32. **ghostly friar's:** Spiritual father's.
33. **close cell:** Small room.
34. **dear hap:** Good fortune.

**18 | Scene iii.** FRIAR LAWRENCE'S *cell.*

[*Enter* FRIAR LAWRENCE *alone, with a basket.*]

**FRIAR.** The gray-eyed morn smiles on the frowning night,
Check'ring the eastern clouds with streaks of light;
And fleckèd[1] darkness like a drunkard reels
From forth day's path and Titan's burning wheels.[2]
5 Now, ere the sun advance his burning eye
The day to cheer and night's dank dew to dry,
I must upfill this osier cage[3] of ours
With baleful[4] weeds and precious-juicèd flowers.
The earth that's nature's mother is her tomb.
10 What is her burying grave, that is her womb;
And from her womb children of divers kind[5]
We sucking on her natural bosom find,
Many for many virtues excellent,
None but for some, and yet all different.
15 O, mickle[6] is the powerful grace[7] that lies
In plants, herbs, stones, and their true qualities;
For naught so vile that on the earth doth live
But to the earth some special good doth give;
Nor aught so good but, strained[8] from that fair use,
20 Revolts from true birth,[9] stumbling on abuse.
Virtue itself turns vice, being misapplied,

1. **flecked:** Spotted.
2. **Titan's burning wheels:** The wheels of the sun god's chariot.

3. **osier cage:** Willow basket.
4. **baleful:** Poisonous.

5. **divers kind:** Different kinds.

6. **mickle:** Great.
7. **grace:** Divine power.

8. **strained:** Turned away.
9. **Revolts . . . birth:** Conflicts with its real purpose.

354  *Drama*

And vice sometime by action dignified.

[*Enter* ROMEO.]

21

Within the infant rind[10] of this weak flower
Poison hath residence and medicine power;[11]
25  For this, being smelt, with that part cheers each
         part;[12]
Being tasted, stays all senses with the heart.[13]
Two such opposèd kings encamp them still[14]
In man as well as herbs—grace and rude will;
And where the worser is predominant,
30  Full soon the canker[15] death eats up that plant.

**ROMEO.** Good morrow, father.

22

**FRIAR.**                    *Benedicite!*[16]
What early tongue so sweet saluteth me?
Young son, it argues a distemperèd head[17]
So soon to bid good morrow to thy bed.
35  Care keeps his watch in every old man's eye,
And where care lodges, sleep will never lie;
But where unbruisèd youth with unstuffed[18] brain
Doth couch his limbs, there golden sleep doth reign.
Therefore thy earliness doth me assure
40  Thou art uproused with some distemp'rature;[19]
Or if not so, then here I hit it right—
Our Romeo hath not been in bed tonight.

**ROMEO.** That last is true. The sweeter rest was mine.

**FRIAR.** God pardon sin! Wast thou with Rosaline?

45  **ROMEO.** With Rosaline, my ghostly father? No.
I have forgot that name and that name's woe.

**FRIAR.** That's my good son! But where hast thou been
then?

**ROMEO.** I'll tell thee ere thou ask it me again.
I have been feasting with mine enemy,
50  Where on a sudden one hath wounded me
That's by me wounded. Both our remedies
Within thy help and holy physic[20] lies.
I bear no hatred, blessèd man, for, lo,
My intercession likewise steads my foe.[21]

55  **FRIAR.** Be plain, good son, and homely in thy drift.[22]
Riddling confession finds but riddling shrift.[23]

**ROMEO.** Then plainly know my heart's dear love is set

*The Tragedy of Romeo and Juliet, Act II, Scene iii*    355

**10. infant rind:** Tender skin.
**11. and medicine power:** And medicinal quality has power.
**12. with . . . part:** With that quality—odor—revives each part of the body.
**13. stays . . . heart:** Kills (stops the working of the five senses along with the heart).
**14. still:** Always.
**15. canker:** A destructive caterpillar.
**16. *Benedicite!*:** God bless you!
**17. distempered head:** Troubled mind.

**18. unstuffed:** Not filled with cares.

**19. distemp'rature:** Illness.

**20. physic** (fĭz' ĭk): Medicine.
**21. My . . . foe:** My plea also helps my enemy (Juliet, a Capulet).
**22. and . . . drift:** And simple in your speech.
**23. Riddling . . . shrift:** A confusing confession will get you uncertain forgiveness. The Friar means that unless Romeo speaks clearly he will not get clear and direct advice.

21 **Discussion** How does Friar Lawrence's knowledge of herbs influence his ideas about people?

22 **Literary Focus** Contrast Friar Lawrence and Romeo.

23 **Reading Strategy** Have students summarize Friar Lawrence's concern about Romeo's change of heart. Why does he mistrust it?

24 **Discussion** Do you think Romeo's argument makes sense? Explain.

25 **Discussion** Why does Friar Lawrence finally agree to marry the couple? Do you think his reason is justified? Explain.

26 **Literary Focus** How do these last two lines of the scene sum up the difference between these two characters?

On the fair daughter of rich Capulet;
As mine on hers, so hers is set on mine,
60  And all combined, save[24] what thou must combine
By holy marriage. When and where and how
We met, we wooed, and made exchange of vow,
I'll tell thee as we pass; but this I pray,
That thou consent to marry us today.

65  **FRIAR.** Holy Saint Francis! What a change is here!
Is Rosaline, that thou didst love so dear,
So soon forsaken? Young men's love then lies
Not truly in their hearts, but in their eyes.
Jesu Maria! What a deal of brine[25]
70  Hath washed thy sallow cheeks for Rosaline!
How much salt water thrown away in waste
To season love, that of it doth not taste!
The sun not yet thy sighs from heaven clears,
Thy old groans ring yet in mine ancient ears.
75  Lo, here upon thy cheek the stain doth sit
Of an old tear that is not washed off yet.
If e'er thou wast thyself, and these woes thine,
Thou and these woes were all for Rosaline.
And art thou changed? Pronounce this sentence then:
80  Women may fall[26] when there's no strength[27] in men.

**ROMEO.** Thou chidst me oft for loving Rosaline.

**FRIAR.** For doting,[28] not for loving, pupil mine.

**ROMEO.** And badst[29] me bury love.

**FRIAR.**                           Not in a grave
To lay one in, another out to have.

85  **ROMEO.** I pray thee chide me not. Her I love now
Doth grace[30] for grace and love for love allow.[31]
The other did not so.

**FRIAR.**                           O, she knew well
Thy love did read by rote, that could not spell.[32]
But come, young waverer, come go with me.
90  In one respect I'll thy assistant be;
For this alliance may so happy prove
To turn your households' rancor[33] to pure love.

**ROMEO.** O, let us hence! I stand on[34] sudden haste.

**FRIAR.** Wisely and slow. They stumble that run fast.    [*Exit.*]

**24. And . . . save:** And we are united in every way, except for (save).

**25. brine:** Salt water (tears).

**26. fall:** Be weak or inconstant.
**27. strength:** Constancy, stability.
**28. doting:** Being infatuated.
**29. badst:** Urged.

**30. grace:** Favor.
**31. allow:** Give.

**32. Thy . . . spell:** Your love was someone who recites words from memory with no understanding of them.

**33. rancor:** Hatred.

**34. stand on:** Insist on.

## Literary Element: Character Traits

Tell students that **character traits** are all of those qualities that make a person unique. Authors give their characters a number of different traits that work together to form their personalities. Often characters will share the same traits. In *Romeo and Juliet,* for example, Mercutio and the Nurse share similar character traits.

Compare and contrast with students the character traits of Mercutio and the Nurse. Ask them in what ways Mercutio and the Nurse are alike. Students might mention, for example, that the nurse is Juliet's best friend and Mercutio is Romeo's. In addition, both characters are comical. On the other hand, Mercutio is young and the Nurse is old. In addition, Mercutio is also eloquent in speech, whereas the Nurse is long-winded and repetitive.

To aid your discussion, have students make a Venn diagram. In Mercutio's circle, students should list his character traits that are different from the Nurse's. Similarly, in the Nurse's circle, students should list her traits that are different from Mercutio's. In the intersecting section of both circles, students should list the traits that the two characters share. Use the following example as a guide.

**Scene iv.** *A street.*

[*Enter* BENVOLIO *and* MERCUTIO.]

**MERCUTIO.** Where the devil should this Romeo be?
    Came he not home tonight?

**BENVOLIO.** Not to his father's. I spoke with his man.

**MERCUTIO.** Why, that same pale hardhearted wench, that
    Rosaline,
5    Torments him so that he will sure run mad.

**BENVOLIO.** Tybalt, the kinsman to old Capulet,
    Hath sent a letter to his father's house.

**MERCUTIO.** A challenge, on my life.

**BENVOLIO.** Romeo will answer it.

10  **MERCUTIO.** Any man that can write may answer a letter.

**BENVOLIO.** Nay, he will answer the letter's master, how he
    dares, being dared.

**MERCUTIO.** Alas, poor Romeo, he is already dead: stabbed
15    with a white wench's black eye; run through the ear
    with a love song; the very pin of his heart cleft with the
    blind bow-boy's butt-shaft;[1] and is he a man to en-
    counter Tybalt?

**BENVOLIO.** Why, what is Tybalt?

**MERCUTIO.** More than Prince of Cats.[2] O, he's the coura-
20    geous captain of compliments.[3] He fights as you sing
    pricksong[4]—keeps time, distance, and proportion; he
    rests his minim rests,[5] one, two, and the third in your
    bosom! The very butcher of a silk button,[6] a duelist, a
    duelist! A gentleman of the very first house,[7] of the first
25    and second cause.[8] Ah, the immortal *passado!* The
    *punto reverso!* The hay![9]

**BENVOLIO.** The what?

**MERCUTIO.** The pox of such antic, lisping, affecting fantas-
30    ticoes—these new tuners of accent![10] By Jesu, a very
    good blade! A very tall man! A very good whore! Why,
    is not this a lamentable thing, grandsir, that we
    should be thus afflicted with these strange flies, these
    fashionmongers, these pardon-me's,[11] who stand so
    much on the new form that they cannot sit at ease on

**1. pin . . . butt-shaft:** Center of his heart pierced by Cupid's blunt arrow.
**2. Prince of Cats:** Tybalt, or a variation of it, is the name of the cat in medieval stories of Reynard the Fox.
**3. captain of compliments:** Master of formal behavior.
**4. as you sing pricksong:** That is to say, with attention to precision and correctness.
**5. rests . . . rests:** Observes all formalities.
**6. button:** An exact spot on his opponent's shirt.
**7. first house:** Finest school of fencing.
**8. the first and second cause:** The reasons that would cause a gentleman to challenge another to a duel.
**9. passado! . . . punto reverso! . . . hay!:** Lunge . . . backhanded stroke . . . home thrust.
**10. The pox . . . accent:** May the plague strike these absurd characters with their phony manners— these men who speak in weird, newfangled ways!
**11. these pardon-me's:** These men who are always saying "Pardon me" (adopting ridiculous manners).

*The Tragedy of Romeo and Juliet, Act II, Scene iv*  357

**27 Enrichment** Point out to students that in comic scenes Shakespeare uses prose rather than blank verse.

**28 Discussion** Why does Mercutio think Romeo is not the person to meet Tybalt?

**29 Discussion** What kind of man is Tybalt?

**Enrichment** Tell students that the name *Benvolio* comes from the Latin words *bene*, meaning "good," and *volo*, meaning "I am willing." Ask students if they think this name matches Benvolio's personality.

    Also tell students that Tybalt, whom Mercutio calls "Prince of Cats" and "King of Cats," is named after a kind of cat. Have students research and name this type of cat and explain how Tybalt is similar to it.

27
28

29

**Student Activity.** Using the same procedure, select two other characters from the play to compare and contrast. You might want to compare and contrast Montague and Capulet, for example.

30 **Clarification** *Roe* is "the egg-laden ovary of a fish." A fish without roe is old and worn out.

31 **Reading Strategy** Have students compare Romeo's mood in this scene with his mood in the first act.

32 **Master Teacher Note** Shakespeare knew that contrast kept an audience's interest, so this humorous scene was included as a change of pace from the previous ones. It is full of allusions and word plays. Tell students that this word play would have been more understandable to Elizabethans than it is to modern readers.

the old bench? O, their bones, their bones!

[*Enter* ROMEO.]

**BENVOLIO.** Here comes Romeo! Here comes Romeo!

30 **MERCUTIO.** Without his roe, like a dried herring.[12] O flesh, flesh, how art thou fishified! Now is he for the numbers[13] that Petrarch flowed in. Laura,[14] to his lady, was a kitchen wench (marry, she had a better love to berhyme her), Dido a dowdy, Cleopatra a gypsy, Helen and Hero hildings and harlots, Thisbe a gray eye or so, but not to the purpose. Signior Romeo, *bon jour!* There's a French salutation to your French slop. You gave us the counterfeit fairly last night.

**ROMEO.** Good morrow to you both. What counterfeit did I give you?

**MERCUTIO.** The slip,[15] sir, the slip. Can you not conceive?

**ROMEO.** Pardon, good Mercutio. My business was great, and in such a case as mine a man may strain courtesy.

**MERCUTIO.** That's as much as to say, such a case as yours constrains a man to bow in the hams.[16]

**ROMEO.** Meaning, to curtsy.

**MERCUTIO.** Thou hast most kindly hit it.

55 **ROMEO.** A most courteous exposition.

**MERCUTIO.** Nay, I am the very pink of courtesy.

**ROMEO.** Pink for flower.

**MERCUTIO.** Right.

**ROMEO.** Why, then is my pump[17] well-flowered.

60 **MERCUTIO.** Sure wit, follow me this jest now till thou hast worn out thy pump, that, when the single sole of it is worn, the jest may remain, after the wearing, solely singular.[18]

**ROMEO.** O single-soled jest, solely singular for the single-
65 ness![19]

**MERCUTIO.** Come between us, good Benvolio! My wits faints.

**ROMEO.** Swits and spurs, swits and spurs; or I'll cry a match.[20]

**12. Without . . . herring:** Worn out.
**13. numbers:** Verses of love poems.
**14. Laura:** Laura and the other ladies mentioned are all notable figures of European love literature. Mercutio is saying that Romeo thinks that none of them compare with Rosaline.

**15. slip:** Escape. *Slip* is also a term for counterfeit coin.

**16. hams:** Hips.

**17. pump:** Shoe.

**18. when . . . singular:** The jest will outwear the shoe and will then be all alone.
**19. O . . . singleness!:** O thin joke, unique for only one thing—weakness!
**20. Swits . . . match:** Drive your wit harder to beat me or else I'll claim victory in this match of wordplay.

358 *Drama*

70 **MERCUTIO.** Nay, if our wits run the wild-goose chase, I
am done; for thou hast more of the wild goose in one of
thy wits than, I am sure, I have in my whole five. Was I
with you there for the goose?

**ROMEO.** Thou wast never with me for anything when thou
75 wast not there for the goose.

**MERCUTIO.** I will bite thee by the ear for that jest.

**ROMEO.** Nay, good goose, bite not!

**MERCUTIO.** Thy wit is a very bitter sweeting;[21] it is a most
sharp sauce.

**21. sweeting:** A kind of apple.

80 **ROMEO.** And is it not, then, well served in to a sweet
goose?

**MERCUTIO.** O, here's a wit of cheveril,[22] that stretches from
an inch narrow to an ell broad!

**22. cheveril:** Easily stretched kid leather.

**ROMEO.** I stretch it out for that word "broad," which added
85 to the goose, proves thee far and wide a broad goose.

**MERCUTIO.** Why, is not this better now than groaning for
love? Now art thou sociable, now art thou Romeo; now
art thou what thou art, by art as well as by nature. For
this driveling love is like a great natural[23] that runs
90 lolling[24] up and down to hide his bauble[25] in a hole.

**23. natural:** Idiot.
**24. lolling:** With tongue hanging out.
**25. bauble:** Toy.

**BENVOLIO.** Stop there, stop there!

**MERCUTIO.** Thou desirest me to stop in my tale against the
hair.[26]

**26. the hair:** Natural inclination.

**Clarification** Nurse uses many "malapropisms"—words that sound somewhat like the ones intended but that are ludicrously wrong. Shakespeare uses this device to indicate she is a servant who is trying to act like a lady.

**BENVOLIO.** Thou wouldst else have made thy tale large.

95   **MERCUTIO.** O, thou art deceived! I would have made it short; for I was come to the whole depth of my tale, and meant indeed to occupy the argument[27] no longer.

**ROMEO.** Here's goodly gear![28]

[*Enter* NURSE *and her Man*, PETER.]

    A sail, a sail!

100   **MERCUTIO.** Two, two! A shirt and a smock.[29]

**NURSE.** Peter!

**PETER.** Anon.

**NURSE.** My fan, Peter.

**MERCUTIO.** Good Peter, to hide her face; for her fan's the
105     fairer face.

**NURSE.** God ye good morrow, gentlemen.

**MERCUTIO.** God ye good-den, fair gentlewoman.

**NURSE.** Is it good-den?

**MERCUTIO.** 'Tis no less, I tell ye; for the bawdy hand of the
110     dial is now upon the prick of noon.

**NURSE.** Out upon you! What a man are you!

**ROMEO.** One, gentlewoman, that God hath made, himself to mar.

**NURSE.** By my troth, it is well said. "For himself to mar,"
115     quoth 'a? Gentlemen, can any of you tell me where I may find the young Romeo?

**ROMEO.** I can tell you; but young Romeo will be older when you have found him than he was when you sought him. I am the youngest of that name, for fault[30] of a
120     worse.

**NURSE.** You say well.

**MERCUTIO.** Yea, is the worst well? Very well took,[31] i' faith! Wisely, wisely.

34   **NURSE.** If you be he, sir, I desire some confidence[32] with
125     you.

**BENVOLIO.** She will endite him to some supper.

**MERCUTIO.** A bawd, a bawd, a bawd! So ho!

*360   Drama*

**27. occupy the argument:** Talk about the matter.
**28. goodly gear:** Good stuff for joking (Romeo sees the Nurse approaching).

**29. A shirt and a smock:** A man and a woman.

**30. fault:** Lack.

**31. took:** Understood.

**32. confidence:** The Nurse means *conference*.

## Primary Source

Shakespeare based this play on *The Tragical History of Romeus and Juliet,* a narrative poem written in 1562 by Arthur Brooke. Following is a portion of Brooke's poem in which Romeus tells the nurse of his plan to marry Juliet.

After you read these lines aloud, discuss with students how Romeo and the nurse in Shakespeare's play are similar to and different from the same characters in Brooke's poem.

"On Saturday," quoth he,
  "if Juliet come to shrift,
She shall be shrived and marrièd;
  how like you, Nurse, this drift?"
"Now, by my troth," quoth she,
  "God's blessing have your heart,
For yet in all my life I have
  not heard of such a part.
Lord, how you young men can
  such crafty wiles devise,
If that you love the daughter well,
  to blear the mother's eyes.

An easy thing it is,
  with cloak of holiness,
To mock the silly mother that
  suspecteth nothing less.
But that it pleasèd you
  to tell me of the case,
For all my many years perhaps
  I should have found it scarce.
Now for the rest let me
  and Juliet alone;
To get her leave, some feat[1] excuse
  I will devise anon:

[1]neat.

**ROMEO.** What hast thou found?

**MERCUTIO.** No hare, sir; unless a hare, sir, in a lenten pie,
130    that is something stale and hoar ere it be spent.

[*He walks by them and sings.*]

> An old hare hoar,
> And an old hare hoar,
> Is very good meat in Lent;
> But a hare that is hoar
> 135    Is too much for a score
> When it hoars ere it be spent.

Romeo, will you come to your father's? We'll to dinner
thither.

**ROMEO.** I will follow you.

140 **MERCUTIO.** Farewell, ancient lady. Farewell, [*singing*]
    "Lady, lady, lady."[33]      [*Exit* MERCUTIO, BENVOLIO.]

**NURSE.** I pray you, sir, what saucy merchant was this that
    was so full of his ropery?[34]

**ROMEO.** A gentleman, nurse, that loves to hear himself talk
145    and will speak more in a minute than he will stand to
    in a month.

**NURSE.** And 'a[35] speak anything against me, I'll take him
    down, and 'a were lustier than he is, and twenty such
    Jacks; and if I cannot, I'll find those that shall. Scurvy
150    knave! I am none of his flirt-gills;[36] I am none of his
    skainsmates.[37] And thou must stand by too, and suffer
    every knave to use me at his pleasure!

**PETER.** I saw no man use you at his pleasure. If I had, my
    weapon should quickly have been out, I warrant you. I
155    dare draw as soon as another man, if I see occasion in
    a good quarrel, and the law on my side.

**NURSE.** Now, afore God, I am so vexed that every part about
    me quivers. Scurvy knave! Pray you, sir, a word; and,
    as I told you, my young lady bid me inquire you out.
160    What she bid me say, I will keep to myself; but first let
    me tell ye, if ye should lead her in a fool's paradise, as
    they say, it were a very gross kind of behavior, as they
    say; for the gentlewoman is young; and therefore, if
    you should deal double with her, truly it were an ill
165    thing to be off'red to any gentlewoman, and very
    weak[38] dealing.

**33. "Lady . . . lady":** A line from an old ballad, "Chaste Susanna."

**34. ropery:** The nurse means *roguery*, the talk and conduct of a rascal.

**35. 'a:** He.

**36. flirt-gills:** Common girls.
**37. skainsmates:** Criminals, cutthroats.

**38. weak:** Unmanly.

35 **Discussion** How does the Nurse reveal unladylike qualities in this passage?

*The Tragedy of Romeo and Juliet, Act II, Scene iv*   361

For that her golden locks
  by sloth have been unkempt,
Or for unwares some wanton dream
  the youthful damsel dreamt,
Or for in thoughts of love
  her idle time she spent,
Or otherwise within her heart
  deservèd to be shent.
I know her mother will
  in no case say her nay,
I warrant you she shall not fail
  to come on Saturday."

And then she swears to him,
  the mother loves her well;
And how she gave her suck in youth
  she leaveth not to tell.
"A pretty babe," quoth she,
  "it was when it was young;
Lord, how it could full prettily
  have prated with its tongue!
A thousand times and more
  I laid her on my lap,
And clapped her on the buttock soft,
  and kissed where I did clap.
And gladder then was I

of such a kiss forsooth,
Than I had been to have a kiss
  of some old lecher's mouth."
And thus of Juliet's youth
  began this prating nurse,
And of her present state to make
  a tedious long discourse.
For though he pleasure took
  in hearing of his love,
The message answer seemed him
  to be of more behoove.
But when these beldams sit
  at ease upon their tale,

The day and eke the candlelight
  before their talk shall fail,
And part they say is true,
  and part they do devise,
Yet boldly do they that of both
  when no man checks their lies.
Then he six crowns of gold
  out of his pocket drew,
And gave them her, "A slight rewa
  quoth he, "and so, adieu."

36 **Discussion** What message does Romeo give the Nurse for Juliet?

37 **Discussion** Do you think the Nurse is good at keeping secrets? Explain.

38 **Clarification** *Rosemary* is "an herb that was considered the emblem of fidelity and remembrance."

**ROMEO.** Nurse, commend[39] me to thy lady and mistress. I protest unto thee—

**NURSE.** Good heart, and i' faith I will tell her as much. Lord, Lord, she will be a joyful woman.

**ROMEO.** What wilt thou tell her, nurse? Thou dost not mark me.

**NURSE.** I will tell her, sir, that you do protest, which, as I take it, is a gentlemanlike offer.

**ROMEO.** Bid her devise
Some means to come to shrift[40] this afternoon;
And there she shall at Friar Lawrence' cell
Be shrived and married. Here is for thy pains.

**NURSE.** No, truly, sir; not a penny.

**ROMEO.** Go to! I say you shall.

**NURSE.** This afternoon, sir? Well, she shall be there.

**ROMEO.** And stay, good nurse, behind the abbey wall.
Within this hour my man shall be with thee
And bring thee cords made like a tackled stair.[41]
Which to the high topgallant[42] of my joy
Must be my convoy[43] in the secret night.
Farewell. Be trusty, and I'll quit[44] thy pains.
Farewell. Commend me to thy mistress.

**NURSE.** Now God in heaven bless thee! Hark you, sir.

**ROMEO.** What say'st thou, my dear nurse?

**NURSE.** Is your man secret? Did you ne'er hear say,
Two may keep counsel, putting one away?[45]

**ROMEO.** Warrant thee my man's as true as steel.

**NURSE.** Well, sir, my mistress is the sweetest lady. Lord, Lord! When 'twas a little prating[46] thing—O, there is a nobleman in town, one Paris, that would fain lay knife aboard;[47] but she, good soul, had as lieve[48] see a toad, a very toad, as see him. I anger her sometimes, and tell her that Paris is the properer man; but I'll warrant you, when I say so, she looks as pale as any clout[49] in the versal world.[50] Doth not rosemary and Romeo begin both with a letter?

**ROMEO.** Ay, nurse; what of that? Both with an *R*.

**NURSE.** Ah, mocker! That's the dog's name.[51] *R* is for the—

**39. commend:** Convey my respect and best wishes.

**40. shrift:** Confession.

**41. tackled stair:** Rope ladder.
**42. topgallant:** Summit.
**43. convoy:** Conveyance.
**44. quit:** Reward, pay you back for.

**45. Two . . . away:** Two can keep a secret if one is ignorant, or out of the way.

**46. prating:** Babbling.
**47. fain . . . aboard:** Eagerly seize Juliet for himself.
**48. had as lieve:** Would as willingly.
**49. clout:** Cloth.
**50. versal world:** Universe.

**51. dog's name:** *R* sounds like a growl.

362  *Drama*

## Primary Source

Tell students that various actresses who have played Juliet have brought their own interpretation of the character to the role. One such actress was Sarah Siddons (1755–1831), who critics claim was the greatest Shakespearean actress of her time.

Siddons began her acting career at the age of eight, playing the spirit Ariel in an adaptation of Shakespeare's *The Tempest*. During her acting career, Siddons played almost every female character in Shakespeare's plays.

Although her greatest achievement was her role as Lady Macbeth, Siddons's portrayal of Juliet was also beautiful and convincing. The *Bath Journal* published the following letter in reference to Siddons's March 4, 1779, performance as Juliet:

I think I never beheld a Juliet till Mrs Siddons showed me one at that time, and yet for these 30 years past I scarce ever miss'd this favourite play, both in London and elsewhere.

The following diary entry written by Mrs. Thrale, a long-standing follower and admirer of Siddons, gives a slightly different critique of Siddons's portrayal as Juliet:

205 No; I know it begins with some other letter; and she
hath the prettiest sententious[52] of it, of you and rosemary, that it would do you good to hear it.

**ROMEO.** Commend me to thy lady.

**NURSE.** Ay, a thousand times. [*Exit* ROMEO.] Peter!

210 **PETER.** Anon.

**NURSE.** Before, and apace.[53]          [*Exit, after* PETER.]

*Scene v.* CAPULET's *orchard.*

[*Enter* JULIET.]

**JULIET.** The clock struck nine when I did send the nurse;
In half an hour she promised to return.
Perchance she cannot meet him. That's not so.
O, she is lame! Love's heralds should be thoughts,
5 Which ten times faster glides than the sun's beams
Driving back shadows over low'ring[1] hills.
Therefore do nimble-pinioned doves draw Love,[2]
And therefore hath the wind-swift Cupid wings.
Now is the sun upon the highmost hill
10 Of this day's journey, and from nine till twelve
Is three long hours; yet she is not come.
Had she affections and warm youthful blood,
She would be as swift in motion as a ball;
My words would bandy her[3] to my sweet love,
15 And his to me.
But old folks, many feign[4] as they were dead—
Unwieldy, slow, heavy and pale as lead.

[*Enter* NURSE *and* PETER.]

O God, she comes! O honey nurse, what news?
Hast thou met with him? Send thy man away.

20 **NURSE.** Peter, stay at the gate.          [*Exit* PETER.]

**JULIET.** Now, good sweet nurse—O Lord, why lookest thou
sad?
Though news be sad, yet tell them merrily;
If good, thou shamest the music of sweet news
By playing it to me with so sour a face.

25 **NURSE.** I am aweary, give me leave[5] awhile.
Fie, how my bones ache! What a jaunce[6] have I!

**JULIET.** I would thou hadst my bones, and I thy news.
Nay, come, I pray thee speak. Good, good nurse, speak.

---

**52. sententious:** The
Nurse means *sentences*—
clever, wise sayings.

**53. Before, and apace:**
Go ahead of me, and
quickly.

**1. low'ring:** Darkening.

**2. Therefore . . . Love:**
Therefore, doves with quick
wings pull the chariot of
Venus, goddess of love.

**3. bandy her:** Send her
rapidly.

**4. feign:** Act.

**5. give me leave:** Excuse
me; give me a moment's
rest.

**6. jaunce:** Rough trip.

*The Tragedy of Romeo and Juliet,* Act II, Scene v    363

---

---

Mrs Siddons acted Juliet last night.—She does it so
*naturally* says someone, so artificially rather said I; but she
is a great Performer. . . . The pouting Scene with the old
Nurse was the cleverest thing I ever saw—so pretty, so
Babyish, *so* charming. . . .

**Student Activity.** Reread Act II, Scene v, of *Romeo and Juliet.* In
groups, discuss how Sarah Siddons might have played this
scene. What gestures, expressions, and movements might she
have used to appear "so babyish and so charming." Write the
stage comments for this scene that Siddons might have noted in
her script. Share and discuss your stage directions with your
classmates. Then as a class, discuss how Siddons's perfor-

mance might be different from other actresses' interpretations of
Juliet, such as Olivia Hussey's Juliet in Franco Zeffirelli's film
version of the play.

41 **Literary Focus** How is the Nurse a dramatic foil in this scene, pointing up Juliet's concerns and state of mind?

**NURSE.** Jesu, what haste? Can you not stay awhile?
30     Do you not see that I am out of breath?

**JULIET.** How art thou out of breath when thou hast breath
    To say to me that thou art out of breath?
    The excuse that thou dost make in this delay
    Is longer than the tale thou dost excuse.
35     Is thy news good or bad? Answer to that.
    Say either, and I'll stay the circumstance.[7]
    Let me be satisfied, is't good or bad?

**7. stay the circumstance:** Wait for the details.

**NURSE.** Well, you have made a simple[8] choice; you know
    not how to choose a man. Romeo? No, not he. Though
40     his face be better than any man's, yet his leg excels all
    men's; and for a hand and a foot, and a body, though
    they be not to be talked on, yet they are past compare.
    He is not the flower of courtesy, but, I'll warrant him,
    as gentle as a lamb. Go thy ways, wench; serve God.
45     What, have you dined at home?

**8. simple:** Foolish; simpleminded.

**JULIET.** No, no. But all this did I know before.
    What says he of our marriage? What of that?

**NURSE.** Lord, how my head aches! What a head have I!
    It beats as it would fall in twenty pieces.
50     My back a[9] t' other side—ah, my back, my back!
    Beshrew[10] your heart for sending me about
    To catch my death with jauncing up and down!

**9. a:** On.

**10. Beshrew:** Shame on.

**JULIET.** I' faith, I am sorry that thou art not well.
    Sweet, sweet, sweet nurse, tell me, what says my love?

55 **NURSE.** Your love says, like an honest gentleman, and a
    courteous, and a kind, and a handsome, and, I warrant, a virtuous—Where is your mother?

**JULIET.** Where is my mother? Why, she is within.
    Where should she be? How oddly thou repliest!
60     "Your love says, like an honest gentleman,
    'Where is your mother?' "

**NURSE.**                O God's Lady dear!
    Are you so hot?[11] Marry come up, I trow.[12]
    Is this the poultice[13] for my aching bones?
    Henceforward do your messages yourself.

**11. hot:** Impatient; hot-tempered.
**12. Marry . . . trow:** Indeed, cool down, I say.
**13. poultice:** Remedy.
**14. coil:** Disturbance.

65 **JULIET.** Here's such a coil![14] Come, what says Romeo?

**NURSE.** Have you got leave to go to shrift today?

## Commentary: Elizabethan Weddings

Tell students that unlike Romeo and Juliet's secret marriage, most Elizabethan weddings were all-day extravaganzas in which almost the whole village or town participated.

Traditionally, the formal betrothal or engagement of the couple was done privately. Afterward, the law required that the banns of marriage be made public. At this time, the priest would announce in church on three consecutive Sundays the couple's engagement and call for any person who knew any cause why the marriage should not be performed to come forward and declare it.

A wedding celebration was usually an all-day event. It began early in the morning when the bridesmaids awakened and dressed the bride. Shortly thereafter, the groom, his groomsmen, friends, relatives, and musicians would arrive at the bride's house to claim her. The entire wedding party then paraded through the town to the church. The bride in her white gown and loose-flowing hair was the center of attraction.

After the ceremony, the wedding party went to the groom's

**JULIET.** I have.

**NURSE.** Then hie you hence to Friar Lawrence' cell;
There stays a husband to make you a wife.
70     Now comes the wanton[15] blood up in your cheeks:
They'll be in scarlet straight at any news.
Hie you to church; I must another way,
To fetch a ladder, by the which your love
Must climb a bird's nest soon when it is dark.
75     I am the drudge, and toil in your delight;
But you shall bear the burden soon at night.
Go; I'll to dinner; hie you to the cell.

**JULIET.** Hie to high fortune! Honest nurse, farewell.   [*Exit.*]

*Scene vi.* Friar Lawrence's cell.

[*Enter* FRIAR LAWRENCE *and* ROMEO.]

**FRIAR.** So smile the heavens upon this holy act
That afterhours with sorrow chide us not![1]

**ROMEO.** Amen, amen! But come what sorrow can,
It cannot countervail[2] the exchange of joy
5     That one short minute gives me in her sight.
Do thou but close our hands with holy words,
Then love-devouring death do what he dare—
It is enough I may but call her mine.

**FRIAR.** These violent delights have violent ends
10     And in their triumph die, like fire and powder,[3]
Which, as they kiss, consume. The sweetest honey
Is loathsome in his own deliciousness
And in the taste confounds[4] the appetite.
Therefore love moderately: long love doth so;
15     Too swift arrives as tardy as too slow.

[*Enter* JULIET.]

Here comes the lady. O, so light a foot
Will ne'er wear out the everlasting flint.[5]
A lover may bestride the gossamers[6]
That idles in the wanton summer air,
20     And yet not fall; so light is vanity.[7]

**JULIET.** Good even to my ghostly confessor.

**FRIAR.** Romeo shall thank thee, daughter, for us both.

**JULIET.** As much to him,[8] else is his thanks too much.

**15. wanton:** Excited.

**1. That . . . not!:** That the future does not punish us with sorrow.
**2. countervail:** Equal.

**3. powder:** Gunpowder.

**4. confounds:** Destroys.

**5. flint:** Stone.
**6. gossamers:** Spider webs.

**7. vanity:** Foolish things that cannot last.

**8. As . . . him:** The same greeting to him.

*The Tragedy of Romeo and Juliet, Act II, Scene vi*   365

**42 Literary Focus** How does Friar Lawrence serve as a dramatic foil for Romeo, pointing up his traits and state of mind?

house for a great feast and celebration. The party lasted the rest of the day with plenty of food, dances, and games.

Sometime during the evening, the bride and groom left the party with their attendants, who would prepare the couple for the night. Later the attendants rejoined the other guests and continued to celebrate until late into the night or early morning.

In the morning on the following day, musicians awakened the couple with a song at their bedroom window. Thereafter, the village considered the couple to be among the married folk. Newlyweds did not have a honeymoon.

**Student Activity.** Shakespeare chose to have Romeo and Juliet's wedding performed in secret and offstage. Imagine you are the director of a new adaptation of this play and want to perform the marriage on stage. In groups, write the script for this scene, developing the dialogue and writing the stage directions for the wedding ceremony as it might have been staged in the sixteenth century. What will Romeo and Juliet's vows be? Who will attend? What events will occur as a result of the marriage? Perform your skits for your classmates.

**Reading Strategy** Paraphrase the speeches of Romeo and Juliet.

**Reader's Response** If you were Romeo, would you renounce your family name for the love of a woman? Explain.

43

**ROMEO.** Ah, Juliet, if the measure of thy joy
25    Be heaped like mine, and that thy skill be more
    To blazon it,[9] then sweeten with thy breath
    This neighbor air, and let rich music's tongue
    Unfold the imagined happiness that both
    Receive in either by this dear encounter.

30 **JULIET.** Conceit, more rich in matter than in words,
    Brags of his substance, not of ornament.[10]
    They are but beggars that can count their worth;
    But my true love is grown to such excess
    I cannot sum up sum of half my wealth.

35 **FRIAR.** Come, come with me, and we will make short work;
    For, by your leaves, you shall not stay alone
    Till Holy Church incorporate two in one.        [*Exit.*]

**9. and . . . it:** And if you are better able to proclaim it.

**10. Conceit . . . ornament:** Understanding does not need to be dressed up in words.

**Closure and Extension**

### *ANSWERS TO THINKING ABOUT THE SELECTION*
*Recalling*

1. She wonders why Romeo has to be a Montague.
2. She fears for his life at the hands of her relatives. She fears that his love is shallow and that he may have a change of heart and turn out to be a liar. She doubts whether he can be sincere in so short a time.
3. She feels that events are moving too fast and that because their love has come so quickly, it is likely to disappear just as fast.
4. He says that Romeo has been too impulsive in falling out of love with one woman and in love with another. Romeo says that Rosaline did not return his love while Juliet does.

## THINKING ABOUT THE SELECTION

### Recalling

1. Why does Juliet cry out in Scene ii "O Romeo, Romeo! Wherefore [Why] art thou Romeo?"
2. What doubts and fears does Juliet express even as she realizes that Romeo loves her?
3. What is her reason for saying, "I have no joy of this contract tonight" (line 118)?
4. What weakness in Romeo's character does Friar Lawrence point out before agreeing to assist the lovers in their plan to wed? How does Romeo defend himself?
5. Why does Friar Lawrence finally agree to marry Romeo and Juliet? Why does the Nurse help them carry out their plan?
6. In Scene iv, what change in Romeo's behavior causes Mercutio to say, "Now art thou sociable, now art thou Romeo . . . "?

### Interpreting

7. Explain the role that darkness plays in helping Romeo and Juliet learn of their love for each other.
8. Describe Juliet's feelings in Scene v as she waits for the Nurse and then as she waits for the Nurse to reveal Romeo's message.
9. Juliet is thirteen years old and Romeo not much older. In what way is their love typical of adolescence, and in what way is it not?

### Applying

10. Why do you think the love scene in Capulet's garden is the most famous one in all of literature?

## ANALYZING LITERATURE

### Understanding the Dramatic Foil

A **dramatic foil** contrasts with another character and helps to highlight this character's traits. Explain how the first character in each of the following pairs is a foil for the other.

1. Mercutio and Romeo
2. the Nurse and Juliet

## UNDERSTANDING LANGUAGE

### Interpreting Personification

**Personification** is a figure of speech in which a quality, idea, or any nonhuman being is represented as having human traits. The following quotations from Act II contain personifications. For each, explain what quality, idea, or nonhuman being is represented and what human trait is applied to it.

1. Arise, fair sun, and kill the envious moon, Who is already sick and pale with grief . . . (Act II, Scene ii, lines 5–6)
2. Sleep dwell upon thine eyes, peace in thy breast!
   Would I were sleep and peace, so sweet to rest! (Act II, Scene ii, lines 187–188)
3. Care keeps his watch in every old man's eye, And where care lodges, sleep will never lie . . . (Act II, Scene iii, lines 35–36)

## THINKING AND WRITING

### Modernizing Dialogue

Rewriting passages of Shakespeare's dialogue in contemporary language is a good way to test your comprehension. Rewrite the dialogue that Romeo and Juliet speak in lines 53 to 84 of Scene ii. (This is the famous balcony scene.) Juliet's first lines might be rewritten as follows:

**JULIET:** Who are you who, under cover of night, overhears my secret thoughts?

Before you begin, make sure you understand Shakespeare's words. Use the marginal notes, and look up in a dictionary any words you still do not know. When you revise your work, try to make the language sound natural enough for actors to speak on stage. Ask two classmates to read your dialogue aloud. How does it sound to you?

*The Tragedy of Romeo and Juliet, Act II* 367

---

(Answers begin on p. 366.)

**Challenge** Some of your **more advanced** students may wish to read the passages from Chaucer's *Canterbury Tales* that describe the Wife of Bath. Have them compare her with the Nurse in this play.

### ANSWERS TO ANALYZING LITERATURE

1. Suggested Response: Mercutio is a carefree, outgoing, and optimistic person to whom almost everything is a joke. He is a good dramatic foil for Romeo, who is sensitive, moody, pessimistic, and romantic.
2. Suggested Response: The Nurse's crude comments and idle chatter make her a good foil for the romantic young Juliet. The Nurse's ramblings, usually in prose, contrast with Juliet's passages in verse. The Nurse is practical in her approach to love, while Juliet is romantic. (Neither Mercutio nor the Nurse can understand the serious commitment the lovers have made to each other.)

### ANSWERS TO UNDERSTANDING LANGUAGE

1. Suggested Response: The sun and moon are depicted as if they were human. Emotions such as envy and grief are attributed to the moon.
2. Suggested Response: Sleep and peace are the qualities. They are said to dwell in the eyes and breast of Juliet.
3. Suggested Response: Care and sleep are the qualities. Care is said to keep watch in old men's eyes; sleep will not lie down "where care lodges."

### THINKING AND WRITING

For help with this assignment, students can refer to Lesson 19, "Writing a Short Dramatic Sketch," in the Handbook of Writing About Literature.

**Publishing Student Writing** You might ask volunteers to present their modernized dialogue to the class.

---

5. Friar Lawrence feels the marriage may end in the feuding. The Nurse is Juliet's confidante and will do whatever makes Juliet happy.
6. Romeo now seems to be his old self. He is relaxed, happy, and sociable.

### Interpreting

7. Suggested Response: Darkness keeps Juliet's relatives from finding Romeo, who has come to be near her. It also hides him from view as she reveals her love for him, a circumstance which leads them to pledge their love for each other.
8. Suggested Response: She is excited and impatient as she waits for the Nurse to return. She is even more impatient and exasperated as she tries to prod the Nurse into giving her the message.
9. Answers will differ, but students may suggest that adolescents make up their minds and rush into things very quickly. In this way, their actions would be typical of others their age. On the other hand, most adolescents are not yet interested in marriage, so in this respect their actions would not be typical.

### Applying

10. Answers will differ, but students may indicate that the romantic words and images, the vivid descriptions, and the expressions of devotion are extremely effective.

## Focus

**Literary Focus** You might have students compare the soliloquy and aside as methods of revealing a character's thoughts with the techniques a novelist uses for this purpose.

**Look For** Consider having students look for evidence of the violence of Romeo's emotions.

**Writing/Prior Knowledge** You might divide the class into small groups and have them discuss these questions before they begin to write.

**Vocabulary** Have your **less advanced** students review the meanings of these words by seeing how many of them they can use in a paragraph.

### The Tragedy of Romeo and Juliet, Act III

**Soliloquy, Aside, and Monologue**

A **soliloquy** is a speech in a play in which a character, alone on stage, expresses his or her thoughts directly to the audience. An **aside** is a brief remark, unheard by the other characters on stage, from a character to the audience. There are two differences between a soliloquy and an aside. One is that a soliloquy is usually a lengthy speech, whereas an aside is brief. The second is that a soliloquy is usually spoken when no other characters are present, whereas an aside is delivered with other characters present but unable to hear. Both devices, however, have the same purpose: to let the audience know what a character is really thinking or feeling. Shakespeare uses soliloquies and asides to reveal character, disclose motives, and advance the plot.

Similar to a soliloquy is a **monologue**, which is a lengthy speech. Unlike a soliloquy, however, a monologue is addressed to other characters, not to the audience.

**Look For**

Near the end of Act II, the Friar warned Romeo: "These violent delights have violent ends. . . ." As you read Act III, look for ways in which the Friar's words turn out to be truer than he expected.

**Writing**

Think of people you know who can be described either as fortunate or as unfortunate. Are happiness and success the result of something called "Fate" (or "Fortune" or "Destiny")? Or are they the result of a person's character? Freewrite, exploring your answer to these questions.

**Vocabulary**

Knowing the following words will help you as you read Act III of *Romeo and Juliet*:

**gallant** (gal′ ənt) *adj.*: Brave and noble (p. 372)
**fray** (frā) *n.*: Noisy fight (p. 373)
**martial** (mär′ shəl) *adj.*: Military (p. 374)
**agile** (aj′ əl) *adj.*: Quick and easy of movement (p. 374)
**exile** (eg′ zīl) *v.*: Banish (p. 374)
**tedious** (tē′ dē əs) *adj.*: Tiresome and boring (p. 375)
**eloquence** (el′ ə kwəns) *n.*: Speech that is vivid, forceful, graceful, and persuasive (p. 375)
**fickle** (fik′ əl) *adj.*: Changeable (p. 386)
**abhors** (əb hôrz′) *v.*: Detests, intensely dislikes (p. 387)

### Objectives
1 To understand dramatic speeches
2 To infer tone in a monologue
3 To understand allusions in a play
4 To write a soliloquy

### Support Material

**Teaching Portfolio**
Teacher Backup, p. 391
Grammar in Action Worksheets, *Using Imagery*, p. 394; *Using Quotation Marks with Other Punctuation*, p. 396
Usage and Mechanics Worksheet, p. 398
Vocabulary Check, p. 399
Critical Thinking and Reading, *Inferring Tone in a Monologue*, p. 401
Language Worksheet, *Understanding Allusions*, p. 402
Selection Test, p. 403

# Act III

*Scene i.* *A public place.*

[*Enter* MERCUTIO, BENVOLIO, *and* MEN.]

**BENVOLIO.** I pray thee, good Mercutio, let's retire.
 The day is hot, the Capels are abroad,
 And, if we meet, we shall not 'scape a brawl,
 For now, these hot days, is the mad blood stirring.

5  **MERCUTIO.** Thou art like one of these fellows that, when he
 enters the confines of a tavern, claps me his sword
 upon the table and says, "God send me no need of
 thee!" and by the operation of the second cup draws
 him on the drawer,¹ when indeed there is no need.

10  **BENVOLIO.** Am I like such a fellow?

**MERCUTIO.** Come, come, thou art as hot a Jack in thy
 mood as any in Italy; and as soon moved to be moody,
 and as soon moody to be moved.²

**BENVOLIO.** And what to?

15  **MERCUTIO.** Nay, and there were two such, we should have
 none shortly, for one would kill the other. Thou! Why,
 thou wilt quarrel with a man that hath a hair more or
 a hair less in his beard than thou hast. Thou wilt
 quarrel with a man for cracking nuts, having no other
20  reason but because thou hast hazel eyes. What eye but
 such an eye would spy out such a quarrel? Thy head
 is as full of quarrels as an egg is full of meat; and
 yet thy head hath been beaten as addle³ as an egg for
 quarreling. Thou hast quarreled with a man for cough-
25  ing in the street, because he hath wakened thy dog
 that hath lain asleep in the sun. Didst thou not fall out
 with a tailor for wearing his new doublet⁴ before Eas-
 ter? With another for tying his new shoes with old rib-
 and?⁵ And yet thou wilt tutor me from quarreling!⁶

30  **BENVOLIO.** And I were so apt to quarrel as thou art, any
 man should buy the fee simple⁷ of my life for an hour
 and a quarter.⁸

**MERCUTIO.** The fee simple? O simple!⁹

[*Enter* TYBALT, PETRUCHIO, *and others.*]

**BENVOLIO.** By my head, here comes the Capulets.

35  **MERCUTIO.** By my heel, I care not.

**1. and . . . drawer:** And
by the effect of the second
drink draws his sword
against the waiter.

**2. and . . . moved:** And as
quickly stirred to anger as
you are eager to be so
stirred.

**3. addle:** Scrambled,
crazy.

**4. doublet:** Jacket.

**5. riband:** Ribbon.
**6. tutor . . . quarreling:**
Instruct me not to quarrel.
**7. fee simple:** Complete
possession.
**8. an hour and a quarter:**
The length of time that a
man with Mercutio's fond-
ness for quarreling may be
expected to live.
**9. O simple!:** O stupid!

*The Tragedy of Romeo and Juliet, Act III, Scene i*   369

3 **Discussion** How does Mercutio interpret Tybalt's phrase "Here comes my man"?

4 **Discussion** Why does Romeo try to call off the duel?

**TYBALT.** Follow me close, for I will speak to them.
  Gentlemen, good-den. A word with one of you.

**MERCUTIO.** And but one word with one of us? Couple it
  with something; make it a word and a blow.

40 **TYBALT.** You shall find me apt enough to that, sir, and you
  will give me occasion.[10]

**MERCUTIO.** Could you not take some occasion without
  giving?

**TYBALT.** Mercutio, thou consortest[11] with Romeo.

45 **MERCUTIO.** Consort?[12] What, dost thou make us minstrels? And thou make minstrels of us, look to hear
  nothing but discords.[13] Here's my fiddlestick; here's
  that shall make you dance. Zounds,[14] consort!

**BENVOLIO.** We talk here in the public haunt of men.
50   Either withdraw unto some private place,
  Or reason coldly of your grievances,
  Or else depart. Here all eyes gaze on us.

**MERCUTIO.** Men's eyes were made to look, and let them
    gaze.
  I will not budge for no man's pleasure, I.

[*Enter* ROMEO.]

55 **TYBALT.** Well, peace be with you, sir. Here comes my
    man.[15]

3

**MERCUTIO.** But I'll be hanged, sir, if he wear your livery.[16]
  Marry, go before to field,[17] he'll be your follower!
  Your worship in that sense may call him man.

**TYBALT.** Romeo, the love I bear thee can afford
60   No better term than this: thou art a villain.[18]

**ROMEO.** Tybalt, the reason that I have to love thee
  Doth much excuse the appertaining[19] rage
  To such a greeting. Villain am I none.
  Therefore farewell. I see thou knowest me not.

4 65 **TYBALT.** Boy, this shall not excuse the injuries
  That thou hast done me; therefore turn and draw.

**ROMEO.** I do protest I never injured thee,
  But love thee better than thou canst devise[20]
  Till thou shalt know the reason of my love;
70   And so, good Capulet, which name I tender[21]
  As dearly as mine own, be satisfied.

**10. occasion:** Cause, reason.

**11. consortest:** Associate with.
**12. Consort:** Associate with; *consort* also meant a group of musicians.
**13. discords:** Harsh sounds.
**14. Zounds:** An exclamation of surprise or anger ("By God's wounds").

**15. man:** The man I'm looking for; *man* also meant "manservant."
**16. livery:** Servant's uniform.
**17. field:** Dueling place.

**18. villain:** A low, vulgar person.

**19. appertaining:** Appropriate.

**20. devise:** Understand; imagine.

**21. tender:** Value.

370   *Drama*

**MERCUTIO.** O calm, dishonorable, vile submission!

5      *Alla stoccata*²² carries it away.      [*Draws.*]

     Tybalt, you ratcatcher, will you walk?

75  **TYBALT.** What wouldst thou have with me?

**MERCUTIO.** Good King of Cats, nothing but one of your
     nine lives. That I mean to make bold withal,²³ and, as
     you shall use me hereafter, dry-beat²⁴ the rest of the
     eight. Will you pluck your sword out of his pilcher²⁵ by
80     the ears? Make haste, lest mine be about your ears ere
     it be out.

**TYBALT.** I am for you.      [*Draws.*]

**ROMEO.** Gentle Mercutio, put thy rapier up.

**MERCUTIO.** Come, sir, your *passado*!      [*They fight.*]

85  **ROMEO.** Draw, Benvolio; beat down their weapons.
     Gentlemen, for shame! Forbear this outrage!
     Tybalt, Mercutio, the Prince expressly hath
     Forbid this bandying in Verona streets.
     Hold, Tybalt! Good Mercutio!

[TYBALT *under* ROMEO's *arms thrusts* MERCUTIO *in, and flies.*]

**MERCUTIO.**                I am hurt.
90     A plague a²⁶ both houses! I am sped.²⁷
     Is he gone and hath nothing?

**BENVOLIO.**              What, art thou hurt?

**MERCUTIO.** Ay, ay, a scratch, a scratch. Marry, 'tis enough.
     Where is my page? Go, villain, fetch a surgeon.

                             [*Exit* PAGE.]

**ROMEO.** Courage, man. The hurt cannot be much.

95  **MERCUTIO.** No, 'tis not so deep as a well, nor so wide as a
     church door; but 'tis enough, 'twill serve. Ask for me
     tomorrow, and you shall find me a grave man. I am
     peppered,²⁸ I warrant, for this world. A plague a both
     your houses! Zounds, a dog, a rat, a mouse, a cat, to
100    scratch a man to death! A braggart, a rogue, a villain,
     that fights by the book of arithmetic!²⁹ Why the devil
     came you between us? I was hurt under your arm.

**ROMEO.** I thought all for the best.

**MERCUTIO.** Help me into some house, Benvolio,
105    Or I shall faint. A plague a both your houses!

*The Tragedy of Romeo and Juliet, Act III, Scene i   371*

**22. *Alla stoccata:*** At the
thrust—an Italian fencing
term that Mercutio uses as
a nickname for Tybalt.

**23. make bold withal:**
Make bold with; take.
**24. dry-beat:** Thrash.
**25. pilcher:** Scabbard.

**26. a:** On.
**27. sped:** Wounded, done
for.

**28. peppered:** Finished
off.

**29. by . . . arithmetic:** By
formal rules.

**5 Discussion** How does Mercutio
interpret Romeo's reluctance to
fight?

**6 Discussion** How are Mercutio's
comments about his wound in
keeping with his character?

**7 Discussion** What does Mercutio
mean by "a plague a both your
houses"?

They have made worms' meat of me. I have it,[30]
And soundly too. Your houses!

[*Exit* MERCUTIO *and* BENVOLIO.]

**30. I have it:** I've got my deathblow.

**ROMEO.** This gentleman, the Prince's near ally,[31]
My very friend, hath got his mortal hurt
110  In my behalf—my reputation stained
With Tybalt's slander—Tybalt, that an hour
Hath been my cousin. O sweet Juliet,
Thy beauty hath made me effeminate
And in my temper soft'ned valor's steel!

**31. ally:** Relative.

[*Enter* BENVOLIO.]

115  **BENVOLIO.** O Romeo, Romeo, brave Mercutio is dead!
That gallant spirit hath aspired[32] the clouds,
Which too untimely here did scorn the earth.

**32. aspired:** Climbed to.

**ROMEO.** This day's black fate on moe[33] days doth
depend;[34]
This but begins the woe others must end.

**33. moe:** More.
**34. depend:** Hang over.

[*Enter* TYBALT.]

120  **BENVOLIO.** Here comes the furious Tybalt back again.

**ROMEO.** Alive in triumph, and Mercutio slain?
Away to heaven respective lenity,[35]
And fire-eyed fury be my conduct[36] now!
Now, Tybalt, take the "villain" back again
125  That late thou gavest me; for Mercutio's soul
Is but a little way above our heads,
Staying for thine to keep him company.
Either thou or I, or both, must go with him.

**35. respective lenity:** Thoughtful mercy.
**36. conduct:** Guide.

**TYBALT.** Thou, wretched boy, that didst consort him
here,
Shalt with him hence.

130  **ROMEO.**                     This shall determine that.

[*They fight.* TYBALT *falls.*]

**BENVOLIO.** Romeo, away, be gone!
The citizens are up, and Tybalt slain.
Stand not amazed. The Prince will doom thee death
If thou art taken. Hence, be gone, away!

**ROMEO.** O, I am fortune's fool![37]

**37. fool:** Plaything.

135  **BENVOLIO.**                     Why dost thou stay?

[*Exit* ROMEO.]

*372  Drama*

## Primary Source

Historians and scholars generally believe that stage directions in Elizabethan plays were the author's notations and not the director's or prompter's. We can assume, therefore, that the stage directions, which were found in the original first and second quartos of *Romeo and Juliet,* were written by Shakespeare himself. A quarto is a published manuscript made up of sheets each of which is folded twice to form four leaves, or eight pages. The first quarto for *Romeo and Juliet* was printed in London in 1597, approximately two years after Shakespeare wrote the play.

Read the following passages from the introduction of *Shakespeare, The Complete Works,* edited by G. B. Harrison, to your students. The stage directions from the first quarto are shown in italics and single quotation marks; those from the second quarto are shown in italics and double quotation marks. The other directions are purely conjectural; Harrison is showing how the rest of the scene might have been staged. "RIGHT" means as the actor faces the audience—the viewer's left.

Act III, Scene i:
*"Enter Mercutio, Benvolio and men,"* by the LEFT door. By the RIGHT door, enter Tybalt and others. Romeo enters through the RECESS curtains. Tybalt draws attention to his

9 **Reading Strategy** Ask students to recall the Prince's comments about public brawling. Have them predict what will happen to Romeo now.

[*Enter* CITIZENS.]

    **CITIZEN.** Which way ran he that killed Mercutio?
      Tybalt, that murderer, which way ran he?

    **BENVOLIO.** There lies that Tybalt.

    **CITIZEN.**                       Up, sir, go with me.
      I charge thee in the Prince's name obey.

9  [*Enter* PRINCE, *old* MONTAGUE, CAPULET, *their* WIVES, *and all.*]

140  **PRINCE.** Where are the vile beginners of this fray?

    **BENVOLIO.** O noble Prince, I can discover[38] all
      The unlucky manage[39] of this fatal brawl.
      There lies the man, slain by young Romeo,
      That slew thy kinsman, brave Mercutio.

**38. discover:** Reveal.
**39. manage:** Course.

145  **LADY CAPULET.** Tybalt, my cousin! O my brother's child!
      O Prince! O cousin! Husband! Oh, the blood is spilled
      Of my dear kinsman! Prince, as thou art true,
      For blood of ours shed blood of Montague.
      O cousin, cousin!

150  **PRINCE.** Benvolio, who began this bloody fray?

    **BENVOLIO.** Tybalt, here slain, whom Romeo's hand did
      slay.
      Romeo, that spoke him fair, bid him bethink

10

*The Tragedy of Romeo and Juliet, Act III, Scene i*   373

entry with "Here comes my man." Tybalt and Mercutio fight; *'Tybalt under Romeo's arm thrusts Mercutio, in and flies'* through the RIGHT door. The page goes out by the LEFT door. Mercutio, supported by Benvolio, goes out through the LEFT door, whence Benvolio emerges to say that Mercutio is dead. Tybalt reenters by the RIGHT door. Romeo and Tybalt fight and Tybalt is slain. Romeo runs out by the LEFT door. The citizens enter through the curtains of the RECESS, followed by the Prince. Capulet and his wife enter by the RIGHT door. Montague and his wife enter by the LEFT. At the end of the scene, all go out by the ways in which they have entered, the body of Tybalt being carried out through the RIGHT door.

Act III, Scene ii
The curtains of the CHAMBER above are opened, revealing Juliet alone. *'Enter Nurse, wringing her hands, with the ladder of the cords in her lap.'* At the end of the scene the curtains of the CHAMBER are closed.

**Student Activity.** Choose a scene from the play and write the stage directions for it, keeping in mind the structure and layout of the Elizabethan theater (see pages 318–319 in the student book).

**10** **Literary Focus** Benvolio's monologue reviews the previous events. Do you think his account is accurate? Why or why not?

**11** **Critical Thinking and Reading** Contrast the views of Lady Capulet and Montague. Why do you think they differ?

**12** **Clarification** Today Romeo would be tried for murder. In earlier times, however, revenge was more common and accepted. Montague says that Romeo only did what the law would have done anyway.

**13** **Critical Thinking and Reading** Why do you think the Prince does not impose the death penalty, as he threatened in Act I?

How nice[40] the quarrel was, and urged withal
Your high displeasure. All this—utterèd
With gentle breath, calm look, knees humbly bowed—
Could not take truce with the unruly spleen[41]
Of Tybalt deaf to peace, but that he tilts[42]
With piercing steel at bold Mercutio's breast;
Who, all as hot, turns deadly point to point,
And, with a martial scorn, with one hand beats
Cold death aside and with the other sends
It back to Tybalt, whose dexterity
Retorts it. Romeo he cries aloud,
"Hold, friends! Friends, part!" and swifter than his tongue,
His agile arm beats down their fatal points,
And 'twixt them rushes; underneath whose arm
An envious[43] thrust from Tybalt hit the life
Of stout Mercutio, and then Tybalt fled;
But by and by comes back to Romeo,
Who had but newly entertained[44] revenge,
And to't they go like lightning; for, ere I
Could draw to part them, was stout Tybalt slain;
And, as he fell, did Romeo turn and fly.
This is the truth, or let Benvolio die.

**LADY CAPULET.** He is a kinsman to the Montague;
Affection makes him false, he speaks not true.
Some twenty of them fought in this black strife,
And all those twenty could but kill one life.
I beg for justice, which thou, Prince, must give.
Romeo slew Tybalt; Romeo must not live.

**PRINCE.** Romeo slew him; he slew Mercutio.
Who now the price of his dear blood doth owe?

**CAPULET.** Not Romeo, Prince; he was Mercutio's friend;
His fault concludes but what the law should end,
The life of Tybalt.[45]

**PRINCE.**                    And for that offense
Immediately we do exile him hence.
I have an interest in your hate's proceeding.
My blood[46] for your rude brawls doth lie a-bleeding;
But I'll amerce[47] you with so strong a fine
That you shall all repent the loss of mine.
I will be deaf to pleading and excuses;
Nor tears nor prayers shall purchase out abuses.
Therefore use none. Let Romeo hence in haste,

**40. nice:** Trivial.

**41. spleen:** Angry nature.
**42. tilts:** Thrusts.

**43. envious:** Full of hatred.

**44. entertained:** Considered.

**45. His fault . . . Tybalt:** By killing Tybalt, he did what the law would have done.

**46. My blood:** Mercutio was related to the Prince.
**47. amerce:** Punish.

374    Drama

## Grammar in Action

Writers use **images** to create pictures for the readers. Using images in your own work will make your writing interesting and come alive for your audience. An image is a word or phrase that appeals to one of the five senses—sight, hearing, touch, taste, smell. By appealing to the reader's senses, use of image, or **imagery** allows that reader to experience what is being described. Study these lines from the play:

JULIET: Come, night; come, Romeo; come, thou day in night;
For thou wilt lie upon the wings of night
Whiter than new snow upon a raven's back.
Come gentle night; come, loving, black-browed night;
Give me my Romeo; and, when he shall die,
Take him and cut him out in little stars,
And he will make the face of heaven so fine
That all the world will be in love with night
And pay no worship to the garish sun.

Images in these lines appeal to the sense of sight. Notice the number and variety of these images: Romeo is compared to snow on a raven's back (lines 2 and 3). Night is given the

Else, when he is found, that hour is his last.

195 Bear hence this body and attend our will.[48]
Mercy but murders, pardoning those that kill.

[Exit with others.]

**48. attend our will:** Await my decision.

**Scene ii.** CAPULET'S orchard.

[Enter JULIET alone.]

JULIET. Gallop apace, you fiery-footed steeds,[1]
Towards Phoebus' lodging![2] Such a wagoner
As Phaëton[3] would whip you to the west
And bring in cloudy night immediately.

5 Spread thy close curtain, love-performing night,
That runaways' eyes may wink,[4] and Romeo
Leap to these arms untalked of and unseen.
Lovers can see to do their amorous rites,
And by their own beauties; or, if love be blind,

10 It best agrees with night. Come, civil night,
Thou sober-suited matron all in black,
And learn me how to lose a winning match,
Played for a pair of stainless maidenhoods.
Hood my unmanned blood, bating in my cheeks.[5]

15 With thy black mantle till strange[6] love grow bold,
Think true love acted simple modesty,
Come, night; come, Romeo; come, thou day in night;
For thou wilt lie upon the wings of night
Whiter than new snow upon a raven's back.

20 Come, gentle night; come, loving, black-browed night;
Give me my Romeo; and, when I shall die,
Take him and cut him out in little stars,
And he will make the face of heaven so fine
That all the world will be in love with night

25 And pay no worship to the garish sun.
O, I have bought the mansion of a love,
But not possessed it; and though I am sold,
Not yet enjoyed. So tedious is this day
As is the night before some festival

30 To an impatient child that hath new robes
And may not wear them. O, here comes my nurse,

[Enter NURSE, with cords.]

And she brings news; and every tongue that speaks
But Romeo's name speaks heavenly eloquence.
Now, nurse, what news? What hast thou there, the cords
That Romeo bid thee fetch?

1. **fiery-footed steeds:** Horses of the sun god, Phoebus.

2. **Phoebus' lodging:** Below the horizon.

3. **Phaëton:** Phoebus' son, who tried to drive his father's horses but was unable to control them.

4. **That runaways' eyes may wink:** So that the eyes of busybodies may not see.

5. **Hood . . . cheeks:** Hide the untamed blood that makes me blush.

6. **strange:** Unfamiliar.

*The Tragedy of Romeo and Juliet, Act III, Scene ii* 375

14 **Literary Focus** This soliloquy gives the audience a glimpse into Juliet's thoughts. Ask students to describe her mood. Why is this soliloquy especially touching after the dramatic events that have just occurred?

qualities of a person—"gentle," "loving, black-browed" (line 4). The image of the stars (lines 5–8) indicates the intensity of Juliet's love. And the use of the word *garish* to describe the sun (line 9) allows readers to not only visualize it but also to see it as Juliet does.

**Student Activity 1.** Find another passage that contains imagery, and discuss your choice with a classmate. Talk about which sense is appealed to and the effect of the image. (If more than one sense is appealed to, be sure to discuss each one.)

**Student Activity 2.** Write several sentences that contain imagery. Read these aloud to a partner, and discuss ways in which they are effective and how they might be improved.

**Critical Thinking and Reading**
These next two scenes show
how Juliet and Romeo act in the
face of bad news. As students
read, have them compare and
contrast the ways in which the
two handle their grief.

35   **NURSE.**                      Ay, ay, the cords.

**JULIET.** Ay me! What news? Why dost thou wring thy
    hands?

15   **NURSE.** Ah, weraday![7] He's dead, he's dead, he's dead!
    We are undone, lady, we are undone!
    Alack the day! He's gone, he's killed, he's dead!

    **7. Ah, weraday!:** Alas!

**JULIET.** Can heaven be so envious?

40   **NURSE.**                       Romeo can,
    Though heaven cannot. O Romeo, Romeo!
    Who ever would have thought it? Romeo!

**JULIET.** What devil art thou that dost torment me thus?
    This torture should be roared in dismal hell.
45     Hath Romeo slain himself? Say thou but "Ay,"
    And that bare vowel "I" shall poison more
    Than the death-darting eye of cockatrice.[8]
    I am not I, if there be such an "Ay,"[9]
    Or those eyes' shot[10] that makes thee answer "Ay."
50     If he be slain, say "Ay"; or if not, "No."
    Brief sounds determine of my weal or woe.

    **8. cockatrice:** A serpent
    that, in fables, could kill
    with its glance.
    **9. "Ay":** Yes.
    **10. eyes' shot:** The
    nurse's glance.

**NURSE.** I saw the wound, I saw it with mine eyes,
    (God save the mark![11]) here on his manly breast.
    A piteous corse,[12] a bloody piteous corse;
55     Pale, pale as ashes, all bedaubed in blood,
    All in gore-blood. I sounded[13] at the sight.

    **11. God save the mark!:**
    May God save us from evil!
    **12. corse:** Corpse.
    **13. sounded:** Swooned,
    fainted.

**JULIET.** O, break, my heart! Poor bankrout,[14] break at
    once!
    To prison, eyes; ne'er look on liberty!
    Vile earth, to earth resign;[15] end motion here,
60     And thou and Romeo press one heavy bier![16]

    **14. bankrout:** Bankrupt.

    **15. Vile . . . resign:** Let
    my body return to the
    earth.
    **16. bier:** A platform on
    which a corpse is displayed
    before burial.

**NURSE.** O Tybalt, Tybalt, the best friend I had!
    O courteous Tybalt! Honest gentleman!
    That ever I should live to see thee dead!

**JULIET.** What storm is this that blows so contrary?[17]
65     Is Romeo slaught'red, and is Tybalt dead?
    My dearest cousin, and my dearer lord?
    Then, dreadful trumpet, sound the general doom![18]
    For who is living, if those two are gone?

    **17. contrary:** In opposite
    directions.

    **18. dreadful . . . doom:**
    Let the trumpet that an-
    nounces doomsday be
    sounded.

**NURSE.** Tybalt is gone, and Romeo banishèd;
70     Romeo that killed him, he is banishèd.

**JULIET.** O God! Did Romeo's hand shed Tybalt's blood?

*376 Drama*

**NURSE.** It did, it did! Alas the day, it did!

**JULIET.** O serpent heart, hid with a flow'ring face!
75 Did ever dragon keep so fair a cave?
Beautiful tyrant! Fiend angelical!
Dove-feathered raven! Wolvish-ravening lamb!
Despisèd substance of divinest show!
Just opposite to what thou justly seem'st—
A damnèd saint, an honorable villain!
80 O nature, what hadst thou to do in hell
When thou didst bower the spirit of a fiend
In mortal paradise of such sweet flesh?
Was ever book containing such vile matter
So fairly bound? O, that deceit should dwell
In such a gorgeous palace!

85 **NURSE.**                              There's no trust,
No faith, no honesty in men; all perjured,
All forsworn,[19] all naught, all dissemblers.[20]
Ah, where's my man? Give me some *aqua vitae.*[21]
These griefs, these woes, these sorrows make me old.
Shame come to Romeo!

90 **JULIET.**                          Blistered be thy tongue
For such a wish! He was not born to shame.
Upon his brow shame is ashamed to sit;
For 'tis a throne where honor may be crowned
Sole monarch of the universal earth.
95 O, what a beast was I to chide at him!

**NURSE.** Will you speak well of him that killed your cousin?

**JULIET.** Shall I speak ill of him that is my husband?
Ah, poor my lord, what tongue shall smooth thy name
When I, thy three-hours wife, have mangled it?
100 But wherefore, villain, didst thou kill my cousin?
That villain cousin would have killed my husband.
Back, foolish tears, back to your native spring!
Your tributary[22] drops belong to woe,
Which you, mistaking, offer up to joy.
105 My husband lives, that Tybalt would have slain;
And Tybalt's dead, that would have slain my husband.
All this is comfort; wherefore weep I then?
Some word there was, worser than Tybalt's death,
That murd'red me. I would forget it fain;
110 But O, it presses to my memory
Like damnèd guilty deeds to sinners' minds!
"Tybalt is dead, and Romeo—banishèd."

*The Tragedy of Romeo and Juliet, Act III, Scene ii   377*

**19. forsworn:** Are liars.
**20. dissemblers:** Hypocrites.
**21. aqua vitae:** Brandy.

**22. tributary:** In tribute.

16 **Discussion** How do Juliet's words reflect her divided feelings?

17 **Discussion** What word would Juliet like to forget but cannot?

18 **Literary Focus** Remind students that a monologue tells how a character is thinking or feeling at that moment. Ask them how the soliloquy beginning the scene prepared for this monologue.

19 **Clarification** Since the days of the Romans, a ring has been a sign of betrothal and marriage.

That "banishèd," that one word "banishèd,"
Hath slain ten thousand Tybalts. Tybalt's death
115  Was woe enough, if it had ended there;
Or, if sour woe delights in fellowship
And needly will be ranked with[23] other griefs,
Why followed not, when she said "Tybalt's dead,"
Thy father, or thy mother, nay, or both,
120  Which modern[24] lamentation might have moved?
But with a rearward[25] following Tybalt's death,
"Romeo is banishèd"—to speak that word
Is father, mother, Tybalt, Romeo, Juliet,
All slain, all dead. "Romeo is banishèd"—
125  There is no end, no limit, measure, bound,
In that word's death; no words can that woe sound.
Where is my father and my mother, nurse?

**NURSE.** Weeping and wailing over Tybalt's corse.
Will you go to them? I will bring you thither.

**JULIET.** Wash they his wounds with tears? Mine shall be
130      spent,
When theirs are dry, for Romeo's banishment.
Take up those cords. Poor ropes, you are beguiled,
Both you and I, for Romeo is exiled.
He made you for a highway to my bed;
135  But I, a maid, die maiden-widowèd.
Come, cords; come, nurse. I'll to my wedding bed;
And death, not Romeo, take my maidenhead!

**NURSE.** Hie to your chamber. I'll find Romeo
To comfort you. I wot[26] well where he is.
140  Hark ye, your Romeo will be here at night.
I'll to him; he is hid at Lawrence' cell.

**JULIET.** O, find him! Give this ring to my true knight
And bid him come to take his last farewell.

[*Exit with* NURSE.]

**23. needly . . . with:** Must be accompanied by.

**24. modern:** Ordinary.
**25. rearward:** Follow up; literally, a rear guard.

**26. wot:** Know.

*Scene iii.* FRIAR LAWRENCE'S *cell.*

[*Enter* FRIAR LAWRENCE.]

**FRIAR.** Romeo, come forth; come forth, thou fearful man.
Affliction is enamored of thy parts.[1]
And thou art wedded to calamity.

[*Enter* ROMEO.]

**1. Affliction . . . parts:** Misery is in love with your attractive qualities.

378  *Drama*

**ROMEO.** Father, what news? What is the Prince's doom?[2]

5     What sorrow craves acquaintance at my hand
    That I yet know not?

**FRIAR.**                     Too familiar
    Is my dear son with such sour company.
    I bring thee tidings of the Prince's doom.

**ROMEO.** What less than doomsday[3] is the Prince's doom?

10 **FRIAR.** A gentler judgment vanished[4] from his lips—
    Not body's death, but body's banishment.

**ROMEO.** Ha, banishment? Be merciful, say "death";
    For exile hath more terror in his look,
    Much more than death. Do not say "banishment."

15 **FRIAR.** Here from Verona art thou banishèd.
    Be patient, for the world is broad and wide.

**ROMEO.** There is no world without[5] Verona walls,
    But purgatory, torture, hell itself.
    Hence banishèd is banished from the world,
20     And world's exile is death. Then "banishèd"
    Is death mistermed. Calling death "banishèd,"
    Thou cut'st my head off with a golden ax
    And smilest upon the stroke that murders me.

**FRIAR.** O deadly sin! O rude unthankfulness!
25     Thy fault our law calls death;[6] but the kind Prince,
    Taking thy part, hath rushed[7] aside the law,
    And turned that black word "death" to "banishment."
    This is dear mercy, and thou seest it not.

**ROMEO.** 'Tis torture, and not mercy. Heaven is here,
30     Where Juliet lives; and every cat and dog
    And little mouse, every unworthy thing,
    Live here in heaven and may look on her;
    But Romeo may not. More validity,[8]
    More honorable state, more courtship lives
35     In carrion flies than Romeo. They may seize
    On the white wonder of dear Juliet's hand
    And steal immortal blessing from her lips,
    Who, even in pure and vestal modesty,
    Still blush, as thinking their own kisses sin;
40     But Romeo may not, he is banishèd.
    Flies may do this but I from this must fly;
    They are freemen, but I am banishèd.
    And sayest thou yet that exile is not death?

*The Tragedy of Romeo and Juliet, Act III, Scene iii*   379

---

**2. doom:** Final decision.

**3. doomsday:** My death.

**4. vanished:** Escaped, came forth.

**5. without:** Outside.

**6. Thy fault . . . death:** For what you did our law demands the death penalty.
**7. rushed:** Pushed.

**8. validity:** Value.

---

**20 Discussion** Is Romeo's reaction to his punishment unreasonable? Explain.

**21 Clarification** Verona and Mantua are only about twenty-five miles apart, less than a day's walk.

**22 Discussion** Why does Friar Lawrence disagree with Romeo?

**23 Literary Focus** How does this monologue reveal a flaw in Romeo's character?

**24 Critical Thinking and Reading**
If you were directing this scene, how would you instruct the actors to move and behave?

**25 Critical Thinking and Reading**
How would you describe Romeo's tone of voice in this speech?

Hadst thou no poison mixed, no sharp-ground knife,
45      No sudden mean[9] of death, though ne'er so mean,[10]
But "banishèd" to kill me—"banishèd"?
O friar, the damnèd use that word in hell;
Howling attends it! How hast thou the heart,
Being a divine, a ghostly confessor,
50      A sin-absolver, and my friend professed,
To mangle me with that word "banishèd"?

**9. mean:** Method.
**10. mean:** Humiliating.

**24**

**FRIAR.** Thou fond mad man, hear me a little speak.

**ROMEO.** O, thou wilt speak again of banishment.

**FRIAR.** I'll give thee armor to keep off that word;
55      Adversity's sweet milk, philosophy,
To comfort thee, though thou art banishèd.

**25**

**ROMEO.** Yet "banishèd"? Hang up philosophy!
Unless philosophy can make a Juliet,
Displant a town, reverse a prince's doom,
60      It helps not, it prevails not. Talk no more.

**FRIAR.** O, then I see that madmen have no ears.

**ROMEO.** How should they, when that wise men have no eyes?

**FRIAR.** Let me dispute[11] with thee of thy estate.[12]

**11. dispute:** Discuss.
**12. estate:** Condition, situation.

380   *Drama*

## Grammar in Action

The placement of **quotation marks with other punctuation** causes some confusion among beginning writers. The question mark or exclamation mark is placed *inside* the final quotation mark if the end mark is part of the quotation:

The teacher asked, "Have you done your homework?"
He exclaimed, "I can't believe I won; I really won!"

The question mark or exclamation mark is placed *outside* the final quotation mark if the end mark is *not* part of the quotation:

Who said: "I'm going to do better next time"?
I was ecstatic when he droned, "Nam Hee Chin, first place"!

Notice how Shakespeare observes these rules in the following excerpts from *Romeo and Juliet:*

But "banished" to kill me—"banishèd"?
. . . How hast thou the heart,/To mangle me with that word 'banishèd"?
Yet "banishèd"? Hang up philosophy!

The quotation marks around *banished* show the exact wording of the Prince's sentence. The questions are Romeo's; therefore, the question marks appear outside the quotation marks.

**ROMEO.** Thou canst not speak of that thou dost not feel.
65    Wert thou as young as I, Juliet thy love,
      An hour but married, Tybalt murderèd,
      Doting like me, and like me banishèd,
      Then mightst thou speak, then mightst thou tear thy
           hair,
      And fall upon the ground, as I do now,
70    Taking the measure of an unmade grave.

[*Enter* NURSE *and knock.*]

**FRIAR.** Arise, one knocks. Good Romeo, hide thyself.

**ROMEO.** Not I; unless the breath of heartsick groans
      Mistlike infold me from the search of eyes.    [*Knock.*]

**FRIAR.** Hark, how they knock! Who's there? Romeo, arise;
75    Thou wilt be taken.—Stay awhile!—Stand up; [*Knock.*]
      Run to my study.—By and by![13]—God's will,
      What simpleness[14] is this.—I come, I come!    [*Knock.*]
      Who knocks so hard? Whence come you? What's your
           will?

[*Enter* NURSE.]

**NURSE.** Let me come in, and you shall know my errand.
      I come from Lady Juliet.

80    **FRIAR.**                      Welcome then.

**NURSE.** O holy friar, O, tell me, holy friar,
      Where is my lady's lord, where's Romeo?

**FRIAR.** There on the ground, with his own tears made
      drunk.

**NURSE.** O, he is even in my mistress' case,
85    Just in her case! O woeful sympathy!
      Piteous predicament! Even so lies she,
      Blubb'ring and weeping, weeping and blubb'ring.
      Stand up, stand up! Stand, and you be a man.
      For Juliet's sake, for her sake, rise and stand!
90    Why should you fall into so deep an O?[15]

**ROMEO.** [*Rises.*] Nurse—

**NURSE.** Ah sir, ah sir! Death's the end of all.

**ROMEO.** Spakest thou of Juliet? How is it with her?
      Doth not she think me an old murderer,
95    Now I have stained the childhood of our joy
      With blood removed but little from her own?

**13. By and by!:** In a minute! (said to the person knocking).
**14. simpleness:** Silly behavior (Romeo does not move).

**15. O:** Cry of grief.

*The Tragedy of Romeo and Juliet*, Act III, Scene iii    381

**26 Discussion** Do you think Romeo's argument is valid? Explain.

**Student Activity 1.** Add end marks either inside or outside the quotation marks in the following sentences:
1. Did he say, "I'm planning a weekend party"
2. At the final buzzer, he screamed, "We did it"
3. Mr. Gaddis asked, "Who's on the newspaper staff"
4. Did you read "The Interlopers" and "The Necklace"

**Student Activity 2.** Write four sentences, two using end marks inside quotation marks and two using them outside.

**27 Discussion** Does Romeo really intend to stab himself?

Where is she? And how doth she? And what says
My concealed lady[16] to our canceled love?

**NURSE.** O, she says nothing, sir, but weeps and weeps;
100 And now falls on her bed, and then starts up,
And Tybalt calls; and then on Romeo cries,
And then down falls again.

**ROMEO.** As if that name,
Shot from the deadly level[17] of a gun,
Did murder her; as that name's cursèd hand
105 Murdered her kinsman. O, tell me, friar, tell me,
In what vile part of this anatomy
Doth my name lodge? Tell me, that I may sack[18]
The hateful mansion.

[*He offers to stab himself, and* NURSE
*snatches the dagger away.*]

**27**

110 **FRIAR.** Hold thy desperate hand.
Art thou a man? Thy form cries out thou art;
Thy tears are womanish, thy wild acts denote
The unreasonable fury of a beast.
Unseemly[19] woman in a seeming man!
And ill-beseeming beast in seeming both![20]
Thou hast amazed me. By my holy order,
115 I thought thy disposition better tempered.
Hast thou slain Tybalt? Wilt thou slay thyself?
And slay thy lady that in thy life lives,
By doing damnèd hate upon thyself?
Why railest thou on thy birth, the heaven, and earth?
120 Since birth and heaven and earth, all three do meet
In thee at once; which thou at once wouldst lose.
Fie, fie, thou shamest thy shape, thy love, thy wit,[21]
Which, like a usurer,[22] abound'st in all,
And usest none in that true use indeed
125 Which should bedeck[23] thy shape, thy love, thy wit.
Thy noble shape is but a form of wax,
Digressing from the valor of a man;
Thy dear love sworn but hollow perjury,
Killing that love which thou hast vowed to cherish;
130 Thy wit, that ornament to shape and love,
Misshapen in the conduct[24] of them both,
Like powder in a skilless soldier's flask,[25]
Is set afire by thine own ignorance,
And thou dismemb'red with thine own defense.[26]
135 What, rouse thee, man! Thy Juliet is alive,

382 *Drama*

16. **concealed lady:** Secret bride.

17. **level:** Aim.

18. **sack:** Plunder.

19. **Unseemly:** Inappropriate (because unnatural).
20. **And . . . both!:** That is, Romeo inappropriately has lost his human nature because he seems like a man and woman combined.

21. **wit:** Mind, intellect.
22. **Which, like a usurer:** Who, like a rich money-lender.
23. **bedeck:** Do honor to.

24. **conduct:** Management.
25. **flask:** Powder flask.
26. **And thou . . . defense:** The friar is saying that Romeo's mind, which is now irrational, is destroying rather than aiding him.

For whose dear sake thou wast but lately dead.[27]
There art thou happy.[28] Tybalt would kill thee,
But thou slewest Tybalt. There art thou happy.
The law, that threat'ned death, becomes thy friend
140 And turns it into exile. There art thou happy.
A pack of blessings light upon thy back;
Happiness courts thee in her best array;
But, like a misbehaved and sullen wench,[29]
Thou puts up[30] thy fortune and thy love.
145 Take heed, take heed, for such die miserable.
Go get thee to thy love, as was decreed,
Ascend her chamber, hence and comfort her.
But look thou stay not till the watch be set,[31]
For then thou canst not pass to Mantua,
150 Where thou shalt live till we can find a time
To blaze[32] your marriage, reconcile your friends,
Beg pardon of the Prince, and call thee back
With twenty hundred thousand times more joy
Than thou went'st forth in lamentation.
155 Go before, nurse. Commend me to thy lady,
And bid her hasten all the house to bed,
Which heavy sorrow makes them apt unto.[33]
Romeo is coming.

**NURSE.** O Lord, I could have stayed here all the night
160 To hear good counsel. O, what learning is!
My lord, I'll tell my lady you will come.

**ROMEO.** Do so, and bid my sweet prepare to chide.[34]
[NURSE *offers to go in and turns again.*]

**NURSE.** Here, sir, a ring she bid me give you, sir.
Hie you, make haste, for it grows very late.          [*Exit.*]

165 **ROMEO.** How well my comfort is revived by this!

**FRIAR.** Go hence; good night; and here stands all your
     state:[35]
Either be gone before the watch be set,
Or by the break of day disguised from hence.
Sojourn[36] in Mantua. I'll find out your man,
170 And he shall signify[37] from time to time
Every good hap to you that chances here.
Give me thy hand. 'Tis late. Farewell; good night.

**ROMEO.** But that a joy past joy calls out on me,
It were a grief so brief to part with thee.
175 Farewell.                                         [*Exit.*]

*The Tragedy of Romeo and Juliet,* Act III, Scene iii   383

---

**27. but lately dead:** Only recently declaring yourself dead.
**28. happy:** Fortunate.

**29. wench:** Low, common girl.
**30. puts up:** Pouts over.

**31. watch be set:** The watchmen go on duty.

**32. blaze:** Announce publicly.

**33. apt unto:** Likely to do.

**34. chide:** Rebuke me (for slaying Tybalt).

**35. here ... state:** This is your situation.

**36. Sojourn:** Remain.
**37. signify:** Let you know.

---

28 **Reading Strategy** Ask students to predict whether these events will occur.

29 **Discussion** What are Friar Lawrence's instructions to Romeo?

**30 Critical Thinking and Reading** Why does Capulet think that Juliet is grieving?

**31 Reading Strategy** Have students predict how Juliet will react to this news.

*Scene iv.* A room in CAPULET's house.

[*Enter old* CAPULET, *his* WIFE, *and* PARIS.]

**CAPULET.** Things have fall'n out, sir, so unluckily
That we have had no time to move¹ our daughter.
Look you, she loved her kinsman Tybalt dearly,
And so did I. Well, we were born to die.
5    'Tis very late; she'll not come down tonight.
I promise you, but for your company,
I would have been abed an hour ago.

**PARIS.** These times of woe afford no times to woo.
Madam, good night. Commend me to your daughter.

10  **LADY.** I will, and know her mind early tomorrow;
Tonight she's mewed up to her heaviness.²

**CAPULET.** Sir, Paris, I will make a desperate tender³
Of my child's love. I think she will be ruled
In all respects by me; nay more, I doubt it not.
15    Wife, go you to her ere you go to bed;
Acquaint her here of my son⁴ Paris' love
And bid her (mark you me?) on Wednesday next—
But soft! What day is this?

**PARIS.**                              Monday, my lord.

**CAPULET.** Monday! Ha, ha! Well, Wednesday is too soon.
20    A⁵ Thursday let it be—a Thursday, tell her,
She shall be married to this noble earl.
Will you be ready? Do you like this haste?
We'll keep no great ado⁶—a friend or two;
For hark you, Tybalt being slain so late,
25    It may be thought we held him carelessly,⁷
Being our kinsman, if we revel much.
Therefore we'll have some half a dozen friends,
And there an end. But what say you to Thursday?

**PARIS.** My lord, I would that Thursday were tomorrow.

30  **CAPULET.** Well, get you gone. A Thursday be it then.
Go you to Juliet ere you go to bed;
Prepare her, wife, against⁸ this wedding day.
Farewell, my lord.—Light to my chamber, ho!
Afore me,⁹ it is so very late
35    That we may call it early by and by.
Good night.                              [*Exit.*]

**1. move:** Discuss your proposal with.

**2. mewed . . . heaviness:** Locked up with her sorrow.
**3. desperate tender:** Risky offer.

**4. son:** Son-in-law.

**5. A:** On.

**6. We'll . . . ado:** We won't make a great fuss.
**7. held him carelessly:** Did not respect him enough.

**8. against:** For.

**9. Afore me:** Indeed (a mild oath).

384   *Drama*

***Scene v.*** CAPULET'S *orchard.*

[*Enter* ROMEO *and* JULIET *aloft.*]

**JULIET.** Wilt thou be gone? It is not yet near day.
It was the nightingale, and not the lark,[1]
That pierced the fearful hollow of thine ear.
Nightly she sings on yond pomegranate tree.
5    Believe me, love, it was the nightingale.

**ROMEO.** It was the lark, the herald of the morn;
No nightingale. Look, love, what envious streaks
Do lace the severing[2] clouds in yonder East.
Night's candles[3] are burnt out, and jocund day
10   Stands tiptoe on the misty mountaintops.
I must be gone and live, or stay and die.

**JULIET.** Yond light is not daylight; I know it, I.
It is some meteor that the sun exhales[4]
To be to thee this night a torchbearer
15   And light thee on thy way to Mantua.
Therefore stay yet; thou need'st not to be gone.

**ROMEO.** Let me be ta'en, let me be put to death.
I am content, so thou wilt have it so.
I'll say yon gray is not the morning's eye,
20   'Tis but the pale reflex of Cynthia's brow;[5]
Nor that is not the lark whose notes do beat
The vaulty heaven so high above our heads.
I have more care to stay than will to go.
Come, death, and welcome! Juliet wills it so.
25   How is't, my soul? Let's talk; it is not day.

**JULIET.** It is, it is! Hie hence, be gone, away!
It is the lark that sings so out of tune,
Straining harsh discords and unpleasing sharps.[6]
Some say the lark makes sweet division;[7]
30   This doth not so, for she divideth us.
Some say the lark and loathèd toad change eyes;[8]
O, now I would they had changed voices too,
Since arm from arm that voice doth us affray,[9]
Hunting thee hence with hunt's-up[10] to the day.
35   O, now be gone! More light and light it grows.

**ROMEO.** More light and light—more dark and dark our
woes.

[*Enter* NURSE.]

**1. nightingale . . . lark:**
The nightingale was associated with the night, the lark with dawn.

**2. severing:** Parting.
**3. Night's candles:** The stars.

**4. exhales:** Sends out.

**5. reflex . . . brow:** Reflection of the moon (Cynthia was a name for the moon goddess).

**6. sharps:** Shrill high notes.
**7. division:** Melody.

**8. change eyes:** Exchange eyes (because the lark has a beautiful body with ugly eyes and the toad has an ugly body with beautiful eyes).
**9. affray:** Frighten.
**10. hunt's-up:** A morning song for hunters.

*The Tragedy of Romeo and Juliet, Act III, Scene v*   385

**33 Discussion** Compare their farewells. Who seems to be more optimistic about the future now?

**34 Reading Strategy** As students read the rest of the scene, have them look for the irony in the exchanges between Juliet and her parents.

**NURSE.** Madam!

**JULIET.** Nurse?

**NURSE.** Your lady mother is coming to your chamber.
40          The day is broke; be wary, look about.                    [*Exit.*]

**JULIET.** Then, window, let day in, and let life out.

**ROMEO.** Farewell, farewell! One kiss, and I'll descend.
                                        [*He goeth down.*]

**JULIET.** Art thou gone so, love-lord, ay husband-friend?
          I must hear from thee every day in the hour,
45          For in a minute there are many days.
          O, by this count I shall be much in years[11]
          Ere I again behold my Romeo!

**ROMEO.** Farewell!
          I will omit no opportunity
50          That may convey my greetings, love, to thee.

**JULIET.** O, think'st thou we shall ever meet again?

**ROMEO.** I doubt it not; and all these woes shall serve
          For sweet discourses[12] in our times to come.

**JULIET.** O God, I have an ill-divining[13] soul!
55          Methinks I see thee, now thou art so low,
          As one dead in the bottom of a tomb.
          Either my eyesight fails, or thou lookest pale.

**ROMEO.** And trust me, love, in my eye so do you.
          Dry sorrow drinks our blood.[14] Adieu, adieu!          [*Exit.*]

60   **JULIET.** O Fortune, Fortune! All men call thee fickle.
          If thou art fickle, what dost thou[15] with him
          That is renowned for faith? Be fickle, Fortune,
          For then I hope thou wilt not keep him long
          But send him back.

[*Enter* MOTHER.]

65   **LADY CAPULET.** Ho, daughter! Are you up?

**JULIET.** Who is't that calls? It is my lady mother.
          Is she not down so late,[16] or up so early?
          What unaccustomed cause procures her hither?[17]

**LADY CAPULET.** Why, how now, Juliet?

**JULIET.**                         Madam, I am not well.

70   **LADY CAPULET.** Evermore weeping for your cousin's death?

**11. much in years:** Much older.

**12. discourses:** Conversations.
**13. ill-divining:** Predicting evil.

**14. Dry sorrow . . . blood:** It was once believed that sorrow drained away the blood.
**15. dost thou:** Do you have to do.

**16. Is she . . . late:** Has she stayed up so late?
**17. What . . . hither?:** What unusual reason brings her here?

386   *Drama*

What, wilt thou wash him from his grave with tears?
And if thou couldst, thou couldst not make him live.
Therefore have done. Some grief shows much of love;
But much of grief shows still some want of wit.

75 **JULIET.** Yet let me weep for such a feeling[18] loss.

    18. **feeling:** Deeply felt.

**LADY CAPULET.** So shall you feel the loss, but not the friend
    Which you weep for.

**JULIET.**                Feeling so the loss,
    I cannot choose but ever weep the friend.

**LADY CAPULET.** Well, girl, thou weep'st not so much for his
    death
80   As that the villain lives which slaughtered him.

**JULIET.** What villain, madam?

**35**

**LADY CAPULET.**            That same villain Romeo.

**JULIET.** [*Aside*] Villain and he be many miles asunder.[19]—
    God pardon him! I do, with all my heart;
    And yet no man like he doth grieve my heart.

    19. **asunder:** Apart.

85 **LADY CAPULET.** That is because the traitor murderer lives.

**JULIET.** Ay, madam, from the reach of these my hands.
    Would none but I might venge my cousin's death!

**LADY CAPULET.** We will have vengeance for it, fear thou
    not.
    Then weep no more. I'll send to one in Mantua,
**36** 90   Where that same banished runagate[20] doth live,
    Shall give him such an unaccustomed dram[21]
    That he shall soon keep Tybalt company;
    And then I hope thou wilt be satisfied.

    20. **runagate:** Renegade;
runaway.
    21. **unaccustomed dram:**
Unexpected dose of poison.

**JULIET.** Indeed I never shall be satisfied
**37** 95   With Romeo till I behold him—dead[22]—
    Is my poor heart so for a kinsman vexed.
    Madam, if you could find out but a man
    To bear a poison, I would temper[23] it;
    That Romeo should, upon receipt thereof,
100   Soon sleep in quiet. O, how my heart abhors
    To hear him named and cannot come to him,
    To wreak[24] the love I bore my cousin
    Upon his body that hath slaughtered him!

    22. **dead:** Juliet is deliber-
ately ambiguous here. Her
mother thinks *dead* refers
to Romeo. But Juliet is using the word with the following line, in reference to
her heart.
    23. **temper:** Mix; weaken.
    24. **wreak** (rēek): Avenge;
express.

**LADY CAPULET.** Find thou the means, and I'll find such a
    man.
105   But now I'll tell thee joyful tidings, girl.

*The Tragedy of Romeo and Juliet, Act III, Scene v*   **387**

**35 Literary Focus** Why is an aside an especially effective device when a character says one thing but means another?

**36 Discussion** Why is Lady Capulet so intent on revenge?

**37 Clarification** Have students read this sentence aloud, pausing before the word *dead*, to show what Juliet really means; then read it again, pausing after the word *dead*, to indicate what her mother thinks she is saying.

38 **Discussion** How does this speech reflect the growth in Juliet's character since the beginning of the play?

39 **Clarification** Young girls were expected to obey their parents and to accept their choice of husbands without question.

**JULIET.** And joy comes well in such a needy time.
What are they, beseech your ladyship?

**LADY CAPULET.** Well, well, thou hast a careful[25] father,
child;
One who, to put thee from thy heaviness,
110 Hath sorted out[26] a sudden day of joy
That thou expects not nor I looked not for.

**25. careful:** Considerate.

**26. sorted out:** Selected.

**JULIET.** Madam, in happy time![27] What day is that?

**27. in happy time:** Just in time.

**LADY CAPULET.** Marry, my child, early next Thursday morn
The gallant, young, and noble gentleman,
115 The County Paris, at Saint Peter's Church,
Shall happily make thee there a joyful bride.

38 | 120

**JULIET.** Now by Saint Peter's Church, and Peter too,
He shall not make me there a joyful bride!
I wonder at this haste, that I must wed
Ere he that should be husband comes to woo.
I pray you tell my lord and father, madam,
I will not marry yet; and when I do, I swear
It shall be Romeo, whom you know I hate,
Rather than Paris. These are news indeed!

39 | 125

**LADY CAPULET.** Here comes your father. Tell him so
yourself,
And see how he will take it at your hands.

[*Enter* CAPULET *and* NURSE.]

**CAPULET.** When the sun sets the earth doth drizzle dew,
But for the sunset of my brother's son
It rains downright.
130 How now? A conduit,[28] girl? What, still in tears?
Evermore show'ring? In one little body
Thou counterfeits a bark,[29] a sea, a wind:
For still thy eyes, which I may call the sea,
Do ebb and flow with tears; the bark thy body is,
135 Sailing in this salt flood; the winds, thy sighs,
Who, raging with thy tears and they with them,
Without a sudden calm will overset
Thy tempest-tossèd body. How now, wife?
Have you delivered to her our decree?

**28. conduit:** Water pipe.

**29. bark:** Boat.

**LADY CAPULET.** Ay, sir; but she will none, she gives you
140 thanks.[30]
I would the fool were married to her grave!

**CAPULET.** Soft! Take me with you,[31] take me with you, wife.

**30. she . . . thanks:** She'll have nothing to do with it, thank you.
**31. Soft! Take . . . you:** Wait a minute. Let me understand you.

388 *Drama*

How? Will she none? Doth she not give us thanks?
Is she not proud?[32] Doth she not count her blest,
145 Unworthy as she is, that we have wrought[33]
So worthy a gentleman to be her bride?

**JULIET.** Not proud you have, but thankful that you have.
Proud can I never be of what I hate,
But thankful even for hate that is meant love.

**CAPULET.** How, how, how, how, chopped-logic?[34] What is
150 this?
"Proud"—and "I thank you"—and "I thank you not"—
And yet "not proud"? Mistress minion[35] you,
Thank me no thankings, nor proud me no prouds,
But fettle[36] your fine joints 'gainst Thursday next
155 To go with Paris to Saint Peter's Church,
Or I will drag thee on a hurdle[37] thither.
Out, you greensickness carrion![38] Out, you baggage![39]
You tallow-face![40]

**LADY CAPULET.** Fie, fie! What, are you mad?

**32. proud:** Pleased.
**33. wrought:** Arranged.

**34. chopped-logic:** Contradictory, unsound thought and speech.

**35. Mistress minion:** Miss Uppity.

**36. fettle:** Prepare.
**37. hurdle:** Sled on which prisoners were taken to their execution.
**38. greensickness carrion:** Anemic lump of flesh.
**39. baggage:** Naughty girl.
**40. tallow-face:** Wax-pale face.

**40 Discussion** How is this speech similar to Capulet's outburst at Tybalt at the party? What do both speeches reveal about Capulet?

**41** **Discussion** Ask students to consider how events might have turned out differently if Capulet had been more patient and understanding.

**42** **Discussion** Many analyses of this play mention the rashness of the adolescents, Romeo and Juliet. What does this speech suggest about the rashness of an adult character?

**JULIET.** Good father, I beseech you on my knees,
160   Hear me with patience but to speak a word.

**CAPULET.** Hang thee, young baggage! Disobedient wretch!
   I tell thee what—get thee to church a Thursday
   Or never after look me in the face.
   Speak not, reply not, do not answer me!
165   My fingers itch. Wife, we scarce thought us blest
   That God had lent us but this only child;
   But now I see this one is one too much,
   And that we have a curse in having her.
   Out on her, hilding!⁴¹

41. **hilding:** Worthless person.

**NURSE.**                    God in heaven bless her!
170   You are to blame, my lord, to rate⁴² her so.

42. **rate:** Scold, berate.

**CAPULET.** And why, my Lady Wisdom? Hold your tongue,
   Good Prudence. Smatter with your gossips, go!⁴³

43. **Smatter . . . go:** Go chatter with the other old women.

**NURSE.** I speak no treason.

**CAPULET.**                    O, God-i-god-en!

**NURSE.** May not one speak?

**CAPULET.**                    Peace, you mumbling fool!
175   Utter your gravity⁴⁴ o'er a gossip's bowl,
   For here we need it not.

44. **gravity:** Wisdom.

**LADY CAPULET.**                    You are too hot.

**CAPULET.** God's bread!⁴⁵ It makes me mad.
   Day, night; hour, tide, time; work, play;
   Alone, in company; still my care hath been
180   To have her matched; and having now provided
   A gentleman of noble parentage,
   Of fair demesnes,⁴⁶ youthful, and nobly trained,
   Stuffed, as they say, with honorable parts,⁴⁷
   Proportioned as one's thought would wish a man—
185   And then to have a wretched puling⁴⁸ fool,
   A whining mammet,⁴⁹ in her fortune's tender,⁵⁰
   To answer "I'll not wed, I cannot love;
   I am too young, I pray you pardon me"!
   But, and you will not wed, I'll pardon you!
190   Graze where you will, you shall not house with me.
   Look to't, think on't; I do not use to jest.
   Thursday is near; lay hand on heart, advise:⁵¹
   And you be mine, I'll give you to my friend;
   And you be not, hang, beg, starve, die in the streets,
195   For, by my soul, I'll ne'er acknowledge thee,

45. **God's bread:** By the holy Eucharist!

46. **demesnes:** Property.
47. **parts:** Qualities.
48. **puling:** Whining.
49. **mammet:** Doll.
50. **tender:** When good fortune is offered her.

51. **advise:** Consider.

Nor what is mine shall never do thee good.
Trust to't. Bethink you. I'll not be forsworn.[52]          [*Exit.*]

**JULIET.** Is there no pity sitting in the clouds
That sees into the bottom of my grief?
200    O sweet my mother, cast me not away!
Delay this marriage for a month, a week;
Or if you do not, make the bridal bed
In that dim monument where Tybalt lies.

**LADY CAPULET.** Talk not to me, for I'll not speak a word.
205    Do as thou wilt, for I have done with thee.          [*Exit.*]

**JULIET.** O God!—O nurse, how shall this be prevented?
My husband is on earth, my faith in heaven.[53]
How shall that faith return again to earth
Unless that husband send it me from heaven
210    By leaving earth?[54] Comfort me, counsel me.
Alack, alack, that heaven should practice stratagems[55]
Upon so soft a subject as myself!
What say'st thou? Hast thou not a word of joy?
Some comfort, nurse.

**NURSE.**                    Faith, here it is.
215    Romeo is banished; and all the world to nothing[56]
That he dares ne'er come back to challenge[57] you;
Or if he do, it needs must be by stealth.
Then, since the case so stands as now it doth,
I think it best you married with the County.
220    O, he's a lovely gentleman!
Romeo's a dishclout to him.[58] An eagle, madam,
Hath not so green, so quick, so fair an eye
As Paris hath. Beshrew my very heart,
I think you are happy in this second match,
225    For it excels your first; or if it did not,
Your first is dead—or 'twere as good he were
As living here and you no use of him.

**JULIET.** Speak'st thou from thy heart?

**NURSE.** And from my soul too; else beshrew them both.

230    **JULIET.** Amen!

**NURSE.** What?

**JULIET.** Well, thou hast comforted me marvelous much.
Go in; and tell my lady I am gone,
Having displeased my father, to Lawrence' cell,
235    To make confession and to be absolved.[59]

**52. forsworn:** Made to violate my promise.

**53. my faith in heaven:** My marriage vow is recorded in heaven.

**54. leaving earth:** Dying.
**55. stratagems:** Tricks, plots.

**56. all . . . nothing:** The odds are overwhelming.
**57. challenge:** Claim.

**58. A dishclout to him:** A dishcloth compared with him.

**59. absolved:** Receive forgiveness for my sins.

*The Tragedy of Romeo and Juliet, Act III, Scene v* 391

**43 Discussion** What does the Nurse's change of heart reveal about her approach to life?

**44 Clarification** When Nurse says she speaks from the heart and from the soul or else they are both cursed, Juliet's *"Amen,"* is a curse of the Nurse.

45

**45 Literary Focus** Juliet's final soliloquy is really addressed to the absent Nurse. Why can she no longer confide in the Nurse?

**46 Critical Thinking and Reading** How does her decision not to confide in the Nurse mark a change in her character? How might her reliance on Friar Lawrence affect the plot?

**Reader's Response** Do you think that the Nurse and Friar Lawrence have acted responsibly and appropriately? If so, why? If not, what would you have done differently?

**Closure and Extension**

***ANSWERS TO THINKING ABOUT THE SELECTION***
*Recalling*

1. Romeo controls his anger and tries to make light of the challenge to a duel. Mercutio becomes angry and begins to fight with Tybalt. As Romeo tries to separate them, Tybalt kills Mercutio and runs away. When Tybalt returns, Romeo avenges his friend's death by killing Tybalt. Romeo runs away.

---

**NURSE.** Marry, I will; and this is wisely done.  [*Exit.*]

**JULIET.** Ancient damnation![60] O most wicked fiend!
Is it more sin to wish me thus forsworn,
Or to dispraise my lord with that same tongue
Which she hath praised him with above compare
So many thousand times? Go, counselor!
Thou and my bosom henceforth shall be twain.[61]
I'll to the friar to know his remedy.
If all else fail, myself have power to die.  [*Exit.*]

240

**60. Ancient damnation:** Old devil.

**61. Thou . . . twain:** You will from now on be separated from my trust.

---

## THINKING ABOUT THE SELECTION
### Recalling

1. Trace the sequence of events that begins with Tybalt's insult to Romeo and ends with Tybalt's death and Romeo's banishment.
2. Describe the clashing emotions Juliet feels when the Nurse reports Tybalt's death and Romeo's banishment.
3. How does Romeo respond to the news of his banishment and Juliet's grief?
4. In his long speech to Romeo, Friar Lawrence mentions three things for which Romeo should consider himself fortunate. What are they?
5. What decision concerning Paris and Juliet does Lord Capulet make in Scene iv? Describe Juliet's reaction to this plan.
6. As Romeo and Juliet are about to part, how do they differ in their views of the future? What advice does the Nurse give Juliet at the end of Act III? Describe Juliet's reaction to this advice.

### Interpreting

7. What does Romeo mean when he says, after killing Tybalt, "O, I am fortune's fool!"?

8. Why did Escalus not sentence Romeo to death, in keeping with his speech in Act I?
9. Explain why you think Romeo and Juliet's troubles do or do not result primarily from fate. Support your answer with details from the play.

### Applying

10. Up to this point, the Nurse has acted as a counselor for Juliet. What qualities should a counselor have?

## ANALYZING LITERATURE
### Understanding Dramatic Speeches

A **soliloquy** is a speech in which a character, alone on stage, speaks directly to the audience. An **aside** is a brief remark to the audience, uttered while other characters are nearby but unable to hear. A **monologue** is a lengthy speech addressed to other characters, rather than to the audience.

1. What thoughts and feelings does Juliet reveal in her soliloquy that opens Scene ii?

*392 Drama*

---

The Prince banishes Romeo.
2. At first Juliet believes Romeo is evil and begins to speak against him, although she can only half-curse him. But when the Nurse also attacks Romeo, Juliet defends him, feeling guilty that she had even thought he was villainous. She is upset for both Tybalt and Romeo because one is dead and the other is banished.
3. Romeo is distressed to hear of his banishment. He feels that the death he expected would be bet-

ter than banishment to a city where he cannot see Juliet. When he hears how Juliet feels, he asks the Friar what part of his body holds his name, so he can destroy it, and he tries to stab himself.
4. Friar Lawrence thinks Romeo should feel fortunate because Juliet is alive, he is alive, and he has only been banished—not sentenced to death.
5. Capulet has decided that Paris and Juliet will marry in two days. Juliet's reaction is explosive and

definite. She will not marry Paris.
6. Juliet is pessimistic, Romeo more positive. She is wondering if they will ever see each other again. Romeo assures her that they will and then all their sorrows will be gone. The Nurse advises Juliet to forget Romeo and marry Paris. Juliet reacts by secretly rejecting the Nurse as a confidante.

*Interpreting*

7. Suggested Response: Romeo feels he is a victim of fate.

2. When Lady Capulet, in Scene v, refers to Romeo as a villain, Juliet utters the aside "Villain and he be many miles asunder." In your own words, what is Juliet saying? Why is it important that the audience, but not Lady Capulet, hear this remark?

3. Reread Friar Lawrence's monologue in Scene iii beginning "Hold thy desperate hand." What criticisms is he addressing to Romeo?

## CRITICAL THINKING AND READING
### Inferring Tone in a Monologue

**Tone** in a monologue is the feelings and emotions that accompany the words. When you attend a play, the tone of a speech is conveyed by the voice of the speaker. When you read a play, however, you must infer the tone. When reading Shakespeare, first do your best to understand what the words and sentences mean. Read again Benvolio's monologue in Scene i beginning "Tybalt, here slain, whom Romeo's hand did slay" (lines 151–174). Then answer the following questions:

1. What situation is the speaker in?
2. To whom is he or she speaking?
3. Why is the speaker uttering these words?
4. In view of the answers to these three questions, what feelings and emotions seem appropriate to the monologue?

## UNDERSTANDING LANGUAGE
### Understanding Allusions

An **allusion** is a reference to something in another work of literature, mythology, or history. For example, Juliet alludes to Phoebus Apollo, the sun god in classical mythology, in her soliloquy at the start of Scene ii ("Gallop apace, you fiery-footed steeds,/ Towards Phoebus' lodging!"). An allusion will enrich or reinforce a statement by drawing on the ideas, feelings, or images associated with the reference.

Allusions are plentiful in Shakespeare's plays. To understand and appreciate them, pay attention to the marginal notes that point them out and explain them. Reference books such as an encyclopedia and a dictionary of mythology will also prove helpful.

1. When Juliet alludes to Phoebus Apollo, she is wishing that the sun would set and night would come. How does the allusion enrich the lines in which it occurs?
2. Near the beginning of Scene v, Romeo sees the first light of dawn and says, "I'll say yon gray is not the morning's eye,/ 'Tis but the pale reflex of Cynthia's brow. . . . " Explain the allusion here.

## CRITICAL THINKING AND WRITING
### Writing a Soliloquy

At the end of Act III, Juliet delivers a brief soliloquy. She expresses anger with the Nurse for suggesting that she should forget Romeo and marry Paris. Then she announces that she will go to the Friar to see how he might help her.

Write a brief soliloquy either in prose or blank verse such as Juliet might speak just before she meets with the Friar. First think of the thoughts that might be on her mind. What might she be thinking about all that has happened since she met Romeo? What might be her thoughts of the future? What feelings would her words convey? Try to suggest the personality and emotional state of a thirteen-year-old girl in such a situation. When you revise your soliloquy, check that it is in harmony with the events of the play to this point and with Juliet's character. Read your finished soliloquy to some of your classmates and ask them if it sounds like the kind of speech Juliet might give.

*The Tragedy of Romeo and Juliet, Act III* 393

(Answers begin on p. 392.)

rence thinks that Romeo is acting irrationally and self-destructively.

### ANSWERS TO CRITICAL THINKING AND READING

1. Suggested Response: The speaker has observed the previous action and knows precisely what has happened.
2. Suggested Response: He is recounting the events to the Prince and all others present.
3. Suggested Response: He is serving as a witness, because no one else was there and the facts of the situation need to be explained.
4. Suggested Response: His tone of voice would be sad and agitated, because he was a friend of Mercutio and is close with Romeo. However, he would try to control his emotions in order to give an accurate account.

### ANSWERS TO UNDERSTANDING LANGUAGE

1. Suggested Response: To anyone who knows the allusion, it gives a vivid picture of horses pulling the sun's chariot—or, in the case of Phaëton, of the sun's chariot hurtling out of control.
2. Suggested Response: Neither Romeo nor Juliet wants the dawn to arrive. Romeo tries to deny daylight has come by calling it instead a reflection of moonlight. Cynthia was the moon goddess.

### THINKING AND WRITING
For help with this assignment, students can consult Lesson 19, "Writing a Short Dramatic Sketch," in the Handbook of Writing About Literature.

### Writing Across the Curriculum
You might have students research and report on some aspect of Italian life during the renaissance, the era in which this play is set. Inform the social studies department of this assignment, so that teachers can help students find resource materials.

8. Suggested Response: The Prince was more lenient because Romeo killed a person who had himself killed the Prince's relative.
9. Answers will differ, but many students will conclude that most of the troubles arise from the fact that their families have been feuding; as a result, their love is dangerous and bound to lead to trouble. Tybalt's anger at Romeo and the need to keep the marriage a secret are the result of the feud. Capulet might easily have approved a marriage to Romeo instead of Paris, if there had not been a feud between the families.

### Applying

10. Answers will differ, but many students may feel that a good counselor should be consistent, intelligent, and not afraid to speak his or her mind.

### ANSWERS TO ANALYZING LITERATURE

1. Suggested Response: Juliet is impatient for the night to arrive, so that she can be with her new husband.
2. Suggested Response: Juliet says there is a big difference between Romeo and a villain. It is important that Lady Capulet not hear how she feels but also important that the audience knows that she does not think that Romeo is a villain.
3. Suggested Response: Friar Law-

**Literary Focus** You might point out other examples of dramatic irony. For example, when Tybalt and Romeo fight, they are kinsmen—though Tybalt is unaware of this fact.

**Look For** Lead students to see that their knowing the true state of affairs can have several effects. It can make them feel superior to the characters, and it can also make them feel helpless to change the course of events.

**Writing/Prior Knowledge** Have students discuss some of the pros and cons of this question before they write. Most students will not see the advantage of an arranged marriage.

**Vocabulary** Have your **less advanced** students read the words and their meanings. Then have them write a paragraph using all the words on the list.

## The Tragedy of Romeo and Juliet, Act IV

**Dramatic Irony**

**Dramatic irony** is a device whereby a character's words or actions have one meaning for the character and a quite different meaning for the audience or reader. For example in Act III, Scene iv, Lord Capulet decides to have Juliet wed Paris on Thursday. He does not know what you know—that Juliet is already married. Such dramatic irony is a powerful device. It adds suspense or tension. It involves us emotionally in the action. It can even make us want to step into the world of the play and give the characters a correct understanding of the situation they are in.

**Look For**

As you read Act IV, notice the dramatic irony of those scenes in which the characters speak and act in ignorance of the true state of affairs. How does your knowing the true state of affairs affect your appreciation of the play?

**Writing**

In the past, marriages were often arranged by parents. They still are in many societies today. On one side of a piece of paper, list some of the things that might be said in favor of an arranged marriage. On the other side, list some of the objections to it. You might proceed by asking yourself, "What problems might an arranged marriage eliminate (or create)? What benefits might it bring (or prevent)?"

**Vocabulary**

Knowing the following words will help you as you read Act IV of *Romeo and Juliet.*

**pensive** (pen′ siv) *adj.*: Thinking deeply or seriously (p. 396)

**vial** (vī′ əl) *n.*: A small bottle containing medicine or other liquids (p. 397)

**enjoined** (in joind′) *v.*: Ordered (p. 399)

**dismal** (diz′ m'l) *adj.*: Causing gloom or misery (p. 400)

**loathsome** (lōth′ səm) *adj.*: Disgusting (p. 401)

**pilgrimage** (pil′ grəm ij) *n.*: Long journey (p. 404)

394   *Drama*

# Act IV

**Scene i.** FRIAR LAWRENCE'S *cell.*

[*Enter* FRIAR LAWRENCE *and* COUNTY PARIS.]

    **FRIAR.** On Thursday, sir? The time is very short.

    **PARIS.** My father[1] Capulet will have it so,
      And I am nothing slow to slack his haste.[2]

    **FRIAR.** You say you do not know the lady's mind.
5    Uneven is the course;[3] I like it not.

    **PARIS.** Immoderately she weeps for Tybalt's death,
      And therefore have I little talked of love;
      For Venus smiles not in a house of tears.
      Now, sir, her father counts it dangerous
10   That she do give her sorrow so much sway,
      And in his wisdom hastes our marriage
      To stop the inundation[4] of her tears,
      Which, too much minded[5] by herself alone,
      May be put from her by society.
15   Now do you know the reason of this haste.

    **FRIAR.** [*Aside*] I would I knew not why it should be
      slowed.—
      Look, sir, here comes the lady toward my cell.

[*Enter* JULIET.]

    **PARIS.** Happily met, my lady and my wife!

    **JULIET.** That may be, sir, when I may be a wife.

20 **PARIS.** That "may be" must be, love, on Thursday next.

    **JULIET.** What must be shall be.

    **FRIAR.**                    That's a certain text.[6]

    **PARIS.** Come you to make confession to this father?

    **JULIET.** To answer that, I should confess to you.

    **PARIS.** Do not deny to him that you love me.

25 **JULIET.** I will confess to you that I love him.

    **PARIS.** So will ye, I am sure, that you love me.

    **JULIET.** If I do so, it will be of more price,[7]
      Being spoke behind your back, than to your face.

    **PARIS.** Poor soul, thy face is much abused with tears.

*The Tragedy of Romeo and Juliet, Act IV, Scene i*   395

**1. father:** Future father-in-law.
**2. I . . . haste:** I won't slow him down by being slow myself.
**3. Uneven . . . course:** Irregular is the plan.

**4. inundation:** Flood.
**5. minded:** Thought about.

**6. That's . . . text:** That's a certain truth.

**7. price:** Value.

4 **Reading Strategy** Have students predict what Juliet might do if there is no way to postpone the wedding.

5 **Discussion** How do Juliet's words echo an earlier speech by Romeo?

30 **JULIET.** The tears have got small victory by that,
 For it was bad enough before their spite.[8]

**PARIS.** Thou wrong'st it more than tears with that report.

**JULIET.** That is no slander, sir, which is a truth;
 And what I spake, I spake it to my face.

35 **PARIS.** Thy face is mine, and thou hast sland'red it.

**JULIET.** It may be so, for it is not mine own.
 Are you at leisure, holy father, now,
 Or shall I come to you at evening mass?

**FRIAR.** My leisure serves me, pensive daughter, now.
40  My lord, we must entreat the time alone.[9]

**PARIS.** God shield[10] I should disturb devotion!
 Juliet, on Thursday early will I rouse ye.
 Till then, adieu, and keep this holy kiss.  [*Exit.*]

**JULIET.** O, shut the door, and when thou hast done so,
45  Come weep with me—past hope, past care, past help!

**FRIAR.** O Juliet, I already know thy grief;
 It strains me past the compass of my wits.[11]
 I hear thou must, and nothing may prorogue[12] it,
 On Thursday next be married to this County.

50 **JULIET.** Tell me not, friar, that thou hearest of this,
 Unless thou tell me how I may prevent it.
 If in thy wisdom thou canst give no help,
 Do thou but call my resolution wise
 And with this knife I'll help it presently.[13]
55  God joined my heart and Romeo's, thou our hands;
 And ere this hand, by thee to Romeo's sealed,
 Shall be the label to another deed,[14]
 Or my true heart with treacherous revolt
 Turn to another, this shall slay them both.
60  Therefore, out of thy long-experienced time,
 Give me some present counsel; or, behold,
 'Twixt my extremes and me[15] this bloody knife
 Shall play the umpire, arbitrating[16] that
 Which the commission of thy years and art
65  Could to no issue of true honor bring.[17]
 Be not so long to speak. I long to die
 If what thou speak'st speak not of remedy.

**FRIAR.** Hold, daughter. I do spy a kind of hope,
 Which craves[18] as desperate an execution
70  As that is desperate which we would prevent.

8. **before their spite:** Before the harm that the tears did.

9. **entreat . . . alone:** Ask to have this time to ourselves.
10. **shield:** Forbid.

11. **past . . . wits:** Beyond the ability of my mind to find a remedy.
12. **prorogue:** Delay.

13. **presently:** At once.

14. **Shall . . . deed:** Shall give the seal of approval to another marriage contract.

15. **'Twixt . . . me:** Between my misfortunes and me.
16. **arbitrating:** Deciding.
17. **Which . . . bring:** Which the authority that derives from your age and ability could not solve honorably.
18. **craves:** Requires.

## Commentary: The Role of Friar Lawrence

Discuss with students Friar Lawrence's role in *Romeo and Juliet*. Point out that literary critics see Friar Lawrence in basically two opposing ways: In one view, the Friar is a surrogate father figure to Romeo who aids and counsels him—he is Romeo's confidant. In the other view, the Friar is a well-meaning but incompetent counselor who leads Romeo and Juliet to their deaths.

Critic Edward Dowden is one who regards Friar Lawrence as an interfering, middle-aged busybody. He states in the introduction of the Arden publication of *Romeo and Juliet* that "the amiable critic of life as seen from the cloister does not understand life or hate or love . . . [he is] an actor whose wisdom is of a kind which may easily lead himself and others astray."

Ask students with which view of Friar Lawrence they agree. Is he a middle-aged busybody who knows nothing about life or love, or does he give Romeo good advice? Or does chance and fate determine the deaths of the "star-crossed lovers"? Students should back up their statements with evidence from the play.

Also ask students if they think that Romeo and Juliet would have been better off had they not followed the advice of Friar Lawrence. What other options were open to Romeo and Juliet? Could their deaths have been avoided? How?

If, rather than to marry County Paris,
Thou hast the strength of will to slay thyself,
Then is it likely thou wilt undertake
A thing like death to chide away this shame,
75  That cop'st with death himself to scape from it;[19]
And, if thou darest, I'll give thee remedy.

JULIET. O, bid me leap, rather than marry Paris,
From off the battlements of any tower,
Or walk in thievish ways,[20] or bid me lurk
80  Where serpents are; chain me with roaring bears,
Or hide me nightly in a charnel house,[21]
O'ercovered quite with dead men's rattling bones,
With reeky[22] shanks and yellow chapless[23] skulls;
Or bid me go into a new-made grave
85  And hide me with a dead man in his shroud—
Things that, to hear them told, have made me
    tremble—
And I will do it without fear or doubt,
To live an unstained wife to my sweet love.

FRIAR. Hold, then. Go home, be merry, give consent
90  To marry Paris. Wednesday is tomorrow.
Tomorrow night look that thou lie alone;
Let not the nurse lie with thee in thy chamber.
Take thou this vial, being then in bed,
And this distilling liquor drink thou off;
95  When presently through all thy veins shall run
A cold and drowsy humor;[24] for no pulse
Shall keep his native[25] progress, but surcease:[26]
No warmth, no breath, shall testify thou livest;
The roses in thy lips and cheeks shall fade
100  To wanny ashes,[27] thy eyes' windows[28] fall
Like death when he shuts up the day of life;
Each part, deprived of supple government,[29]
Shall, stiff and stark and cold, appear like death;
And in this borrowed likeness of shrunk death
105  Thou shalt continue two-and-forty hours,
And then awake as from a pleasant sleep.
Now, when the bridegroom in the morning comes
To rouse thee from thy bed, there art thou dead.
Then, as the manner of our country is,
110  In thy best robes uncovered on the bier[30]
Thou shalt be borne to that same ancient vault
Where all the kindred of the Capulets lie.
In the meantime, against[31] thou shalt awake,

19. **That cop'st . . . it:**
That bargains with death
itself to escape from it.

20. **thievish ways:** Roads
where criminals lurk.

21. **charnel house:** Vault
for bones removed from
graves to be reused.
22. **reeky:** Foul-smelling.
23. **chapless:** Jawless.

24. **humor:** Fluid, liquid.
25. **native:** Natural.
26. **surcease:** Stop.

27. **wanny ashes:** To the
color of pale ashes.
28. **eyes' windows:** Eyelids.
29. **supple government:**
Ability for maintaining
motion.

30. **uncovered on the
bier:** Displayed on the
funeral platform.

31. **against:** Before.

*The Tragedy of Romeo and Juliet, Act IV, Scene i*  397

6 **Discussion** Why does Friar Lawrence suggest such a desperate
solution?

7 **Critical Thinking and Reading**
How does this speech reflect a
change in Juliet?

8 **Discussion** Is Friar Lawrence's
plan a good one? Why or why
not?

**Student Activity.** At some point in time we all need to confide in
someone and seek advice and counsel. Imagine that Romeo or
Juliet approaches you with his or her problem. What advice
would you give? In a letter to either Romeo or Juliet, express how
you believe he or she should handle the situation.

**9 Discussion** What kind of a wedding is Capulet planning?

Shall Romeo by my letters know our drift;[32]
115　And hither shall he come; and he and I
Will watch thy waking, and that very night
Shall Romeo bear thee hence to Mantua.
And this shall free thee from this present shame,
If no inconstant toy[33] nor womanish fear
120　Abate thy valor[34] in the acting it.

**JULIET.** Give me, give me! O, tell not me of fear!

**FRIAR.** Hold! Get you gone, be strong and prosperous
In this resolve. I'll send a friar with speed
To Mantua, with my letters to thy lord.

**JULIET.** Love give me strength, and strength shall help
125　　afford.
Farewell, dear father.　　　　　　[*Exit with* FRIAR.]

**Scene ii.** *Hall in* CAPULET's *house.*

[*Enter* FATHER CAPULET, MOTHER, NURSE, *and* SERVINGMEN, *two
or three.*]

**CAPULET.** So many guests invite as here are writ.
　　　　　　　　　　　　[*Exit a* SERVINGMAN.]
Sirrah, go hire me twenty cunning[1] cooks.

**SERVINGMAN.** You shall have none ill, sir; for I'll try[2] if
they can lick their fingers.

5　**CAPULET.** How canst thou try them so?

**SERVINGMAN.** Marry, sir, 'tis an ill cook that cannot lick
his own fingers.[3] Therefore he that cannot lick his
fingers goes not with me.

**CAPULET.** Go, begone.　　　　　　[*Exit* SERVINGMAN.]
10　We shall be much unfurnished[4] for this time.
What, is my daughter gone to Friar Lawrence?

**NURSE.** Ay, forsooth.[5]

**CAPULET.** Well, he may chance to do some good on her.
A peevish self-willed harlotry it is.[6]

[*Enter* JULIET.]

15　**NURSE.** See where she comes from shrift with merry look.

**CAPULET.** How now, my headstrong? Where have you been
gadding?

**32. drift:** Purpose, plan.

**33. inconstant toy:**
Passing whim.
**34. Abate thy valor:**
Lessen your courage.

**1. cunning:** Skillful.
**2. try:** Test.

**3. 'tis . . . fingers:** It's a
bad cook that won't taste
his own cooking.

**4. unfurnished:** Unprepared.

**5. forsooth:** In truth.

**6. A peevish . . .
harlotry:** It is the ill-tempered, selfish behavior of a
woman without good
breeding.

398　*Drama*

**JULIET.** Where I have learnt me to repent the sin
    Of disobedient opposition
20    To you and your behests,[7] and am enjoined
    By holy Lawrence to fall prostrate[8] here
    To beg your pardon. Pardon, I beseech you!
    Henceforward I am ever ruled by you.

**CAPULET.** Send for the County. Go tell him of this.
25    I'll have this knot knit up tomorrow morning.

**JULIET.** I met the youthful lord at Lawrence' cell
    And gave him what becomèd[9] love I might,
    Not stepping o'er the bounds of modesty.

**CAPULET.** Why, I am glad on't. This is well. Stand up.
30    This is as't should be. Let me see the County.
    Ay, marry, go, I say, and fetch him hither.
    Now, afore God, this reverend holy friar,
    All our whole city is much bound[10] to him.

**JULIET.** Nurse, will you go with me into my closet[11]
35    To help me sort such needful ornaments[12]
    As you think fit to furnish me tomorrow?

**LADY CAPULET.** No, not till Thursday. There is time
    enough.

**CAPULET.** Go, nurse, go with her. We'll to church
    tomorrow.        [*Exit* JULIET *and* NURSE.]

**LADY CAPULET.** We shall be short in our provision.[13]
    'Tis now near night.

40 **CAPULET.**          Tush, I will stir about,
    And all things shall be well, I warrant thee, wife.
    Go thou to Juliet, help to deck up her.[14]
    I'll not to bed tonight; let me alone.
    I'll play the housewife for this once. What, ho![15]
45    They are all forth; well, I will walk myself
    To County Paris, to prepare up him
    Against tomorrow. My heart is wondrous light,
    Since this same wayward girl is so reclaimed.
                     [*Exit with* MOTHER.]

**Scene iii.** JULIET's *chamber.*

[*Enter* JULIET *and* NURSE.]

**JULIET.** Ay, those attires are best; but, gentle nurse,
    I pray thee leave me to myself tonight;

*The Tragedy of Romeo and Juliet, Act IV, Scene iii*   **399**

7. **behests:** Requests.

8. **fall prostrate:** Lie face down in humble submission.

9. **becomèd:** Suitable, proper.

10. **bound:** Indebted.

11. **closet:** Private room.
12. **ornaments:** Clothes.

13. **short . . . provision:** Lacking time for preparation.

14. **deck her up:** Dress her; get her ready.

15. **What, ho!:** Capulet is calling for his servants.

**10 Literary Focus** How is Capulet's bustle and activity an example of dramatic irony?

For I have need of many orisons[1]
To move the heavens to smile upon my state,[2]
5   Which, well thou knowest, is cross[3] and full of sin.

**1. orisons:** Prayers.
**2. state:** Condition.
**3. cross:** Selfish, disobedient.

[*Enter* MOTHER.]

**LADY CAPULET.** What are you busy, ho? Need you my help?

**JULIET.** No, madam; we have culled[4] such necessaries
As are behoveful[5] for our state tomorrow.
So please you, let me now be left alone,
10   And let the nurse this night sit up with you;
For I am sure you have your hands full all
In this so sudden business.

**4. culled:** Chosen.
**5. behoveful:** Desirable, appropriate.

**LADY CAPULET.**                    Good night.
Get thee to bed, and rest; for thou hast need.
                              [*Exit* MOTHER *and* NURSE.]

**JULIET.** Farewell! God knows when we shall meet again.
15   I have a faint cold fear thrills through my veins
That almost freezes up the heat of life.
I'll call them back again to comfort me.
Nurse!—What should she do here?
My dismal scene I needs must act alone.
20   Come, vial.
What if this mixture do not work at all?
Shall I be married then tomorrow morning?
No, no! This shall forbid it. Lie thou there.
                              [*Lays down a dagger.*]
What if it be a poison which the friar
25   Subtly hath minist'red[6] to have me dead,
Lest in this marriage he should be dishonored
Because he married me before to Romeo?
I fear it is; and yet methinks it should not,
For he hath still been tried[7] a holy man.
30   How if, when I am laid into the tomb,
I wake before the time that Romeo
Come to redeem me? There's a fearful point!
Shall I not then be stifled in the vault,
**11**   To whose foul mouth no healthsome air breathes in,
35   And there die strangled ere my Romeo comes?
Or, if I live, is it not very like
The horrible conceit[8] of death and night,
Together with the terror of the place—
As in a vault, an ancient receptacle
40   Where for this many hundred years the bones

**6. minist'red:** Given me.

**7. tried:** Proved.

**8. conceit:** Idea, thought.

**12 Discussion** is Juliet's drinking of the potion foolhardy or courageous? Explain.

**13 Literary Focus** Point out to students that this scene is a powerful example of dramatic irony. The excitement of the household and the humor between Capulet and his wife contrast sharply with the desperation of the true situation.

Of all my buried ancestors are packed;
Where bloody Tybalt, yet but green in earth,[9]
Lies fest'ring in his shroud; where, as they say,
At some hours in the night spirits resort—
45   Alack, alack, is it not like[10] that I,
So early waking—what with loathsome smells,
And shrieks like mandrakes[11] torn out of the earth,
That living mortals, hearing them, run mad—
O, if I wake, shall I not be distraught,[12]
50   Environèd[13] with all these hideous fears,
And madly play with my forefathers' joints,
And pluck the mangled Tybalt from his shroud,
And, in this rage, with some great kinsman's bone
As with a club dash out my desp'rate brains?
55   O, look! Methinks I see my cousin's ghost
Seeking out Romeo, that did spit his body
Upon a rapier's point. Stay, Tybalt, stay!
Romeo, Romeo, Romeo, I drink to thee.
    [*She falls upon her bed within the curtains.*]

**9. green in earth:** Newly entombed.

**10. like:** Likely.

**11. mandrakes:** Plants with forked roots that resemble human legs. The mandrake was believed to shriek when uprooted and cause the hearer to go mad.
**12. distraught:** Insane.
**13. Environèd:** Surrounded.

**Scene iv.** *Hall in* CAPULET's *house.*

[*Enter* LADY OF THE HOUSE *and* NURSE.]

    **LADY CAPULET.** Hold, take these keys and fetch more
      spices, nurse.

*The Tragedy of Romeo and Juliet, Act IV, Scene iv*   401

**NURSE.** They call for dates and quinces[1] in the pastry.[2]

[*Enter old* CAPULET.]

5
**CAPULET.** Come, stir, stir, stir! The second cock hath
    crowed,
The curfew bell hath rung, 'tis three o'clock.
Look to the baked meats, good Angelica;[3]
Spare not for cost.

**NURSE.**               Go, you cotquean,[4] go,
Get you to bed! Faith, you'll be sick tomorrow
For this night's watching.[5]

10 **CAPULET.** No, not a whit. What, I have watched ere now
All night for lesser cause, and ne'er been sick.

**LADY CAPULET.** Ay, you have been a mouse hunt[6] in your
    time;
But I will watch you from such watching now.
                 [*Exit* LADY *and* NURSE.]

**CAPULET.** A jealous hood,[7] a jealous hood!

[*Enter three or four* FELLOWS *with spits and logs and baskets.*]

                 Now, fellow,
15 What is there?

**FIRST FELLOW.** Things for the cook, sir; but I know not
    what.

**CAPULET.** Make haste, make haste.     [*Exit first* FELLOW.]
Sirrah, fetch drier logs.
Call Peter; he will show thee where they are.

20 **SECOND FELLOW.** I have a head, sir, that will find out logs
And never trouble Peter for the matter.

**CAPULET.** Mass,[8] and well said; a merry whoreson, ha!
Thou shalt be loggerhead.[9] [*Exit second* FELLOW, *with
    the others.*] Good faith, 'tis day.
The County will be here with music straight,
For so he said he would.           [*Play music.*]
25                 I hear him near.
Nurse! Wife! What, ho! What, nurse, I say!

[*Enter* NURSE.]

Go waken Juliet; go and trim her up.
I'll go and chat with Paris. Hie, make haste,
Make haste! The bridegroom he is come already:
30 Make haste, I say.             [*Exit.*]

---

**1. quinces:** Golden, apple-shaped fruit.
**2. pastry:** Baking room.

**3. Angelica:** This is probably the Nurse's name.

**4. cotquean** (kät′ kwēn): Man who does housework.
**5. watching:** Staying awake.

**6. mouse hunt:** Woman chaser.

**7. jealous hood:** Jealousy.

**8. Mass:** By the Mass (an oath).
**9. loggerhead:** Blockhead.

***Scene v.*** JULIET'S *chamber.*

**NURSE.** Mistress! What, mistress! Juliet! Fast,[1] I warrant
    her, she.
Why, lamb! Why, lady! Fie, you slugabed.[2]
Why, love, I say! Madam; Sweetheart! Why, bride!
What, not a word? You take your pennyworths now;
5  Sleep for a week; for the next night, I warrant,
The County Paris hath set up his rest
That you shall rest but little. God forgive me!
Marry, and amen. How sound is she asleep!
I needs must wake her. Madam, madam, madam!
10  Ay, let the County take you in your bed;
He'll fright you up, i' faith. Will it not be?
I needs must wake her. Madam, madam, madam!
               [*Draws aside the curtains.*]
What, dressed, and in your clothes, and down again?[3]
I must needs wake you. Lady! Lady! Lady!
15  Alas, alas! Help, help! My lady's dead!
O weraday that ever I was born!
Some *aqua vitae*, ho! My lord! My lady!

[*Enter* MOTHER.]

**LADY CAPULET.** What noise is here?

**NURSE.**                     O lamentable day!

**LADY CAPULET.** What is the matter?

**NURSE.**                Look, look! O heavy day!

20 **LADY CAPULET.** O me, O me! My child, my only life!
Revive, look up, or I will die with thee!
Help, help! Call help.

[*Enter* FATHER.]

**CAPULET.** For shame, bring Juliet forth; her lord is come.

**NURSE.** She's dead, deceased; she's dead, alack the day!

**LADY CAPULET.** Alack the day, she's dead, she's dead, she's
25  dead!

**CAPULET.** Ha! Let me see her. Out alas! She's cold,
Her blood is settled, and her joints are stiff;
Life and these lips have long been separated.
Death lies on her like an untimely frost
30  Upon the sweetest flower of all the field.

**NURSE.** O lamentable day!

*The Tragedy of Romeo and Juliet, Act IV, Scene v*   403

**1. Fast:** Fast asleep.

**2. slugabed:** Sleepy head.

**3. down again:** Back in bed.

**14 Critical Thinking and Reading**
Contrast the ways in which Lady Capulet and her husband verify that Juliet is dead.

15 **Literary Focus** What makes Friar Lawrence's question so ironic?

16 **Critical Thinking and Reading** Have students compare and contrast these speeches of lament.

**LADY CAPULET.**                    O woeful time!

**CAPULET.** Death, that hath ta'en her hence to make me wail,
Ties up my tongue and will not let me speak.

[*Enter* FRIAR LAWRENCE *and the* COUNTY PARIS, *with Musicians.*]

15     **FRIAR.** Come, is the bride ready to go to church?

35 **CAPULET.** Ready to go, but never to return.
    O son, the night before thy wedding day
    Hath Death lain with thy wife. There she lies,
    Flower as she was, deflowerèd by him.
    Death is my son-in-law, Death is my heir;
40     My daughter he hath wedded. I will die
    And leave him all. Life, living, all is Death's.

**PARIS.** Have I thought, love, to see this morning's face,
    And doth it give me such a sight as this?

**LADY CAPULET.** Accursed, unhappy, wretched, hateful day!
45     Most miserable hour that e'er time saw
    In lasting labor of his pilgrimage!
    But one, poor one, one poor and loving child,
    But one thing to rejoice and solace[4] in,
    And cruel Death hath catched it from my sight.

50 **NURSE.** O woe! O woeful, woeful, woeful day!
    Most lamentable day, most woeful day
    That ever ever I did yet behold!
    O day, O day, O day! O hateful day!
    Never was seen so black a day as this.
55     O woeful day! O woeful day!

**PARIS.** Beguiled,[5] divorcèd, wrongèd, spited, slain!
    Most detestable Death, by thee beguiled,
    By cruel, cruel thee quite overthrown.
    O love! O life!—not life, but love in death!

60 **CAPULET.** Despised, distressèd, hated, martyred, killed!
    Uncomfortable[6] time, why cam'st thou now
    To murder, murder our solemnity?[7]
    O child, O child! My soul, and not my child!
    Dead art thou—alack, my child is dead,
65     And with my child my joys are burièd!

**FRIAR.** Peace, ho, for shame! Confusion's cure lives not
    In these confusions.[8] Heaven and yourself

**4. solace:** Find comfort.

**5. Beguiled:** Cheated.

**6. Uncomfortable:** Painful, upsetting.
**7. solemnity:** Solemn rites.

**8. Confusion's . . . confusions:** The remedy for this calamity is not to be found in these outcries.

## Grammar in Action

**Apostrophes** are used with nouns to show possession, or ownership. To form the possessive of most singular nouns, add an apostrophe and -s. To form the possessive of plural nouns ending in -s or -es, add an apostrophe.

    Possessive, singular:   *Martin's* garage, my best *friend's* car
    Possessive, plural:   *teachers'* grading scales, *boys'* teams

Apostrophes also show where a letter is left out in a contraction.

Contractions:   can't (cannot), we'd (we would)

    Shakespeare uses the apostrophe both to show ownership and to show where letters are left out. Because of the poetic form of *Romeo and Juliet*, he uses contractions often. Many of the contractions are uncommon in modern English. The following lines illustrate his use of apostrophes:

    Death, that hath *ta'en* her hence to make me wail . . . .
    Life, living, all is *Death's*
    Most miserable hour that *e'er* time saw . . . .

Had part in this fair maid—now heaven hath all,
And all the better is it for the maid.

70 Your part in her you could not keep from death,
But heaven keeps his part in eternal life.
The most you sought was her promotion,
For 'twas your heaven she should be advanced;
And weep ye now, seeing she is advanced

75 Above the clouds, as high as heaven itself?
O, in this love, you love your child so ill
That you run mad, seeing that she is well.[9]
She's not well married that lives married long,
But she's best married that dies married young.

80 Dry up your tears and stick your rosemary[10]
On this fair corse, and, as the custom is,
And in her best array bear her to church;
For though fond nature[11] bids us all lament,
Yet nature's tears are reason's merriment.[12]

85 **CAPULET.** All things that we ordainèd festival[13]
Turn from their office to black funeral—
Our instruments to melancholy bells,
Our wedding cheer to a sad burial feast;
Our solemn hymns to sullen dirges[14] change;

90 Our bridal flowers serve for a buried corse;
And all things change them to the contrary.

**FRIAR.** Sir, go you in; and, madam, go with him;
And go, Sir Paris. Everyone prepare
To follow this fair corse unto her grave.

95 The heavens do low'r[15] upon you for some ill;
Move them no more by crossing their high will.

[*Exit, casting rosemary on her and shutting the curtains.
The* NURSE *and* MUSICIANS *remain.*]

**FIRST MUSICIAN.** Faith, we may put up our pipes and be
gone.

**NURSE.** Honest good fellows, ah, put up, put up!
For well you know this is a pitiful case.[16]            [*Exit.*]

100 **FIRST MUSICIAN.** Ay, by my troth, the case may be
amended.

[*Enter* PETER.]

**PETER.** Musicians, O, musicians, "Heart's ease," "Heart's
ease"! O, and you will have me live, play "Heart's ease."

*The Tragedy of Romeo and Juliet, Act IV, Scene v*   405

**9. well:** Blessed in heaven.

**10. rosemary:** An evergreen signifying love and remembrance.

**11. fond nature:** Mistake-prone human nature.
**12. Yet . . . merriment:** While human nature causes us to weep for Juliet, reason should cause us to be happy (since she is in heaven).
**13. ordainèd festival:** Planned to be part of a celebration.
**14. dirges:** Funeral hymns.

**15. low'r:** Frown.

**16. case:** Situation; instrument case.

**17 Discussion** What knowledge might help Friar Lawrence offer this consolation?

**18 Reading Strategy** Have students predict whether Friar Lawrence's plan will succeed.

For 'twas your heaven she should be advanced. . . .
The heavens do *low'r* upon you for some ill. . . .
Musicians, O, musicians, *"Heart's* ease," *"Heart's* ease"!

Two instances above show possession: *Death's* and *Heart's.* The others are all contractions, which Shakespeare used to make his verse run smoothly.

**Student Activity 1.** Study each of the contractions in the illustration above. Decide which letter or letters each apostrophe represents.

**Student Activity 2.** Write a series of sentences in which you use both possessive nouns and contractions. Be sure to put apostrophes in the right places.

19 **Discussion** Why do you think Shakespeare ends this act with a comic scene?

**Reader's Response** To what lengths would you go for a loved one? Explain.

**FIRST MUSICIAN.** Why "Heart's ease"?

**PETER.** O, musicians, because my heart itself plays "My
105 heart is full." O, play me some merry dump[17] to comfort
me.

**FIRST MUSICIAN.** Not a dump we! 'Tis no time to play now.

**PETER.** You will not then?

**FIRST MUSICIAN.** No.

**PETER.** I will then give it you soundly.

110 **FIRST MUSICIAN.** What will you give us?

**PETER.** No money, on my faith, but the gleek.[18] I will give
you[19] the minstrel.[20]

**FIRST MUSICIAN.** Then will I give you the serving-creature.

**PETER.** Then will I lay the serving-creature's dagger on
115 your pate. I will carry no crotchets.[21] I'll *re* you, I'll *fa*
you. Do you note me?

**FIRST MUSICIAN.** And you *re* us and *fa* us, you note us.

**SECOND MUSICIAN.** Pray you put up your dagger, and put
out your wit. Then have at you with my wit!

120 **PETER.** I will dry-beat you with an iron wit, and put up my
iron dagger. Answer me like men.

"When griping grief the heart doth wound,
And doleful dumps the mind oppress,
Then music with her silver sound"—

125 Why "silver sound"? Why "music with her silver
sound"? What say you, Simon Catling?

**FIRST MUSICIAN.** Marry, sir, because silver hath a sweet
sound.

**PETER.** Pretty! What say you, Hugh Rebeck?

130 **SECOND MUSICIAN.** I say "silver sound" because musicians
sound for silver.

**PETER.** Pretty too! What say you, James Soundpost?

**THIRD MUSICIAN.** Faith, I know not what to say.

**PETER.** O, I cry you mercy,[22] you are the singer. I will say
135 for you. It is "music with her silver sound" because musicians have no gold for sounding.

**17. dump:** Sad tune.

**18. gleek:** Scornful speech.
**19. give you:** Call you.
**20. minstrel:** A contemptuous term (as opposed to *musician*).

**21. crotchets:** Whims; quarter notes.

**22. cry you mercy:** Beg your pardon.

406 *Drama*

## Closure and Extension

### ANSWERS TO THINKING ABOUT THE SELECTION
*Recalling*

1. Friar Lawrence will give her a potion to make her fall into a coma for forty-two hours. She will be placed in the tomb. Friar Lawrence will call Romeo and they will be in the tomb when she wakes. Romeo will then take her back to Mantua.

2. Instead of preparing for a small wedding, he plans a large celebration.

3. The potion may not work; it may kill her; she may wake up before Romeo comes.

4. Everyone is happy, busy, full of good humor, and ready to meet the bridegroom.

"Then music with her silver sound
With speedy help doth lend redress." [*Exit.*]

**FIRST MUSICIAN.** What a pestilent knave is this same!

140 **SECOND MUSICIAN.** Hang him, Jack! Come, we'll in here,
tarry for the mourners, and stay dinner.

[*Exit with others.*]

## THINKING ABOUT THE SELECTION

### Recalling

1. Describe Friar Lawrence's plan for Juliet.
2. In Scene ii, what change does Capulet make in the wedding plans?
3. What three fears rise up in Juliet just before she drinks the potion?
4. Describe the atmosphere in Capulet's house in Scene iv.

### Interpreting

5. How has Juliet's character developed since the start of the play?
6. Describe Friar Lawrence's character. Why do you think he concocts his plan rather than tell the Capulets of Romeo and Juliet's marriage?

### Applying

7. Compare and contrast marriage in the society that Romeo and Juliet belonged to and marriage in contemporary society.

## ANALYZING LITERATURE

### Understanding Dramatic Irony

**Dramatic irony** is a device whereby an audience's understanding of a character's words or actions is quite different from the character's understanding. The audience's special knowledge enables it to view the characters with superior understanding.

1. How is Juliet's meeting with Paris in Friar Lawrence's cell an example of dramatic irony?
2. Review Scene iv, in which Capulet is preparing for Juliet's wedding to Paris. What makes this scene an example of dramatic irony?
3. Find at least one other example of dramatic irony in the first four acts.

## CRITICAL THINKING AND READING

### Predicting Outcomes

To predict a story's outcome you need to be alert to **foreshadowings**—the hints and preparations for later events. In *Romeo and Juliet,* foreshadowings appear from the very start. In the Prologue to Act I, for example, Romeo and Juliet are described as "star-crossed," their love as "death-marked."

1. What foreshadowings are present in Act IV?
2. Find two other examples of foreshadowing in the first four acts.

## THINKING AND WRITING

### Writing an Ending for the Play

If you were to write your own ending to *Romeo and Juliet,* what would it be? Write a narrative of the events that would occur in your version of Act V. First answer such questions as these: Will Romeo and Juliet live and be reunited? Or will one, or both, die? What events will lead up to and bring about the happy (or tragic) ending? What will be the settings of these events? When you revise the narrative, make sure that it develops naturally out of Acts I–IV.

Then ask some classmates if your ending is convincing.

*The Tragedy of Romeo and Juliet, Act IV* 407

*ANSWERS TO ANALYZING LITERATURE*

1. Suggested Response: When Juliet goes to Friar Lawrence for help in avoiding a marriage with Paris, she finds him there arranging for the ceremony.
2. Suggested Response: The entire household is busy and in good humor, getting ready for a large and happy wedding. They do not know, as the audience does, that Juliet has taken the drug and that the wedding will turn into a funeral.
3. Answers will differ. One possibility is the scene at the beginning of Act II, when Romeo goes to the orchard to be near Juliet and Mercutio teases him by talking about Rosaline.

*ANSWERS TO CRITICAL THINKING AND READING*

1. Answers will differ, but some possibilities are: Juliet's fears concerning Friar Lawrence's plan may foreshadow real difficulties; the lament over Juliet's supposed death may hint at her real death at the end of the play.
2. Answers will differ, but two possibilities from Act I are: Tybalt's promise that he will challenge Romeo, and the fears that Romeo and Juliet express when they learn each other's identities.

*THINKING AND WRITING*

For help with this assignment, students can refer to Lesson 19, "Writing a Short Dramatic Sketch," in the Handbook of Writing About Literature.

**Publishing Student Writing**

Have volunteers present their endings to the class.

**Writing Across the Curriculum**

You might have students research and report on the biology of hibernation—this would be the closest modern analogue to Friar Lawrence's potion. Consider informing the science department of this assignment, so that teachers can refer students to appropriate books and articles.

*Interpreting*

5. Suggested Response: Juliet has developed a more mature and serious outlook. She is no longer a little girl, but a woman in love and determined not to be married to someone other than Romeo.

6. Suggested Response: Friar Lawrence is well-meaning but unrealistic and perhaps in a way as rash as the young couple. He hopes to unite the families through the marriage of Romeo and Juliet, but he does not foresee the difficulties. He might concoct his plan to have Juliet drink the potion because he is afraid of revealing the marriage and his part in it.

*Applying*

7. Answers will differ, but most students will realize that today marriages are no longer arranged and people tend to marry when they are older. As in the time of Romeo and Juliet, however, we often celebrate marriages with religious rituals and feasts.

**Challenge** Romeo does not appear in this act. Have students plan a scene set in Mantua. This outline or plan should indicate how Romeo is spending his time and what he is thinking and feeling.

## Focus

**Literary Focus** You may want to ask students to consider, as they read the final act, what distinguishes a tragedy from a story that is merely sad. For example, what are the differences between this tragedy and a newspaper story about a fire or an automobile crash?

**Look For** Some critics feel Romeo was not noble enough or did not suffer enough to be a tragic hero. You might want to ask students to compare and contrast the nobility and suffering of Romeo and Juliet.

**Writing/Prior Knowledge** You might list the headings on the chalkboard and add the details as a class activity, discussing which elements belong under which headings as students suggest them.

**Vocabulary** Have your **less advanced** students study the words carefully. Then have them look up synonyms for each word in a thesaurus.

## The Tragedy of Romeo and Juliet, Act V

**Tragedy and Theme**

A **tragedy** is a drama in which the central character meets with disaster or great misfortune. In the great tragedies of the past, including Shakespeare's, the central character's downfall is usually the result of fate or a serious character flaw or a combination of the two. Other causes, however, may also be involved. Though flawed, the tragic hero or heroine is usually of noble stature and basically good. The downfall, therefore, always seems worse than what the character deserves. Yet a great tragedy is not depressing. It uplifts the audience by showing what greatness of spirit human beings are capable of.

A **theme** is the central idea or insight about life revealed in a work of literature. In a tragedy, the theme will concern the downfall of the hero or heroine—or both, as in *Romeo and Juliet*. It will be an idea or insight that explains why the central character suffers a downfall.

**Look For**

George Orwell wrote: "A tragic situation exists precisely when virtue does *not* triumph but when it is still felt that man is nobler than the forces which destroy him." As you read the last act of this play, look for the way the fates of Romeo and Juliet are worked out. How do they prove to be nobler than the forces that bring about their downfall?

**Writing**

Divide a paper into three columns headed as follows:

CHARACTER TRAITS
FATE/CHANCE
OTHER CAUSES AND CIRCUMSTANCES

In the appropriate column, briefly note the character traits, examples of fate and chance, and any other causes and circumstances that you feel have been operating in the lives of Romeo and Juliet.

**Vocabulary**

Knowing the following words will help you as you read Act V of *Romeo and Juliet*.

**remnants** (rem′ nənts) *n.*: Remaining persons or things (p. 410)

**penury** (pen′ yə rē) *n.*: Extreme poverty (p. 410)

**haughty** (hôt′ ē) *adj.*: Arrogant (p. 414)

**sepulcher** (sep′ əl kər) *n.*: Tomb (p. 417)

**ambiguities** (am′ bə gyōō′ ə tēz) *n.*: Statements or events whose meanings are unclear (p. 420)

**scourge** (skʉrj) *n.*: Whip or other instrument for inflicting punishment (p. 422)

### Objectives

1 To understand tragedy and theme
2 To interpret metaphorical language
3 To respond to literary criticism

## Support Material

**Teaching Portfolio**
Teacher Backup, p. 417
Grammar in Action Worksheet, *Using Nouns of Direct Address,* p. 420
Usage and Mechanics Worksheet, p. 422
Vocabulary Check, p. 423
Critical Thinking and Reading Worksheet, *Interpreting Metaphorical Language,* p. 424

Language Worksheet, *Using the Context to Find the Meaning,* p. 425
Selection Test, p. 426

# Act V

**Scene i.** *Mantua. A street.*

[*Enter* ROMEO.]

> **ROMEO.** If I may trust the flattering truth of sleep,[1]
> My dreams presage[2] some joyful news at hand.
> My bosom's lord[3] sits lightly in his throne,
> And all this day an unaccustomed spirit
> 5  Lifts me above the ground with cheerful thoughts.
> I dreamt my lady came and found me dead
> (Strange dream that gives a dead man leave to think!)
> And breathed such life with kisses in my lips
> That I revived and was an emperor.
> 10  Ah me! How sweet is love itself possessed,
> When but love's shadows[4] are so rich in joy!

[*Enter* ROMEO'S MAN, BALTHASAR, *booted.*]

> News from Verona! How now, Balthasar?
> Dost thou not bring me letters from the friar?
> How doth my lady? Is my father well?
> 15  How fares my Juliet? That I ask again,
> For nothing can be ill if she be well.

> **MAN.** Then she is well, and nothing can be ill.
> Her body sleeps in Capels' monument,[5]
> And her immortal part with angels lives.
> 20  I saw her laid low in her kindred's vault
> And presently took post[6] to tell it you.
> O, pardon me for bringing these ill news,
> Since you did leave it for my office,[7] sir.

> **ROMEO.** Is it e'en so? Then I defy you, stars!
> 25  Thou knowest my lodging. Get me ink and paper
> And hire post horses. I will hence tonight.

> **MAN.** I do beseech you, sir, have patience.
> Your looks are pale and wild and do import
> Some misadventure.[8]

> **ROMEO.**                    Tush, thou art deceived.
> 30  Leave me and do the thing I bid thee do.
> Hast thou no letters to me from the friar?

> **MAN.** No, my good lord.

> **ROMEO.**                No matter. Get thee gone.
> And hire those horses. I'll be with thee straight.

[*Exit* BALTHASAR.]

*The Tragedy of Romeo and Juliet, Act V, Scene i* 409

---

**1. flattering . . . sleep:** Pleasing illusions of dreams.

**2. presage:** Foretell.

**3. bosom's lord:** Heart.

**4. shadows:** Dreams; unreal images.

**5. Capels' monument:** The Capulets' burial vault.

**6. presently took post:** Immediately set out on horseback.

**7. office:** Duty.

**8. import/Some misadventure:** Suggest some misfortune.

---

**4 Discussion** What is Romeo about to do? How is this in keeping with his nature?

**5 Discussion** Have students explain why he picked this particular apothecary.

**6 Discussion** Why does the apothecary not wish to sell the poison? What argument does Romeo use to convince him?

**Enrichment** Point out to students that early in his career, Shakespeare developed his acting talents, working for perhaps more than one theater company at a time. His shift from acting to writing may have been because of the outbreak of the plague in 1592. The plague—which also lurks in Verona in *Romeo and Juliet*—almost entirely closed all of London's theaters and forced actors to find other employment. Some of London's theaters remained open for a few performances each week.

---

**4**

35　Well, Juliet, I will lie with thee tonight.<br>
Let's see for means. O mischief, thou art swift<br>
To enter in the thoughts of desperate men!<br>
I do remember an apothecary,[9]<br>
And hereabouts 'a dwells, which late I noted<br>
In tatt'red weeds, with overwhelming brows,<br>
40　Culling of simples.[10] Meager were his looks,<br>
Sharp misery had worn him to the bones;<br>
And in his needy shop a tortoise hung,<br>
An alligator stuffed, and other skins<br>
Of ill-shaped fishes; and about his shelves<br>
45　A beggarly account[11] of empty boxes,<br>
Green earthen pots, bladders, and musty seeds,<br>
Remnants of packthread, and old cakes of roses[12]<br>
Were thinly scattered, to make up a show.<br>
Noting this penury, to myself I said,<br>
50　"And if a man did need a poison now<br>
Whose sale is present death in Mantua,<br>
Here lives a caitiff[13] wretch would sell it him."

**5**

O, this same thought did but forerun my need,<br>
And this same needy man must sell it me.<br>
55　As I remember, this should be the house.<br>
Being holiday, the beggar's shop is shut.<br>
What, ho! Apothecary!

[*Enter* APOTHECARY.]

**APOTHECARY.**　　　　Who calls so loud?

**ROMEO.** Come hither, man. I see that thou art poor.<br>
Hold, there is forty ducats.[14] Let me have<br>
60　A dram of poison, such soon-speeding gear[15]<br>
As will disperse itself through all the veins<br>
That the life-weary taker may fall dead,<br>
And that the trunk[16] may be discharged of breath<br>
As violently as hasty powder fired<br>
65　Doth hurry from the fatal cannon's womb.

**APOTHECARY.** Such mortal drugs I have; but Mantua's law<br>
Is death to any he that utters[17] them.

**ROMEO.** Art thou so bare and full of wretchedness<br>
And fearest to die? Famine is in thy cheeks,<br>
**6**　70　Need and oppression starveth in thy eyes,<br>
Contempt and beggary hangs upon thy back:<br>
The world is not thy friend, nor the world's law;<br>
The world affords no law to make thee rich;<br>
Then be not poor, but break it and take this.

**9. apothecary:** One who prepares and sells drugs and medicines.

**10. In tatt'red . . . simples:** In torn clothing, with overhanging eyebrows, sorting out herbs.

**11. beggarly account:** Small number.

**12. cakes of roses:** Pressed rose petals (used for perfume).

**13. caitiff:** Miserable.

**14. ducats:** Gold coins.

**15. soon-speeding gear:** Fast-working stuff.

**16. trunk:** Body.

**17. utters:** Sells.

410　*Drama*

---

## Primary Source

Tell students that playing a part in one of Shakespeare's plays can present some problems for the actor. One problem for Laurence Olivier (1907–1989)—a well-known stage and screen actor—was in delivering Shakespeare's lines in verse. Olivier wrote in his autobiography, *Laurence Olivier On Acting,* that it was always his intention to modernize Shakespeare's language—in other words, deemphasize the verse. Critics, however, attacked Olivier, claiming that he could not speak the verse.

Olivier did not buckle under the critics' reviews and stuck to his "modern" speech, always hoping, however, the critics would soon accept him.

In his autobiography, Olivier wrote the following about the production of *Romeo and Juliet* he did with John Gielgud—also a well-known stage and screen actor.

It's very easy, looking back, to criticize, but in those days there was a way of doing things. That was how they were done, and that was what the public came to see. They wanted their verse spoken beautifully, and if that was not how you delivered it, you were considered an upstart, an outsider. . . .

**75 APOTHECARY.** My poverty but not my will consents.

**ROMEO.** I pay thy poverty and not thy will.

**APOTHECARY.** Put this in any liquid thing you will
And drink it off, and if you had the strength
Of twenty men, it would dispatch you straight.

**80 ROMEO.** There is thy gold—worse poison to men's souls,
Doing more murder in this loathsome world,
Than these poor compounds[18] that thou mayst not sell.
I sell thee poison; thou hast sold me none.
Farewell. Buy food and get thyself in flesh.
85 Come, cordial[19] and not poison, go with me
To Juliet's grave; for there must I use thee.          [*Exit.*]

**18. compounds:**
Mixtures.

**19. cordial:** Health-giving
drink.

*Scene ii.* FRIAR LAWRENCE's *cell.*

[*Enter* FRIAR JOHN *to* FRIAR LAWRENCE.]

**JOHN.** Holy Franciscan friar, brother, ho!

[*Enter* FRIAR LAWRENCE.]

**LAWRENCE.** This same should be the voice of Friar John.
Welcome from Mantua. What says Romeo?
Or, if his mind be writ, give me his letter.

**JOHN.** Going to find a barefoot brother out,
5     One of our order, to associate[1] me
Here in this city visiting the sick,
And finding him, the searchers[2] of the town,
Suspecting that we both were in a house
Where the infectious pestilence did reign,
10    Sealed up the doors, and would not let us forth,
So that my speed to Mantua there was stayed.

**LAWRENCE.** Who bare my letter, then, to Romeo?

**JOHN.** I could not send it—here it is again—
Nor get a messenger to bring it thee,
15    So fearful were they of infection.

**LAWRENCE.** Unhappy fortune! By my brotherhood,
The letter was not nice,[3] but full of charge,
Of dear import;[4] and the neglecting it
May do much danger. Friar John, go hence,
20    Get me an iron crow and bring it straight
Unto my cell.

**JOHN.**          Brother, I'll go and bring it thee.     [*Exit.*]

**1. associate:** Accompany.

**2. searchers:** Health officers who search for victims of the plague.

**3. nice:** Trivial.
**4. full of charge, Of dear import:** Urgent and important.

*The Tragedy of Romeo and Juliet, Act V, Scene ii   411*

**7 Literary Focus** There are many unfortunate coincidences in this act that could change the end of the play. As students read, have them keep track of these mischances.

**8 Clarification** Bubonic plague was a feared disease. In the Middle Ages, it had killed millions of people in Europe. By Shakespeare's time, people still had not realized that the plague was transmitted from rats to humans by fleas. In a misguided attempt to prevent the spread of the disease, houses and whole towns were closed off or quarantined. The quarantine of humans, of course, did not hinder the movement of rats and fleas!

[John Gielgud's] voice, of course was musical enough to sell his performance to the people on the old grounds. He was giving the familiar tradition fresh life, whereas I was completely disregarding the old in favor of something new. . . . By the time we did Romeo, I was considered by the Establishment to be his opponent. Everybody was in his favor, while I might have been from another planet. I can still remember some of the awful headlines. You always do, don't you? The good ones dance through your head and are forgotten in a day; the bad ones become indelibly stamped forever. Here's one from the *Evening News*: "A beautiful Juliet but . . ." Another said, "Mr. Olivier can play many parts; Romeo is not one of them. His blank verse is the blankest I've ever heard."

I made a terrible flop as Romeo because they said I couldn't speak verse. . . .

**Student Activity.** In small groups, select a scene in Act V to perform for the class. Half of the groups should modernize the verse; the other half should read the lines in verse as written. Perform your scenes for your classmates. Then, as a class compare and contrast the performances. What difficulties did each way present? What are the pros and cons of each way?

9 **Discussion** Do you think Friar Lawrence's new plan will work? Explain.

10 **Master Teacher Note** The actions in this scene move along quickly and clearly. Help your students follow the swift steps by having them read the entire scene with few or no interruptions. Then, if you wish, you can go over the scene again in greater depth.

11 **Reading Strategy** As they read this scene, have students remember the order in which characters come to the churchyard.

12 **Discussion** Does Paris's sorrow seem genuine? Why or why not?

**LAWRENCE.** Now must I to the monument alone.
Within this three hours will fair Juliet wake.
She will beshrew⁵ me much that Romeo
25  Hath had no notice of these accidents;⁶
But I will write again to Mantua,
And keep her at my cell till Romeo come—
Poor living corse, closed in a dead man's tomb!  [*Exit.*]

5. **beshrew:** Blame.
6. **accidents:** Happenings.

**Scene iii.** *A churchyard; in it a monument belonging to the* CAPULETS.

[*Enter* PARIS *and his* PAGE *with flowers and sweet water.*]

**PARIS.** Give me thy torch, boy. Hence, and stand aloof.¹
Yet put it out, for I would not be seen.
Under yond yew trees lay thee all along,²
Holding thy ear close to the hollow ground.
5  So shall no foot upon the churchyard tread
(Being loose, unfirm, with digging up of graves)
But thou shalt hear it. Whistle then to me,
As signal that thou hearest something approach.
Give me those flowers. Do as I bid thee, go.

1. **aloof:** Apart.

2. **lay . . . along:** Lie down flat.

10 **PAGE.** [*Aside*] I am almost afraid to stand alone
Here in the churchyard; yet I will adventure.³  [*Retires.*]

3. **adventure:** Chance it.

**PARIS.** Sweet flower, with flowers thy bridal bed I strew
(O woe! thy canopy is dust and stones)
Which with sweet⁴ water nightly I will dew;
15  Or, wanting that, with tears distilled by moans.
The obsequies⁵ that I for thee will keep
Nightly shall be to strew thy grave and weep.

4. **sweet:** Perfumed.

5. **obsequies:** Memorial ceremonies.

[*Whistle* BOY.]

The boy gives warning something doth approach.
What cursèd foot wanders this way tonight
20  To cross⁶ my obsequies and true love's rite?
What, with a torch? Muffle me, night, awhile.  [*Retires.*]

6. **cross:** Interrupt.

[*Enter* ROMEO, *and* BALTHASAR *with a torch, a mattock, and a crow of iron.*]

**ROMEO.** Give me that mattock and the wrenching iron.
Hold, take this letter. Early in the morning
See thou deliver it to my lord and father.
25  Give me the light. Upon thy life I charge thee,
Whate'er thou hearest or seest, stand all aloof
And do not interrupt me in my course.
Why I descend into this bed of death

412   Drama

Is partly to behold my lady's face,
30 But chiefly to take thence from her dead finger
A precious ring—a ring that I must use
In dear employment.[7] Therefore hence, be gone.
But if thou, jealous,[8] dost return to pry
In what I farther shall intend to do,
35 By heaven, I will tear thee joint by joint
And strew this hungry churchyard with thy limbs.
The time and my intents are savage-wild,
More fierce and more inexorable[9] far
Than empty[10] tigers or the roaring sea.

40 **BALTHASAR.** I will be gone, sir, and not trouble ye.

**ROMEO.** So shalt thou show me friendship. Take thou
    that.
    Live, and be prosperous; and farewell, good fellow.

**BALTHASAR.** [*Aside*] For all this same, I'll hide me
    hereabout.
    His looks I fear, and his intents I doubt.    [*Retires.*]

45 **ROMEO.** Thou detestable maw,[11] thou womb of death,
    Gorged with the dearest morsel of the earth,
    Thus I enforce thy rotten jaws to open,
    And in despite[12] I'll cram thee with more food.
                [ROMEO *opens the tomb.*]

**7. dear employment:**
Important business.
**8. jealous:** Curious.

**9. inexorable:** Uncontrollable.
**10. empty:** Hungry.

**11. maw:** Stomach.

**12. despite:** Scorn.

13

14

**13 Critical Thinking and Reading**
What do you think Balthasar fears?

**14 Critical Thinking and Reading**
This play contains many examples of metaphorical language. What rotten jaws is Romeo opening? What is the food he will cram in them?

**Enrichment** You might want to tell students that David Garrick and Spranger Barry, both eighteenth-century actors, simultaneously played Romeo in competing theaters in London. At each of twelve shows, each actor tried to outdo the other's performance. Critics coined the two actors the rivaling Romeos. "Such a contest had never been known before in the history of the stage, and merits of the rival Romeos were discussed and compared for many years afterwards," Margaret Barton wrote in *David Garrick,* her biography of the actor.

My kind propitious stars o'erpay me now
For all my sorrows past. Rise, rise, my Juliet,
And from this cave of death, this house of horror,
Quick let me snatch thee to thy Romeo's arms.
There breathe a vital spirit in thy lips,
And call thee back to life and love! (*Takes her hand.*)—
Author Margaret Barton wrote in *David Garrick,* her biography of the actor, this description of the changes he made in his production of *Romeo and Juliet:*

'No play ever received greater advantage from alteration than this tragedy,' wrote Francis Gentleman, a distinguished critic of the day, 'especially in the last act. Bringing

Juliet to life before Romeo dies is undoubtedly a change of infinite merit. The whole dying scene does Mr. Garrick great credit.' And generation after generation of playgoers agreed with him. It was not until 1845 that Garrick's additions to the play were scrapped.

**Student Activity.** Form two debating teams: One team will argue that Shakespeare's plays can and should be "refashioned"; the other team will argue that the plays cannot and should not be altered for any reason. After you have prepared and organized your arguments, hold a debate.

15 **Discussion** Why is this statement ironical?

16 **Literary Focus** Romeo's weakness is his rash and impulsive
nature, but he is not bent on murder. Have students recall how he
tried to avoid a fight with Tybalt in
Act III.

17 **Discussion** How has Romeo
ironically fulfilled his promise to
give the tomb "more food"?

**PARIS.** This is that banished haughty Montague
50   That murd'red my love's cousin—with which grief
  It is supposed the fair creature died—
  And here is come to do some villainous shame
  To the dead bodies. I will apprehend[13] him.
  Stop thy unhallowèd toil, vile Montague!
55   Can vengeance be pursued further than death?
  Condemnèd villain, I do apprehend thee.
  Obey, and go with me; for thou must die.

**ROMEO.** I must indeed; and therefore came I hither.
  Good gentle youth, tempt not a desp'rate man.
60   Fly hence and leave me. Think upon these gone;
  Let them affright thee. I beseech thee, youth,
  Put not another sin upon my head
  By urging me to fury. O, be gone!
  By heaven, I love thee better than myself,
65   For I come hither armed against myself.
  Stay not, be gone. Live, and hereafter say
  A madman's mercy bid thee run away.

**PARIS.** I do defy thy conjurations.[14]
  And apprehend thee for a felon[15] here.

70 **ROMEO.** Wilt thou provoke me? Then have at thee, boy!

*[They fight.]*

**PAGE.** O Lord, they fight! I will go call the watch.

*[Exit. PARIS falls.]*

**PARIS.** O, I am slain! If thou be merciful,
  Open the tomb, lay me with Juliet.     *[Dies.]*

**ROMEO.** In faith, I will. Let me peruse[16] this face.
75   Mercutio's kinsman, noble County Paris!
  What said my man when my betossèd[17] soul
  Did not attend[18] him as we rode? I think
  He told me Paris should have married Juliet.
  Said he not so, or did I dream it so?
80   Or am I mad, hearing him talk of Juliet,
  To think it was so? O, give me thy hand,
  One writ with me in sour misfortune's book!
  I'll bury thee in a triumphant grave.
  A grave? O, no, a lanthorn,[19] slaught'red youth,
85   For here lies Juliet, and her beauty makes
  This vault a feasting presence[20] full of light.
  Death, lie thou there, by a dead man interred.

*[Lays him in the tomb.]*

**13. apprehend:** Seize, arrest.

**14. conjurations:** Solemn appeals.
**15. felon:** Criminal.

**16. peruse:** Look over.

**17. betossèd:** Upset.
**18. attend:** Give attention to.

**19. lanthorn:** Windowed structure on top of a room to admit light; also, a lantern.
**20. feasting presence:** Chamber fit for a celebration.

414   *Drama*

## Grammar in Action

**A noun of direct address** is the name of the person being spoken to, or addressed. Daily conversation regularly includes nouns of direct address:

"*Fred*, did you phone in our order?"
"Come on, *Valda*, we'll catch the first bus."
"So I ask you, *fellow classmates*, to vote for me tomorrow."
"Is this, *Madam Chairman*, in keeping with our bylaws?"

Notice that the noun of direct address may be a proper name (*Fred, Valda*), a common noun (*classmates*), or a title (*Madam Chairman*). In each case, the noun of direct address is set apart from the rest of the sentence with commas.

Shakespeare uses the noun of direct address regularly. The following examples illustrate:

*Condemnèd villain*, I do apprehend thee.
*Good gentle youth*, tempt not a desp'rate man.

18 **Discussion** If Romeo had been thinking more calmly, what would he have realized from Juliet's appearance?

    How oft when men are at the point of death
    Have they been merry! Which their keepers[21] call     **21. keepers:** Jailers.
90   A lightning before death. O, how may I
    Call this a lightning? O my love, my wife!
    Death, that hath sucked the honey of thy breath,
    Hath had no power yet upon thy beauty.
    Thou art not conquered. Beauty's ensign[22] yet      **22. ensign:** Banner.
95   Is crimson in thy lips and in thy cheeks,
    And death's pale flag is not advancèd there.
    Tybalt, liest thou there in thy bloody sheet?
    O, what more favor can I do to thee
    Than with that hand that cut thy youth in twain
100  To sunder[23] his that was thine enemy?             **23. sunder:** Cut off.
    Forgive me, cousin!, Ah, dear Juliet,

*The Tragedy of Romeo and Juliet, Act V, Scene iii* 415

Let them affright thee. I beseech thee, youth. . . .
*Death,* lie thou there, by a dead man interred.
*Tybalt,* liest thou there in thy bloody sheet?
Forgive me, *cousin!* Ah, *dear Juliet,* . . .

Shakespeare uses a variety of nouns of direct address. Each is set off with commas.

**Student Activity 1.** Suggest possible substitute nouns for each noun of address that Shakespeare uses in the quoted lines.

**Student Activity 2.** Write five sentences, each with a noun of address. Vary the kinds of nouns you use. Be sure to set each off with commas.

**19 Literary Focus** How is Friar Lawrence's late arrival another example of chance contributing to this tragedy?

Why art thou yet so fair? Shall I believe
That unsubstantial Death is amorous,[24]
And that the lean abhorrèd monster keeps
105 Thee here in dark to be his paramour?
For fear of that I still will stay with thee
And never from this pallet[25] of dim night
Depart again. Here, here will I remain
With worms that are thy chambermaids. O, here
110 Will I set up my everlasting rest
And shake the yoke of inauspicious[26] stars
From this world-wearied flesh. Eyes, look your last!
Arms, take your last embrace! And, lips, O you
The doors of breath, seal with a righteous kiss
115 A dateless[27] bargain to engrossing[28] death!
Come, bitter conduct;[29] come, unsavory guide!
Thou desperate pilot,[30] now at once run on
The dashing rocks thy seasick weary bark!
Here's to my love! [*Drinks.*] O true apothecary!
120 Thy drugs are quick. Thus with a kiss I die.   [*Falls.*]

[*Enter* FRIAR LAWRENCE, *with lanthorn, crow, and spade.*]

19

**FRIAR.** Saint Francis be my speed![31] How oft tonight
Have my old feet stumbled[32] at graves! Who's there?

**BALTHASAR.** Here's one, a friend, and one that knows you
well.

**FRIAR.** Bliss be upon you! Tell me, good my friend,
125 What torch is yond that vainly lends his light
To grubs[33] and eyeless skulls? As I discern,
It burneth in the Capels' monument.

**BALTHASAR.** It doth so, holy sir; and there's my master,
One that you love.

**FRIAR.**                Who is it?

**BALTHASAR.**                     Romeo.

**FRIAR.** How long hath he been there?

130 **BALTHASAR.**                          Full half an hour.

**FRIAR.** Go with me to the vault.

**BALTHASAR.**                     I dare not, sir.
My master knows not but I am gone hence,
And fearfully did menace me with death
If I did stay to look on his intents.

24. **amorous:** Full of love.

25. **pallet:** Bed.

26. **inauspicious:** Promising misfortune.

27. **dateless:** Eternal.
28. **engrossing:** All-encompassing.
29. **conduct:** Guide (poison).
30. **pilot:** Captain (Romeo himself).

31. **speed:** Help.
32. **stumbled:** Stumbling was thought to be a bad omen.

33. **grubs:** Worms.

135 **FRIAR.** Stay then; I'll go alone. Fear comes upon me.
O, much I fear some ill unthrifty[34] thing.

**BALTHASAR.** As I did sleep under this yew tree here,
I dreamt my master and another fought,
And that my master slew him.

**FRIAR.**                                   Romeo!
140 Alack, alack, what blood is this which stains
The stony entrance of this sepulcher?
What mean these masterless[35] and gory swords
To lie discolored by this place of peace?
                                        [*Enters the tomb.*]
Romeo! O, pale! Who else? What, Paris too?
145 And steeped in blood? Ah, what an unkind[36] hour
Is guilty of this lamentable chance!
The lady stirs.                      [JULIET *rises.*]

**JULIET.** O comfortable[37] friar! Where is my lord?
I do remember well where I should be,
150 And there I am. Where is my Romeo?

**FRIAR.** I hear some noise. Lady, come from that nest
Of death, contagion, and unnatural sleep.
A greater power than we can contradict
Hath thwarted our intents. Come, come away.
155 Thy husband in thy bosom there lies dead;
And Paris too. Come, I'll dispose of thee
Among a sisterhood of holy nuns.
Stay not to question, for the watch is coming.
Come, go, good Juliet. I dare no longer stay.

160 **JULIET.** Go, get thee hence, for I will not away.     [*Exit* FRIAR.]
What's here? A cup, closed in my truelove's hand?
Poison, I see, hath been his timeless[38] end.
O churl![39] Drunk all, and left no friendly drop
To help me after? I will kiss thy lips.
165 Haply some poison yet doth hang on them
To make me die with a restorative.[40]        [*Kisses him.*]
Thy lips are warm!

**CHIEF WATCHMAN.** [*Within*] Lead, boy. Which way?

**JULIET.** Yea, noise? Then I'll be brief. O happy[41] dagger!
                    [*Snatches* ROMEO'S *dagger.*]
This is thy sheath; there rust, and let me die.
                    [*She stabs herself and falls.*]

*The Tragedy of Romeo and Juliet, Act V, Scene iii  417*

**34. unthrifty:** Unlucky.

**35. masterless:** Discarded (without masters).

**36. unkind:** Unnatural.

**37. comfortable:** Comforting.

**38. timeless:** Untimely; too soon.
**39. churl:** Rude fellow.

**40. restorative:** Medicine.

**41. happy:** Convenient; opportune.

**20 Discussion** What is Friar Lawrence's final solution for Juliet?

**21 Critical Thinking and Reading** Why do you think that Friar Lawrence is so quick to leave at the appearance of the watch?

**22 Discussion** How does this passage echo lines 85-100?

23 **Literary Focus** How might the outcome have been different if the characters had come to the churchyard in a different order?

**Enrichment** *Romeo and Juliet* was written four or five years before the first Globe Theater was built. It is possible that Shakespeare wrote *Romeo and Juliet* for the Rose while acting with the Lord Admiral's Men.

[*Enter* PARIS' BOY *and* WATCH.]

170 **BOY.** This is the place. There, where the torch doth burn.

    **CHIEF WATCHMAN.** The ground is bloody. Search about the
      churchyard.
    Go, some of you; whoe'er you find attach.[42]        **42: attach:** Arrest.
                  [*Exit some of the* WATCH.]

23    Pitiful sight! Here lies the County slain;
      And Juliet bleeding, warm, and newly dead,
175   Who here hath lain this two days burièd.
      Go, tell the Prince; run to the Capulets;
      Raise up the Montagues; some others search.
               [*Exit others of the* WATCH.]

418   *Drama*

## Commentary: The Rose Theater

Tell students that although scholars and historians have been able to piece together a fairly accurate picture of Elizabethan theater, it was not until in June, 1989, when archaeologists discovered the actual Rose Theater—believed to be where Shakespeare first performed—that they could confirm and update their information and conjectures. Scholars, for example, had believed that 2,000 people could fit into the standing area of the Globe Theater. Based on the size of the Rose, however, they now think that their estimate is too high; it appears that the Rose could only accommodate a few hundred people.

What is confirmed is that the Rose and Globe theaters were within close proximity of each other. Because of this, the two theaters competed for their audiences. At the height of the competition, the Rose brought in a packed house every day with its production of *The Spanish Tragedy* by Thomas Kyd. As an attempt to cash in on the success of the Rose's monopoly of the most popular play of the age, Shakespeare wrote for the Globe a tragedy—which appears to have been lost—entitled *Hamlet, Revenge!*

Once the popularity of *The Spanish Tragedy* began to wane, audiences began noticing that the theater was decaying and

We see the ground whereon these woes do lie,
But the true ground[43] of all these piteous woes
180    We cannot without circumstance descry.[44]

[*Enter some of the* WATCH, *with* ROMEO'S MAN, BALTHASAR.]

**SECOND WATCHMAN.** Here's Romeo's man. We found him in
the churchyard.

**CHIEF WATCHMAN.** Hold him in safety till the Prince come
hither.

[*Enter* FRIAR LAWRENCE *and another* WATCHMAN.]

**THIRD WATCHMAN.** Here is a friar that trembles, sighs, and
185    weeps.
We took this mattock and this spade from him
As he was coming from this churchyard's side.

**CHIEF WATCHMAN.** A great suspicion! Stay the friar too.

[*Enter the* PRINCE *and Attendants.*]

**PRINCE.** What misadventure is so early up,
That calls our person from our morning rest?

[*Enter* CAPULET *and his* WIFE *with others.*]

190 **CAPULET.** What should it be, that is so shrieked abroad?

**LADY CAPULET.** O, the people in the street cry "Romeo,"
Some "Juliet," and some "Paris"; and all run
With open outcry toward our monument.

**PRINCE.** What fear is this which startles in your ears?

**CHIEF WATCHMAN.** Sovereign, here lies the County Paris
195    slain;
And Romeo dead; and Juliet, dead before,
Warm and new killed.

**PRINCE.** Search, seek, and know how this foul murder
comes.

**CHIEF WATCHMAN.** Here is a friar, and slaughtered Romeo's
man,
200    With instruments upon them fit to open
These dead men's tombs.

**CAPULET.** O heavens! O wife, look how our daughter
bleeds!
This dagger hath mista'en, for, lo, his house[45]
Is empty on the back of Montague,
205    And it missheathèd in my daughter's bosom!

*The Tragedy of Romeo and Juliet, Act V, Scene iii*    419

---

**43. ground:** Cause.
**44. without circumstance descry:** See clearly without details.

**45. house:** Sheath.

---

24 **Master Teacher Note** Consider telling students that at this point everyone is brought on stage for the denouement (the outcome or final solution of a complex sequence of events). All the pieces come together and, for the first time, everyone knows the whole story. Have students think of instances, at the end of modern film and television mysteries, where similar scenes are enacted.

25 **Discussion** What does Capulet think has happened?

---

was too small to accommodate the number of people wanting to see its productions. The Globe, on the other hand, offered audiences the latest in theatrical architecture and a larger capacity.

In the end, the Globe won the competition, leaving the Rose in a state of neglect and decay. In 1613 the Globe burned down.

**Student Activity.** Research Elizabethan audiences and give an oral presentation of your findings. You might, for example, report on the occupations of those who attended the theater or report on the class status of those who went to the theater and where each class was expected to sit. Present your research to the class.

**LADY CAPULET.** O me, this sight of death is as a bell
    That warns my old age to a sepulcher.

[*Enter* MONTAGUE *and others.*]

**PRINCE.** Come, Montague; for thou art early up
    To see thy son and heir more early down.

210 **MONTAGUE.** Alas, my liege,[46] my wife is dead tonight!
    Grief of my son's exile hath stopped her breath.
    What further woe conspires against mine age?

**PRINCE.** Look, and thou shalt see.

**MONTAGUE.** O thou untaught! What manners is in this,
215     To press before thy father to a grave?

**PRINCE.** Seal up the mouth of outrage[47] for a while,
    Till we can clear these ambiguities
    And know their spring, their head, their true descent;
    And then will I be general of your woes[48]
220     And lead you even to death. Meantime forbear,
    And let mischance be slave to patience.[49]
    Bring forth the parties of suspicion.

**FRIAR.** I am the greatest, able to do least,
    Yet most suspected, as the time and place
225     Doth make against me, of this direful[50] murder;
    And here I stand, both to impeach and purge[51]
    Myself condemnèd and myself excused.

**PRINCE.** Then say at once what thou dost know in this.

**FRIAR.** I will be brief, for my short date of breath[52]
230     Is not so long as is a tedious tale.
    Romeo, there dead, was husband to that Juliet;
    And she, there dead, that's Romeo's faithful wife.
    I married them; and their stol'n marriage day
    Was Tybalt's doomsday, whose untimely death
235     Banished the new-made bridegroom from this city;
    For whom, and not for Tybalt, Juliet pined.
    You, to remove that siege of grief from her,
    Betrothed and would have married her perforce
    To County Paris. Then comes she to me
240     And with wild looks bid me devise some mean
    To rid her from this second marriage,
    Or in my cell there would she kill herself.
    Then gave I her (so tutored by my art)
    A sleeping potion; which so took effect
245     As I intended, for it wrought on her

**46. liege** (lēj): Lord.

**47. mouth of outrage:** Violent cries.

**48. general . . . woes:** Leader in your sorrowing.

**49. let . . . patience:** Be patient in the face of misfortune.

**50. direful:** Terrible.
**51. impeach and purge:** Accuse and declare blameless.

**52. date of breath:** Term of life.

The form of death. Meantime I writ to Romeo
That he should hither come as<sup>53</sup> this dire night
To help to take her from her borrowed grave,
Being the time the potion's force should cease,
250  But he which bore my letter, Friar John,
Was stayed by accident, and yesternight
Returned my letter back. Then all alone
At the prefixèd hour of her waking
Came I to take her from her kindred's vault;
255  Meaning to keep her closely<sup>54</sup> at my cell
Till I conveniently could send to Romeo.
But when I came, some minute ere the time
Of her awakening, here untimely lay
The noble Paris and true Romeo dead.
260  She wakes; and I entreated her come forth
And bear this work of heaven with patience;
But then a noise did scare me from the tomb,
And she, too desperate, would not go with me,
But, as it seems, did violence on herself.
265  All this I know, and to the marriage
Her nurse is privy;<sup>55</sup> and if aught in this
Miscarried by my fault, let my old life
Be sacrificed some hour before his time
Unto the rigor<sup>56</sup> of severest law.

270  **PRINCE.** We still have known thee for a holy man.
Where's Romeo's man? What can he say to this?

**BALTHASAR.** I brought my master news of Juliet's death;
And then in post he came from Mantua
To this same place, to this same monument.
275  This letter he early bid me give his father,
And threat'ned me with death, going in the vault,
If I departed not and left him there.

**PRINCE.** Give me the letter. I will look on it.
Where is the County's page that raised the watch?
280  Sirrah, what made your master<sup>57</sup> in this place?

**BOY.** He came with flowers to strew his lady's grave;
And bid me stand aloof, and so I did.
Anon comes one with light to ope the tomb;
And by and by my master drew on him;
285  And then I ran away to call the watch.

**PRINCE.** This letter doth make good the friar's words,
Their course of love, the tidings of her death;
And here he writes that he did buy a poison

**53. as:** On.

**54. closely:** Hidden; secretly.

**55. privy:** Secretly informed about.

**56. rigor:** Strictness.

**57. made your master:** Was your master doing.

*The Tragedy of Romeo and Juliet,* Act V, Scene iii  421

27 **Reading Strategy** Have students compare and contrast the account of events in the Friar's monologue with the events as they remember them. (This passage—when combined with the comments of Balthasar and the Boy, and the contents of the letter—is an excellent synopsis of the play.)

28 **Discussion** Why does the Prince blame himself? How has he been punished?

29 **Discussion** How does the tragedy resolve the feud?

30 **Discussion** If you were the Prince, whom would you pardon and whom punish? What types of punishment would you decree?

**Reader's Response** Do you believe Romeo and Juliet's ending was due to fate—as the stars predicted? Explain.

Of a poor pothecary and therewithal
290 Came to this vault to die and lie with Juliet.
Where be these enemies? Capulet, Montague,
See what a scourge is laid upon your hate,
That heaven finds means to kill your joys with love.
And I, for winking at⁵⁸ your discords too,
295 Have lost a brace⁵⁹ of kinsmen. All are punished.

**CAPULET.** O brother Montague, give me thy hand.
This is my daughter's jointure,⁶⁰ for no more
Can I demand.

**MONTAGUE.**           But I can give thee more;
For I will raise her statue in pure gold,
300 That whiles Verona by that name is known,
There shall no figure at such rate⁶¹ be set
As that of true and faithful Juliet.

**CAPULET.** As rich shall Romeo's by his lady's lie—
Poor sacrifices of our enmity!⁶²

305 **PRINCE.** A glooming⁶³ peace this morning with it brings.
The sun for sorrow will not show his head.
Go hence, to have more talk of these sad things;
Some shall be pardoned, and some punishèd;
For never was a story of more woe
310 Than this of Juliet and her Romeo.          [*Exit all.*]

**58. winking at:** Closing my eyes to.

**59. brace:** Pair (Mercutio and Paris).

**60. jointure:** Wedding gift; marriage settlement.

**61. rate:** Value.

**62. enmity:** Hostility.

**63. glooming:** Cloudy, gloomy.

---

## THINKING ABOUT THE SELECTION
### Recalling

1. At the start of Scene i, why is Romeo happy and expecting joyful news?
2. What unforeseen occurrence revealed in Scene ii ruins Friar Lawrence's plan?
3. Why does the Friar go to Juliet's tomb?
4. What causes Paris and Romeo to fight?
5. How do Romeo and Juliet die?
6. How does the relationship of the feuding families change at the end of the play?

### Interpreting

7. Hearing Balthasar's report of Juliet's death (Scene i), Romeo exclaims, "Then I defy you,

stars!" What might he mean by this? How are his words consistent with what you know of his character?
8. Explain why the following words of Romeo over Juliet's body are ironic:

Death, that hath sucked the honey of thy breath,
Hath had no power yet upon thy beauty.
Thou art not conquered. Beauty's ensign yet
Is crimson in thy lips and in thy cheeks,
And death's pale flag is not advancèd there.

9. Tell why you think that either character or

**Closure and Extension**

***ANSWERS TO THINKING ABOUT THE SELECTION***
*Recalling*

1. Throughout the play, Romeo has believed in dreams. He says that his dreams have predicted some joyful news.
2. The friar who was to take the letter to Romeo was stopped and quar-

antined by the health authorities. He could not give the letter to Romeo.
3. He wants to be there when she wakes up so he can take her to his cell until he can send for Romeo.
4. Paris believes that Juliet died because she was heartbroken about Tybalt, who was killed by Romeo. He suspects that Romeo has come to vandalize the tomb.
5. Believing Juliet dead, Romeo takes

chance plays the greater role in bringing about the deaths of Romeo and Juliet.

## Applying

10. In a good play, the ending develops from the preceding action. How would preceding events have to be changed so that *Romeo and Juliet* could have a happy ending?

## ANALYZING LITERATURE
### Understanding Tragedy and Theme

A **tragedy** is a drama in which the central character or characters suffer disaster or great misfortune. In many tragedies, the downfall results from fate, a serious character flaw, or a combination of the two. Other contributing causes may be present as well. The **theme** of a tragedy is the central idea or insight about life that explains why the downfall occurred.

1. What character traits of the lovers may have led to their destruction?
2. What events reveal the tragic influence of fate or chance?
3. What other causes or conditions are important to the way events turn out?
4. Using your answers to the preceding questions, write a one-sentence statement of the theme of *Romeo and Juliet*. You might put your sentence in a form like the following: "The theme of the play is that _____ leads to the destruction of _____."

## CRITICAL THINKING AND READING
### Interpreting Metaphorical Language

**Metaphorical language** involves a comparison of unlike things. For example, when Paris is standing over the apparently lifeless body of Juliet, he says, "Sweet flower, with flowers thy bridal bed I strew . . ." He is comparing Juliet to a flower and her tomb to a bridal bed. Such metaphorical language deepens meaning and expresses feelings and emotions in a way that ordinary, plain language often cannot.

To interpret metaphorical language, first clarify what the subject of the comparison is—what is the writer writing about? Then clarify what the subject is being compared to. Finally ask yourself, "What ideas, feelings, and emotions are suggested by the comparison?"

Interpret the following examples of metaphorical language from Act V.

1. "My bosom's lord sits lightly in his throne . . ." (Romeo, Scene i, line 3)
2. "There is thy gold—worse poison to men's souls . . ." (Romeo to the Apothecary, Scene i, line 80)
3. "Thou detestable maw, . . . /Gorged with the dearest morsel of the earth . . ." (Romeo opening Juliet's tomb, Scene iii, lines 45–46)

## THINKING AND WRITING
### Responding to Criticism

A well-known poet and critic, W. H. Auden, has said of *Romeo and Juliet* that it "is not simply a tragedy of two individuals, but the tragedy of a city. Everybody in the city is in one way or another involved in and responsible for what happens."

Write a brief essay in which you explain why you agree or disagree with this statement. First think about the many characters that appear in the play: the Prince, the Friar, Lords Capulet and Montague, their wives, relatives, and servants, and so on. Are all such characters "involved in and responsible for what happens"? Then decide in what sense the play can be thought the tragedy of a city, since the city does not lie slain at the end.

When you write your essay, deal directly with such issues as these to support your opinion of Auden's criticism. When you revise, check that you have included enough references to what is actually in the play to make your own views convincing.

---

poison. Juliet wakes up and sees the dead Romeo, so she stabs herself with his dagger.
6. The fathers shake hands and end their feud. Each says he will erect a monument in memory of the other man's child.

### Interpreting
7. Suggested Response: Romeo says he is challenging fate, that nothing can keep him from Juliet. They are the angry words of a rash and impulsive person.
8. Suggested Response: Romeo sees the evidence that Juliet is not really dead, but ironically he is too distracted to understand what he himself sees and says.
9. Answers will differ. Students should select episodes from the play to prove their point. There are many mischances that suggest the role of fate in the tragedy. However, there are also instances of rash and impulsive behavior, especially on Romeo's part.

### Applying
10. Answers will differ. Students might respond that if the Friar's plan had not gone amiss, the ending could have been happy.

### ANSWERS TO ANALYZING LITERATURE
1. Suggested Response: The lovers are impulsive, quick to act, stubborn, and insistent on having their way.
2. Answers will differ. Some events might be: the chance meeting of Romeo and Juliet as he overhears her speaking from the balcony, or the circumstances that keep Friar John from delivering the letter.
3. Answers will differ. A key cause is: the feud between the two families.
4. Answers will differ. Students may respond that a combination of fate and character flaws leads to the destruction of the hero and heroine.

### ANSWERS TO CRITICAL THINKING AND READING
1. Suggested Response: My heart feels light in my breast—I am happy.
2. Suggested Response: Gold is a more powerful corrupter of men's souls than poison is a destroyer of their bodies.
3. Suggested Response: The tomb is like a mouth or stomach into which Juliet has been placed. This metaphor suggests Romeo's feelings of disgust and horror.

### THINKING AND WRITING
Before they begin this assignment, students can consult Lesson 14, "Writing About Drama," in the Handbook of Writing About Literature.

**Publishing Student Writing** Divide the opinions into those that agree and those that disagree. Make a class list of reasons for each opinion. Do most students agree or disagree? Which list of reasons seems stronger?

**Writing Across the Curriculum** A feud is an important factor in this tragedy. Have students research and report on famous feuds, such as the conflict involving the Hatfields and McCoys in West Virginia. Consider informing the social studies department of this assignment, so that teachers can guide students to appropriate resource materials.

Mapping
Ask for two or three pairs of student volunteers to create a semantic map on the board using
characters from *The Boor*. Have
members of the class suggest
character traits of the major characters to the pairs at the board so
that they can add to their maps.
After they have finished, have the
class discuss the maps.

Answers to the Activity
Have the students compare their
answers. Allow them to add to or
alter their maps if they discover
more information. Have them discuss what they learned as they
mapped *The Miracle Worker*.

# Mapping

Visual aids can be very useful in studying. One especially helpful visual aid is the semantic map. A **semantic map** clearly illustrates the relationship between ideas.

**Steps**

To make a semantic map, first decide what is the important information in the material you have read. Identify the major concepts that
you want to cover. For example, after reading a play, you might want
to organize details of the plot, setting, and characters. Or you may
choose to map the character traits of several characters or to show
the development of one or more characters throughout the play.

The next step is to organize the information into main ideas and
relevant details. Draw lines indicating main ideas. Draw branches indicating relevant details that back up these main ideas. Skim the play
to find the information you need. Then use this information to fill in the
lines and branches.

Remember that a map is fluid. Feel free to change and add information as you think about the play.

**Guidelines**

• Select the important information or concepts to organize.
• Identify the main ideas and pertinent details.
• Determine the best shape to show the relationship between this in-
formation.
• Construct the map.
• Fill in the map from memory.
• Fill in gaps by skimming material.
• Review the map to recall information.

**Activity**

Using the information from *The Miracle Worker*, fill in the following semantic map. Carefully think about how you will organize your
information. Identify characters to include on your map, the time
frame in which the play occurred, the conflict that keeps the plot moving, and the themes of the play.

Remember that a map is flexible. Feel free to change the form of
these map skeletons to fit your needs. When you have completely
filled out your map, compare your answers with your classmates'.

424    *Drama*

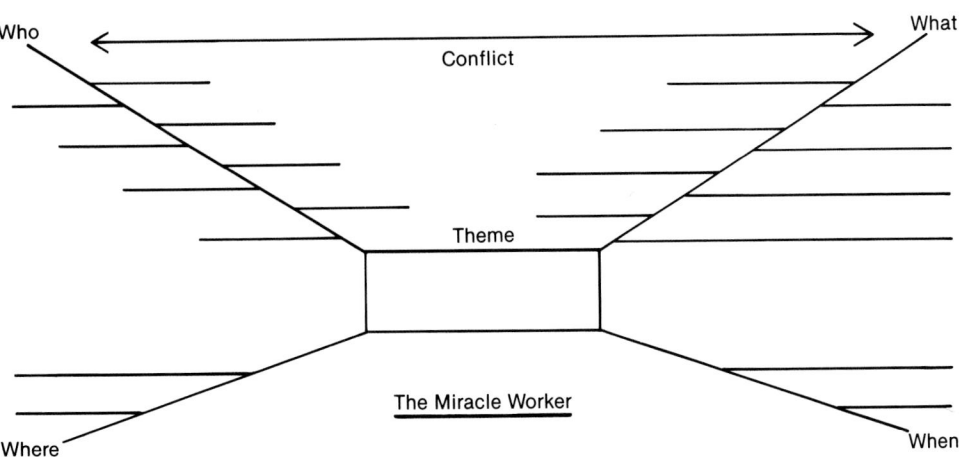

Who

What

Conflict

Theme

The Miracle Worker

Where

When

**Activity**

Now you are going to create your own map for *The Tragedy of Romeo and Juliet*. Brainstorm with your classmates to list the three most appropriate character traits for each of the major characters. Brainstorm some more to decide how you could organize this information so that your map would show which characters were most similar and which least alike. When you have created and filled in your map, compare it with those of your classmates.

The writing assignments on page 426 have students write creatively, while those on page 427 have them think about the plays and write critically.

## YOU THE WRITER
### Guidelines for Evaluating Assignment 1

1. Has the student written a monologue in which a misunderstood character has the opportunity to tell his or her side of the story?
2. Has the student captured the voice of the character?
3. Has the student arranged the monologue in a logical order?
4. Is the monologue free from grammar, usage, and mechanics errors?

### Guidelines for Evaluating Assignment 2

1. Does the scene advance the story?
2. Does the scene capture the flavor of the characters?
3. Does the scene follow the conventions of drama, using the speakers' names, stage directions, and dialogue?
4. Is the scene free from grammar, usage, and mechanics errors?

### Guidelines for Evaluating Assignment 3

1. Does the new ending proceed logically from the previous events in the play?
2. Are the new events presented in the order in which they would happen?
3. Does the new ending follow the conventions of drama, using the speakers' names, stage directions, and dialogue?
4. Is the ending free from grammar, usage, and mechanics errors?

# ▌YOU THE WRITER▐

**Assignment**

**1.** Write a dramatic monologue for one of the characters, in which this character tells his or her side of the story.

**Prewriting.** Think about the plays you have read in this unit. Choose a character who you think was misunderstood. Pretending to be this character, quickly jot down the things you would like the audience to know.

**Writing.** Write the first draft of a dramatic monologue, presenting your character's side of the story.

**Revising.** When you revise, make sure you have presented your story in a logical order. Have you captured the special "voice" of your character? Prepare a final draft and present it to your classmates.

**Assignment**

**2.** Write another scene for a play. Make sure that the scene is consistent with the rest of the play.

**Prewriting.** Choose a play that you particularly liked. Freewrite about what might have happened in this play on another day.

**Writing.** Write the first draft of your play. Remember to follow the conventions of drama.

**Revising.** When you revise, make sure you have written dialogue that accurately captures the flavor of the characters and that advances the story. Prepare a final draft.

**Assignment**

**3.** The ending of one of the plays you read may have seemed wrong to you. You may have felt that the rest of the story seemed possible but that the ending brought in impossible events. Perhaps you felt that the ending was too sad or left too many loose ends. Decide at what point you would begin to change the play. Then write your own ending, beginning at that point.

**Prewriting.** Skim the last few pages of the play you chose and list specific events that would not occur in your new ending. Then decide on a series of different events that would make the ending more to your liking. Arrange the events in the order they would happen.

**Writing.** Follow your plan, unless you think of better ideas as you write. Make any changes that would improve it. If you do change your plan, make sure the new events follow logically.

**Revising.** Read over your ending and make any changes that would improve it. Make sure you have followed the conventions of play writing. Share your new endings with your classmates.

# YOU THE CRITIC

**Assignment**

1. Choose a character from a play in this unit. The way that the characters act should be a key to the theme. Write an essay explaining how theme is revealed through the character you chose. Show how the character's actions help shape the theme.

    **Prewriting.** Brainstorm to form a list of the personality traits of the character you chose.

    **Writing.** Begin your essay with an introductory paragraph stating your premise. Then discuss the character's actions. Conclude with an explanation of how the character's actions reveal the theme.

    **Revising.** Revise your essay. Add any information you think will strengthen it. Edit your sentences. Then proofread your final draft.

**Assignment**

2. Think about heroes and heroines. Is there a man or woman in the plays you have read who you feel is heroic? What makes that character a hero? Is it courage, intelligence, humor, or some special talent? Write an essay about your hero or heroine.

    **Prewriting.** List the qualities of this character that you admire. Find passages where he or she displays these qualities.

    **Writing.** Write your first draft. Include at least three reasons why this person is heroic. Organize your essay according to order of importance.

    **Revising.** Check over your writing. Make sure you have adequately supported your main idea. Proofread your essay and prepare a final draft.

**Assignment**

3. Many plays deal with the search for justice and dignity. Write an essay explaining what you think one of the plays in this unit reveals about this topic.

    **Prewriting.** First select a play. Then jot down actions, words, phrases, and actual quotations from the play that reveal the theme. Cluster these items.

    **Writing.** Write the first draft of your essay. State your thesis in your first paragraph. Use examples, details, and quotations from the play to support your thesis. End with a statement that summarizes your points.

    **Revising.** When you revise, make sure you have organized your supporting information in a logical and effective order. Proofread your essay and prepare a final draft.

*You the Critic*    427

---

**YOU THE CRITIC**
*Guidelines for Evaluating Assignment 1*

1. Does the introductory paragraph state the student's premise about how the theme is revealed through the actions of a character?
2. Does the body of the essay contain enough information to discuss thoroughly the character's actions?
3. Does the conclusion contain an explanation of how the character's actions reveal the theme?
4. Is the essay free from grammar, usage, and mechanics errors?

*Guidelines for Evaluating Assignment 2*

1. Does the essay present a thesis about what makes a character heroic?
2. Are there at least three reasons that adequately explain why this person is heroic?
3. Is the essay organized by order of importance?
4. Is the essay free from grammar, usage, and mechanics errors?

*Guidelines for Evaluating Assignment 3*

1. Does the first paragraph present a thesis about the search for justice and dignity in a play?
2. Does the body of the essay use examples, details, and quotations from the play to support the thesis?
3. Does the conclusion include a statement that summarizes the student's points?
4. Is the essay well-organized and free from grammar, usage, and mechanics errors?

## Humanities Note

Fine Art, *Office in a Small City*, 1953, Edward Hopper. Edward Hopper (1882-1967), painted evocative urban scenes and rural landscapes in a simple, realistic style. Hopper studied painting in New York City with the important realist painter Robert Henri. Despite the influence of this teacher, Hopper developed his own unique style. His objective paintings are diffused with mood and colored by harsh light.

Edward Hopper would have insisted that the mood created by *Office in a Small City*, was unintentional on his part. He claimed that he painted buildings and rooms merely to study the effects of light, space, and color. However, this poignant, stark painting of a modern office looking out on the older architecture of a small city is more than that to the viewer, who must wonder about the life of the lone figure in the painting. The scene might also prompt a viewer to contemplate human isolation and the impersonality of the business world as well. Hopper's compelling paintings show American scenes with uncompromising truth and clarity.

**OFFICE IN A SMALL CITY, 1953**
*Edward Hopper*
The Metropolitan Museum of Art

428   Nonfiction

# NONFICTION

Nonfiction is concerned with real life, rather than with people and events drawn from the imagination. Autobiographies and biographies tell about the lives of people who once lived or who are now living. An autobiography is written by the person whose life is being related, while a biography is written by someone other than the subject. An essay is a type of musing upon a subject. The form gives a writer the opportunity to think aloud on paper and explore one or even all aspects of the topic.

Nonfiction is written for a variety of purposes. Its purpose may be to inform, to describe, to persuade, and even to entertain. It also comes in a variety of types, called forms of discourse. Narrative essays relate stories, while descriptive essays primarily describe and present sensory impressions. Expository essays set forth information, while persuasive essays influence people and may even change the course of their actions.

In this unit you will encounter each of these types of essays as well as autobiographies and biographies. In addition, you will take a special look at essays on subjects in the arts and sciences.

429

**Reading Actively** The strategies
outlined here for reading actively
are based on research into the
ways that effective readers derive meaning from nonfiction.

Introduce these strategies to
your students, pointing out that
they are similar to those used in
reading fiction. You might emphasize the importance of interaction with the text while reading.

Encourage students to use
these strategies when reading
the other nonfiction selections in
this unit. To give them further
practice with these strategies,
you might use the selection in the
Teaching Portfolio, "Talent," by
Annie Dillard, page 446, which
students can annotate themselves.

# READING ACTIVELY

## Nonfiction

What are active readers? People who relate the information the author provides to their own experiences and react to the text as they read are active readers. They interact with the text by questioning what they read, predicting what will come, and clarifying as their questions are answered. By using these techniques of active reading, they gain better understanding and comprehension of what they read.

To become an active reader, review the following active-reading strategies carefully.

**Question**    Pause and ask questions about information that is presented. What does the author reveal about the topic? What is the author's purpose? Are conclusions based on information that has been given? Do the conclusions support the purpose? Is the author's purpose to persuade, to explain, or to tell a story?

**Predict**    Filter the information through your own experiences and make predictions about the author's conclusions. Based on what you already know about the subject, what conclusions is the author leading to? You will discover the accuracy of these predictions as you read on.

**Clarify**    As you are reading, answer the questions you raised and find out if your predictions are accurate. This will help to guide any other questions and predictions you might have, as well as help you to understand the information presented. If there are any words you do not understand, look them up in a dictionary. If any information is unclear or seems inaccurate, check it in a reference book.

**Summarize**    Periodically, summarize the information the author has presented so far. Review the important points the author has made. How have these points been supported?

**Pull It Together**    Determine the main idea, or purpose, of the entire selection. What have you learned? How was the information presented and supported? What are your reactions to the information?

On the following page, you will find a model of how to read an essay actively.

**Objectives**
1  To understand anecdotes
2  To recognize generalizations
3  To practice sentence
completion
4  To write about a profession

**Support Material**

**Teaching Portfolio**
Teacher Backup, p. 443
Reading Actively, "Talent," by
Annie Dillard, p. 446
Usage and Mechanics Work-
sheet, p. 448
Analyzing Literature Worksheet,
*Understanding Anecdotes,* p.
449
Critical Thinking and Reading

# A Neighbor of Mine

## Dorothy Canfield Fisher

A much-experienced cosmopolitan visitor to our region sat chatting the other day on the bench overlooking our garden. The talk chanced to turn to books, and after a moment's silence, he said to me abruptly, "Maybe you can give me the answer. You must know authors through and through. *What's the matter with them?*"

I knew perfectly well what he meant, but I was nettled, and pretended not to. "Matter?" I asked.

"Well, why is it that after you meet a famous writer, you usually decide his books can't be as good as you thought? Why are authors harder to talk to than a professional beauty? In my line of business I've met dozens of them," and he rattled off a list of glittering names. "They're simply impossible, all of them. Clammy as dead fish on any subject you can bring up if it's not going to get them more publicity. They don't seem to have any natural interests, as other human beings do, that take them out of themselves. And every word they say sounds like a move in a game, not an expression of what they think. What can there be about writing that turns a man into a posing self-conscious—I tell you, every time I've had to talk to one I go off and hunt me up a nice garage hand—"

I thought he had said about enough and interrupted him, "It's not writing. There's no more occupational risk in authorship than in farming or plumbing. The trouble is this lionizing business. Put your farmers or your plumbers or your nice, natural, unself-conscious garage hands into the damp hotness that lionizers create around authors—around any famous people—they'd spindle up the same sickly way, and put out shoots in the one direction that flattery comes from. But it's absurd to lump authors all together. You just notice any author who lives in ordinary, honest, human relationships with other people and with the earth—"

*A Neighbor of Mine* 431

"I'd like fine to notice such an author!" broke in my interlocutor dryly.

A Chevrolet car began to climb the road up our hill. "I beg your pardon," I said. "Those are some neighbors of mine, and they're coming here to get some roots out of our garden. They've moved lately, from the farm where they lived to another one, and are starting a new perennial garden. I offered them some of the overflow from ours. You know how phlox and iris multiply."

The small car stopped. A middle-aged man and woman and a little boy got out from it. "Oh, they've brought along one of their grandchildren," I said. "That's fine. They have such lovely grandchildren. Come on, won't you, and help us dig roots?"

We were soon at it, spades and trowels in hand, the fair-haired five-year-old tagging tirelessly beside his grandfather, half listening to the talk, half dreamily soaking up the spring sunshine. There was plenty of talk to listen to, as, Yankee-fashion, it ranged from local gossip, zestfully passed along, to pungent comments on world news. My city visitor was evidently greatly taken with my Vermont neighbors, laughed out several times at a shrewd comical fancy of the husband, and after a brief, wise comment on life from the wife, looked with a quick pleasure of appreciation into her serene face and quiet eyes.

We finished, brushed the drying earth from our fingers, knocked off most of the mud from our shoes, and walked back to the bench for a rest. The little boy came to lean against his grandfather's knee. "You two are great friends, I see," said the city man.

My neighbor bent his graying head to look down at his grandson, who responded by nestling a little closer. "We get along together all right," said the grandfather.

The talk ran from one subject to another, baseball, politics, India, and fell on forestry—always a subject of interest to Vermonters. My neighbor knew all about white-pine plantations, and on being questioned by the man from the city, gave a disquisition on how to plant them and what they do for poor land, which made his listener reach for a notebook and jot down some pointers. It was his turn later to talk at length, when, someone happening to mention Ireland, it came out

**Summarize:** The visitor is enjoying the company of the neighbors, especially the perceptive and inquisitive grandfather, a great deal.

that he had just returned from a summer there. My country neighbor began at once to ask searching questions about the situation under the Free-State regime. At first the city man answered with caution, the cynical caution of experience which has found out that nobody ever really wants to hear about another person's travels. But he was soon enthusiastically recounting what he had seen, having found, apparently, the exception to his cynical rule in the countryman who sat next to him, his shirt open at the throat, his gray hair ruffled by the breeze, his hand stained with earth hanging relaxed between his knees. He fixed intent blue eyes on the speaker, and with question and creative attention drew out the best of what the other had to give. I learned a great deal about Ireland in the five minutes that followed.

Just then another neighbor came across through the pine plantation back of us, looking for a strayed cow, and asked if we had seen her. After we said we hadn't he stood there in his overalls, for a chat. "Have folks down your way got their oats in yet?" he asked the farmer from down the road, and they were off on farm talk, swapping stories about lost cows, laughing, comparing notes about firewood. He nodded, finally, and went his way, and so did the three who had come in the Chevrolet, which departed loaded to the gunwales with roots and seedlings.

**Clarification:** The visitor has not forgotten about the previous conversation and now uses the farmer as an example to support his argument.

"There," said my city visitor, "that's a good example of what I was talking about. Why can't authors be like that farmer? Did you notice how *natural* he was? Nothing said for effect, not a word. And open to the world outside himself. Do you know why his questions about Ireland were so intelligent, went to the heart of the matter? I'll tell you why. It was because he was thinking about Ireland, and not about himself. Because he really wanted to find out something about it—he wasn't just making me talk as one way of soft-soaping me. The way he listened! Just show me an author who's as fine a human being as that gray-haired farmer—who's moved out of himself into a bigger place as that countryman has, who can talk on equal terms with another farmer and with a transatlantic traveler, who's grown to be one with a fine wife as a man can only after years of deep living, who has time to live with his grandchildren, and who never once in a long conversation brings the talk around to himself. Why, just the way that man looks at a person, sees that he's there, as much a human being as he is! No author—" He stopped, staring at me. I imagine I was looking rather odd.

"You didn't, I take it," I said, "catch his name, when I introduced you."

"No, I don't believe I did."

"His name," I said, "is Robert Frost."

**Clarification:** In using the farmer, the author's neighbor, as an example, the visitor has unwittingly disproved his claim about authors. The author has proved her point by the fact that her neighbor, the famous writer Robert Frost, is as natural as ordinary people.

**Pulling It Together:** Many people make hasty generalizations about others based on limited experiences. There are always exceptions to these generalizations. In the case of authors, many of them are judged by their appearance in the spotlight of publicity. To judge them, as well as other groups of people, you must see them as they appear out of the public eye and in their own element.

**Dorothy Canfield Fisher** (1879–1958) was born in Lawrence, Kansas. She became well known for her novels about the problems of married couples and their children. She also published short stories, essays, plays, and books for children. For much of her life, Canfield lived on a farm near Arlington, Vermont. Many of her stories reflect her admiration for the character of the people of New England.

**Enrichment** Robert Frost was a very popular poet during the latter part of his life. Part of his popularity was based on his reputation as a New England poet close to the land. He seemed to exemplify the New England "Yankee" character—individualistic, independent, yet reserved. Frost received many literary, academic, and public honors, including an invitation to speak at the inauguration of President John F. Kennedy in 1960.

For an example of his poetry see "The Runaway," page 584.

**Critical Thinking and Reading** You might point out the author's effective use of irony. By withholding the identity of the neighbor while the visitor develops his case against authors, she is able to present a clear contrast between the visitor's views and reality.

**More About the Author** Because of the cogency of her views, Dorothy Canfield Fisher was nominated by Mrs. Eleanor Roosevelt as one of the ten most influential women in the United States.

Ask students to discuss whom they would consider among the most important or influential women in the United States today.

**Reader's Response** How do you feel when generalizations are made about you?

**Closure and Extension**

*(Questions begin on p. 436.)*

**ANSWERS TO THINKING ABOUT THE SELECTION**
*Recalling*

1. The visitor believes that authors do not have any natural interests outside of themselves.

2. The neighbors visit in order to get some roots of perennial flowers from the garden.
3. The visitor thinks that the neighbors are wonderful, natural human beings, alive to their own environment and interested in the world beyond their locality.

4. The farmer is the famous poet Robert Frost.

## Interpreting

5. Suggested Response:Lionizing celebrities focuses excessive attention on them and makes it difficult for them to act naturally and show concern about other things.
6. Suggested Response: The author allows her visitor to go on at length before countering his argument. Naturally she does not accept his negative view of authors because she is an author herself.
7. Frost was a person with very real interests in farming and the world in general. He was also a devoted family man.

## Applying

8. Suggested Response: People are so varied. Within any group of people there is a range of personalities. Generalizations about a group, therefore, are usually not valid because they only apply to some members of that group.

## ANSWERS TO ANALYZING LITERATURE

1. Suggested Response: The author is interested in her neighbors but also has a wider view of life. She is clever and knows how to win an argument.
2. Suggested Response: The point the author makes is that generalizations about groups of people usually are invalid and unfair. The author also stresses that the lionization of celebrities in general and authors in particular may be the cause of their self-interest and egotism.

## ANSWERS TO CRITICAL THINKING AND READING

1. Suggested Response: The visitor generalizes that all authors are concerned only about themselves and do not have other interests.
2. Suggested Response:Frost demonstrates his interest in his grandson, in farming, and in other outside topics, such as Ireland.
3. Suggested Response: The author demonstrates her interest in her neighbors and in a variety of conversational topics.

## THINKING ABOUT THE SELECTION

### Recalling

1. Why is the visitor upset with the way authors act?
2. What is the reason for the neighbors' visit?
3. How do the farmer and his wife impress the visitor?
4. Who is the farmer?

### Interpreting

5. Why does "lionizing" people make them act unnaturally?
6. Explain how the author reacts to her visitor's complaints.
7. What do you learn about Frost's character?

### Applying

8. Why are generalizations about people often misleading?

## ANALYZING LITERATURE

### Understanding Anecdotes

Writers often use brief personal accounts, or anecdotes, to illustrate a point or to teach a lesson. Anecdotes are often written from the first-person point of view and generally reveal something about the author.

1. What does the anecdote reveal about Fisher's personality ?
2. What is the point, or lesson, of this anecdote?

## CRITICAL THINKING AND READING

### Recognizing Generalizations

A **generalization** is a broad conclusion emphasizing common rather than specific details. People often use generalizations without sufficient information to support them. These generalizations may be untrue because they overlook exceptions.

1. What generalization does the visitor make?
2. How does Frost's character refute this generalization?
3. How does the author's personality refute the generalization?

## UNDERSTANDING LANGUAGE

### Using Sentence Completion

Many aptitude tests include **Sentence Completion** sections that test context, structure, and vocabulary skills. The following sentences are incomplete. From the four words listed below each, choose the word that best completes the meaning of the sentence.

1. Because of his great talent, the actor was . . . for the lead.
   a. chosen          c. adored
   b. rejected        d. anxious
2. The high winds and driving rain . . . the explorers to find shelter.
   a. discussed       c. forced
   b persuading       d. asked
3. He asked many . . . questions, each one probing deeper and deeper.
   a. searching       c. meaningless
   b. ridiculous      d. confused

## THINKING AND WRITING

### Writing About a Profession

Select a profession such as teaching or medicine, and list the qualities you think are needed for this profession. Then write an essay explaining why a person needs these qualities to be successful. When you revise, make sure you have arranged your details according to order of importance, saving the quality you consider the most important for last. Proofread your essay and share it with the class.

## ANSWERS TO UNDERSTANDING LANGUAGE

1. a. chosen
2. c. forced
3. a. searching

**Challenge** How might the visitor have behaved if he had known that the farmer was Robert Frost?

## THINKING AND WRITING

For help with this assignment, students may consult Lesson 20, "Writing a Personal Essay," in the Handbook of Writing About Literature.

## Publishing Student Writing

Have students send a copy of their essays to a person in that profession and ask for comments on the importance of the qualities described.

### Writing Across the Curriculum

You might have students interview teachers in different disciplines about the qualities needed in their fields. After students have gathered their information, they could use it to create a vocational handbook.

# Biographies and Personal Accounts

**MY WIFE, SACKVILLE RIVER,**
**NOVA SCOTIA, 1918**
*Arthur Lismer*
Art Gallery of Ontario, Toronto

## Humanities Note

Fine Art, *My Wife, Sackville River*, Arthur Lismer. Arthur Lismer (1885-1969), emigrated to Canada from England. He became a part of the Group of Seven, Canadian nationalist artists who sought to glorify the rugged beauty of their country in a modern painting style. Lismer and these other artist changed the face of Canadian painting.

*My Wife, Sackville River* was painted on one of the many sketching trips Lismer made into the Canadian wilderness. Painted in a decorative Fauve-like style, the painting serves as a partial account of the trip. Later in his career, Lismer became an innovative teacher of art to children. His innovative techniques are still in use today to open children's eyes and imaginations to beauty.

## *from* A Lincoln Preface

**Carl Sandburg** (1878–1967) was born in Galesburg, Illinois, of Swedish immigrant parents. He won Pulitzer prizes both for his poetry and for his biography of Abraham Lincoln, from which this preface comes. His six-volume biography describes Lincoln's life from his early years in the West to his presidency during the Civil War. Sandburg believed that this war was our nation's most desperate crisis and Lincoln our greatest leader.

**Biography**

The word *biography* comes from two Greek words, *bios* (life) and *graphein* (to write). These Greek words are reflected in the meaning of **biography**: an account of a person's life written by someone else.

Anyone can be the subject of a biography, from a world leader to a person next door. Writers of biography, called **biographers**, carefully research the facts of their subjects' lives. However, biographers also present their own interpretation of these facts. They explain both the reasons for their subjects' actions and the meaning of their lives. In "A Lincoln Preface," for example, Sandburg weaves together insights and stories to present Lincoln's many-sided personality.

**Look For**

Look for the way that Lincoln's "life, mind and heart ran in contrasts," as Sandburg puts it. As you read, try to identify the different, and sometimes opposite, sides of Lincoln's personality.

**Writing**

Do you think a great leader must have a public face as well as a private face? Freewrite exploring your answer.

**Vocabulary**

Knowing the following words will help you as you read "A Lincoln Preface."

**despotic** (de spät′ ik) *adj.*: Absolute; unlimited (p. 439)

**chattel** (chat′'l) *n.*: A movable item of personal property (p. 439)

**cipher** (sī′ fər) *adj.*: Code (usually a noun or verb) (p. 441)

**slouching** (slouch′ iŋ) *adj.*: Drooping (usually a verb) (p. 441)

**censure** (sen′ shər) *n.*: Strong disapproval (p. 442)

**gaunt** (gônt) *adj.*: Thin and bony (p. 444)

**droll** (drōl) *adj.*: Comic and amusing in an odd way (p. 444)

**raillery** (rāl′ ər ē) *n.*: Good-natured teasing (p. 444)

438    *Nonfiction*

# *from* **A Lincoln Preface**

## Carl Sandburg

In the time of the April lilacs in the year 1865, a man in the City of Washington, D. C., trusted a guard to watch at a door, and the guard was careless, left the door, and the man was shot, lingered a night, passed away, was laid in a box, and carried north and west a thousand miles; bells sobbed; cities wore crepe[1]; people stood with hats off as the railroad burial car came past at midnight, dawn or noon.

During the four years of time before he gave up the ghost, this man was clothed with despotic power, commanding the most powerful armies till then assembled in modern warfare, enforcing drafts of soldiers, abolishing the right of habeas corpus[2], directing politically and spiritually the wild, massive forces loosed in civil war.

Four billion dollars' worth of property was taken from those who had been legal owners of it, confiscated, wiped out as by fire, at his instigation and executive direction; a class of chattel property recognized as lawful for two hundred years went to the scrap pile.

When the woman who wrote *Uncle Tom's Cabin*[3] came to see him in the White House, he greeted her, "So you're the little woman who wrote the book that made this great war," and as they seated themselves at a fireplace, "I do love an open fire; I always had one at home." As they were finishing their talk of the days of blood, he said, "I shan't last long after it's over."

An Illinois Congressman looked in on him as he had his face lathered for a shave in the White House, and remarked, "If anybody had told me that in a great crisis like this the people were going out to a little one-horse town and pick out a one-horse lawyer for president, I wouldn't have believed it." The answer was, "Neither would I. But it was a time when a man with a policy would have been fatal to the country. I never had a policy. I have simply tried to do what seemed best each day, as each day came."

"I don't intend precisely to throw the Constitution overboard, but I will stick it in a hole if I can," he told a Cabinet officer. The enemy was violating the Constitution to destroy the Union, he argued, and therefore, "I will violate the Constitution, if necessary, to save the Union." He instructed a messenger to the Secretary of the Treasury, "Tell him not to bother himself about the Constitution. Say that I have that sacred instrument here at the White House, and I am guarding it with great care."

When he was renominated, it was by the device of seating delegates from Tennessee,

---

**1. crepe** (krāp) *n.*: Thin, black cloth worn to show mourning.
**2. habeas corpus** (hā′ bē əs kôr′ pəs): Right of an imprisoned person to have a court hearing.
**3. woman . . . Cabin:** Harriet Beecher Stowe (1811–1896), whose novel stirred up opinion against slavery.

**Presentation**

**Motivation/Prior Knowledge** Ask students what qualities a national leader must possess during a time of crisis. Then tell them that, by reading this selection, they can learn whether Abraham Lincoln displayed any of the qualities they have mentioned.

**Master Teacher Note** You might remind students that Abraham Lincoln was born in Kentucky on February 12, 1809. A Republican candidate, he was elected President of the United States in November 1860. The first battle of the Civil War was fought at Bull Run in July 1861. Lincoln was elected to a second term in November 1864. The Civil War officially ended on April 9, 1865, and on April 15, 1865, Lincoln was assassinated by John Wilkes Booth at the Ford Theater in Washington, D.C.

**Thematic Idea** Another selection that deals with a great and original personality is "Georgia O'Keefe," page 511.

**Purpose-Setting Question** What qualities made Lincoln the right man to lead our country during one of its worst crises?

1 **Clarification** The expression *gave up the ghost* means "died or passed away."

2 **Clarification** During Lincoln's presidency, the right to own slaves, a practice which had existed for 200 years, was abolished.

3 **Discussion** How would you characterize Lincoln's attitude toward the Constitution?

**LINCOLN PROCLAIMING THANKSGIVING**
*Dean Cornwell*
*Louis A. Warren Lincoln Library and Museum, Fort Wayne, Indiana*

which gave enough added votes to seat favorable delegates from Kentucky, Missouri, Louisiana, Arkansas, and from one county in Florida. Until late in that campaign of 1864, he expected to lose the November election; military victories brought the tide his way; the vote was 2,200,000 for him and 1,800,000 against him. Among those who bitterly fought him politically, and accused him of blunders or crimes, were Franklin Pierce, a former president of the United States; Horatio Seymour, the Governor of New York; Samuel F. B. Morse, inventor of the telegraph; Cyrus H. McCormick, inventor of the farm reaper; General George B. Mc-

Clellan, a Democrat who had commanded the Army of the Potomac; and the Chicago *Times,* a daily newspaper. In all its essential propositions the Southern Confederacy had the moral support of powerful, respectable elements throughout the North, probably more than a million votes believing in the justice of the cause of the South as compared with the North.

While propagandas raged, and the war winds howled, he sat in the White House, the Stubborn Man of History, writing that the Mississippi was one river and could not belong to two countries, that the plans for railroad connection from coast to coast must

his white kid gloves broke into tatters while shaking hands at a White House reception, he remarked, "This looks like a general bustification." When he talked with an Ohio friend one day during the 1864 campaign, he mentioned one public man and murmured, "He's a thistle! I don't see why God lets him live." Of a devious senator, he said, "He's too crooked to lie still!" And of a New York editor, "In early life in the West, we used to make our shoes last a great while with much mending, and sometimes, when far gone, we found the leather so rotten the stitches would not hold. Greely is so rotten that nothing can be done with him. He is not truthful; the stitches all tear out." As he sat in the telegraph be pushed through and the Union Pacific[4] realized.

His life, mind and heart ran in contrasts. When his white kid gloves broke into tatters while shaking hands at a White House reception, he remarked, "This looks like a general bustification." When he talked with an Ohio friend one day during the 1864 campaign, he mentioned one public man, and murmured, "He's a thistle! I don't see why God lets him live." Of a devious Senator, he said, "He's too crooked to lie still!" And of a New York editor, "In early life in the West, we used to make our shoes last a great while with much mending, and sometimes, when far gone, we found the leather so rotten the stitches would not hold. Greeley is so rotten that nothing can be done with him. He is not truthful; the stitches all tear out." As he sat in the telegraph office of the War Department, reading cipher dispatches, and came to the words, Hosanna and Husband, he would chuckle, "Jeffy D.,"[5] and at the words, Hunter and Happy, "Bobby Lee."[6]

While the luck of war wavered and broke and came again, as generals failed and campaigns were lost, he held enough forces of the Union together to raise new armies and supply them, until generals were found who made war as victorious war has always been made, with terror, frightfulness, destruction, and valor and sacrifice past words of man to tell.

**4** A slouching, gray-headed poet,[7] haunting the hospitals at Washington, characterized him as "the grandest figure on the crowded canvas of the drama of the nineteenth century—a Hoosier Michael Angelo."[8]

His own speeches, letters, telegrams and official messages during that war form the most significant and enduring document from any one man on why the war began, why it went on, and the dangers beyond its end. He mentioned "the politicians," over and again "the politicians," with scorn and blame. As the platoons filed before him at a review of an army corps, he asked, "What is to become of these boys when the war is over?"

**5** He was a chosen spokesman; yet there were times he was silent; nothing but silence could at those times have fitted a chosen spokesman; in the mixed shame and blame of the immense wrongs of two crashing civilizations, with nothing to say, he said nothing, slept not at all, and wept at those times in a way that made weeping appropriate, decent, majestic.

**6** His hat was shot off as he rode alone one night in Washington; a son he loved died as he watched at the bed; his wife was accused of betraying information to the enemy, until denials from him were necessary; his best companion was a fine-hearted and brilliant son with a deformed palate and an impediment of speech; when a Pennsylvania Congressman told him the enemy had declared they would break into the city and hang him to a lamppost, he said he had considered "the violent preliminaries" to such a scene; on his left thumb was a scar where an ax had nearly chopped the thumb off when he was a boy; over one eye was a scar where he had been hit with a club in the hands of a man trying to steal the cargo off a Mississippi River flatboat; he threw a cashiered[9]

---

**4. Union Pacific:** Railroad chartered by Congress in 1862 to form part of a transcontinental system.
**5. "Jeffy D.":** Jefferson Davis (1808–1889), president of the Confederacy.
**6. "Bobby Lee":** Robert E. Lee (1807–1870), commander in chief of the Confederate army.
**7. slouching . . . poet:** Walt Whitman (1819–1892).

**8. Michael Angelo:** Michelangelo (mī′ k′l an′ jə lō′), a famous Italian artist (1475–1564).
**9. cashiered** (ka shird′) v.: Dishonorably discharged.

from *A Lincoln Preface*  441

**4 Enrichment** Walt Whitman's poem "When Lilacs Last in the Dooryard Bloom'd" mourns Lincoln's death.

**5 Literary Focus** Sandburg portrays Lincoln as a man of contrasts. Ask students what contrast in Lincoln's personality is revealed in this passage.

**6 Discussion** We rarely think of the President as someone who weeps. Ask students how their knowledge that Lincoln wept affects their opinion of him.

office of the War Department, reading cipher dispatches, and came to the words Hosanna and Husband, he would chuckle, "Jeffy D.," and at the words Hunter and Happy, "Bobby Lee." Notice that the first sentence states that Lincoln's character "ran to contrasts." The rest of the paragraph supports this statement with specific examples from Lincoln's life. These examples serve as **supporting details,** details provided to prove the accuracy of the main idea. Notice that the supporting details show on the one hand a gentle, almost playful side to the man's character and on the other, an indignation and anger that is awe-inspiring—and perhaps a bit frightening—in its righteousness.

**Student Activity 1.** With your classmates, examine the supporting details in the paragraph, and then classify these according to which side of Lincoln's character they describe.

**Student Activity 2.** Discuss the overall effect of this paragraph. Do the details adequately support the main idea? Explain your opinion.

**Critical Thinking and Reading** Why do you think this woman's action provoked such an angry response from Lincoln?

8 **Discussion** Abraham Lincoln is often referred to as "Honest Abe." Does the information in these two paragraphs undercut that nickname? Do you think that rules should be bent to benefit an important cause? Why or why not?

officer out of his room in the White House, crying, "I can bear censure, but not insult. I never wish to see your face again."

As he shook hands with the correspondent of the London *Times*, he drawled, "Well, I guess the London *Times* is about the greatest power on earth—unless perhaps it is the Mississippi River." He rebuked with anger a woman who got on her knees to thank him for a pardon that saved her son from being shot at sunrise; and when an Iowa woman said she had journeyed out of her way to Washington just for a look at him, he grinned, "Well, in the matter of looking at one another, I have altogether the advantage."

He asked his Cabinet to vote on the high military command, and after the vote, told them the appointment had already been made; one Cabinet officer, who had been governor of Ohio, came away personally baffled and frustrated from an interview, to exclaim, to a private secretary, "That man is the most cunning person I ever saw in my life"; an Illinois lawyer who had been sent on errands carrying his political secrets, said, "He is a trimmer[10] and such a trimmer as the world has never seen."

He manipulated the admission of Nevada as a state in the Union, when her votes were needed for the Emancipation Proclamation,[11] saying, "It is easier to admit Nevada than to raise another million of soldiers." At the same time he went to the office of a former New York editor, who had become Assistant Secretary of War, and said the votes of three congressmen were wanted for the required three-quarters of votes in the House of Representatives, advising, "There are

---

**10. trimmer** (trim' ər) *n.*: Person who changes his opinion to suit the circumstances.
**11. Emancipation Proclamation:** Document issued by President Lincoln freeing the slaves in all territories still at war with the Union.

three that you can deal with better than anybody else. . . . Whatever promise you make to those men, I will perform it." And in the same week, he said to a Massachusetts politician that two votes were lacking, and, "Those two votes must be procured. I leave it to you to determine how it shall be done; but remember that I am President of the United States and clothed with immense power, and I expect you to procure those votes." And while he was thus employing every last resource and device of practical politics to constitutionally abolish slavery, the abolitionist[12] Henry Ward Beecher attacked him with javelins of scorn and detestation in a series of editorials that brought from him the single comment, "Is thy servant a dog?"

When the King of Siam sent him a costly sword of exquisite embellishment, and two elephant tusks, along with letters and a photograph of the King, he acknowledged the gifts in a manner as lavish as the Orientals. Addressing the King of Siam as "Great and Good Friend," he wrote thanks for each of the gifts, including "also two elephant's tusks of length and magnitude, such as indicate they could have belonged only to an animal which was a native of Siam." After further thanks for the tokens received, he closed the letter to the King of Siam with strange grace and humor, saying, "I appreciate most highly your Majesty's tender of good offices in forwarding to this Government a stock from which a supply of elephants might be raised on our soil. . . . Our political jurisdiction, however, does not reach a latitude so low as to favor the multiplication of the elephant, and steam on land as well as water has been our best agent of transportation. . . . Meantime, wishing for your Majesty a long and happy life, and, for the

---

**12. abolitionist** (ab' ə lish' ən ist) *n.*: Person in favor of doing away with slavery in the United States.

PECULIARSOME ABE
N. C. Wyeth
The Free Library of Philadelphia

Fine art, *Peculiarsome Abe*, by N.C. Wyeth (1882–1945). Wyeth, who received his training at the prestigious Howard Pyle School of Art in Delaware, became widely known as an illustrator. However, he also left a legacy of paintings that celebrate American history.

This painting shows Lincoln as a young man, leaning against a corn shock in a field. He has chosen to spend the noontime break reading a book instead of chatting with the others shown in the picture.

1. How does Wyeth show Lincoln's interest in what he is reading?
2. Do you think that this picture has a message? Explain.

from *A Lincoln Preface*    443

9 **Discussion** What does Lincoln's preference for this story reveal about him?

10 **Reading Strategy** Ask students to summarize this paragraph in their own words.

**Reader's Response** If you were to write a biography of a famous political figure you admired, who would it be? Why?

**Closure and Extension**

**ANSWERS TO THINKING ABOUT THE SELECTION**
*Recalling*

1. Lincoln felt he was justified in violating the Constitution to preserve the Union, because he felt the enemy was violating it to destroy the Union.
2. As the luck of the war changed, Lincoln managed to hold enough forces of the union together to raise new armies until effective generals could be found.
3. Lincoln had a number of family tragedies—his son died, his wife was accused of giving information to the enemy, and another son had a speech impediment and a deformed palate.

generous and emulous people of Siam, the highest possible prosperity, I commend both to the blessing of Almighty God."

He sent hundreds of telegrams, "Suspend death sentence" or "Suspend execution" of So-and-So, who was to be shot at sunrise. The telegrams varied oddly at times, as in one, "If Thomas Samplogh, of the First Delaware Regiment, has been sentenced to death, and is not yet executed, suspend and report the case to me." And another, "Is it Lieut. Samuel B. Davis whose death sentence is commuted? If not done, let it be done."

9 | While the war drums beat, he liked best of all the stories told of him, one of two Quakeresses[13] heard talking in a railway car. "I think that Jefferson will succeed." "Why does thee think so?" "Because Jefferson is a praying man." "And so is Abraham a praying man." "Yes, but the Lord will think Abraham is joking."

An Indiana man at the White House heard him say, "Voorhees, don't it seem strange to you that I, who could never so much as cut off the head of a chicken, should be elected, or selected, into the midst of all this blood?"

A party of American citizens, standing in the ruins of the Forum in Rome, Italy, heard there the news of the first assassination of the first American dictator, and took it as a sign of the growing up and the aging of the civilization on the North American continent. Far out in Coles County, Illinois, a beautiful, gaunt old woman in a log cabin said, "I knowed he'd never come back."

Of men taking too fat profits out of the war, he said, "Where the carcass is there will the eagles be gathered together."

---

**13. Quakeresses** (kwāk′ ər es əz) *n.*: Female members of the religious group known as the Society of Friends, or Quakers.

An enemy general, Longstreet, after the war, declared him to have been "the one matchless man in forty millions of people," while one of his private secretaries, Hay, declared his life to have been the most perfect in its relationships and adjustments since that of Christ.

Between the days in which he crawled as a baby on the dirt floor of a Kentucky cabin, and the time when he gave his final breath in Washington, he packed a rich life with work, thought, laughter, tears, hate, love.

With vast reservoirs of the comic and the droll, and notwithstanding a mastery of mirth and nonsense, he delivered a volume of addresses and letters of terrible and serious appeal, with import beyond his own day, shot through here and there with far, thin ironics, with paragraphs having raillery of the quality of the Book of Job,[14] and echoes as subtle as the whispers of wind in prairie grass.

Perhaps no human clay pot has held more laughter and tears.

10 | The facts and myths of his life are to be an American possession, shared widely over the world, for thousands of years, as the tradition of Knute or Alfred, Lao-tse or Diogenes, Pericles or Caesar,[15] are kept. This because he was not only a genius in the science of neighborly human relationships and an artist in the personal handling of life from day to day, but a strange friend and a friendly stranger to all forms of life that he met.

He lived fifty-six years of which fifty-two were lived in the West—the prairie years.

---

**14. Book of Job** (jōb): Book of the Old Testament in which a man named Job is tested by God.
**15. Knute** (k' nōōt′) **or Alfred, Lao-tse** (lou′dzu′) **or Diogenes** (dī äj′ ə nēz′), **Pericles** (per′ ə klēz′) **or Caesar** (sē′ zər): Well-known thinkers and leaders from different eras and places.

4. "He manipulated the admission of Nevada as a state in the Union" in order to obtain votes for the Emancipation Proclamation. He also procured additional Congressional votes by exercising his great power as President.

*Interpreting*

5. Suggested Response: Lincoln's most important goal during the Civil War was to hold the country together.

6. Answers will differ, but most students will realize that Sandburg portrays Lincoln as an active, thoughtful, sensitive, many-sided man. Lincoln's life was eventful before he became President, and afterward he was at the center of the greatest crisis in the history of the United States.

7. Suggested Response: Sandburg describes Lincoln as a man of contrasts. He could be angry and compassionate, sad and humor-

ous. Also, he was a "man of the people" who exercised an almost despotic power.

*Applying*

8. Answers may differ. A positive response would be that no limits should be placed on achieving a goal that results in a greater common good. A negative response would be that certain laws and restrictions are necessary and that adherence to these rules prevents

## THINKING ABOUT THE SELECTION

### Recalling

1. How did Lincoln justify his violating the Constitution?
2. How did he show his leadership as "the luck of war" changed?
3. Describe the family tragedies that he experienced.
4. How did he use "practical politics" to end slavery?

### Interpreting

5. What was Lincoln's most important goal during the Civil War?
6. How does Sandburg show that Lincoln "packed a rich life with work, thought, laughter, tears, hate, love"?
7. In what ways does Sandburg describe Lincoln as a complex man?

### Applying

8. Do you think the ends ever justify the means? Support your answer with evidence from current events or history.

## ANALYZING LITERATURE

### Understanding Biography

A **biography** is the story of a person's life written by someone else. In "A Lincoln Preface," Sandburg combines facts, anecdotes, and his own insights to produce a vivid portrait of Lincoln.

1. Why is Lincoln a good subject for a biography?
2. Sandburg tells you that Lincoln was shot in 1865. Find three other key facts about Lincoln that he includes.
3. Select three of the many anecdotes that he tells about his subject. Why did you find each of these anecdotes effective?
4. Summarize Sandburg's opinion of Lincoln. On the basis of this biography, do you agree with it? Explain your answer.

## CRITICAL THINKING AND READING

### Evaluating the Subject of a Biography

Sandburg tells many little stories about Lincoln that reveal different sides of his personality. For example, you learn that he once said when reviewing troops, "What is to become of these boys when the war is over?" This indicates that he was a thoughtful person, concerned about others.

1. Sandburg tells how Lincoln obtained votes to pass the Emancipation Proclamation. What do these stories reveal about him?
2. What can you learn about him from the story of Harriet Beecher Stowe's visit?
3. Why has Lincoln been called many-sided? Do you agree with this estimation? Why?

## UNDERSTANDING LANGUAGE

### Completing Verbal Analogies

A **verbal analogy** is a comparison of relationships between words. Choose the lettered pair of words that expresses the same relationship as that between the capitalized pair.

1. DROLL : SERIOUS : :
   - a. joyful : glad
   - b. shoes : sneakers
   - c. sick : well
   - d. fork : rake
2. SIMPLE : COMPLEX : :
   - a. ground : building
   - b. high : lofty
   - c. shirt : pants
   - d. happy : sad

## THINKING AND WRITING

### Writing a Biographical Sketch

Imagine that your school newspaper wants you to write a biographical sketch. First select your subject. It could be someone you know or someone you have read about. List the facts and anecdotes that readers should know about your subject. Then write a short biography of your subject that your schoolmates will enjoy. As you revise, check to see that you have included your own insights into your subject's life.

about Lincoln's methods of obtaining votes to pass the Emancipation Proclamation reveal that he was relentless in the pursuit of his goals.
2. Suggested Response: His meeting with Stowe reveals his wit, sentimentality, and sense of mortality.
3. Answers will differ. However, most students will realize that Lincoln was a person of contrasts. For example, he could pardon a soldier out of compassion and then rebuke the soldier's mother for thanking him on her knees. He could write a proclamation freeing the slaves and then use every trick of practical politics to get it adopted.

## ANSWERS TO UNDERSTANDING LANGUAGE

1. c
2. d

**Challenge** The highly controversial novel *Uncle Tom's Cabin*, by Harriet Beecher Stowe, was published in 1852. Many people feel that it greatly contributed to the election of President Lincoln and created a strong antislavery sentiment throughout the country. How do controversial books and the media affect social and political issues today?

## THINKING AND WRITING

For help with this assignment, students may consult Lesson 2, "Drafting and Revising," in the Handbook of Writing About Literature.

**Publishing Student Writing** You might have students submit their sketches to the school newspaper.

**Writing Across the Curriculum** Ask students to research and report on Lincoln's most famous speeches. Consider informing the social studies department of this assignment so that teachers can direct students to the appropriate resource materials.

the abuse of power. Students may consider such historical and current events as the rise and fall of Hitler, the Bay of Pigs invasion, Watergate, and the Iran-Contra scandal to support their answers.

## ANSWERS TO ANALYZING LITERATURE

1. Suggested Response: Lincoln is a good subject for a biography because of his complex personality and central role in American history.

2. Suggested Response: Sandburg also tells us that Lincoln was born in Kentucky and lived in a log cabin, lived to be fifty-six years old, and won the 1864 election with 2,200,000 votes.
3. Answers may differ, but might include the meeting between Lincoln and Harriet Beecher Stowe (this anecdote shows his humility and foreshadows his death); Lincoln's response to the woman whose son he had pardoned (this anecdote shows the contradictions in his nature); and the opinions of the

Quaker women (this anecdote shows his ability to laugh at himself).
4. Answers will differ. Most students will realize that Sandburg thinks Lincoln was one of the greatest men in history. Many students will also realize that Sandburg tends to present facts that support his thesis.

## ANSWERS TO CRITICAL THINKING AND READING

1. Suggested Response: The stories

**More About the Author** One of Uchida's goals as a writer is "to dispel the stereotype image still held by many non-Asians about . . . Japanese Americans. . . ." Ask students why stereotypes—simplified or distorted images of a people or group—can be harmful. What can a writer do to correct such false images?

**Literary Focus** You might have students consider the advantages and disadvantages of the different methods of characterization.

**Look For** You might also want students to look for the ways that Mr. Shimada was a leader and model for other Japanese-Americans.

**Writing/Prior Knowledge** Discuss with students various personality traits they find admirable. Students should consider famous people as well as those they know personally.

**Vocabulary** For the benefit of **less advanced** students, assign students to work in pairs to write a brief story that includes all the listed vocabulary words.

## Of Dry Goods and Black Bow Ties

**Yoshiko Uchida** (1921–     ) was born in Alameda, California, the daughter of a Japanese businessman. As a girl, she made books out of brown wrapping paper and filled them with her own stories. Today she is a full-time writer, known for her prize-winning collections of Japanese folk tales and her descriptions of the Japanese experience in the United States. Ms. Uchida has said that she hopes "to give young Asians a sense of their own history." She also wants to write about Japanese-Americans so that non-Asians see them "as real people."

**Biography: Characterization**

**Characterization** refers to the way that writers make people in their narratives come alive for readers. Biographers use many of the same methods as fiction writers to accomplish this goal. Often they will describe how a character looks and behaves, letting you draw your own conclusions about his or her personality. Sometimes they will tell you directly that the person has certain traits, such as pride or intelligence. Finally, they might show how other characters react to this person. In "Of Dry Goods and Black Bow Ties," Yoshiko Uchida uses all these techniques to create a touching portrait of Mr. Shimada.

**Look For**

In the following selection, Mr. Shimada comes to the United States with dreams for the future. As you read, look for the way his dreams change.

**Writing**

Uchida's father was very impressed by Mr. Shimada, the subject of this biographical sketch. Recall someone you have looked up to, and freewrite about the qualities in this person that caused you to admire him or her.

**Vocabulary**

Knowing the following words will help you as you read "Of Dry Goods and Black Bow Ties."

**expediency** (ik spē′ dē ən sē) n.: Practicality (p. 447)
**confidant** (kän′ fə dant′) n.: A close friend to whom one tells secrets (p. 448)
**repository** (ri päz′ ə tôr′ ē) n.: Place for safekeeping (p. 448)
**tycoon** (tī kōōn′) n.: Wealthy

and powerful person (p. 449)
**awe** (ô) n.: Mixed feeling of fear and wonder (p. 449)
**exhilarated** (ig zil′ ə rāt′ əd) adj.: Lively (p. 450)
**typhoon** (tī fōōn′) n.: Violent tropical storm (p. 451)

446  *Nonfiction*

### Objectives
1 To understand characterization in biography
2 To separate fact from opinion in biography
3 To write about characterization in biography

### Support Material

**Teaching Portfolio**
Teacher Backup, p. 465
Grammar in Action Worksheet, *Using Transitions,* p. 469
Usage and Mechanics Worksheet, p. 471
Vocabulary Check, p. 472
Analyzing Literature Worksheet, *Understanding Characterization,* p. 473

Language Worksheet, *Understanding Synonyms,* p. 474
Selection Test, p. 475

# Of Dry Goods[1]
# and Black Bow Ties

Yoshiko Uchida

Long after reaching the age of sixty, when my father was persuaded at last to wear a conservative four-in-hand tie,[2] it was not because of his family's urging, but because Mr. Shimada (s*h*i mä′ də) (I shall call him that) had died. Until then, for some forty years, my father had always worn a plain black bow tie, a formality which was required on his first job in America and which he had continued to observe as faithfully as his father before him had worn his samurai[3] sword.

My father came to America in 1906 when he was not yet twenty-one. Sailing from Japan on a small six-thousand-ton ship which was buffeted all the way by rough seas, he landed in Seattle on a bleak January day. He revived himself with the first solid meal he had enjoyed in many days, and then allowed himself one day of rest to restore his sagging spirits. Early on the second morning, wearing a stiff new bowler,[4] he went to see Mr. Shozo Shimada to whom he carried a letter of introduction.

At that time, Shozo Shimada was Seattle's most successful Japanese business man. He owned a chain of dry goods stores which extended not only from Vancouver to Portland, but to cities in Japan as well. He had come to America in 1880, penniless but enterprising, and sought work as a laborer. It wasn't long, however, before he saw the futility of trying to compete with American laborers whose bodies were twice his in muscle and bulk. He knew he would never go far as a laborer, but he did possess another skill that could give him a start toward better things. He knew how to sew. It was a matter of expediency over masculine pride. He set aside his shovel, bought a second-hand sewing machine, and hung a dressmaker's sign in his window. He was in business.

In those days, there were some Japanese women in Seattle who had neither homes nor families nor sewing machines, and were delighted to find a friendly Japanese person to do some sewing for them. They flocked to Mr. Shimada with bolts of cloth, elated to discover a dressmaker who could speak their native tongue and, although a male, sew western-styled dresses for them.

Mr. Shimada acquainted himself with the fine points of turning a seam, fitting sleeves, and coping with the slippery folds of satin, and soon the women ordered enough dresses to keep him thriving and able to es-

---

1. **dry goods:** Cloth, lace, thread, buttons, and so forth.
2. **four-in-hand tie:** Necktie.
3. **samurai** (sam′ ə rī′): Members of a military class in feudal Japan who wore two swords.
4. **bowler** (bōl′ ər) *n.*: Derby hat.

tablish a healthy bank account. He became a trusted friend and confidant to many of them and soon they began to bring him what money they earned for safekeeping.

"Keep our money for us, Shimada-san,"[5] they urged, refusing to go to American banks whose tellers spoke in a language they could not understand.

---

5. **-san** (sän): Respectful Japanese suffix added to names and titles.

At first the money accumulated slowly and Mr. Shimada used a pair of old socks as a repository, stuffing them into a far corner of his drawer beneath his union suits. But after a time, Mr. Shimada's private bank began to overflow and he soon found it necessary to replenish his supply of socks.

He went to a small dry goods store downtown, and as he glanced about at the buttons, threads, needles and laces, it occurred to him that he owed it to the women to in-

448    *Nonfiction*

## Grammar in Action

A smooth writing style results from making clear connections between ideas. Words that make connections are called **transitions.** They clarify relationships such as time, contrast, result, and addition. Subordinating and coordinating conjunctions are specific kinds of transitions.

> *Afterwards,* we walked home. (transition showing time)
> *After the game ended,* we walked home. (subordinate clause)

> Some drove home, *but we walked. (coordinating conjunction)*

The following illustrate transitions in Uchida's work:

> *At first* the money accumulated slowly *and* Mr. Shimada used a pair of old socks as a repository . . . (transition indicating time; coordinator)
> *By the time my father appeared,* Mr. Shimada had long since abandoned his sewing machine . . . (subordinate clause)

vest their savings in a business venture with more future than the dark recesses of his bureau drawer. That night he called a group of them together.

"Think, ladies," he began. "What are the two basic needs of the Japanese living in Seattle? Clothes to wear and food to eat," he answered himself. "Is that not right? Every man must buy a shirt to put on his back and pickles and rice for his stomach."

The women marveled at Mr. Shimada's cleverness as he spread before them his fine plans for a Japanese dry goods store that would not only carry everything available in an American dry goods store, but Japanese foodstuff as well. That was the beginning of the first Shimada Dry Goods Store on State Street.

By the time my father appeared, Mr. Shimada had long since abandoned his sewing machine and was well on his way to becoming a business tycoon. Although he had opened cautiously with such stock items as ginghams, flannel, handkerchiefs, socks, shirts, overalls, umbrellas and ladies' silk and cotton stockings, he now carried tins of salt rice crackers, bottles of soy sauce, vinegar, ginger root, fish-paste cakes, bean paste, Japanese pickles, dried mushrooms, salt fish, red beans, and just about every item of canned food that could be shipped from Japan. In addition, his was the first Japanese store to install a U.S. Post Office Station, and he therefore flew an American flag in front of the large sign that bore the name of his shop.

When my father first saw the big American flag fluttering in front of Mr. Shimada's shop, he was overcome with admiration and awe. He expected that Mr. Shozo Shimada would be the finest of Americanized Japanese gentlemen, and when he met him, he was not disappointed.

Although Mr. Shimada was not very tall,

he gave the illusion of height because of his erect carriage. He wore a spotless black alpaca suit, an immaculate white shirt and a white collar so stiff it might have overcome a lesser man. He also wore a black bow tie, black shoes that buttoned up the side and a gold watch whose thick chain looped grandly on his vest. He was probably in his fifties then, a ruddy-faced man whose hair, already turning white, was parted carefully in the center. He was an imposing figure to confront a young man fresh from Japan with scarcely a future to look forward to. My father bowed, summoned as much dignity as he could muster, and presented the letter of introduction he carried to him.

Mr. Shimada was quick to sense his need. "Do you know anything about bookkeeping?" he inquired.

"I intend to go to night school to learn this very skill," my father answered.

Mr. Shimada could assess a man's qualities in a very few minutes. He looked my father straight in the eye and said, "Consider yourself hired." Then he added, "I have a few basic rules. My employees must at all times wear a clean white shirt and a black bow tie. They must answer the telephone promptly with the words, 'Good morning or good afternoon, Shimada's Dry Goods,' and they must always treat each customer with respect. It never hurts to be polite," he said thoughtfully. "One never knows when one might be indebted to even the lowliest of beggars."

My father was impressed with these modest words from a man of such success. He accepted them with a sense of mission and from that day was committed to white shirts and black bow ties, and treated every customer, no matter how humble, with respect and courtesy. When, in later years, he had his own home, he never failed to answer the phone before it could ring twice if at all possible.

*Of Dry Goods and Black Bow Ties* 449

2 **Discussion** Why do you think this priviledge was important to Mr. Shimada?

3 **Enrichment** What symbols of success does Mr. Shimada display? Compare and contrast these with current status symbols.

4 **Discussion** Is it wise to make quick decisions on a person's character? Explain.

. . . he *therefore* flew an American flag . . . (transition indicating result)
He *also* wore a black bow tie . . . (transition indicating addition)
*In spite of his phenomenal success, however,* Mr. Shimada never forgot his early friends . . . (transitions indicating contrast)
By using a variety of transitions, you will allow readers to understand the relationships among your ideas.

**Student Activity 1.** Tell whether the following transitions show time, contrast, result, or addition:
1. moreover          4. because
2. consequently      5. on the other hand
3. nevertheless      6. earlier

**Student Activity 2.** Write a paragraph of at least six sentences. Use transitions to join your ideas. Mark each transition.

My father worked with Mr. Shimada for ten years, becoming first the buyer for his Seattle store and later, manager of the Portland branch. During this time Mr. Shimada continued on a course of exhilarated expansion. He established two Japanese banks in Seattle, bought a fifteen-room house outside the dreary confines of the Japanese community and dressed his wife and daughter in velvets and ostrich feathers. When his daughter became eighteen, he sent her to study in Paris, and the party he gave on the eve of her departure, with musicians, as well as caterers to serve roast turkey, venison,

*Nippon Kan Heritage Association*

baked ham and champagne, seemed to verify rumors that he had become one of the first Japanese millionaires of America.

In spite of his phenomenal success, however, Mr. Shimada never forgot his early friends nor lost any of his generosity, and this, ironically enough, was his undoing. Many of the women for whom he had once sewn dresses were now well established, and they came to him requesting loans with which they and their husbands might open grocery stores and laundries and shoe repair shops. Mr. Shimada helped them all and never demanded any collateral. He operated his banks on faith and trust and gave no thought to such common prudence as maintaining a reserve.

When my father was called to a new position with a large Japanese firm in San Francisco, Mr. Shimada came down to Portland to extend personally his good wishes. He took Father to a Chinese dinner and told him over the peanut duck and chow mein that he would like always to be considered a friend.

"If I can ever be of assistance to you," he said, "don't ever hesitate to call." And with a firm shake of the hand, he wished my father well.

That was in 1916. My father wrote regularly to Mr. Shimada telling him of his new job, of his bride, and later, of his two children. Mr. Shimada did not write often, but each Christmas he sent a box of Oregon apples and pears, and at New Year's a slab of heavy white rice paste from his Seattle shop.

In 1929 the letters and gifts stopped coming and Father learned from friends in Seattle that both of Mr. Shimada's banks had failed.[6] He immediately dispatched a letter to Mr. Shimada, but it was returned unopened. The next news he had was that Mr.

Shimada had had to sell all of his shops. My father was now manager of the San Francisco branch of his firm. He wrote once more asking Mr. Shimada if there was anything he could do to help. The letter did not come back, but there was no reply, and my father did not write again. After all, how do you offer help to the head of a fallen empire? It seemed almost irreverent.

It was many years later that Mr. Shimada appeared one night at our home in Berkeley.[7] In the dim light of the front porch my mother was startled to see an elderly gentleman wearing striped pants, a morning coat[8] and a shabby black hat. In his hand he carried a small black satchel. When she invited him inside, she saw that the morning coat was faded, and his shoes badly in need of a shine.

"I am Shimada," he announced with a courtly bow, and it was my mother who felt inadequate to the occasion. She hurriedly pulled off her apron and went to call my father. When he heard who was in the living room, he put on his coat and tie before going out to greet his old friend.

Mr. Shimada spoke to them about Father's friends in Seattle and about his daughter who was now married and living in Denver. He spoke of a typhoon that had recently swept over Japan, and he drank the tea my mother served and ate a piece of her chocolate cake. Only then did he open his black satchel.

"I thought your girls might enjoy these books," he said, as he drew out a brochure describing *The Book of Knowledge*.

"Fourteen volumes that will tell them of the wonders of this world." He spread his arms in a magnificent gesture that recalled his eloquence of the past. "I wish I could give

---

**6. In 1929 . . . failed:** This was the year that the Great Depression began.

**7. Berkeley** (bur′ klē): City in California, on San Francisco Bay.
**8. morning coat:** Jacket with tails, used for formal occasions.

*Of Dry Goods and Black Bow Ties* 451

5 **Reading Strategy** Ask students to predict whether the writer's father and Mr. Shimada will continue to be close friends.

6 **Clarification** The expression *almost irreverent* means "almost disrespectful."

7 **Critical Thinking and Reading** How has Mr. Shimada's appearance changed? What does this change indicate?

them to your children as a personal gift," he added softly.

Without asking the price of the set, my father wrote a check for one hundred dollars and gave it to Mr. Shimada.

Mr. Shimada glanced at the check and said, "You have given me fifty dollars too much." He seemed troubled for only a moment, however, and quickly added, "Ah, the balance is for a deposit, is it? Very well, yours will be the first deposit in my next bank."

"Is your home still in Seattle then?" Father asked cautiously.

"I am living there, yes," Mr. Shimada answered.

And then, suddenly overcome with memories of the past, he spoke in a voice so low he could scarcely be heard.

"I paid back every cent," he murmured. "It took ten years, but I paid it back. All of it. I owe nothing."

"You are a true gentleman, Shimada-san," Father said. "You always will be." Then he pointed to the black tie he wore, saying, "You see, I am still one of the Shimada men."

That was the last time my father saw Shozo Shimada. Some time later he heard that he had returned to Japan as penniless as the day he set out for America.

It wasn't until the Christmas after we heard of Mr. Shimada's death that I ventured to give my father a silk four-in-hand tie. It was charcoal gray and flecked with threads of silver. My father looked at it for a long time before he tried it on, and then fingering it gently, he said, "Well, perhaps it is time now that I put away my black bow ties."

**Closure and Extension**

**ANSWERS TO THINKING ABOUT THE SELECTION**
*Recalling*

1. Mr. Shimada advanced himself by starting a dressmaker's business, safeguarding money for his clients, and then opening a dry goods store that catered to American and Japanese needs.
2. Mr. Shimada hired Uchida's father as a bookkeeper, then promoted him to other positions, and finally made him manager of one of his branch stores.
3. Mr. Shimada helped all the people who came to him for loans, neither asking for collateral nor maintaining a reserve of funds.
4. Mr. Shimada has lost his business

## THINKING ABOUT THE SELECTION

### Recalling

1. Explain how Mr. Shimada advanced from a laborer to a successful business person.
2. Explain how Mr. Shimada helped Yoshiko Uchida's father.
3. Why does Mr. Shimada's generosity lead to his downfall?
4. In what ways is he a changed man when he visits the Uchidas years later?

### Interpreting

5. What did Mr. Shimada symbolize for Uchida's father when they first met?
6. In what important ways did Mr. Shimada affect the life of Uchida's father?
7. (a) Why does Uchida's father consider Mr. Shimada "a true gentleman"? (b) What does he mean when he says, "You see, I am still one of the Shimada men"?
8. Why did Uchida give her father a four-in-hand tie only after Mr. Shimada died?

### Applying

9. Uchida's father looked up to Mr. Shimada as a model. Why do you think people search out models to imitate?

## ANALYZING LITERATURE

### Understanding Characterization

**Characterization** refers to the way that writers make a person in a narrative come alive for the reader. In "Of Dry Goods and Black Bow Ties," the writer creates a portrait of a man who deeply influenced her father. She tells you directly what Mr. Shimada was like, describes his appearance, recounts his history, and shows how others reacted to him.

1. Find two examples where Uchida tells you directly what Mr. Shimada was like.
2. Explain how Mr. Shimada demonstrates pride, cleverness, and generosity.

3. Compare and contrast Mr. Shimada in his first and last meetings with Uchida's father.
4. The Japanese add -*san* to the end of a name to show respect. Explain how the writer has created a character who is worthy of being called "Shimada-san."

## CRITICAL THINKING AND READING

### Separating Fact from Opinion

A **statement of fact** can be proved to be true or false. For example, Uchida says that her "father came to America in 1906." You could verify this fact through research. A **statement of opinion,** however, expresses a person's belief or attitude. Such a statement can be supported by arguments, but it cannot be proved absolutely true or false. When Uchida says that Mr. Shimada was generous, she is expressing an opinion.

Identify which of the following statements from the essay are facts and which are opinions.

1. ". . . his was the first Japanese store to install a U.S. Post Office Station. . . ."
2. "Mr. Shimada could assess a man's qualities in a very few minutes."
3. "My father worked with Mr. Shimada for ten years. . . ."

## THINKING AND WRITING

### Writing About Characterization

Imagine that a friend of yours is writing a biographical sketch for a class assignment and has asked for your advice. First, list the methods that Uchida uses to make Mr. Shimada such a memorable character. Then use this list to write a note to your friend explaining how to make a subject come alive. In revising your note, check to see that your advice is clear and specific.

*Of Dry Goods and Black Bow Ties* 453

### ANSWERS TO ANALYZING LITERATURE

1. Answers will differ. However, students may respond that the writer says that Mr. Shimada could assess a man's qualities in a very few minutes and that Mr. Shimada never forgot his early friends.
2. Suggested Response: Shimada demonstrates pride when he tells Uchida's father that he paid back all he owed even though it took ten years. Mr. Shimada shows cleverness in planning his dry goods store. Shimada shows generosity by making loans to everyone who needed them.
3. Suggested Response: In both the first and last meetings, Shimada is a man of pride who commands respect. At their first meeting however, Uchida's father is a poor young man looking for a job with the successful Shimada. When they meet for the final time, Shimada is penniless and Uchida's father is a succcessful manager of a Japanese firm.
4. Suggested Response: Throughout the entire essay, the author has given examples of Shimada's integrity, honesty, and dignity—all of which are worthy of respect.

### ANSWERS TO CRITICAL THINKING AND READING

1. This is a statement of fact.
2. This is a statement of opinion.
3. This is a statement of fact.

### THINKING AND WRITING

For help with this assignment, students can refer to Lesson 9, "Writing About Character," in the Handbook of Writing About Literature.

**Publishing Student Writing** You might want to divide the class into small groups and have students share their notes with fellow group members.

**Writing Across the Curriculum** Have students research and report on the Japanese who came to the United States at the beginning of the century. Consider informing the social studies department of this assignment, so teachers can provide guidance to students.

---

empire and now must sell encyclopedias to support himself.

### Interpreting

5. Suggested Response: Mr. Shimada symbolized the possibility of achieving success in America and retaining one's Japanese identity.
6. Suggested Response: Mr. Shimada gave Uchida's father a start in business as well as a sense of pride in himself.

7. Suggested Responses: Part a: Uchida's father feels Shimada is "a true gentleman" because he treats everyone with respect and courtesy. Part b: Uchida's father means that he still upholds the virtues that Shimada had taught him.
8. Suggested Response: She gave him the tie after Shimada's death because it symbolized the end of an era in his life. He would no longer wear bow ties exclusively.

### Applying

9. Answers will differ. Students may respond that people need direction in their lives. It is easier to imitate a real person than to live by abstract standards.

**Challenge** What do you think are the main concerns of immigrants who have just arrived in the United States? If possible, give examples to support your answer.

**More About the Author** Agnes De Mille compared her role as choreographer to that of a playwright, saying, "I tell a story, and I tell it well." Ask students how dance movements can tell a story.

**Literary Focus** You might tell students that through vivid personal accounts, the author tells of the grueling preparation and total commitment necessary to become an accomplished ballet dancer. De Mille's devotion is enhanced by her respect for the tradition associated with this enduring art form.

**Look For** Have students note words and phrases De Mille uses to communicate the atmosphere of practice sessions.

**Writing/Prior Knowledge** Have students discuss what motivates a person to continue a certain activity when they are tired.

**Vocabulary** For the benefit of less advanced students, assign each of several students a vocabulary word. Ask each student to define the word for the class, to use the word in a sentence, and to give a synonym and antonym for the assigned word.

## *from* Dance to the Piper

**Agnes De Mille** (1905–     ) is the niece of Cecil B. De Mille, the well-known producer of major movies like *The Ten Commandments*. She studied dancing from an early age and made her first professional appearance in her early twenties. Later she became famous as a choreographer as well, creating dances for the 1936 film version of *Romeo and Juliet* and for the popular Broadway show *Oklahoma*. As you will see from this selection, dancing is more than a profession for Agnes De Mille—it is a way of life!

### Autobiography

An **autobiography** is an account of a person's life written by that person. It differs from a **biography,** which is the story of a person's life written by someone else. There is no single reason that explains why people choose to write about themselves. However, one important motivation may be the wish to share with others the story of how they struggled against odds to achieve their goals. In *Dance to the Piper,* Agnes De Mille writes about her difficulties as a young dancer with humor and honesty.

### Look For

Look for how De Mille not only explains ballet but gives you the feel of what it is like to train as a ballet dancer. She conveys the appearance and even the smells of the studio, and she describes practice sessions so that your own muscles seem to ache.

### Writing

Recall a time when you have engaged in difficult physical work or exercise. Freewrite about the way your body felt during and just after your efforts.

### Vocabulary

Knowing the following words will help you as you read this selection from *Dance to the Piper.*

**inviolable** (in vī′ ə lə b′l) *adj.* Not to be changed (p. 456)

**complacent** (kəm plās′′nt) *adj.*: Self-satisfied (p. 456)

**masochistic** (mas′ ə kiz′ tik) *adj.*: Getting pleasure from pain (p. 456)

**paradoxically** (par′ ə däk′ si k′lē) *adj.*: In a way that seems

opposite or contradictory (p. 458)

**deportment** (di pôrt′ mənt) *n.*: Way of holding oneself or behaving (p. 458)

**flag** (flag) *v.*: Grow weak or tired (p. 459)

**flout** (flout) *v.*: Show scorn or contempt for (p. 460)

### Objectives

1 To understand autobiography
2 To separate subjective from objective details
3 To choose the meaning that fits the context
4 To write an autobiographical sketch

## Support Material

**Teaching Portfolio**
Teacher Backup, p. 477
Grammar in Action Worksheet, *Varying Word Order,* p. 480
Usage and Mechanics Worksheet, p. 482
Vocabulary Check, p. 483
Critical Thinking and Reading Worksheet, *Separating Details,* p. 484

Language Worksheet, *Fitting the Context,* p. 485
Selection Test, p. 486

# *from* **Dance to the Piper**

## Agnes De Mille

Kosloff agreed to take us as pupils and out of courtesy to Uncle Cecil[1] he took us free without pay of any sort for as long or as often as we wished to go to his school.

We went down for our audition on a summer morning. The studio was an enormous bare room with folding chairs pushed against the white walls for the mothers to sit on while they watched their daughters sweat. Across one end of the hall hung a large mirror. Around the other three sides stretched the traditional barre.[2] I gave my audition in a bathing suit. Kosloff himself put me through the test. He did not say how talented I was or how naturally graceful. He said my knees were weak, my spine curved, that I was heavy for my age and had "no juice." By this he meant, I came to learn, that my muscles were dry, stubborn and unresilient. He said I was a bit old to start training; I was at the time thirteen. I looked at him in mild surprise. I hardly knew what emotion to give way to, the astonishment of hurt vanity or gratitude for professional help. I was sent off (I keep saying "I"—my sister of course was with me but from the start I took for granted that these lessons were mine. She just came along). We were sent off to buy blocked toe slippers, fitted right to the very ends of our toes, and to prepare proper practice dresses.

The first lesson was a private one conducted by Miss Fredova. Miss Fredova was born Winifred Edwards and had received her training in London from Anna Pavlova.[3] She was as slim as a sapling and always wore white like a trained nurse. She parted her dark hair in the center and drew it to the nape of her neck in glossy wings, Russian style. She was shod in low-heeled sandals. She taught standing erect as a guardsman, and beat time with a long pole. First she picked up a watering can and sprinkled water on the floor in a sunny corner by the barre. This she explained was so that we should not slip. Then she placed our hands on the barre and showed us how to turn out our feet ninety degrees from their normal walking stance into first position. Then she told us to *plier*[4] or bend our knees deeply, keeping our heels as long as possible on the floor. I naturally stuck out behind. I found the pole placed rigidly against my spine. I naturally pressed forward on my insteps. Her leg and knee planted against my foot curbed this tendency. "I can't move," I said, laughing with winning helplessness.

---

**1. Uncle Cecil:** Cecil B. De Mille (1881–1959), well-known American movie producer.
**2. barre** (bár) *n.*: Handrail held onto while doing ballet exercises.

---

**3. Anna Pavlova** (päv' lŏ vä): Famous Russian ballerina.
**4. *plier*** (plē ā'): French for "bend."

from *Dance to the Piper*  455

## Presentation

**Motivation/Prior Knowledge**
You might tell students that professional athletes sometimes take ballet lessons to become more agile and graceful. Tell students that this selection will demonstrate both the value and difficulty of ballet training.

**Master Teacher Note** Consider telling students that Agnes De Mille, who choreographed many famous Broadway shows, felt that she could reveal a character's personality with a few well-chosen gestures. Lead students to see that the body language we use in everyday life communicates much about us and that choreographers like De Mille base their work on such an understanding.

**Purpose-Setting Question** Why does De Mille persist in striving toward her goal despite setbacks?

**Discussion** What do you conclude about De Mille as a person from her comment that ". . . from the start I took for granted that these lessons were mine"?

**2 Clarification** De Mille provides the reader with an historical perspective on ballet. Many forms of dance fade out of style, are modified, or are updated. Ballet, however, has stayed very much the same for hundreds of years.

**3 Discussion** What does De Mille mean when she says that she "inherited the labor of centuries"?

"Don't talk," she said. "Down-ee, two-ee, three-ee, four-ee. Down the heels, don't rock on your feet."

At the end of ten minutes the sweat stuck in beads on my forehead. "May I sit down?" I asked.

"You must never sit during practice. It ruins the thigh muscles. If you sit down you may not continue with class." I of course would have submitted to a beating with whips rather than stop. I was taking the first steps into the promised land. The path might be thorny but it led straight to Paradise. "Down-ee, two-ee, three-ee, four-ee. *Nuca.*[5] Give me this fourth position. Repeat the exercise."

So she began every lesson. So I have begun every practice period since. It is part of the inviolable ritual of ballet dancing. Every ballet student that has ever trained in the classic technique in any part of the world begins just this way, never any other. They were dreary exercises and I was very bad at them but these were the exercises that built Taglioni's[6] leg. These repeated stretches and pulls gave Pavlova her magic foot and Legnani hers and Kchessinska[7] hers. This was the very secret of how to dance, the tradition handed down from teacher to pupil for three hundred years. A king had patterned the style and named the steps, the king who built Versailles.[8] Here was an ancient and enduring art whose technique stood like the rules of harmony. All other kinds of performance in our Western theater had faded or

---

**5. *Nuca*:** Informal Russian expression meaning "come on."
**6. Taglioni's** (tä lyō′ nēz): Maria Taglioni (1804–1884), an Italian ballerina.
**7. Legnani** (lā nyä′ nē) **. . . Kchessinska** (che sēn′ skä): Pierina Legnani (1863–1923), an Italian ballerina; Mathilda Kchessinska, a Polish ballerina.
**8. king . . . Versailles** (vər sī′): King Louis XIV of France (1638–1715) built a splendid palace in Versailles, near Paris.

changed. What were movies to this? Or Broadway plays?

I, a complacent child, who had been flattered into believing I could do without what had gone before, now inherited the labor of centuries. I had come into my birthright. I was fourteen, and I had found my life's work. I felt superior to other adolescents as I stood beside the adults serene and strong, reassured by my vision.

I bent to the discipline. I learned to relax with my head between my knees when I felt sick or faint. I learned how to rest my insteps by lying on my back with my feet vertically up against the wall. I learned how to bind up my toes so that they would not bleed through the satin shoes. But I never sat down. I learned the first and all-important dictate of ballet dancing—never to miss the daily practice, hell or high water, sickness or health, never to miss the barre practice; to miss meals, sleep, rehearsals even but not the practice, not for one day ever under any circumstances, except on Sundays and during childbirth.

I seemed, however, to have little aptitude for the business. What had all this talk about God-given talent amounted to? It was like trying to wiggle my ears. I strained and strained. Nothing perceptible happened. A terrible sense of frustration drove me to striving with masochistic frenzy. Twice I fainted in class. My calves used to ache until tears stuck in my eyes. I learned every possible manipulation of the shoe to ease the aching tendons of my insteps. I used to get abominable stitches in my sides from attempting continuous jumps. But I never sat down. I learned to cool my forehead against the plaster of the walls. I licked the perspiration off from around my mouth. I breathed through my nose though my eyes bugged. But I did not sit and I did not stop.

Ballet technique is arbitrary and very dif-

AGNES DE MILLE IN COSTUME FOR "STAGEFRIGHT"
*Performing Arts Research Center*
The New York Public Library at Lincoln Center

DANCER IN PINK
*Edgar Degas*
Three Lions

4 **Discussion** A paradox is a state-ment that seems to contain a contradiction. Explain the para-dox in this statement.

5 **Reading Strategy** Ask students to summarize the background information on pages 458 and 459.

ficult. It never becomes easy; it becomes pos-sible. The effort involved in making a dancer's body is so long and relentless, in many instances so painful, the effort to maintain the technique so grueling that un-less a certain satisfaction is derived from the disciplining and punishing, the pace could not be maintained. Most dancers are to an extent masochists. "What a good pain! What a profitable pain!" said Miss Fredova as she stretched her insteps in her two strong hands. "I have practiced for three hours. I am exhausted, and I feel wonderful."

My strongest impression of the Kosloff studio was, beside the sunlight on the floor and the white walls, the smell of sweat, the salty smell of clean sweat, the musty smell of old sweat on unwashed dresses, the smell of kitchen soap and sweat on the fresh dresses. Every dance studio smells of this—moist flesh, moist hair, hot glue in the shoes, hot socks and feet, and soap.

4 Paradoxically enough ballet dancing is designed to give the impression of lightness and ease. Nothing in classic dancing should be convulsive or tormented. Derived from the seventeenth- and eighteenth-century court

5 dances the style is kingly, a series of har-monious and balanced postures linked by serene movement. The style involves a total defiance of gravity, and because this must perforce be an illusion, the effect is achieved first by an enormous strengthening of the legs and feet to produce great resilient jumps and second by a coordination of arms and head in a rhythm slower than the rhythm of the legs which have no choice but to take the weight of the body when the body falls. But the slow relaxed movement of head and arms gives the illusion of sustained flight, gives the sense of effortless ease. The lungs may be bursting, the heart pounding in the throat, sweat springing from every pore, but hands must float in repose, the head stir

gently as though swooning in delight. The diaphragm must be lifted to expand the chest fully, proudly, the abdomen pulled in flat. The knees must be taut and flat to give the extended leg every inch of length. The leg must be turned outward forty-five degrees in the hip socket so that the side of the knee and the long unbroken line of the leg are pre-sented to view and never the lax, droopy line of a bent knee. The leg must look like a sword. The foot arches to prolong the line of extension. The supporting foot turns out forty-five degrees to enhance the line of the supporting leg, to keep the hips even, and to ensure the broadest possible base for the support and balancing of the body.

It should always be remembered that the court, and therefore the first, ballet dances were performed by expert swordsmen and derive much of their style from fencing posi-tions. The discipline embraces the whole de-portment. The lifted foot springs to attention the minute it leaves the floor. The support-ing foot endures all; the instep must never give way even when the whole weight of the body drops and grinds on the single slim arch. The legs can be held in their turned position by the great muscles across the but-tocks only by pulling the buttocks in flat. The spine should be steady, the expression of the face noble, the face of a king to whom all things are possible. The eyebrows may not go up, the shoulders may not lift, the neck may not stiffen, nor the mouth open like a hooked fish.

The five classic positions and the basic arm postures and steps were named at the request of Louis XIV by his great ballet mas-ter, Pécourt, Lully's[9] collaborator, codified, described and fixed in the regimen of daily exercise which has become almost ceremo-

---

**9. Lully's:** Jean Baptiste Lully (zhän bä tēst' lü lē'), a French composer (1632–1687).

## Grammar in Action

Writers often change **word order** to emphasize key words or phrases. For example, writers know that the word or phrase in the final portion of a sentence usually receives the most emphasis. The word or phrase that begins a sentence receives the second greatest emphasis. Note the effect of word order in the following sentences:

A vicious storm, growing in intensity, howled across the hills from the southwest.

Growing in intensity, roaring across the hills from the south-west, a vicious storm howled.

The first sentence buries in the middle words like *intensity* and *howled*; the emphasis is on the words *southwest* and *vicious storm*. In the second sentence, the emphasis is on the word *howled* and the participial phrase *growing in intensity*.

nial with time. Since then the technique has expanded and diversified but the fundamental steps and nomenclature remain unchanged. The "Royale" is still the faked beaten jump it was when Louis XIV, not as nimble in the legs as he would have liked to appear, failed to achieve a proper *entrechat quatre.*[10]

The ideal ballet body is long limbed with a small compact torso. This makes for beauty of line; the longer the arms and legs the more exciting the body line. The ideal ballet foot has a high taut instep and a wide stretch in the Achilles' tendon.[11] This tendon is the spring on which a dancer pushes for his jump, the hinge on which he takes the shock of landing. If there is one tendon in a dancer's body more important than any other, it is this tendon. It is, I should say, the prerequisite for all great technique. When the heel does not stretch easily and softly like a cat's, as mine did not, almost to the point of malformation, the shock of running or jumping must be taken somewhere in the spine by sticking out behind, for instance, in a sitting posture after every jump. I seemed to be all rusty wire and safety pins. My torso was long with unusually broad hips, my legs and arms abnormally short, my hands and feet broad and short. I was besides fat. What I did not know was that I was constructed for endurance and that I developed through effort alone a capacity for outperforming far, far better technicians. Because I was built like a mustang, stocky, mettlesome and sturdy, I became a good jumper, growing special compensating muscles up the front of my shins for the lack of a helpful heel. But the long, cool, serene classic line was forever denied me.

---

10. *entrechat quatre* (än′ trə shä′ kä′ tr′): French term for a difficult ballet leap.
11. **Achilles' tendon:** Cord of tissue connecting the back of the heel to the calf muscles.

And at first, of course, the compensations and adjustments were neither present nor indicated. Every dancer makes his own body. He is born only with certain physical tendencies. This making of a ballet leg takes approximately ten years and the initial stages are almost entirely discouraging, for even the best look awkward and paralyzed at the beginning.

My predicament was intensified by the fact that Mother and Father had no intention of permitting me to slight my other studies for this new enthusiasm. I was allowed one private lesson a week (forty-five minutes) and one class lesson (one hour). In between times I practiced at home alone, something no dancer, pupil or professional, ever does. One needs company to overcome the almost irresistible tendency to flag. One needs someone else's eye on awkward parts impossible to see. It is an unnatural and unprofitable strain for a child to practice without supervision. I practiced in Mother's bathroom where she had a little barre fitted for me. The floor was slippery and there was no mirror. And I hated to practice there. I flagellated myself into the daily grind. Mother thought I was overworking and forbade me to practice more than forty-five minutes. When I showed signs of resisting, she persuaded Kosloff to order me not to exceed this limit. All the other children practiced one hour a day in the studio and had a daily class lesson besides. They practically lived at the studio, practicing in the morning, taking lessons in the afternoon, sewing costumes and talking dancing in between times. Some of them even came back at night to practice alone. I cried myself to sleep because of the restraints imposed on me. Mother answered that dancing technique was not as important as education and health. We reached an impasse.

Why did I not simply disobey Mother?

*from* Dance to the Piper   459

6 **Discussion** De Mille gives insight into the tenacity required to develop the physical characteristics necessary for ballet. Have students compare and contrast ballet practice and athletic training.

7 **Clarification** Tell students that *to flag* means "to grow weak."

8 **Clarification** *Flagellated* means "whipped or punished."

9 **Reading Strategy** How do you think this conflict will be resolved?

---

Now observe how Agnes De Mille uses word order:

The eyebrows may not go up, the shoulders may not lift, the neck may not stiffen, nor the mouth open like a hooked fish. My torso was long with unusually broad hips, my legs and arms abnormally short, my hands and feet broad and short. Mother answered that dancing technique was not as important as education and health.

**Student Activity 1.** Rearrange the word order in the sentences from Dance to the Piper that were used as examples, and explain how the new order changes the emphasis.

**Student Activity 2.** Write a sentence about an activity or hobby of your own. Then revise the sentence to change the words or phrases that are emphasized. Choose the version you like best and explain your choice.

**10 Clarification** To *flout* is "to show contempt for."

**11 Discussion** What does this response reveal about De Mille's mother?

**12 Discussion** Compare and contrast the approaches of Kosloff and Fredova.

Because I cannot remember disobeying her in any single instance after the age of ten, never at any time. And because behind my mother stood my father, whom I loved with all my heart and whom I did not wish to flout.

Since I could not practice long, obviously I must practice harder. I strained and strained. Between the Monday lesson and the Thursday lesson, I developed and matured rigid bad habits. Every week I developed a new bad habit.

The plain truth is I was the worst pupil in the class. Having grown into adolescence feeling that I was remarkably gifted and destined to be great (I remember a friend asking Mother, "But do you want her to be a professional dancer?" and Mother's cool reply, "If she can be a Pavlova—not otherwise"), I now found I could not hold my own with any of the girls standing on the floor beside me. So I crept about at the rear of the group, found matters wrong with my shoes, with my knees, with my hair, resorted to any device to get away from the dreadful exposure.

Furthermore, the Kosloff method of teaching rather accentuated my dilemma. The accent was placed on force and duration instead of harmony. He was intent on disciplining the feet and legs, and paid almost no attention to the co-ordination of arms and facial expression. The girls grew as vigorous as Cossacks,[12] leaping prodigiously, whirling without cease, flailing and thrashing as they went and contorting their necks and faces in a hideous effort to show the master how altogether hell-bent for beauty they were. The exercises he devised were little miracles of perverse difficulty, muscle-locking gutbusters, all of them. I have never since seen healthy girls faint in class, but in Kosloff's class they went down quite regularly and

were dragged off with their heels bumping on the floor behind them. Kosloff barely stopped counting. He used to sit in a great armchair facing the room, stamping and roaring, whacking a cane in measure to the music. In the corner sat the man with the balalaika[13] barely audible through the noise. All the girls adored the master and gladly fainted for him. It was Miss Fredova, however, who gave me my private lessons, quietly, patiently, kindly. Kosloff occasionally walked in, looked for a minute, said, "No juice, no juice. More *plié*. Do you know? More expression, more sowl,"[14] grinned suddenly with Tartar[15] glee and lost interest. "Don't be discouraged," said the angel Fredova, "I wish though you could practice more regularly."

I was always late for class. We had a piano lesson before the dancing lesson and the traveling between required at least forty minutes and getting into practice clothes another ten. Mother allowed twenty minutes exactly from keyboard to barre and in three years she refused to adjust her timetable, always hoping that geography would somehow give way. As a consequence I always missed the preliminary warming-up exercises and started every class half through, cold and unprepared. I was not permitted ever to make the trip into town alone so I could not better the situation. Mother gave up two afternoons a week, a noteworthy sacrifice in a busy life, to driving us downtown. She never put off one class in three years, but she also was never on time.

Only once did I have a small bit of my share of success. On a single occasion Kosloff gave exercises in pantomime. He suddenly stopped the class and called me out from my position in the back of the room. I

12

11

12. **Cossacks** (käs′ aks): A people of southern Russia known for their fierceness.

13. **balalaika** (bal′ ə līk′ ə): Russian stringed instrument somewhat like a guitar.
14. **sowl:** Soul.
15. **Tartar** (tär′ tər): Fierce Mongol or Turk.

demonstrated the exercise to a hushed and watching group. I did, of course, the best I could, trembling a little. They applauded. Kosloff beamed on me. He told Uncle Cecil that I showed the finest talent for pantomime of any pupil he had ever taught. This remark was naturally not repeated to me until long after.

Ah but there was a glory in that room! Each day's class was important and a little frightening. When the master praised a pupil we shivered with envy and excitement. When he roared and denounced we blanched. When he made jokes we laughed although we rarely understood what he was saying—it nearly always had to do with teasing some wretch. When he talked about expression and "sowl" I, for one, wept. When he talked about fame, galas, "applows," and *réclame*,[16] I slept poorly for nights after. We curtsied formally at the end of class. We were never late—that is, the others never were, I always was. When he talked of his triumphs with Diaghilev[17] in Paris and how the pupils practice in Moscow with butter on the floor to make it harder, and how as a young man he could easily turn twenty pirouettes[18] with a single push, we listened round-eyed, grabbing the chance to get our breaths before the next frantic series of jumps.

At Christmas there was a table covered with gifts, photographs for the first year pupils, gold pins for the second year, and pins with additional diamonds and wreaths and bars for the veterans. We were called out singly by name and given our gift. We then made a reverence,[19] said "thank you" in Russian and retired. Kosloff kept open house on

**AGNES DE MILLE IN "RODEO"**
*Performing Arts Research Center*
*The New York Public Library at Lincoln Center*

Christmas with magnificent Russian food and boundless Russian welcome.

There were books on a side table in the studio filled with pictures of the great ballerinas. We pored over them between classes. As I stood shifting from one weary foot to the other trying to ease my cramped muscles, Miss Fredova used to tell about Legnani, the great Italian ballerina, who brought the *fouetté* pirouette[20] to Russia—how a ruble[21] used to be placed on the floor and a circle drawn around it—how she placed the toe of her left foot in this mark and then performed sixty-four consecutive *fouetté* pirouettes, stopping in perfect fifth position, the toe of her left foot exactly in the ruble mark; how

---

**16. *réclame*** (rā kläm´): French for "publicity."
**17. Diaghilev:** Sergei Pavlovich Diaghilev (syer gyä´ i päv lō´ vich dyä´ gi lyef), Famous Russian ballet producer (1872–1929).
**18. pirouettes** (pir´oo wetz) *n.*: Rapid turns on one foot or the point of the toe.
**19. reverence** (rev´ ər əns) *n.*: Curtsy or bow.

**20. *fouetté*** (fwe tā´) **pirouette:** French term for a turn combined with a kick.
**21. ruble** (rōo´ b'l) *n.*: Russian coin.

from *Dance to the Piper*   461

**13 Discussion** As she practiced ballet steps, De Mille also learned about great ballerinas of the past. Why do you think such stories were important to her?

13

14 **Discussion** Ask students why De Mille might have chosen to call her autobiography *Dance to the Piper?*

**Reader's Response** What art or hobby do you feel as passionately about as De Mille does about ballet in this selection? Why?

her turnout was so extraordinary that she could balance a glass of wine on the flat of her instep as she revolved in second position—how her balance was so peerless that she could perform a complete adage,[22] thirty-two measures long, standing in the middle of the floor on one point without support of any sort. "Will I be able to do this?" I asked breathlessly. "I doubt if you will be that good," she said smiling. "Oh," I sighed with deep disappointment, not realizing that no one else has ever been able to duplicate this feat, not realizing that it is unlikely indeed that Legnani herself performed it. But the legend spurred me on. "*Nuca,*" said Miss Fredova, "give me this one pirouette and stop in some recognizable position."

My weeks were divided into two sections, the three days I prepared for the class lesson, and the three days I prepared for the private lesson. I woke on Monday saying happily, "Today I have a lesson, today I need not practice alone." I woke most blissfully on Thursday saying, "Today I have a lesson with Miss Fredova." Friday entailed disappointment since it introduced a whole week before the next private lesson. Three times during the first winter, Miss Fredova said "very good" and I recorded the event duly in my diary. On those nights I drove home with a singing heart and stood in the bedroom in the dark gripping the edge of my desk in excitement, so in love with dancing, so in love with her.

"Oh God," I prayed, "let me be like her. Let me be a fine dancer." I took to wearing sandals because she did, even to parties, and when my schoolmates teased, I scoffed at their fashionably distorted toes and said proudly, "I have a use for *my* feet."

My well-filled curriculum—classes, homework, tennis, piano, editing—was ordered with just one thought: to make room for the dance practice. I rose at six-thirty and I studied and practiced at breakneck concentration until six in the evening when I was at last free to put on dancing dress and walk—to Mother's bathroom.

All through the lonely, drab exercises beside Mother's tub, without music or beat, proper floor or mirror, I had the joy of looking forward to dinner with Father, to hearing him talk about his scenarios[23] and what was going on at the studio. Sometimes he talked about music and literature. Once he said he thought I was an artist. Sometimes after dinner he sang and I accompanied him. These evenings my cup ran over. I went to bed early planning next day's practice, praying to do better in class. And as I lay waiting for sleep, breathing in the moist garden smells with my fox terrier slowly pressing me from the comfortable center of the bed, I used to dream about dancing on the stage with Pavlova, dancing until I dropped in a faint at her feet so that she would notice me and say, "That girl has talent."

14

---

**22. adage** (ə däj'): Slow, sustained movement.

**23. scenarios** (si ner' ē ōz): Scripts for movies.

## Closure and Extension

### ANSWERS TO THINKING ABOUT THE SELECTION
*Recalling*

1. Kosloff was very critical of De Mille's audition. He felt her muscles were unresilient, dry, and stubborn.
2. She had pains in her calves, insteps, and abdomen. She sometimes felt sick and faint.
3. Her parents would allow her to practice only forty-five minutes per day, with only one private and one class lesson per week. This limited De Mille's practice considerably. Her parents felt that dancing was not as important as education and health. Since she could not practice long, she practiced hard.
4. Kosloff praised De Mille for her talent for pantomime.

## THINKING ABOUT THE SELECTION

### Recalling

1. How did Kosloff rate De Mille's audition?
2. What aches and pains did she feel as she "drove" herself to try harder in class?
3. Explain why her parents' attitude was an obstacle to her study of dance. How did she overcome this obstacle?
4. Why did Kosloff praise De Mille?
5. Explain how dance started to fill her whole life.

### Interpreting

6. Why is ballet "a . . . defiance of gravity"?
7. Compare and contrast Fredova and Kosloff as teachers.
8. What do you think De Mille liked so much about ballet?

### Applying

9. Is it worth experiencing a great deal of pain to achieve a dream? Why or why not?

## ANALYZING LITERATURE

### Understanding Autobiography

An **autobiography** is an account of a person's life written by that person. Since Agnes De Mille is writing about herself, you learn much about her thoughts and feelings as well as the facts of her life. In this section of *Dance to the Piper*, she conveys both her excitement at discovering ballet and her frustration at being a beginner.

1. How did the difficulty of learning ballet challenge her ideas about herself?
2. Why do you think that she kept at it despite all the pain and frustration?
3. How might this account have been different if she had written it as a teenager instead of years later?

## CRITICAL THINKING AND READING

### Separating Details

A **subjective detail** is an account of what a writer feels or thinks. An **objective detail** is a fact or a description of something outside the writer. Most autobiographies contain both types of details. When De Mille says that "frustration drove me to striving with masochistic frenzy," she is reporting a subjective detail. However, her description of the studio as "an enormous bare room" is an objective detail.

Find three subjective details and three objective details in this selection.

## UNDERSTANDING LANGUAGE

### Fitting the Context

Many words have more than one meaning. You can determine the meaning the writer intends by examining the **context,** or the surrounding words. De Mille writes, "One needs company to overcome the almost irresistible tendency to flag." The word *flag* has several meanings, but the one that fits best here is "to weaken or tire."

For each italicized word identify the meaning that works best in the context.
1. The boxer tried to *steel* himself against his opponent's blows.
2. Why do you always *crow* over your victories?

## THINKING AND WRITING

### Writing an Autobiographical Sketch

Imagine that you are competing for a summer job. To get the job, you must write an autobiographical sketch telling how you became interested in this type of work. First outline the steps by which your interest developed. Then turn this outline into an autobiographical sketch. In revising your sketch, make sure that you have included both objective and subjective details.

from *Dance to the Piper* 463

(Answers begin on p.462.)

learned the difficulties involved in pursuing an art and, over a period of time, gained true self-confidence.

2. Suggested Response: She continued because she felt she had found her life's work and was determined to be successful.
3. Suggested Response: If she had written it as a teen-ager, she might not have taken such a humorous tone about her difficulties.

**Challenge** Write a paragraph describing De Mille's involvement with ballet from her mother's point of view.

### ANSWERS TO CRITICAL THINKING AND READING

1. Suggested Responses: Objective details include the facts that she first auditioned on a summer morning, that Miss Fredova was her teacher, and that the students received gifts each Christmas. Subjective details include her report that she was a complacent child, her statement that she hated to practice in the bathroom, and her assertion that she loved her father.

### ANSWERS TO UNDERSTANDING LANGUAGE

1. *Steel* in this context means "to harden or strengthen."
2. *Crow* in this context means "to brag or boast."

### THINKING AND WRITING

For help with this assignment, students can refer to Lesson 20, "Writing a Personal Essay," in the Handbook of Writing About Literature.

**Publishing Student Writing** You might want to have volunteers read their sketches to the class.

**Writing Across the Curriculum** You might want to have students research and report on ballet. Such research might even include attending a ballet performance.

---

5. De Mille thought and fantasized about dance all the time.

### Interpreting

6. Suggested Response: Ballet is "a... defiance of gravity" because the feet and legs become so strong for jumping and because the slow relaxed movement of head and arms gives an aura of weightlessness.
7. Suggested Response: Kosloff appears critical, negative and

highly disciplined. Fredova was more supportive and demonstrative. De Mille idolized Fredova and feared, yet admired, Kosloff.
8. Suggested Response: De Mille felt that ballet was an enduring art that she had been born to pursue.

### Applying

9. Answers will differ. One response would be that a dream is worth achieving at any cost and that

strength of conviction is an admirable quality. Another response might be that the goal may not be all that you expect it to be after you have made a rigorous and painful effort.

### ANSWERS TO ANALYZING LITERATURE

1. Suggested Response: When she began ballet, she was complacent about her abilities. She soon

**More About the Author** Heyerdahl also sailed a boat made of
papyrus reeds from Morocco to
the West Indies. The purpose of
this trip was to prove that the
ancient Egyptians could have
made similar voyages. Ask students why such a voyage would
have been even more daring for
an ancient Egyptian than it was
for Heyerdahl.

**Literary Focus** You may want to
have students note the passages
in which Heyerdahl describes
the dangers that lie ahead.

**Look For** Have students look for
the attitudes of the men as catastrophe is imminent. How do the
men prepare for disaster? How
do the preparations increase the
suspense?

**Writing/Prior Knowledge** Consider having students discuss
this issue in small groups before
they begin to freewrite.

**Vocabulary** For the benefit of
**less advanced** students, assign
each of several students a vocabulary word. Ask students to
define the word and then use it in
proper context within a sentence.

# GUIDE FOR READING

## *from* Kon-Tiki

**Thor Heyerdahl** (1914–    ), born in Larvik, Norway, has won fame
as an anthropologist and explorer. His expeditions have taken him to
many different parts of the globe, from the Polynesian Islands in the
Pacific Ocean to Africa and Asia. One of the many honors he has
received for his work is membership in the Royal Norwegian Academy
of Sciences. This selection comes from his book *Kon-Tiki*, an account
of his daring trip across the Pacific on a specially designed raft.

**Suspense in
Autobiography**

**Suspense** is the quality of a work that makes you wonder what will
happen next. The two main ingredients of suspense are uncertainty—
the Latin word from which *suspense* comes means "uncertain"—and
danger. You tend to feel suspense, therefore, when someone is in a
dangerous situation and you do not know how events will turn out. In
this episode from *Kon-Tiki,* Heyerdahl and his crew face the dangers
of shipwreck.

**Look For**

As you read, look for how the writer increases the suspense by constantly telling you about the risks that lie ahead.

**Writing**

Some people dream of adventure while others dream of home. Freewrite, exploring what you see as the difference between the two different types of personalities.

**Vocabulary**

Knowing the following words will help you as you read this selection
from *Kon-Tiki*.

**ominous** (äm′ ə nəs) *adj.*:
Threatening; dangerous (p.
465)
**idyllic** (ī dil′ ik) *adj.*: Pleasing
and simple; peaceful (p. 466)
**laconic** (lə kän′ ik) *adj.*: Not
speaking much (p. 468)

**lagoon** (lə go͞on′) *n.*: Water enclosed by a circular coral reef
(p. 469)
**elation** (i lā′ shən) *n.*: Feeling of
great joy (p. 470)
**plaiting** (plāt′ iŋ) *n.*: Braiding
(p. 472)

464    *Nonfiction*

---

| Objectives | Support Material | |
|---|---|---|
| 1  To understand suspense in autobiography<br>2  To understand the sequence of events in autobiography<br>3  To learn seafaring terms<br>4  To write about autobiography | **Teaching Portfolio**<br>Teacher Backup, p. 489<br>Grammar in Action Worksheets, *Appreciating Narrative Writing,* p. 493; *Using Semicolons,* p. 495<br>Usage and Mechanics Worksheet, p. 497<br>Vocabulary Check, p. 498<br>Analyzing Literature Worksheet, | *Understanding Suspense,* p. 499<br>Critical Thinking and Reading Worksheet, *Understanding the Sequence of Events,* p. 500<br>Selection Test, p. 501<br>Art Transparency 7: *The Lookout "All's Well,"* by Winslow Homer |

# from Kon-Tiki

## Thor Heyerdahl

For three days we drifted across the sea without a sight of land.

We were drifting straight toward the ominous Takume and Raroia reefs, which together blocked up forty to fifty miles of the sea ahead of us. We made desperate efforts to steer clear, to the north of these dangerous reefs, and things seemed to be going well till one night the watch came hurrying in and called us all out.

The wind had changed. We were heading straight for the Takume reef. It had begun to rain, and there was no visibility at all. The reef could not be far off.

In the middle of night we held a council of war. It was a question of saving our lives now. To get past on the north side was now hopeless; we must try to get through on the south side instead. We trimmed the sail, laid the oar over, and began a dangerous piece of sailing with the uncertain north wind behind us. If the east wind came back before we passed the whole façade of the fifty-mile-long reefs, we should be hurled in among the breakers, at their mercy.

We agreed on all that should be done if shipwreck was imminent. We would stay on board the Kon-Tiki at all costs. We would not climb up the mast, from which we should be shaken down like rotten fruit, but would cling tight to the stays[1] of the mast when the

seas poured over us. We laid the rubber raft loose on the deck and made fast to it a small watertight radio transmitter, a small quantity of provisions, waterbottles, and medical stores. This would be washed ashore independently of us if we ourselves should get over the reef safe but empty-handed. In the stern of the Kon-Tiki we made fast a long rope with a float which also would be washed ashore, so that we could try to pull in the raft if she were stranded out on the reef. And so we crept into bed and left the watch to the helmsman out in the rain.

As long as the north wind held, we glided slowly but surely down along the façade of the coral reefs which lay in ambush below the horizon. But then one afternoon the wind died away, and when it returned it had gone round into the east. According to Erik's position we were already so far down that we now had some hope of steering clear of the southernmost point of the Raroia reef. We would try to get round it and into shelter before going on to other reefs beyond it.

When night came, we had been a hundred days at sea.

Late in the night I woke, feeling restless and uneasy. There was something unusual in the movement of the waves. The Kon-Tiki's motion was a little different from what it usually was in such conditions. We had become sensitive to changes in the rhythm of the logs. I thought at once of suction from a coast, which was drawing near, and was

---

1. **stays** (stāz) n.: A heavy rope or cable used for support.

from Kon-Tiki   465

**Presentation**

**Motivation/Prior Knowledge**
Heyerdahl risked his life to prove that ancient Peruvians could have migrated to Pacific islands in small boats. Tell the students that the risks he took are especially evident in this excerpt.

**Master Teacher Note** Use the overhead projector to show students Art Transparency 7, *The Lookout "All's Well,"* by Winslow Homer. Ask them how this picture conveys the sense of an ocean voyage.

Tell students that Heyerdahl traveled on a much smaller craft than the one suggested in Homer's picture. It was a raft made of nine fresh balsa logs fastened together with hemp ropes. This raft was named in memory of an Incan god.

**Purpose-Setting Question** What different types of danger do Heyerdahl and his crew encounter?

**Thematic Idea** Another selection that deals with the courage required of individuals who stretch themselves to their limits is "Dance to the Piper," page 455.

You might also want to teach the *Odyssey*, page 681, with this selection. Like Heyerdahl, Odysseus had to face the dangers of a long sea voyage.

1 **Literary Focus** How does this passage create suspense?

2 **Clarification** *Facade* means "the main face or front."

3 **Reading Strategy** Heyerdahl has given a vivid sense of impending danger and vulnerability. Ask students to predict what is in store for the crew of the *Kon-Tiki*.

4 **Clarification** *Islets* means "small islands."

5 **Discussion** What is the importance of preparing in advance for emergencies?

continually out on deck and up the mast. Nothing but sea was visible. But I could get no quiet sleep. Time passed.

At dawn, just before six, Torstein came hurrying down from the masthead.[2] He could see a whole line of small palm-clad islands far ahead. Before doing anything else we laid the oar over to southward as far as we could. What Torstein had seen must be the small coral islands which lay strewn like pearls on a string behind the Raroia reef. A northward current must have caught us.

At half-past seven palm-clad islets had appeared in a row all along the horizon to westward. The southernmost lay roughly ahead of our bow, and thence there were islands and clumps of palms all along the horizon on our starboard[3] side till they disappeared as dots away to northward. The nearest were four or five sea miles away.

A survey from the masthead showed that, even if our bow pointed toward the bottom island in the chain, our drift sideways was so great that we were not advancing in the direction in which our bow pointed. We were drifting diagonally right in toward the reef. With fixed centerboards[4] we should still have had some hope of steering clear. But sharks were following close astern, so that it was impossible to dive under the raft and tighten up the loose centerboards with fresh guy[5] ropes.

We saw that we had now only a few hours more on board the *Kon-Tiki*. They must be used in preparation for our inevitable wreck on the coral reef. Every man learned what he had to do when the moment came; each one of us knew where his own limited sphere of responsibility lay, so that we should not fly round treading on one another's toes when the time came and seconds counted. The *Kon-Tiki* pitched up and down, up and down, as the wind forced us in. There was no doubt that here was the turmoil of waves created by the reef—some waves advancing while others were hurled back after beating vainly against the surrounding wall.

We were still under full sail in the hope of even now being able to steer clear. As we gradually drifted nearer, half sideways, we saw from the mast how the whole string of palm-clad isles was connected with a coral reef, part above and part under water, which lay like a mole where the sea was white with foam and leaped high into the air. The Raroia atoll[6] is oval in shape and has a diameter of twenty-five miles, not counting the adjoining reefs of Takume. The whole of its longer side faces the sea to eastward, where we came pitching in. The reef itself, which runs in one line from horizon to horizon, is only a few hundred yards clear, and behind it idyllic islets lie in a string round the still lagoon inside.

It was with mixed feelings that we saw the blue Pacific being ruthlessly torn up and hurled into the air all along the horizon ahead of us. I knew what awaited us; I had visited the Tuamotu group before and had stood safe on land looking out over the immense spectacle in the east, where the surf from the open Pacific broke in over the reef. New reefs and islands kept on gradually appearing to southward. We must be lying off the middle of the façade of the coral wall.

On board the *Kon-Tiki* all preparations for the end of the voyage were being made. Everything of value was carried into the

---

**2. masthead:** The top part of the mast.
**3. starboard:** The right-hand side of a ship, as opposed to *port*, the left-hand side.
**4. centerboards:** Boards lowered through the bottom of a sailing vessel to prevent drifting.
**5. guy** (gī) *adj.*: Used for steadying or guiding.

---

**6. atoll** (a′ tôl) *n.*: A ring-shaped coral island.

466  Nonfiction

cabin and lashed fast. Documents and papers were packed into watertight bags, along with films and other things which would not stand a dip in the sea. The whole bamboo cabin was covered with canvas, and especially strong ropes were lashed across it. When we saw that all hope was gone, we opened up the bamboo deck and cut off with machete knives all the ropes which held the centerboards down. It was a hard job to get

from *Kon-Tiki*   467

6 **Critical Thinking and Reading**
Why do you think the men put on their shoes?

7 **Literary Focus** Why is the quoting of entries from the log an effective way to build suspense?

the centerboards drawn up, because they were all thickly covered with stout barnacles. With the centerboards up the draft[7] of our vessel was no deeper than to the bottom of the timber logs, and we would therefore be more easily washed in over the reef. With no centerboards and with the sail down, the raft lay completely sideways on and was entirely at the mercy of wind and sea.

We tied the longest rope we had to the homemade anchor and made it fast to the step of the port mast, so that the *Kon-Tiki* would go into the surf stern first when the anchor was thrown overboard. The anchor itself consisted of empty water cans filled with used radio batteries and heavy scrap, and solid mangrove-wood sticks projected from it, set crosswise.

Order number one, which came first and last, was: Hold on to the raft! Whatever happened, we must hang on tight on board and let the nine great logs take the pressure from the reef. We ourselves had more than enough to do to withstand the weight of the water. If we jumped overboard, we should become helpless victims of the suction which would fling us in and out over the sharp corals. The rubber raft would capsize in the steep seas or, heavily loaded with us in it, it would be torn to ribbons against the reef. But the wooden logs would sooner or later be cast ashore, and we with them, if we only managed to hold fast.

6 Next, all hands were told to put on their shoes for the first time in a hundred days and to have their life belts ready. The last precaution, however, was not of much value, for if a man fell overboard he would be battered to death, not drowned. We had time, too, to put our passports and such few dollars as we had left into our pockets. But it was not lack of time that was troubling us.

_____
**7. draft** *n.*: The depth of water that a ship displaces.

Those were anxious hours in which we lay drifting helplessly sideways, step after step, in toward the reef. It was noticeably quiet on board; we all crept in and out from cabin to bamboo deck, silent or laconic, and carried on with our jobs. Our serious faces showed that no one was in doubt as to what awaited us, and the absence of nervousness showed that we had all gradually acquired an unshakable confidence in the raft. If it had brought us across the sea, it would also manage to bring us ashore alive.

Inside the cabin there was a complete chaos of provision cartons and cargo, lashed fast. Torstein had barely found room for himself in the radio corner, where he had got the shortwave transmitter working. We were now over 4,000 sea miles from our old base at Callao,[8] where the Peruvian Naval War School had maintained regular contact with us, and still farther from Hal and Frank and the other radio amateurs in the United States. But, as chance willed, we had on the previous day got in touch with a capable radio "ham" who had a set on Rarotonga in the Cook Islands,[9] and the operators, quite contrary to all our usual practice, had arranged for an extra contact with him early in the morning. All the time we were drifting closer and closer in to the reef, Torstein was sitting tapping his key and calling Rarotonga.

Entries in the *Kon-Tiki's* log ran:

—8:15: We are slowly approaching land. We can now make out with the naked eye the separate palm trees inside on the starboard side.

—8:45: The wind has veered into a still more unfavorable quarter for us, so

7

_____
**8. Callao** (kä yä' ō̌) *n.*: A seaport in western Peru.
**9. Cook Islands:** A group of islands of New Zealand, in the South Pacific.

## Grammar in Action

**Narrative writing** relates an event or tells a story. Most fiction is narrative, but the narrative form can also be used to develop a topic in a work of nonfiction. Some subjects for works of nonfiction lend themselves particularly well to the narrative form. When a nonfiction work is about an event, as "Kon-Tiki" is, the logical form to use is the form of the narrative, or story. Look at this passage from the selection.

A few minutes later the anchor rushed overboard and caught hold of the bottom, so that the Kon-Tiki swung around and turned her stern inward toward the breakers. It held us for a few valuable minutes, while Thorstein sat hammering like mad on the key. He had got Rarotonga now. The breakers thundered in the air and the sea rose and fell furiously. All hands were at work on deck, and now Thorstein got his message through. He said we were drifting toward the Raroia reef. He asked Rarotonga to listen in on the same wave length every hour. If we were silent for more than thirty-six hours, Rarotonga must let the we have no hope of getting clear. No nervousness on board, but hectic preparations on deck. There is something lying on the reef ahead of us which looks like the wreck of a sailing vessel, but it may be only a heap of driftwood.

—9:45: The wind is taking us straight toward the last island but one we see behind the reef. We can now see the whole coral reef clearly; here it is built up like a white and red speckled wall which barely sticks up out of the water as a belt in front of all the islands. All along the reef white foaming surf is flung up toward the sky. Bengt is just serving up a good hot meal, the last before the great action!

It *is* a wreck lying in there on the reef. We are so close now that we can see right across the shining lagoon behind the reef and see the outlines of other islands on the other side of the lagoon.

As this was written, the dull drone of the surf came near again; it came from the whole reef and filled the air like thrilling rolls of the drum, heralding the exciting last act of the *Kon-Tiki*.

—9:50: Very close now. Drifting along the reef. Only a hundred yards or so away. Torstein is talking to the man on Rarotonga. All clear. Must pack up log now. All in good spirits; it looks bad, *but we shall make it!*

A few minutes later the anchor rushed overboard and caught hold of the bottom, so that the *Kon-Tiki* swung around and turned her stern inward toward the breakers. It held us for a few valuable minutes, while Torstein sat hammering like mad on the key. He had got Rarotonga now. The breakers thundered in the air and the sea rose and fell furiously. All hands were at work on deck, and now Torstein got his message through. He said we were drifting toward the Raroia reef. He asked Rarotonga to listen in on the same wave length every hour. If we were silent for more than thirty-six hours, Rarotonga must let the Norwegian Embassy in Washington know. Torstein's last words were:

"O.K. Fifty yards left. Here we go. Good-by."

Then he closed down the station, Knut sealed up the papers, and both crawled out on deck as fast as they could to join the rest of us, for it was clear now that the anchor was giving way.

The swell grew heavier and heavier, with deep troughs between the waves, and we felt the raft being swung up and down, up and down, higher and higher.

Again the order was shouted: "Hold on, never mind about the cargo, hold on!"

We were now so near the waterfall inside that we no longer heard the steady continuous roar from all along the reef. We now heard only a separate boom each time the nearest breaker crashed down on the rocks.

All hands stood in readiness, each clinging fast to the rope he thought the most secure. Only Erik crept into the cabin at the last moment; there was one part of the program he had not yet carried out—he had not found his shoes!

No one stood aft, for it was there the shock from the reef would come. Nor were the two firm stays which ran from the masthead down to the stern safe. For if the mast fell they would be left hanging overboard, over the reef. Herman, Bengt, and Torstein had climbed up on some boxes which were lashed fast forward of the cabin wall, and, while Herman clung on to the guy ropes

8

8 **Discussion** What are some of the camera shots you would use if you were filming this episode of the story?

Norwegian Embassy in Washington know. Torstein's final words were:

"O.K. Fifty yards left. Here we go. Good-by."

Note that events are told as a narrative, in chronological order the order in which they actually happen. Use of the narrative form allows readers to experience the events as the crew of the raft does. At this point in the narrative, what is the effect of the description in the fourth sentence? What is the effect of Thorstein's message?

**Student Activity 1.** Find two other narrative passages from the selection and share these with a classmate. Discuss whether you think the narrative conveys the events as Heyerdahl and the crew experienced them.

**Student Activity 2.** Write a brief narrative about an event that you or someone you know experienced. Include in the narrative details that will help your readers experience the event. Share your composition with the class.

9 **Clarification** *Ramshackle* means "shoddily constructed or rickety."

10 **Discussion** What can you infer about the crew based on their behavior?

from the ridge of the roof, the other two held on to the ropes from the masthead by which the sail at other times was hauled up. Knut and I chose the stay running from the bow up to the masthead, for, if mast and cabin and everything else went overboard, we thought the rope from the bow would nevertheless remain lying inboard, as we were now head on to the seas.

When we realized that the seas had got hold of us, the anchor rope was cut and we were off. A sea rose straight up under us, and we felt the *Kon-Tiki* being lifted up in the air. The great moment had come; we were riding on the wave back at breathless speed, our ramshackle craft creaking and groaning as she quivered under us. The excitement made one's blood boil. I remember that, having no other inspiration, I waved my arm and bellowed "Hurrah!" at the top of my lungs; it afforded a certain relief and could do no harm anyway. The others certainly thought I had gone mad, but they all beamed and grinned enthusiastically. On we ran with the seas rushing in behind us; this was the *Kon-Tiki's* baptism of fire. All must and would go well.

But our elation was soon dampened. A new sea rose high up astern of us like a glittering, green glass wall. As we sank down it came rolling after us, and, in the same second in which I saw it high above me, I felt a violent blow and was submerged under floods of water. I felt the suction through my whole body, with such great power that I had to strain every single muscle in my frame and think of one thing only—hold on, hold on! I think that in such a desperate situation the arms will be torn off before the brain consents to let go, evident as the outcome is. Then I felt that the mountain of water was passing on and relaxing its devilish grip of my body. When the whole mountain had

rushed on, with an ear-splitting roaring and crashing, I saw Knut again hanging on beside me, doubled up into a ball. Seen from behind, the great sea was almost flat and gray. As it rushed on, it swept over the ridge of the cabin roof which projected from the water, and there hung the three others, pressed against the cabin roof as the water passed over them.

We were still afloat.

In an instant I renewed my hold, with arms and legs bent round the strong rope. Knut let himself down and with a tiger's leap joined the others on the boxes, where the cabin took the strain. I heard reassuring exclamations from them, but at the same time I saw a new green wall rise up and come towering toward us. I shouted a warning and made myself as small and hard as I could where I hung. In an instant the *Kon-Tiki* disappeared completely under the masses of water. The sea tugged and pulled with all the force it could bring to bear at the poor little bundles of human bodies. The second sea rushed over us, to be followed by a third like it.

Then I heard a triumphant shout from Knut, who was now hanging on to the rope ladder:

"Look at the raft—she's holding!"

After three seas only the double mast and the cabin had been knocked a bit crooked. Again we had a feeling of triumph over the elements, and the elation of victory gave us new strength.

Then I saw the next sea coming towering up, higher than all the rest, and again I bellowed a warning aft to the others as I climbed up the stay, as high as I could get in a hurry, and hung on fast. Then I myself disappeared sideways into the midst of the green wall which towered high over us. The others, who were farther aft and saw me dis-

## Grammar in Action

A **semicolon** can be used to separate closely related independent clauses not joined by a coordinating conjunction. The semicolon is sometimes preferable to a period because it stresses the close relationship between two clauses and does not break the flow as a period would. You should not use a semicolon to connect clauses, however, unless they are closely related.

Notice Heyerdahl's effective use of the semicolon in the following sentences from *Kon-Tiki*:

The great moment had come; we were riding on the wave back at breathless speed, our ramshackle craft creaking and groaning as she quivered under us.
The vessel we knew from weeks and months at sea was no more; in a few seconds our pleasant world had become a shattered wreck.

In each of these passages, a period would have introduced too sharp a break, slowing the dramatic action.

appear first, estimated the height of the wall of water at twenty-five feet, while the foaming crest passed by fifteen feet above the part of the glassy wall into which I had vanished. Then the great wave reached them, and we had all one single thought—hold on, hold on, hold, hold, hold!

We must have hit the reef that time. I myself felt only the strain on the stay, which seemed to bend and slacken jerkily. But whether the bumps came from above or below I could not tell, hanging there. The whole submersion lasted only seconds, but it demanded more endurance than we usually have in our bodies. There is greater strength in the human mechanism than that of the muscles alone. I determined that, if I was to die, I would die in this position, like a knot on the stay. The sea thundered on, over and past, and as it roared by it revealed a hideous sight. The *Kon-Tiki* was wholly changed, as by the stroke of a magic wand. The vessel we knew from weeks and months at sea was no more; in a few seconds our pleasant world had become a shattered wreck.

I saw only one man on board besides myself. He lay pressed flat across the ridge of

11 **Discussion** What does this statement mean?

from *Kon-Tiki* 471

**Student Activity 1.** Find two other examples where Heyerdahl uses semicolons to connect related, independent clauses. Explain why each sentence is effective.

**Student Activity 2.** Write a paragraph describing a dramatic action. Use at least two sentences with semicolons.

the cabin roof, face downward with his arms stretched out on both sides, while the cabin itself was crushed in, like a house of cards, toward the stern and toward the starboard side. The motionless figure was Herman. There was no other sign of life, while the hill of water thundered by, in across the reef. The hardwood mast on the starboard side was broken like a match, and the upper stump, in its fall, had smashed right through the cabin roof, so that the mast and all its gear slanted at a low angle over the reef on the starboard side. Astern, the steering block was twisted round lengthways and the crossbeam broken, while the steering oar was smashed to splinters. The splashboards at the bow were broken like cigar boxes, and the whole deck was torn up and pasted like wet paper against the forward wall of the cabin, along with boxes, cans, canvas, and other cargo. Bamboo sticks and rope ends stuck up everywhere, and the general effect was of complete chaos.

**12** I felt cold fear run through my whole body. What was the good of my holding on? If I lost one single man here, in the run in, the whole thing would be ruined, and for the moment there was only one human figure to be seen after the last buffet. In that second Torstein's hunched-up form appeared outside the raft. He was hanging like a monkey in the ropes from the masthead and managed to get on to the logs again, where he crawled up on to the debris forward of the cabin. Herman, too, now turned his head and gave me a forced grin of encouragement, but did not move. I bellowed in the faint hope of locating the others and heard Bengt's calm voice call out that all hands were aboard. They were lying holding on to the ropes behind the tangled barricade which the tough plaiting from the bamboo deck had built up.

All this happened in the course of a few seconds, while the *Kon-Tiki* was being drawn out of the witches' caldron by the backwash, and a fresh sea came rolling over her. For the last time I bellowed "Hang on!" at the top of my lungs amid the uproar, and that was all I myself did; I hung on and disappeared in the masses of water which rushed over and past in those endless two or three seconds. That was enough for me. I saw the ends of the logs knocking and bumping against a sharp step in the coral reef without going over it. Then we were sucked out again. I also saw the two men who lay stretched out across the ridge of the cabin roof, but none of us smiled any longer. Behind the chaos of bamboo I heard a calm voice call out:

"This won't do."

I myself felt equally discouraged. As the masthead sank farther and farther out over the starboard side, I found myself hanging on to a slack line outside the raft. The next sea came. When it had gone by I was dead tired, and my only thought was to get up on to the logs and lie behind the barricade. When the backwash retreated, I saw for the first time the rugged red reef naked beneath us and perceived Torstein standing, bent double, on gleaming red corals, holding on to a bunch of rope ends from the mast. Knut, standing aft, was about to jump. I shouted that we must all keep on the logs, and Torstein, who had been washed overboard by the pressure of water, sprang up again like a cat.

Two or three more seas rolled over us with diminishing force, and what happened then I do not remember, except that water foamed in and out and I myself sank lower and lower toward the red reef over which we were being lifted in. Then only crests of foam full of salt spray came whirling in, and I was

472    *Nonfiction*

able to work my way in on to the raft, where we all made for the after end of the logs which was highest up on the reef.

At the same moment Knut crouched down and sprang up on to the reef with the line which lay clear astern. While the backwash was running out, he waded through the whirling water some thirty yards in and stood safely at the end of the line when the next sea foamed in toward him, died down, and ran back from the flat reef like a broad stream.

Then Erik came crawling out of the collapsed cabin, with his shoes on. If we had all done as he did, we should have got off cheaply. As the cabin had not been washed overboard but had been pressed down pretty flat under the canvas, Erik lay quietly stretched out among the cargo and heard the peals of thunder crashing above him while the collapsed bamboo walls curved downward. Bengt had had a slight concussion when the mast fell but had managed to crawl under the wrecked cabin alongside Erik. We should all of us have been lying there if we had realized in advance how firmly the countless lashings and plaited bamboo sheets would hang on to the main logs under the pressure of the water.

Erik was now standing ready on the logs aft, and when the sea retired he, too, jumped up on to the reef. It was Herman's turn next, and then Bengt's. Each time the raft was pushed a bit farther in, and, when Torstein's turn and my own came, the raft already lay so far in on the reef that there was no longer any ground for abandoning her. All hands began the work of salvage.

13

13 **Reading Strategy** Ask students to summarize the sequence of events from the moment the raft hits the reef.

**Reader's Response** What do you think was the most suspenseful part of this story? the most exciting? Why?

## ANSWERS TO THINKING ABOUT THE SELECTION
### Recalling

1. The raft was drifting toward a forty-to fifty-mile expanse of reefs with coral and tumultuous waves.
2. "Order number one" for the men was to hold on to the raft no matter what happened.
3. After the anchor rope was cut, the *Kon-Tiki* was caught by the waves and tossed about. The men managed to hang on. The *Kon-Tiki* was shattered and carried in over the reef, and all the men survived.

### Interpreting

4. Answers will differ, but should include the necessity of hanging on to the raft and a knowledge of their responsibilities so that order would be maintained.
5. Suggested Response: Heyerdahl demonstrates courage and determination.
6. Suggested Response: Heyerdahl creates an impression of the sea as an awesome and powerful adversary.

### Applying

7. Answers will differ, but most students will realize that this goal suggests a courageous pursuit of adventure. It applies to Heyerdahl because he set out to prove his theory and nothing, not even powerful natural forces, deterred him.

**Challenge** Describe an act of courage that does *not* involve facing physical danger.

## ANSWERS TO ANALYZING LITERATURE

1. Suggested Response: The description of the emergency preparations keeps you wondering what will happen.
2. Suggested Response: This explanation creates suspense by vividly describing the dangers that the crew faces.
3. Suggested Response: The minute-by-minute accounts give readers a sense of living through the dangerous situation. Readers

## THINKING ABOUT THE SELECTION
### Recalling

1. Explain the danger toward which the raft was drifting.
2. What is "Order number one" for the men?
3. Briefly summarize what happens after they cut the anchor rope.

### Interpreting

4. In your own words, explain the men's plan for surviving the shipwreck.
5. Identify two character traits that Heyerdahl demonstrates in this account.
6. Explain the overall impression that Heyerdahl creates of the sea.

### Applying

7. One of the most famous adventurers is Odysseus, a Greek king who wandered the seas for ten years in search of home. (See Homer's *Odyssey,* page 676). In his poem about Odysseus, Tennyson has him express his goal as "To strive, to seek, to find, and not to yield." Discuss the meaning of this goal. Then explain how it applies to Heyerdahl as well.

## ANALYZING LITERATURE
### Understanding Suspense

**Suspense** is the quality of a work that makes you wonder what will happen next. In this selection from *Kon-Tiki,* for example, Heyerdahl builds suspense by describing the crew's repeated "efforts to steer clear" of the reef. This account makes you think about the danger and wonder whether the men will escape it.

Explain how each of the following elements also adds to the suspense.
1. The description of the emergency "preparations for the end of the voyage. . . ."
2. The explanation of the reason for "Order number one . . . Hold on to the raft!"
3. The minute-by-minute entries from the ship's log.

474   *Nonfiction*

## CRITICAL THINKING AND READING
### Understanding the Sequence of Events

To appreciate the suspense of a narrative, you must have a clear understanding of the sequence of events. The following is a scrambled version of some of the key events from this selection. Rearrange the list so that the events appear in the order in which they actually occurred.
1. The anchor rope is cut and the *Kon-Tiki* rides "at breathless speed."
2. The cabin of the raft is destroyed.
3. Sharks make it impossible to fix the centerboards under the raft.
4. They try to steer north of the reefs.

## UNDERSTANDING LANGUAGE
### Learning Seafaring Terms

In this narrative, Heyerdahl uses many special terms that relate to seafaring. By learning these terms, you will better understand the exciting action in this episode. Look up the following words in a dictionary, find where they appear in the selection, and use each in a sentence.

1. stern      4. aft
2. bow       5. starboard
3. port

## THINKING AND WRITING
### Writing About Autobiography

Autobiographies often appear on best-seller lists. Do you read autobiographies on your own? Do your friends? Why? Jot down the ingredients that make an autobiography valuable and interesting. Then use this list to write an essay explaining why people enjoy reading autobiographies. When revising, make sure that you have provided adequate support for your opinion. Proofread your essay and prepare a final draft.

can feel like crew members, wondering what will happen.

## ANSWERS TO CRITICAL THINKING AND READING

The sentence order would be 4, 3, 1, 2.

## ANSWERS TO UNDERSTANDING LANGUAGE

1. stern: the rear of a ship or boat.
2. bow: the front of a ship or boat.
3. port: the left-hand side of a ship (for a person facing the bow).
4. aft: toward the stern of a ship.
5. starboard: the right-hand side of a ship (for a person facing the bow).

## THINKING AND WRITING

For help with this assignment, students may refer to Lesson 20, "Writing a Personal Essay," in the Handbook of Writing About Literature.

**Publishing Student Writing** You might ask students to submit their essays to the school newspaper or literary magazine.

**Writing Across the Curriculum** You might ask students to research and report on theories that ancient peoples made long sea voyages.

# Types of Essays

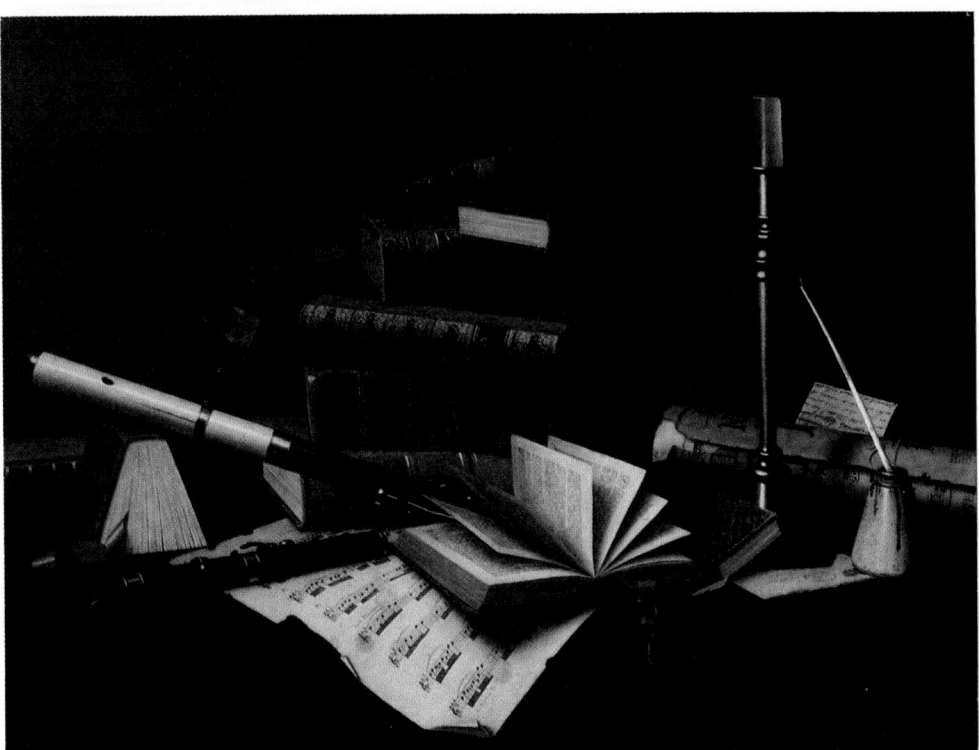

**MUSIC AND LITERATURE, 1878**
*William Harnett*
Albright-Knox Art Gallery,
Buffalo, New York

**Humanities Note**
Fine Art, *Music and Literature*, 1878, William Harnett. The American still-life painter William Harnett (1848-1892), began his career as a silver engraver in Philadelphia. His interest in painting induced him to devote every spare moment to it. He originally used still life as his subject to avoid the cost of a model. As his skill increased, he found he preferred still life and set about exploring it in depth. The style of William Harnett is known as "trompe l'oeil" or "fool-the-eye."

*Music and Literature* is composed with remarkable natural skill. Here Harnett groups a selection of objects in a manner that creates a mood of peace and nostalgia. Painted with minute detail, the objects attain a three dimensionality that is almost super-real. Harnett did not intend to deceive the viewer for more than a first glance. His purpose instead was to delight and charm with the magic of his realistic skill.

**Master Teacher Note** Use the overhead projector to show students Art Transparency 8, *Fats Domino* by Red Grooms. This picture is a portrait of Fats Domino, the great rock and roll and blues singer. You might want to point out to students that whether an essay is narrative, descriptive, expository, or persuasive, it has an unmistakable personal quality. Similarly, a work of art like this portrait of Fats Domino reflects the artist's interpretation of his subject. Ask students what seems to be unique about Red Grooms's style. How has Grooms conveyed the spirit of Fats Domino's music?

**More About the Author** William Least Heat Moon left a teaching position at a major university to set out on a journey through America. Ask students whether it would be worth leaving a good job to go on such a trip.

**Literary Focus** You might want to ask students to consider, as they read, how the narrative element creates suspense and interest. How would a descriptive or expository essay about Nameless differ from this piece of writing?

**Look For** Consider telling students that Moon uses dialect and careful descriptions of objects—the food, the record player, the stove in the store—to enhance his narrative.

**Writing/Prior Knowledge** Before students begin writing, have them discuss with classmates the stories they will record.

**Vocabulary** Have less advanced students work in pairs to test each other on the vocabulary words.

## Nameless, Tennessee

**William Least Heat Moon** (1939–    ) is the Sioux pen name of William Trogdon, a Native American teacher and author. In 1978 he toured the country in his van, traveling back roads in search of the "real" America. The book he wrote about his trip is entitled *Blue Highways* because these smaller roads are colored blue on highway maps. One of the places he stopped was "Nameless, Tennessee," a tiny town he visited out of simple curiosity about its name.

**Narrative Essay**

An **essay** is a work of nonfiction in which a writer expresses a personal view of a topic. In a **narrative essay,** a writer tells a story. The narrative essay "Nameless, Tennessee," for example, recounts William Least Heat Moon's visit to a town that is little more than "a dozen houses along the road. " Within this narrative, there are other stories as well. The residents of Nameless entertain the writer with their own tales, including a recital of "how Nameless come to be Nameless."

**Look For**

As you read, notice how the stories told by the residents of Nameless, Tennessee, recall an older—now vanishing—United States. Also, look for the passage where the writer seems to discover the essential qualities of this older way of life in a single, precious moment.

**Writing**

Recall a story that an adult told you about his or her past or about the history of your region. Discuss the details in this story that indicate how life was different years ago.

**Vocabulary**

Knowing the following words will help you as you read "Nameless, Tennessee."

**salves** (savs) *n.*: Ointments that soothe or heal skin irritations, burns, or wounds (p. 478)
**blight** (blīt) *n.*: A plant disease (p. 478)

**lore** (lôr) *n.*: Knowledge of a particular subject (p. 479)
**gaunt** (gônt) *adj.*: Thin and bony (p. 479)

---

### Objectives
1 To understand the narrative essay
2 To summarize an essay
3 To understand dialect
4 To write a narrative essay

### Support Material

**Teaching Portfolio**
Teacher Backup, p. 503
Grammar in Action Worksheet, *Recognizing Supporting Information,* p. 506
Usage and Mechanics Worksheet, p. 508
Vocabulary Check, p. 509
Analyzing Literature Worksheet, *Understanding the Narrative Essay,* p. 510

Critical Thinking and Reading Worksheet, *Summarizing an Essay,* p. 511
Selection Test, p. 512

# Nameless, Tennessee

*from* **Blue Highways**

**William Least Heat Moon**

Nameless, Tennessee, was a town of maybe ninety people if you pushed it, a dozen houses along the road, a couple of barns, same number of churches, a general merchandise store selling Fire Chief gasoline, and a community center with a lighted volleyball court. Behind the center was an open-roof, rusting metal privy with PAINT ME on the door. From the houses, the odor of coal smoke.

Next to a red tobacco barn stood the general merchandise with a poster of Senator Albert Gore, Jr., smiling from the window. I knocked. The door opened partway. A tall, thin man said, "Closed up. For good," and started to shut the door.

"Don't want to buy anything. Just a question for Mr. Thurmond Watts."

The man peered through the slight opening. He looked me over. "What question would that be?"

"If this is Nameless, Tennessee, could he tell me how it got that name?"

The man turned back into the store and called out, "Miss Ginny! Somebody here wants to know how Nameless come to be Nameless."

Miss Ginny edged to the door and looked me and my truck over. Clearly, she didn't approve. She said, "You know as well as I do, Thurmond. Don't keep him on the stoop in the damp to tell him." Miss Ginny, I found out, was Mrs. Virginia Watts, Thurmond's wife.

I stepped in and they both began telling the story, adding a detail here, the other correcting a fact there, both smiling at the foolishness of it all. It seems the hilltop settlement went for years without a name. Then one day the Post Office Department told the people if they wanted mail up on the mountain they would have to give the place a name you could properly address a letter to. The community met; there were only a handful, but they commenced debating. Some wanted patriotic names, some names from nature, one man recommended in all seriousness his own name. They couldn't agree, and they ran out of names to argue about. Finally, a fellow tired of the talk; he didn't like the mail he received anyway. "Forget the durn Post Office," he said. "This here's a nameless place if I ever seen one, so leave it be." And that's just what they did.

Watts pointed out the window. "We used to have signs on the road, but the Halloween boys keep tearin' them down."

"You think Nameless is a funny name," Miss Ginny said. "I see it plain in your eyes. Well, you take yourself up north a piece to Difficult or Defeated or Shake Rag. Now them are silly names."

## Presentation

**Motivation/Prior Knowledge**
Ask students to imagine being given the opportunity to travel freely for a year. Where would they go? How would they travel? Then tell them that Moon decided to travel across the United States in his van.

**Master Teacher Note** This essay comes from an unusual book by William Least Heat Moon. The author describes his visits to smaller, mostly rural communities throughout America rather than exotic or spectacular places. Moon's skill lies in his ability to capture meaningful nuances of appearance and speech so that his very "ordinary" places seem extremely interesting.

**Purpose-Setting Question** What is the writer searching for in Nameless, Tennessee?

**Thematic Idea** Another selection that deals with the benefits of the simple life is "The Ballad of William Sycamore," page 557.

1 **Discussion** What impression of Nameless does this paragraph convey?

2 **Discussion** Do you think the town made the right decision? Explain.

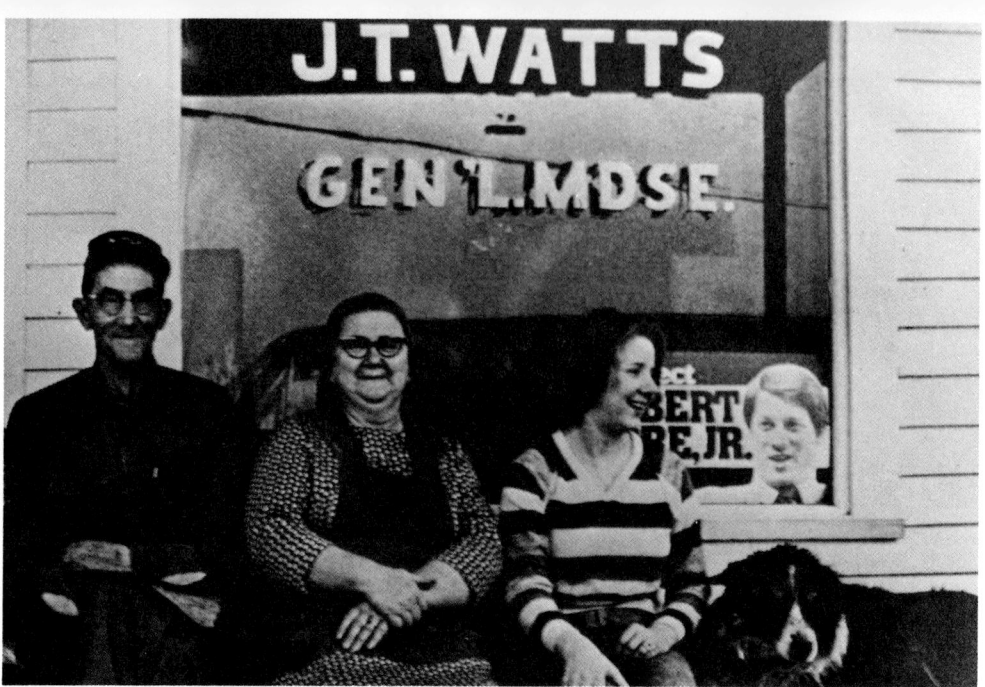

The old store, lighted only by three fifty-watt bulbs, smelled of coal oil and baking bread. In the middle of the rectangular room, where the oak floor sagged a little, stood an iron stove. To the right was a wooden table with an unfinished game of checkers and a stool made from an apple-tree stump. On shelves around the walls sat earthen jugs with corncob stoppers, a few canned goods, and some of the two thousand old clocks and clockworks Thurmond Watts owned. Only one was ticking; the others he just looked at. I asked how long he'd been in the store.

"Thirty-five years, but we closed the first day of the year. We're hopin' to sell it to a churchly couple. Upright people. No athians."[1]

_____
**1. athians:** Atheists, people who do not believe in God.

478  *Nonfiction*

"Did you build this store?"

"I built this one, but it's the third general store on the ground. I fear it'll be the last. I take no pleasure in that. Once you could come in here for a gallon of paint, a pickle, a pair of shoes, and a can of corn."

"Or horehound candy," Miss Ginny said. "Or corsets and salves. We had cough syrups and all that for the body. In season, we'd buy and sell blackberries and walnuts and chestnuts, before the blight got them. And outside, Thurmond milled corn and sharpened plows. Even shoed a horse sometimes."

"We could fix up a horse or a man or a baby," Watts said.

"Thurmond, tell him we had a doctor on the ridge in them days."

"We had a doctor on the ridge in them days. As good as any doctor alivin'. He'd cut a crooked toenail or deliver a woman. Dead these last years."

3

## Grammar in Action

Writers clarify their ideas and enliven their descriptions by using **supporting information.** The basic kinds of supporting information include examples, details, facts, reasons, and incidents.

The following passages illustrate William Least Heat Moon's use of this technique:

1. In the middle of the rectangular room, where the oak floor sagged a little, stood an iron stove. To the right was a wooden table with an unfinished game of checkers and a stool made from an apple tree stump.  (details, facts)

2. "Once you could come in here for a gallon of paint, a pickle, a pair of shoes, and a can of corn."  (example)

3. "I got some bad ham meat one day . . . and took to vomitin' . . . . I said to Thurmond, 'Thurmond unless you want shut of me, call the doctor.'"  (incident)

Without specific details, William Least Heat Moon's passages may have sounded as general and uninteresting as this:

"I got some bad ham meat one day," Miss Ginny said, "and took to vomitin'. All day, all night. Hangin' on the drop edge of yonder. I said to Thurmond, 'Thurmond, unless you want shut of me, call the doctor.' "

"I studied on it," Watts said.

"You never did. You got him right now. He come over and put three drops of iodeen[2] in half a glass of well water. I drank it down and the vomitin' stopped with the last swallow. Would you think iodeen could do that?"

"He put Miss Ginny on one teaspoon of spirits of ammonia in well water for her nerves. Ain't nothin' works better for her to this day."

"Calms me like the hand of the Lord."

Hilda, the Wattses' daughter, came out of the backroom. "I remember him," she said. "I was just a baby. Y'all were talkin' to him, and he lifted me up on the counter and gave me a stick of Juicy Fruit and a piece of cheese."

"Knew the old medicines," Watts said. "Only drugstore he needed was a good kitchen cabinet. None of them anteebeeotics[3] that hit you worsen your ailment. Forgotten lore now, the old medicines, because they ain't profit in iodeen."

Miss Ginny started back to the side room where she and her sister Marilyn were taking apart a duck-down mattress to make bolsters. She stopped at the window for another look at Ghost Dancing.[4] "How do you sleep in that thing? Ain't you all cramped and cold?"

"How does the clam sleep in his shell?" Watts said in my defense.

"Thurmond, get the boy a piece of buttermilk pie afore he goes on."

---

2. **iodeen:** Iodine.
3. **antee-beeotics:** Antibiotics (an' ti bī ät' iks), medicines like penicillin.
4. **Ghost Dancing:** The name of the author's van.

"Hilda, get him some buttermilk pie." He looked at me. "You like good music?" I said I did. He cranked up an old Edison phonograph, the kind with the big morning-glory blossom for a speaker, and put on a wax cylinder. "This will be 'My Mother's Prayer,' " he said.

While I ate buttermilk pie, Watts served as disc jockey of Nameless, Tennessee. "Here's 'Mountain Rose.' " It was one of those moments that you know at the time will stay with you to the grave: the sweet pie, the gaunt man playing the old music, the coals in the stove glowing orange, the scent of kerosene and hot bread. "Here's 'Evening Rhapsody.' " The music was so heavily romantic we both laughed. I thought: It is for this I have come.

Feathered over and giggling, Miss Ginny stepped from the side room. She knew she was a sight. "Thurmond, give him some lunch. Still looks hungry."

Hilda pulled food off the woodstove in the backroom: home-butchered and canned whole-hog sausage, home-canned June apples, turnip greens, cole slaw, potatoes, stuffing, hot cornbread. All delicious.

Watts and Hilda sat and talked while I ate. "Wish you would join me."

"We've ate," Watts said. "Cain't beat a woodstove for flavorful cookin'."

He told me he was raised in a one-hundred-fifty-year-old cabin still standing in one of the hollows. "How many's left," he said, "that grew up in a log cabin? I ain't the last surely, but I must be climbin' on the list."

Hilda cleared the table. "You Watts ladies know how to cook."

"She's in nursin' school at Tennessee Tech. I went over for one of them football games last year there at Coevul." To say *Cookeville,* you let the word collapse in upon itself so that it comes out "Coevul."

"Do you like football?" I asked.

*Nameless, Tennessee,* from *Blue Highways*   479

4 **Discussion** What effect does the writer's visit seem to be having on the Watts family?

5 **Critical Thinking and Reading** In your own words, explain the purpose of the writer's visit.

1. The old store was rather primitive and plain.
2. They used to carry a wide variety of things.
3. "One day I got sick and needed a doctor."

The use of specific supporting detail is a sign of good writing.

**Student Activity 1.** Find four more pieces of supporting information in this selection. Decide whether each is an example, fact, detail, reason, incident, or a combination of these types of support.

**Student Activity 2.** Write two sentences which lack supporting information. Then expand each with examples, facts, details, reasons, incidents, or a combination of specifics.

**Reader's Response** If you were to write a narrative essay about an unusual place, what would it be? Why?

"Don't know. I was so high up in that stadium, I never opened my eyes."

Watts went to the back and returned with a fat spiral notebook that he set on the table. His expression had changed. "Miss Ginny's *Deathbook*."

The thing startled me. Was it something I was supposed to sign? He opened it but said nothing. There were scads of names written in a tidy hand over pages incised to crinkliness by a ballpoint. Chronologically, the names had piled up: wives, grandparents, a stillborn infant, relatives, friends close and distant. Names, names. After each, the date of *the* unknown finally known and transcribed. The last entry bore yesterday's date.

"She's wrote out twenty years' worth. Ever day she listens to the hospital report on the radio and puts the names in. Folks come by to check a date. Or they just turn through the books. Read them like a scrapbook."

Hilda said, "Like Saint Peter at the gates inscribin' the names."

Watts took my arm. "Come along." He led me to the fruit cellar under the store. As we went down, he said, "Always take a newborn baby upstairs afore you take him downstairs, otherwise you'll incline him downwards."

The cellar was dry and full of cobwebs and jar after jar of home-canned food, the bottles organized as a shopkeeper would: sausage, pumpkin, sweet pickles, tomatoes, corn relish, blackberries, peppers, squash, jellies. He held a hand out toward the dusty bottles. "Our tomorrows."

Upstairs again, he said, "Hope to sell the store to the right folk. I see now, though, it'll be somebody offen the ridge. I've studied on it, and maybe it's the end of our place." He stirred the coals. "This store could give a comfortable livin', but not likely get you rich. But just gettin' by is dice rollin' to people nowadays. I never did see my day guaranteed."

When it was time to go, Watts said, "If you find anyone along your way wants a good store—on the road to Cordell Hull Lake—tell them about us."

I said I would. Miss Ginny and Hilda and Marilyn came out to say goodbye. It was cold and drizzling again. "Weather to give a man the weary dismals," Watts grumbled. "Where you headed from here?"

"I don't know."

"Cain't get lost then."

Miss Ginny looked again at my rig. It had worried her from the first as it had my mother. "I hope you don't get yourself kilt in that durn thing gallivantin' around the country."

"Come back when the hills dry off," Watts said. "We'll go lookin' for some of them round rocks all sparkly inside."

I thought a moment. "Geodes?"

"Them's the ones. The county's properly full of them."

## Closure and Extension

### ANSWERS TO THINKING ABOUT THE SELECTION
*Recalling*

1. He wants to know how the town got its name.
2. The Post Office Department requested that the people name their community so that letters could be properly addressed and delivered. People met and debated about a name but could not agree on one. Finally, one person said they should forget the Post Office since it was a nameless place anyway. The people left it that way.
3. The Watts family owns a general store that is old and dimly lit. It has a cast-iron stove in the center of the room, and its shelves hold earthen jugs, canned goods, and old clocks that Watts collected.
4. In an earlier time, people were more inclined to trust home remedies, and indeed preferred them to manufactured medicines.
5. Mr. Watts plays old songs on an old-fashioned record player. He also shows Moon the rows and rows of canned goods in his cellar.

### Interpreting

6. Suggested Response: He is able to

## THINKING ABOUT THE SELECTION

### Recalling

1. What question brings the writer to the little town of Nameless, Tennessee?
2. Recount the story that Mr. and Mrs. Watts tell to answer this question.
3. Describe the Wattses' "old store."
4. How does the story about the doctor show the customs of an older time?
5. Find two ways other than storytelling in which Mr. Watts reveals his past.

### Interpreting

6. Why does the writer find his visit to this tiny town so satisfying?
7. What clues to the writer's personality can you find in this essay?

### Applying

8. What features of a past way of life would you like to preserve or imitate? Explain.

## ANALYZING LITERATURE

### Understanding the Narrative Essay

An **essay** is a work of nonfiction in which a writer expresses a personal view of a topic. In a **narrative essay**, a writer tells a story. "Nameless, Tennessee" is the story of a writer's visit to a small southern town for which no one could agree on a name.

1. Why is telling a story an effective way of involving readers in this essay?
2. What do the stories told by the people in the town add to the writer's account?

## CRITICAL THINKING AND READING

### Summarizing an Essay

**Summarizing** means briefly stating the main points and key details of a work in your own words. A summary of a narrative essay would include the important events, the narrator's principal thoughts or comments, and a few essential descriptions of people and places. For example, the following is a summary of the first five paragraphs of "Nameless, Tennessee": The writer visits the general store in Nameless, Tennessee, a town that is not much more than a few houses. He tells a tall, thin man who comes to the door that he wants to ask Thurmond Watts how the town got its name.

1. Summarize the next five paragraphs.
2. Review your summary to make sure it captures the main points.

## UNDERSTANDING LANGUAGE

### Understanding Dialect

**Dialect** is the form of a spoken language used in a certain region. William Least Heat Moon conveys the flavor of rural Tennessee by including the dialect that the Wattses use. For instance, Miss Ginny says that when she ate some bad meat she was "Hangin' on the drop edge of yonder." This expression means that she felt as if she were going to die.

Figure out the meaning of the following examples of dialect from the essay.

1. "I studied on it. . . ." (page 479)
2. "Weather to give a man the weary dismals . . . ." (page 480)

## THINKING AND WRITING

### Writing a Narrative Essay

Recall a time when your curiosity led you to visit a person or a place. Write what you wanted to find out, and list the events that occurred during your visit. Then, using these notes, write a narrative essay like "Nameless, Tennessee" about this experience. In revising your essay, make sure that you have explained whether your curiosity about this person or place was satisfied. Also, you may want to add details—like the description of the store in "Nameless, Tennessee"—to make your account more vivid. When you are finished, share your essay with your classmates.

(Answers begin on p. 480.)

2. Suggested Response: Moon preserves many features of their dialect, so that their speech adds color and richness to his account. Their stories also make them seem more real than a mere description of them would.

### ANSWERS TO CRITICAL THINKING AND READING

1. Mr. Watts calls his wife, Miss Ginny, and together they tell the story of how the town got its name. The Post Office Department requested that the community have a name so that mail could be addressed and delivered. The people debated but could not agree on a name. One person said that it was a nameless place anyway, and so they left it that way. Miss Ginny defends the name by saying that Nameless is not as funny a name as those some other towns have.

### ANSWERS TO UNDERSTANDING LANGUAGE

1. I thought about it, or I considered it.
2. The weather is dreary enough to make me gloomy.

### THINKING AND WRITING

For help with this assignment, students can consult Lesson 20, "Writing a Personal Essay," in the Handbook of Writing About Literature.

**Publishing Student Writing**
When students have finished their essays, have them compile their work in a class book or in several brochures suggesting interesting places for other people to visit. This booklet, or the brochures, can be shown to students from other classes, parents, and other teachers in the school.

**Writing Across the Curriculum**
You might want to have students research and report on economic conditions in Appalachia. Consider informing the social studies department of this assignment, so that teachers can provide guidance to students.

---

meet long-time residents of the town, talk with them, and gain insight into an older way of life.
7. Suggested Response: His interest in the town reveals his curiosity. His behavior toward the Watts family shows he is respectful and capable of warmth.

### Applying

8. Answers will differ, but some students might mention the fact that many people were once able to grow and preserve all their own food. They might mention that life might have been simpler then and that it would have been possible to know most of the people living around one's home.

**Challenge** Have students locate a copy of *Blue Highways* and read all or parts of it. Then have them discuss Moon's visit to Nameless Tennessee, in relation to other places he visited. How was it the same? How was it different?

### ANSWERS TO ANALYZING LITERATURE

1. Suggested Response: The reader has the sense of accompanying Moon on his visit to the Watts family's store and can experience some of what he experienced while he was there.

**More About the Author** Anne Morrow Lindbergh was the first woman in America to obtain a glider-pilot's license. She studied navigation and accompanied her husband as a radio operator on survey flights to Asia and Europe. Ask students to imagine what it was like to fly long distances in the airplanes of the 1920's and 1930's.

**Literary Focus** You might ask students to consider the different senses to which Lindbergh appeals in her descriptive passages.

**Look For** Consider telling students that a key to Lindbergh's technique is the general impression of movement that she creates. Ask them to pinpoint words and phrases that contribute to this impression.

**Writing/Prior Knowledge** Consider dividing the class into small groups and having students describe the scene they remember to group members before writing about it.

**Vocabulary** Ask students to write a sentence for each of these words.

### "Sayonara"

**Anne Morrow Lindbergh** (1906–    ) is the widow of Charles Lindbergh, who in 1927 made the first solo flight across the Atlantic. Several years later Anne Morrow Lindbergh accompanied her famous husband as a copilot and radio operator on a 40,000-mile flight over five continents. In addition to her flying exploits, she has written many books—poetry, fiction, and nonfiction. "Sayonara" comes from *North to the Orient,* her account of a trip she took with her husband to the Far East in 1931.

**Descriptive Essay**

In a **descriptive essay,** a writer does not tell a story but depicts a person, place, object, or scene. By focusing on vivid details and using lively comparisons, writers give you the sensation of actually witnessing what they are describing. Often writers choose details that contribute to a unified effect. In "Sayonara," for example, Anne Morrow Lindbergh wants to convey the feeling of saying farewell to Japan. The scenes and objects that she describes combine to express a single idea: Sayonara—or Goodbye.

**Look For**

As you read, look for the vivid descriptions of sights and sounds that make these farewell scenes so effective. Also, be aware of how every detail in these descriptions conveys a sense of parting.

**Writing**

Recall a time when you said goodbye to someone who was either leaving on a trip or who stayed behind while you departed. List some of the details of this scene that stand out in your mind.

**Vocabulary**

Knowing the following words will help you as you read "Sayonara."
**conglomerate** (kən gläm′ ə rāt′) *adj.*: Whole made up of parts (p. 483) (usually a noun)
**kimonos** (ko mō′ nəs) *n.*: Loose-fitting gowns, part of the traditional costume of Japanese men and women (p. 484)
**doggerel** (dôg′ ər əl) *adj.*: Dull verse that sounds like a jingle (p. 485) (usually a noun)
**intricately** (in′ tri kit lē) *adv.*: With complicated detail (p. 485)

**raveled** (rav′′ld) *adj.*: Untwisted; unwoven (p. 485)
**bravado** (brə vä′ dō) *n.*: Pretended courage (p. 485)
**sedative** (sed′ ə tiv) *n.*: Something that soothes or quiets (p. 485)
**admonition** (ad′ mə nish′ ən) *n.*: Warning (p. 485)

# "Sayonara"[1]

### Anne Morrow Lindbergh

"Sayonara, Sayonara!" I was in my stateroom[2] but I could hear them, outside on the deck of the Japanese boat, calling to friends and relatives on the dock at Shanghai.[3] "Sayonara"—up and down the gangplank and over the rails. A boatload of Japanese were leaving China for home, as we were. "Sayonara," the chains clanked and the warning whistle shook the boat. The voices outside rose in a flurry of noise, like a flock of frightened birds. But above the conglomerate sound there was always one voice, clean and sharp and individual and yet representative of the mass like that one face in the front line that holds the meaning of the whole crowd—one cry, "Sayonara." The impression was intensified perhaps because it was the one word of Japanese I understood—"Sayonara" ("Good-bye").

I was to hear it again, all along our trip home. For we crossed Japan by train from the southern tip to Yokohama,[4] where we boarded the boat for America.

"Sayonara": the clatter of wooden clogs

---

1. **"Sayonara"** (sä′ yô̄ nä′ rä): Japanese for "farewell."
2. **stateroom** (stāt′ rōōm) *n.*: Private cabin on a ship.
3. **Shanghai** (shaŋ′ hī): Seaport in eastern China.

4. **Yokohama** (yō′ kə hä′ mə): Seaport south of Tokyo, Japan.

"Sayonara" 483

## Presentation

**Motivation/Prior Knowledge** Ask students to list words and phrases they use when parting from friends or acquaintances. Have them briefly compare and contrast the connotations of some of these expressions. Then tell them that Lindbergh shows how the Japanese word for goodbye, *Sayonara,* sums up a whole philosophy of life.

**Master Teacher Note** You might want to tell students that Lindbergh describes her impressions of Japan just as she is leaving the country. Have students speculate how this descriptive essay might have been different if Lindbergh had recorded her impressions upon arriving in Japan.

**Purpose-Setting Question** How does the brevity of this essay contribute to its effectiveness?

**Thematic Idea** You might want to have students compare the philosophy embodied in the word *Sayonara* with that reflected in the passage from Ecclesiastes, page 645.

1 **Discussion** Why do you think Lindbergh repeats the word "Sayonara" so many times at the very start of the essay?

**2 Clarification** A *kimono* is "a long robe with wide sleeves that may be worn by men or women."

**3 Literary Focus** Here Lindbergh is providing rich visual detail. Ask students which of the impressions Lindbergh is describing stand out in their minds. Have them identify the words and phrases that help create the images.

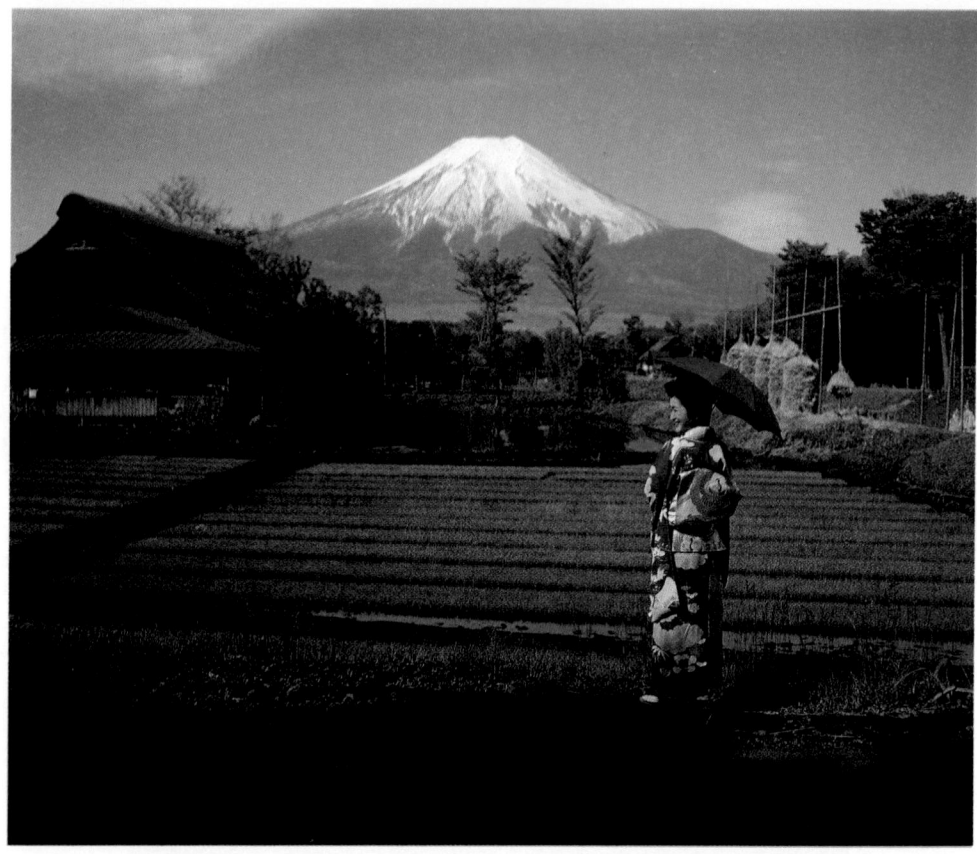

2 along the station platform; the flutter of kimonos; babies jogging on their mother's backs; men carrying four or five small bundles tied up in different-colored furoshiki (squares of parti-colored silk or cotton); old women knocking along with their sticks, their brown faces hidden under enormous 3 rooflike hats of straw; a man shouting his wares. We leaned out of the window at one of these stations and motioned to a vender for some tea. He poured out of his big tin into a little brown clay teapot like a child's toy, with a saucer for a lid and an inverted cup on top.

"Two! Two!" we shouted and signaled as the train jerked forward, starting to pull out. The vender ran after us with another teapot swinging from its wire handle and pushed it in our window.

"Sayonara—Sayonara!" cried the passengers who had just stepped on board. A Japanese family across the aisle from us leaned out of the window to say a few last words. They occupied two long seats raised on a slight platform, separated from the next family by a partition. The mother and nurse (or older sister) were dressed in Japanese kimo-

## Grammar in Action

Items in a series are usually separated by commas, but **semicolons** are used to avoid confusion when items in a series already contain commas.

Simple series:    *Flowering crab trees, apple trees*, and *dogwoods* bloomed simultaneously. (commas)

Complicated series:    The orchard was abloom with *flowering crab trees; apple trees, separated by kind*; and *dogwoods, both pink and white.* (semicolons)

The second and third items of the complicated series include commas within the items. As a result, semicolons are necessary to separate the three items. The following passage shows how Lindbergh uses semicolons to avoid confusion in a complicated series:

nos, the father in Western business suit, the two little girls in green challis[5] suits with Irish-lace collars, and the baby in woolens. They had already kicked off their shoes, in Japanese fashion, and were squatting on their feet on the blue plush seats. They held the baby up to the window for the last good-bye—"Sayonara"; and then the monotonous doggerel rhythm of the train, quickening to a roar, drowned all noise. We were off.

It was good-bye for us too, as we rushed through Japan on our way to the boat. Good-bye to the rice fields terraced up a narrow gully in the hills; to thatched roofs and paper walls; to heavy-headed grain bent to a curve; to a field of awkward lotus leaves, like big elephant ears, flapping on their tall stalks; to a white road leading up a hill to a pine grove and the flicker of red of a shrine gate. Good-bye to the little towns we rattled through, with their narrow cobbled streets lined with shops, open to the passer-by except for fluttering blue-toweling curtains or bright paper and cloth flag-signs. Good-bye to blue paper umbrellas in the rain and little boys chasing dragon flies.

Our real good-bye was not until the boat pulled out of the dock at Yokohama, when the crowd of Japanese leaning over the rails of the decks shot twirling strands of serpentine[6] across to those they had left behind on shore—a rain of bright fireworks. One end of these colored paper ribbons was held in the hands of those on deck, the other, by those on shore, until a brilliant multicolored web was spun between ship and shore. This and the shouts of conversation, unintelligible to me, interlacing back and forth across the gap, made up a finely woven band—a tissue, intricately patterned and rich in texture which held together for a few more seconds those remaining and those departing. Then the gap of water slowly widening between dock and ship, the ribbons tautened and snapped, the broken and raveled ends twirling off idly into the water, floating away with the unfinished ends of sentences. And nothing could bridge the gap but "Sayonara!"

For *Sayonara*, literally translated, "Since it must be so," of all the good-byes I have heard is the most beautiful. Unlike the *Auf Wiedersehens* and *Au revoirs*,[7] it does not try to cheat itself by any bravado "Till we meet again," any sedative to postpone the pain of separation. It does not evade the issue like the sturdy blinking *Farewell*. *Farewell* is a father's *good-bye*. It is—"Go out in the world and do well, my son." It is encouragement and admonition. It is hope and faith. But it passes over the significance of the moment; of parting it says nothing. It hides its emotion. It says too little. While *Good-bye* ("God be with you") and *Adios*[8] say too much. They try to bridge the distance, almost to deny it. *Good-bye* is a prayer, a ringing cry. "You must not go—I cannot bear to have you go! But you shall not go alone, unwatched. God will be with you. God's hand will be over you" and even—underneath, hidden, but it is there, incorrigible—"I will be with you; I will watch you—always." It is a mother's *good-bye*. But *Sayonara* says neither too much nor too little. It is a simple acceptance of fact. All understanding of life lies in its limits. All emotion, smoldering, is banked up behind it. But it says nothing. It is really the unspoken good-bye, the pressure of a hand, "Sayonara."

---

5. **challis** (shal′ ē) *n.*: Soft, lightweight fabric, usually printed with a design.
6. **serpentine** (sʉr′ pən tēn′) *n.*: Coils of thin paper that unwind as they are thrown.

7. **Auf Wiedersehens** (ouf vē′ dər zā′ ənz) **and Au revoirs** (ō′ rə vwärz′): "Till we meet again" in German and French, respectively.
8. **Adios** (a′ dē ōs′): Spanish for "good-bye."

---

It was good-bye for us too, as we rushed through Japan on our way to the boat. Good-bye to the rice fields terraced up a narrow gully in the hills; to thatched roofs and paper walls; to heavy-headed grain bent to a curve; to a field of awkward lotus leaves, like big elephant ears, flapping on their tall stalks; to a white road leading up a hill to a pine grove and the flicker of red of a shrine gate.

**Student Activity 1.** Change some of the commas to semicolons in order to punctuate the following complicated series (remember that semicolons go outside of quotation marks): *Sayonara*, the Japanese good-bye, is different from the German *Auf Wiede-* rsehen, meaning "Till we meet again," the French *Au revoir*, which resembles the German good-bye, and the English *Good-bye*, which suggests a prayer, a ringing cry.

**Student Activity 2.** Write two sentences that include a complicated series. Use accurate punctuation to avoid confusion.

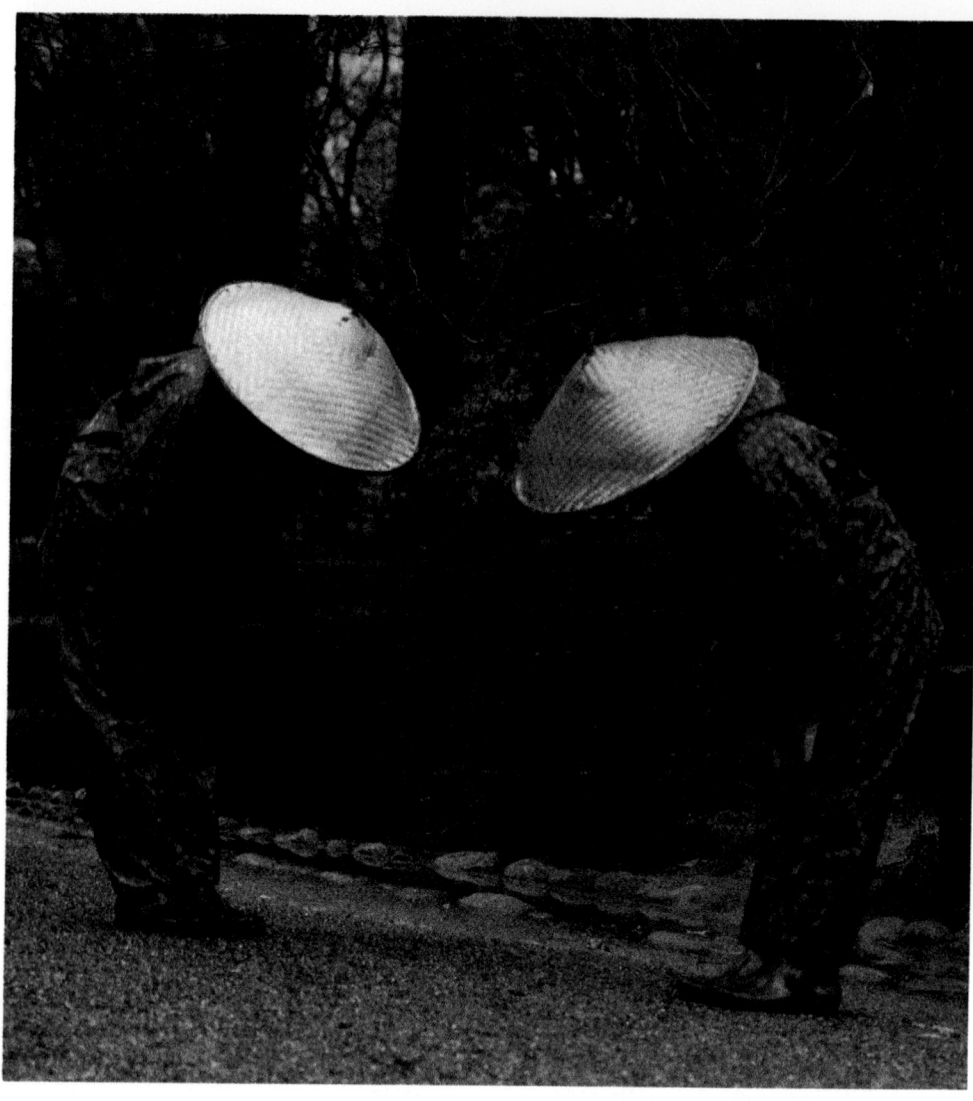

## Closure and Extension

### ANSWERS TO THINKING ABOUT THE SELECTION
*Recalling*

1. Answers might include: The clatter of wooden clogs, the flutter of kimonos, men carrying bundles, old women walking with sticks, the man selling tea in clay teapots, the little girls in challis suits with shoes off.

2. The literal translation is: "Since it must be so."

3. She feels it says neither too much nor too little.

### Interpreting

4. Suggested Response: Lindbergh is expressing the thought that parting is one of the facts of human existence and that the word *sayonara* implies acceptance of this fact.

## THINKING ABOUT THE SELECTION

### Recalling

1. Name four vivid details that the writer includes in her descriptions of farewells.
2. According to Lindbergh, what is the literal translation of *Sayonara*?
3. Why does the writer like this Japanese word of farewell?

### Interpreting

4. What does the writer mean when she says that "All understanding of life . . ." is contained within the word *Sayonara*?
5. How do you think she felt about leaving Japan? Explain.

### Applying

6. Basing your answer on Lindbergh's insights into the meaning of *Sayonara*, what can you infer about Japanese culture in general?

## ANALYZING LITERATURE

### Understanding the Descriptive Essay

In a **descriptive essay,** a writer does not tell a story but depicts a person, place, or scene. All the details that Anne Morrow Lindbergh describes in "Sayonara" contribute to the feeling of leaving a place. For example, many of the vivid sights that she sees are only glimpsed through the window of a moving train. Even when the train has stopped briefly at a station, the people on the platform are in hurried motion: "the clatter of wooden clogs . . . the flutter of kimonos . . . babies jogging on their mothers' backs. . . ." Even the voices she overhears on the boat at Shanghai move "like a flock of frightened birds."

1. Reread the paragraph beginning, "It was good-bye for us, too . . ." Identify three ways in which Lindbergh conveys a sense of hurried motion in this paragraph.
2. How does the description of the web of ribbons

at Yokohama relate to the theme of departure?
3. What overall impression of Japan do you form based on Lindbergh's descriptions?

## CRITICAL THINKING AND READING

### Comparing and Contrasting Words

**Comparing** means finding similarities, while **contrasting** means showing differences. In "Sayonara," Lindbergh reaches conclusions about different expressions of farewell by comparing and contrasting them. For example, she finds that *farewell* "is a father's *good-bye*," which encourages and warns the person leaving. *Good-bye,* on the other hand, is a mother's word for leave-taking. It is both a prayer—"God be with you"—and a promise that the person left behind will watch over the one who is departing.

Compare and contrast the following expressions of farewell with each other and with the words that Lindbergh discusses. Consider the situations in which a person would use each expression, the idea that each expresses, and any attitudes that it reflects.

1. Take care
2. Catch you later
3. Godspeed
4. Don't work too hard

## THINKING AND WRITING

### Writing a Descriptive Essay

Recall the details of the farewell scene that you listed before reading this selection. Using this list, write a descriptive essay about the parting for your classmates. Where possible, include descriptions of sounds and vivid sights, as Lindbergh does. In revising your essay, make sure that the details you have included convey the feeling of departure. For example, you might want to describe objects that are moving apart. Share your essay with your classmates when you are done.

the others. Close friends use this expression when they part for a short period of time.

2. Catch you later—This expression is informal. It might be used by friends who know they are likely to see each other again soon. It does not suggest the same concern or affection that the other expressions do, nor does it resemble any of the examples Lindbergh includes.
3. Godspeed—This expression might have been used in the past as people invoked God's protection for the departing person. This is a much more serious expression than the others; our contemporary "goodbye" derives from it, although the religious connotations once associated with "goodbye" have been lost.
4. Don't work too hard—This is a somewhat humorous expression that does not suggest the concern of "Take care" or "Godspeed." This phrase might be used by friends or companions who have no particular reason to worry about one another.

**Challenge** Compare and contrast three different words or phrases of greeting in our language.

### THINKING AND WRITING

For help with this assignment, students may consult Lesson 2, "Drafting and Revising," and Lesson 20, "Writing a Personal Essay," in the Handbook of Writing About Literature.

### Publishing Student Writing

When students have finished, some might wish to submit their essays to the school newspaper or magazine or to another literary publication.

### Writing Across the Curriculum

Have students research and report on some aspect of Japanese culture. Consider informing the social studies department of this assignment, so that teachers can help students narrow their topics and find resource materials.

---

5. Suggested Response: Lindbergh seems to have felt reluctant to leave Japan.

### Applying

6. Answers will differ. However, many students will realize that Lindbergh suggests that the Japanese express emotion in an understated fashion. She also seems to suggest that the Japanese are fatalistic,

recognizing that some things cannot be changed.

### ANSWERS TO ANALYZING LITERATURE

1. Suggested Response: She repeats the word "good-bye"; she describes one scene right after another, as it might be glimpsed from a moving train; and she describes many little towns as if they were blurring into a single place.

2. Suggested Response: The web of ribbons symbolizes the stretching and snapping of connections as people depart.
3. Suggested Response: She conveys an impression of an exotic, delicately beautiful country.

### ANSWERS TO CRITICAL THINKING AND READING

Suggested Responses:
1. Take care—These words express more fondness and concern than

# GUIDE FOR READING

## The Loch Ness Monster

**John McPhee** (1931–    ) was a television writer from 1955 to 1957, during the early years of that medium. After that experience he became an associate editor for *Time* magazine. However, he is best known as an essayist for *The New Yorker,* a weekly magazine famous for its excellent writing. McPhee has also written books on various subjects, including Alaska and the Pine Barrens of New Jersey. In "The Loch Ness Monster," he turns his attention to a creature that some believe is a throwback to the dinosaurs.

**Expository Essay**

The purpose of an **expository essay** is to explain a concept, event, or process by presenting information. Such essays usually contain details, examples, and facts conveyed in an informative tone. As "The Loch Ness Monster" shows, however, an expository piece can be personal and entertaining as well as informative. In this essay, John McPhee tells about an organization that gathers data on a shy, forty-foot monster living in a deep Scottish lake.

**Look For**

As you read, look for the ways in which McPhee gives this expository essay a personal flavor. Ask yourself how such details make the essay more interesting to read.

**Writing**

The Loch Ness Monster seems to be a form of reptile. Tell why you think that reptiles—a category including snakes, lizards, crocodiles, and dinosaurs—both fascinate and repel many people.

**Vocabulary**

Knowing the following words will help you as you read "The Loch Ness Monster."

**panorama** (pan' ə ram' ə) *n.*: Unlimited view in all directions (p. 490)

**depot** (dē' pō) *n.*: Railroad or bus station (p. 490)

**milieu** (mēl yoo') *n.*: Environment; setting (p. 491)

**fanatical** (fə nat' ik'l) *adj.*: Unreasonably enthusiastic (p. 492)

**hoax** (hōks) *n.*: Trick; fraud (p. 493)

**nocturnal** (näk tur' n'l) *adj.*: Happening in the night (p. 494)

**undulates** (un' joo lāts') *v.*: Moves in waves (p. 496)

**impediment** (im ped'ə mənt) *n.*: Obstruction; hindrance (p. 496)

# The Loch Ness Monster

## John McPhee

The road—the A-82—stayed close to the
lake, often on ledges that had been blasted
into the mountainsides. The steep forests
continued, broken now and again, on one
shore or the other, by fields of fern, clumps
of bright-yellow whin,[1] and isolated stands of
cedar. Along the far shore were widely separated houses and farms, which to the eyes of
a traveller appeared almost unbelievably lux-
uriant after the spare desolation of some of
the higher glens.[2] We came to the top of the
rise and suddenly saw, on the right-hand
side of the road, on the edge of a high
meadow that sloped sharply a considerable
distance to the lake, a cluster of caravans[3]
and other vehicles, arranged in the shape of
a C, with an opening toward the road—
much like a circle of prairie schooners,
formed for protection against savage attack.
All but one or two of the vehicles were
painted bright lily-pad green. The compound, in its compact half acre, was surrounded by a fence, to keep out, among
other things, sheep, which were grazing all
over the slope in deep-green turf among buttercups, daisies, and thistles. Gulls above
beat hard into the wind, then turned and
planed toward the south. Gulls are inland
birds in Scotland, there being so little dis-

1. **whin** (hwin) *n.*: Prickly, evergreen shrub.
2. **glens** *n.*: Narrow, secluded, mountain valleys.
3. **caravans** *n.*: In Great Britain, camping trailers.

*The Loch Ness Monster* 489

tance from anywhere to the sea. A big fireplace had been made from rocks of the sort that were scattered all over the meadow. And on the lakeward side a platform had been built, its level eminence[4] emphasizing the declivity[5] of the hill, which dropped away below it. Mounted on the platform was a thirty-five-millimeter motion-picture camera with an enormous telephoto lens. From its point of view, two hundred feet above the lake and protruding like a gargoyle, the camera could take in a bedazzling panorama that covered thousands of acres of water.

This was Expedition Headquarters, the principal field station of the Loch Ness Phenomena Investigation Bureau—dues five pounds per annum,[6] life membership one hundred pounds, tax on donations recoverable under covenant.[7] Those who join the bureau receive newsletters and annual reports, and are eligible to participate in the fieldwork if they so desire. I turned into the compound and parked between two bright-green reconditioned old London taxis. The central area had long since been worn grassless, and was covered at this moment with fine-grain dust. People were coming and going. The place seemed rather public, as if it were a depot. No one even halfway interested in the natural history of the Great Glen would think of driving up the A-82 without stopping in there. Since the A-82 is the principal route between Glasgow and Inverness,[8] it is not surprising that the apparently amphibious creature as yet unnamed, the so-called Loch Ness Monster, has been seen not only from the highway but on it.

----

4. **eminence** (em'ə nəns) *n.*: High or lofty place.
5. **declivity** (di kliv'ə tē) *n.*: Downward slope.
6. **dues five pounds per annum:** Amount of British money per year that it costs to belong.
7. **tax on donations recoverable by covenant:** Taxes paid on donations will be refunded.
8. **Glasgow and Inverness:** Cities in southern and northern Scotland.

The atmosphere around the headquarters suggested a scientific frontier and also a boom town, much as Cape Canaveral and Cocoa Beach do. There were, as well, cirrus[9] wisps of show business and fine arts. Probably the one word that might have been applied to everyone present was adventurer. There was, at any rate, nothing emphatically laboratorial about the place, although the prevailing mood seemed to be one not of holiday but of matter-of-fact application and patient dedication. A telephone call came in that day, to the caravan that served as an office, from a woman who owned an inn south of Inverarigaig, on the other side of the lake. She said that she had seen the creature that morning just forty yards offshore—three humps, nothing else to report, and being very busy just now, thank you very much, good day. This was recorded, with no particular display of excitement, by an extremely attractive young woman who appeared to be in her late twenties, an artist from London who had missed but one summer at Loch Ness in seven years. She wore sandals, dungarees, a black pullover, and gold earrings. Her name was Mary Piercy, and her toes were painted pink. The bulletin board where she recorded the sighting resembled the kind used in railway stations for the listing of incoming trains.

The office walls were decorated with photographs of the monster in various postures—basking,[10] cruising, diving, splashing, looking up inquisitively. A counter was covered with some of the essential bibliography: the bureau's annual report (twenty-nine sightings the previous year), J. A. Carruth's *Loch Ness and Its Monster* (The Abbey Press, Fort Augustus), Tim Dinsdale's *Loch Ness Monster* (Routledge and Kegan

----

9. **cirrus** (sir'əs) *adj.*: Feathery.
10. **basking** (bask'iŋ) *n.*: Warming oneself pleasantly, as in sunlight.

----

## Grammar in Action

**Descriptive writing** gives the reader a picture of a person, a thing, or a place. Look at this passage from "The Loch Ness Monster."

The atmosphere around the headquarters suggested a scientific frontier and also a boom town, much as Cape Canaveral and Cocoa Beach do. There were, as well, cirrus whisps of show business and fine arts. Probably the word that might have been applied to everyone present was adventurer. There was, at any rate, nothing emphatically laboratorial about the place, although the prevailing mood seemed to be one not of holiday but of matter-of-fact application and patient dedication.

In the passage John McPhee describes the Expedition Headquarters of the Loch Ness Phenomena Investigation Bureau. Notice that he describes both the physical detail of the place as well as its mood, or emotional atmosphere.

Now read this description:

This [call] was recorded, with no particular display of excitement, by an extremely attractive young woman who appeared to be in her late twenties, an artist from London

Paul, London), and a report by the Joint Air Reconnaissance Center of the Royal Air Force on a motion picture of the monster swimming about half a mile on the lake's surface. These books and documents could, in turn, lead the interested reader to less available but nonetheless highly relevant works such as R. T. Gould's *The Loch Ness Monster and Others* and Constance Whyte's *More Than a Legend.*

My children looked over the photographs with absorption but not a great deal of awe, and they bought about a dozen postcards with glossy prints of a picture of the monster—three humps showing, much the same sight that the innkeeper had described—that had been taken by a man named Stuart, directly across the lake from Urquhart Castle. The three younger girls then ran out into the meadow and began to pick daisies and buttercups. Their mother and sister sat down in the sun to read about the creature in the lake, and to write postcards. We were on our way to Inverness, but with no need to hurry. "Dear Grammy, we came to see the monster today."

From the office to the camera-observation platform to the caravan that served as a pocket mess hall, I wandered around among the crew, was offered and accepted tea, and squinted with imaginary experience up and down the lake, where the whitecaps had, if anything, increased. Among the crew at the time were two Canadians, a Swede, an Australian, three Americans, two Englishmen, a Welshman, and one Scot. Two were women. When I asked one of the crew members if he knew what some of the others did, vocationally, when they were not at Loch Ness, he said, "I'm not sure what they are. We don't go into that." This was obviously a place where now was all that mattered, and in such a milieu it is distinctly pleasant to accept that approach to things. Nonetheless, I found that I couldn't adhere completely to this principle, and I did find out that one man was a medical doctor, another a farmer, another a retired naval officer, and that several, inevitably, were students. The daily watch begins at four in the morning and goes on, as one fellow put it, "as long as we can stand up." It has been the pattern among the hundreds of sightings reported that the early-morning hours are the most promising ones. Camera stations are manned until ten at night, dawn and sunset being so close to midnight at that latitude in summer, but the sentries tend to thin out with the lengthening of the day. During the autumn, the size of the crew reduces precipitously[11] toward one.

One man lives at the headquarters all year long. His name is Clem Lister Skelton. "I've been staring at that piece of water since five o'clock," he said, while he drank tea in the mess caravan.

"Is there a technique?" I asked him.

"Just look," he said. "Look. Run your eye over the water in one quick skim. What we're looking for is not hard to see. You just sit and sort of gaze at the loch, that's all. Mutter a few incantations.[12] That's all there is to do. In wintertime, very often, it's just myself. And of course one keeps a very much more perfunctory[13] watch in the winter. I saw it once in a snowstorm, though, and that was the only time I've had a clear view of the head and neck. The neck is obviously very mobile. The creature was quite big, but it wasn't as big as a seventy-foot MFV. Motor fishing vessel. I'd been closer to it, but I hadn't seen as much of it before. I've seen it eight times. The last time was in September. Only the

---

11. **precipitously** (pri sip′ə təs lē) *adv.*: Steeply.
12. **incantations** (in′kan tā′shəns) *n.*: Spells.
13. **perfunctory** (pər fuŋk′tər ē) *adj.*: Routine; superficial.

6 **Discussion** Why do you think McPhee includes this personal information?

7 **Literary Focus** How does McPhee heighten a reader's interest by letting Skelton speak for himself? Why might this passage have been less interesting if McPhee had summarized Skelton's words?

who had missed but one summer at Loch Ness in seven years. She wore sandals, dungarees, a black pullover, and gold earrings. Her name was Mary Piercy, and her toes were painted pink.

Keep in mind that these passages of description are from an expository essay, one written to explain a concept or event by providing information. Why might the author have included the descriptive passages? What do they add to the essay?

**Student Activity 1.** Find several other passages of descriptive writing in the essay, and share these with a partner. Discuss what they add to the essay.

**Student Activity 2.** Write a paragraph in which you describe a person, an object, or a place. Try to convey in this composition your own feelings about the subject.

**8 Critical Thinking and Reading**
As this paragraph opens, it is clear that McPhee will give a personal reaction to Skelton. Ask students to notice, as they read on, if they are able to judge how Skelton affected McPhee.

**9 Discussion** Why do you think the place might make someone think of a carnival?

back. Just the sort of upturned boat, which is the classic view of it."

Skelton drank some more tea, and refilled a cup he had given me. "I must know what it is," he went on. "I shall never rest peacefully until I know what it is. Some of the largest creatures in the world are out there, and we can't name them. It may take ten years, but we're going to identify the genus.[14] Most people are not as fanatical as I, but I would like to see this through to the end, if I don't get too broke first."

Skelton is a tall, offhand[15] man, English, with reddish hair that is disheveled[16] in long strings from the thinning crown of his head. In outline, Skelton's life there in the caravan on the edge of the high meadow over the lake, in a place that must be uncorrectably gloomy during the wet rains of winter, seemed cagelike and hopeless to me—unacceptably lonely. The impression he gave was of a man who had drawn a circle around himself many hundreds of miles from the rest of his life. But how could I know? He was saying that he had flown Supermarine Spitfires for the R.A.F.[17] during the Second World War. His father had been a soldier, and when Skelton was a boy, he lived, as he put it, "all over the place." As an adult, he became first an actor, later a writer and director of films. He acted in London in plays like *March Hare* and *Saraband for Dead Lovers*. One film he directed was, in his words, "a dreadful thing called *Saul and David*." These appearances on the surface apparently did not occur so frequently that he needed to do nothing else for a livelihood. He also directed, in the course of many

years, several hundred educational films. The publisher who distributed some of these films was David James, a friend of Skelton's, and at that time a Member of Parliament.[18] James happened to be, as well, the founder of the Loch Ness Phenomena Investigation Bureau—phenomena, because, for breeding purposes, there would have to be at least two monsters living in the lake at any one time, probably more, and in fact two had on occasion been sighted simultaneously. James asked Skelton if he would go up to the lake and give the bureau the benefit of his technical knowledge of movie cameras. "Anything for a laugh," Skelton had said to James. This was in the early nineteen-sixties. "I came for a fortnight,"[19] Skelton said now, in the caravan. "And I saw it. I wanted to know what it was, and I've wanted to know what it was ever since. I thought I'd have time to write up here, but I haven't. I don't do anything now except hunt this beast."

Skelton talked on about what the monster might be—a magnified newt,[20] a long-necked variety of giant seal, an unextinct *Elasmosaurus*. Visitors wandered by in groups outside the caravan, and unexplained strangers kept coming in for tea. In the air was a feeling, utterly belied by the relative permanence of the place, of a country carnival on a two-night stand. The caravans themselves, in their alignment, suggested a section of a midway. I remembered a woman shouting to attract people to a big caravan on a carnival midway one night in May in New Jersey. That was some time ago. I must have been nineteen. The woman, who was standing on a small platform, was fifty or sixty, and she was trying to get people to go

---

**14. genus** (jē′ nəs) *n.*: Main subdivision of a family of closely related species.
**15. offhand** *adj.*: Casual; informal.
**16. disheveled** (di shev′ ′ld) *adj.*: Untidy; tousled.
**17. Supermarine Spitfires for the R.A.F.:** Fighter planes for the British Royal Air Force.

**18. Parliament** (pär′ lə mənt) *n.*: The national legislative body of Great Britain.
**19. fortnight** (fôrt′ nīt′) *n.*: Two weeks.
**20. newt** (nōot) *n.*: Salamander.

into the caravan to see big jungle cats, I suppose, and brown bears—"Ferocious Beasts," at any rate, according to block lettering on the side of the caravan. A steel cage containing a small black bear had been set up on two sawhorses outside the caravan—a fragment to imply what might be found on a larger scale inside.

So young that it was no more than two feet from nose to tail, the bear was engaged in desperate motion, racing along one side of the cage from corner to corner, striking the steel bars bluntly with its nose. Whirling then, tossing its head over its shoulder like a racing swimmer, it turned and bolted crazily for the opposite end. Its eyes were deep red, and shining in a kind of full-sighted blindness. It had gone mad there in the cage, and its motion, rhythmic and tortured, never ceased, back and forth, back and forth, the head tossing with each jarring turn. The animal abraded its flanks on the steel bars as it ran. Hair and skin had scraped from its sides so that pink flesh showed in the downpour of the carnival arc lights. Blood drained freely through the thinned hair of its belly and dropped onto the floor of the cage. What had a paralyzing effect on me was the animal's almost perfect and now involuntary rhythm—the wild toss of the head after the crash into the corner, the turn, the scraping run, the crash again at the other end, never stopping, metronomic—the exposed interior of some brutal and organic timepiece.

Beside the cage, the plump, impervious woman, red-faced, red-nosed, kept shouting to the crowds, but she said to me, leaning down, her own eyes bloodshot, "Why don't you move on, sonny, if you ain't going to buy a ticket? Beat it. Come on, now. Move on."

"We argue about what it is," Skelton said. "I'm inclined to think it's a giant slug, but there is an amazingly impressive theory for its being a worm. You can't rule out that it's one of the big dinosaurs, but I think this is more wishful thinking than anything else." In the late nineteen-thirties, a large and exotic footprint was found along the shore of Loch Ness. It was meticulously studied by various people and was assumed, for a time, to be an impression from a foot or flipper of the monster. Eventually, the print was identified. Someone who owned the preserved foot of a hippopotamus had successfully brought off a hoax that put layers of mockery and incredibility over the creature in the lake for many years. The Second World War further diverted any serious interest that amateurs or naturalists might have taken. Sightings continued, however, in a consistent pattern, and finally, in the early nineteen-sixties, the Loch Ness Phenomena Investigation Bureau was established. "I have no plans whatever for leaving," Skelton said. "I am prepared to stay here ad infinitum.[21] All my worldly goods are here."

A dark-haired young woman had stepped into the caravan and poured herself a cup of tea. Skelton, introducing her to me, said, "If the beast has done nothing else, it has brought me a wife. She was studying Gaelic[22] and Scottish history at Edinburgh University, and she walked into the glen one day, and I said, 'That is the girl I am going to marry.' " He gestured toward a window of the caravan, which framed a view of the hills and the lake. "The Great Glen is one of the most beautiful places in the world," he continued. "It is peaceful here. I'd be happy here all my life, even if there were nothing in the loch. I've even committed the unforgivable

---

**21. ad infinitum** (ad in′ fə nīt′ əm): Latin phrase meaning *forever*.
**22. Gaelic** (gāl′ ik) *adj.*: A Celtic language spoken in Scotland and Ireland.

**10 Critical Thinking and Reading** How do you think this memory relates to the rest of the essay?

**11 Clarification** Some students, particularly those who have taken piano lessons, will know that a *metronome* is a "mechanical device for establishing the regular intervals of a rhythm."

**12 Discussion** How does the inclusion of the information about Skelton's wife add to the reader's understanding of Skelton's character?

13 **Literary Focus** How does McPhee shift the focus of the essay in this section?

14 **Discussion** How reliable is this older report? Explain.

sin of going to sleep in the sun during a flat calm. With enough time, we could shoot the beast with a crossbow and a line, and get a bit of skin. We could also shoot a small transmitter into its hide and learn more than we know now about its habits and characteristics."

13 The creature swims with remarkable speed, as much as ten or fifteen knots when it is really moving. It makes no noise other than seismic splashes, but it is apparently responsive in a highly sensitive way to sound. A shout, an approaching engine, any loud report, will send it into an immediate dive, and this shyness is in large part the cause of its inaccessibility, and therefore of its mystery. Curiously, though, reverberate sound was what apparently brought the creature widespread attention, for the first sequence of frequent sightings occurred in 1933, when the A-82 was blasted into the cliffsides of the western shore of the lake. Immense boulders kept falling into the depths, and shock waves from dynamite repeatedly ran through the water, causing the creature to lose confidence in its environment and to alter, at least temporarily, its shy and preferentially nocturnal life. In that year it was first observed on land, perhaps attempting to seek a way out forever from the detonations that had alarmed it. A couple named Spicer saw it, near Inverarigaig, and later described its long, serpentine neck, followed by an ungainly hulk of body, lurching toward the lake and disappearing into high undergrowth as they approached.

14 With the exception of one report recorded in the sixth century, which said that a monster (fitting the description of the contemporary creatures in the lake) had killed a man with a single bite, there have been no other examples of savagery on its part. To the contrary, its sensitivity to people seems to be acute, and it keeps a wide margin between itself and mankind. In all likelihood, it feeds on fish and particularly on eels, of which there are millions in the lake. Loch Ness is unparalleled in eel-fishing circles, and has drawn commercial eel fishermen from all over the United Kingdom. The monster has been observed with its neck bent down in the water, like a swan feeding. When the creatures die, they apparently settle into the seven-hundred-foot floor of the lake, where the temperature is always forty-

494 *Nonfiction*

## Grammar in Action

Good writers vary their sentence structure, and one means of doing so is to use different **sentence openers.** If all sentences begin the same way, readers soon tire of the repetition.

In addition to its subject, a sentence can begin with one-word modifiers, phrases, clauses, or a combination of these openers:

*Exhausted*, the racer collapsed. (one-word modifier)
*Sensing danger*, the snake coiled. (phrase)

*Yesterday, when the mail arrived*, the check was missing. (one-word modifier and clause)

Variety results from the many kinds of one-word modifiers, phrases, and clauses writers can use: adjectives, adverbs, participles, infinitives, gerunds, prepositional phrases, adverb clauses, adjective clauses, and so forth.

John McPhee uses many different types of sentence openers in "The Loch Ness Monster":

two degrees Fahrenheit—so cold that the lake is known for never giving up its dead. Loch Ness never freezes, despite its high latitude, so if the creature breathes air, as has seemed apparent from the reports of observers who have watched its mouth rhythmically opening and closing, it does not lose access to the surface in winter. It clearly prefers the smooth, sunbaked waterscapes of summer, however, for it seems to love to bask in the sun, like an upturned boat, slowly rolling, plunging, squirming around

with what can only be taken as pleasure. By observers' reports, the creature has two pairs of lateral[23] flippers, and when it swims off, tail thrashing, it leaves behind it a wake as impressive as the wake of a small warship. When it dives from a still position, it inexplicably[24] goes down without leaving a bubble. When it dives as it swims, it leaves on the surface a churning signature of foam.

Skelton leaned back against the wall of the caravan in a slouched and nonchalant posture. He was wearing a dark blue tie that was monogrammed in small block letters sewn with white thread—L.N.I. (Loch Ness Investigation). Above the monogram and embroidered also in white thread was a small depiction of the monster—humps undulant, head high, tail extending astern. Skelton gave the tie a flick with one hand. "You get this with a five-pound membership," he said.

The sea-serpent effect given by the white thread on the tie was less a stylization than an attempt toward a naturalistic sketch. As I studied it there, framed on Skelton's chest, the thought occurred to me that there was something inconvenient about the monster's actual appearance. In every sense except possibly the sense that involves cruelty, the creature in Loch Ness is indeed a monster. An average taken from many films and sightings gives its mature length at about forty feet. Its general appearance is repulsive, in the instant and radical sense in which reptiles are repulsive to many human beings, and any number of people might find difficulty in accepting a creature that looks like the one that was slain by St. George. Its neck, about six feet long, columnar, powerfully muscled, is the neck of a serpent. Its

---

**23. lateral** (lat′ ər əl) *adj.:* On the side.
**24. inexplicably** (in eks′ pli kə blē) *adv.:* Unexplainably.

*The Loch Ness Monster* 495

15 **Reading Strategy** Ask students to summarize the important information about the monster.

16 **Clarification** St. George was a Christian martyr who died in the year 303. He became the patron saint of England, and during the Middle Ages his name became associated with many legends. According to one tale, he slew a great dragon.

---

The *sea-serpent* effect given by the white thread . . . (subject with adjective modifier)

*As I studied it there, framed on Skeleton's chest,* the thought occurred to me . . . (clause, participial phrase)

*In every sense except possibly the sense that involves cruelty,* the creature . . . (prepositional phrase, prepositional phrase that includes an adjective clause)

Good writers like McPhee will rarely begin two successive sentences with the same kind of opener.

**Student Activity 1.** Select three other successive sentences from this selection. Name the kind of sentence opener used in each.

**Student Activity 2.** Write a paragraph describing your thoughts about the Loch Ness Monster. Use a different opener for each sentence.

**17 Critical Thinking and Reading**
Why is the resemblance of the monster to the creature of legend an impediment to the investigation?

**18 Discussion** Ask students to identify the parallels between the incident with the garden snake and the investigation of the Loch Ness Monster.

**Reader's Response** Do you believe the Loch Ness Monster exists? Explain.

head, scarcely broader than the neck, is a serpent's head, with uncompromising, lenticular[25] eyes. Sometimes as it swims it holds its head and neck erect. The creature's mouth is at least a foot wide. Its body undulates. Its skin glistens when wet and appears coarse, mottled, gray, and elephantine when exposed to the air long enough to become dry. The tail, long and columnar, stretches back to something of a point. It seemed to me, sitting there at Headquarters, that the classical, mythical, dragon likeness of this animate thing—the modified dinosaur, the fantastically exaggerated newt—was an impediment to the work of the investigation bureau, which has no pertinent interest in what the monster resembles or calls to mind but a great deal in what it actually is, the goal being a final and positive identification of the genus.

"What we need is a good, lengthy, basking sighting," Skelton said. "We've had one long surfacing—twenty-five minutes. I saw it. Opposite Urquhart Castle. We only had a twelve-inch lens then, at four and a half miles. We have thirty-six-inch lenses now. We need a long, clear, close-up—in color."

My children had watched, some months earlier, the killing of a small snake on a lawn in Maryland. About eighteen inches long, it came out from a basement-window well, through a covering lattice of redwood, and

25. **lenticular** (len tik′ yoo lər) *adj*.: Shaped like a lentil bean.

was noticed with shouts and shrieks by the children and a young retriever that barked at the snake and leaped about it in a circle. We were the weekend guests of another family, and eight children in all crowded around the snake, which had been gliding slowly across the lawn during the moments after it had been seen, but had now stopped and was turning its head from side to side in apparent indecision. Our host hurried into his garage and came running back to the lawn with a long shovel. Before he killed the snake, his wife urged him not to. She said the snake could not possibly be poisonous. He said, "How do you know?" The children, mine and theirs, looked back and forth from him to her. The dog began to bark more rapidly and at a higher pitch.

"It has none of the markings. There is nothing triangular about its head," she told him.

"That may very well be," he said. "But you can't be sure."

"It is *not* poisonous. Leave it alone. Look at all these children."

"I can't help that."

"It is *not* poisonous."

"How do you know?"

"I know."

He hit the snake with the flat of the shovel, and it writhed. He hit it again. It kept moving. He hit it a third time, and it stopped. Its underside, whitish green, segmental, turned up. The children moved in for a closer look.

## Closure and Extension

### ANSWERS TO THINKING ABOUT THE SELECTION
*Recalling*

1. The bureau conducts field work to investigate the monster's behavior and appearance; it also publishes a newsletter and annual reports about its findings.

2. A caravan serves as the headquarters' office; the atmosphere suggests both a scientific frontier and a boom town.

3. One staff member is Mary Piercy, an artist from London who had spent all but one of the past seven summers at Loch Ness. Another is Clem Skelton; before coming to Loch Ness, Skelton had first been a

## THINKING ABOUT THE SELECTION

### Recalling

1. What is the purpose of the Loch Ness Phenomena Investigation Bureau?
2. Describe the layout and atmosphere of the organization.
3. Recount the background of two of the staff.
4. Summarize what is known about the Loch Ness Monster's habits and appearance.

### Interpreting

5. How are the crew members being adventurers even though they are not risking their lives?
6. What does McPhee mean by calling the bureau a place "where now was all that mattered"?
7. Why does he include the story about "the killing of a small snake"?

### Applying

8. How can investigators find out more about the Loch Ness Monster?

## ANALYZING LITERATURE

### Understanding the Expository Essay

The purpose of an **expository essay** is to explain a concept, event, or process by presenting information. Skilled writers can make an expository essay fun to read as well as informative. In "The Loch Ness Monster," for instance, McPhee creates interest by dealing with a fascinating topic, holding back information until the end, and introducing personal details.

1. How does McPhee's delay in describing the monster make the essay more interesting?
2. Identify three ways in which he gives the essay a personal flavor.
3. Why do personal details create interest?

## CRITICAL THINKING AND READING

### Finding Relevant Evidence

**Relevant evidence** is pertinent to or supports the matter being studied. It bears a close logical relationship to this issue. For example, a photograph of the Loch Ness Monster is relevant to proving its existence.

Make a list of five pieces of evidence you think would be relevant to proving or disproving the existence of this creature.

## UNDERSTANDING LANGUAGE

### Understanding Words with the Suffix *ity*

A **suffix** is one or more syllables added at the end of a root to form a word. The suffix *ity* means "state of being, character, or condition." In this essay, *ity* appears in the word *declivity*—"the state or condition of being a downward slope." You can also find this common suffix in the word *equality*—"the state of being equal."

Explain how this suffix contributes to the meaning of the following words. You may use a dictionary if you wish.

1. integrity      3. hospitality
2. parity         4. originality

## THINKING AND WRITING

### Writing an Expository Essay

Think of a company, club, team, or any other organization that you know about. List some important facts regarding this group, including its goal, the location of its headquarters, and the type of people who work for it. Then, using this list, write an expository essay about the group for your classmates. Remember that such an essay does not tell a story but presents information in an interesting way. You will find it helpful to give the main ideas in your first paragraph, with the other paragraphs providing further details. In revising your essay, you may want to include some of your personal experiences with the group, as McPhee does in his piece. When you are done, show the essay to your classmates.

---

scribing the monster immediately, McPhee keeps readers wondering about it.

2. Suggested Response: McPhee talks about his children and their response to the visit. He also describes the incident with the garden snake and he describes the carnival incident that he recalls from his youth.
3. Suggested Response: Personal details allow the reader to identify more closely with the writer.

### ANSWERS TO CRITICAL THINKING AND READING

Answers will differ, but students might include the following in their list of evidence: a footprint or other trace; a clear film or videotape; the dead body of a monster; a diver's clear sighting of the monster; and the actual capture of one of these creatures.

### ANSWERS TO UNDERSTANDING LANGUAGE

1. integrity—having the character of wholeness or honesty.
2. parity—the state of being equal or having equal status.
3. hospitality—the quality of being welcoming.
4. originality—the condition or quality of being new and different.

### THINKING AND WRITING

For help with this assignment, students might consult Lesson 2, "Drafting and Revising," in the Handbook of Writing About Literature.

**Publishing Student Writing** You might have students submit their essays to the school newspaper.

**Writing Across the Curriculum** You might have students research and report on scientists—like Jane Goodall—who study animal behavior in the wild. Consider informing the science department of this assignment so that teachers can guide students to appropriate resource materials.

---

writer and then an actor. He had also directed several hundred educational films.

4. The Loch Ness Monster is about forty feet long with two fins, a long tail that stretches into a point, and a mouth at least a foot wide. Its appearance is repulsive. The skin is coarse and gray. The monster prefers summer to winter and seems to like to bask in the sun. It is highly sensitive to sound, seems to be shy, and swims with remarkable speed.

### Interpreting

5. Suggested Response: They do not know what will happen next, or when it will happen. Like adventurers, they must be prepared for anything.
6. Suggested Response: Everyone is united in the task of looking for current evidence of the monster's activity.
7. Suggested Response: The fascination, fear, and repulsion that the snake calls up are the same feelings evoked by the monster.

### Applying

8. Answers will differ, but students might suggest that divers look for the creature.

**Challenge** What do you think would happen if the monster were captured?

### ANSWERS TO ANALYZING LITERATURE

1. Suggested Response: By not de-

## Focus

**More About the Author** Martin Luther King, Jr., an American clergyman and civil-rights leader, was awarded the Nobel Peace Prize in 1964. At 35 he was the youngest man and only the third black man to be awarded this prestigious honor. Ask students why they think Dr. King received this award. You might also ask students whether Dr. King's goals have been achieved.

**Literary Focus** In a persuasive essay, the writer must choose examples carefully to appeal to the reader in particular ways. In his speech, King shows the same concern as the persuasive essayist. He appeals to the audience's respect for the Bible, their traditional American values, and their familiarity with a song well-known to most from their schooldays. Collectively, these make a powerful appeal to the American reader or listener.

**Look For** Consider pointing out to students that while some of the details of King's dream are literal, others are meant in a more metaphorical sense.

**Writing/Prior Knowledge** You may want to explain to students that Aristotle (384-322 B.C.), a Greek philosopher and scientist, had a tremendous influence on Western culture. During the Middle Ages, Christian and Arabic scholars regarded him as the greatest of all thinkers.

**Vocabulary** Have students read the list of words and their definitions. Ask them to use each one in a sentence that indicates its meaning and compare their use of the word with King's.

## "I Have a Dream"

**Persuasive Essay**

**Martin Luther King, Jr.** (1929–1968) was a minister and civil rights leader who struggled to bring black Americans into the political and economic mainstream of American life. He was born in Atlanta, Georgia, the son of a minister. Inspired by Christian ideals and the philosophy of the Indian leader Mohandas K. Gandhi, King led marches and sit-ins to protest discrimination against black people. "I Have a Dream" comes from a speech he gave to a massive civil rights demonstration in Washington, D.C., in 1963.

The purpose of a **persuasive essay** is to convince an audience to accept or consider an opinion or recommended course of action. Usually the writer states the opinion or recommendation at the start of the essay and then supports it with convincing evidence. While Martin Luther King, Jr.'s speech, "I Have a Dream," is not strictly a persuasive essay, it does share qualities with this type of writing. Like an essayist, for example, King tries to convince his audience to accept and work for his dream of equality.

**Look For**

What are dreams? Why do people need to dream of the future? As you read, look for King's statement of his "dream" at the beginning of the speech. Then be aware of the way in which he adds further details to make his vision seem like a worthwhile goal.

**Writing**

The great Greek philosopher Aristotle wrote, "Equality consists in the same treatment of similar persons." Write your own definition of equality.

**Vocabulary**

Knowing the following words will help you as you read "I Have a Dream."

**creed** (krēd) *n.*: Statement of belief (p. 499)
**oppression** (ə presh′ ən) *n.*: Keeping others down by the unjust use of power (p. 499)
**oasis** (ō ā′ sis) *n.*: Fertile place in the desert (p. 499)

**exalted** (ig zôlt′ əd) *v.*: Lifted up (p. 499)
**prodigious** (prə dij′ əs) *adj.*: Wonderful; of great size (p. 500)
**hamlet** (ham′ lit) *n.*: Very small village (p. 501)

## Objectives

1 To understand the persuasive essay
2 To recognize persuasive techniques
3 To deliver a speech
4 To write about persuasion

## Support Material

**Teaching Portfolio**
Teacher Backup, p. 543
Grammar in Action Worksheet, *Using Parallel Structure,* p. 546
Usage and Mechanics Worksheet, p. 548
Vocabulary Check, p. 549
Analyzing Literature Worksheet, *Understanding the Persuasive Essay,* p. 550
Language Worksheet, *Under-standing Synonyms and Antonyms,* p. 551
Selection Test, p. 552

# "I Have a Dream"

## Martin Luther King, Jr.

. . . I say to you today, my friends, that in spite of the difficulties and frustrations of the moment I still have a dream. It is a dream deeply rooted in the American dream.

I have a dream that one day this nation will rise up and live out the true meaning of its creed: "We hold these truths to be self-evident; that all men are created equal."

I have a dream that one day on the red hills of Georgia the sons of former slaves and the sons of former slaveowners will be able to sit down together at the table of brotherhood.

I have a dream that one day even the state of Mississippi, a desert state sweltering with the heat of injustice and oppression, will be transformed into an oasis of freedom and justice.

I have a dream that my four little children will one day live in a nation where they will not be judged by the color of their skin but by the content of their character.

I have a dream today.

I have a dream that one day the state of Alabama, whose governor's lips are presently dripping with the words of interposition and nullification,[1] will be transformed into a situation where little black boys and black girls will be able to join hands with little white boys and white girls and walk together as sisters and brothers.

I have a dream today.

I have a dream that one day every valley shall be exalted, every hill and mountain shall be made low, the rough places will be made plains, and the crooked places will be made straight, and the glory of the Lord shall be revealed, and all flesh shall see it together.[2]

This is our hope. This is the faith with which I return to the South. With this faith we will be able to transform the jangling discords of our nation into a beautiful symphony of brotherhood. With this faith we will be able to work together, to pray together, to struggle together, to go to jail together, to stand up for freedom together, knowing that we will be free one day.

This will be the day when all of God's children will be able to sing with new meaning "My country 'tis of thee, sweet land of liberty, of thee I sing. Land where my fathers died, land of the pilgrim's pride, from every mountainside, let freedom ring."

And if America is to be a great nation

---

1. **interposition** (in' tər pə zish ən) **and nullification** (nul' ə fi kā' shən): The disputed doctrine that a state can reject federal laws considered to be violations of its rights.

2. **every valley . . . all flesh shall see it together:** Refers to a Biblical passage (Isaiah 40:4 and 5).

*"I Have a Dream"* 499

**4 Clarification** *Prodigious* means "wonderful; enormous."

**5 Critical Thinking and Reading** Where else does King use vivid words like *curvaceous?* Why are these words effective?

4 this must become true. So let freedom ring from the prodigious hilltops of New Hampshire. Let freedom ring from the mighty mountains of New York. Let freedom ring from the heightening Alleghenies of Pennsylvania!

Let freedom ring from the snowcapped Rockies of Colorado!

Let freedom ring from the curvaceous peaks of California! 5

But not only that; let freedom ring from Stone Mountain of Georgia!

*500   Nonfiction*

## Grammar in Action

**Parallelism** is the repetition of similar grammatical structures to create emphasis and show the equality of ideas. One type of parallelism occurs when parts of a sentence are similar in structure. The following sentence, for example, has a compound predicate with each part consisting of the verb and a direct object with adjectives.

The freshman class *earned the best attendance record,* *achieved the highest grade-point average,* and *won the interclass softball tournament.*

Martin Luther King, Jr., used parallel structures in different sentences to create a rousing speech. The parallelism helps listeners hear the emphasis:

Let freedom ring from the mighty mountains of New York. Let freedom ring from the heightening Alleghenies of Pennsylvania! Let freedom ring from the snowcapped Rockies of

6 **Literary Focus** Is King's use of the phrase "let freedom ring" similar to the earlier use of the phrase "I have a dream"? Explain.

7 **Critical Thinking and Reading** Why do you think King suggests that other groups will not be truly free until black people are?

8 **Discussion** Explain how the conclusion of the speech—"Free at last"—relates to the beginning—"I have a dream. . . ."

**Reader's Response** Do you think King's dream will come true? Why or why not?

6

Let freedom ring from every hill and molehill of Mississippi. From every mountainside, let freedom ring.

When we let freedom ring, when we let it ring from every village and every hamlet, from every state and every city, we will be able to speed up that day when all of God's children, black men and white men, Jews and Gentiles, Protestants and Catholics, will be able to join hands and sing in the words of that old Negro spiritual, "Free at last! Free at last! Thank God almighty, we are free at last!"

7

8

*"I Have a Dream"* 501

Colorado! Let freedom ring from the curvaceous peaks of California! But not only that; let freedom ring from Stone Mountain of Georgia.

Each sentence begins with the same words, "Let freedom ring." In each sentence, two prepositional phrases follow: "from" followed by an adjective and a noun, and "of" followed by a state's name. Variation in the last sentence underscores the parallelism.

**Student Activity 1.** Find another series of parallel structures in the speech.

**Student Activity 2.** Write three sentences, each of which includes parallelism. Vary the parts of the sentences which are parallel.

## ANSWERS TO THINKING ABOUT THE SELECTION
### Recalling

1. King's dream is that one day Americans of all races, creeds, and religions will live together in peace and equality.
2. The sources of King's dream are the Bible and the Declaration of Independence.
3. He hopes that one day they will be able to sing "My Country 'Tis of Thee" believing that it applies to them and that they will not be judged by the color of their skin.
4. King will be able to return to the South and work towards brotherhood.

### Interpreting

5. Suggested Response: King wants to suggest that civil rights are the concern of all Americans no matter where they live. He also wants to indicate the size and diversity of the United States.
6. Suggested Response: When King repeats this phrase, he emphasizes his conviction and recalls the repetitions in a sermon.

### Applying

7. Answers will differ. Most students will realize that Kennedy meant all people should have the *same* chance to develop their *different* talents and abilities.

## ANSWERS TO ANALYZING LITERATURE

1. Suggested Response: He uses the image of sons of slaves sitting down together with the sons of slaveowners. He also uses the image of white and black children joining hands in Alabama.
2. Answers will differ. Many students will respond that the speech is passionate in its repetition of the phrases "I have a dream" and "let freedom ring" and appeals to traditional American values. This quality makes the speech very persuasive.

## THINKING ABOUT THE SELECTION
### Recalling

1. In your own words, briefly state King's dream.
2. What are the roots, or sources, of this dream?
3. What does King want for his own children?
4. What will the hope of realizing his dream enable him to do?

### Interpreting

5. Why does King mention the names of so many states in his speech?
6. Explain the effect of repeating the phrase, "I have a dream."

### Applying

7. Discuss the following statement by John F. Kennedy: "All of us do not have equal talent, but all of us should have equal opportunity to develop our talents."

## ANALYZING LITERATURE
### Understanding the Persuasive Essay

The purpose of a **persuasive essay** is to convince an audience to accept or consider an opinion or recommended course of action. In "I Have a Dream," Martin Luther King, Jr. urges his audience to accept his dream of the United States transformed "into a beautiful symphony of brotherhood."

1. King paints many vivid word pictures of his dream, in addition to calling brotherhood a "symphony." Find two examples of the powerful images that he uses.
2. The success of a persuasive essay depends on its effect on its audience. Does King convince you to accept or work for his dream? Explain.

## CRITICAL THINKING AND READING
### Recognizing Persuasive Techniques

One technique that writers of persuasive essays or speeches use is to associate their goals

with a familiar and honored document, phrase, or person. In "I Have a Dream," for instance, Martin Luther King, Jr. describes his dream using words from the Bible: ". . . every valley shall be exalted . . ." He wants the audience to transfer to his cause their positive feelings about the Bible.

1. Identify two other examples where King quotes from honored and familiar sources.
2. In each case explain whether King has chosen inspiring words to identify with his cause.

## SPEAKING AND LISTENING
### Delivering a Speech

When delivering a speech, you should remember to speak in a natural way rather than in a singsong voice. Also, you should make your voice loud or soft according to the meaning of the words. Keep in mind, however, that even the words you speak softly should be audible to your listeners.

1. Your teacher will divide you into small groups. Practice delivering "I Have a Dream" in your group. Take suggestions from listeners for improving your delivery.
2. Each group will choose a speaker to deliver a portion of the speech to the class.

## THINKING AND WRITING
### Writing About Persuasion

Imagine that two of your good friends have had an argument. List some of the ways in which you could persuade them to settle their dispute. For instance, you might want to consider appealing to a source or authority they respect, or showing them the benefits of making up. Then, using your list, write an essay further detailing your persuasive techniques. In revising the essay, make sure that you have explained why your persuasive techniques would be effective.

## ANSWERS TO CRITICAL THINKING AND READING

1. Suggested Response: King quotes from the song "My Country 'Tis of Thee" and from an old Negro spiritual.
2. Suggested Response: In each case, King has chosen inspiring words to identify with his cause. The familiar words from "My Country 'Tis of Thee" take on a new power in the context of the civil-rights movement. Also, the words from the spiritual powerfully express the longing of blacks for freedom.

## THINKING AND WRITING
For help with this assignment, students may refer to Lesson 1, "Prewriting," in the Handbook of Writing About Literature.

**Publishing Student Writing** Divide the class into small groups and have students read and discuss the compositions of fellow group members.

**Writing Across the Curriculum** You might want to have students research and report on some aspect of the civil-rights movement —perhaps the March on Washington that was the occasion of this famous speech. Consider informing the social studies department of this assignment, so that teachers can provide guidance for students.

# Essays in the Arts and Sciences

**WOMAN WITH VIOLIN**
*Henri Matisse*
Musée de l'Orangerie, Paris

**Humanities Note**

Fine Art, *Woman with Violin*, Henri Matisse. The French painter Henri Matisse (1869-1954), was the leader of the Fauvist movement in painting, which glorified line and rhythm and the free use of vibrant color. His work created a new way of thinking in twentieth-century art and had a lasting influence on subsequent trends.

In *Woman with Violin*, Matisse uses distortion of form to attain a decorative effect. The color has no relation to reality but is expressive of the way the artist feels about his subject. The color combinations are unusual but are made to work through sensitive handling. As in all of his works, detail is kept at a minimum. Matisse felt that any element included in a composition that did not contribute to the overall decorative effect was, in fact, a detriment.

### The Death of a Tree

**Edwin Way Teale** (1899–1980) was a naturalist, illustrator, and photographer. He was also a staff writer for *Popular Science* magazine and the author of nearly thirty books. The most popular of these are his studies of the seasons in the United States, like *North with the Spring* and *Journey Into Summer.* In 1966 he won the Pulitzer Prize for a volume in this series, *Wandering Through Winter.* Like his other works, "The Death of a Tree" shows Teale's great knowledge of nature, as well as his love for it.

**Transformation**

For most of us, the death of a tree may seem like a change that occurs all at once. To a naturalist like Edwin Way Teale, however, the death of a tree is a process that occurs in slow, and sometimes hardly visible, stages. His knowledge of nature enables him to explain these changes in detail. As he traces the passing of an oak, you will see how one transformation grows out of another and how the death of a tree can sustain many smaller plants and creatures.

**Look For**

As you read, notice the way in which each stage of the tree's death leads to the next stage. Also be aware of how Teale expresses his feeling for the tree as well as his knowledge of it.

**Writing**

Recall a natural process that you have witnessed. It could be the growth of a plant or animal, or any similar change over time. List the main stages of this change.

**Vocabulary**

Knowing the following words will help you as you read "The Death of a Tree."

**ebbs** (ebs) *v.*: Lessens; weakens (p. 505)

**venerable** (ven' ərə b'l) *adj.*: Old and respected (p. 505)

**dissolution** (dis' ə loo' shən) *n.*: Disintegration; death (p. 505)

**gilded** (gild' əd) *v.*: Overlaid with gold; made bright and attractive (p. 506)

**resiliency** (ri zil' yən sē) *n.*: Ability to bounce or spring back (p. 506)

**protozoa** (prōt' ə zō' ə) *n.*: Microscopic animals (p. 506)

**tumult** (too' mult) *n.*: Noisy commotion (p. 508)

**prostrate** (präs' trāt) *adj.*: Lying flat (p. 508)

# The Death of a Tree

### Edwin Way Teale

For a great tree death comes as a gradual transformation. Its vitality ebbs slowly. Even when life has abandoned it entirely it remains a majestic thing. On some hilltop a dead tree may dominate the landscape for miles around. Alone among living things it retains its character and dignity after death. Plants wither; animals disintegrate. But a dead tree may be as arresting, as filled with personality, in death as it is in life. Even in its final moments, when the massive trunk lies prone and it has moldered[1] into a ridge covered with mosses and fungi,[2] it arrives at a fitting and a noble end. It enriches and refreshes the earth. And later, as part of other green and growing things, it rises again.

The death of the great white oak which gave our Indiana homestead its name and which played such an important part in our daily lives was so gentle a transition that we never knew just when it ceased to be a living organism.

It had stood there, toward the sunset from the farmhouse, rooted in that same spot for 200 years or more. How many generations of red squirrels had rattled up and down its gray-black bark! How many genera-tions of robins had sung from its upper branches! How many humans, from how many lands, had paused beneath its shade!

The passing of this venerable giant made a profound impression upon my young mind. Just what caused its death was then a mystery. Looking back, I believe the deep drainage ditches, which had been cut through the dune-country[3] marshes a few years before, had lowered the water table[4] just sufficiently to affect the roots of the old oak. Millions of delicate root-tips were injured. As they began to wither, the whole vast underground system of nourishment broke down and the tree was no longer able to send sap to the upper branches.

Like a river flowing into a desert, the life stream of the tree dwindled and disappeared before it reached the topmost twigs. They died first. The leaf at the tip of each twig, the last to unfold, was the first to wither and fall. Then, little by little, the twig itself became dead and dry. This process of dissolution, in the manner of a movie run backward, reversed the development of growth. Just as, cell by cell, the twig had grown outward toward the tip, so now death spread, cell by cell, backward from the tip.

---

**1. moldered** (mōl′ dərd) v.: Crumbled into dust; decayed.
**2. fungi** (fun′ jī) n., plural of *fungus*: Parasites such as molds, mildews, and mushrooms, which feed on dead organic material and lack chlorophyll.

**3. dune-country:** Sandy, hilly area in Indiana near Lake Michigan.
**4. water table:** The level below which the ground is saturated with water.

*The Death of a Tree*   505

## Presentation

**Motivation/Prior Knowledge**
Suggest to the students that most of us feel closely related to some aspect of the natural world—a particular tree, mountain, river, or animal. Tell students that in this essay Teale describes the slow changes in a great tree he loved.

**Master Teacher Note** You might explain to students that Teale is especially adroit at combining factual scientific detail and personal recollection. Much of what he knew about the process of decay he came to understand more fully after he had left childhood. He was then able to use this knowledge to elaborate and dignify an important event in his early life.

**Thematic Idea** Teale's essay shows the importance of accurate observation. Another selection that stresses observation is "Single Room, Earth View," page 517.

**Purpose-Setting Question** What are the main stages in the death of a tree?

1 **Discussion** Teale uses the phrase "a great tree." Ask students what makes a tree great.

2 **Discussion** The author, in describing the process of death, brings to light a positive aspect of nature's recycling. This is the idea that new life is created from the old. Have students give other examples of nature's recycling process.

3 **Discussion** Why is this an effective image?

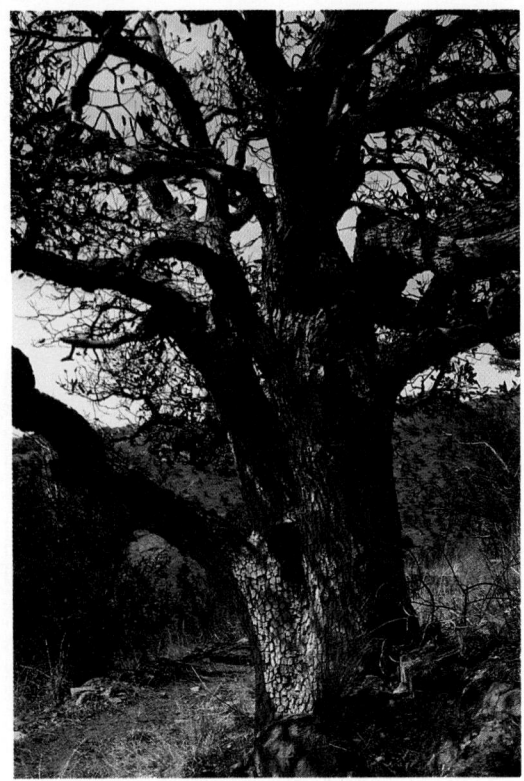

after the purple of advancing dusk filled the spaces below.

Then, one by one, their resiliency gone, the topmost limbs crashed to earth, carried away by the fury of stormwinds. In fragments and patches, bark from the upper trunk littered the ground below. The protecting skin of the tree was broken. In through the gaps poured a host of microscopic enemies, the organisms of decay.

Ghostly white fungus penetrated into the sapwood. It worked its way downward along the unused tubes, those vertical channels through which had flowed the life-blood of the oak. The continued flow of this sap might have kept out the fungus. But sap rises only to branches clothed with leaves. As each limb became blighted and leafless, the sap level dropped to the next living branch below. And close on the heels of this descending fluid followed the fungus. From branch to branch its silent, deadly descent continued.

Soft and flabby, so unsubstantial it can be crushed without apparent pressure between a thumb and forefinger, this pale fungus is yet able to penetrate through the hardest of woods. This amazing and paradoxical[7] feat is accomplished by means of digestive enzymes[8] which the fungus secretes and which dissolve the wood as strong acids might do. These fungus-enzymes, science has learned, are virtually the same as those produced by the single-celled protozoa which live in the bodies of the termites and enable those insects to digest the cellulose[9] in wood.

Advancing in the form of thin white threads, which branch again and again, the

4  Sadly we watched the blight[5] work from twig to branch, from smaller branch to larger branch, until the whole top of the tree was dead and bare. For years those dry, barkless upper branches remained intact. Their wood became gray and polished by the winds. When thunderstorms rolled over the farm from the northwest the dead branches shone like silver against the black and swollen sky. Robins and veeries[6] sang from these lofty perches, gilded by the sunset long

---

**5. blight** (blīt) *n.*: Plant diseases that result in the death of leaves or whole plants.
**6. veeries** (vir′ ēs) *n.*: Brown and cream-colored thrushes.

---

**7. paradoxical** (par ə däk′ si k'l) *adj.*: Contradictory.
**8. enzymes** (en′ zīmz) *n.*: Various proteinlike substances, formed in plant and animal cells, that act to start or speed up specific chemical reactions.
**9. cellulose** (sel′ yoo lōs′) *n.*: The chief substance composing the cell walls or fibers of all plant tissue.

*506   Nonfiction*

## Grammar in Action

**Sensory impressions** are created by words that describe sights, sounds, smells, tastes, and textures. In other words, sensory impressions stimulate the five senses. The use of sensory impressions helps writers create specific images in their readers' minds.

  drab, brown, box-like car  (sense of sight)
  water gurgling over boulders  (sense of hearing)
  tart pucker of sour pickles  (sense of taste)
  hot, raw, sunburned back  (sense of touch)
  musty odor of a wet dog  (sense of smell)

The use of sensory impressions enhances description. Note how Teale uses sensory impressions in "The Death of a Tree":

  *Soft and flabby,* so *unsubstantial* it can be *crushed without apparent pressure* between a thumb and forefinger, this *pale* fungus is yet able to *penetrate* through the *hardest* of woods. . . .

fungus works its way from side to side as well as downward through the trunk of a dying tree. Beyond the reach of our eyes the fungus kept spreading within the body of the old oak, branching into a kind of vast, interlacing root system of its own, pale and ghostly.

Behind the fungus, along the dead upper trunk, yellow-hammers drummed on the dry wood. I saw them, with their chisel-bills, hewing out nesting holes which, in turn, admitted new organisms of decay. In effect, the dissolution of a great tree is like the slow turning of an immense wheel of life. Each stage of its decline and decay brings a whole new, interdependent population of dwellers and their parasites.

Even while the lower branches of the oak were still green, insect wreckers were already at work above them. First to arrive were the bark beetles. In the earliest stages their fare was the tender inner layer of the bark, the living bond between the trunk and its covering. As death spread downward in the oak, as freezing and storms loosened the bark, the beetles descended, foot by foot. Some of them left behind elaborate patterns, branching mazes of tunnels that took on the appearance of fantastic "thousand-leggers" engraved on wood.

During the winter when I was twelve years old a gale of abnormal force swept the Great Lakes region. Gusts reached almost hurricane proportions. Weakened by the work of the fungus, bacteria, woodpeckers, and beetles, the whole top of the tree snapped off some seventy feet from the ground. After that the progress of its dissolution was rapid.

Finally the last of the lower leaves disappeared. The green badge of life returned no more. On summer days the sound of the wind sweeping through the old oak had a winter shrillness. No more was there the rustling of a multitude of leaves above our hammock; no more was there the "plump!" of falling acorns. Leaves and acorns, life and progress, were at an end.

In the days that followed, as the bark loosened to the base, the wheel of life, which had its hub in the now dead oak, grew larger.

I saw carpenter ants hurrying this way and that over the lower tree-trunk. Ichneumon flies,[10] trailing deadly, drill-like ovipositors,[11] hovered above the bark in search of buried larvae on which to lay their eggs. Carpenter bees, their black abdomens glistening like patent leather, bit their way into the dry wood of the dead branches. Click beetles and sow-bugs and small spiders found security beneath fragments of the loosened bark. And around the base of the tree swift-legged carabid beetles hunted their insect prey under cover of darkness.

Yellowish brown, the wood-flour of the powder-post beetles began to sift about the foot of the oak. It, in turn, attracted the larvae of the darkling beetles. Thus, link by link, the chain of life expanded. To the expert eye the condition of the wood, the bark, the ground about the base of the oak—all told of the action of the interrelated forms of life attracted by the death and decay of a tree.

But below all this activity, beyond the power of human sight to detect, other changes were taking place. The underground root system, comprising almost as much wood as was visible in the tree rising above-ground, was also altering.

Fungus, entering the damaged root-tips or working downward from the infected

---

10. **Ichneumon** (ik nyo͞o′ mən) **flies:** Insects whose larvae live as parasites in or on other insect larvae.
11. **ovipositors** (ō′ vi päz′ i tərs) n.: Tubular structures of many female insects, usually at the end of the abdomen, for depositing eggs.

*The Death of a Tree*   507

5 **Discussion** Why do you think Teale lists again the organisms that caused the tree to decay?

6 **Discussion** What does this statement mean?

---

Behind the fungus . . . yellow-hammers *drummed* on the *dry* wood. I saw them, with their *chisel-bills, hewing* out nesting holes . . .

On summer days the sound of the wind *sweeping* through the old oak had a *winter shrillness* . . . no more was there the *"plump!"* of falling acorns . . .

Readers hear, see, and feel the decay because of Teale's use of words that convey vivid sensory impressions.

**Student Activity 1.** Identify each of the sensory impressions in the passage quoted from "The Death of a Tree" and tell which of the five senses it stimulates.

**Student Activity 2.** Write a description of a landmark in your neighborhood. Use words that appeal to as many of the five senses as possible.

**7 Clarification** Some students may not know that the word *pliancy* means "flexibility."

**8 Discussion** Why is this image effective? Ask students to give examples of such an impression from their own experience.

**9 Discussion** Would the essay be better or worse without this final paragraph? Explain.

**Reader's Response** If Teale were alive today, on what topic might he choose to write? Why?

## Closure and Extension

### ANSWERS TO THINKING ABOUT THE SELECTION
*Recalling*

1. The Indiana homestead where Teale grew up was named for this tree; he remembers it as part of his daily life as a child.
2. Teale thinks that the water supply to the tree's roots was reduced enough by the digging of drainage ditches to cause the tree to begin dying.
3. The water available to the tree was too limited to reach the top of the tree.
4. The fungus reached into the sapwood where there was not enough sap left to keep the fungus from spreading through the tree; the fungus then acted to dissolve the wood of the tree. The yellow-hammers drilled holes in the tree with their bills; insects could then enter the tree through the holes and attack the wood of the tree. Insects such as bark beetles ate the bark of the tree and destroyed the tree's protective covering.
5. Teale's grandfather had planned the felling of the tree. He sawed where he had chopped a v-shaped bite. Then the tree "arced downward" marking a swooshing sound as it fell to the ground.

trunk, followed the sap channels and hastened decay. The great main roots, spreading out as far as the widest branches of the tree itself, altered rapidly. Their fibers grew brittle; their old pliancy disappeared; their bark split and loosened. The breakdown of the upper tree found its counterpart, within the darkness of the earth, in the dissolution of the lower roots.

I remember well the day the great oak came down. I was fourteen at the time. Gramp had measured distances and planned his cutting operations in advance. He chopped away for fully half an hour before he had a V-shaped bite cut exactly in position to bring the trunk crashing in the place desired. Hours filled with the whine of the crosscut saw followed.

Then came the great moment. A few last, quick strokes. A slow, deliberate swaying. The crack of parting fibers. Then a long "swo-o-sh!" that rose in pitch as the towering trunk arced downward at increasing speed. There followed a vast tumult of crashing, crackling sound; the dance of splintered branches; a haze of dead, swirling grass. Then a slow settling of small objects and silence. All was over. Lone oak was gone.

Gram, I remember, brushed away what she remarked was dust in her eyes with a corner of her apron and went inside. She had known and loved that one great tree since she had come to the farm as a bride of sixteen. She had seen it under all conditions and through eyes colored by many moods. Her children had grown up under its shadow and I, a grandchild, had known its shade. Its passing was like the passing of an old, old friend. For all of us there seemed an empty space in our sky in the days that followed.

Gramp and I set to work, attacking the fallen giant. Great piles of cordwood, mounds of broken branches for kindling, grew around the prostrate trunk as the weeks went by. Eventually only the huge, circular table of the low stump remained—reddish brown and slowly dissolving into dust.

For two winters wood from the old oak fed the kitchen range and the dining-room stove. It had a clean, well-seasoned smell. And it burned with a clear and leaping flame, continuing—unlike the quickly consumed poplar and elm—for an admirable length of time. Like the old tree itself, the fibers of these sticks had character and endurance to the very end.

*Interpreting*

6. Suggested Response: Teale uses this phrase to indicate the interdependence of organisms in a continuing cycle of growth and decay. Some organisms, such as the fungus and the insects, were able to survive by feeding on the tree.
7. Suggested Responses: Sight— He says the decay of the tree is like "a movie run backward." Also, he says the wood became gray. Hearing—He says the limbs "crashed to earth." He also mentions the "crack of parting fibers" and "a vast tumult of crashing, crackling sound." Touch—He says that the fungus is "Soft and flabby."
8. Suggested Response: Gram might have cried and then left because she was embarrassed.

*Applying*

9. Answers will differ, but many students will probably be able to describe a similar attachment.

**Challenge** Imagine an account of the tree's death written by Teale's grandparents. How would it have differed from this essay?

### ANSWERS TO READING IN THE ARTS AND SCIENCES

1. Suggested Response: First the upper twigs and branches began to die because not enough water was reaching them from the damaged root system. These broke and

## THINKING ABOUT THE SELECTION

### Recalling

1. Why was this tree special for Teale?
2. What does he think caused its death?
3. Why did the topmost twigs begin to die?
4. How did fungus, yellowhammers, and insects contribute to the tree's death?
5. Briefly describe "the day the great oak came down."

### Interpreting

6. Why does Teale describe the tree's *death* as the turning of a wheel of *life*?
7. Show how he uses language that appeals to your senses of sight, hearing, and touch.
8. What else beside the dust might explain Gram's wiping her eyes and leaving?

### Applying

9. Have you ever felt affection for a plant or animal, as Teale did for this oak? Explain.

## READING IN THE ARTS AND SCIENCES

### Understanding Transformation

All of nature is a process of change, with new organisms emerging into life while old ones die. A naturalist such as Edwin Way Teale can show you the truth of these words in detail. In "The Death of a Tree," he indicates how the transformation we call by a single name—death—really involves many interrelated changes. This process may begin, for example, with a slight lowering of the water table.

1. Trace the changes that lead from a reduced water supply to the death of the treetop.
2. Show how each change causes the next one as death spreads downward from the treetop.
3. Tell how five organisms benefit from this death.

## CRITICAL THINKING AND READING

### Creating a Flow Chart

A **flow chart** is a diagram that shows the different stages of a process. This type of chart is used in many fields, including computer studies, because it clearly indicates how each stage flows into the next one. A flow chart showing the death of Teale's oak tree would look as follows:

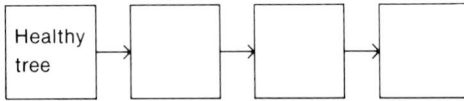

1. Draw a larger version of this chart and fill in the empty boxes from left to right showing the key stages in the process. (If you need another box, you may draw it.)
2. Below each arrow list the causes leading to the stage at which the arrow points.

## UNDERSTANDING LANGUAGE

### Understanding Terms from Biology

Writers who describe the natural world must often use terms from **biology,** the science that studies living organisms, to make their meaning clear. Teale uses the word *blight,* which means "plant diseases." The following biological terms also appear in "The Death of a Tree." Look up each in a dictionary and explain the role it plays in the process that Teale is describing.

1. sap   2. parasites   3. larvae   4. bacteria

## THINKING AND WRITING

### Writing About Transformation

Recall the natural process whose stages you listed before reading this selection. Use your list to write an essay about this process. Give your audience a clear picture of the different stages. Whenever possible, explain how each stage led to the next. Also, like Teale, express what you felt as you witnessed these changes. In revising your work, include some lively descriptions that will appeal to your readers' senses.

*The Death of a Tree* 509

(Answers begin on p. 508.)

water table lowers, roots are damaged; b) fungus enters, yellowhammers drum on wood, beetles enter tree, gale winds blow; c) other insects enter tree, fungus penetrates damaged root-tips

### ANSWERS TO UNDERSTANDING LANGUAGE

1. Suggested Response: sap—a fluid that nourishes plant tissue as it circulates; the sap level dropped as leaves and branches died, allowing the fungus to penetrate the sapwood more easily.
2. Suggested Response: parasites—often harmful organisms that live on another organism; the fungus is an example of a parasite—it survived inside the tree and grew by dissolving the wood of the tree. The insects mentioned were also parasites.
3. Suggested Response: larvae—the wingless, often wormlike form of a newly hatched insect; ichneumon flies lay their eggs on larvae buried in the decaying wood of the tree.
4. Suggested Response: bacteria—one-celled organisms that multiply by division and have no chlorophyll; these entered the tree and served to weaken it further.

### THINKING AND WRITING

For help with this assignment, students may consult Lesson 2, "Drafting and Revising," in the Handbook of Writing About Literature.

**Publishing Student Writing** You might want to collect and organize the essays in a class book.

**Writing Across the Curriculum** You might want to ask students to read and report on the works of other well-known naturalists or scientists, such as Lewis Thomas, Konrad Lorenz, or Loren Eiseley. Consider informing the science department of this assignment, so that teachers can suggest books and help students with difficult passages.

fell to the ground. Then a fungus entered through the openings and began to spread downward through the tree. The fungus acted to dissolve and kill the wood that was still living. Then beetles and other insects entered the tree through holes drilled by birds. These insects fed on the bark, loosening the protective covering of the tree, and weakened the wood still further by digging tunnels through it.

2. Suggested Response: The top branches break off, creating openings for fungus to enter and spread. Where fungus has damaged the tree, birds can drill holes. Other insects are then able to enter the trunk through these holes. Freezing and storms which loosen the bark also make it possible for bark beetles to descend the tree.
3. Suggested Response: The fungus thrives as it spreads through the tree; the yellow-hammers are able

to drill nesting holes; the bark beetles feed on the bark; carpenter bees feed on the wood of the dead branches; and ichneumon flies lay their eggs on buried larvae.

### ANSWERS TO CRITICAL THINKING AND READING

1. Suggested Response: labels—a) top of tree dies; b) top of tree falls; c) lower roots break down
2. Suggested Response: arrows—a)

**More About the Author** Joan Didion's second novel, *Play It As It Lays,* was made into a movie. Also, Didion and her husband collaborated on the script for the Barbra Streisand version of *A Star is Born.* Ask students to discuss the differences between writing a novel and writing a script for a film.

**Literary Focus** Help students understand how one might begin to formulate ideas in order to write a character analysis. Have students suggest a famous person whom most students know. Then have them suggest adjectives that describe this person and tell anecdotes about this person to illustrate these characteristics. Help students understand how this brainstorming of ideas can help in the writing of a character analysis.

**Look For** Didion clearly admires O'Keeffe, although she does not always express this admiration directly. As students read, have them look for the ways that Didion conveys her attitude toward O'Keefe.

**Writing/Prior Knowledge** Before students begin writing, have them suggest words that they associate with the character trait "hardness." Then have them imagine how they would feel about a person referred to as "hard."

**Vocabulary** Have your less advanced students read the words and their definitions. Then have them use the words in a conversation with two or three other classmates.

## Georgia O'Keeffe

**Joan Didion** (1934–    ) descends from a long line of pioneers. Her great-great-grandmother came West in a covered wagon in 1846. Didion grew up in California and, as a young woman, won a writing contest sponsored by *Vogue.* Eventually she rose to become an editor of that well-known magazine. Her reputation in the literary world, however, is based on her novels and collections of essays. The essay "Georgia O'Keeffe," which comes from *The White Album,* pays tribute to an artist who displayed a strong pioneer spirit.

**Character Analysis**

In a **character analysis,** the writer tries to reveal the key traits that give a person his or her identity. This type of essay is different from a biography in several ways. It is usually briefer and more focused than an account of a person's life, and it does not necessarily follow a chronological sequence. In "Georgia O'Keeffe," for example, Joan Didion begins by identifying an important quality of the artist Georgia O'Keeffe: "Hardness." Didion then gives examples from O'Keeffe's work and life to clarify what she means by this descriptive word.

**Look For**

What is "hardness"? As you read, look for the ways in which Didion clarifies the meaning of O'Keeffe's "hardness" by quoting this artist's words and telling about her life.

**Writing**

Consider the personality trait that Didion calls "hardness." Freewrite about your idea of a hard person.

**Vocabulary**

Knowing the following words will help you as you read "Georgia O'Keeffe."

**condescending** (kän′ də sen′ diŋ) *adj.*: Characterized by looking down on someone (p. 511)
**tonic** (tän′ ik) *adj.*: Stimulating; invigorating (p. 512)
**indulged** (in dulj′′d) *v.*: Accepted in a belittling way (p. 512)
**sentimental** (sen′ tə men′ t′l) *adj.*: Foolishly emotional (p. 512)

**genesis** (jen′ ə sis) *n.*: Birth; origin; beginning (p. 512)
**derisive** (di rī′ siv) *adj.*: Scornful; mocking (p. 512)
**rancor** (raŋ′ kər) *n.*: Hatred; spite (p. 514)
**contempt** (kən tempt′) *n.*: Scorn; disrespect (p. 514)
**immutable** (i myo͞ot′ ə b'l) *adj.*: Never changing (p. 514)

**Objectives**

1 To appreciate character analysis
2 To evaluate conclusions about art
3 To understand art terms
4 To write about art

**Support Material**

**Teaching Portfolio**
Teacher Backup, p. 567
Grammar in Action Worksheet, *Using Coordination,* p. 571
Usage and Mechanics Worksheet, p. 573
Vocabulary Check, p. 574
Analyzing Literature Worksheet, *Character Analysis,* p. 576

Critical Thinking and Reading Worksheet, *Evaluating Conclusions About Art,* p. 577
Selection Test, p. 578
Art Trasparency 9: *Self-portrait* by Joan Miró

# Georgia O'Keeffe

### Joan Didion

"Where I was born and where and how I have lived is unimportant," Georgia O'Keeffe told us in the book of paintings and words published in her ninetieth year on earth. She seemed to be advising us to forget the beautiful face in the Stieglitz[1] photographs. She appeared to be dismissing the rather condescending romance that had attached to her by then, the romance of extreme good looks and advanced age and deliberate isolation. "It is what I have done with where I have been that should be of interest." I recall an August afternoon in Chicago in 1973 when I took my daughter, then seven, to see what Georgia O'Keeffe had done with where she had been. One of the vast O'Keeffe "Sky Above Clouds" canvases floated over the back stairs in the Chicago Art Institute that day, dominating what seemed to be several stories of empty light, and my daughter looked at it once, ran to the landing, and kept on looking. "Who drew it," she whispered after a while. I told her. "I need to talk to her," she said finally.

My daughter was making, that day in Chicago, an entirely unconscious but quite basic assumption about people and the work they do. She was assuming that the glory she saw in the work reflected a glory in its maker, that the painting was the painter as the poem is the poet, that every choice one made alone—every word chosen or rejected, every brush stroke laid or not laid down—betrayed one's character. *Style is character.* It seemed to me that afternoon that I had

---

1. **Stieglitz:** Alfred Stieglitz (1864–1946), U.S. photographer and husband of Georgia O'Keeffe.

**THE WHITE TRUMPET FLOWER, 1932**
*Georgia O'Keeffe*
*San Diego Museum of Art*

*Georgia O'Keeffe* 511

## Presentation

**Motivation/Prior Knowledge** Ask students to mention artists, writers, or musicians whose style they would recognize. Ask them what qualities make a style distinctive. Then tell them that Georgia O'Keeffe, the artist they will read about, developed an inimitable style of her own.

**Master Teacher Note** Use the overheard projector to show students Art Transparency 9, *Self-portrait,* by Joan Miró. Ask them what qualities the artist has revealed. Have them specify the details that suggest these qualities.

Then tell them that Didion's essay is like a portrait in words of the artist Georgia O'Keeffe. Have them look for the way that Didion uses words and phrases to reveal O'Keeffe's important qualities.

**Purpose-Setting Question** What does Didion mean when she attributes the quality of "Hardness" to O'Keeffe?

**Thematic Idea** Another selection that deals with a person of integrity is "A Lincoln Preface," page 439.

**1 Discussion** What insights into O'Keeffe's personality does Didion convey in this first paragraph?

**2 Enrichment** *Sky Above Clouds,* which O'Keeffe began in 1965 at the age of seventy-seven, was 28′ × 8′. It was her largest painting.

**3 Critical Thinking and Reading** The author italicized *"Style is character"* to draw attention to and emphasize the importance of that statement. What do you think she meant by it?

## Humanities Note

Fine art, *The White Trumpet Flower,* by Georgia O'Keeffe (1887-1986).
1. Why do you think O'Keeffe chose to focus on a single flower?
2. What kinds of shapes and lines did O'Keeffe emphasize in this painting?
3. What associations or feelings does this painting call up?

**4 Discussion** What does this paragraph reveal about O'Keeffe? Refer to lines in the paragraph to support your answer.

**5 Discussion** Who are the "city men"? What words and phrases in this paragraph tell you how O'Keeffe feels about the "city men"?

rarely seen so instinctive an application of this familiar principle, and I recall being pleased not only that my daughter responded to style as character but that it was Georgia O'Keeffe's particular style to which she responded: this was a hard woman who had imposed her 192 square feet of clouds on Chicago.

"Hardness" has not been in our century a quality much admired in women, nor in the past twenty years has it even been in official favor for men. When hardness surfaces in the very old we tend to transform it into "crustiness" or eccentricity, some tonic pepperiness to be indulged at a distance. On the evidence of her work and what she has said about it, Georgia O'Keeffe is neither "crusty" nor eccentric. She is simply hard, a straight shooter, a woman clean of received wisdom and open to what she sees. This is a woman who could early on dismiss most of her contemporaries as "dreamy," and would later single out one she liked as "a very poor painter." (And then add, apparently by way of softening the judgment: "I guess he wasn't a painter at all. He had no courage and I believe that to create one's own world in any of the arts takes courage.") This is a woman who in 1939 could advise her admirers that they were missing her point, that their appreciation of her famous flowers was merely sentimental. "When I paint a red hill," she observed coolly in the catalogue for an exhibition that year, "you say it is too bad that I don't always paint flowers. A flower touches almost everyone's heart. A red hill doesn't touch everyone's heart." This is a woman who could describe the genesis of one of her most well-known paintings—the "Cow's Skull: Red, White and Blue" owned by the Metropolitan[2]—as an act of quite deliberate and derisive orneriness. "I thought of the city men I had been seeing in the East," she wrote. "They talked so often of writing the Great American Novel—the Great American Play—the Great American Poetry. . . . So as I was painting my cow's head on blue I thought to myself, 'I'll make it an American painting. They will not think it great with the red stripes down the sides—Red, White and Blue—but they will notice it.' "

*The city men. The men. They.* The words crop up again and again as this astonishingly aggressive woman tells us what was on her mind when she was making her astonishingly aggressive paintings. It was those city men who stood accused of sentimentalizing her flowers: "I made you take time to look at what I saw and when you took time to really notice my flower you hung all your associations with flowers on my flower and you write about my flower as if I think and see what you think and see—and I don't." *And I don't.* Imagine those words spoken, and the sound you hear is *don't tread on me.*[3] "The men" believed it impossible to paint New York, so Georgia O'Keeffe painted New York. "The men" didn't think much of her bright color, so she made it brighter. The men yearned toward Europe so she went to Texas, and then New Mexico. The men talked about Cézanne,[4] "long involved remarks about the 'plastic quality' of his form and color," and took one another's long involved remarks, in the view of this angelic rattlesnake in their midst, altogether too seriously. "I can paint one of those dismal-colored paintings like the men," the woman who regarded herself always as an outsider remembers thinking one day in 1922, and she did: a painting of a shed "all low-toned

**2. Metropolitan:** Metropolitan Museum of Art in New York City.

**3. Don't tread on me:** Motto of the first official American flag that was first flown by a naval vessel on December 3, 1775.
**4. Cézanne:** Paul Cézanne (1839–1906), French impressionist and postimpressionist painter.

## Grammar in Action

**Coordination** is the use of conjunctions to connect equally important ideas smoothly and clearly. Among the most common coordinating conjunctions are: *and, but, or, nor, for, yet,* and *so.* By using these conjunctions, writers can avoid choppy sentences and clarify the relationship between ideas:

Unconnected:     Mother wants a cat. She knows it may sometimes claw on furniture.

With Coordination:    Mother wants a cat, *yet* she knows it may sometimes claw on furniture.

The following sentences from "Georgia O'Keeffe" illustrate effective coordination:

Imagine those words spoken, *and* the sound you hear is *don't tread on me.* "The men" believed it impossible to paint New York, *so* Georgia O'Keeffe painted New York. "The

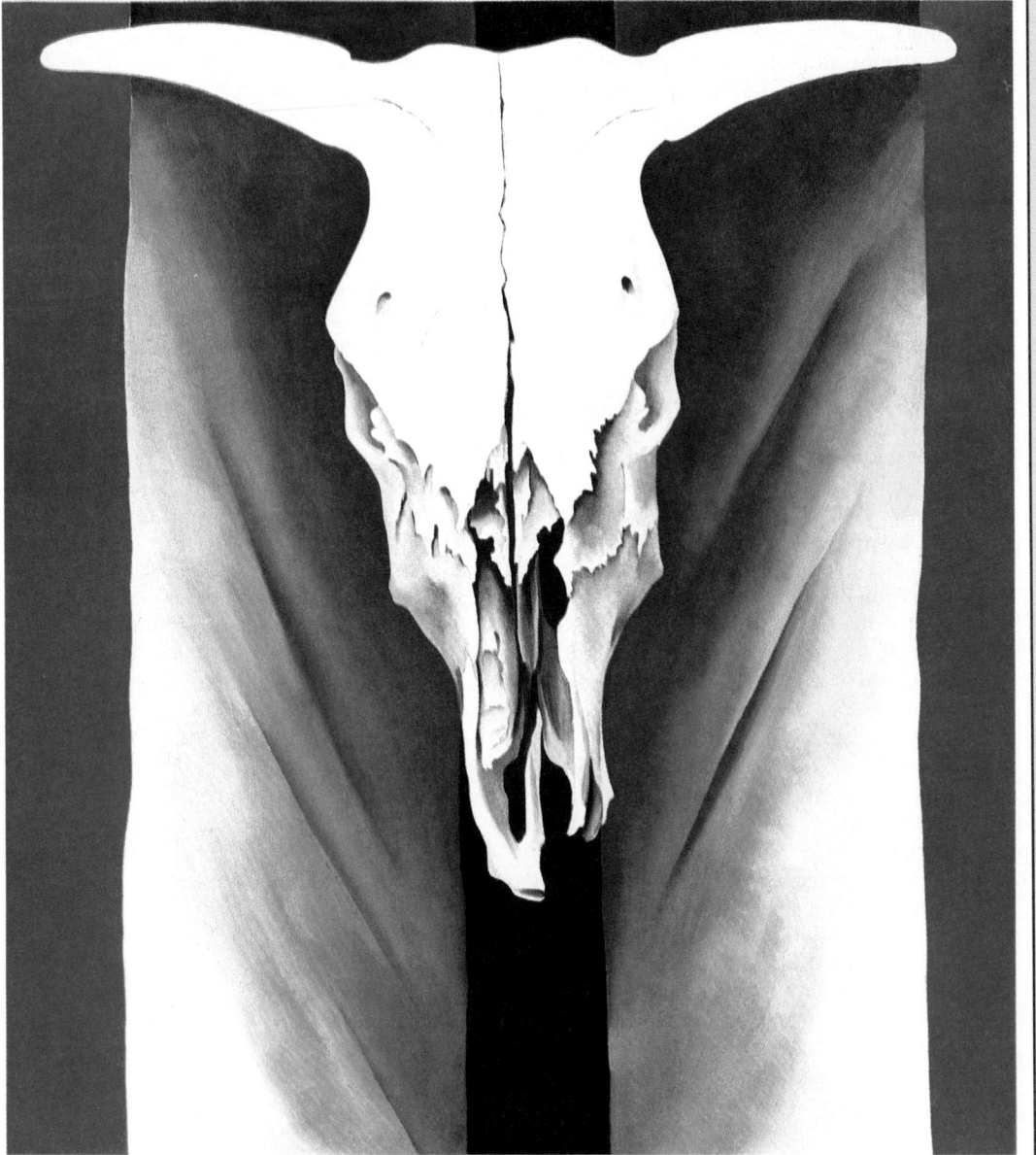

COW'S SKULL: RED, WHITE AND BLUE, 1931
*Georgia O'Keeffe*
*The Metropolitan Museum of Art*

## Humanities Note

Fine art, *Cow's Skull: Red, White, and Blue,* by Georgia O'Keeffe. In 1949, Georgia O'Keeffe settled in New Mexico. Many of her paintings, like this one, are based on subjects and themes of the Southwest. O'Keeffe's use of colors and contrasts, in addition to the striking subject, make this a very dramatic work.

1. What mood does this painting create?
2. How does it reflect O'Keeffe's "Hardness"?
3. What is daring about this painting?

men" didn't think much of her bright color, so she made it brighter.

The men yearned toward Europe, *so* she went to Texas, *and* then New Mexico. . . . "I can paint one of those dismal-colored paintings like the men," the woman who regarded herself always as an outsider remembers thinking one day in 1922, *and* she did: a painting of a shed. . . .

**Student Activity 1.** Find three other sentences in "Georgia O'Keeffe" that use coordination.

**Student Activity 2.** Write three sentences using coordination. Try to use a different coordinating conjunction in each, but be sure the meaning is clear and the relationship between the clauses or phrases logical.

6 **Critical Thinking and Reading**
What do you think the first sentence of the paragraph means? What is the relationship between this sentence and the one that follows it?

7 **Enrichment** The O'Keeffe family lived near Sun Prairie in the southern part of Wisconsin. Georgia lived there with her family until she was thirteen; at thirteen she was enrolled in Sacred Heart Academy, a convent boarding school outside of Madison, Wisconsin.

8 **Reading Strategy** Ask students to summarize O'Keeffe's development as an artist.

9 **Discussion** Why does Didion end the essay with this image? What does the image suggest about O'Keeffe and her sister?

**Reader's Response** Conduct your own character analysis. What one word would you use to describe yourself? Why is this word appropriate?

and dreary with the tree beside the door." She called this act of rancor "The Shanty" and hung it in her next show. "The men seemed to approve of it," she reported fifty-four years later, her contempt undimmed. "They seemed to think that maybe I was beginning to paint. That was my only low-toned dismal-colored painting."

Some women fight and others do not. Like so many successful guerrillas in the war between the sexes, Georgia O'Keeffe seems to have been equipped early with an immutable sense of who she was and a fairly clear understanding that she would be required to prove it. On the surface her upbringing was conventional. She was a child on the Wisconsin prairie who played with china dolls and painted watercolors with cloudy skies because sunlight was too hard to paint and, with her brother and sisters, listened every night to her mother read stories of the Wild West, of Texas, of Kit Carson and Billy the Kid. She told adults that she wanted to be an artist and was embarrassed when they asked what kind of artist she wanted to be: she had no idea "what kind." She had no idea what artists did. She had never seen a picture that interested her, other than a pen-and-ink Maid of Athens in one of her mother's books, some Mother Goose illustrations printed on cloth, a tablet cover that showed a little girl with pink roses, and the painting of Arabs on horseback that hung in her grandmother's parlor. At thirteen, in a Dominican convent, she was mortified when the sister corrected her drawing. At Chatham Episcopal Institute in Virginia she

painted lilacs and sneaked time alone to walk out to where she could see the line of the Blue Ridge Mountains on the horizon. At the Art Institute in Chicago she was shocked by the presence of live models and wanted to abandon anatomy lessons. At the Art Students League in New York one of her fellow students advised her that, since he would be a great painter and she would end up teaching painting in a girls' school, any work of hers was less important than modeling for him. Another painted over her work to show her how the Impressionists did trees. She had not before heard how the Impressionists did trees and she did not much care.

At twenty-four she left all these opinions behind and went for the first time to live in Texas, where there were no trees to paint and no one to tell her how not to paint them. In Texas there was only the horizon she craved. In Texas she had her sister Claudia with her for a while, and in the late afternoons they would walk away from town and toward the horizon and watch the evening star come out. "That evening star fascinated me," she wrote. "It was in some way very exciting to me. My sister had a gun, and as we walked she would throw bottles into the air and shoot as many as she could before they hit the ground. I had nothing but to walk into nowhere and the wide sunset space with the star. Ten watercolors were made from that star." In a way one's interest is compelled as much by the sister Claudia with the gun as by the painter Georgia with the star, but only the painter left us this shining record. Ten watercolors were made from that star.

**Closure and Extension**

**ANSWERS TO THINKING ABOUT THE SELECTION**
*Recalling*

1. One's artistic style is a reflection of one's character.
2. O'Keeffe is described as a direct, open, and original person.
3. O'Keeffe retained her individuality, painting only those things she wanted to paint, regardless of what others thought or said about her work.

## THINKING ABOUT THE SELECTION

### Recalling

1. Explain the statement, *"Style is character."*
2. Describe O'Keeffe's character as it is portrayed in this essay.
3. How did O'Keeffe assert herself among the male artists whom she knew?
4. What signs of her character did she show in growing up?

### Interpreting

5. Explain what Didion means by saying O'Keeffe had "an immutable sense of who she was"?
6. What do you think O'Keeffe found attractive about Texas?

### Applying

7. O'Keeffe said "that to create one's own world in any of the arts takes courage." Comment on this remark.

## READING IN THE ARTS AND SCIENCES

### Character Analysis

In a **character analysis,** the writer tries to reveal the key traits that give a person his or her identity. According to Joan Didion, one of Georgia O'Keeffe's important traits was "hardness." An example of this quality was her insistence on using bright colors when other artists favored dull ones.

1. Explain how O'Keeffe demonstrated this trait in two other ways.
2. What is the difference between hardness and crustiness?
3. Explain how O'Keeffe's hardness was the opposite of sentimentality.

## CRITICAL THINKING AND READING

### Evaluating Conclusions About Art

You can evaluate a writer's conclusions about a painting by carefully studying the work yourself.

For example, you will want to look at O'Keeffe's "The White Trumpet Flower" (page 511) before evaluating Didion's remark that O'Keeffe's flowers are not "sentimental." Here are some questions you might ask yourself before reaching a conclusion: Why did O'Keeffe focus in on just one flower? Why did she stress the curved lines? Did she convey a sense of how the flower might feel?

1. After considering these matters, explain some of the usual feelings about flowers that Didion might be referring to as "sentimental."
2. Is O'Keeffe's flower sentimental? Why or why not?

## UNDERSTANDING LANGUAGE

### Understanding Art Terms

In "Georgia O'Keeffe," Joan Didion uses a number of art terms. She refers to O'Keeffe's "canvases," for example, in the first paragraph. A *canvas* is "heavy woven cloth on which artists paint." Look up the following terms from the essay and explain how each relates to the world of art.

1. catalogue
2. exhibition
3. watercolors
4. Impressionists

## THINKING AND WRITING

### Writing About Art

Imagine that you have to write about the painting "Cow's Skull: Red, White and Blue" (page 513) for a catalogue. Before beginning, reread what Didion says about this painting and look at it carefully. List the points that you want to make. For instance, you might want to tell readers why O'Keeffe used red, white, and blue. You might also discuss the choice of subject and the feelings it calls up. In revising make sure that your catalogue entry will help readers to understand the work. When you are done, share what you have written with your classmates.

(Answers begin on p. 514.)

people. It implies eccentricity and rigidity.
3. Suggested Response: Sentimentality is associated with soft and conventional emotions like an easy "love" of flowers and other "beautiful" objects. O'Keeffe however, was hard and unconventional. She did not pretend to experience what others expected her to experience.

### ANSWERS TO CRITICAL THINKING AND READING

1. Suggested Response: Flowers are usually thought of as soft, gentle, pleasing and beautiful in a conventional way.
2. Answers will differ, but students might suggest that O'Keeffe's flowers are bold, arresting, and vibrant—characteristics not often associated with sentimentality.

### ANSWERS TO UNDERSTANDING LANGUAGE

1. A *catalogue* is "a publication listing the art pieces being exhibited in a show."
2. An *exhibition* is "a display of one's works for the public to view."
3. *Watercolors* are "paints composed of a water-soluble substance."
4. *Impressionists* are "artists who tried to record fleeting impressions created by effects of light rather than the more permanent shapes of objects."

### THINKING AND WRITING

For help with this assignment, students may refer to Lesson 1, "Prewriting," in the Handbook of Writing About Literature.

### Publishing Student Writing

Have students design a catalogue. Once it is designed, have students incorporate their writing into it.

### Writing Across the Curriculum

Have students research and report on criticism of O'Keeffe's work. Consider informing the art department of this assignment, so that teachers can provide guidance for students.

---

4. In growing up, she decided early that she wanted to be an artist and stuck to her decision.

### Interpreting

5. Answers will differ, but students might say that O'Keeffe was not very influenced by what others thought about her or by what others wanted for her.
6. Answers will differ, but students might say that she was attracted to the open spaces of the prairie.

### Applying

7. Answers will differ. Students may realize, however, that art involves two main risks: failing to express one's vision adequately and having one's vision rejected by others.

**Challenge** Georgia O'Keeffe has said, "Still—in a way—nobody sees a flower—really—it is so small—we haven't time—and to see takes time, like to have a friend takes time." Have students comment on the meaning of this quote.

### ANSWERS TO READING IN THE ARTS AND SCIENCES

1. Suggested Response: She demonstrated this trait in her comments regarding *Cow's Skull: Red, White and Blue* and in her criticism of her contemporaries and their art.
2. Suggested Response: Crustiness is more often associated with older

**More About the Author** Sally Ride, the first woman astronaut in the United States, was a member of the Presidential Commission that investigated the *Challenger* disaster. Ask students why they think Ride was chosen for this job.

**Literary Focus** You might want to ask students if they think they are good observers. Have them give examples of their ability. Then ask them how they would train people to be better observers. Also ask them what training in this skill they think scientists receive.

**Look For** Since only a limited number of people have been to outer space, Sally Ride tries to describe this experience for readers. Tell students to visualize or create pictures in their minds as they read. This will help them better understand the sights, sounds, and sensations that Ride is trying to convey.

**Writing/Prior Knowledge** You might want to divide the class into small groups and have students discuss with their group members what they might see as astronauts.

**Vocabulary** Have your less advanced students read the words and their definitions. Then have them create a meaningful sentence for each of the words.

## Single Room, Earth View

**Sally Ride** (1951–　) graduated from Stanford University in 1973 with a bachelor's degree in English and physics. She went on to earn a doctorate in physics from Stanford, specializing in X-ray astronomy and lasers. In June 1983 she became the third woman to orbit the earth and the first American woman to travel in a spacecraft. Ride tells how our planet looks from 200 miles up in her essay "Single Room, Earth View."

### Scientific Observation

**Scientific observation** is the act of carefully noting facts and events. This manner of observing is a skill that scientists must learn. It is more precise and systematic than the way we usually look at people and events in everyday life.

When Sally Ride became the first American woman in space, she was already a trained scientist. In this selection her descriptions of the Earth from orbit show her skill as a scientific observer.

### Look For

As you read, look for the many careful observations that Ride made from her orbiting spacecraft. Also notice the way she uses lively language and comparisons to describe these observations.

### Writing

Imagine that you are an astronaut orbiting the Earth. Describe what our planet looks like from such a great height. Also tell about the experience of seeing the sun rise every ninety minutes as you travel at five miles a second!

### Vocabulary

Knowing the following words will help you as you read "Single Room, Earth View."

**articulate** (är tik′ yə lit) *adj.*: Expressing oneself well (p. 517)

**surreal** (sə rē′ əl) *adj.*: Strange (p. 517)

**ominous** (äm′ ə nəs) *adj.*: Threatening (p. 517)

**novice** (näv′ is) *adj.*: Beginner (p. 517)

**muted** (myo͞ot əd) *adj.*: Weaker; less intense (p. 519)

**subtle** (sut′ ′l) *adj.*: Small (p. 519)

**eddies** (ed′ ēs) *n.*: Circular currents (p. 519)

**eerie** (ir′ ē) *adj.* Mysterious (p. 519)

**diffused** (di fyo͞osd′) *v.*: Spread out (p. 520)

**extrapolating** (ik strap′ ə lāt′ iŋ) *v.*: Arriving at a conclusion by making inferences based on known facts (p. 520)

### Objectives

1 To understand scientific observation
2 To find the main idea of a paragraph
3 To understand scientific terms
4 To write up an observation

### Support Material

**Teaching Portfolio**
Teacher Backup, p. 581
Grammar in Action Worksheet, *Using* like *and* as, p. 584
Usage and Mechanics Worksheet, p. 586
Vocabulary Check, p. 587
Analyzing Literature Worksheet, *Understanding Scientific Observation*, p. 589

Critical Thinking and Reading Worksheet, *Finding the Main Idea of a Paragraph*, p. 590
Selection Test, p. 591

# Single Room, Earth View

## Sally Ride

Everyone I've met has a glittering, if vague, mental image of space travel. And naturally enough, people want to hear about it from an astronaut: "How did it feel. . . ?" "What did it look like. . . ?" "Were you scared?" Sometimes, the questions come from reporters, their pens poised and their tape recorders silently reeling in the words; sometimes, it's wide-eyed, ten-year-old girls who want answers. I find a way to answer all of them, but it's not easy.

Imagine trying to describe an airplane ride to someone who has never flown. An articulate traveler could describe the sights but would find it much harder to explain the difference in perspective provided by the new view from a greater distance, along with the feelings, impressions, and insights that go with the new perspective. And the difference is enormous: Space flight moves the traveler another giant step farther away. Eight and one-half thunderous minutes after launch, an astronaut is orbiting high above the Earth, suddenly able to watch typhoons form, volcanoes smolder, and meteors streak through the atmosphere below.

While flying over the Hawaiian Islands, several astronauts have marveled that the islands look just as they do on a map. When people first hear that, they wonder what should be so surprising about Hawaii looking the way it does in the atlas. Yet, to the astronauts it is an absolutely startling sensation: The islands really *do* look as if that part of the world has been carpeted with a big page torn out of Rand-McNally,[1] and all we can do is try to convey the surreal quality of that scene.

In orbit, racing along at five miles per second, the space shuttle circles the Earth once every 90 minutes. I found that at this speed, unless I kept my nose pressed to the window, it was almost impossible to keep track of where we were at any given moment—the world below simply changes too fast. If I turned my concentration away for too long, even just to change film in a camera, I could miss an entire land mass. It's embarrassing to float up to a window, glance outside, and then have to ask a crewmate, "What continent is this?"

We could see smoke rising from fires that dotted the entire east coast of Africa, and in the same orbit only moments later, ice floes jostling for position in the Antarctic. We could see the Ganges River dumping its murky, sediment-laden water into the Indian Ocean and watch ominous hurricane clouds expanding and rising like biscuits in the oven of the Caribbean.

Mountain ranges, volcanoes, and river deltas appeared in salt-and-flour relief, all leading me to assume the role of a novice geologist. In such moments, it was easy to imagine the dynamic upheavals that created jutting mountain ranges and the internal

---

1. **Rand-McNally:** Publishers of atlases.

*Single Room, Earth View*   517

**Motivation/Prior Knowledge**
Have students imagine what it might be like to travel to outer space. Have them consider the speed at which they would be traveling and the distance they would be from Earth. Ask students what they think they would be able to see in outer space and on the surface of the Earth.

**Master Teacher Note** You might want to tell students that Sally Kristen Ride, the first American woman astronaut, traveled in space in June of 1983 and again in October of 1984. On her first six-day flight on the *Challenger,* she and four other astronauts successfully launched communications satellites and conducted experiments. On her second flight, she assisted in launching a satellite to measure the sun's effect on the Earth's weather.

**Thematic Idea** Another selection that stresses the importance of observation is "The Death of a Tree," page 505.

**Purpose-Setting Question**
What are Ride's most important observations from orbit?

1 **Discussion** Is Ride successful in explaining the difficulty of describing space flight? Why or why not?

2 **Discussion** How does Ride use humor to make her point?

3 **Clarification** You might tell students that a *relief map* "shows the different heights of land forms."

4 **Discussion** What does Sally Ride mean when she says that "the view . . . makes theory come alive"?

5 **Discussion** What land forms would you be most interested in observing from orbit?

6 **Discussion** Why is the term "signatures" especially appropriate for what Ride means?

wrenchings that created rifts and seas. I also became an instant believer in plate tectonics;[2] India really *is* crashing into Asia, and Saudi Arabia and Egypt really *are* pulling apart, making the Red Sea wider. Even though their respective motion is really no more than mere inches a year, the view from overhead makes theory come alive.

Spectacular as the view is from 200 miles up, the Earth is not the awe-inspiring "blue marble" made famous by the photos from the moon. From space shuttle height, we can't see the entire globe at a glance, but we can look down the entire boot of Italy, or up the East Coast of the United States from Cape Hatteras to Cape Cod. The panoramic view inspires an appreciation for the scale of some of nature's phenomena. One day, as I scanned the sandy expanse of Northern Af-

---

**2. plate tectonics:** The theory that the earth's surface consists of plates whose constant motion explains continental drift, mountain building, large earthquakes, and so forth.

rica, I couldn't find any of the familiar landmarks—colorful outcroppings of rock in Chad, irrigated patches of the Sahara. Then I realized they were obscured by a huge dust storm, a cloud of sand that enveloped the continent from Morocco to the Sudan.

Since the space shuttle flies fairly low (at least by orbital standards; it's more than 22,000 miles lower than a typical TV satellite), we can make out both natural and manmade features in surprising detail. Familiar geographical features like San Francisco Bay, Long Island, and Lake Michigan are easy to recognize, as are many cities, bridges, and airports. The Great Wall of China is *not* the only manmade object visible from space.

The signatures of civilization are usually seen in straight lines (bridges or runways) or sharp delineations (abrupt transitions from desert to irrigated land, as in California's Imperial Valley). A modern city like New York doesn't leap from the canvas of its surround-

---

## Grammar in Action

Skillful writers usually avoid common usage problems like the **confusion between *like* and *as.*** *Like* is a preposition meaning "similar to" or "such as." Except in informal usage, it should not be used in place of the conjunction *as* or *as if.* (*As* can also be an adverb.)

Nonstandard:     She walks *like* she talks—quickly.
Standard:         She walks *as* she talks—quickly.

Nonstandard:     The students looked *like* they were bored.
Standard:         The students looked *as if* they were bored.

Notice how Sally Ride uses the two words:

Familiar geographical features *like* San Fransisco Bay, Long Island, and Lake Michigan are easy to recognize. . . . (*like* used correctly as a preposition) ings, but its straight piers and concrete runways catch the eye—and around them, the city materializes. I found Salina, Kansas (and pleased my in-laws, who live there) by spotting its long runway amid the wheat fields near the city. Over Florida, I could see the launch pad where we had begun our trip, and the landing strip, where we would eventually land.

Some of civilization's more unfortunate effects on the environment are also evident from orbit. Oil slicks glisten on the surface of the Persian Gulf, patches of pollution-damaged trees dot the forests of central Europe. Some cities look out of focus, and their colors muted, when viewed through a pollutant haze. Not surprisingly, the effects are more noticeable now than they were a decade ago. An astronaut who has flown in both Skylab and the space shuttle reported that the horizon didn't seem quite as sharp, or the colors quite as bright, in 1983 as they had in 1973.

Of course, informal observations by individual astronauts are one thing, but more precise measurements are continually being made from space: The space shuttle has carried infrared film to document damage to citrus trees in Florida and in rain forests along the Amazon. It has carried even more sophisticated sensors in the payload bay. Here is one example: sensors used to measure atmospheric carbon monoxide levels, allowing scientists to study the environmental effects of city emissions and land-clearing fires.

Most of the Earth's surface is covered with water, and at first glance it all looks the same: blue. But with the right lighting conditions and a couple of orbits of practice, it's possible to make out the intricate patterns in the oceans—eddies and spirals become visible because of the subtle differences in water color or reflectivity.

Observations and photographs by astronauts have contributed significantly to the understanding of ocean dynamics, and some of the more intriguing discoveries prompted the National Aeronautics and Space Administration to fly an oceanographic observer for the express purpose of studying the ocean from orbit. Scientists' understanding of the energy balance in the oceans has increased significantly as a result of the discoveries of circular and spiral eddies tens of kilometers in diameter, of standing waves hundreds of kilometers long, and of spiral eddies that sometimes trail into one another for thousands of kilometers. If a scientist wants to study features on this scale, it's much easier from an orbiting vehicle than from the vantage point of a boat.

Believe it or not, an astronaut can also see the wakes of large ships and the contrails[3] of airplanes. The sun angle has to be just right, but when the lighting conditions are perfect, you can follow otherwise invisible oil tankers on the Persian Gulf and trace major shipping lanes through the Mediterranean Sea. Similarly, when atmospheric conditions allow contrail formation, the thousand-mile-long condensation trails let astronauts trace the major air routes across the northern Pacific Ocean.

Part of every orbit takes us to the dark side of the planet. In space, night is very, very black—but that doesn't mean there's nothing to look at. The lights of cities sparkle; on nights when there was no moon, it was difficult for me to tell the Earth from the sky—the twinkling lights could be stars or they could be small cities. On one nighttime pass from Cuba to Nova Scotia, the entire East Coast of the United States appeared in twinkling outline.

When the moon is full, it casts an eerie light on the Earth. In its light, we see ghostly

---

3. **contrails** (kän' trāls) *n*.: White trails of condensed water vapor that sometimes form in the wake of aircraft.

7 **Critical Thinking and Reading** What are the implications of this observation?

8 **Literary Focus** What do Ride's comments suggest about the way to become a better observer?

. . . the horizon didn't seem quite *as* sharp, or the colors quite *as* bright, in 1983 *as* they had in 1973. (*as* used correctly as an adverb—twice—and then as a conjunction)

**Student Activity 1.** Choose the correct word in the following sentences:
1. Kaylen wrote (like, as) a veteran reporter.
2. Misunderstandings (like, as) those he illustrated can cause serious public-relations problems.
3. Gnats were flying (like, as if) they were guided toward my eyes.
4. Report cards went out (like, as) teachers planned.

**Student Activity 2.** Write two sentences correctly using *like* and two correctly using *as* or *as if*.

9 **Discussion** How does Ride make her description lively and dramatic?

10 **Critical Thinking and Reading** Ride contends that one cannot liken the experience of space flight to familiar experiences. What are some examples from her essay that support this view?

**Reader's Response** Would you like to travel in space? Why or why not?

clouds and bright reflections on the water. One night, the Mississippi River flashed into view, and because of our viewing angle and orbital path, the reflected moonlight seemed to flow downstream—as if Huck Finn[4] had tied a candle to his raft.

Of all the sights from orbit, the most spectacular may be the magnificent displays of lightning that ignite the clouds at night. On Earth, we see lightning from below the clouds; in orbit, we see it from above. Bolts of lightning are diffused by the clouds into bursting balls of light. Sometimes, when a storm extends hundreds of miles, it looks like a transcontinental brigade is tossing fireworks from cloud to cloud.

As the shuttle races the sun around the Earth, we pass from day to night and back again during a single orbit—hurtling into darkness, then bursting into daylight. The sun's appearance unleashes spectacular blue and orange bands along the horizon, a clockwork miracle that astronauts witness every 90 minutes. But, I really can't describe a sunrise in orbit. The drama set against the black backdrop of space and the magic of the materializing colors can't be captured in an astronomer's equations or an astronaut's photographs.

I once heard someone (not an astronaut) suggest that it's possible to imagine what spaceflight is like by simply extrapolating from the sensations you experience on an airplane. All you have to do, he said, is mentally raise the airplane 200 miles, mentally eliminate the air noise and the turbulence, and you get an accurate mental picture of a trip in the space shuttle.

Not true. And while it's natural to try to liken space flight to familiar experiences, it can't be brought "down to Earth"—not in the final sense. The environment is different, the perspective is different. Part of the fascination with space travel is the element of the unknown—the conviction that it's different from earthbound experiences. And it is.

9

10

---

**4. Huck Finn:** Hero of Mark Twain's novel *The Adventures of Huckleberry Finn.*

520 *Nonfiction*

**Closure and Extension**

**ANSWERS TO THINKING ABOUT THE SELECTION**
*Recalling*

1. Ride was able to see mountain ranges, volcanoes, river deltas, ice floes, rocks, deserts, and oceans.
2. Ride was able to see bridges, piers, runways, oil slicks, and

## THINKING ABOUT THE SELECTION

### Recalling

1. Name three natural features that Ride saw from orbit.
2. Identify three examples that she observed of humans' effect on the environment.
3. How have observations and photographs by astronauts contributed to science?

### Interpreting

4. What does the essay's title mean?
5. Why do you think that Ride found it easier to imagine the forces of geology when she was in orbital flight?
6. An astronaut reported that colors did not seem as bright in 1983 as in 1973. What conclusion does this fact suggest?

### Applying

7. How have Ride's descriptions of the Earth from 200 miles up affected your thoughts and feelings about our planet?

## READING IN THE ARTS AND SCIENCES

### Understanding Scientific Observation

**Scientific observation** is the act of carefully noting facts and events. Sally Ride made such observations as she orbited around the Earth. For example, she was able to see some of the effects of pollution on the environment—"Oil slicks . . . on the surface of the Persian Gulf" and "patches of pollution-damaged trees" in central European forests.

1. How does Ride show her talent for observation in finding civilization's "signatures"?
2. How does she prove herself to be a careful observer of the Earth's oceans?

## CRITICAL THINKING AND READING

### Finding the Main Idea of a Paragraph

The **main idea** of a paragraph is the most important idea about the subject on which the paragraph focuses. This idea is stated in the **topic sentence,** which can appear at the beginning, end, or middle of the paragraph. For example, in the paragraph beginning, "The signatures of civilization are usually seen in straight lines . . . ," Ride places the topic sentence at the start of the paragraph. The other sentences contain examples of this idea.

Identify the topic sentence in each of the following paragraphs from the essay. (The quoted words indicate the beginning of each paragraph.)

1. "Some of civilization's . . ." (page 519)
2. "Observations and photographs . . ." (page 519)
3. "Believe it or not . . ." (page 519)

## UNDERSTANDING LANGUAGE

### Understanding Scientific Terms

Sally Ride uses a number of scientific terms in describing her observations from the shuttle. For instance, she refers to "wrenchings that created rifts and seas." A *rift* is "a break in a rock formation caused by a shift in the Earth's crust."

The following scientific terms also appear in the essay. Look up each in a dictionary and use it in a sentence.

1. outcroppings
2. rain forests
3. carbon monoxide
4. oceanographic

## THINKING AND WRITING

### Writing up an Observation

Recall a person, object, or scene that fascinated you and that you observed carefully. List some of your observations. Then using this list, write a description of what you saw for your classmates. Try to be as careful an observer as Sally Ride. For example, do not simply say that a person's shirt was red. Tell exactly what shade of red it was. In revising, you may want to include some vivid images, like Ride's description of lightning as "fireworks." When you are done, share your observation with your classmates.

*Single Room, Earth View* 521

(Answers begin on p. 520.)

more intricate patterns like eddies and spirals.

## ANSWERS TO CRITICAL THINKING AND READING

1. "Some of civilization's more unfortunate effects on the environment are also evident from orbit."
2. "Observations and photographs by astronauts have contributed significantly to the understanding of ocean dynamics. . . ."
3. "... an astronaut can also see the wakes of large ships and the contrails of airplanes."

## ANSWERS TO UNDERSTANDING LANGUAGE

1. *Outcroppings* are "bedrock or other layers of material emerging through the soil level."
2. A *rain forest* is "a tropical woodland area that has a rainfall of at least 100 inches (2500 mm) a year and is rich with vegetation and animal life."
3. *Carbon monoxide* is "a highly poisonous gas formed when carbon burns with insufficient air."
4. *Oceanography* is "the exploratory and scientific study of the ocean and things related to the ocean." *Oceanographic* means "relating to oceanography."

## THINKING AND WRITING

For help with this assignment, students may refer to Lesson 2, "Drafting and Revising," in the Handbook of Writing About Literature.

**Publishing Student Writing** You might want to have students read their descriptions without mentioning the actual person, object, or scene being described. Classmates can then guess what is being described.

**Writing Across the Curriculum** You might want to have students research and report on the United States space program. Consider informing the science department of this assignment, so that teachers can provide guidance for students.

patches of pollution-damaged trees.

3. Observation and photographs have increased our understanding of ocean dynamics.

### Interpreting

4. Answers will differ, but students might relate the title to a typical expression referring to a hotel room— "single room, ocean view." The single room in this case, of course, is the shuttle.

5. Answers will differ. Many students will realize that from the vantage point of outer space, Ride could better see the effects of such forces.
6. Suggested Response: Pollution has increased.

### Applying

7. Responses will differ, but students might say that the essay has given them a new sense of the unity of our planet.

**Challenge** Start a notebook in which you record daily observations of a familiar place or pet.

## ANSWERS TO READING IN THE ARTS AND SCIENCES

1. Suggested Response: She was able to spot the straight lines of bridges and runways.
2. Suggested Response: Ride says that at first glance the ocean is blue. But with experience and the right lighting, Ride is able to report

**More About the Author** James Thurber became blind in one eye from an accident he suffered in childhood. However, he did not let this injury slow him down. Ask students what qualities a person must have to overcome such a handicap.

**Literary Focus** Suggest to students a topic sentence—for example, "The United States has an abundance of beautiful land formations." Have students give examples related to the topic sentence. Have them use descriptive language that clearly illustrates the topic sentence.

**Look For** As students read, have them consider the main idea of Thurber's essay. Then have them be attentive to the examples in the essay that support this idea.

**Writing/Prior Knowledge** Before students begin to write have them suggest other words or phrases used today that Thurber might consider "mindless repetition." Have students give examples of the way these words or phrases are used.

**Vocabulary** Have your **less advanced** students read the words and their definitions. Have them write a paragraph that incorporates all three words, demonstrating their understanding of the words' meanings.

# GUIDE FOR READING

## The Spreading *"You Know"*

**James Thurber** (1894–1961) became famous as a humorous writer for *The New Yorker* magazine. Many of his amusing essays are collected in books such as *My Life and Hard Times* and *The Middle-Aged Man on the Flying Trapeze*. In addition to being a witty writer and a talented cartoonist, Thurber earned a reputation as an author who chose his words with care. "The Spreading '*You* Know' " is a humorous essay about the importance of choosing words carefully in conversation.

**Illustration**

**Illustration** is the process by which writers clarify and support their ideas through examples. This practice of introducing a well-timed example to support a more general argument is so natural that most skilled writers do it almost automatically. They know from experience that the mention of an actual case or situation can enliven a discussion and increase a reader's interest. James Thurber, for instance, uses this technique in "The Spreading '*You* Know' " to ridicule the mindless repetition of a phrase.

**Look For**

Look for the examples that Thurber uses to make his case against the overuse of the phrase "*you* know" in conversation. Also notice how he exaggerates the problem, describing it as a "blight" and "curse" to make it seem more humorous.

**Writing**

Think of a similar conversational habit that you have noticed, such as the repetition of the word *like*. Freewrite, telling how you think this habit first started and why it became popular.

**Vocabulary**

Knowing the following words will help you as you read "The Spreading '*You* Know.' "
**blight** (blīt) *n.*: Anything that destroys (p. 523)
**reiteration** (rē it′ ər ā′ shən) *n.*: Repetition (p. 523)
**hapless** (hap′ lis) *adj.*: Unlucky (p. 523)

## Objectives

1 To understand illustration
2 To infer a writer's purpose
3 To understand speech habits
4 To write about spoken language

## Support Material

**Teaching Portfolio**
Teacher Backup, p. 593
Usage and Mechanics Worksheet, p. 596
Vocabulary Check, p. 597
Critical Thinking and Reading Worksheet, *Inferring a Writer's Purpose,* p. 598
Language Worksheet, *Understanding Words with the Prefix* over, p. 599

Selection Test, p. 600

# The Spreading "You Know"

### James Thurber

The latest blight to afflict the spoken word in the United States is the rapidly spreading reiteration of the phrase "*you know.*" I don't know just when it began moving like a rainstorm through the language, but I tremble at its increasing garbling[1] of meaning, ruining of rhythm, and drumming upon my hapless ears. One man, in a phone conversation with me last summer, used the phrase thirty-four times in about five minutes, by my own count; a young matron in Chicago got seven "*you knows*" into one wavy sentence, and I have also heard it as far west as Denver, where an otherwise charming woman at a garden party in August said it almost as often as a whippoorwill says, "Whippoorwill." Once, speaking of whippoorwills, I was waked after midnight by one of those feathered hellions[2] and lay there counting his chants. He got up to one hundred and fifty-eight and then suddenly said, "Whip—" and stopped dead. I like to believe that his mate, at the end of her patience, finally let him have it.

---

**1. garbling** (gär'b'liŋ) *n.*: Confusion, mix-up.

**2. hellions** (hel'yənz) *n.*: Mischievous troublemakers.

*The Spreading "You Know"* 523

---

## Humanities Note

Illustration by James Thurber. This is another of Thurber's illustrations of his own work. Have students note the simple lines and lack of detail.

1. How does Thurber convey humor with such simple drawing?
2. What is the point of this cartoon?
3. Do Thurber's humorous cartoons make his essay more effective? Why or why not?

5 **Discussion** What is Thurber's attitude toward Broadway and Hollywood? Do you share that attitude? Explain.

6 **Literary Focus** How does Thurber use humor and exaggeration to make his point in this last paragraph?

**Reader's Response** If you were to write an essay similar to Thurber's, what current colloquial phrase would you ridicule? Why?

Copyright © **1961 JAMES THURBER.**
From Lanterns and Lances, published by Harper & Row

My unfortunate tendency to count "*you knows*" is practically making a female whippoorwill out of me. Listening to a radio commentator, not long ago, discussing the recent meeting of the United Nations, I thought I was going mad when I heard him using "you know" as a noun, until I realized that he had shortened United Nations Organizations to UNO and was pronouncing it, you know, as if it were "*you* know."

A typical example of speech *you*-knowed to death goes like this. "The other day I saw, you know, Harry Johnson, the, you know, former publicity man for, you know, the Charteriss Publishing Company, and, you know, what he wanted to talk about, strangely enough, was, you know, something you'd never guess. . . ."

5 This curse may have originated simultaneously on Broadway and in Hollywood, where such curses often originate. About twenty-five years ago, or perhaps longer, theater and movie people jammed their sentences with "you know what I mean?" which was soon shortened to "you *know*?" That had followed the overuse, in the 1920s, of

"you see?" or just plain "see?" These blights often disappear finally, but a few have stayed and will continue to stay, such as "Well" and "I mean to say" and "I mean" and "The fact is." Others seem to have mercifully passed out of lingo into limbo,[3] such as, to go back a long way, "Twenty-three, skiddoo" and "So's your old man" and "I don't know nothin' from nothin' " and "Believe you me." About five years ago both men and women were saying things like "He has a new Cadillac job with a built-in bar deal in the back seat" and in 1958 almost everything anybody mentioned, or even wrote about, was "triggered." Arguments were triggered, and allergies, and divorces, and even love affairs. This gun-and-bomb verb seemed to make the jumpiest of the jumpy even jumpier, but it has almost died out now, and I trust that I have not triggered its revival.

It was in Paris, from late 1918 until early 1920, that there was a glut—an American glut, to be sure—of "You said it" and "You can say that again," and an American Marine I knew, from Montana, could not speak any sentence of agreement or concurrence without saying, "It *is*, you *know*." Fortunately, that perhaps original use of "*you* know" did not seem to be imported into America.

6 I am reluctantly making notes for a possible future volume to be called *A Farewell to Speech* or *The Decline and Fall of the King's English.* I hope and pray that I shall not have to write the book. Maybe everything, or at least the language, will clear up before it is too late. Let's face it, it better had, that's for sure, and I don't mean maybe.

---

**3. out of lingo** (liŋ'gō) **into limbo** (lim'bō): From substandard language into neglect and nonuse.

## THINKING ABOUT THE SELECTION

### Recalling

1. What does Thurber object to about the repetition of the phrase "you know"?
2. Find an example he gives to show the overuse of this phrase.
3. According to Thurber, how might this bad habit have started?
4. Identify three other words or phrases that he complains about.

### Interpreting

5. Explain the techniques Thurber uses to make this essay humorous.
6. Why does Thurber say he is taking notes for a book to be called *A Farewell to Speech*?
7. Explain the joke in the final sentence of this essay.
8. What is the true topic of this essay? What main idea does Thurber express about this topic?

### Applying

9. Someone once wrote that there are fashions in language just as in clothing. Comment on this remark.

## READING IN THE ARTS AND SCIENCES

### Understanding Illustration

**Illustration** is the process by which writers clarify and support their ideas through examples. In "The Spreading '*You* Know,'" Thurber ridicules the overuse of the phrase "*you* know" by giving examples of this bad habit. He tells, for instance, about the man who used this "phrase thirty-four times in about five minutes."

1. What is the effect of Thurber's giving three quick examples of this habit in the very first paragraph?
2. Why does he save his longest example of "speech *you*-knowed to death" for later in the essay?
3. How might this essay have been different if Thurber had not used any examples?

## CRITICAL THINKING AND READING

### Inferring a Writer's Purpose

**Inferring** means reaching a conclusion based on evidence. You can often infer a writer's purpose by paying close attention to his or her opening and closing statements. For example, if a writer begins by criticizing companies that pollute the air, you can infer that the writer's purpose is to halt this form of pollution.

Carefully reread the first and last paragraphs of "The Spreading '*You* Know.'" State Thurber's purpose in your own words.

## SPEAKING AND LISTENING

### Understanding Speech Habits

In this essay Thurber tells about a speech habit common in his time. By conferring with your classmates, you can decide which words and phrases are overused today.

1. Your teacher will divide the class into small groups. Brainstorm with your group to create a list of words, similar to Thurber's "*you* know," that are repeated again and again.
2. Share your group's list with the class.

## THINKING AND WRITING

### Writing About Spoken Language

Write a humorous essay like Thurber's for your classmates, making fun of an overused word or phrase. First, choose the word or phrase that you want to focus on. The list of words that you compiled with your group will assist you. Note some ways in which people mindlessly repeat this word or phrase. Then, using your notes, write an essay poking fun at this speech habit. Remember to include examples, as Thurber does. In revising your essay, you might want to exaggerate these examples to make them more humorous. Share your essay with your classmates when you are finished.

*The Spreading "You Know"* 525

and provides humorous examples of it.
6. Suggested Response: Thurber believes that language is deteriorating.
7. Suggested Response: The joke is that Thurber uses the types of phrases that he hates.
8. Suggested Response: The true topic of the essay is Thurber's belief that improper or careless use of language reflects imprecise and careless thought.

### Applying

9. Answers will differ. Students might agree that words, expressions, and phrases become popular for a time and then drop out of common usage.

**Challenge** Ask an adult to list some of the colloquial expressions that were popular when he or she was younger.

### ANSWERS TO READING IN THE ARTS AND SCIENCES

1. Suggested Response: The three quick examples give readers a clear example of the habit and make it seem that it is overrunning the country.
2. Answers will differ, but students might say that Thurber waits to engage and interest the reader, before giving a longer example.
3. Answers will differ, but students may say that the essay might have been less humorous and persuasive.

### ANSWERS TO CRITICAL THINKING AND READING

Suggested Response: Thurber wants to convince the reader that the spoken word is on the decline. He wants to stop this deterioration, if possible.

### THINKING AND WRITING

For help with this assignment, students can refer to Lesson 3, "Proofreading and Publishing," in the Handbook of Writing About Literature.

**Publishing Student Writing** You might want to display students' essays or collect them in a class book.

525

## Closure and Extension

### ANSWERS TO THINKING ABOUT THE SELECTION
*Recalling*

1. Thurber objects to the phrase because it is overused and garbles meaning.
2. Student responses might include the man in a phone conversation who used it thirty-four times; the two women, one from Chicago and one from Denver; the radio commentator; and the conversation about Harry Johnson.
3. The "curse," according to Thurber, may have started on Broadway or in Hollywood.
4. Other phrases he complains about include "Man," "I mean to say," "you see?," "see?," and "The fact is."

*Interpreting*

5. Suggested Response: Thurber exaggerates the effect of the habit

**More About the Author** In addition to biographies and historical accounts of famous and important English literary figures, Marchette Chute also writes children's poetry. Ask students to discuss what would motivate a writer to produce such different types of work.

**Literary Focus** Have students consider how they would find information about an historical period of particular interest to them. Ask them to evaluate the usefulness of the following resources for this purpose—old newspapers; books by scholars of our own time; paintings; records of births, marriages, and deaths; diaries; and accounts by travelers. Have them suggest additional resources as well.

**Look For** Have students consider the list of resources that they have suggested. As they read, have them refer to the list to determine which resources Chute might have used.

**Writing/Prior Knowledge** Before students begin writing, have them discuss actors and actresses they have seen in current movies, plays, or television programs.

**Vocabulary** Have your less advanced students read the words and their definitions. Have them use each of the words in a sentence about an historical person or period.

## *from* Shakespeare of London

**Marchette Chute** (1909–     ) was born in Minnesota and attended the Minneapolis School of Art and the University of Minnesota. She is primarily known as a writer of biographies and historical studies. Among her award-winning books about great English authors are *Geoffrey Chaucer of England* and *Ben Jonson of Westminster*. In these and in *Shakespeare of London,* she shows her ability to recreate the flavor of an era.

### Historical Inference

**Historical inference** is the technique of arriving at reasonable conclusions about a person or time in history based on limited evidence. In making their inferences, or educated guesses, historians use such sources as district records, pamphlets, books, and written accounts by travelers. They assemble as much information as possible and then draw conclusions from it to paint a more complete picture of the person or time they are studying. In this excerpt from *Shakespeare of London,* Chute uses historical inference to portray the greatest poet and playwright in the English language, William Shakespeare.

### Look For

As you read, look for the sources of evidence about Shakespeare and his time that Chute uses. Also be aware of the conclusions she reaches. Ask yourself whether these conclusions make sense.

### Writing

In this essay, Chute discusses some of the qualities that a successful actor needed about four hundred years ago. Freewrite about the skills that an actor or actress must have today.

### Vocabulary

Knowing the following words will help you as you read "Shakespeare of London."

**strenuous** (stren′ yōō wəs) *adj.*: Requiring great effort (p. 527)

**parrying** (par′ ē iŋ) *v.*: Warding off a sword-thrust (p. 527)

**entrails** (en′ trālz) *n.*: Intestines; guts (p. 528)

**sleight of hand** (slīt): Skill in deceiving onlookers (p. 528)

**susceptible** (sə sep′ tə b'l) *adj.*:

Receptive (p. 529)

**intricate** (in′ tri kit) *adj.*: Complex (p. 529)

**supple** (sup′'l) *adj.*: Flexible; adaptable (p. 530)

**collaborated** (kə lab′ ə rāt′ ed) *v.*: Worked together (p. 530)

**exacting** (ig zakt′ iŋ) *adj.*: Demanding (p. 530)

---

### Objectives
1  To understand historical inference
2  To evaluate historical inferences
3  To understand theater terms
4  To write about inference

### Support Material

**Teaching Portfolio**
Teacher Backup, p. 603
Grammar in Action Worksheet, *Understanding Infinitives,* p. 607
Usage and Mechanics Worksheet, p. 609
Vocabulary Check, p. 610
Analyzing Literature Worksheet, *Understanding Historical Inference,* p. 612

Language Worksheet, *Understanding Theater Terms,* p. 613
Selection Test, p. 614

# *from* Shakespeare of London

## Marchette Chute

Acting was not an easy profession on the Elizabethan[1] stage or one to be taken up lightly. An actor went through a strenuous period of training before he could be entrusted with an important part by one of the great city companies. He worked on a raised stage in the glare of the afternoon sun, with none of the softening illusions that can be achieved in the modern theater, and in plays that made strenuous demands upon his skill as a fencer, a dancer and an acrobat.

Many of the men in the London companies had been "trained up from their childhood" in the art, and an actor like Shakespeare, who entered the profession in his twenties, had an initial handicap that could only be overcome by intelligence and rigorous discipline. Since he was a well-known actor by 1592 and Chettle[2] says he was an excellent one, he must have had the initial advantages of a strong body and a good voice and have taught himself in the hard school of the Elizabethan theater how to use them to advantage.

One of the most famous of the London companies, that of Lord Strange, began its career as a company of tumblers, and a standard production like "The Forces of Hercules" was at least half acrobatics. Training of this kind was extremely useful to the actors, for the normal London stage consisted of several different levels. Battles and sieges were very popular with the audiences, with the upper levels of the stage used as the town walls and turrets, and an actor had to know how to take violent falls without damaging either himself or his expensive costume.

Nearly all plays involved some kind of fighting, and in staging hand-to-hand combats the actor's training had to be excellent. The average Londoner was an expert on the subject of fencing, and he did not pay his penny to see two professional actors make ineffectual dabs at each other with rapiers[3] when the script claimed they were fighting to the death. A young actor like Shakespeare must have gone through long, grueling hours of practice to learn the ruthless technique of Elizabethan fencing. He had to learn how to handle a long, heavy rapier in one hand, with a dagger for parrying in the other, and to make a series of savage, calculated thrusts at close quarters from the wrist and forearm, aiming either at his opponent's eyes or below the ribs. The actor had to achieve the brutal reality of an actual Elizabethan duel without injuring himself or his opponent, a problem that required a high degree of training and of physical coordination. The theaters and the inn-yards were frequently rented by the fencing societies to

---

**1. Elizabethan** (i liz′ ə bē′ thən) *adj.*: Concerning the period 1558 to 1603, when Elizabeth I ruled England.

**2. Chettle:** Henry Chettle (died 1607?), an English playwright, publisher, and poet.

**3. rapiers** (rā′ pē ərz) *n.*: Slender, two-edged swords with cuplike handles.

from *Shakespeare of London*   527

## Presentation

**Motivation/Prior Knowledge**
Ask students what sources of information future historians might use in writing about our own era. Have them consider which of these sources would be most valuable in giving people of the future the true flavor of our times. Then tell them that, in this essay, Marchette Chute tries to recreate one aspect of Elizabethan life—the experience of actors.

**Master Teacher Note** You might want to tell students that Shakespeare owned a financial share of the theater company for which he acted and wrote plays. In the early 1600's he was able to retire to Stratford, his place of birth, with the money he had earned.

**Purpose-Setting Question**
What do you learn about William Shakespeare from this essay?

**Thematic Idea** Another selection that deals with a journey to personal fulfillment through the arts is "Georgia O'Keeffe," page 511.

1 **Discussion** What does the writer mean by the phrase "trained up from their childhood"?

2 **Enrichment** The opening of Laurence Olivier's movie, *Henry V*, presents the stage and players as an Elizabethan might have seen them.

3 **Discussion** You might want to have students compare such "combats" with stunts and special effects in today's movies. Are contemporary audiences just as demanding in this respect as Elizabethan audiences were?

Fine art, *Reconstruction of the Second Globe Theatre at London.* This drawing shows a view of the stage of the Globe Theatre. The stage juts out into the yard, surrounded on three sides by seats or standing room for spectators. Over the stage and supported by pillars is the "shadow," which protected players from the rain. Behind the stage is an inner recess, often called the "tiring house," used for indoor scenes. On the second level is the "chamber," with a balcony. This chamber was used to represent a bedchamber in a dwelling or the walls of a castle or town. On the third level is another chamber, usually used by musicians. The fourth level is the turret, known as "the heavens," containing a bell and other means of creating sound effects.

In this scene, actors are performing a play by Christopher Marlowe, a contemporary of Shakespeare.

1. Notice how the stage extends into the section where some of the audience stands. What advantages does this extended stage give the performer?

2. How might the fact that the audience surrounds the actor affect the way that an actor would portray his character?

4 **Discussion** Does advanced technology—for example, computerized lighting, visual projections, and audio tapes—make it unnecessary for actors to have such skills today?

**RECONSTRUCTION OF THE SECOND GLOBE THEATRE AT LONDON**
*The Granger Collection*

put on exhibition matches, and on one such occasion at the Swan[4] a fencer was run through the eye and died, an indication of the risks this sort of work involved even with trained, experienced fencers. The actors had to be extremely skilled, since they faced precisely the same audience. Richard Tarleton, a comic actor of the 80's who was the first great popular star of the Elizabethan theater, was made Master of Fence the year before he died and this was the highest degree the fencing schools could award.

Not being content with savage, realistic fights in its theater productions, the London audience also expected to see bloody deaths and mutilations; and it was necessary to find some way to run a sword through an actor's head or tear out his entrails without impair-

ing his usefulness for the next afternoon's performance. This involved not only agility but a thorough knowledge of sleight of hand, since the players were working close to the audience and in broad daylight. Elizabethan stage management was not slavishly interested in realism but it was always concerned with good stage effects and when bloodshed was involved it gave the audience real blood. It had been found by experience that ox blood was too thick to run well, and sheep's blood was generally used. To stage a realistic stabbing one actor would use a knife with a hollow handle into which the blade would slip back when it was pressed home, and his fellow actor would be equipped with a bladder of blood inside his white leather jerkin,[5] which could be painted to look like skin.

4

_____
**4. the Swan:** A London theater of the time.

_____
**5. jerkin** (jur' kin) *n.*: Short, closefitting jacket.

## Grammar in Action

An **infinitive** is a form of a verb that generally appears with the word *to* and acts as a noun, adjective, or adverb:

*To win the gold medal* is his goal. (noun, subject)
Paula planned *to visit her aunt.* (noun, direct object)
The plan is *to work until noon.* (noun, predicate nominative)
The name *to call* appears below. (adjective, modifies *name*)
He spoke *to be understood.* (adverb, modifies *spoke*)

The sentence variety achieved with the use of infinitives helps add interest to a piece of writing. Note how Chute uses them:

It had been found by experience that ox blood was too thick *to run well*, and sheep's blood was generally used. *To stage a realistic stabbing* one actor would use a knife with a hollow handle . . . and his fellow actor would be equipped with a bladder of blood . . . painted *to look like skin.*

. . . beginning actors were expected *to handle several roles in an afternoon* instead of only one. A major company . . .

When the bladder was pricked and the actor arched himself at the moment of contact, the blood spurted out in a most satisfactory manner.

Another test of an actor's physical control was in dancing. Apart from the dances that were written into the actual texts of the plays, it was usual to end the performance with a dance performed by some of the members of the company. A traveler from abroad who saw Shakespeare's company act *Julius Caesar* said that "when the play was over they danced very marvelously and gracefully together," and when the English actors traveled abroad special mention was always made of their ability as dancers. The fashion of the time was for violent, spectacular dances and the schools in London taught intricate steps like those of the galliard,[6] the exaggerated leap called the "capriole" and the violent lifting of one's partner high into the air that was the "volte." A visitor to one of these dancing schools of London watched a performer do a galliard and noted how "wonderfully he leaped, flung and took on"; and if amateurs were talented at this kind of work, professionals on the stage were expected to be very much better.

In addition to all this, subordinate or beginning actors were expected to handle several roles in an afternoon instead of only one. A major company seldom had more than twelve actors in it and could not afford to hire an indefinite number of extra ones for a single production. This meant that the men who had short speaking parts or none were constantly racing about and leaping into different costumes to get onstage with a different characterization as soon as they heard their cues. In one of Alleyn's[7] productions a single actor played a Tartar[8] noble-man, a spirit, an attendant, a hostage, a ghost, a child, a captain and a Persian; and while none of the parts made any special demands on his acting ability he must have had very little time to catch his breath. The London theater was no place for physical weaklings; and, in the same way it is safe to assume that John Shakespeare must have had a strong, well-made body or he would not have been appointed a constable in Stratford, it is safe to assume that he must have passed the inheritance on to his eldest son.

There was one more physical qualification an Elizabethan actor had to possess, and this was perhaps more important than any of the others. He had to have a good voice. An Elizabethan play was full of action, but in the final analysis it was not the physical activity that caught and held the emotions of the audience; it was the words. An audience was an assembly of listeners and it was through the ear, not the eye, that the audience learned the location of each of the scenes, the emotions of each of the characters and the poetry and excitement of the play as a whole. More especially, since the actors were men and boys and close physical contact could not carry the illusion of love-making, words had to be depended upon in the parts that were written for women.

An Elizabethan audience had become highly susceptible to the use of words, trained and alert to catch their exact meaning and full of joy if they were used well. But this meant, as the basis of any successful stage production, that all the words had to be heard clearly. The actors used a fairly rapid delivery of their lines and this meant that breath control, emphasis and enunciation had to be perfect if the link that was being forged between the emotions of the audience and the action on the stage was not to be broken. When Shakespeare first came to London, the problem of effective stage de-

---

6. **galliard** (gal′ yərd) *n.*: Lively French dance.
7. **Alleyn's:** Edward Alleyn (1566–1626), an English actor and theater owner.
8. **Tartar** (tär′ tər): Turk or Mongol.

from *Shakespeare of London*   529

5 **Enrichment** Jerome Robbins created jazzy dances for the teenage gangs in *West Side Story*, a contemporary musical version of *Romeo and Juliet*. Ask students how dance numbers can contribute to a drama.

6 **Clarification** There are well over twelve speaking parts in Shakespeare's *Julius Caesar*. The practice of giving actors more than one role in this and other plays was called *doubling*.

7 **Master Teacher Note** Elizabethan actors often spoke twenty-five or more lines per minute in performing a play. Have students consider what kinds of problems this might have created for actors. You might want to give students a Shakespearean script of twenty-five lines to read so that they can appreciate the demands of this task.

8 **Discussion** What does Chute mean by this statement?

could not afford *to hire an indefinite number of extra ones for a single production*

The first infinitive functions as an adverb (modifies *thick*); the second as an adverb (modifies *use*); the third as an adverb (modifies *painted*); the fourth as a noun (direct object); and the fifth as a noun (direct object).

**Student Activity 1.** Identify the use of the following infinitives:
1. They raced *to get onstage as a different character.*
2. It is safe *to assume that John Shakespeare was big.*
3. An Elizabethan actor had *to have a good voice.*
4. Elizabethan audiences were trained *to catch the words' exact meaning.*

**Student Activity 2.** Write four sentences using infinitives in a variety of ways.

**9 Enrichment** Shakespeare himself commented on the competitiveness in the acting profession in his day in the tragedy *Hamlet*. In Act II, Scene ii, Rosencrantz tells Hamlet that it is much more difficult for actors today because of a new fad—companies of child actors! Rosencrantz says, "But there is, sir, an eyrie of children . . . that cry out on the top of question and are most tyranically clapped for't."

**10 Critical Thinking and Reading** Throughout this historical essay, Chute seems to imply that acting today is much less demanding than it was in Elizabethan times. Compare and contrast the difficulties faced by modern and Elizabethan actors.

**11 Literary Focus** Explain the process of inference by which Chute arrives at her conclusion.

**Reader's Response** How do you think Chute's essay would differ if she were writing about contemporary actors and acting?

livery was made somewhat easier by the use of a heavily end-stopped line,[9] where the actor could draw his breath at regular intervals and proceed at a kind of jog-trot. But during the following decade this kind of writing became increasingly old-fashioned, giving way to an intricate and supple blank verse[10] that was much more difficult to handle intelligently; and no one was more instrumental in bringing the new way of writing into general use than Shakespeare himself.

Even with all the assistance given him by the old way of writing, with mechanical accenting and heavy use of rhyme, an Elizabethan actor had no easy time remembering his part. A repertory system[11] was used and no play was given two days in succession. The actor played a different part every night and he had no opportunity to settle into a comfortable routine while the lines of the part became second nature to him. He could expect very little help from the prompter, for that overworked individual was chiefly occupied in seeing that the actors came on in proper order, that they had their properties available and that the intricate stage arrangements that controlled the pulleys from the "heavens"[12] and the springs to the trap doors were worked with quick, accurate timing. These stage effects, which naturally had to be changed each afternoon for each new play, were extremely complicated. A single play in which Greene and Lodge[13] collaborated required the descent of a prophet and an angel let down on a throne, a woman blackened by a thunder stroke, sailors coming in wet from the sea, a serpent devouring

---

**9. end-stopped line:** Line of poetry read with a pause at the end.
**10. blank verse:** Unrhymed iambic pentameter (see Guide to Literary Terms).
**11. repertory system:** The alternate presentation of several plays by the same theater company.
**12. the "heavens":** A canopy above the stage.
**13. Greene and Lodge:** Robert Greene (1558–1592) and Thomas Lodge (1557–1625), English playwrights.

a vine, a hand with a burning sword emerging from a cloud and "Jonah the prophet cast out of the whale's belly upon the stage." Any production that had to wrestle with as many complications as this had no room for an actor who could not remember his lines.

Moreover, an actor who forgot his lines would not have lasted long in what was a highly competitive profession. There were more actors than there were parts for them, judging by the number of people who were listed as players in the parish registers.[14] Even the actor who had achieved the position of a sharer in one of the large London companies was not secure. Richard Jones, for instance, was the owner of costumes and properties and playbooks worth nearly forty pounds, which was an enormous sum in those days, and yet three years later he was working in the theater at whatever stray acting jobs he could get. "Sometimes I have a shilling a day and sometimes nothing," he told Edward Alleyn, asking for help in getting his suit and cloak out of pawn.

The usual solution for an actor who could not keep his place in the competitive London theater was to join one of the country companies, where the standards were less exacting, or to go abroad. English actors were extravagantly admired abroad and even a second-string company with poor equipment became the hit of the Frankfort[15] Fair, so that "both men and women flocked wonderfully" to see them. An actor like Shakespeare who maintained his position on the London stage for two decades could legitimately be praised, as Chettle praised him, for being "excellent in the quality he professes." If it had been otherwise, he would not have remained for long on the London stage.

---

**14. parish registers:** District records.
**15. Frankfort:** Frankfurt, Germany.

## THINKING ABOUT THE SELECTION

### Recalling

1. What "initial handicap" as an actor did Shakespeare have?
2. Identify three skills that an Elizabethan actor had to learn. Explain why each of these skills was important.
3. What evidence is there that Shakespeare had these skills?

### Interpreting

4. Basing your answer on this essay, what can you infer about the tastes of Elizabethan theater-goers?
5. What can you infer about Elizabethan life in general?

### Applying

6. Would you like to have lived during the Elizabethan Age? Explain.

## READING IN THE ARTS AND SCIENCES

### Understanding Historical Inference

**Historical inference** is the technique of arriving at reasonable conclusions about a person or time in history based on limited evidence. In "Shakespeare of London," for example, Chute infers that, during Elizabethan times, acting "was . . . highly competitive." One piece of evidence for this conclusion is the fact that many people were listed as actors in district records, "more actors than there were parts for them."

1. What conclusion does Chute reach about Shakespeare and other Elizabethan actors in the paragraph beginning, "Nearly all plays . . ."? (page 527)
2. What evidence does she give to support her inference?

## CRITICAL THINKING AND READING

### Evaluating Historical Inferences

You can evaluate an historical inference by asking yourself whether the evidence suggests other possible conclusions. Then you can decide which of these conclusions is the most reasonable. For instance, Chute infers that acting was competitive because so many actors were listed in district records. Another possible conclusion from this evidence is that the records were inaccurate and exaggerated the number of actors. However, in the absence of information about the inaccuracy of the records, Chute's conclusion seems correct.

Examine the following inferences from the essay and determine whether each is reasonable.
1. "The London theater was no place for physical weaklings. . . ." (page 529)
2. "John Shakespeare must have had a strong, well-made body. . . ." (page 529)

## UNDERSTANDING LANGUAGE

### Understanding Theater Terms

In this essay on Shakespeare and Elizabethan drama, Chute uses several theater terms. One such term is *prompter,* "a person who helps actors with their lines and performs various other tasks." Look up the following words and explain how each relates to the theater.
1. companies
2. production
3. characterization
4. cues

## THINKING AND WRITING

### Writing About Inference

Recall a time in your life when you had to make an inference, or educated guess, based on limited evidence. Briefly note the evidence that was available and the conclusion you reached. Then, using these notes, write an essay for your classmates describing this situation. Make sure that you explain in detail the way in which you evaluated the evidence and reached your conclusion. In revising check to see that you have told your readers whether your inference was correct. Share your essay with your classmates when you have finished.

*from Shakespeare of London   531*

531

**Putting It Together** The purpose
of this page is to review the major
elements of nonfiction and to
show how a writer uses them in
constructing a work of nonfiction.
Students should be able to use
the points outlined on this page
to "put together" the elements of
nonfiction.

The selection on the following pages, an excerpt from *In
Patagonia* by Bruce Chatwin, is a
model for "putting it together."
The notes in the side column
show how one reader might analyze the elements of this essay
and then put them together to
understand the work as a whole.

To give students further
practice with this process, use
the essay "On Excellence" by
Cynthia Ozick, in the Teaching
Portfolio on page 621, which students can annotate themselves.

# PUTTING IT TOGETHER

## Nonfiction

Nonfiction deals with actual people, places, things, and events. Some nonfiction reports facts and conveys information, and some expresses a writer's thoughts, beliefs, and feelings. If fiction refers to short stories and novels, then nonfiction refers to all prose literature except short stories and novels. A writer of nonfiction usually has a main purpose: to narrate, to describe, to explain, or to argue or persuade. With a main purpose in mind, the nonfiction writer will then use an assortment of literary techniques to achieve the main purpose.

**Purpose**

A writer may have both a general purpose and a specific purpose. If the main purpose is to narrate, for example, the writer may tell the story of his or her own life, or of someone else's life, or of an event. The specific purpose, however, may be to explain how or why incidents and events occurred as they did and the effect they had on the writer. Understanding a writer's purposes should be a main concern of every reader.

**Techniques**

Nonfiction writers achieve their purposes by means of two general kinds of techniques: organizational and stylistic. They are free to arrange the parts and paragraphs of their work so as to increase the effectiveness of their narration, description, explanation, or argumentation. They can also choose words, expressions, sentence structures, images, and so on, to achieve the greatest expressiveness.

**Support**

Nonfiction deals with thoughts and ideas that need to be supported, clarified, or illustrated. Therefore, the paragraphs or sections of a piece of nonfiction will consist largely of details, facts, reasons, incidents, and so on. A careful reader will try to understand the writer's purpose and then see why the supporting details have been included.

**Arrangement**

To further help a reader understand a work of nonfiction, a writer will arrange the material in chronological order, comparison-and-contrast order, cause-and-effect order, order of importance, or spatial order. Such an arrangement helps a reader to follow and grasp all the details that are presented.

The annotations that accompany the following selection will suggest how an active reader might read a work of nonfiction.

532   *Nonfiction*

# Butch Cassidy
## from *In Patagonia*
### Bruce Chatwin

Purpose: The title suggests that the author will be discussing Butch Cassidy and perhaps also his exploits in Patagonia. Will this be a narrative account? What will the specific purpose of this essay be?

He was a nice boy, a lively friendly-faced boy, who loved his Mormon family and the cabin in the cottonwoods. Both his parents came out from England as children and trekked the Plains, with Brigham Young's[1] handcart companies, from Iowa City to the Salt Lake. Anne Parker was a nervous and highly strung Scotswoman; her husband, Max, a simple soul, who had a hard time squeezing a living from the homestead and made a little extra in timber haulage.

The two-room cabin is still standing at Circleville, Utah. The corrals are there, and the paddock where Robert Leroy rode his first calf. The poplars he planted still line the irrigation ditch between the orchard and the sage. He was the oldest of eleven children, a boy of precise loyalties and a sense of fair play. He dreamed of being a cowboy and, in dime novels, read the ongoing saga of Jesse James.

At eighteen he identified as his natural enemies the cattle companies, the railroads and the banks, and convinced himself that right lay the wrong side of the law. One June morning in 1884, awkwardly and ashamed, he told his mother he was going to work in a mine at Telluride. She gave him her father's blue traveling blanket and a pot of blueberry preserves. He kissed his baby sister, Lula, crying in her cradle, and rode out of their lives. The truth came out when Max Parker returned to the homestead. His son had rustled some cattle with a young outlaw called Mike Cassidy. The law was after them both.

Bob Parker took the name Cassidy and rode into a new life of wide horizons and the scent of horse leather. (Butch was the name of a borrowed gun.) His apprentice years, the 1880's, were years of the Beef Bonanza; of Texas longhorns peppering the range; of cowboys "livin' the life of a buck nun" (one woman to ten men); of the Cattle Barons who paid mi-

---

1. **Brigham Young:** 1801–1877; United States Mormon leader.

*Butch Cassidy*  533

Technique: In this description, the author reveals information about Cassidy's family life and background, his home, and his upbringing.

Arrangement: The author jumps from when Cassidy was a boy to when he was eighteen years old and leaving home. It appears that the essay will be chronologically arranged.

Purpose: Here it is clear that the essay will focus on Cassidy's life.

Technique: The author summarizes the events of Cassidy's early years as an outlaw in a series of short phrases. This technique gives the impression of time passing quickly.

## Presentation

**Motivation/Prior Knowledge** Ask students to name famous historical figures about whom they would like to know more. Have them imagine that they have the opportunity to interview people who knew this person. What questions would they ask? Tell the class that Chatwin's travels to Argentina gave him the opportunity to delve into the life of the famous outlaw, Butch Cassidy.

**Purpose-Setting Question** What is Chatwin's attitude toward Butch Cassidy—sympathetic, condemning, or nonjudgmental?

**Enrichment** Patagonia is a section of Argentina in the southwestern part of South America.

**Discussion** What would you imagine Robert Leroy Parker's life in Circleville, Utah, to have been like?

**Enrichment** Jesse James was the leader of a band of bank and trains robbers. He was born in Clay County, Missouri, in 1847, and, like Butch Cassidy, grew up on a farm.

**Reading Strategy** Can you predict the effect the novels about Jesse James might have on young Robert Parker?

**Enrichment** Telluride is a mining town in Colorado.

**Literary Focus** What does the anecdote about how Butch Cassidy left home reveal about his character? What function does the anecdote serve with regard to plot?

**Discussion** How would you compare Cassidy's new life with his old life?

**Master Teacher Note** Ask students to name famous outlaws. (You might suggest Jesse James, Billy the Kid, Bonnie and Clyde.) Ask the class to conjecture why people who committed crimes such as robbery and murder would become romantic folk heroes. Why do we find such figures appealing?

**Thematic Idea** The narrator of "The Ballad of William Sycamore," on page 557, lived about the same time as Butch Cassidy. The poem offers a different perspective on life in the west. You may want to pair the two selections.

**Enrichment** With the completion of the Union Pacific and Central Pacific railroad lines in 1869 and the end of the Civil War came the period of the "cattle kingdom." Ranchers could drive their cattle to the railroads and ship them north.

**Critical Thinking and Reading** What does the author mean by saying that Cassidy's prison sentence "soured him to any further dealing with the law"?

**Enrichment** Mormons are members of the Church of Jesus Christ of Latter-day Saints. Some Mormons practiced polygamy as a religious principle during the mid-1800, but the church outlawed the practice in 1890 after the Supreme Court ruled it illegal.

**Discussion** Why does Chatwin say that today, Cassidy would be classed as a revolutionary? According to Chatwin's description, with what character in folklore could Cassidy be compared?

Technique: This quotation establishes the tone of the essay. The cowboy's dialect adds humor and authenticity.

Support: The first sentence in this paragraph gives a sense of who Cassidy was. The remainder of the paragraph supports the first sentence by explaining the effect Cassidy had on those around him and describing the activities he and other outlaws engaged in.

Technique: What can be inferred about Cassidy from this statement?

serly wages and dividends of 40 per cent to their shareholders; of champagne breakfasts at the Cheyenne Club and the English dukes who called their cowboys "cow-servants" and whose cowboys called them "dudes." There were plenty of Englishmen knocking round the West: one cowboy wrote to his Yankee employer: "That Inglishman yu lef in charge at the other ranch got to fresh and we had to kil him. Nothing much has hapened since yu lef . . ."

Then the great white winter of 1886–7 wiped out three-quarters of the stock. Greed combined with natural catastrophe to breed a new type, the cowboy-outlaw, men driven by unemployment and blacklisting into criminal hideouts and the rustling game. At Brown's Hole or Hole-in-the-Wall they joined up with professional desperadoes; men like Black Jack Ketchum, or the psychopath Harry Tracy, or Flat-Nose George Curry, or Harvey Logan, the diarist of his own murders.

Butch Cassidy, in those years, was drover, horse-wrangler, mavericker,[2] part-time bank-robber, and leader of men; the sheriffs feared him most for the last of these accomplishments. In 1894 they gave him two years in the Wyoming State Penitentiary for stealing a horse he hadn't stolen, valued at five dollars. The sentence soured him to any further dealing with the law. And, from 1896 to 1901, his Train Robbers' Syndicate, better known as The Wild Bunch, performed the string of perfect hold-ups that kept lawmen, Pinkerton detectives and the railroad in perpetual jitters. The stories of his antics are endless; breathless rides along the Outlaw Trail; shooting glass conductors from telegraph poles; or paying a poor widow's rent by robbing the rent man. The homesteaders loved him. Many were Mormons, outlawed themselves for polygamy.[3] They gave him food, shelter, alibis, and occasionally their daughters. Today, he would be classed as a revolutionary. But he had no sense of political organization.

Butch Cassidy never killed a man. Yet his friends were seasoned killers; their murders drove him to fits of remorse. He hated having to rely on the deadly aim of Harry Longabaugh, the Pennsylvania German with evil blue eyes and a foul temper. He tried to go straight, but there was too much on his

---

**2. mavericker** (mav′ ər ik ər) *n.*: A Texas rancher who did not brand his cattle.

**3. polygamy** (pə lig′ ə mē) *n.*: The state or practice of having two or more spouses at the same time.

## Grammar in Action

Writers rely on the **semicolon** to separate closely related independent clauses not joined by a coordinating conjunction such as *and, but, or, for.* While a period interrupts the flow of ideas and distances the connection between clauses, a semicolon shows the close relationship between two independent clauses. Examine, for example, the following sentence from "Butch Cassidy":

"Butch Cassidy, in those years, was drover, horsewrangler, mavericker, part-time bank-robber, and leader of men; the sheriffs feared him most for the last of these accomplishments."

By connecting the two independent clauses with a semicolon, Chatwin shows the close relationship between Cassidy's talent as a leader and the fear that he instilled in the sheriffs. If the author had chosen to use a period instead of a semicolon, the connection would not have been as strong. In addition, the period would have created too sharp a break in the narration.

A semicolon may also separate longer phrases in a series. The following sentence from the selection demonstrates this use of the semicolon:

Pinkerton card and his pleas for amnesty went unheard. Each new robbery spawned another and added years to his sentence. The costs of operating became unbearable. The story goes that the Wild Bunch frittered their hauls on women and the gaming table, but this is only half true. They had another, far greater expense: horseflesh.

The art of the hold-up depends on a quick getaway and Butch Cassidy's hold-ups depended on relays of fine thoroughbreds. His horse dealer was a man called Cleophas Dowd, the son of Irish immigrants to San Francisco, dedicated to the Jesuit priesthood, and forced as a boy to grovel to altar and confessional. Immediately after his ordination,[4] Dowd startled his parents and the Fathers by riding past on his new racehorse, a brace of six-shooters strapped over his cassock. That night, in Sausalito, he had the pleasure—a pleasure he had long savored—of giving last rites to the first man he shot. Dowd fled from California and settled at Sheep Creek Canyon, Utah, where he raised horses for outlaws. A Dowd horse was ready for sale when its rider could balance a gun between its ears and fire. The necessary speed he purchased from the Cavendish Stud at Nashville, Tennessee, and relayed the cost to his clients.

Technique: The author uses anecdotes to increase reader interest and to add a touch of humor.

Around 1900 law and order settled in on the last American frontier. The lawmen bought their own fine bloodstock, solved the problem of outpacing the outlaws, and organized crime hid in the cities. Posses flushed out Brown's Hole; the Pinkertons put mounted rangers in box cars, and Butch saw his friends die in saloon brawls, picked off by hired gunmen, or disappear behind bars. Some of the gang signed on in the U.S. Armed Forces and exported their talents to Cuba and the Philippines. But for him the choices were a stiff sentence—or Argentina.

Technique: Interrupting the last sentence with a dash emphasizes the last part of the sentence. This technique provides a transition to the remainder of the essay.

Word was out among the cowboys that the land of the gaucho[5] offered the lawless freedom of Wyoming in the 1870's. The artist-cowboy Will Rogers wrote: "They wanted North American riders for foremen over the natives. The natives was too slow." Butch believed he was safe from extradition[6] there, and his last two hold-ups were to raise funds for the journey.

---

**4. ordination** (ôr' d'n ā' shən) n.: The ceremony during which a person is admitted to the priesthood.

**5. gaucho** (gou' chō) n.: A South American cowboy.

**6. extradition** (eks' trə dish' ən) n.: Being turned over to stand trial in the United States where the crimes were committed.

---

**Enrichment** Allan Pinkerton (1819-1884) established one of the first detective agencies in the United States. After the Civil War, Pinkerton organized groups of armed men who were available for hire.

**Reading Strategy** Summarize Cassidy's reasons for going to Argentina.

**Enrichment** Will Rogers (1879-1935) was an American humorist and social critic. In 1902, Rogers went to seek adventure in Argentina, (two years after Cassidy), and then to South Africa to join Texas Jack's Wild West Show doing rope tricks. He returned to the U.S. in 1904 and began his career as a vaudeville humorist, gaining fame as "the cowboy philosopher."

**Critical Thinking and Reading** Compare the tone of the quotation from Will Rogers with Chatwin's tone in this selection. How are they similar?

---

The stories of his antics are endless: breathless rides along the Outlaw Trail; shooting glass conductors from telegraph poles; or paying a poor widow's rent by robbing the rent man.

**Student Activity 1.** Find one example in "Butch Cassidy" in which Chatwin uses a semicolon to join closely related independent clauses. Also find one example in which he uses a semicolon to separate phrases in a series.

**Student Activity 2.** Write a paragraph about a person whose life interests you. Use at least two sentences in which you use a semicolon to join closely related independent clauses or to separate phrases in a series.

Seated, left to right: *Harry Longabaugh (The Sundance Kid), Ben Kilpatrick (The Tall Texan), and Robert Leroy Parker (Butch Cassidy).* Standing: *Will Carver, Harvey Logan (Kid Curry).*

After the Winnemucca raid, the five ringleaders, in a mood of high spirits, had their group portrait taken in Fort Worth and sent a copy to the manager. (The photo is still in the office.)

In the fall of 1901 Butch met the Sundance Kid and his girl, Etta Place, in New York. She was young, beautiful and intelligent, and she kept her men to heel. Her Pinkerton card says she was a school teacher in Denver; one rumor has it she was the daughter of an English remittance man called George Capel, hence Place. Under the names of James Ryan and Mr. and Mrs. Harry A. Place, the "family of 3" went to operas and theaters. (The Sundance Kid was a keen Wagnerian.[7]) They bought Etta a gold watch at Tiffany's and sailed for Buenos Aires on S.S. *Soldier Prince.* On landing they stayed at the Hotel Europa, called on the Director of the Land Department, and secured 12,000 acres of rough camp in Chubut.

"Are there any bandits?" they asked. They were glad to hear there were none.

A few weeks later, Milton Roberts, the Welsh police commissioner from Esquel, found them under canvas at Cholila; their fine light thoroughbreds, already saddled up, struck him as rather odd. Butch, as we know from the letter, was alone the first winter. He stocked the farm with sheep bought from an English neighbor. The cabin, modeled on Circleville but bigger, was up by June.

In the following year, a Pinkerton detective, Frank Dimaio, tracked them to Cholila with the Winnemucca photograph, but was put off going to Patagonia by stories of snakes and jungles, perhaps invented for his benefit. The "family of 3" used Cholila as a base for five years without interference. They built a brick house and a country store (now owned by an Arab trader) and put "another North American" in charge.

The locals thought they were peaceable citizens. At Cholila I met the grandchildren of their neighbor, Señora Blanca de Gérez, who left this note when she died three years ago:

They were not good mixers, but whatever they did was correct. They often slept in our house. Ryan was more sociable than Place and joined in the festivities of the settlement. On the first visit of Governor Lezana, Place

---

7. **Wagnerian** (väg nir' ē ən) *adj.*: An admirer or follower of Richard Wagner's music and theories.

played the samba on his guitar and Ryan danced with the daughter of Don Ventura Solís. No one suspected they were criminals.

The Pinkerton Agency wrote to the Chief of Police in Buenos Aires: "It is only a question of time until these men commit some desperate robbery in the Argentine Republic." They were right. Apart from running low in funds, "the family of 3" were addicted to the art of the hold-up, without which life itself became a bore. Perhaps they were spurred on by the arrival of their friend Harvey Logan. In 1903 he had wormed his way out of jail in Knoxville, Tennessee, after all but throttling his warder with the coil of wire he kept hidden in his boot. He turned up in Patagonia under the name of Andrew Duffy, an alias he had already used in Montana.

In 1905 the reconstituted Wild Bunch broke out and robbed a bank in Southern Santa Cruz. They repeated the performance on the *Banco de la Nación* at Villa Mercedes in San Luis in the summer of 1907. It seems that Harvey Logan shot the manager through the head. Etta was there, dressed as a man—a fact obliquely confirmed by Blanca de Gérez: "The Señora cropped her hair short and wore a wig."

In December 1907 they sold Cholila, in a hurry, to a beef syndicate, and scattered into the Cordillera. None of their neighbors ever heard of them again. I have heard a number of reasons for their departure. But the most usual explanation is that Etta was bored, had a grumbling appendix and insisted on going to Denver for the operation. There is another possibility: that appendix was a euphemism for baby and that the father was a young Englishman, John Gardner, who was ranching in Patagonia for his health. The story goes that Harvey Logan had to get him out of the Kid's way, back to his family estate in Ireland.

Etta was apparently living in Denver in 1924. (Her daughter may have been a competitive girl called Betty Weaver, who pulled fifteen spectacular bank robberies before her arrest and jail-sentence at Belleplaine, Kansas, in 1932.) In the Ashley Valley in Utah, I met an old man, rocking on his porch, who remembered Butch Cassidy in 1908. But if they did come back that summer, the pace was too hot; for by December both outlaws were in Bolivia working for a man called Siebert at the Concordia tin mine.

Technique: The author deviates from the chronological order of the piece to finish the narrative of Etta Place.

*Butch Cassidy* 537

The classic account of their death, at San Vicente, Bolivia, in December 1909, following their theft of a mine payroll, was first set down in *Elk's Magazine* for 1930 by the Western poet, Arthur Chapman. It was an ideal scenario for the moviemakers; the brave cavalry captain shot while trying to arrest the gringos[8]; the mud-walled courtyard full of dead mules; the impossible odds; the Kid first wounded, then shot through the head by Butch, who, having now killed a man, reserves the last bullet for himself. The episode ends with the Bolivian soldiers finding Etta's Tiffany watch on one of the bodies.

No one knows where Chapman got the story: Butch Cassidy could have invented it himself. His aim, after all, was to "die" in South America and re-emerge under a new name. The shooting at San Vicente was investigated by the late President René Barrientos, Ché Guevara's killer, himself an ardent Western history buff. He put a team on to solving the mystery, grilled the villagers personally, exhumed corpses in the cemetery, checked the army and police files, and concluded that the whole thing was a fabrication. Nor did Pinkertons believe it. They have their own version, based on the skimpiest evidence, that the "family of 3" died together in a shoot-out with the Uruguayan police in 1911. Three years later they assumed Butch Cassidy dead—which, if he were alive, was exactly what he wanted.

"Bunkum!" his friends said when they heard the stories coming out of South America. Butch didn't go in for shoot-outs. And from 1915 on, hundreds of people saw—or thought they saw—him; running guns for Pancho Villa in Mexico; prospecting with Wyatt Earp in Alaska; touring the West in a Model T Ford; calling on old girlfriends (who remember him as gotten rather fat); or turning up at a Wild West Show in San Francisco.

I went to see the star witness to his return; his sister, Mrs. Lula Parker Betenson, a forthright and energetic woman in her nineties, with a lifetime of service to the Democratic Party. She has no doubts: her brother came back and ate blueberry pie with the family at Circleville in the fall of 1925. She believes he died of pneumonia in Washington State in the late 1930's. Another version puts his death in an Eastern city, a retired railroad engineer with two married daughters.

---

**8. gringos** (griŋ′ gōs) *n.:* In Latin America, a contemptuous term for a foreigner, especially an American or Englishman.

538    *Nonfiction*

**Bruce Chatwin** (1940–1989), who was born in England, traveled extensively. His travels took him all over the world, from Afghanistan to Argentina and Brazil. *In Patagonia*—Chatwin's most highly acclaimed travel book—is a South American quest story. The book revolves around the narrator's search for a giant sloth skin and his encounters with other people whose stories, such as this one about Butch Cassidy, delay his journey. His last travel book, *Songlines*, is a study of Australia's nomadic aborigines.

## THINKING ABOUT THE SELECTION

### Interpreting

1. What is the meaning of the statement that Cassidy "convinced himself that right lay the wrong side of the law"?
2. Why did the sheriffs fear Cassidy more for being a "leader of men" than for the crimes he committed?
3. Describe Cassidy's life in Argentina. How did it parallel his life in America?

### Applying

4. Cassidy and many other outlaws believed that "right lay the wrong side of the law." Why might they have adopted this philosophy? What happens when civilians take the law into their own hands?

## ANALYZING LITERATURE

### Understanding Anecdotes

An anecdote is a brief story about an interesting, amusing, or strange event. In "Butch Cassidy," Chatwin writes about the outlaw's life in Argentina and the events that led up to his arrival in the country. Chatwin effectively embellishes the account of Cassidy's life with anecdotes from many sources. These anecdotes are what give the reader a sense of who Butch Cassidy was.

1. Describe three anecdotes Chatwin uses to reveal the character of Butch Cassidy.
2. What does each anecdote illustrate?

## CRITICAL THINKING AND READING

### Appreciating Tone

A writer's style reflects the tone, or the writer's attitude toward a subject. The tone of a literary piece might be described as formal, informal, serious, playful, bitter, or ironic. *In Patagonia*, Chatwin's travel narrative, could have been written much like a travel brochure or a history textbook. Instead, he wrote in a humorous, informal tone that makes this book light and interesting to read.

1. Compare and contrast the tone of Chatwin's essay with that of another essay in the unit.
2. List two passages in which Chatwin conveys a light, humorous touch. Is the humor appropriate? Why or why not? What effect do these passages have on the reader?

## THINKING AND WRITING

### Writing a Travel Narrative

Think of a specific incident that occurred during one of your travels. The incident could have occurred during a vacation, an excursion to a new part of your hometown, a field trip, and so on. Then think of several anecdotes, or brief stories, that relate an interesting, amusing, or strange event that led up to, followed, or occurred during the incident you chose. These anecdotes should either entertain, make a point, or tell more about you or someone else who was involved in the incident.

*Butch Cassidy* 539

**FOCUS ON READING**
*Reading Diagrams, Graphs,
and Statistical Information*

# FOCUS ON READING

# Reading Diagrams, Graphs, and Statistical Information

When you read nonfiction, you often encounter diagrams, graphs, and statistical information. Each provides a visual representation of information.

**Diagrams**

A diagram is a drawing that explains a thing by outlining its parts and their relationships. For example, imagine that a writer wants to describe playing street games when she was a child. One common street game is hopscotch. A diagram for a hopscotch game would look like this:

**Activity**

Think of a game you played when you were a child. Prepare a diagram that explains this game.

**Activity**

Many scientific articles contain diagrams. Thumb through a newspaper or article in a science magazine to find a diagram—perhaps of the space shuttle or of the human circulatory system. Bring it into class. Explain to your classmates what information the diagram reveals.

**Graphs**

A graph is a special kind of diagram. Usually it is prepared on a grid, a framework of horizontal and vertical bars. Line graphs present their information with lines drawn against this grid, bar graphs with bars. For example, if a researcher wanted to show the number of people who have claimed to have sighted the Loch Ness monster over the course of a year, his graph might look like this.

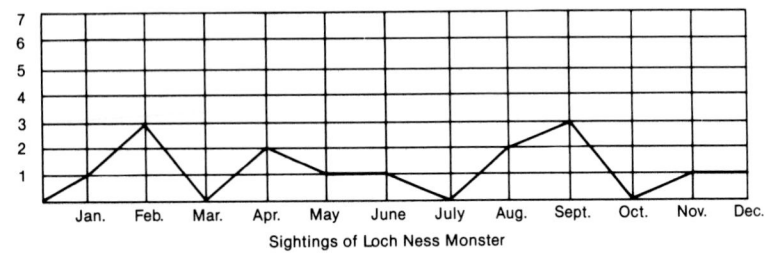

Sightings of Loch Ness Monster

**Activity**

Imagine that like James Thurber you wanted to show the widespread use of an expression like "*you* know." Over the course of a week, keep track of how many times you hear this expression. Prepare a line graph showing your findings. Share your graph and report your findings to your classmates.

**Statistical Information**

Statistical information consists of facts or data presented in tabular form. For example, after preparing a graph of the number of sightings of the Loch Ness monster, a researcher might arrange the information in tabular form as follows. The researcher might further arrange the information to show the number of sightings during the day and the number at night. The table clearly shows that more sightings occur during the night than during the day.

| 1988 | Day | Night | Total |
|------|-----|-------|-------|
| Jan. | 0 | 1 | 1 |
| Feb. | 1 | 2 | 3 |
| Mar. | 0 | 0 | 0 |
| Apr. | 1 | 1 | 2 |
| May | 0 | 1 | 1 |
| June | 0 | 1 | 1 |
| July | 0 | 0 | 0 |
| Aug. | 0 | 2 | 2 |
| Sept. | 1 | 3 | 4 |
| Oct. | 0 | 0 | 0 |
| Nov. | 0 | 1 | 1 |
| Dec. | 0 | 1 | 1 |
| Total | 3 | 13 | 16 |

**Activity**

Present the information shown in your graph in tabular form. Arrange your table to show how many occurrences happen at home and how many in school. Have a third category labeled miscellaneous for occurrences that take place neither at home nor at school.

*Answers to the Activity*
You might wish to post the graphs after asking the students to write a brief paragraph explaining what they were researching and how they interpreted their findings.

*Answers to the Activity*
If you chose to have students' graphs posted, you might also include the tabular form.

## YOU THE WRITER

**Assignment**

**1.** Write an autobiographical account that relates a memorable experience you have had and also conveys a strong sense of yourself.

**Prewriting.** Brainstorm about different events or periods of your life. Concentrate on one that would make an interesting story. Make sure it is one that will reveal definite traits and attitudes.

**Writing.** Begin your autobiography by stating clearly what the event or period of your life was. Describe what happened, using specific details. Focus on one or two dominant personality traits, but include any others that are relevant to the event. Finally, state any conclusions you have formed about this time of your life.

**Revising.** In reading over your personal account, replace some of the passive verbs with more active ones. Could more colorful or descriptive adjectives and adverbs help to make your account more interesting?

**Assignment**

**2.** Essays are often used to persuade someone to believe in a specific point of view. Write a persuasive essay that defends a viewpoint.

**Prewriting.** Choose an issue, question, or topic you know well and have a strong feeling about. This may be a social issue such as world hunger or drunk driving, or a more private topic such as why you feel strongly for or against a local curfew. List details about your topic.

**Writing.** Begin your essay with a strong thesis statement. Use your first paragraph to define clearly what the issue is, then use the next paragraphs to list the details, facts, examples, and historical data that support your statement. Sum up your strongest points in a solid, concluding paragraph.

**Revising.** Revise your essay carefully for any problems in the development or organization of your ideas.

**Assignment**

**3.** Biographies provide interesting information about people we perhaps would not otherwise know about. Write a biographical sketch.

**Prewriting.** Gather as much information about the person as you can. Make notes as you research. Prepare an outline.

**Writing.** Begin writing your profile by introducing your subject. Focus on one or two dominant traits and support these throughout the profile. Continue your profile with background facts that influenced the shaping of his or her character. Conclude with an anecdote that expresses what he or she is like.

**Revising.** Check your profile for accurate descriptions and interpretations of the person you have chosen to write about.

### YOU THE WRITER
#### Guidelines for Evaluating Assignment 1

1. Has the student written an autobiographical account of a memorable experience, which reveals the student's traits?
2. Does the autobiographical account indicate the event or period of the writer's life?
3. Has the student described the event with specific details?
4. Has the student revealed conclusions formed during this period or as a result of this event?
5. Has the student used active voice verbs, and is the account free from grammar, usage, and mechanics errors?

#### Guidelines for Evaluating Assignment 2

1. Has the student clearly stated the issue and included a thesis statement in the first paragraph?
2. Has the student supported the thesis statement with details, facts, examples, or historical data in the body paragraphs?
3. Has the student summarized the persuasive points in a concluding paragraph?
4. Is the essay free from grammar, usage, and mechanics errors?

#### Guidelines for Evaluating Assignment 3

1. Has the student written a profile of the subject that focuses on one or two dominant traits?
2. Has the student included background facts that illustrate the subject's character?
3. Has the student concluded with an anecdote?
4. Is the essay free from grammar, usage, and mechanics errors?

# YOU THE CRITIC

**Assignment**

1. Write a review of a biography or autobiography you have read, analyzing the presentation of the subject's life and expressing what you learned from the book.

**Prewriting.** Narrow your focus by concentrating on the subject of the book. Outline the chronological events of his/her life.

**Writing.** Begin your critical evaluation by writing a thesis statement. Then develop a brief personality profile of the subject. Evaluate the author's portrayal of the subject's life.

**Revising.** Check your review carefully for any weak, unsubstantiated statements. Do not simply say you felt "this or that" without providing specific details to support your opinion.

**Assignment**

2. A précis is a synopsis or summary of a piece of writing, usually an essay, article, or chapter of a book. Write a précis of one of the essays in the section "Essays in the Arts and Sciences."

**Prewriting.** Carefully read the essay you have chosen. Take notes or make an outline of the main ideas and major details.

**Writing.** As you write, use your notes to form the basis of your work. Use language that captures the tone of the original.

**Revising.** As you revise, check your précis for length. It should never be too long to be used as a tool for evaluation.

**Assignment**

3. As you read nonfiction, you must always remember that, though it is based on facts, these facts can be challenged. Write a critical evaluation of an essay to determine whether it contains author bias or any misrepresentation of facts.

**Prewriting.** After choosing your article, break down the facts it presents into the following categories: *who, what, where, when, why* and *how*. List any questions you have concerning any of the facts.

**Writing.** Begin writing your evaluation of the article by briefly summarizing it. State what you feel are the author's strong points. These are what you have determined to be valid statements. Show how the author made these points, using direct quotes. Point out what you feel might be author bias. Summarize the strong and weak points of the article and your own feelings about it.

**Revising.** Read over your material to make sure you have not made any hasty generalizations yourself. If the author gives any references, try to verify some of them. Are the quotes correct? Use clear, logical arguments to support your opinions and to refute those of the author.

---

## YOU THE CRITIC

### Guidelines for Evaluating Assignment 1

1. Has the student begun the review with a thesis statement?
2. Does the review develop a personality profile of the subject?
3. Does the student support all opinions offered in the review?
4. Is the review free from grammar, usage, and mechanics errors?

### Guidelines for Evaluating Assignment 2

1. Has the student written a précis of one of the essays in the Arts and Sciences?
2. Does the student's précis capture the tone of the original essay?
3. Is the précis free from grammar, usage, and mechanics errors?

### Guidelines for Evaluating Assignment 3

1. Does the student's evaluation begin with a brief summary?
2. Has the student stated the author's strong points, and supported them with quotations from the essay?
3. Has the student identified any examples of author bias?
4. Has the student supported his or her points with logical arguments?
5. Is the essay free from grammar, usage, and mechanics errors?

## Humanities Note

Fine art, *Mist Fantasy*, J.E.H. MacDonald. James Edward Harvey MacDonald (1873-1932), a Canadian painter and illustrator, was an important member of the band of Canadian nationalist artists known as the "Group of Seven." Their aim was to capture the magnificence of the landscape of their country on canvas. Their works, modern in approach, were considered radical and brought about far-reaching changes in Canadian art.

The Canadian countryside provided endless subjects for MacDonald to paint. *Mist Fantasy* is painted in thick, pure color. The simplified shapes of the boats riding on the reflective surface of the water, beneath the swirling mist, is bold and evocative, suggesting a poetic image. This is J.E.H. MacDonald's rugged version of Impressionism. He sought to express the power and raw beauty of his country in terms that could not be confused with the art of any other country on earth.

**MIST FANTASY**
*J.E.H. MacDonald*
*Art Gallery of Ontario, Toronto*

*544   Poetry*

# POETRY

"If I read a book," wrote the poet Emily Dickinson, "and it makes my whole body so cold no fire can ever warm me, I know that is poetry. If I feel physically as if the top of my head were taken off, I know that is poetry."

Poetry is a highly charged form of literature in which every word is packed with meaning. It has a musical quality that may be achieved through the use of rhythm and rhyme or through repetition. A poem is written in lines, which do not always signal the end of sentences, and the lines are arranged in stanzas.

There are several types of poetry. Narrative poetry tells a story, while dramatic poetry is poetry in which one or more characters speak. Lyric poetry expresses a strong emotional response toward its subject.

In this unit you will encounter poems on a variety of subjects and in a variety of forms. You will also develop strategies for gaining the fullest appreciation of each poem.

545

Because poetry is more musical than prose, it is important to read it slowly and to read it several times—aloud as well as silently. You might tell students that the sound of a poem—its music—often reinforces its meaning. A poem like "The Charge of the Light Brigade," for example, has a galloping rhythm, which emphasizes the action in the poem.

You might also emphasize the strategy of paraphrasing. Students are sometimes intimidated by poetry. If they can put a poem into their own words, they will feel more comfortable with it. Caution them, however, that a paraphrase is not a substitute for a poem. A paraphrase can be useful in understanding meaning, but it ignores the poem's music.

After discussing these strategies with students, turn to the poem, "Sympathy," on the next page. It is a model for active reading. The annotations show how an active reader might construct meaning from this poem.

Ask students to pay attention to these annotations as they read. Suggest that they also add their own comments and responses as they read.

For further practice with this process, use the poem on page 652 of the Teaching Portfolio, "Your World," which students can annotate themselves.

# READING ACTIVELY

## Poetry

The poet Walt Whitman has written, "To have great poetry, there must be great audiences, too." What does this mean? It means that to gain the most from poetry, you must approach each poem as an active reader.

The following strategies will help you read poetry actively.

**Question**

An active reader becomes involved. Ask questions as you read. If the poem tells a story, ask questions about the characters and events. If the poem relates strong feelings, ask questions about what is evoking these feelings. Stop to think about the use of language and imagery. What does the language make you see and feel?

**Clarify**

Most poetry is written economically, which means that each word packs a lot of meaning. Take time to clarify the meaning of words. Monitor your reading by checking the answers to your questions.

**Listen**

Poetry has a musical quality. To fully appreciate it, listen to the music of the words. What effect is created by musical devices such as rhythm, rhyme, and repetition.

**Summarize**

Narrative poems tell a story. If the poem you are reading relates events, stop at appropriate points to summarize.

**Paraphrase**

Put the poem in your own words. By doing this, you will make its meaning clear.

**Pull It Together**

The poet Robert Frost has written, "A poem begins in delight but ends in wisdom." Start reading the poem by reacting to it with your emotions; but at the end, pull the details together and find what the poem has to say to you.

On the facing page is a poem with annotations in the side column showing how an active reader might read it.

**Objectives**
1  To learn to read poetry actively
2  To understand symbols
3  To understand shades of difference
4  To write an extended definition

**Support Material**

**Teaching Portfolio**
Teacher Backup, p. 649
Reading Actively, "Your World," by Georgia Douglas Johnson, p. 652
Usage and Mechanics Worksheet, p. 653
Analyzing Literature Worksheet, *Understanding Symbols,* p. 654
Language Worksheet, *Under-* *standing Shades of Difference,* p. 655
Selection Test, p. 656

# Sympathy
## Paul Laurence Dunbar

I know what the caged bird feels, alas!
    When the sun is bright on the upland slopes;
When the wind stirs soft through the springing grass,
And the river flows like a stream of glass;
5    When the first bird sings and the first bud opes,
And the faint perfume from its chalice[1] steals—
I know what the caged bird feels!

I know why the caged bird beats his wing
    Till its blood is red on the cruel bars;
10 For he must fly back to his perch and cling
When he fain[2] would be on the bough a-swing;
    And a pain still throbs in the old, old scars
And they pulse again with a keener sting—
I know why he beats his wing!

15 I know why the caged bird sings, ah me,
    When his wing is bruised and his bosom sore,—
When he beats his bars and he would be free;
It is not a carol of joy or glee,
    But a prayer that he sends from his heart's deep core,
20 But a plea, that upward to Heaven he flings—
I know why the caged bird sings!

---

**1. chalice** (chăl′ is) *n.*: A cup or goblet; here, the cup-shaped part of a budding flower.
**2. fain** (fān) *adv.*: Gladly; eagerly.

**Paul Laurence Dunbar** (1872–1906) was born in Dayton, Ohio, the son of former slaves who had been freed before the outbreak of the Civil War. He was the first black writer to support himself entirely through his writing. He wrote poems, short stories, and novels. In "Sympathy," Dunbar expresses the frustration of not being free.

---

**Question:** Why does the poet call the poem "Sympathy"? What does the title suggest about the theme?

**Question:** Is the poet simply expressing sympathy for the caged bird or does the caged bird seem to stand for something larger than itself?

**Clarify:** The poet gives to the bird emotions that are more likely to be felt by human beings. It seems that the caged bird represents human beings that have been trapped in some way.

**Listen:** Hear the rhyme pattern. Notice that the poet emphasizes the last two lines in each stanza by having them rhyme.

**Paraphrase:** The caged bird's song is a plea for freedom.

**Pulling It Together:** The poet sees human beings who are trapped by circumstances as caged birds—bruised and sore, and crying for freedom.

---

---

## Closure and Extension

*(Questions begin on p. 548)*

### ANSWERS TO THINKING ABOUT THE SELECTION
*Recalling*

1. The speaker identifies with the bird in these five situations: "When the sun is bright on the upland slopes," "When the wind stirs soft through the springing grass," when "the river flows like a stream of glass," "When the first bird sings and the first bud" opens, and when "the perfume from the bud is released."

2. The bird beats its wings on the cage because it wants desperately to be free but is imprisoned in its cage.

3. The caged bird's song is a prayer or plea for freedom.

## Interpreting

4. Suggested Response: The poet describes the beauty of life by depicting scenes of spring. The bird, however, trapped in its cage, is unable to experience this beauty.
5. Suggested Response: The "old, old scars" refer to the bird's previous injuries from attempts to escape. For the speaker, the scars refer to past injustices and slavery. Time has neither erased nor soothed the pain of these memories, and the speaker remembers them with increased emotion.
6. Answers will differ. Most students will realize that the speaker feels sympathy with the bird because they have both experienced similar emotions as a result of their lack of freedom.

## Applying

7. Answers will differ. Students may respond that a feeling of frustration comes from wanting something you cannot have. Seeing others that are free gives the bird and the speaker a vision of what they want and cannot have.

## ANSWERS TO ANALYZING LITERATURE

1. Suggested Response: The cage represents restrictions in life. Often social, political, and economic conditions result in such restrictions and constraints.
2. Suggested Response: The woodland scenes represent the beauty of life. We are surrounded by life's gifts and joys but if we are not free to enjoy them we can only feel frustrated, not blessed.
3. Suggested Response: The bird represents people who encounter restrictions. Social, political, and economic constraints deprive people of their freedom, and are like the bars of a cage.
4. Answers will differ. Many students may respond that life offers many exciting possibilities, but people must be free to pursue and enjoy

## THINKING ABOUT THE SELECTION

### Recalling

1. In the first stanza, the speaker identifies with, or knows, how the caged bird feels, in what five situations?
2. In the second stanza, why does the caged bird beat his wings?
3. In the last stanza, why does the caged bird sing?

### Interpreting

4. In the first stanza, compare the circumstances of the bird with the situations the poet describes.
5. In the second stanza, what do you think are the "old, old scars"? Why do they "pulse again with a keener sting"?
6. Why does the poet call this poem "Sympathy"?

### Applying

7. Do you think the caged bird's frustration is greater because it sees creatures that aren't caged? Explain your answer.

## ANALYZING LITERATURE

### Understanding Symbols

A **symbol** is something that has its own meaning but that also represents something else. For example, an oak tree is a thing in itself, but it can also serve as a symbol of strength and endurance.

1. What do you think the cage represents? Explain your answer.
2. What do you think the woodland scenes represent? Explain your answer.
3. What do you think the bird represents? Explain your answer.
4. Keeping these symbols in mind, what insight into life do you think the poem provides?

## UNDERSTANDING LANGUAGE

### Understanding Shades of Difference

Words may be synonyms, but mean slightly different things. For example, consider the words *plead, appeal,* and *pray. Plead* suggests the making of an urgent request that is based on reasoning while *appeal* suggests a request based on moral values. *Pray* suggests a request directed toward God or a higher authority.

1. Use your dictionary to help you explain the difference between the words *sympathy, pity,* and *compassion.*
2. Would the title "Pity" or "Compassion" have been appropriate for this poem? Explain your answer.

## THINKING AND WRITING

### Writing an Extended Definition

An extended definition both provides the meaning of a word and describes its distinguishing characteristics. Some abstract words require more than a simple dictionary definition. For example, think about the word *sympathy.* First jot down the dictionary definition of the word. Then freewrite about what the word means to you. Explore your thoughts about what sympathy is and is *not,* why it is important, and how you can recognize it. Then write the first draft of an extended definition. Start by defining the word as a dictionary would. Then use the ideas in your freewriting to expand on your definition by describing the word, or getting at the heart of its meaning. When you revise your definition, make sure you have included enough details to make its meaning clear. Proofread your definition and compare it with the definitions of your classmates.

them or they feel as frustrated as a caged bird.

## ANSWERS TO UNDERSTANDING LANGUAGE

1. Suggested Response: *Pity* is a feeling of grief aroused by the misfortunes of others. *Sympathy* implies an experiencing of the same feelings as the one pitied. *Compassion* adds a feeling of tenderness to the expression of pity.

2. Suggested Response: No. The point of the poem is to express how the speaker is experiencing the same feelings as the caged bird. Only the word *sympathy* provides this meaning. *Compassion* would have implied a superiority on the part of the speaker.

**Challenge** The speaker in the poem feels sympathy for the caged bird because the speaker has had similar emotions. Identify

other situations with which a person might feel sympathy.

### THINKING AND WRITING

For help with this assignment, students may consult Lesson 2, "Drafting and Revising," in the Handbook of Writing About Literature.

### Publishing Student Writing

Have students collect their extended definitions in a class "writer's handbook."

# Narrative Poetry

**BUFFALO CHASE**
*George Catlin*
*Smithsonian Institution*

**Humanities Note**

Fine art, *Buffalo Chase*, George Catlin. George Catlin (1796-1872), a self-taught American painter and anthropologist, enjoyed some success in Philadelphia as a portraitist. Seeing a traveling "Wild West" show convinced him to leave the settled East and pursue his life-long interest in recording the features, customs, and dwellings of Native Americans. He is one of the foremost painters of Native American tribes.

Catlin's epic journey through the West to paint the various tribes necessitated concessions in equipment to portability. His paints were premixed in large batches, which gives his paintings a uniform color quality. The canvases themselves were painted ahead with general landscape backgrounds upon which he could superimpose details and action scenes from Native American life. These backgrounds, usually of rolling green hills, at times create a strangely unrealistic effect in some of his scenes.

This type of background can be seen in *Buffalo Chase*; however, in this case, it becomes subordinate to the action of the painting. Done in characteristic rapid, sketchy brushwork, this scene has a brisk immediacy that suits the subject.

## Casey at the Bat

**Ernest Lawrence Thayer** (1863–1940) was born in California. He worked there and in New York as a newspaper writer and often published his poems in the newspapers on which he worked. Today, Thayer is remembered best for one work, "Casey at the Bat." This humorous poem grew out of his love of baseball, with its style at least partly reflecting Thayer's work as a reporter. In fact, you could almost read it as a sports story in verse. "Casey at the Bat" was popularized by a comedian, De Wolf Hopper, who recited it in theaters.

**Narrative Poetry**

**Narrative poetry** is poetry that tells a story. Like a short story, a narrative poem has a plot, characters, a setting, and a theme. Unlike a short story, it is written in verse, language with a definite rhythm, or "beat." In many, but not all narrative poems, the verses rhyme. Narrative poems, like other kinds of poetry, are often divided into stanzas, or groups of lines that form a unit, rather like paragraphs in prose. The stanzas of a poem usually have the same number of lines and the same rhyme pattern.

**Look For**

In baseball it's three strikes and you're out. As you read this poem, look for what happens when Casey comes up to bat.

**Writing**

Imagine that it is the second half of the ninth inning of a baseball game. The home team is losing by two runs. The players representing the tying runs are on base. The team's best hitter comes to bat with two men out. Use your imagination and freewrite about what happens in this situation, indicating how the game ends and the reaction of the fans.

**Vocabulary**

Knowing the following words will help you as you read "Casey at the Bat."

**pallor** (pal′ ər) *n.*: Paleness (p. 551)

**wreathed** (rētﬣd) *v.*: Curled around (p. 551)

**writhing** (rītﬣ′ iŋ) *v.*: Twisting, turning (p. 553)

**tumult** (too′ məlt) *n.*: Noisy commotion (p. 553)

**Objectives**

1 To enjoy narrative poetry
2 To paraphrase poetry
3 To recognize jargon
4 To write narrative verse

**Support Material**

**Teaching Portfolio**
Teacher Backup, p. 659
Usage and Mechanics Worksheet, p. 662
Vocabulary Check, p. 663
Critical Thinking and Reading Worksheet, *Paraphrasing Poetry*, p. 664

Language Worksheet, *Recognizing Jargon*, p. 665
Selection Test, p. 666

# Casey at the Bat

**Ernest Lawrence Thayer**

1
It looked extremely rocky for the Mudville nine that day;
The score stood two to four, with but an inning left to play.
So, when Cooney died at second, and Burrows did the
    same,
A pallor wreathed the features of the patrons of the game.

2
5    A straggling few got up to go, leaving there the rest,
With that hope which springs eternal within the human
    breast.
For they thought: "If only Casey could get a whack at that,"
They'd put even money now, with Casey at the bat.
But Flynn preceded Casey, and likewise so did Blake,
10  And the former was a pudd'n, and the latter was a fake.
So on that stricken multitude a deathlike silence sat;
For there seemed but little chance of Casey's getting to the
    bat.

3
But Flynn let drive a "single," to the wonderment of all.
And the much-despised Blakey "tore the cover off the ball."
15  And when the dust had lifted, and they saw what had
    occurred,
There was Blakey safe at second, and Flynn a-huggin' third.

Then from the gladdened multitude went up a joyous yell—
It rumbled in the mountaintops, it rattled in the dell;[1]
It struck upon the hillside and rebounded on the flat;
20  For Casey, mighty Casey, was advancing to the bat.

There was ease in Casey's manner as he stepped into his
    place,
There was pride in Casey's bearing and a smile on Casey's
    face;
And when responding to the cheers he lightly doffed[2] his
    hat,
No stranger in the crowd could doubt 'twas Casey at the
    bat.

---

**1. dell** (del) *n*.: Small, secluded valley.
**2. doffed** (däft) *v*.: Lifted.

**Motivation/Prior Knowledge**
Ask students to recall a sports event in which their team had a good chance to win, but lost. Have them describe their emotions at the time they still had a chance to win. What were their feelings at the end of the game?

**Master Teacher Note** To involve students in this poem, you might want to read the poem aloud, play a recording of the poem, or ask a talented student to read it to the class. Ask students to bring in a clipping from a sports magazine or newspaper about a difficult defeat for an athlete or team.

**Purpose-Setting Question**
What can you infer about Casey's character from this poem?

1 **Discussion** What must the Mudville team do to win at this point?

2 **Discussion** What does this well-known phrase mean?

3 **Discussion** Why are these events surprising?

**BASEBALL PLAYERS PRACTICING, 1875**
*Thomas Eakins*
Museum of Art, Rhode Island School of Design

25 Ten thousand eyes were on him as he rubbed his hands
        with dirt,
     Five thousand tongues applauded when he wiped them on
        his shirt;
     Then when the writhing pitcher ground the ball into his
        hip,
     Defiance glanced in Casey's eye, a sneer curled Casey's lip.

     And now the leather-covered sphere came hurtling through
        the air,
30 And Casey stood a-watching it in haughty grandeur there.
     Close by the sturdy batsman the ball unheeded sped;
     "That ain't my style," said Casey. "Strike one," the umpire
        said.

     From the benches, black with people, there went up a
        muffled roar,
     Like the beating of the storm waves on the stern and
        distant shore.
35 "Kill him! kill the umpire!" shouted someone on the stand;
     And it's likely they'd have killed him had not Casey raised
        his hand.

     With a smile of Christian charity great Casey's visage[3]
        shone;
     He stilled the rising tumult, he made the game go on;
     He signaled to the pitcher, and once more the spheroid
        flew;
40 But Casey still ignored it, and the umpire said, "Strike
        two."

     "Fraud!" cried the maddened thousands, and the echo
        answered "Fraud!"
     But one scornful look from Casey and the audience was
        awed;
     They saw his face grow stern and cold, they saw his
        muscles strain,
     And they knew that Casey wouldn't let the ball go by again.

_____

**3. visage** (viz′ ij) *n.*: Face.

*Casey at the Bat*   553

4 **Critical Thinking and Reading**
What can you infer about Casey's
past performance?

5 **Discussion** How does the crowd
feel about Casey? What evidence
is there of Casey's power over the
crowd?

6 **Reading Strategy** Ask students
to predict what will happen next.

**Literary Focus** Narrative poems rely on suspense just as stories or novels do. How does the poet heighten the suspense in the final stanza?

**Reader's Response** How did your reactions change as you read the poem? Explain.

45　The sneer is gone from Casey's lips, his teeth are clenched
　　　in hate,
　　He pounds with cruel vengeance his bat upon the plate;
　　And now the pitcher holds the ball, and now he lets it go,
　　And now the air is shattered by the force of Casey's blow.

　　Oh, somewhere in this favored land the sun is shining
　　　bright,
50　The band is playing somewhere, and somewhere hearts are
　　　light;
7　And somewhere men are laughing, and somewhere children
　　　shout,
　　But there is no joy in Mudville: Mighty Casey has struck
　　　out.

## Closure and Extension

### ANSWERS TO THINKING ABOUT THE SELECTION
*Recalling*

1. Flynn hits a single. Blake then hits a double, and Flynn advances to third base.
2. When Casey comes to bat, the crowd gives out a joyous yell that reverberates over the surrounding landscape. After the first strike, the crowd roars angrily; after the second strike, the crowd cries, "Fraud!"
3. Casey strikes out and the Mudville team loses, four to two.

*Interpreting*

4. Suggested Response: Casey is proud, defiant, and overconfident.
5. Answers will differ, but most students will realize that the tone is personal and involved and the

## THINKING ABOUT THE SELECTION

### Recalling

1. What do Flynn and Blake do when they bat?
2. Describe the crowd's response to Casey's coming up to bat. How does the crowd respond after each of the first two pitches to him?
3. How does the game conclude?

### Interpreting

4. Describe Casey's personality.
5. Describe the tone and style of the poem. How is it different from a typical sports report in a newspaper?
6. Explain how the poet heightens suspense in this poem.

### Applying

7. Why do you think baseball has become our national pastime? What is it about the game that captures our imagination?

## ANALYZING LITERATURE

### Enjoying Narrative Poetry

A **narrative poem** offers two kinds of pleasure, the pleasure of a story and the pleasure of poetry. To get the most out of a narrative poem, you might have to read it over more than once to make sure you understand what all the lines mean and what all the words and phrases suggest. You also need to read with attention to the rhythm and rhyme.

1. What do you think is the chief source of pleasure in the poem, the suspenseful story or the rhythm, rhyme, and colorful language? Explain your answer.
2. If this narrative poem were retold as a typical realistic short story, what kinds of details would probably be added to it?

## CRITICAL THINKING AND READING

### Paraphrasing Poetry

A **paraphrase** is a restatement of a poem in the reader's own words. Paraphrasing is the best way to clarify passages that are hard to understand because of unfamiliar words, unusual sentence structure, or other difficulties presented by poetical language. The following is a paraphrase of the first stanza: The Mudville team's situation was bad. They were losing 4–2 in the ninth inning. When two of their baserunners were called out at second base, their fans became pale with gloom.

Paraphrase stanzas 5, 8, 9, and 10.

## UNDERSTANDING LANGUAGE

### Recognizing Jargon

**Jargon** is the special words and phrasing used by people who do the same work, share the same interests, and so on. It is very common in sports writing and broadcasts, often adding color to a sports story. For example, the phrase *the hot corner* is baseball jargon meaning "third base" as a fielding position.

1. What does the jargon "died at second" mean?
2. What does the jargon "tore the cover off the ball" mean?
3. Point out any other examples of jargon you see in the poem.
4. Brainstorm with your classmates to form a list of colorful baseball jargon.

## THINKING AND WRITING

### Writing Narrative Verse

Use the freewriting you did before reading "Casey at the Bat" to write a stanza or two that presents your own ending to the poem. You may change Thayer's ending if you wish, or you may add to it. (For example, you might want to describe Casey after he has struck out.) Follow Thayer's stanza pattern: four lines, with six or seven "beats" per line and rhymes in the pattern *day/play, same/game*. When you revise, try to make your verses sound as much as possible like those in the poem. Proofread your ending and share it with your classmates.

(Answers begin on p. 554.)

Stanza 8: Casey watched the first pitch go by because it was not the pitch he wanted. The umpire called a strike.

Stanza 9: When the crowd roared, "Kill the umpire!," Casey raised his hand to quiet them.

Stanza 10: After quieting the crowd, Casey had the game continue. Casey let the second pitch go by without attempting to hit it, and the umpire called a second strike on him.

### ANSWERS TO UNDERSTANDING LANGUAGE

1. The runner was called out at second base.
2. The batter hit the ball so hard he almost tore its cover off.
3. Suggested Response: Examples of jargon include "get a whack at that," "put even money," and "Flynn a-huggin' third."
4. Answers will vary, but the list might include such phrases as "the batter is in a slump," "the pitcher is in a hole," and "the fielder was under it for the out."

### THINKING AND WRITING

For help with this assignment, students may refer to Lesson 18, "Writing A Poem," in the Handbook of Writing About Literature.

**Publishing Student Writing**
Ask students to read a part of "Casey at the Bat" aloud to the class and insert their new stanza(s) at the proper place.

**Challenge** The poem was written from a third person point of view. Ask students to describe what the poem would be like if Casey had narrated it himself.

**Writing Across the Curriculum**
Invite a physical education teacher or coach to be interviewed by the class on the manager's view of preparing for a big game. Students may want to write up the interview as a feature story for the school newspaper.

---

style humorously lyrical. In these respects, it is unlike a typical newspaper sports story.

6. Suggested Response: The poet builds suspense by reflecting the anticipation of the crowd, first for Flynn, then for Blake, and finally for Casey. The descriptions of Casey's manner also build suspense.

### Applying

7. Answers will differ, but many students will say that baseball involves skill and strategy, is suspenseful, and can be played by people who are not physical giants.

### ANSWERS TO ANALYZING LITERATURE

1. Answers will differ, but many students will probably point to the suspenseful story. Especially insightful students may mention the humor.
2. Answers will differ, but most students will say that there would be more exposition in the beginning to set the scene.

### ANSWERS TO CRITICAL THINKING AND READING

Suggested Responses: Stanza 5: The crowd yelled so joyously when Casey came up to bat that you could hear their shouting reverberate from the hills and mountains and valleys around the stadium.

# GUIDE FOR READING

## The Ballad of William Sycamore

**Stephen Vincent Benét** (1898–1943) was born in Bethlehem, Pennsylvania, where his father, an army officer, was stationed. As a boy, Benét read a great deal of history with his father. His love of reading inspired him to write, and he published his first book of poems before his graduation from Yale, in 1919. His devotion to American history and legends was the inspiration for "The Ballad of William Sycamore," his powerful portrait of the life of a frontiersman.

**Ballad**

A **ballad** is a poem that tells a story, often of a single historical or legendary person. Ballads are usually made up of four-line stanzas, and the stanzas normally have the same rhythm and rhyme scheme throughout the entire poem. In Benét's ballad the first and third lines have four rhythmic beats each and rhyme with each other. The second and fourth lines have three beats, and they, too, rhyme. This rhyme scheme may be signified by the letters _abab_. Because of their strong rhythm and rhyme, ballads are often set to music.

**Look For**

As you read "The Ballad of William Sycamore," look for the lively, song-like effect created by the rhythm and rhymes. Also, notice the vivid images—word pictures—Benét uses to express the quality of William Sycamore's life.

**Writing**

Benét's poem is partly about the changes in American life during the nineteenth century. Think about some changes you have noticed in your community. Freewrite about them and your reactions to them.

**Vocabulary**

Knowing the following words will help you as you read "The Ballad of William Sycamore."
**trifles** (trī' fəlz) _n._: Small, unimportant things (p. 557, l. 18)
**lend** (lend) _v._: Pass along, as from parent to child (p. 559, l. 34)

**flagons** (flag' ənz) _n._: Pitchers for water or wine (p. 559, l. 46)

# The Ballad of William Sycamore
## (1790–1871)

Stephen Vincent Benét

My father, he was a mountaineer,
His fist was a knotty hammer;
He was quick on his feet as a running deer,
And he spoke with a Yankee stammer.

5 My mother, she was merry and brave,
And so she came to her labor,
With a tall green fir for her doctor grave
And a stream for her comforting neighbor.

And some are wrapped in the linen fine,
10 And some like a godling's scion;[1]
But I was cradled on twigs of pine
In the skin of a mountain lion.

And some remember a white, starched lap
And a ewer[2] with silver handles;
15 But I remember a coonskin cap
And the smell of bayberry candles.

The cabin logs, with the bark still rough,
And my mother who laughed at trifles,
And the tall, lank visitors, brown as snuff,
20 With their long, straight squirrel-rifles.

I can hear them dance, like a foggy song,
Through the deepest one of my slumbers,
The fiddle squeaking the boots along
And my father calling the numbers.[3]

---

1. **a godling's scion** (sī′ ən): The descendant or child of a god.
2. **ewer** (yōō′ ər) *n.*: A large water pitcher.
3. **numbers:** The different steps in a square dance.

## Presentation

**Motivation/Prior Knowledge**
Ask students to recall any songs they have heard that tell a story. Who are the characters in these songs? What kind of people are they? What is their story? If recordings of any of these songs are available, play them in class as a part of the discussion.

**Master Teacher Note** Point out to students that many of the narrative songs they listen to are a form of ballad. Two characteristics of ballads are that they often are about everyday people and they often deal with themes of courage or love. Do these characteristics apply to the narrative songs with which students are familiar?

**Purpose-Setting    Question**
What characteristics of a ballad does this poem contain?

**Thematic Idea** Another selection that deals with the benefits of a simple life in tune with nature is "Nameless, Tennessee" by William Least Heat Moon, page 477.

1 **Discussion** Have students discuss the effect of the poet using the construction "My father, he . . ."

2 **Discussion** Ask students to discuss the two figures of speech in these lines.

3 **Clarification** The word *grave* is used as an adjective and not as a noun in this line. If this is not pointed out, students could misunderstand the meaning.

*I Got a Gal on Sourwood Mountain,* by Thomas Hart Benton. Thomas Hart Benton (1889-1975) was an American known for his regionalist paintings. Although he studied art in Paris, he felt his true education came from the years he spent roaming the United States.

You might want to use these questions for discussion:

1. In what region of the country might this scene have taken place?
2. How does Benton capture the flavor of the music in his painting?
3. How does the picture provide insight into Benét's intentions or catch the central meaning of the poem?

I GOT A GAL ON SOURWOOD MOUNTAIN, 1938
*Thomas Hart Benton*
Art Resource

558 Poetry

## Grammar in Action

Skillful writers observe the rules of **capitalization.** In addition to the usual rules about capitalizing the first word of a sentence and capitalizing proper nouns and adjectives, most (but not all) poets follow the rule that calls for capitalizing the first word of each line of poetry. Benét does that:

When I grew as tall as the Indian corn,
My father had little to lend me,

But he gave me his great, old powder-horn
And his woodsman's skill to befriend me.

In addition, Benét's ballad illustrates other rules for capitalization, specifically the capitalization of proper names:

For I cut my teeth on "Money Musk." (name of a dance tune)
A girl like a Salem clipper! (name of a city)
With eyes as bright as the Dipper! (name of a constellation)
On the trail of the Western wagons (name of a geographic area)

25    The quick feet shaking the puncheon-floor,[4]
    And the fiddle squealing and squealing,
    Till the dried herbs rattled above the door
    And the dust went up to the ceiling.

    There are children lucky from dawn till dusk,
30    But never a child so lucky!
    For I cut my teeth on "Money Musk"[5]
    In the Bloody Ground of Kentucky!

    When I grew tall as the Indian corn,
    My father had little to lend me,
35    But he gave me his great, old powder-horn
    And his woodsman's skill to befriend me.

    With a leather shirt to cover my back,
    And a redskin nose to unravel
    Each forest sign, I carried my pack
40    As far as a scout could travel.

    Till I lost my boyhood and found my wife,
    A girl like a Salem clipper![6]
    A woman straight as a hunting-knife
    With eyes as bright as the Dipper![7]

45    We cleared our camp where the buffalo feed,
    Unheard-of streams were our flagons;
    And I sowed my sons like the apple-seed
    On the trail of the Western wagons.

    They were right, tight boys, never sulky or slow,
50    A fruitful, a goodly muster.[8]
    The eldest died at the Alamo.[9]
    The youngest fell with Custer.[10]

---

**4. puncheon-floor** (pun′ chən flor) *n.*: A floor made of heavy, broad pieces of timber.
**5. "Money Musk":** A square-dance tune.
**6. a Salem clipper:** A tall-masted sailing ship from Salem, Massachusetts, noted for speed.
**7. the Dipper:** The Big Dipper, a dipper-shaped group of stars.
**8. muster** (mus′ tər) *n.*: An assembly, especially of soldiers.
**9. the Alamo:** A fort in San Antonio, Texas, where 188 Texans were killed by 2,500 Mexican soldiers in 1836.
**10. Custer:** General George Armstrong Custer and all his men were killed at the Battle of the Little Bighorn in 1876.

*The Ballad of William Sycamore* 559

4 **Reading Strategy** Ask students to summarize what they have learned about the narrator's childhood. Have them predict what might happen to him in manhood.

5 **Discussion** Have students discuss what the narrator possessed to start his own adult life. Ask them to include both inner resources and personal possessions.

6 **Reading Strategy** Ask students to summarize the story so far. What do they predict will happen to the narrator now?

The eldest died at the Alamo. (name of a fort)
The youngest fell with Custer. (name of a man)

By observing the rules of capitalization, writers help readers to understand the meaning of a poem, story, or essay. For example, if Benét had not capitalized the *D* of Dipper, readers might think of a kitchen implement rather than a constellation!

**Student Activity.** Write a four-line stanza that could be added to "The Ballad of William Sycamore." Capitalize as necessary.

7    55   
The letter that told it burned my hand.
Yet we smiled and said, "So be it!"
But I could not live when they fenced the land,
For it broke my heart to see it.

8    60   
I saddled a red, unbroken colt
And rode him into the day there;
And he threw me down like a thunderbolt
And rolled on me as I lay there.

The hunter's whistle hummed in my ear
As the city-men tried to move me,
And I died in my boots like a pioneer
With the whole wide sky above me.

65   
Now I lie in the heart of the fat, black soil,
Like the seed of a prairie-thistle;
It has washed my bones with honey and oil
And picked them clean as a whistle.

70   
And my youth returns, like the rains of Spring,
And my sons, like the wild-geese flying;
And I lie and hear the meadow-lark sing
And have much content in my dying.

9    75   
Go play with the towns you have built of blocks,
The towns where you would have bound me!
I sleep in my earth like a tired fox,
And my buffalo have found me.

## THINKING ABOUT THE SELECTION
### Recalling

1. What skills did William's father pass along to William?
2. Explain what happened to William's oldest and youngest sons.
3. How did he feel about the fencing of the land?
4. Explain how William Sycamore died.

### Interpreting

5. Describe the kind of people William Sycamore, his wife, and his parents were.
6. In line 53, William speaks of a letter burning his hand. What does he mean?
7. What does he mean by "the towns you have built of blocks" (line 73)?

### Applying

8. If you could ask William Sycamore, "What is your idea of a good and happy life?" how might he reply?

## ANALYZING LITERATURE
### Understanding Ballads

A **ballad** is a poem that tells a story, usually about a historical or legendary person. Ballads are written with a rhythm and rhyme that make them song-like—therefore, many are set to music.

1. What is the story that Benét's ballad tells? Summarize it in a brief paragraph.
2. What do you think that Benét saw in the lives and characters of frontiersmen like William Sycamore that inspired him to write this ballad?

## CRITICAL THINKING AND READING
### Inferring the Theme of a Ballad

The **theme** of a literary work is the central idea or insight into life that it presents. The theme of a ballad must be inferred from the plot, charac-ters, and setting, and also from the spirit or tone of the poem.

1. What does the poem imply about the changes that civilization has caused?
2. What does it imply about the United States as it was known by the frontiersmen?
3. How would you describe the spirit or tone of the poem?
4. State the theme of the poem.

## UNDERSTANDING LANGUAGE
### Completing Word Analogies

Word analogies show the relationships be-tween pairs of words. Usually on a word analogy test, you are given the first pair of words and asked to complete the second pair with a word showing the same relationship. For example,

FIDDLE : INSTRUMENT : : BALLAD:

a. singer  b. poetry  c. dance  d. voting

The first pair of words shows the relationship between an item in a category and the category itself. *Ballad* is an item in the category poetry. Therefore, the second pair should be completed by b. poetry.

The first word in the first pair in each item be-low is from "The Ballad of William Sycamore." Find the relationship between the first pair. Then complete the second pair. Use your dictionary for help.

1. REMEMBER : FORGET : : FUTILE:
   a. useless  b. futuristic  c. sorry  d. useful
2. SCION : DESCENDANT : : FLAGON:
   a. pitcher  b. banner  c. weapon  d. candle
3. BAYBERRY : CANDLE : : COONSKIN:
   a. frontiersman  b. animal  c. cap  d. warmth
4. FENCE : LAND : : DAM:
   a. conservation        b. water
   c. flood               d. drought
5. DIPPER : CONSTELLATION : : CONESTOGA:
   a. wagon               b. pioneers
   c. travel              d. frontier

*The Ballad of William Sycamore* 561

(Answers begin on p. 560.)

## ANSWERS TO ANALYZING LITERATURE

1. Suggested Response: William Sycamore grew up on the frontier, and he remembers the good times his parents had with their neigh-bors. He left home, married, and had two sons who were killed in wars. He kept moving west and lived on the frontier all his life. When civilization and its fences caught up with him, he died trying to ride an unbroken horse. He is buried in the land he loved so much.
2. Suggested Response: Benét rec-ognized the spirit of the westward movement in the United States in these people who lived on the fron-tier. He admired their courage, determination, fun-loving spirit, and zest for life.

## ANSWERS TO CRITICAL THINKING AND READING

1. Suggested Response: Civilization brought restrictions to the brave people of the frontier; they could not accept these constraints as a part of their way of life.
2. Suggested Response: The United States at the time of William Syca-more was a changing land. As people moved west to live on the frontier, civilization always followed them.
3. Suggested Response: Benét cre-ates a tone of respect for the people of the frontier. The poem conveys their zest for living, their courage, and their rough and ready ways.
4. Suggested Response: We in the United States today have a valu-able legacy in the hard work, cour-age, and zest for life of the men and women who were pioneers.

---

his youngest son died fighting the Indians with Custer.
3. The fencing of the land broke William's heart.
4. William was killed trying to ride an unbroken horse, which threw him off and rolled over on him.

### Interpreting

5. Suggested Response: The Syca-mores were happy, fun-loving people who had a zest for the hard-working, but free and uncharted life of the frontier.
6. Suggested Response: William's emotional response to the letter that told of his son's death made him feel like the letter was burning his hand.
7. Suggested Response: The rectan-gular buildings in the towns all looked like blocks to William. He thinks that what others regard as progress is silly child's play.

### Applying

8. Answers will differ, but students might respond as follows: The best life is one in which a family can have friends but also have a lot of open land, without fences, to make pro-ductive and to enjoy. Work hard and play hard would be his motto.

## ANSWERS TO UNDERSTANDING LANGUAGE

1. d. useful
2. a. pitcher
3. c. cap
4. b. water
5. a. wagon

**More About the Author** Edgar Allan Poe's life was plagued by numerous personal and professional conflicts, as well as illness. "The Raven," which is considered one of the most popular poems in the English language, is memorable for its haunting and eerie tone. Ask students how Poe's personal life may have influenced his literary preference for the supernatural.

**Literary Focus** The concept of repetition in literature should be familiar to students from their earliest experiences with stories and poems. From the "I'll huff and I'll puff, and I'll blow your house down" of the *Three Little Pigs* to the final line of each stanza in "The Raven," students have anticipated the ringing of familiar sounds as they read. When their expectancy is fulfilled, readers have a satisfied feeling. Repetition is a key in making some stories and poems memorable.

**Look For** Have students note the effect of repetition. Why is it pleasing? Is it easier to "hear" the poem even when it is read silently? Will they remember this poem better as a result? How does it increase the rhythmical values of the poem?

**Writing/Prior Knowledge** Many excellent stories students have read or seen on film or television deal with the theme of loss. Encourage a brief discussion of stories students can recall. What do they remember best about their favorite story? The discussion should generate some ideas that students can use in their writing assignment.

**Vocabulary** Have less advanced students write a sentence for each of the words on the list.

# GUIDE FOR READING

## The Raven

**Edgar Allan Poe** (1809–1849) was born in Boston, Massachusetts. As a young man, he drifted for a while before he found a home with an aunt, Maria Poe Clemm, whose young daughter, Virginia, he secretly married in 1835. His wife died in 1847. Misfortunes such as his young wife's death and his own poverty and illnesses at least partly inspired his haunting, sometimes mournful poems. Of these, "The Raven" is perhaps the most unforgettable.

### Repetition and Refrain

**Repetition** in poetry is the use, again and again, of a word or phrase. When the word or phrase appears in the same position in all or many of the stanzas of a poem, it is termed a **refrain**. In "The Raven," for example, the words "Lenore" and "Nevermore" are prominently repeated. Repetitions and refrains can create powerful effects. They contribute to the music of poetry, emphasize ideas and feelings, and establish mood and tone.

### Look For

As you read "The Raven," look for the repetition of words and phrases. Which repetitions are refrains? How would you describe the effect of these repetitions?

### Writing

"The Raven" is largely about the effects of the loss of a loved one. Think of a book you have read or movie you have seen in which someone experienced a permanent loss. The loss can involve a person, an animal, an object, or an ideal. Freewrite about the time just after the loss. How did the person act? What thoughts did the person have?

### Vocabulary

Knowing the following words will help you as you read "The Raven."

**quaint** (kwānt) *adj.*: Strange, unusual (p. 563, l. 2)
**beguiling** (bi gīl' iŋ) *v.*: Tricking; charming (p. 565, l. 67)
**respite** (res' pit) *n.*: Rest, relief (p. 566, l. 82)

**desolate** (des' ə lit) *adj.*: Deserted, abandoned (p. 566, l. 87)
**pallid** (pal' id) *adj.*: Pale (p. 566, l. 104)

### Objectives

1 To understand the use of repetition and refrain in poetry
2 To make inferences about the speaker of a poem
3 To respond to criticism of a poem

## Support Material

**Teaching Portfolio**
Teacher Backup, p. 681
Grammar in Action Worksheet, *Using Alliteration,* p. 684
Usage and Mechanics Worksheet, p. 686
Vocabulary Check, p. 687
Analyzing Literature Worksheet, *Understanding Repetition and Refrain,* p. 688
Critical Thinking and Reading

Worksheet, *Making Inferences About the Speaker,* p. 689
Selection Test, p. 690
Art Transparency 10: *Crows and Sycamores,* by James Cook

# The Raven

Edgar Allan Poe

1
Once upon a midnight dreary, while I pondered, weak and weary,
Over many a quaint and curious volume of forgotten lore,[1]
While I nodded, nearly napping, suddenly there came a tapping,
As of someone gently rapping, rapping at my chamber door.
5 " 'Tis some visitor," I muttered, "tapping at my chamber door—
    Only this, and nothing more."

2
Ah, distinctly I remember it was in the bleak December,
And each separate dying ember wrought its ghost upon the floor.
Eagerly I wished the morrow—vainly I had tried to borrow
10 From my books surcease[2] of sorrow—sorrow for the lost Lenore—
For the rare and radiant maiden whom the angels name Lenore—
    Nameless here for evermore.

And the silken, sad, uncertain rustling of each purple curtain
Thrilled me—filled me with fantastic terrors never felt before;
15 So that now, to still the beating of my heart, I stood repeating
" 'Tis some visitor entreating entrance at my chamber door—
Some late visitor entreating entrance at my chamber door—
    This it is and nothing more."

3
Presently my soul grew stronger; hesitating then no longer,
20 "Sir," said I, "or Madam, truly your forgiveness I implore;
But the fact is I was napping, and so gently you came rapping,
And so faintly you came tapping, tapping at my chamber door,
That I scarce was sure I heard you"—here I opened wide the door—
    Darkness there, and nothing more.

25 Deep into that darkness peering, long I stood there wondering, fearing,
Doubting, dreaming dreams no mortal ever dared to dream before;
But the silence was unbroken, and the darkness gave no token,[3]
And the only word there spoken was the whispered word, "Lenore!"
This *I* whispered, and an echo murmured back the word, "Lenore!"
30     Merely this, and nothing more.

---

**1. quaint . . . lore:** Strange book of ancient learning.
**2. surcease** (sur sēs') *n.:* End.
**3. token** (tō' k'n) *n.:* Sign.

4 **Discussion** Do you agree with the narrator's solution to the mystery?

5 **Discussion** Describe the raven based on the evidence provided in this stanza.

6 **Reading Strategy** Have students note the first question the narrator puts to the raven. What is its answer? Ask students to predict other questions the narrator will ask the raven. What will be the raven's responses?

7 **Master Teacher Note** Point out to students the two allusions in these stanzas—Pallas and Plutonian shore. Discuss with them the irony of a bird speaking from above the goddess of wisdom and the effect on the poem's atmosphere of referring to the underworld.

8 **Reading Strategy** Have students note the literal acceptance by the narrator of the raven's response to his question. What predictions can they make about the narrator's responses to the raven?

9 **Discussion** Do you think that the raven is responding to the narrator's thought? Explain.

4

35
Then into the chamber turning, all my soul within me burning,
Soon I heard again a tapping somewhat louder than before.
"Surely," said I, "surely that is something at my window lattice;[4]
Let me see, then, what thereat[5] is, and this mystery explore—
Let my heart be still a moment and this mystery explore—
    'Tis the wind, and nothing more!"

5

40
Open here I flung the shutter, when, with many a flirt[6] and flutter,
In there stepped a stately raven of the saintly days of yore;
Not the least obeisance[7] made he; not an instant stopped or stayed he;
But, with mien[8] of lord or lady, perched above my chamber door—
Perched upon a bust of Pallas[9] just above my chamber door—
    Perched, and sat, and nothing more.

6
7
45
Then this ebony bird beguiling my sad fancy[10] into smiling,
By the grave and stern decorum of the countenance[11] it wore,
"Though thy crest be shorn and shaven, thou," I said, "art sure no craven,[12]
Ghastly grim and ancient raven wandering from the Nightly shore—
Tell me what thy lordly name is on the Night's Plutonian[13] shore!"
    Quoth[14] the raven, "Nevermore."

8
50
Much I marveled this ungainly fowl to hear discourse so plainly,
Though its answer little meaning—little relevancy bore;
For we cannot help agreeing that no sublunary[15] being
Ever yet was blessed with seeing bird above his chamber door—
Bird or beast upon the sculptured bust above his chamber door,
    With such name as "Nevermore."

9
55

60
But the raven, sitting lonely on the placid bust, spoke only
That one word, as if his soul in that one word he did outpour.
Nothing farther then he uttered—not a feather then he fluttered—
Till I scarcely more than muttered, "Other friends have flown before—
On the morrow *he* will leave me, as my hopes have flown before."
    Quoth the raven, "Nevermore."

---

**4. lattice** (lat' is) *n.*: Framework of wood or metal.
**5. thereat** (*th*er at') *adv.*: There.
**6. flirt** (flurt) *n.*: Quick, uneven movement.
**7. obeisance** (ō bā' s'ns) *n.*: A bow or another sign of respect.
**8. mien** (mēn) *n.*: Manner.
**9. bust of Pallas** (pal' əs): Sculpture of the head and shoulders of Pallas Athena (ə thē' nə), the ancient Greek goddess of wisdom.
**10. fancy** (fan' sē) *n.*: Imagination.
**11. countenance** (koun' tə nəns) *n.*: Facial appearance.
**12. craven** (krā' vən) *n.*: Coward (usually an adjective).
**13. Plutonian** (ploo tō' nē ən) *adj.*: Like the underworld, ruled over by the ancient Roman god Pluto.
**14. quoth** (kwōth) *v.*: Said.
**15. sublunary** (sub' loo ner' ē) *adj.*: Earthly.

## Grammar in Action

**Alliteration** is the repetition of initial consonant sounds. Writers, and especially poets, use this device to give emphasis to particular words, to imitate sounds, and to create musical effects. Poe makes use of alliteration throughout "The Raven." Look at the repetition of the initial *fl* and *s* sounds in these lines:

   Open here I *fl*ung the shutter, when, with many a *fl*irt and *fl*utter,
   In there *s*tepped a *s*tately raven of the *s*aintly
      days of yore;

Now look at this stanza from the poem. How many different initial sounds are repeated? (The best way to begin determining this is either to read the stanza aloud to yourself or listen as it is read aloud.)

   Then this ebony bird beguiling my sad fancy into smiling,
   By the grave and stern decorum of the countenance it
      wore,
   "Though thy crest be shorn and shaven, thou, I said, "art
      sure no craven.
   Ghastly, grim, and ancient raven wandering from the
      Nightly shore—
   Tell me what thine lordly name is on the Night's Plutonian
      shore!"

Wondering at the stillness broken by reply so aptly spoken,
"Doubtless," said I, "what it utters is its only stock and store,
Caught from some unhappy master whom unmerciful Disaster
Followed fast and followed faster—so, when Hope he would adjure,[16]
65    Stern Despair returned, instead of the sweet Hope he dared adjure—
            That sad answer, "Nevermore!"

But the raven still beguiling all my sad soul into smiling,
Straight I wheeled a cushioned seat in front of bird, and bust, and door;
Then upon the velvet sinking, I betook myself to linking
70    Fancy unto fancy, thinking what this ominous bird of yore—
What this grim, ungainly, ghastly, gaunt, and ominous bird of yore
            Meant in croaking "Nevermore."

This I sat engaged in guessing, but no syllable expressing
To the fowl whose fiery eyes now burned into my bosom's core;
75    This and more I sat divining,[17] with my head at ease reclining
On the cushion's velvet lining that the lamplight gloated o'er,
But whose velvet violet lining with the lamplight gloating o'er,
            *She* shall press, ah, nevermore!

---

**16. adjure** (ə joor') v.: Appeal to.
**17. divining** (də vīn' iŋ) v.: Guessing.

**THE RAVEN**
*Edouard Manet*
Museum of Fine Arts, Boston

10 **Discussion** What is the mood of the narrator in these lines?

11 **Reading Strategy** Ask students to predict how the narrator's questions will be resolved.

12 **Discussion** Who is the woman that comes to the narrator's mind? Why is it the narrator, rather than the bird, who says "nevermore"?

## Humanities Note

Fine art, *The Raven,* by Edouard Manet. Manet (1832–1883) broke with tradition by emphasizing the pictorial qualities of his paintings rather than their story-telling aspects. He is often linked with the impressionists, whom he influenced and learned from.

You might use the following questions:
1. Does this picture capture the mood of the poem? Explain.
2. Which adjectives applied to the speaker and the raven in the poem might also fit the picture?

---

    Quoth the raven, "Nevermore."
The sounds of initial *b, s, q, th,* and *sh* are repeated throughout the lines. This repetition, together with the rhythm of the lines, creates a unique and musical effect.

**Student Activity 1.** Find three additional examples of alliteration in the poem and share these with a small group of classmates. Discuss the effect of the alliteration.

**Student Activity 2.** Work with a classmate to compose four lines of verse in which you use at least two different alliterative sounds.

13 **Discussion** Is the raven merely repeating this word like a parrot, or is it really responding to the narrator?

14 **Discussion** In what way does the raven serve as a part of the narrator's own personality?

**Reader's Response** Why do you think this poem is considered an American classic?

Then, methought, the air grew denser, perfumed from an unseen censer[18]
80 Swung by angels whose faint footfalls tinkled on the tufted floor.
"Wretch," I cried, "thy God hath lent thee—by these angels he hath sent thee
Respite—respite and Nepenthe[19] from thy memories of Lenore!
Let me quaff[20] this kind Nepenthe and forget this lost Lenore!"
        Quoth the raven, "Nevermore."

85 "Prophet!" said I, "thing of evil!—prophet still, if bird or devil!—
Whether Tempter[21] sent, or whether tempest tossed thee here ashore,
Desolate, yet all undaunted, on this desert land enchanted—
On this home by Horror haunted—tell me truly, I implore—
Is there—*is* there balm in Gilead?[22]—tell me—tell me, I implore!"
90        Quoth the raven, "Nevermore."

"Prophet!" said I, "thing of evil!—prophet still, if bird or devil!
By that Heaven that bends above us—by that God we both adore—
Tell this soul with sorrow laden if, within the distant Aidenn,[23]
It shall clasp a sainted maiden whom the angels name Lenore—
95 Clasp a rare and radiant maiden whom the angels name Lenore."
        Quoth the raven, "Nevermore."

"Be that word our sign of parting, bird or fiend!" I shrieked, upstarting—
"Get thee back into the tempest and the Night's Plutonian shore!
Leave no black plume as a token of that lie thy soul hath spoken!
100 Leave my loneliness unbroken!—quit the bust above my door!
Take thy beak from out my heart, and take thy form from off my door!"
        Quoth the raven, "Nevermore."

And the raven, never flitting, still is sitting, still is sitting
On the pallid bust of Pallas just above my chamber door;
105 And his eyes have all the seeming of a demon that is dreaming,
And the lamplight o'er him streaming throws his shadow on the floor;
And my soul from out that shadow that lies floating on the floor
        Shall be lifted—nevermore!

---

**18. censer** (sen' sər) *n.*: Container for burning incense.
**19. Nepenthe** (ni pen' thē) *n.*: A drug used in ancient times to cause forgetfulness of sorrow.
**20. quaff** (kwäf) *v.*: Drink.
**21. Tempter:** The Devil.
**22. balm** (bäm) **in Gilead** (gil' ē əd): Cure for suffering; the Bible refers to a medicinal ointment, or balm, made in a region called Gilead.
**23. Aidenn:** A name meant to suggest Eden or paradise.

## Closure and Extension

### ANSWERS TO THINKING ABOUT THE SELECTION
*Recalling*

1. The speaker is in his study at midnight nearly going to sleep reading an old book.
2. He thinks it is a visitor knocking at his door.
3. At first the speaker thinks the raven is merely repeating a word it had been taught, but later he accuses it of being a prophet and a thing of evil.
4. At the end of the poem, the raven still is sitting on the statue above the speaker's chamber door.

*Interpreting*

5. Suggested Response: The raven has told the speaker that he shall

## THINKING ABOUT THE SELECTION

### Recalling

1. Describe the speaker's situation at the start of the poem.
2. What are his thoughts when he hears the noise at his door and window?
3. Describe his changing thoughts as the raven keeps repeating "Nevermore."
4. Describe the situation at the end of the poem.

### Interpreting

5. "Lenore" and "Nevermore" rhyme. By the end of the poem, what meaning connects the two words?
6. What can you infer about Lenore and the speaker's relationship with her?
7. Describe how your impression of the raven changes as the poem progresses. What is your first impression of the bird? What is your final one?
8. Summarize the story of "The Raven," including the speaker's changing thoughts and feelings.
9. When Poe set out to write this poem, he thought of having a parrot repeat the word "Nevermore." Do you think this poem would have been as effective if Poe had used a parrot instead of a raven? Explain your answer.

### Applying

10. Might the raven be a figment of the speaker's unsound imagination? Give reasons for your opinion.

## ANALYZING LITERATURE

### Understanding Repetition and Refrain

In poetry, **repetition** refers to the repeated use of a word or phrase. A **refrain** is a repeated word or phrase that occurs in the same position in the stanzas of a poem. These devices contribute to the music of a poem, emphasize ideas and feelings, and establish mood and tone.

1. What ideas and feelings are expressed by the refrain "Nevermore"?
2. What mood does it create or deepen?

3. Choose two other important examples of repetition in "The Raven" and tell what they contribute to its meaning and mood.

## CRITICAL THINKING AND READING

### Making Inferences About the Speaker

**Making inferences** about the speaker of a poem like "The Raven" means seeing what is suggested about him by his own words. When, for example, the speaker says, "Eagerly I wished the morrow—vainly I had tried to borrow/From my books surcease of sorrow . . .," you can infer that he is sorrowful, that the night worsens the way he feels, and that he is trying to escape from sorrow by reading.

1. What can you infer about the speaker's breeding, education, or social class by the way he speaks throughout the poem?
2. What do you infer about him from the line "Let me quaff this kind Nepenthe and forget this lost Lenore!"?
3. What else could you infer about him from other details of the poem?

## THINKING AND WRITING

### Responding to Criticism

The poet and critic W. H. Auden once said, "The trouble with 'The Raven' . . . is that the thematic interest and the prosodic [rhythmic] interest . . . do not combine and are even often at odds." In other words, the rhythm of the poem is not suitable to the subject matter. Write an essay in which you tell why you agree or disagree with Auden's statement. Before you write, answer such questions as these: What is the subject matter of "The Raven"? What mood or spirit should a work have that deals with such a subject? What mood or spirit is created by the rhythm of "The Raven"? Is the rhythm suitable or not? When you write your essay, give full and complete reasons in support of your view. When you revise, be sure that your argument has been presented clearly and convincingly.

*The Raven* 567

(Answers begin on p. 566.)

**Challenge** In what sense is this a poem about all types of loss?

## ANSWERS TO ANALYZING LITERATURE

1. Suggested Response: "Nevermore" expresses the sad and dreary feelings of loss in the poem and introduces the idea of mystery.
2. Suggested Response: The refrain deepens and extends the oppressive mood of the setting and the situation.
3. Answers will differ, but students may refer to the tapping sound repeated in the opening of the poem, and the speaker's repetition of *Lenore*. The first makes the strange visitor seem persistent, implying that it has a purpose in being there, and the second reinforces the sad mood of the speaker.

## ANSWERS TO CRITICAL THINKING AND READING

1. Suggested Response: The speaker is well-educated and has enough wealth to support the kind of home he describes.
2. Suggested Response: He is desperate to forget his pain at losing Lenore. Also, he has probably received a classical education.
3. Suggested Response: The speaker is a reader, has gentlemanly manners, and is highly suggestible, unhappy, and imaginative.

## THINKING AND WRITING

For help with this assignment, students may consult Lesson 13, "Writing About a Poem," in the Handbook of Writing About Literature.

**Publishing Student Writing**
When students have completed a first draft have them meet in one of two groups—those who agreed with Poe and those who disagreed. Ask them to select the strongest arguments to support their position and plan for a debate with students from another group who have taken the opposite point of view.

nevermore forget or nevermore see Lenore, even in the next world.

6. Suggested Response: The speaker was in love with Lenore before she died.
7. Suggested Response: At first the reader is amused at the strange bird who talks, but as the poem goes on the reader sees the raven as more and more threatening.
8. Suggested Response: Answering a strange knock, the speaker finally

opens the window and a raven flies in and sits above his study door. At first he does not take seriously the bird's repetition of the word "Nevermore," but gradually he becomes obsessed with its responses to his questions. To him the raven is now a thing of evil as it continues to sit above his door.

9. Suggested Response: Because of its bright colors and humorous

associations, the parrot would not have provided the dark and dreary mood needed in this poem.

### Applying

10. Answers will vary, but students may note several possibilities. The raven could be part of a dream, or its presence might be imagined by the speaker. If it is real, its responses could be imagined.

**More About the Author** Alfred,
Lord Tennyson had strong political convictions that are expressed in "The Charge of the
Light Brigade." Ask students
whether they think poetry is an
effective medium for expressing
a person's political ideas and
opinions. Why or why not? Would
the answers for the nineteenth
and twentieth centuries be different?

**Literary Focus** Rhythm is a familiar concept to most students
because of the music they listen
to. It may help them to understand rhythm in poetry by comparing the musical beat of the
percussionist to the pattern of
stresses in a line of poetry.

**Look For** The rhythm in "The
Charge of the Light Brigade" reflects the battle scene itself.
Have students note the heavy
beat at the beginning of each
line. Does it remind them of the
cannon fire during the battle?

**Motivation/Prior Knowledge**
"Bravely" is only one adverb to
use in describing how soldiers
meet death. Ask students to discuss some others. What about
"quietly," or "reluctantly"? Do
these adverbs take away from
the sacrifice the person is making? This discussion should help
set the stage for the writing assignment.

**Vocabulary** Ask less advanced
students to add these words to
the paragraph they wrote for the
writing assignment. They might
insert them appropriately as they
revise the paragraph, or they
might extend the paragraph with
sentences that include these
words.

# GUIDE FOR READING

**Rhythm in Poetry**

**Look For**

**Writing**

**Vocabulary**

## The Charge of the Light Brigade

**Alfred, Lord Tennyson** (1809–1892) was born in Lincolnshire, England. He studied at Cambridge, where he formed a close friendship
with Arthur Hallam. Hallam's sudden death in 1833 inspired Tennyson's great elegy *In Memoriam*. Tennyson was intensely concerned
with the vital issues of his day. His political responsibility and interests
led him to write "The Charge of the Light Brigade," based on a newspaper account of a battle between British cavalrymen and Russian
artillery forces.

In poetry, **rhythm** is the arrangement, or pattern, of accented and unaccented syllables—in a word, "the beat." For example, if you read
the following lines from Tennyson's poem aloud, you will hear the
forceful rhythm of the lines.

> Theirs not to make reply,
> Theirs not to reason why,
> Theirs but to do and die.

Like songs, different poems have different rhythms. Usually a poet
will use a rhythm that is appropriate to the subject and the poet's feelings about it. When you read a poem, your first concern should be
with understanding what the lines mean. Your next concern should
be with "catching the beat" and responding to it.

As you read "The Charge of the Light Brigade," notice the rhythm.
You might read a stanza or two aloud to help you hear and feel the
pattern Tennyson uses. How would you describe the rhythm? What
does it contribute to the total effect of the poem?

What does it mean to be a soldier? Freewrite, exploring your answer
to this question.

Knowing the following words will help you as you read "The Charge
of the Light Brigade."
**dismayed** (dis mād') *v.*: Discouraged, made afraid (p. 569,
l. 10)
**volleyed** (väl' ēd) *v.*: Fired at
the same time (p. 569, l. 21)

**reeled** (rēld) *v.*: Fell back, staggered (p. 569, l. 35)
**sundered** (sun' dərd) *v.*: Broken apart (p. 569, l. 36)

# The Charge of the Light Brigade[1]

## Alfred, Lord Tennyson

**1**

Half a league,[2] half a league,
Half a league onward,
All in the valley of Death
   Rode the six hundred.
5 "Forward the Light Brigade!
Charge for the guns!" he said.
Into the valley of Death
   Rode the six hundred.

**2**

"Forward, the Light Brigade!"
10 Was there a man dismayed?
Not though the soldier knew
   Someone had blundered.
Theirs not to make reply,
Theirs not to reason why,
15 Theirs but to do and die.
Into the valley of Death
   Rode the six hundred.

**3**

Cannon to right of them,
Cannon to left of them,
20 Cannon in front of them
   Volleyed and thundered;

Stormed at with shot and shell,
Boldly they rode and well,
Into the jaws of Death,
25 Into the mouth of hell
   Rode the six hundred.

**4**

Flashed all their sabers bare,
Flashed as they turned in air
Sab'ring the gunners there,
30 Charging an army, while
   All the world wondered.
Plunged in the battery[3] smoke
Right through the line they broke;
Cossack[4] and Russian
35 Reeled from the saber stroke
   Shattered and sundered.
Then they rode back, but not,
   Not the six hundred.

**5**

Cannon to right of them,
40 Cannon to left of them,
Cannon behind them
   Volleyed and thundered;
Stormed at with shot and shell,
While horse and hero fell.

---

**1.** During the Crimean War (1854–1856), six hundred lightly armed British cavalrymen charged a heavily armed Russian fortification. The charge was the result of a confusion in orders. Three-fourths of the cavalrymen were killed.
**2. league** (lēg) *n.*: Three miles.

---

**3. battery:** A fortification equipped with heavy guns.
**4. Cossack** (käs′ ak): A people of southern Russia famous as horsemen and cavalrymen.

*The Charge of the Light Brigade* 569

## Presentation

**Motivation/Prior Knowledge** Have students recall any war movies they have seen in which soldiers participated in a dangerous action. Then tell students that the cavalry charge described in this poem was particularly perilous.

**Master Teacher Note** Have students consider what kind of rhythm would be most appropriate to describe a cavalry charge. To reinforce this point, also have them consider inappropriate rhythms.

**Purpose-Setting Question** What was the author's purpose in writing this poem?

**Thematic Idea** Another selection that deals with wartime experiences is "Beware of the Dog," page 147.

1 **Discussion** Ask students to paraphrase and discuss the significance of these lines.

2 **Discussion** What is the effect of the repetition of these lines?

Fine art, *Charge of the Light Brigade at the Battle of Balaclava*, artist unknown.

As students look at the action in this painting, you might ask the following questions:

1. What is happening in this picture?
2. What attitude toward the charge does the artist seem to take?
3. How is the artist's point of view different from or similar to that of the poet?

**CHARGE OF THE LIGHT BRIGADE AT THE BATTLE OF BALAKLAVA, 1854**
*Unknown*
*Three Lions*

570   *Poetry*

45 They that had fought so well
Came through the jaws of Death,
Back from the mouth of hell,
All that was left of them,
  Left of six hundred.

**6**

50 When can their glory fade?
O the wild charge they made!
  All the world wondered.
Honor the charge they made!
Honor the Light Brigade,
55 Noble six hundred!

3 **Reading Strategy** Ask students what happened in this battle.

4 **Discussion** Ask students to discuss the poet's attitude toward the men of the light brigade? Do they agree or disagree with his evaluation? Why?

**Reader's Response** If Tennyson were alive today, whom do you think he would want to honor as he does the Light Brigade in this poem? Explain.

## ANSWERS TO THINKING ABOUT THE SELECTION
### Recalling

1. They go into battle because they believe that their role as soldiers is to follow orders.
2. They charged right at the cannon and broke through the line, but very few of them returned.
3. The outcome was that only a few of the cavalrymen survived.

### Interpreting

4. Suggested Response: The cavalrymen go boldly forth without question and do what they were told to do.
5. Suggested Response: The speaker thinks that their brave deed is worth celebrating.
6. Suggested Response: The rhythm of the poem is punctuated with a heavily accented syllable at the beginning of each line. It reflects the cannon fire of the battle and the stirring spirit of a cavalry charge.

### Applying

7. Answers will differ, but most students will realize that modern-day warfare relies more on air power and on the "super weapons" of the atomic age. Cavalrymen do not play a major role. Bloody hand-to-hand skirmishes and sniper attacks, however, still play a role in remote areas like the southeast Asian jungles. Nevertheless, a frontal attack against a heavily armed position probably would not occur today.

**Challenge** This poem is clearly written from the British point of view. Describe what a Russian poem about the same event might be like? How would the content and point of view differ?

## ANSWERS TO ANALYZING LITERATURE

1. Suggested Response: Students' answers will differ. Each stanza contains three-beat and two-beat lines.

## THINKING ABOUT THE SELECTION
### Recalling

1. Although the soldiers realize someone had blundered, why do they still go into battle?
2. Describe the charge of the cavalrymen.
3. What is the outcome of the battle?

### Interpreting

4. What is the spirit of the cavalrymen as they make their charge?
5. Describe the speaker's feelings about them.
6. Describe the rhythm of the poem. Does it suggest any aspect of the battle?

### Applying

7. Could a poem like this be written about a battle in a modern-day war? Tell why you think it likely or unlikely.

## ANALYZING LITERATURE
### Understanding Rhythm in Poetry

**Rhythm** is the pattern of accented and unaccented syllables in a poem—its beat. After meaning, rhythm is the most important element of a poem. In fact rhythm is often closely linked to meaning. It can reinforce it by creating an appropriate spirit and by affecting a reader's response.
1. Choose any stanza of the poem and read it aloud. Tell how many accented syllables, or beats, each line of the stanza has.
2. What does the rhythm suggest about the speaker's feelings toward the cavalrymen and their charge?

## CRITICAL THINKING AND READING
### Understanding Cause and Effect

A **cause** is the reason why something happens. An **effect** is the result of the cause. For example, the cause of the military slaughter described in "The Charge of the Light Brigade" is a confusion of orders. The effect is the death of three fourths of the cavalrymen.

Do some library research to find the results of this battle between the British and Russians. Report your findings to your classmates.

## SPEAKING AND LISTENING
### Reading with Expression

Poems like "The Charge of the Light Brigade" were meant to be read aloud—and read with expression. To read with expression, you must vary the speed, volume, and tone of your voice. Like an actor studying a role, the reader of a poem should study the lines and decide where and how his or her reading should speed up, get louder, change tone, and so on. Follow this suggestion and practice reading Tennyson's poem aloud. Aim to achieve a style of reading appropriate to each part of it.

## THINKING AND WRITING
### Writing a News Report

"The Charge of the Light Brigade" is based on a newspaper report of the Battle of Balaklava. Write your own newspaper report based on the poem. First find the facts contained in the poem. You might next turn to an encyclopedia for more information about the battle, which was part of the Crimean War. Write your report as a real reporter might. Begin with a one-sentence "lead" that presents the most important fact. Then present the supporting details. When you revise, check that you have included all the facts that may be inferred from the poem as well as any key ones you found in the encyclopedia.

2. Suggested Response: The galloping rhythm suggests that the speaker is inspired by the cavalry charge.

## ANSWERS TO CRITICAL THINKING AND READING

Suggested Response: You might ask a social studies teacher to suggest appropriate books and articles about the battle. Make sure that students present both the military and political results of this engagement.

## THINKING AND WRITING

For help with this assignment, students can consult Lesson 2, "Drafting and Revising," in the Handbook of Writing About Literature.

**Publishing Student Writing** After the news reports are filed, ask students to write headlines for their story and construct a dummy for the front page of the newspaper. The dummies, the headlines, and the stories can be used for a bulletin board display of several newspapers of that day.

# Dramatic Poetry and the Speaker

**PORTRAIT OF MME. MATISSE**
*Henri Matisse*
The Hermitage, Leningrad

**Humanities Note**

Fine Art, *Portrait of Mme. Matisse*, Henri Matisse. In 1890 Henri Matisse (1869-1954), gave up the practice of law to study painting at the Academie Julien in Paris. During his early years, he associated with modern artists working in Paris, while he traveled and worked as a decorator. With the painter Derain, Matisse led the Fauve movement—characterized by the unorthodox and free use of vibrant color. His paintings are personal expressions, which display a remarkable sensitivity for color relationships.

In this portrait of his wife, Matisse does not rely on shadow and light to model the features of his subject. Rather, in the innovative way that is peculiar to him, he uses color variations to describe the forms of the features. The feelings of the artist for his subject are also apparent in his expressive use of color. Color was art to Henri Matisse, and through it he expressed harmony and order in a bright unusual way.

**Master Teacher Note** Use an overhead projector to show students Art Transparency 11, *The Postman Joseph Roulin*, by Vincent Van Gogh. It is a portrait of a nineteenth-century French postman in his uniform. Tell students that just as artists attempt to portray the character of their subjects, poets also strive to make fictional characters come alive for their readers. Have students discuss this postman's personality, as Van Gogh has depicted it. What qualities do they see in his face? What message does his body language communicate? Why do they think that he has posed in his uniform?

## Focus

**More About the Author** Donald Justice selected an ancient dialogue form for his poem "Incident in a Rose Garden." It seems surprising to hear the speakers in the poem being so polite and civil when discussing death. Ask students why it is effective for Justice to use an old poetic form in a surprising way.

**Literary Focus** Readers of dramatic poetry should bring with them the skills they apply to the reading of plays. All conclusions about character and situation must be inferred from what characters say in the dialogue. The poet cannot describe characters directly and tell the reader they are brave or fun-loving or cruel. The alert reader must learn all this from a careful study of the dialogue.

**Look For** Visualization is a skill good readers apply to gain greater comprehension. It is of special importance in the reading of plays and dramatic poetry. Have students picture in their mind's eye the three characters and the scene in the garden.

**Writing/Prior Knowledge** Hold a brief class discussion to help students recall portrayals of Death before they begin their writing. Invite them to consider movies and television films as well as fine art and literature.

**Vocabulary** Ask less advanced students if they have heard the expression, the "grim reaper." To whom does it refer? Why is it an appropriate expression? Have them write a sentence or two explaining why the "grim reaper" is usually pictured carrying a scythe.

## Incident in a Rose Garden

**Donald Justice** (1925–     ), a native of Florida, has experimented with different types of poetry, and sometimes takes ancient poetic forms and uses them in startling new ways. "Incident in a Rose Garden" is such a poem. It is written in the very old dialogue form. Though all the speakers in the poem are polite and civil, the poem conveys the dread of death.

**Dramatic Poetry**

**Dramatic poetry** is poetry in which the speaker is clearly someone other than the poet. Some of the best dramatic poetry consists of dialogue in which more than one character speaks.

**Look For**

As you read this poem, look for the way in which death becomes a character. If death were a person, what would you expect it to be like?

**Writing**

Look at the painting on page 575. Freewrite about portrayals of Death you have encountered in art and literature.

**Vocabulary**

Knowing the following word will help you as you read "Incident in a Rose Garden."
**scythe** (sīth) *n.*: A tool used for cutting down tall grass (p. 575, l. 3)

THE RACE TRACK OR DEATH ON A PALE HORSE
*Albert Pinkham Ryder*
*The Cleveland Museum of Art*

# Incident in
# a Rose Garden

## Donald Justice

*Gardener:* Sir, I encountered Death
Just now among our roses.
Thin as a scythe he stood there.

I knew him by his pictures.
He had his black coat on,
Black gloves, a broad black hat.

**Presentation**

**Humanities Note**

Fine Art, *The Race Track or Death on a Pale Horse,* by Albert Pinkham Ryder. Ryder (1847–1917) is an American artist known for his original, often mystical paintings. He used simple designs and applied paint thickly on his canvases. Ryder said that he got the idea for *The Race Track* in a dream.

You might ask students the following questions:
1. What might have prompted Ryder to paint Death on a racetrack?
2. Compare and contrast the gardener's description of Death with the image of Death in the painting.

**Motivation/Prior Knowledge** Death is an event or process that occurs to all living beings. Poets and artists, however, sometimes personify Death. Ask students to imagine that they are casting a movie in which Death is a character. What actor or actress might they choose for this role? What would Death look like? Invite them to compare their description with the character of Death in this poem.

**Purpose-Setting Question** How does the poet create suspense?

1 **Discussion** Ask students to discuss the effectiveness of this simile. How does it contribute to the picture of Death? How does it match their image of Death? Why is the word *scythe* appropriate?

**Thematic Idea** Another selection that deals with the inescapability of death is "The Seven Ages of Man," by Shakespeare, page 579.

**Master Teacher Note** Help students to understand why a poet might choose this topic. Through discussion the class might suggest that the poet could be fearing his or her own death, that the poet might have experienced the death of someone close, that the poet has an awareness of death's final claim on all of us, and that the poet had an appreciation of the dramatic possibilities of the subject.

2 **Reading Strategy** Ask students to predict what Death would have said if he had spoken.

3 **Discussion** Have students discuss the significance of these details.

4 **Discussion** Ask students to decide why Death does not speak to the gardener. Why does the gardener run to see his master?

5 **Reading Strategy** What does the master assume is Death's reason for seeking out his gardener? Do students think he is correct? Ask students to predict how the poem will end.

6 **Discussion** What does Death mean?

7 **Reading Strategy** Ask students to think about the gardener's mistake. Have they changed their predictions about the end of the poem? How?

8 **Discussion** What is the irony in the last stanza of this poem?

**Reader's Response** Imagine you were to meet Death as the gardener does in this poem. How would you react? What would you want to do before you die?

2
3
I think he would have spoken,
Seeing his mouth stood open.
Big it was, with white teeth.

10
4
As soon as he beckoned, I ran.
I ran until I found you.
Sir, I am quitting my job.

15
I want to see my sons
Once more before I die.
I want to see California.

5
Master: Sir, you must be that stranger
Who threatened my gardener.
This is my property, sir.

I welcome only friends here.
6 20 Death: Sir, I knew your father.
And we were friends at the end.

7
As for your gardener,
I did not threaten him.
Old men mistake my gestures.

25
8
I only meant to ask him
To show me to his master.
I take it you are he?

## THINKING ABOUT THE SELECTION

### Recalling

1. How does the gardener recognize Death?
2. Why does he run away?
3. According to Death, why was the gardener mistaken in running away?

### Interpreting

4. Describe Death's personality.
5. Interpret the lines "Sir, I knew your father. / And we were friends at the end."
6. What is implied by the final line?
7. In what way is the ending of the poem ironic, or the opposite of what was expected?

### Applying

8. If the poet had continued the poem, what might the master's reply to Death be?

## ANALYZING LITERATURE

### Understanding Dramatic Poetry

In **dramatic poetry,** the speaker is someone other than the poet—a character, like one in a play or story. In many dramatic poems, not only is there a speaker but there may be indications of other characters, a setting, and even a developing situation.

1. Tell how Justice's poem illustrates the characteristics of dramatic poetry.
2. What developing situation is suggested?

## CRITICAL THINKING AND READING

### Interpreting Personification

**Personification** means giving human quality to nonhuman objects or ideas. In this poem death is personified as a man.

1. Why is it appropriate that Death is wearing black?
2. Why is it appropriate that Death is "Thin as a scythe. . . ."?
3. How would you personify death?

## THINKING AND WRITING

### Continuing a Poem

Using your answer to the Applying question, write one or two three-line stanzas in which the master replies to Death. Then write another stanza or two in which Death speaks. If Death has the last word, what might he say? When you write your continuation, try to follow the poet's verse pattern: short lines, with three accented syllables, or beats, in each line. When you revise and polish your work, try to make the speakers sound as they do in the poem as Justice wrote it. Compare your continuation with those written by your classmates.

*Incident in a Rose Garden*   577

## The Seven Ages of Man

**William Shakespeare** (1564–1616) came to maturity when the English language was rapidly developing into a rich and powerful means of expression. Theater-goers were eager to hear impressive, fully developed speeches modeled on those in classical drama. Shakespeare's genius, therefore, was perfectly suited for his era. All of his plays include speeches in which thought and feeling are expressed with a brilliance unequaled by any other poet or dramatist. "The Seven Ages of Man" is one of the best of them.

**Dramatic Monologue**

Another kind of dramatic poetry is the **dramatic monologue**: a speech in which a fictional character expresses his or her thoughts and feelings within a developing situation. The word monologue is based on the root *mono,* meaning "one"—in other words, only one character speaks. Some of the best dramatic monologues come from verse plays, such as Shakespeare's, and can stand by themselves as complete poems.

**Look For**

As you read "The Seven Ages of Man," look for the stages of life the speaker reveals.

**Writing**

What stages of life do you think a person passes through? Freewrite, exploring your answer.

**Vocabulary**

Knowing the following words will help you as you read "The Seven Ages of Man."

**woeful** (wō′ fəl) *adj.*: Full of sorrow (p. 580, l. 10)

**treble** (treb′ 'l) *n.*: High-pitched voice (p. 580, l. 24)

# The Seven Ages of Man

## William Shakespeare

All the world's a stage,
And all the men and women merely players:[1]
They have their exits and their entrances;
And one man in his time plays many parts,
His acts being seven ages.[2] At first the infant,

5

1. **players:** Actors.
2. **ages:** Periods of life.

THE SEVEN AGES OF MAN
*Milton Glaser*
Signet Classic, New American Library

*The Seven Ages of Man*   579

## Presentation

**Motivation/Prior Knowledge** Ask students to summarize the main stages they have passed through in their own lives so far. Tell them that Shakespeare describes the stages of human life in this poem.

**Master Teacher Note** You might want to tell students that Shakespeare frequently compared life to acting. In this speech, however, he extends the comparison for many lines. Explain to students that "The Seven Ages of Man" is an excerpt from Shakespeare's play *As You Like It,* and its opening lines are frequently quoted.

**Thematic Idea** Another selection you might want to use with this one is Marchette Chute's essay from *Shakespeare of London,* page 527. This essay describes the kind of theatrical training that Shakespeare received.

**Purpose-Setting Question** How accurate is the description of each stage of life?

1 **Discussion** How can one person play many parts?

2 **Reading Strategy** Ask students to predict what the stages will be.

## Humanities Note

Fine art, illustration by Milton Glaser. Milton Glaser is a well-known graphic artist. This illustration appears on the cover of an edition of Shakespeare's works.

You might want to use the following questions:
1. What scene does the illustration depict?
2. Is the illustration suitable for this poem? Explain.

3 **Discussion** Ask students to identify the simile in this description. Is the comparison a good one?

4 **Discussion** Ask students to identify the simile in line 10. Is it effective?

5 **Discussion** What does Shakespeare mean by the phrase "the bubble reputation"?

6 **Discussion** How does this phase of life relate to an earlier phase?

7 **Discussion** What mood do these lines create?

**Reader's Response** In "The Seven Ages of Man" Shakespeare states, "And one man in his time plays many parts." What parts have you played in your life so far?

Mewling[3] and puking in the nurse's arms.
And then the whining schoolboy, with his satchel,
And shining morning face, creeping like snail
Unwillingly to school. And then the lover,
10  Sighing like furnace, with a woeful ballad
Made to his mistress' eyebrow. Then a soldier,
Full of strange oaths, and bearded like the pard,[4]
Jealous in honor,[5] sudden and quick in quarrel,
Seeking the bubble reputation
15  Even in the cannon's mouth. And then the justice,[6]
In fair round belly with good capon[7] lined,
With eyes severe and beard of formal cut,
Full of wise saws and modern instances;[8]
And so he plays his part. The sixth age shifts
20  Into the lean and slippered pantaloon,[9]
With spectacles on nose and pouch on side,
His youthful hose[10] well saved, a world too wide
For his shrunk shank;[11] and his big manly voice,
Turning again toward childish treble, pipes
25  And whistles in his sound. Last scene of all,
That ends this strange eventful history,
Is second childishness, and mere oblivion,
Sans[12] teeth, sans eyes, sans taste, sans everything.

---

**3. mewling** (myo͞ol' iŋ) *v.*: Whimpering, crying like a baby.
**4. pard** (pärd) *n.*: A leopard or panther.
**5. Jealous in honor:** Very concerned about his honor.
**6. justice:** A judge.
**7. capon** (kā' pän) *n.*: A roasted chicken. The speaker is implying that the judge has been bribed with the present of a fat chicken.
**8. wise saws and modern instances:** Wise sayings and modern examples that show the truth of the sayings.
**9. pantaloon** (pan' t'l o͞on') *n.*: A thin, foolish old man—originally a character in old comedies.
**10. hose** (hōz) *n.*: Stockings.
**11. shank** (shank) *n.*: Leg.
**12. sans** (sanz) *prep.*: Without, lacking.

## THINKING ABOUT THE SELECTION

### Recalling

1. List the seven types of persons the speaker uses to represent the seven ages of life.

### Interpreting

2. What period of life does each of these persons represent?
3. If the speaker compares the world to a stage and people to actors, then what might people's "exits and . . . entrances" represent?
4. What is the "bubble reputation" that the soldier seeks?
5. What are the qualities or characteristics of the periods of life represented by the soldier and the judge?
6. How does the last age bring us full circle back to the start?
7. What attitude toward life does the speaker seem to be expressing? Support your answer.

### Applying

8. Do you think that most people who live long lives pass through seven periods similar to those described in the poem? Give reasons for your opinion.

## ANALYZING LITERATURE

### Appreciating Poems from Plays

**Poems from plays** are speeches, songs, or other passages that can be read and enjoyed by themselves. Shakespeare's plays are filled with such passages, and many consider them to be his finest poetry. Such poems are dramatic in that they are found in dramas. Many, however, are dramatic in another sense: they depict a character reacting to other characters in the midst of a developing situation or conflict.

1. "The Seven Ages of Man" is from Shakespeare's play *As You Like It.* Tell why you think

the poem is or is not clear and complete by itself, apart from the rest of the play.

2. Describe the organization of the poem. How are the various details arranged in relation to one another?

## UNDERSTANDING LANGUAGE

### Appreciating Vivid Words

In poetry **vivid words** are those that arouse rich or striking mental images in a reader. The speaker in "The Seven Ages of Man," for example, describes the infant as "Mewling and puking in the nurse's arms." The words *mewling* and *puking* create a vividly unpleasant impression of the infant.

1. Find four words that describe the schoolboy. What impression do they create?
2. Which three words vividly describe the lover? What impression do they create?
3. What contrasts do you find in the words that describe the sixth age? Why are these contrasts appropriate?

## THINKING AND WRITING

### Imitating Shakespeare

Write an essay titled "The Stages of Life." Like Shakespeare, choose a type of person (or, if you wish, a kind of activity) to represent each stage of life. Into how many stages will you divide life? What characteristics will each stage have? When you write your essay, use a systematic organization like the one in "The Seven Ages of Man." When you revise, make sure that each person or activity you have selected is described in a way that clearly suggests a stage of life. Compare your essay with your classmates'. Into how many stages did they divide life? How are their stages similar to or different from yours?

8. Answers will differ, but most students will say that people do pass through phases similar to the ones that Shakespeare describes.

**Challenge** The poem presents the seven ages of life. What other processes might be divided into stages?

## ANSWERS TO ANALYZING LITERATURE

1. Suggested Response: The poem is clear by itself because it does not refer to any specific action or character in the play. The idea it presents can stand by itself.
2. Suggested Response: The poem has a four-line introduction followed by a chronological description of each of the seven ages.

## ANSWERS TO UNDERSTANDING LANGUAGE

1. Suggested Response: Four words that describe the schoolboy are *"whining . . . shining morning face . . . creeping . . ."* These words suggest a fresh-faced youngster who does not want to go to school.
2. Suggested Response: Three words that describe the lover are *"Sighing like furnace."* These words create a humorous impression of a smitten lover.
3. Suggested Response: The contrasts are between the "youthful hose" and "shrunk shank," the "big manly voice" and the "childish treble." These contrasts indicate a decline in life and a coming full circle back to childhood.

## THINKING AND WRITING

For help with this assignment, students can consult Lesson 2, "Drafting and Revising," in the Handbook of Writing About Literature.

**Closure and Extension**

## ANSWERS TO THINKING ABOUT THE SELECTION
### Recalling

1. The seven ages are represented by a baby, a schoolboy, a lover, a soldier, a judge, an old man with spectacles, and an even older, now childish, man without teeth, sight, or taste.

### Interpreting

2. Suggested Response: They represent infancy, school age, youth, adulthood, advanced middle age, old age, and senility.
3. Suggested Response: Entrance might be birth and exit death.
4. Suggested Response: This phrase might refer to glory and fame.
5. The soldier is a bearded man, very proud and quarrelsome, who acts bravely to gain fame. The

judge is a fat man with a trim beard who likes to display his wisdom.

6. Suggested Response: During this last stage, humans resemble children again.
7. Suggested Response: The speaker seems to be expressing a detached, somewhat cynical, and ironical view of life. He seems to be laughing at the reluctance of the schoolchildren, the earnestness of the lover, and the soldier's pursuit of glory.

**More About the Authors** Although **Robert Frost's** poems usually portray New England settings, they are appreciated by people all over the world. Ask students how the appreciation and understanding of Frost's work by people from New England may differ from that of people from other geographic locations.

**Sara Henderson Hay** is known for her convincing characterizations. Ask students how a poet can make a character come alive for the reader and how the technique for accomplishing this goal may differ in a novel, short story, or biography.

You might want to tell students that **Edgar Lee Masters** was one of the first American authors to portray small-town life in a realistic manner. Ask students why such an achievement might be important.

### The Runaway

**Robert Frost** (1874–1963) was born in California and, as a struggling young poet, lived in England for a time. It is New England, however, that gave Frost the subjects of his finest poems—New England scenes, characters, and events that he depicted in clear, memorable verse. "The Runaway" presents a vivid picture of a little horse in a mountain pasture. The poem conveys affection, amusement, and compassion—feelings that run through many of Frost's memorable nature poems.

### The Princess

**Sara Henderson Hay** (1906–    ) was born in Pittsburgh, Pennsylvania. "The Princess" illustrates the unusual way she sometimes approaches poetry. She takes a character from a legend—in this case a princess—and presents her as a real person. She can similarly treat everyday subjects and scenes from an imaginative and striking point of view.

### George Gray

**Edgar Lee Masters** (1868–1950) was born in Kansas and raised in two small Illinois towns. His observations of life there are the basis of his masterpiece, *Spoon River Anthology*. This book is a collection of monologues by various characters—all of them dead—who speak honestly and wtih intense feeling about their lives. "George Gray" illustrates Masters's ability to condense the meaning of an entire life in a brief, powerful speech.

582   *Poetry*

**Objectives**

1  To understand point of view when reading poetry
2  To read aloud a dramatic dialogue
3  To recognize assertions

**Support Material**

**Teaching Portfolio**
Teacher Backup, p. 719
Grammar in Action Worksheet, *Using Colons,* p. 723
Usage and Mechanics Worksheet, p. 725
Vocabulary Check, p. 726
Analyzing Literature Worksheet, *Understanding a Dramatic Monologue,* p. 727
Language Worksheet, *Language*

*of Contrast,* p. 728
Selection Test, p. 729
Art Transparency 12: *The Birthplace of Herbert Hoover,* by Grant Wood

## The Speaker

In dramatic poetry, the **speaker** should not be confused with the author of the poems. Speakers are characters with their own points of view—their own attitudes, backgrounds, and ways of looking at reality. Their thoughts and feelings may be similar to those of the author, or they may be utterly different.

## Look For

As you read the poems in this section, look for indications that the speakers are created characters. What do you learn about their personalities? What do you learn about their lives?

## Writing

Write a brief letter to yourself from a well-known person whom you admire. Let the letter say whatever you wish this person would say to you in an actual letter.

## Vocabulary

Knowing the following words will help you as you read these poems.
**suitors** (sōōt′ ərs) *n.*: Men courting a woman (p. 587, l. 12)
**furled** (furld) *v.*: Rolled up and tied (p. 588, l. 3)
**disillusionment** (dis i lōō′ zhən mənt) *n.*: Disappointment (p. 588, l. 6)

---

**Literary Focus** It will be easier for students to understand the concept of the speaker in poetry by comparing it to the first-person point of view in fiction. When a character narrates the action in a story, it is usually clear that the character is not the author. The narrator describes events from his or her own point of view.

**Look For** The author's attitude is revealed through the tone of the story or poem and may be different from or similar to the feelings of the character. In dramatic poetry as in first-person fiction, the author's feelings are never directly stated and the reader must infer from the words what the author's attitude is toward the characters and events. Consider telling students to look first for the speaker's feelings and then compare those with the attitude of the author, as it can be inferred from other elements of the poem.

**Writing/Prior Knowledge** Before writing, students should consider what interest they might share with the person they have selected. This common interest could then be the topic of the letter.

**Vocabulary** Have the less advanced students select a synonym for each of the words. Then ask them to write a sentence for each word that includes both the word and its synonym.

**Spelling Tip** Have students find the word *illusion* in *disillusionment*. Point out that *illusion* is spelled with one *s*, not two.

# The Runaway

## Robert Frost

Once when the snow of the year was beginning to fall,
We stopped by a mountain pasture to say, "Whose colt?"
A little Morgan[1] had one forefoot on the wall,
The other curled at his breast. He dipped his head
5   And snorted at us. And then he had to bolt.
We heard the miniature thunder where he fled,
And we saw him, or thought we saw him, dim and gray,
Like a shadow against the curtain of falling flakes.
"I think the little fellow's afraid of the snow.
10   He isn't winter-broken. It isn't play
With the little fellow at all. He's running away.
I doubt if even his mother could tell him, 'Sakes,
It's only weather.' He'd think she didn't know!
Where is his mother? He can't be out alone."
15   And now he comes again with clatter of stone,

---

**1. Morgan** (môr′ gən) *n.*: A breed of saddle horse that originated in New England.

584

3 And mounts the wall again with whited eyes
And all his tail that isn't hair up straight.
He shudders his coat as if to throw off flies.
"Whoever it is that leaves him out so late,
4 20 When other creatures have gone to stall and bin,
Ought to be told to come and take him in."

## THINKING ABOUT THE SELECTION
### Recalling

1. Describe the actions of the colt.
2. According to the person whose remarks are quoted, why is the colt acting as he is?

### Interpreting

3. Find three descriptive phrases that suggest the colt's feelings and tell the feelings suggested.
4. Find two phrases that vividly suggest the sound of the running colt. Why are they especially effective as description?
5. The last three lines express disapproval of whoever has left the colt outside. Do you think these lines express the theme, or point, of the poem? Tell why you do or do not think so.

### Applying

6. What is it about human beings that makes us want to aid creatures we see as helpless or in need of protection? Explain your answer.

## ANALYZING LITERATURE
### Understanding Point of View

In dramatic poetry, **point of view** refers to the speaker's attitudes, opinions, and ways of looking at reality or the situation presented in the poem. Even if the speaker's thoughts and feelings should be the same as the poet's, the speaker presents them in his or her own way and from within the situation presented in the poem. You should, therefore, not equate the speaker of a dramatic poem with the author of the poem.

1. The speaker of "The Runaway" twice quotes someone's remarks, once in lines 9–14 and again in lines 19–21. Are these two pairs of remarks uttered by the same person? Tell why you feel that they are or are not.
2. Do you think that the speaker of the entire poem is quoting himself or herself in these pairs of remarks? To answer this question, compare the tone of voice in the quoted lines with the tone of the rest of the poem.

*The Runaway*   585

THE FAIRY MORGANA
*Howard Pyle*
Delaware Art Museum

586  *Poetry*

# The Princess

## Sara Henderson Hay

1
I'll ask for a red rose blossoming in the snow,
A music box hid in a walnut shell,
Nine golden apples on a silver bough,
A mirror that can speak, and cast a spell.
5  I'll send them East of the Moon, and West of the Sun
For a wishing ring made of a dragon's claw. . . .

2
And they will fail, just as the rest have done,
And I can stay at home, with dear Papa.

3
Oh sometimes in my silken bed I wake
10  All of a shiver, and my hair on end,
Because again the terrible dream occurred:
What if one of those suitors *should* come back
With the impossible trophy in his hand,

4
And I should have to keep my foolish word!

---

1 **Discussion** Why do you think she will ask for such gifts?

2 **Reading Strategy** Have students paraphrase the thought that goes through the mind of the princess in these lines.

3 **Discussion** Ask students to explain what the phrase "fear of the unknown" means to them. How does this idea relate to the poem?

4 **Reading Strategy** Ask students to predict what will happen to the princess.

## Closure and Extension

### ANSWERS TO THINKING ABOUT THE SELECTION
*Recalling*

1. The princess wants to stay home with her "dear Papa."
2. Her one fear is that one of the suitors will return with "the impossible trophy" and she will have to marry him and leave her father.

*Interpreting*

3. Suggested Response: Each of the gifts is impossible to find.
4. Suggested Response: These places are impossible to reach.
5. Answers will differ, but most students will realize that she is afraid of leaving home and cruel to the men who pursue her.

*Applying*

6. Answers will differ, but most students will realize that the poet is describing a certain type of person rather than trying to depict a typical princess.

**Challenge** Write a description of the princess from the point of view of a suitor who has failed. Then write a description of her from the perspective of a suitor who has just arrived at court.

## THINKING ABOUT THE SELECTION

### Recalling

1. What is the one thing the princess wants to do?
2. What is her one fear?

### Interpreting

3. What do the requested gifts described in lines 1–4 all have in common?
4. What do the destinations mentioned in line 5 have in common with the gifts?
5. Describe the character and personality of the princess.

### Applying

6. Do you think the purpose of the poem is to show what a typical princess is like? Or could it be to represent a certain kind of personality?

Tell what you think the purpose is and give your reasons.

## SPEAKING AND LISTENING

### Reading Aloud a Dramatic Monologue

When you read a dramatic monologue aloud, think of yourself as an actor playing a part. Like an actor rehearsing a role, think about the character you are representing. For "The Princess" ask yourself: "What is she like? What is going on in her life when she speaks these words? What are her feelings and mood? How will her voice change in the course of the poem?" When you have answered these questions, practice reciting the poem. If you have studied and rehearsed your "role" thoroughly, you should be able to read "The Princess" with only an occasional glance at the text.

*The Princess*  587

**Motivation/Prior Knowledge**
Have students imagine that they are invited to go on a great and potentially dangerous adventure. It could be mountain climbing in the Himalayas, a safari in deepest Africa, a voyage in a space shuttle into the unknown, or whatever else they might imagine. What would be the dangers involved? What would be the possible rewards? What would determine whether or not they would accept the invitation? Then tell them that this poem is spoken by a man who was afraid to take risks and strive for his goals.

**Master Teacher Note** Use the overhead projector to show students Art Transparency 12, *The Birthplace of Herbert Hoover,* by Grant Wood. Tell students that Hoover served as the thirty-first President of the United States (1929–1933). Ask students why we honor presidents and other famous figures by making their birthplaces into museums. Lead them to see that these figures, through their willingness to strive for their goals, can serve as role models for us. Then tell them that Masters's poem "George Gray" is about a person who was afraid to work for a goal.

**Purpose-Setting Question**
What are George Gray's main fear and main desire?

1 **Discussion** What feelings do you have when you see a sailboat running before the wind? What feelings does a boat with furled sails suggest?

2 **Discussion** What can you infer about his life based on his comment?

3 **Discussion** How might his life be different if he could live it again? What is the effect of your knowledge that he will not have a second chance?

# George Gray

**Edgar Lee Masters**

I have studied many times
The marble which was chiseled for me—
1 A boat with a furled sail at rest in a harbor.
In truth it pictures not my destination
2 5 But my life.
For love was offered me, and I shrank from its
 disillusionment;
Sorrow knocked at my door, but I was afraid;
Ambition called to me, but I dreaded the chances.
Yet all the while I hungered for meaning in my life
10 And now I know that we must lift the sail
And catch the winds of destiny
Wherever they drive the boat.
To put meaning in one's life may end in madness,
But life without meaning is the torture
3 15 Of restlessness and vague desire—
It is a boat longing for the sea and yet afraid.

## THINKING ABOUT THE SELECTION

### Recalling

1. What did the speaker turn away from in life, yet what did he want?

### Interpreting

2. Why is the carving on the speaker's tombstone a fitting image of his life?
3. What does the speaker now know?
4. Interpret the last three lines. What is "life without meaning"?

### Applying

5. If you could ask the speaker "What should people do to put meaning in their lives?" what answer do you think he would give?

## CRITICAL THINKING AND READING

### Recognizing Assertions

An **assertion** is a positive statement made with great confidence but with little or no proof to support it. An assertion may be true or false, reasonable or unreasonable. In "George Gray" the speaker says "And now I know that we must lift the sail/And catch the winds of destiny/Wherever they drive the boat."
1. What does this assertion mean? Rephrase it in plain, simple language.
2. Evaluate the assertion. Is it true and reasonable or not? Does it contain good advice? Give reasons for your opinion.

**ANSWERS TO THINKING ABOUT THE SELECTION**
*Recalling*

1. George Gray turned away from love, sorrow, and ambition. He wanted meaning in his life.

*Interpreting*

2. Suggested Response: The sails on the boat are furled, so it can go nowhere. This boat symbolizes the lack of any adventure in his life.
3. Suggested Response: He now knows that in order to have meaning in one's life, one must take risks.
4. Suggested Response: The words "life without meaning" refer to a life in which nothing is risked, so a person experiences "vague desire" without fulfillment.

*Applying*

5. Answers will differ. However, most students will realize that the speaker would advise them to pursue love, risk sorrow, and work toward their ambition.

**ANSWERS TO CRITICAL THINKING AND READING**

1. Suggested Response: We must risk going out into life and living it fully no matter what happens.
2. Answers will differ. Most students will realize that it is good advice if it is tempered with some caution.

# Lyric Poetry

**QUINTET**
*Samuel Reindorf*

**Humanities Note**

Fine Art, *Quintet*, 1961, Samuel Reindorf. Samuel Reindorf, born in 1914, is a Mexican painter of Polish origins. He studied art at the Toronto School of Art in Canada and the American Artists School in New York City. He presently resides in Mexico.

*Quintet* is the artist's salute to jazz and the musicians who perform it. The harmonious colors of this abstract composition add to its lively charm.

**More About the Authors Shakespeare's** reputation as a lyric poet is also based on his series of sonnets—fourteen-line poems with a set rhythm and rhyme scheme. Scholars are still arguing about the identities of the young nobleman and the mysterious "dark lady" mentioned in these poems. Ask students what kind of detective-work scholars might do to solve this puzzle.

Many people remember **Edwin Arlington Robinson** for his portraits of unfortunate people who led lives of tragedy and frustration. "Miniver Cheevey" and "Richard Cory" stand out as centerpieces of this poet's art. Ask students if a poet's choice of moral theme or subject matter clearly marks the type of person he or she is.

In addition to writing poetry, **Gordon Parks** has careers as an eminent photographer and motion picture director. He directed and wrote the score for the film *The Learning Tree*. Ask students for the names of other creative people who are or were multi-talented. Also discuss the different ways in which creativity is manifested in people.

**Christina Rossetti** was the youngest child in a family of four children and was overshadowed by both her brothers. Ask students what a younger sibling, who has older brothers or sisters with strong egos, might do to assert her own identity?

Consider telling students that **James Joyce** seldom returned to Ireland once he had left. Ask them what factors might cause a writer to live and write in another country.

# GUIDE FOR READING

## Winter

**William Shakespeare** (1564–1616) was a lyric poet as well as an author of poetic dramas. Among his most famous lyrics are his sonnets. Even Shakespeare's plays, however, contain lyric poems. "Winter," for example, appears at the end of the comedy *Love's Labor's Lost*. Like many of the lyrics in his plays, it was probably sung to music. The boy actors in the theater companies of the time were skilled singers, and many acting troupes had a variety of musical instruments.

## The Dark Hills

**Edwin Arlington Robinson** (1869–1935) was considered the major poet of his time in America. He led a difficult life, plagued by ill health and money problems. These experiences probably contributed to the depiction of suffering in his poems about small-town life. Tilbury Town, the fictional small town of his work, was actually based on the place where he grew up—Gardiner, Maine. Robinson's lyric "The Dark Hills" reflects a yearning for the end of war and conflict.

## Funeral

**Gordon Parks** (1912–     ) achieved an important breakthrough as the first black film director in the history of Hollywood. However, Parks is best known for his work as a photographer and writer. These two careers are summed up in the title of his book *A Poet and His Camera* (1968). In his poem "The Funeral," he writes about a universal theme—how the world you knew as a child seems different when you are older.

## Uphill

**Christina Rossetti** (1830–1894) is considered by some critics to be the best female poet in English literature. She was the daughter of an Italian father (her mother is to the right in the picture), who had come to live in England, and her brother was the famous poet and painter Dante Gabriel Rossetti. Today Christina Rossetti's best-known work is the long poem "Goblin Market," a kind of supernatural fairy tale. Many of her other poems, however, reflect her concern with religion. A number of them, like "Uphill," deal with the theme of death.

### Objectives

1 To understand lyric poetry
2 To write a lyric poem
3 To interpret connotative meaning in a lyric poem
4 To write about a lyric poem
5 To interpret symbols in lyric poetry
6 To interpret sensory words
7 To write about fine art

### Support Material

**Teaching Portfolio**
Teacher Backup, p. 731
Usage and Mechanics Worksheet, p. 737
Vocabulary Check, p. 738

Critical Thinking and Reading Worksheet, *Interpreting Symbols in Lyric Poetry*, p. 740
Language Worksheet, *Using General and Specific Words*, p. 741
Selection Test, p. 742
Art Transparency 13: *War Series: Casualty—The Secretary of War Regrets,* by Jacob Lawrence

# I Hear an Army

**James Joyce** (1882–1941) was born in Dublin, Ireland. He was educated in Catholic schools and almost became a priest, but he chose to be a writer instead. Rebelling against traditional values, he left Ireland to live abroad after graduating from college. Joyce is primarily known for his daring, experimental works of fiction, such as *Portrait of the Artist as a Young Man* and *Ulysses.* However, he also published an excellent volume of lyrics, *Pomes Penyeach,* from which "I Hear an Army" comes.

**Lyric Poetry**

In **lyric poetry** writers express their thoughts and feelings about a subject in a brief but musical way. The reference to music in this definition is a key point. Of all the different types of poetry, lyrics are most closely related to song. In ancient times lyric poetry was accompanied by the stringed instrument called a lyre—which explains the term *lyric.* Today such poems are not usually set to music, but they still have a songlike quality.

Lyric poems can take many different forms. "The Dark Hills" uses rhymes and regular rhythms. "Funeral," on the other hand, does not use these devices. Almost all lyric poems, however, convey the writer's thoughts and feelings in lively language.

**Look For**

Look for the vivid words that these poets use to communicate their feelings and thoughts. Also, ask yourself which of the following poems could best be set to music.

**Writing**

In "Winter" Shakespeare describes sights, sounds, and feelings associated with that season. Choose your favorite season and list some sights, sounds, feelings, tastes, and smells that are typical of that time of year.

**Vocabulary**

Knowing the following words will help you as you read these poems.

**brooding** (brood ĭŋ) *v.:* Thinking about something in a troubled way (p. 592, l. 12)

**legions** (lē′ jəns) *n.:* Groups of soldiers (p. 594, l. 6)

**whittled** (hwit′ld) *v.:* Reduced gradually, as if cut away in slices by a knife (p. 595, l. 2)

**wayfarers** (wā′ fer ərz) *n.:* Travelers (p. 596, l. 9)

**arrogant** (ar′ ə gənt) *adj.:* Proud; haughty (p. 597, l. 3)

**disdaining** (dis dān′ iŋ) *v.:* Rejecting with scorn (p. 597, l. 4)

**cleave** (klēv) *v.:* Split (p. 597, l. 7)

**Literary Focus** Readers of lyric poetry must be alert to the concentration of language in the poems they read. Authors of novels and stories and plays have many more words with which to create their effects, but the poet makes use of every word, connotation, syllable, and mark of punctuation. Because there is so much the poet does not say and so much the poet implies, the reader must be able to make inferences. Because the poet creates so many images, all the reader's sensory powers must be in gear. The reader must be active and alert to get the full experience and meaning from lyric poetry.

**Look For** A writer once described a boxing match as a sea of faces rising and falling, threatening to overcome the canvas island at its center. Lyric poets specialize in new ways to view experience. Their unique and vivid images provide a fountain from which new ideas flow. Readers of lyric poetry need to be alert to these intriguing images and to the new ideas they engender.

**Writing/Prior Knowledge** If students are familiar with the construction of semantic maps, have them divide into groups and construct such a map for one of the seasons of the year. The maps can then serve as a springboard for students to use in their writing assignment.

**Vocabulary** Ask less advanced students to create an analogy around each of the words on the list; for example, *brooding* is to *rejoicing* as *frowning* is to *smiling.*

**Spelling Tip** Point out that *arrogant* ends with an *ant,* not *ent.*

**Motivation/Prior Knowledge**
Ask students to name their favorite season of the year. What associations do they have with that season? What is their least favorite season? What do they dislike about that time of year?

**Master Teacher Note** Students' reactions to the different seasons depend on their experiences. These experiences vary widely depending, in part, on where they have lived. Winter in one climate is very different from winter in another. For those who have never experienced winter in a northern climate, it would be of help to discuss vicarious experiences they might have had through motion pictures, television, or reading. Experience with the seasons also is different through the centuries. Establish with students the problems of coping with the weather 300 years ago compared with their experiences today.

**Thematic Ideas** Other selections that you might use with "Winter" are "The Seven Ages of Man," page 579, a monologue from *As You Like It,* and Marchette Chute's essay from *Shakespeare of London,* page 527. This essay describes the training that Shakespeare received as an actor.

You may teach "The Raven," page 563, with "I Hear an Army." Both these poems deal with loss of love.

**Purpose-Setting Question**
What is the attitude of the poet toward winter?

1 **Discussion** Are Shakespeare's winter scenes realistic? Explain.

2 **Discussion** How do you think Shakespeare felt about the winter?

3 **Literary Focus** What is the effect of repetition in this poem?

# Winter

### William Shakespeare

1
When icicles hang by the wall
    And Dick the shepherd blows his nail[1]
And Tom bears logs into the hall
    And milk comes frozen home in pail,
5 When blood is nipp'd[2] and ways be foul,
Then nightly sings the staring owl,
        Tu-whit;
Tu-who, a merry note,
While greasy Joan doth keel the pot.[3]

10 When all around the wind doth blow
    And coughing drowns the parson's saw[4]
2
And birds sit brooding in the snow
    And Marian's nose looks red and raw,
When roasted crabs[5] hiss in the bowl,
3
15 Then nightly sings the staring owl,
        Tu-whit;
Tu-who, a merry note,
While greasy Joan doth keel the pot.

---

1. **blows his nail:** Blows on his fingernails to warm his hands.
2. **nipp'd:** Stung with cold.
3. **keel the pot:** Stir the pot to cool its contents.
4. **saw:** Sermon.
5. **crabs:** Here, crab apples.

**Reader's Response** How is your vision of winter similar to or different from that of Shakespeare?

## THINKING ABOUT THE SELECTION
### Recalling
1. Identify four of the little winter scenes that Shakespeare depicts.

### Interpreting
2. Why is the scene described in line 11 especially typical of the winter?
3. What is the mood of this poem?

### Applying
4. Why do you think that lyric poets often write about a particular season?

## ANALYZING LITERATURE
### Understanding Lyric Poetry
In **lyric poetry** writers express their thoughts and feelings about a subject in a brief but musical way. Shakespeare's "Winter," like a number of his lyrics, was actually written as a song for a play. The repeated lines are similar to the repeated words and phrases you hear in today's popular songs. This lyric, however, is less an expression of Shakespeare's personal feelings than a vivid description of winter scenes.
1. Identify the refrain, or repeated lines, of this lyric poem.
2. What different senses does Shakespeare appeal to in his descriptions? Explain.
3. If you were adding to this poem, what winter scenes would you include?

## THINKING AND WRITING
### Writing a Lyric Poem
Recall the sights, sounds, tastes, and smells that you listed as you thought about your favorite season. Add to this list some of the thoughts and feelings that this season calls up in you. Using these notes, write a lyric poem about this season. It can present little scenes, as "Winter" does, but it does not have to use rhyme or definite rhythms. However, you might want to imitate Shakespeare's use of a refrain. Write a first draft of this poem and then read it aloud to several classmates. Ask them how you can make your descriptions more vivid. Then revise the poem and share it with your classmates.

*Winter* 593

# The Dark Hills

### Edwin Arlington Robinson

1
Dark hills at evening in the west,
Where sunset hovers like a sound
Of golden horns that sang to rest
Old bones of warriors under ground,

2
5 Far now from all the bannered ways
Where flash the legions of the sun,
You fade—as if the last of days
Were fading, and all wars were done.

## THINKING ABOUT THE SELECTION

### Recalling

1. Describe the scene at which the poet is looking.
2. What scene from the past does the sunset recall?
3. In the last two lines, what does the poet imagine is happening?

### Interpreting

4. What is the main difference between the "bones of warriors under ground" and "the legions of the sun"?
5. How is the sunset "like a sound"?
6. Whom or what is the poet addressing in the next-to-last line?
7. A critic has called this poem a wish for the end of war. Comment on this interpretation.

### Applying

8. Why do you think that times of dramatic changes in light, like sunset, call up many thoughts and feelings in people?

## CRITICAL THINKING AND READING

### Interpreting Connotative Meaning

The **connotations** of words are the emotions and associations that they suggest, beyond their plain dictionary meaning. For example, the dictionary meaning of *dark,* which appears in the title and first line of Robinson's poem, is "the absence of light." However, this word also suggests peace, mystery, and even danger—these are some of its connotations. Poets use the connotations of words to create moods and reveal deeper meanings in their lyrics.

1. Explain how some of the connotations of *dark* contribute to the mood and meaning of "The Dark Hills."
2. What associations does the word "sunset" in line 2 bring to mind?
3. What are some of the connotations of the word "golden" in line 3?
4. What are some of the connotations of the word "sun" in line 6?
5. What do the connotations of these words add to the meaning of the poem?

# The Funeral

## Gordon Parks

1
5

After many snows I was home again.
Time had whittled down to mere hills
The great mountains of my childhood.
Raging rivers I once swam trickled now like gentle streams.
And the wide road curving on to China or Kansas City or
    perhaps Calcutta,[1]
Had withered to a crooked path of dust
Ending abruptly at the county burying ground.

2
10

Only the giant who was my father remained the same.
A hundred strong men strained beneath his coffin
When they bore him to his grave.

---

**1. Calcutta** (kal kut′ ə) *n.*: A major city of India.

---

## THINKING ABOUT THE SELECTION

### Recalling

1. Identify three ways in which the place where the speaker grew up seems different to him.
2. What is the only event that occurs in this poem?

### Interpreting

3. Why did the rivers seem "Raging" and the mountains "great" when he was a child?
4. Why has the speaker returned home?
5. Do the last three lines record a child's or an adult's perception? Explain.

### Applying

6. Discuss one way in which your perception of familiar surroundings has changed as you have grown up. How do you account for the difference?

## THINKING AND WRITING

### Writing About a Lyric Poem

You can perform an experiment with Parks's poem "The Funeral" to show the effects of vivid language in a lyric. Rewrite the poem making the following changes: line 1—change "snows" to *years;* line 2—change "whittled" to *worn;* line 4—change "Raging" to *Wide* and "trickled" to *ran;* line 5—eliminate "wide" and change "curving" to *going;* line 6—change "withered" to *changed;* line 7—eliminate "abruptly." Compare and contrast the original poem with the one you have just created. Briefly note the differences between the two. Consider the effect of removing some of the vivid language. How do the descriptions and mood of the new poem compare with those of the original? Then, using your notes, write a comparison and contrast of the two poems.

*The Funeral* 595

## Presentation

**Motivation/Prior Knowledge**
Have students recall the longest trip they have taken. What was their feeling at the beginning of the journey? Ask them to contrast it with their feeling midway and just before they arrived at their destination. Tell them that this poem is about the longest possible journey.

**Purpose-Setting Question**
What is the destination of the journey in this poem?

**1 Reading Strategy** Have the students note that questions and answers alternate throughout the poem. Ask students to predict what the line of questioning will be.

**2 Reading Strategy** Have students summarize the literal description of the journey.

**3 Discussion** Ask students to discuss the possible figurative meaning of the journey. What is the final destination?

## Closure and Extension

### ANSWERS TO THINKING ABOUT THE SELECTION
*Recalling*

1. The speaker learns that the road winds uphill; the trip takes a full day; there is an inn at the top where other wayfarers are staying; one can see the inn after dark; it will be easy to get in; and beds are available for a good rest.

*Interpreting*

2. Suggested Response: The inn at the end of the journey is most unusual in that all who have gone before are still there, and yet there are beds available for all who come.
3. Suggested Response: The first and third line of each stanza are

# Uphill

## Christina Rossetti

1 ⌈ Does the road wind uphill all the way?
    Yes, to the very end.
⌈ Will the day's journey take the whole long day?
    From morn to night, my friend.

5 ⌈ But is there for the night a restingplace?
    A roof for when the slow dark hours begin.
May not the darkness hide it from my face?
    You cannot miss that inn.

2

Shall I meet other wayfarers at night?
10     Those who have gone before.
Then must I knock, or call when just in sight?
    They will not keep you standing at that door.

Shall I find comfort, travel-sore and weak?
    Of labor you shall find the sum.
3 ⌈ 15 Will there be beds for me and all who seek?
    Yea, beds for all who come.

---

## THINKING ABOUT THE SELECTION
### Recalling

1. Summarize what the questioner in this poem learns about the journey that he or she is taking.

### Interpreting

2. What evidence is there that this journey is not just an ordinary trip?
3. Show how the lines of the poem are divided between two speakers.
4. Who do you think these speakers are?

### Applying

5. If you were the questioner in this poem, how would you respond to the answers you received? Explain.

*596   Poetry*

## CRITICAL THINKING AND READING
### Interpreting Symbols in Lyric Poetry

A **symbol** is something which is itself and yet suggests or represents another thing as well. The advantage of a symbol is that it focuses a complex idea or experience onto an object or experience that can be readily understood. In "Uphill," for instance, Rossetti symbolizes life and death as a journey and rest. Once you understand this symbolism, the meaning of the poem becomes clear.

1. Why is a journey along a road a good symbol for life?
2. What might the uphill winding represent?
3. Explain what the "roof" and "slow dark hours" could symbolize.
4. Who are "Those who have gone before"?

spoken by the questioner, and second and fourth lines are spoken by the answerer.
4. Suggested Response: The questioner is a person approaching death, and the answerer could be Death itself.

*Applying*

5. Answers will differ, but students may have a difficult time identifying with an older person who is approaching the end of life.

### ANSWERS TO CRITICAL THINKING AND READING

1. Suggested Response: In a sense life is a trip through many stages and experiences from birth to death.
2. Suggested Response: The struggles of life and its frustrations are symbolized by the winding uphill road.
3. Suggested Response: The roof may be the earth over the grave

and the slow dark hours Death itself.
4. Suggested Response: "Those who have gone before" are all the people who have lived and died.

HORSES OF NEPTUNE, 1892
*Walter Crane*
*Bayerische Staatsgemäldesammlungen*

# I Hear an Army

## James Joyce

1
    I hear an army charging upon the land,
       And the thunder of horses plunging, foam about their
          knees:
    Arrogant, in black armor, behind them stand,
       Disdaining the reins, with fluttering whips, the
          charioteers.

2
5   They cry unto the night their battle-name:
       I moan in sleep when I hear afar their whirling
          laughter.
    They cleave the gloom of dreams, a blinding flame,
       Clanging, clanging upon the heart as upon an anvil.

    They come shaking in triumph their long, green hair:
10      They come out of the sea and run shouting by the
          shore.

3
    My heart, have you no wisdom thus to despair?
       My love, my love, my love, why have you left me alone?

*I Hear an Army*   597

## Closure and Extension

### ANSWERS TO THINKING ABOUT THE SELECTION
*Recalling*

1. An army of thundering horses and arrogant charioteers with green hair and black armor come charging out of the sea.
2. The speaker is sleeping and dreaming when he hears the army.
3. The speaker's love has departed and left the speaker alone.

*Interpreting*

4. Suggested Response: The army is not real. The charioteers have green hair and the horses come thundering from out of the sea.
5. Suggested Response: "Plunging," "fluttering," and "whirling" provide visual images of movement and force. The word "clanging" provides an aural image.

*Applying*

6. Answers will differ, but students may comment that heartbreak lends itself to images that are dramatic such as the ones in this poem. Happiness suggests images that are pleasant, but not as exciting.

### ANSWERS TO CRITICAL THINKING AND READING

1. Suggested Responses: You can hear the sounds of horses' hoofs and the splashing of water.
2. Suggested Response: You can hear the cracking of whips.
3. Suggested Response: The word that names this sound is *clanging*.

### THINKING AND WRITING

For help with this assignment, students may consult Lesson 2, "Drafting and Revising," in the Handbook of Writing About Literature.

**Publishing Student Writing** You may want to display students' memos alongside a Xerox of the picture.

### THINKING ABOUT THE SELECTION
**Recalling**

1. Describe the army that the poet hears.
2. What is the speaker doing when he hears this army?
3. What has the speaker's love done to him?

**Interpreting**

4. Is the army that the poet describes real? Explain.
5. How do verbs like "plunging," "fluttering," "whirling," and "clanging" contribute to the mood of the poem?

**Applying**

6. A famous poet once said that it is easier to write about heartbreak than about happiness in love. Comment on this remark.

### CRITICAL THINKING AND READING
**Interpreting Sensory Words**

**Sensory words** appeal to one or more of the five senses. Since Joyce's poem is called "I Hear an Army," many of the words he chose appeal to the sense of hearing.

1. What sounds do you hear when you read the words "charging upon the land"?
2. What sounds do you hear when you read of the "fluttering whips."?
3. Joyce uses onomatopoeia, or words that imitate sounds, to describe the army's effect on the heart. What word names this sound?

### THINKING AND WRITING
**Writing About Fine Art**

Imagine that you are an editor working on a book of Joyce's poems. A fellow editor has suggested illustrating "I Hear an Army" with the painting "Neptune" (p. 597). First, reread the poem and look carefully at the painting. Then list your reactions to this idea, considering whether the subject and mood of the picture are in harmony with the poem. Using your list, write a memo to your co-worker accepting or rejecting the proposal. In revising this memo, make sure that you have been specific in pointing out qualities of the picture that enhance or conflict with the poem. Share your memo with your classmates when you are finished.

# Word Choice and Tone

**ORION IN DECEMBER, 1959**
*Charles Burchfield*
*National Museum of American Art,
Smithsonian Institution*

**Humanities Note**

Fine art, *Orion in December*, 1959, Charles Burchfield. The American artist Charles Burchfield (1893-1967), was educated at the Cleveland institute of Art. His teacher there, Henry Keller, encouraged him to develop an individualistic style of painting. Burchfield worked at many things to finance his painting career, including designing wallpaper, illustrating and teaching art classes. He eventually gained fame for his intense and imaginative paintings of nature and haunted buildings.

*Orion in December* is a mystical interpretation of a starry winter night. Energy seems to emanate from the natural forms, and the forces of nature vibrate through the elements of the painting. Burchfield wanted the viewer to experience looking at the stars on a cold, clear evening.

# GUIDE FOR READING

## Meeting at Night

**Robert Browning** (1812–1889) was one of the greatest English poets of the 19th century. Though he lacked a formal college education, his parents instilled in him a love of art and literature. Browning had a special fondness for Italy, where he lived for a time with his wife and fellow poet Elizabeth Barrett. That country is the setting for some of his most famous dramatic monologues, poems in which a character speaks to a silent listener. "Meeting at Night" is not a monologue, but it does show Browning's gift for vivid language.

## Jabberwocky

**Lewis Carroll** (1832–1898) was the pen name of Charles Lutwidge Dodgson, a mathematics teacher at an English university. Dodgson wrote his most famous works, *Alice's Adventures in Wonderland* and *Through the Looking Glass,* for the young daughters of the dean of his college. One of the girls, Alice Liddell, was the model for Dodgson's Alice. In the course of her adventures in Wonderland, Alice encounters a poem that can only be read when held up to a mirror. Its name is "Jabberwocky."

## Macavity: The Mystery Cat

**T. S. Eliot** (1888–1965) was born in St. Louis, Missouri, but went to England as a young man and lived there for most of his life. Eliot was an extremely influential poet and wrote one of the greatest poems of our time, "The Waste Land." Even on a first reading, this difficult poem conveys a sense of excitement. However, Eliot wrote humorous poems as well. His *Old Possum's Book of Practical Cats,* from which "Macavity: the Mystery Cat" comes, was the basis for the Broadway play *Cats.*

## Solace

**Dorothy Parker** (1893–1967) was an important personality in the New York literary world for many years. She was the book critic for *The New Yorker,* a famous literary magazine, but quit this job when her first volume of poems became a best seller. Parker was known for her witty conversation as much as for her poetry. She was one of a group of humorists and writers who met regularly at the Algonquin Hotel in New York City. "Solace" combines poetic skill with a bitter but compassionate wit.

600   *Poetry*

## Word Choice

What difference does it make whether a poet uses one or another of synonyms such as *bond, tie, link,* or *connection*? The answer is that it can matter a great deal. In addition to their denotations, or dictionary meanings, words have different connotations, or emotional associations, that result from their different histories. Choosing a word with the wrong connotation for your purposes is the same as singing a song out of tune. For example, would you describe a friendship as a *link* or *connection*? The word *bond* is better able to convey the warm feelings that friends have for each other.

As the poem "Jabberwocky" demonstrates, even made-up words have connotations. These emotional associations come mostly from the way that the writer uses the made-up words and the resemblance of these words to more familiar ones.

Mood and tone also depend on a poet's choice of words. **Mood** is the feeling that a poem creates, while **tone** is the attitude that a poet takes toward his or her subject and readers. If a poet calls a friendship a *connection,* he or she may be creating a tone of disapproval toward it. This choice of words may also call up a mood of coldness and a lack of caring. Other factors besides word choice, however, can influence mood and tone. If a poem has jingly rhymes and a bouncy rhythm, for instance, it is clear that the poet is not being serious.

## Look For

As you read these poems, pay special attention to the poets' choice of words and to the mood and tone that these words create. Whenever a word seems particularly effective, ask yourself why it works better than any of its synonyms.

## Writing

Choose three synonyms that have roughly the same dictionary meaning and freewrite about the differences in their connotations. Tell some of the situations in which you would use each of these words.

## Vocabulary

Knowing the following word will help you as you read these poems.
**prow** (prou) *n.*: Forward part of
a ship (p. 602, l. 5)

## Humanities Note

Fine art, *Moonlit Cove,* by Albert Pinkham Ryder. Ryder (1847-1917) was born in the whaling port of New Bedford, Massachusetts, and was deeply influenced by his boyhood contact with the sea.

You might want to use the following questions:
1. How does Ryder make the scene mysterious and inviting?
2. Does the picture show the type of beach you imagined while reading the poem? Explain.

## Presentation

**Motivation/Prior Knowledge** Have students recall a time when they were outdoors at night. What sounds did they hear? How were familiar objects changed by the night? In what ways is the world different at night than it is during the day? Tell them that Browning's poem contains vivid nighttime images.

**Master Teacher Note** Use the overhead projector to show students Art Transparency 14, *The Voice,* by Edvard Munch. Ask students to describe the mood of this picture. Also ask them whom the girl might be waiting to meet. Then tell them that Browning's poem describes a rendezvous between lovers.

**Thematic Idea** Another selection that deals with anticipation is "Great Expectations" by Dickens, page 757.

**Purpose-Setting Question** What mood does the poet create?

1 **Literary Focus** Poets create images with words that evoke responses from the five senses. The more vividly descriptive the poet's word choices are, the better the image is. Ask students to

**MOONLIT COVE, 1880–90**
*Albert Pinkham Ryder*
The Phillips Collection, Washington D.C.

# Meeting at Night

### Robert Browning

**I**

The gray sea and the long black land;
And the yellow half-moon large and low;
And the startled little waves that leap
In fiery ringlets from their sleep,
5   As I gain the cove with pushing prow,
And quench its speed i' the slushy sand.

602   *Poetry*

identify several images in "Meeting at Night" and explain to which senses these images appeal.

## II

Then a mile of warm sea-scented beach;
Three fields to cross till a farm appears;
A tap at the pane, the quick sharp scratch
10 And blue spurt of a lighted match,
And a voice less loud, through its joys and fears,
Than the two hearts beating each to each!

2

## THINKING ABOUT THE SELECTION
### Recalling

1. Describe the setting in each part of the poem.
2. Give a chronological account of the actions that occur in this poem.

### Interpreting

3. Explain the title of this poem. What "Meeting at Night" does the poem describe?

### Applying

4. Why do you think some poets try to appeal to as many of the reader's senses as possible?

## ANALYZING LITERATURE
### Understanding Word Choice

In choosing words, poets pay as much attention to their connotations, or emotional associa-

tions, as to their denotations, or dictionary meanings. Poets also take into account the sounds of words and try to select words whose sounds harmonize with those of the words around them. You might wonder, for instance, why Browning chooses the word "black" rather than *dark* in line 1. The answer may be that the *l* and *a* sounds of "black" go better with similar sounds in "land." Also, the word *black* has a more vivid feeling than *dark*. Browning may have been looking for a livelier word to contrast with "gray," which appears earlier in the line.

1. Explain why Browning might have chosen the word "pushing" rather than *moving* in line 5.

2. In line 7, why does "sea-scented" have better connotations for Browning's purposes than *salty-smelling*?

*Meeting at Night*   603

## Motivation/Prior Knowledge

Ask students if they have ever read works by Lewis Carroll, such as *Alice in Wonderland.* What were their favorite characters or scenes? If students are not familiar with Carroll, explain that he is famous for his imaginative, often witty, fantasy stories. Tell them that "Jabberwocky" is from Carroll's book, *Through the Looking Glass.* The poem is very famous for the "nonsense" language found in it.

## Master Teacher Note

Because of the nature of the created language used in "Jabberwocky," it would be most useful for the students to hear a recording of it. Have students listen to the recording once before they read the poem and then listen to it again as they read the selection themselves.

## Purpose-Setting Question

What do you think a "Jabberwocky" is?

**1 Discussion** You might want to remind students that rhyme is the repetition of the accented vowel and all subsequent sounds. Rhyme is usually found at the end of two or more lines; this is called end rhyme. However, rhyme can occur within a line, in which case it is called internal rhyme. Find examples of end rhyme and internal rhyme in "Jabberwocky."

**2 Critical Thinking and Reading** Who do students think might be speaking here and in stanza six?

**3 Discussion** Many descriptive words in this poem do not make literal sense. They are inventions or, as Carroll called them, "portmanteau words." For example, "slithy" is a combination of the words "lithe" and "slimy." Despite these inventions, we can still understand the poem. Why does the poet use made-up

**THE JABBERWOCK, 1872**
*John Tenniel*
*The Granger Collection*

# Jabberwocky

## Lewis Carroll

'Twas brillig, and the slithy toves
    Did gyre and gimble in the wabe;
All mimsy were the borogoves,
    And the mome raths outgrabe.

  5  "Beware the Jabberwock, my son!
    The jaws that bite, the claws that
      catch!
Beware the Jubjub bird, and shun
    The frumious Bandersnatch!"

He took his vorpal sword in hand:
 10  Long time the manxome foe he
      sought—
So rested he by the Tumtum tree,
    And stood awhile in thought.

And as in uffish thought he stood,
    The Jabberwock, with eyes of flame,
 15  Came whiffling through the tulgey wood,
    And burbled as it came!

One, two! One, two! And through and
    through
    The vorpal blade went snicker-snack!
He left it dead, and with its head
 20  He went galumphing back.

"And hast thou slain the Jabberwock?
    Come to my arms, my beamish boy!
O frabjous day! Callooh! Callay!"
    He chortled in his joy.

 25  'Twas brillig, and the slithy toves
    Did gyre and gimble in the wabe;
All mimsy were the borogoves,
    And the mome raths outgrabe.

*604   Poetry*

words? What effect do these words have on the poem? What qualities might the poem lack if the poet had used ordinary language?

**4 Reading Strategy** Have the students explain the action in "Jabberwocky" using quotations from the text.

**Reader's Response** Do you like the poem "Jabberwocky?" Why or why not?

## Humanities Note

Fine Art illustration, *The Jabberwock,* by John Tenniel. Tenniel (1820-1914) illustrated the original version of *Through the Looking Glass,* from which this poem comes.

You might want to use the following questions:
1. Describe what is happening in this picture.
2. Does Tenniel's version of the monster satisfy you? Explain.

## THINKING ABOUT THE SELECTION

### Recalling

1. Reread lines 5–8. In your own words, express the warning that the hero receives.
2. Reread lines 9–20. Tell the key events that occur in this section of the poem.
3. Describe the reception that the hero receives from the person who warned him.

### Interpreting

4. A critic has said that, despite its many strange words, the story of "Jabberwocky" is similar to many legends about knights and dragons. Comment on this remark.
5. You can often tell the part of speech of a word even if you do not understand it. Identify the part of speech of three of the made-up words in this poem. Explain how you arrived at each answer.
6. Explain how a real word that is part of the title is a clue to the poem's style.
7. What mood, or atmosphere, is created by the events in this poem? Explain your answer.

### Applying

8. How can a poem like "Jabberwocky" give you a better understanding of language?

## ANALYZING LITERATURE

### Understanding Made-up Words

Lewis Carroll created the made-up words in "Jabberwocky" in several ways. Some are portmanteau words—a *portmanteau* is "a large, leather suitcase"—because they have "two meanings packed up into one word." *Mimsy* is such a word because it is made up of *flimsy* and *miserable* with some of the meaning of each. Other made-up words in the poem are parts of familiar words. For example, to "gyre" means "to go round and round like a gyroscope." Still other made-up words are just plain nonsense. Carroll says that "toves," for instance, are a combination of badgers, lizards, and corkscrews!

1. Fill in the missing half of the following portmanteau words and then figure out the meaning of each.
   a. *Chortled* is what word plus *snorted*? (Look this word up in the dictionary to check your answer. It became a part of our language as a result of this poem.)
   b. *Slithy* is what word plus *lithe*?
2. A gimlet is a small tool. What do you think the word *gimble* means?

## THINKING AND WRITING

### Writing a Poem Using Made-up Words

Write a poem like Carroll's "Jabberwocky," using a combination of made-up words and ordinary words. The subject of your poem can also be the hunting of a strange monster. However, you do not have to use rhymes or write the same number of lines that Carroll did. First, think of a name for your monster that will be as memorable as Carroll's Jabberwock. Some of your made-up words can be portmanteau words, while others can be parts of regular words, like *gyre* in Carroll's poem. You can also use words that are pure nonsense. However, write your poem so that your classmates can understand and enjoy it even if they cannot immediately define each word. When you finish your first draft, read it aloud to several classmates. If they have trouble understanding it, try to make it clearer. Share your poem with the class when you are finished.

---

### ANSWERS TO THINKING ABOUT THE SELECTION
*Recalling*

1. Answers will differ, but should express a warning from an older adult to a young person about the danger of these beasts.
2. Answers will differ, but most students should indicate that the young man takes up his sword and goes into the woods to look for the Jabberwock. He stands by a tree for a few moments, thinking. Then the Jabberwock appears. The young man fights and kills the monster, cuts off its head, and returns home.
3. The person who warned the young man gives the hero a warm, affectionate, and joyous welcome.

*Interpreting*

4. Answers will differ, but should include the fact that the hero goes in search of a dangerous monster, alone, and kills it with his sword; this is exactly the behavior of many chivalric heroes.
5. Answers will differ, but "uffish" and "vorpal" are adjectives, while "galumphing" is a verb. The first two words describe recognizable nouns, and the third has a recognizable verb ending—*ing*.
6. *Jabber* is the real word in the title. It means "to speak gibberish," or nonsense, which gives us a clue about the language that will appear in the poem.
7. Suggested Response: A mood of silliness is created by the made-up words.

*Applying*

8. Answers will differ, but might include the fact that Carroll's pretend language makes the reader think about how words can have meaning outside of their literal meanings.

**Challenge** Why do you think this poem has remained popular?

### ANSWERS TO ANALYZING LITERATURE

Suggested Responses:
1. a. chuckle
   b. slimy
2. It means "move through and penetrate the waves," as a gimlet might penetrate wood.

### THINKING AND WRITING

For help with this assignment, students can refer to Lesson 18, "Writing a Poem," in the Handbook of Writing About Literature.

**Publishing Student Writing** Ask some students who are artistically inclined to draw the monster they describe. Students' poems can be assembled into a collection of illustrated "Monster Nonsense" poems.

Illustrations, by Edward Gorey.
Tell students that the illustrations
on this page and page 608 appear in *Old Possum's Book of
Practical Cats,* in which this
poem appears.

You might want to use the
following questions:
1. Can you relate the illustrations
   to particular lines?
2. Do the illustrations capture
   the poem's spirit? Explain.

## Presentation

**Motivation/Prior Knowledge**
Ask students to think about their
favorite pets, or about other animals in which they are interested.
Have they ever imagined these
animals behaving like people?
Do the animals possess any
characteristics, good or bad, that
remind the students of people?
Tell students that this poem is
about a cat with some extraordinary abilities.

**Purpose-Setting Question** What
is so mysterious about Macavity?

**Discussion** How does Eliot immediately set the tone of this
poem?

*Edward Gorey*

# Macavity: The Mystery Cat

## T. S. Eliot

1

Macavity's a Mystery Cat: he's called the Hidden Paw—
For he's the master criminal who can defy the Law.
He's the bafflement of Scotland Yard,[1] the Flying Squad's[2] despair;
For when they reach the scene of crime—*Macavity's not there!*

---

**1. Scotland Yard:** The London police.
**2. Flying Squad:** A criminal-investigation department.

## Grammar in Action

**Coordinating conjunctions** include *and, but, or, nor, for, yet,*
and *so.* They are used to connect equally important ideas
smoothly and clearly. They can connect words, phrases, clauses, or complete ideas, as follows:

Put the lamp on the table *or* on the mat. (joins two
prepositional phrases)
Andrew dieted *and* exercised to lose weight. (joins two
verbs)

Friends came to visit me at the hospital, *but* the nurse sent
them home. (joins two independent clauses)
Members may pay dues when they join *or* when they renew
membership. (joins two subordinate adverb clauses)

Poets, too, use coordinating conjunctions to join words, phrases,
clauses and sentences. Study these illustrations from "Macavity:
The Mystery Cat":

Macavity's a Mystery Cat: he's called the Hidden Paw
*For* he's the master criminal who can defy the Law.
You'll be sure to find him resting, or a-licking of his thumbs,
*Or* engaged in doing complicated long-division sums.

Macavity, Macavity, there's no one like Macavity,
He's broken every human law, he breaks the law of gravity.
His powers of levitation³ would make a fakir⁴ stare,
And when you reach the scene of crime—*Macavity's not there!*
You may seek him in the basement, you may look up in the air—
10 But I tell you once and once again, *Macavity's not there!*

Macavity's a ginger cat, he's very tall and thin;
You would know him if you saw him, for his eyes are sunken in.
His brow is deeply lined with thought, his head is highly domed;
His coat is dusty from neglect, his whiskers are uncombed.
15 He sways his head from side to side, with movements like a snake;
And when you think he's half asleep, he's always wide awake.

Macavity, Macavity, there's no one like Macavity,
For he's a fiend in feline shape, a monster of depravity.
You may meet him in a by-street, you may see him in the square—
20 But when a crime's discovered, then *Macavity's not there!*

He's outwardly respectable. (They say he cheats at cards.)
And his footprints are not found in any file of Scotland Yard's.
And when the larder's looted, or the jewel-case is rifled,
Or when the milk is missing, or another Peke's⁵ been stifled,
25 Or the greenhouse glass is broken, and the trellis past repair—
Ay, there's the wonder of the thing! *Macavity's not there!*

And when the Foreign Office⁶ find a Treaty's gone astray,
Or the Admiralty⁷ lose some plans and drawings by the way,
There may be a scrap of paper in the hall or on the stair—
30 But it's useless to investigate—*Macavity's not there!*
And when the loss has been disclosed, the Secret Service say:
"It *must* have been Macavity!"—but he's a mile away.
You'll be sure to find him resting, or a-licking of his thumbs,
Or engaged in doing complicated long-division sums.

---

**3. levitation** (lev′ ə tā′ shən) *n.*: Remaining in air with no physical support.
**4. fakir** (fə kir′) *n.*: A Moslem or Hindu beggar who claims to perform miracles.
**5. Peke:** Short for Pekingese, a small dog with long silky hair and a pug nose.
**6. Foreign Office:** The British equivalent of the U.S. Department of State.
**7. Admiralty:** The British governmental department in charge of naval affairs.

*Macavity: The Mystery Cat* 607

**2 Discussion** What human characteristics does Macavity possess? Do students have trouble imagining Macavity? What effect do his human qualities have on their images of him?

**3 Critical Thinking and Reading** What is the effect of the repeated phrase "Macavity's not there"?

**4 Critical Thinking and Reading** How does Eliot heighten the sense of absurdity in this stanza?

**Reader's Response** What do you like most and least about Macavity the cat? Explain.

The conjunction joins two independent clauses, while *or* (used twice) joins three participles, two of them with modifiers.

**Student Activity 1.** Find four or more coordinating conjunctions in the poem. Tell what each joins.

**Student Activity 2.** Write four sentences about Macavity that include coordinating conjunctions. Use the conjunctions to join words, phrases, and clauses.

5 **Enrichment** Mungojerrie and Griddlebone are two of several remarkable felines described, along with Macavity, in Eliot's *Old Possum's Book of Practical Cats.* "Old Possum" was a nickname for Eliot created by some of his literary friends. *Old Possum's Book of Practical Cats* was the basis for Andrew Lloyd Webber's immensely popular musical, *Cats.*

6 **Discussion** How is Macavity the "Napoleon of Crime"?

Edward Gorey

35    Macavity, Macavity, there's no one like Macavity,
There never was a Cat of such deceitfulness and suavity.[8]
He always has an alibi, and one or two to spare:
At whatever time the deed took place—MACAVITY WASN'T THERE!
And they say that all the Cats whose wicked deeds are widely known
40    (I might mention Mungojerrie, I might mention Griddlebone)
Are nothing more than agents for the Cat who all the time
Just controls their operations: the Napoleon of Crime!

---

**8. suavity** (swa' və tē) *n.*: Graceful politeness.

608   *Poetry*

## THINKING ABOUT THE SELECTION

### Recalling

1. Why is Macavity "a Mystery Cat"?
2. Describe his appearance.
3. Give four examples of his misdeeds.
4. Why can't the police charge him with a crime?
5. Why is Macavity known as "the Napoleon of Crime"?

### Interpreting

6. Give three clues that indicate Eliot is taking a humorous tone in this poem.
7. What word in the name *Macavity* explains this cat's ability to evade the law? Explain.

### Applying

8. What qualities do cats have that might humorously suggest criminal activities?


## UNDERSTANDING LANGUAGE

### Finding Antonyms

**Antonyms** are words that have opposite, or nearly opposite, meanings. For example, Macavity engages in *complicated* long-division sums. The opposite of *complicated* is simple.

Imagine that in a parallel world Macavity has an opposite.

Answer each of the following questions by finding an opposite for the italicized word.

1. Since Macavity *defies* the law, what would his opposite do?
2. Macavity is the Flying Squad's *despair*. What would his opposite be?
3. Macavity *neglects* his coat. What would his opposite do?
4. Macavity is a *fiend* in feline shape. What would his opposite be?
5. Macavity is *deceitful*. What would his opposite be?


## THINKING AND WRITING

### Writing about Tone

You have probably heard of people who are deaf to the tones in music. Imagine a reader who, in a similar way, cannot understand the tone that a writer is taking toward his or her subject. List some of the humorous *mistakes* that such a reader would make in trying to understand "Macavity: The Mystery Cat." Then, using your list, write an interpretation of the poem from this reader's point of view. (Of course, your tone will be ironic because you really understand Eliot's humor.) Try to make this reader's *mis*understandings of the tone as funny as possible. Show your first draft to several classmates and ask them for suggestions to make the misinterpretations of tone even more ridiculous. When you are finished, share your essay with the class.

### ANSWERS TO THINKING ABOUT THE SELECTION
#### Recalling

1. Macavity is a "Mystery Cat" because he is never found at the scenes of his crimes.
2. Answers may differ but should include information from the third stanza of the poem.
3. Answers will differ, but students might include theft of jewels, milk, food, and treaties.
4. Macavity is never around after he commits his crimes; the police cannot catch him.
5. Macavity is a criminal mastermind, just as Napoleon was a military genius.

#### Interpreting

6. Answers will differ, but might include the fact that Macavity can outwit Scotland Yard, that he can fly, or that he cheats at cards, all of which are beyond the capabilities of cats.
7. Suggested Response: The word *cavity* in Macavity's name means "a hole" or "emptiness." This is appropriate for Macavity since he can never be found.

#### Applying

8. Answers will differ, but might include the ideas that cats are quiet, appear sneaky, like to go out at night, seem aloof, and can never be found when something has been broken or when the curtains are torn.

### ANSWERS TO UNDERSTANDING LANGUAGE

Suggested Responses:
1. He would *obey* the law.
2. He would be the Flying Squad's *joy*.
3. His opposite would *tend* his coat.
4. His opposite would be an *angel*.
5. His opposite would be *truthful*.

### THINKING AND WRITING

Refer students to Lesson 13, "Writing About a Poem," in the Handbook of Writing About Literature.

**Motivation/Prior Knowledge**
Have students think about a time when they felt badly about something and were told "Every cloud has a silver lining," or the like. How did they feel about this sort of consolation? Then tell them that Dorothy Parker's poem deals with this kind of "Solace."

**Master Teacher Note** To generate interest in this poem, ask students, "What are some of the dumb things that people say to those who have just broken up with a boyfriend or girlfriend?" Elicit various responses from the class and discuss them. Tell the students to keep this discussion in mind as they read "Solace."

**Purpose-Setting Question** What is the author's opinion of this variety of "solace"?

1 **Literary Focus** A poet will often arrange the meter of a poem to help clarify or deliver the message. In each stanza of this poem, Parker presents four lines of iambic tetrameter (eight syllables with the accent on every other syllable) and two lines of iambic trimeter (six syllables with the accent on every other syllable). This arrangement causes the short lines to stand out. Why are lines 3, 6, 9, and 12 given such emphasis?

2 **Discussion** Personal pain, particularly the pain of abandonment, can sometimes be too intense for philosophical consolation. Why is this so?

# Solace

## Dorothy Parker

1
There was a rose that faded young;
I saw its shattered beauty hung
    Upon a broken stem.
I heard them say, "What need to care
5 With roses budding everywhere?"
    I did not answer them.

There was a bird, brought down to die;
They said, "A hundred fill the sky—
    What reason to be sad?"
2
10 There was a girl, whose lover fled;
I did not wait, the while they said,
    "There's many another lad."

## THINKING ABOUT THE SELECTION

### Recalling

1. What kind of solace do people give for the faded rose, dying bird, and abandoned girl?
2. Identify the different ways in which the narrator reacts to this solace.

### Interpreting

3. How do you think the narrator feels about the solace that she hears?
4. Why might the narrator feel this way?
5. Why do you think she mentions the rose first, the bird second, and the girl last?

### Applying

6. What are the qualities of a more genuine response to another person's loss?

## ANALYZING LITERATURE

### Understanding an Ironical Tone

A writer is taking an **ironical tone** toward a subject when there is a difference between what he or she is saying and what is really meant. You are probably familiar with an ironical tone in everyday situations. For example, if you enter a house with your raincoat dripping and someone asks you if it is raining, you might reply, "Not at all!" While it seems that you are saying that the weather is fine, you are really answering—Can't you see for yourself that it is raining?

1. What does the title of this poem *seem* to say that the people in the poem are offering?
2. What clues are there that Parker means the title ironically?

**ANSWERS TO THINKING ABOUT THE SELECTION**
*Recalling*
1. People say that the loss is not so bad because there are many more lost "things" in the world.
2. Her first reaction is simply not to answer; her second response is to leave.

*Interpreting*
3. Answers will differ, but students should show that they understand that the poet feels negatively.
4. Answers will differ, but students might indicate that she has possibly been in a similar situation and received similar "solace" which she found empty and useless.
5. Suggested Response: The poet is stressing the irony of the solace in the last stanza by comparing it to the solace offered when a rose and then a bird die; all three consoling statements are basically the same, but the events they refer to differ in their significance.

*Applying*
6. Answers will differ, but might include the idea that true "solace" considers the often very deep pain of the person being consoled. A person offering sympathy needs to understand that superficial "solace" ignores the pain of the person being consoled.

**ANSWERS TO ANALYZING LITERATURE**
1. Suggested Response: It suggests that the people in the poem are offering real support to an unhappy person.
2. Suggested Response: By comparing the solace offered when a rose dies or a bird dies with the solace offered to a young woman whose lover has left her, Parker shows how empty and useless this type of solace is.

# Imagery

**PINK SHELL WITH SEAWEED, c. 1938**
*Georgia O'Keeffe*
*San Diego Museum of Art*

**Humanities Note**

Fine Art, *Pink Shell With Seaweed*, c. 1938, Georgia O'Keeffe. Probably the best known female American artist, Georgia O'Keeffe (1887-1986), acquired her formal art education at the Art Institute of Chicago and The Art Student League in New York City. She worked in commercial art and taught before deciding to devote her life to painting. O'Keeffe's work places her as a pioneer modern American artist. She was discovered by Alfred Stieglitz, a major exhibitor of "new" art in New York City.

O'Keeffe's hallmark in art is her abstraction of natural forms. *Pink Shell With Seaweed* in pastels, is just that. Done while living in the desert in New Mexico, this work was perhaps inspired by the direct relationship between desert and ocean, the former being the remains of the latter. The gentle curve of the shell lends itself to the softness of the medium. The luminous colors recall the ocean. Taken out of context and viewed close up, the image of the shell assumes a greater importance and so becomes a symbol of the circular nature of life itself.

## Focus

**More About the Authors**
**Margaret Walker** was born in Birmingham, Alabama in 1915. She studied at Northwestern University in the 1930's, and in her volume *For My People,* she expresses disillusionment at discovering that racial prejudice was just as strong in the Midwest as in the South. Ask students how a writer's disillusionment with society could be turned into something positive.

You might want to tell students that **Theodore Roethke's** father raised plants and that, as a boy, Roethke played in and around his father's greenhouse. Later he wrote many excellent poems about growing plants. Ask students why childhood experience is often so important for a writer.

During most of her life, **Marge Piercy** has been politically active in civil rights, the antiwar movement, and the women's movement. In addition, she has contributed many articles and stories to underground newspapers and magazines. Currently she travels all over the country giving poetry readings, lectures, and writing workshops.

**Gary Soto** attended California State University. He is currently an associate professor at the University of California at Berkeley. He is an award-winning writer; his first collection of poems, *The Element of San Joaquin,* won the United States Award from International Poetry Forum. Other awards include the Academy of American Poets Prize for his poem "The Discovery" and the American Book Award for *Living up the Street.*

612

# GUIDE FOR READING

## Memory

**Margaret Walker** (1915–    ) was born in Birmingham, Alabama. The daughter of a minister, she received her earliest education at Methodist Church schools. She earned degrees from Northwestern University and the State University of Iowa. She then taught college. Her first book of poetry won the Yale University Younger Poets competition. As an artist, she focuses on the experiences and hardships of black people in America. "Memory" is a powerful example of her artistic commitment to her people.

## The Meadow Mouse

**Theodore Roethke** (1908–1963) was born in Saginaw, Michigan. He won a Pulitzer Prize, a National Book Award, and a Guggenheim Fellowship. He writes of the natural world and its creatures with precision, tenderness, and even, sometimes, poetic splendor. In some of his poems, the outer world of nature becomes an external representation of his own deepest feelings. "The Meadow Mouse" shows how sensitive, perceptive, and tender Roethke's best nature poetry is.

## To be of use

**Marge Piercy** (1936–    ), who was born in Detroit, Michigan, is both a poet and a novelist. Her books of poetry include *Breaking Camp, Hard Loving,* and *Circles on the Water,* from which "To be of use" was taken. She also has a book of essays, short stories, and reviews entitled *Parti-Colored Blocks for a Quilt.*

## The Space

**Gary Soto** (1952–    ) was born in Fresno, California. Both his poetry and prose exhibit a style and content influenced by his working-class Mexican-American background. When he was a child, he worked as a migrant worker. Soto said, in an interview about his desire to become a poet, "I don't think I had any literary aspirations when I was a kid. . . . So my wanting to write poetry was a sort of fluke."

612    Poetry

### Objectives

1 To write a poem entitled "Memory"
2 To understand imagery
3 To write about imagery
4 To appreciate the effects of imagery
5 To write a poem with imagery

### Support Material

**Teaching Portfolio**
Teacher Backup, p. 759
Grammar in Action Worksheet, *Using Commas,* p. 766
Usage and Mechanics Worksheet, p. 768
Vocabulary Check, p. 769
Analyzing Literature Worksheet, *Studying Imagery,* p. 770
Language Worksheet, *Appreciating Vivid Verbs,* p. 771

Selection Test, p. 772
Art Transparency 15: *Automat,* by Edward Hopper

# The Creation

**James Weldon Johnson** (1871–1938) was born in Florida. He was a lawyer, a song writer, a United States consul to Venezuela and Nicaragua, an executive secretary of the NAACP, and a college professor. "The Creation" is from his most famous book, *God's Trombones*. This volume is both a collection of poetry and a collection of folk sermons. It represents art drawn and shaped from the rich depths of black American spirituality.

**Imagery**

**Imagery** means a poet's use of words to create mental pictures, or images, that communicate experience. An image may appeal to any one of the five senses, though in literature visual images are the most common. When Theodore Roethke describes a meadow mouse as "Wriggling like a miniscule puppy," he is using visual imagery to give you a mental picture of the mouse. When Margaret Walker, in "Memory," speaks of "wind-swept streets of cities/on cold and blustery nights," she is using imagery that appeals to our sense of touch, or physical sensation. Imagery is one of the most important resources poets make use of to capture and express experience.

**Look For**

As you read "Memory," "The Meadow Mouse," "To be of use," "The Space," and "The Creation," look for the images these poems contain. Try to infer the ideas, feelings, or qualities of experience they aim to express.

**Writing**

Think of a moment in your life that is vivid in your memory. What feelings does this moment stir up? Freewrite about the moment by describing what you saw, heard, touched, tasted, or smelled. See if you can communicate your feelings without naming them.

**Vocabulary**

Knowing the following words will help you as you read the poems in this section.

**sinister** (sin′ is tər) *adj.*: Threatening harm or evil (p. 614, l. 6)
**paralytic** (par ə lit′ ik) *n.*: A paralyzed person (p. 616, l. 28)
**forsaken** (fər sāk′ ən) *adj.*:

Abandoned, without hope (p. 616, l. 29)
**ecstatic** (ek stat′ ik) *adj.*: In a state of extreme emotion (p. 618, l. 8)

*Guide for Reading* 613

**Motivation/Prior Knowledge**
Ask students what it might be like to live without hope of bettering oneself. Then tell them that, in this poem, Margaret Walker writes about the inhabitants of a black ghetto whose lives are bleak and hopeless.

**Purpose-Setting Question** How does the poet use adjectives to create a troubling mood?

**Master Teacher Note** Use the overhead projector to show students Art Transparency 15, *Automat,* by Edward Hopper. Ask students to describe the feelings that this scene calls up. Have them speculate about the thoughts and memories of the woman sitting at the table. Then tell them that Margaret Walker's poem "Memory" deals with recollections that are bitter and disturbing.

Vivid adjectives can help set the mood of a poem, and they are used skillfully here by Walker. Ask the students to point out the adjectives that they believe create a feeling of despair or distress in "Memory."

**1 Discussion** The poet recalls the despondency of the people she sees on the streets. She senses their dissatisfaction and resentment. Ask the students who these people are. Why might they be angry?

# Memory

## Margaret Walker

I can remember wind-swept streets of cities
on cold and blustery nights, on rainy days;
heads under shabby felts[1] and parasols
and shoulders hunched against a sharp concern;
5  seeing hurt bewilderment on poor faces,
smelling a deep and sinister unrest
these brooding people cautiously caress;
hearing ghostly marching on pavement stones
and closing fast around their squares of hate.
10  I can remember seeing them alone,
at work, and in their tenements at home.
I can remember hearing all they said:
their muttering protests, their whispered oaths,
and all that spells their living in distress.

---

**1. felts:** Felt hats.

---

**THINKING ABOUT THE SELECTION**
**Recalling**

1. Describe in general terms the kind of memories the speaker presents in the poem.

**Interpreting**

2. What kind of lives do the people lead whom the poet remembers?
3. Pick out three phrases that suggest the feelings or spirit of these people. What do these phrases suggest?
4. Pick out three vivid images. Tell what each suggests to you.
5. Do you think that the imagery in the poem is primarily intended to create a picture of the external world—what you could see and hear if you were in it? Or is it intended to communicate the inner lives of the people there? Give reasons for your opinion.

**Applying**

6. Tell why you think that this poem is or is not a poem of social protest; that is, one that criticizes an injustice in society.

**THINKING AND WRITING**
**Writing Your Own "Memory"**

Using the freewriting you did before you read Walker's poem, write a poem titled "Memory." If you wish, imitate Walker's pattern. Her poem has fourteen lines. Most of the lines have five accented syllables. Three times she uses the phrase "I can remember." Try to fit your imagery into this or a similar pattern. When you revise, see if you can think of sharper or more vivid images to suggest your feelings about the experience you are treating. Share your poem with your classmates.

**ANSWERS TO THINKING ABOUT THE SELECTION**
*Recalling*

1. Answers may differ but should include such things as memories of the city, of poverty, of anger, and of the cold.

*Interpreting*

2. Answers will differ but should show that the students understand the difficulties of the people's lives and the anger and resentment they feel.
3. Answers will differ. Students should choose phrases that suggest hurt, anger, and suffering.
4. Answers will differ. Students should include vivid images that suggest anger or suffering.
5. Suggested Response: The poem

contains descriptions of the outer world, but it mostly communicates feelings—with words such as "hurt," "brooding," and "hate."

*Applying*

6. Answers will differ. Most students will realize that the descriptions in the poem are an indirect form of protest.

**THINKING AND WRITING**

For help with this assignment, students can consult Lesson 18, "Writing a Poem," in the Handbook of Writing About Literature.

**Publishing Student Writing** You may want to have students publish a magazine with their poems and distribute it to other classes.

# The Meadow Mouse

Theodore Roethke

## I

In a shoe box stuffed in an old nylon stocking
Sleeps the baby mouse I found in the meadow,
Where he trembled and shook beneath a stick
Till I caught him up by the tail and brought him in,
5  Cradled in my hand,
A little quaker, the whole body of him trembling,
His absurd whiskers sticking out like a cartoon-mouse,
His feet like small leaves,
Little lizard-feet,
10  Whitish and spread wide when he tried to struggle away,
Wriggling like a miniscule[1] puppy.

Now he's eaten his three kinds of cheese and drunk from
      his bottle-cap watering-trough—
So much he just lies in one corner,
His tail curled under him, his belly big
15  As his head; his bat-like ears
Twitching, tilting toward the least sound.

Do I imagine he no longer trembles
When I come close to him?
He seems no longer to tremble.

## II

20  But this morning the shoe-box house on the back porch is
      empty.
Where has he gone, my meadow mouse,
My thumb of a child that nuzzled in my palm?—
To run under the hawk's wing,
Under the eye of the great owl watching from the elm-tree,
25  To live by courtesy of the shrike,[2] the snake, the tom-cat.

---

**1. miniscule** (min′ ə skyōōl′) adj.: Very small. The normal spelling
is *minuscule*, but the poet chose to use the spelling that appears
here.
**2. shrike** (shrīk) n.: A shrill-voiced bird that feeds on small
animals.

**Presentation**

**Motivation/Prior Knowledge**
Have students ever rescued and nursed a wild, baby animal? How did they feel about the animal while they were taking care of it? What did it feel like to return the animal to the wild? Tell them that this poem is about such a situation.

**Purpose-Setting Question**
What does the meadow mouse in the title symbolize?

1 **Literary Focus** How does the poet use comparisons to create an image of the little mouse? What words especially help the reader to visualize the mouse?

2 **Critical Thinking and Reading** What is the poet saying in this stanza? What is he hoping?

3 **Discussion** What feelings does the poet express here? How does he feel about the mouse?

I think of the nestling fallen into the deep grass,
The turtle gasping in the dusty rubble of the highway,
The paralytic stunned in the tub, and the water rising—
All things innocent, hapless,³ forsaken.

———

**3. hapless** (hap′ lis) *adj.*: Unfortunate, luckless.

---

**4 Discussion** The poet has used his experience with the meadow mouse to illustrate a more universal issue, which he addresses in the final stanza. What is the "message" of this poem?

## THINKING ABOUT THE SELECTION
### Recalling

1. Briefly describe the meadow mouse that the speaker has found.
2. What happens to it?

### Interpreting

3. Describe the speaker's feelings about the meadow mouse.
4. What new feelings are expressed in the second part of the poem?
5. What is the connection between the last four lines and the rest of the poem?
6. Pick out what you feel is the single most effective image used to describe the mouse. Why did you select this particular image?

### Applying

7. Do you think that the speaker's feelings about the meadow mouse are in any way unusual or out of the ordinary? Or are they the feelings of any kind person taking care of a delicate little pet? Discuss this issue.

## ANALYZING LITERATURE
### Understanding Imagery

**Imagery** is the use of words to create word pictures—images—that capture and communicate experience. Though visual imagery is the most common kind of imagery found in literature,

a poet may use imagery that appeals to any of the five senses. Imagery may be used to communicate the sights, sounds, and sensations of the external world. It may also, however, be used to express the inner world of thought and emotion.

1. The speaker creates an image of the meadow mouse that appeals to the senses of sight and touch. He calls it "A little quaker, the whole body of him trembling" and describes it as "wriggling like a miniscule puppy." What feelings does this image arouse?
2. The word *nuzzled* in the second section also appeals to these senses. What feelings does it arouse?
3. What feelings are aroused by the images in the last four lines.

## THINKING AND WRITING
### Writing About Imagery

Write an essay that begins with and develops the following sentence: In the second part of "The Meadow Mouse," the speaker never talks about his feelings, but he nevertheless expresses them forcefully through images. Develop your essay by pointing out the feelings implied in the various images. When you revise the essay, check your interpretations by asking, "If the speaker used this image, what must he have felt?" Compare your interpretations with those of other students.

*616    Poetry*

---

**Closure and Extension**

**ANSWERS TO THINKING ABOUT THE SELECTION**
*Recalling*

1. Answers may differ but should include some of the descriptive information found in the first stanza.
2. The meadow mouse escapes from the shoebox.

*Interpreting*

3. Suggested Response: The speaker is fond of the little mouse and cares about it. He hopes that the mouse has come to trust him. He is concerned about the mouse after it has gone.
4. Suggested Response: The speaker expresses fear for the mouse's safety after it has gone. He also expresses concern for all helpless creatures.
5. Suggested Response: The mouse is symbolic of all the innocent,

616

gentle creatures, including humans, that exist alone and unprotected in the world.
6. Answers will differ, but students should fully explain why they think a particular image is the most effective.

*Applying*

7. Answers will differ, but students should be able to support their conclusions with evidence from the text, as well as their own opinions.

**ANSWERS TO ANALYZING LITERATURE**

1. Suggested Response: These images make the reader feel protective of the mouse.
2. Suggested Response: This word makes the reader feel as if the mouse is a little human baby.
3. Suggested Response: The images of the last four lines make the reader feel protective of all helpless creatures.

**THINKING AND WRITING**

For help with this assignment, students may refer to Lesson 13, "Writing About a Poem," in the Handbook of Writing About Literature.

**Publishing Student Writing** You might want to divide the class into small groups and have students read their essays to their fellow group members.

# To be of use

Marge Piercy

The people I love the best
jump into work head first
without dallying in the shallows
and swim off with sure strokes almost
    out of sight.
5   They seem to become natives of that
    element,
the black sleek heads of seals
bouncing like half-submerged balls.

I love people who harness themselves,
    an ox to a heavy cart,
who pull like water buffalo, with
    massive patience,
who strain in the mud and the muck to
10    move things forward,
who do what has to be done, again and
    again.
I want to be with people who submerge
in the task, who go into the fields to
    harvest
and work in a row and pass the bags
    along,

who are not parlor generals and field
15    deserters
but move in a common rhythm
when the food must come in or the fire be
    put out.

The work of the world is common as mud.
Botched, it smears the hands, crumbles to
    dust.
20  But the thing worth doing well done
has a shape that satisfies, clean and evident.
Greek amphoras[1] for wine or oil,
Hopi[2] vases that held corn, are put in
    museums
but you know they were made to be used.
25  The pitcher cries for water to carry
and a person for work that is real.

---

**1. amphoras** (am′ fər əz) *n.*: Tall jars that have a narrow neck and base and two handles, used by the ancient Greeks and Romans.
**2. Hopi** (hō′ pē) *n.*: A Pueblo tribe of Indians in northeastern Arizona.

## THINKING ABOUT THE SELECTION

### Recalling

1. What kind of people does the speaker like?
2. Give two images the author uses to describe these people.

### Interpreting

3. Why does the speaker appreciate such people?
4. Explain the meaning of line 18. Do you agree with it? Why or why not?
5. Explain what lines 22–24 suggest about working. How do these lines relate to the title of the poem?

### Applying

6. This poem suggests living and working according to a work ethic—an attitude about and a set of values one has toward work. What is your work ethic, or your attitude about work?

*To be of use* 617

**Motivation/Prior Knowledge**
Many students may not be familiar with the scenes of the American Southwest that Soto describes in "The Space." You
might consider displaying photographs and paintings of the
Southwest to familiarize students
with the region and to pique their
curiosity about the poem. Painters you might consider displaying include Georgia O'Keeffe,
Edward Hopper, Marsden Hart-
ley, and Walter Ufer.

**Purpose-Setting Question** Why
is the space important to the
poem's speaker?

**Discussion** What type of lessons might the birds teach? Why
might these lessons be of interest to the speaker?

**ANSWERS TO THINKING
ABOUT THE SELECTION**
*Recalling*

1. The speaker sleeps in a place with
avocado trees, cane, spider-
grass, chula, and banana trees. It
is also a peaceful place where
animals and lizards freely roam.

*Interpreting*

2. The space is his personal sanctu-
ary. With the exception of nature,
the speaker is free and alone in his
place.

3. The repetition of the phrase, "it is
enough" suggests that the speaker is satisfied with his surroundings and his freedom—he requires nothing more to make him
happy.

4. Answers will differ. Because the
speaker is content with what he
has, he is probably quite happy
with his space and loves where he
is.

618

# The Space

## Gary Soto

West of town,
Near Hermosa's well,
I sleep sometimes—
In a hammock of course—
5   Among avocado trees,
Cane, spider-grass,
The hatchet-faced chula,[1]
The banana's umbrella
Of leaves.
10   It is here
In the spiny brush
Where cocks gabble,
Where the javelina[2]
Lies on its side
15   Like an overturned high-heel.
I say it is enough
To be where the smells
Of creatures
Braid like rope
20   And to know if
The grasses' rustle
Is only
A lizard passing.
It is enough, brother,
25   Listening to a bird coo
A leash of parables,[3]
Keeping an eye
On the moon,
The space
30   Between cork trees
Where the sun first appears.

---

**1. chula** (chōō′ lə) *n.*: Prickly pear, the pear-shaped
fruit of a cactus.
**2. javelina** (ha′ və lē′ nə) *n.*: A wild sow; literally a
female mountain pig.
**3. parables** (par′ ə b'lz) *n.*: Short, simple stories
that illustrate a moral or religious lesson.

**THINKING ABOUT THE SELECTION**
**Recalling**

1. Describe the place where the speaker sometimes likes to sleep.

**Interpreting**

2. Other than the physical space the speaker describes, what other meaning of space is suggested in the poem?
3. The speaker twice uses the phrase, "it is
enough." What is the impact of repeating this
statement?
4. What is the speaker's attitude about the space
he describes?

**Applying**

5. Whether you live in the country or a city, you
can have a space that is your own. Describe
your special space and your attitude toward it.
Then explain why it is important to have a private space.

**CRITICAL THINKING AND READING**
**Appreciating the Effects of Imagery**

An image is a word or phrase that appeals to
one or more of the five senses. Writers use images to re-create sensory experiences with words
and to aid the reader in understanding the poem.
In "The Space," Soto creates images that appeal
to four of the five senses: sight, sound, touch, and
smell. For example, the line "In the spiny brush"
appeals to the sense of touch; "spiny" suggests
that the brush is prickly and full of thorns.

1. Name at least one image from the poem that
appeals to each of the following senses: sight,
sound, touch, and smell.
2. What effect do these images have on your understanding of the poem?

*Applying*

5. Answers will differ. Many students
will express the need to have a
space of one's own, a place
where they can think about and
enjoy life.

**ANSWERS TO CRITICAL
THINKING AND READING**

1. Images of sight include the "avocado tree," "spider-grass,"
"hatchet-faced chula," and so on.
Images of sound are "gabble,"
"rustle," and "coo." Images of
touch are "spiny," "braid like
rope." An image of smell is
"smells of creatures."

2. The speaker's attention to the
smallest details of his surroundings suggests that he is content
and at peace with his environment
and is free to enjoy what his space
has to offer. These images reveal
his attitude toward his private
space.

# The Creation

James Weldon Johnson

1

And God stepped out on space,
And he looked around and said:
I'm lonely—
I'll make me a world.

5 And far as the eye of God could see
Darkness covered everything,
Blacker than a hundred midnights
Down in a cypress swamp.

Then God smiled,
10 And the light broke,
And the darkness rolled up on one side,
And the light stood shining on the other,
And God said: That's good!

Then God reached out and took the light in his hands,
15 And God rolled the light around in his hands
Until he made the sun;
And he set that sun a-blazing in the heavens.

2

And the light that was left from making the sun
God gathered it up in a shining ball
20 And flung it against the darkness,
Spangling the night with the moon and stars.
Then down between
The darkness and the light
He hurled the world;
25 And God said: That's good!

Then God himself stepped down—
And the sun was on his right hand,
And the moon was on his left;
The stars were clustered about his head,
30 And the earth was under his feet.
And God walked, and where he trod
His footsteps hollowed the valleys out
And bulged the mountains up.

*The Creation*   619

## Presentation

**Motivation/Prior Knowledge**
Briefly retell the story of creation to the class, or read the first two chapters from Genesis. Ask the students to think about creation stories from other cultures that they may have heard or read. Then tell them that this poem describes the creation of the world.

**Purpose-Setting Question**
What motivates God to create the world and humans?

1 **Literary Focus** What image does Johnson use to convey the state of things before creation?

2 **Discussion** How does the phrase "Spangling the night with the moon and stars" give the reader an extraordinary image of God's creation of the heavens?

Fine art, *The Creation*, 1935, by Aaron Douglas. Aaron Douglass (1899-1979) was an Afro-American painter who came to Harlem in 1924 in search of a more meaningful outlet for his art than teaching. During his years there, he gave up his attachment to academic realism and devoted his painting to the expression of the Black experience, using African motifs and a modern style. His example inspired many Black artists of that time to turn toward their African roots.

*The Creation* shows the unique "Synthetic Cubist" style favored by Douglas. He divides his canvas geometrically—here with a circle—defined by flatly painted variations of color. An image of a man with recognizable Black features dominates the stylized landscape, validating the place of Blacks in God's creation of the human race.

You might ask students the following questions:

1. What feelings does this painting capture?
2. What shapes are important in this picture?
3. Why do you think Douglas did not choose to make his painting more realistic?
4. Does this picture go well with the poem? Explain.

**3 Critical Thinking and Reading**
What image of God does this stanza present?

THE CREATION
*Aaron Douglas*
*Studio Museum of Harlem*

> Then he stopped and looked and saw
> 35  That the earth was hot and barren.
> So God stepped over to the edge of the world
> And he spat out the seven seas—
> He batted his eyes, and the lightnings flashed—
> He clapped his hands, and the thunders rolled—
> 40  And the waters above the earth came down,
> The cooling waters came down.

3

## Grammar in Action

**Commas** are used to separate adjectives of equal rank. To test whether adjectives are of equal rank, you can insert *and* between them to see if the sentence still makes sense. Another test is to see whether the adjectives can be reversed.

Sentence:    The *rugged, jagged* incline was difficult to climb.
Test 1:    The *rugged and jagged* incline was difficult to climb. (makes sense)

Test 2:    The *jagged, rugged* incline was difficult to climb. (makes sense)
Result:    The adjectives are coordinate; use a comma between them.

Do not use commas between adjectives if they must stay in a specific order, if they make sense when joined by *and*, or if they are joined by *and* already.

Sentence:    After *several long* days, the job was finished.
Nonsense:    After *long several* days. . . .

Then the green grass sprouted,
And the little red flowers blossomed,
The pine tree pointed his finger to the sky,
45 And the oak spread out his arms,
The lakes cuddled down in the hollows of the ground,
And the rivers ran down to the sea;
And God smiled again,
And the rainbow appeared,
50 And curled itself around his shoulder.

Then God raised his arm and he waved his hand
Over the sea and over the land,
And he said: Bring forth! Bring forth!
And quicker than God could drop his hand,
55 Fishes and fowls
And beasts and birds
Swam the rivers and the seas,
Roamed the forests and the woods,
And split the air with their wings.
60 And God said: That's good!

Then God walked around,
And God looked around
On all that he had made.
He looked at his sun,
65 And he looked at his moon,
And he looked at his little stars;
He looked on his world
With all its living things,
And God said: I'm lonely still.

70 Then God sat down—
On the side of a hill where he could think;
By a deep, wide river he sat down;
With his head in his hands,
God thought and thought,
75 Till he thought: I'll make me a man!

Up from the bed of the river
God scooped the clay;
And by the bank of the river
He kneeled him down;
80 And there the great God Almighty
Who lit the sun and fixed it in the sky,

*The Creation*   621

4 **Critical Thinking and Reading** Have the students explain what they imagine as they read this section. What makes Johnson's images work so well?

5 **Discussion** Ask the students why God was still dissatisfied after His immense acts of creation. Why was He still lonely?

Nonsense: After *several and long* days. . . .
   Result: The adjectives are not coordinate; do not use a comma between them.

The following lines from "The Creation" show adjectives being used together:

. . . the earth was *hot and barren* . . .

And the *little red* flowers blossomed. . . .

By a *deep, wide* river, he sat down. . . .

**Student Activity 1.** Explain whether or not Johnson followed these rules in the two lines quoted from "The Creation."

**Student Activity 2.** Write a short paragraph describing someone making something. Use at least two sentences in which adjectives are correctly combined.

**Reader's Response** Which image in "The Creation" did you think was the most effective? Why?

## Closure and Extension

### ANSWERS TO THINKING ABOUT THE SELECTION
*Recalling*

1. In "The Creation," God first creates the earth, then light, the sun, moon, and stars, the physical features of the earth, the oceans, bodies of fresh water, plants, animals, and finally, mankind.
2. Answers will differ, but should express a logical reason for this chain of events.

*Interpreting*

3. Answers will differ, but should include all the items from question 1. There is clearly a movement from inanimate to animate and also from creatures of lesser intelligence to man.
4. Answers will differ, but may include impressions of strength, creativity, kindness, loneliness, power, majesty, or humanity.
5. Answers will differ, but students should include specific images found in the text to illustrate the impressions they described in question 4.

*Applying*

6. Answers will differ, but students will most likely feel that the poem would become more serious if it were presented as a sermon. Also, they may feel that the poet would then be more concerned with getting a message across in addition to capturing the imagination of the listener.

### THINKING AND WRITING

For help with this assignment, students can consult Lesson 18, "Writing a Poem," in the Handbook of Writing About Literature.

---

Who flung the stars to the most far corner of the night,
Who rounded the earth in the middle of his hand;
This Great God,
85  Like a mammy bending over her baby,
Kneeled down in the dust
Toiling over a lump of clay
6  Till he shaped it in his own image;

Then into it he blew the breath of life,
90  And man became a living soul.
Amen. Amen.

---

## THINKING ABOUT THE SELECTION
### Recalling

1. Describe the progression God follows in creating the world. What did he create first, what next, and so on?
2. Why did he create the world and, finally, man?

### Interpreting

3. After reviewing your answer to question 1, describe the system or kind of order God followed in creating the world.
4. Describe the impression of God created by the poem. Explain how specific images contributed to this impression.
5. Select one image applied to God that you consider especially imaginative and effective. What does this image suggest? Why do you consider it effective?

### Applying

6. Johnson considered "The Creation" a sermon as well as a poem. Does the effect or meaning of "The Creation" change if it is read as a sermon? Give reasons for your opinion.

### THINKING AND WRITING
**Writing a Poem with Imagery**

Write a brief poem that describes somebody doing or making something. Like Johnson and the other poets in this section, use vivid, imaginative images to make your subject come alive for the reader. When you have selected a subject, you might first write a clear description in prose. Then, when you describe the subject in verse, concentrate on using effective images. When you revise, see if you can improve the imagery in any way. Share your completed poem with your classmates.

**Publishing Student Writing** You might want to have volunteers read their poems to the class.

# Figurative Language

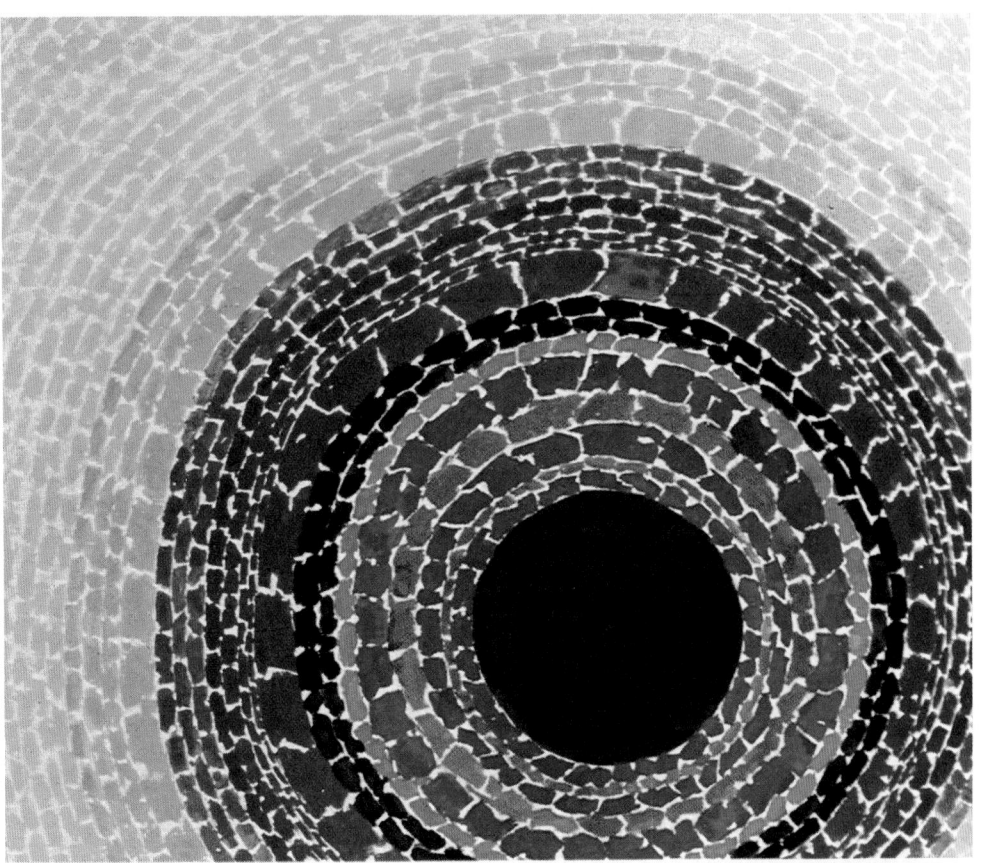

**ECLIPSE, MARCH 1970**
*A. W. Thomas*
*National Museum of American Art,
Smithsonian Institution*

**Humanities Note**
Fine art, *Eclipse*, A.W. Thomas. The contemporary American artist A.W. Thomas has presented a decorative interpretation of a total eclipse. Concentric bands of color radiate from the black center of the sun. The fields of color are fragmented into a mosaic-like pattern. Thomas has rendered the simple observation of a natural phenomenon with dynamic energy.

**More About the Authors** You might want to tell students that, of all nineteenth-century poets, Alfred, Lord Tennyson was perhaps the most familiar with science. He was familiar, for instance, with the latest discoveries in astronomy and geology. Ask students whether they believe breakthroughs in science today can be a source of inspiration for poets.

William Wordsworth is regarded as one of England's great nature poets. Ask students to name the authors and poets they have read whose love of and interest in nature has made an impression on them. Ask why some poets have affected them more than others.

Consider telling students that Langston Hughes was an excellent reciter of poetry and that he wrote many of his poems with public performance in mind. Ask students whether they have ever attended a poetry reading. Also, ask them why a reading might be a good introduction to a poet's work.

You might want to tell students that Emily Dickinson did not write for publication—only eight of her poems appeared in print during her lifetime. Have students consider the advantages and disadvantages of such a situation.

You may want to tell students that Carl Sandburg had a great deal of rough and ready experience. He served as a soldier, and worked as a salesman, fireman, and newspaper reporter, to name only a few of the trades he followed. Have students consider whether such experience is necessary or helpful for a poet.

624

# GUIDE FOR READING

### The Eagle

**Alfred, Lord Tennyson** (1809–1892) took an early interest in the classical literature of Greece and Rome. Later, he carefully studied the great English poets of the early nineteenth century. Their nature poetry inspired such impressive works as "The Eagle." This short lyric illustrates Tennyson's ability to recreate a natural scene so that it almost becomes the expression of a state of mind and feeling.

### I Wandered Lonely as a Cloud

**William Wordsworth** (1770–1850) was born on the northern fringe of the Lake District of England. This rural area inspired most of his outstanding nature poetry, and his fame in turn transformed the area into the poetic center of England. Wordsworth thought of poetry as "emotion recollected in tranquility"—a concept perfectly illustrated in "I Wandered Lonely as a Cloud." Written in 1804, the poem is a recollection, or remembrance, of an experience the poet had two years earlier.

### A Dream Deferred, Dreams

**Langston Hughes** (1902–1967) was born in Joplin, MIssouri. As a young man he held a variety of jobs—teacher, ranch hand, farmer, seaman, and night-club cook, among others. He drew on all these experiences and, above all, on the experience of being a black man in America to create his great body of literary work. "A Dream Deferred" and "Dreams" illustrate his ability to express the spirit of black America.

### The Sky Is Low

**Emily Dickinson** (1830–1886) was born and lived most of her life in Amherst, Massachusetts. Outwardly, her life was uneventful. The range and depth of her inner life, however, is suggested by the fact that she wrote at least 1,775 poems. The subjects of her poems—God, nature, love, death, and others—were conventional ones for her time. What makes the poems outstanding is her genius. "The Sky Is Low" illustrates the imaginative power with which Dickinson could describe a passing moment of New England weather.

*624    Poetry*

### Objectives
1  To understand similes
2  To write a poem using a simile
3  To analyze a poem
4  To understand metaphors
5  To understand personification
6  To respond to literary criticism
7  To write a poem

### Support Material

**Teaching Portfolio**
Teacher Backup, p. 775
Grammar in Action Worksheet, *Using Punctuation in Poetry,* p. 782
Usage and Mechanics Worksheet, p. 784
Vocabulary Check, p. 785
Analyzing Literature Worksheet, *Understanding Figurative Language,* p. 787
Language Worksheet, *Using Context Clues,* p. 788
Selection Test, p. 789
Art Transparency 16: *The Thankful Poor,* by Henry O. Tanner

## Splinter

**Carl Sandburg** (1878–1967) was born in Illinois to Swedish immigrants. Much of his poetry was inspired by the spirit and tempo of city life. "Splinter," however, shows the kind of poetry he wrote when inspired by the prairies of America. The brevity of the poem and the imaginative image of the last line show the influence of the Imagist poets, who relied on sharp, clear visual images to carry the meaning of a poem.

**Figurative Language**

**Figurative language** is language that uses figures of speech. A figure of speech is a way of saying one thing and meaning another. For example, when Tennyson says that the eagle "clasps the crag with crooked hands" he means that the eagle's claws are angular, bent, and bony-looking—reminding him of mangled human hands.

Three of the most important figures of speech are simile, metaphor, and personification. A **simile** compares one thing to another using the word *like* or *as;* for example, "This bread is like rubber." A **metaphor** compares one thing to another without using *like* or *as*—"Genius is a fountain." **Personification** gives human characteristics to an animal, object, or idea—"The sun's a wizard."

**Look For**

As you read the poems in this section, look for the figures of speech. Notice how they enrich meaning and add vividness and force to expression.

**Writing**

List five things or experiences about which you have strong reactions. For each one, write a simile, metaphor, or personification that implies your reaction. For example, "From here the river looks like an endlessly long snake."

**Vocabulary**

Knowing the following words will help you as you read the poems in this section.

**azure** (azh′ ər) *adj.*: Blue (p. 627, l. 3)
**host** (hōst) *n.*: A great number (p. 628, l. 4)
**glee** (glē) *n.*: Lively joy, merriment (p. 628, l. 14)
**pensive** (pen′ siv) *adj.*: Think-

ing deeply (p. 628, l. 20)
**bliss** (blis) *n.*: Great joy or happiness (p. 628, l. 22)
**deferred** (di furd′) *v.*: Put off until a future time (p. 630, l. 1)
**fester** (fes′ tər) *v.*: Form pus (p. 630, l. 4)

Fine art, *Eagle in a Snowstorm,* by Katsushika Hokusai (1760-1849). Tell students that Hokusai produced a tremendous number of works and that his landscapes are known for their sense of drama.

You might want to ask students the following questions:

1. What is dramatic about Hokusai's eagle?
2. Compare and contrast this eagle with Tennyson's.

**EAGLE IN A SNOWSTORM**
*Hokusai*
*The Harari Collection of Japanese Paintings
and Drawings*

626 *Poetry*

## ANSWERS TO THINKING ABOUT THE SELECTION
*Recalling*

1. The eagle is perched on a high seaside cliff, watching for his prey. He then dives down to catch a small animal or fish.

# The Eagle
## Alfred, Lord Tennyson

He clasps the crag with crooked hands;
Close to the sun in lonely lands,
Ring'd with the azure world, he stands.

The wrinkled sea beneath him crawls;
He watches from his mountain walls,
And like a thunderbolt he falls.

---

## THINKING ABOUT THE SELECTION

### Recalling

1. Describe the scene "The Eagle" presents.

### Interpreting

2. Since no spot on earth is literally "Close to the sun," how would you interpret this phrase figuratively?
3. Interpret the phrase "Ring'd with the azure world."
4. Why is the sea described as "wrinkled" and crawling?

### Applying

5. Compare "The Eagle" with the following paragraph from the *World Book Encyclopedia*. What does the poem express that the prose description does not?

   The eagle is one of the largest and most powerful birds in the world. At close range, eagles look fierce and proud. As a result, they are pictured as fierce, courageous hunters. Some eagles soar high in the air hunting for food. Because of this, eagles have long been symbols of grace and power.

## ANALYZING LITERATURE
### Understanding Similes

A **simile** is a figure of speech in which one thing is compared to another using the word *like* or *as*. Like other figures of speech, similes enable poets to suggest a great deal in a very few words.

1. The last line of "The Eagle" consists of the simile "And like a thunderbolt he falls." Tell at least four qualities that a swooping eagle and a thunderbolt have in common.
2. In view of your answer to question 1, explain why this simile is an effective figure of speech.

*The Eagle* 627

---

# I Wandered Lonely as a Cloud

**William Wordsworth**

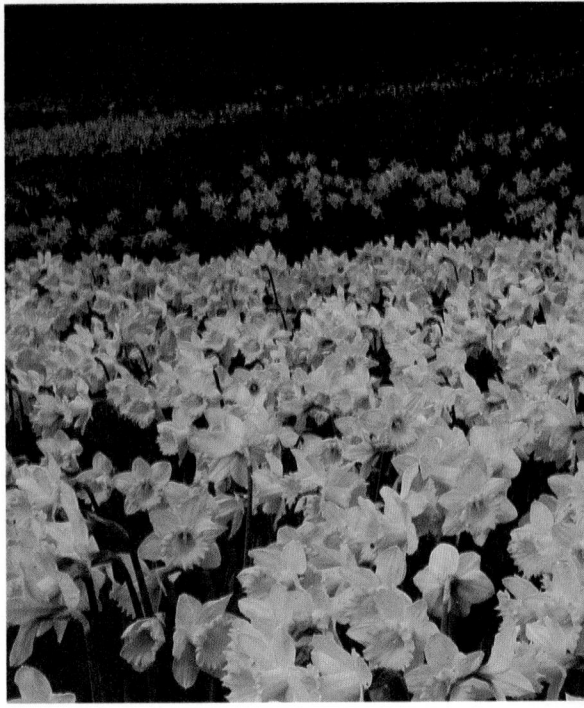

1    I wandered lonely as a cloud
That floats on high o'er vales¹ and hills,
When all at once I saw a crowd,
A host, of golden daffodils;
5  Beside the lake, beneath the trees,
Fluttering and dancing in the breeze.

Continuous as the stars that shine
And twinkle on the milky way,
They stretched in never-ending line
10  Along the margin of a bay:
Ten thousand saw I at a glance,
Tossing their heads in sprightly dance.

The waves beside them danced; but they
Outdid the sparkling waves in glee;
15  A poet could not but be gay,
In such a jocund² company;
I gazed—and gazed—but little thought
What wealth the show to me had brought:

2    For oft,³ when on my couch I lie
20  In vacant or in pensive mood,
They flash upon that inward eye
Which is the bliss of solitude;
And then my heart with pleasure fills,
And dances with the daffodils.

---

**1. o'er vales:** Over valleys.
**2. jocund** (jäk′ ənd) *adj.*: Cheerful.
**3. oft:** Often.

## Grammar in Action

Poets sometimes take liberties with **punctuation** to clarify their meaning or to emphasize an idea. This practice can be effective if done carefully and with moderation. Poets, for instance, will use a comma at the end of a line where a comma would not appear in prose, or they will put a period at the end of a word group that is not a sentence.

Generally, in poetry, commas suggest a pause; semicolons, a longer pause; periods, full stops. Dashes usually set off items for emphasis, and colons show that an explanation follows. Study these lines from the Wordsworth poem:

13  The waves beside them danced; but they
14  Outdid the sparkling waves in glee;
15  A poet could not but be gay,
16  In such a jocund company;
17  I gazed—and gazed—but little thought
18  What wealth the show to me had brought:

## THINKING ABOUT THE SELECTION

### Recalling

1. Describe the scene the speaker suddenly comes upon in his wandering.
2. What happens when he recollects the scene?

### Interpreting

3. Find two similes in which the comparison is indicated by the word *as*. In each simile, what is compared to what? What is suggested by each simile?
4. What effect does the scene have on the speaker while he is present?
5. What "wealth" is he later aware of?

### Applying

6. Of what value to human beings are natural scenes such as the one this poem presents?

## THINKING AND WRITING

### Writing a Poem Using a Simile

Review the list you made before reading "The Eagle." Select one of the experiences from it (or, if you wish, a different one). Write a short poem that leads up to a simile that suggests your view of or feeling about the experience. You might begin with a simple literal description of the experience, and then use the simile to convey its meaning. Be sure to let your imagination suggest an appropriate, effective simile. When you revise, remove unnecessary or ineffective details from the poem. Try to make each word count. Read your poem to your classmates, and invite them to read their poems.

*I Wandered Lonely as a Cloud* 629

### ANSWERS TO THINKING ABOUT THE SELECTION
#### Recalling

1. The speaker sees many daffodils fluttering in the breeze beside a lake and underneath some trees.
2. He is always cheered by the vision he had of the daffodils.

#### Interpreting

3. Suggested Response: "I wandered lonely as a cloud" is a comparison of the poet's walk to a single cloud floating in the sky. The phrase "Continuous as the stars that shine" compares the many daffodils to the appearance of the stars in the Milky Way at night.
4. Suggested Response: The poet is amazed, surprised, and overcome by the beauty of the daffodils. He gazes at them and feels happy.
5. Suggested Response: "Wealth" refers to the fact that the poet now has a beautiful memory which he can use to cheer himself up when he is bored or unhappy.

#### Applying

6. Answers will differ, but most students will indicate that the beauty of such scenes can be inspiring.

### THINKING AND WRITING

Refer students to Lesson 18, "Writing a Poem," in the Handbook of Writing About Literature.

**Publishing Student Writing**
You might divide the class into small groups and have students present their poems to fellow group members.

The semicolons in lines 13, 14, and 16 separate four main clauses and show their equality. The comma at the end of line 15, though not required by punctuation rules, suggests a brief pause. The dashes in line 17, also not required by the rules, emphasize the repeated verb. Notice that Wordsworth always has a good reason for taking liberties with punctuation.

**Student Activity 1.** Examine other marks of punctuation in this poem. Which marks follow the rules and which are added by the poet to emphasize or clarify an idea?

**Student Activity 2.** Add a stanza of your own to Wordsworth's poem. Take liberties with punctuation to emphasize or clarify your meaning. Then write a brief paragraph justifying your violation of the rules.

# A Dream Deferred

## Langston Hughes

*Harlem*

         What happens to a dream deferred?

      Does it dry up
      like a raisin in the sun?
      Or fester like a sore—
5    And then run?
      Does it stink like rotten meat?
      Or crust and sugar over—
      like a syrupy sweet?

      Maybe it just sags
10   like a heavy load.

      *Or does it explode?*

---

## THINKING ABOUT THE SELECTION

### Recalling

1. List the verbs used to indicate what can happen to "a dream deferred."

### Interpreting

2. Harlem, in New York City, is one of the largest and most famous black communities in the world. What does the mention of Harlem imply about the subject of this poem?
3. With what kind of dream do you think the poem is concerned?
4. In view of your answers to the preceding questions, interpret the five similes. What do you think the speaker is suggesting in each?
5. Interpret the last line.

### Applying

6. Discuss why people need to feel they can fulfill their dreams.

## THINKING AND WRITING

### Analyzing a Poem

Write an essay for your school literary magazine in which you interpret the meaning of Hughes's poem. Since the poem is written entirely in figurative language, primarily similes, your interpretation should be based on a careful analysis of these figures of speech. When you have written a satisfactory first draft, revise it so that all your separate thoughts and suggestions support a single idea.

630   Poetry

# Dreams

### Langston Hughes

1
> Hold fast to dreams
> For if dreams die
> Life is a broken-winged bird
> That cannot fly.

2  5
> Hold fast to dreams
> For when dreams go
> Life is a barren field
> Frozen with snow.

## THINKING ABOUT THE SELECTION

### Recalling

1. To what does the speaker compare life in the first stanza and in the second stanza?

### Interpreting

2. Interpret the metaphors. What does each suggest about life?
3. Restate in your own words the advice that this poem offers.

### Applying

4. The American poet Delmore Schwartz once wrote, "In dreams begin responsibilities." How might Langston Hughes interpret this statement? Base your answer on the two poems you have just read.

## ANALYZING LITERATURE

### Understanding Metaphors

A **metaphor** is a comparison of one thing to another without the use of *like* or *as* or a similar word. In a metaphor, one thing is said *to be* another—for example, "Life *is* a broken-winged bird . . ."

1. Hughes might have written "Dreams" entirely in literal language, without the metaphors in lines 3–4 and 7–8. What do these metaphors contribute to the meaning of the poem?
2. Change the two metaphors into similes by adding *like*. Tell why this change does or does not alter the effect or meaning of "Dreams."

*Dreams*   631

# The Sky Is Low

**Emily Dickinson**

The Sky is low—the Clouds are mean.
A Traveling Flake of Snow
Across a Barn or through a Rut
Debates if it will go—

5  A Narrow Wind complains all Day
How some one treated him.
Nature, like Us is sometimes caught
Without her Diadem.[1]

———————

**1. diadem** (dī′ ə dem) *n.*: Crown.

## THINKING ABOUT THE SELECTION

### Recalling

1. Describe the scene.

### Interpreting

2. What does "mean" suggest about the clouds?
3. What does "debates" suggest about the movement of the snowflake?
4. What impression of the wind do you get from lines 5–6?
5. Restate in your own words the meaning of lines 7–8.

### Applying

6. How would you reply to someone who said that this poem is merely a weather report in rhyme?

## ANALYZING LITERATURE

### Understanding Personification

**Personification** is a figure of speech that represents nonhuman or lifeless things as if they had the qualities of living human beings. When Wordsworth, in "I Wandered Lonely as a Cloud," describes the daffodils as "Tossing their heads in sprightly dance," he is using personification.

1. Point out at least two examples of personification in "The Sky Is Low," and explain how each
   fulfills the definition of this figure of speech.
2. Explain why Dickinson's use of personification
   is so effective. Could she have written an
   equally effective poem in plain, literal language?

632  *Poetry*

CAP BON AMI, 1961 (detail)
Samuel Reindorf

## Humanities Note

Fine Art, *Cap Bon Ami,* 1961 (detail), by Samuel Reindorf. Born in Poland, Reindorf (1914- ) immigrated to the United States and now lives in Mexico. He studied at the American Artists School, New York City, and has won many prizes for his work.

In *Cap Bon Ami,* Reindorf depicts a seaside scene, skillfully contrasting the textures of earth, water, stone, and sky.

You might want to use the following questions with this picture:
1. What kind of weather does the artist depict?
2. Does this picture go well with Dickinson's poem? Explain.

## THINKING AND WRITING

### Responding to Criticism

The poet and critic Conrad Aiken once wrote that Emily Dickinson's nature poems "are often superficial, a mere affectionate playing with the smaller things that give her delight . . ." Write an essay in which you explain why you think that Aiken's remark can or cannot be fairly applied to "The Sky Is Low." Before you write, decide whether or not the poem is superficial. Your reasons should be based squarely on the poem. Your first draft should consist of your judgment about the poem and your supporting reasons. When you revise the draft, check that you have not supported your opinion merely by restating it in different words. Compare your essay with those of your classmates. How many agreed with Aiken? How many disagreed?

*The Sky Is Low*   633

### ANSWERS TO ANALYZING LITERATURE

1. Answers will differ, but might include the images that the clouds are mean, that the snowflake debates, and that the wind complains; all of these are examples of personification because they describe non-human things in terms of human behavior.
2. Answers will differ, but should express the idea that the poem could not have been as effectively written without some use of figurative language, especially personification, because the poet is using the behavior of the weather to comment on the behavior of people.

### THINKING AND WRITING

Refer students to Lesson 15, "Evaluating a Literary Work," in the Handbook of Writing About Literature.

**Publishing Student Writing** You might want to collect the essays in a looseleaf book.

## Closure and Extension

### ANSWERS TO THINKING ABOUT THE SELECTION
#### Recalling

1. The scene is of an overcast, somewhat windy, winter day with snow flurries.

#### Interpreting

2. Suggested Response: "mean" suggests that the clouds are gray and threatening snow.
3. Suggested Response: "Debates" suggests that the snowflake is being tossed about by the wind before it settles.
4. Answers may differ, but might include the concept that the wind is light, but sharp and cold.
5. Answers will differ, but should express the idea that Nature, like human beings, is not always perfect.

#### Applying

6. Answers will differ, but students should realize that there is another purpose to the poem besides the description of a winter day. Dickinson is also commenting on human behavior.

633

1
2

The voice of the last cricket
across the first frost
is one kind of good-by.
It is so thin a splinter of singing.

---

## Presentation

**Motivation/Prior Knowledge**
Ask students to tell how they know when the summer is over and the fall has begun. Is the first cold day a sign? Is it the first red leaves they see on the trees? How do they feel when seasons change? Tell them that this poem is about such a transition.

**Purpose-Setting Question** What images does the title of this poem bring to mind?

1 **Discussion** How does Sandburg capture the exact moment when one season ends and another begins? What is the literal meaning of the metaphor in the last line?

2 **Enrichment** Tell students that Japanese *haiku* often express images like the one in "Splinter." Explain to students that a *haiku* is made of three lines, with a total of seventeen syllables, arranged in a five-seven-five syllable pattern.

## THINKING ABOUT THE SELECTION

### Recalling

1. What real-life experience could be the basis of "Splinter"?

### Interpreting

2. In what sense is the cricket's voice a "kind of good-by"?
3. Interpret the last line.

### Applying

4. Does Sandburg in "Splinter" use personification in the same way Dickinson does in "The Sky Is Low"? Explain your answer.

## THINKING AND WRITING

### Writing a Poem

Sandburg provides one kind of good-by—"the voice of the last cricket." Brainstorm to list other images that make fitting pictures of good-by. Choose the one you consider most appropriate. Then, patterning Sandburg's poem, write a four-line poem describing this kind of good-by. When you revise, make sure you have ended your poem with a powerful descriptive sentence.

634    Poetry

---

634

## Closure and Extension

### ANSWERS TO THINKING ABOUT THE SELECTION
#### Recalling

1. The poem is about the changing of the seasons from fall to winter.

### Interpreting

2. Suggested Response: The cricket will die in the cold; his chirping is a farewell song.
3. Answers may differ, but one response might be that the cricket's song is like a thin splinter of wood.

### Applying

4. Answers will differ, but students may indicate that Sandburg's use of personification is more subtle than Dickinson's; it is also not as complete a use of that figure of speech because crickets do have a "voice" and they do "sing." Dickinson's use of personification creates an amusing tone, while Sandburg's use of personification is more gentle and serious.

### THINKING AND WRITING

Have students refer to Lesson 18, "Writing a Poem," in the Handbook of Writing About Literature.

# Musical Devices

**THREE MUSICIANS, 1921**
*Pablo Picasso*
Collection, The Museum of Modern Art,
New York

## Humanities Note

Fine Art, *Three Musicians*, 1921, Pablo Picasso. Pablo Picasso (1881-1973), is a name synonymous with modern art. This Spanish artist is perhaps the greatest of the twentieth century. The child of an artist, he was encouraged in his interest in drawing and painting. He later studied at his father's school in Barcelona, The La Llonja Art School. In 1901, he settled in Paris and immediately became a leader of the artistic avant garde there. His influence on other artists with his continuous invention and exploration of many of the styles and trends of modern art cannot be overemphaszed.

*Three Musicians* is an example of Picasso's stepping away from his own style—Cubism, invented in collaboration with George Braque—to explore a new direction—Synthetic Cubism. Cubism is the reduction of form into geometric shapes. Feeling that it became confining in its analytic approach to form, Picasso looked for greater freedom in color, texture, and spatial relationships. In *Three Musicians* the forms are treated flatly with an almost paper cutout appearance. The colors are brighter and varied, quite unlike the monochromatic greys and browns of Cubism. The rhythm of the shapes and dissonant textures are reminiscent of those of modern music.

*Musical Devices*   635

**Master Teacher Note** Place Art Transparency 17, *Traveling Carnival, Santa Fe*, by John Sloan, on the overhead projector. This painting depicts a night-time carnival scene. You might point out to students that just as poets use musical devices to call up certain moods, painters can evoke moods through their use of movement. Ask students to identify the different types of movement that Sloan has portrayed. Then ask them what feelings the artist communicates through his depiction of the whirling merry-go-round, the turning ferris wheel, and the flowing crowd.

## The Listeners

**Walter de la Mare** (1873–1956) was born in Kent, England, and lived much of his life in and around London. Many of his poems are imaginative journeys into the shadowy world between the real and the unreal. His mastery of eerie moods and dreamlike situations is well illustrated by "The Listeners," one of his best-known poems.

## The Bells

**Edgar Allan Poe** (1809–1849) lived a life marked by one misfortune after another. Ill health frequently afflicted him. Fortunately, Mrs. Marie Louise Shew, a woman with medical training, treated Poe. He expressed his gratitude by writing several poems to her. "The Bells" is one of these. Some scholars believe that this poem originated in an idea that Mrs. Shew suggested to him.

## Ecclesiastes 3: 1–8

**The King James, or Authorized, Version of the Bible** was published in 1611. It was the work of a committee of English churchmen led by Lancelot Andrewes. The language of the King James Version is so beautiful that the Bible is ranked in English literature with the works of Shakespeare. According to tradition, Ecclesiastes was written by Solomon, the Hebrew king who died around 932 BC.

## I Hear America Singing

**Walt Whitman** (1819–1892) was born on Long Island, near New York City. His ability to absorb and comprehend all that he observed of his growing country provided him with the subject matter of his major work, *Leaves of Grass*. Part of Whitman's mission as a poet was to inspire and vitalize the United States through the ecstatic vision of democratic life that *Leaves* projected. His expansive vision and spirit may be glimpsed in "I Hear America Singing."

636   *Poetry*

## Musical Devices

The term **musical devices** refers to the various ways poets use the sound of words to enrich their poetry. One of the most frequently used musical devices is *alliteration,* the repetition of the same consonant sound, usually at the start of words. When de la Mare writes of the "*forest's ferny floor,*" he is using this device. A similar device is *assonance,* the repetition of vowel sounds. Poe uses this device in line 3 of "The Bells": "What a world of merriment their melody foretells!" In the same poem, he uses another musical device, *onomatopoeia.* This is the use of a word whose sound imitates or suggests sound— "How they tinkle, tinkle, tinkle," he says of the bells.

Alliteration, assonance, and—often—onomatopoeia are forms of the most basic musical device of all: *repetition.* This device is found not only in particular words or sounds but also in the structure of entire lines of verse. In the passage from Ecclesiastes, all the lines after the first are structured the same way. Each has two pairs of contrasting phrases: "A time to be born, and a time to die; a time to plant and a time to pluck up that which is planted . . ." Such repetition of similarly structured lines is called *parallelism.* This device is fundamental to the kind of verse Whitman wrote, free verse.

## Look For

As you read the poems in this section, look for the musical devices and notice how they enhance the sound of the poetry.

## Writing

"I Hear America Singing" presents a catalogue of ordinary people going about their occupations. Prepare a list of activities that various people in your school or neighborhood do every day. Try to list activities that, taken together, make up a "group picture."

## Vocabulary

Knowing the following words will help you as you read the poems in this section.

**thronging** (throŋ′ iŋ) *v.:* Crowding into (p. 638, l. 17)
**voluminously** (və lo͞o′ mə nəs lē) *adv.:* Fully, in great volume (p. 640, l. 26)

**palpitating** (pal′ pə tāt′ iŋ) *v.:* Beating rapidly, throbbing (p. 642, l. 56)
**paean** (pē ən) *n.:* Song of joy, triumph, etc. (p. 643, l. 92)

**Literary Focus** The world is alive with sound. Birds sing, dogs bark, trains whistle and chug, and wheels click and clack. Even when we read, we listen to the sounds of letters and words that we see on the page. Poets have a number of sound effects they can use to help us hear the sounds in their poems. A poet chooses words not only to communicate, but also to create a distinct sound.

**Look For** As students read each poem, have them pay attention to each poet's use of sound. For example, in Poe's poem, "The Bells," have them listen for words which tell how the various bells sound.

**Writing/Prior Knowledge** Have students discuss the different types of work talked about in the poem "I Hear America Singing." Have students name other kinds of work not mentioned in the poem. Then have them complete the writing assignment.

**Vocabulary** Have less advanced students read the words aloud. Then have them use the words in sentences to reflect their meanings.

**Spelling Tip** Point out the *ae* combination in *paean.*

**HET BLINDE HUIS**
*William Degouve de Nunques*
*State Museum, Kroller-Muller, Otterlo, The Netherlands*

# The Listeners

## Walter de la Mare

'Is there anybody there?' said the Traveler,
    Knocking on the moonlit door;
And his horse in the silence champed[1]
    the grasses
    Of the forest's ferny floor:
5  And a bird flew up out of the turret,
    Above the Traveler's head:
And he smote[2] upon the door again a
    second time;
    'Is there anybody there?' he said.
But no one descended to the Traveler;
10  No head from the leaf-fringed sill
Leaned over and looked into his gray eyes,
    Where he stood perplexed and still.
But only a host of phantom listeners
    That dwelt in the lone house then
15  Stood listening in the quiet of the moonlight
    To that voice from the world of men:
Stood thronging the faint moonbeams on
    the dark stair,
    That goes down to the empty hall,
Hearkening in an air stirred and shaken
20  By the lonely Traveler's call.
And he felt in his heart their strangeness,
    Their stillness answering his cry,
While his horse moved, cropping the dark
    turf,
    'Neath the starred and leafy sky;
25  For he suddenly smote on the door, even
    Louder, and lifted his head:—
'Tell them I came, and no one answered,
    That I kept my word,' he said.
Never the least stir made the listeners,
30  Though every word he spake[3]

---

**1. champed** (champt) *v.*: Chewed.
**2. smote** (smōt) *v.*: Struck hard.
**3. spake** (spāk) *v.*: Spoke.

Fell echoing through the shadowiness of
    the still house
From the one man left awake:
Ay, they heard his foot upon the stirrup,
    And the sound of iron on stone,
35   And how the silence surged softly backward,  **2**
    When the plunging hoofs were gone.

## THINKING ABOUT THE SELECTION

### Recalling

1. Briefly tell what happens in this poem.
2. Who are the listeners?

### Interpreting

3. What details create the eerie, dreamlike atmosphere of the poem?
4. What unanswered questions does the poem leave you with?

### Applying

5. What are some possible answers to these questions?

## ANALYZING LITERATURE

### Recognizing Alliteration

    **Alliteration** is the repetition of the same consonant sound, usually at the start of words—as in the "*forest's ferny floor*." In "The Listeners," the alliteration is light. Though you may have hardly noticed it, it contributes to the "music" and mood of the poem.

1. Find at least three lines with alliteration based on the *s* sound.
2. Find two lines with alliteration based on the *l* sound.
3. How important do you think such alliteration is to the mysterious mood of the poem?

## Closure and Extension

### ANSWERS TO THINKING ABOUT THE SELECTION
*Recalling*

1. A traveler comes to a house and knocks on the door. There seems to be no one in the house. When no one answers the door, the traveler tells whoever is listening to let someone know that he has kept his word.
2. It is not clear who the listeners are. Perhaps they are phantoms.

*Interpreting*

3. Answers will differ, but the following phrases might be suggested: "phantom listeners"; "lone house"; "empty hall"; "stillness answering his cry."
4. Answers will differ, but students might suggest that the questions left unanswered are: Who is the traveler? Why was he supposed to come to the house? Who had told him to come to the house? Who or what are the listeners?

*Applying*

5. Answers will differ, but the following might be suggested: The traveler could have been a person coming to pay off a debt or redeem a promise.

### ANSWERS TO ANALYZING LITERATURE

1. Suggested Response: Lines 7, 25 and 28-29.
2. Suggested Response: Lines 11 and 26.
3. Answers will differ, but might suggest that it helps to create a whispering eeriness.

# The Bells

Edgar Allan Poe

## I

Hear the sledges[1] with the bells—
Silver bells!
What a world of merriment their melody foretells!
How they tinkle, tinkle, tinkle,
5    In the icy air of night!
While the stars, that oversprinkle
All the heavens, seem to twinkle
With a crystalline delight;
Keeping time, time, time,
10    In a sort of Runic[2] rhyme,
To the tintinnabulation[3] that so musically wells
From the bells, bells, bells, bells,
Bells, bells, bells—
From the jingling and the tinkling of the bells.

## II

15    Hear the mellow wedding bells,
Golden bells!
What a world of happiness their harmony foretells!
Through the balmy air of night
How they ring out their delight!
20    From the molten golden-notes,
And all in tune,
What a liquid ditty[4] floats
To the turtle-dove[5] that listens, while she gloats
On the moon!
25    Oh, from out the sounding cells,
What a gush of euphony[6] voluminously wells!
How it swells!
How it dwells

---

1. **sledges** (slej′ əz) *n.*: Sleighs.
2. **Runic** (rōō′ nik) *adj.*: Songlike; poetical.
3. **tintinnabulation** (tin ti nab yōō lā′ shən) *n.*: The ringing of bells.
4. **ditty** (dit′ ē) *n.*: A song.
5. **turtle-dove:** The turtle-dove is traditionally associated with love.
6. **euphony** (yōō′ fə nē) *n.*: Pleasing sound.

640   *Poetry*

# Grammar in Action

Poetry is such a concentrated form that there is no room for words that don't quite do the jobs they are supposed to do. Poets must make every word count. Poets must always choose **precise words,** words that state exactly the idea being conveyed.

For a poet, the precise word might be one that imitates a particular sound. Using words that imitate sounds is called *onomatopoeia. (Buzz, murmur, hiss, hum* are onomatopoetic words.) Poe uses precise words and words that suggest sound to convey ideas about several different kinds of bells. Look at these lines:

> While the stars that oversprinkle
> All the heavens, seem to twinkle
>    With a chrystaline delight;
> Keeping time, time, time,
> In a sort of Runic rhyme,
> To the tintinnabulation that so musically swells
>    From the bells, bells, bells, bells,
>      Bells, bells, bells—
> From the jingling and the twinkling of the bells.

In this passage, what words suggest that the poet is writing of

**THE BELLS**
*Edmund Dulac*
*New York Public Library*

*The Bells* 641

## Humanities Note

Fine art, *The Bells,* by Edmund Dulac (1882–1953). Dulac was a French illustrator known for the color and imagination of his work.

You might want to use the following questions:

1. Does the mood of the illustration suit that of the poem?
2. How else could this poem be illustrated?

sleigh bells and not the fire bells described in a later stanza? What examples of onomatopoeia do the lines contain?

**Student Activity 1.** Read aloud one of the stanzas to a partner, but begin the stanza after the poet has identified the kind of bell being described. Have your partner listen for words that precisely convey the kind of bell that is ringing. After the reading, discuss the words and the use of onomatopoeia in the passage.

**Student Activity 2.** In either a poem or a short paragraph, describe a place, an object, or an experience. Use precise words. Make use of onomatopoeia to convey the sound of what you are describing.

On the future! how it tells
30     Of the rapture that impels
To the swinging and the ringing
Of the bells, bells, bells,
Of the bells, bells, bells, bells,
Bells, bells, bells—
35     To the rhyming and the chiming of the bells!

### III

Hear the loud alarum[7] bells!
Brazen[8] bells!
What a tale of terror now their turbulency tells!
In the startled ear of night
40     How they scream out their affright!
Too much horrified to speak,
They can only shriek, shriek,
Out of tune,
In a clamorous appealing to the mercy of the fire,
45     In a mad expostulation[9] with the deaf and frantic fire
Leaping higher, higher, higher,
With a desperate desire,
And a resolute endeavor
Now—now to sit or never,
50     By the side of the pale-faced moon.
Oh, the bells, bells, bells!
What a tale their terror tells
Of Despair!
How they clang, and clash, and roar!
55     What a horror they outpour
On the bosom of the palpitating air!
Yet the ear it fully knows,
By the twanging
And the clanging,
60     How the danger ebbs and flows;
Yet the ear distinctly tells,
In the jangling,
And the wrangling,
How the danger sinks and swells,
65     By the sinking or the swelling in the anger of the bells—
Of the bells—

---

**7. alarum** (ə ler′ əm) *n*.: A sudden call to arms; alarm.
**8. brazen** (brā′ z′n) *adj*.: Made of brass; having the sound of brass.
**9. expostulation** (ik späs chə lā′ sh′n) *n*.: Objection; complaint.

## Grammar in Action

Poets choose words carefully, not only for their denotation, but also for their connotation. The **denotation** of a word is its dictionary meaning; the **connotation** refers to a range of emotional and cultural associations that the word calls up. For instance, the words *home*, *house*, and *residence* all refer to a structure in which a family lives. That is their denotative meaning. The connotative meaning of *residence*, however, suggests something cold and impersonal, while *home* has connotations of warmth and comfort. The word *house* still emphasizes the structure rather than the people, but its connotative meaning is not so cold as *residence*.

Poe takes full advantage of connotative meanings, as this passage shows:

Hear the *loud alarum* bells!
*Brazen* bells!
What a tale of *terror* now their *turbulency* tells!

Of the bells, bells, bells, bells,
   Bells, bells, bells—
In the clamor and the clangor of the bells!

## IV

70    Hear the tolling of the bells—
               Iron bells!
What a world of solemn thought their monody[10] compels!
            In the silence of the night,
            How we shiver with affright
75   At the melancholy menace of their tone!
            For every sound that floats
            From the rust within their throats
                  Is a groan.
            And the people—ah, the people—
80   They that dwell up in the steeple,
                  All alone,
            And who tolling, tolling, tolling,
               In that muffled monotone,
            Feel a glory in so rolling
85         On the human heart a stone—
      They are neither man nor woman—
      They are neither brute nor human—
                  They are Ghouls:[11]
            And their king it is who tolls;
90   And he rolls, rolls, rolls,
                     Rolls
            A pæan from the bells!
            And his merry bosom swells
               With the pæan of the bells!
95         And he dances and he yells;
            Keeping time, time, time,
            In a sort of Runic rhyme,
               To the pæan of the bells—
                  Of the bells:
100        Keeping time, time, time,
            In a sort of Runic rhyme,
               To the throbbing of the bells—
      Of the bells, bells, bells—

---

**10. monody** (män′ ə dē) *n.*: A poem of mourning; a steady sound;
music in which one instrument or voice is dominant.
**11. Ghouls** (go͞olz) *n.*: Evil spirits that rob graves.

*The Bells*    643

4 **Discussion** Why do you think Poe varies the length of his lines in this poem?

In the *startled* ear of night
   How they *scream* out their *affright*!
The italicized words have especially vivid connotative meanings. Poe chose them to call up in the reader feelings of danger, alarm, disturbance, and horror.

**Student Activity 1.** Reread the first six lines of section IV of "The Bells." Identify the words with especially vivid connotative meanings and explain the feelings and associations they call up.

**Student Activity 2.** Suppose you were planning to write a poem about the sound of an alarm clock. List 3-5 words with vivid connotations that would enhance your poem. Explain why each word would be effective.

## Closure and Extension

### ANSWERS TO THINKING ABOUT THE SELECTION
*Recalling*

1. Answers should include sleigh bells; wedding bells; alarm bells; and church bells.
2. Suggested Response: Each stanza begins with the same two words. The rhythm in the first five lines is the same in each stanza. The next-to-last line of each stanza is "Bells, bells, bells." There are other similarities as well.

### *Interpreting*

3. Suggested Response: The first stanza suggests a sleigh ride on a winter night. The second suggests a wedding right after the ceremony. The third suggests a fire. The fourth suggests a nighttime scene.
4. Suggested Response: The mood varies. In the first stanza, the mood is merry; in the second stanza the mood is happy; in the third stanza the mood is turbulent; in the fourth stanza the mood is wild and sad.

### *Applying*

5. Answers will differ, but students might suggest that what Eliot says can be applied to the poem "The Bells" because a person reading or listening to the poem gets caught up in its sounds and the moods it creates.

### ANSWERS TO ANALYZING LITERATURE

1. Suggested Response: You can find assonance in lines 3 and 14 and alliteration in lines 3 and 10. Other forms of repetition are rhyme and the repeating of words like *bells* and *time.*
2. Suggested Response: Comparison of stanzas 1 and 2—The poet

---

105 To the sobbing of the bells:
Keeping time, time, time,
As he knells, knells, knells,
In a happy Runic rhyme,
To the rolling of the bells—
110 Of the bells, bells, bells—
To the tolling of the bells,
Of the bells, bells, bells, bells,
Bells, bells, bells—
To the moaning and the groaning of the bells.

---

## THINKING ABOUT THE SELECTION
### Recalling

1. What kind of bells are described in each of the four sections?
2. What similarities among the four sections do you see? Describe at least three.

### Interpreting

3. What scene or situation is suggested in each of the sections?
4. Does the mood or spirit of the poem vary from one section to another, or is it basically the same throughout? Give reasons for your opinion.

### Applying

5. The poet T. S. Eliot once suggested that poetry can be enjoyed before it is understood. Could "The Bells" be used as evidence in support of this idea? Give reasons for your opinion.

## ANALYZING LITERATURE
### Recognizing Forms of Repetition

The **repetition** of sounds, patterns of rhythm, words, phrases, and so on is the primary source of the music of poetry. A number of different forms of repetition are found in "The Bells." Besides *alliteration,* Poe uses assonance (the repetition of vowel sounds), as in the phrase "the mellow wedding bells . . ." He also uses repetition to achieve the effect of *onomatopoeia,* as in "How they tinkle, tinkle, tinkle . . ."

1. Point out all the different kinds of repetition you can find in the first section of "The Bells."
2. Compare any two stanzas of the poem. Point out two examples of Poe's repeating in one stanza words or phrases found in the other.
3. Usually, rhymes, which are a kind of repetition, consist of words at the ends of lines. Point out examples of rhymes within the same line of verse.

## SPEAKING AND LISTENING
### Reading Aloud "The Bells"

"The Bells" is a perfect example of a poem that was meant to be read aloud. In fact, it is far more enjoyable read aloud than read silently. It is also a good example of a poem that must be gone over carefully before it can be recited smoothly and easily. Review the poem for its sense. Try to figure out just what the longer or more complex sentences are saying. Then go back to those parts you may have stumbled over when you first read them. Decide how they should be read. Finally, when you feel comfortable with the whole poem read it aloud and notice how it comes alive.

*644   Poetry*

---

repeats the word "delight," the phrases "air of night," and "what a world," and the word "wells." The word "bells" is also repeated in each stanza.
3. Suggested Response: Internal rhymes can be found in lines 31 and 35 of Stanza 2 and line 113 of Stanza 4.

# Ecclesiastes 3:1-8

## (King James Version)

1 To every thing there is a season, and a time to every purpose under the heaven:
A time to be born, and a time to die; a time to plant, and a time to pluck up that
    which is planted;
A time to kill, and a time to heal; a time to break down, and a time to build up;
A time to weep, and a time to laugh; a time to mourn, and a time to dance;

2  5 A time to cast away stones, and a time to gather stones together; a time to
    embrace, and a time to refrain from embracing;
A time to get, and a time to lose; a time to keep, and a time to cast away;
A time to rend,[1] and a time to sew; a time to keep silence, and a time to speak;
A time to love, and a time to hate; a time of war, and a time of peace.

---

1. **rend** (rend) v.: Tear.

---

## THINKING ABOUT THE SELECTION

### Recalling

1. What verse contains the main idea of the passage?
2. How would you describe the way this passage is organized?

### Interpreting

3. What activity is suggested by the words "A time to cast away stones, and a time to gather stones together . . ."?
4. What is suggested by "A time to rend, and a time to sew . . ."?
5. Describe the tone or mood of this passage. Would you call it happy, sad, optimistic, calm? What other words might you use to describe it? Give reasons for your view.

### Applying

6. What comfort or guidance can a person of to-day find in these verses written more than 2,200 years ago in ancient Israel?

## ANALYZING LITERATURE
### Understanding Parallelism

In poetry, **parallelism** is the use of similar grammatical structures in succeeding lines of verse. Often, as in Ecclesiastes, a single line of verse will contain balanced and coordinated phrases. The lines that follow will also contain such phrases. In line 2, for example, the phrase "A time to be born" is balanced with "a time to die," and "a time to plant" is balanced with "a time to pluck up that which is planted . . . ."

1. Read the passage aloud. Do all the lines have the same rhythm, or does the rhythm vary somewhat? Explain your answer.
2. "The Bells" represents one kind of poetic music; Ecclesiastes represents another kind. Which kind do you prefer, and why?

*Ecclesiastes 3:1–8*   645

Fine Art, *Coal*, 1920, Thomas Hart Benton. Thomas Hart Benton (1889-1975) was an American painter and muralist. Benton attended the Art Institute of Chicago and Academie Julien in Paris; however, he said that his true education came from the years he spent roaming the United States. He became the primary force behind the American Regionalist movement in painting, a movement that glorified the hard-working farmers and laborers of the American heartland.

*Coal* is part of a series of murals glorifying contemporary America, done for the New School for Social Research in New York City. This vigorous, animated mural depicts the mining and industrial use of coal, showing the workers who make this whole process possible. Benton used an innovative montage of images separated by stylized architectural elements, a technique that revolutionized mural design in America.

You might want to use the following questions:

1. How does this mural depict the mining and use of coal?
2. What mood does Benton's mural call up?
3. Compare and contrast Benton's treatment of work with Whitman's.

**COAL (*from America Today*), 1920**
*Thomas Hart Benton*
Courtesy of The Equitable Life Assurance Society of the U.S.

# I Hear America Singing

**Walt Whitman**

1 I hear America singing, the varied carols I hear,
Those of mechanics, each one singing his as it should be
  blithe and strong,
The carpenter singing his as he measures his plank or
  beam,
The mason singing his as he makes ready for work, or
  leaves off work,
5 The boatman singing what belongs to him in his boat, the
  deckhand singing on the steamboat deck,
The shoemaker singing as he sits on his bench, the hatter[1]
  singing as he stands,
The wood-cutter's song, the ploughboy's on his way in the
  morning, or at noon intermission or at sundown,
The delicious singing of the mother, or of the young wife at
  work, or of the girl sewing or washing,
Each singing what belongs to him or her and to none else,
10 The day what belongs to the day—at night the party of
  young fellows, robust, friendly,
Singing with open mouths their strong melodious songs.

---

**1. hatter:** A person who makes, sells, or cleans hats.

## Presentation

**Motivation/Prior Knowledge**
Ask students if it is possible to characterize the mood and spirit of a country. How might they accomplish such a task? Tell them that Whitman presents *his* vision of the United States in this poem.

**Purpose-Setting Question** Is Whitman's reference to song and singing literal, figurative, or both?

1 **Enrichment** Whitman loved to attend the opera and heard many of the great singers of his day. He was very susceptible to the powers of song.

2 **Discussion** What images are associated with each worker mentioned?

3 **Enrichment** Have artistic students choose one of the workers mentioned and illustrate the passage about him or her. Try to have all twelve occupations illustrated. Display the illustrations as a mural.

**Reader's Response** If Whitman were to write this poem today, how do you think he would change it? Do you think his message would be the same? Explain.

### ANSWERS TO THINKING ABOUT THE SELECTION
*Recalling*

1. The people are mostly manual workers.

*Interpreting*

2. Suggested Response: Singing should be interpreted both literally and figuratively. In addition to literal song, singing refers to each worker's expression of himself or herself through work.
3. Suggested Response: The images of the various workers create a vision of what America is and represents. People can work at what they want. The poem implies that all of these individuals work for the common good.
4. Suggested Response: The spirit is one of togetherness. It is one of happiness and optimism.

*Applying*

5. Answers will differ, but students might suggest that Whitman was trying to depict a nation of individuals freely expressing themselves and yet working for the common good.

### ANSWERS TO ANALYZING LITERATURE

1. Answers will differ. Students may respond that if another poet tried to treat the content of this poem with a regular rhythmic pattern, it might alter the free and expansive mood.
2. Suggested Response: Both poems use parallel structure. While the Biblical passage is distanced and unemotional, Whitman's poem is optimistic.

### THINKING AND WRITING

Refer students to Lesson 2, "Drafting and Revising," in the Handbook of Writing About Literature.

**Publishing Student Writing** You might want to have students use their essays in a classroom de-

---

## THINKING ABOUT THE SELECTION
### Recalling

1. In general, what are the various people mentioned in the poem doing?

### Interpreting

2. Are the people literally singing, or should "singing" be interpreted figuratively? Give reasons for your opinion.
3. Explain the title. In what sense does the speaker hear America singing?
4. Describe the tone and spirit of the poem.

### Applying

5. What do you think Whitman was trying to express in this poem?

## ANALYZING LITERATURE
### Understanding Free Verse

**Free verse** is verse without a regular arrangement of accented and unaccented syllables. It is "free" of the restrictions of a set rhythmical pattern for each line. However, since free-verse poetry is divided into lines, the movement from one line to the next establishes a kind of rhythm. In the hands of a poet such as Whitman, free verse can be an instrument of rich and varied music.

1. Another poet might have treated the subject matter of "I Hear America Singing" in rhymed verse with a regular rhythmic pattern. Tell why you think such a treatment would or would not have resulted in a more effective poem than Whitman's.
2. Compare the rhythm of Whitman's poem with that of Ecclesiastes 3:1–8. What similarities and what differences do you find?

## THINKING AND WRITING
### Responding to Criticism

The Whitman scholar James E. Miller, Jr., has written that " 'I Hear America Singing' presents an image of America that America would like to believe true—an image of proud and healthy individualists engaged in productive and happy labor." Miller implies that Whitman's image of America may be untrue.

Do you think it is untrue? Write an essay in which you discuss this question. First gather evidence in support of your opinion. Then write it up in a well-organized first draft. When you revise the draft, check that all your statements are relevant to your main idea. Compare your opinion and supporting arguments with those of your classmates.

*648    Poetry*

bate to answer the question: Was Whitman's image of America in the poem "I Hear America Singing" untrue? This will give students an opportunity to share their essays with the class.

# Structure

HARMONY IN RED, 1908–09
*Henri Matisse*
*The Hermitage, Leningrad/Art Resource*

## Humanities Note

Fine art, *Harmony in Red*, 1908, Henri Matisse. The French artist Henri Matisse (1869-1954), was a Post-impressionist painter. He headed the Fauvist group, artists whose work was characterized by simplification of form and the use of brilliant, often incongruous colors.

*Harmony in Red* is a large decorative composition painted at the height of Matisse's development as an artist. This joyous painting is a study in contrasts: cool colors against warm; straight lines against curved; close distance against far. The painting appears flat but achieves spatial depth with line direction and subtle color change. Matisse always painted cheerful subjects, as he felt art should be a pleasure, not a chore.

*Structure*   *649*

**More About the Authors** Tell students that, in many of her love poems, **Sara Teasdale** left out the specifics of who, when, and why. She felt that the poems would be more powerful without this concrete information. Have students discuss this device.

**E.E. Cummings's** method of working was to sleep until noon, work for hours on his writing, and then socialize in the evening. Ask students if they would enjoy a similar routine.

**John Masefield** was named "Poet Laureate" of England because his poetic skills, insights, and spirit were thought to carry forward the British heritage and to represent the concerns dearest to the British people. Ask students whom they would choose to be an American "poet laureate." How would this poet echo the talent and ethos of our nation?

**Gabriela Mistral** began teaching elementary school at 15 without having finished school and without a teaching certificate. When she was 21, Mistral obtained her teaching certificate and thereafter taught at the secondary level. At the same time she started her teaching career, Mistral began writing poetry. She submitted her work to local newspapers and international magazines under a variety of pen names. Mistral was the pen name under which she was to become famous. Ask students why being a successful poet may have contributed to Mistral's teaching career.

# GUIDE FOR READING

## "There Will Come Soft Rains"

**Sara Teasdale** (1884–1933) was born in St. Louis, Missouri. Success as a poet came early to her. Her first poems were published when she was still a girl, and her first book appeared before she was 25. Her attachment to the well-known poet Vachel Lindsay ended in grief when he committed suicide. Two years later, she took her own life. Many of Teasdale's poems, such as "There Will Come Soft Rains," are sad, as her life was.

## maggie and milly and molly and may

**E. E. Cummings** (1894–1962) was born in Cambridge, Massachusetts, and educated at Harvard. During World War I, he was an ambulance driver in France and spent three months in a detention camp. The unusual typography of his poems is an expression of his quirky individualism, which is squarely in the tradition of New England writers. The lyrical lightheartedness of "maggie and milly and molly and may" is typical of much, though not all, of his verse.

## Sea-Fever

**John Masefield** (1878–1967) was born in Herefordshire, England. As a boy, he went to sea and for many years wandered the globe working at odd jobs. His life at sea is the source of his best-known poems. Of these, "Sea-Fever" is the most famous. Masefield was the twenty-second poet laureate of England.

## Cradle Song

**Gabriela Mistral** (1889–1957), whose real name is Lucila Godoy Alcayaga, was born in Vicuña, Chile. Mistral changed her name when she was a young teacher because she feared the content of her poetry might lead to the loss of her job. Her first name comes from the archangel Gabriel; her last name comes from the name of a sea wind. Mistral won the Nobel Prize for Literature in 1945; she was the first South American to receive this award. Mistral wrote many poems about children and motherhood, such as "Cradle Song."

### Objectives

1 To understand structure in poetry
2 To compare structures
3 To understand meter
4 To write a critical evaluation of a poem

### Support Material

**Teaching Portfolio**
Teacher Backup, p. 807
Usage and Mechanics Worksheet, p. 813
Vocabulary Check, p. 814
Analyzing Literature Worksheet, *Understanding Structure*, p. 815
Language Worksheet, *Recognizing Related Words*, p. 816

Selection Test, p. 817
Art Transparency 18: *Trees and Rocks*, by Emile Branchard

# My Father's Song

**Simon J. Ortiz** (1941–    )—an Acoma Pueblo Indian from New Mexico—writes poems and stories about the universal experiences of Native Americans. Embedded in his work are Indian history, mythology, philosophy, and contemporary social concerns. In "My Father's Song," Ortiz pays tribute to and remembers his dead father. Ortiz has a strong belief in the importance of education, and because of this he devotes much of his free time to educating fellow Native Americans.

**Structure**

The **structure** of a poem may be described in terms of its stanza form and its meter. A *stanza* is a unit with a set number of lines. For example, the stanza form in a couplet is made up of two rhymed lines. Another form is the *quatrain*: a stanza of four lines with any one of several rhyme patterns.

An important part of a poem's structure is its meter—the pattern of accented and unaccented syllables that form the basis of a poem's rhythm. Meter signifies the number of rhythmic beats, or "feet," in a line and the arrangement of accented and unaccented syllables in each foot. For example, a line that has five beats, or feet, is called a pentameter. If each foot consists of an unaccented syllable followed by an accented one, it is called an iamb. The meter of the poem would then be iambic pentameter. A poem that does not have a regular meter is called free verse.

**Look For**

Look for examples of couplets, quatrains, and free verse in the following set of poems. Try to determine the number of feet per line in each poem.

**Writing**

Each poem in this section is a lyric poem—a type of poem that expresses personal thoughts and feelings. Think of a person, place, or event that has special significance to you and freewrite about it.

**Vocabulary**

Knowing the following words will help you as you read the poems in this section.

**tremulous** (trem′ yə ləs) *adj.*: Quivering (p. 652, l. 4)
**languid** (lan′ gwid) *adj.*: Drooping, weak (p. 653, l. 6)

**spume** (spyo͞om) *n.*: Foam, froth (p. 654, l. 8)
**whetted** (hwet′ əd) *v.*: Sharpened (p. 654, l. 11)

*Guide for Reading* 651

# "There Will Come Soft Rains"
## (War Time)
### Sara Teasdale

There will come soft rains and the smell of the ground,
And swallows circling with their shimmering sound;

And frogs in the pools singing at night,
And wild plum-trees in tremulous white;

5  Robins will wear their feathery fire
Whistling their whims on a low fence-wire;

And not one will know of the war, not one
Will care at last when it is done.

Not one would mind, neither bird nor tree
10 If mankind perished utterly;

And Spring herself, when she woke at dawn,
Would scarcely know that we were gone.

1

---

## THINKING ABOUT THE SELECTION

### Recalling

1. What is the topic of this poem?

### Interpreting

2. Describe nature's attitude, as the speaker imagines it, toward human self-destruction.
3. What does the poem suggest about the effect of war on nature?
4. What seem to be the speaker's feelings about the situation described in the poem?

### Applying

5. Teasdale died in 1933. How might her poem be different had she written it in the age of nuclear weapons?

652   Poetry

## ANALYZING LITERATURE
### Understanding Structure

   Many poems have a **structure** that may be described in terms of *stanza, form,* and *meter,* or the pattern of accented and unaccented syllables. Teasdale's poem consists of *couplets*—that is, pairs of rhyming lines. Each line has four heavily accented syllables, or four feet. A line of four feet is called a tetrameter. So the structure of the poem may be described as tetrameter couplets.

1. Read the poem aloud. How does the structure of couplets and tetrameter lines affect the spirit or mood of what is said?
2. Change one of the rhymed words in each couplet (for example, change "ground" to "soil" in line 1). How does the absence of rhyme change the poem's overall effect?

# maggie and milly
# and molly and may

### E. E. Cummings

maggie and milly and molly and may
went down to the beach(to play one day)

1

and maggie discovered a shell that sang
so sweetly she couldn't remember her troubles,and

5  milly befriended a stranded star
whose rays five languid fingers were;

and molly was chased by a horrible thing
which raced sideways while blowing bubbles:and

may came home with a smooth round stone
10  as small as a world and as large as alone.

2

For whatever we lose(like a you or a me)
it's always ourselves we find in the sea

---

## THINKING ABOUT THE SELECTION

### Recalling

1. Describe each girl's experience on the beach.

### Interpreting

2. What creature did milly befriend?
3. Do you think that the "horrible thing" that chases molly can be identified? Explain.
4. Describe the tone and spirit of the poem.

### Applying

5. Is this poem in any way serious, or is it just an amusement in verse? Discuss what you think the purpose of the poem might be.

## THINKING AND WRITING
### Comparing Structures

You are frequently asked on tests to write an essay of comparison and contrast. To practice for such a question, write a brief essay in which you compare and contrast the couplet structure of Cummings's poem and that of "There Will Come Soft Rains." Look closely at the two poems. What similarities do you see in the couplets, and what differences? Make sure you quote from the poems to support your judgments. When your essay is finished, see what some of your classmates had to say in their essays. Did anyone notice a similarity or difference that you missed?

*maggie and milly and molly and may*   653

**Motivation/Prior Knowledge**
Ask students to recall their visits to the shore of a lake, river, or ocean. Have them describe any interesting objects they found. Then tell them that each of the girls in this poem discovers something about herself at the beach.

**Purpose-Setting Question** How does each girl gain insight into herself?

1 **Discussion** What does each girl's discovery suggest about her?

2 **Discussion** How do we find ourselves at the sea?

## Closure and Extension

### ANSWERS TO THINKING ABOUT THE SELECTION
*Recalling*

1. One girl finds a shell that sings to her. Another befriends a starfish. Another is chased by a sea creature. Another finds a smooth round stone.

*Interpreting*

2. She befriended a starfish.
3. Suggested Response: No. The only description given is that it raced sideways and blew bubbles.
4. Suggested Response: The tone and spirit are playful.

*Applying*

5. Answers will differ, but might suggest that the poem has a serious theme—people's experience with nature reveals their deeper selves.

### THINKING AND WRITING

For help with this assignment, students can refer to Lesson 13, "Writing About a Poem," in the Handbook of Writing About Literature.

# Sea-Fever

## John Masefield

1
I must go down to the seas again, to the lonely sea and the
  sky,
And all I ask is a tall ship and a star to steer her by,
And the wheel's kick and the wind's song and the white
  sail's shaking,
And a gray mist on the sea's face and a gray dawn
  breaking.

5 I must go down to the seas again, for the call of the
  running tide
Is a wild call and a clear call that may not be denied;
And all I ask is a windy day with the white clouds flying,
And the flung spray and the blown spume, and the seagulls
  crying.

I must go down to the seas again to the vagrant gypsy life,
10 To the gull's way and the whale's way where the wind's like
  a whetted knife;
And all I ask is a merry yarn from a laughing fellow-rover
2 And quiet sleep and a sweet dream when the long trick's[1]
  over.

————————
**1. trick:** A shift of duty, as on a ship.

---

## THINKING ABOUT THE SELECTION

### Recalling

1. What reason does the speaker give for the statement that he "must go down to the seas again"?
2. Identify at least four of the things he asks for.

### Interpreting

3. Explain the kind of appeal the sea has for the speaker.
4. What figurative or symbolic meaning might the final line have?
5. Discuss the title. In particular, what is suggested by the word "fever"?

### Applying

6. What other ways of life have a powerful hold on some people?

## ANALYZING LITERATURE

### Understanding Meter

**Meter** is the pattern of accented and unac-

654    *Poetry*

THE MUCH RESOUNDING SEA, 1884
*Thomas Moran*
*National Gallery of Art, Washington*

## Humanities Note

Fine art, *The Much Resounding Sea*, by Thomas Moran (1837–1926). Moran was an American landscape painter. He went on an early expedition down the Colorado River and illustrated the report made by the explorers.

You might want to use the following questions:
1. What aspect of the sea does the painting express?
2. Does the painting express the same love of the sea that the poem does? Explain.

cented syllables that form the basis of a poem's rhythm. Here is the first line of "Sea Fever" with the accented syllables indicated by an accent mark and the unaccented syllables indicated by an *x*. The separate feet are marked by vertical lines.

> x   ′   x   ′   x   x   ′   x   ′   x   x
> I must|go down|to the seas|again,|to the
> ′   x   ′   x   ′   x
> lone|ly sea|and the sky . . .

Notice that the line has seven accented syllables. Such a line is called a heptameter. This particular heptameter has two different kinds of feet. Those made up of one unaccented syllable followed by an accented one are called iambs (for example, "I must"). Those made up of two unaccented syllables followed by one accented syllable are called anapests (for example, "to the seas"). This kind of analysis and identification of meter is called *scansion*.

1. Reread "Sea Fever" noting the pattern of accented and unaccented syllables in each line. How many feet, or beats, do you find in each line?
2. Is the pattern of accented and unaccented syllables the same for all the lines, or does it vary? Explain.
3. How would you describe the connection between the meter or rhythm and the content of the poem?

*Sea-Fever* 655

**Motivation/Prior Knowledge**
Ask students to think about the one person whom they consider the most important to them. What do they remember about this person? What would they say to this person to express how they feel about him or her? Then tell students that in "My Father's Song" Ortiz expresses his feelings to the most important person to him—his father.

**Purpose-Setting Question**
What does the speaker of the poem learn from his father?

1 **Discussion** What might be preventing the speaker from saying things?

2 **Discussion** The speaker remembers the very specific characteristics of his father's voice. What might this suggest about the speaker? About the speaker's relationship with his father?

3 **Clarification** Students may be unfamiliar with the word *furrow*. A furrow is a narrow grove in the ground made by a plow.

4 **Discussion** What "things" might the father have said to his son?

## Humanities Note

# My Father's Song

## Simon J. Ortiz

1 Wanting to say things,
I miss my father tonight.
His voice, the slight catch,
the depth from his thin chest,
2 5 the tremble of emotion
in something he has just said
to his son, his song:

We planted corn one Spring at Acu—
we planted several times
10 but this one particular time
I remember the soft damp sand
in my hand.

My father had stopped at one point
to show me an overturned furrow;
3 15 the plowshare had unearthed
the burrow nest of a mouse
in the soft moist sand.

Very gently, he scooped tiny pink
animals
into the palm of his hand
20 and told me to touch them.
We took them to the edge
of the field and put them in the shade
of a sand moist clod.

I remember the very softness
of cool and warm sand and tiny alive
25 mice
4 and my father saying things.

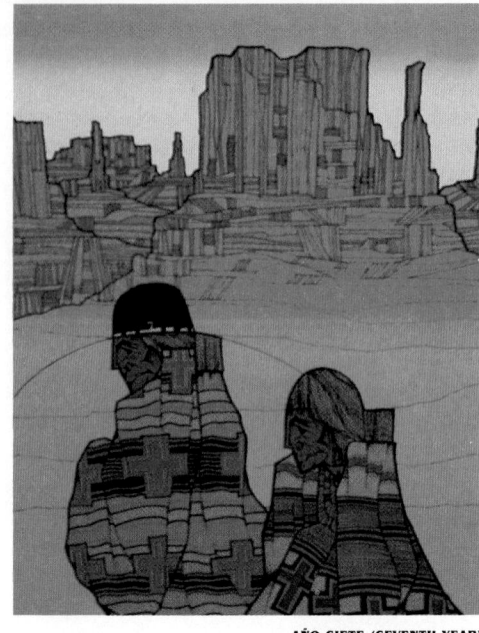

AÑO SIETE (SEVENTH YEAR)
*Amato Peka*

## READING ABOUT THE SELECTION

### Recalling

1. What emotion leads the speaker to write this poem?

### Interpreting

2. Explain the similarity between the first line of the poem and the last line.
3. What values does the boy learn from his father?

### Applying

4. Imagine that your children years in the future remember you "saying things." What understandings about life would you want them to remember?

## ANSWERS TO THINKING ABOUT THE SELECTION
### Recalling

1. The speaker appears to have written this poem out of his fondness and love for his father. The poem commemorates his father's life and the influence he had on the speaker.

### Interpreting

2. Answers may vary. The first and last lines are similar, yet they suggest a difference between the speaker and his father. In the first line, the speaker expresses his desire to say something to or about his father. In the last line, the speaker remembers the words that his father was able to say.
3. The speaker learned to value the time he spent with his father. He also learned to appreciate life and the land on which they live.

### Applying

4. Answers will differ. Students should express their own personal feelings. Many students may express similar values as those expressed in this poem.

# Meciendo ("Cradle Song")

Gabriela Mistral    translated by Langston Hughes (1957)

El mar sus millares de olas
mece, divino
Oyendo a los mares amantes,
mezo a mi niño.

5   El viento errabundo en la noche
mece a los trigos.
Oyendo a los vientos amantes,
mezo a mi niño.

Dios Padre sus miles de mundos
10  mece sin ruido.
Sintiendo su mano en la sombra,
mezo a mi niño.

The sea cradles
its millions of stars divine.
Listening to the seas in love,
I cradle the one who is mine.

5   The errant[1] wind in the night
cradles the wheat.
Listening to the winds in love,
I cradle my sweet.

God Our Father cradles
10  His thousands of worlds without sound.
Feeling His hand in the darkness,
I cradle the babe I have found.

**1.** **errant** (erʹ ənt) *adj.*: Roving or wandering; shifting about.

## THINKING ABOUT THE SELECTION

### Recalling

1. Whom is the speaker cradling or rocking?
2. Which two lines in each stanza rhyme? What is the rhyme scheme of the poem?

### Interpreting

3. Other poets have translated "Meciendo," the title of the poem, as "rocking"; Hughes translates it as "cradle song." What are the different connotations of each translation of the title? Which is a more appropriate title? Why?
4. Mistral never had children of her own, yet she often wrote of children and motherhood. What attitude about children and motherhood does she convey in "Cradle Song"?

### Applying

5. What universal truths about motherhood do you think Mistral is addressing in her poem?

## THINKING AND WRITING

### Writing a Critical Evaluation

Laurence Perrine, a notable teacher of poetry, once wrote, "Great poetry seeks not merely to entertain the reader but to bring him, along with pure pleasure, fresh insights . . . into the nature of human experience. Great poetry, we might say, gives its reader a broader and deeper understanding of life. . . ."

Which of the poems in this section best meets Perrine's requirement for great poetry? Write an essay in which you argue for the poem of your choice. Make sure you explain why you feel that the four other poems are less successful. Before you submit your work, review your arguments. Are they reasonable? Are they based on what is in the poems and not merely on personal preference? Revise your essay as necessary to strengthen your argument. Then compare your essay with those of your classmates.

*Meciendo* 657

## The Sound of the Sea

**Henry Wadsworth Longfellow** (1807–1882) was born in Portland, Maine, and educated at Bowdoin College. His knowledge of foreign languages gained him a professorship at Bowdoin and later at Harvard. The deaths of his first wife and child and of his second wife had a profound effect on his poetry. The thoughtful, serious brooding on life found in such poems as "The Sound of the Sea" is the result of these personal tragedies. Longfellow remains one of the most popular of American poets.

## Sonnet 30

**William Shakespeare** (1564–1616) is revered not only for his thirty-seven plays but also for his 154 splendid sonnets. Taken together, the sonnets seem to tell a story. The "plot" is hard to follow, but it is clear that the main characters are a young nobleman, a lady, a poet (probably Shakespeare himself), and a rival poet. Some of the best sonnets, like Sonnet 30, are addressed to the young nobleman. In these, Shakespeare expresses his devotion to the man and urges him to marry and have children so that his virtues will live on in his offspring.

## The Sonnet

A **sonnet** is a lyric poem of fourteen lines with a set rhyme scheme. It is normally written in iambic pentameter, a line of ten syllables in which every second syllable is accented. This meter can be seen in the first line of Longfellow's sonnet.

> The sea awoke at midnight from its sleep . . .

Here the accented syllables are marked by ´, the unaccented by ˘. "The Sound of the Sea" is an example of a *Petrarchan sonnet,* named after the great Italian poet Petrarch. This kind of sonnet consists of an octave (eight lines of verse) and a sestet (six lines). The octave of a Petrarchan sonnet always uses two rhymes, in the pattern *abbaabba.* The rhyme scheme of the sestet can vary. The Shakespearean sonnet consists of three quatrains and a couplet. The rhyme scheme is *abab cdcd efef gg.*

## Look For

As you read "The Sound of the Sea" and Sonnet 30, look for the features of the sonnet form described above. Also, notice how the thought content of each poem is divided into units that match the stanza structure.

## Writing

To prepare for writing your own sonnet, write three short paragraphs, each of two or three sentences. Let the first paragraph begin with the word *Yesterday,* the second paragraph with *Today,* the third with *Tomorrow.* Briefly describe your thoughts about the past, present, and future.

## Vocabulary

Knowing the following words will help you as you read Longfellow's and Shakespeare's sonnets.

**cataract** (kat′ ə rakt) *n.:* A large waterfall (p. 660, l. 7)
**inaccessible** (in ək ses′ ə b'l) *adj.:* Impossible to reach or enter (p. 660, l. 10)

**deem** (dēm) *v.:* Consider (p. 660, l. 12)
**foreshadowing** (fôr shad′ ō iŋ) *n.:* Sign of something to come (p. 660, l. 13)

*Guide for Reading* 659

**Literary Focus** The sonnet is a challenge to both poets and readers because of the controlled form of the poem. Both Longfellow and Shakespeare knew how to use this controlled form with ease and power. It takes a great deal of skill and thought to interpret a sonnet because a sonnet says a great deal in few words.

**Look For** As students read "The Sound of the Sea," lead them to see that the poem consists of two sentences. The octave—the first eight lines—is one sentence. The sextet—the last six lines—is another sentence.

**Writing/Prior Knowledge** Consider dividing the class into small groups so that students can discuss their thoughts with fellow group members before beginning the assignment.

**Vocabulary** Have your **less advanced** students discuss the meaning of each word and then use each word in a sentence reflecting its meaning.

**Spelling Tip** Point out the double *c* and double *s* in *inaccessible.*

**Motivation/Prior Knowledge**
Have students close their eyes and imagine they are at the sea. What does the sea look like? What sounds can they hear? Then tell them that Longfellow describes the sea in order to convey his theme.

**Master Teacher Note** Consider telling students that the form of the sonnet contributes to the shape of the argument or statement that the poet is making. A Petrarchan sonnet, like Longfellow's "The Sound of the Sea," is divided into an octet and a sextet. The poet divides his statement into two parts, according to these divisions.

**Thematic Ideas** You might want to use Joyce's "I Hear an Army," page 597, and Masefield's "Sea-Fever," page 654, with "The Sound of the Sea." Like Longfellow, Joyce gives the sea a symbolic meaning. Masefield's sea does not have this symbolic dimension, except perhaps at the end.

You may want to teach "Sonnet 30" with Margaret Walker's "Memory," page 614. While memory can be both destructive and healing for Shakespeare, it seems to have little consolation for Walker.

**Purpose-Setting Question** What is the theme of this sonnet?

1 **Clarification** "The sea awoke at midnight from its sleep" is a good example of personification.

2 **Discussion** Was the voice that was heard loud or soft? Which words provide the answer to this question?

3 **Discussion** This poem compares the sound of the sea to an inner voice of intuition that guides our decisions. In what ways are the two sounds alike?

660

# The Sound of the Sea

## Henry Wadsworth Longfellow

1    The sea awoke at midnight from its sleep,
     And round the pebbly beaches far and wide
     I heard the first wave of the rising tide
     Rush onward with uninterrupted sweep;
5    A voice out of the silence of the deep,
2      A sound mysteriously multiplied
     As of a cataract from the mountain's side,
     Or roar of winds upon a wooded steep.[1]
   So comes to us at times, from the unknown
10    And inaccessible solitudes of being,
3      The rushing of the sea-tides of the soul;
   And inspirations that we deem our own,
     Are some divine foreshadowing and foreseeing
     Of things beyond our reason or control.

---

**1. steep** (stĕp) *n.*: A mountain slope.

---

### THINKING ABOUT THE SELECTION

#### Recalling

1. Describe what the speaker sees and hears in the first four lines.
2. In lines 5–8, to what two things does he compare the sound he hears?

#### Interpreting

3. The word "so" at the start of the sestet signals a comparison between the octave and the sestet. What is being compared to what?
4. What are "the unknown/And inaccessible solitudes of being"?
5. What are the "sea-tides" of the soul?

*660 Poetry*

#### Applying

6. Since the theme of this poem is contained in the sestet, what artistic purpose is served by the description of the sea in the octet?

### ANALYZING LITERATURE

#### Understanding a Petrarchan Sonnet

A **Petrarchan sonnet** consists of an octave (eight lines) and a sestet (six lines).
1. Using letters, describe the rhyme scheme of the sestet.
2. How does the content of the sonnet reflect the two-part structure of octave and sestet?

**ANSWERS TO THINKING ABOUT THE SELECTION**
*Recalling*
1. The speaker sees and hears the tide coming in.
2. He compares the sound he hears to the sounds of a mountain waterfall and winds roaring in a mountain forest.

*Interpreting*
3. Suggested Response: The speaker is comparing the voice of the sea to a person's inner voice.
4. Answers will differ, but students might realize this phrase refers to our inmost self or subconscious mind.
5. Answers will differ, but students might feel this phrase refers to inspirations or deep feelings.

*Applying*
6. Answers will differ, however, students may realize that, since the poet is comparing the voice of inspiration to the voice of the sea, the description of the sea in the octet gives the poet's intangible idea a greater reality.

**ANSWERS TO ANALYZING LITERATURE**
1. The rhyme scheme is *cdecde*.
2. Suggested Response: The two-part structure of the sonnet reflects the comparison of the two "voices."

# Sonnet 30

## William Shakespeare

When to the sessions of sweet silent thought
I summon up remembrance of things past,
I sigh the lack of many a thing I sought,
And with old woes' new wail my dear times waste:[1]
5  Then can I drown an eye, unused to flow,
For precious friends hid in death's dateless[2] night,
And weep afresh love's long since cancelled woe,
And moan the expense[3] of many a vanished sight:
Then can I grieve at grievances foregone,[4]
10  And heavily from woe to woe tell o'er[5]
The sad account of fore-bemoanèd moan,[6]
Which I new pay as if not paid before.
But if the while I think on thee, dear friend,
All losses are restored and sorrows end.

---

1. **And . . . waste:** And by grieving anew for past sorrows ruin the precious present.
2. **dateless:** Endless.
3. **expense:** Loss.
4. **foregone:** Past and done with.
5. **tell o'er:** Count up.
6. **fore-bemoanèd moan:** Sorrows suffered in the past.

---

## THINKING ABOUT THE SELECTION

### Recalling

1. In general, what are the speaker's feelings when he recalls the past?

### Interpreting

2. What does "drown an eye" (line 5) mean?
3. What does line 7 mean?
4. In lines 10–12, the words "tell o'er" (count up), "account," "pay," and "paid" suggest someone going over bills. What action is the speaker describing through this metaphor?

### Applying

5. What does this sonnet imply about the value of friendship?

## ANALYZING LITERATURE

### Understanding a Shakespearean Sonnet

Like a Petrarchan sonnet, a **Shakespearean sonnet** consists of fourteen lines.

1. Can the thought content of Sonnet 30 be divided into units that correspond to the divisions of three quatrains and a couplet? Give reasons for your opinion.
2. Where does the most obvious change in thought and feeling occur?

*Sonnet 30   661*

**More About the Authors** Haiku
are usually poems of great delicacy in which a few key details
suggest a scene or a mood. Ask
students why the form of the
haiku lends itself to this type of
approach.

    **Richard Wright** is best
known for his book *Native Son,*
which tells about a young black
man living in the slums of Chicago. Wright is most famous for his
contemporary realistic fiction.
Ask students why he would also
want to write haiku poetry, which
is known for its subtle, descriptive beauty and its economy of
words. Do the two genres have
anything in common?

    **John Updike** gained valu-
able experience as a staff writer
for *The New Yorker,* a famous
literary magazine. Ask students
what other types of work might
be helpful for a writer.

# GUIDE FOR READING

## Three Haiku

**Bashō** (bash′ō) (1644‑1694) was born near Kyoto, Japan. In his
youth, he was companion to the son of a lord. In later life, he lived
apart and devoted himself to the writing of haiku. Many of his best
poems were inspired by travels in which he observed nature. His
poem printed here illustrates his typical approach to poetry. He looks
for a detail or two that will give the impression of an entire landscape.

**Chiyojo** (chēyō′ jē) (1703‑1775) was the wife of a servant of a samurai. When her husband died, she became a nun. She also studied
poetry with a well-known teacher of haiku. The two poems of hers
printed here illustrate the lightness of spirit for which her work is valued by haiku scholars and critics.

## Hokku Poems

**Richard Wright** (1908–1960) was born on a farm near Natchez, Mississippi. He left school early and worked at low-paying jobs. However,
his interest in books prompted him to try writing, and in 1940 he
published the novel *Native Son,* which describes the life of a boy
raised in the Chicago slums. His wide knowledge of literature enabled
him to experiment with different forms. In the two poems printed here,
Wright shows how well he could write in the traditional haiku form.

## Pendulum

**John Updike** (1932–    ) was born in Shillington, Pennsylvania. A
Harvard graduate, Updike has a remarkable ability to absorb new
knowledge and ideas and make them the basis of his stories and
novels. He often portrays the manners and morals of modern American families in his work. His perceptive interest in the contemporary
social scene is the basis of "Pendulum," a little poem which is representative of the light verse Updike occasionally publishes in magazines.

662   *Poetry*

**Support Material**

**Teaching Portfolio**
Teacher Backup, p. 729
Usage and Mechanics Work-
  sheet, p. 834
Analyzing Literature Worksheet,
  *Understanding Haiku,* p. 835
Language Worksheet, *Appreci-
ating Concrete Words,* p. 836
Selection Test, p. 837

## Haiku and Concrete Poetry

Haiku is a Japanese form of poetry. A **haiku** consists of three lines of verse. The first and third lines have five syllables each. The second line has seven syllables. In this kind of poetry, a detail or two is presented and the reader is left to interpret what they suggest or imply.

**Concrete poetry** is poetry in which the words are arranged to look like, or suggest something about, the subject being presented. Updike's "Pendulum" is an example of the form.

## Look For

As you read the haiku, look for ideas, feelings, and meanings that are suggested by the details presented. It may help if you try to imagine yourself in the poet's place. What was he or she observing? What feelings would you have if you were standing beside the poet? When you read "Pendulum," ask yourself what the arrangement of the words is intended to suggest.

## Writing

List several details of a place or scene you have witnessed that made a lasting impression on you.

## Vocabulary

In haiku, the vocabulary is normally quite simple. The haiku poet chooses words for their vividness and their suggestive power.

**Literary Focus** Although the haiku looks as though it might be easy to write, it is a restrictive form of poetry. The word choice is dictated by the number of syllables necessary on a given line and by the descriptive, sensory nature of haiku. In concrete poetry, the poet arranges the words to form a picture related to the poem's subject.

**Look For** Have students try to identify the speakers of the haiku poems and to pay attention to the aptness of the word choice. Then have students compare and contrast Wright's versions of haiku with those by Japanese writers. Once students understand the arrangement of Updike's poem, have them suggest other, equally plausible, arrangements.

**Writing/Prior Knowledge** Have students divide into small groups and discuss the assignment before they begin writing.

**Motivation/Prior Knowledge**
Ask students to remember the sounds, sights, and smells of a calm evening. Then tell them that Bashō tries to suggest such an evening in the first haiku.

**Purpose-Setting Question** How do these writers suggest their meanings with only seventeen syllables?

**1 Reading Strategy** Each poem presents a single image and each image suggests a subtle message. What is the poet suggesting in each poem?

**2 Discussion** What images in each poem appeal to sight, sound, or smell?

## Humanities Note

Fine art, *Girl With a Lantern on a Balcony at Night,* by Suzuki Harunobu. Suzuki Harunobu (c. 1724-1770) was a major Japanese print artist known for his portrayals of frail, feminine beauty. The colored woodcut print was an art form perfected by the Japanese in the seventeenth century. Designs were cut into wooden blocks, inked, then pressed onto paper to print an image. A different block was cut for each color and superimposed on the same paper. As many as ten separate blocks were used for a single print. Harunobu took his technique to its limits, producing pictures called "brocade prints" for their opulent variety of colors. Harunobu's innovative work influenced print artists in Japan through the nineteenth century.

In the print *Girl With a Lantern on a Balcony at Night,* Harunobu typically chose a poetic setting to emphasize the delicate beauty of the young woman. The perfect balance of the composition and the magical mood of the scene enhance this vision.

# Three Haiku

Temple bells die out.
The fragrant blossoms remain.
A perfect evening!

—BASHŌ

1 Dragonfly catcher,
2 How far have you gone today
In your wandering?

—CHIYOJO

Bearing no flowers,
I am free to toss madly
Like the willow tree.

—CHIYOJO

**GIRL WITH LANTERN ON A BALCONY AT NIGHT,** c. 1768
*Suzuki Harunobu*
*The Metropolitan Museum of Art*

664 *Poetry*

You might ask students the following questions:
1. What feeling does this scene call up?
2. Does the picture go well with the haiku? Explain.

# Hokku Poems

### Richard Wright

1

Make up your mind snail!
You are half inside your house
And halfway out!

In the falling snow
A laughing boy holds out his palms
Until they are white

Keep straight down this block
Then turn right where you will find
A peach tree blooming

2

Whose town did you leave
O wild and drowning spring rain
And where do you go?

---

## THINKING ABOUT THE SELECTION

### Recalling

1. If an artist were to paint the scene that Bashō's haiku suggests, what details might the painting include?
2. What scene do you think Chiyojo was observing in the first of her two haiku?
3. Describe the image presented in her second haiku.

### Interpreting

4. Describe the kind of evening that you imagine inspired Bashō's haiku.
5. What feelings does Chiyojo's first haiku suggest to you?
6. In her second haiku, what might the speaker be suggesting about herself?
7. What is the "house" in Wright's first haiku?
8. What feelings are stirred in you by the scene Wright depicts in his second haiku?

### Applying

9. "Poetry," Robert Frost said, "is what gets lost in translation." Do the three Japanese poems seem less effective than Wright's two haiku? What do you suppose Bashō's and Chiyojo's haiku may have lost in translation?

## THINKING AND WRITING

### Writing Haiku

Using the details you listed before reading the poems in this section, write your own haiku. First decide what effect you want to create and what feelings you wish to suggest. Then select the details that will enable you to achieve your purpose. Follow the traditional haiku form: three lines of five, seven, and five syllables. When you revise, try to eliminate any unnecessary word.

You and your classmates might consider collecting your haiku and making them into a little volume of poetry.

*Hokku Poems* 665

---

# Pendulum

### John Updike

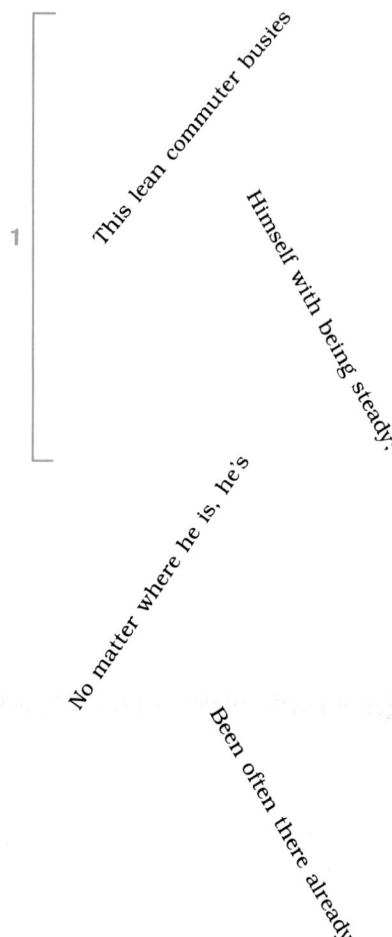

1

This lean commuter busies

Himself with being steady;

No matter where he is, he's

Been often there already.

## THINKING ABOUT THE SELECTION

### Recalling

1. Describe the scene that the speaker is observing.

### Interpreting

2. What two meanings do you see in "lean"?
3. How do you interpret the last two lines?
4. Why are the lines arranged as they are?

### Applying

5. In what way is a poet's choice of subject matter limited if he or she wishes to write concrete poetry?

## ANALYZING LITERATURE

### Understanding Concrete Poetry

A concrete poem uses the physical shape of the poem as well as the words to convey meaning. In "Pendulum" John Updike found the back-and-forth movement of a pendulum appropriate for picturing the daily movement of a commuter.

For each of the following items, find a shape that would be appropriate for conveying its meaning.

1. a typist
2. a rainstorm
3. a runner
4. a pilot
5. a rainbow
6. a doctor
7. a student
8. a computer expert
9. a rock-and-roll singer
10. a writer

## THINKING AND WRITING

### Writing a Concrete Poem

Create a sketch of an object such as an umbrella or a computer scene. Describe in words the object you drew, and arrange the words so that they resemble the drawing. (You might want to use one of the topics and pictures from the Analyzing Literature assignment.) When you revise your poem, try to make the language as expressive as it might be in a poem of the ordinary kind. You and your classmates might wish to mount your concrete poems on a bulletin board.

### ANSWERS TO THINKING ABOUT THE SELECTION
*Recalling*

1. The speaker is observing a commuter who has to stand while riding a train or bus.

*Interpreting*

2. *Lean* could mean "thin" or "bent slightly."
3. Answers will differ, but students might say that the commuter takes the same route to and from work every day. Also, the commuter moves back and forth in the same way as the train or bus shifts.
4. Answers will differ, but students might argue that the appearance of the poem mimics the shifting of a person trying to stand still in a moving vehicle.

*Applying*

5. Answers will differ. Students will probably realize that there is a limit to the subjects that can be easily imitated by a poem's appearance.

### ANSWERS TO ANALYZING LITERATURE

Answers will differ, but make sure students have selected shapes that will suitably illustrate the subject.

### THINKING AND WRITING

Students may want to consult Lesson 18, "Writing a Poem," in the Handbook of Writing About Literature.

### Publishing Student Writing

Have students submit their poems to the school newspaper to see if they can be published or publish them in a class newspaper.

**Putting It Together** After reading many poems and studying the elements of poetry, students should be able to read a poem and recognize how the elements of poetry work together to convey a unified effect.

This lesson reviews the major elements of poetry, using the poem "A Red, Red Rose" as a model for "putting it together."

You may first want to review the elements of poetry, using the points suggested on this page. Then you can read "A Red, Red, Rose" with students, discussing the annotations and having them make other critical comments.

To give students further practice in putting together the elements of a poem, use the poem "Our Fathers Had Powerful Songs" by Natalia Belting, following the Teacher Backup, in the Teaching Portfolio, page 843, which students can annotate themselves.

# ◼PUTTING IT TOGETHER◼

| | |
|---|---|
| **Poetry** | There is no generally accepted definition for poetry. However, poetry can be characterized by its musicality, imaginativeness, and compactness. Poems also share a number of common elements. To fully appreciate a poem, you must look for these elements and take note of how they work together. |
| **Types of Poetry** | There are three types of poetry: narrative poetry, dramatic poetry, and lyric poetry. Narrative poetry tells a story. Dramatic poetry dramatizes action through dialogue or monologue. Lyric poetry expresses personal thoughts and emotions. |
| **Speaker and Tone** | The **speaker** is the voice of the poem. While the speaker may be the poet himself or herself, it may also be a fictional character, an animal, or even an inanimate object. The **tone** is the poet's attitude toward the subject and/or the characters. |
| **Figurative Language** | **Figurative language** is language that is not intended to be interpreted literally. Three common types of figurative language are metaphor, simile, and personification. A simile is a figurative comparison that uses the word *like* or *as.* A metaphor is a figurative comparison that does not use the word *like* or *as.* Personification is the giving of human characteristics to nonhuman things. |
| **Imagery** | **Imagery** refers to language that creates mental pictures, or images, that appeal to one or more of the five senses. |
| **Musical Devices** | **Musical devices** refer to the techniques used by poets to give their work a musical quality. Rhythm, rhyme, alliteration, assonance, consonance, and onomatapoeia are among the most common musical devices. |
| **Forms** | **Poetry** can be written in a wide variety of different forms. The sonnet and the haiku are two common forms. |
| **Theme** | Poems often convey an important idea or insight about life. This idea or insight is the poem's **theme**. |

On the following pages is a model with annotations in the margin showing how an active reader might put together the elements of the poem.

1  To recognize musical devices in poetry
2  To analyze the effect of musical devices
3  To interpret dialect
4  To write a lyric poem

**Teaching Portfolio**
Teacher Backup, p. 739
Putting It Together, "Our Fathers Had Powerful Songs," by Natalia Belting, p. 843
Usage and Mechanics Worksheet, p. 845
Analyzing Literature Worksheet, *Analyzing Musical Devices,* p. 846

Language Worksheet, *Interpreting Dialect,* p. 847
Selection Test, p. 848

## Presentation

**Motivation/Prior Knowledge** Have students identify for themselves someone or something they love very much—a person, a pet, a thing, or even an activity. Then have them list items to which they might compare the loved person, pet, or thing. Then tell them that this love poem by Burns makes use of comparisons.

**Thematic Idea** Another selection that deals with the endurance of love is *The Tragedy of Romeo and Juliet,* page 321.

**Purpose-Setting Question** Point out the model question with the title. Let it provide a purpose for reading.

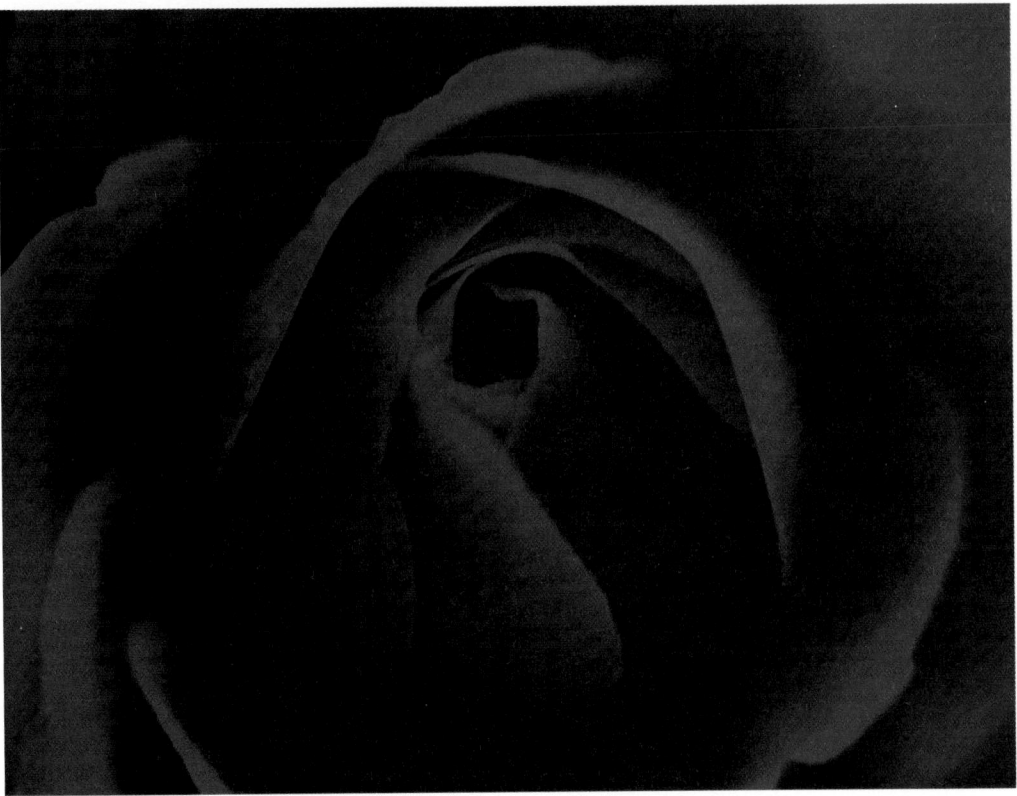

# A Red, Red Rose

**Robert Burns**

**Theme:** The title often provides a clue to the theme. What might a red rose represent?

### I

5  O, my love is like a red, red rose,
    That's newly sprung in June,
O, my love is like the melody,
    That's sweetly played in tune.

**Types of Poetry:** This poem is a lyric. What emotions is the speaker expressing?

**Figurative Language:** The speaker is using similes. How do these similes help to express his feelings?

*A Red, Red Rose*   669

**II**

5   As fair art thou, my bonny[1] lass,
      So deep in love am I,
  And I will love thee still, my dear,
      Till a' the seas gang[2] dry.

**III**

  Till a' the seas gang dry, my dear,
10      And the rocks melt wi' the sun!
  And I will love thee still, my dear,
     While the sands o' life shall run.

**IV**

  And fare thee weel,[3] my only love,
     And fare thee weel a while!
15   And I will come again, my love,
     Tho' it were ten thousand mile!

---

**1. bonny** (bän' ē) *adj.*: Pretty.
**2. gang** (gaŋ) *v.*: Go.
**3. weel** (wēl) *adv.*: Well.

**Robert Burns** (1759–1796) was born in southwestern Scotland. As a child he learned many traditional Scottish songs and stories, which he later used as material for his poetry. He first achieved success as a poet in 1786 when he published *Poems: Chiefly in Scottish Dialect*, a collection of poems that captured the essence of Scottish peasant life. Unfortunately, Burns's success was short-lived. He developed a serious heart condition and died at the early age of thirty-seven.

## THINKING ABOUT THE SELECTION

### Recalling

1. How does the speaker describe his love in the first stanza?
2. According to the second and third stanzas, how long will the speaker love his "bonny lass"?
3. What does the speaker vow to do in the final stanza?

### Interpreting

4. What do the similes, or explicit comparisons, in the first stanza suggest about the speaker's feelings?
5. How does the speaker use concrete images, or word pictures, to help express his feelings in the third stanza?
6. What does the vow that the speaker makes in the final stanza reveal about the depth of his love for his "bonny lass"?

### Applying

7. Why do you think that a red rose is often used to symbolize, or represent, love?

## ANALYZING LITERATURE

### Musical Devices

Alliteration and assonance are two **musical devices** used in poetry. Alliteration is the repetition of similar sounds, usually consonants, at the beginnings of words or accented syllables. For example, Burns repeats the *r* sound in the first line of "A Red, Red Rose": "My love is like a *r*ed, *r*ed *r*ose". Assonance is the repetition of vowel sounds within words. Notice the repetition of the *ea* sound in line 9 of "A Red, Red Rose": "Till a' the s*ea*s gang dry, my d*ea*r".

1. Find two more examples of alliteration in "A Red, Red Rose."
2. Find two more examples of assonance.

## CRITICAL THINKING AND READING

### Analyzing the Effect of Musical Devices

Poets use musical devices to give their work a musical quality. The repetition of sounds can also reinforce the meaning of a poem by adding emphasis to important words. For example, Burns's use of alliteration in line 1 of "A Red, Red Rose" adds emphasis to the image of the rose.

1. Find two other instances in which Burns's use of alliteration or assonance adds emphasis to important words.
2. Explain how his use of musical devices helps to reinforce the overall meaning of the poem.

## UNDERSTANDING LANGUAGE

### Interpreting Dialect

**Dialect** is the colloquial language of people living in a certain region. "A Red, Red Rose" is written in the dialect of Scottish peasants.

Rewrite each of the following lines in standard English. Then explain why the poem would or would not be as effective if it had been written in standard English.

1. "As fair art thou, my bonny lass"
2. "Till a' the seas gang dry"

## THINKING AND WRITING

### Writing a Lyric

Write a lyric poem in which the speaker expresses his or her thoughts and feelings concerning a specific subject. Choose a subject. Then prepare a list of thoughts and feelings associated with this subject. When you write your poem, link these thoughts and feelings to concrete images. After you finish writing, revise and proofread your poem and share it with your classmates.

*A Red, Red Rose* 671

# FOCUS ON READING

## Making Inferences

An **inference** is a conclusion you reach after examining the evidence. In other words, an inference is a type of intelligent guess. Ideas in poetry are often implied or suggested rather than stated outright. Since this is so, making inferences is an especially useful skill for reading poetry, where so much of the meaning lies just below the surface.

**Character**

Often, as you read poetry, you make inferences about **characters.** You determine what they feel and what they are like based on what they say and do and what others say and think about them. For example, when you read "Sympathy," you probably inferred that the speaker felt trapped by the circumstances of his life. You based this inference on evidence: He identified with the caged bird and understood its song. When you read "Casey at the Bat," you probably inferred that Casey was a pretty good ballplayer. You based this inference on evidence: The crowd wishes that Casey will get a chance at bat; when he does come up to bat, they let out a joyous yell.

**Past and Present Events**

When you read, you make inferences about what has happened in the past and what will happen in the future. For example, when you read "Incident in a Rose Garden," you probably inferred that Death had taken off the Master's father and that the father had come to accept his fate. You based your inference on evidence: Death says, "Sir, I knew your father. / And we were friends at the end." Probably you also inferred that the Master is about to die. Death says, "I only meant to ask him / To show me to his master. / I take it you are he?"

**Tone**

**Tone** is the attitude toward the subject that the poet conveys through the poem. Tone is rarely stated directly but is revealed through what the poet says and how he or she says it. For example, when you read "The Charge of the Light Brigade," you probably inferred that the poet's tone was admiring and somewhat reverential. You based your inference on evidence: The speaker says that we should honor the charge and honor the Light Brigade. He uses words like *glory* and *noble* when referring to the Light Brigade.

**Activity**

Read the following poem. Then use your inference-making skills to answer the questions that follow it.

### Penelope

Dorothy Parker

In the pathway of the sun,
   In the footsteps of the breeze,
Where the world and sky are one,
   He shall ride the silver seas,
5     He shall cut the glittering wave.
I shall sit at home, and rock;
Rise, to heed a neighbor's knock;
Brew my tea, and snip my thread;
Bleach the linen for my bed.
10     They will call him brave.

1. Who is the *he* in this poem? Who is the speaker? How do you know?
2. What has he done?
3. How is Penelope's life different from his life?
4. Reread the last line. What is Penelope's attitude toward him? If you were reading this poem aloud, what tone of voice would you use for the last line?
5. What is the poet's attitude toward the role of woman in society, as portrayed through this poem? Support your answer with details from the poem.

---

**Answers to the Activity**

Suggested Responses:

1. The *he* is Odysseus and the speaker is Penelope. These inferences are based on the title and the references to the Odyssey.
2. Odysseus is sailing the seas.
3. Penelope stays home, leading what would seem to be an unexciting life.
4. A suggested response would indicate that Penelope seems to be somewhat bitter and resentful. A sarcastic tone might be appropriate.
5. Women's role in society is less exciting and less acknowledged than men's. Parker indicates that Odysseus is living a glamorous life in the pathway of the sun, on silver seas and glittering waves, while his wife must stay at home rocking in her chair, snipping thread, and keeping house. The diction supports the differences.

## YOU THE WRITER
### Guidelines for Evaluating Assignment 1

1. Has the student written a descriptive poem?
2. Has the student included details that appeal to different senses?
3. Has the student used vivid language to create effective imagery?
4. Is the poem free from grammar, usage, and mechanics errors?

### Guidelines for Evaluating Assignment 2

1. Has the student written a poem describing a scene of destruction?
2. Does the poem successfully convey the writer's feeling about the scene?
3. Has the writer constructed sentences that help convey the intended tone?
4. Is the poem free from grammar, usage, and mechanics errors?

### Guidelines for Evaluating Assignment 3

1. Has the student written a poem effectively personifying something?
2. Has the student included a simile and a metaphor?
3. Does the poem make sense?
4. Is the poem constructed with effective sentences, and is it free from grammar, usage, and mechanics errors?

# YOU THE WRITER

**Assignment**

**1.** Write a poem, using imagery, that describes a part of the community you live in. Have your poem convey the characteristics of an area you know well.

**Prewriting.** Choose a segment of your town or a nearby environment to describe in a poem. Under the headings Sight, Sound, Taste, Smell and Touch, list all of the words connected with this place.

**Writing.** Write a brief descriptive poem about the place you selected. The sharpness and vividness of your imagery will depend on how specific it is and how effective the detail is.

**Revising.** As you read over your poem, replace words that you feel could be strengthened by more vivid language.

**Assignment**

**2.** The tone in a poem is the writer's or speaker's attitude toward his subject, his audience, or himself. Patterning "There Will Come Soft Rains" by Sara Teasdale, write a poem that describes a scene of destruction, whether through nature or by man, that has a definite tone of waste, awe, despair, or hope.

**Prewriting.** Review the Teasdale poem. Brainstorm for an idea for a poem that describes a scene of destruction. Then write the five W's of the situation—*who, what, where, when, why* (and *how*).

**Writing.** Write the first draft of your poem. Try to convey the feeling you have toward what has been destroyed. Experiment with the use of different words to create the desired tone. Different connotations can lend different meanings, so try several variations of words before you settle on any one.

**Revising.** Check your poem to see if the sentence construction and pattern lends itself to the intended tone.

**Assignment**

**3.** Poet Robert Frost said, "Poetry provides the one permissible way of saying one thing and meaning another." After experimenting with different forms of figurative language, write a poem using at least one metaphor or simile and one example of personification.

**Prewriting.** Choose a topic for your poem: the sea, the sunset, a parkway. Practice writing ten similes, ten metaphors, and five examples of personification describing your topic.

**Writing.** Write a short poem describing your topic. Try breathing a form of life into it. Once you have personified your topic, add to the figurative language of your poem by using a simile or metaphor that will enhance it.

**Revising.** As you read over your poem, check to see if you have used the most vivid and accurate comparison you can. Does it make sense? Check your poem for sentence structure and pattern.

# YOU THE CRITIC

**Assignment**

1. Laurence Perrine, a well-known poetic critic, has called poetry a "universal" and "multi-dimensional" language. Choose a poem you feel would appeal to people in different places and times.

**Prewriting.** Freewrite, exploring why you consider this poem a type of universal language.

**Writing.** Explain why you feel this poem could be considered universal in its appeal. Evaluate the experience the poem creates. Lastly, conclude by describing how the poem made you feel.

**Revising.** When you revise, add any direct quotes from the poem that will help support your viewpoint.

**Assignment**

2. Choose a poem and analyze its sound content. Concentrate on the elements of the poem that appeal to the ear.

**Prewriting.** Begin by reading aloud the poem you have chosen. Try reading it in different ways. If this poem were set to music, what type of song would it be? Happy? Sad? Pensive? Angry? Hurt?

**Writing.** Begin your analysis of the sound of your poem by stating why you chose that poem. Break the remainder of your analysis into specific areas such as rhyming pattern, repetition of sounds, sentence and stanza length, imagery, meter, word choice, and tone. Does the meaning of the poem correspond to how it sounds?

**Revising.** Check your analysis to see if you have covered all the elements that determine a poem's sound.

**Assignment**

3. Occasionally you will need to paraphrase a poem quickly in order to check on your understanding of it. When you paraphrase, you are restating what the poem means in simpler, more direct language. The paraphrase is written in prose rather than poetry. A good paraphrase should contain all the ideas in the poem, but stated in a clear manner and in your own language. Choose a poem that contains at least three stanzas and paraphrase it for its meaning and content.

**Prewriting.** List what you feel the poem means to you. Include in this list who is the speaker in the poem and what is the occasion. It is also helpful to determine who may be the intended audience. Next, determine what is the central purpose of the poem and how it is achieved.

**Writing.** Begin writing your paraphrase of the poem by stating its title and author, if known. Then restate what the poem means in clear, simple language. You will want to rephrase figurative language into literal language. Be sure to include all the ideas in the poem.

**Revising.** Check your paraphrase to make sure it contains all the ideas in the poem.

*Guidelines for Evaluating Assignment 1*
1. Does the student explain why he or she considers the poem to be universal?
2. Has the student evaluated the experience the poem creates?
3. Does the student conclude by explaining how the poem makes him or her feel?
4. Is the essay free from grammar, usage, and mechanics errors?

*Guidelines for Evaluating Assignment 2*
1. Has the student stated why he or she chose the poem?
2. Has the student discussed all the elements that determine a poem's sound?
3. Has the student discussed how the meaning of the poem corresponds to how it sounds?
4. Is the essay free from grammar, usage, and mechanics errors?

*Guidelines for Evaluating Assignment 3*
1. Has the student restated the meaning of the poem in clear, simple language?
2. Has the student rephrased figurative language into literal language?
3. Has the student's paraphrase included all the ideas in the poem?
4. Is the paraphrase free from grammar, usage, and mechanics errors?

## Humanities Note

Fine Art, *Ulysses Deriding Polyphemus*, J.M.W. Turner. Joseph Mallord William Turner (1775-1851), was a premier British landscape painter. His extreme talent was obvious at a very young age. At fifteen he exhibited a painting at the Royal Academy, well before he graduated from the Schools of the Royal Academy — an unusual occurrence. Today he is remembered for his landscape and marine paintings of poetic vision in which he studied the effects of light and atmosphere to the point of near abstraction.

*Ulysses Deriding Polyphemus* is one of Turner's complex mythological paintings. It was exhibited at the Royal Academy in 1829. The almost impressionistic treatment of this marine subject gives the scene the appearance of being painted in "colored steam." Turner's interest in the effects of light and weather result in the golden atmosphere, aglow with the rays of the setting sun. The romantic turmoil and grandeur of this scene won Turner critical acclaim.

**ULYSSES DERIDING POLYPHEMUS**
*J. M. W. Turner*
The National Gallery, London

676 *The Epic*

# THE EPIC

Have you ever said that a problem was so large it was of epic proportions? What are epics, and what do we mean when we describe something as having epic proportions?

An epic is a long narrative poem about the deeds of a hero. This epic hero often portrays the goals and values of the society. Typically, epics are based in part on historical fact, blending legend with truth. Gods and goddesses often play a part in epics, guiding the hero or thwarting his actions.

Two of the greatest epics are the *Iliad* and the *Odyssey*. Both are part of our oral tradition. They were passed down through word of mouth by wandering Greek minstrels until they were finally written down by Homer, probably around 800 B.C.

677

# The Odyssey

**Master Teacher Note** Before students begin reading the *Odyssey,* you might discuss the Trojan War. Perhaps you could summarized the *Iliad,* which depicts the events immediately preceding those depicted in the *Odyssey.*

**Reading Strategies** Point out that the *Odyssey* is a long narrative poem. You might have students review the section on narrative poetry beginning on page 551.

Emphasize that an epic is more difficult to read than a shorter narrative poem. Help students to read the lines as sentences rather than simply as lines. Encourage them to clarify and summarize regularly to ensure comprehension.

**Background**

In primitive societies stories were passed from one person to another by word of mouth. Storytellers, arriving in a village, court, or camp, would entertain eager listeners with tales of the gods or great heroes. The longer stories, now called epics, might be told over a series of days. To help the storytellers remember these lengthy pieces, the tales were composed in poetic lines and were often recited to the accompaniment of stringed instruments. Although these stories were filled with incredible deeds and fantastic exploits, many were based on historical events and were accepted as fact by the listeners. Two epics, the *Iliad* and the *Odyssey,* had their roots in the events of the Trojan War, which occurred about 1200 B.C. While legend credits the abduction of Helen as the cause, most probably economic conflict over control of trade in the Aegean Sea was the reason for the war.

Although a major purpose for telling and retelling the myths and legends was entertainment, another goal was to teach important lessons about religion and society. Myths about Zeus, Athena, and Apollo were many, but there were also stories about great human heroes such as Hector, Odysseus, and Penelope, who served as examples of ideal human qualities. In fact, Alexander the Great credited Homer's *Iliad* as the source of his ideas about valor and nobility.

**Reading Strategies**

As you read the *Odyssey,* remember you are reading an epic that was composed to be heard by an audience, so you and your classmates might try reading the poem aloud. You may find a few areas that might cause some difficulty when you read. The Greek names of the gods and humans might seem to be a problem at first. However, if you familiarize yourself with the names and pronunciations before you read, you will have less difficulty with the epic. Second, the poetic form of the *Odyssey* might cause you a problem at first. Try reading the sentences according to the punctuation, instead of line by poetic line, for an easier time. Also remember that epics are written with elevated style and epic similes, which are long, involved, and ornate comparisons. You might choose to skim through these on your first reading so that you do not lose the plot line. Later, reread the epic similes to appreciate their imagery. Finally, interact with the literature by using the active reading strategies: question, predict, clarify, summarize, pull together.

678　The Epic

## Themes

You will encounter the following themes in the *Odyssey:*

- loyalty, devotion, and fortitude
- the Greek ideal of a strong body and a strong intellect
- the wandering hero
- the triumph of good over evil
- obedience to the laws of the gods

## Characters

Become familiar with the following characters from the *Odyssey:*

Alcinoüs (al sin′ ə wəs)—king of the Phaecians to whom Odysseus tells his story

Odysseus (ō dis′ ē əs)—king of Ithaca

Calypso (kə lip′ so)—a sea goddess who loved Odysseus

Circe (sur′ sē) An enchantress who helped Odysseus

Zeus (Zoos)—king of the gods

Apollo (ə päl′ ō)—god of music, poetry, and medicine

Agamemnon (ag′ə mem′ nän)—king and leader of Greek forces in Trojan War

Poseidon (pō sī′ d′n)—god of sea and earthquakes

Athena (ə thē′ nə)—goddess of wisdom, skills, and warfare

Polyphemus (päl′ ə fē′ məs)—the cyclops who imprisoned the Greeks

Laertes (lā ur′ tēz)—Odysseus' father

Cronus (krō′ nəs)—Titan ruler of the universe, father of Zeus

Perimedes (per′ə mē′ dēz)—a member of Odysseus' crew

Eurylochus (yoo ril′ə kəs)—another member of the crew

Tiresias (tī rē′ sē əs)–a blind prophet who advised Odysseus from the underworld

Persephone (pər səf′ ə nē)—wife of Hades

Telemachus (tə lem′ ə kəs)—Odysseus and Penelope's son

sirens (sī′ rənz)—creatures whose songs lure sailors to their deaths

Scylla (sil′ ə)—a sea monster of gray rock

Charybdis (kə rib′ dis)—an enormous and dangerous whirlpool

Lampetia (lam pē′ shə)—a nymph

Hermes (hur′ mēz)—herald and messenger of the gods

Eumaeus (yoo mē′ əs)—an old swineherd and friend of Odysseus

Antinous (an tin′ ə wəs)—a leader among the suitors

Eurynome (yoo rin′ ə mē)—a housekeeper for Penelope

Penelope (pə nel′ ə pē)—Odysseus' wife

Eurymachus (yoo rim′ə kəs)—a suitor

Amphinomis (am fin′ ə məs)—a suitor

**Master Teacher Note** You might have students prepare a theme chart in their notebooks. Under each theme, have them jot down thoughts and comments as they read. They might also jot down appropriate quotations from the *Odyssey.*

You might also have students prepare a character chart, keeping a list of personality traits for each of the major characters.

**More About the Author** Oral poets like Homer composed their works from memory as they recited them to an audience. They organized narrative songs according to key themes or scenes —such as a wedding celebration, the arming of a hero for battle, and so forth—which they shortened, lengthened, and combined in different ways. Ask students to consider how the widespread use of writing may have affected this oral tradition of poetry.

**Literary Focus** Discuss with students the elevated and extraordinary qualities associated with an epic hero—for example, a national or international reputation for heroic deeds and a close relationship with the gods. In the opening lines of the poem, Homer describes two specific characteristics of Odysseus— his guile, during both peace and war, and his love of his native Greece. As students read, have them look for evidence of these characteristics in addition to others that emerge as the journey continues.

**Look For** Because the feats of epic heroes are often so extraordinary, it is sometimes difficult to accept their very human qualities. As the character of Odysseus develops, have students note under what circumstances he is prone to be human, rather than superhuman.

**Writing/Prior Knowledge** You might want to have students imagine some of these "perils and challenges" before they begin to write.

**Vocabulary** Have more advanced students write a brief paragraph using five of the seven words.

## The Odyssey, Part 1

**Homer** is thought to have been born sometime between 700 B.C. and 1000 B.C., possibly in western Asia Minor. According to tradition, he was blind. He did not write his two great epics, the *Iliad* and the *Odyssey*, as a modern novelist writes a novel. Rather, he composed them orally by assembling a number of earlier and shorter narrative songs. He probably traveled around Greece reciting them on many occasions. In later centuries the two epics were the basis of Greek and Roman education.

### The Epic Hero

The **epic hero** is the central hero of an epic—a figure of great, sometimes larger-than-life stature. His importance is national, international, or even cosmic. He may be a character from history or from legend. His most remarkable traits are generally the ones most valued by the society in which the epic originated. Odysseus, the epic hero of the *Odyssey*, is probably the most famous of all epic heroes.

### Look For

As you read the first part of the *Odyssey*, look for the character traits Odysseus exhibits. What are they? At what points of the story does he seem larger than life? At what points does he seem more like an ordinary man?

### Writing

Odysseus is a man trying to return home from war, but it is taking him years to do so. He endures one extraordinary and dangerous adventure after another. If you were continually facing perils and challenges in strange places, what qualities would you need to survive? List several, and tell which would be the most valuable one of all.

### Vocabulary

Knowing the following words will help you as you read Part I of the *Odyssey*.

**plunder** (plun′ dər) *n.*: Goods taken by force, loot (p. 683)

**squall** (skwôl) *n.*: A brief, violent storm (p. 685)

**dispatched** (dis pachd′) *v.*: Finished quickly (p. 690)

**mammoth** (mam′ əth) *adj.*: Enormous (p. 693)

**bereft** (bi reft′) *v.*: Left in a sad and lonely state (p. 703)

**cherishes** (cher′ ish əs) *v.*: Holds dear, feels love for (p. 710)

**insidious** (in sid′e əs) *adj.*: Characterized by treachery (p. 711)

680    *The Epic*

### Objectives

1 To understand the qualities of the epic hero
2 To interpret epithets
3 To recognize allusions
4 To write about the epic hero

### Support Material

**Teaching Portfolio**

Teacher Backup, p. 871
Grammar in Action Worksheets, *Using Figurative Language*, p. 874, and *Using Appositives and Appositive Phrases*, p. 876
Usage and Mechanics Worksheet, p. 878
Vocabulary Check, p. 879

Analyzing Literature Worksheet, *Understanding the Epic Hero*, p. 880
Language Worksheet, *Recognizing Allusions*, p. 881
Selection Test, p. 882

# The Odyssey

## Homer

### translated by Robert Fitzgerald

*In the opening verses, Homer addresses the muse
of epic poetry. He asks her help in telling the tale of
Odysseus.*

Sing in me, Muse,[1] and through me tell the story
of that man skilled in all ways of contending,
the wanderer, harried for years on end,
after he plundered the stronghold
5  on the proud height of Troy.[2]
⠀⠀⠀⠀⠀⠀⠀⠀⠀⠀⠀⠀⠀⠀He saw the townlands
and learned the minds of many distant men,
and weathered many bitter nights and days
in his deep heart at sea, while he fought only
to save his life, to bring his shipmates home.
10  But not by will nor valor could he save them,
for their own recklessness destroyed them all—
children and fools, they killed and feasted on
the cattle of Lord Helios,[3] the Sun,
and he who moves all day through heaven
15  took from their eyes the dawn of their return.

Of these adventures, Muse, daughter of Zeus,[4]
tell us in our time, lift the great song again.

**1. Muse** (myōōz): Any of
the nine goddesses of the
arts, literature, and the sciences.

**2. Troy** (troi): City in
northwest Asia Minor, site
of the Trojan War.

**3. Helios** (hē′ lē ās′): The
sun god.

**4. Zeus** (zōōs): King of the
gods.

Note: In his translation of the *Odyssey*, Fitzgerald spelled Greek names in a
way that suggests the sound and flavor of the original Greek. In the excerpts
included here, more familiar spellings have been used. Where, for example,
Fitzgerald wrote "Kirkê," "Kyklops," and "Seirênês," you will here find
"Circe," "Cyclops," and "Sirens."

## Presentation

**Motivation/Prior Knowledge**
Ask students what positive associations the word *home* calls up.
Have them explain how these
associations might affect them if
they were traveling in a foreign
country. Then tell them that
Odysseus, the hero of the epic
they are about to read, is strongly
motivated by thoughts of home.

**Master Teacher Note** You might
want to explain to students that
the *Iliad* and the *Odyssey* were
the keystones of Greek and Roman education. Ask students to
consider, as they read, what values and attitudes toward life this
epic teaches. Also, have students speculate about the values
that a modern epic might teach.

**Thematic Ideas** Other selections
that deal with themes and characters from the *Odyssey* are the
modern poems "Siren Song,"
page 745, and "Ithaca," page
746.

**Purpose-Setting Question** The
*Odyssey* is rich with figurative
language. How does this language contribute to the story?

1 **Clarification** Scholars still debate whether or not the legendary Homer existed. They do
agree, however, that the *Iliad* and
the *Odyssey* were composed by
a poet or poets working in an oral
tradition.

2 **Reading Strategy** Have students summarize these lines.

3 **Clarification** This is probably a
reference to Calliope, the muse
of epic poetry.

## Humanities Note

Fine Art, *La Nef de Telemachus* (The Ship of Telemachus). This picture is an illustration for the *Odyssey* of Homer. The modern style of this rendering in no way interferes with its ancient flavor. The illustration was inspired by motifs from statues, urns, and frescoes of ancient Greece. The rich blue of the sea is a striking frame for the massive black ship. Powered by sail and oar, this craft is the kind on which Odysseus and his men would have sailed to and from Troy.

You might use these questions for discussion:

1. How do you think this ship compares in size with Columbus's vessels or with a modern ocean liner?
2. How do you think this ship would fare in a storm? Explain.

**LA NEF DE TELEMACHUS**
*The New York Public Library
Picture Collection*

682   *The Epic*

## PART I  THE ADVENTURES OF ODYSSEUS

### Sailing from Troy

*Ten years after the Trojan War, Odysseus departs from the goddess Calypso's island. He arrives in Phaeacia, ruled by Alcinous. Alcinous offers a ship to Odysseus and asks him to tell of his adventures.*

"I am Laertes'[5] son, Odysseus.

                      Men hold me
formidable for guile in peace and war:
20  this fame has gone abroad to the sky's rim.

My home is on the peaked sea-mark of Ithaca[6]
under Mount Neion's wind-blown robe of leaves,
in sight of other islands—Dulichium,
Same, wooded Zacynthus—Ithaca
25  being most lofty in that coastal sea,
and northwest, while the rest lie east and south.
A rocky isle, but good for a boy's training;
I shall not see on earth a place more dear,
though I have been detained long by Calypso,[7]
30  loveliest among goddesses, who held me
in her smooth caves, to be her heart's delight,
as Circe of Aeaea,[8] the enchantress,
desired me, and detained me in her hall.
But in my heart I never gave consent.
35  Where shall a man find sweetness to surpass
his own home and his parents? In far lands
he shall not, though he find a house of gold.

What of my sailing, then, from Troy?

                    What of those years
of rough adventure, weathered under Zeus?
40  The wind that carried west from Ilium[9]
brought me to Ismarus, on the far shore,
a strongpoint on the coast of Cicones.[10]
I stormed that place and killed the men who fought.
Plunder we took, and we enslaved the women,
45  to make division, equal shares to all—
but on the spot I told them: 'Back, and quickly!
Out to sea again!' My men were mutinous,
fools, on stores of wine. Sheep after sheep
they butchered by the surf, and shambling cattle,

**5. Laertes** (lā ûr' tēz)

**6. Ithaca** (ith' ə kə): An island off the west coast of Greece.

**7. Calypso** (kə lip' sō)

**8. Circe** (sûr' sē) of **Aeaea** (ē' ē ə)

**9. Ilium** (il' ē əm): Troy.

**10. Cicones** (si kō' nēz)

---

4 **Clarification** The *Iliad*, also attributed to Homer, is the epic poem detailing the events of the Trojan War.

5 **Enrichment** Hyperbole, or exaggeration, is used often throughout the poem.

6 **Discussion** Why did Odysseus not give in to the charms of Circe?

## Closure and Extension

### ANSWERS TO THINKING ABOUT THE SELECTION
*Recalling*

1. Odysseus and his men attack the island—killing, plundering, and enslaving its women. When Odysseus orders his men to leave, they rebel (having had too much to drink) and continue slaughtering livestock. Survivors run to the main force of Cicones for help. This army soundly defeats Odysseus and his men, killing many of them.

*Interpreting*

2. Although Odysseus recognizes the beauty of Calypso and Circe, he is homesick for Ithaca.
3. The army of the Cicones is trained to fight on horseback or on foot; also it outnumbers Odysseus' army.

*Applying*

4. Answers will differ, but most students will include the influence of the gods in everyday life as the greatest difference.

---

50  feasting,—while fugitives went inland, running
to call to arms the main force of Cicones.
This was an army, trained to fight on horseback
or, where the ground required, on foot. They came
with dawn over that terrain like the leaves
55  and blades of spring. So doom appeared to us,
dark word of Zeus for us, our evil days.
My men stood up and made a fight of it—
backed on the ships, with lances kept in play,
from bright morning through the blaze of noon
60  holding our beach, although so far outnumbered;
but when the sun passed toward unyoking time,
then the Achaeans,[11] one by one, gave way.
Six benches were left empty in every ship
that evening when we pulled away from death.
65  And this new grief we bore with us to sea:
our precious lives we had, but not our friends.
No ship made sail next day until some shipmate
had raised a cry, three times, for each poor ghost
unfleshed by the Cicones on that field.

7

**11. Achaeans** (ə kē′ ənz): Greeks; here referring to Odysseus' men.

---

## THINKING ABOUT THE SELECTION
### Recalling

1. Describe the events on Ismarus.

### Interpreting

2. What were Odysseus' feelings when he was held captive by Calypso and Circe?
3. Why were Odysseus and his men defeated by the Cicones?

### Applying

4. What impression do you have of the differences between the world of the *Odyssey* and our own world?

684    *The Epic*

## The Lotus-Eaters

70    Now Zeus the lord of cloud roused in the north
     a storm against the ships, and driving veils
     of squall moved down like night on land and sea.
     The bows went plunging at the gust; sails
     cracked and lashed out strips in the big wind.

75    We saw death in that fury, dropped the yards,
     unshipped the oars, and pulled for the nearest lee:[12]
     then two long days and nights we lay offshore
     worn out and sick at heart, tasting our grief,
     until a third Dawn came with ringlets shining.

80    Then we put up our masts, hauled sail, and rested,
     letting the steersmen and the breeze take over.

     I might have made it safely home, that time,
     but as I came round Malea the current
     took me out to sea, and from the north

85    a fresh gale drove me on, past Cythera.
     Nine days I drifted on the teeming sea
     before dangerous high winds. Upon the tenth
     we came to the coastline of the Lotus-Eaters,
     who live upon that flower. We landed there

90    to take on water. All ships' companies
     mustered alongside for the midday meal.
     Then I sent out two picked men and a runner
     to learn what race of men that land sustained.
     They fell in, soon enough, with Lotus-Eaters,

95    who showed no will to do us harm, only
     offering the sweet Lotus to our friends—
     but those who ate this honeyed plant, the Lotus,
     never cared to report, nor to return:
     they longed to stay forever, browsing on

100   that native bloom, forgetful of their homeland.
     I drove them, all three wailing, to the ships,
     tied them down under their rowing benches,
     and called the rest: 'All hands aboard;
     come, clear the beach and no one taste

105   the Lotus, or you lose your hope of home.'
     Filing in to their places by the rowlocks
     my oarsmen dipped their long oars in the surf,
     and we moved out again on our seafaring.

**12. lee** (lē) *n.*: An area sheltered from the wind.

8 **Clarification** In this instance, *yards* means "thick poles used to support rigging."

9 **Discussion** Why did Odysseus not allow his men to eat "the sweet Lotus"?

## Closure and Extension

### THINKING ABOUT THE SELECTION

#### Recalling

1. What keeps Odysseus from reaching home?
2. What happens to the crew members who eat the Lotus?

#### Interpreting

3. The third dawn after the storm is described as coming "with ringlets shining." What impression of the dawn does this image give you?
4. What does this episode suggest about the kinds of problems Odysseus has with his men?

#### Applying

5. Brief as it is, the episode of the Lotus-Eaters is one of the most famous parts of the Odyssey. Why do you think readers have found it so interesting?

---

### The Cyclops

In the next land we found were Cyclopes,[13]

110   giants, louts, without a law to bless them.
In ignorance leaving the fruitage of the earth in
    mystery
to the immortal gods, they neither plow
nor sow by hand, nor till the ground, though
    grain—
wild wheat and barley—grows untended, and

115   wine grapes, in clusters, ripen in heaven's rains.
Cyclopes have no muster and no meeting,
no consultation or old tribal ways,
but each one dwells in his own mountain cave
dealing out rough justice to wife and child,

120   indifferent to what the others do. . . .

As we rowed on, and nearer to the mainland,
at one end of the bay, we saw a cavern
yawning above the water, screened with laurel,
and many rams and goats about the place

125   inside a sheepfold—made from slabs of stone
earthfast between tall trunks of pine and rugged
towering oak trees.
                 A prodigious[14] man
slept in this cave alone, and took his flocks
to graze afield—remote from all companions,

130   knowing none but savage ways, a brute
so huge, he seemed no man at all of those
who eat good wheaten bread; but he seemed rather

**13. Cyclopes** (sī klō′ pēz) *n.*: Plural form of Cyclops (sī′ kläps), a race of giants with one eye in the middle of the forehead.

**14. prodigious** (prə dij′ əs) *adj.*: Enormous.

686   *The Epic*

**THE CYCLOPS (detail)**
*Odilon Redon*
*Rijksmuseum, Kröller Müller Otterloo*

## Humanities Note

Fine art, *The Cyclops* (detail) by Odilon Redon. Odilon Redon (1840–1916) was a French painter and lithographer. Critics have said that he was born too soon. Redon's visionary and highly imaginative work is a precursor to Surrealism, a revolutionary art movement which did not begin until after his death.

The painting *The Cyclops*, executed during the period 1898–1900, marks the beginning of a new phase in Redon's art. He discarded the sinister subjects in black and white that he had favored in previous years for bright, colorful paintings of mythological scenes and flowers. This radical change reflects the change in his life from an obscure unknown to a prominent, recognized artist. Reality is put aside in this dream-like interpretation of the Cyclops. The odd fusing of green and purple in the sky frame the countenance of the creature, whose single eye regards the viewer from an ochre-colored face. The purple vegetation in the foreground vibrates with a strange energy.

You might use these questions for class discussion:
1. How does Redon's interpretation of the cyclops compare with that of N. C. Wyeth on page 696?
2. Which interpretation do you prefer? Explain your reasons.

a shaggy mountain reared in solitude.
We beached there, and I told the crew
135  to stand by and keep watch over the ship;
as for myself I took my twelve best fighters
and went ahead. I had a goatskin full
of that sweet liquor that Euanthes' son,
Maron, had given me. He kept Apollo's[15]
140  holy grove at Ismarus; for kindness
we showed him there, and showed his wife and child,
he gave me seven shining golden talents[16]
perfectly formed, a solid silver winebowl,
and then this liquor—twelve two-handled jars
145  of brandy, pure and fiery. Not a slave
in Maron's household knew this drink; only
he, his wife and the storeroom mistress knew;

**15. Apollo** (ə päl' ō): The god of music, poetry, prophecy, and medicine.

**16. talents:** Units of money in ancient Greece.

*The Odyssey*   687

**12**

13 **Discussion** What use would the wine and victuals be if they met a Cyclops?

14 **Reading Strategy** Based on what you know so far about Odysseus, predict whether he will honor his men's request.

15 **Clarification** The Greek laws of hospitality mandated an exchange of gifts. A host was expected to welcome his guests *and* give them gifts.

16 **Enrichment** Tell the students that the legendary Titan Atlas was so strong that he could support the world on his shoulders. Then ask students to recall some other literary characters renowned for their extraordinary strength.

and they would put one cupful—ruby-colored,
honey-smooth—in twenty more of water,
150 but still the sweet scent hovered like a fume
over the winebowl. No man turned away
when cups of this came round.
                                          A wineskin full
**13** I brought along, and victuals in a bag,
for in my bones I knew some towering brute
155 would be upon us soon—all outward power,
a wild man, ignorant of civility.

We climbed, then, briskly to the cave. But Cyclops
had gone afield, to pasture his fat sheep,
so we looked round at everything inside:
160 a drying rack that sagged with cheeses, pens
crowded with lambs and kids, each in its class:
firstlings apart from middlings, and the 'dewdrops,'
or newborn lambkins, penned apart from both.
And vessels full of whey[17] were brimming there—
165 bowls of earthenware and pails for milking.
My men came pressing round me, pleading:

                                          'Why not
**14** take these cheeses, get them stowed, come back,
throw open all the pens, and make a run for it?
We'll drive the kids and lambs aboard. We say
170 put out again on good salt water!'

                                          Ah,
**15** how sound that was! Yet I refused. I wished
to see the cave man, what he had to offer—
no pretty sight, it turned out, for my friends.
We lit a fire, burnt an offering,
175 and took some cheese to eat; then sat in silence
around the embers, waiting. When he came
he had a load of dry boughs on his shoulder
to stoke his fire at suppertime. He dumped it
with a great crash into that hollow cave,
180 and we all scattered fast to the far wall.
Then over the broad cavern floor he ushered
the ewes he meant to milk. He left his rams
**16** and he-goats in the yard outside, and swung
high overhead a slab of solid rock
185 to close the cave. Two dozen four-wheeled wagons,
with heaving wagon teams, could not have stirred

**17. whey** (wā) *n.*: The thin, watery part of milk separated from the thicker curds.

688    *The Epic*

## Grammar in Action

**Figurative language** is writing or speech that is not meant to be interpreted literally. Figurative expressions often involve comparisons between two basically unlike things. Look at this figurative expression in a speech by the Cyclops in the *Odyssey:*

> 'Strangers,' he said, 'who are you? And where from?
>     What brings you here by seaways—a fair traffic?
>     Or are you wandering rogues, who cast their lives like
> dice, and ravage other folk by sea?'

Dice are thrown in games of chance or by gamblers. In asking whether Odysseus and his men cast their lives as people do the dice, in search of a quick fortune, the speaker uses figurative language, comparing the lives of pirates and other marauders to the behavior of gamblers.

Writers use figurative language to create for the reader vivid impressions of what they are describing.

Now look at this expression. What two things are being compared?

> . . . then two long days and nights we lay offshore tasting
>     our grief,
>         until a third Dawn came with ringlets shining.

the tonnage of that rock from where he wedged it
over the doorsill. Next he took his seat
and milked his bleating ewes. A practiced job
190 he made of it, giving each ewe her suckling;
thickened his milk, then, into curds and whey,
sieved out the curds to drip in withy[18] baskets,
and poured the whey to stand in bowls
cooling until he drank it for his supper.
195 When all these chores were done, he poked the fire,
heaping on brushwood. In the glare he saw us.

'Strangers,' he said, 'who are you? And where from?
What brings you here by seaways—a fair traffic?
Or are you wandering rogues, who cast your lives
200 like dice, and ravage other folk by sea?'

We felt a pressure on our hearts, in dread
of that deep rumble and that mighty man.
But all the same I spoke up in reply:

'We are from Troy, Achaeans, blown off course
205 by shifting gales on the Great South Sea;
homeward bound, but taking routes and ways
uncommon; so the will of Zeus would have it.
We served under Agamemnon,[19] son of Atreus—
the whole world knows what city
210 he laid waste, what armies he destroyed.
It was our luck to come here; here we stand,
beholden for your help, or any gifts
you give—as custom is to honor strangers.
We would entreat you, great Sir, have a care
215 for the gods' courtesy; Zeus will avenge
the unoffending guest.'

He answered this
from his brute chest, unmoved:

'You are a ninny,
or else you come from the other end of nowhere,
telling me, mind the gods! We Cyclopes
220 care not a whistle for your thundering Zeus
or all the gods in bliss; we have more force by far.
I would not let you go for fear of Zeus—
you or your friends—unless I had a whim to.
Tell me, where was it, now, you left your ship—

**18. withy** (with' ē) *adj.*: Tough, flexible twigs.

**19. Agamemnon** (ag'ə mem' nän): the King who led the Greek army during the Trojan War.

**17 Discussion** What kind of welcome does the Cyclops give Odysseus and his men?

**18 Discussion** What values could a Greek or Roman student have learned from this passage?

**19 Clarification** The word *ninny* means "a person who is a fool."

While the comparison in the first example is stated directly, the comparison in this one is implied, or suggested. Homer indirectly compares the dawn of day with a person by capitalizing the word as if it were a proper name and by alluding to Dawn's ringlets, or curly hair.

**Student Activity 1.** Find four other examples of figurative language in the epic and write these on your paper. Read your choices to the class, discussing the comparison in each expression as well as the effect of that expression on the reader.

**Student Activity 2.** Work with a partner to write five original figurative expressions. Share your work with the rest of the class.

**20 Clarification** Poseidon is a brother of Zeus.

**21 Discussion** What does Odysseus' change of mind tell about his character?

**22 Clarification** Legend has it that Athena emerged, in full armor, from the head of Zeus. She was the goddess of wisdom and the special protector of Odysseus.

225   around the point, or down the shore, I wonder?'

He thought he'd find out, but I saw through this,
and answered with a ready lie:

'My ship?

**20** Poseidon[20] Lord, who sets the earth a-tremble,
broke it up on the rocks at your land's end.
230   A wind from seaward served him, drove us there.
We are survivors, these good men and I.'

Neither reply nor pity came from him,
but in one stride he clutched at my companions
and caught two in his hands like squirming puppies
235   to beat their brains out, spattering the floor.
Then he dismembered them and made his meal,
gaping and crunching like a mountain lion—
everything: innards, flesh, and marrow bones.
We cried aloud, lifting our hands to Zeus,
240   powerless, looking on at this, appalled;
but Cyclops went on filling up his belly
with manflesh and great gulps of whey,
then lay down like a mast among his sheep.

**21** My heart beat high now at the chance of action,
245   and drawing the sharp sword from my hip I went
along his flank to stab him where the midriff
holds the liver. I had touched the spot
when sudden fear stayed me: if I killed him
we perished there as well, for we could never
250   move his ponderous doorway slab aside.
So we were left to groan and wait for morning.

When the young Dawn with fingertips of rose
lit up the world, the Cyclops built a fire
and milked his handsome ewes, all in due order,
255   putting the sucklings to the mothers. Then,
his chores being all dispatched, he caught
another brace[21] of men to make his breakfast,
and whisked away his great door slab
to let his sheep go through—but he, behind,
260   reset the stone as one would cap a quiver.
There was a din of whistling as the Cyclops
rounded his flock to higher ground, then stillness.
And now I pondered how to hurt him worst,
**22** if but Athena[22] granted what I prayed for.

690   *The Epic*

**20. Poseidon** (pō sī′ d'n): God of the sea and of earthquakes.

**21. brace** (brās) *n.*: A pair.

**22. Athena** (ə thē′ nə): The goddess of wisdom, skills, and warfare.

265 Here are the means I thought would serve my turn:

a club, or staff, lay there along the fold—
an olive tree, felled green and left to season
for Cyclops' hand. And it was like a mast
a lugger[23] of twenty oars, broad in the beam—
270 a deep-sea-going craft—might carry:
so long, so big around, it seemed. Now I
chopped out a six foot section of this pole
and set it down before my men, who scraped it;
and when they had it smooth, I hewed again
275 to make a stake with pointed end. I held this
in the fire's heart and turned it, toughening it,
then hid it, well back in the cavern, under
one of the dung piles in profusion there.
Now came the time to toss for it: who ventured
280 along with me? whose hand could bear to thrust
and grind that spike in Cyclops' eye, when mild
sleep had mastered him? As luck would have it,
the men I would have chosen won the toss—
four strong men, and I made five as captain.

23 285 At evening came the shepherd with his flock,
his woolly flock. The rams as well this time,
entered the cave: by some sheepherding whim—
or a god's bidding—none were left outside.
He hefted his great boulder into place
290 and sat him down to milk the bleating ewes
in proper order, put the lambs to suck,
and swiftly ran through all his evening chores.
Then he caught two more men and feasted on them.
My moment was at hand, and I went forward
295 holding an ivy bowl of my dark drink,
looking up, saying:

'Cyclops, try some wine.
Here's liquor to wash down your scraps of men.
Taste it, and see the kind of drink we carried
24 under our planks. I meant it for an offering
300 if you would help us home. But you are mad,
unbearable, a bloody monster! After this,
will any other traveler come to see you?'

He seized and drained the bowl, and it went down
so fiery and smooth he called for more:

23. **lugger** (lug′ ər) n.: A ship equipped with a four-sided sail.

23 **Clarification** The "shepherd" is the Cyclops.

24 **Discussion** What does Odysseus hope to achieve by offering the Cyclops his wine?

The Odyssey   691

**25 Clarification** The word *fuddle* means "muddle or confusion."

**26 Discussion** What do you think Odysseus believed was the source of this "more than natural" strength?

**27 Discussion** What does this simile contribute to the description?

305 'Give me another, thank you kindly. Tell me,
how are you called? I'll make a gift will please you.
Even Cyclopes know the wine grapes grow
out of grassland and loam in heaven's rain,
but here's a bit of nectar and ambrosia!'[24]

310 Three bowls I brought him, and he poured them
       down.

[25]     I saw the fuddle and flush come over him,
then I sang out in cordial tones:

                                    'Cyclops,
you ask my honorable name? Remember
the gift you promised me, and I shall tell you.
315 My name is Nohbdy: mother, father, and friends,
everyone calls me Nohbdy.'

                                And he said:
'Nohbdy's my meat, then, after I eat his friends.
Others come first. There's a noble gift, now.'

Even as he spoke, he reeled and tumbled backward,
320 his great head lolling to one side; and sleep
took him like any creature. Drunk, hiccuping,
he dribbled streams of liquor and bits of men.

Now, by the gods, I drove my big hand spike
deep in the embers, charring it again,
325 and cheered my men along with battle talk
to keep their courage up: no quitting now.
The pike of olive, green though it had been,
reddened and glowed as if about to catch.
I drew it from the coals and my four fellows
330 gave me a hand, lugging it near the Cyclops
[26]     as more than natural force nerved them; straight
forward they sprinted, lifted it, and rammed it
[27]     deep in his crater eye, and I leaned on it
turning it as a shipwright turns a drill
335 in planking, having men below to swing
the two-handled strap that spins it in the groove.
So with our brand we bored that great eye socket
while blood ran out around the red-hot bar.
Eyelid and lash were seared; the pierced ball
340 hissed broiling, and the roots popped.

**24. nectar** (nek′ tər) **and ambrosia** (am brō′ zhə): Drink and food of the gods.

692    *The Epic*

                                    In a smithy
one sees a white-hot axhead or an adze
plunged and wrung in a cold tub, screeching steam—
the way they make soft iron hale and hard—:
just so that eyeball hissed around the spike.
345　The Cyclops bellowed and the rock roared round him,
and we fell back in fear. Clawing his face
he tugged the bloody spike out of his eye,
threw it away, and his wild hands went groping;
then he set up a howl for Cyclopes
350　who lived in caves on windy peaks nearby.
Some heard him; and they came by divers[25] ways
to clump around outside and call:

                                    'What ails you,
Polyphemus?[26] Why do you cry so sore
in the starry night? You will not let us sleep.
355　Sure no man's driving off your flock? No man
has tricked you, ruined you?'

                                    Out of the cave
the mammoth Polyphemus roared in answer:
29　'Nohbdy, Nohbdy's tricked me, Nohbdy's ruined me!'
To this rough shout they made a sage reply:
360　'Ah well, if nobody has played you foul
there in your lonely bed, we are no use in pain
given by great Zeus. Let it be your father,
Poseidon Lord, to whom you pray.'
                                    So saying
they trailed away. And I was filled with laughter
365　to see how like a charm the name deceived them.
Now Cyclops, wheezing as the pain came on him,
fumbled to wrench away the great doorstone
and squatted in the breach with arms thrown wide
for any silly beast or man who bolted—
370　hoping somehow I might be such a fool.
But I kept thinking how to win the game:
death sat there huge; how could we slip away?
30　I drew on all my wits, and ran through tactics,
reasoning as a man will for dear life,
375　until a trick came—and it pleased me well.
The Cyclops' rams were handsome, fat, with heavy
fleeces, a dark violet.

**25. divers** (dī′ vərz) *adj.*:
Several, various.

**26. Polyphemus** (päl′ ə fē məs).

**28 Clarification** The word *smithy* means "the forge of a blacksmith."

**29 Discussion** How do you know that Odysseus anticipated this reply?

**30 Discussion** What personality trait is implied here? When else have we seen it displayed?

*The Odyssey*　693

**31 Clarification** The word *kinky* means "tightly curled hair or fleece."

**32 Discussion** How does the reference to Dawn's "fingertips" contrast with the description of Odysseus' fingers in the previous passage?

**33 Discussion** Homer states that the ram is weighted down, in part by Odysseus' meditations. What does Homer mean?

**34 Discussion** How does the use of the double negative make this statement ironic?

I tied them silently together, twining
cords of willow from the ogre's bed
380  then slung a man under each middle one
to ride there safely, shielded left and right.
So three sheep could convey each man. I took
the woolliest ram, the choicest of the flock,
and hung myself under his kinky belly,
385  pulled up tight, with fingers twisted deep
in sheepskin ringlets for an iron grip.
So, breathing hard, we waited until morning.

When Dawn spead out her fingertips of rose
the rams began to stir, moving for pasture,
390  and peals of bleating echoed round the pens
where dams with udders full called for a milking.
Blinded, and sick with pain from his head wound,
the master stroked each ram, then let it pass,
but my men riding on the pectoral[27] fleece
395  the giant's blind hands blundering never found.
Last of them all my ram, the leader, came,
weighted by wool and me with my meditations.
The Cyclops patted him, and then he said:

'Sweet cousin ram, why lag behind the rest
400  in the night cave? You never linger so,
but graze before them all, and go afar
to crop sweet grass, and take your stately way
leading along the streams, until at evening
you run to be the first one in the fold.
405  Why, now, so far behind? Can you be grieving
over your Master's eye? That carrion rogue[28]
and his accurst companions burnt it out
when he had conquered all my wits with wine.
Nohbdy will not get out alive, I swear.
410  Oh, had you brain and voice to tell
where he may be now, dodging all my fury!
Bashed by this hand and bashed on this rock wall
his brains would strew the floor, and I should have
rest from the outrage Nohbdy worked upon me.'

415  He sent us into the open, then. Close by,
I dropped and rolled clear of the ram's belly,
going this way and that to untie the men.

**27. pectoral** (pek′ tər əl) *adj.*: Located on the chest.

**28. carrion** (kar′ ē ən) **rogue** (rōg): Repulsive scoundrel.

With many glances back, we rounded up
his fat, stiff-legged sheep to take aboard,
420 and drove them down to where the good ship lay.
We saw, as we came near, our fellows' faces
shining; then we saw them turn to grief
tallying those who had not fled from death.
I hushed them, jerking head and eyebrows up,
425 and in a low voice told them: 'Load this herd;
move fast, and put the ship's head toward the
     breakers.'
They all pitched in at loading, then embarked
and struck their oars into the sea. Far out,
as far offshore as shouted words would carry,
430 I sent a few back to the adversary:
'O Cyclops! Would you feast on my companions?
Puny, am I, in a cave man's hands?
How do you like the beating that we gave you,
you damned cannibal? Eater of guests
435 under your roof! Zeus and the gods have paid you!'

The blind thing in his doubled fury broke
a hilltop in his hands and heaved it after us.
Ahead of our black prow it struck and sank
whelmed in a spuming geyser, a giant wave
440 that washed the ship stern foremost back to shore.
I got the longest boathook out and stood
fending us off, with furious nods to all
to put their backs into a racing stroke—
row, row, or perish. So the long oars bent
445 kicking the foam sternward, making head
until we drew away, and twice as far.
Now when I cupped my hands I heard the crew
in low voices protesting:

                         'Godsake, Captain!
Why bait the beast again? Let him alone!'

450 'That tidal wave he made on the first throw
all but beached us.'

                         'All but stove us in!'
'Give him our bearing with your trumpeting,
he'll get the range and lob a boulder.'

                         'Aye
He'll smash our timbers and our heads together!'

35 **Clarification** Notice that Odysseus is especially furious at the Cyclops for violating the bond between host and guest.

36 **Clarification** The word *whelmed* means "submerged."

37 **Discussion** What characteristics does Odysseus display here? Where did he show them before?

## Humanities Note

Fine art, *Polyphemus, the Cyclops*, 1929, by N. C. Wyeth. Wyeth (1882–1945) was a renowned American illustrator, muralist, and painter. As a young man, he attended various art schools in his native Massachusetts but learned little that could help him. At the urging of a friend, Wyeth sent examples of his work to the elite Howard Pyle School of Art in Delaware. Acceptance by the school and subsequent contact with the artist and teacher Howard Pyle changed the course of N. C. Wyeth's life. Eventually, he came to be regarded as America's foremost illustrator.

The illustration *Polyphemus, the Cyclops* was done for a luxury edition of the *Odyssey* published in 1929. This illustrated book was very popular and has been reissued many times. The illustration demonstrates the skill with which Wyeth was able to depict fantastic creatures. The Cyclops he paints is fearsome and huge, yet believable.

You might use these questions for discussion:
1. What mood does this picture call up?
2. What details in this illustration contribute to this mood?
3. How does N. C. Wyeth's depiction of the Cyclops compare with the creature you imagined?

---

455 I would not heed them in my glorying spirit,
but let my anger flare and yelled:

                              'Cyclops,
if ever mortal man inquire
how you were put to shame and blinded, tell him
Odysseus, raider of cities, took your eye:
460 Laertes' son, whose home's on Ithaca!'

At this he gave a mighty sob and rumbled:

'Now comes the weird[29] upon me, spoken of old.
A wizard, grand and wondrous, lived here—Telemus,
a son of Eurymus; great length of days
465 he had in wizardry among the Cyclopes,

**29. weird** (wird) *n.:* Fate or destiny.

POLYPHEMUS, THE CYCLOPS
*N. C. Wyeth*
*Delaware Art Museum*

---

## Grammar in Action

An **appositive** is a noun or pronoun placed next to another noun or pronoun to identify, rename, or explain it. An appositive phrase is an appositive with modifiers; it performs the same function as an appositive.

Appositives are used to develop the meaning of nouns and pronouns. In epic poetry, writers often use appositives to give brief but appropriate descriptions of gods and heroes. Notice how Homer adds information to his lines by using appositives:

"O hear me, lord, *blue girdler of the islands*,
if I am thine indeed, and thou art father:
grant that Odysseus, *raider of cities*, never
see his home. . . .

Notice that the appositives in this example are set off by commas. These commas indicate that the appositives are nonessential to the sentence because they could be eliminated without changing the sentence's meaning. If an appositive is essential to the under-

and these things he foretold for time to come:
my great eye lost, and at Odysseus' hands.
Always I had in mind some giant, armed
in giant force, would come against me here.

470 But this, but you—small, pitiful and twiggy—
you put me down with wine, you blinded me.

38 Come back, Odysseus, and I'll treat you well,
praying the god of earthquake[30] to befriend you—
his son I am, for he by his avowal

475 fathered me, and, if he will, he may
heal me of this black wound—he and no other
of all the happy gods or mortal men.'

Few words I shouted in reply to him:

'If I could take your life I would and take
480 your time away, and hurl you down to hell!
The god of earthquake could not heal you there!'

At this he stretched his hands out in the darkness
toward the sky of stars, and prayed Poseidon:

'O hear me, lord, blue girdler of the islands,
485 if I am thine indeed, and thou art father:
grant that Odysseus, raider of cities, never
see his home: Laertes' son, I mean,
who kept his hall on Ithaca. Should destiny
intend that he shall see his roof again
490 among his family in his father land,
far be that day, and dark the years between.
Let him lose all companions, and return
under strange sail to bitter days at home.'

39 In these words he prayed, and the god heard him.
495 Now he laid hands upon a bigger stone
and wheeled around, titanic for the cast,
to let it fly in the black-prowed vessel's track.
But it fell short, just aft the steering oar,
and whelming seas rose giant above the stone
500 to bear us onward toward the island.

There
as we ran in we saw the squadron waiting,
the trim ships drawn up side by side, and all
our troubled friends who waited, looking seaward.

*The Odyssey*  697

**30. god of earthquake:** Poseidon.

38 **Discussion** At this point, why would the Cyclops want to treat Odysseus well?

39 **Discussion** What is the implication of the phrase "and the god heard him"?

standing of the sentence because it defines the noun before it, it is not separated by commas.

**Student Activity 1.** Find three other lines in which Homer uses appositives.

**Student Activity 2.** Write a brief addition to Odysseus' adventure with the Cyclops. Use appositives to identify or explain some of the nouns and pronouns. You may want to think of your own appositive phrases for Odysseus (like "raider of cities") or one of the gods.

**41 Reading Strategy** A number of times Homer foreshadows or hints at events to come. What does this passage foreshadow?

## Closure and Extension

### ANSWERS TO THINKING ABOUT THE SELECTION
*Recalling*

1. Polyphemus is a savage, enormous brute who lives in solitude among the other Cyclopes. He spends his days tending his flocks of sheep. His home is a cave closed off by a huge rock. He has great disdain for men and for the gods.
2. If Odysseus had killed the giant at the first opportunity, he and his men would not have been able to escape from the cave because of the door slab.
3. He stabs Polyphemus in the eye with a burning spike.
4. He expected Odysseus to be a giant who would overcome him with force, rather than a man who would overcome him with guile.

### Interpreting

5. Suggested Response: He displays guile, caution, and a tendency to think before he acts.

### Applying

6. Answers will differ. Some students may cite the importance of considering the consequences of actions before they are taken; others may cite the importance of not letting victory go to your head.

---

We beached her, grinding keel in the soft sand,
505  and waded in, ourselves, on the sandy beach.
Then we unloaded all of Cyclops' flock
to make division, share and share alike,
only my fighters voted that my ram,
the prize of all, should go to me. I slew him
510  by the seaside and burnt his long thighbones
to Zeus beyond the stormcloud, Cronus'[31] son,
who rules the world. But Zeus disdained my
        offering;
destruction for my ships he had in store
and death for those who sailed them, my
        companions.
515  Now all day long until the sun went down
we made our feast on mutton and sweet wine,
till after sunset in the gathering dark
we went to sleep above the wash of ripples.

When the young Dawn with fingertips of rose
520  touched the world, I roused the men, gave orders
to man the ships, cast off the mooring lines;
and filing in to sit beside the rowlocks
oarsmen in line dipped oars in the gray sea.
So we moved out, sad in the vast offing,[32]
525  having our precious lives, but not our friends.

**31. Cronus** (krō' nəs): A titan who was ruler of the universe until he was overthrown by his son Zeus.

**32. offing** (ôf' iŋ) *n.*: The distant part of the sea visible from the shore.

---

## THINKING ABOUT THE SELECTION
### Recalling

1. Describe Polyphemus and his home.
2. Why does Odysseus not kill Polyphemus when he first gets an opportunity to do so?
3. What does Odysseus do to blind Polyphemus and ultimately escape from him?

4. Polyphemus did not expect Odysseus to be as he is. What did he expect?

### Interpreting

5. What survival qualities does Odysseus exhibit in his conflict with Polyphemus?

### Applying

6. What might a young person in ancient Greece have learned from the Cyclops episode?

---

### The Land of the Dead

*Odysseus and his men sail to Aeolia, where Aeolus, king of the winds, sends Odysseus on his way with a gift: a sack containing all the winds except the favorable west wind. When they are near home, Odysseus' men open the sack, let-*

698    The Epic

*ting loose a storm that drives them back to Aeolia. Aeolus casts them out, having decided that they are detested by the gods. They sail seven days and arrive in the land of the Laestrygonians, a race of cannibals. These creatures destroy all of Odysseus' ships except the one he is sailing in. Odysseus and his reduced crew escape and reach Aeaea, the island ruled by the sorceress-goddess Circe. She transforms half of the men into swine. Protected by a magic herb, Odysseus demands that Circe change his men back into human form. Before Odysseus departs from the island a year later, Circe informs him that in order to reach home he must journey to the land of the dead, Hades, and consult the blind prophet Tiresias.*

We bore down on the ship at the sea's edge
and launched her on the salt immortal sea,
stepping our mast and spar in the black ship;
embarked the ram and ewe and went aboard
530    in tears, with bitter and sore dread upon us.
But now a breeze came up for us astern—
a canvas-bellying land breeze, hale shipmate
sent by the singing nymph with sunbright hair;[33]
  so we made fast the braces, took our thwarts,
535    and let the wind and steersman work the ship
with full sail spread all day above our coursing,
till the sun dipped, and all the ways grew dark
upon the fathomless unresting sea.
                      By night
our ship ran onward toward the Ocean's bourn,
540    the realm and region of the Men of Winter,
hidden in mist and cloud. Never the flaming
eye of Helios lights on those men
at morning, when he climbs the sky of stars,
nor in descending earthward out of heaven;
545    ruinous night being rove over those wretches.
We made the land, put ram and ewe ashore,
and took our way along the Ocean stream
to find the place foretold for us by Circe.
There Perimedes and Eurylochus,[34]
550    pinioned[35] the sacred beasts. With my drawn blade
I spaded up the votive[36] pit, and poured
libations[37] round it to the unnumbered dead:
sweet milk and honey, then sweet wine, and last
clear water; and I scattered barley down.
555    Then I addressed the blurred and breathless dead,

**42**

**43**

**33. singing nymph . . . hair.:** Circe.

**34. Perimedes** (per′ə mē′ dēz) **and Eurylochus** (yoo ril′ ə kəs).
**35. pinioned** (pin′ yən d) *v.*: confined or shackled.
**36. votive** (vōt′ iv) *adj.*: Done in fulfillment of a vow or pledge.
**37. libations** (lī bā′ shənz) *n.*: Wine or other liquids poured upon the ground as a sacrifice.

*The Odyssey*   699

**42 Clarification** The word *thwarts* refers to rowers' seats in a boat.

**43 Clarification** According to the Greek concept of the universe, the Ocean was a stream or river flowing around the earth.

vowing to slaughter my best heifer for them
before she calved, at home in Ithaca,
and burn the choice bits on the altar fire;

44      as for Tiresias, I swore to sacrifice
560    a black lamb, handsomest of all our flock.
Thus to assuage the nations of the dead
I pledged these rites, then slashed the lamb and
      ewe,
letting their black blood stream into the wellpit.
Now the souls gathered, stirring out of Erebus,[38]
565   brides and young men, and men grown old in pain,
and tender girls whose hearts were new to grief;
many were there, too, torn by brazen lanceheads,

**38. Erebus** (er′ ə bəs): The dark region under the earth through which the dead pass before entering the realm of Hades.

ODYSSEUS IN THE LAND OF THE DEAD
*N. C. Wyeth*
*Delaware Art Museum*

700    *The Epic*

battle-slain, bearing still their bloody gear.
From every side they came and sought the pit
570 with rustling cries; and I grew sick with fear.
But presently I gave command to my officers
to flay those sheep the bronze cut down, and make
burnt offerings of flesh to the gods below—
to sovereign Death, to pale Persephone.[39]
575 Meanwhile I crouched with my drawn sword to keep
the surging phantoms from the bloody pit
till I should know the presence of Tiresias.

One shade came first—Elpenor, of our company,
who lay unburied still on the wide earth
580 as we had left him—dead in Circe's hall,
untouched, unmourned, when other cares compelled us.
Now when I saw him there I wept for pity
and called out to him:

          'How is this, Elpenor,
how could you journey to the western gloom
585 swifter afoot than I in the black lugger?'
He sighed, and answered:

          'Son of great Laertes,
Odysseus, master mariner and soldier,
bad luck shadowed me, and no kindly power;
ignoble death I drank with so much wine.
590 I slept on Circe's roof, then could not see
the long steep backward ladder, coming down,
and fell that height. My neckbone, buckled under,
snapped, and my spirit found this well of dark.
Now hear the grace I pray for, in the name
595 of those back in the world, not here—your wife
and father, he who gave you bread in childhood,
and your own child, your only son, Telemachus,[40]
long ago left at home.

          When you make sail
and put these lodgings of dim Death behind,
600 you will moor ship, I know, upon Aeaea Island;
there, O my lord, remember me, I pray,
do not abandon me unwept, unburied,
to tempt the gods' wrath, while you sail for home;
but fire my corpse, and all the gear I had,
605 and build a cairn[41] for me above the breakers—
an unknown sailor's mark for men to come.

**39. Persephone** (pər səf′ ə nē): Wife of Hades.

**40. Telemachus** (tə lem′ ə kəs)

**41. cairn** (kern) *n.*: A conical heap of stones built as a monument.

*The Odyssey* 701

---

**45 Clarification** The word *flay* means "to skin."

**46 Discussion** Why is Odysseus waiting for Tiresias?

**47 Clarification** The word *lugger* means "a small sailing vessel."

**48 Enrichment** To the ancients, it was a disgrace to die and not be buried or cremated with appropriate ceremony. Accordingly, it was customary to deny the rites of burial to traitors or enemies. In Sophocles' tragedy *Antigone*, Creon's denial of burial rites for Antigone's brother Polynices is the cause of the central conflict. Antigone defies Creon, her uncle, by performing this ceremony.

**Clarification** This word *barrow* means "a mound of stones covering the remains of the dead."

**Clarification** Recall from lines 362–363 that Cyclops is the son of Poseidon. Although Poseidon is best known as god of the sea, he also controlled thunder.

**Reading Strategy** Keep Tiresias' warning in mind as you read about the next stage of Odysseus' journey.

Heap up the mound there, and implant upon it
the oar I pulled in life with my companions.'

He ceased, and I replied:

           'Unhappy spirit,
**49** 610 I promise you the barrow and the burial.'

So we conversed, and grimly, at a distance,
with my long sword between, guarding the blood,
while the faint image of the lad spoke on.
Now came the soul of Anticlea, dead,
615 my mother, daughter of Autolycus,
dead now, though living still when I took ship
for holy Troy. Seeing this ghost I grieved,
but held her off, through pang on pang of tears,
till I should know the presence of Tiresias.
620 Soon from the dark that prince of Thebes came
  forward
bearing a golden staff; and he addressed me:

'Son of Laertes and the gods of old,
Odysseus, master of landways and seaways,
why leave the blazing sun, O man of woe,
625 to see the cold dead and the joyless region?
Stand clear, put up your sword;
let me but taste the blood, I shall speak true.'

At this I stepped aside, and in the scabbard
let my long sword ring home to the pommel silver,
630 as he bent down to the somber blood. Then spoke
the prince of those with gift of speech:

          'Great captain,
a fair wind and the honey lights of home
are all you seek. But anguish lies ahead;
the god who thunders on the land prepares it,
**50** 635 not to be shaken from your track, implacable,
in rancor for the son whose eye you blinded.
**51** One narrow strait may take you through his blows:
denial of yourself, restraint of shipmates.
When you make landfall on Thrinacia first
640 and quit the violet sea, dark on the land
you'll find the grazing herds of Helios
by whom all things are seen, all speech is known.

702 *The Epic*

Avoid these kine,[42] hold fast to your intent,
and hard seafaring brings you all to Ithaca.

**52** | 645 | But if you raid the beeves, I see destruction
for ship and crew. Though you survive alone,
bereft of all companions, lost for years,
under strange sail shall you come home, to find
your own house filled with trouble: insolent men

650 | eating your livestock as they court your lady.
Aye, you shall make those men atone in blood!
But after you have dealt out death—in open
combat or by stealth—to all the suitors,
go overland on foot, and take an oar,

655 | until one day you come where men have lived
with meat unsalted, never known the sea,
nor seen seagoing ships, with crimson bows
and oars that fledge light hulls for dipping flight.
The spot will soon be plain to you, and I

660 | can tell you how: some passerby will say,
'What winnowing fan is that upon your shoulder?'
Halt, and implant your smooth oar in the turf
and make fair sacrifice to Lord Poseidon:
a ram, a bull, a great buck boar; turn back,

665 | and carry out pure hecatombs[43] at home
to all wide heaven's lords, the undying gods,
to each in order. Then a seaborne death

**53** | soft as this hand of mist will come upon you
when you are wearied out with rich old age,

670 | your country folk in blessed peace around you.
And all this shall be just as I foretell.'

42. **kine** (kīn) *n.pl.*: cattle.

43. **hecatombs** (hek' ə tōmz') *n.*: Large-scale sacrifices; often the slaughter of 100 cattle at one time.

---

## THINKING ABOUT THE SELECTION

### Recalling

1. What is the purpose of the rites Odysseus performs in the land of the Men of Winter?
2. What does the ghost of Elpenor request?
3. What does Tiresias foretell?
4. What directions and warnings does he give?

### Interpreting

5. What character traits does Odysseus display in this episode that he did not reveal in his adventure with the Cyclops?
6. Describe his reaction to the appearance of his mother's ghost.

### Applying

7. What events and adventures do you expect to read about in the remaining excerpts from the *Odyssey*?

*The Odyssey* 703

**52 Clarification** The word *beeves* is a variation of the plural for "beef," a reference to the herds of Helios.

**53 Critical Thinking and Reading** Notice Homer's personification of an aspect of nature. Compare it with lines 252 and 388. How is this type of personification also reflected in the tendency of the ancient Greeks to identify natural forces with gods?

## Closure and Extension

### ANSWERS TO THINKING ABOUT THE SELECTION
*Recalling*

1. The rites are performed to appease the dead.
2. Elpenor requests that Odysseus give him a proper burial, which he never had, and that a monument be built to him.
3. Tiresias warns that Poseidon will seek revenge against Odysseus for killing Polyphemus, by tempting him and his men with the herds of Helios. If the herds are destroyed, Odysseus' army will also be destroyed—though he will survive.
4. Tiresias advises Odysseus to practice self-denial and restrain his shipmates.

*Interpreting*

5. Suggested Response: He displays compassion for both Elpenor and his mother.
6. Suggested Response: Odysseus openly grieves when he sees his mother's ghost.

*Applying*

7. Answers will differ. However, students may speculate whether Odysseus and his men will be able to avoid the herds of Helios and kill the suitors.

Fine art, *"Circe Meanwhile Had Gone Her Ways . . ."* by William Russell Flint. The Scottish painter and illustrator William Russell Flint (1880–1969) was the son of landscape painter F. Wighton Flint. In 1900, the young artist became interested in the medium of watercolor. For many years this was his favorite medium, and his watercolors were exhibited in both England and Europe with great success. He also began to create designs to illustrate various literary works. His subsequent success as an illustrator added another dimension to his work.

The watercolor *"Circe Meanwhile Had Gone Her Ways . . ."* was executed in 1924 for an edition of the *Odyssey.* Combining his skill as a watercolorist with his narrative ability, W. Russell Flint created a beautiful Circe who looks as if she has stepped from a Grecian urn. In keeping with this effect, the perspective of the painting is flat. The predominantly blue coloring creates an air of mystery.

You might use these questions for discussion:

1. What is the nature or personality of the woman in this painting?
2. What special abilities does she seem to have?

**CIRCE MEANWHILE HAD GONE HER WAYS . . ., 1924**
*William Russell Flint*
Collection of the New York Public Library,
Astor, Lenox and Tilden Foundations

704   *The Epic*

### The Sirens

*Odysseus returns to Circe's island. The goddess reveals his course to him and gives advice on how to avoid the dangers he will face: the Sirens, who lure sailors to their destruction; the Wandering Rocks, sea rocks that destroy even birds in flight; the perils of the sea monster Scylla and, nearby, the whirlpool Charybdis; and the cattle of the sun god, which Tiresias has warned Odysseus not to harm.*

As Circe spoke, Dawn mounted her golden throne,
and on the first rays Circe left me, taking
her way like a great goddess up the island.
675  I made straight for the ship, roused up the men
to get aboard and cast off at the stern.
They scrambled to their places by the rowlocks
and all in line dipped oars in the gray sea.
But soon an offshore breeze blew to our liking—
680  a canvas-bellying breeze, a lusty shipmate
sent by the singing nymph with sunbright hair.
So we made fast the braces, and we rested,
letting the wind and steersman work the ship.
The crew being now silent before me, I
685  addressed them, sore at heart:

                     'Dear friends,
more than one man, or two, should know those
    things
Circe foresaw for us and shared with me,
so let me tell her forecast: then we die
with our eyes open, if we are going to die,
690  or know what death we baffle if we can. Sirens
weaving a haunting song over the sea
we are to shun, she said, and their green shore
all sweet with clover; yet she urged that I
alone should listen to their song. Therefore
695  you are to tie me up, tight as a splint,
erect along the mast, lashed to the mast,
and if I shout and beg to be untied,
take more turns of the rope to muffle me.'

I rather dwelt on this part of the forecast,
700  while our good ship made time, bound outward
    down
the wind for the strange island of Sirens.
Then all at once the wind fell, and a calm

*The Odyssey*   705

---

**54**  **Discussion** Compare and contrast the personifications of Dawn that Homer has included in the *Odyssey*.

**55**  **Discussion** Why does Odysseus not want to be the only man to know Circe's forecast?

**56**  **Clarification** The name Sirens comes from the Greek word *sirenes*, which means "entanglers." Today, the word refers to any woman who is dangerous and alluring.

57 **Enrichment** Homer refers to only two Sirens; later writers describe three.

58 **Discussion** What do the Sirens promise?

came over all the sea, as though some power
lulled the swell.

                    The crew were on their feet
705    briskly, to furl the sail, and stow it; then
each in place, they poised the smooth oar blades
and sent the white foam scudding by. I carved
a massive cake of beeswax into bits
and rolled them in my hands until they softened—
710    no long task, for a burning heat came down
from Helios, lord of high noon. Going forward
I carried wax along the line, and laid it
thick on their ears. They tied me up, then, plumb
amidships, back to the mast, lashed to the mast,
715    and took themselves again to rowing. Soon,
as we came smartly within hailing distance,
the two Sirens, noting our fast ship
off their point, made ready, and they sang:

720            *This way, oh turn your bows,*
                 *Achaea's glory,*
            *As all the world allows—*
                 *Moor and be merry.*

            *Sweet coupled airs we sing.*
                 *No lonely seafarer*
725          *Holds clear of entering*
                 *Our green mirror.*

           *Pleased by each purling note*
                 *Like honey twining*
          *From her throat and my throat,*
730            *Who lies a-pining?*

           *Sea rovers here take joy*
                 *Voyaging onward,*
           *As from our song of Troy*
          *Graybeard and rower-boy*
735            *Goeth more learnèd.*

          *All feats on that great field*
                 *In the long warfare,*
        *Dark days the bright gods willed,*
               *Wounds you bore there,*

706   *The Epic*

740          *Argos' old soldiery*[44]
            *On Troy beach teeming,*
            *Charmed out of time we see.*
            *No life on earth can be*
            *Hid from our dreaming.*

745   The lovely voices in ardor appealing over the water
      made me crave to listen, and I tried to say
      'Untie me!' to the crew, jerking my brows;
      but they bent steady to the oars. Then Perimedes
      got to his feet, he and Eurylochus,
750   and passed more line about, to hold me still.
      So all rowed on, until the Sirens
      dropped under the sea rim, and their singing
      dwindled away.
                        My faithful company
      rested on their oars now, peeling off
755   the wax that I had laid thick on their ears;
      then set me free.

**44. Argos' old soldiery:** Soldiers from Argos, a city in ancient Greece..

## THINKING ABOUT THE SELECTION
### Recalling

1. What does Odysseus have his crew do to him so that he can listen to the Sirens' song?
2. What does Odysseus do to protect his men?
3. How does he react to the song?

### Interpreting

4. Summarize what the Sirens say in the song.
5. Compare and contrast the peril of the Sirens and the peril of the Lotus-Eaters.

### Applying

6. Why do you think Homer decided to let only Odysseus hear the Sirens' song?

*The Odyssey*   707

**Scylla and Charybdis**

                                        But scarcely had that island
faded in blue air than I saw smoke
and white water, with sound of waves in tumult—
a sound the men heard, and it terrified them.
760  Oars flew from their hands; the blades went
            knocking
wild alongside till the ship lost way,
with no oar blades to drive her through the water.

Well, I walked up and down from bow to stern,
trying to put heart into them, standing over
765  every oarsman, saying gently,

                                        'Friends,
have we never been in danger before this?
More fearsome, is it now, than when the Cyclops
penned us in his cave? What power he had!
Did I not keep my nerve, and use my wits
770  to find a way out for us?

                                        Now I say
by hook or crook this peril too shall be
something that we remember.

                                        Heads up, lads!
We must obey the orders as I give them.
Get the oar shafts in your hands, and lay back
775  hard on your benches; hit these breaking seas.
Zeus help us pull away before we founder.
You at the tiller, listen, and take in
all that I say—the rudders are your duty;
keep her out of the combers and the smoke;
780  steer for that headland; watch the drift, or we
fetch up in the smother, and you drown us.'

That was all, and it brought them round to action.
But as I sent them on toward Scylla,[45] I
told them nothing, as they could do nothing.
785  They would have dropped their oars again, in panic,
to roll for cover under the decking. Circe's
bidding against arms had slipped my mind,
so I tied on my cuirass[46] and took up
two heavy spears, then made my way along
790  to the foredeck—thinking to see her first from there,
the monster of the gray rock, harboring

**45. Scylla** (sil'a)

**46. cuirass** (kwi ras') *n.*: armor for the upper body.

708    *The Epic*

torment for my friends. I strained my eyes
upon the cliffside veiled in cloud, but nowhere
could I catch sight of her.

                    And all this time,
795  in travail, sobbing, gaining on the current,
we rowed into the strait—Scylla to port
and on our starboard beam Charybdis,[47] dire
gorge[48] of the salt-sea tide. By heaven! when she
800  vomited, all the sea was like a cauldron
seething over intense fire, when the mixture
suddenly heaves and rises.

                   The shot spume
soared to the landside heights, and fell like rain.

But when she swallowed the sea water down
we saw the funnel of the maelstrom,[49] heard
805  the rock bellowing all around, and dark
sand raged on the bottom far below.
My men all blanched against the gloom, our eyes
were fixed upon that yawning mouth in fear
of being devoured.

               Then Scylla made her strike,
810  whisking six of my best men from the ship.
I happened to glance aft at ship and oarsmen
and caught sight of their arms and legs, dangling
high overhead. Voices came down to me
in anguish, calling my name for the last time.

815  A man surfcasting on a point of rock
for bass or mackerel, whipping his long rod
to drop the sinker and the bait far out,
will hook a fish and rip it from the surface
to dangle wriggling through the air:
                      so these
820  were borne aloft in spasms toward the cliff.

She ate them as they shrieked there, in her den,
in the dire grapple, reaching still for me—
and deathly pity ran me through
at that sight—far the worst I ever suffered,
825  questing the passes of the strange sea.
                   We rowed on.
The Rocks were now behind; Charybdis, too,
and Scylla dropped astern. . . .

**47. Charybdis** (ka rib′ dis)

**48. gorge** (gôrj) *n.*: Voracious, consuming mouth.

**49. maelstrom** (māl′ strəm) *n.*: A large, violent whirlpool.

**61 Enrichment** Legend has it that Charybdis swallowed and threw up the sea three times a day.

**62 Enrichment** Artistic representations of Scylla show her with twelve feet and six heads, each with three rows of canine teeth.

**63 Discussion** To what does Homer compare the death of these men?

**64 Discussion** The expression "to pass between Scylla and Charybdis" is still used. What does it mean?

*The Odyssey* 709

**ANSWERS TO THINKING ABOUT THE SELECTION**
*Recalling*

1. They are terrified and lose control of the ship until Odysseus encourages them.
2. Syclla grabs them from the ship, hurls them into the air, and finally eats them.

*Interpreting*

3. Suggested Response: Despite the panic of his men, Odysseus is able to rally them back to their senses.
4. Suggested Response: He may have made the choice because Scylla looked less violent than Charybdis, and therefore he considered it the lesser of two evils.

*Applying*

5. Answers will differ, but many students may agree with Odysseus' reasoning that the less the men knew about their destination, the less opportunity they would have to panic.

---

**65** **Enrichment** The sacred cattle of Helios symbolized the days in one's life. Thus, it was believed that by killing them, Greeks cut short their own lives.

## THINKING ABOUT THE SELECTION

### Recalling

1. As Odysseus and his crew near Scylla and Charybdis, how do the men react?
2. Describe how Scylla kills six of the men.

### Interpreting

3. How does Odysseus show himself to be an effective leader of men?
4. Why do you think Odysseus chooses to sail toward Scylla rather than Charybdis?

### Applying

5. Is Odysseus right to keep his decision to sail toward Scylla a secret from his men? Give reasons for your opinion.

---

### The Cattle of the Sun God

In the small hours of the third watch, when stars
that shone out in the first dusk of evening
830  had gone down to their setting, a giant wind
blew from heaven, and clouds driven by Zeus
shrouded land and sea in a night of storm;
so, just as Dawn with fingertips of rose
touched the windy world, we dragged our ship
835  to cover in a grotto, a sea cave
where nymphs had chairs of rock and sanded floors.
I mustered all the crew and said:

>       'Old shipmates,
our stores are in the ship's hold, food and drink;
the cattle here are not for our provision,
840  or we pay dearly for it.
>       Fierce the god is
who cherishes these heifers and these sheep:
Helios; and no man avoids his eye.'

To this my fighters nodded. Yes. But now
we had a month of onshore gales, blowing
845  day in, day out—south winds, or south by east.
As long as bread and good red wine remained

710  *The Epic*

to keep the men up, and appease their craving,
they would not touch the cattle. But in the end,
when all the barley in the ship was gone,
850   hunger drove them to scour the wild shore
with angling hooks, for fishes and seafowl,
whatever fell into their hands; and lean days
wore their bellies thin.

                    The storms continued.
So one day I withdrew to the interior
855   to pray the gods in solitude, for hope
that one might show me some way of salvation.
Slipping away, I struck across the island
to a sheltered spot, out of the driving gale.
I washed my hands there, and made supplication

**66**

860   to the gods who own Olympus,[50] all the gods—
but they, for answer, only closed my eyes
under slow drops of sleep.
                   Now on the shore Eurylochus
made his insidious plea:

                    'Comrades,' he said,
'You've gone through everything; listen to what I say.
865   All deaths are hateful to us, mortal wretches,
but famine is the most pitiful, the worst
end that a man can come to.
                   Will you fight it?

**67**

Come, we'll cut out the noblest of these cattle
for sacrifice to the gods who own the sky;
870   and once at home, in the old country of Ithaca,
if ever that day comes—
we'll build a costly temple and adorn it
with every beauty for the Lord of Noon.[51]
But if he flares up over his heifers lost,
875   wishing our ship destroyed, and if the gods
make cause with him, why, then I say: Better
open your lungs to a big sea once for all
than waste to skin and bones on a lonely island!'

Thus Eurylochus; and they murmered 'Aye!'
880   trooping away at once to round up heifers.
Now, that day tranquil cattle with broad brows
were gazing near, and soon the men drew up
around their chosen beasts in ceremony.
They plucked the leaves that shone on a tall oak—

**50. Olympus** (ō lim′ pəs): Mount Olympus, home of the gods.

**51. Lord of Noon:** Helios.

*The Odyssey*   711

**66 Discussion** Why, at this point, does Odysseus pray to all the gods?

**67 Discussion** If you were one of Odysseus' men in this situation, would you take Eurylochus' advice? Why?

**68 Discussion** Is it a coincidence that Odysseus wakes up at this point? Explain.

**69 Clarification** This word *overweening* means "arrogant and presumptuous."

**70 Discussion** Explain Helios' threat.

885 having no barley meal—to strew the victims,
performed the prayers and ritual, knifed the kine
and flayed each carcass, cutting thighbones free
to wrap in double folds of fat. These offerings,
with strips of meat, were laid upon the fire.
890 Then, as they had no wine, they made libation
with clear spring water, broiling the entrails first;
and when the bones were burnt and tripes shared,
they spitted the carved meat.

Just then my slumber

68 left me in a rush, my eyes opened,
895 and I went down the seaward path. No sooner
had I caught sight of our black hull, than savory
odors of burnt fat eddied around me;
grief took hold of me, and I cried aloud:

'O Father Zeus and gods in bliss forever,
900 you made me sleep away this day of mischief!
O cruel drowsing, in the evil hour!
Here they sat, and a great work they contrived.'

Lampetia[52] in her long gown meanwhile
had borne swift word to the Overlord of Noon:

905 'They have killed your kine.'

And the Lord Helios
burst into angry speech amid the immortals:

'O Father Zeus and gods in bliss forever,
69 punish Odysseus' men! So overweening,
now they have killed my peaceful kine, my joy
910 at morning when I climbed the sky of stars,
and evening, when I bore westward from heaven.
Restitution or penalty they shall pay—
70 and pay in full—or I go down forever
to light the dead men in the underworld.'

915 Then Zeus who drives the stormcloud made reply:

'Peace, Helios: shine on among the gods,
shine over mortals in the fields of grain.
Let me throw down one white-hot bolt, and make
splinters of their ship in the winedark sea.'

**52. Lampetia** (lam pē′ shə): A nymph.

*712   The Epic*

920  —Calypso later told me of this exchange,
  as she declared that Hermes[53] had told her.
  Well, when I reached the sea cave and the ship,
  I faced each man, and had it out; but where
  could any remedy be found? There was none.
925  The silken beeves of Helios were dead.
  The gods, moreover, made queer signs appear:
  cowhides began to crawl, and beef, both raw
  and roasted, lowed like kine upon the spits.
  Now six full days my gallant crew could feast
930  upon the prime beef they had marked for slaughter
  from Helios' herd; and Zeus, the son of Cronus,
  added one fine morning.

         All the gales
  had ceased, blown out, and with an offshore breeze
  we launched again, stepping the mast and sail,
935  to make for the open sea. Astern of us
  the island coastline faded, and no land
  showed anywhere, but only sea and heaven,
  when Zeus Cronion piled a thunderhead
  above the ship, while gloom spread on the ocean.
940  We held our course, but briefly. Then the squall
  struck whining from the west, with gale force,
    breaking
  both forestays, and the mast came toppling aft
  along the ship's length, so the running rigging
  showered into the bilge.

        On the afterdeck
945  the mast had hit the steersman a slant blow
  bashing the skull in, knocking him overside,
  as the brave soul fled the body, like a diver.
  With crack on crack of thunder, Zeus let fly
  a bolt against the ship, a direct hit,
950  so that she bucked, in reeking fumes of sulphur,
  and all the men were flung into the sea.
  They came up 'round the wreck, bobbing awhile
  like petrels[54] on the waves.

        No more seafaring
  homeward for these, no sweet day of return;
955  the god had turned his face from them.

         I clambered
  fore and aft my hulk until a comber
  split her, keel from ribs, and the big timber
  floated free; the mast, too, broke away.

**53. Hermes** (hur′ mēz):
The herald and messenger
of the gods.

**54. petrels** (pet′ rəlz):
Small, dark sea birds.

**71 Reading Strategy** Ask students
to predict what will happen.

**72 Clarification** The Greeks believed that, upon death, the soul
departed the body.

**73 Clarification** A *comber* is "a long
curling ocean wave."

*The Odyssey*   713

74 **Clarification** According to Homer, Charybdis lived under this enormous fig tree.

75 **Enrichment** According to classical mythology, Calypso kept Odysseus on the island for seven years and promised him eternal youth if he remained forever.

**Reader's Response** Which of Odysseus' adventures did you find most exciting or perilous? Explain.

A backstay floated dangling from it, stout
960     rawhide rope, and I used this for lashing
mast and keel together. These I straddled,
riding the frightful storm.

                   Nor had I yet
seen the worst of it: for now the west wind
dropped, and a southeast gale came on—one more
965     twist of the knife—taking me north again,
straight for Charybdis. All that night I drifted,
and in the sunrise, sure enough, I lay
off Scylla mountain and Charybdis deep.
There, as the whirlpool drank the tide, a billow
970     tossed me, and I sprang for the great fig tree,
catching on like a bat under a bough.
Nowhere had I to stand, no way of climbing,
the root and bole[55] being far below, and far
above my head the branches and their leaves,
975     massed, overshadowing Charybdis pool.
But I clung grimly, thinking my mast and keel
would come back to the surface when she spouted.
And ah! how long, with what desire, I waited!
till, at the twilight hour, when one who hears
980     and judges pleas in the marketplace all day
between contentious men, goes home to supper,
the long poles at last reared from the sea.

Now I let go with hands and feet, plunging
straight into the foam beside the timbers,
985     pulled astride, and rowed hard with my hands
to pass by Scylla. Never could I have passed her
had not the Father of gods and men,[56] this time,
kept me from her eyes. Once through the strait,
nine days I drifted in the open sea
990     before I made shore, buoyed up by the gods,
upon Ogygia[57] Isle. The dangerous nymph
Calypso lives and sings there, in her beauty,
and she received me, loved me.

                   But why tell
the same tale that I told last night in hall
995     to you and to your lady? Those adventures
made a long evening, and I do not hold
with tiresome repetition of a story."

**55. bole** (bōl) *n*.: A tree trunk.

**56. Father . . . men:** Zeus.

**57. Ogygia** (o jij′ i a).

## THINKING ABOUT THE SELECTION

### Recalling

1. What does Eurylochus say to persuade Odysseus' men to slaughter and eat the cattle of Helios, the sun god?
2. What is Zeus' response to Helios' demand for revenge?
3. How does Odysseus manage to escape death?

### Interpreting

4. Do the men obey Eurylochus because his speech is more persuasive than Odysseus' or because Odysseus is not present to stop them? Give reasons for your opinion.
5. What impression of the gods do you get from the conference between Helios and Zeus?

### Applying

6. Tell why you do or do not think that the punishment Zeus inflicts on the men is the right one for their offense?

## ANALYZING LITERATURE

### Understanding the Epic Hero

The **epic hero** is the central character of an epic. He possesses qualities superior to those of most men, yet he remains recognizably human.

1. In what ways does Odysseus stand out from ordinary men?
2. At what points in the story does he seem more like an ordinary man, with weaknesses and limitations?
3. Do you like and admire Odysseus? Tell why you do or do not?

## CRITICAL THINKING AND READING

### Interpreting Epithets

In epic poetry, an **epithet** is a word or phrase used repeatedly to characterize or describe someone or something. Odysseus, for example, is frequently described as "raider of cities" and "Laertes' son." Epithets are one of the distinctive aspects of epic style. They add formality and dignity to the poetry and emphasize basic qualities of the person or thing to which they are applied.

Describe the effect of each of the following frequently used epithets, and tell what quality it emphasizes.

1. "fingertips of rose" (applied to dawn)
2. "raider of cities" (applied to Odysseus)
3. "lord of cloud" (applied to Zeus)

## UNDERSTANDING LANGUAGE

### Recognizing Allusions

An **allusion** is a reference to a person, place, thing, or event from myth, history, earlier literature, or some other such source. The *Odyssey* is one of the richest sources of allusions in world literature. For example, the common expression "between Scylla and Charybdis," meaning *caught between two equally undesirable alternatives,* is an allusion to the Scylla and Charybdis episode of the *Odyssey.*

1. Voyages and journeys are often called odysseys. Considering what Homer's epic is about, for what kind of voyage or journey would you use the word *odyssey?*
2. In the past, Hollywood actresses famed for their beauty were sometimes termed sirens. Explain the allusion.

## THINKING AND WRITING

### Writing About the Epic Hero

Write an essay on Odysseus that expresses how rich and complex his character is. First review your answers to the questions under the heading "Understanding the Epic Hero." Then select several traits to focus on. Refer to events in the *Odyssey* where the traits are displayed. When you revise your essay, concentrate on creating a sense of the living personality of Odysseus.

*The Odyssey* 715

## ANSWERS TO THINKING ABOUT THE SELECTION

### Recalling

1. Eurylochus convinces his shipmates that starvation is the worst form of death.
2. Zeus overrules Helios' plan for revenge, saying that he wants Helios to continue shining on earth and heaven. The destruction of Odysseus' ship will avenge the stolen cattle.
3. Odysseus clings to the fig tree above Charybdis and waits patiently for the pieces of the ship's mast and keel to resurface. Once Odysseus climbs back on his raft, Zeus helps him pass by Scylla unharmed.

### Interpreting

4. Answers will differ; however, most students will see Odysseus' absence as a factor.
5. Suggested Response: It is Zeus who makes the final decisions.

### Applying

6. Answers will differ. Many students may think that the punishment is harsh.

## ANSWERS TO ANALYZING LITERATURE

1. Answers will differ. Possible answers include that he is both protected and punished by the gods; he shows caution and restraint when ordinary men cannot; he survives extraordinary tests of courage. Also, he is exceptionally clever.
2. Suggested Response: Odysseus is more like ordinary men when he shows fear during his encounter with the dead; when he is proud of escaping from Polyphemus; and when he openly shows his emotions toward his family.
3. Answers will differ. However, many students will probably admire his courage and intelligence.

## ANSWERS TO CRITICAL THINKING AND READING

1. Suggested Response: This epithet emphasizes the delicacy and beauty of dawn.
2. Suggested Response: This epithet emphasizes Odysseus' combative side. The effect is to characterize him as a merciless warrior.
3. Suggested Response: This epithet emphasizes the loftiness and majesty of Zeus.

## ANSWERS TO UNDERSTANDING LANGUAGE

1. Suggested Response: The word would be applied to an extended journey consisting of many tests of courage.
2. Suggested Response: Among their other characteristics, the Sirens were exceptionally alluring.

## THINKING AND WRITING

For help with this assignment, students can refer to Lesson 9, "Writing About Character," in the Handbook of Writing About Literature.

### Publishing Student Writing

This assignment should produce an impressive variety of character studies. You might want to collect the finished assignments in a looseleaf notebook, so students can read them at their leisure.

715

**Literary Focus** Point out that, although the plot of the *Odyssey* is episodic (that is, made up of a series of discrete incidents), it has definite recurring themes. As students read the poem, have them think about the themes that dominate, as well as the different ways Homer illustrates and dramatizes them.

**Look For** In some ways, Part II, "The Return of Odysseus," is less episodic than Part I. Rather than being a series of separate incidents connected only by some common themes, the incidents point toward a definite outcome.

**Writing/Prior Knowledge** Before they write, have students discuss some of their own homecoming experiences. Students may also discuss the homecoming of others or imaginary homecoming experiences.

**Vocabulary** Ask less advanced students to give examples of situations where each of these words might apply. For example, a ballet or a gymnastics exhibition is a time when you would see people who are *lithe*.

## The Odyssey, Part II

**Plot in the Epic**

The **plot** of an epic is made up of a series of stories. They are based on myths and legends that are central to the history and culture of a people. The plot of the *Odyssey* in its entirety has three broad divisions. The first consists of the adventures of Telemachus, Odysseus' son. The second presents the travels and adventures of Odysseus. The third is about the return of Odysseus to Ithaca. Homer, being a great poet, was able to weave all the separate stories of all three parts into a unified poem. Nevertheless, the plot of the *Odyssey* remains episodic—made up of distinct episodes.

**Look For**

As you read the second part of the *Odyssey,* look for the way all the episodes advance the plot toward Odysseus' final conflict, with the suitors who have taken over his home.

**Writing**

The events you will read about in Part II of the *Odyssey* all take place in Ithaca, Odysseus' homeland. What might some of these events be? What scenes can you imagine? Briefly describe three of the scenes or events you expect to read about.

**Vocabulary**

Knowing the following words will help you as you read Part II of the *Odyssey.*

**dissemble** (di sem′b'l) *v.*: Conceal with false appearances; disguise (p. 717)

**lithe** (li*th*) *adj.*: Supple, limber (p. 718)

**incredulity** (in′krə doo′lə té) *n.*: Inability to believe (p. 719)

**bemusing** (bi myoo′ziŋ) *v.*: Stupefying or muddling (p. 722)

**glowering** (glou′ər iŋ) *v.*: Star-ing with sullen anger; scowling (p. 725)

**maudlin** (môd′lin) *adj.*: Tearfully sentimental from too much liquor (p. 727)

**contempt** (kən tempt′) *n.*: Actions or attitude of a person toward someone or something he or she considers low or worthless (p. 734)

1 To understand the plot of an epic
2 To infer customs and beliefs of ancient peoples from an epic
3 To interpret Homeric similes
4 To write an essay responding to literary criticism

**Teaching Portfolio**
Teacher Backup, p. 885
Grammar in Action Worksheets, *Using Parenthetical Expressions,* p. 888, and *Using Vivid Verbs,* p. 890
Usage and Mechanics Worksheet, p. 892
Vocabulary Check, p. 893
Critical Thinking and Reading Worksheet, *Inferring Customs and Beliefs,* p. 894
Language Worksheet, *Interpreting Homeric Similes,* p. 895
Selection Test, p. 896
Art Transparency 19: *Odysseus and Penelope Reunited,* by Romare Bearden

## PART 2   THE RETURN OF ODYSSEUS

### "Twenty years gone, and I am back again"

*Odysseus has ended his story to the Phaeacians. The next day, young Phaeacian noblemen conduct him home by ship. He arrives in Ithaca after an absence of twenty years. The goddess Athena appears and informs him of the situation at home. Numerous suitors, believing Odysseus to be dead, have been continually seeking the hand of his wife, Penelope, in marriage, while overrunning Odysseus' palace and enjoying themselves at Penelope's expense. Moreover, they are plotting to murder Odysseus' son, Telemachus, before he can inherit his father's lands. Telemachus, who, like Penelope, still hopes for his father's return, has journeyed to Pylos and Sparta to learn what he can about his father's fate. Athena disguises Odysseus as a beggar and directs him to the hut of Eumaeus, his old and faithful swineherd. While Odysseus and Eumaeus are eating breakfast, Telemachus arrives. Athena then appears to Odysseus.*

            . . . . From the air
she walked, taking the form of a tall woman,
handsome and clever at her craft, and stood

1000    beyond the gate in plain sight of Odysseus,
unseen, though, by Telemachus, unguessed,
for not to everyone will gods appear.
Odysseus noticed her; so did the dogs,
who cowered whimpering away from her. She only

1005    nodded, signing to him with her brows,
a sign he recognized. Crossing the yard,
he passed out through the gate in the stockade
to face the goddess. There she said to him:

"Son of Laertes and the gods of old,

1010    Odysseus, master of landways and seaways,
dissemble to your son no longer now.
The time has come: tell him how you together
will bring doom on the suitors in the town.
I shall not be far distant then, for I

1015    myself desire battle."

                Saying no more,
she tipped her golden wand upon the man,
making his cloak pure white, and the knit tunic

*The Odyssey*   717

**3** **Clarification** Unexplainable events were often attributed to the gods.

## Humanities Note

Fine art, *Eumaeus, the Swineherd*, 1929, by N. C. Wyeth. In the 1920's the art of the American illustrator N. C. Wyeth (1882–1945) was very much in demand. During these years he illustrated a total of fourteen books, among them a 1929 edition of the *Odyssey*. This illustration, *Eumaeus, the Swineherd*, was one of sixteen N. C. Wyeth painted for this book.

You might use these questions for discussion:

1. What do the stance and attitude of this character suggest to you?

2. Homer calls Eumaeus "the noble swineherd." How does Wyeth depict the noble qualities of Eumaeus?

fresh around him. Lithe and young she made him,
ruddy with sun, his jawline clean, the beard
1020 no longer gray upon his chin. And she
withdrew when she had done.

                    Then Lord Odysseus
reappeared—and his son was thunderstruck.
**3** Fear in his eyes, he looked down and away
as though it were a god, and whispered:

                        "Stranger,
1025 you are no longer what you were just now!
Your cloak is new; even your skin! You are
one of the gods who rule the sweep of heaven!
Be kind to us, we'll make you fair oblation[1]
and gifts of hammered gold. Have mercy on us!"

**1. oblation** (ä blā′ sh∂n) *n.*: An offering to a god.

**EUMAEUS, THE SWINEHERD**
*N. C. Wyeth*
*Delaware Art Museum*

1030   The noble and enduring man replied:

"No god. Why take me for a god? No, no.
I am that father whom your boyhood lacked
and suffered pain for lack of. I am he."

4  Held back too long, the tears ran down his cheeks
1035  as he embraced his son.

                              Only Telemachus,
uncomprehending, wild
with incredulity, cried out:

                              "You cannot
be my father Odysseus! Meddling spirits
conceived this trick to twist the knife in me!
1040  No man of woman born could work these wonders
by his own craft, unless a god came into it
with ease to turn him young or old at will.
I swear you were in rags and old,
and here you stand like one of the immortals!"

1045  Odysseus brought his ranging mind to bear
and said:

                              "This is not princely, to be swept
away by wonder at your father's presence.
No other Odysseus will ever come,
for he and I are one, the same; his bitter
1050  fortune and his wanderings are mine.
Twenty years gone, and I am back again
on my own island.

                              As for my change of skin,
that is a charm Athena, Hope of Soldiers,
uses as she will; she has the knack
1055  to make me seem a beggar man sometimes
and sometimes young, with finer clothes about me.
5  It is no hard thing for the gods of heaven
to glorify a man or bring him low."

When he had spoken, down he sat.
                              Then, throwing
1060  his arms around this marvel of a father
Telemachus began to weep. Salt tears
rose from the wells of longing in both men,
and cries burst from both as keen and fluttering

*The Odyssey*   719

**4 Discussion** Does this behavior make you think better or worse of Odysseus? Why?

**5 Clarification** Homer summarizes one of the underlying themes of the poem—the omnipotence of the gods.

6 **Discussion** Is this simile effective? Why?

7 **Discussion** This is one of the few instances of humor. Where else has Homer used humor?

6
1065
as those of the great taloned hawk,
whose nestlings farmers take before they fly.
So helplessly they cried, pouring out tears,
and might have gone on weeping so till sundown,
had not Telemachus said:

"Dear father! Tell me
what kind of vessel put you here ashore
7 1070
on Ithaca? Your sailors, who were they?
I doubt you made it, walking on the sea!"

Then said Odysseus, who had borne the barren sea:

"Only plain truth shall I tell you, child.
Great seafarers, the Phaeacians, gave me passage
1075
as they give other wanderers. By night
over the open ocean, while I slept,
they brought me in their cutter, set me down
on Ithaca, with gifts of bronze and gold
and stores of woven things. By the gods' will
1080
these lie all hidden in a cave. I came
to this wild place, directed by Athena,
so that we might lay plans to kill our enemies.
Count up the suitors for me, let me know
what men at arms are there, how many men.
1085
I must put all my mind to it, to see
if we two by ourselves can take them on
or if we should look round for help."

Telemachus
replied:

"O Father, all my life your fame
as a fighting man has echoed in my ears—
1090
your skill with weapons and the tricks of war—
but what you speak of is a staggering thing,
beyond imagining, for me. How can two men
do battle with a houseful in their prime?
For I must tell you this is no affair
1095
of ten or even twice ten men, but scores,
throngs of them. You shall see, here and now.
The number from Dulichium alone
is fifty-two, picked men, with armorers,
a half dozen; twenty-four came from Same,

720    The Epic

## Grammar in Action

A **parenthetical expression** is a word or phrase that is only loosely related to the rest of the sentence. Types of parenthetical expressions include names of people being addressed, certain nonessential adverbs, common expressions, and contrasting expressions. Here are some examples:

I'll go to the store, *Mom*, after I finish my other chores. (name of someone being addressed)

We bought the horse, *therefore*, with our savings. (adverb)
My new fountain pen, *not the old ball point*, was missing. (contrasting expression)

Notice that parenthetical expressions are separated from the rest of the sentence by commas.

Writers use parenthetical expressions to add interesting details, vary the length of their sentences, and add to the drama of their accounts. In the following passages from the *Odyssey*, for example, Homer's inclusion of the names of people being addressed makes the story seem more urgent and emotional:

1100   twenty from Zacynthus; our own island
        accounts for twelve, high-ranked, and their
              retainers,
        Medon the crier, and the Master Harper,
        besides a pair of handymen at feasts.
        If we go in against all these
1105   I fear we pay in salt blood for your vengeance.
        You must think hard if you would conjure up
        the fighting strength to take us through."
                                    Odysseus
        who had endured the long war and the sea
        answered:

                              "I'll tell you now.
1110   Suppose Athena's arm is over us, and Zeus
        her father's, must I rack my brains for more?"

        Clearheaded Telemachus looked hard and said:

        "Those two are great defenders, no one doubts it,
        but throned in the serene clouds overhead;
1115   other affairs of men and gods they have
        to rule over."

                              And the hero answered:
        "Before long they will stand to right and left of us
        in combat, in the shouting, when the test comes—
        our nerve against the suitors' in my hall.
1120   Here is your part: at break of day tomorrow
        home with you, go mingle with our princes.
        The swineherd later on will take me down
        the port-side trail—a beggar, by my looks,
        hangdog and old. If they make fun of me
1125   in my own courtyard, let your ribs cage up
        your springing heart, no matter what I suffer,
        no matter if they pull me by the heels
        or practice shots at me, to drive me out.
        Look on, hold down your anger. You may even
1130   plead with them, by heaven! in gentle terms
        to quit their horseplay—not that they will heed you,
        rash as they are, facing their day of wrath.
        Now fix the next step in your mind.
                                    Athena,
        counseling me, will give me word, and I

8 **Discussion** What does this dialogue reveal about each man's experience with the gods?

9 **Reading Strategy** Summarize Odysseus' advice to his son. Where else has Odysseus given similar advice?

"Only plain truth shall I tell you, *child. . . .*"
                                    Telemachus
replied:
        "*O Father,* all my life your fame. . . ."

**Student Activity 1.** Find five other lines in which Homer uses parenthetical expressions. Explain how each contributes to the story.

**Student Activity 2.** Write a brief scene in which the goddess Athena appears to Penelope before Odysseus returns to Ithaca. Use parenthetical expressions to heighten the drama.

10 **Reading Strategy** Summarize the steps in Odysseus' plan for overpowering Penelope's suitors.

11 **Discussion** Why does Odysseus want Telemachus to keep his return a secret?

1135 shall signal to you, nodding: at that point
round up all armor, lances, gear of war
left in our hall, and stow the lot away
back in the vaulted storeroom. When the suitors
miss those arms and question you, be soft
1140 in what you say: answer:

          'I thought I'd move them
out of the smoke. They seemed no longer those
bright arms Odysseus left us years ago
when he went off to Troy. Here where the fire's
hot breath came, they had grown black and drear.
1145 One better reason, too, I had from Zeus:
suppose a brawl starts up when you are drunk,
you might be crazed and bloody one another,
and that would stain your feast, your courtship.
    Tempered
iron can magnetize a man.'
              Say that

**10** 1150 But put aside two broadswords and two spears
for our own use, two oxhide shields nearby
when we go into action. Pallas Athena
and Zeus All-Provident will see you through,
bemusing our young friends.
              Now one thing more.

**11** 1155 If son of mine you are and blood of mine,
let no one hear Odysseus is about.
Neither Laertes, nor the swineherd here,
nor any slave, nor even Penelope.
But you and I alone must learn how far
1160 the women are corrupted; we should know
how to locate good men among our hands,
the loyal and respectful, and the shirkers
who take you lightly, as alone and young."

---

## THINKING ABOUT THE SELECTION

### Recalling

1. What does Athena say and do to Odysseus?
2. Describe Telemachus' reactions when Odysseus reveals himself.
3. What does Odysseus direct his son to do in preparation for an attack on the suitors?
4. Why does Odysseus not want his presence revealed even to his family and household?

### Interpreting

5. Compare Odysseus' emotions with Telemachus' when they are reunited.
6. What is Odysseus' relationship with Athena and Zeus?

### Applying

7. When you look ahead to Odysseus' reunion with his wife, what scene do you imagine?

722    *The Epic*

**Closure and Extension**

## ANSWERS TO THINKING ABOUT THE SELECTION
*Recalling*

1. Athena disguises herself as a mortal, and she instructs Odysseus to reveal his identity to his son and prepare to kill Penelope's suitors.
2. Initially Telemachus does not believe that this man is really his father. However, after Odysseus explains his odd appearance, Telemachus is convinced and is overwhelmed with joy.
3. Odysseus tells his son to collect all the armor left in the great hall and stow it away in a storeroom. He is to tell the suitors that he put it away to move it out of the smoke and to keep the men from harming each other in case a brawl starts. Telemachus is also instructed to put aside certain gear for himself and his father to use when necessary.
4. Odysseus does not want his true identity revealed until he knows who has been loyal and who has betrayed him.

*Interpreting*

5. Suggested Response: Telemachus and Odysseus are equally moved when they are reunited.
6. Suggested Response: Athena is Odysseus' protector at all times. Zeus sometimes helps him.

*Applying*

7. Answers may differ, but most students will anticipate an emotional reunion.

**Argus**

*Odysseus heads for town with Eumaeus.[2] Out-
side the palace, Odysseus' old dog, Argus, is lying at
rest as his long-absent master approaches.*

2. **Eumaeus** (ū mē′ us)

                              While he spoke
an old hound, lying near, pricked up his ears
1165    and lifted up his muzzle. This was Argus,
        trained as a puppy by Odysseus,
        but never taken on a hunt before
        his master sailed for Troy. The young men, afterward,
        hunted wild goats with him, and hare, and deer,
1170    but he had grown old in his master's absence.
        Treated as rubbish now, he lay at last
        upon a mass of dung before the gates—
        manure of mules and cows, piled there until
        fieldhands could spread it on the king's estate.
1175    Abandoned there, and half destroyed with flies,
        old Argus lay.

                          But when he knew he heard
        Odysseus' voice nearby, he did his best
        to wag his tail, nose down, with flattened ears,
        having no strength to move nearer his master.
1180    And the man looked away,
        wiping a salt tear from his cheek; but he
        hid this from Eumaeus. Then he said:

        "I marvel that they leave this hound to lie
        here on the dung pile;
1185    he would have been a fine dog, from the look of
              him,
        though I can't say as to his power and speed
        when he was young. You find the same good build
        in house dogs, table dogs landowners keep
        all for style."

                        And you replied, Eumaeus:
1190    "A hunter owned him—but the man is dead
        in some far place. If this old hound could show
        the form he had when Lord Odysseus left him,
        going to Troy, you'd see him swift and strong.
        He never shrank from any savage thing
1195    he'd brought to bay in the deep woods; on the scent
        no other dog kept up with him. Now misery
        has him in leash. His owner died abroad,
        and here the women slaves will take no care of him.

*The Odyssey*    723

**12 Enrichment** Argus' lying on the
dung heap may symbolize the
decay and ruin of Odysseus' kingdom.

**13 Discussion** Odysseus has wept
several times. What kinds of
things make him sad?

You know how servants are: without a master
1200  they have no will to labor, or excel.
For Zeus who views the wide world takes away
half the manhood of a man, that day
he goes into captivity and slavery."

**14**

Eumaeus crossed the court and went straight forward
1205  into the megaron among the suitors;
but death and darkness in that instant closed
the eyes of Argus, who had seen his master,
Odysseus, after twenty years.

---

## THINKING ABOUT THE SELECTION
### Recalling

1. What was Argus like in his youth?

### Interpreting

2. Why doesn't Odysseus greet Argus?

3. Is Argus' death just when Odysseus returns a coincidence? Tell why you do or do not think so.

### Applying

4. How would this scene be different if Argus were younger and more vigorous?

---

### The Suitors

*Still disguised as a beggar, Odysseus enters his home. He is confronted by the haughty suitor Antinous.*

But here Antinous[3] broke in, shouting:

"God!

**15**

1210  What evil wind blew in this pest?

Get over,
stand in the passage! Nudge my table, will you?
Egyptian whips are sweet
to what you'll come to here, you nosing rat,
making your pitch to everyone!
1215  These men have bread to throw away on you
because it is not theirs. Who cares? Who spares
another's food, when he has more than plenty?"

With guile Odysseus drew away, then said:

**3. Antinous** (an tin′ ō us)

724  *The Epic*

"A pity that you have more looks than heart.
You'd grudge a pinch of salt from your own larder
to your own handyman. You sit here, fat
on others' meat, and cannot bring yourself
to rummage out a crust of bread for me!"

Then anger made Antinous' heart beat hard,
and, glowering under his brows, he answered:

                                    "Now!
You think you'll shuffle off and get away
after that impudence? Oh, no you don't!"

The stool he let fly hit the man's right shoulder
on the packed muscle under the shoulder blade—
like solid rock, for all the effect one saw.
Odysseus only shook his head, containing
thoughts of bloody work, as he walked on,
then sat, and dropped his loaded bag again
upon the door sill. Facing the whole crowd
he said, and eyed them all:

                                    "One word only,
my lords, and suitors of the famous queen.
One thing I have to say.
There is no pain, no burden for the heart
when blows come to a man, and he defending
his own cattle—his own cows and lambs.
Here it was otherwise. Antinous
hit me for being driven on by hunger—
how many bitter seas men cross for hunger!
If beggars interest the gods, if there are Furies[4]
pent in the dark to avenge a poor man's wrong, then may
Antinous meet his death before his wedding day!"

Then said Eupeithes' son, Antinous:

                                    "Enough.
Eat and be quiet where you are, or shamble
      elsewhere,
unless you want these lads to stop your mouth
pulling you by the heels, or hands and feet,
over the whole floor, till your back is peeled!"

But now the rest were mortified, and someone
spoke from the crowd of young bucks to rebuke him:

4. **Furies** (fyoor′ ēz):
Three terrible spirits who
punish those whose crimes
have not been avenged.

*The Odyssey*  725

16 **Clarification** By enjoying the hospitality of Odysseus' home and refusing to help a beggar, Antinous is breaking the laws of hospitality. By law, Odysseus is justified in his remarks.

17 **Reading Strategy** What do you think will happen to Antinous?

18 **Critical Thinking** Homer gives further evidence of how intimately involved the gods are in the every-day lives of the Greeks.

19 **Discussion** What does Homer accomplish by having Antinous mistreat Odysseus?

18

"A poor show, that—hitting this famished tramp—
1255 bad business, if he happened to be a god.
You know they go in foreign guise, the gods do,
looking like strangers, turning up
in towns and settlements to keep an eye
on manners, good or bad."

But at this notion
1260 Antinous only shrugged.

Telemachus,
after the blow his father bore, sat still
without a tear, though his heart felt the blow.
Slowly he shook his head from side to side,
containing murderous thoughts.

Penelope
1265 on the higher level of her room had heard
the blow, and knew who gave it. Now she murmured:

"Would god you could be hit yourself, Antinous—
hit by Apollo's bowshot!"

And Eurynome[5]
her housekeeper, put in:

"He and no other?
1270 If all we pray for came to pass, not one
would live till dawn!"

Her gentle mistress said:

"Oh, Nan, they are a bad lot; they intend
ruin for all of us; but Antinous
appears a blacker-hearted hound than any.
1275 Here is a poor man come, a wanderer,
driven by want to beg his bread, and everyone
in hall gave bits, to cram his bag—only
Antinous threw a stool, and banged his shoulder!"

19

So she described it, sitting in her chamber
1280 among her maids—while her true lord was eating.
Then she called in the forester and said:

"Go to that man on my behalf, Eumaeus,
and send him here, so I can greet and question him.
Abroad in the great world, he may have heard
1285 rumors about Odysseus—may have known him!"

5. **Eurynome:** (yoo rin' ə mē)

**Recalling**

1. Describe Antinous' treatment of Odysseus.
2. What fate does Odysseus wish for Antinous?
3. Why do the other suitors speak against Antinous?

**Interpreting**

4. Compare Telemachus' behavior and Odysseus'. How are they similar? How are they different?
5. Compare Penelope's and Eurynome's reactions to the events in the hall below.

**Applying**

6. Dramatic irony consists of actions and speeches that readers understand in a way that characters cannot. Explain the dramatic irony in this scene.

**20 Clarification** In complimenting Penelope, his hostess, Odysseus not only speaks from his heart but also abides by the Greek rules of hospitality.

**21 Discussion** What excuse does Odysseus give for not revealing his background?

**22 Clarification** The word *maudlin* as used here means "weak or sentimental."

---

**Penelope**

> *In the evening, Penelope questions the old beggar about himself.*

"Friend, let me ask you first of all:
who are you, where do you come from, of what
    nation
and parents were you born?"

          And he replied:

"My lady, never a man in the wide world
1290  should have a fault to find with you. Your name
has gone out under heaven like the sweet
honor of some god-fearing king, who rules
in equity over the strong: his black lands bear
both wheat and barley, fruit trees laden bright,
1295  new lambs at lambing time—and the deep sea
gives great hauls of fish by his good strategy,
so that his folk fare well.
          O my dear lady,
this being so, let it suffice to ask me
of other matters—not my blood, my homeland.
1300  Do not enforce me to recall my pain.
My heart is sore; but I must not be found
sitting in tears here, in another's house:
it is not well forever to be grieving.
One of the maids might say—or you might think—
1305  I had got maudlin over cups of wine."

And Penelope replied:

          "Stranger, my looks,
my face, my carriage, were soon lost or faded

*The Odyssey* 727

---

## Closure and Extension

### ANSWERS TO THINKING ABOUT THE SELECTION
**Recalling**

1. Antinous insults and abuses Odysseus.
2. Odysseus predicts that Antinous will die before he can marry.
3. The other suitors are embarrassed by his behavior. They are also afraid that Odysseus is one of the gods disguised as a mortal.

**Interpreting**

4. Suggested Response: Odysseus has more faith that the gods will help him defeat the suitors. Also, when Antinous attacks Odysseus, Telemachus thinks murderous thoughts, but Odysseus speaks up against his assailant.

5. Suggested Response: Penelope hopes that Antinous will be struck by Apollo's bow. Eurynome hopes that all the suitors will die.

**Applying**

6. Answers will differ. One source of dramatic irony is that Penelope asks to speak to the beggar in hopes that he may have heard something about Odysseus. Another is that the abused beggar is really the master of the house.

23 **Enrichment** The expression "a web of Penelope" refers to work that is always in progress but never done.

24 **Discussion** What does Homer accomplish by including this conversation between Penelope and Odysseus?

when the Achaeans crossed the sea to Troy,
Odysseus my lord among the rest.

1310 If he returned, if he were here to care for me,
I might be happily renowned!
But grief instead heaven sent me—years of pain.
Sons of the noblest families on the islands,
Dulichium, Same, wooded Zacynthus,

1315 with native Ithacans, are here to court me,
against my wish; and they consume this house.
Can I give proper heed to guest or suppliant
or herald on the realm's affairs?

                             How could I?
wasted with longing for Odysseus, while here

1320 they press for marriage.

                           Ruses served my turn
to draw the time out—first a close-grained web
I had the happy thought to set up weaving
on my big loom in hall. I said, that day:
'Young men—my suitors, now my lord is dead,

1325 let me finish my weaving before I marry,
or else my thread will have been spun in vain.
It is a shroud I weave for Lord Laertes
when cold Death comes to lay him on his bier.
The country wives would hold me in dishonor

1330 if he, with all his fortune, lay unshrouded.'
I reached their hearts that way, and they agreed.
So every day I wove on the great loom,
but every night by torchlight I unwove it;
and so for three years I deceived the Achaeans.

1335 But when the seasons brought a fourth year on,
as long months waned, and the long days were spent,
through impudent folly in the slinking maids
they caught me—clamored up to me at night;
I had no choice then but to finish it.

1340 And now, as matters stand at last,
I have no strength left to evade a marriage,
cannot find any further way; my parents
urge it upon me, and my son
will not stand by while they eat up his property.

1345 He comprehends it, being a man full-grown,
able to oversee the kind of house
Zeus would endow with honor.

                               But you too
confide in me, tell me your ancestry.
You were not born of mythic oak or stone."

728   *The Epic*

**PENELOPE**
*Henry Fuseli*
Courtesy of Stiftung für Kunst,
Kultur und Geschichte, Küsnacht

**Humanities Note**

Fine Art, *Penelope*, by Henry Fuseli. Fuseli (1741–1825), an English artist, was born in Switzerland. In the classic way of an artist of his time, Fuseli spent eight years in Rome studying the Italian masters. This study gave his painting a classic style, but his style was more admired for its emotional content than its artistic merit. His eccentric paintings appear to be almost surreal. He was fascinated by the strange, the romantic, and the psychologically complex. Psychological studies of figures from history and myth were among his subjects.

In the painting *Penelope*, Fuseli tries to capture the emotion of this moment in Penelope's life. The sorrow of Penelope is intensified by the dark, gloomy background of the painting.

You might use these questions for class discussion:
1. What is the overwhelming mood of this painting?
2. What physical, emotional, and psychological characteristics does this woman display?
3. How does Fuseli's portrayal of Penelope compare with Homer's.

25 **Discussion** Why does Odysseus take this oath?

*Penelope again asks the beggar to tell about himself. He makes up a tale in which Odysseus is mentioned and declares that Penelope's husband will soon be home.*

1350 You see, then, he is alive and well, and headed
homeward now, no more to be abroad
far from his island, his dear wife and son.
Here is my sworn word for it. Witness this,
god of the zenith, noblest of the gods,[6]
1355 and Lord Odysseus' hearthfire, now before me:
I swear these things shall turn out as I say.
Between this present dark and one day's ebb,
after the wane, before the crescent moon,
Odysseus will come."

**6. god of the zenith, noblest of the gods:** Zeus.

*The Odyssey*   729

1. Odysseus says that recalling his background is too painful, and he does not want to cry in her presence.
2. Penelope said she would choose a husband when she finished her weaving, but each night she would undo that day's progress.

### Interpreting

3. Suggested Response: Odysseus is no doubt overjoyed that his wife has waited for him all these years. He also sympathizes with her plight and wants to help her.
4. Suggested Response: Penelope is evidently very much in love with her husband. She is also clever.

### Applying

5. Answers will differ. Students may feel that Odysseus believes that confiding in Penelope may interfere with the revenge he plans.

---

26 **Clarification** Termite damage would weaken the bow.

27 **Discussion** What is ironic about this statement?

## THINKING ABOUT THE SELECTION
### Recalling

1. What reason does Odysseus give for not answering Penelope's questions about his background?
2. Describe the trick Penelope used to delay choosing a husband from among the suitors.

### Interpreting

3. What would Odysseus' hidden feelings most likely be during this scene?
4. What impression of Penelope do you get from her speech?

### Applying

5. Why do you think Odysseus chooses not to reveal his identity to his wife now?

---

### The Challenge

*Pressed by the suitors to choose a husband from among them, Penelope says she will marry whoever can string Odysseus' bow and shoot an arrow through twelve ax-handle sockets. The suitors try and fail. Still in disguise, Odysseus asks for a turn and gets it.*

. . . . And Odysseus took his time,

1360 turning the bow, tapping it, every inch,
for borings that termites might have made
while the master of the weapon was abroad.
The suitors were now watching him, and some
jested among themselves:

"A bow lover!"

1365 "Dealer in old bows!"

"Maybe he has one like it
at home!"

"Or has an itch to make one for himself."

"See how he handles it, the sly old buzzard!"

And one disdainful suitor added this:

"May his fortune grow an inch for every inch he
bends it!"
1370 But the man skilled in all ways of contending,
satisfied by the great bow's look and heft,

730   *The Epic*

**THE TRIAL OF THE BOW**
*N. C. Wyeth*
*Delaware Art Museum*

> 28
>
> like a musician, like a harper, when
> with quiet hand upon his instrument
> he draws between his thumb and forefinger
> 1375  a sweet new string upon a peg: so effortlessly
> Odysseus in one motion strung the bow.
> Then slid his right hand down the cord and plucked it,
> so the taut gut vibrating hummed and sang
> a swallow's note.

*The Odyssey*  731

**29 Discussion** Why does Odysseus not laugh out loud at the thunder clap?

**30 Literary Focus** What is ironic about this statement?

In the hushed hall it smote the suitors
1380 and all their faces changed. Then Zeus thundered
overhead, one loud crack for a sign.
**29**
And Odysseus laughed within him that the son
of crooked-minded Cronus had flung that omen down.
He picked one ready arrow from his table
1385 where it lay bare: the rest were waiting still
in the quiver for the young men's turn to come.
He nocked[7] it, let it rest across the handgrip,
and drew the string and grooved butt of the arrow,
aiming from where he sat upon the stool.
Now flashed
1390 arrow from twanging bow clean as a whistle
through every socket ring, and grazed not one,
to thud with heavy brazen head beyond.
Then quietly
Odysseus said:

"Telemachus, the stranger
you welcomed in your hall has not disgraced you.
1395 I did not miss, neither did I take all day
stringing the bow. My hand and eye are sound,
not so contemptible as the young men say.
**30** The hour has come to cook their lordships' mutton—
supper by daylight. Other amusements later,
1400 with song and harping that adorn a feast."

He dropped his eyes and nodded, and the prince
Telemachus, true son of King Odysseus,
belted his sword on, clapped hand to his spear,
and with a clink and glitter of keen bronze
1405 stood by his chair, in the forefront near his father.

**7. nocked:** Set an arrow against the bowstring.

---

## THINKING ABOUT THE SELECTION
### Recalling

1. What is the suitors' reaction when Odysseus, still in disguise, takes up the bow?

### Interpreting

2. What might be the meaning of the sign that Zeus gives?

3. What does Odysseus mean when he says, "The hour has come to cook their lordships' mutton—/supper by daylight"?

### Applying

4. Does Odysseus' success in the contest show that he is an extraordinary archer or merely that he has a god on his side? Give reasons for your opinion.

---

**Closure and Extension**

**ANSWERS TO THINKING ABOUT THE SELECTION**
*Recalling*

1. At first the suitors are disdainful, but soon they are amazed at Odysseus' skill.

*Interpreting*

2. Suggested Response: The sign is probably a warning that the time of revenge is at hand.
3. Suggested Response: Odysseus is referring to his imminent attack on the suitors—they will be the source of his feast.

*Applying*

4. Answers will differ, but students would be correct in answering that it shows both. Being an epic hero, Odysseus is undoubtedly a skilled archer, but it is also true that the gods often assist him.

### Odysseus' Revenge

Now shrugging off his rags the wiliest fighter of the
    islands
leapt and stood on the broad doorsill, his own bow
    in his hand.
He poured out at his feet a rain of arrows from the
    quiver
and spoke to the crowd:
        "So much for that. Your clean-cut game is over.

1410  Now watch me hit a target that no man has hit
    before,
if I can make this shot. Help me, Apollo."

He drew to his fist the cruel head of an arrow for
    Antinous
just as the young man leaned to lift his beautiful
    drinking cup,
embossed, two-handled, golden: the cup was in his
    fingers:
1415  the wine was even at his lips: and did he dream of
    death?
How could he? In that revelry amid his throng of
    friends
who would imagine a single foe—though a strong foe
    indeed—
could dare to bring death's pain on him and
    darkness on his eyes?
Odysseus' arrow hit him under the chin
1420  and punched up to the feathers through his throat.

Backward and down he went, letting the winecup fall
from his shocked hand. Like pipes his nostrils jetted
crimson runnels, a river of mortal red,
and one last kick upset his table
1425  knocking the bread and meat to soak in dusty blood.
Now as they craned to see their champion where he lay
the suitors jostled in uproar down the hall,
everyone on his feet. Wildly they turned and scanned
the walls in the long room for arms; but not a shield,
1430  not a good ashen spear was there for a man to take
    and throw.
All they could do was yell in outrage at Odysseus:
"Foul! to shoot at a man! That was your last shot!"

"Your own throat will be slit for this!"
                    "Our finest lad is down!
You killed the best on Ithaca."
          "Buzzards will tear your eyes out!"

*The Odyssey*   733

**31 Discussion** Why do you think Homer includes this description of Antinous' life just before his death?

**32 Discussion** Why do you think Homer includes such vivid descriptions of death?

33 **Discussion** Why does Odysseus choose to reveal his identity under these circumstances?

34 **Reading Strategy** How do you think Odysseus will respond to Eurymachus' speech?

35 **Clarification** The word *glower* means "to frown with annoyance and anger."

1435 For they imagined as they wished—that it was a wild shot,
an unintended killing—fools, not to comprehend
they were already in the grip of death.
But glaring under his brows Odysseus answered:

33 "You yellow dogs, you thought I'd never make it
1440 home from the land of Troy. You took my house to plunder.
. . . You dared
bid for my wife while I was still alive.
Contempt was all you had for the gods who rule
     wide heaven,
contempt for what men say of you hereafter.
Your last hour has come. You die in blood."

1445 As they all took this in, sickly green fear
pulled at their entrails, and their eyes flickered
looking for some hatch or hideaway from death.
Eurymachus[8] alone could speak. He said:

**8. Eurymachus** (yoo ri´ mə kəs)

"If you are Odysseus of Ithaca come back,
1450 all that you say these men have done is true.
Rash actions, many here, more in the countryside.
But here he lies, the man who caused them all.
Antinous was the ringleader, he whipped us on
to do these things. He cared less for a marriage
1455 than for the power Cronion has denied him
as king of Ithaca. For that
he tried to trap your son and would have killed him.
34 He is dead now and has his portion. Spare
your own people. As for ourselves, we'll make
1460 restitution of wine and meat consumed,
and add, each one, a tithe of twenty oxen
with gifts of bronze and gold to warm your heart.
Meanwhile we cannot blame you for your anger."

35 Odysseus glowered under his black brows
1465 and said:

          "Not for the whole treasure of your fathers,
all you enjoy, lands, flocks, or any gold
put up by others, would I hold my hand.
There will be killing till the score is paid.
You forced yourselves upon this house. Fight your way out,
1470 or run for it, if you think you'll escape death.
I doubt one man of you skins by."

*734   The Epic*

## Grammar in Action

Many verbs show action, and **vivid verbs** are ones that paint a particularly clear picture of that action. Look at some of the verbs Eurymachus uses to call his men to action in these lines from the *Odyssey:*

*Fight,* I say,
let's remember the joy of it. Swords out!
*Hold* up your tables to *deflect* his arrows.
After me, everyone, *rush* him where he *stands*.

If we *can budge* him from the door, if we *can pass* into the town, we'll *call out* men to *chase* him. This fellow with his bow *will shoot* no more.

Compare this with a similar passage that does not use these verbs:

Move, I say,
let's remember the joy of it. Swords out!
Use your tables to shield you from his arrows.
After me, everyone, get him where he is now.
If we can move him from the door, if we then go into the town, we'll get men to go find him. This fellow with the bow will be no more.

They felt their knees fail, and their hearts—but heard
Eurymachus for the last time rallying them.

"Friends," he said, "the man is implacable.
1475 Now that he's got his hands on bow and quiver
he'll shoot from the big doorstone there
until he kills us to the last man.
                              Fight, I say,
let's remember the joy of it. Swords out!
Hold up your tables to deflect his arrows.
1480 After me, everyone: rush him where he stands.
If we can budge him from the door, if we can pass
into the town, we'll call out men to chase him.
This fellow with his bow will shoot no more."

He drew his own sword as he spoke, a broadsword
    of fine bronze,
1485 honed like a razor on either edge. Then crying
    hoarse and loud
he hurled himself at Odysseus. But the kingly man
    let fly
an arrow at that instant, and the quivering
    feathered butt
sprang to the nipple of his breast as the barb stuck
    in his liver.
The bright broadsword clanged down. He lurched
    and fell aside,
1490 pitching across his table. His cup, his bread and meat,
were spilt and scattered far and wide, and his head
    slammed on the ground.
Revulsion, anguish in his heart, with both feet
    kicking out,
he downed his chair, while the shrouding wave of
    mist closed on his eyes.

Amphinomus now came running at Odysseus,
1495 broadsword naked in his hand. He thought to make
the great soldier give way at the door.
But with a spear throw from behind Telemachus hit him
between the shoulders, and the lancehead drove
clear through his chest. He left his feet and fell
1500 forward, thudding, forehead against the ground.
Telemachus swerved around him, leaving the long
    dark spear
planted in Amphinomus. If he paused to yank it out
someone might jump him from behind or cut him
    down with a sword

*The Odyssey*   735

36 **Discussion** What do you think of Eurymachus' plan? What is it motivated by?

37 **Discussion** What other metaphors for dying has Homer used?

38 **Discussion** What quality does Telemachus show here? Who else has demonstrated this same quality?

Notice how what began as a rousing speech becomes colorless and far less rousing when robbed of its vivid action words.

**Student Activity 1.** Find five other sentences in the epic that contain vivid verbs, and talk about these with your classmates.

**Student Activity 2.** Write four sentences about the illustration on page 736. Use vivid verbs in these.

Fine art, *The Slaughter of the Suitors*, 1929, N. C. Wyeth. N. C. Wyeth, America's foremost illustrator of children's books and of the classics, created this illustration for a 1929 edition of the *Odyssey*.

Wyeth's illustrations add elements of drama and imagination to this already exciting story. His animation of the figures in this illustration is a marvel of painterly skill. The intensity of the movement and the play of light and dark both serve to accentuate this dynamic composition.

You might use the following questions for discussion:
1. Which lines from the *Odyssey* does this scene illustrate?
2. Which details contribute to the realism of the scene?

**39 Discussion** Odysseus agrees with his son's plan. What does this suggest about Odysseus' confidence in his son?

THE SLAUGHTER OF THE SUITORS
*N. C. Wyeth*
*Delaware Art Museum*

at the moment he bent over. So he ran—ran from
    the tables
1505  to his father's side and halted, panting, saying:

"Father let me bring you a shield and spear,
a pair of spears, a helmet.
I can arm on the run myself; I'll give
outfits to Eumaeus and this cowherd.
1510  Better to have equipment."

                   Said Odysseus:

**39**    "Run then, while I hold them off with arrows
as long as the arrows last. When all are gone
if I'm alone they can dislodge me."

                      Quick
upon his father's word Telemachus
1515  ran to the room where spears and armor lay.
He caught up four light shields, four pairs of spears,

736  *The Epic*

four helms of war high-plumed with flowing manes,
and ran back, loaded down, to his father's side.
He was the first to pull a helmet on
1520 and slide his bare arm in a buckler strap.
The servants armed themselves, and all three took
their stand
beside the master of battle.
While he had arrows
he aimed and shot, and every shot brought down
one of his huddling enemies.
1525 But when all barbs had flown from the bowman's fist,
he leaned his bow in the bright entryway
beside the door, and armed: a four-ply shield
hard on his shoulder, and a crested helm,
horsetailed, nodding stormy upon his head,
1530 then took his tough and bronze-shod spears. . . .

*Aided by Athena, Odysseus, Telemachus, Eu-*
*maeus, and another faithful herdsman kill all the*
*suitors.*

And Odysseus looked around him, narrow-eyed,
for any others who had lain hidden
while death's black fury passed.
In blood and dust
he saw that crowd all fallen, many and many slain.

1535 Think of a catch that fishermen haul in to a half-
moon bay
in a fine-meshed net from the whitecaps of the sea:
how all are poured out on the sand, in throes for
the salt sea,
twitching their cold lives away in Helios' fiery air:
so lay the suitors heaped on one another.

## THINKING ABOUT THE SELECTION

### Recalling

1. Describe the immediate reaction of the suitors
   to the killing of Antinous.
2. What arguments does Eurymachus use to try
   to persuade Odysseus to spare him and the
   others?

3. How does Telemachus aid his father in the
   battle?

### Interpreting

4. Discuss Odysseus' judgment on the suitors.
   What are his reasons for slaying them all?

### Applying

5. Compare justice at the hands of Odysseus
   with justice in a modern society.

*The Odyssey* 737

40 **Discussion** To whom does the
description "master of battle" refer? What does it imply?

41 **Reading Strategy** Homer uses a
similar image earlier to describe
dying men. Ask students to recall
the incident.

## Closure and Extension

### ANSWERS TO THINKING ABOUT THE SELECTION
*Recalling*

1. The suitors are outraged at the
   cold-blooded murder.
2. Eurymachus tells Odysseus that
   Antinous was their ringleader and
   forced them to behave as they
   did.
3. Telemachus kills one of Odysseus'
   attackers just as he is about to kill
   Odysseus. Then he runs to fetch
   armor and a spear for his father so
   he can better defend himself.

*Interpreting*

4. Answers will differ. Students may
   respond that Odysseus' justification for slaying all the suitors is that
   all were guilty of forcing themselves into his household.

*Applying*

5. Answers will differ. Most students
   will realize that we do not permit
   such individual revenge today.

42 **Literary Focus** Odysseus is described as more godlike than human.

43 **Clarification** Athena was also the goddess of crafts and techniques that uphold civilization.

**Penelope's Test**

*Penelope tests Odysseus to prove that he really is her husband.*

1540 Greathearted Odysseus, home at last,
was being bathed now by Eurynome
and rubbed with golden oil, and clothed again
in a fresh tunic and a cloak. Athena
lent him beauty, head to foot. She made him
1545 taller, and massive, too, with crisping hair
in curls like petals of wild hyacinth
but all red-golden. Think of gold infused
on silver by a craftsman, whose fine art
Hephaestus[9] taught him, or Athena: one
1550 whose work moves to delight: just so she lavished
beauty over Odysseus' head and shoulders.
He sat then in the same chair by the pillar,
facing his silent wife, and said:

　　　　　　　　　　"Strange woman,
the immortals of Olympus made you hard,
1555 harder than any. Who else in the world
would keep aloof as you do from her husband
if he returned to her from years of trouble,
cast on his own land in the twentieth year?

Nurse, make up a bed for me to sleep on.
1560 Her heart is iron in her breast."

　　　　　　　　　　　　　　Penelope
spoke to Odysseus now. She said:

　　　　　　　　　　"Strange man,
if man you are . . . This is no pride on my part
nor scorn for you—not even wonder, merely.
I know so well how you—how he—appeared
1565 boarding the ship for Troy. But all the same . . .

Make up his bed for him, Eurycleia.
Place it outside the bedchamber my lord
built with his own hands. Pile the big bed
with fleeces, rugs, and sheets of purest linen."

1570 With this she tried him to the breaking point,
and he turned on her in a flash raging:

**9. Hephaestus** (hi fes′ təs): God of fire and the forge and of metalworking.

738　*The Epic*

"Woman, by heaven you've stung me now!
Who dared to move my bed?
No builder had the skill for that—unless
1575 a god came down to turn the trick. No mortal
in his best days could budge it with a crowbar.
There is our pact and pledge, our secret sign,
built into that bed—my handiwork
and no one else's!
                                    An old trunk of olive
1580 grew like a pillar on the building plot,
and I laid out our bedroom round that tree,
lined up the stone walls, built the walls and roof,
gave it a doorway and smooth-fitting doors.
Then I lopped off the silvery leaves and branches,
1585 hewed and shaped that stump from the roots up
into a bedpost, drilled it, let it serve
as model for the rest. I planed them all,
inlaid them all with silver, gold and ivory,
and stretched a bed between—a pliant web
1590 of oxhide thongs dyed crimson.
                                    There's our sign!
I know no more. Could someone else's hand
have sawn that trunk and dragged the frame away?"

Their secret! as she heard it told, her knees
grew tremulous and weak, her heart failed her.
1595 With eyes brimming tears she ran to him,
throwing her arms around his neck, and kissed
    him,
murmuring:

                                    "Do not rage at me, Odysseus!
No one ever matched your caution! Think
what difficulty the gods gave: they denied us
1600 life together in our prime and flowering years,
kept us from crossing into age together.
Forgive me, don't be angry. I could not
welcome you with love on sight! I armed myself
long ago against the frauds of men,
1605 impostors who might come—and all those many
whose underhanded ways bring evil on! . . .
But here and now, what sign could be so clear
as this of our own bed?
No other man has ever laid eyes on it—
1610 only my own slave, Actoris, that my father

44

*The Odyssey*   739

45 **Reading Strategy** Compare and contrast this reunion with the reunion with Telemachus.

46 **Master Teacher Note** Use the overhead projector to show students Art Transparency 19 *Odysseus and Penelope Reunited,* by Romare Bearden. Ask students how this picture reflects the happy reunion of husband and wife in a peaceful kingdom. Also, how do they think Bearden's identity as a black artist has influenced his depiction of this scene?

47 **Enrichment** You might want to ask students to read Tennyson's "Ulysses," which presents Odysseus at the end of his life. Then have them compare Homer's hero with Tennyson's.

**Reader's Response** How would you have handled Odysseus' situation at home when he returns from war? Would you have acted differently? Explain.

sent with me as a gift—she kept our door.
You make my stiff heart know that I am yours."

Now from his breast into his eyes the ache
of longing mounted, and he wept at last,
his dear wife, clear and faithful, in his arms,
longed for as the sunwarmed earth is longed for by a swimmer
spent in rough water where his ship went down
under Poseidon's blows, gale winds and tons of sea.
Few men can keep alive through a big surf
to crawl, clotted with brine, on kindly beaches
in joy, in joy, knowing the abyss behind:
and so she too rejoiced, her gaze upon her husband,
her white arms round him pressed as though
forever.

1615

1620

**The Ending**

*Odysseus is reunited with his father. Athena commands that peace prevail between Odysseus and the relatives of the slain suitors. Odysseus has regained his family and his kingdom.*

## THINKING ABOUT THE SELECTION

### Recalling

1. Why is Odysseus displeased with Penelope?
2. What is her response to his complaint?
3. What is Penelope's test, and how does Odysseus "pass" it?

### Interpreting

4. Since Odysseus has abandoned his disguise, why does Penelope doubt his identity?
5. Describe the mood of this scene. Is it altogether happy, or does it include some sadness? Give reasons for your opinion.

### Applying

6. Some scholars believe the events that follow the reunion of Odysseus and Penelope were added to the Odyssey by someone other than Homer. Tell why you think that these events ("The Ending") do or do not make up an appropriate conclusion to the epic.

## ANALYZING LITERATURE

### Understanding the Plot of an Epic

The **plot** of an epic is made up of a series of episodes in which the hero performs extraordinary deeds. In classical epics such as the *Odyssey,* the outcomes of these episodes may depend on the influence of the gods as well as on the strengths and weaknesses of the human characters.

1. Give three examples of a god or goddess influencing the events of the *Odyssey.*

**Closure and Extension**

*ANSWERS TO THINKING ABOUT THE SELECTION*
*Recalling*

1. Odysseus is displeased with Penelope's aloofness after such a long separation.
2. Penelope explains that she is still uncertain about Odysseus' identity and that she has had to guard against imposters.
3. Penelope tells her servant to move

2. Do Odysseus' deeds seem less heroic because the gods sometimes enter into the action? Give reasons for your opinion.
3. In which episode is Odysseus' character most fully displayed? Tell what traits are revealed in it.

## CRITICAL THINKING AND READING
### Inferring Ways of Life from Epics

A chief source of our knowledge of ancient peoples is their literature. The *Odyssey* reveals a great deal about the civilization in which it was composed. From what characters say and the way they act, you can infer some of the customs and beliefs of Homer's world. For example, you can infer that it was customary for wealthier families to keep servants and slaves.
1. What does the *Odyssey* suggest about Greek customs of hospitality?
2. What attitudes toward the gods are upheld as appropriate?
3. What beliefs concerning death can you infer from the *Odyssey*?
4. What other customs or beliefs seemed to you very much different from those of today?

## UNDERSTANDING LANGUAGE
### Interpreting Homeric Similes

A *Homeric simile* is a lengthy and elaborate comparison of one thing to another. For example, when Odysseus is stringing his bow for the ax-handle contest he is compared to a musician: "like a musician, like a harper, when/with quiet hand upon his instrument/he draws between his thumb and forefinger/a sweet new string upon a peg . . ." Such a simile gives you a brief glimpse of something altogether unrelated to the subject of the comparison. But at the same time you see the subject revealed in a startling new way, with some aspect or quality vividly emphasized.

Reread the Homeric similes indicated below by their line numbers. For each, tell what the subject of the comparison is and what the subject is compared to. Then describe the effect of the simile.
1. lines 1061–1065
2. lines 1290–1297
3. lines 1535–1539
4. lines 1616–1621

## THINKING AND WRITING
### Responding to Criticism

The poet and critic W. H. Auden once made the following comment about Homer's heroes.

Though it would be unfair to describe the Homeric hero as a mere puppet of the gods, his area of free choice and responsibility is pretty circumscribed. In the first place he is born, not made . . . so that though he does brave deeds, he cannot be called brave in our sense of the word because he never feels fear.

Write an essay in which you tell why you agree or disagree with this comment. First find those episodes or parts of episodes that support your opinion. Refer to them when you write your draft. When you revise make sure that you have addressed the key questions about Odysseus that Auden's comment suggests: Does he act freely or not? Does he feel fear or not? Is he brave or not?

*The Odyssey* 741

(Answers begin on p. 740.)

argue that the episode in which Odysseus blinds the Cyclops best shows Odysseus' cleverness.

## ANSWERS TO CRITICAL THINKING AND READING
1. Suggested Response: Everyone, regardless of class, should be made welcome. In addition, not only were guests obliged to offer gifts to their hosts, but hosts were supposed to provide gifts for the guests as well.
2. Suggested Response: Deference, respect, and fear were appropriate attitudes toward the gods.
3. Suggested Response: The Greeks believed that upon death, the soul departed from the body and went to the Underworld, a place of gloom.
4. Answers will differ. Some students may respond that the Greek belief that many gods control different aspects of nature seems strange.

## ANSWERS TO UNDERSTANDING LANGUAGE
1. Suggested Response: The weeping of Odysseus and Telemachus is compared to the cries of a hawk whose nestlings have been taken. The simile dramatizes the powerful relationship between parents and their young.
2. Suggested Response: Penelope's reputation is compared to that of a king who prospers because of his respect for the gods. This simile shows how much she is respected for her faithfulness.
3. Suggested Response: The massacre of the suitors is compared to a fisherman's catch. The effect is to diminish the importance of the suitors, even in death.
4. Suggested Response: Odysseus' longing for his wife is compared to the longing of a swimmer for sun-warmed earth. The effect is to recapitulate in one image all of Odysseus' adventures and to show how much he has longed for this reunion.

the bed, a suggestion that enrages Odysseus, who built the bed himself. He passes her test by describing the unique bed in detail.

### Interpreting
4. Suggested Response: She doubts his identity because he has changed so dramatically.
5. Suggested Response: The scene is one of conflicting emotions: suspicion, joy at being reunited, and sorrow for their long separation.

### Applying
6. Answers will differ. Students should give reasons for their responses, indicating whether this ending is a satisfying climax.

## ANSWERS TO ANALYZING LITERATURE
1. Suggested Response: Poseidon sinks Odysseus' ship; Athena tells Odysseus to reveal himself to his son; and Athena helps Odysseus kill the suitors.

2. Answers will differ. Some students might argue that the assistance of the gods does not detract from Odysseus' skill and courage. For example, he is obviously a skillful archer.
3. Answers will differ. Some students may argue that Odysseus' humanity is most clearly revealed in his sadness at seeing his mother's shade; his joy at being reunited with Telemachus; or his mixed joy, sadness, and anger in the reunion with Penelope. Other students may

## THINKING AND WRITING
For help with this assignment, students may consult Lesson 9, "Writing About Character," in the Handbook of Writing About Literature.

**More About the Author** As a girl, Margaret Atwood grew up in a rural section of Canada. What advantages or disadvantages might a writer gain from growing up in the country rather than in a large city?

**More About the Author** Critics have commented on Cavafy's almost uncanny ability to make the past come alive. Even though he writes about people and events of long ago, he makes them seem as real as the newspaper stories of today. Ask students what factors might account for this ability.

# GUIDE FOR READING

## Siren Song and Ithaca

**Margaret Atwood** (1939–    ) was born in Ottawa, Ontario, and has lived in Canada most of her life. She writes fiction, poetry, and screenplays. Her concern with what it means to be a woman in a period of social change is reflected in her startling re-creation of Homer's sirens in "Siren Song."

**Constantine Cavafy** (1863–1933) was born in Alexandria, Egypt, of Greek Parents. In "Ithaca," you can see his basic creative method– to use the classical Greek mythological world to write poems that speak to the reader of today.

742    *The Epic*

### Objectives

1 To understand interpretations of the *Odyssey*
2 To interpret the *Odyssey* creatively

### Support Material

**Teaching Portfolio**
Teacher Backup, p. 899
Usage and Mechanics Worksheet, p. 902
Vocabulary Check, p. 903
Analyzing Literature Worksheet, *Understanding Interpretations of the Odyssey,* p. 904

Language Worksheet, *Recognizing Modern Allusions to the Odyssey,* p. 905
Selection Test, p. 906

742

## Modern Interpretations of the *Odyssey*

The characters and events of the *Odyssey* are timeless and universal in their interest and significance. They are so rich in meaning that every generation sees in them ideas and values relevant to the present. Hence countless writers have mined the *Odyssey* for material to create original poems, plays, novels, and essays. Though these "interpretations" differ widely in purpose, theme, and artistic method, they usually have two features in common. They present persons, places, and events whose origins are in Homer, but they use Homer's material in original ways to express contemporary thoughts, values, beliefs, and feelings.

### Look For

As you read "Siren Song" and "Ithaca," look for the material that Atwood and Cavafy took from the *Odyssey.* Then decide what is original about the way they treated it.

### Writing

Imagine that you are either Telemachus or Penelope. Odysseus has spent an entire day and evening telling you of his travels and adventures. Freewrite about all that you have heard. How might your view of your father (or husband) change? How might your ideas about yourself and your future change?

### Vocabulary

Knowing the following words will help you as you read "Siren Song" and "Ithaca."

**beached** (bēcht) *adj.*: Washed up and lying on a beach (p. 745) (usually a verb)

**picturesque** (pik′ chə resk′) *adj.*: Like or suggesting a picture (p. 745)

**amber** (am′ bər) *n.*: A yellowish resin used in jewelry (p. 746)

**ebony** (eb′ ə nē) *n.*: A hard, dark wood used for furniture (p. 746)

**defrauded** (di frôd′ əd) *v.*: Cheated (p. 747)

Fine art, *Ulysses and the Siren*, by Pablo Picasso. The Spanish artist Pablo Picasso (1881–1973) was one of the greatest artists of the twentieth century. As the child of an artist and teacher, Picasso was given every encouragement when he showed an interest in drawing. When he was fifteen, he attended La Llonja Art School in Barcelona, where he studied painting and drawing under his father. He then worked as an illustrator and later as an art editor. In 1901, he settled in Paris. There he came into contact with the avant garde of the French art world. His role in influencing these artists and changing the face of twentieth century art cannot be overstated.

While figures from mythology are not a common subject in Picasso's work, they do recur throughout his working years. In *Ulysses and the Sirens*, Picasso does not let a strictly realistic approach limit his interpretation.

You might use these questions for discussion:

1. How does this work interpret Homer's Sirens?
2. How does the artist convey the reaction of Ulysses (Odysseus) to the Sirens?

**ULYSSES AND THE SIRENS**
*Pablo Picasso*
Musée Picasso

744    The Epic

# Siren Song

## Margaret Atwood

1
This is the one song everyone
would like to learn: the song
that is irresistible:

the song that forces men
5   to leap overboard in squadrons
even though they see the beached skulls

2
the song nobody knows
because anyone who has heard it
is dead, and the others can't remember.

10   Shall I tell you the secret
and if I do, will you get me
out of this bird suit?[1]

I don't enjoy it here
squatting on this island
15   looking picturesque and mythical

3
with these two feathery maniacs,
I don't enjoy singing
this trio, fatal and valuable.

I will tell the secret to you,
20   to you, only to you.
Come closer. This song

is a cry for help: Help me!
Only you, only you can,
you are unique

4  25   at last. Alas
it is a boring song
but it works every time.

---
**1. bird suit:** The sirens are usually represented as
half bird and half woman.

## Presentation

**Motivation/Prior Knowledge**
Ask students how it might feel to
be one of the Sirens in the *Odyssey*. Then tell them that Atwood
offers an imaginative answer to
this question.

**Master Teacher Note** Although
Atwood's poem is based on well-
known figures from Homer's
classic, the poem offers a contemporary message. As students
read, ask them to consider the
effect of using a classical figure
to make a point about a contemporary issue.

**Purpose-Setting    Question**
What trick does the narrator of
Atwood's poem use to get men's
attention?

1 **Discussion** To whom do you
think "everyone" refers?

2 **Literary Focus** To what characteristics of Homer's Sirens
does this refer?

3 **Discussion** Why do you think the
speaker refers to the Sirens as
maniacs?

4 **Discussion** Notice Atwood's
play on words. How does it contribute to the meaning?

## THINKING ABOUT THE SELECTION

### Recalling

1. What does the Siren reveal about the song?
2. What does she reveal about herself?

### Interpreting

3. Who might the "others" be who have heard the
   song but "can't remember"?
4. The siren describes the song as "fatal and
   valuable." In what sense is it valuable?
5. To whom might the siren be speaking? Give
   reaons for your opinion.

### Applying

6. How much of "Siren Song" is based on Homer,
   and how much is Atwood's original creation?

---

## Closure and Extension

### ANSWERS TO THINKING ABOUT THE SELECTION

**Recalling**

1. She says that the secret song is
   irresistible and forces men to leap
   overboard to their death.
2. The Siren reveals that she is unhappy in her role, "looking picturesque and mythical," that she
   does not enjoy singing, and that
   her song is a cry for help.

**Interpreting**

3. Answers will differ. Students may
   respond that the "others" are men
   who have not yet heard the Sirens
   sing.
4. Suggested Response: It may be
   valuable because it "is irresistible."
5. Answers will differ. Students may
   even indicate that she is speaking
   to herself.

**Applying**

6. Answers will differ. Most students
   will realize that the character and
   situation are Homeric but that the
   modern speech and interpretation
   are Atwood's.

When you start on your journey to Ithaca,
then pray that the road is long,
full of adventure, full of knowledge.
Do not fear the Lestrygonians[1]
5  and the Cyclopes and the angry Poseidon.
You will never meet such as these on your path,
if your thoughts remain lofty, if a fine
emotion touches your body and your spirit.
You will never meet the Lestrygonians,
10  the Cyclopes and the fierce Poseidon,
if you do not carry them within your soul,
if your soul does not raise them up before you.

Then pray that the road is long.
That the summer mornings are many,
15  that you will enter ports seen for the first time
with such pleasure, with such joy!
Stop at Phoenician markets,
and purchase fine merchandise,
mother-of-pearl and corals, amber and ebony,
20  and pleasurable perfumes of all kinds,
buy as many pleasurable perfumes as you can;
visit hosts of Egyptian cities,
to learn and learn from those who have knowledge.

Always keep Ithaca fixed in your mind.
25  To arrive there is your ultimate goal.
But do not hurry the voyage at all.
It is better to let it last for long years;
and even to anchor at the isle when you are old,
rich with all that you have gained on the way,
30  not expecting that Ithaca will offer you riches.

Ithaca has given you the beautiful voyage.
Without her you would never have taken the road.
But she has nothing more to give you.

---

**1. Lestrygonians** (les tri gō' nē ənz): Cannibals who destroy all of Odysseus' ships except his own and kill the crews.

And if you find her poor, Ithaca has not defrauded you.
35 With the great wisdom you have gained, with so much experience,
you must surely have understood by then what Ithacas mean.

---

## THINKING ABOUT THE SELECTION

### Recalling

1. What benefits await the traveler to Ithaca if the road, or journey, is long?
2. What does the speaker say directly about the meaning and value of Ithaca?

### Interpreting

3. What might the journey to Ithaca symbolize?
4. What might Ithaca symbolize?
5. What might the Lestrygonians, Cyclopes, and "fierce Poseidon" symbolize?

### Applying

6. In what way could a person carry the Lestrygonians, Cyclopes, and angry Poseidon within his or her own soul?

## ANALYZING LITERATURE

### Understanding Interpretations

When modern writers interpret the *Odyssey* or some part of it creatively, they frequently use it to organize and express their own feelings, beliefs, and experiences. Atwood, for example, uses the sirens to say something about women. Cavafy uses a basic plot thread of the *Odyssey*—the journey home of Odysseus—to say something about life and living. Therefore, in the hands of modern writers Homer's subject matter takes on new meanings according to the special purpose of each artist.

1. What resemblance do you see between Atwood's siren and some contemporary women?
2. Why is Odysseus' journey home such excellent material for a literary work concerned with the course of human life?

## THINKING AND WRITING

### Interpreting the *Odyssey* Creatively

Write a monologue in prose or poetry such as Telemachus or Penelope might utter after listening to Odysseus recount his adventures. Use the freewriting you did before you read Atwood's and Cavafy's poems. Let the character you chose express some of your own thoughts and feelings about life. When you revise your monologue, try to make your speaker sound the way Telemachus or Penelope might sound. Compare your monologue with those of your classmates. In how many different ways was Homer's material used?

*Ithaca*   747

# FOCUS ON READING

## Reading a Map

Maps often make clear a character's journey in a story. By studying a map, you can understand how far a character has traveled and, often, draw conclusions about the obstacles that the character had to overcome in the course of the journey. Understanding the geography of the area is crucial to understanding Homer's *Odyssey*.

**Information**

The map you will be using will help you to trace Odysseus' journey. Although the adventures of Odysseus are fictional, many of the places mentioned in the *Odyssey* actually exist. This suggests that Homer had some knowledge of the geography of the Mediterranean region. Homer often uses the ancient names of Italian, Greek, and Turkish locations, but these locations are associated with identifiable modern locations, which you will see on the map.

**Layout**

Although there are many different types of maps providing different types of information, most maps are laid out the same way in terms of their north, south, east, and west directions. On a map, north is up, south is down, east is right, and west is left. Many maps include a symbol that looks like a cross, to show *N, S, E,* and *W* directions. This is a standard orientation.

**Guidelines**

- Understand the purpose of a map.
- Understand the standard orientation.
- Identify geographical features.
- Identify specific places.

## Activity

Use the map of the Mediterranean region to answer the following questions.

1. Troy, or Ilium, the site of the Trojan War, was uncovered in what is now Turkey. Locate Turkey on the map. What body of water borders it on the north?

2. Ithaca is the island homeland from which Odysseus begins his journey. Locate Ithaca off the western coast of Greece. (It is the middle one of the three islands.) What body of water did Odysseus have to navigate upon leaving Ithaca?

3. Scylla, the six-headed monster, is thought to be located at the passage between Sicily and the toe of the boot of Italy. The Ionian Sea is on the east. What sea is on the west?

4. The entrance to the Underworld, or Land of the Dead, is believed to be at the Strait of Gibraltar. Why would people of the Mediterranean area living during Odysseus' time consider anything beyond this point frightening?

# YOU THE WRITER

**Assignment**

**1.** The strange, the unusual, the incredible—these words describe the creatures Odysseus met on his voyage. Describe a creature Odysseus might have met but didn't.

**Prewriting.** Freewrite, describing your incredible creature. Explore as many aspects of this creature's appearance and personality as you can. Let your mind roam freely. Do not worry about how all the parts of your description will work together yet.

**Writing.** Review your freewriting. Underline the physical descriptions of your character that you want to use in your sketch. Star the personality traits you will include. Then write your description. Begin by describing the creature's appearance and end by describing its personality.

**Revising.** Read over your description. Can you picture that creature based on the details you have included? If not, include additional details now. Proofread your description and prepare a final draft.

**Assignment**

**2.** Imagine that you are one of the creatures Odysseus met. Retell one of the adventures from this creature's point of view.

**Prewriting.** First choose your character. For example, you might choose the Cyclops or Scylla. List the major events in this episode in chronological order.

**Writing.** Write the first draft of your adventure. Include in your retelling thoughts and feelings the creature would have. Relate the events in chronological order.

**Revising.** When you revise, make sure you have maintained a consistent point of view. Have you made the creature come alive for your readers? Have you included the creature's thoughts and feelings? Proofread your tale and prepare a final draft.

**Assignment**

**3.** The content of the song the Sirens sang has intrigued writers throughout the centuries. Write your own Siren's Song.

**Prewriting.** Freewrite, exploring your ideas for what song might hold the seamen.

**Writing.** Write a short, lyric poem singing the song of the Sirens. Perhaps you will want to include rhythm and rhyme to give your poem a musical quality.

**Revising.** When you revise, make sure your song has a musical quality. If you were at sea, would this song hold you? Prepare a final draft and share your poem with your classmates.

750    *The Epic*

# YOU THE CRITIC

Assignment

**1.** Choose the character other than Odysseus whom you think was best developed. Write an essay explaining why you chose this character.

**Prewriting.** Make a word bank listing words or ideas about the character you chose. Then categorize your list.

**Writing.** Write your first draft using words from your word bank. Make sure you support your statements with details from the story.

**Revising.** Make sure you have provided adequate support for your opinion. Proofread your essay and prepare a final draft.

Assignment

**2.** Choose one of the adventures from the *Odyssey* that had, for you, an unsatisfactory ending. Show why it was unsatisfactory. Describe how characters could have acted to effect a different outcome.

**Prewriting.** Use a cueing technique to generate ideas. Answer the questions *Who? What? Where? When?* and *Why?*

**Writing.** Begin your essay with a description of the plot. Go on to describe how the adventure ended. Then discuss how the characters could have acted to produce the "ideal" ending. Explain how the characters would have to be different from the way they are.

**Revising.** Read over your essay. Make sure your introduction will arouse your readers' interest. Check to see that you have presented your ideas clearly and arranged them in logical order. Edit your sentences and proofread your essay.

Assignment

**3.** The characters in epics often embody the character traits held in esteem by a certain society. Choose one of the characters from the *Odyssey* and show how this character represents a trait the ancient Greeks valued.

**Prewriting.** List the major characters in the *Odyssey*. By each character's name, list the trait or traits you think this character best represents. For example, by Penelope's name you might list loyalty and by Odysseus' name, cunning. Then choose the character about whom you will write your essay. Jot down details showing how this character displays this trait.

**Writing.** Write the first draft of your essay. Begin by explaining what trait the ancient Greeks valued. Then show how the character you have chosen embodies this trait. End your essay by restating your main idea.

**Revising.** When you revise your essay, make sure you have included details from the *Odyssey* that back up your main idea. Proofread your essay and prepare a final draft.

*You the Critic* 751

---

*YOU THE CRITIC*
## *Guidelines for Evaluating Assignment 1*

1. Has the student expressed an opinion about the development of a character?
2. Has the student used strong and effective words to describe the character?
3. Has the student provided adequate support for his or her opinion?
4. Is the essay free from grammar, usage, and mechanics errors?

## *Guidelines for Evaluating Assignment 2*

1. Has the student briefly summarized an episode in the plot and offered a different ending?
2. Has the essay explained how the characters would have behaved differently to effect this ending?
3. Does the essay include a strong introduction that will capture a reader's interest?
4. Is the essay free from grammar, usage, and mechanics errors?

## *Guidelines for Evaluating Assignment 3*

1. Has the student clearly described a trait valued by the ancient Greeks?
2. Has the student given examples from the *Odyssey* that show how the character embodies that trait?
3. Does the essay conclude with a restatement of the main idea?
4. Is the essay free from grammar, usage, and mechanics errors?

## Humanities Note

Fine Art, *Mid-Victorian Father Reading to Entire Family.* This work is a colored lithograph. Lithography, a process for printing unlimited multiple images, involves drawing a design on a smooth stone with a grease crayon, applying an oily ink which will adhere only to the crayon, and pressing paper onto the stone to transfer the design. This black and white image can then be hand-colored with transparent ink or watercolor. This process allowed inexpensive decorative pictures, such as this scene of the Victorian family, to become readily available to the public.

The father in this print might very well be reading a serialized novel of the Victorian period. Long novels, like those of Charles Dickens and others, were published in monthly installments, which were eagerly awaited by the reading public.

MID-VICTORIAN FATHER READING TO ENTIRE FAMILY
*Three Lions*

752

# THE NOVEL

A novel is an extended fictional work written in prose. The novel presents plot, character, setting, theme, point of view, tone, symbol, and irony with greater breadth and freedom than does a short story. A novel can encompass a wide range of narratives and time spans, and can present more involved conflicts than a short story can. Although we are all familiar with novels, the novel is a relatively new form of literature. It has existed for only about three hundred years.

Novels provide us with a wealth of experience and understanding. The novelist William Styron has written, "A great book should leave you with many experiences, and slightly exhausted at the end. You live several lives while reading it."

# Great Expectations

**Background**

Charles Dickens himself described the era in which he lived, the period of the Industrial Revolution, as a time of "machinery and tall chimneys, out of which interminable serpents of smoke trailed themselves for ever and ever, and never got uncoiled. . . . a black canal . . . and a river that ran purple with ill-smelling dye. . . ." These terrible conditions resulted from a long slow process of change in the means of production that brought, in the beginning, exploitation of workers and social disruptions. Working conditions were miserable. Sixteen-hour days and six-day weeks combined with the monotony of factory work and lack of any safety standards to make working conditions unbearable, yet those in positions of wealth led lives of incredible luxury. In fact, Dickens's father had been sent to debtors' prison, which forced the writer to work in a factory at the age of twelve. It was against this background of the early Industrial Revolution that Dickens wrote *Great Expectations*.

**Reading Strategies**

When you read *Great Expectations,* you might encounter some difficulty with Dickens's sentence structure and vocabulary. His sentences can be complex, and occasionally his choice of words is difficult for the modern reader. Try reading the sentences rapidly. Pay attention to the punctuation, for it will guide you as you read. Often, in long sentences, you can consider a semicolon to be a period. Use contextual clues to discover the meanings of words, but use a dictionary if you are really stuck. Dickens enjoyed using irony and caricature, so, as you read, be aware of these elements. Sometimes you will find them both in characters' names. Finally, interact with the literature by using the active reading strategies: question, predict, clarify, summarize, pull together. Because this novel was originally conceived as a serial, you will have numerous opportunities to question and predict.

**Themes**

You will encounter the following themes in *Great Expectations*.
• the struggle between good and evil, both internal and external
• self-discovery and maturing
• inner worth as the source of true goodness
• loyalty and responsibility
• how wealth and position corrupt

754   *The Novel*

# Great Expectations

**THE ACQUITTAL**
*Abraham Solomon*
From the collection of
Barbara and Norman S. Namerow,
Beverly Hills, California

**Humanities Note**

Fine Art, *The Acquittal*, Abraham Solomon. Abraham Solomon (1824-1862), was a British painter. A student of the Royal Academy, Solomon became a painter of narrative subjects in the great Victorian tradition. His paintings, obvious and sentimental, were extremely popular with the public. They were issued for circulation as wood engravings and as so were likely to be found displayed in many British parlors.

*The Acquittal*, also called *Not Guilty*, is the sequel to Abraham Solomon's painting *Waiting For the Verdict* (see page 928). Together these paintings established Solomon's reputation as a narrative painter. The Victorian public considered the heartwarming joy of the accused man's family a suitable happy ending to the story revealed by the first painting.

**Master Teacher Note** Use the overhead projector to show students Art Transparency 20, *St. Pancras Hotel and Pentonville Road*, by John Arthur O'Connor. This painting depicts a street scene from nineteenth-century London. You might tell students that much of *Great Expectations* takes place in nineteenth-century London. What impression of the city does this painting convey? Does the city seem large and crowded? What methods of transportation are people using? How are they dressed? How does the quality of the light affect the mood that the picture communicates?

## Focus

**More About the Author** Charles Dickens spent a happy childhood in Chatham, but this period was followed by an intensely sad one. His father was imprisoned for his debts, and Dickens had to go to work in a factory. Memories of this painful period inspired much of his fiction. Ask pupils to what extent early experiences affect an author's work.

**Literary Focus** Students will need to be aware of the subtle shifts between a child's and an adult's perspective that constantly occur in this novel. Pip may seem to be almost a "naive narrator" at the beginning of the novel, but his intense awareness of his motives discloses the older man who is looking through the child's eyes.

**Look For** *Great Expectations* is a work about the growing-up of a sensitive young person who is trying to discover the meaning of life and his purpose and goals. Ask students to be alert for signs of Pip's growth throughout the work, beginning with his first encounter with Magwitch.

**Writing/Prior Knowledge** Write the words *anticipation, hope,* and *expectation* on the board. Ask students to list actions, events, emotions, and other associations that come to mind when they think of these words. Ask them to consider the subtle differences between these three apparent synonyms. Then have them proceed with the freewriting.

**Vocabulary** Even in a somewhat abridged text, Dickens's use of polysyllabic words may give some students difficulty. Encourage students to note any words that they do not understand. If possible, provide students with desk copies of a good dictionary.

## Great Expectations, Chapters 1–8

**Charles Dickens** (1812–1870) is one of the greatest English novelists. He is known for creating lively works that are enjoyed by people of all ages and backgrounds. Dickens was raised in London and lived most of his life there. His passion for reading and his keen eye for observation prepared him for a career as a writer. Among his well-known novels are *Oliver Twist, David Copperfield, A Tale of Two Cities,* and *Great Expectations.* In these and other books, he created memorable characters and criticized the injustices of his time.

**Point of View**

**Point of view** is the perspective or angle from which the events of a story or novel are told. In a **first-person narrative,** a character in the novel tells you his or her story directly. This narrator refers to himself or herself as "I" or "me." What you learn immediately is limited to what that character observes or thinks. However, by reading between the lines, you may understand things the narrator does not.

The point of view in *Great Expectations* is that of the first-person narrator, Pip. You learn about the world of this novel through him.

**Look For**

At the opening of the novel, Pip has a frightening encounter, which has long-term results. As you read Chapters 1–8, look for Pip's perception of this and other events. Also, when does Pip's adult perspective influence this account of his childhood?

**Writing**

One of the themes of this novel concerns expectations for the future. George Eliot has written: "Nothing is so good as it seems beforehand." Freewrite, expressing your reaction to this statement.

**Vocabulary**

Knowing the following words will help you as you read *Great Expectations.*

**consternation** (kän stər nā′ shən) *n.:* Great fear or shock that confuses or bewilders (p. 760)
**imprecations** (im′ prə kā′ shənz) *n.:* Curses (p. 764)
**vicariously** (vī ker′ ē əs lē) *adv.:* Experiencing something by imagined participation in another's experience (p. 765)

**presentiment** (pri zen′ tə mənt) *n.:* A feeling that something bad will occur (p. 765)
**disdainfully** (dis dān′ fəl lē) *adv.:* Scornfully (p. 769)
**melancholy** (mel′ ən käl′ ē) *adj.:* Sad; gloomy (p. 779)

### Objectives

1 To understand theme when reading a novel
2 To paraphrase key statements when reading a novel
3 To respond to the theme of a novel

## Support Material

**Teaching Portfolio**
Teacher Backup, p. 919
Grammar in Action Worksheets, *Using Direct Quotations,* p. 924; *Using Gerunds,* p. 926
Usage and Mechanics Worksheet, p. 928
Vocabulary Check, p. 929
Analyzing Literature Worksheet, *Understanding Point of View,* p. 930

Language Worksheet, *Appreciating Word Histories,* p. 931
Selection Test, p. 932
Art Transparency 20: *St. Pancras Hotel and Pentonville Road,* by John Arthur O'Connor
**Library of Video Classics,** *Great Expectations*

# Great Expectations

## Charles Dickens

### Chapter 1

My father's family name being Pirrip, and my Christian name Philip, my infant tongue could make of both names nothing longer or more explicit than Pip. So I called myself Pip, and came to be called Pip.

I give Pirrip as my father's family name on the authority of his tombstone and my sister—Mrs. Joe Gargery, who married the blacksmith. As I never saw my father or my mother, and never saw any likeness of either of them (for their days were long before the days of photographs), my first fancies regarding what they were like were unreasonably derived from their tombstones. The shape of the letters on my father's gave me an odd idea that he was a square, stout, dark man, with curly black hair. From the character and turn of the inscription, *"Also Georgiana Wife of the Above,"* I drew a childish conclusion that my mother was freckled and sickly. To five little stone lozenges,[1] each about a foot and a half long, which were arranged in a neat row beside their grave, and were sacred to the memory of five little brothers of mine—who gave up trying to get a living exceedingly early in that universal struggle—I am indebted for a belief I religiously entertained that they had all been born on their backs with their hands in their trousers pockets.

---

1. **lozenges** (läz′ ′nj iz) *n.*: Diamond-shaped objects.

Ours was the marsh country, down by the river, within, as the river wound, twenty miles of the sea. My first most vivid and broad impression of the identity of things seems to me to have been gained on a memorable raw afternoon towards evening. At such a time I found out for certain that this bleak place overgrown with nettles was the churchyard; and that Philip Pirrip, Late of this Parish, and Also Georgiana Wife of the Above, were dead and buried; and that Alexander, Bartholomew, Abraham, Tobias, and Roger, infant children of the aforesaid, were also dead and buried; and that the dark flat wilderness beyond the churchyard, intersected with dikes and mounds and gates, with scattered cattle feeding on it, was the marshes; and that the low leaden line beyond was the river; and that the distant savage lair from which the wind was rushing was the sea; and that the small bundle of shivers growing afraid of it all and beginning to cry was Pip.

"Hold your noise!" cried a terrible voice, as a man started up from among the graves at the side of the church porch. "Keep still, you little devil, or I'll cut your throat!"

A fearful man, all in coarse gray, with a great iron on his leg. A man with no hat, and with broken shoes, and with an old rag tied around his head. A man who had been soaked in water, and smothered in mud, and lamed by stones, and cut by flints, and stung

*Great Expectations* 757

by nettles, and torn by briars; who limped, and shivered, and glared, and growled; and whose teeth chattered in his head, as he seized me by the chin.

"Oh! Don't cut my throat, sir," I pleaded in terror. "Pray don't do it, sir."

"Tell us your name!" said the man. "Quick!"

"Pip, sir."

"Once more," said the man, staring at me. "Give it mouth!"

"Pip. Pip, sir."

"Show us where you live," said the man. "Pint out the place!"

I pointed to where our village lay, on the flat in-shore among the alder trees and pollards,[2] a mile or more from the church.

The man, after looking at me for a moment, turned me upside down, and emptied my pockets. There was nothing in them but a piece of bread. When the church came to itself—for he was so sudden and strong that he made it go head over heels before me, and I saw the steeple under my feet—when the church came to itself, I say, I was seated on a high tombstone, trembling, while he ate the bread ravenously.

"You young dog," said the man, licking his lips, "what fat cheeks you ha' got."

I believe they were fat, though I was at that time undersized, for my years, and not strong.

"Darn me if I couldn't eat 'em," said the man, with a threatening shake of his head, "and if I han't half a mind to't!"

I earnestly expressed my hope that he wouldn't, and held tighter to the tombstone on which he had put me; partly to keep myself upon it; partly to keep myself from crying.

"Now lookee here!" said the man. "Where's your mother?"

"There, sir!" said I.

He started, made a short run, and stopped and looked over his shoulder.

"There, sir!" I timidly explained. "Also Georgiana. That's my mother."

"Oh!" said he, coming back. "And is that your father alonger your mother?"

"Yes, sir," said I; "him, too; late of this parish."

"Ha!" he muttered then, considering. "Who d'ye live with—supposin' ye're kindly let to live, which I han't made up my mind about?"

"My sister, sir—Mrs. Joe Gargery—wife of Joe Gargery, the blacksmith, sir."

"Blacksmith, eh?" said he. And looked down at his leg.

After darkly looking at his leg and at me several times, he came closer to my tombstone, took me by both arms, and tilted me back as far as he could hold me.

"Now lookee here," he said, "the question being whether you're to be let to live. You know what a file is?"

"Yes, sir."

"And you know what wittles[3] is?"

"Yes, sir."

After each question he tilted me over a little more, so as to give me a greater sense of helplessness and danger.

"You get me a file." He tilted me again. "And you get me wittles." He tilted me again. "You bring 'em both to me." He tilted me again. "Or I'll have your heart and liver out." He tilted me again.

I was dreadfully frightened, and so giddy that I clung to him with both hands.

"You bring me, to-morrow morning early, that file and them wittles. You bring the lot to me at that old battery[4] over yonder. You do it, and you never dare to say a word

---

**2. pollards** (päl' ərdz) *n.*: Trees with their top branches cut back to the trunk.

**3. wittles:** Victuals (vit' 'lz), food; some characters pronounce *v* as *w*.

**4. battery** (bat' ər ē) *n.*: Mound of earth on which cannons are placed.

758   *The Novel*

or dare to make a sign concerning your having seen such a person as me, or any person sumever, and you shall be let to live. You fail, or you go from my words in any partickler, no matter how small it is, and your heart and your liver shall be tore out, roasted, and ate.

I said that I would get him the file, and I would get him what broken bits of food I could, and I would come to him at the battery, early in the morning.

"Say, Lord strike you dead if you don't!" said the man. I said so, and he took me down.

"Goo-good night sir," I faltered.

"Much of that!" said he, glancing about him over the cold wet flat. "I wish I was a frog. Or a eel!"

At the same time, he hugged his shuddering body in both his arms—clasping himself, as if to hold himself together—and limped towards the low church wall.

When he came to the low church wall, he got over it like a man whose legs were numbed and stiff, and then turned round to look for me. When I saw him turning, I set my face towards home, and made the best use of my legs.

**Chapter 2**

My sister, Mrs. Joe Gargery, was more than twenty years older than I, and had established a great reputation with herself and the neighbors because she had brought me up "by hand." Having at that time to find out for myself what the expression meant, and knowing her to have a hard and heavy hand, and to be much in the habit of laying it upon her husband as well as upon me, I supposed that Joe Gargery and I were both brought up by hand.

She was not a good-looking woman, my sister, and I had a general impression that she must have made Joe Gargery marry her by hand. Joe was a fair man, with curls of flaxen hair on each side of his smooth face, and with eyes of such a very undecided blue that they seemed to have somehow got mixed with their own whites. He was a mild, good-natured, sweet-tempered, easy-going, foolish, dear fellow—a sort of Hercules[1] in strength, and also in weakness.

My sister, Mrs. Joe, with black hair and eyes, had such a prevailing redness of skin that I sometimes used to wonder whether it was possible she washed herself with a nutmeg-grater instead of soap. She was tall and bony, and almost always wore a coarse apron, fastened over her figure behind with two loops.

Joe's forge adjoined our house, which was a wooden house, as many of the dwellings in our country were—most of them, at that time. When I ran home from the churchyard, the forge was shut up, and Joe was sitting alone in the kitchen. Joe and I being fellow-sufferers, and having confidences as such, Joe imparted a confidence to me the moment I raised the latch of the door and peeped in at him.

"Mrs. Joe has been out a dozen times, looking for you, Pip. And she's out now, making it a baker's dozen."

"Is she?"

"Yes, Pip," said Joe; "and what's worse, she's got Tickler with her."

At this dismal intelligence,[2] I twisted the only button on my waistcoat round and round, and looked in great depression at the fire. Tickler was a wax-ended piece of cane, worn smooth by collision with my tickled frame.

"She sot down," said Joe, "and she got up, and she made a grab at Tickler, and she

---

**1. Hercules** (hʉr′ kyə lēz′): A character from Greek and Roman mythology, famous for his strength.
**2. intelligence** (in tel′ ə jəns) n.: Here, it means news.

6 **Critical Thinking and Reading** What do you think Pip's sister means by this expression? Why is Pip's interpretation of the phrase ironical?

7 **Discussion** What impression of his sister does Pip convey?

8 **Discussion** Who is in charge of the Gargery household? Explain.

**9 Critical Thinking and Reading**
Why does Joe fence Pip up?

**10 Discussion** How do Mrs. Joe's mannerisms and gestures reveal her character?

ram-paged[3] out. That's what she did," said Joe, "she ram-paged out, Pip."

"Has she been gone long, Joe?" I always treated him as a larger species of child, and as no more than my equal.

"Well," said Joe, "she's been on the rampage, this last spell, about five minutes, Pip. She's a-coming! Get behind the door, old chap."

I took the advice. My sister, Mrs. Joe, throwing the door wide open, and finding an obstruction behind it, immediately divined the cause, and applied Tickler to its further investigation. She concluded by throwing me at Joe, who passed me on into the chimney and quietly fenced me up there with his great leg.

"Where have you been, you young monkey?" said Mrs. Joe, stamping her foot. "Tell me directly what you've been doing to wear me away with fret and fright and worrit, or I'd have you out of that corner if you was fifty Pips, and he was five hundred Gargerys."

"I have only been to the churchyard."

"Churchyard!" repeated my sister. "If it warn't for me, you'd have been to the churchyard long ago, and stayed there. Who brought you up by hand?"

"You did," said I.

"And why did I do it, I should like to know?"

I whimpered, "I don't know."

"*I* don't!" said my sister. "I'd never do it again! I know that. I may truly say I've never had this apron of mine off, since born you were. It's bad enough to be a blacksmith's wife (and him a Gargery) without being your mother."

My thoughts strayed from that question as I looked disconsolately at the fire. For the fugitive out on the marshes with the ironed

leg, the file, the food, and the dreadful pledge I was under to commit a larceny on those sheltering premises rose before me in the avenging coals.

"Hah!" said Mrs. Joe, restoring Tickler to his station. "Churchyard, indeed! You may well say churchyard, you two." One of us, by-the-bye, had not said it at all. "You'll drive *me* to the churchyard betwixt you, one of these days, and oh, a pr-r-recious pair you'd be without me!"

My sister had a trenchant way of cutting our bread-and-butter for us that never varied. First, with her left hand she jammed the loaf hard and fast against her bib. Then she took some butter (not too much) on a knife and spread it on the loaf, using both sides of the knife with a slapping dexterity, and trimming and molding the butter off round the crust. Then she gave the knife a final smart wipe and then sawed a very thick round off the loaf; which she finally, before separating from the loaf, hewed into two halves, of which Joe got one, and I the other.

On the present occasion, though I was hungry, I dared not eat my slice. I felt that I must have something in reserve for my dreadful acquaintance. Therefore I resolved to put my hunk of bread-and-butter down the leg of my trousers. I took advantage of a moment when Joe had just looked at me, and got my bread-and-butter down my leg.

When Joe saw that my bread-and-butter was gone, the wonder and consternation with which he stopped on the threshold of his bite and stared at me were too evident to escape my sister's observation.

"What's the matter now?" said she smartly, as she put down her cup.

"I say, you know!" muttered Joe, shaking his head at me in a very serious remonstrance. "Pip, old chap! You'll do yourself a mischief. It'll stick somewhere. You can't have chawed it, Pip."

---

**3. ram-paged:** Rampaged (ram pāj′ ′d), rushed about in wild anger.

---

## Grammar in Action

**Direct quotations** represent a person's exact speech or thoughts and are enclosed in quotation marks. Only the actual words of a person or character can be used in a direct quotation. Sentences in which quotations appear often include expressions that indicate the speaker. These expressions can introduce, conclude, or interrupt a direct quotation. Use a comma or colon after an introductory expression. Use a comma, question mark, or exclamation mark after a quotation followed by a concluding expres-

sion. If an expression interrupts a quoted sentence, use another comma after the expression.

Authors use direct quotations in order to make their characters seem real to readers. Notice how Charles Dickens uses quotations in the following conversation between Pip, his sister, and Joe Gargery:

"Lord bless the boy!" exclaimed my sister, as if she didn't quite mean that, but rather the contrary. "From the Hulks!"
"Oh-h!" said I, looking at Joe. "Hulks!"

"What's the matter *now*?" repeated my sister more sharply than before.

"If you can cough any trifle on it up, Pip, I'd recommend you to do it," said Joe, all aghast. "Manners is manners, but still your 'elth's your 'elth."

By this time, my sister was quite desperate, so she pounced on Joe, and, taking him by the two whiskers, knocked his head for a little while against the wall behind him—while I sat in the corner, looking guiltily on.

"Now, perhaps you'll mention what's the matter," said my sister, out of breath, "you staring great stuck pig."

Joe looked at her in a helpless way, then took a helpless bite, and looked at me again.

"You know, Pip," said Joe, "you and me is always friends, and I'd be the last to tell upon you, any time. But such a—such a most uncommon bolt as that!"

"Been bolting his food, has he?" cried my sister.

"You know, old chap," said Joe, "I bolted, myself, when I was your age—frequent—and as a boy I've been among a many bolters; but I never see your bolting equal yet, Pip, and it's a mercy you ain't bolted dead."

My sister made a dive at me, and fished me up by the hair: saying nothing more than the awful words, "You come along and be dosed."

Some medical beast had revived tar-water in those days as a fine medicine, and Mrs. Joe always kept a supply of it in the cupboard, having a belief in its virtues correspondent to its nastiness. A pint of this mixture was poured down my throat, for my greater comfort, while Mrs. Joe held my head under her arm.

Conscience is a dreadful thing. The guilty knowledge that I was going to rob Mrs. Joe—I never thought I was going to rob Joe, for I never thought of any of the housekeeping property as his—united to the necessity of always keeping one hand on my bread-and-butter as I sat or when I was ordered about the kitchen on any small errand, almost drove me out of my mind.

It was Christmas Eve, and I had to stir the pudding for next day with a copper-stick, from seven to eight by the Dutch clock. I tried it with the load upon my leg (and that made me think afresh of the man with the load on *his* leg), and found the tendency of exercise to bring the bread-and-butter out at my ankle quite unmanageable. Happily I slipped away, and deposited that part of my conscience in my garret bedroom.

"Hark!" said I, when I had done my stirring, and was taking a final warm in the chimney-corner before being sent up to bed; "was that great guns, Joe?"

"Ah!" said Joe. "There's another conwict off."

"What does that mean, Joe?" said I.

Mrs. Joe, who always took explanations upon herself, said snappishly, "Escaped. Escaped," administering the definition like tar-water.

"There was a conwict off last night" said Joe, aloud, "after sunset-gun. And they fired warning of him. And now it appears they're firing warning of another."

"*Who's* firing?" said I.

"Drat that boy," interposed my sister, "what a questioner he is. Ask no questions, and you'll be told no lies."

"Mrs. Joe," said I, "I should like to know—if you wouldn't much mind—where the firing comes from."

"Lord bless the boy!" exclaimed my sister, as if she didn't quite mean that, but rather the contrary. "From the Hulks!"

"Oh-h!" said I, looking at Joe. "Hulks!"

Joe gave a reproachful cough, as much as to say, "Well, I told you so."

"And please, what's Hulks?" said I.

"That's the way with this boy!" exclaimed

*Great Expectations* 761

**11 Critical Thinking and Reading** What can be inferred about Pip's moral values from his judgment of his own behavior?

**12 Reading Strategy** Ask students to predict how this new development will affect Pip.

Joe gave a reproachful cough, as much as to say, "Well, I told you so."

**Student Activity 1.** In the passage from *Great Expectations,* find an example of a quoted statement followed by a concluding expression. What punctuation mark separates the quotation from the concluding expression?

**Student Activity 2.** Write three direct quotations: one with an introductory expression, one with a concluding expression, and one with an interrupting expression.

my sister. "Answer him one question, and he'll ask you a dozen directly. Hulks are prison-ships, right 'cross th' meshes." We always used that name for marshes in our country.

"I wonder who's put into prison-ships, and why they're put there?" said I, in a general way, and with quiet desperation.

It was too much for Mrs. Joe, who immediately rose. "I tell you what, young fellow," said she, "I didn't bring you up by hand to badger people's lives out. People are put in the Hulks because they murder, and because they rob, and forge, and do all sorts of bad; and they always begin by asking questions. Now you get along to bed!"

I was never allowed a candle to light me to bed, and, as I went upstairs in the dark, I felt fearfully sensible of the great convenience that the Hulks were handy for me. I was clearly on my way there. I had begun by asking questions, and I was going to rob Mrs. Joe.

If I slept at all that night, it was only to imagine myself drifting down the river on a strong spring-tide, to the Hulks. As soon as the great black velvet pall outside my little window was shot with gray, I got up and went downstairs; every board upon the way, and every crack in every board, calling after me, "Stop thief!" and "Get up, Mrs. Joe!" I stole some bread, some rind of cheese, about half a jar of mincemeat, some brandy from a stone bottle (diluting the stone bottle from a jug in the kitchen cupboard), a meat bone with very little on it, and a beautiful round compact pork-pie.

There was a door in the kitchen communicating with the forge; I unlocked and unbolted that door, and got a file from among Joe's tools. Then I put the fastenings as I had found them, opened the door at which I had entered when I ran home last night, shut it, and ran for the misty marshes.

### Chapter 3

It was a rimy morning, and very damp. On every rail and gate, wet lay clammy, and the marsh-mist was so thick that the wooden finger on the post directing people to our village—a direction which they never accepted, for they never came there—was invisible to me until I was quite close under it. However fast I went, I couldn't warm my feet, to which the damp cold seemed riveted, as the iron was riveted to the leg of the man I was running to meet. I had just crossed a ditch which I knew to be very near the battery, and had just scrambled up the mound beyond the ditch, when I saw the man sitting before me. His back was towards me, and he had his arms folded, and was nodding forward, heavy with sleep. I went forward softly and touched him on the shoulder. He instantly jumped up, and it was not the same man, but another man!

And yet this man was dressed in coarse gray, too, and had a great iron on his leg, and was lame, and hoarse, and cold, and was everything that the other man was; except that he had not the same face, and had a flat, broad-brimmed, low-crowned felt hat on. All this I saw in a moment, for I had only a moment to see it in: he swore an oath at me, made a hit at me—it was a round, weak blow that missed me and almost knocked himself down, for it made him stumble—and then he ran into the mist, stumbling twice as he went, and I lost him.

I was soon at the battery, after that, and there was the right man waiting for me. He was obviously cold, and his eyes looked awfully hungry. He did not turn me upside down, this time, to get at what I had, but left me right side upwards while I opened the bundle and emptied my pockets.

"What's in the bottle, boy?" said he.

"Brandy," said I.

13

**THE STONE-BREAKER (1857–58)**
*Henry Wallis*
*Birmingham Museums and Art Gallery*

**Humanities Note**

Fine Art, *The Stone Breaker*, 1857-1858, by Henry Wallis. Henry Wallis (1830-1916) was a British painter and a member of the Pre-Raphaelite brotherhood—a group of artists who sought a return to the realism and honesty of the Italian painters before Raphael (1483-1520). As you discuss this painting, you might want to point out to students that it is Wallis's most famous work. Also, it demonstrates the Pre-Raphaelites' fondness for paintings that tell a story.

Consider asking students the following questions:
1. Do the sharp details increase your interest in this scene? Explain.
2. Explain what is happening in this picture.
3. What story does the picture suggest?

He was already handing mincemeat down his throat in the most curious manner—more like a man who was putting it away somewhere in a violent hurry, than a man who was eating it—but he left off to take some of the liquor. He shivered all the while so violently that it was quite as much as he could do to keep the neck of the bottle between his teeth, without biting it off.

"I think you have got the ague,[1]" said I.

"I'm much of your opinion, boy," said he.

---

1. **ague** (ā′ gyo͞o) *n.*: Chills and fever.

"It's bad about here," I told him. "You've been lying out on the meshes."

"I'll eat my breakfast afore they're the death of me," said he. "I'd do that if I was going to be strung up to that there gallows as there is over there, directly arterwards. I'll beat the shivers so far, *I'll* bet you."

He was gobbling mincemeat, meatbone, bread, cheese, and pork pie all at once, staring distrustfully while he did so at the mist all round us, and often stopping—even stopping his jaws—to listen. Some real or fancied sound, some clink upon the river or breath-

*Great Expectations* 763

14 **Discussion** What qualities does Pip reveal in this exchange?

15 **Critical Thinking and Reading** What can you infer from this convict's eager interest in the other one?

ing of beast upon the marsh, now gave him a start, and he said suddenly:

"You're not a deceiving imp? You brought no one with you?"

"No, sir! No!"

"Nor giv' no one the office to follow you?"

"No!"

"Well," said he, "I believe you. You'd be but a fierce young hound indeed, if at your time of life you could help to hunt a wretched warmint,[2] hunted as near death and dunghill as this poor wretched warmint is!"

Something clicked in his throat as if he had works in him like a clock, and was going to strike. And he smeared his ragged rough sleeve over his eyes.

Pitying his desolation, and watching him as he gradually settled down upon the pie, I made bold to say, "I am glad you enjoy it."

"Did you speak?"

"I said, I was glad you enjoyed it."

"Thankee, my boy. I do."

"I am afraid you won't leave any of it for him," said I timidly.

"Leave any for him? Who's him?" said my friend, stopping in his crunching of pie-crust.

"The young man," said I, pointing; "over there, where I found him nodding asleep, and thought it was you."

He held me by the collar and stared at me so that I began to think his first idea about cutting my throat had revived.

"Dressed like you, you know, only with a hat," I explained, trembling; "and—and"—I was very anxious to put this delicately—"and with—the same reason for wanting to borrow a file. Didn't you hear the cannon last night?"

"Then, there *was* firing!" he said to himself.

---

**2. warmint:** Varmint (vär′ mənt), an undesirable or troublesome person.

"This man"—he had said all the rest as if he had forgotten my being there—"did you notice anything in him?"

"He had a badly bruised face," said I, recalling what I hardly knew I knew.

"Not here?" exclaimed the man, striking his left cheek mercilessly with the flat of his hand.

"Yes, there!"

"Where is he?" He crammed what little food was left into the breast of his gray jacket. "Show me the way he went. I'll pull him down, like a bloodhound. Curse this iron on my sore leg! Give us hold of the file, boy."

I indicated in what direction the mist had shrouded the other man, and he looked up at it for an instant. But he was down on the rank wet grass, filing at his iron like a madman, and not minding me or minding his own leg, which had an old chafe upon it, and was bloody, but which he handled as roughly as if it had no more feeling in it than the file. I was very much afraid of him again, now that he had worked himself into this fierce hurry, and I was likewise very much afraid of keeping away from home any longer. I told him I must go, but he took no notice, so I thought the best thing I could do was to slip off. The last I saw of him, his head was bent over his knee and he was working hard at his fetter, muttering impatient imprecations at it and his leg. The last I heard of him, I stopped in the mist to listen, and the file was still going.

## Chapter 4

I fully expected to find a constable in the kitchen, waiting to take me up. But not only was there no constable there, but no discovery had yet been made of the robbery.

"And where the deuce ha' *you* been?" was Mrs. Joe's Christmas salutation, when I and my conscience showed ourselves.

## Commentary: More About Charles Dickens

Charles John Huffam Dickens was born in Portsea, Portsmouth on February 7, 1812. Dickens was a sickly child, but when his father, who was a clerk in the Navy Pay Office was transferred in 1817 to the government dockyard at Chatham, Dickens was able to enjoy a happy and carefree childhood that allowed him to grow strong and healthy. In 1822 his father was again transferred, this time to London, where Dickens was to spend the next thirty-eight years. In 1860 he moved near Chatham, where he died.

At twelve, Dickens's father was imprisoned. As the oldest child, Dickens was pulled out of school to support his family. He worked in a blacking warehouse at which he worked twelve hours a day and earned six shillings a week. Both his father's imprisonment and his experience in the factory affected Dickens deeply. His experience in the factory, however, provided him with knowledge about and experience with the lower class.

When Dickens was seventeen he worked as a court stenographer. His experience in this job aroused his contempt for law and the parliament. It, however, eventually led to and heightened his affection for journalism. From 1834 to 1836, Dickens worked as a reporter for the *Morning Chronicle*. Under the pen name

I said I had been down to hear the carols. "Ah! well!" observed Mrs. Joe. "You might ha' done worse."

We were to have a superb dinner, consisting of a leg of pickled pork and greens, and a pair of roast stuffed fowls. A handsome mince pie had been made yesterday morning (which accounted for the mincemeat not being missed), and the pudding was already on the boil.

My sister having so much to do, was going to church vicariously; that is to say, Joe and I were going. In his working clothes, Joe was a well-knit characteristic-looking blacksmith; in his holiday clothes, he was more like a scarecrow in good circumstances than anything else. Nothing that he wore then fitted him or seemed to belong to him. I was always treated as if I had insisted on being born in opposition to the dictates of reason, religion, and morality, and against the dissuading arguments of my best friends. Even when I was taken to have a new suit of clothes, the tailor had orders to make them like a kind of reformatory, and on no account to let me have the free use of my limbs.

Mr. Wopsle, the clerk[1] at church, was to dine with us; and Mr. Hubble, the wheelwright,[2] and Mrs. Hubble; and Uncle Pumblechook (Joe's uncle, but Mrs. Joe appropriated him), who was a well-to-do corn chandler[3] in the nearest town, and drove his own chaise-cart.[4] The dinner hour was half-past one. When Joe and I got home, we found the table laid, and Mrs. Joe dressed, and the dinner dressing, and the front door unlocked (it never was at any other time) for the company to enter by, and everything most splendid. And still, not a word of the robbery.

The time came, without bringing with it any relief to my feelings, and the company came. I opened the door—making believe that it was a habit of ours to open that door—and I opened it first to Mr. Wopsle, next to Mr. and Mrs. Hubble, and last of all to Uncle Pumblechook. N.B.[5] *I* was not allowed to call him uncle, under the severest penalties.

"Mrs. Joe," said Uncle Pumblechook—a large hard-breathing middle-aged slow man, with a mouth like a fish, dull staring eyes, and sandy hair standing upright on his head, so that he looked as if he had just been all but choked, and had that moment come to—"I have brought you as the compliments of the season—I have brought you, mum, a bottle of sherry wine—and I have brought you, mum, a bottle of port wine."

We dined on these occasions in the kitchen, and adjourned, for the nuts and oranges and apples, to the parlor. My sister was uncommonly lively on the present occasion, and indeed was generally more gracious in the society of Mrs. Hubble than in other company. When we sat down to dinner, Mr. Wopsle said grace with theatrical declamation and ended with the very proper aspiration that we might be truly grateful. Upon which my sister fixed me with her eye, and said, in a low reproachful voice, "Do you hear that? Be grateful."

"Especially," said Mr. Pumblechook, "be grateful, boy, of them which brought you up by hand."

Mrs. Hubble shook her head, and contemplating me with a mournful presentiment that I should come to no good, asked,

---

**1. clerk** (klʉrk) *n*.: Official who has minor duties in a church.
**2. wheelwright** (hwēl' rīt') *n*.: Person who makes and repairs wheels and wheeled vehicles.
**3. corn chandler** (chan' dlər): Corn merchant.
**4. chaise-cart** (shāz' kärt') *n*.: Lightweight carriage drawn by one or two horses.

---

**5. N.B.:** *Nota bene*, Latin for "note well."

16

16 **Discussion** Does Dickens give you a favorable or unfavorable impression of Uncle Pumblechook? Explain.

---

Boz, Dickens wrote brief descriptions of life in London. His sketches began appearing in periodicals, and by 1836 *Sketches by Boz* was a great success.

Dickens became the most popular English novelist in his day. He wrote his novels rapidly and sometimes worked on more than one book. He usually rushed his completed installment to his publishers just in the nick of time on the due date.

In Europe and the United States, Dickens's characters have become household names. References to such characters as Mr. Pickwick (*Pickwick Papers*), Uriah Heep (*David Copperfield*), Mrs. Havisham, and Ebenezer Scrooge (*A Christmas Carol*) are heard even today. Despite his colorful and memorable characters, much of Dickens's success was from his ability to bring to life the sights, sounds, and smells of London and the customs of his day.

17 **Enrichment** Speech characteristics—choice of wording, grammar, pronunciation, intonation, and so forth—reflect social and regional differences. Dickens had a keen ear for speech patterns, which he imitated with great skill. If students "listen" as they read, they may be able to tell much about characters from the way they speak.

18 **Discussion** How does Dickens heighten the suspense and tension?

17 "Why is it that the young are never grateful?" This moral mystery seemed too much for the company until Mr. Hubble tersely solved it by saying, "Naterally wicious." Everybody then murmured "True!" and looked at me in a particularly unpleasant and personal manner.

Joe's station and influence were something feebler (if possible) when there was company than when there was none. But he always aided and comforted me when he could, in some way of his own, and he always did so at dinner-time by giving me gravy, if there were any. There being plenty of gravy to-day, Joe spooned into my plate, at this point, about half a pint.

The guests continued discussing how ungrateful I was and how much trouble I had been to my sister as they finished the main course. Then my sister offered some brandy to Uncle Pumblechook, and I was sure my time had come. He would find it was weak, he would say it was weak, and I was lost! I held tight to the leg of the table under the cloth, with both hands, and awaited my fate.

My sister went for the stone bottle, came back with the stone bottle, and poured his brandy out; no one else taking any. The wretched man trifled with his glass—took it up, looked at it through the light, put it down—prolonged my misery. All this time Mrs. Joe and Joe were briskly clearing the table for the pie and pudding.

I watched the miserable creature finger his glass playfully, take it up, smile, throw his head back, and drink the brandy off. Instantly afterwards, the company were seized with unspeakable consternation, owing to his springing to his feet, turning round several times in an appalling spasmodic whooping-cough dance, and rushing out at the door; he then became visible through the window, violently plunging and expectorat-ing,[6] making the most hideous faces and apparently out of his mind.

I held on tight, while Mrs. Joe and Joe ran to him. I didn't know how I had done it, but I had no doubt I had murdered him somehow. In my dreadful situation, it was a relief when he was brought back, and, surveying the company all round as if *they* had disagreed with him, sank down into his chair with the one significant gasp, "Tar!"

I had filled up the bottle from the tar-water jug. I knew he would be worse by-and-by.

"Tar!" cried my sister, in amazement. "Why, how ever could tar come there?"

But Uncle Pumblechook, who was omnipotent in that kitchen, wouldn't hear the word, wouldn't hear of the subject, imperiously waved it all away with his hand, and asked for hot gin-and-water. My sister, who had begun to be alarmingly meditative, had to employ herself actively in getting the gin, the hot water, the sugar, and the lemon-peel, and mixing them. For the time at least, I was saved.

All partook of pudding. The course terminated, and Mr. Pumblechook had begun to beam under the genial influence of gin-and-water. I began to think I should get over the day, when my sister said to Joe, "Clean plates—cold."

I clutched the leg of the table again immediately, and pressed it to my bosom as if it had been the companion of my youth and friend of my soul. I foresaw what was coming, and I felt that this time I really was gone. 18

"You must taste," said my sister, addressing the guests with her best grace, "You must taste, to finish with, such a delightful and delicious present of Uncle Pumblechook's!"

---

**6. expectorating** (ik spek′ tə rāt′ iŋ) *v.*: Spitting.

Must they! Let them not hope to taste it!

"You must know," said my sister, rising, "it's a pie—a savory pork pie."

My sister went out to get it. I heard her steps proceed to the pantry. I heard Joe say, "You shall have some, Pip." I have never been absolutely certain whether I uttered a shrill yell of terror, merely in spirit, or in the bodily hearing of the company. I felt that I could bear no more, and that I must run away. I released the leg of the table, and ran for my life.

But I ran no further than the house door, for there I ran head foremost into a party of soldiers with their muskets; one of whom held out a pair of handcuffs to me, saying, "Here you are, look sharp, come on!"

## Chapter 5

The apparition of a file of soldiers ringing down the butt-ends of their loaded muskets on our doorstep caused the dinner party to rise from the table in confusion, and caused Mrs. Joe, reentering the kitchen empty-handed, to stop short and stare, in her wondering lament of "Gracious goodness me, what's gone—with the—pie!"

"Excuse me, ladies and gentlemen," said the sergeant, "but as I have mentioned at the door to this smart young shaver"—which he hadn't—"I am on a chase in the name of the King, and I want the blacksmith."

"You see, blacksmith," continued the sergeant, who had by this time picked out Joe with his eye, "we have had an accident with these, and I find the lock of one of 'em goes wrong, and the coupling don't act pretty. As they are wanted for immediate service, will you throw your eye over them?"

Joe threw his eye over them, and pronounced that the job would necessitate the lighting of his forge fire, and would take nearer two hours than one. "Will it? Then will you set about it at once, blacksmith?" said the off-hand sergeant, "as it's on his Majesty's service. And if my men can bear a hand anywhere, they'll make themselves useful." With that he called to his men, who came trooping into the kitchen one after another, and piled their arms in a corner.

I was in an agony of apprehension. But, beginning to perceive that the handcuffs were not for me, and that the military had so far got the better of the pie as to put it in the background, I collected a little more of my scattered wits.

"How far might you call yourselves from the marshes, hereabouts?" asked the sergeant, reflecting. "Not above a mile, I reckon?"

"Just a mile," said Mrs. Joe.

"That'll do. We begin to close in upon 'em about dusk. A little before dusk, my orders are. That'll do."

"Convicts, sergeant?" asked Mr. Wopsle.

"Aye!" returned the sergeant, "two. They're pretty well known to be out on the marshes still, and they won't try to get clear of 'em before dusk. Anybody here seen anything of any such game?"

Everybody, myself excepted, said no, with confidence. Nobody thought of me.

"Well," said the sergeant, "they'll find themselves trapped in a circle, I expect, sooner than they count on. Now, blacksmith! If you're ready, his Majesty the King is."

Joe had got his coat and waistcoat and cravat[1] off, and his leather apron on, and passed into the forge. One of the soldiers opened its wooden windows, another lighted the fire, another turned to at the bellows, the rest stood round the blaze, which was soon roaring. Then Joe began to hammer and clink, hammer and clink, and we all looked on.

---

**1. cravat** (krə vat') *n.*: Necktie.

*Great Expectations* 767

19 **Enrichment** This story, like others Dickens wrote, appeared first as a serial in a monthly magazine. As is common with serial stories, each installment ended at a particularly suspenseful moment in order to hold the reader's interest until the next installment. The first installment of the story ended here. Tell students that critics disagree about the effectiveness of this device—some consider it melodramatic. Then ask students to express their opinions of this technique.

20 **Critical Thinking and Reading** Why did Pip assume that the handcuffs were for him?

When Joe's job was done, the ringing and roaring stopped. As Joe got on his coat, he mustered courage to propose that some of us should go down with the soldiers and see what came of the hunt. Mr. Pumblechook and Mr. Hubble declined, on the plea of a pipe and ladies' society; but Mr. Wopsle said he would go, if Joe would. Joe said he was agreeable, and would take me.

The sergeant took a polite leave of the ladies, and parted from Mr. Pumblechook as from a comrade.

His men resumed their muskets and fell in. Mr. Wopsle, Joe, and I received strict charge to keep in the rear, and to speak no word after we reached the marshes. When we were all out in the raw air and were steadily **21** moving towards our business, I treasonably whispered to Joe, "I hope, Joe, we sha'n't find them." And Joe whispered to me, "I'd give a shilling if they had cut and run, Pip."

We struck out on the open marshes, through the gate at the side of the churchyard. A bitter sleet came rattling against us here on the east wind, and Joe took me on his back.

Now that we were out upon the dismal wilderness where they little thought I had been within eight or nine hours, and had seen both men hiding, I considered for the first time, with great dread, if we should come upon them, would my particular convict suppose that it was I who had brought the soldiers there? He had asked me if I was a deceiving imp, and he said I should be a fierce young hound if I joined the hunt against him. Would he believe that I was both imp and hound in treacherous earnest, and had betrayed him?

With my heart thumping like a blacksmith at Joe's broad shoulder, I looked all about for any sign of the convicts. I could see none, I could hear none. The soldiers were moving on in the direction of the old battery, and we were moving on a little way behind

them, when, all of a sudden, we all stopped. For, there had reached us, on the wings of the wind and rain, a long shout. It was repeated. It was at a distance towards the east, but it was long and loud.

The sergeant, a decisive man, ordered that the sound should not be answered, but that the course should be changed, and that his men should make towards it "at the double." So we started to the right (where the east was), and Joe pounded away so wonderfully that I had to hold on tight to keep my seat.

It was a run indeed now, and what Joe called, in the only two words he spoke all the time, "a winder." Down banks and up banks, and over gates, and splashing into dikes, and breaking among coarse rushes: no man cared where he went. As we came nearer to the shouting, it became more and more apparent that it was made by more than one voice. After a while, we had so run it down that we could hear one voice calling "Murder!" and another voice, "Convicts! Runaways! Guard! This way for the runaway convicts!" Then both voices would seem to be stifled in a struggle, and then would break out again. And when it had come to this, the soldiers ran like deer, and Joe too.

The sergeant ran in first, when we had run the noise quite down, and two of his men ran in close upon him. Their pieces[2] were cocked and leveled when we all ran in.

"Here are both men!" panted the sergeant, struggling at the bottom of a ditch. "Surrender, you two! And confound you for two wild beasts! Come asunder!"

Water was splashing, and mud was flying, and oaths were being sworn, and blows were being struck, when some more men went down into the ditch to help the sergeant; and dragged out, separately, my convict and the other one. Both were bleeding

---

**2. pieces** *n.*: Rifles.

## Grammar in Action

A **gerund** is a verb form that ends in *ing* and is used as a noun:

When Joe's job was done, the *ringing* and *roaring* stopped.

Use of gerunds allows writers to vary sentence style within a work of literature.

These forms of the verb can be used anywhere that nouns are. Notice that in this sentence from the novel, the two gerunds act as the compound subject of the verb *stopped*.

Don't confuse gerunds with other verb forms that end in *ing*.

**Participle:** He asked me if I was a *deceiving* imp, and he said I would be a fierce young hound if I joined the hunt against him.

**Verb phrase:** The soldiers were *moving* on in the direction of the old battery, and we were *moving* on a little way behind them.

**Gerund:** As we came nearer to the *shouting,* it became more and more apparent that it was made by more than one voice.

In the first sentence the *deceiving* acts as an adjective modifying *imp;* it is a participle, not a gerund. In the second sentence, *moving* is part of a verb phrase. In the last sentence, and panting and execrating and struggling; but of course I knew them both directly.

"Mind!" said my convict, wiping blood from his face with his ragged sleeves, and shaking torn hair from his fingers; "I took him! I give him up to you! Mind that!"

"It's not much to be particular about," said the sergeant; "it'll do you small good, my man, being in the same plight yourself. Handcuffs there!"

"I don't expect it to do me any good. I don't want it to do me more good than it does now," said my convict, with a greedy laugh. "I took him. He knows it. That's enough for me."

The other convict was livid to look at, and, in addition to the old bruised left side of his face, seemed to be bruised and torn all over. He could not so much as get his breath to speak until they were both separately handcuffed, but leaned upon a soldier to keep himself from falling.

"Take notice, guard—he tried to murder me," were his first words.

"Tried to murder him?" said my convict disdainfully. "Try, and not do it? I took him, and giv' him up; that's what I done. I not only prevented him getting off the marshes, but I dragged him here—dragged him this far on his way back. He's a gentleman, if you please, this villain. Now, the Hulks has got its gentleman again, through me. Murder him? Worth my while, too, to murder him, when I could do worse and drag him back!"

The other one still gasped, "He tried—he tried—to—murder me. Bear—bear witness."

"Lookee here!" said my convict to the sergeant. "Single-handed I got clear of the prison-ship; I made a dash and I done it. I could ha' got clear of these death-cold flats likewise—look at my leg: you won't find much iron on it—if I hadn't made discovery that *he* was here. Let *him* go free? Let *him* profit by the means as I found out? Let *him* make a tool of me afresh and again? Once

more? No, no, no. If I had died at the bottom there"—and he made an emphatic swing at the ditch with his manacled hands—"I'd have held to him with that grip, that you should have been safe to find him in my hold."

The other fugitive, who was evidently in extreme horror of his companion, repeated, "He tried to murder me. I should have been a dead man if you had not come up."

"He lies!" said my convict, with fierce energy. "He's a liar born, and he'll die a liar. Look at his face; ain't it written there? Let him turn those eyes of his on me. I defy him to do it."

The other, with an effort at a scornful smile, looked at the soldiers, and looked about at the marshes and at the sky, but certainly did not look at the speaker.

"Do you see him?" pursued my convict. "Do you see what a villain he is? Do you see those groveling and wandering eyes? That's how he looked when we were tried together. He never looked at me."

The other, always working and working his dry lips and turning his eyes restlessly about him far and near, did at last turn them for a moment on the speaker, with the words, "You are not much to look at," and with a half-taunting glance at the bound hands. At that point, my convict became so frantically exasperated that he would have rushed upon him but for the interposition of the soldiers. "Didn't I tell you," said the other convict then, "that he would murder me, if he could?"

"Enough of this parley," said the sergeant. "Light those torches."

As one of the soldiers, who carried a basket in lieu[3] of a gun, went down on his knee to open it, my convict looked round him for the first time, and saw me. I had alighted from Joe's back on the brink of the ditch

_____
**3. in lieu** (loō): Instead.

*Great Expectations* 769

**22 Critical Thinking and Reading** What can you infer from the behavior of the first convict toward the second one?

**23 Reading Strategy** Have students summarize the events in the story of the escape and capture of the convicts.

**24 Critical Thinking and Reading** Why do you think the first convict is so set on vengeance that he forfeits his own freedom in order to see the second convict returned to prison?

*shouting* acts as the object of a preposition. In this sentence, *shouting* is a gerund.

**Student Activity 1.** Find and copy three more examples of Dickens's use of gerunds. Share and discuss these with a partner.

**Student Activity 2.** Write five sentences containing gerunds. Discuss these with a group of classmates, noting the part of speech that the gerund functions as in each sentence.

when we came up, and had not moved since. I looked at him eagerly when he looked at me, and slightly moved my hands and shook my head. He gave me a look that I did not understand, and it all passed in a moment. But if he had looked at me for an hour or for a day, I could not have remembered his face ever afterwards as having been more attentive.

The soldier with the basket soon got a light, and lighted three or four torches. Before we departed from that spot, four soldiers standing in a ring fired twice into the air. Presently we saw other torches kindled at some distance behind us, and others on the marshes on the opposite bank of the river. "All right," said the sergeant. "March."

We had not gone far when three cannon were fired ahead of us with a sound that seemed to burst something inside my ear. "You are expected on board," said the sergeant to my convict; "they know you are coming. Don't straggle, my man. Close up here."

The two were kept apart, and each walked surrounded by a separate guard. I had hold of Joe's hand now, and Joe carried one of the torches. Mr. Wopsle had been for going back, but Joe was resolved to see it out, so we went on with the party. When I looked round, I could see the other lights coming in after us. Our lights warmed the air about us with their pitchy blaze, and the two prisoners seemed rather to like that, as they limped along in the midst of the muskets. We could not go fast because of their lameness; and they were so spent that two or three times we had to halt while they rested.

After an hour or so of this traveling, we came to a rough wooden hut and a landing place. There was a guard in the hut, and they challenged, and the sergeant answered. Then, we went into the hut. The sergeant made some kind of report, and some entry in a book, and then the convict whom I call the other convict was drafted off with his guard, to go on board first.

My convict never looked at me, except that once. While we stood in the hut, he turned to the sergeant, and remarked:

"I wish to say something respecting this escape. It may prevent some persons laying under suspicion alonger me."

"You can say what you like," returned the sergeant, "but you have no call to say it here. You'll have opportunity enough to say about it, and hear about it, before it's done with, you know."

"I know, but this is another pint, a separate matter. A man can't starve; at least *I* can't. I took some wittles, up at the willage over yonder."

"You mean stole," said the sergeant.

"And I'll tell you where from. From the blacksmith's."

"Halloa!" said the sergeant, staring at Joe.

"Halloa, Pip!" said Joe, staring at me.

"It was some broken wittles—that's what it was—and a dram of liquor, and a pie."

"Have you happened to miss such an article as a pie, blacksmith?" asked the sergeant confidentially.

"My wife did, at the very moment when you came in. Don't you know, Pip?"

"So," said my convict, turning his eyes on Joe in a moody manner, and without the least glance at me; "so you're the blacksmith, are you? Then I'm sorry to say I've eat your pie."

"God knows you're welcome to it—so far as it was ever mine," returned Joe, with a saving remembrance of Mrs. Joe. "We don't know what you have done, but we wouldn't have you starved to death for it, poor miserable fellow-creatur. Would us, Pip?"

The something that I had noticed before clicked in the man's throat again, and he turned his back. The boat had returned, and his guard were ready, so we followed him to

770   *The Novel*

the landing-place made of rough stakes and stones, and saw him put into the boat, which was rowed by a crew of convicts like himself. No one seemed surprised to see him, or interested in seeing him, or glad to see him, or sorry to see him, or spoke a word, except that somebody in the boat growled as if to dogs, "Give way, you!" which was the signal for the dip of the oars. By the light of the torches, we saw the black Hulk lying out a little way from the mud of the shore, like a wicked Noah's ark. We saw the boat go alongside, and we saw him taken up the side and disappear. Then, the ends of the torches were flung hissing into the water, and went out, as if it were all over with him.

## Chapter 6

I do not recall that I felt any tenderness of conscience in reference to Mrs. Joe, when the fear of being found out was lifted off me. But I loved Joe—perhaps for no better reason in those early days than because the dear fellow let me love him—and as to him my inner self was not so easily composed. It was much upon my mind (particularly when I first saw him looking about for his file) that I ought to tell Joe the whole truth. Yet I did not. The fear of losing Joe's confidence, and of thenceforth sitting in the chimney-corner at night staring drearily at my for ever lost companion and friend, tied up my tongue. I was too cowardly to do what I knew to be right, as I had been too cowardly to avoid doing what I knew to be wrong.

By that time, I was staggering on the kitchen floor, through having been newly set upon my feet, and through having been fast asleep, and through waking in the heat and lights and noise of tongues. As I came to myself I found Joe telling them about the convict's confession, and all the visitors sug-gesting different ways by which he had got into the pantry.

This was all I heard that night before my sister clutched me, as a slumberous offense to the company's eyesight, and assisted me up to bed with such a strong hand that I seemed to have fifty boots on, and to be dangling them all against the edges of the stairs.

## Chapter 7

When I was old enough, I was to be apprenticed to Joe, and until I could assume that dignity I was not to be what Mrs. Joe called "pompeyed," or (as I render it) pampered. Therefore, I was not only odd-boy about the forge, but if any neighbor happened to want an extra boy to frighten birds, or pick up stones, or do any such job, I was favored with the employment. In order, however, that our superior position might not be compromised thereby, a money-box was kept on the kitchen mantel shelf, into which it was publicly made known that all my earnings were dropped. I have an impression that they were to be contributed eventually towards the liquidation of the national debt, but I know I had no hope of any personal participation in the treasure.

Mr. Wopsle's great-aunt kept an evening school in the village. She rented a small cottage, and Mr. Wopsle had the room upstairs, where we students used to overhear him reading aloud in a most dignified and terrific manner, and occasionally bumping on the ceiling. There was a fiction that Mr. Wopsle "examined" the scholars once a quarter. What he did on those occasions was to turn up his cuffs, stick up his hair, and give us Mark Antony's oration over the body of Caesar.[1]

---

**1. give us . . . Caesar:** Recite a famous speech from Shakespeare's play *Julius Caesar*.

26 **Discussion** Why is this image effective?

27 **Literary Focus** Explain how this passage might reflect an adult's point of view as well as a child's.

28 **Discussion** How does this comment reveal the nature of Pip's relationship with his sister?

**29 Enrichment** Dickens often wrote about inadequate schools and incompetent or cruel teachers. He describes such schools, for example, in *Nicholas Nickleby*, *David Copperfield*, and *Hard Times*.

**30 Discussion** What do these details reveal about Biddy?

**31 Discussion** What does Pip mean by this statement?

**29** Mr. Wopsle's great-aunt, besides keeping this educational institution, kept in the same room—a little general shop. She had no idea what stock she had, or what the price of anything in it was; but here was a little greasy memorandum book kept in a drawer which served as a catalogue of prices, and by this oracle[2] Biddy arranged all the shop transactions. Biddy was Mr. Wopsle's great-aunt's granddaughter; I confess myself quite unequal to the working out of the problem, what relation she was to Mr. Wopsle. She was an orphan like myself; like me, too, had been brought up by hand. She was **30** most noticeable, I thought, in respect of her extremities; for her hair always wanted brushing, her hands always wanted washing, and her shoes always wanted mending and pulling up at heel.

Much of my unassisted self, and more by the help of Biddy than of Mr. Wopsle's great-aunt, I struggled through the alphabet as if it had been a bramble bush, getting considerably worried and scratched by every letter. After that, I fell among those thieves, the **31** nine figures, who seemed every evening to do something new to disguise themselves and baffle recognition. But, at last I began, in a purblind groping way, to read, write, and cipher[3] on the very smallest scale.

One night, I was sitting in the chimney corner with my slate, expending great efforts on the production of a letter to Joe. I think it must have been a full year after our hunt upon the marshes, for it was a long time after, and it was winter and a hard frost. With an alphabet on the hearth at my feet for reference, I contrived in an hour or two to print and smear this epistle:

"MI DEER JO i OPE U R KRWITE WELL i OPE i SHAL SON B HABELL 4 2 TEEDGE U JO AN THEN WE SHORL B SO GLODD AN WEN i M PRENGTD 2 U JO WOT LARX AN BLEVE ME INF XN PIP."

There was no indispensable necessity for my communicating with Joe by letter, inasmuch as he sat beside me and we were alone. But I delivered this written communication (slate and all) with my own hand, and Joe received it as a miracle of erudition.

"I say, Pip, old chap!" cried Joe, opening his blue eyes wide, "what a scholar you are! Ain't you?"

"I should like to be," said I, glancing at the slate as he held it—with a misgiving that the writing was rather hilly.

"Why, here's a J," said Joe, "and a O equal to anythink! Here's a J and a O, Pip, and a J-O, Joe."

I had never heard Joe read aloud to any greater extent than this monosyllable, and I had observed at church last Sunday, when I accidentally held our prayer book upside down, that it seemed to suit his convenience quite as well as if it had been all right. Wishing to embrace the present occasion of finding out whether, in teaching Joe, I should have to begin quite at the beginning, I said, "Ah! But read the rest, Joe."

"The rest, eh, Pip?" said Joe, looking at it with a slowly searching eye, "One, two, three. Why, here's three Js, and three Os, and three J-O, Joes, in it, Pip!"

I leaned over Joe, and, with the aid of my forefinger, read him the whole letter.

"Astonishing!" said Joe, when I had finished. "You ARE a scholar."

"How do you spell Gargery, Joe?" I asked him, with a modest patronage.[4]

"I don't spell it at all," said Joe.

"But supposing you did?"

"It *can't* be supposed," said Joe. "Tho' I'm oncommon fond of reading, too."

"Are you, Joe?"

---

**2. oracle** (ôr′ ə k'l) *n.*: Source of wisdom.
**3. cipher** (sī′ fər) *v.*: Do arithmetic.

**4. patronage** (pā′ trən ij) *n.*: Encouragement shown to someone inferior.

772 *The Novel*

**RUSTIC GIRL SEATED**
*John Constable*
Victoria and Albert Museum
Trustees, London

"Oncommon. Give me," said Joe, "a good book, or a good newspaper, and sit me down afore a good fire, and I ask no better. Lord!" he continued, after rubbing his knees a little "when you *do* come to a J and a O, and says you, 'Here, at last, is a J-O, Joe,' how interesting reading is!"

I derived from this last that Joe's education, like steam, was yet in its infancy. Pursuing the subject, I inquired:

32

*Great Expectations* 773

33 **Reading Strategy** Have students summarize the story that Joe tells Pip.

34 **Critical Thinking and Reading** Why do you think Joe has a high opinion of his wife despite her faults?

"Didn't you ever go to school, Joe, when you were as little as me?"

"No, Pip."

"Why didn't you ever go to school, Joe, when you were as little as me?"

"Well, Pip," said Joe, taking up the poker, and settling himself to his usual occupation when he was thoughtful, of slowly raking the fire between the lower bars, "I'll tell you. My father, Pip, he were given to drink, and when he were overtook with drink, he hammered away at my mother most onmerciful. It were a'most the only hammering he did, indeed, 'xcepting at myself. And he hammered at me with a wigor only to be equaled by the wigor with which he didn't hammer at his anwil. You're a-listening and understanding, Pip?"

"Yes, Joe."

" 'Consequence, my mother and me we ran away from my father several times; and then my mother she'd go out to work, and she'd say, 'Joe,' she'd say, 'now, please God, you shall have some schooling, child,' and she'd put me to school. But my father were that good in his hart that he couldn't a-bear to be without us. So, he'd come with a most tremenjous crowd and make such a row at the doors of the houses where we was that they used to be obligated to have no more to do with us and to give us up to him. And then he took us home and hammered us. Which, you see, Pip," said Joe, pausing in his meditative raking of the fire, and looking at me, "were a drawback on my learning."

"Certainly, poor Joe!"

"Though mind you, Pip," said Joe, with a judicial touch or two of the poker on the top bar, "rendering unto all their doo, and maintaining equal justice betwixt man and man, my father were that good in his hart, don't you see?"

I didn't see, but I didn't say so.

"Well!" Joe pursued, "somebody must keep the pot a-biling, Pip, or the pot won't bile, don't you know?"

I saw that, and said so.

" 'Consequence, my father didn't make objections to my going to work; so I went to work at my present calling, which were his, too, if he would have followed it, and I worked tolerable hard, I assure *you*, Pip. In time I were able to keep him, and I kep him till he went off in a purple 'leptic fit.[5] Then all the money that could be spared were wanted for my mother. She were in poor 'elth, and quite broke. She waren't long of following, poor soul, and her share of peace came round at last."

"It were but lonesome then," said Joe, "living here alone, and I got acquainted with your sister. Now, Pip"—Joe looked firmly at me, as if he knew I was not going to agree with him—"your sister is a fine figure of a woman."

I could not help looking at the fire, in an obvious state of doubt.

"Whatever family opinions, or whatever the world's opinions, on that subject may be, Pip, your sister is"—Joe tapped the top bar with the poker after every word following—"a—fine—figure—of—a—woman!"

I could think of nothing better to say than, "I am glad you think so, Joe."

"So am I," returned Joe, catching me up. "*I* am glad I think so, Pip. When I got acquainted with your sister," said Joe, "it were the talk how she was bringing you up by hand. Very kind of her, too, all the folks said, and I said, along with all the folks. As to you, if you could have been aware how small and flabby and mean you was, dear me, you'd have formed the most contemptible opinions of yourself!"

---

**5. purple 'leptic fit:** Joe means an apoplectic (ap' ə plek' tik) fit, a sudden paralysis and partial or complete loss of consciousness.

Not exactly relishing this, I said, "Never mind me, Joe."

"But I did mind you, Pip," he returned, with tender simplicity. "When I offered to your sister to keep company, and to be asked in church, at such times as she was willing and ready to come to the forge, I said to her, 'And bring the poor little child. God bless the poor little child,' I said to your sister, 'there's room for *him* at the forge!'"

I broke out crying and begging pardon, and hugged Joe round the neck: who dropped the poker to hug me, and to say, "Ever the best of friends; ain't us, Pip? Don't cry, old chap!"

When this little interruption was over, Joe resumed:

"Well, you see, Pip, and here we are! That's about where it lights; here we are! Now, when you take me in hand in my learning, Pip (and I tell you beforehand I am awful dull, most awful dull), Mrs. Joe mustn't see too much of what we're up to. It must be done, as I may say, on the sly. And why on the sly? I'll tell you why, Pip. Your sister is given to government."

"Given to government, Joe?"

"Given to government," said Joe. "Which I meantersay the government of you and myself."

"Oh!"

"And she ain't over partial to having scholars on the premises," Joe continued, "and in partickler would not be over partial to my being a scholar, for fear as I might rise. Like a sort of rebel."

"Your sister is a mastermind. And I ain't a mastermind. And last of all, Pip—and this I want to say very serous to you, old chap—I see so much in my poor mother, of a woman drudging and slaving and breaking her honest hart and never getting no peace in her mortal days, that I'm dead afeerd of going wrong in the way of not doing what's right by a woman, and I'd fur rather of the two go wrong the t'other way, and be a little ill-conwenienced myself. I wish it was only me that got put out, Pip; I wish there warn't no Tickler for you, old chap; I wish I could take it all on myself; but this is the up-and-down-straight on it, Pip, and I hope you'll overlook shortcomings."

Young as I was, I believe that I dated a new admiration of Joe from that night. We were equals afterwards, as we had been before; but, afterwards at quiet times when I sat looking at Joe and thinking about him, I had a new sensation of feeling conscious that I was looking up to Joe in my heart.

"However," said Joe, rising to replenish the fire, "here's the Dutch clock a-working himself up to being equal to strike eight of 'em, and she's not come home yet! I hope Uncle Pumblechook's mare mayn't have set a fore-foot on a piece o' ice, and gone down."

Mrs. Joe made occasional trips with Uncle Pumblechook on market days, to assist him in buying such household stuffs and goods as required a woman's judgment; Uncle Pumblechook being a bachelor and reposing no confidences in his domestic servant. This was market day, and Mrs. Joe was out on one of these expeditions.

Joe made the fire and swept the hearth, and then we went to the door to listen for the chaise-cart. "Here comes the mare," said Joe, "ringing like a peal of bells!"

Mrs. Joe was soon landed, and Uncle Pumblechook was soon down too, covering the mare with a cloth, and we were soon all in the kitchen, carrying so much cold air with us that it seemed to drive all the heat out of the fire.

"Now," said Mrs. Joe, unwrapping herself with haste and excitement, and throwing her bonnet back on her shoulders where it hung by the strings, "if this boy ain't grateful this night, he never will be!"

*Great Expectations* 775

35

35 **Discussion** Why would Mrs. Joe object to Pip's teaching Joe to read and write?

I looked as grateful as any boy possibly could who was wholly uninformed why he ought to assume that expression.

"It's only to be hoped," said my sister, "that he won't be pompeyed. But I have my fears."

"She ain't in that line, mum," said Mr. Pumblechook. "She knows better."

She? I looked at Joe, making the motion with my lips and eyebrows, "She?" Joe looked at me, making the motion with *his* lips and eyebrows, "She?" My sister catching him in the act, he drew the back of his hand across his nose with his usual conciliatory air on such occasions, and looked at her.

"Well?" said my sister, in her snappish way. "What are you staring at? Is the house afire?"

"—Which some individual," Joe politely hinted, "mentioned she."

"And she is a she, I suppose?" said my sister. "Unless you call Miss Havisham a he. And I doubt if even you'll go so far as that."

"Miss Havisham up town?" said Joe.

"Is there any Miss Havisham down town?" returned my sister. "She wants this boy to go and play there. And of course he's going. And he had better play there," said my sister, "or I'll work him."

I had heard of Miss Havisham up town as an immensely rich and grim lady who lived in a large and dismal house barricaded against robbers, and who led a life of seclusion.

"Well, to be sure!" said Joe, astounded. "I wonder how she comes to know Pip!"

"Noodle!" cried my sister. "Who said she knew him?"

"—Which some individual," Joe again politely hinted, "mentioned that she wanted him to go and play there."

"And couldn't she ask Uncle Pumblechook if he knew of a boy to go and play there? Isn't it just barely possible that Uncle Pumblechook may be a tenant of hers, and that he may sometimes go there to pay his rent? And couldn't she then ask Uncle Pumblechook if he knew of a boy to go and play there? And couldn't Uncle Pumblechook, being always considerate and thoughtful for us—though you may not think it, Joseph," in a tone of the deepest reproach, "then mention this boy that I have for ever been a willing slave to?"

"Uncle Pumblechook, being sensible that for anything we can tell, this boy's fortune may be made by his going to Miss Havisham's, has offered to take him into town tonight in his own chaise-cart, and to keep him tonight, and to take him with his own hands to Miss Havisham's tomorrow morning. And Lor-a-mussy me!" cried my sister, casting off her bonnet in sudden desperation, "here I stand talking to mere mooncalfs, with Uncle Pumblechook waiting, and the mare catching cold at the door, and the boy grimed with crock and dirt from the hair of his head to the sole of his foot!"

With that, she pounced on me, like an eagle on a lamb, and my face was squeezed into wooden bowls in sinks, and my head was put under taps of water-butts, and I was soaped, and kneaded, and toweled, and thumped, and harrowed, and rasped, until I really was quite beside myself.

When my ablutions were completed, I was put into clean linen of the stiffest character, like a young penitent into sackcloth, and was trussed up in my tightest and fearfullest suit. I was then delivered over to Mr. Pumblechook, who formally received me as if he were the sheriff, and who let off upon me the speech that I knew he had been dying to make all along: "Boy, be for ever grateful to all friends, but especially unto them which brought you up by hand!"

"Good-bye, Joe!"

"God bless you, Pip, old chap!"

I had never parted from him before, and what with my feelings and what with soap-suds, I could at first see no stars from the chaise-cart. But they twinkled out one by one, without throwing any light on the questions why on earth I was going to play at Miss Havisham's, and what on earth I was expected to play at.

## Chapter 8

Mr. Pumblechook's premises in the High Street of the market town were of a pepper-corny and farinaceous character, as the premises of a corn chandler and seedsman should be.

Mr. Pumblechook and I breakfasted at eight o'clock in the parlor behind his shop. I considered Mr. Pumblechook wretched company. Besides being possessed by my sister's idea that a mortifying and penitential character ought to be imparted to my diet—besides giving me as much crumb as possible in combination with as little butter, and putting such a quantity of warm water into my milk that it would have been more candid to have left the milk out altogether—his conversation consisted of nothing but arithmetic. On my politely bidding him good morning, he said pompously, "Seven times nine, boy?" And how should *I* be able to answer, dodged in that way, in a strange place, on an empty stomach! I was hungry, but before I had swallowed a morsel, he began a running sum that lasted all through the breakfast. "Seven?" "And four?" "And eight?" "And six?" "And two?" "And ten?" And so on.

For such reasons I was very glad when ten o'clock came and we started for Miss Havisham's. Within a quarter of an hour we came to Miss Havisham's house, which was of old brick, and dismal, and had a great many iron bars to it. Some of the windows had been walled up; of those that remained, all the lower were rustily barred. There was a courtyard in front, and that was barred; so, we had to wait, after ringing the bell, until some one should come to open it. While we waited at the gate, I peeped in and saw that at the side of the house there was a large brewery.[1] No brewing was going on in it, and none seemed to have gone on for a long time.

A window was raised, and a clear voice demanded "What name?" To which my conductor replied, "Pumblechook." The voice returned, "Quite right," and the window was shut again, and a young lady came across the courtyard, with keys in her hand.

"This," said Mr. Pumblechook, "is Pip."

"This is Pip, is it?" returned the young lady, who was very pretty and seemed very proud; "come in, Pip."

Mr. Pumblechook was coming in also, when she stopped him with the gate.

"Oh!" she said. "Did you wish to see Miss Havisham?"

"If Miss Havisham wished to see me," returned Mr. Pumblechook, discomfited.

"Ah!" said the girl; "but you see, she don't."

She said it so finally that Mr. Pumblechook, though in a condition of ruffled dignity, could not protest. But he eyed me severely—as if *I* had done anything to him!—and departed with the words reproachfully delivered: "Boy! Let your behavior here be a credit unto them which brought you up by hand!"

My young conductress locked the gate, and we went across the courtyard. It was paved and clean, but grass was growing in every crevice. The brewery buildings had a little lane of communication with it; and the wooden gates of that lane stood open, and all

---

**1. brewery** (br$\overline{oo}'$ ər ē) *n*.: Establishment where beer and similar beverages are made.

37 **Discussion** How do you think Pip feels as he leaves Joe?

38 **Discussion** What mood does this description call up?

**39 Discussion** What is the irony in the name Satis House?

**40 Discussion** How does Pip view the girl? How does he view himself in relationship to her?

**41 Reading Strategy** Have students summarize Pip's impressions of Miss Havisham's room.

**42 Discussion** What does this passage reveal about Miss Havisham?

the brewery beyond stood open, away to the high enclosing wall; and all was empty and disused.

"What is the name of this house, miss?"

"Its name was Satis; which is Greek, or Latin, or Hebrew, or all three—or all one to me—for enough."

"Enough House!" said I; "that's a curious name, miss."

"Yes," she replied; "but it meant more than it said. It meant, when it was given, that whoever had this house could want nothing else. They must have been easily satisfied in those days, I should think. But don't loiter, boy."

Though she called me "boy" so often, and with a carelessness that was far from complimentary, she was of about my own age. She seemed much older than I, of course, being a girl, and beautiful and self-possessed; and she was as scornful of me as if she had been one-and-twenty, and a queen.

We went into the house by a side door— the great front entrance had two chains across it outside—and the first thing I noticed was that the passages were all dark, and she had left a candle burning there. She took it up, and we went through more passages and up a staircase, and still it was all dark, and only the candle lighted us.

At last we came to the door of a room, and she said, "Go in."

I answered, more in shyness than politeness, "After you, miss."

To this, she returned: "Don't be ridiculous, boy; I am not going in." And scornfully walked away, and—what was worse—took the candle with her.

This was very uncomfortable, and I was half-afraid. However, the only thing to be done being to knock at the door, I knocked, and was told from within to enter. I entered, therefore, and found myself in a pretty large room, well lighted with wax candles. No glimpse of daylight was to be seen in it. It was a dressing room, as I supposed from the furniture, though much of it was of forms and uses then quite unknown to me. But prominent in it was a draped table with a gilded looking glass, and that I made out at first sight to be a fine lady's dressing-table.

Whether I should have made out this object so soon if there had been no fine lady sitting at it, I cannot say. In an arm-chair, with an elbow resting on the table and her head leaning on that hand, sat the strangest lady I have ever seen, or shall ever see.

She was dressed in rich materials—satins, and lace, and silks—all of white. Her shoes were white. And she had a long white veil dependent from her hair, and she had bridal flowers in her hair, but her hair was white. Some bright jewels sparkled on her neck and on her hands, and some other jewels lay sparkling on the table. Dresses less splendid than the dress she wore, and half-packed trunks, were scattered about. She had not quite finished dressing, for she had but one shoe on—the other was on the table near her hand—her veil was but half arranged, her watch and chain were not put on, and some lace for her bosom lay with those trinkets, and with her handkerchief, and gloves, and some flowers, and a prayer book, all confusedly heaped about the looking glass.

I saw that everything within my view which ought to be white, had been white long ago, and had lost its luster, and was faded and yellow. I saw that the bride within the bridal dress had withered like the dress, and like the flowers, and had no brightness left but the brightness of her sunken eyes. I saw that the dress had been put upon the rounded figure of a young woman, and that the figure upon which it now hung loose had shrunk to skin and bone.

"Who is it?" said the lady at the table.

"Pip, ma'am."

"Pip?"

"Mr. Pumblechook's boy, ma'am. Come—to play."

"Come nearer; let me look at you. Come close."

It was when I stood before her, avoiding her eyes, that I took note of the surrounding objects in detail, and saw that her watch had stopped at twenty minutes to nine, and that a clock in the room had stopped at twenty minutes to nine.

"Look at me," said Miss Havisham. "You are not afraid of a woman who has never seen the sun since you were born?"

I regret to state that I was not afraid of telling the enormous lie comprehended in the answer "No."

"Do you know what I touch here?" she said, laying her hands, one upon the other, on her left side.

"Yes, ma'am."

"What do I touch?"

"Your heart."

"Broken!"

She uttered the word with an eager look, and with strong emphasis, and with a weird smile that had a kind of boast in it. Afterwards, she kept her hands there for a little while, and slowly took them away as if they were heavy.

"I am tired," said Miss Havisham. "I want diversion, and I have done with men and women. Play."

I think it will be conceded by my most disputatious reader that she could hardly have directed an unfortunate boy to do anything in the wide world more difficult to be done under the circumstances.

"I sometimes have sick fancies," she went on, "and I have a sick fancy that I want to see some play. There, there!" with an impatient movement of the fingers of her right hand; "play, play, play!"

I had a desperate idea of starting round the room in the assumed character of Mr. Pumblechook's chaise-cart. But I felt myself so unequal to the performance that I gave it up, and stood looking at Miss Havisham in what I suppose she took for a dogged manner, inasmuch as she said, when we had taken a good look at each other: "Are you sullen and obstinate?"

"No, ma'am, I am very sorry for you, and very sorry I can't play just now. If you complain of me I shall get into trouble with my sister, so I would do it if I could; but it's so new here, and so strange, and so fine—and melancholy—" I stopped, fearing I might say too much, or had already said it, and we took another look at each other.

"So new to him," she muttered, "so old to me; so strange to him, so familiar to me; so melancholy to both of us! Call Estella."

I thought she was still talking to herself, and kept quiet.

"Call Estella," she repeated, flashing a look at me. "You can do that. Call Estella. At the door."

To stand in the dark in a mysterious passage of an unknown house, bawling Estella to a scornful young lady neither visible nor responsive, and feeling it a dreadful liberty so to roar out her name, was almost as bad as playing to order. But she answered at last, and her light came along the dark passage like a star.

Miss Havisham beckoned her to come close, and took up a jewel from the table, and tried its effect against her pretty brown hair. "Your own, one day, my dear, and you will use it well. Let me see you play cards with this boy."

"With this boy! Why, he is a common laboring boy!"

I thought I overheard Miss Havisham answer—only it seemed so unlikely, "Well? You can break his heart."

43

43 **Critical Thinking and Reading** What does Estella say about Pip that makes her opinion of him very clear? What does Miss Havisham's response mean? Is there a relationship between her response and her disclosure about her own broken heart?

*Great Expectations*   779

## Humanities Note

Fine art, *Miss Cicely Alexander: Harmony in Grey and Green*, 1872–4, by James McNeill Whistler. James McNeill Whistler (1834–1903) was an American artist who lived and worked in England, where he became known for his distinctive landscapes and portraits.

This particular portrait was commissioned by a wealthy British patron. The simplicity of form and subtle blending of color suggest the influence of Japanese prints. Whistler often included musical references in his titles—like *Harmony in Grey and Green*—to stress the lyricism of his work.

You might want to use the following questions in a class discussion:

1. What is the personality and social status of this young girl?
2. Which details in the picture reveal this information?
3. Do you think the subject of this portrait resembles Estella? Explain.

**MISS CICELY ALEXANDER: HARMONY IN GREY AND GREEN**
*James McNeill Whistler*
The Tate Gallery, London

"What do you play, boy?" asked Estella of myself, with the greatest disdain.

"Nothing but Beggar my Neighbor, miss."

"Beggar him," said Miss Havisham to Estella. So we sat down to cards.

It was then I began to understand that everything in the room had stopped, like the watch and the clock, a long time ago. As Estella dealt the cards, I glanced at the dressing table again, and saw that the shoe upon it, once white, now yellow, had never been worn. I glanced down at the foot from which the shoe was absent, and saw that the silk stocking on it, once white, now yellow, had been trodden ragged.

"He calls the knaves, jacks, this boy!" said Estella with disdain, before our first game was out. "And what coarse hands he has! And what thick boots!"

I never thought of being ashamed of my hands before; but I began to consider them a very indifferent pair. Her contempt for me was so strong that it became infectious, and I caught it.

She won the game, and I dealt. I misdealt, as was only natural, when I knew she was lying in wait for me to do wrong; and she denounced me for a stupid, clumsy laboring boy.

"You say nothing of her," remarked Miss Havisham to me, as she looked on. "She says many hard things of you, yet you say nothing of her. What do you think of her?"

"I don't like to say," I stammered.

"Tell me in my ear," said Miss Havisham, bending down.

"I think she is very proud," I replied, in a whisper.

"Anything else?"

"I think she is very pretty."

"Anything else?"

"I think she is very insulting." (She was looking at me then with a look of supreme aversion.)

"Anything else?"

"I think I should like to go home."

"And never see her again, though she is so pretty?"

"I am not sure that I shouldn't like to see her again, but I should like to go home now."

"You shall go soon," said Miss Havisham aloud. "Play the game out."

I played the game to an end with Estella, and she beggared me. She threw the cards down on the table when she had won them all, as if she despised them for having been won of me.

"When shall I have you here again?" said Miss Havisham. "Let me think."

I was beginning to remind her that today was Wednesday when she checked me with her former impatient movement of the fingers of her right hand.

"There, there! I know nothing of the days of the week; I know nothing of the weeks of the year. Come again after six days. You hear?"

"Yes, ma'am."

"Estella, take him down. Let him have something to eat, and let him roam and look about him while he eats. Go, Pip."

I followed the candle down, as I had followed the candle up, and she stood it in the place where we had found it. Until she opened the side entrance, I had fancied, without thinking about it, that it must necessarily be nighttime. The rush of daylight quite confounded me, and made me feel as if I had been in the candlelight of the strange room many hours.

"You are to wait here, you boy," said Estella, and disappeared and closed the door.

I took the opportunity of being alone in the courtyard to look at my coarse hands and my common boots. My opinion of those accessories was not favorable. They had never troubled me before, but they troubled me now. I determined to ask Joe why he had ever taught me to call those picture cards

**44 Discussion** How does the name of the card game take on extra meaning?

**45 Discussion** What is it about Estella that would make Pip want to see her again, although she has scorned and insulted him?

**46 Discussion** How has this visit affected Pip's opinion of himself?

47 **Reading Strategy** Have students predict how Pip's life will change as a result of this visit.

**Reader's Response** Pip was threatened by the convict and forced to steal food for him. Do you think this justifies Pip's actions and frees him from blame? Explain.

jacks which ought to be called knaves. I wished Joe had been rather more genteelly brought up, and then I should have been so, too.

She came back with some bread and meat and a little mug of beer. She put the mug down on the stones of the yard, and gave me the bread and meat without looking at me, as insolently as if I were a dog in disgrace. I was so humiliated, hurt, spurned, offended, angry, sorry—I cannot hit upon the right name for the smart—God knows what its name was—that tears started to my eyes. The moment they sprang there, the girl looked at me with a quick delight in having been the cause of them. This gave me power to keep them back and to look at her: so, she gave a contemptuous toss—but with a sense, I thought, of having made too sure that I was so wounded—and left me.

But, when she was gone, I looked about me for a place to hide my face in, and got behind one of the gates in the brewery lane, and leaned my sleeve against the wall there, and leaned my forehead on it and cried. As I cried, I kicked the wall, and took a hard twist at my hair.

I got rid of my injured feelings for the time by kicking them into the brewery wall, and twisting them out of my hair, and then I smoothed my face with my sleeve, and

came from behind the gate. The bread and meat were acceptable, and I was soon in spirits to look about me.

Then I saw Estella approaching with the keys, to let me out. She gave me a triumphant glance in passing me, as if she rejoiced that my hands were so coarse and my boots were so thick, and she opened the gate, and stood holding it. I was passing out without looking at her, when she touched me with a taunting hand.

"Why don't you cry?"

"Because I don't want to."

"You do," said she. "You have been crying till you were half-blind, and you are near crying again now."

She laughed contemptuously, pushed me out, and locked the gate upon me. I went straight to Mr. Pumblechook's, and was immensely relieved to find him not at home. So, leaving word with the shopman on what day I was wanted at Miss Havisham's again, I set off on the four-mile walk to our forge, pondering, as I went along, on all I had seen, and deeply revolving that I was a common laboring boy; that my hands were coarse; that my boots were thick; that I had fallen into a despicable habit of calling knaves jacks; that I was much more ignorant than I had considered myself last night; and generally that I was in a low-lived bad way.

47

**Closure and Extension**

**ANSWERS TO THINKING ABOUT THE SELECTION**
*Recalling*

1. Pip is suddenly confronted by a terrifying figure rising out of the mist. This man, an escaped convict, orders him to bring him food and a file early the next morning, and swears him to secrecy. As soon as the convict climbs over the wall, Pip runs home.

2. Pip steals food and drink from Mrs. Joe's larder and a file from the forge, and he brings them to the convict.

3. Miss Havisham is an old lady dressed in a yellowed bridal gown, with faded flowers in her hair, a tattered veil, and bright jewels on her neck and fingers. Her bright eyes shine from sunken sockets. She is the strangest person Pip has ever seen.

   The house is a decaying mansion of brick behind a high wall, with many barred or walled-

## THINKING ABOUT THE SELECTION

### Recalling

1. Describe Pip's encounter in the cemetery.
2. In what two ways does Pip help the convict?
3. Describe Miss Havishman and her house.
4. What conclusion does Pip draw about himself after his visit with Miss Havisham?

### Interpreting

5. Explain why the convict claims to have taken the items that Pip actually took.
6. Explain the relationship between Pip and Joe. Explain the relationship that they have with Pip's sister.
7. How would you characterize Estella's behavior toward Pip? What does her behavior indicate about her?

### Applying

8. Based on the conversation between Joe and Pip in chapter 7, what conclusions do you draw about education in England at the time of this novel?
9. Pip shows great determination and a growing ambition to change. How does determination play a role in change? Give examples.

## ANALYZING LITERATURE

### Understanding Point of View

**Point of view** is the angle or perspective from which a story is told. *Great Expectations* is told in the **first person.** The narrator is Pip, an orphan being raised by his sister and her husband in a small, nineteenth-century English town. However, Pip is not telling the events at the time they happen. He tells them as an adult looking back on his past. From his adult perspective, he is able to have insight into his childhood actions.

1. Why is the meeting with the convict more effective in a first-person narrative than it would be if it were told by the author?
2. How does Pip as narrator get the reader's sympathy? Would you feel as sympathetic to him if another character were telling the story? Explain your answer.
3. Give an example in which Pip judges his own behavior.
4. Explain how the novel would be different if Pip were writing about events at the time they occurred.

## UNDERSTANDING LANGUAGE

### Appreciating Word Histories

Most English words come from words in other languages. You can find a word's history in a dictionary in the etymology, the information in brackets. Abbreviations—like *Fr.* for French, *Ger.* for German, and *L.* for Latin—indicate the language or languages from which the word comes.

Look up the following words from *Great Expectations* and identify the languages from which they came.

1. parley       3. dexterity
2. timid        4. manacle

## THINKING AND WRITING

### Writing from Another Point of View

We have Pip's point of view on his meeting with Estella. Put yourself in the place of Estella meeting Pip. What does she think of him? How does she feel playing cards with him? Rewrite the incident from Estella's point of view. When you have written a draft, revise it, making sure you have used "I" as Estella. Add details that would be known only by Estella.

difficult and determination is required to overcome obstacles.

### ANSWERS TO ANALYZING LITERATURE

1. Suggested Response: The first-person narrative allows us to feel more powerfully the fear that Pip experiences.
2. Suggested Response: Pip gets our sympathy because he is bright, perceptive, good-hearted, and oppressed. We would probably not feel quite as sympathetic toward him if the story were narrated by another character, because we would not know as much about Pip's thoughts and feelings.
3. Suggested Response: Pip feels guilty about stealing Joe's file.
4. Suggested Response: If Pip were writing as a child, he would not be able to explain his conflicts and feelings as well.

### ANSWERS TO UNDERSTANDING LANGUAGE

1. parley—French
2. timid—Latin
3. dexterity—Latin
4. manacle—Latin

### THINKING AND WRITING

For help with this assignment, students can refer to Lesson 2, "Drafting and Revising," in the Handbook of Writing About Literature.

**Publishing Student Writing**
You might want to have volunteers read their accounts to the class.

**Challenge** Write an account of the graveyard scene from the first convict's point of view.

**Writing Across the Curriculum**
Have students work with the social studies department to research and report on education in nineteenth-century England.

up windows. There is a barred courtyard in front and an abandoned brewery at the side. The front doors are heavily chained.
4. Pip feels that he is the "common clod" Estella had called him, that his boots are too thick, that he is more ignorant than he had thought, and that he is altogether a low sort of person.

### Interpreting

5. Suggested Response: Since Pip probably saved the convict's life,

the convict wants to protect him from the punishment that will follow the knowledge of the theft.
6. Suggested Response: Pip has a warm relationship with Joe; however, they are more like equals than adult and child. Both are under the thumb of Mrs. Joe, Pip's sister and Joe's wife. She is a hot-tempered and domineering person.
7. Suggested Response: Estella is proud and haughty. She assumes she is better than Pip and treats him cruelly.

### Applying

8. Answers will differ; however, many students will probably respond that village schools were private establishments and therefore not available to every child. Books were scarce, primary-grade children wrote on slates instead of paper, and reading and basic arithmetic were taught. Children from wealthy backgrounds were probably privately tutored.
9. Answers will differ, but most students will realize that change is

**Literary Focus** You might want to tell students that Dickens created a whole world of memorable characters in his novels. His major characters, like Pip, are convincing, complex, and round. But Dickens also created many flat characters—eccentric, fascinating near-caricatures who are essential to the plot.

**Look For** Have students list all of the characters in the novel under the headings "Round" and "Flat." Have them list the key traits for each character and the changes, if any, these characters undergo. Remind them that every character, however obscure, plays some role in the plot.

**Writing/Prior Knowledge** You might want to divide the class into small groups and have students tell their stories to fellow group members before they begin to write.

**Vocabulary** Have less advanced students identify the prefixes and suffixes of the polysyllabic words. Then have them find additional words in these chapters with these same prefixes and suffixes.

## Great Expectations, Chapters 9–15

### Characterization

**Characterization** refers to the methods by which writers reveal the personalities of their fictional characters. When writers use **direct characterization,** they openly tell you about the traits of their characters. **Indirect characterization** is the technique of revealing characters' personalities through their own words or actions or what others say about them. In *Great Expectations,* Dickens cannot tell you directly about the characters because Pip is narrating the story. Although Pip is sensitive and intelligent, his information is limited, and he himself changes over the course of the book. You therefore cannot assume that Pip's evaluations of himself or others at any point are those of Dickens. Yet you learn a great deal about Pip because you know how he responds and what he thinks in given situations.

In novels as well as short stories, **round characters** are those who have many traits and are capable of growth. Pip is a good example of a round character. Dickens also uses **flat characters,** with only one or two traits, to contrast with the round ones. Mr. Pumblechook, for example, is little more than a bundle of bullying self-importance.

### Look For

One outstanding feature of the novels of Dickens is the memorable characters he creates. What makes Miss Havisham and Estella interesting? How do you learn what they're like? Look for the ways that Dickens reveals his characters' personalities.

### Writing

In this section of the novel, Pip meets someone who is to become his very good friend. Tell the story of how you first met one of your good friends. Include details that reveal your friend's personality.

### Vocabulary

Knowing the following words will help you as you read Chapters 9–15 of *Great Expectations.*

**felicitous** (fə lis′ ə təs) *adj.*: Suitable to the occasion (p. 787)
**superciliously** (soo̅ pər sil′ ē əs lē) *adv.*: Haughtily (p. 789)
**plaintively** (plān′ tiv lē) *adv.*: Sadly (p. 793)
**condescend** (kän′ də send′)
*v.*: Lower oneself to another's level (p. 794)
**alluded** (ə loo̅d′əd) *v.*: Referred to indirectly (p. 797)
**unscrupulous** (un skroo̅p′ yə ləs) *adj.*: Without principles (p. 803)

## Objectives
1 To understand characterization
2 To draw conclusions about characters
3 To write about art

## Support Material

**Teaching Portfolio**
Teacher Backup, p. 935
Grammar in Action Worksheets, *Writing Dialogue,* p. 938; *Appreciating Details of Setting that Suggest Time,* p. 940
Usage and Mechanics Worksheet, p. 942
Vocabulary Check, p. 943
Analyzing Literature Worksheet, *Understanding Characterization,* p. 944
Language Worksheet, *Understanding Context Clues,* p. 945
Selection Test, p. 946

**Chapter 9**

When I reached home, my sister was very curious to know all about Miss Havisham's, and asked a number of questions. And I soon found myself getting heavily bumped from behind in the nape of the neck and the small of the back, and having my face ignominiously shoved against the kitchen wall, because I did not answer those questions at sufficient length.

I felt convinced that if I described Miss Havisham's as my eyes had seen it, I should not be understood. Not only that, but I felt convinced that Miss Havisham, too, would not be understood; and although she was perfectly incomprehensible to me, I entertained an impression that there would be something coarse and treacherous in my dragging her as she really was (to say nothing of Miss Estella) before the contemplation of Mrs. Joe. Consequently, I said as little as I could, and had my face shoved against the kitchen wall.

The worst of it was that that bullying old Pumblechook, preyed upon by a devouring curiosity to be informed of all I had seen and heard, came gaping over in his chaise-cart at tea-time to have the details divulged to him.

"Well, boy," Uncle Pumblechook began, "how did you get on up town?"

I answered, "Pretty well, sir," and my sister shook her fist at me.

"Pretty well?" Mr. Pumblechook repeated. "Pretty well is no answer. Tell us what you mean by pretty well, boy."

"I mean pretty well."

My sister with an exclamation of impatience was going to fly at me—I had no shadow of defense, for Joe was busy in the forge—when Mr. Pumblechook interposed with "No! Don't lose your temper. Leave this lad to me, ma'am; leave this lad to me." Mr. Pumblechook then turned me towards him as if he were going to cut my hair, and said:

"Boy! What like is Miss Havisham?"

"Very tall and dark," I told him.

"Is she, Uncle?" asked my sister.

Mr. Pumblechook winked assent; from which I at once inferred that he had never seen Miss Havisham, for she was nothing of the kind.

"Good!" said Mr. Pumblechook conceitedly.

"I am sure, Uncle," returned Mrs. Joe, "I wish you had him always: you know so well how to deal with him."

"Now, boy! What was she a-doing of, when you went in today?" asked Mr. Pumblechook.

"She was sitting," I answered, "in a black velvet coach."

Mr. Pumblechook and Mrs. Joe stared at one another—as they well might—and both repeated, "In a black velvet coach?"

"Was anybody else there?" asked Mr. Pumblechook.

"Four dogs," said I.

"Large or small?"

"Immense," said I. "And they fought for veal-cutlets out of a silver basket."

Mr. Pumblechook and Mrs. Joe stared at one another again, in utter amazement. I was perfectly frantic—a reckless witness under the torture—and would have told them anything.

"Where *was* this coach, in the name of gracious?" asked my sister.

"In Miss Havisham's room." They stared again. "But there weren't any horses to it." I added this saving clause, in the moment of rejecting four richly caparisoned coursers,[1] which I had had wild thoughts of harnessing.

"Did you ever see her in it, Uncle?" asked Mrs. Joe.

---

1. **caparisoned** (kə par' ə s'nd) **coursers:** Horses with ornamented coverings.

**Motivation/Prior Knowledge**
Ask students to recall a childhood dream of what they most wanted to be or what person they hoped to imitate. What has happened to that dream? Is it still alive? Does it no longer seem attainable or desirable? Has it been replaced by another? Then tell them that in the next section of the book Pip begins to see his dreams come true.

**Master Teacher Note** Consider telling students that in Dickens's England, the public house—a bar or inn—was an important social gathering place for the working-class community. In the larger cities, intellectuals gathered in coffee-houses and upperclass gentlemen met in private clubs.

**Purpose-Setting Question** How does Pip's encounter with Miss Havisham and Estella continue to influence him?

**1 Literary Focus** What does this thought suggest about Pip?

**2 Critical Thinking and Reading** Why do you think Pip tells such an outrageous lie?

**3 Literary Focus** What does this passage reveal about Pip's imagination?

4 **Critical Thinking and Reading**
Why does Pip feel penitent only
with regard to Joe?

"How could I," he returned, forced to the admission, "when I never see her in my life?"

"Goodness, Uncle! And yet you have spoken to her?"

"Why, don't you know," said Mr. Pumblechook testily, "that when I have been there, I have been took up to the outside of her door, and the door has stood ajar, and she has spoken to me that way. Don't say you don't know *that*, mum. Howsever, the boy went there to play. What did you play at, boy?"

"We played with flags," I said.

"Flags!" echoed my sister.

"Yes," said I. "Estella waved a blue flag, and I waved a red one, and Miss Havisham waved one sprinkled all over with little gold stars, out at the coach-window. And then we all waved our swords and hurrahed."

"Swords!" repeated my sister. "Where did you get swords from?"

"Out of the cupboard," said I. "And I saw pistols in it—and jam—and pills. And there was no daylight in the room, but it was all lighted up with candles."

"That's true, mum," said Mr. Pumblechook, with a grave nod. "That's the state of the case, for that much I've seen myself." When Joe came in, they were occupied in discussing the marvels I had already presented for their consideration. More for the relief of her own mind than for the gratification of his, my sister related my pretended experiences to Joe.

4  Now when I saw Joe open his blue eyes and roll them all round the kitchen in helpless amazement, I was overtaken by penitence; but only as regarded him—not in the least as regarded the other two. Towards Joe, and Joe only, I considered myself a young monster, while they sat debating what results would come to me from Miss Havisham's acquaintance and favor.

After Mr. Pumblechook had driven off, and when my sister was washing up, I stole into the forge to Joe, and remained by him until he had done for the night. Then I said, "Before the fire goes out, Joe, I should like to tell you something."

"Should you, Pip?" said Joe, drawing his shoeing-stool near the forge. "Then tell us. What is it, Pip?"

"Joe," said I, taking hold of his rolled-up shirt-sleeve, and twisting it between my finger and thumb, "you remember all that about Miss Havisham's?"

"Remember?" said Joe. "I believe you! Wonderful!"

"It's a terrible thing, Joe; it ain't true."

"What are you telling of, Pip?" cried Joe, falling back in the greatest amazement. "You don't mean to say it's—"

"Yes, I do; it's lies, Joe."

As I fixed my eyes hopelessly on Joe, Joe contemplated me in dismay. "Pip, old chap! This won't do, old fellow! I say! Where do you expect to go to?"

"It's terrible, Joe; ain't it?"

"Terrible?" cried Joe. "Awful! What possessed you?"

"I don't know what possessed me, Joe," I replied, letting his shirt-sleeve go, and sitting down in the ashes at his feet, hanging my head; "but I wish you hadn't taught me to call knaves at cards jacks; and I wish my boots weren't so thick nor my hands so coarse."

And then I told Joe that I felt very miserable, and that I hadn't been able to explain myself to Mrs. Joe and Pumblechook, who were so rude to me, and that there had been a beautiful young lady at Miss Havisham's who was dreadfully proud, and that she had said I was common, and that I knew I was common, and that I wished I was not common, and that the lies had come of it somehow, though I didn't know how.

"There's one thing you may be sure of,

Pip," said Joe, after some rumination, "namely, that lies is lies. Howsever they come, they didn't ought to come. Don't you tell no more of 'em, Pip. *That* ain't the way to get out of being common, old chap. And as to being common, I don't make it out at all clear. You are oncommon in some things. You're oncommon small. Likewise you're a oncommon scholar."

"No, I am ignorant and backward, Joe."

"Why, see what a letter you wrote last night! Wrote in print even! I've seen letters—ah! and from gentlefolks!—that I'll swear weren't wrote in print," said Joe.

"I have learnt next to nothing, Joe. You think much of me. It's only that."

"Well, Pip," said Joe, "be it so, be it son't, you must be a common scholar afore you can be a oncommon one, I should hope!"

There was some hope in this piece of wisdom, and it rather encouraged me.

"If you can't get to be oncommon through going straight," pursued Joe, "you'll never get to do it through going crooked. So don't tell no more on 'em, Pip, and live well and die happy."

"You are not angry with me, Joe?"

"No, old chap. But bearing in mind that them were which I meantersay of a stunning and outdacious sort—alluding to them which bordered on weal-cutlets and dog-fighting—a sincere well-wisher would advise, Pip, their being dropped into your meditations, when you go upstairs to bed. That's all, old chap, and don't never do it no more."

When I got up to my little room and said my prayers, I did not forget Joe's recommendation, and yet my young mind was in that disturbed and unthankful state that I thought long after I laid me down, how common Estella would consider Joe, a mere blacksmith: how thick his boots, and how coarse his hands.

## Chapter 10

The felicitous idea occurred to me a morning or two later when I woke that the best step I could take towards making myself uncommon was to get out of Biddy everything she knew. In pursuance of this luminous conception, I mentioned to Biddy when I went to Mr. Wopsle's great-aunt's at night that I had a particular reason for wishing to get on in life, and that I should feel very much obliged to her if she would impart all her learning to me. Biddy, who was the most obliging of girls, immediately said she would, and indeed began to carry out her promise within five minutes.

Biddy entered on our special agreement by imparting some information from her little catalogue of prices under the head of moist sugar, and lending me, to copy at home, a large old English D which she had imitated from the heading of some newspaper, and which I supposed, until she told me what it was, to be a design for a buckle.

Of course there was a public house[1] in the village, and of course Joe liked sometimes to smoke his pipe there. I had received strict orders from my sister to call for him at the Three Jolly Bargemen that evening, on my way from school, and bring him home at my peril. To the Three Jolly Bargemen, therefore, I directed my steps.

I wished the landlord good evening and passed into the common room at the end of the passage, where there was a bright large kitchen fire, and where Joe was smoking his pipe in company with Mr. Wopsle and a stranger. Joe greeted me as usual with "Halloa, Pip, old chap!" and the moment he said that, the stranger turned his head and looked at me.

He was a secret-looking man whom I had

_____
1. **public house:** Bar or inn.

5 **Literary Focus** What new aspects of Joe's character do these statements reveal?

6 **Literary Focus** Explain the inner conflict that Pip experiences.

7 **Discussion** What is Pip's reason for wanting to "get on"?

never seen before. His head was all on one side, and one of his eyes was half-shut up, as if he were taking aim at something with an invisible gun. He had a pipe in his mouth, and he took it out, and, after slowly blowing all his smoke away and looking hard at me all the time, nodded. So, I nodded, and then he nodded again, and made room on the settle[2] beside him that I might sit down there.

But, as I was used to sit beside Joe whenever I entered that place of resort, I said "No, thank you, sir," and fell into the space Joe made for me on the opposite settle. The strange man, after glancing at Joe, and seeing that his attention was otherwise engaged, nodded to me again when I had taken my seat, and then rubbed his leg—in a very odd way, as it struck me.

"You was saying," said the strange man, turning to Joe, "that you was a blacksmith."

"Yes. I said it, you know," said Joe.

**8** The stranger, with a comfortable kind of grunt over his pipe, put his legs up on the settle that he had to himself. He wore a flapping broad-brimmed traveler's hat, and under it a handkerchief tied over his head in the manner of a cap, so that he showed no hair. As he looked at the fire, I thought I saw a cunning expression, followed by a half-laugh, come into his face.

"I am not acquainted with this country, gentlemen, but it seems a solitary country towards the river."

"Most marshes is solitary," said Joe.

"No doubt, no doubt. Do you find any gypsies, now, or tramps, or vagrants of any sort, out there?"

"No," said Joe; "none but a runaway convict now and then. And we don't find *them*, easy. Eh, Mr. Wopsle?"

Mr. Wopsle, with a majestic remembrance of old discomfiture, assented, but not warmly.

"Seems you have been out after such?" asked the stranger.

"Once," returned Joe. "Not that we wanted to take them, you understand; we went out as lookers on; me and Mr. Wopsle, and Pip. Didn't us, Pip?"

"Yes, Joe."

The stranger looked at me again—still cocking his eye, as if he were expressly taking aim at me with his invisible gun—and said, "He's a likely young parcel of bones that. What is it you call him?"

"Pip," said Joe.

"Christened Pip?"

"No, not christened Pip."

"Surname Pip?"

"No," said Joe; "It's a kind of family name what he gave himself when an infant, and is called by."

"Son of yours?"

"Well," said Joe, "well, no. No, he ain't."

"Nevvy?"[3] said the strange man.

"Well," said Joe, "he is not—no, not to deceive you, he is *not*—my nevvy."

"What the blue blazes is he?" asked the stranger.

Mr. Wopsle struck in upon that—and expounded the ties between me and Joe. Having his hand in, Mr. Wopsle finished off with a most terrifically snarling passage from *Richard the Third*,[4] and seemed to think he had done quite enough to account for it when he added, "as the poet says."

All this while, the strange man looked at nobody but me, and looked at me as if he were determined to have a shot at me at last, and bring me down. But he said nothing after offering his blue blazes observation, until the glasses of rum-and-water were brought:

---

**2. settle** (set' 'l) *n.*: Bench.

**3. nevvy:** Nephew.
**4. Richard the Third:** Play by William Shakespeare.

and then he made his shot, and a most extraordinary shot it was.

It was not a verbal remark, but a proceeding in dumb show, and was pointedly addressed to me. He stirred his rum-and-water pointedly at me, and he tasted his rum-and-water pointedly at me. And he stirred it and he tasted it: not with a spoon that was brought to him, but *with a file.*

He did this so that nobody but I saw the file; and when he had done it, he wiped the file and put it in a breast-pocket. I knew it to be Joe's file, and I knew that he knew my convict, the moment I saw the instrument. I sat gazing at him, spell-bound. But he now reclined on his settle, taking very little notice of me, and talking principally about turnips.

Joe got up to go, and took me by the hand. "Stop half a moment, Mr. Gargery," said the strange man. "I think I've got a bright new shilling somewhere in my pocket, and if I have, the boy shall have it."

He looked it out from a handful of small change, folded it in some crumpled paper, and gave it to me. "Yours!" said he. "Mind! Your own."

I thanked him, staring at him far beyond the bounds of good manners, and holding tight to Joe. He gave Joe good night, and he gave Mr. Wopsle good night (who went out with us), and he gave me only a look with his aiming eye—no, not a look, for he shut it up, but wonders may be done with an eye by hiding it.

My sister was not in a very bad temper when we presented ourselves in the kitchen, and Joe was encouraged by that unusual circumstance to tell her about the bright shilling. "A bad un, I'll be bound," said Mrs. Joe triumphantly, "or he wouldn't have given it to the boy. Let's look at it."

I took it out of the paper, and it proved to be a good one. "But what's this?" said Mrs. Joe, throwing down the shilling and catching up the paper. "Two one-pound notes?"[5]

Nothing less than two fat sweltering one-pound notes that seemed to have been on terms of the warmest intimacy with all the cattle markets in the county. Joe caught up his hat again, and ran with them to the Jolly Bargmen to restore them to their owner. While he was gone I sat down on my usual stool and looked vacantly at my sister, feeling pretty sure that the man would not be there.

Presently, Joe came back, saying that the man was gone, but that he, Joe, had left word at the Three Jolly Bargemen concerning the notes. Then my sister sealed them up in a piece of paper, and put them under some dried rose-leaves in an ornamental tea-pot on the top of a press in the state parlor. There they remained a nightmare to me many and many a night and day.

## Chapter 11

At the appointed time I returned to Miss Havisham's, and my hesitating ring at the gate brought out Estella. She locked it after admitting me, as she had done before, and again preceded me into the dark passage where her candle stood. She took no notice of me until she had the candle in her hand, when she looked over her shoulder, superciliously saying, "You are to come this way today," and took me to quite another part of the house.

The passage was a long one, and seemed to pervade the whole square basement of the Manor House. We traversed but one side of the square, however, and at the end of it she stopped and put her candle down and opened a door. Here, the daylight reap-

---

**5. two one-pound notes:** The pound is the basic unit of British currency, equal to twenty shillings.

**9 Discussion** Why is Pip sure that the man will not be there? What was the purpose of the man's visit?

**10 Discussion** Why do you think Pip's ring is "hesitating"?

peared, and I found myself in a small paved courtyard, the opposite side of which was formed by a detached dwelling house that looked as if it had once belonged to the manager or head clerk of the extinct brewery. There was a clock in the outer wall of this house. Like the clock in Miss Havisham's room, and like Miss Havisham's watch, it had stopped at twenty minutes to nine.

We went in at the door, which stood open, and into a gloomy room with a low ceiling, on the ground floor at the back. There was some company in the room, and Estella said to me as she joined it, "You are to go and stand there, boy, till you are wanted." "There" being the window, I crossed to it, and stood "there" in a very uncomfortable state of mind, looking out.

It opened to the ground, and looked into a most miserable corner of the neglected garden, upon a rank ruin of cabbage-stalks, and one box-tree that had been clipped round long ago, like a pudding, and had a new growth at the top of it, out of shape and of a different color, as if that part of the pudding had stuck to the saucepan and got burnt.

I divined that my coming had stopped conversation in the room, and that its other occupants were looking at me. There were three ladies in the room and one gentleman. Before I had been standing at the window five minutes, they somehow conveyed to me that they were all toadies and humbugs[1], but that each of them pretended not to know that the others were toadies and humbugs, because the admission that he or she did know it would have made him or her out to be a toady and humbug.

They all had a listless and dreary air of waiting somebody's pleasure, and the most talkative of the ladies had to speak quite rig-

idly to suppress a yawn. This lady, whose name was Camilla, very much reminded me of my sister, with the difference that she was older.

"Poor dear soul!" said this lady, with an abruptness of manner quite my sister's. "Nobody's enemy but his own!"

"It would be much more commendable to be somebody else's enemy," said the gentleman; "far more natural."

"Cousin Raymond," observed another lady, "we are to love our neighbor."

"Sarah Pocket," returned Cousin Raymond, "if a man is not his own neighbor, who is?"

"Poor soul!" Camilla presently went on (I knew they had all been looking at me in the meantime), "he is so very strange! Would any one believe that when Tom's wife died, he actually could not be induced to see the importance of the children's having the deepest of trimmings to their mourning? 'Good Lord!' says he, 'Camilla, what can it signify so long as the poor bereaved little things are in black?' So like Matthew! The idea!"

"Good points in him, good points in him," said Cousin Raymond; "Heaven forbid I should deny good points in him; but he never had, and he never will have, any sense of the proprieties."[2]

The ringing of a distant bell, combined with the echoing of some cry or call along the passage by which I had come, interrupted the conversation and caused Estella to say to me, "Now, boy!" On my turning round, they all looked at me with the utmost contempt, and, as I went out, I heard Sarah Pocket say, "Well I am sure! What next!" and Camilla add, with indignation, "Was there ever such a fancy! The i-de-a!"

As we were going with our candle along the dark passage, Estella stopped all of a

---

**1. toadies** (tōd′ ēz) **and humbugs:** Flatterers and deceivers.

**2. proprieties** (prə prī′ ə tēz) *n.:* Proper manners or behavior.

## Grammar in Action

**Dialogue** is direct conversation between two or more people. When writing dialogue for a story or essay, most authors use a new paragraph to indicate a change of speaker. Notice that by beginning new paragraphs as he changes speakers, Dickens makes it easier for the reader to follow the conversation between Estella and Pip:

"Now?" said she. "You little coarse monster, what do you think of me now?"

"I shall not tell you."
"Because you are going to tell upstairs. Is that it?"
"No," said I, "that's not it."
"Why don't you cry again, you little wretch?"
"Because I'll never cry for you again," said I.

In addition to changing paragraphs with speakers, Dickens punctuates each sentence according to the rules governing direct quotations.

THE SCHOOLMASTER'S DAUGHTER
*James Sant, R.A.*
*Royal Academy of Arts, London*

sudden, and, facing round, said in her taunting manner, with her face quite close to mine:

"Well?"

"Well, miss," I answered, almost falling over her and checking myself.

She stood looking at me, and of course I stood looking at her.

"Am I pretty?"

"Yes, I think you are very pretty."

"Am I insulting?"

"Not so much so as you were last time," said I.

"Not so much so?"

"No."

She fired when she asked the last question, and she slapped my face with such force as she had, when I answered it.

"Now?" said she. "You little coarse monster, what do you think of me now?"

"I shall not tell you."

"Because you are going to tell upstairs. Is that it?"

"No," said I, "that's not it."

"Why don't you cry again, you little wretch?"

"Because I'll never cry for you again," said I. Which was, I suppose, as false a declaration as ever was made; for I was inwardly crying for her then, and I know what I know of the pain she cost me afterwards.

We went on our way upstairs after this

*Great Expectations* 791

**Student Activity.** Read again several other passages of dialogue in this chapter. Then use one you like as a model and write your own conversation between two of Dickens's characters. It should have at least five changes of speaker.

**13 Literary Focus** What inferences can you make about the personality of this new character?

**14 Critical Thinking and Reading** What does the state of this room reveal about Miss Havisham?

episode, and as we were going up, we met a gentleman groping his way down.

"Whom have we here?" asked the gentleman, stopping and looking at me.

"A boy," said Estella.

He was a burly man of an exceedingly dark complexion, with an exceedingly large head and a corresponding large hand. He took my chin in his large hand and turned up my face to have a look at me by the light of the candle. He was prematurely bald on the top of his head, and had bushy black eyebrows that wouldn't lie down, but stood up bristling. His eyes were set very deep in his head, and were disagreeably sharp and suspicious. He was nothing to me, and I could have had no foresight then that he ever would be anything to me, but it happened that I had this opportunity of observing him well.

"Boy of the neighborhood? Hey?" said he.

"Yes, sir," said I.

"How do *you* come here?"

"Miss Havisham sent for me, sir," I explained.

"Well! Behave yourself. I have a pretty large experience of boys, and you're a bad set of fellows. Now mind!" said he, biting the side of his great forefinger as he frowned at me, "you behave yourself!"

With these words he released me—which I was glad of, for his hand smelt of scented soap—and went his way downstairs. We were soon in Miss Havisham's room, where she and everything else were just as I had left them. Estella left me standing near the door, and I stood there until Miss Havisham cast her eyes upon me from the dressing table.

"So!" she said, without being startled or surprised; "the days have worn away, have they?"

"Yes, ma'am. Today is—"

"There, there, there!" with the impatient movement of her fingers. "I don't want to know. Are you ready to play?"

"I don't think I am, ma'am."

"Not at cards again?" she demanded with a searching look.

"Yes, ma'am; I could do that, if I was wanted."

"Since this house strikes you old and grave, boy," said Miss Havisham impatiently, "and you are unwilling to play, are you willing to work?"

I said I was quite willing.

"Then go into that opposite room," said she, pointing at the door behind me with her withered hand, "and wait there till I come."

I crossed the staircase landing, and entered the room she indicated. From that room too, the daylight was completely excluded, and it had an airless smell that was oppressive. A fire had been lately kindled in the damp old-fashioned grate, and it was more disposed to go out than to burn up, and the reluctant smoke which hung in the room seemed colder than the clearer air—like our own marsh mist. Certain wintry branches of candles on the high chimney piece faintly lighted the chamber, or, it would be more expressive to say, faintly troubled its darkness. It was spacious, and I dare say had once been handsome, but every discernible thing in it was covered with dust and mold, and dropping to pieces. The most prominent object was a long table with a tablecloth spread on it, as if a feast had been in preparation when the house and the clocks all stopped together. An épergne or centerpiece of some kind was in the middle of this cloth; it was so heavily overhung with cobwebs that its form was quite undistinguishable; and, as I looked along the yellow expanse out of which I remember its seeming to grow, like a black fungus, I saw speckled-legged spiders with blotchy bodies running home to it, and running out from it, as if some circumstance of the greatest public importance had just transpired in the spider community.

But, the black beetles took no notice of the agitation, and groped about the hearth in a ponderous elderly way, as if they were shortsighted and hard of hearing, and not on terms with one another.

These crawling things had fascinated my attention, and I was watching them from a distance, when Miss Havisham laid a hand upon my shoulder. In her other hand she had a crutch-headed stick on which she leaned, and she looked like the witch of the place.

"This," said she, pointing to the long table with her stick, "is where I will be laid when I am dead. They shall come and look at me here."

"What do you think that is?" she asked me, again pointing with her stick; "that, where those cobwebs are?"

"I can't guess what it is, ma'am."

"It's a great cake. A bride-cake. Mine!"

She looked all round the room in a glaring manner, and then said, leaning on me while her hand twitched my shoulder, "Come, come, come! Walk me, walk me!"

I made out from this that the work I had to do was to walk Miss Havisham round and round the room. Accordingly, I started at once, and she leaned upon my shoulder, and we went away at a pace that might have been an imitation (founded on my first impulse under that roof) of Mr. Pumblechook's chaise-cart.

After a while she said, "Call Estella!" so I went out on the landing and roared that name as I had done on the previous occasion. When her light appeared, I returned to Miss Havisham, and we started away again round and round the room.

If only Estella had come to be a spectator of our proceedings, I should have felt suffi-ciently discontented; but, as she brought with her the three ladies and the gentleman whom I had seen below, I didn't know what to do.

"Dear Miss Havisham," said Miss Sarah Pocket. "How well you look!"

"I do not," returned Miss Havisham. "I am yellow skin and bone."

Camilla brightened when Miss Pocket met with this rebuff; and she murmured, as she plaintively contemplated Miss Havisham, "Poor dear soul! Certainly not to be expected to look well, poor thing. The idea!"

"And how are *you*?" said Miss Havisham to Camilla. As we were close to Camilla then, I would have stopped as a matter of course, only Miss Havisham wouldn't stop.

"Thank you, Miss Havisham," she re-turned, "I am as well as can be expected."

"Why, what's the matter with you?" asked Miss Havisham, with exceeding sharp-ness.

"Nothing worth mentioning," replied Ca-milla. "I don't wish to make a display of my feelings, but I have habitually thought of you more in the night than I am quite equal to."

"Then don't think of me," retorted Miss Havisham.

"Very easily said!" remarked Camilla, amiably repressing a sob, while a hitch came into her upper lip, and her tears overflowed. "It's a weakness to be so affectionate, but I can't help it."

Miss Havisham and I kept going round and round the room; now brushing against the skirts of the visitors, now giving them the whole length of the dismal chamber.

"There's Matthew!" said Camilla. "Never mixing with any natural ties, never coming here to see how Miss Havisham is!"

When Matthew was mentioned, Miss Havisham stopped me and herself, and stood looking at the speaker.

"Matthew will come and see me at last,"

15

15 **Discussion** Why does Camilla brighten when Miss Havisham rebuffs Sarah Pocket?

**16 Critical Thinking and Reading**
What does Miss Havisham mean when she speaks of "sharper teeth than teeth of mice"?

**17 Discussion** Why does Miss Havisham want Pip to notice Estella's beauty?

said Miss Havisham sternly, "when I am laid on that table. That will be his place—there," striking the table with her stick, "at my head! And yours will be there! And your husband's there! And Sarah Pocket's there! And Georgiana's there! Now you all know where to take your stations when you come to feast upon me.[3] And now go!"

At the mention of each name, she had struck the table with her stick in a new place. She now said, "Walk me, walk me!" and we went on again.

"I suppose there's nothing to be done," exclaimed Camilla, "but comply and depart. It's something to have seen the object of one's love and duty, even for so short a time. I shall think of it with a melancholy satisfaction when I wake up in the night. I wish Matthew could have that comfort, but he sets it at defiance."

While Estella was away lighting them down, Miss Havisham still walked with her hand on my shoulder, but more and more slowly. At last she stopped before the fire, and said, after muttering and looking at it some seconds:

"This is my birthday, Pip."

I was going to wish her many happy returns, when she lifted her stick.

"I don't suffer it to be spoken of. I don't suffer those who were here just now, or any one, to speak of it. They come here on the day, but they dare not refer to it."

Of course I made no further effort to refer to it.

"On this day of the year, long before you were born, this heap of decay," stabbing with her crutched stick at the pile of cobwebs on the table, but not touching it, "was brought here. It and I have worn away together. The mice have gnawed at it, and sharper teeth than teeth of mice have gnawed at me."

---

3. **feast upon me:** Claim your inheritance when I die.

"When the ruin is complete," said she, with a ghastly look, "and when they lay me dead, in my bride's dress on the bride's table—which shall be done, and which will be the finished curse upon him—so much the better if it is done on this day!"

She stood looking at the table as if she stood looking at her own figure lying there. I remained quiet. Estella returned, and she, too, remained quiet. It seemed to me that we continued thus a long time.

At length, not coming out of her distraught state by degrees, but in an instant, Miss Havisham said, "Let me see you two play at cards; why have you not begun?" With that we returned to her room, and sat down as before; I was beggared, as before; and again, as before, Miss Havisham watched us all the time, directed my attention to Estella's beauty, and made me notice it the more by trying her jewels on Estella.

Estella, for her part, likewise treated me as before; except that she did not condescend to speak. When we had played some half-dozen games, a day was appointed for my return, and I was taken down into the yard to be fed in the former dog-like manner. There, too, I was again left to wander about as I liked.

When I had exhausted the garden and a greenhouse with nothing in it but a fallen-down grape-vine and some bottles, I found myself in the dismal corner upon which I had looked out of the window. Never questioning for a moment that the house was now empty, I looked in at another window, and found myself, to my great surprise, exchanging a broad stare with a pale young gentleman with red eyelids and light hair.

This pale young gentleman quickly disappeared, and reappeared beside me.

"Halloa!" said he, "young fellow!"

I said "Halloa!" politely omitting young fellow.

"Who let *you* in?" said he.

**JOHN RANDOLPH**
*Gilbert Stuart*
National Gallery of Art, Washington

**Humanities Note**

Fine art, *John Randolph*, 1805, by Gilbert Stuart. Gilbert Stuart (1755–1828) was the premier portraitist of the new American Republic. Stuart painted nearly one thousand portraits in his lifetime, the most famous of which is the picture of George Washington that is reproduced on the one-dollar bill.

*John Randolph* (1805) is a charming study of a young man in a casual pose. The background is left sketchy in the manner of Reynolds or Gainsborough, directing the focus of the viewer to the sitter.

You may want to use the following questions to prompt a discussion:

1. To which social class do you think this young man belongs?
2. Describe his personality, as the artist reveals it.
3. Do you think he resembles the "pale young gentleman" whom Pip sees? Why or why not?

**18 Discussion** Does Dickens intend that readers take this character seriously? Explain.

"Miss Estella."

"Who gave you leave to prowl about?"

"Miss Estella."

"Come and fight," said the pale young gentleman.

What could I do but follow him? I have often asked myself the question since; but what else could I do? His manner was so final, and I was so astonished, that I followed where he led, as if I had been under a spell.

"Stop a minute, though," he said, wheeling round before we had gone many paces. "I ought to give you a reason for fighting, too. There it is!" In a most irritating manner he instantly slapped his hands against one another, daintily flung one of his legs up behind him, pulled my hair, slapped his hands again, dipped his head, and butted it into my stomach.

I hit out at him, and was going to hit out again, when he said, "Aha! Would you?" and began dancing backwards and forwards in a manner quite unparalleled within my limited experience.

"Laws of the game!" said he. Here, he skipped from his left leg on to his right. "Regular rules!" Here, he skipped from his right leg on to his left. "Come to the ground, and go through the preliminaries!" Here, he dodged backwards and forwards, and did all sorts of things while I looked helplessly at him.

*Great Expectations*  795

19 **Critical Thinking and Reading**
What do you think accounts for this change in Estella's behavior toward Pip?

20 **Discussion** When else has Pip shown signs of guilt?

I was secretly afraid of him when I saw him so dexterous, but I followed him, without a word, to a retired nook of the garden. On his asking me if I was satisfied with the ground, and on my replying Yes, he begged my leave to absent himself for a moment, and quickly returned with a bottle of water and a sponge dipped in vinegar. "Available for both," he said, placing these against the wall. And then fell to pulling off, not only his jacket and waistcoat, but his shirt too, in a manner at once light-hearted, business-like, and bloodthirsty.

My heart failed me when I saw him squaring at me with every demonstration of mechanical nicety, and eyeing my anatomy as if he were minutely choosing his bone. I never have been so surprised in my life as I was when I let out the first blow, and saw him lying on his back, looking up at me with a bloody nose and his face exceedingly foreshortened.

But, he was on his feet directly, and after sponging himself with a great show of dexterity, began squaring again. The second greatest surprise I have ever had in my life was seeing him on his back again, looking up at me out of a black eye.

His spirit inspired me with great respect. He seemed to have no strength, and he never once hit me hard, and he was always knocked down; but, he would be up again in a moment sponging himself or drinking out of the water bottle, with the greatest satisfaction in seconding himself according to form, and then came at me with an air and a show that made me believe he really was going to do for me at last. He got heavily bruised, for I am sorry to record that the more I hit him, the harder I hit him; but, he came up again and again and again, until at last he got a bad fall with the back of his head against the wall. Even after that crisis in our affairs, he got up and turned round and round confusedly a few times, not know-

ing where I was; but finally went on his knees to his sponge and threw it up: at the same time panting out, "That means you have won."

He seemed so brave and innocent that, although I had not proposed the contest, I felt but a gloomy satisfaction in my victory. However, I got dressed, darkly wiping my sanguinary face at intervals, and, I said, "Can I help you?" and he said, "No thankee," and I said, "Good afternoon," and *he* said, "Same to you."

When I got into the courtyard, I found Estella waiting with the keys. But she neither asked me where I had been, nor why I had kept her waiting; and there was a bright flush upon her face, as though something had happened to delight her. Instead of going straight to the gate too, she stepped back into the passage, and beckoned me.

"Come here! You may kiss me if you like."

I kissed her cheek as she turned it to me. I think I would have gone through a great deal to kiss her cheek. But I felt that the kiss was given to the coarse common boy as a piece of money might have been, and that it was worth nothing.

What with the birthday visitors, and what with the cards, and what with the fight, my stay had lasted so long that, when I neared home, the light on the spit of sand off the point on the marshes was gleaming against a black night sky, and Joe's furnace was flinging a path of fire across the road.

### Chapter 12

My mind grew very uneasy on the subject of the pale young gentleman. The more I thought of the fight, and recalled the pale young gentleman on his back, the more certain it appeared that something would be done to me. I felt that the pale young gentle-

## Primary Source

Much has been written about Charles Dickens. He is, in fact, one of the authors most often written about among biographers and literary critics. Much is now known about Dickens, his work, and his life in London. In what is considered the most comprehensive and authoritative biography of Charles Dickens, *Charles Dickens: His Tragedy and Triumph,* Edgar Johnson states this about Dickens's character and his life:

Dickens was himself a Dickens character, bursting with an inordinate and fantastic vitality. The world in which his spirit dwelt was identical with the world of his novels, brilliant in hue, violent in movement, crammed with people all furiously alive and with places as alive as the people. 'The Dickens world' was his everyday world. He found his own intimates as funny as Mr. Micawber [(*David Copperfield*)], Mr. Toots [(*Dombey and Son*)], and Flora Finching [(*Little Dorrit*)], and felt their joys and sorrows as deeply as he did those of the characters in his fictions. His adventures and misadventures were as hilarious or painful as those of Mr. Pickwick or David Copperfield or Pip. And Dickens was not man's blood was on my head, and that the law would avenge it.

When the day came round for my return to the scene of the deed of violence, my terrors reached their height. However, go to Miss Havisham's I must, and go I did. And behold! nothing came of the late struggle. It was not alluded to in any way, and no pale young gentleman was to be discovered on the premises.

On the broad landing between Miss Havisham's own room and that other room in which the long table was laid out, I saw a garden chair—a light chair on wheels, that you pushed from behind. It had been placed there since my last visit, and I entered, that same day, on a regular occupation of pushing Miss Havisham in this chair (when she was tired of walking with her hand upon my shoulder) round her own room, and across the landing, and round the other room. Over and over and over again, we would make these journeys, and sometimes they would last as long as three hours at a stretch. I insensibly fall into a general mention of these journeys as numerous, because it was at once settled that I should return every alternate day at noon for these purposes, and because I am now going to sum up a period of at least eight or ten months.

As we began to be more used to one another, Miss Havisham talked more to me, and asked me such questions as what had I learnt and what was I going to be? I told her I was going to be apprenticed to Joe, I believed; and I enlarged upon my knowing nothing and wanting to know everything, in the hope that she might offer some help towards that desirable end. But she did not; on the contrary, she seemed to prefer my being ignorant. Neither did she ever give me any money or anything but my daily dinner—nor even stipulate that I should be paid for my services.

Estella was always about, and always let me in and out, but never told me I might kiss her again. Miss Havisham would often ask me in a whisper, or when we were alone, "Does she grow prettier and prettier, Pip?" And when I said Yes (for indeed she did), would seem to enjoy it greedily. Also, when we played at cards, Miss Havisham would look on, with a miserly relish of Estella's moods, whatever they were. And sometimes, when her moods were so many and so contradictory of one another that I was puzzled what to say or do, Miss Havisham would embrace her with lavish fondness, murmuring something in her ear that sounded like, "Break their hearts, my pride and hope, break their hearts and have no mercy!"

Perhaps I might have told Joe about the pale young gentleman, if I had not previously been betrayed into those enormous inventions to which I had confessed. Under the circumstances, I felt that Joe could hardly fail to discern in the pale young gentleman an appropriate passenger to be put into the black velvet coach; therefore, I said nothing of him. I reposed complete confidence in no one but Biddy; but I told poor Biddy everything. Why, it came natural for me to do so, and why Biddy had a deep concern in everything I told her, I did not know then, though I think I know now.

Meanwhile, councils went on in the kitchen at home. Pumblechook used often to come over of a night for the purpose of discussing my prospects. He and my sister would pair off in such nonsensical speculations about Miss Havisham, and about what she would do with me and for me, that I used to want—quite painfully—to burst into spiteful tears. In these discussions, Joe bore no part. But he was often talked at, while they were in progress, by reason of Mrs. Joe's perceiving that he was not favorable to my being taken from the forge.

We went on in this way for a long time, and it seemed likely that we should continue

*Great Expectations*  797

21 **Discussion** Do you think Pip is correct in thinking that Miss Havisham would prefer him to remain ignorant? If so, what explains her attitude?

22 **Critical Thinking and Reading** What can you infer about the relationship between Miss Havisham and Estella?

23 **Discussion** What do you think provokes Biddy's concern?

one of those frugal authors who save all their good things for their books. In the profusion of his creativity, in his prodigal exuberance, he poured out through his thousands of letters a wealth of psychological observation and comic episode, a depth of feeling and a vividness of language, that might have enriched a dozen more novels. . . .

24 **Clarification** The indenture system was a means of training young men for a trade or occupation. The master, or teacher, would usually be paid a fee and he would specify the number of years it would take to complete the training. The indenture papers were a binding contract.

25 **Critical Thinking and Reading** Why is Mrs. Joe so upset?

26 **Discussion** Why do you think Joe refuses to address Miss Havisham directly?

to go on in this way for a long time, when, one day, Miss Havisham stopped short as she and I were walking—she leaning on my shoulder—and said, with some displeasure:

"You are growing tall, Pip!"

She said no more at the time; but she presently stopped and looked at me again; and presently again; and after that, looked frowning and moody. On the next day of my attendance, she stayed me with a movement of her impatient fingers:

"Tell me the name again of that blacksmith of yours."

"Joe Gargery, ma'am."

"Meaning the master you were to be apprenticed to?"

"Yes, Miss Havisham."

24 "You had better be apprenticed at once. Would Gargery come here with you, and bring your indentures,[1] do you think?"

I signified that I had no doubt he would take it as an honor to be asked.

"Then let him come."

"At any particular time, Miss Havisham?"

"There, there! I know nothing about times. Let him come soon, and come alone with you."

25 When I got home at night, and delivered this message for Joe, my sister "went on the rampage" in a more alarming degree than at any previous period.

### Chapter 13

It was a trial to my feelings, on the next day but one, to see Joe arraying himself in his Sunday clothes to accompany me to Miss Havisham's. However, as he thought his court suit necessary to the occasion, it was not for me to tell him that he looked far better in his working dress; the rather, because

---

**1. indentures** (in den′ chərz) *n.*: A contract binding an apprentice to a master.

I knew he made himself so dreadfully uncomfortable entirely on my account, and that it was for me he pulled up his shirt-collar so very high behind that it made the hair on the crown of his head stand up like a tuft of feathers.

At breakfast-time, my sister declared her intention of going to town with us, and being left at Uncle Pumblechook's, and called for "when we had done with our fine ladies." The forge was shut up for the day, and Joe inscribed in chalk upon the door (as it was his custom to do on the very rare occasions when he was not at work) the monosyllable HOUT, accompanied by a sketch of an arrow supposed to be flying in the direction he had taken.

When we came to Pumblechook's, my sister bounced in and left us. As it was almost noon, Joe and I held straight on to Miss Havisham's house. Estella opened the gate as usual, and, the moment she appeared, Joe took his hat off and stood weighing it by the brim in both his hands.

Estella took no notice of either of us, but led us the way that I knew so well. I followed next to her, and Joe came last. Estella told me we were both to go in, so I took Joe by the coat cuff and conducted him into Miss Havisham's presence. She was seated at her dressing table, and looked round at us immediately.

"Oh!" said she to Joe. "You are the husband of the sister of this boy?"

I could hardly have imagined dear old Joe looking so unlike himself or so like some extraordinary bird, standing, as he did, speechless, with his tuft of feathers ruffled, and his mouth open as if he wanted a worm.

"You are the husband," repeated Miss Havisham, "of the sister of this boy?"

26 It was very aggravating; but, throughout the interview, Joe persisted in addressing me instead of Miss Havisham.

"Which I meantersay, Pip," Joe now

observed, in a manner that was at once expressive of forcible argumentation, strict confidence, and great politeness, "as I hup and married your sister, and I were at the time what you might call (if you was any ways inclined) a single man."

"Well!" said Miss Havisham. "And you have reared the boy, with the intention of taking him for your apprentice; is that so, Mr. Gargery?"

"You know, Pip," replied Joe, "as you and me were ever friends, and it were looked for'ard to betwixt us, as being calc'lated to lead to larks.[1] Not but what, Pip, if you had ever made objections to the business—such as its being open to black and sut, or such-like—not but what they would have been attended to, don't you see?"

"Has the boy," said Miss Havisham, "ever made any objection? Does he like the trade?"

"Which it is well beknown to yourself, Pip," returned Joe, "that it were the wish of your own hart."

It was quite in vain for me to endeavor to make him sensible that he ought to speak to Miss Havisham. The more I made faces and gestures to him to do it, the more confidential, argumentative, and polite he persisted in being to me.

"Have you brought his indentures with you?" asked Miss Havisham.

"Well, Pip, you know," replied Joe, as if that were a little unreasonable, "you yourself see me put 'em in my 'at, and therefore you know as they are here." With which he took them out, and gave them, not to Miss Havisham, but to me. I am afraid I was ashamed of the dear good fellow—I *know* I was ashamed of him—when I saw that Estella stood at the back of Miss Havisham's chair, and that her eyes laughed mischievously. I took the indentures out of his hand and gave them to Miss Havisham.

---

**1. larks:** Fun.

"You expected," said Miss Havisham, as she looked them over, "no premium[2] with the boy?"

"Joe!" I remonstrated; for he made no reply at all. "Why don't you answer—"

"Pip," returned Joe, cutting me short as if he were hurt, "which I meantersay that were not a question requiring a answer betwixt yourself and me, and which you know the answer to be full well No. You know it to be No, Pip, and wherefore should I say it?"

Miss Havisham glanced at him as if she understood what he really was better than I had thought possible, seeing what he was there, and took up a little bag from the table beside her.

"Pip has earned a premium here," she said, "and here it is. There are five-and-twenty guineas[3] in this bag. Give it to your master, Pip."

As if he were absolutely out of his mind with the wonder awakened in him by her strange figure and the strange room, Joe, even at this pass, persisted in addressing me.

"This is very liberal on your part, Pip," said Joe, "and it is as such received and grateful welcome, though never looked for, far nor near nor nowheres. And now, old chap," said Joe, "and now, old chap, may we do our duty! May you and me do our duty, both on us by one and another, and by them which your liberal present—have—conweyed—to be—for the satisfaction of mind—of—them as never—" here Joe showed that he felt he had fallen into frightful difficulties, until he triumphantly rescued himself with the words, "and from myself far be it!"

"Good-bye, Pip!" said Miss Havisham. "Let them out, Estella."

---

**2. premium** (prē′ mē əm) *n.*: A fee paid by an apprentice to a master.
**3. guineas** (gin′ ēz) *n.*: Gold coins worth about one pound each.

*Great Expectations*  799

27 **Discussion** There have been many indications that Pip's views of "common" people are changing. How do you think Pip's association with Miss Havisham and Estella has influenced his reaction to Joe's awkward behavior?

**28 Literary Focus** How are Pumblechook and Mrs. Joe similar?

**29 Discussion** Why is Pip no longer pleased at the thought of becoming a blacksmith?

"Am I to come again, Miss Havisham?" I asked.

"No. Gargery is your master now. Gargery! One word!"

Thus calling him back as I went out of the door, I heard her say to Joe, in a distinct emphatic voice, "The boy has been a good boy here, and that is his reward. Of course, as an honest man, you will expect no other and no more."

In another minute we were outside the gate, and it was locked, and Estella was gone. Joe backed up against a wall, and said to me, "Astonishing!" And there he remained so long, saying "Astonishing" at intervals so often that I began to think his senses were never coming back. At length, he prolonged his remark into "Pip, I do assure *you* this is as-TON-ishing!" and so, by degrees, became conversational and able to walk away.

I have reason to think that Joe's intellects were brightened by the encounter they had passed through, and that on our way to Pumblechook's, he invented a subtle and deep design. My reason is to be found in what took place in Mr. Pumblechook's parlor: where, on our presenting ourselves, my sister sat in conference with that detested seedsman.

"Well!" cried my sister, "what did Miss Havisham give young Rantipole[4] here?"

"She giv' him," said Joe, "nothing."

Mrs. Joe was going to break out, but Joe went on.

"What she giv'," said Joe, "she giv' to his friends. 'And by his friends,' were her explanation, 'I mean into the hands of his sister, Mrs. J. Gargery.'"

"And how much have you got?" asked my sister, laughing. Positively, laughing!

"Five-and-twenty pound," said Joe, de-

lightedly handing the bag to my sister.

"It's five-and-twenty pound, mum," echoed that basest of swindlers, Pumblechook, rising to shake hands with her; "and it's no more than your merits (as I said when my opinion was asked), and I wish you joy of the money!"

"Goodness knows, Uncle Pumblechook," said my sister (grasping the money), "we're deeply beholden to you."

"Never mind me, mum," returned that diabolical corn chandler. "A pleasure's a pleasure all the world over. But this boy, you know; we must have him bound. I said I'd see to it—to tell you the truth."

The justices were sitting in the Town Hall near at hand, and we at once went over to have me bound apprentice to Joe in the magisterial presence. I say, we went over, but I was pushed over by Pumblechook, exactly as if I had that moment picked a pocket or fired a rick.[5] My indentures were duly signed and attested, and I was "bound," Mr. Pumblechook holding me all the while as if we had looked in on our way to the scaffold[6] to have those little preliminaries disposed of.

When I got into my little bedroom that night, I was truly wretched, and had a strong conviction on me that I should never like Joe's trade. I had liked it once, but once was not now.

## Chapter 14

Once it had seemed to me that when I should at last roll up my shirt-sleeves and go into the forge, Joe's 'prentice, I should be distinguished and happy. Now the reality was in my hold, I only felt that I was dusty with the dust of the small coal, and that I had a weight upon my daily remembrance to

---

**4. rantipole** (ran' tē pōl) *n*.: Wild and reckless person.

---

**5. fired a rick:** Set fire to a stack of hay or straw.
**6. scaffold** (skaf' 'ld) *n*.: Raised platform on which criminals are executed.

which the anvil was a feather. There have been occasions in my later life (I suppose as in most lives) when I have felt for a time as if a thick curtain had fallen on all its interest and romance, to shut me out from anything save dull endurance any more. Never has that curtain dropped so heavy and blank as when my way in life stretched out straight before me through the newly-entered road of apprenticeship to Joe.

I was dejected on the first working day of my apprenticeship; but I am glad to know that I never breathed a murmur to Joe while my indentures lasted. It is about the only thing I *am* glad to know of myself in that connection.

For, though it includes what I proceed to add, all the merit of what I proceed to add was Joe's. It was not because I was faithful, but because Joe was faithful, that I never ran away and went for a soldier or a sailor. It is not possible to know how far the influence of any amiable honest-hearted duty-doing man flies out into the world, but it is very possible to know how it has touched one's self in going by, and I know right well that any good that intermixed itself with my apprenticeship came of plain contented Joe, and not of restless aspiring discontented me.

What I wanted, who can say? How can *I* say, when I never knew? What I dreaded was that in some unlucky hour I, being at my grimiest and commonest, should lift up my eyes and see Estella looking in at one of the wooden windows of the forge. I was haunted by the fear that she would, sooner or later, find me out, with a black face and hands, doing the coarsest part of my work, and would exult over me and despise me.

## Chapter 15

As I was getting too big for Mr. Wopsle's great-aunt's room, my education under that preposterous female terminated. Not, how-

ever, until Biddy had imparted to me every-thing she knew, from the little catalogue of prices. In my hunger for information, I also made proposals to Mr. Wopsle to bestow some intellectual crumbs upon me; with which he kindly complied.

Whatever I acquired, I tried to impart to Joe. This statement sounds so well that I cannot in my conscience let it pass unex-plained. I wanted to make Joe less ignorant and common, that he might be worthier of my society and less open to Estella's re-proach.

The old battery out on the marshes was our place of study, and a broken slate and a short piece of slate pencil were our educa-tional implements: to which Joe always added a pipe of tobacco. I never knew Joe to remember anything from one Sunday to an-other, or to acquire, under my tuition, any piece of information whatever. Yet he would smoke his pipe at the battery with a far more sagacious air than anywhere else—even with a learned air—as if he considered himself to be advancing immensely. Dear fellow, I hope he did.

It was pleasant and quiet, out there with the sails on the river passing beyond the earth-work, and sometimes, when the tide was low, looking as if they belonged to sunken ships that were still sailing on at the bottom of the water. Whenever I watched the vessels standing out to sea with their white sails spread, I somehow thought of Miss Havi-sham and Estella. One Sunday I resolved to mention a thought concerning them that had been much in my head.

"Joe," said I, "don't you think I ought to pay Miss Havisham a visit?"

"Well, Pip," returned Joe, slowly consid-ering. "What for?"

"What for, Joe? What is any visit made for?"

"There is some wisits p'r'aps," said Joe, "as for ever remains open to the question,

*Great Expectations* 801

30

**30 Critical Thinking and Reading**
How does this statement reveal the perspective of the adult Pip as well as the boy?

Pip. But in regard of wisiting Miss Havisham. She might think you wanted something—expected something of her."

"Don't you think I might say that I did not, Joe?"

"You might, old chap," said Joe. "And she might credit it. Similarly, she mightn't."

Joe felt, as I did, that he had made a point there, and he pulled hard at his pipe to keep himself from weakening it by repetition.

"You see, Pip," Joe pursued, as soon as he was past that danger,"Miss Havisham done the handsome thing by you. When Miss Havisham done the handsome thing by you, she called me back to say to me as that were all."

"Yes, Joe. I heard her."

"Which I meantersay, Pip, it might be that her meaning were—Make a end on it!—As you was!—Me to the North, and you to the South!—Keep in sunders!"

I had thought of that too, and it was very far from comforting to me to find that he had thought of it; for it seemed to render it more probable.

"But, Joe."

"Yes, old chap."

"Here am I, getting on in the first year of my time, and, since the day of my being bound I have never thanked Miss Havisham, or asked after her, or shown that I remembered her."

"That's true, Pip; and unless you were to turn her out a set of shoes all four round—and which I meantersay as even a set of shoes all four round might not act acceptable as a present in a total wacancy of hoofs—"

"I don't mean that sort of remembrance, Joe; I don't mean a present."

But Joe had got the idea of a present in his head and must harp upon it."Or even," said he, "if you was helped to knocking her

up a new chain for the front door—or say a gross or two of shark-headed screws for general use—or some light fancy article, such as a toasting-fork when she took her muffins.

"My dear Joe," I cried in desperation, taking hold of his coat, "don't go on in that way. I never thought of making Miss Havisham any present."

"No, Pip," Joe assented, as if he had been contending for that all along, "and what I say to you is, you are right, Pip."

"Yes, Joe; but what I wanted to say was that, as we are rather slack just now, if you would give me a half-holiday tomorrow, I think I would go up town and make a call on Miss Est—Havisham."

"Which her name," said Joe gravely, "ain't Estavisham, Pip, unless she have been rechris'ended."

"I know, Joe, I know. It was a slip of mine. What do you think of it, Joe?"

In brief, Joe thought that if I thought well of it, he thought well of it. But, he was particular in stipulating that if I were not received with cordiality, then this experimental trip should have no successor. By these conditions I promised to abide.

Now Joe kept a journeyman[1] at weekly wages whose name was Orlick. He was a broad-shouldered loose-limbed swarthy fellow of great strength, never in a hurry, and always slouching. He never even seemed to come to his work on purpose, but would slouch in as if by mere accident; and when he went to the Jolly Bargemen to eat his dinner, or went away at night, he would slouch out as if he had no idea where he was going, and no intention of ever coming back. He lodged at a sluice-keeper's[2] out on the marshes, and on working days would come

31

---

1. **journeyman** (jʉr′ nē mən) *n.*: Person who has learned a trade but still works for a master.
2. **sluice** (slo͞os)-**keeper**: Person in charge of regulating the flow of water in an artificial stream.

## Grammar in Action

When reading a work of literature, look for specific details that help determine the time in which that work takes place. Details of setting that indicate time suggest to the reader the general historical period of a work. Look at these details from *Great Expectations:*

"Or even," [said Joe] "—or some light fancy article, such as a toasting fork when she took her muffins."

Joe, a blacksmith, is suggesting that he and Pip make a toasting fork for Miss Havisham to spear muffins in order to toast them over an open flame. Today, blacksmiths devote their time to shoeing horses for riding stables or mounted police, and most toast is made in an electric toaster or a gas or electric oven. This detail from the novel indicates that it takes place in an earlier time.

What does the following passage tell you about the historical time of the setting?

He [Orlick] and Joe had got a piece of hot iron between them, and I was at the bellows.

slouching from his hermitage,[3] with his hands in his pockets and his dinner loosely tied in a bundle round his neck and dangling on his back. He always slouched, locomotively, with his eyes on the ground; and, when accosted or otherwise required to raise them, he looked up in a half-resentful, half-puzzled way.

This morose journeyman had no liking for me. When I became Joe's 'prentice, Orlick was perhaps confirmed in some suspicion that I should displace him.

Orlick was at work and present, next day, when I reminded Joe of my half-holiday. He said nothing at the moment, for he and Joe had just got a piece of hot iron between them, and I was at the bellows;[4] but by-and-by he said, leaning on his hammer:

"Now, master! Sure you're not a going to favor only one of us. If young Pip has a half-holiday, do as much for Old Orlick." I suppose he was about five-and-twenty, but he usually spoke of himself as an ancient person.

"Why, what'll you do with a half-holiday, if you get it?" said Joe.

"What'll *I* do with it? What'll *he* do with it? I'll do as much with it as *him*," said Orlick.

"As to Pip, he's going up town," said Joe.

"Well, then, as to Old Orlick, *he's* a-going up town," retorted that worthy. "Two can go up town. Tain't only one wot can go up town."

"Don't lose your temper," said Joe.

"Shall if I like," growled Orlick. "Some and their up towning! Now, master! Come. No favoring in this shop. Be a man!"

"All right, as in general you stick to your work as well as most men," said Joe, "let it be a half-holiday for all."

My sister had been standing silent in the yard, within hearing—she was a most unscrupulous spy and listener—and she instantly looked in at one of the windows.

"Like you, you fool!" said she to Joe, "giving holidays to great idle hulkers like that. You are a rich man, upon my life, to waste wages in that way. I wish *I* was his master!"

"You'd be everybody's master if you durst," retorted Orlick, with an ill-favored grin.

("Let her alone," said Joe.)

"I'd be a match for all noodles and all rogues," returned my sister, beginning to work herself into a mighty rage. "And I couldn't be a match for the noodles without being a match for your master, who's the dunderheaded king of the noodles. And I couldn't be a match for the rogues without being a match for you, who are the blackest-looking and the worst rogue between this and France. Now!"

"You're a foul shrew, Mother Gargery," growled the journeyman. "If that makes a judge of rogues, you ought to be a good 'un."

("Let her alone, will you?" said Joe.)

"What did you say?" cried my sister, beginning to scream. "What did you say? What did that fellow Orlick say to me, Pip? What did he call me, with my husband standing by? Oh! Oh! Oh!" Each of these exclamations was a shriek. "What was the name that he gave me before the base man who swore to defend me? Oh! Hold me! Oh!"

"Ah-h-h!" growled the journeyman, between his teeth, "I'd hold you, if you was my wife. I'd hold you under the pump, and choke it out of you."

("I tell you, let her alone," said Joe.)

"Oh! To hear him!" cried my sister, with a clap of her hands and a scream together—which was her next stage. "To hear the

------

3. **hermitage** (hur' mit ij) *n.*: Secluded and solitary dwelling.

4. **bellows** (bel' ōz) *n.*: Device for blowing air on a fire.

**32 Discussion** Why is Mrs. Joe so upset by Joe's decision?

*Great Expectations* 803

Knowledge of details of setting that suggest the period will add to your understanding and enjoyment of a work of literature.

**Student Activity 1.** Find three or four more passages that contain details that suggest the time period in which the novel is set. Explain what you learned from each passage for your classmates and teacher.

**Student Activity 2.** With a partner or small group of classmates, decide on a time period other than the present and brainstorm a list of details which suggest that period. Discuss how you might work such details of setting into a short story set at the time you chose.

## Humanities Note

Fine Art, *Pat Lyon at the Forge*, 1826-27, by John Neagle. John Neagle (1796-1865) was an American portrait painter trained by the famous painter of presidents, Gilbert Stuart. John Neagle and his father-in-law Thomas Sully were the most fashionable portrait painters in Philadelphia.

There is an interesting story connected with *Pat Lyon at the Forge*. Lyon, a Philadelphia blacksmith, was imprisoned for a bank robbery he did not commit. Released after three months, he sued the city and won a great deal of money. He immediately commissioned John Neagle to paint his portrait, not as a gentleman but as a working man.

You might ask students the following questions:

1. Which details reveal the trade and social status of the subject?
2. Do you think Pat Lyon resembles Dickens's character Joe Gargery? Why or why not?

**PAT LYON AT THE FORGE 1826–27**
*John Neagle*
The Museum of Fine Arts, Boston

804　The Novel

names he's giving me! That Orlick! In my own house! Me, a married woman! With my husband standing by! Oh! Oh!"

What could the wretched Joe do now, after his disregarded parenthetical interruptions, but stand up to his journeyman? Old Orlick felt that the situation admitted of nothing less than coming on, and was on his defense straightway, so, without so much as pulling off their singed and burnt aprons, they went at one another, like two giants. But if any man in that neighborhood could stand up long against Joe, I never saw the man. Orlick, as if he had been of no more account than the pale young gentleman, was very soon among the coal dust, and in no hurry to come out of it. Then Joe unlocked the door and picked up my sister, who had dropped insensible at the window (but who had seen the fight first I think), and who was carried into the house.

I went upstairs to dress myself. When I came down again, I found Joe and Orlick sweeping up, without any other traces of discomposure than a slit in one of Orlick's nostrils.

**33** With what absurd emotions (for we think the feelings that are very serious in a man quite comical in a boy) I found myself again going to Miss Havisham's matters little here. Nor how I passed and repassed the gate many times before I could make up my mind to ring.

Miss Sarah Pocket came to the gate. No Estella.

"How, then? You here again?" said Miss Pocket. "What do you want?"

When I said that I only came to see how Miss Havisham was, Sarah evidently deliberated whether or no she should send me about my business. But, unwilling to hazard the responsibility, she let me in, and presently brought the sharp message that I was to "come up."

Everything was unchanged, and Miss Havisham was alone. "Well!" said she, fixing her eyes upon me. "I hope you want nothing? You'll get nothing."

"No, indeed, Miss Havisham. I only wanted you to know that I am doing very well in my apprenticeship, and am always much obliged to you."

"There, there!" with the old restless fingers. "Come now and then; come on your birthday. Aye!" she cried suddenly, turning herself and her chair towards me, "You are looking round for Estella? Hey?"

I had been looking round—in fact, for Estella—and I stammered that I hoped she was well.

"Abroad," said Miss Havisham; "educating for a lady. Do you feel that you have lost her?"

There was such a malignant enjoyment in her utterance of the last words, and she broke into such a disagreeable laugh that I was at a loss what to say. She spared me the trouble of considering, by dismissing me. When the gate was closed upon me by Sarah of the walnut-shell countenance, I felt more than ever dissatisfied with my home and with my trade and with everything.

As I was loitering along the High Street, looking in disconsolately at the shop windows, and thinking what I would buy if I were a gentleman, who should come out of the bookshop but Mr. Wopsle. Mr. Wopsle had in his hand the affecting tragedy of George Barnwell, in which he had that moment invested sixpence, with the view of heaping every word of it on the head of Pumblechook, with whom he was going to drink tea. No sooner did he see me than he appeared to consider that a special Providence had put a 'prentice in his way to be read at; and he laid hold of me, and insisted on my accompanying him to the Pumblechookian parlor. As I knew it would be miserable at

**33 Discussion** What do you think the "absurd emotions" were?

home, and as the nights were dark and the way was dreary, and almost any companionship on the road was better than none, I made no great resistance; consequently, we turned into Pumblechook's just as the street and the shops were lighting up.

It was a very dark night when it was all over, and when I set out with Mr. Wopsle on the walk home. Beyond town, we found a heavy mist out, and it fell wet and thick. The turnpike lamp was a blur, and its rays looked solid substance on the fog. We were noticing this, when we came upon a man, slouching under the lee of the turnpike house.

"Halloa!" we said, stopping. "Orlick there?"

"Ah!" he answered, slouching out. "I was standing by, a minute, on the chance of company."

"You are late," I remarked.

Orlick not unnaturally answered, "Well? And *you're* late."

"We have been," said Mr. Wopsle, exalted with his late performance, "we have been indulging, Mr. Orlick, in an intellectual evening."

Old Orlick growled, as if he had nothing to say about that, and we all went on together. I asked him presently whether he had been spending his half-holiday up and down town?

"Yes," said he, "all of it. I come in behind yourself. I didn't see you, but I must have been pretty close behind you. By-the-bye, the guns is going again."

"At the Hulks?" said I.

"Aye! There's some of the birds flown from the cages. The guns have been going since dark, about. You'll hear one presently."

In effect, we had not walked many yards

further, when the well-remembered boom came towards us, deadened by the mist.

"A good night for cutting off in," said Orlick. "We'd be puzzled how to bring down a jailbird on the wing tonight."

We came to the village. The way by which we approached it took us past the Three Jolly Bargemen, which we were surprised to find—it being eleven o'clock—in a state of commotion, with the door wide open, and unwonted lights that had been hastily caught up and put down scattered about. Mr. Wopsle dropped in to ask what was the matter (surmising that a convict had been taken), but came running out in a great hurry.

"There's something wrong," said he, without stopping, "up at your place, Pip. Run all!"

"What is it?" I asked, keeping up with him. So did Orlick, at my side.

"I can't quite understand. The house seems to have been violently entered when Joe Gargery was out. Supposed by convicts. Somebody has been attacked and hurt."

We were running too fast to admit of more being said, and we made no stop until we got into our kitchen. It was full of people; the whole village was there, or in the yard; and there was a surgeon, and there was Joe, and there was a group of women, all on the floor in the midst of the kitchen. The unemployed bystanders drew back when they saw me, and so I became aware of my sister—lying without sense or movement on the bare boards where she had been knocked down by a tremendous blow on the back of the head, dealt by some unknown hand when her face was turned towards the fire—destined never to be on the rampage again while she was the wife of Joe.

34

## Closure and Extension

### ANSWERS TO THINKING ABOUT THE SELECTION
*Recalling*

1. Pip cannot bring himself to tell the truth because he does not think that Pumblechook and Mrs. Joe would understand him. Also, he thinks that it would be "treacherous" to reveal information about Miss Havisham to Mrs. Joe.

2. Pip plans to be educated, and he asks Biddy to teach him everything she knows.

3. Pip meets Miss Havisham's relatives, who are gossiping about an absent family member and waiting to be summoned by Miss Havisham. Then Miss Havisham shows the assembly the large table on which she wishes to be laid out when she dies and tells her relatives what positions to take on that occasion.

4. For his meeting with Miss Havisham, Joe dresses in his Sunday best, looking stiff and uncomfortable, his hair tousled and his mouth open as he faces her. Her purpose is to ask Joe whether he intends to apprentice Pip as a blacksmith. Joe will not answer her questions directly, but persists in turning to Pip and giving the answers to him, much to Pip's annoyance and embarrassment.

5. Estella has gone abroad to be educated as a lady, and Mrs. Joe has been struck down by an assailant and badly injured.

## THINKING ABOUT THE SELECTION

### Recalling

1. Why does Pip lie to Mrs. Joe and Pumblechook about Miss Havisham?
2. How does Pip plan to make himself "uncommon"?
3. What important events occur during Pip's second visit to Miss Havisham?
4. Describe Miss Havisham's meeting with Joe. What is its purpose?
5. What two pieces of distressing news does Pip hear at the end of this section?

### Interpreting

6. What does the visitor to the Three Jolly Bargemen want to communicate to Pip?
7. What does Joe's meeting with Miss Havisham reveal about his feelings for Pip?
8. Explain how Pip changes after his visit to Miss Havisham.
   What do you predict about his future based on this change?
9. Why does Miss Havisham take satisfaction in Estella's beauty and arrogance?
10. Based on what you know of Miss Havisham, what role do you think she will play in Pip's achieving his expectations?

### Applying

11. What advice would you give to Pip in planning for his future?

## ANALYZING LITERATURE

### Understanding Characterization

**Direct characterization** refers to statements by the writer about the characters. **Indirect characterization** is the method by which the writer reveals the characters' personalities through what they say or do or what others say about them. Since Pip rather than Dickens is the narrator of *Great Expectations,* all of the characterization in this novel is indirect.

Pip is a **round** rather than a **flat character** because he displays many traits and is capable of changing. He begins to change, in fact, as a result of his visit to Satis House.

1. How does this visit cause him to change?
2. Identify three of Pip's traits and indicate whether you learned about each through his words or actions, or what others say.
3. Name a flat character besides Mr. Pumblechook and explain your choice.

## CRITICAL THINKING AND READING

### Drawing Conclusions about Characters

You must often reach conclusions about characters based on what they say or do or what others say about them. For example, Pip does not mind lying to Mrs. Joe and Mr. Pumblechook about his visit to Miss Havisham, but he feels guilty about deceiving Joe. These different reactions indicate that he has less respect for Mrs. Joe and Pumblechook than he does for Joe.

Explain what conclusions the following facts suggest about each of the characters.

1. Miss Havisham has allowed her bridal feast to become a "heap of decay."
2. The young gentleman that Pip meets provokes a fight but proves to be a terrible boxer.

## THINKING AND WRITING

### Writing About Art

Look at the fine art on any of the following pages: 791, 795, or 804. Choose one of these paintings and write a characterization of the person in the art. First, examine carefully the painting you choose and list outstanding points or details about the person in it. Then make inferences about the traits or qualities of that person based on the details you see. Finally, if you think the portrait resembles one of the characters in *Great Expectations,* tell which character and give your reasons. Revise your draft, adding as much specific detail about the art as you need to support your points. Then prepare a final copy.

*Great Expectations* 807

### ANSWERS TO ANALYZING LITERATURE

1. Suggested Response: Pip is ashamed of his appearance and ignorance. He wants to rise in life so that he can be with Estella.
2. Suggested Response: Pip is conscientious because he cares deeply about how he behaves toward others and often says how guilty he feels about some action or thought (revealed through his thoughts); he is ambitious, because he wants to improve his education (revealed through his words and actions); and he is self-divided because his contact with Estella leads him to think of himself as "common" (revealed through his thoughts).
3. Suggested Response: Sarah Pocket is another flat character. There is little to her personality besides her hypocrisy and greed. She is one of the greedy hangers-on at Satis House.

### ANSWERS TO CRITICAL THINKING AND READING

1. Suggested Response: The decayed bridal feast symbolizes Miss Havisham's decay and withdrawal from life. It also symbolizes the death of her hopes caused by her fiancé's betrayal.
2. Suggested Response: The young gentleman is not very objective about his own skills and abilities.

### THINKING AND WRITING

Before beginning this assignment, students may want to refer to Lesson 9, "Writing About Character," in the Handbook of Writing About Literature.

**Publishing Student Writing**
You might want to display students' work on the bulletin board.

**Writing Across the Curriculum**
You might want to have students research and report on manual apprenticeship during the nineteenth century. Consider informing the social studies department of this assignment, so that teachers can provide guidance for students.

### Interpreting

6. Suggested Response: The stranger wants Pip to know that he has been sent by "Pip's convict," and feeling assured that Pip has understood, he slips Pip a shilling wrapped in two one-pound notes.
7. Suggested Response: We learn from the meeting that Joe is very fond of Pip, is looking forward to working with him, and is not motivated by greed.
8. Suggested Response: Pip is no longer content to be a blacksmith and wants to rise in life. He will probably find some way to obtain more education.
9. Suggested Response: Estella's beauty will attract men, and her arrogance will break their hearts. Miss Havisham may want to use Estella as a means for revenging herself on men.
10. Answers will differ. Some students may respond that Miss Havisham is a self-centered person. She says that there will be no more money coming to Pip after she has paid his indenture fee. It is not probable, therefore, that she will help him further.

### Applying

11. Answers will differ. Some students might advise Pip to go to London and work as a junior clerk, while continuing to study on his own.

**Challenge** Do you think Pip will meet Estella again? Explain.

**Literary Focus** You might want
to point out to students that the
various subplots include Abel
Magwitch's conflict with Compeyson and Biddy's rise from
servant to Joe's wife. Have students explain how these and other subplots are related to the
main plot.

**Look For** As students look for
Pip's conflicting motives, have
them pay special attention to his
thoughts about Joe.

**Writing/Prior Knowledge** You
might want to divide the class
into small groups and have students discuss the change they
will write about.

**Vocabulary** Have less advanced
students find the vocabulary
words in the text and replace
each one with an appropriate
synonym.

# GUIDE FOR READING

## Great Expectations, Chapters 16–23

**Plot and Subplot**

The **plot** is the sequence of interrelated events in a work of fiction. In novels and short stories, the plot often centers on one or more **conflicts,** the struggles between opposing forces. Since a novel is longer than a short story, novelists can develop their plots more fully. They can take more time to introduce the characters and conflicts, and they can build suspense more gradually. There may be both external and internal conflicts. Dickens does not resolve the main conflict of *Great Expectations,* Pip's internal conflict, until the book is nearly over.

A novel may contain **subplots,** which are minor, secondary plots running through the novel. Subplots are related to the main plot through the characters, who have parts in both. Subplots are also based on conflicts that must be resolved. Dickens skillfully weaves a number of subplots into *Great Expectations;* for example, one subplot involves the career of "the pale young gentleman," whom Pip meets again in London.

**Look For**

Pip must deal with conflicting motives. How does Dickens point up Pip's conflict between a love and respect for his origins and a fear of being "common"? Also, look for the comparisons and contrasts between the careers and "expectations" of Pip and "the pale young gentleman."

**Writing**

In these chapters of *Great Expectations,* Pip experiences a great change as he moves from his small town to London. Freewrite about a time when you experienced an important change in your life, such as entering a new school or grade, or coming to a new neighborhood.

**Vocabulary**

Knowing the following words will help you as you read Chapters 16–23 of *Great Expectations.*

**corroborated** (kə räb′ ə rāt′ əd) *v.*: Confirmed (p. 809)

**extract** (ik strakt′) *v.*: Draw out with special effort (p. 809)

**aberration** (ab′ər ā′ sʰən) *n.*: Mental derangement (p. 810)

**latent** (lāt′ 'nt) *adj.*: Hidden (p. 812)

**audacious** (ô dā′ sʰəs) *adj.*: Brave; without fear (p. 820)

**alleviated** (ə lē′ vē āt əd) *v.*: Lessened; relieved (p. 826)

**languor** (laŋ′ gər) *n.*: Weakness; sluggishness (p. 829)

**perplexity** (pər plek′ sə tē) *n.*: State of being confused (p. 831)

808    *The Novel*

---

**Objectives**

1 To understand plot and subplot in a novel
2 To predict outcomes
3 To understand the Latin root *spect*
4 To extend the story of a novel

**Support Material**

**Teaching Portfolio**
Teacher Backup, p. 949
Grammar in Action Worksheets, *Using Who and Whom,* p. 953; *Using Participial Phrases,* p. 955
Usage and Mechanics Worksheet, p. 957
Vocabulary Check, p. 958
Critical Thinking and Reading

Worksheet, *Predicting Outcomes,* p. 960
Language Worksheet, *Understanding the Latin Root* spect, p. 961
Selection Test, p. 962

## Chapter 16

Joe had been at the Three Jolly Bargemen, smoking his pipe, from a quarter after eight o'clock to a quarter before ten. While he was there, my sister had been seen standing at the kitchen door and had exchanged good night with a farm laborer going home. When Joe went home at five minutes before ten, he found her struck down on the floor, and promptly called in assistance. The fire had not then burnt unusually low, nor was the snuff[1] of the candle very long; the candle, however, had been blown out.

Nothing had been taken away from any part of the house. But, there was one remarkable piece of evidence on the spot. She had been struck with something blunt and heavy, on the head and spine; after the blows were dealt, something heavy had been thrown down at her with considerable violence, as she lay on her face. And on the ground beside her, when Joe picked her up, was a convict's leg iron which had been filed asunder.

Now, Joe, examining this iron with a smith's eye, declared it to have been filed asunder some time ago. The hue and cry going off to the Hulks, and people coming thence to examine the iron, Joe's opinion was corroborated. They did not undertake to say when it had left the prison ships to which it undoubtedly had once belonged, but they claimed to know for certain that that particular manacle had not been worn by either of two convicts who had escaped last night. Further, one of those two was already retaken, and had not freed himself of his iron.

Knowing what I knew, I set up an inference of my own here. I believed the iron to be my convict's iron—the iron I had seen and heard him filing at, on the marshes—but my mind did not accuse him of having put it to its latest use. For, I believed one of two other persons to have become possessed of it, and to have turned it to this cruel account. Either Orlick, or the strange man who had shown me the file.

Now, as to Orlick; he had gone to town exactly as he told us when we picked him up at the turnpike, he had been seen about town all the evening, he had been in divers[2] companies in several public houses, and he had come back with myself and Mr. Wopsle. There was nothing against him, save the quarrel; and my sister had quarrelled with him, and with everybody else about her, ten thousand times. As to the strange man, if he had come back for his two bank notes, there could have been no dispute about them, because my sister was fully prepared to restore them. Besides, there had been no altercation; the assailant had come in so silently and suddenly that she had been felled before she could look round.

The constables, and the Bow Street men from London—for, this happened in the days of the extinct red-waistcoated police—were about the house for a week or two, and did pretty much what I have heard and read of like authorities doing in other such cases. They took up several obviously wrong people, and they ran their heads very hard against wrong ideas, and persisted in trying to fit the circumstances to the ideas, instead of trying to extract ideas from the circumstances.

Long after these constitutional powers had dispersed, my sister lay very ill in bed. Her sight was disturbed, so that she saw objects multiplied, and grasped at visionary

---

**1. snuff** *n*.: Charred end of the candlewick.

**2. divers** (dī′ vərz) *adj*.: Several, various.

teacups and wineglasses instead of the realities; her hearing was greatly impaired; her memory also; and her speech was unintelligible. When, at last, she came round so far as to be helped downstairs, it was still necessary to keep my slate always by her, that she might indicate in writing what she could not indicate in speech. As she was (very bad handwriting apart) a more than indifferent speller, and as Joe was a more than indifferent reader, extraordinary complications arose between them, which I was always called in to solve.

However, her temper was greatly improved, and she was patient. A tremulous uncertainty of the action of all her limbs soon became a part of her regular state, and afterwards, at intervals of two or three months, she would often put her hands to her head, and would then remain for about a week at a time in some gloomy aberration of mind. We were at a loss to find a suitable attendant for her, until a circumstance happened conveniently to relieve us. Mr. Wopsle's great-aunt conquered a confirmed habit of living into which she had fallen,[3] and Biddy became a part of our establishment.

It may have been about a month after my sister's reappearance in the kitchen when Biddy came to us with a small speckled box containing the whole of her worldly effects, and became a blessing to the household. Above all she was a blessing to Joe, for the dear old fellow was sadly cut up by the constant contemplation of the wreck of his wife, and had been accustomed, while attending on her of an evening, to turn to me every now and then and say, with his blue eyes moistened, "Such a fine figure of a woman as she once were, Pip!" Biddy instantly taking the cleverest charge of her as though she

_____
**3. conquered . . . fallen:** Died.

had studied her from infancy, Joe became able in some sort to appreciate the greater quiet of his life, and to get down to the Jolly Bargemen now and then for a change that did him good.

Biddy's first triumph in her new office was to solve a difficulty that had completely vanquished me. I had tried hard at it, but had made nothing of it. Thus it was:

Again and again and again, my sister had traced upon the slate a character that looked like a curious T, and then with the utmost eagerness had called our attention to it as everything she particularly wanted. I had in vain tried everything producible that began with a T, from tar to toast and tub. At length it had come into my head that the sign looked like a hammer, and on my lustily calling that word in my sister's ear, she had begun to hammer on the table and had expressed a qualified assent. Thereupon, I had brought in all our hammers, one after another, but without avail.

When my sister found that Biddy was very quick to understand her, this mysterious sign reappeared on the slate. Biddy looked thoughtfully at it, heard my explanation, looked thoughtfully at my sister, looked thoughtfully at Joe (who was always represented on the slate by his initial letter), and ran into the forge, followed by Joe and me.

"Why, of course!" cried Biddy, with an exultant face. "Don't you see? It's _him_!"

Orlick, without a doubt! She had lost his name, and could only signify him by his hammer. We told him why we wanted him to come into the kitchen, and he slowly laid down his hammer, wiped his brow with his arm, took another wipe at it with his apron, and came slouching out.

I confess that I expected to see my sister denounce him, and that I was disappointed by the different result. She manifested the greatest anxiety to be on good terms with him, was evidently much pleased by his being at length produced, and motioned that she would have him given something to drink. After that day, a day rarely passed without her drawing the hammer on her slate, and without Orlick's slouching in and standing doggedly before her, as if he knew no more than I did what to make of it.

**Chapter 17**

I now fell into a regular routine of apprenticeship life, which was varied, beyond the limits of the village and the marshes, by no more remarkable circumstance than the arrival of my birthday and my paying another visit to Miss Havisham. I found Miss Havisham just as I had left her, and she spoke of Estella in the very same way, if not in the very same words. The interview lasted but a few minutes, and she gave me a guinea when I was going, and told me to come again on my next birthday. I may mention at once that this became an annual custom.

So unchanging was the dull old house that I felt as if the stopping of the clocks had stopped time in that mysterious place. It bewildered me, and under its influence I continued at heart to hate my trade and to be ashamed of home.

Imperceptibly I became conscious of a change in Biddy, however. Her shoes came up at the heel, her hair grew bright and neat, her hands were always clean. She was not beautiful—she was common, and could not be like Estella—but she was pleasant and wholesome and sweet-tempered. I observed to myself one evening that she had curiously thoughtful and attentive eyes; eyes that were very pretty and very good.

It came of my lifting up my own eyes from a task I was poring at—writing some passages from a book, to improve myself in two ways at once by a sort of stratagem—and seeing Biddy observant of what I was about. I laid down my pen, and Biddy stopped in her needlework without laying it down.

"How do you manage, Biddy," said I, "to learn everything that I learn, and always to keep up with me?" I was beginning to be rather vain of my knowledge, for I spent my birthday guineas on it, and set aside the greater part of my pocket-money for similar investment; though I have no doubt, now, that the little I knew was extremely dear at the price.

"I might as well ask you," said Biddy, "how *you* manage?"

"No; because when I come in from the forge of a night anyone can see me turning to at it. But you never turn to at it, Biddy."

"I suppose I must catch it—like a cough," said Biddy, quietly, and went on with her sewing.

Pursuing my idea as I leaned back in my wooden chair and looked at Biddy sewing away with her head on one side, I began to think her rather an extraordinary girl. For, I called to mind now that she was equally accomplished in the terms of our trade, and the names of our different sorts of work, and our various tools. In short, whatever I knew, Biddy knew. Theoretically, she was already as good a blacksmith as I, or better.

"You are one of those, Biddy," said I, "who make the most of every chance. You never had a chance before you came here, and see how improved you are!"

Biddy looked at me for an instant, and went on with her sewing. "I was your first teacher though, wasn't I?" said she, as she sewed.

I recalled the hopeless circumstances by which she had been surrounded in the miserable little shop and the miserable little

**4 Critical Thinking and Reading**
What might motivate Mrs. Joe's behavior?

**5 Critical Thinking and Reading**
How much of this change results from a real change in Biddy and how much from an alteration in Pip's perception of her? Explain.

6 **Discussion** Why is the word *you* emphasized? Who else might Pip have in mind?

7 **Discussion** Why is this an insightful question?

noisy evening school, with that miserable old bundle of incompetence always to be dragged and shouldered. I reflected that even in those untoward times there must have been latent in Biddy what was now developing, for, in my first uneasiness and discontent, I had turned to her for help as a matter of course. Biddy sat quietly sewing, and while I looked at her and thought about it all, it occurred to me that perhaps I had not been sufficiently grateful to Biddy.

"Yes, Biddy," I observed, "you were my first teacher, and that at a time when we little thought of ever being together like this, in this kitchen. Let us have a quiet walk on the marshes next Sunday, Biddy, and a long chat."

My sister was never left alone now; but Joe more than readily undertook the care of her on that Sunday afternoon, and Biddy and I went out together. When we came to the riverside and sat down on the bank, I resolved that it was a good time and place for the admission of Biddy into my inner confidence.

"Biddy," said I, after binding her to secrecy, "I want to be a gentleman."

"Oh, I wouldn't, if I was you!" she returned. "I don't think it would answer."

"Biddy," said I, with some severity, "I have particular reasons for wanting to be a gentleman."

"You know best, Pip; but don't you think you are happier as you are?"

"Biddy," I exclaimed impatiently, "I am not at all happy as I am. I am disgusted with my calling and with my life. I have never taken to either since I was bound. Don't be absurd."

"Was I absurd?" said Biddy, quietly raising her eyebrows; "I am sorry for that; I didn't mean to be. I only want you to do well, and be comfortable."

"Well, then, understand once for all that I never shall or can be comfortable—or anything but miserable—there, Biddy!—unless I can lead a very different sort of life from the life I lead now."

"That's a pity!" said Biddy, shaking her head with a sorrowful air.

"If I could have settled down," I said to Biddy, "and been but half as fond of the forge as I was when I was little, I know it would have been much better for me. You and I and Joe would have wanted nothing then, and Joe and I would perhaps have gone partners when I was out of my time, and I might even have grown up to keep company with you, and we might have sat on this very bank on a fine Sunday, quite different people. I should have been good enough for *you*; shouldn't I, Biddy?"

Biddy sighed as she looked at the ships sailing on, and returned for answer, "Yes, I am not over-particular." It scarcely sounded flattering, but I knew she meant well.

"Instead of that," said I, "see how I am going on. Dissatisfied, and uncomfortable, and—what would it signify to me, being coarse and common, if nobody had told me so?"

"It was neither a very true nor a very polite thing to say," she remarked. "Who said it?"

"The beautiful young lady at Miss Havisham's, and she's more beautiful than anybody ever was, and I admire her dreadfully, and I want to be a gentleman on her account."

"Do you want to be a gentleman to spite her or to gain her over?" Biddy quietly asked me, after a pause.

"I don't know," I moodily answered.

"Because, if it is to spite her," Biddy pursued, "I should think—but you know best—that might be better and more independently done by caring nothing for her words. And if it is to gain her over, I should think—but you know best—she was not worth gaining over."

Exactly what I myself had thought, many times. Exactly what was perfectly manifest to me at the moment. But how could I, a poor dazed village lad, avoid that wonderful inconsistency into which the best and wisest of men fall every day?

"It may be all quite true," said I to Biddy, "but I admire her dreadfully."

Biddy was the wisest of girls, and she tried to reason no more with me. She softly patted my shoulder in a soothing way, while with my face upon my sleeve I cried a little—exactly as I had done in the brewery-yard—and felt vaguely convinced that I was very much ill-used by somebody, or by everybody; I can't say which.

"I am glad of one thing," said Biddy, "and that is that you have felt you could give me your confidence, Pip."

"Biddy," I cried, getting up, putting my arm around her neck, and giving her a kiss, "I shall always tell you everything."

"Till you're a gentleman," said Biddy.

"You know I never shall be, so that's always."

## Chapter 18

It was in the fourth year of my apprenticeship to Joe, and it was a Saturday night. There was a group assembled round the fire at the Three Jolly Bargemen, attentive to Mr. Wopsle as he read the newspaper aloud. Of that group, I was one.

A highly popular murder had been committed, and Mr. Wopsle was imbrued in blood to the eyebrows. He gloated over every abhorrent adjective in the description, and identified himself with every witness at the inquest. He enjoyed himself thoroughly, and we all enjoyed ourselves, and were delightfully comfortable. In this cozy state of mind we came to the verdict of willful murder.

Then, and not sooner, I became aware of a strange gentleman leaning over the back of the settle opposite me, looking on. There was an expression of contempt on his face, and he bit the side of a great forefinger as he watched the group of faces.

"Well!" said the stranger to Mr. Wopsle, when the reading was done, "you have settled it all to your own satisfaction, I have no doubt?"

The strange gentleman, with an air of authority not to be disputed, and with a manner expressive of knowing something secret about every one of us that would effectually do for each individual if he chose to disclose it, left the back of the settle, and came into the space between the two settles, in front of the fire.

"From information I have received," said he, looking round at us as we all quailed before him, "I have reason to believe there is a blacksmith among you, by name Joseph—or Joe—Gargery. Which is the man?"

"Here is the man," said Joe.

The strange gentleman beckoned him out of his place, and Joe went.

"You have an apprentice," pursued the stranger, "commonly known as Pip? Is he here?"

"I am here!" I cried.

The stranger did not recognize me, but I recognized him as the gentleman I had met on the stairs on the occasion of my second visit to Miss Havisham. I had known him the moment I saw him looking over the settle, and now that I stood confronting him with his hand upon my shoulder, I checked off again in detail, his large head, his dark complexion, his deep-set eyes, his bushy black

*Great Expectations* 813

8 **Discussion** Why is Pip unable to follow advice he knows to be true?

9 **Critical Thinking and Reading** How does the description of the strange gentleman looking contemptuously at the unpretentious villagers suggest the ideas that Pip and Biddy discussed in the previous chapter?

**MORTLAKE TERRACE**
*J. M. W. Turner*
*National Gallery of Art, Washington*

eyebrows, his large watch chain, his strong black dots of beard and whisker, and even the smell of scented soap on his great hand.

"I wish to have a private conference with you two," said he, when he had surveyed me at his leisure. "It will take a little time. Perhaps we had better go to your place of residence."

Amidst a wondering silence, we three walked out of the Jolly Bargemen, and in a wondering silence walked home.

Our conference began with the strange gentleman's sitting down at the table, drawing the candle to him, and looking over some entries in his pocket book. He then put up the pocket book and set the candle a little

814    *The Novel*

aside, after peering round it into the darkness at Joe and me to ascertain which was which.

"My name," he said, "is Jaggers, and I am a lawyer in London. I am pretty well known. I have unusual business to transact with you, and I commence by explaining that it is not of my originating. If my advice had been asked, I should not have been here. It was not asked, and you see me here. What I have to do as the confidential agent of another, I do. No less, no more.

"Now, Joseph Gargery, I am the bearer of an offer to relieve you of this young fellow, your apprentice. You would not object to cancel his indentures at his request and for his good? You would want nothing for so doing?"

"Lord forbid that I should want anything for not standing in Pip's way," said Joe, staring.

"Lord forbidding is pious, but not to the purpose," returned Mr. Jaggers. "The question is, would you want anything? Do you want anything?"

"The answer is," returned Joe sternly, "No."

I thought Mr. Jaggers glanced at Joe as if he considered him a fool for his disinterestedness. But I was too much bewildered between breathless curiosity and surprise to be sure of it.

"Very well," said Mr. Jaggers. "Recollect the admission you have made, and don't try to go from it presently."

"Who's a-going to try?" retorted Joe.

"I don't say anybody is. Do you keep a dog?"

"Yes, I do keep a dog."

"Bear in mind then, that Brag is a good dog, but that Holdfast is a better. Bear that in mind, will you?" repeated Mr. Jaggers, shutting his eyes and nodding his head at Joe, as if he were forgiving him something. "Now, I return to this young fellow. And the communication I have got to make is that he has great expectations."

Joe and I gasped, and looked at one another.

"I am instructed to communicate to him," said Mr. Jaggers, throwing his finger at me sideways, "that he will come into a handsome property. Further, that it is the desire of the present possessor of that property that he be immediately removed from his present sphere of life and from this place, and be brought up as a gentleman—in a word, as a young fellow of great expectations."

My dream was out; my wild fancy was surpassed by sober reality; Miss Havisham was going to make my fortune on a grand scale.

"Now, Mr. Pip," pursued the lawyer, "I address the rest of what I have to say to you. You are to understand, first, that it is the request of the person from whom I take my instructions that you always bear the name of Pip. You will have no objection, I dare say, to your great expectations being encumbered with that easy condition. But if you have any objection, this is the time to mention it."

My heart was beating so fast, and there was such a singing in my ears, that I could scarcely stammer I had no objection.

"I should think not! Now you are to understand, secondly, Mr. Pip, that the name of the person who is your liberal benefactor remains a profound secret, until the person chooses to reveal it. I am empowered to mention that it is the intention of the person to reveal it at first hand by word of mouth to yourself. When or where that intention may be carried out, I cannot say; no one can say. It may be years hence. Now, you are distinctly to understand that you are most posi-

10 **Discussion** What does Mr. Jaggers's opening statement reveal about him?

11 **Discussion** Compare and contrast Mr. Jaggers and Joe.

12 **Critical Thinking and Reading** What makes Pip believe Miss Havisham is his benefactress? Is this a reasonable assumption? Explain.

**13 Discussion** Why is it important that Pip be better educated?

**14 Discussion** How has Mr. Jaggers's profession influenced the way he talks?

**15 Discussion** How does Mr. Jaggers's mention of Matthew Pocket as tutor support Pip's belief that Miss Havisham is the benefactress?

tively prohibited from making any inquiry on this head, in all the communications you may have with me. Your acceptance of this, and your observance of it as binding, is the only remaining condition that I am charged with by the person from whom I take my instructions, and for whom I am not otherwise responsible. That person is the person from whom you derive your expectations, and the secret is solely held by that person and by me. Again, not a very difficult condition with which to encumber such a rise in fortune; but if you have any objection to it, this is the time to mention it. Speak out."

Once more, I stammered with difficulty that I had no objection.

"I should think not! Now, Mr. Pip, I have done with stipulations. We come next to mere details of arrangement. You must know that although I use the term 'expectations' more than once, you are not endowed with expectations only. There is already lodged in my hands a sum of money amply sufficient for your suitable education and maintenance. You will please consider me your guardian. Oh!" for I was going to thank him, "I tell you at once, I am paid for my services, or I shouldn't render them. It is considered that you must be better educated, in accordance with your altered position, and that you will be alive to the importance and necessity of at once entering on that advantage."

I said I had always longed for it.

"Never mind what you have always longed for, Mr. Pip," he retorted; "keep to the record. If you long for it now, that's enough. Am I answered that you are ready to be placed at once under some proper tutor? Is that it?"

I stammered yes, that was it.

"Good. Now, your inclinations are to be consulted. I don't think that wise, mind, but it's my trust. Have you ever heard of any tutor whom you would prefer to another?"

I had never heard of any tutor but Biddy, and Mr. Wopsle's great-aunt, so I replied in the negative.

"There is a certain tutor, of whom I have some knowledge, who I think might suit the purpose," said Mr. Jaggers. "I don't recommend him, observe; because I never recommended anybody. The gentleman I speak of is one Mr. Matthew Pocket."

Ah! I caught at the name directly. Miss Havisham's relation. The Matthew whom Mr. and Mrs. Camilla had spoken of. The Matthew whose place was to be at Miss Havisham's head, when she lay dead, in her bride's dress on the bride's table.

"You know the name?" said Mr. Jaggers, looking shrewdly at me, and then shutting up his eyes while he waited for my answer.

My answer was that I had heard of the name.

"Oh!" said he. "You have heard of the name! But the question is, what do you say of it?"

I said, or tried to say, that I was much obliged to him for his mention of Matthew Pocket, and that I would gladly try that gentleman.

"Good. You had better try him in his own house. The way shall be prepared for you, and you can see his son first, who is in London. When will you come to London?"

I said (glancing at Joe, who stood looking on, motionless), that I supposed I could come directly.

"First," said Mr. Jaggers, "you should have some new clothes to come in, and they should not be working clothes. Say this day week.[1] You'll want some money. Shall I leave you twenty guineas?"

_____
**1. this day week:** One week from today.

## Grammar in Action

In informal speech and often in informal writing, the pronouns *who* and *whoever* are frequently used for *whom* and *whomever*.

Who is this?
Who did you call?
Whoever left the ice cream out?
Whoever did you give that information to?

more formal written or spoken English, however, a distinction is between these pronouns:

The way will be prepared for you, and you will see his son first, *who* is in London.

Your acceptance of this, and your observation of it as binding, is the only remaining condition that I am charged with by the person from *whom* I take my instructions, and for *whom* I am not otherwise responsible.

In these examples from *Great Expectations,* the formal rules for using these pronouns apply: *Who* is in the nominative case, and so is used as subject and subject complement. *Whom* is in the objective case, and so is used as direct object and object of a preposition. In the first sentence above, *who* is the subject of the verb *is.* In the second sentence, both examples of *whom* are

He produced a long purse, with the greatest coolness, and counted them out on the table and pushed them over to me.

"Well, Joseph Gargery? You look dumbfounded!"

"I *am*!" said Joe, in a very decided manner.

"It was understood that you wanted nothing for yourself, remember?"

"It were understood," said Joe. "And it are understood. And it ever will be similar according."

"But what," said Mr. Jaggers, swinging his purse, "what if it was in my instructions to make you a present, as compensation?"

"As compensation what for?" Joe demanded.

"For the loss of his services."

Joe laid his hand upon my shoulder with the touch of a woman. "Pip is that hearty welcome," said Joe, "to go free with his services, to honor and fortun', as no words can tell him. But if you think as money can make compensation to me for the loss of the little child—what come to the forge—and ever the best of friends!—"

Oh, dear good Joe, whom I was so ready to leave and so unthankful to, I see you again, with your muscular blacksmith's arm before your eyes, and your broad chest heaving, and your voice dying away.

But I encouraged Joe at the time. I was lost in the mazes of my future fortunes, and could not retrace the bypaths we had trodden together. I begged Joe to be comforted, for (as he said) we had ever been the best of friends, and (as I said) we ever would be so. Joe scooped his eyes with his disengaged wrist, as if he were bent on gouging himself, but said not another word.

Mr. Jaggers had looked on at this as one who recognized in Joe the village idiot, and in me his keeper. When it was over, he said, weighing in his hand the purse he had ceased to swing:

"Now, Joseph Gargery, I warn you this is your last chance. No half-measures with me. If you mean to take a present that I have it in charge to make you, speak out, and you shall have it. If on the contrary you mean to say—" Here, to his great amazement, he was stopped by Joe's suddenly working round him with every demonstration of a fell pugilistic purpose.[2]

"Which I meantersay," cried Joe, "that if you come into my place bull-baiting and badgering me, come out! Which I meantersay as sech if you're a man, come on! Which I meantersay that what I say, I meantersay and stand or fall by!"

I drew Joe away, and he immediately became placable, merely stating to me, in an obliging manner and as a polite expostulatory notice to any one whom it might happen to concern, that he were not a-going to be bull-baited and badgered in his own place. Mr. Jaggers had risen when Joe demonstrated, and had backed near the door. Without evincing any inclination to come in again, he there delivered his valedictory remarks. They were these:

"Well, Mr. Pip, I think the sooner you leave here—as you are to be a gentleman—the better. Let it stand for this day week, and you shall receive my printed address in the meantime. You can take a hackney coach at the stagecoach office in London, and come straight to me. Understand that I express no opinion, one way or other, on the trust I undertake. I am paid for undertaking it, and I do so. Now, understand that finally. Understand that!"

---

**2. pugilistic** (pyoo' jəl is' tik) **purpose:** Intention to start a fistfight.

**16 Discussion** How does this passage reflect two different perspectives on the same events?

**17 Discussion** Why do you think Joe is so angry?

objects of prepositions; therefore, the objective case is necessary.

**Student Activity 1.** Find five other examples of sentences using *who* and *whom* in the novel, and copy these. Share the sentences with a small group, discussing how the pronouns are used in each.

**Student Activity 2.** Write three sentences containing *who* and three containing *whom*. Trade papers with a partner and discuss your sentences.

**18** **Clarification** A comment by Jesus in the gospels indicates that it will be more difficult for a rich man to enter the kingdom of heaven than for a camel to pass through the eye of a needle. What does Pip's reaction to this statement reveal about his state of mind?

He was throwing his finger at both of us, and I think would have gone on, but for his seeming to think Joe dangerous, and going off.

## Chapter 19

The next morning, after breakfast, Joe brought out my indentures from the press in the best parlor, and we put them in the fire, and I felt that I was free. With all the novelty of my emancipation on me, I went to church with Joe, and thought perhaps the clergyman wouldn't have read that about the rich man and the kingdom of Heaven, if he had known all.

After our early dinner, I strolled out alone, proposing to finish off the marshes at once, and get them done with. As I passed the church, I felt (as I had felt during service in the morning) a sublime compassion for the poor creatures who were destined to go there, Sunday after Sunday, all their lives through, and to lie obscurely at last among the low green mounds. I promised myself that I would do something for them one of these days, and formed a plan in outline for bestowing a dinner of roast beef and plum pudding, a pint of ale, and a gallon of condescension upon everybody in the village.

I made my exultant way to the old battery, and, lying down there to consider the question whether Miss Havisham intended me for Estella, fell asleep. When I awoke, I was much surprised to find Joe sitting beside me, smoking his pipe. He greeted me with a cheerful smile on my opening my eyes, and said:

"As being the last time, Pip, I thought I'd foller."

"And Joe, I am very glad you did so."

"Thankee, Pip."

"You may be sure, dear Joe," I went on, after we had shaken hands, "that I shall never forget you."

"No, no, Pip!" said Joe, in a comfortable tone, "I'm sure of that. Aye, aye, old chap! Bless you, it were only necessary to get it well round in a man's mind to be certain on it. But it took a bit of time to get it well round, the change come so oncommon plump; didn't it?"

I made no remark on Joe's first head, merely saying as to his second that the tidings had indeed come suddenly, but that I had always wanted to be a gentleman, and had often and often speculated on what I would do if I were one.

"Have you though?" said Joe. "Astonishing!"

"It's a pity now, Joe," said I, "that you did not get on a little more, when we had our lessons here; isn't it?"

"Well, I don't know," returned Joe. "I'm so awful dull. I'm only master of my own trade. It were always a pity as I was so awful dull; but it's no more of a pity now, than it was—this day twelvemonth[1]—don't you see!"

What I had meant was that when I came into my property and was able to do something for Joe, it would have been much more agreeable if he had been better qualified for a rise in station. He was so perfectly innocent of my meaning, however, that I thought I would mention it to Biddy in preference.

So, when we had walked home and had had tea, I took Biddy into our little garden by the side of the lane, and, after throwing out in a general way for the elevation of her spirits, that I should never forget her, said I had a favor to ask of her.

"And it is, Biddy," said I, "that you will not omit any opportunity of helping Joe on, a little."

———————
**1. this day twelvemonth:** One year ago today.

"How helping him on?" asked Biddy.

"Well! Joe is a dear good fellow—in fact, I think he is the dearest fellow that ever lived—but he is rather backward in some things. For instance, Biddy, in his learning and his manners."

Although I was looking at Biddy as I spoke, and although she opened her eyes very wide when I had spoken, she did not look at me.

"Oh, his manners! Won't his manners do, then?" asked Biddy.

"My dear Biddy, they do very well here—"

"Oh! They *do* very well here?" interrupted Biddy.

"Hear me out—but if I were to remove Joe into a higher sphere, as I shall hope to remove him when I fully come into my property, they would hardly do him justice."

"And don't you think he knows that?" asked Biddy.

It was such a provoking question (for it had never in the most distant manner occurred to me) that I said snappishly, "Biddy, what do you mean?"

Biddy said, "Have you never considered that he may be proud?"

"Proud?" I repeated, with disdainful emphasis.

"Oh, there are many kinds of pride," said Biddy, looking full at me and shaking her head; "pride is not all of one kind—"

"Well? What are you stopping for?" said I.

"Not all of one kind," resumed Biddy. "He may be too proud to let any one take him out of a place that he is competent to fill, and fills well and with respect. To tell you the truth, I think he is—though it sounds bold in me to say so, for you must know him far better than I do."

"Now, Biddy," said I, "I am very sorry to see this in you. You are envious, Biddy, and grudging. You are dissatisfied on account of my rise in fortune, and you can't help showing it."

"If you have the heart to think so," returned Biddy, "say so. Say so over and over again, if you have the heart to think so."

"If you have the heart to be so, you mean, Biddy," said I, in a virtuous and superior tone; "don't put it off upon me. I am very sorry to see it, and it's a—it's a bad side of human nature. I did intend to ask you to use any little opportunities you might have after I was gone of improving dear Joe. But after this, I ask you nothing. I am extremely sorry to see this in you, Biddy," I repeated. "It's a—it's a bad side of human nature."

"Whether you scold me or approve of me," returned poor Biddy, "you may equally depend upon my trying to do all that lies in my power, here, at all times. And whatever opinion you take away of me shall make no difference in my remembrance of you. Yet a gentleman should not be unjust neither," said Biddy, turning away her head.

I again warmly repeated that it was a bad side of human nature, and I walked down the little path away from Biddy, and Biddy went into the house, and I went out at the garden gate and took a dejected stroll until suppertime.

But morning once more brightened my view, and I extended my clemency to Biddy, and we dropped the subject. Putting on the best clothes I had, I went into town as early as I could hope to find the shops open, and presented myself before Mr. Trabb, the tailor; who was having his breakfast in the parlor behind his shop, and who did not think it worth his while to come out to me, but called me in to him.

"Well!" said Mr. Trabb, in a hail-fellow-well-met kind of way. "How are you, and what can I do for you?"

"Mr. Trabb," said I, "it's an unpleasant

**19 Discussion** How would you describe Pip's attitude toward Joe? How might Pip's attitude have been influenced by his "expectations"?

**20 Critical Thinking and Reading** Do you agree with Pip? Why or why not?

**21 Discussion** How has Trabb's behavior toward Pip changed? What does this change indicate about Trabb's character?

**22 Discussion** What does this memory suggest about Pip's state of mind at the time?

thing to have to mention, because it looks like boasting, but I have come into a handsome property."

A change passed over Mr. Trabb. He got up from the bedside and wiped his fingers on the table-cloth, exclaiming, "Lord bless my soul!"

"I am going up to my guardian in London," said I, casually drawing some guineas out of my pocket and looking at them; "and I want a fashionable suit of clothes to go in. I wish to pay for them," I added—otherwise I thought he might only pretend to make them—"with ready money."

"My dear sir," said Mr. Trabb, "don't hurt me by mentioning that. May I venture to congratulate you? Would you do me the favor of stepping into the shop?"

Mr. Trabb's boy was the most audacious boy in all that countryside. When I had entered he was sweeping the shop, and he had sweetened his labors by sweeping over me. He was still sweeping when I came out into the shop with Mr. Trabb, and he knocked the broom against all possible corners and obstacles to express (as I understood it) equality with any blacksmith, alive or dead.

"Hold that noise," said Mr. Trabb, with the greatest sternness, "or I'll knock your head off! Do me the favor to be seated, sir."

I selected the materials for a suit, with the assistance of Mr. Trabb's judgment, and reentered the parlor to be measured. When he had at last done and had appointed to send the articles to Mr. Pumblechook's on the Thursday evening, he said, with his hand upon the parlor lock, "I know, sir, that London gentlemen cannot be expected to patronize local work, as a rule; but if you would give me a turn now and then in the quality of a townsman, I should greatly esteem it. Good morning, sir, much obliged. Door!"

The last word was flung at the boy, who had not the least notion what it meant. But I saw him collapse as his master rubbed me out with his hands, and my first decided experience of the stupendous power of money was that it had morally laid upon his back, Trabb's boy.

After this memorable event, I went to the hatter's, and the bootmaker's, and the hosier's. I also went to the coach office and took my place for seven o'clock on Saturday morning. When I had ordered everything I wanted, I directed my steps towards Pumblechook's, and, as I approached that gentleman's place of business, I saw him standing at his door.

He was waiting for me with great impatience. He had been out early with the chaise-cart, and had called at the forge and heard the news. He had prepared a collation[2] for me in the Barnwell parlor, and he too ordered his shopman to "come out of the gangway" as my sacred person passed.

"To think," said Mr. Pumblechook, after snorting admiration at me for some moments, "that I should have been the humble instrument of leading up to this is a proud reward."

I begged Mr. Pumblechook to remember that nothing was to be ever said or hinted on that point.

I mentioned to him that I wished to have my new clothes sent to his house, and he was ecstatic on my so distinguishing him. I mentioned my reason for desiring to avoid observation in the village, and he lauded it to the skies. There was nobody but himself, he intimated, worthy of my confidence. Then he asked me tenderly if I remembered our boyish games at sums, and how we had gone together to have me bound apprentice, and, in effect, how he had ever been my favorite fancy and my chosen friend? I remember

2. **collation** (kä lä′ shən) n.: Light meal.

feeling convinced that I had been much mistaken in him, and that he was a sensible practical good-hearted prime fellow.

So Tuesday, Wednesday, and Thursday passed; and on Friday morning I went to Mr. Pumblechook's, to put on my new clothes and pay my visit to Miss Havisham. Mr. Pumblechook's own room was given up to me to dress in, and was decorated with clean towels expressly for the event. My clothes were rather a disappointment, of course. Probably every new and eagerly expected garment ever put on since clothes came in fell a trifle short of the wearer's expectation. But after I had had my new suit on some half an hour, it seemed to fit me better.

I went circuitously to Miss Havisham's by all the back ways, and rang at the bell. Sarah Pocket came to the gate, and positively reeled back when she saw me so changed.

"You?" said she. "You? Good gracious! What do you want?"

"I am going to London, Miss Pocket," said I, "and want to say good-bye to Miss Havisham."

I was not expected, for she left me locked in the yard, while she went to ask if I were to be admitted. After a very short delay, she returned and took me up, staring at me all the way.

Miss Havisham was taking exercise in the room with the long spread table, leaning on her crutch stick. The room was lighted as of yore, and at the sound of our entrance, she stopped and turned. She was then just abreast of the rotted bride-cake.

"Don't go, Sarah," she said. "Well, Pip?"

"I start for London, Miss Havisham, tomorrow," I was exceedingly careful what I said, "and I thought you would kindly not mind my taking leave of you."

"This is a gay figure, Pip," said she, making her crutch stick play round me, as if she, the fairy godmother who had changed me, were bestowing the finishing gift.

"I have come into such good fortune since I saw you last, Miss Havisham," I murmured. "And I am so grateful for it, Miss Havisham!"

"Aye, aye!" said she, looking at the discomfited and envious Sarah, with delight. "I have seen Mr. Jaggers. I have heard about it, Pip. So you go tomorrow?"

"Yes, Miss Havisham."

"And you are adopted by a rich person?"

"Yes, Miss Havisham."

"Not named?"

"No, Miss Havisham."

"And Mr. Jaggers is made your guardian?"

"Yes, Miss Havisham."

She quite gloated on these questions and answers, so keen was her enjoyment of Sarah Pocket's jealous dismay. "Well!" she went on; "you have a promising career before you. Be good—deserve it—and abide by Mr. Jaggers's instructions." She looked at me, and looked at Sarah, and Sarah's countenance wrung out of her watchful face a cruel smile. "Good-bye, Pip! You will always keep the name of Pip, you know."

"Yes, Miss Havisham."

"Good-bye, Pip!"

She stretched out her hand, and I went down on my knee and put it to my lips. I had not considered how I should take leave of her; it came naturally to me at the moment, to do this. She looked at Sarah Pocket with triumph in her weird eyes, and so I left my fairy godmother, with both her hands on her crutch stick, standing in the midst of the dimly lighted room beside the rotten bride-cake that was hidden in cobwebs.

And now those six days which were to have run out so slowly had run out fast and

23 **Discussion** Why does he refer to Miss Havisham as his "fairy godmother"?

23

24 **Discussion** What is the source of Pip's inner conflict?

25 **Clarification** Joe and Biddy throw old shoes after Pip as a way of wishing him good luck.

were gone, and tomorrow looked me in the face more steadily than I could look at it. As the six evenings had dwindled away to five, to four, to three, to two, I had become more and more appreciative of the society of Joe and Biddy. On this last evening, I dressed myself out in my new clothes for their delight, and sat in my splendor until bedtime. We had a hot supper on the occasion, graced by the inevitable roast fowl. We were all very low, and none the higher for pretending to be in spirits.

I was to leave our village at five in the morning, and I had told Joe that I wished to walk away all alone. I am afraid—sore afraid—that this purpose originated in my sense of the contrast there would be between me and Joe, if we went to the coach together. I had pretended with myself that there was nothing of this taint in the arrangement; but when I went up to my little room on this last night, I felt compelled to admit that it might be done so, and had an impulse upon me to go down again and entreat Joe to walk with me in the morning. I did not.

Biddy was astir so early to get my breakfast that, although I did not sleep at the window an hour, I smelt the smoke of the kitchen fire when I started up with a terrible idea that it must be late in the afternoon. But long after that, and long after I heard the clinking of the teacups and was quite ready, I wanted the resolution to go downstairs. After all, I remained up there, repeatedly unlocking and unstrapping my small portmanteau and locking and strapping it up again, until Biddy called to me that I was late.

It was a hurried breakfast with no taste in it. I got up from the meal, saying with a sort of briskness, as if it had only just occurred to me, "Well! I suppose I must be off!"

and then I kissed my sister, who was laughing, and nodding and shaking in her usual chair, and kissed Biddy, and threw my arms around Joe's neck. Then I took up my little portmanteau and walked out. The last I saw of them was when I presently heard a scuffle behind me, and looking back, saw Joe throwing an old shoe after me and Biddy throwing another old shoe. I stopped then, to wave my hat, and dear old Joe waved his strong right arm above his head, crying huskily, "Hooroar!" and Biddy put her apron to her face.

I walked away at a good pace, thinking it was easier to go than I had supposed it would be. I whistled and made nothing of going. But the village was very peaceful and quiet, and the light mists were solemnly rising, as if to show me the world, and I had been so innocent and little there, and all beyond was so unknown and great, that in a moment with a strong heave and sob I broke into tears. It was by the finger-post at the end of the village, and I laid my hand upon it, and said, "Good-bye, O my dear, dear friend!"

So subdued I was by those tears, and by their breaking out again in the course of the quiet walk, that when I was on the coach, and it was clear of the town, I deliberated with an aching heart whether I would not get down when we changed horses and walk back, and have another evening at home, and a better parting.

We changed again, and yet again, and it was now too late and too far to go back, and I went on. And the mists had all solemnly risen now, and the world lay spread before me.

THIS IS THE END OF THE FIRST STAGE OF
PIP'S EXPECTATIONS

## nar in Action

rb forms, called verbals, can function as other parts of e of these verbals is the **participle.** Participles function s to modify nouns or pronouns. Participles usually end y, but some also have irregular endings. Because verb forms, they can have modifiers and comple- is occurs, the entire **participial phrase** acts as an

Using participles and participial phrases adds variety to your sentences and helps hold the reader's interest. Participles and participial phrases are especially useful for adding details to sentences. Notice Dickens's use of participial phrases in the following passage:

Then I stepped outside and turned into a street where I saw the great black dome of Saint Paul's *bulging at me* from behind a grim stone building which a bystander said was

## Chapter 20

The journey from our town to the metropolis was a journey of about five hours. It was a little past midday when the four-horse stagecoach by which I was a passenger got into the ravel of traffic frayed out about the Cross Keys, Wood Street, Cheapside, London.

Mr. Jaggers had duly sent me his address; it was Little Britain, and he had written after it on his card, "just out of Smithfield, and close by the coach-office." Nevertheless, a hackney coachman, who seemed to have as many capes to his greasy greatcoat as he was years old, packed me up in his coach and hemmed me in with a folding and jingling barrier of steps, as if he were going to take me fifty miles.

I had scarcely had time to enjoy the coach and to think how like a straw yard it was, and yet how like a rag shop, and to wonder why the horses' nose bags were kept inside, when I observed the coachman beginning to get down, as if we were going to stop presently. And stop we presently did, in a gloomy street, at certain offices with an open door, whereon was painted MR. JAGGERS.

I went into the front office with my little portmanteau in my hand, and asked, was Mr. Jaggers at home?

"He is not," returned the clerk. "He is in court at present. Am I addressing Mr. Pip?"

I signified that he was addressing Mr. Pip.

"Mr. Jaggers left word would you wait in his room. He couldn't say how long he might be, having a case on. But it stands to reason, his time being valuable, that he won't be longer than he can help."

With those words, the clerk opened a door, and ushered me into an inner chamber at the back. Mr. Jaggers's room was lighted by a skylight only, and was a most dismal place. I sat down in the cliental chair placed over against Mr. Jaggers's chair. After I had sat wondering and waiting in Mr. Jaggers's close room for some time, I got up and went out.

I told the clerk that I would take a turn in the air while I waited. Then I stepped outside and turned into a street where I saw the great black dome of Saint Paul's[1] bulging at me from behind a grim stone building which a bystander said was Newgate Prison. Following the wall of the jail, I found the roadway covered with straw to deaden the noise of passing vehicles; and from this, and from the quantity of people standing about, I inferred that the trials were on.

I dropped into the office to ask if Mr. Jaggers had come in yet, and I found he had not, and I strolled out again. This time I made the tour of Little Britain, and now I became aware that other people were waiting about for Mr. Jaggers, as well as I. There were two men of secret appearance lounging, and thoughtfully fitting their feet into the cracks of the pavement as they talked together, one of whom said to the other when they first passed me that "Jaggers would do it if it was to be done." There was a knot of three men and two women standing at a corner, and one of the women was crying on her dirty shawl, and the other comforted her by saying, as she pulled her own shawl over her shoulders, "Jaggers is for him, 'Melia, and what more *could* you have?" These testimonies to the popularity of my guardian made a deep impression on me, and I admired and wondered more than ever.

At length, I saw Mr. Jaggers coming across the road towards me. All the others who were waiting saw him at the same time,

---

**1. Saint Paul's:** Famous cathedral in London.

26

*Great Expectations* 823

---

Newgate Prison. *Following the wall of the jail,* I found the roadway *covered with straw* to deaden the noise of *passing vehicles;* and from the quantity of people *standing about,* I inferred that the trials were on.

In addition to adding details, participles and participial phrases can furnish you with a variety of sentence openers. Notice Dickens's use of a participial phrase to begin the final sentence in the paragraph.

**Student Activity 1.** What details does Dickens add to the paragraph by using participles and participial phrases?

**Student Activity 2.** Write an original paragraph describing a place you have visited. Use five participles or participial phrases to add details to your description.

Fine art, *Ludgate Hill*, by Gustave Doré. Gustave Doré (1832–1883) was a French painter, engraver, and lithographer. He learned to draw without a teacher, and at age 16 he was employed as a caricaturist by a Paris newspaper—an achievement that won him the nickname "child genius" from older artists. His work for the newspaper, combined with his study of engravings and etchings at the National Library, made him a superb wood engraver. Wood engraving is a printing technique in which lines are incised into a wooden block and then the block is inked and pressed onto paper to record the image.

*Ludgate Hill* is from a series of engravings by Doré entitled *The City of London in the 1860's*. Have students note the mire of people and animals—the sheep sharing the same roadway as the coaches, wagons, and carts. The intense crowding is heightened by the stone buildings framing and defining the flow of traffic, as though making everyone march through a vise-like canyon, and by the vast numbers of people coming from beyond the arched roadway, on which the train moves.

You might want to use the following questions to provoke a discussion:

1. What impression of London does this engraving convey?
2. Which details contribute to this impression?
3. How would such a scene affect a young man like Pip, who had never been to the city before?

**LUDGATE HILL**
*Gustave Doré*
*Reproduced by courtesy of the Trustees of The British Museum*

824  *The Novel*

and there was quite a rush at him. Mr. Jaggers, putting a hand on my shoulder and walking me on at his side without saying anything to me, addressed himself to his followers.

First, he took the two secret men.

"Now, I have nothing to say to *you*," said Mr. Jaggers, throwing his finger at them. "I want to know no more than I know. As to the result, it's a toss-up. I told you from the first it was a toss-up. Have you paid Wemmick?"

"Yes, sir," said both the men together.

"Very well; then you may go. Now, I won't have it!" said Mr. Jaggers, waving his hand at them to put them behind him. "If you say a word to me, I'll throw up the case."

"We thought, Mr. Jaggers—" one of the men began, pulling off his hat.

"That's what I told you not to do," said Mr. Jaggers. "*You* thought! I think for you; that's enough for you.

"And now *you*!" said Mr. Jaggers, suddenly stopping, and turning on the two women with the shawls. "Once for all. If you don't know that your Bill's in good hands, I know it. And if you come here bothering about your Bill, I'll make an example of both your Bill and you, and let him slip through my fingers. Have you paid Wemmick?"

"Oh, yes, sir!"

"Very well. Then you have done all you have got to do. Say another word—one single word—and Wemmick shall give you your money back."

This terrible threat caused the two women to fall off immediately. Without further interruption, we reached the front office.

My guardian then took me into his own room, and while he lunched, standing, from a sandwich-box, informed me what arrangements he had made for me. I was to go to "Barnard's Inn," to young Mr. Pocket's rooms, where a bed had been sent in for my accommodation; I was to remain with young Mr. Pocket until Monday; on Monday I was to go with him to his father's house on a visit, that I might try how I liked it. Also, I was told what my allowance was to be—it was a very liberal one—and had handed to me from one of my guardian's drawers the cards of certain tradesmen with whom I was to deal for all kinds of clothes, and such other things as I could in reason want. "You will find your credit good, Mr. Pip," said my guardian, "but I shall by this means be able to check your bills, and to pull you up if I find you outrunning the constable. Of course you'll go wrong somehow, but that's no fault of mine."

After I had pondered a little over this encouraging sentiment, I asked Mr. Jaggers if I could send for a coach. He said it was not worthwhile, I was so near my destination; Wemmick should walk round with me, if I pleased.

I then found that Wemmick was the clerk in the next room. Another clerk was rung down from upstairs to take his place while he was out, and I accompanied him into the street, after shaking hands with my guardian. We found a new set of people lingering outside, but Wemmick made a way among them by saying coolly yet decisively, "I tell you it's no use; he won't have a word to say to one of you"; and we soon got clear of them, and went on side by side.

## Chapter 21

Casting my eyes on Mr. Wemmick as we went along, to see what he was like in the light of day, I found him to be a dry man, rather short in stature, with a square wooden face, whose expression seemed to have been imperfectly chipped out with a dull-edged chisel. There were some marks in it that might have been dimples, if the mate-

*Great Expectations* 825

27 **Discussion** What does Mr. Jaggers's attitude toward his clients reveal about him?

28 **Critical Thinking and Reading** What inferences can you make about Mr. Wemmick based on this description?

rial had been softer and the instrument finer, but which, as it was, were only dints. He had glittering eyes—small, keen, and black—and thin wide mottled lips. He had had them, to the best of my belief, from forty to fifty years.

"Do you know where Mr. Matthew Pocket lives?" I asked Mr. Wemmick.

"Yes," said he, nodding in the direction. "At Hammersmith, west of London."

"Is that far?"

"Well! Say five miles."

"Do you know him?"

"Why, you are a regular cross-examiner!" said Mr. Wemmick, looking at me with an approving air. "Yes, I know him. *I* know him!"

There was an air of toleration or depreciation about his utterance of these words that rather depressed me; and I was still looking sideways at his block of a face in search of any encouraging note to the text, when he said here we were at Barnard's Inn. My depression was not alleviated by the announcement, for I had supposed that establishment to be a hotel kept by Mr. Barnard, to which the Blue Boar in our town was a mere public house. Whereas I now found Barnard to be a disembodied spirit, or a fiction, and his inn the dingiest collection of shabby buildings ever squeezed together in a rank corner as a club for tomcats.

So imperfect was this realization of the first of my great expectations that I looked in dismay at Mr. Wemmick. "Ah!" said he, mistaking me, "the retirement reminds you of the country. So it does me."

He led me into a corner and conducted me up a flight of stairs—which appeared to me to be slowly collapsing into sawdust, so that one of those days the upper lodgers would look out at their doors and find themselves without the means of coming down—to a set of chambers on the top floor. MR.

POCKET, JUN., was painted on the door, and there was a label on the letter box, "Return shortly."

"He hardly thought you'd come so soon," Mr. Wemmick explained. "You don't want me any more?"

"No, thank you," said I.

"As I keep the cash," Mr. Wemmick observed, "we shall most likely meet pretty often. Good day."

"Good day."

When he was gone, I opened the staircase window and had nearly beheaded myself, for the lines had rotted away, and it came down like the guillotine.[1] After this escape, I was content to take a foggy view of the Inn through the window's encrusting dirt, and to stand dolefully looking out, saying to myself that London was decidedly overrated.

Mr. Pocket, Junior's, idea of shortly was not mine, for I had nearly maddened myself with looking out for half an hour, and had written my name with my finger several times in the dirt of every pane in the window, before I heard footsteps on the stairs. Gradually there arose before me the hat, head, neckcloth, waistcoat, trousers, boots, of a member of society of about my own standing. He had a paper bag under each arm and a pottle[2] of strawberries in one hand, and was out of breath.

"Mr. Pip?" said he.

"Mr. Pocket?" said I.

"Dear me!" he exclaimed. "I am extremely sorry; but I knew there was a coach from your part of the country at midday, and I thought you would come by that one. The fact is, I have been out on your account—not that that is any excuse—for I thought, com-

---

**1. guillotine** (gil′ ə tēn′) *n.*: Instrument that beheads a victim with a falling blade.
**2. pottle** (pät′ l) *n.*: Pot that holds two quarts.

COVENT GARDEN, LONDON
*John Wykeham Archer*
Bridgeman/Art Resource British Library, London

## Humanities Note

Fine art, *Covent Garden, London*, by John Wykeham Archer. John Wykeham Archer (1808–1864) was a British etcher and painter. A student of the celebrated engraver, John Scott, Archer devoted most of his life to print making. He did many etchings of London life and architecture, which he used to illustrate the books he wrote on that subject.

In *Covent Garden, London*, his constant study and drawing of the London scene served him well in capturing the raucous flavor of this busy produce market.

You might want to use the following questions to help students appreciate the picture:

1. Which details indicate that Covent Garden was a produce market?
2. Compare and contrast this London scene with the one shown in Gustave Doré's *Ludgate Hill*, page 824.

**30 Discussion** How is this remark in keeping with Herbert's character, as it was previously revealed?

ing from the country, you might like a little fruit after dinner, and I went to Covent Garden Market to get it good."

For a reason that I had, I felt as if my eyes would start out of my head. I began to think this was a dream.

As I stood opposite to Mr. Pocket, Junior, I saw the starting appearance come into his own eyes that I knew to be in mine, and he said, falling back:

"Lord bless me, you're the prowling boy!"

"And you," said I, "are the pale young gentleman!"

## Chapter 22

The pale young gentleman and I stood contemplating one another in Barnard's Inn, until we both burst out laughing. "The idea of its being you!" said he. "The idea of its being *you!*" said I. And then we contemplated one another afresh, and laughed again. "Well!" said the pale young gentleman, reaching out his hand good-humoredly, "it's all over now, I hope, and it will be magnanimous in you if you'll forgive me for having knocked you about so."

30

*Great Expectations* 827

I derived from this speech that Mr. Herbert Pocket (for Herbert was the pale young gentleman's name) still rather confounded his intention with his execution. But I made a modest reply, and we shook hands warmly.

"You hadn't come into your good fortune at that time?" said Herbert Pocket.

"No," said I.

"No," he acquiesced. "I heard it had happened very lately. *I* was rather on the lookout for good fortune then."

"Indeed?"

"Yes. Miss Havisham had sent for me, to see if she could take a fancy to me. But she couldn't—at all events, she didn't."

I thought it polite to remark that I was surprised to hear that.

"Bad taste," said Herbert, laughing, "but a fact. Yes, she had sent for me on a trial visit, and if I had come out of it successfully, I suppose I should have been provided for, perhaps I should have been what-you-may-called it to Estella."

"What's that?" I asked, with sudden gravity.

He was arranging his fruit in plates while we talked, which divided his attention, and was the cause of his having made this lapse of a word. "Affianced," he explained, still busy with the fruit. "Betrothed. Engaged. What's-his-named. Any word of that sort."

"How did you bear your disappointment?" I asked.

"Pooh!" said he, "I didn't care much for it. *She's* a Tartar."[1]

"Miss Havisham?"

"I don't say no to that, but I meant Estella. That girl's hard and haughty and capricious to the last degree, and has been brought up by Miss Havisham to wreak revenge on all the male sex."

"What relation is she to Miss Havisham?"

"None," said he. "Only adopted."

"Why should she wreak revenge on all the male sex? What revenge?"

"Lord, Mr. Pip!" said he. "Don't you know?"

"No," said I.

"Dear me! It's quite a story, and shall be saved till dinner time. And now let me take the liberty of asking you a question. How did you come there, that day?"

I told him, and he was attentive until I had finished, and then burst out laughing again, and asked me if I was sore afterwards? I didn't ask him if *he* was, for my conviction on that point was perfectly established.

"Mr. Jaggers is your guardian, I understand?" he went on.

"Yes."

"You know he is Miss Havisham's man of business and solicitor,[2] and has her confidence when nobody else has?"

This was bringing me (I felt) towards dangerous ground. I answered with a constraint I made no attempt to disguise, that I had seen Mr. Jaggers in Miss Havisham's house on the very day of our combat, but never at any other time, and that I believed he had no recollection of having ever seen me there.

"He was so obliging as to suggest my father for your tutor, and he called on my father to propose it. Of course he knew about my father from his connection with Miss Havisham. My father is Miss Havisham's

**31**

---

**1. Tartar** (tär' tər) *n*.: Ferocious, unmanageable person.

**2. solicitor** (sə lis' it ər) *n*.: British lawyer who can assist clients but cannot plead cases in the higher courts.

## Primary Source

Much of Dickens's life has been revealed through his letters which he wrote frequently and which were detailed accounts of his life, current events, and his social philosophy. Dickens kept up a continual correspondence with family and friends which are now in print; his letters were published in a three-volume collection, comprising twenty-five hundred pages and over a million words. He wrote more than five hundred letters to Miss Angela Burdett Coutts, the wife of Sir Francis Burdett, in which he discussed his involvement in charities, slum improvements, and reform movements. He also often wrote about his work and the ideas that were brewing in his mind. The following letter, which is published in *The Heart of Charles Dickens* by Edgar Johnson, was written to Angela Burdett Coutts on November 12, 1842. In it Dickens wrote about his state of mind as he embarked on the writing of a new book:

> Your most kind note found me in the agonies of plotting and contriving a new book [*Martin Chuzzlewit*], in which stage of the tremendous process, I am accustomed to walk up and down the house, smiting my forehead dejectedly; and to be so horribly cross and surly, that the boldest fly at my

cousin; not that that implies familiar intercourse between them, for he is a bad courtier and will not propitiate her."

Herbert Pocket had a frank and easy way with him that was very taking. I had never seen any one then, and I have never seen any one since, who more strongly expressed to me, in every look and tone, a natural incapacity to do anything secret and mean. There was something wonderfully hopeful about his general air, and something that at the same time whispered to me he would never be very successful or rich. I don't know how this was.

He was still a pale young gentleman, and had a certain conquered languor about him in the midst of his spirits and briskness, that did not seem indicative of natural strength. He had not a handsome face, but it was better than handsome, being extremely amiable and cheerful.

I told him my small story, and laid stress on my being forbidden to inquire who my benefactor was. I further mentioned that as I had been brought up by a blacksmith in a country place, and knew very little of the ways of politeness, I would take it as a great kindness in him if he would give me a hint whenever he saw me at a loss or going wrong.

"With pleasure," said he, "though I venture to prophesy that you'll want very few hints. Will you do me the favor to begin at once to call me by my Christian name, Herbert?"

I thanked him, and said I would. I informed him in exchange that my Christian name was Philip.

"I don't take to Philip," said he, smiling, "for it sounds like a moral boy out of the spelling book. I tell you what I should like. We are so harmonious, and you have been a blacksmith. Would you mind Handel for a familiar name? There's a charming piece of music by Handel[3] called 'The Harmonious Blacksmith.' "

"I should like it very much."

"Then, my dear Handel," said he, turning round as the door opened, "here is the dinner."

We had made some progress in the dinner when I reminded Herbert of his promise to tell me about Miss Havisham.

"True," he replied. "I'll redeem it at once. Let me introduce the topic, Handel, by mentioning that in London it is not the custom to put the knife in the mouth—for fear of accidents—and that while the fork is reserved for that use, it is not put further in than necessary. It is scarcely worth mentioning, only it's as well to do as other people do. Also, the spoon is not generally used overhand, but under. This has two advantages. You get at your mouth better (which after all is the object), and you save a good deal of the attitude of opening oysters on the part of the right elbow."

He offered these friendly suggestions in such a lively way that we both laughed and I scarcely blushed.

"Now," he pursued, "concerning Miss Havisham. Miss Havisham, you must know, was a spoiled child. Her mother died when she was a baby, and her father denied her nothing. Her father was a country gentleman down in your part of the world, and was a brewer. Well! Mr. Havisham was very rich and very proud. So was his daughter."

"Miss Havisham was an only child?" I hazarded.

"Stop a moment, I am coming to that. No, she was not an only child; she had a

---

**3. Handel** (han' d'l): George Frederick Handel (1685–1759), a German-born English composer.

**32 Discussion** Why do you think Pip believes Herbert will not be successful?

**33 Discussion** Why do you think Pip allows Herbert to rename him?

approach. At such times, even the Postman knocks at the door with a mild feebleness, and my publishers always come two together, lest I should fall upon a single invader and do murder on his intrusive body. . . .

. . . In starting a work which is to last for twenty months, there are so many little things to attend to, which require my personal superintendence, that I am obliged to be constantly on the watch; and I may add seriously, that unless I were to shut myself up, obstinately and sullenly in my own room for a great many days without writing a word, I don't think I ever should make a beginning. . . .

half-brother. Her father privately married again—his cook, I rather think."

"I thought he was proud," said I.

"My good Handel, so he was. He married his second wife privately because he was proud, and in course of time *she* died. When she was dead, I apprehend he first told his daughter what he had done, and then the son became a part of the family, residing in the house you are acquainted with. As the son grew a young man, he turned out riotous, extravagant, undutiful—altogether bad. At last his father disinherited him; but he softened when he was dying, and left him well off, though not nearly so well off as Miss Havisham.

"Miss Havisham was now an heiress, and you may suppose was looked after as a great match. Her half-brother had now ample means again, but what with debts and what with new madness, wasted them again. There were stronger differences between him and her than there had been between him and his father, and it is suspected that he cherished a deep and mortal grudge against her as having influenced the father's anger. Now, I come to the cruel part of the story.

"There appeared upon the scene a certain man who made love to Miss Havisham. I have heard my father mention that he was a showy man, and the kind of man for the purpose. But he was not to be, without ignorance or prejudice, mistaken for a gentleman. Well! This man pursued Miss Havisham closely, and professed to be devoted to her. I believe she had not shown much susceptibility up to that time, but all the susceptibility she possessed certainly came out then, and she passionately loved him. There is no doubt that she perfectly idolized him. He got great sums of money from her, and he induced her to buy her brother out of a share in the brewery (which had been weakly left him by his father) at an immense price,

on the plea that when he was her husband he must hold and manage it all. Your guardian was not at that time in Miss Havisham's councils, and she was too haughty and too much in love to be advised by any one. Her relations were poor and scheming, with the exception of my father; he was poor enough, but not time-serving or jealous. The only independent one among them, he warned her that she was doing too much for this man, and was placing herself too unreservedly in his power. She took the first opportunity of angrily ordering my father out of the house, in his presence, and my father has never seen her since."

I thought of her having said, "Matthew will come and see me at last when I am laid dead upon that table."

"To return to the man and make an end of him. The marriage day was fixed, the wedding dresses were bought, the wedding tour was planned out, the wedding guests were invited. The day came, but not the bridegroom. He wrote a letter—"

"Which she received," I struck in, "when she was dressing for her marriage? At twenty minutes to nine?"

"At the hour and minute," said Herbert, nodding, "at which she afterwards stopped all the clocks. What was in it, further than that it most heartlessly broke the marriage off, I can't tell you, because I don't know. When she recovered from a bad illness that she had, she laid the whole place waste, as you have seen it, and she has never since looked upon the light of day."

"Is that all the story?" I asked, after considering it.

"All I know of it. But I have forgotten one thing. It has been supposed that the man to whom she gave her misplaced confidence acted throughout in concert with her half-brother; that it was a conspiracy between them; and that they shared the profits."

"What became of the two men?" I asked, after again considering the subject.

"They fell into deeper shame and degradation—if there can be deeper—and ruin."

"Are they alive, now?"

"I don't know."

"You said just now that Estella was not related to Miss Havisham, but adopted. When adopted?"

Herbert shrugged his shoulders. "There has always been an Estella, since I have heard of a Miss Havisham. I know no more."

"And all I know," I retorted, "you know."

"I fully believe it. So there can be no competition or perplexity between you and me. And as to the condition on which you hold your advancement in life—namely, that you are not to inquire or discuss to whom you owe it—you may be very sure that it will never be encroached upon, or even approached, by me."

35

He said this with so much meaning that I felt he as perfectly understood Miss Havisham to be my benefactress as I understood the fact myself.

We were very gay and sociable, and I asked him, in the course of conversation, what he was? He replied, "A capitalist—an insurer of ships. However, I shall not rest satisfied with merely employing my capital in insuring ships. I think I shall trade," said he, leaning back in his chair, "to the East Indies, for silks, shawls, spices, dyes, drugs, and precious woods. It's an interesting trade."

36

"I think I shall trade, also," said he, putting his thumbs in his waistcoat pockets, "to the West Indies, for sugar, tobacco, and rum. Also to Ceylon, especially for elephants' tusks."

"You will want a good many ships," said I.

"A perfect fleet," said he.

Quite overpowered by the magnificence of these transactions, I asked him where the ships he insured mostly traded to at present?

"I haven't begun insuring yet," he replied. "I am looking about me."

Somehow that pursuit seemed more in keeping with Barnard's Inn. I said (in a tone of conviction), "Ah-h!"

"Yes. I am in a countinghouse,[4] and looking about me."

"Is a countinghouse profitable?" I asked.

"Why, n-no; not to me. Not directly profitable. That is, it doesn't pay me anything, and I have to—keep myself. But the thing is that you look about you. *That's* the grand thing. You are in a countinghouse, you know, and you look about you."

This was very like his way of conducting that encounter in the garden; very like. His manner of bearing his poverty, too, exactly corresponded to his manner of bearing that defeat. It seemed to me that he took all blows and buffets now with just the same air as he had taken mine then. It was evident that he had nothing around him but the simplest necessaries, for everything that I remarked upon turned out to have been sent in on my account from the coffee-house or somewhere else.

Yet, having already made his fortune in his own mind, he was so unassuming with it that I felt quite grateful to him for not being puffed up. It was a pleasant addition to his naturally pleasant ways, and we got on famously.

On Monday, we took coach for Hammersmith. We arrived there at two or three o'clock in the afternoon, and had very little way to walk to Mr. Pocket's house. Lifting the latch of a gate, we passed direct into a

---

**4. countinghouse** (koun' tiŋ hous') *n.*: Office where a firm keeps business records and handles correspondence.

*Great Expectations* 831

**35 Critical Thinking and Reading**
Do you agree with Pip's reasoning? Explain.

**36 Critical Thinking and Reading**
What do Herbert Pocket's dreams reveal about him?

37 **Discussion** Why is Pip "not much surprised" by Mr. Pocket's expression and appearance?

**Reader's Response** If you suddenly acquired a great deal of wealth, how do you think you would change? How would you spend your time and money?

little garden overlooking the river, where Mr. Pocket's children were playing about. And, unless I deceive myself on a point where my interests or prepossessions are certainly not concerned, I saw that Mr. and Mrs. Pocket's children were not growing up or being brought up, but were tumbling up.

Mrs. Pocket was sitting on a garden chair under a tree, reading, with her legs upon another garden chair, and Mrs. Pocket's two nursemaids were looking about them while the children played. "Mamma," said Herbert, "this is young Mr. Pip." Upon which Mrs. Pocket received me with an appearance of amiable dignity.

Mr. Pocket came out to make my acquaintance, and I was not much surprised to find that Mr. Pocket was a gentleman with a rather perplexed expression of face, and with his very gray hair disordered on his head, as if he didn't quite see his way to putting anything straight.

## Chapter 23

Mr. Pocket said he was glad to see me, and he hoped I was not sorry to see him. "For, I really am not," he added, with his son's smile, "an alarming personage." He was a young-looking man, in spite of his perplexities and his very gray hair, and his manner seemed quite natural.

Mr. Pocket took me into the house and showed me my room, which was a pleasant one. He then knocked at the doors of two other similar rooms, and introduced me to their occupants, by name Drummle and Startop. Drummle, an old-looking young man of a heavy order of architecture, was whistling. Startop, younger in years and appearance, was reading and holding his head, as if he thought himself in danger of exploding it with too strong a charge of knowledge.

By degrees I learned, and chiefly from Herbert, that Mr. Pocket had been educated at Harrow and at Cambridge,[1] where he had distinguished himself. He had come to London, and after gradually failing in loftier hopes, he had turned his acquirements to the account of literary compilation[2] and correction.

In the evening there was rowing on the river. As Drummle and Startop had each a boat, I resolved to set up mine, and to cut them both out. I was pretty good at most exercises in which country boys are adepts, but, as I was conscious of wanting elegance of style for the Thames[3]—not to say for other waters—I at once engaged to place myself under the tuition of the winner of a prize wherry[4] who plied at our stairs, and to whom I was introduced by my new allies.

---

**1. Harrow and Cambridge:** A famous English preparatory school and university, respectively.
**2. compilation** (käm′ pə lā′ shən) *n.*: Making collections or anthologies.
**3. Thames** (temz): River that flows through London into the North Sea.
**4. wherry** (hwer′ ē) *n.*: Light rowboat used on rivers.

**Closure and Extension**

## ANSWERS TO THINKING ABOUT THE SELECTION
*Recalling*

1. Biddy brings peace and order to the household. She is able to understand Mrs. Joe better than Joe or Pip can.
2. Pip learns that an unknown benefactor has left him a fortune, on the following conditions: that he bear the name of Pip, that the name of his benefactor remain a secret until his benefactor chooses to reveal it, that Pip never ask Mr. Jaggers to reveal any information about this benefactor, and that Mr. Jaggers act as his guardian.
3. Mr. Trabb greets Pip in an offhanded manner until he learns that Pip has come into a fortune; then he is effusively pleased to serve Pip. Uncle Pumblechook flatters Pip excessively when he learns of Pip's fortune.
4. Mr. Jaggers is Pip's "man of business" and his guardian. Wemmick makes out the drafts of money for Pip and gives him advice. Herbert is Pip's best friend and confidant.
5. Pip learns from Herbert that Miss Havisham was the daughter of a wealthy father and her mother died when Miss Havisham was still a baby. When Miss Havisham grew up, she was courted by a handsome man with whom she fell in love, but he abandoned her on their wedding day. Jaggers was Miss Havisham's lawyer, and Miss Havisham adopted Estella as a baby.

### Interpreting

6. Suggested Response: Pip leaves with mixed feelings of regret for the past and longing for his future expectations. Pip attempts to instill in Joe and Biddy the idea that they

## THINKING ABOUT THE SELECTION

### Recalling

1. Why is Biddy a good nurse and housekeeper?
2. What does Pip learn from Mr. Jaggers about his "great expectations"? What conditions are attached?
3. What are Trabb's and Pumblechook's reactions when they hear of Pip's good fortune?
4. Summarize the roles that Jaggers, Wemmick, and Herbert each play in Pip's new life.
5. What important facts does Pip learn about Miss Havisham?

### Interpreting

6. What are Pip's conflicting feelings about his good fortune? How do Pip's "expectations" affect his relationship with Biddy and Joe?
7. On what basis does Pip believe that Miss Havisham is his benefactor?

### Applying

8. Why do sudden wealth or good luck often change people?

## ANALYZING LITERATURE

### Understanding Plot and Subplot

The **plot** is the sequence of interrelated events in a work of fiction. These events are often based on a **conflict.** A long novel may also have **subplots,** or secondary plots, to complicate and mirror the action of the main plot.

The plot of *Great Expectations* focuses on Pip's conflict about the importance of money and success compared to love and devotion. Various subplots—involving Orlick, Herbert, and Wemmick—introduce conflicts that relate to the struggle within Pip.

1. Which feelings seem to be gaining in the conflict that Pip is experiencing? Explain.
2. One subplot concerns the "expectations" of Herbert Pocket. Contrast the attitudes, back-

ground, and prospects of Pip and Herbert.
3. Identify another subplot of the novel.

## CRITICAL THINKING AND READING

### Predicting Outcomes

Once the central conflict is clear and certain situations and relationships are established in a novel, you can make predictions about the outcome. For example, you know that Pip is experiencing two opposite feelings: wanting to embrace Joe, Biddy, and his old life and wanting to reject them as "coarse and common." The outcome of the story will depend, in part, on which of these two feelings becomes stronger. If Pip decides to reject his old way of life, for instance, he may settle in London and marry a rich woman.

1. How do you think Pip will resolve his inner conflict? Support you answer with details from the novel.
2. What does this resolution suggest about the life that Pip will lead?

## UNDERSTANDING LANGUAGE

### Understanding the Latin Root *spect*

The word *expectations,* meaning "something to look forward to," is based on the Latin root *spect* (from *spectare*—"to look"). This root also appears in the following words. Find each in a dictionary and tell how it relates to the idea of looking.

1. inspect    2. specter    3. spectacle

## THINKING AND WRITING

### Extending the Story

Recall the predictions you made about the outcome of the central conflict. List additional details that you would include if you were finishing the story based on your prediction. Then, using your notes, write an ending to the story that resolves the conflict. Discuss your first draft with classmates. Use their ideas to revise your work.

*Great Expectations* 833

(Answers begin on p. 832.)

Herbert is a gentleman, though he comes from a poor family. Pip's social status is lower, though he is being trained to be a gentleman.
3. Suggested Response: Another subplot involves the relationship between Biddy and Joe.

## ANSWERS TO CRITICAL THINKING AND READING

1. Suggested Response: Pip's conflict will not be resolved until he relinquishes his dream and faces the realities of life. His longing for Estella and all she symbolizes, however, is so strong—witness his conversation with Herbert on this subject—that his disillusionment will probably be painful.
2. Suggested Response: Once Pip gets over the pain of giving up his illusions, he will have a chance to lead a happy life.

## ANSWERS TO UNDERSTANDING LANGUAGE

1. *Inspect* means "to look upon, to examine closely."
2. *Spectacle* means "a public performance or display, appealing to the eye."
3. *Specter* means "a ghost, or visible spirit."

## THINKING AND WRITING

For help with this assignment, students may consult Lesson 17, "Writing a Short Story," in the Handbook of Writing About Literature.

### Publishing Student Writing

Have students keep the endings they write so they can compare them with the final chapters of the novel.

### Writing Across the Curriculum

Have students research and report on London life in the middle of the nineteenth century. Consider informing the social studies department of this assignment so that teachers can direct students to appropriate resource materials.

should get more education and raise their station. Joe tolerates him placidly, but Biddy is offended by his presumed superiority.
7. Suggested Response: Pip bases his conclusion on the following facts—he met Mr. Jaggers at Miss Havisham's house, her cousin was suggested as his tutor, and Jaggers is Miss Havisham's lawyer. He wants to believe that Miss Havisham intends him for Estella and is raising him as a gentleman for that purpose.

### Applying

8. Answers will differ. Students may respond that sudden wealth or good luck may cause a person to feel superior, insecure, or distrustful.

## ANSWERS TO ANALYZING LITERATURE

1. Suggested Response: Pip seems to be more concerned with money and success than with love and devotion. He is becoming ab-

sorbed in his new way of life and is obsessed by winning Estella's hand and showing her he is a gentleman.
2. Suggested Response: Herbert is more realistic about the prospect and desirability of winning Estella; however, he is unrealistic about his chances of obtaining a fleet of ships and becoming an important merchant. Pip sees that Herbert is a dreamer but does not realize that he himself is unrealistic in his dreams of winning Estella's hand.

## Focus

**Literary Focus** Consider pointing out to students that Victorian England is so vivid for us today in part because novelists described it. Dickens is particularly famous for his descriptions of London, a city whose streets he walked incessantly.

**Look For** Dickens is a master of detail. Have students choose one specific setting in the novel and make a list of all the details used by Dickens to evoke that place for the reader.

**Writing/Prior Knowledge** Consider playing for the class a composition like Beethoven's "Moonlight Sonata" (RCA-LSC-4001) or Tchaikovsky's *Violin Concerto* (Columbia-35126). Have students close their eyes and visualize a place that has been important in their lives. Have them think about where it was, who has been there with them, when it was important to them—season or time of their lives—and why it was so important. Then follow up with the writing exercise.

**Vocabulary** You might want to call out vocabulary words from the first four sections and have students give synonyms and antonyms for them.

**Spelling Tip** Point out that three words in this list—*cupidity, incongruity,* and *disparity*—have the same ending sound spelled *ity.*

# GUIDE FOR READING

## Setting and Atmosphere

### Great Expectations, Chapters 24–31

The **setting** of a novel refers to the time and place of the events, as well as the clothing, customs, and occupations that reflect this time and place. *Great Expectations,* for example, is set in England during the nineteenth century. More specifically, the events of the novel alternate between Pip's small town in the marsh country and the great city of London. The stagecoach that journeys between these two places, the blacksmith's forge, and Jaggers's law office are all part of the setting.

Through careful description of details such as these, Dickens creates an **atmosphere,** or mood, which gives a special flavor to each part of the story. The description of the cemetery near the marsh, for instance, calls up a feeling of mystery and fear. This atmosphere prepares you for a key incident in the plot, the first appearance of the convict.

## Look For

Look for the details that Dickens includes to make a setting come alive. For instance, he describes the neighborhood surrounding Wemmick's house, notes the house's special features, and even estimates the size of the ditch around it. Notice, too, how these descriptions create a different atmosphere for each setting. Wemmick's house, for example, has a much different atmosphere than does Jaggers's office.

## Writing

Recall a place you have visited that had a definite atmosphere. Describe this place, including details—like the quality of light, certain colors, or even a particular odor—that will communicate this atmosphere to a reader.

## Vocabulary

Knowing the following words will help you as you read Chapters 24–31 of *Great Expectations.*

**discomfiture** (dis kum′ fi chər) *n.*: Unease; confusion (p. 835)

**cupidity** (kyo͞o pid′ ə tē) *n.*: Greed (p. 836)

**dexterously** (dek′ strəs lē) *adv.*: With skillful use of the hands (p. 841)

**incongruity** (in′ kən gro͞o′ ə tē) *n.*: Quality of being out of place (p. 841)

**lethargic** (li thär′ jik) *adj.*: Drowsy; without energy (p. 845)

**disparity** (dis par′ ə tē) *n.*: Condition of inequality (p. 848)

### Objectives

1 To understand setting and atmosphere
2 To identify details that create setting
3 To compare and contrast settings

## Support Material

**Teaching Portfolio**
Teacher Backup, p. 965
Grammar in Action Worksheets, *Using Prepositional Phrases,* p. 969; *Using Parallelism,* p. 971
Usage and Mechanics Worksheet, p. 973
Vocabulary Check, p. 974
Analyzing Literature Worksheet, *Understanding Setting and Atmosphere,* p. 975

Language Worksheet, *Exploring Connotations,* p. 976
Selection Test, p. 977

## Chapter 24

After two or three days, when I had established myself in my room and had gone backwards and forwards to London several times, and had ordered all I wanted of my tradesmen, Mr. Pocket and I had a long talk together. He knew more of my intended career than I knew myself, for he referred to his having been told by Mr. Jaggers that I was not designed for any profession, and that I should be well enough educated for my destiny if I could "hold my own" with the average of young men in prosperous circumstances.

When I had begun to work in earnest, it occurred to me that if I could retain my bedroom in Barnard's Inn, my life would be agreeably varied, while my manners would be none the worse for Herbert's society. Mr. Pocket did not object to this arrangement, but urged that before any step could possibly be taken in it, it must be submitted to my guardian. I felt that his delicacy[1] arose out of the consideration that the plan would save Herbert some expense, so I went off to Little Britain and imparted my wish to Mr. Jaggers.

"If I could buy the furniture now hired for me," said I, "and one or two other little things, I should be quite at home there."

"Go it!" said Mr. Jaggers, with a short laugh. "I told you you'd get on. Well! How much do you want?"

I said I didn't know how much.

"Come!" retorted Mr. Jaggers. "How much? Fifty pounds?"

"Oh, not nearly so much."

"Five pounds?" said Mr. Jaggers.

This was such a great fall that I said in discomfiture, "Oh! more than that."

---

**1. delicacy** (del' i kə sē) *n.*: Regard for what is proper.

"More than that, eh!" retorted Mr. Jaggers. "How much more?"

"It is so difficult to fix a sum," said I, hesitating.

"Come!" said Mr. Jaggers. "Let's get at it. Twice five; will that do? Three times five; will that do? Four times five; will that do?"

I said I thought that would do handsomely.

"Four times five will do handsomely, will it?" said Mr. Jaggers, knitting his brows. "Now, what do you make of four times five?"

"Twenty pounds, of course."

"Wemmick!" said Mr. Jaggers, opening his office door. "Take Mr. Pip's written order, and pay him twenty pounds."

This strongly marked way of doing business made a strongly marked impression on me, and that not of an agreeable kind. As Mr. Jaggers happened to go out now, and as Wemmick was brisk and talkative, I said to Wemmick that I hardly knew what to make of Mr. Jaggers's manner.

"Tell him that, and he'll take it as a compliment," answered Wemmick; "he don't mean that you *should* know what to make of it. Oh!" for I looked surprised, "it's not personal; it's professional, only professional."

Then he went on to say in a friendly manner:

"If at any odd time when you have nothing better to do, you wouldn't mind coming over to see me at Walworth, I could offer you a bed, and I should consider it an honor. I have not much to show you; but such two or three curiosities as I have got, you might like to look over; and I am fond of a bit of garden and a summer house."

I said I should be delighted to accept his hospitality.

"Thankee," said he: ' then we'll consider that it's to come off, when convenient to you. Have you dined with Mr. Jaggers yet?"

"Not yet."

*Great Expectations* 835

**3 Discussion** How does Wemmick's comment add to the suspense of the story?

**4 Discussion** What is the irony in the description of how Bentley Drummle reads a book? How does Dickens compare his reading a book and meeting a new acquaintance?

**5 Discussion** Consider what has already been noted about Mr. Wemmick. Although putting his key "down his back" appears to be unusual behavior, how does it fit in with his already portrayed personality?

**3** "Well," said Wemmick, "I'll tell you something. When you go to dine with Mr. Jaggers, look at his housekeeper."

"Shall I see something very uncommon?"

"Well," said Wemmick, "you'll see a wild beast tamed. It won't lower your opinion of Mr. Jaggers's powers. Keep your eye on it."

I told him I would do so, with all the interest and curiosity that his preparation awakened.

### Chapter 25

**4** Bentley Drummle, who was so sulky a fellow that he even took up a book as if its writer had done him an injury, did not take up an acquaintance in a more agreeable spirit. Heavy in figure, movement, and comprehension, he was idle, proud, niggardly, reserved, and suspicious.

Startop had been spoiled by a weak mother, and kept at home when he ought to have been at school, but he was devotedly attached to her, and admired her beyond measure. He had a woman's delicacy of feature, and was—"as you may see, though you never saw her," said Herbert to me—"exactly like his mother." It was but natural that I should take to him much more kindly than to Drummle, and that, even in the earliest evenings of our boating, he and I should pull homeward abreast of one another conversing from boat to boat, while Bentley Drummle came up in our wake alone.

Herbert was my intimate companion and friend. I presented him with a half share in my boat, which was the occasion of his often coming down to Hammersmith; and my possession of a half share in his chambers often took me up to London. We used to walk between the two places at all hours.

When I had been in Mr. Pocket's family a month or two, Mr. and Mrs. Camilla turned up. Camilla was Mr. Pocket's sister. Georgiana, whom I had seen at Miss Havisham's on the same occasion, also turned up. These people hated me with the hatred of cupidity and disappointment. As a matter of course, they fawned upon me in my prosperity with the basest meanness.

These were the surroundings among which I settled down, and applied myself to my education. I soon contracted expensive habits, and began to spend an amount of money that within a few short months I should have thought almost fabulous; but through good and evil I stuck to my books.

**5** I had not seen Mr. Wemmick for some weeks, when I thought I would write him a note and propose to go home with him on a certain evening. He replied that it would give him much pleasure, and that he would expect me at the office at six o'clock. Thither I went, and there I found him, putting the key of his safe down his back as the clock struck.

"Did you think of walking down to Walworth?" said he.

"Certainly," said I, "if you approve."

"Very much," was Wemmick's reply, "for I have had my legs under the desk all day, and shall be glad to stretch them. Now I'll tell you what I've got for supper, Mr. Pip. I have got a stewed steak—which is of home preparation—and a cold roast fowl—which is from the cook's shop. You don't object to an aged parent, I hope?"

I really thought he was still speaking of the fowl, until he added, "Because I have got an aged parent at my place." I then said what politeness required.

"So you haven't dined with Mr. Jaggers yet?" he pursued, as we walked along.

"Not yet."

"He told me so this afternoon when he heard you were coming. I expect you'll have an invitation tomorrow. He's going to ask your pals, too."

## Primary Source

According to Edgar Johnson in *The Heart of Charles Dickens:*

During the opening dozen years of Dickens's career his rise was rapid and dazzling. Almost every novel he wrote represented an advance over its predecessors in structural skill and intellectual grasp. With his glowing enjoyment of all the rich variety of existence, his delight in the varicolored aspects of human nature, and his zeal for the welfare of mankind, he developed as both a literary artist of brilliant genius and social reformer of penetrating insight. In long explorations through London's slums and in repeated journeys through the manufacturing towns of England he learned how an industrial civilization was affecting the lives of the poor, and in innumerable parliamentary blue books he studied its consequences in child labor, conditions in mines and factories, filth and disease in people's homes, illiteracy, brutality, and crime in their lives.

His knowledge made him both a compassionate advocate of social betterment in all his written works and a man of action, laboring persistently to help all victims of misfor-

**DAVID JOHNSTON**
*Pierre-Paul Prud'hon*
*National Gallery of Art, Washington, D.C.*

**Humanities Note**

Fine art, *David Johnston,* Pierre-Paul Prud'hon. The French painter Pierre-Paul Prud'hon (1758–1823) taught himself the elements of oil painting. A prize won in a competition enabled him to go to Italy where he studied the old masters, particularly da Vinci. Prud'hon drew illustrations, designed stationery, and painted portraits to support his family. He attributed the grace and emotional quality of his paintings to his study of da Vinci. Pierre-Paul Prud'hon gained recognition late in life and was given the honor of painting a ceiling in the Louvre.

*David Johnston* shows Prud'hon's considerable skill as a portraitist. The clean lines and sensitivity of the rendering show the classicism of his style. You might want to use the following questions:

1. How would you describe the personality of this subject?
2. Which details convey his personality?
3. Do you think this subject is similar to Bentley Drummle in *Great Expectations*? Why or why not?

6 **Literary Focus** Mr. Wemmick has something in common with Pip when it comes to living in a fantasy world. What are the details of his home that create this special atmosphere?

Mr. Wemmick and I beguiled the time and the road, until he gave me to understand that we had arrived in the district of Walworth.

It appeared to be a collection of black lanes, ditches, and little gardens, and to present the aspect of a rather dull retirement. Wemmick's house was a little wooden cottage in the midst of plots of garden, and the top of it was cut out and painted like a battery mounted with guns.

"My own doing," said Wemmick. "Looks pretty, don't it?"

I highly commended it. I think it was the smallest house I ever saw, with the queerest Gothic[1] windows, and a Gothic door, almost too small to get in at.

"That's a real flagstaff, you see," said Wemmick, "and on Sundays I run up a real flag. Then look here. After I have crossed this bridge, I hoist it up—so—and cut off the communication."

The bridge was a plank, and it crossed a chasm about four feet wide and two deep. But it was very pleasant to see the pride with

---

**1. Gothic** (gäth′ ik) *adj.*: Style of architecture that makes use of pointed arches.

tune upon whom he came, seeking out still others, and tirelessly devising ways of dealing with specific evils to which he devoted hours of effort beyond those he spent at his desk. [The letters he wrote to Miss Burdett Coutts] reveal Dickens in action, moved by a most warmhearted social conscience to the most practical efforts, not only in behalf of individuals but in striking at the ignorance and dirt that degraded the lives of whole classes of the poor and fostered every social evil.

**7 Discussion** What do you infer about Mr. Wemmick's character from his manner with his father?

**8 Clarification** "Proud as Punch" is a familiar expression that refers to the character in a favorite puppet show in Dickens's day—*Punch and Judy.*

**9 Critical Thinking and Reading** Why does Mr. Wemmick tell Pip he wants to keep his private life totally separate from his business life at Mr. Jaggers's office?

**10 Critical Thinking and Reading** Why does the nightly entertainment appeal to the Aged? Have students cite examples from the story that support their responses.

which he hoisted it up, and made it fast; smiling as he did so, with a relish, and not merely mechanically.

"At nine o'clock every night, Greenwich time,"[2] said Wemmick, "the gun fires. There he is, you see! And when you hear him go, I think you'll say he's a stinger."

The piece of ordnance referred to was mounted in a separate fortress, constructed of latticework. It was protected from the weather by an ingenious little tarpaulin contrivance in the nature of an umbrella.

"Then, at the back," said Wemmick, "there's a pig, and there are fowls and rabbits; then I knock together my own little frame, you see, and grow cucumbers; and you'll judge at supper what sort of a salad I can raise. So, sir," said Wemmick, "if you can suppose the little place besieged, it would hold out a devil of a time in point of provisions.

"I am my own engineer, and my own carpenter, and my own plumber, and my own gardener, and my own jack of all trades," said Wemmick. "Well, it's a good thing, you know. It brushes the Newgate[3] cobwebs away, and pleases the Aged. You wouldn't mind being at once introduced to the Aged, would you? It wouldn't put you out?"

I expressed the readiness I felt, and we went into the castle. There, we found sitting by a fire, a very old man in a flannel coat—clean, cheerful, comfortable, and well cared for, but intensely deaf.

"Well, aged parent," said Wemmick, shaking hands with him in a cordial and jocose way, "how am you?"

"All right, John; all right!" replied the old man.

---

**2. Greenwich** (gren′ ich) **time:** Solar time at Greenwich, England, is the basis for standard time throughout most of the world.
**3. Newgate:** Newgate Prison in London.

"Here's Mr. Pip, aged parent," said Wemmick, "and I wish you could hear his name. Nod away at him, Mr. Pip; that's what he likes. Nod away at him, if you please."

"This is a fine place of my son's, sir," cried the old man, while I nodded as hard as I possibly could.

"You're as proud of it as Punch; ain't you, Aged?" said Wemmick, contemplating the old man, with his hard face really softened. "*There's* a nod for you"—giving him a tremendous one. "You like that, don't you? If you're not tired, Mr. Pip—though I know it's tiring to strangers—would you tip him one more? You can't think how it pleases him."

I tipped him several more, and he was in great spirits. We left him bestirring himself to feed the fowls, and we sat down to our punch in the arbor, where Wemmick told me as he smoked a pipe that it had taken him a good many years to bring the property up to its present pitch of perfection.

"Is it your own, Mr. Wemmick?"

"Oh, yes," said Wemmick.

"Is it, indeed? I hope Mr. Jaggers admires it?"

"Never seen it," said Wemmick. "Never heard of it. Never seen the Aged. Never heard of him. No; the office is one thing, and private life is another. When I go into the office, I leave the castle behind me, and when I come into the castle, I leave the office behind me. If it's not in any way disagreeable to you, you'll oblige me by doing the same. I don't wish it professionally spoken about."

Of course I felt my good faith involved in the observance of his request. The punch being very nice, we sat there drinking it and talking, until it was almost nine o'clock. "Getting near gun-fire," said Wemmick then, as he laid down his pipe; "it's the Aged's treat."

Proceeding into the castle again, we found the Aged heating the poker, with expectant eyes, as a preliminary to the performance of this great nightly ceremony. Wemmick stood with his watch in his hand until the moment was come for him to take the red-hot poker from the Aged, and repair to the battery. He took it, and went out, and presently the stinger went off with a bang that shook the crazy little box of a cottage as if it must fall to pieces, and made every glass and tea-cup in it ring. Upon this the Aged—who I believed would have been blown out of his armchair but for holding on by the elbows—cried out exultingly, "He's fired! I heerd him!" and I nodded at the old gentleman until I absolutely could not see him.

The supper was excellent, and I was heartily pleased with my whole entertainment. Nor was there any drawback on my little turret bedroom.

Our breakfast was as good as the supper, and at half-past eight precisely we started for Little Britain. By degrees, Wemmick got dryer and harder as we went along. At last, when we got to his place of business and he pulled out his key from his coat collar, he looked as unconscious of his Walworth property as if the castle and the drawbridge and the arbor and the lake and the fountain and the Aged had all been blown into space together by the last discharge of the stinger.

## Chapter 26

It fell out, as Wemmick had told me it would, that I had an early opportunity of comparing my guardian's establishment with that of his cashier and clerk. My guardian was in his room, washing his hands with his scented soap, when I went into the office from Walworth; and he called me to him, and gave me the invitation for myself and friends which Wemmick had prepared me to receive. "No ceremony," he stipulated, "and no dinner dress, and say tomorrow."

When I and my friends repaired[1] to him at six o'clock next day, he conducted us to Gerrard Street, Soho, to a house on the south side of that street, rather a stately house of its kind, but dolefully in want of painting, and with dirty windows. He took out his key and opened the door, and we all went into a stone hall, bare, gloomy, and little used. So up a dark brown staircase into a series of three dark brown rooms on the first floor.

As he had scarcely seen my three companions until now—for he and I had walked together—he stood on the hearth rug, after ringing the bell, and took a searching look at them. To my surprise, he seemed at once to be principally, if not solely, interested in Drummle.

"Pip," said he, putting his large hand on my shoulder and moving me to the window, "I don't know one from the other. Who's the spider?"

"The spider?" said I.

"The blotchy, sprawly, sulky fellow."

"That's Bentley Drummle," I replied; "the one with the delicate face is Startop."

Not making the least account of "the one with the delicate face," he returned, "Bentley Drummle is his name, is it? I like the look of that fellow."

He immediately began to talk to Drummle. I was looking at the two, when there came between me and them, the housekeeper, with the first dish for the table.

She was a woman of about forty, I supposed—but I may have thought her younger than she was. Rather tall, of a lithe nimble figure, extremely pale, with large faded eyes, and a quantity of streaming hair. She set the dish on, touched my guardian quietly on the arm with a finger to notify that dinner was ready, and vanished.

---

**1. repaired** (ri perd') *v.*: Went.

11

**11 Critical Thinking and Reading** Drummle's attitudes and qualities are not portrayed as appealing ones. Why, then, might Mr. Jaggers select him from among the others for his special attention?

*Great Expectations* 839

**12 Discussion** Why does Jaggers revel in his control over Molly? What important aspects of his character are revealed in this scene?

**13 Discussion** How does Mr. Jaggers's behavior toward Drummle relate to his behavior toward Molly?

**14 Reading Strategy** Have students note Drummle's behavior at the dinner party. What action indicates that there might be further trouble from him in a later chapter?

Induced to take particular notice of the housekeeper, both by her own striking appearance and by Wemmick's preparation, I observed that whenever she was in the room, she kept her eyes attentively on my guardian. I fancied that I could detect in his manner a consciousness of this, and a purpose of always holding her in suspense.

Dinner went off gaily, and, although my guardian seemed to follow rather than originate subjects, I knew that he wrenched the weakest part of our dispositions out of us. It was not then, but when we had got to the cheese, that our conversation turned upon our rowing feats, and that Drummle was rallied for coming up behind of a night in that slow amphibious way of his. Drummle, upon this, informed our host that he much preferred our room to our company, and that as to skill he was more than our master, and that as to strength he could scatter us like chaff. By some invisible agency, my guardian wound him up to a pitch little short of ferocity about this trifle, and he fell to baring and spanning his arm to show how muscular it was, and we all fell to baring and spanning our arms in a ridiculous manner.

Now the housekeeper was at that time clearing the table; my guardian, taking no heed of her, but with the side of his face turned from her, was leaning back in his chair, biting the side of his forefinger and showing an interest in Drummle that, to me, was quite inexplicable. Suddenly, he clapped his large hand on the housekeeper's, like a trap, as she stretched it across the table.

"If you talk of strength," said Mr. Jaggers, "I'll show you a wrist. Molly, let them see your wrist."

Her entrapped hand was on the table, but she had already put her other hand behind her waist: "Master," she said, in a low voice, "don't."

"I'll show you a wrist," repeated Mr. Jag-

gers, with an immovable determination to show it. "Molly, let them see your wrist."

"Master," she again murmured. "Please!"

"Molly," said Mr. Jaggers, "let them see *both* your wrists. Show them. Come!"

He took his hand from hers, and turned that wrist up on the table. She brought her other hand from behind her, and held the two out side by side. The last wrist was much disfigured—deeply scarred and scarred across and across. When she held her hands out, she took her eyes from Mr. Jaggers, and turned them watchfully on every one of the rest of us in succession.

"There's power here," said Mr. Jaggers, coolly tracing out the sinews with his forefinger. "Very few men have the power of wrist that this woman has. It's remarkable what mere force of grip there is in these hands. I have had occasion to notice many hands; but I never saw stronger in that respect, man's or woman's, than these."

"That'll do, Molly," said Mr. Jaggers, giving her a slight nod; "you have been admired, and can go." She withdrew her hands and went out of the room.

"At half-past nine, gentlemen," said he, "we must break up. Pray make the best use of your time. I am glad to see you all. Mr. Drummle, I drink to you."

If his object in singling out Drummle were to bring him out still more, it perfectly succeeded. In a sulky triumph, Drummle showed his morose depreciation of the rest of us in a more and more offensive degree, until he became downright intolerable. Through all his stages, Mr. Jaggers followed him with the same strange interest.

We became particularly hot upon some boorish sneer of Drummle's to the effect that we were too free with our money. It led to my remarking, with more zeal than discretion, that it came with a bad grace from him, to whom Startop had lent money in my pres-

A **prepositional phrase** is a group of words that includes a preposition, a noun or pronoun, and any modifiers. Writers use such phrases to add descriptive details and create longer, more interesting sentences.

Notice the use that Dickens makes of prepositional phrases in the following passage from *Great Expectations*:

Now the housekeeper was *at that time* clearing the table; my guardian, taking no heed *of her*, but *with the side of his face* turned *from her*, was leaning back *in his chair*, biting the side *of his forefinger* and showing an interest *in Drummle* that, *to me*, was quite inexplicable. Suddenly, he clapped his large hand *on the housekeeper's* like a trap, as she stretched it *across the table*.

As you can see, the prepositional phrases add many details that make the description lively and specific. Some prepositions, like *across* in the final line, almost seem as if they were action verbs.

ence but a week or so before. Startop tried to turn the discussion aside with some small pleasantry that made us all laugh. Resenting this little success more than anything, Drummle, without any threat or warning, pulled his hands out of his pockets, dropped his round shoulders, swore, took up a large glass, and would have flung it at his adversary's head, but for our entertainer's dexterously seizing it at the instant when it was raised for that purpose.

"Gentlemen," said Mr. Jaggers, deliberately putting down the glass, "I am exceedingly sorry to announce that it's half-past nine."

On this hint we all rose to depart. Before we got to the street door, Startop was cheerily calling Drummle "old boy," as if nothing had happened. But the old boy was so far from responding that he would not even walk to Hammersmith on the same side of the way, so Herbert and I, who remained in town, saw them going down the street on opposite sides; Startop leading, and Drummle lagging behind in the shadow of the houses, much as he was wont to follow in his boat.

In about a month after that, the spider's time with Mr. Pocket was up for good, and, to the great relief of all the house but Mrs. Pocket, he went home to the family hole.

### Chapter 27

My dear Mr. Pip,

I write this by request of Mr. Gargery, for to let you know that he is going to London in company with Mr. Wopsle and would be glad if agreeable to be allowed to see you. He would call at Barnard's Hotel Tuesday morning at nine o'clock, when if not agreeable please leave word. Your poor sister is much the same as when you left. We talk of you in the kitchen every night, and wonder what you are saying and doing. If now considered in the light of a liberty, excuse it for the love of poor old days. No more, dear Mr. Pip, from

Your ever obliged, and affectionate servant,

Biddy.

P.S. He wishes me most particular to write *what larks*. He says you will understand. I hope and do not doubt it will be agreeable to see him even though a gentleman, for you had ever a good heart, and he is a worthy worthy man. I have read him all excepting only the last little sentence, and he wishes me most particular to write again *what larks*.

I received this letter by post on Monday morning, and therefore its appointment was for the next day. Let me confess exactly with what feelings I looked forward to Joe's coming.

Not with pleasure, though I was bound to him by so many ties; no; with considerable disturbance, some mortification, and a keen sense of incongruity. If I could have kept him away by paying money, I certainly would have paid money. My greatest reassurance was that he was coming to Barnard's Inn, not the Hammersmith. I had little objection to his being seen by Herbert or his father, for both of whom I had a respect, but I had the sharpest sensitiveness as to his being seen by Drummle, whom I held in contempt. So throughout life our worst weaknesses and meannesses are usually committed for the sake of the people whom we most despise.

I had got on so fast of late that I had even

**15 Critical Thinking and Reading** Pip has been to two dinner parties, one at Wemmick's house and the other at Mr. Jaggers's. Compare and contrast the atmosphere and events at each.

**16 Discussion** What is Pip's reaction to the letter from Biddy, and what are his reasons for feeling as he does?

**Student Activity 1.** Identify four other prepositional phrases that Dickens uses in this chapter.

**Student Activity 2.** Write a one-paragraph description of a sudden or surprising occurrence. Use prepositional phrases to make your description more detailed and dramatic.

17 **Discussion** Dickens uses figurative language to describe how Joe carries his hat when he comes to visit Pip. Have students discuss the effectiveness of his use of figurative language. Have students paraphrase the sentence to demonstrate their understanding of it.

18 **Discussion** How does Joe's behavior toward Herbert resemble his earlier behavior toward Miss Havisham?

started a boy in boots[1]—top boots—and had clothed him with a blue coat, canary waistcoat, white cravat, creamy breeches, and the boots already mentioned, I had to find him a little to do and a great deal to eat; and with both of these horrible requirements he haunted my existence.

I came into town on the Monday night to be ready for Joe, and I got up early in the morning, and caused the sitting room and breakfast table to assume their most splendid appearance.

As the time approached I should have liked to run away, but presently I heard Joe on the staircase. I knew it was Joe by his clumsy manner of coming upstairs. When at last he stopped outside our door, I could hear his finger tracing over the painted letters of my name. Finally he gave a faint single rap, and Pepper—such was the compromising name of the boy—announced "Mr. Gargery!"

"Joe, how are you, Joe?"

"Pip, how AIR you, Pip?"

With his good honest face all glowing and shining, and his hat put down on the floor between us, he caught both my hands and worked them straight up and down.

"I am glad to see you, Joe. Give me your hat."

But Joe, taking it up carefully with both hands, like a bird's-nest with eggs in it, wouldn't hear of parting with that piece of property.

"Which you have that growed," said Joe, "and that swelled and that gentle-folked"—Joe considered a little before he discovered this word—"as to be sure you are a honor to your king and country."

"And you, Joe, look wonderfully well."

"Thank God," said Joe, "I'm ekerval to most. And your sister, she's no worse than she were. And Biddy, she's ever right and ready. And all friends is no backerder, if not no forarder. 'Ceptin' Wopsle; he's had a drop."

All this time (still with both hands taking great care of the bird's-nest), Joe was rolling his eyes round and round the room, and round and round the flowered pattern of my dressing-gown.

"Had a drop, Joe?"

"Why, yes," said Joe, lowering his voice, "he's left the Church and went into the play-acting. Which the play-acting have likewise brought him to London along with me. And his wish were," said Joe, getting the bird's-nest under his left arm for the moment, and groping in it for an egg with his right, "if no offense, as I would 'and you that."

I took what Joe gave me, and found it to be the crumpled playbill of a small metropolitan theater, announcing the first appearance, in that very week, of "the celebrated provincial amateur, whose unique performance in the highest tragic walk of our national bard[2] has lately occasioned so great a sensation in local dramatic circles."

"Were you at his performance, Joe?" I inquired.

"I *were*," said Joe, with emphasis and solemnity.

"Was there a great sensation?"

"Why," said Joe, "yes, there certainly were a peck of orange-peel. Partickler when he see the ghost."

A ghost-seeing effect in Joe's own countenance informed me that Herbert had entered the room. So, I presented Joe to Herbert, who held out his hand; but Joe backed from it, and held on by the bird's-nest.

Joe, being invited to sit down to table, looked all round the room for a suitable spot

1. **started a boy in boots:** Hired a servant.

2. **our national bard:** William Shakespeare.

on which to deposit his hat and ultimately stood it on an extreme corner of the chimney piece, from which it ever afterwards fell off at intervals.

"Do you take tea, or coffee, Mr. Gargery?" asked Herbert, who always presided of a morning.

"Thankee, sir," said Joe, stiff from head to foot, "I'll take whichever is most agreeable to yourself."

"What do you say to coffee?"

"Thankee, sir," returned Joe, evidently dispirited by the proposal, "since you *are* so kind as make chice of coffee, I will not run contrairy to your own opinions. But don't you never find it a little 'eating?"

"Say tea, then," said Herbert, pouring it out.

Here Joe's hat tumbled off the mantle-piece, and he started out of his chair and picked it up, and fitted it to the same exact spot.

"When did you come to town, Mr. Gargery?"

"Were it yesterday afternoon?" said Joe. "No, it were not. Yes, it were. Yes. It were yesterday afternoon."

19 "Have you seen anything of London yet?"

"Why, yes, sir," said Joe, "me and Wopsle went off straight to look at the Blacking Ware'us. But we didn't find that it come up to its likeness in the red bills at the shop doors."

Then he fell into such unaccountable fits of meditation, with his fork midway between his plate and his mouth; had his eyes attracted in such strange directions; was afflicted with such remarkable coughs; sat so far from the table, and dropped so much more than he ate, and pretended that he hadn't dropped it; that I was heartily glad when Herbert left us for the City.

20 I had neither the good sense nor the good feeling to know that this was all my fault, and that if I had been easier with Joe, Joe would have been easier with me. I felt impatient of him and out of temper with him.

"Us two being now alone, sir"—began Joe.

"Joe," I interrupted, pettishly, "how can you call me sir?"

Joe looked at me for a single instant with something faintly like reproach. Utterly preposterous as his cravat was, and as his collars were, I was conscious of a sort of dignity in the look.

"Us two being now alone," resumed Joe, "and me having the intentions and abilities to stay not many minutes more, I will now conclude—leastways begin—to mention what have led to my having had the present honor.

"Well, sir," pursued Joe, "this is how it were. I were at the Bargemen t'other night, Pip"—whenever he subsided into affection, he called me Pip, and whenever he relapsed into politeness he called me sir—"when there come up in his shay cart Pumblechook. Which that same identical come to me at the Bargemen, and his word were, 'Joseph, Miss Havisham she wish to speak to you.' "

"Miss Havisham, Joe?"

" 'She wished,' were Pumblechook's word, 'to speak to you.' " Joe sat and rolled his eyes at the ceiling.

"Yes, Joe? Go on, please."

"Next day, sir," said Joe, "having cleaned myself, I go and I see Miss A."

"Miss A., Joe? Miss Havisham?"

"Which I say, sir," replied Joe, "Miss A., or otherways Havisham. Her expression air then as follering: 'Mr. Gargery. You air in correspondence with Mr. Pip?' Having had a letter from you, I were able to say 'I am.' 'Would you tell him, then,' said she, 'that which Estella has come home, and would be glad to see him.' "

19 **Enrichment** Joe reports that he and Mr. Wopsle have gone walking in London and visited the Blacking Ware'us. This could be a reference to the factory where Dickens worked as a child. Dickens was ashamed of having worked in such a factory. Years afterward Dickens avoided the smells and sights of blacking corks because they reminded him of this experience.

20 **Discussion** Why does Pip reproach himself for Joe's obvious discomfort during his visit?

21 **Discussion** Joe's sound judgments on human relationships are disclosed in this passage. How does he explain to Pip that he will not prolong his visit or try to visit Pip again?

22 **Discussion** Pip, too, understands what Joe is saying, but cannot bring himself to act to make theirs a more satisfactory parting. Why?

23 **Critical Thinking and Reading** When Pip returns to the village in response to Miss Havisham's request, what reasons does he give for not staying with Joe at the forge on the visit? Basing your answer on what you know about Pip, why do you think he does not want to stay at the forge?

I felt my face fire up as I looked at Joe. I hope one remote cause of its firing, may have been my consciousness that if I had known his errand, I should have given him more encouragement.

"Biddy," pursued Joe, "when I got home and asked her fur to write the message to you, a little hung back. Biddy says, 'I know he will be very glad to have it by word of mouth, it is holiday time, you want to see him, go!' I have now concluded, sir," said Joe, rising from his chair, "and, Pip, I wish you ever well and ever prospering to a greater and greater height."

"But you are not going now, Joe?"

"Yes, I am," said Joe.

"But you are coming back to dinner, Joe?"

"No, I am not," said Joe.

Our eyes met, and all the "sir" melted out of that manly heart as he gave me his hand.

"Pip, dear old chap, life is made of ever so many partings welded together, as I may say, and one man's a blacksmith, and one's a whitesmith,[3] and one's a goldsmith, and one's a coppersmith. Diwisions among such must come, and must be met as they come. If there's been any fault at all today, it's mine. You and me is not two figures to be together in London; nor yet anywheres else but what is private, and beknown, and understood among friends. It ain't that I am proud, but that I want to be right, as you shall never see me no more in these clothes. I'm wrong in these clothes. I'm wrong out of the forge, the kitchen, or off th' meshes. You won't find half so much fault in me if you think of me in my forge dress, with my hammer in my hand, or even my pipe. You won't find half so much fault in me if, supposing as you should ever wish to see me, you come and put your head in at the forge window

---
**3. whitesmith** (hwīt′ smith′) *n.*: Tinsmith.

and see Joe the blacksmith there at the old anwil, in the old burnt apron, sticking to the old work. I'm awful dull, but I hope I've beat out something nigh the rights of this at last. And so GOD bless you, dear old Pip, old chap, GOD bless you!"

I had not been mistaken in my fancy that there was a simple dignity in him. The fashion of his dress could no more come in its way when he spoke these words than it could come in its way in Heaven. He touched me gently on the forehead, and went out. As soon as I could recover myself sufficiently, I hurried out after him and looked for him in the neighboring streets, but he was gone.

## Chapter 28

It was clear that I must repair to our town next day, and in the first flow of my repentance it was equally clear that I must stay at Joe's. But when I had secured my box place by tomorrow's coach, and had been down to Mr. Pocket's and back, I was not by any means convinced on the last point, and began to invent reasons and make excuses for putting up at the Blue Boar. I should be an inconvenience at Joe's; I was not expected, and my bed would not be ready; I should be too far from Miss Havisham's, and she was exacting and mightn't like it. All other swindlers upon earth are nothing to the self-swindlers, and with such pretenses did I cheat myself. I settled that I must go to the Blue Boar.

At that time it was customary to carry convicts down to the dockyards by stagecoach. As I had often heard of them in the capacity of outside passengers, and had more than once seen them on the high road dangling their ironed legs over the coach roof, I had no cause to be surprised when

Herbert, meeting me in the yard, came up and told me there were two convicts going down with me. But I had a reason that was an old reason now for constitutionally faltering whenever I heard the word convict.

"You don't mind them, Handel?" said Herbert.

"Oh, no!"

"I thought you seemed as if you didn't like them."

"I can't pretend that I do like them, and I suppose you don't particularly. But I don't mind them."

"See! There they are," said Herbert, "coming out of the tap. What a degraded and vile sight it is!"

The two convicts were handcuffed together, and had irons on their legs—irons of a pattern that I knew well. They wore the dress that I likewise knew well. One was a taller and stouter man than the other, and appeared to have had allotted to him the smaller suit of clothes. His attire disguised him absurdly; but I knew his half-closed eye at one glance. There stood the man whom I had seen on the settle at the Three Jolly Bargemen on a Saturday night.

But this was not the worst of it. It came out that the whole of the back of the coach had been taken by a family removing from London, and that there were no places for the two prisoners but on the seat in front, behind the coachman. The convict I had recognized sat behind me with his breath on the hair of my head.

24 "Good-bye, Handel!" Herbert called out as we started. I thought what a blessed fortune it was that he had found another name for me than Pip.

The weather was miserably raw, and the two cursed the cold. It made us all lethargic before we had gone far, and when we had left the Half-way House behind, we habitually dozed and shivered and were silent. I dozed off, myself, in considering the question whether I ought to restore a couple of pounds sterling to this creature before losing sight of him, and how it could best be done. In the act of dipping forward, as if I were going to bathe among the horses, I woke in a fright and took the question up again.

Cowering forward for warmth and to make me a screen against the wind, the convicts were closer to me than before. The very first words I heard them interchange as I became conscious were the words of my own thought, "Two one-pound notes."

"How did he get 'em?" said the convict I had never seen.

"How should I know?" returned the other. "He had 'em stowed away somehows. Giv him by friends, I expect."

"I wish," said the other, "that I had 'em here."

"Two one-pound notes, or friends?"

"Two one-pound notes. I'd sell all the friends I ever had, for one, and think it a blessed good bargain. Well? So he says—?"

"So he says," resumed the convict I had recognized, "—it was all said and done in half a minute, behind a pile of timber in the dockyard—'You're a-going to be discharged!' Yes, I was. Would I find out that boy that had fed him and kep' his secret, and give him them two one-pound notes? Yes I would. And I did."

"More fool you," growled the other. "I'd have spent 'em on a man, in wittles and drink. He must have been a green one. Mean to say he knowed nothing of you?"

"Not a ha'porth.[1] Different gangs and different ships. He was tried again for prison breaking, and got made a lifer.[2]"

25

---

1. **Not a ha'porth:** Not a half-penny's worth.
2. **got made a lifer:** Was given a life sentence in prison.

24 **Discussion** What reason does Pip have for being grateful to Herbert for calling him by another name?

25 **Discussion** Pip is astonished at the news the convict he knows is revealing to the other convict. What is this news and how does it solve a mystery?

## Humanities Note

Fine art, *Omnibus Life in London,* 1859, William Maw Egley. William Maw Egley (1826–1916) was a British painter of genre and historical scenes. A genre scene shows common or everyday activities. William Egley is especially remembered for anecdotal scenes of London life, which show his fine touch and sense of humor.

The influence of the Pre-Raphaelites is apparent in the detail, realism and intense color of the painting *Omnibus Life in London.*

You might want to use the following questions:

1. What impression of this mode of travel does the picture convey?
2. Compare and contrast this omnibus with a modern bus or train.

**OMNIBUS LIFE IN LONDON, 1859**
*William Maw Egley*
The Tate Gallery, London

846   *The Novel*

"And was that—Honor!—the only time you worked out, in this part of the country?"

"The only time."

"What might have been your opinion of the place?"

"A most beastly place. Mudbank, mist, swamp, and work: work, swamp, mist, and mudbank."

They both execrated the place in very strong language, and gradually growled themselves out, and had nothing left to say.

After overhearing this dialogue, I resolved to alight as soon as we touched the town. This device I executed successfully. As to the convicts, they went their way with the coach, and I knew at what point they would be spirited off to the river. In my fancy, I saw the boat with its convict crew waiting for them at the slime-washed stairs; again heard the gruff "Give way, you!" like an order to dogs; again saw the wicked Noah's Ark lying out on the black water.

**Chapter 29**

Betimes in the morning I was up and out. It was too early yet to go to Miss Havisham's, so I loitered into the country on Miss Havisham's side of town—which was not Joe's side; I could go there tomorrow—thinking about my patroness, and painting brilliant pictures of her plans for me.

26 | I so shaped out my walk as to arrive at the gate at my old time. When I had rung at the bell with an unsteady hand, I turned my back upon the gate. I heard the side door open, and steps come across the courtyard; but I pretended not to hear, even when the gate swung on its rusty hinges.

Being at last touched on the shoulder, I started and turned. I started much more naturally, then, to find myself confronted by a man in a sober gray dress. The last man I should have expected to see in that place of porter at Miss Havisham's door.

"Orlick!"

"Ah, young master, there's more changes than yours. But come in, come in. It's opposed to my orders to hold the gate open."

I entered, and he swung it, and locked it, and took the key out. "Yes!" said he, facing round, after doggedly preceding me a few steps towards the house. "Here I am!"

"How did you come here?"

"I come here," he retorted, "on my legs."

"Are you here for good?"

"I ain't here for harm, young master, I suppose."

"Then you have left the forge?" I said.

"Do this look like a forge?" replied Orlick.

By this time we had come to the house, where I found his room to be one just within the side door, with a little window in it looking on the courtyard.

"I never saw this room before," I remarked; "but there used to be no porter here."

"No," said he, "not till it got about that there was no protection on the premises, and it come to be considered dangerous, with convicts and tag and rag and bobtail going up and down. And then I was recommended to the place as a man who could give another man as good as he brought, and I took it. It's easier than bellowsing and hammering. That's loaded, that is."

My eye had been caught by a gun with a brass-bound stock over the chimney piece, and his eye had followed mine.

"Well," said I, not desirous of more conversation, "shall I go up to Miss Havisham?"

"Burn me, if I know!" he retorted, first stretching himself and then shaking himself; "my orders ends here, young master. I give this here bell a rap with this here ham-

26 **Discussion** Why does Pip turn his back and pretend not to hear the footsteps approach the gate?

**27 Clarification** The colors *green* and *yellow* are used symbolically here to describe Sarah Pocket's feelings. Green and yellow together stand for *jealousy* or *envy*, and also *bitterness* or *spite*.

**28 Discussion** What surprise awaits Pip when he is ushered into Miss Havisham's room?

**29 Discussion** Although greatly attracted by Estella's beauty, Pip begins to feel awkward with her. Why?

**30 Discussion** What changes do both Pip and Estella see in each other?

mer, and you go on along the passage till you meet somebody."

Upon that I turned down the long passage which I had first trodden in my thick boots, and he made his bell sound. At the end of the passage, I found Sarah Pocket, who appeared to have now become constitutionally green and yellow by reason of me.

"Oh!" said she. "You, is it, Mr. Pip?"

"It is, Miss Pocket. I am glad to tell you that Mr. Pocket and family are all well."

"Are they any wiser?" said Sarah, with a dismal shake of the head; "they had better be wiser than well. Ah, Matthew, Matthew! You know your way, sir?"

Tolerably, for I had gone up the staircase in the dark, many a time. I ascended it now, in lighter boots than of yore, and tapped in my old way at the door of Miss Havisham's room. "Pip's rap," I heard her say immediately; "come in, Pip."

She was in her chair near the old table, in the old dress, with her two hands crossed on her stick, her chin resting on them, and her eyes on the fire. Sitting near her, with the white shoe that had never been worn in her hand, and her head bent as she looked at it, was an elegant lady whom I had never seen.

"Come in, Pip," Miss Havisham continued to mutter, without looking round or up; "come in, Pip; how do you do, Pip?"

"I heard, Miss Havisham," said I, "that you were so kind as to wish me to come and see you, and I came directly."

The lady whom I had never seen before lifted up her eyes and looked archly at me, and then I saw that the eyes were Estella's eyes. But she was so much changed, was so much more beautiful, so much more womanly, in all things winning admiration had made such wonderful advance, that I seemed to have made none. I fancied, as I looked at her, that I slipped hopelessly back into the coarse and common boy again. Oh, the sense of distance and disparity that came upon me, and the inaccessibility that came about her!

"Do you find her much changed, Pip?" asked Miss Havisham.

"When I came in, Miss Havisham, I thought there was nothing of Estella in the face or figure; but now it all settles down so curiously into the old—"

"What? You are not going to say into the old Estella?" Miss Havisham interrupted. "She was proud and insulting, and you wanted to go away from her. Don't you remember?"

I said confusedly that that was long ago, and that I knew no better then, and the like. Estella smiled with perfect composure, and said she had no doubt of my having been quite right, and of her having been very disagreeable.

"Is *he* changed?" Miss Havisham asked her.

"Very much," said Estella, looking at me.

"Less coarse and common?" said Miss Havisham, playing with Estella's hair.

Estella laughed, and looked at the shoe in her hand, and laughed again, and looked at me, and put the shoe down. She treated me as a boy still, but she lured me on.

We sat in the dreamy room among the old strange influences which had so wrought upon me, and I learned that she had but just come home from France, and that she was going to London.

It was settled that I should stay there all the rest of the day, and return to the hotel at night, and to London tomorrow. When we had conversed for a while, Miss Havisham sent us two out to walk in the neglected garden.

The garden was too overgrown and rank for walking in with ease, and after we had made the round of it twice or thrice, we

## Grammar in Action

**Parallelism** is the arrangement of equal ideas in equivalent grammatical structures. A writer's careful use of parallelism adds balance, emphasis, and clarity to sentences and paragraphs. Look at this example of parallelism from *Great Expectations.*

Estella smiled with perfect composure, and said she had no doubt *of my having been quite right,* and *of her having been very disagreeable.* [parallel prepositional phrases with gerunds as objects]

Parallelism may also extend through more than one sentence:

I have not bestowed my tenderness anywhere. I have never had any such thing. [parallel sentences made up of subject-verb-direct object, beginning with *I have*]

Parallel structure adds a dignity and a pleasant rhythm to many passages but it may also help clarify long and involved sentences:

I verily believe that her *not remembering* and *not minding* in the least, made me cry again inwardly—and that is the sharpest crying of all.

came out again into the brewery yard. I showed her to a nicety where I had seen her walking on the casks that first old day, and she said with a cold and careless look in that direction, "Did I?" I reminded her where she had come out of the house and given me my meat and drink, and she said, "I don't remember." "Not remember that you made me cry?" said I. "No," said she, and shook her head and looked about her. I verily believe that her not remembering and not minding in the least, made me cry again, inwardly—and that is the sharpest crying of all.

"You must know," said Estella, condescending to me as a brilliant and beautiful woman might, "that I have no heart—if that has anything to do with my memory."

I got through some jargon to the effect that I took the liberty of doubting that. That I knew better. That there could be no such beauty without it.

"I am serious," said Estella, not so much with a frown (for her brow was smooth) as with a darkening of her face; "if we are to be thrown much together, you had better believe it at once. No!" imperiously stopping me as I opened my lips. "I have not bestowed my tenderness anywhere. I have never had any such thing."

We went back into the house, and there I heard, with surprise, that my guardian had come down to see Miss Havisham on business, and would come back to dinner. The old wintry branches of chandeliers in the room where the moldering table was spread had been lighted while we were out, and Miss Havisham was in her chair and waiting for me.

It was like pushing the chair itself back into the past, when we began the old slow circuit round about the ashes of the bridal feast. The time so melted away that our early dinner-hour drew close at hand, and Estella left us to prepare herself.

Then, Estella being gone and we two left alone, she turned to me and said in a whisper:

"Is she beautiful, graceful, well-grown? Do you admire her?"

"Everybody must who sees her, Miss Havisham."

She drew an arm round my neck, and drew my head close down to hers as she sat in the chair. "Love her, love her, love her! How does she use you?"

Before I could answer (if I could have answered so difficult a question at all), she repeated, "Love her, love her, love her! If she favors you, love her. If she wounds you, love her. If she tears your heart to pieces—and as it gets older and stronger it will tear deeper—love her, love her, love her!"

"I'll tell you," said she, in the same hurried passionate whisper, "what real love is. It is blind devotion, unquestioning self-humiliation, utter submission, trust and belief against yourself and against the whole world, giving up your whole heart and soul to the smiter[1]—as I did!"

When she came to that, and to a wild cry that followed that, I caught her round the waist. For she rose up in the chair, in her shroud of a dress, and struck at the air as if she would as soon have struck herself against the wall and fallen dead.

All this passed in a few seconds. As I drew her down into her chair, I was conscious of a scent that I knew, and turning, saw my guardian in the room.

Miss Havisham had seen him as soon as I, and was (like everybody else) afraid of him. She made a strong attempt to compose herself, and stammered that he was as punctual as ever.

"As punctual as ever," he repeated, coming up to us. "And so you are here, Pip?"

_____
**1. smiter** (smīt′ ər) *n.*: One who hurts you.

31 **Reading Strategy** Summarize the interaction between Estella and Pip.

32 **Discussion** What reply of Estella's makes Pip want to cry all over again, as he did when a child?

33 **Discussion** Miss Havisham is virtually unchanged since the beginning of the novel. How does her conversation with Pip indicate this and how is her attitude toward her adopted daughter, Estella, unchanged?

34 **Discussion** What is Miss Havisham's definition of love? How does it reflect her own experiences?

We sat in the dreamy room among the old strange influences which had so wrought upon me, and I learned *that she had but just come home from France* and *that she was going to London.*

**Student Activity 1.** Find five other examples of parallelism in the novel, and copy these. Share them with the class, explaining why they are parallel.

**Student Activity 2.** Use the passages you copied as models for writing five passage of your own, each passage containing an example of parallelism. Exchange papers with a partner and discuss improvements.

**35 Literary Focus** How would you describe the atmosphere at Miss Havisham's dinner table?

I told him when I had arrived, and how Miss Havisham wished me to come and see Estella. To which he replied, "Ah! Very fine young lady!"

"Well, Pip! How often have you seen Miss Estella before?" said he.

"How often?"

"Ah! How many times? Ten thousand times?"

"Oh! Certainly not so many."

"Twice?"

"Jaggers," interposed Miss Havisham, much to my relief, "leave my Pip alone, and go with him to your dinner."

He complied, and we groped our way down the dark stairs together.

"Pray, sir," said I, "may I ask you a question?"

"You may," said he, "and I may decline to answer it. Put your question."

"Estella's name, is it Havisham or—?" I had nothing to add.

"Or what?" said he.

"Is it Havisham?"

"It is Havisham."

This brought us to the dinner table, where she and Sarah Pocket awaited us. Mr. Jaggers presided, Estella sat opposite to him, I faced my green and yellow friend. We dined very well, and were waited on by a maidservant whom I had never seen in all my comings and goings, but who, ·for anything I know, had been in that mysterious house the whole time.

Anything to equal the determined reticence of Mr. Jaggers under that roof I never saw elsewhere, even in him. He kept his very looks to himself, and scarcely directed his eyes to Estella's face once during dinner. When she spoke to him, he listened, and in due course, answered, but never looked at her that I could see. On the other hand, she often looked at him with interest and curiosity, if not distrust, but his face never showed the least consciousness. Throughout dinner, he took a dry delight in making Sarah Pocket greener and yellower by often referring in conversation with me to my expectations.

I think Miss Pocket was conscious that the sight of me involved her in the danger of being goaded to madness. She did not appear when we afterwards went up to Miss Havisham's room, and we four played at whist.[2] We played until nine o'clock, and then it was arranged that when Estella came to London I should be forewarned of her coming and should meet her at the coach; and then I took leave of her, and touched her, and left her.

My guardian lay at the Boar in the next room to mine. Far into the night, Miss Havisham's words, "Love her, love her, love her!" sounded in my ears. I adapted them for my own repetition, and said to my pillow, "I love her, I love her, I love her!" hundreds of times.

Ah me! I thought those were high and great emotions. But I never thought there was anything low and small in my keeping away from Joe, because I knew she would be contemptuous of him. It was but a day gone, and Joe had brought the tears into my eyes; they had soon dried—God forgive me!—soon dried.

**Chapter 30**

After well considering the matter while I was dressing at the Blue Boar in the morning, I resolved to tell my guardian that I doubted Orlick's being the right sort of man to fill a post of trust at Miss Havisham's. "Why, of course he is not the right sort of man, Pip," said my guardian, comfortably

---

2. **whist** (hwist) *n.:* A card game like bridge.

**THE WHITE GIRL
(SYMPHONY IN WHITE NO. 1)**
*James McNeill Whistler*
*National Gallery of Art, Washington, D.C.*

## Humanities Note

Fine art, *The White Girl: Symphony in White, No. 1,* by James McNeill Whistler. The American artist James McNeill Whistler (1834-1903) lived and worked in London. His eccentric and controversial style resulted from the influence of French painters in Paris, Japanese prints, and his own radical views of painting.

*The White Girl: Symphony in White, No. 1* is a portrait of Joanna Heffernan, a friend of Whistler's. Shown at a French exhibition in 1863, it was derided by the public and highly praised by critics. The sensation it created established Whistler as the first American painter to gain recognition in Europe.

Point out to students how the dark hair falling on the right shoulder frames and contrasts with the face, heightening its beauty. Then ask students the following questions:

1. What is the personality of this young woman?
2. Compare and contrast her with Estella.

**36 Discussion** Why does Pip choose to walk along the London road and let the coach catch up with him instead of going to the station with Mr. Jaggers?

**37 Discussion** When Pip confesses his love for Estella to Herbert, how does Herbert prove to be a true friend?

satisfied beforehand on the general head, "because the man who fills the post of trust never is the right sort of man." It seemed quite to put him in spirits to find that this particular post was not exceptionally held by the right sort of man, and he listened in a satisfied manner while I told him what knowledge I had of Orlick. "Very good, Pip," he observed, when I had concluded, "I'll go round presently, and pay our friend off." Rather alarmed by this summary action, I was for a little delay, and even hinted that our friend himself might be difficult to deal with. "Oh, no, he won't," said my guardian, with perfect confidence: "I should like to see him argue the question with *me*."

**36** As we were going back together to London by the midday coach, and as I breakfasted under such terrors of Pumblechook that I could scarcely hold my cup, this gave me an opportunity of saying that I wanted a walk, and that I would go on along the London road while Mr. Jaggers was occupied, if he would let the coachman know that I would get into my place when overtaken.

The coach, with Mr. Jaggers inside, came up in due time, and I took my box seat again, and arrived in London safe—but not sound, for my heart was gone. As soon as I arrived, I sent a penitential codfish and barrel of oysters to Joe (as reparation for not having gone myself), and then went on to Barnard's Inn.

I found Herbert delighted to welcome me back, and I felt that I must open my breast that very evening to my friend and chum.

Dinner done and we sitting with our feet upon the fender, I said to Herbert, "My dear Herbert, I have something very particular to tell you."

"My dear Handel," he returned, "I shall esteem and respect your confidence."

**37** "Herbert," said I, laying my hand upon his knee, "I love—I adore—Estella."

Instead of being transfixed, Herbert replied in an easy matter-of-course way, "Exactly. Well?"

"Well, Herbert. Is that all you say? Well?"

"What next, I mean?" said Herbert. "Of course I know *that*."

"How do you know it?" said I.

"How do I know it, Handel? Why, from you."

"I never told you."

"Told me! You have never told me when you have got your hair cut, but I have had senses to perceive it. You have always adored her, ever since I have known you. Have you any idea yet of Estella's views on the adoration question?"

I shook my head gloomily. "Oh! She is thousands of miles away from me," said I.

"Patience, my dear Handel—time enough, time enough. But you have something more to say?"

"I am ashamed to say it," I returned, "and yet it's no worse to say it than to think it. You call me a lucky fellow. Of course I am. I was a blacksmith's boy but yesterday; I am—what shall I say I am today?"

"Say, a good fellow, if you want a phrase," returned Herbert, smiling, and clapping his hand on the back of mine: "a good fellow, with impetuosity and hesitation, boldness and diffidence, action and dreaming curiously mixed in him."

"When I ask what I am to call myself today, Herbert," I went on, "I suggest what I have in my thoughts. You say I am lucky. I know I have done nothing to raise myself in life, and that fortune alone has raised me; that is being very lucky. And yet, when I think of Estella—

"—Then, my dear Herbert, I cannot tell you how dependent and uncertain I feel, and how exposed to hundreds of chances. Avoiding forbidden ground, as you did just now, I may still say that on the constancy of one person (naming no person) all my expectations depend. And at the best, how indefinite and unsatisfactory only to know so vaguely what they are!"

"Now, Handel," Herbert replied, in his gay hopeful way, "it seems to me that in the despondency of the tender passion, we are looking into our gift horse's mouth with a magnifying glass. Didn't you tell me that your guardian, Mr. Jaggers, told you in the beginning that you were not endowed with expectations only? And even if he had not told you so—though that is a very large if, I grant—could you believe that of all men in London, Mr. Jaggers is the man to hold his present relations towards you unless he was sure of his ground?"

I said I could not deny that this was a strong point.

"I should think it *was* a strong point," said Herbert. "You'll be one-and-twenty before you know where you are, and then perhaps you'll get some further enlightenment. At all events, you'll be nearer getting it, for it must come at last."

"What a hopeful disposition you have!" said I.

"I ought to have," said Herbert, "for I have not much else. And now, I want to make myself seriously disagreeable to you for a moment—positively repulsive."

"You won't succeed," said I.

"Oh, yes, I shall!" said he. "Handel, my good fellow, I have been thinking since we have been talking with our feet on this fender that Estella cannot surely be a condition of your inheritance, if she was never referred to by your guardian. Am I right in so understanding what you have told me, as that he never referred to her, directly or indirectly, in any way? Never even hinted, for instance, that your patron might have views as to your marriage ultimately?"

"Never."

"Now, Handel, I am quite free from the flavor of sour grapes, upon my soul and honor! Not being bound to her, can you not detach yourself from her? I told you I should be disagreeable."

I turned my head aside and there was silence between us for a little while.

"Yes; but my dear Handel," Herbert went on, as if we had been talking instead of silent, "think of her bringing-up, and think of Miss Havisham. Think of what she is herself. This may lead to miserable things."

"I know it, Herbert," said I, with my head still turned away, "but I can't help it."

"Well!" said Herbert, getting up with a lively shake as if he had been asleep, and stirring the fire; "now I'll endeavor to make myself agreeable again! I was going to say a word or two, Handel, concerning my father and my father's son. May I ask you if you have ever had an opportunity of remarking, down in your part of the country, that the children of not exactly suitable marriages are always most particularly anxious to be married?"

This was such a singular question that I asked him, in return, "Is it so?"

"I don't know," said Herbert; "that's what I want to know. Because it is decidedly the case with us. I think we are all engaged, except the baby."

"Then you are?" said I.

"I am," said Herbert; "but it's a secret."

I assured him of my keeping the secret, and begged to be favored with further particulars. He had spoken so sensibly and feelingly of my weakness that I wanted to know something about his strength.

"May I ask the name?" I said.

"Name of Clara," said Herbert.

"Live in London?"

"Yes. Perhaps I ought to mention," said Herbert, "that she is rather below my mother's nonsensical family notions. Her fa-

**38 Discussion** Why is Pip in a state of uncertainty as this chapter ends?

**39 Reading Strategy** Ask students to predict whether Pip will continue to be frustrated by Estella.

**Reader's Response** If you were Pip, how would you feel when you found out that a convict had given you the two one-pound notes? Why?

ther had to do with the victualling[1] of passenger-ships. I think he was a species of purser."

"What is he now?" said I.

"He's an invalid now," replied Herbert.

"Living on—?"

"On the first floor," said Herbert. Which was not at all what I meant, for I had intended my question to apply to his means. "I have never seen him, for he has always kept his room overhead, since I have known Clara. But I have heard him constantly. He makes tremendous rows—roars, and pegs at the floor with some frightful instrument."

"Don't you expect to see him?" said I.

"Oh, yes, I constantly expect to see him," returned Herbert, "because I never hear him without expecting him to come tumbling through the ceiling. But I don't know how long the rafters may hold."

When he had once more laughed heartily, he became meek again, and told me that the moment he began to realize capital,[2] it was his intention to marry this young lady. He added as a self-evident proposition, engendering low spirits, "But you *can't* marry, you know, while you're looking about you."

---

**1. victualling** (vit' 'l iŋ) *v*.: Supplying victuals, or food.
**2. realize capital:** Make money.

**Chapter 31**

One day when I was busy with my books and Mr. Pocket, I received a note by the post. It had no set beginning, as Dear Mr. Pip, or Dear Pip, or Dear Sir, or Dear Anything, but ran thus:

> I am to come to London the day after tomorrow by the midday coach. I believe it was settled you should meet me? At all events Miss Havisham has that impression, and I write in obedience to it. She sends you her regard.
>
> Yours,
> ESTELLA.

My appetite vanished instantly, and I knew no peace or rest until the day arrived. Not that its arrival brought me either, for then I was worse than ever, and began haunting the coach office in Wood Street, Cheapside, before the coach had left the Blue Boar in our town. For all that I knew this perfectly well, I still felt as if it were not safe to let the coach office be out of my sight longer than five minutes at a time. **38**

The coach came quickly after all, and I saw her face at the coach window and her hand waving to me. **39**

## Closure and Extension

### ANSWERS TO THINKING ABOUT THE SELECTION
#### Recalling

1. Her wrist is scarred and powerful. Wemmick says she is an example of Jaggers's powers.
2. Pip feels shame, thinking Joe will seem a comic figure in London's polite society, and dreads that people will scorn Joe. Joe is stiff and awkward, and Pip is impatient and upset at his manner. Later he realizes it was his own fault for not being easy with Joe.
3. Pip learns that the convict whom he had helped in the cemetery was the one who had sent him the two one-pound bank notes.
4. Whenever Pip and Estella are together and Estella turns cool toward him, he is unhappy. When he leaves her at Richmond, realizing she will attract many admirers, he is jealous and wretched. He also realizes that he has never been happy in their relationship.
5. He learns that Herbert is engaged to a young woman and plans to marry her as soon as he makes some money.

#### Interpreting

6. Suggested Response: Mr. Wemmick lives in a tiny wooden cottage which he has built to look like a miniature castle. He lives comfortably with his aged father, who is

## THINKING ABOUT THE SELECTION

### Recalling

1. What is remarkable about Mr. Jaggers's housekeeper ?
2. Describe the mixed feelings that Joe's visit calls up in Pip.
3. What does Pip learn from the two convicts he overhears on the stagecoach?
4. Explain how Pip's relationship with Estella continues to disappoint him.
5. What does Pip learn about Herbert's plans?

### Interpreting

6. Compare and contrast Wemmick's home life with that of Jaggers.
7. How do Pip's mixed feelings about Joe's visit reveal an inner conflict?
8. Why does Estella say she has "no heart"? Do you agree with her judgment of herself? Find evidence that supports your answer.

### Applying

9. Miss Havisham says that "real love is . . . blind devotion, unquestioning self-humiliation. . . ." Comment on this remark.

## ANALYZING LITERATURE

### Understanding Setting and Atmosphere

**Setting** refers to the time and place in which the events of a work of fiction occur. **Atmosphere** is the mood that a setting calls up. In *Great Expectations,* the story unfolds in a number of places and over a period of years. Each of these places has its own atmosphere. Satis House, for instance, is haunted and decaying, while Mr. Jaggers's office is cold and businesslike.

What atmosphere is suggested by each of the following settings?

a. the marshes     c. Pip's rooms
b. Wemmick's house     d. London

## CRITICAL THINKING AND READING

### Identifying Details that Create Setting

Even in a long novel, writers do not have the space to describe every aspect of a setting. They must therefore sketch in a few details and leave the rest to your imagination. By observing which details they choose to describe, you can learn how they create an atmosphere or reveal character. If a writer stresses the pleasant colors in an apartment, for instance, he or she may be trying to create a joyful mood. These colors may also reveal that the person who lives there is happy. Dickens makes a definite association between certain characters and the settings in which they are found.

What do the following settings reveal about the characters associated with them?
1. Satis House—Miss Havisham
2. Jaggers's office—Jaggers
3. Wemmick's house—Wemmick

## THINKING AND WRITING

### Comparing and Contrasting Settings

**Comparing** settings means showing how they are similar, while **contrasting** them means indicating how they are different. Compare and contrast Satis House with Wemmick's home. List the details that Dickens uses to describe each. Briefly note the atmosphere of each house and the way it reveals its owner's personality. Using your notes, write a comparison and contrast of these two settings, with an introduction and a conclusion. In your introduction, tell whether the houses are mostly similar or different. Support your view in the body of your paper. When you revise, make sure you have discussed both houses for each point of comparison or contrast.

b. Wemmick's house suggests a whimsical, warm, peaceful, and orderly atmosphere.
c. Pip's rooms seem to be a comfortable, pleasant apartment for two bachelors.
d. London is dense with people. Its atmosphere is lively and exciting, though much of it is also dingy and poor.

## ANSWERS TO CRITICAL THINKING AND READING

1. Suggested Response: The Satis House setting reveals Miss Havisham's own state of decay and withdrawal.
2. Suggested Response: Jaggers's office setting reveals his single-minded devotion to business and his coldness.
3. Suggested Response: Wemmick's house reveals the pleasant and whimsical nature he hides beneath his business exterior. It also reveals his devotion to his father.

## THINKING AND WRITING

For help with this assignment, students may want to consult Lesson 7, "Writing About Setting," in the Handbook of Writing About Literature.

## Publishing Student Writing

You might want to display these essays, along with illustrations of the various settings.

## Writing Across the Curriculum

You might want to have students research and report on stage-coach travel in nineteenth-century England. Consider informing the social studies department of this assignment, so that teachers can provide guidance for students.

cared for by a young girl. Mr. Wemmick caters to his father's needs. There is a warm, cheerful atmosphere in the house. By contrast, Mr. Jaggers's home is rather dignified and much larger than Mr. Wemmick's but is badly in need of paint, has dirty windows, a bare and cold stone hallway, and a dark-brown staircase; all these features produce a gloomy atmosphere. He is cared for by an efficient housekeeper, Molly, whom he bullies.
7. Suggested Response: Pip is both

devoted to Joe and ashamed of him. These divided feelings reflect his inner conflict regarding the worth of advancement and status versus that of love.
8. Suggested Response: Estella says she has "no heart" because she never bestows affection on anyone. Estella made Pip cry on his first visit to Satis House. When she is asked if she remembers making Pip cry on that visit, she replies in such a casual way that Pip feels hurt.

### Applying

9. Answers will differ. Most students will respond that Miss Havisham's definition of love is unrealistic and distorted, reflecting her own unfortunate experience.

## ANSWERS TO ANALYZING LITERATURE

Suggested Responses:
a. The marshes suggest an atmosphere of melancholy, brooding, and romance.

**Literary Focus** In *Great Expectations,* the central theme concerns Pip's resolution of the conflicts in his life, trapped as he is between Miss Havisham's vindictiveness and Magwitch's gratitude. As always in Dickens, the abstract concepts are personified in larger-than-life figures of good and evil, with good ultimately prevailing.

**Look For** Remind students that it is conflict which creates both interest and suspense in a plot. Have the class discuss the many conflicts that arise for Pip with the appearance of Magwitch at this point in the novel.

**Writing/Prior Knowledge** Put the word *snob* on the board and ask students to list all the characteristics of a person who is a snob. Discuss how the word applies to Pip at this point in the novel. Then have students proceed with the writing assignment.

**Vocabulary** Have more advanced students write original sentences using each of the vocabulary words in this section. Ask them to imitate Dickens's style.

## Great Expectations, Chapters 32–44

**Theme**

A **theme** is the central idea or insight into life revealed in a work of literature. Sometimes writers will state the theme directly, but often you must read between the lines to find it. A good clue to the theme of a novel is its main conflict. Imagine, for example, a novel that describes a woman's attempt to climb a steep and dangerous mountain. If she succeeds against all odds, the theme of the book might be the importance of facing challenges with courage.

Short stories and novels can have equally important themes. The size of a work does not limit its ability to treat matters of universal concern. The theme of a novel, however, may have a greater emotional effect than that of a short story. In reading a novel, you have more time to become involved with the characters and therefore may be more receptive to the insight that their struggles reveal.

**Look For**

Look for the way in which the sudden appearance of Pip's benefactor heightens Pip's inner conflict. Recall other events that added to this conflict and ask yourself what idea about life Dickens wants to illustrate through Pip's inner struggles.

**Writing**

In this section Pip suffers a shock when something unexpected happens to him. Make up a situation in which you have a similar experience. First describe the way you expected events to turn out and the reasons for your expectations. Then recount what actually happened and your reaction to the surprise.

**Vocabulary**

Knowing the following words will help you as you read Chapters 32–44 of *Great Expectations*.

**chronic** (krön′ ik) *adj.*: Constant (p. 859)

**pacific** (pə sif′ ik) *adj.*: Peaceful (p. 866)

**sundry** (sun′ drē) *adj.*: Various; several (p. 868)

**abhorrence** (əb hôr′ ə ns) *n.*: Hatred and disgust (p. 876)

**dubiously** (dōō′ bē əs lē) *adv.*: Uncertainly; doubtfully (p. 880)

**extricate** (eks′ trə kāt) *v.*: Free or disentangle (p. 885)

**feign** (fān) *v.*: Pretend (p. 889)

**haggard** (hag′ ərd) *adj.*: Worn; gaunt (p. 891)

856    The Novel

## Objectives

1 To understand theme when reading a novel
2 To paraphrase key statements when reading a novel
3 To respond to the theme of a novel

## Support Material

**Teaching Portfolio**
Teacher Backup, p. 979
Grammar in Action Worksheets, *Using Subordination,* p. 984; *Appreciating Dialect,* p. 986
Usage and Mechanics Worksheet, p. 988
Vocabulary Check, p. 989
Critical Thinking and Reading Worksheet, *Paraphrasing Key Statements,* p. 991

Language Worksheet, *Completing Analogies,* p. 992
Selection Test, p. 993

## Chapter 32

In her furred traveling-dress, Estella seemed more delicately beautiful than she had ever seemed yet, even in my eyes. Her manner was more winning than she had cared to let it be to me before, and I thought I saw Miss Havisham's influence in the change.

We stood in the inn yard while she pointed out her luggage to me, and when it was all collected I remembered—having forgotten everything but herself in the meanwhile—that I knew nothing of her destination.

"I am going to Richmond," she told me. "The distance is ten miles. I am to have a carriage, and you are to take me. This is my purse, and you are to pay my charges out of it. Oh, you must take the purse! We have no choice, you and I, but to obey our instructions. We are not free to follow our own devices, you and I."

As she looked at me in giving me the purse, I hoped there was an inner meaning in her words. She said them slightingly, but not with displeasure.

"A carriage will have to be sent for, Estella. Will you rest here a little?"

"Yes, I am to rest here a little, and I am to drink some tea, and you are to take care of me the while."

She drew her arm through mine, as if it must be done, and I requested a waiter to show us a private sitting-room. He led us to the black hole of the establishment: fitted up with a diminishing mirror, an anchovy sauce cruet, and somebody's pattens.[1] On my objecting to this retreat, he took us into another room with a dinner table for thirty. Then he took my order—which, proving to

be merely "Some tea for the lady," sent him out of the room in a very low state of mind.

I was sensible that the air of this chamber, in its strong combination of stable with soup stock, might have led one to infer that the coaching department was not doing well, and that the enterprising proprietor was boiling down the horses for the refreshment department. Yet the room was all in all to me, Estella being in it. I thought that with her I could have been happy there for life. (I was not at all happy there at the time, observe, and I knew it well.)

"Where are you going to at Richmond?" I asked Estella.

"I am going to live," said she, "at a great expense, with a lady there, who has the power—or says she has—of taking me about, and introducing me, and showing people to me and showing me to people. How do you thrive with Mr. Pocket?"

"I live quite pleasantly there; at least—" It appeared to me that I was losing a chance.

"At least?" repeated Estella.

"As pleasantly as I could anywhere, away from you."

"You silly boy," said Estella quite composedly, "how can you talk such nonsense? Your friend Mr. Matthew, I believe, is superior to the rest of his family?"

"Very superior indeed."

"He really is disinterested, and above small jealousy and spite, I have heard?"

"I am sure I have every reason to say so."

"You have not every reason to say so of the rest of his people," said Estella, "for they beset Miss Havisham with reports and insinuations to your disadvantage. They watch you, misrepresent you, write letters about you (anonymous sometimes), and you are the torment and occupation of their lives. You can scarcely realize to yourself the hatred those people feel for you."

"They do me no harm, I hope?"

---

1. **an anchovy sauce cruet . . . pattens:** A bottle for anchovy sauce; thick, wooden sandals.

*Great Expectations*   857

---

## Presentation

**Motivation/Prior Knowledge** Explain to students that knowing characters and their traits can help in predicting the outcome of a story. In this segment of *Great Expectations,* Dickens reveals who is responsible for Pip's wealth, who Miss Havisham's fiancé was, and who Estella's prospective husband is. Each of these is a character students have already met. Have students make predictions about these unsolved mysteries and verify their predictions as they read.

**Master Teacher Note** Up to this point, Dickens has woven an intricate web of characters, events, and settings. In these chapters the plot becomes even more interwoven and complex. It may be helpful for students to summarize the major events of the story thus far, noting the main characters and their involvement in the major events.

**Purpose-Setting Question** Describe the changing relationships between Pip and each of the following characters: Estella, Miss Havisham, Joe, and Magwitch.

**1 Reading Strategy** In this chapter, Pip and Estella are alone together as they travel to Richmond. Pip alternates between hope and despair in his desire to have Estella love him. As students read, have them identify Pip's emotional reactions and use this information to predict his future success with Estella.

**2 Discussion** What is Estella's attitude toward Pip as they start off on their journey?

**3 Discussion** Why does Estella refuse to take Pip's statement seriously?

4 **Discussion** What information does Pip learn from Estella that might raise his hopes?

5 **Discussion** What does Estella try to make Pip understand about her when she says, "...will you never take warning"? Why does Pip not understand?

6 **Reading Strategy** Summarize Pip's account of his relationship with Estella.

Instead of answering, Estella burst out laughing.

"I hope I may suppose that you would not be amused if they did me any harm?"

"No, no, you may be sure of that," said Estella. "You may be certain that I laugh because they fail. It is not easy for even you to know what satisfaction it gives me to see those people thwarted. For you were not brought up in that strange house from a mere baby—I was. You had not your little wits sharpened by their intriguing against you, suppressed and defenseless, under the mask of sympathy and pity and what not that is soft and soothing—I had. You did not gradually open your round childish eyes wider and wider to the discovery of that impostor of a woman who calculates her stores of peace of mind for when she wakes up in the night—I did.

"Two things I can tell you. First, these people never will—never would in a hundred years—impair your ground with Miss Havisham, in any particular, great or small. Second, I am beholden to you as the cause of their being so busy and so mean in vain, and there is my hand upon it."

As she gave it me playfully—for her darker mood had been but momentary—I held it and put it to my lips. "You ridiculous boy," said Estella, "will you never take warning? Or do you kiss my hand in the same spirit in which I once let you kiss my cheek?"

"What spirit was that?" said I.

"A spirit of contempt for the fawners and plotters."

"If I say yes, may I kiss the cheek again?"

"You should have asked before you touched the hand. But, yes, if you like."

I leaned down, and her calm face was like a statue's. "Now," said Estella, gliding away the instant I touched her cheek, "you are to take care that I have some tea, and you are to take me to Richmond."

Her reverting to this tone, as if our association were forced upon us and we were mere puppets, gave me pain; but everything in our intercourse did give me pain. Whatever her tone with me happened to be, I could put no trust in it, and build no hope on it; and yet I went on against trust and against hope.

I rang for the tea, and the waiter brought in by degrees some fifty adjuncts to that refreshment, but of tea not a glimpse. Then, after a prolonged absence, he at length came back with a casket of precious appearance containing twigs. These I steeped in hot water, and so from the whole of these appliances extracted one cup of I don't know what for Estella.

The bill paid, and the waiter remembered, we got into our post coach and drove away.

When we passed through Hammersmith, I showed her where Mr. Matthew Pocket lived, and said it was no great way from Richmond, and that I hoped I should see her sometimes.

"Oh, yes, you are to see me; you are to come when you think proper; you are to be mentioned to the family; indeed, you are already mentioned."

I inquired, was it a large household she was going to be a member of?

"No, there are only two; mother and daughter. The mother is a lady of some station, though not averse to increasing her income."

"I wonder Miss Havisham could part with you again so soon."

"It is a part of Miss Havisham's plans for me, Pip," said Estella, with a sigh, as if she were tired; "I am to write to her constantly and see her regularly, and report how I go on—I and the jewels—for they are nearly all mine now."

It was the first time she had ever called me by my name. Of course she did so pur-

**THE SEAT OF MAJOR NORICE, MAIDSTONE**
*George Sidney Shepherd*
*Maidstone Museums and Art Gallery*

posely, and knew that I should treasure it up.

We came to Richmond all too soon, and our destination there was a house by the green—a staid old house, where hoops and powder and patches, embroidered coats, rolled stockings, ruffles, and swords had had their court days many a time. Some ancient trees before the house were still cut into fashions as formal and unnatural as the hoops and wigs and stiff skirts.

Two cherry-colored maids came fluttering out to receive Estella. The doorway soon absorbed her boxes, and she gave me her hand and a smile, and said good night, and was absorbed likewise. And still I stood looking at the house, thinking how happy I should be if I lived there with her, and knowing that I never was happy with her, but always miserable.

## Chapter 33

As I had grown accustomed to my expectations, I had insensibly begun to notice their effect upon myself and those around me. Their influence on my own character I disguised from my recognition as much as possible, but I knew very well that it was not all good. I lived in a state of chronic uneasiness respecting my behavior to Joe. My conscience was not by any means comfortable

*Great Expectations* 859

---

## Humanities Note

Fine art, *The Seat of Major Norice, Maidstone*, by George Sidney Shepherd. George Sidney Shepherd (active 1821–1861) was a British topographical painter. Topographical painting includes views of estates, country homes, churches, antiquities, sporting events, and fairs. Painters such as George Sidney Shepherd were hired by wealthy patrons to paint these subjects.

The picture entitled *The Seat of Major Norice, Maidstone* was commissioned by such a patron. Painted in watercolor, it is a charming example of this successful topographer's work.

You might want to ask students the following questions:
1. What is the social status of the owner of this house?
2. Why do you think the owner wanted this picture painted?
3. Do you think this house resembles the one in Richmond to which Estella travels? Why or why not?

**7 Discussion** Dickens gives a description of the house where Estella will be living. What details convey its setting and atmosphere?

**8 Reading Strategy** In this chapter, Pip reflects on how his "great expectations" have affected the lives of the people close to him, as well as his relationships with them. Have students keep Pip's reflections in mind as they read the chapter.

**9 Discussion** In his unhappy mood, how does Pip's conscience bother him with respect to Joe?

**10 Discussion** What depresses Pip when he thinks about what might have been had he never met Miss Havisham?

**11 Discussion** What is ironic about Herbert's estimate of Pip's business ability?

10

about Biddy. When I woke up in the night, I used to think, with a weariness of my spirits, that I should have been happier and better if I had never seen Miss Havisham's face, and had risen to manhood content to be partners with Joe in the honest old forge. Many a time of an evening, when I sat alone looking at the fire, I thought, after all, there was no fire like the forge fire and the kitchen fire at home.

Now, concerning the influence of my position on others, I perceived that it was not beneficial to anybody, and above all, that it was not beneficial to Herbert. My lavish habits led his easy nature into expenses that he could not afford, corrupted the simplicity of his life, and disturbed his peace with anxieties and regrets.

In my confidence in my own resources, I would willingly have taken Herbert's expenses on myself; but Herbert was proud, and I could make no such proposal to him. So, he got into difficulties in every direction, and continued to look about him. When we gradually fell into keeping late hours and late company, I noticed that he looked about him with a desponding eye at breakfast-time; that he began to look about him more hopefully about midday; that he drooped when he came into dinner; that he seemed to descry¹ capital in the distance, rather clearly, after dinner; that he all but realized capital towards midnight; and that about two o'clock in the morning, he became so deeply despondent again as to talk of buying a rifle and going to America, with a general purpose of compelling buffaloes to make his fortune.

At certain times I would say to Herbert, as if it were a remarkable discovery:

"My dear Herbert, we are getting on badly."

"My dear Handel," Herbert would say to

_____
1. **descry** (di skrī′) v.: Catch sight of.

me, in all sincerity, "if you will believe me, those very words were on my lips, by a strange coincidence."

"Then, Herbert," I would respond, "let us look into our affairs."

We always derived profound satisfaction from making an appointment for this purpose. I always thought this was business, this was the way to confront the thing.

I would then take a sheet of paper, and write across the top of it, in a neat hand, the heading, "Memorandum of Pip's debts," with Barnard's Inn and the date very carefully added. Herbert would also take a sheet of paper, and write across it with similar formalities, "Memorandum of Herbert's debts."

Each of us would then refer to a confused heap of papers at his side. The sound of our pens going refreshed us exceedingly, insomuch that I sometimes found it difficult to distinguish between this edifying business proceeding and actually paying the money.

When we had written a little while, I would ask Herbert how he got on.

"They are mounting up, Handel," Herbert would say, "upon my life, they are mounting up."

"Be firm, Herbert," I would retort. "Look the thing in the face. Look into your affairs. Stare them out of countenance."

"So I would, Handel, only they are staring _me_ out of countenance."

However, my determined manner would have its effect, and Herbert would fall to work again. After a time he would give up once more, on the plea that he had not got Cobbs's bill, or Lobbs's, or Nobbs's, as the case might be.

"Then, Herbert, estimate; estimate it in round numbers, and put it down."

"What a fellow of resource you are!" my friend would reply, with admiration. "Really, your business powers are very remarkable."

11

## Grammar in Action

**Subordination** is the process by which writers connect two unequal but related ideas to form a complex sentence. The main clause of such a sentence should be able to stand by itself, but the subordinate clause—which includes a conjunction like _although_, _because_, or _while_—cannot function as an independent sentence:

_Although we went to bed early,_ we could not fall asleep.

_Because he left school without a degree,_ he had trouble finding a job.
_While I want to help you,_ I won't be able to drive to your house tomorrow.

Writers use subordination to vary the structure and length of their sentences and to clarify the the relationship between ideas. The less important idea is placed in the subordinate clause.

Notice how Dickens uses subordinate clauses in the following sentences from _Great Expectations_:

I thought so, too. I established with myself, on these occasions, the reputation of a first-rate man of business—prompt, decisive, energetic, clear, coolheaded. When I had got all my responsibilities down upon my list, I compared each with the bill, and ticked it off. My self-approval when I ticked an entry was quite a luxurious sensation. When I had no more ticks to make, I folded all my bills up uniformly, docketed[2] each on the back, and tied the whole into a symmetrical bundle. Then I did the same for Herbert, and felt that I had brought his affairs into a focus for him.

There was a calm, a rest, a virtuous hush consequent on these examinations of our affairs that gave me, for the time, an admirable opinion of myself. Soothed by my exertions, my method, and Herbert's compliments, I would sit with his symmetrical bundle and my own on the table before me among the stationery, and feel like a bank of some sort, rather than a private individual.

We shut our outer door on these solemn occasions in order that we might not be interrupted. I had fallen into my serene state one evening, when we heard a letter dropped through the slit in the said door, and fall on the ground. "It's for you, Handel," said Herbert, going out and coming back with it, "and I hope there is nothing the matter." This was in allusion to its heavy black seal and border.

The letter was signed TRABB & CO., and its contents were simply that I was an honored sir, and that they begged to inform me that Mrs. J. Gargery had departed this life on Monday last at twenty minutes past six in the evening, and that my attendance was requested at the interment[3] on Monday next at three o'clock in the afternoon.

---

2. **docketed** (däk′ it əd) v.: Labeled.
3. **interment** (in tʉr′ mənt) n.: Burial.

## Chapter 34

It was the first time that a grave had opened in my road of life, and the gap it made in the smooth ground was wonderful.[1] The figure of my sister in her chair by the kitchen fire haunted me night and day. That the place could possibly be without her was something my mind seemed unable to compass, and whereas she had seldom or never been in my thoughts of late, I had now the strangest idea that she was coming towards me in the street, or that she would presently knock at the door.

Whatever my fortunes might have been, I could scarcely have recalled my sister with much tenderness. But I suppose there is a shock of regret which may exist without much tenderness.

Having written to Joe to offer him consolation, and to assure him that I would come to the funeral, I passed the intermediate days in the curious state of mind I have glanced at.[2] I went down early in the morning, and alighted at the Blue Boar in good time to walk over to the forge.

At last I came within sight of the house, and saw that Trabb & Co. had put in a funereal execution and taken possession. Poor dear Joe, entangled in a little black cloak tied in a large bow under his chin, was seated apart at the upper end of the room; where, as chief mourner, he had evidently been stationed by Trabb. When I bent down and said to him, "Dear Joe, how are you?" he said, "Pip, old chap, you know'd her when she were a fine figure of a—" and clasped my hand and said no more.

Biddy, looking very neat and modest in her black dress, went quietly here and there,

---

1. **wonderful** (wun′ dər fəl) adj.: In this case, it means "amazing."
2. **curious state . . . glanced at:** Strange state of mind I have briefly mentioned.

12 **Discussion** How does this system of handling bills affect Pip's spirits?

13 **Reading Strategy** Ask students to predict the changes that will result from this event.

14 **Critical Thinking and Reading** What is the strange experience that Pip has as he thinks about his relationship with his sister and tries to acknowledge the reality of her death? How does this reflect the emotional atmosphere of the funeral?

15 **Discussion** What expression is Joe's way of communicating his feeling about his first wife?

The sounds of our pens going refreshed us exceedingly, *insomuch that I sometimes found it difficult to distinguish between this edifying business and actually paying the money.*

Whatever my fortunes might have been, I could scarcely have recalled my sister with much tenderness.

The somewhat old-fashioned sounding subordinate conjunction *insomuch that* means "to the degree that."

**Student Activity.** Write a one-paragraph description of the most exciting sports event you ever witnessed or heard about. Use subordination in at least two sentences.

16 **Discussion** Why is this simile effective?

17 **Discussion** How does Pip help restore his old relationship with Joe?

18 **Discussion** In his talk with Biddy after the funeral, what attitude does Pip adopt that temporarily strains their relationship?

and was very helpful. When I had spoken to Biddy, as I thought it not a time for talking, I went and sat down near Joe.

"Pocket-handkerchiefs out, all!" cried Mr. Trabb at this point, in a depressed business-like voice. "Pocket-handkerchiefs out! We are ready!"

So, we all put our pocket-handkerchiefs to our faces, as if our noses were bleeding, and filed out two and two; Joe and I; Biddy and Pumblechook; Mr. and Mrs. Hubble. The remains of my poor sister had been brought round by the kitchen door, and it being a point of undertaking ceremony that the six bearers must be stifled and blinded under a horrible black velvet housing with a white border, the whole looked like a blind monster with twelve human legs, shuffling and blundering along under the guidance of two keepers—the post-boy and his comrade. The neighborhood, however, highly approved of these arrangements, and we were much admired as we went through the village.

And now the range of marshes lay clear before us, with the sails of the ships on the river growing out of it; and we went into the churchyard, close to the graves of my unknown parents, Philip Pirrip, Late of this Parish, and Also Georgiana, Wife of the Above. And there my sister was laid quietly in the earth while the larks sang high above it, and the light wind strewed it with beautiful shadows of clouds and trees.

Soon afterwards, Biddy, Joe, and I had a cold dinner together; but we dined in the best parlor, not in the old kitchen, and Joe was so exceedingly particular what he did with his knife and fork and the saltcellar and what not that there was great restraint upon us. But after dinner, when I made him take his pipe, and when I had loitered with him about the forge, and when we sat down together on the great block of stone outside it, we got on better.

He was very much pleased by my asking

if I might sleep in my own little room, and I was pleased, too, for I felt that I had done rather a great thing in making the request. When the shadows of evening were closing in, I took an opportunity of getting into the garden with Biddy for a little talk.

"Biddy," said I, "I think you might have written to me about these sad matters."

"Do you, Mr. Pip?" said Biddy. "I should have written if I had thought that."

She was so quiet, and had such an orderly, good, and pretty way with her that I did not like the thought of making her cry again. After looking a little at her downcast eyes as she walked beside me, I gave up that point.

"I suppose it will be difficult for you to remain here now, Biddy, dear?"

"Oh! I can't do so, Mr. Pip," said Biddy, in a tone of regret, but still of quiet conviction. "I have been speaking to Mrs. Hubble, and I am going to her tomorrow. I hope we shall be able to take some care of Mr. Gargery, together, until he settles down."

"How are you going to live, Biddy? If you want any mo—"

"How am I going to live?" repeated Biddy, striking in, with a momentary flush upon her face. "I'll tell you, Mr. Pip. I am going to try to get the place of mistress in the new school nearly finished here. I can be well recommended by all the neighbors, and I hope I can be industrious and patient, and teach myself while I teach others. The new schools are not like the old, but I learned a good deal from you after that time, and have had time since then to improve."

"I think you would always improve, Biddy, under any circumstances."

Then I thought I would give up that point, too. So, I walked a little further with Biddy, looking silently at her downcast eyes.

"I have not heard the particulars of my sister's death, Biddy."

"They are very slight, poor thing. She

had been in one of her bad states for four days when she came out of it in the evening, just at tea-time, and said quite plainly, 'Joe.' As she had never said any word for a long while, I ran and fetched in Mr. Gargery from the forge. She made signs to me that she wanted him to sit down close to her, and wanted me to put her arms round his neck. So I put them round his neck, and she laid her head down on his shoulder quite content and satisfied. And so she presently said 'Joe' again, and once 'Pardon,' and once 'Pip.' And so she never lifted her head up any more, and it was just an hour later when we laid it down on her own bed, because we found she was gone."

Biddy cried; the darkening garden, and the lane, and the stars that were coming out were blurred in my own sight.

"Nothing was ever discovered, Biddy?"

"Nothing."

"Do you know what is become of Orlick?"

"I should think from the color of his clothes that he is working in the quarries."

"Of course you have seen him then? Why are you looking at that dark tree in the lane?"

"I saw him there, on the night she died."

"That was not the last time either, Biddy?"

"No, I have seen him there since we have been walking here. It is of no use," said Biddy, laying her hand upon my arm, as I was for running out, "you know I would not deceive you; he was not there a minute, and he is gone."

It revived my utmost indignation to find that she was still pursued by this fellow, and I felt inveterate against him. I told her so, and told her that I would spend any money or take any pains to drive him out of that country. By degrees she led me into more temperate talk, and she told me how Joe loved me, and how Joe never complained of anything—she didn't say of me; she had no

need; I knew what she meant—but ever did his duty in his way of life, with a strong hand, a quiet tongue, and a gentle heart.

"Indeed, it would be hard to say too much for him," said I; "and, Biddy, we must often speak of these things, for of course I shall be often down here now. I am not going to leave poor Joe alone."

"Are you quite sure, then, that you *will* come to see him often?" asked Biddy, stopping in the narrow garden walk, and looking at me under the stars with a clear and honest eye.

"Oh, dear me!" said I, as I found myself compelled to give up Biddy in despair. "This really is a very bad side of human nature! Don't say any more, if you please, Biddy. This shocks me very much."

For which cogent reason I kept Biddy at a distance during supper, and when I went up to my own old little room, took as stately a leave of her as I could. As often as I was restless in the night, and that was every quarter of an hour, I reflected what an unkindness, what an injury, what an injustice Biddy had done me.

Early in the morning, I was to go. Early in the morning, I was out, and looking in, unseen, at one of the wooden windows of the forge. There I stood for minutes looking at Joe, already at work with a glow of health and strength upon his face that made it show as if the bright sun of the life in store for him were shining on it.

"Good-bye, dear Joe! No, don't wipe it off—for God's sake, give me your blackened hand! I shall be down soon and often."

"Never too soon, sir," said Joe, "and never too often, Pip!"

Biddy was waiting for me at the kitchen door, with a mug of new milk and a crust of bread. "Biddy," said I, when I gave her my hand at parting, "I am not angry, but I am hurt."

"No, don't be hurt," she pleaded quite

*Great Expectations* 863

19 **Discussion** What do you infer from the information which Biddy imparts about Orlick?

20 **Discussion** Is her view of Joe accurate? Explain.

21 **Discussion** How does Pip react to Biddy's implied criticism of him?

pathetically; "let only me be hurt, if I have been ungenerous."

**22** Once more, the mists were rising as I walked away. If they disclosed to me, as I suspect they did, that I should *not* come back, and that Biddy was quite right, all I can say is—they were quite right, too.

### Chapter 35

**23** Herbert and I went on from bad to worse, in the way of increasing our debts. But we looked forward to my one-and-twentieth birthday, for we had both considered that my guardian could hardly help saying something definite on that occasion.

I had taken care to have it well understood in Little Britain when my birthday was. On the day before it, I received an official note from Wemmick, informing me that Mr. Jaggers would be glad if I would call upon him at five in the afternoon of the auspicious day. This convinced us that something great was to happen, and threw me into an unusual flutter when I repaired to my guardian's office, a model of punctuality.

In the outer office Wemmick offered me his congratulations, and incidentally rubbed the side of his nose with a folded piece of tissue paper that I liked the look of. It was November, and my guardian was standing before his fire leaning his back against the chimneypiece, with his hands under his coat-tails.

"Well, Pip," said he, "I must call you Mr. Pip today. Congratulations, Mr. Pip."

We shook hands—he was always a remarkably short shaker—and I thanked him.

"Take a chair, Mr. Pip," said my guardian.

As I sat down, I felt at a disadvantage, which reminded me of that old time when I had been put upon a tombstone.

**24** "Now, my young friend," my guardian began, as if I were a witness in the box, "I am going to have a word or two with you."

"If you please, sir."

"What do you suppose," said Mr. Jaggers, "you are living at the rate of?"

"At the rate of, sir?"

"At," repeated Mr. Jaggers, "the—rate—of?"

Reluctantly, I confessed myself quite unable to answer the question. This reply seemed agreeable to Mr. Jaggers, who said, "I thought so!"

"Now, I have asked *you* a question, my friend," said Mr. Jaggers. "Have you anything to ask *me*?"

"Of course it would be a great relief to me to ask you several questions, sir; but I remember your prohibition."

"Ask one," said Mr. Jaggers.

"Is my benefactor to be made known to me today?"

"No. Ask another."

"Is that confidence to be imparted to me soon?"

"Waive that, a moment," said Mr. Jaggers, "and ask another."

"Have—I—anything to receive, sir?" On that, Mr. Jaggers said triumphantly, "I thought we should come to it!" and called to Wemmick to give him that piece of paper. Wemmick appeared, handed it in, and disappeared.

"Now, Mr. Pip," said Mr. Jaggers, "attend if you please. You have been drawing pretty freely here; your name occurs pretty often in Wemmick's cash book: but you are in debt, of course?"

"I am afraid I must say yes, sir."

"You know you must say yes, don't you?" said Mr. Jaggers.

"Yes, sir."

"I don't ask you what you owe, because you don't know; and if you did know, you wouldn't tell me; you would say less. Yes, yes, my friend," cried Mr. Jaggers, waving his forefinger to stop me, as I made a show of protesting, "it's likely enough that you think you wouldn't, but you would. You'll excuse me, but I know better than you. Now, take this piece of paper in your hand. You have got it? Very good. Now, unfold it and tell me what it is."

"This is a bank note," said I, "for five hundred pounds."

"You consider it, undoubtedly, a handsome sum of money. Now, that handsome sum of money, Pip, is your own. It is a present to you on this day, in earnest of your expectations. And at the rate of that handsome sum of money per annum,[1] and at no higher rate, you are to live until the donor of the whole appears. That is to say, you will now take your money affairs entirely into your own hands, and you will draw from Wemmick one hundred and twenty-five pounds per quarter, until you are in communication with the fountainhead,[2] and no longer with the mere agent."

After a pause, I hinted:

"There was a question just now, Mr. Jaggers, which you desired me to waive for a moment. I hope I am doing nothing wrong in asking it again?"

"What is it?" said he.

"Is it likely," I said, after hesitating, "that my patron, the fountainhead you have spoken of, Mr. Jaggers, will soon come to London, or summon me anywhere else?"

"Now here," replied Mr. Jaggers, fixing me for the first time with his dark deep-set eyes, "we must revert to the evening when we first encountered one another in your village. What did I tell you then, Pip?"

"You told me, Mr. Jaggers, that it might be years hence when that person appeared."

"Just so," said Mr. Jaggers; "that's my answer."

"Do you suppose it will still be years hence, Mr. Jaggers?"

"Come!" said Mr. Jaggers, "I'll be plain with you, my friend Pip. That's a question I must not be asked. You'll understand that better when I tell you it's a question that might compromise *me*. When that person discloses, you and that person will settle your own affairs. When that person discloses, my part in this business will cease and determine. And that's all I have got to say."

We looked at one another until I withdrew my eyes, and looked thoughtfully at the floor. From this last speech I derived the notion that Miss Havisham, for some reason or no reason, had not taken him into her confidence as to her designing me for Estella; that he resented this, and felt a jealousy about it; or that he really did object to that scheme, and would have nothing to do with it.

"If that is all you have to say, sir," I remarked, "there can be nothing left for me to say."

He nodded assent and asked me where I was going to dine. I replied at my own chambers, with Herbert. As a necessary sequence, I asked him if he would favor us with his company, and he promptly accepted the invitation. But he insisted on walking home with me, in order that I might make no extra preparation for him, and first he had a letter or two to write. So, I said I would go into the outer office and talk to Wemmick.

The fact was that when the five hundred pounds had come into my pocket, a thought had come into my head which had been often there before; and it appeared to me that Wemmick was a good person to advise[3] with, concerning such thought.

"Mr. Wemmick," said I, "I want to ask your opinion. I am very desirous to serve a

---

1. **per annum:** Latin for "yearly."
2. **fountainhead** (foun′ t'n hed′) *n*.: Source.
3. **advise** (əd vīz′) *v*.: Consult.

25 **Critical Thinking and Reading**
What conclusion does Pip draw from Mr. Jaggers's refusal to tell him who his benefactor is?

friend. This friend," I pursued, "is trying to get on in commercial life, but has no money, and finds it difficult and disheartening to make a beginning. Now, I want somehow to help him to a beginning."

"With money down?" said Wemmick, in a tone drier than any sawdust.

"With *some* money down," I replied, for an uneasy remembrance shot across me of that symmetrical bundle of papers at home; "with *some* money down, and perhaps some anticipation of my expectations."

"Choose a bridge, Mr. Pip," returned Wemmick, "and take a walk upon your bridge, and pitch your money into the Thames over the center arch of your bridge, and you know the end of it. Serve a friend with it, and you may know the end of it, too—but it's a less pleasant and profitable end."

"And that," said I, "is your deliberate opinion, Mr. Wemmick?"

"That," he returned, "is my deliberate opinion in this office."

"Ah!" said I, pressing him, for I thought I saw him near a loophole here. "But would that be your opinion at Walworth?"

"Mr. Pip," he replied with gravity, "Walworth is one place, and this office is another. Much as the Aged is one person, and Mr. Jaggers is another. They must not be confounded together. My Walworth sentiments must be taken at Walworth; none but my official sentiments can be taken in this office."

"Very well," said I, much relieved, "then I shall look you up at Walworth, you may depend upon it."

"Mr. Pip," he returned, "you will be welcome there, in a private and personal capacity."

We had held this conversation in a low voice, well knowing my guardian's ears to be the sharpest of the sharp. As he now appeared in his doorway, toweling his hands,

Wemmick got on his greatcoat and stood by to snuff out the candles. We all three went into the street together, and from the doorstep Wemmick turned his way, and Mr. Jaggers and I turned ours.

## Chapter 36

Deeming Sunday the best day for taking Mr. Wemmick's Walworth sentiments, I devoted the next ensuing Sunday afternoon to a pilgrimage to the castle. On arriving before the battlements, I found the Union Jack flying and the drawbridge up, but undeterred by this show of defiance and resistance, I rang at the gate, and was admitted in a most pacific manner by the Aged.

"My son, sir," said the old man, after securing the drawbridge, "left word that he would soon be home from his afternoon's walk."

I nodded at the old gentleman as Wemmick himself might have nodded, and we went in and sat down by the fireside.

"You made acquaintance with my son, sir," said the old man in his chirping way, while he warmed his hands at the blaze, "at his office, I expect?" I nodded. "Hah! I have heerd that my son is a wonderful hand at his business, sir?" I nodded hard. "Yes, so they tell me. His business is the law?" I nodded harder.

I was startled by a sudden click in the wall on one side of the chimney, and the ghostly tumbling open of a little wooden flap with "JOHN" upon it. The old man, following my eyes, cried with great triumph, "My son's come home!" and we both went out to the drawbridge.

It was worth any money to see Wemmick waving a salute to me from the other side of the moat, when we might have shaken hands across it with the greatest ease. The Aged was so delighted to work the draw-

## Primary Source

Literary critics have both praised and criticized Dickens's work. It has fallen under harsh criticism by critics who have claimed that Dickens's characters are flat and can be described in one sentence. Other critics state that although Dickens ought to be considered bad, there is something compelling and appealing about his work. Still others, such as is illustrated in the following example, highly praise Dickens's talent and works. In "The Great

Inimitable," one of the essays in *Charles Dickens 1812–1870, a Centennial Volume* edited by E.W.F. Tomlin, J.B. Priestley quotes literary critic G. K. Chesterton as follows:

The art of Dickens was the most exquisite of arts: it was the art of enjoying everybody. Dickens, being a very human writer, had to be a very human being; he had his faults and sensibilities in a strong degree; and I do not for a moment maintain that he enjoyed everybody in his daily life. But he enjoyed everybody in his books; and everybody has enjoyed everybody in those books even till today. His books are full of baffled villains stalking out or cowardly bullies kicked downstairs. But the villains and the cowards bridge that I made no offer to assist him, but stood quiet until Wemmick had come across, and had presented me to Miss Skiffins, a lady by whom he was accompanied.

Miss Skiffins was of a wooden appearance. The cut of her dress from the waist upward, both before and behind, made her figure very like a boy's kite, and I might have pronounced her gown a little too decidedly orange, and her gloves a little too intensely green. But she seemed to be a good sort of fellow, and showed a high regard for the Aged. I was not long in discovering that she was a frequent visitor at the castle.

While Miss Skiffins was taking off her bonnet, Wemmick invited me to take a walk with him round the property, and see how the island looked in wintertime. Thinking that he did this to give me an opportunity of taking his Walworth sentiments, I seized the opportunity as soon as we were out of the castle.

I informed Wemmick that I was anxious in behalf of Herbert Pocket, and I told him how we had first met, and how we had fought. I alluded to the advantages I had derived in my first rawness and ignorance from his society, and I confessed that I feared I had but ill repaid them, and that he might have done better without me and my expectations. For all these reasons (I told Wemmick), and because he was my young companion and friend, and I had a great affection for him, I wished my own good fortune to reflect some rays upon him, and therefore I sought advice from Wemmick's experience and knowledge of men and affairs, how I could best try with my resources to help Herbert to some present income—say of a hundred a year, to keep him in good hope and heart—and gradually to buy him on to some small partnership. I begged Wemmick, in conclusion, to understand that my help must always be rendered without Her-

bert's knowledge or suspicion, and that there was no one else in the world with whom I could advise. I wound up by laying my hand upon his shoulder, and saying, "I can't help confiding in you, though I know it must be troublesome to you; but that is your fault, in having ever brought me here."

"I'll put on my considering cap," said Wemmick "and I think all you want to do may be done by degrees. Skiffins (that's her brother) is an accountant and agent. I'll look him up and go to work for you."

After a little further conversation to the same effect, we returned into the castle, where we found Miss Skiffins preparing tea. The responsible duty of making the toast was delegated to the Aged, and that excellent old gentleman prepared such a haystack of buttered toast that I could scarcely see him over it.

We ate the whole of the toast, and drank tea in proportion, and it was delightful to see how warm and greasy we all got after it. Then we drew round the fire, and Wemmick said, "Now, Aged Parent, tip us the paper."

Wemmick explained to me while the Aged got his spectacles out that this was according to custom, and that it gave the old gentleman infinite satisfaction to read the news aloud. "I won't offer an apology," said Wemmick, "for he isn't capable of many pleasures—are you, Aged P.?"

"All right, John, all right," returned the old man, seeing himself spoken to.

"Only tip him a nod every now and then when he looks off his paper," said Wemmick, "and he'll be as happy as a king. We are all attention, Aged One."

After awhile the Aged read himself into a light slumber. Then we all had something warm to drink, including the Aged, who was soon awake again. Miss Skiffins mixed, and I observed that she and Wemmick drank out of one glass. Of course I knew better than to

are such delightful people that the reader always hopes the villain will put his head through a side window and make a last remark; or that the bully will say one thing more, even from the bottom of the stairs. . . . Though Mr Pecksniff [*(Martin Chuzzlewit)*] fell to be a borrower of money, and Mr Mantalini [*(Nicholas Nickleby)*] to turning a mangle, the human race has the comfort of thinking they are still alive: and one might have the rapture of receiving a begging letter from Mr Pecksniff, or even of catching Mr Mantalini collecting the washing, if one always lurked about on Monday mornings. . . .

27 **Critical Thinking and Reading** Compare and contrast Miss Skiffins with Biddy, Estella, or Mrs. Joe in appearance and manner. Also compare and contrast the professional Mr. Wemmick with the private Mr. Wemmick.

28 **Discussion** What is Pip's purpose in visiting Mr. Wemmick?

**29 Discussion** How does Mr. Wemmick arrange to improve Herbert's prospects while keeping Pip's part in the scheme anonymous?

**30 Discussion** What effect does Pip's plan have on Herbert and on Pip?

**31 Discussion** Pip becomes aware of Estella's many admirers and her attitude toward them. What effect does this awareness have on Pip?

offer to see Miss Skiffins home, and under the circumstances I thought I had best go first—which I did, taking a cordial leave of the Aged, and having passed a pleasant evening.

Before a week was out, I received a note from Wemmick, dated Walworth, stating that he hoped he had made some advance in that matter appertaining to our private and personal capacities. The upshot was that we found a worthy young merchant or shipping broker, not long established in business, who wanted intelligent help, and who wanted capital, and who in due course of time and receipt would want a partner. Between him and me, secret articles were signed of which Herbert was the subject, and I paid him half of my five hundred pounds down, and engaged for sundry other payments: some, to fall due at certain dates out of my income; some contingent on my coming into my property. Miss Skiffins's brother conducted the negotiation. Wemmick pervaded it throughout, but never appeared in it.

The whole business was so cleverly managed that Herbert had not the least suspicion of my hand being in it. I never shall forget the radiant face with which he came home one afternoon, and told me as a mighty piece of news, of his having fallen in with one Clarriker (the young merchant's name), and of Clarriker's having shown an extraordinary inclination towards him, and of his belief that the opening had come at last. Day by day as his hopes grew stronger and his face brighter, he must have thought me a more and more affectionate friend, for I had the greatest difficulty in restraining my tears of triumph when I saw him so happy.

At length, the thing being done, and he having that day entered Clarriker's House, and he having talked to me for a whole evening in a flush of pleasure and success, I did really cry in good earnest when I went to bed, to think that my expectations had done some good to somebody.

A great event in my life, the turning point of my life, now opens on my view. But before I proceed to narrate it, and before I pass on to all the changes it involved, I must give one chapter to Estella. It is not much to give to the theme that so long filled my heart.

## Chapter 37

The lady with whom Estella was placed, Mrs. Brandley by name, was a widow, with one daughter several years older than Estella. They were in what is called a good position, and visited, and were visited by, numbers of people.

In Mrs. Brandley's house and out of Mrs. Brandley's house, I suffered every kind and degree of torture that Estella could cause me. She made use of me to tease other admirers, and she turned the very familiarity between herself and me to the account of putting a constant slight on my devotion to her.

She had admirers without end. No doubt my jealousy made an admirer of every one who went near her, but there were more than enough of them without that.

I saw her often at Richmond, I heard of her often in town, and I used often to take her and the Brandleys on the water; there were picnics, fête days, plays, operas, concerts, parties, all sorts of pleasures, through which I pursued her—and they were all miseries to me. I never had one hour's happiness in her society, and yet my mind all round the four-and-twenty hours was harping on the happiness of having her with me unto death.

Throughout this part of our intercourse, she habitually reverted to that tone which expressed that our association was forced

**ONLY A LOCK OF HAIR**
*Sir John Everett Millais*
*City of Manchester Art Galleries*

**Humanities Note**

Fine art, *Only a Lock of Hair*, 1859, by Sir John Everett Millais. John Everett Millais (1829–1896) was a British painter. Extremely precocious, Millais entered the Royal Academy at age eleven and won a gold medal for his paintings at seventeen. This exceptionally talented portrait painter worked in the Pre-Raphaelite style, which can be characterized as true to nature, romantic, and emotional.

*Only a Lock of Hair* is a portrait of Ellen Petrie. This lovely painting of a young woman is a study in contrasts: the creamy white of her skin against the dark background and the silky texture of her hair against the velvet of her gown. The white lace collar and cuffs add a demure note to this otherwise sensuous portrait, which is a romantic salute to this young woman's beauty.

You might want to ask students the following questions:
1. Why do you think Millais chose to focus on his subject's face and hands?
2. How do the contrasts between light and dark areas enhance the picture?
3. What overall impression does this portrait convey?

**32 Discussion** Estella has warned Pip on several occasions to use caution in respect to his feelings for her. Why does Pip repeatedly refuse to heed Estella's warnings about herself?

upon us. There were other times when she would come to a sudden check in this tone and in all her many tones, and would seem to pity me.

"Pip, Pip," she said one evening, coming to such a check, when we sat apart at a darkening window of the house in Richmond; "will you never take warning?"

"Of what?"

"Of me."

"Warning not to be attracted by you, do you mean, Estella?"

"Do I mean! If you don't know what I mean, you are blind."

"At any rate," said I, "I have no warning given me just now, for you wrote to me to come to you, this time."

"That's true," said Estella, with a cold careless smile that always chilled me. "The time has come round when Miss Havisham

*Great Expectations* 869

**33 Discussion** How does Miss Havisham intensify her efforts to enchant Pip with Estella's beauty? How does Pip judge Miss Havisham as a result?

**34 Discussion** Why does Estella draw away from Miss Havisham, causing a quarrel?

**35 Discussion** Describe the setting and atmosphere of this scene. What effect do they have on the characters present?

**36 Clarification** The phrase *stock and stone* means "as heartless as an inanimate object."

wishes to have me for a day at Satis. You are to take me there, and bring me back, if you will. She would rather I did not travel alone, and objects to receiving my maid, for she has a sensitive horror of being talked of by such people. Can you take me?"

"Can I take you, Estella!"

"You can then? The day after tomorrow, if you please. You are to pay all charges out of my purse. You hear the condition of your going?"

"And must obey," said I.

This was all the preparation I received for that visit, or for others like it: Miss Havisham never wrote to me, nor had I ever so much as seen her handwriting. We went down on the next day but one, and we found her in the room where I had first beheld her.

She was even more dreadfully fond of Estella than she had been when I last saw them together; I repeat the word advisedly, for there was something positively dreadful in the energy of her looks and embraces. She hung upon Estella's beauty, hung upon her words, hung upon her gestures, and sat mumbling her own trembling fingers while she looked at her, as though she were devouring the beautiful creature she had reared.

From Estella she looked at me, with a searching glance that seemed to pry into my heart and probe its wounds. "How does she use you, Pip, how does she use you?" she asked me again, with her witch-like eagerness, even in Estella's hearing. But, when we sat by her flickering fire at night, she was most weird; for then, keeping Estella's hand drawn through her arm and clutched in her own hand, she extorted from her by dint of referring back to what Estella had told her in her regular letters, the names and conditions of the men whom she had fascinated.

I saw in this that Estella was set to wreak Miss Havisham's revenge on men, and that she was not to be given to me until she had gratified it for a term. I saw in this a reason for her being beforehand assigned to me. Sending her out to attract and torment and do mischief, Miss Havisham sent her with the malicious assurance that she was beyond the reach of all admirers. I saw in this, that I, too, was tormented by a perversion of ingenuity, even while the prize was reserved for me. I saw in this the reason for my being staved off so long, and the reason for my late guardian's declining to commit himself to the formal knowledge of such a scheme.

It happened on the occasion of this visit that some sharp words arose between Estella and Miss Havisham. It was the first time I had ever seen them opposed.

We were seated by the fire, and Miss Havisham still had Estella's arm drawn through her own, and still clutched Estella's hand in hers, when Estella gradually began to detach herself.

"What!" said Miss Havisham, flashing her eyes upon her, "are you tired of me?"

"Only a little tired of myself," replied Estella, disengaging her arm, and moving to the great chimneypiece, where she stood looking down at the fire.

"Speak the truth, you ingrate!" cried Miss Havisham, passionately striking her stick upon the floor; "you are tired of me."

Estella looked at her with perfect composure, and again looked down at the fire. Her graceful figure and her beautiful face expressed a self-possessed indifference to the wild heat of the other that was almost cruel.

"You stock and stone!" exclaimed Miss Havisham. "You cold, cold heart!"

"What!" said Estella. "Do you reproach me for being cold? You?"

"Are you not?" was the fierce retort.

"You should know," said Estella. "I am what you have made me."

"Oh, look at her, look at her!" cried Miss

Havisham bitterly. "Look at her, so hard and thankless, on the hearth where she was reared!"

"You have been very good to me," said Estella "and I owe everything to you. What would you have?"

"Love," replied the other.

"You have it."

"I have not," said Miss Havisham.

"Mother by adoption," retorted Estella, "I have said that I owe everything to you. All I possess is freely yours. All that you have given me is at your command to have again. Beyond that, I have nothing. And if you ask me to give you what you never gave me, my gratitude and duty cannot do impossibilities."

"Did I never give her love!" cried Miss Havisham, turning wildly to me. "Let her call me mad!"

"Why should I call you mad," returned Estella, "I, of all people? Does any one live who knows what set purposes you have half as well as I do? I who have sat on this same hearth on the little stool that is even now beside you there, learning your lessons and looking up into your face."

"Soon forgotten!" moaned Miss Havisham.

"No, not forgotten," retorted Estella. "Not fogotten, but treasured up in my memory. When have you found me false to your teaching? When have you found me unmindful of your lessons?"

"So proud, so proud!" moaned Miss Havisham.

"Who taught me to be proud?" returned Estella.

"So hard, so hard!" moaned Miss Havisham.

"Who taught me to be hard?" returned Estella.

"But to be proud and hard to *me*!" Miss Havisham quite shrieked, as she stretched out her arms. "Estella, Estella, Estella, to be proud and hard to *me*!"

Estella looked at her for a moment with a kind of calm wonder, but was not otherwise disturbed; when the moment was past, she looked down at the fire again.

Miss Havisham settled down, I hardly knew how, upon the floor, among the faded bridal relics with which it was strewn. I took advantage of the moment to leave the room, after beseeching Estella's attention to her with a movement of my hand.

It was with a depressed heart that I walked in the starlight for an hour and more, about the courtyard, and about the ruined garden. When I at last took courage to return to the room, I found Estella sitting at Miss Havisham's knee, taking up some stitches in one of those old articles of dress that were dropping to pieces. Afterwards, Estella and I played at cards, as of yore—only we were skillful now, and played French games—and so the evening wore away, and I went to bed.

Before we left next day, there was no revival of the difference between her and Estella, nor was it ever revived on any similar occasion.

It is impossible to turn this leaf of my life without putting Bentley Drummle's name upon it; or I would, very gladly.

On a certain occasion when the Finches[1] were assembled in force, the presiding Finch called the Grove to order, forasmuch as Mr. Drummle had not yet toasted a lady. What was my indignant surprise when he called upon the company to pledge him to "Estella!"

This was no light thing to me. For I cannot adequately express what pain it gave me to think that Estella should show any favor

---

**1. Finches:** Finches of the Grove, a social club to which Drummle, Herbert, and Pip belong.

**37 Discussion** Why is Estella unable to love Miss Havisham? What has Estella offered her instead?

to a contemptible, clumsy, sulky booby, so very far below the average.

It was easy for me to find out, and I did soon find out, that Drummle had begun to follow her closely, and that she allowed him to do it. A little while, and he was always in pursuit of her. He held on, in a dull persistent way, and Estella held him on; now with encouragement, now with discouragement, now almost flattering him, now openly despising him, now knowing him very well, now scarcely remembering who he was.

The Spider, as Mr. Jaggers had called him, was used to lying in wait, however, and had the patience of his tribe.

At a certain Assembly Ball at Richmond, this blundering Drummle so hung about her, and with so much toleration on her part, that I resolved to speak to her concerning him. I took the next opportunity, which was when she was waiting for Mrs. Brandley to take her home.

"Estella," said I, "look at that fellow in the corner yonder who is looking over here at us."

"Why should I look at him?" returned Estella, with her eyes on me instead. "What is there in that fellow in the corner yonder that I need look at?"

"Indeed, that is the very question I want to ask you," said I. "For he has been hovering about you all night."

"Moths, and all sorts of ugly creatures," replied Estella, with a glance towards him, "hover about a lighted candle. Can the candle help it?"

"No," I returned: "but cannot the Estella help it?"

"Well!" said she, "perhaps. Yes. Anything you like."

"But, Estella, do hear me speak. It makes me wretched that you should encourage a man so generally despised as Drummle. You know he is despised."

"Well?" said she.

"You know he is a deficient, ill-tempered, lowering, stupid fellow."

"Well?" said she.

"You know he has nothing to recommend him but money, don't you?"

"Well?" said she again.

"Well! Then, that is why it makes me wretched."

"Pip," said Estella, "don't be foolish about its effect on you. It may have its effect on others, and may be meant to have. It's not worth discussing."

"Yes it is," said I, "because I cannot bear that people should say, 'She throws away her graces and attractions on a mere boor,[2] the lowest in the crowd.' "

"I can bear it," said Estella.

"Oh, don't be so proud, Estella, and so inflexible."

"Calls me proud and inflexible in this breath!" said Estella. "And in his last breath reproached me for stooping to a boor!"

"There is no doubt you do," said I something hurriedly, "for I have seen you give him looks and smiles this very night, such as you never give to—me."

"Do you want me then," said Estella, turning suddenly with a fixed and serious, if not angry look, "to deceive and entrap you?"

"Do you deceive and entrap him, Estella?"

"Yes, and many others—all of them but you. Here is Mrs. Brandley. I'll say no more."

**Chapter 38**

I was three-and-twenty years of age. Not another word had I heard to enlighten me on the subject of my expectations. We had left Barnard's Inn more than a year, and lived in the Temple.[1] Our chambers were in Garden

---

2. **boor** (boŏr) *n.*: A rude, unpleasant person.
1. **Temple:** Buildings near the Thames River for people associated with the court system.

Court, down by the river. Mr. Pocket and I had for some time parted company as to our original relations, though we continued on the best terms.

Business had taken Herbert on a journey to Marseilles.[2] I was alone, and had a dull sense of being alone. Dispirited and anxious, I sadly missed the cheerful face and ready response of my friend.

It was wretched weather; stormy and wet, stormy and wet; mud, mud, mud, deep in all the streets. Day after day, a vast heavy veil had been driving over London from the east, and it drove still, as if in the east there were an eternity of cloud and wind.

Alterations have been made in that part of the Temple since that time, and it has not now so lonely a character as it had then, nor is it so exposed to the river. We lived at the top of the last house, and the wind rushing up the river shook the house that night, like discharges of cannon, or breakings of a sea. I saw that the lamps in the court were blown out, and that the lamps on the bridges and the shore were shuddering, and that the coal fires in barges on the river were being carried away before the wind like red-hot splashes in the rain.

I read with my watch upon the table, purposing to close my book at eleven o'clock. As I shut it, Saint Paul's, and all the many church-clocks in the City struck that hour. The sound was curiously flawed by the wind; and I was listening, and thinking how the wind assailed and tore it, when I heard a footstep on the stair.

Remembering, then, that the staircase lights were blown out, I took up my reading-lamp and went out to the stair-head. Whoever was below had stopped on seeing my lamp, for all was quiet.

_____
**2. Marseilles** (măr sĕ′ y′): Seaport in southeast France.

"There is some one down there, is there not?" I called out, looking down.

"Yes," said a voice from the darkness beneath.

"What floor do you want?"

"The top. Mr. Pip."

"That is my name. There is nothing the matter?"

"Nothing the matter," returned the voice. And the man came on.

I stood with my lamp held out over the stair-rail, and he came slowly within its light. I saw a face that was strange to me, looking up with an incomprehensible air of being touched and pleased by the sight of me.

Moving the lamp as the man moved, I made out that he was substantially dressed, but roughly, like a voyager by sea. That he had long iron-gray hair. That his age was about sixty. That he was a muscular man, strong on his legs, and that he was browned and hardened by exposure to weather. As he ascended the last stair or two, and the light of my lamp included us both, I saw, with a stupid kind of amazement, that he was holding out both his hands to me.

"Pray what is your business?" I asked him.

"My business?" he repeated, pausing. "Ah! Yes. I will explain my business, by your leave."

"Do you wish to come in?"

"Yes," he replied, "I wish to come in, master."

I took him into the room I had just left, and, having set the lamp on the table, asked him as civilly as I could to explain himself.

He looked about him with the strangest air—an air of wondering pleasure, as if he had some part in the things he admired—and he pulled off a rough outer coat, and his hat. Then, I saw that his head was furrowed and bald, and that the long iron-gray hair grew only on its sides. But I saw nothing

39

**39 Literary Focus** Foreshadowing is a literary device by which writers hint at events to come. How might weather foreshadow future events?

that in the least explained him. On the contrary, I saw him next moment once more holding out both his hands to me.

"What do you mean?" said I, half-suspecting him to be mad.

He stopped in his looking at me and slowly rubbed his right hand over his head. "It's disappointing to a man," he said, in a coarse broken voice, "arter having looked for'ard so distant, and come so fur; but you're not to blame for that—neither on us is to blame for that. I'll speak in half a minute. Give me half a minute, please."

He sat down on a chair that stood before the fire, and covered his forehead with his large brown veinous hands. I looked at him attentively then, and recoiled a little from him; but I did not know him.

"There's no one nigh," said he, looking over his shoulder, "is there?"

"Why do you, a stranger coming into my rooms at this time of the night, ask that question?" said I.

"You're a game one," he returned. "I'm glad you've grow'd up a game one! But don't catch hold of me. You'd be sorry arterwards to have done it."

I relinquished the intention he had detected, for I knew him! Even yet I could not recall a single feature, but I knew him! If the wind and the rain had driven away the intervening years, had scattered all the intervening objects, had swept us to the churchyard where we first stood face to face on such different levels, I could not have known my convict more distinctly than I knew him now, as he sat in the chair before the fire. No need to take a file from his pocket and show it to me; no need to take the handkerchief from his neck and twist it round his head; no need to hug himself with both his arms, and take a shivering turn across the room, looking back at me for recognition. I knew him before he gave me one of those aids, though, a mo-

ment before, I had not been conscious of remotely suspecting his identity.

He came back to where I stood, and again held out both his hands. Not knowing what to do—for, in my astonishment I had lost my self-possession—I reluctantly gave him my hands. He grasped them heartily, raised them to his lips, kissed them, and still held them.

"You acted nobly, my boy," said he. "Noble Pip! And I have never forgot it!"

At a change in his manner as if he were even going to embrace me, I laid a hand upon his breast and put him away.

"Stay!" said I. "Keep off! If you are grateful to me for what I did when I was a little child, I hope you have shown your gratitude by mending your way of life. If you have come here to thank me, it was not necessary. Still, however, you have found me out, there must be something good in the feeling that has brought you here, and I will not repulse you; but surely you must understand—I—"

My attention was so attracted by the singularity of his fixed look at me that the words died away on my tongue.

"You was a-saying," he observed, when we had confronted one another in silence, "that surely I must understand. What, surely must I understand?"

"That I cannot wish to renew that chance intercourse with you of long ago, under these different circumstances. I am glad to believe you have repented and recovered yourself. I am glad to tell you so. I am glad that, thinking I deserve to be thanked, you have come to thank me. But our ways are different ways, none the less. You are wet, and you look weary. Will you drink something before you go?"

He had replaced his neckerchief loosely, and had stood, keenly observant of me, biting a long end of it. "I think," he answered, still with the end at his mouth and still ob-

40

servant of me, "that I *will* drink (I thank you) afore I go." I made him some hot rum-and-water. When I put the glass to him, I saw with amazement that his eyes were full of tears.

"I hope," said I, "that you will not think I spoke harshly to you just now. I had no intention of doing it, and I am sorry for it if I did. I wish you well, and happy!"

As I put my glass to my lips, he stretched out his hand. I gave him mine, and then he drank, and drew his sleeve across his eyes and forehead.

"How are you living?" I asked him.

"I've been a sheep-farmer, stock-breeder, other trades besides, away in the New World,"[3] said he, "many a thousand mile of stormy water off from this."

"I hope you have done well."

"I've done wonderful well. No man has done nigh as well as me. I'm famous for it."

"I am glad to hear it."

"I hope to hear you say so, my dear boy."

Without stopping to try to understand those words or the tone in which they were spoken, I turned off to a point that had just come into my mind.

"Have you ever seen a messenger you once sent to me," I inquired, "since he undertook that trust?"

"Never set eyes upon him. I warn't likely to it."

"He came faithfully, and he brought me the two one-pound notes. I was a poor boy then, as you know, and to a poor boy they were a little fortune. But, like you, I have done well since, and you must let me pay them back. You can put them to some other poor boy's use." I took out my purse.

He watched me as I laid my purse upon the table and opened it, and he watched me as I separated two one-pound notes from its

---

**3. New World:** Australia.

contents. They were clean and new, and I spread them out and handed them over to him. Still watching me, he laid them one upon the other, folded them long-wise, gave them a twist, set fire to them at the lamp, and dropped the ashes into the tray.

"May I make so bold," he said then, "as ask you *how* you have done well, since you and me was out on them lone shivering marshes?"

He emptied his glass, got up, and stood at the side of the fire, with his heavy brown hand on the mantelshelf. He put a foot up to the bars, to dry and warm it, and the wet boot began to steam; but he neither looked at it, nor at the fire, but steadily looked at me. It was only now that I began to tremble.

When my lips had parted, I forced myself to tell him that I had been chosen to succeed to some property.

"Might a mere warmint ask what property?" said he.

I faltered, "I don't know."

"Might a mere warmint ask whose property?" said he.

I faltered again, "I don't know."

"Could I make a guess, I wonder," said the convict, "at your income since you come of age! As to the first figure, now. Five?"

With my heart beating like a heavy hammer of disordered action, I rose out of my chair, and stood with my hand upon the back of it, looking wildly at him.

"Concerning a guardian," he went on. "There ought to have been some guardian or such-like, whiles you was a minor. Some lawyer, maybe. As to the first letter of that lawyer's name, now. Would it be J?"

All the truth of my position came flashing on me, and its disappointments, dangers, disgraces, consequences of all kinds rushed in in such a multitude that I was borne down by them and had to struggle for every breath I drew. "Put it," he resumed, "as

41 **Discussion** What does Pip reveal about himself in his behavior toward the convict?

the employer of that lawyer whose name begun with a J, and might be Jaggers—put it as he had come over sea to Portsmouth,[4] and had landed there, and had wanted to come on to you. 'However, you have found me out,' you says just now. Well, however, did I find you out? Why, I wrote from Portsmouth to a person in London for particulars of your address. That person's name? Why, Wemmick."

I could not have spoken one word, though it had been to save my life. I stood, with a hand on the chair-back and a hand on my breast, where I seemed to be suffocating—I stood so, looking wildly at him, until I grasped at the chair, when the room began to surge and turn. He caught me, drew me to the sofa, put me up against the cushions, and bent on one knee before me; bringing the face that I now well remembered, and that I shuddered at, very near to mine.

"Yes, Pip, dear boy, I've made a gentleman on you! It's me wot has done it! I swore that time, sure as ever I earned a guinea, that guinea should go to you. I swore arterwards, sure as ever I spec'lated and got rich, you should get rich. I lived rough, that you should live smooth; I worked hard that you should be above work. What odds, dear boy? Do I tell it fur you to feel a obligation? Not a bit. I tell it fur you to know as that there hunted dunghill dog wot you kep life in got his head so high that he could make a gentleman—and, Pip, you're him!"

The abhorrence in which I held the man, the dread I had of him, the repugnance with which I shrank from him could not have been exceeded if he had been some terrible beast.

"Look'ee here, Pip. I'm your second father. You're my son—more to me nor any son. I've put away money, only for you to

___
4. **Portsmouth:** Seaport in south England.

spend. When I was a hired-out shepherd in a solitary hut, not seeing no faces but faces of sheep till I half-forgot wot men's and women's faces wos like, I see yourn. I drops my knife many a time in that hut when I was a-eating my dinner or my supper, and I says, 'Here's the boy again, a-looking at me whiles I eats and drinks!' I see you there a many times as plain as ever I see you on them misty marshes. 'Lord strike me dead!' I says each time—and I goes out in the open air to say it under the open heavens—'but wot, if I gets liberty and money, I'll make that boy a gentleman!' And I done it. Why, look at you, dear boy! Look at these here lodgings of yourn, fit for a lord! A lord? Ah! You shall show money with lords for wagers, and beat 'em!"

Again he took both my hands and put them to his lips, while my blood ran cold within me.

"Don't you mind talking, Pip," said he, "You ain't looked slowly forward to this as I have; you wosn't prepared for this, as I wos. But didn't you never think it might be me?"

"Oh, no, no, no," I returned. "Never, never!"

"Well, you see it *wos* me, and single-handed. Never a soul in it but my own self and Mr. Jaggers."

"Was there no one else?" I asked.

"No," said he, with a glance of surprise. "Who else should there be? And, dear boy, how good-looking you have growed! There's bright eyes somewheres—eh? Isn't there bright eyes somewheres, wot you love the thoughts on?"

O Estella, Estella!

"They shall be yourn, dear boy, if money can buy 'em. Not that a gentleman like you, so well set up as you, can't win 'em off of his own game; but money shall back you! Let me finish wot I was a-telling you, dear boy. From that there hut and that there hiring-out, I got money left me by my master (which died, and had been the same as me), and got my liberty and went for myself. In every single thing I went for, I went for you. 'Lord strike a blight upon it,' I says, wotever it was I went for, 'if it ain't for him!' It all prospered wonderful. As I giv' you to understand just now, I'm famous for it. It was the money left me, and the gains of the first few year, wot I sent home to Mr. Jaggers—all for you—when he first come arter you, agreeable to my letter."

O that he had never come! That he had left me at the forge—far from contented, yet, by comparison, happy!

"And then, dear boy, I held steady afore my mind that I would for certain come one day and see my boy, and make myself known to him, on his own ground."

He laid his hand on my shoulder. I shuddered at the thought that for anything I knew, his hand might be stained with blood.

"Where will you put me?" he asked presently. "I must be put somewheres, dear boy."

"To sleep?" said I.

"Yes. And to sleep long and sound," he answered, "for I've been sea-tossed and sea-washed, months and months."

"My friend and companion," said I, rising from the sofa, "is absent; you must have his room."

"He won't come back tomorrow, will he?"

"No," said I, answering almost mechanically, "not tomorrow."

"Because, look'ee here, dear boy," he said, dropping his voice, and laying a long finger on my breast in an impressive manner, "caution is necessary."

"How do you mean, caution?"

"It's death!"

"What's death?"

"I was sent for life. It's death to come back. There's been overmuch coming back of late years, and I should of a certainty be hanged if took."

Nothing was needed but this; the wretched man, after loading me with his wretched gold and silver chains for years, had risked his life to come to me, and I held it there in my keeping!

My first care was to close the shutters, so that no light might be seen from without, and then to close and make fast the doors. While I did so, he stood at the table drinking rum and eating biscuit.

When I had gone into Herbert's room, and had shut off any other communication between it and the staircase than through the room in which our conversation had been held, I asked him if he would go to bed. He said yes, but asked me for some of my "gentleman's linen" to put on in the morning. I brought it out, and laid it ready for him, and my blood again ran cold when he again took me by both hands to give me good night.

I got away from him, without knowing how I did it, and mended the fire in the room where we had been together, and sat down by it, afraid to go to bed. For an hour or more, I remained too stunned to think; and it was not until I began to think that I began fully to know how wrecked I was.

Miss Havisham's intentions towards me, all a mere dream; Estella not designed for me; I only suffered in Satis House as a convenience, a sting for the greedy relations, a model with a mechanical heart to practice on when no other practice was at hand; those were the first smarts I had. But, sharpest and deepest pain of all—it was for the convict, guilty of I knew not what crimes, that I had deserted Joe.

In every rage of wind and rush of rain, I heard pursuers. Twice I could have sworn there was a knocking and whispering at the outer door. With these fears upon me, I began either to imagine or recall that I had had mysterious warnings of this man's ap-

43 **Discussion** Although not part of the action of this novel, the tale Pip's benefactor tells about his life is a dramatic story in itself. What are some important details in this account? What is Pip's reaction to the story?

44 **Discussion** Why would the convict risk death by coming to see Pip?

45 **Discussion** Why is Pip so distressed by what he has learned?

46 **Discussion** What is the "sharpest and deepest pain of all" when Pip realizes that Miss Havisham is not his benefactor?

*Great Expectations*  877

## Humanities Note

Fine art, *Adeline, Seventh Countess of Cardigan*, 1858-1868, by Richard Buckner. The British painter Richard Buckner (active 1840-1879) specialized in full-length portraits.

*Adeline, 7th Countess of Cardigan* is an unusual portrait of a young woman in an evening dress. With her graceful hands, tiny feet, lacy gown, and shy demeanor, she is the embodiment of youthful loveliness. The romance of the balcony setting is accentuated by moonlight.

You might want to use the following questions:

1. Is this young woman as cold and callous as Estella? Explain.
2. Compare and contrast this young woman with the subject of Whistler's *Symphony in White, No. 1*, page 851.

**ADELINE, SEVENTH COUNTESS OF CARDIGAN**
*Richard Buckner*
From the collection of Edmund Brudenell, Esq.

878    *The Novel*

proach. That for weeks gone by I had passed faces in the streets which I had thought like his.

Then came the reflection that I had seen him with my childish eyes to be a desperately violent man; that I had heard that other convict reiterate that he had tried to murder him. Out of such remembrances I brought into the light of the fire, a half-formed terror that it might not be safe to be shut up there with him in the dead of the wild solitary night. This dilated until it filled the room, and impelled me to take a candle and go in and look at my dreadful burden.

He had rolled a handkerchief round his head, and his face was set and lowering in his sleep. But he was asleep, and quietly, too, though he had a pistol lying on the pillow. Assured of this, I softly removed the key to the outside of his door, and turned it on him before I again sat down by the fire. Gradually I slipped from the chair and lay on the floor. When I awoke without having parted in my sleep with the perception of my wretchedness, the clocks of the eastward churches were striking five, the candles were wasted out, the fire was dead, and the wind and rain intensified the thick black darkness.

THIS IS THE END OF THE SECOND STAGE
OF PIP'S EXPECTATIONS

## Chapter 39

The impossibility of keeping my dreaded visitor concealed in the chambers was self-evident. It could not be done, and the attempt to do it would inevitably engender suspicion. True, I had no one in my service now, but I was looked after by an inflammatory old female, assisted by an animated ragbag whom she called her niece, and to keep a room secret from them would be to invite curiosity and exaggeration. So I resolved to announce in the morning that my uncle had unexpectedly come from the country.

This course I decided on while I was yet groping about in the darkness for the means of getting a light. Then in groping my way down the black staircase, I fell over something, and that something was a man crouching in a corner.

As the man made no answer when I asked him what he did there, but eluded my touch in silence, I ran to the lodge and urged the watchman to come quickly, telling him of the incident on the way back. We examined the staircase from the bottom to the top and found no one there.

It troubled me that there should have been a lurker on the stairs, on that night of all nights in the year, and I asked the watchman whether he had admitted at his gate any gentleman who had perceptibly been dining out?

"The night being so bad, sir," said the watchman, "uncommon few have come in at my gate. Besides them three gentlemen that I have named, I don't call to mind another since about eleven o'clock, when a stranger asked for you."

"My uncle," I muttered. "Yes."

"You saw him, sir?"

"Yes. Oh, yes."

"Likewise the person with him?"

"Person with him!" I repeated. "What sort of person?"

The watchman had not particularly noticed; he should say a working person; to the best of his belief, he had a dust-colored kind of clothes on, under a dark coat.

My mind was much troubled by these two circumstances taken together. I lighted my fire, which burnt with a raw pale flare at that time of the morning, and fell into a doze

47 **Discussion** At the end of the second stage of Pip's "great expectations," what new incidents does he dread?

48 **Critical Thinking and Reading** What is Pip's reaction on learning that there was a man "with" his uncle? What might be the significance of this information?

*Great Expectations* 879

before it. I seemed to have been dozing a whole night when the clocks struck six. As there was full an hour and a half between me and daylight, I dozed again; now waking up uneasily, with prolix conversations about nothing, in my ears; now making thunder of the wind in the chimney; at length falling off into a profound sleep from which the daylight woke me with a start.

The old woman and the niece came in and testified surprise at sight of me and the fire. To whom I imparted how my uncle had come in the night and was then asleep, and how the breakfast preparations were to be modified accordingly.

By-and-by, his door opened and he came out. I could not bring myself to bear the sight of him, and I thought he had a worse look by daylight.

"I do not even know," said I, speaking low as he took his seat at the table, "by what name to call you. I have given out that you are my uncle."

"That's it, dear boy! Call me uncle."

"You assumed some name, I suppose, on board ship?"

"Yes, dear boy. I took the name of Provis."

"Do you mean to keep that name?"

"Why, yes, dear boy, it's as good as another—unless you'd like another."

"What is your real name?" I asked him in a whisper.

"Magwitch," he answered, in the same tone; "chrisen'd Abel."

"What were you brought up to be?"

"A warmint, dear boy."

He answered quite seriously, and used the words as if it denoted some profession.

"When you came in at the gate and asked the watchman the way here, had you any one with you?"

"With me? No, dear boy."

"But there was some one there?"

"I didn't take particular notice," he said dubiously, "not knowing the ways of the place. But I think there *was* a person, too, come in alonger me."

"Are you known in London?"

"I hope not!" said he.

"Were you known in London, once?"

"Not over and above, dear boy. I was in the provinces mostly."

"Were you—tried—in London?"

"Which time?" said he, with a sharp look.

"The last time."

He nodded. "First knowed Mr. Jaggers that way. Jaggers was for me."

It was on my lips to ask him what he was tried for, but he took up a knife, gave it a flourish, and with the words, "And what I done is worked out and paid for!" fell to at his breakfast.

I found that I was beginning slowly to settle down to the contemplation of my condition. What I was chained to, and how heavily, became intelligible to me, as I heard his hoarse voice, and sat looking up at his furrowed bald head with its iron-gray hair at the sides.

He took out of his pocket a great thick pocketbook, bursting with papers, and tossed it on the table.

"There's something worth spending in that there book, dear boy. It's yourn. All I've got ain't mine; it's yourn. Don't you be afeered on it. There's more where that come from. I've come to the old country fur to see my gentleman spend his money *like* a gentleman. That'll be my pleasure. *My* pleasure 'ull be fur to see him do it."

"Stop!" said I, almost in a frenzy of fear and dislike, "I want to speak to you. I want to know what is to be done. I want to know how you are to be kept out of danger, how long you are going to stay, what projects you have."

"Look'ee here, Pip," said he, "I forgot myself half a minute ago. What I said was low; that's what it was; low. Look'ee here, Pip. Look over it. I ain't a-going to be low."

"First," I resumed, half-groaning, "what precautions can be taken against your being recognized and seized?"

"Well, dear boy, the danger ain't so great. Without I was informed agen, the danger ain't so much to signify. There's Jaggers, and there's Wemmick, and there's you. Who else is there to inform?"

"Is there no chance person who might identify you in the street?" said I.

"Well," he returned, "there ain't many. Still, look'ee here, Pip. If the danger had been fifty times as great, I should ha' come to see you, mind you, just the same."

"And how long do you remain?"

"How long?" said he. "I'm not a-going back. I've come for good."

"Where are you to live?" said I. "What is to be done with you? Where will you be safe?"

"Dear boy," he returned, "there's disguising wigs can be bought for money, and there's hair powder, and spectacles, and black clothes—shorts and what not. As to the where and how of living, dear boy, give me your own opinions on it."

It appeared to me that I could do no better than secure him some quiet lodging hard by, of which he might take possession when Herbert returned—whom I expected in two or three days. That the secret must be confided to Herbert as a matter of unavoidable necessity, even if I could have put the immense relief I should derive from sharing it with him out of the question, was plain to me. But it was by no means so plain to Mr. Provis (I resolved to call him by that name), who reserved his consent to Herbert's participation until he should have seen him and formed a favorable judgment of his physiognomy. "And even then, dear boy," said he, pulling a greasy little clasped black Testament out of his pocket, "we'll have him on his oath."

There being to my knowledge a respectable lodginghouse in Essex Street, the back of which looked into the Temple, and was almost within hail of my windows, I first of all repaired to that house, and was so fortunate as to secure the second floor for my uncle, Mr. Provis. I then went from shop to shop, making such purchases as were necessary to a change in his appearance. This business transacted, I turned my face, on my own account, to Little Britain. Mr. Jaggers was at his desk, but, seeing me enter, got up immediately and stood before his fire.

"Now, Pip," said he, "be careful."

"I will, sir," I returned.

"Don't commit yourself," said Mr. Jaggers, "and don't commit any one. You understand—any one. Don't tell me anything; I don't want to know anything; I am not curious."

Of course I saw that he knew the man was come.

"I merely want, Mr. Jaggers," said I, "to assure myself what I have been told, is true."

Mr. Jaggers nodded. "But did you say 'told' or 'informed'?" he asked me. "Told would seem to imply verbal communication. You can't have verbal communication with a man in New South Wales,[1] you know."

"I will say informed, Mr. Jaggers."

"Good."

"I have been informed by a person named Abel Magwitch that he is the benefactor so long unknown to me."

---

**1. New South Wales:** A state in southeast Australia.

**50 Discussion** What does Provis believe will be an effective disguise?

**51 Reading Strategy** Summarize the discussion between Mr. Jaggers and Pip.

50

51

*Great Expectations* 881

52 **Discussion** What is the admission Pip makes to Mr. Jaggers about his "mistake"?

53 **Discussion** What advice does Mr. Jaggers give in regard to "appearance" versus "reality" after Pip explains his mistaken conviction that Miss Havisham was his benefactress?

54 **Discussion** What were the cautions Mr. Jaggers told Pip he had communicated to Provis in Australia?

55 **Discussion** How did Provis know how to find Pip's lodgings in London?

"That is the man," said Mr. Jaggers, "—in New South Wales."

"And only he?" said I.

"And only he," said Mr. Jaggers.

"I am not so unreasonable, sir, as to think you at all responsible for my mistakes and wrong conclusions, but I always supposed it was Miss Havisham."

"As you say, Pip," returned Mr. Jaggers, "I am not at all responsible for that."

"And yet it looked so like it, sir," I pleaded with a downcast heart.

"Not a particle of evidence, Pip," said Mr. Jaggers. "Take nothing on its looks; take everything on evidence. There's no better rule."

"I have no more to say," said I. "I have verified my information, and there's an end."

"And Magwitch—in New South Wales—having at last disclosed himself," said Mr. Jaggers, "you will comprehend, Pip, how rigidly throughout my communication with you I have always adhered to the strict line of fact.

"I communicated to Magwitch—in New South Wales—when he first wrote to me—from New South Wales—the caution that he must not expect me ever to deviate from the strict line of fact. I also communicated to him another caution. He appeared to me to have obscurely hinted in his letter at some distant idea of seeing you in England here. I cautioned him that I must hear no more of that; that he was not at all likely to obtain a pardon; that he was expatriated[2] for the term of his natural life; and that his presenting himself in this country would be an act of felony, rendering him liable to the extreme penalty of the law. I gave Magwitch that caution," said Mr. Jaggers, looking hard at me; "I wrote it to New South Wales. He guided himself by it, no doubt."

---

2. **expatriated** (eks pā' trē āt' əd) v.: Exiled.

"No doubt," said I.

"I have been informed by Wemmick," pursued Mr. Jaggers, "that he has received a letter, under date Portsmouth, from a colonist of the name of Purvis, or—"

"Or Provis," I suggested.

"Or Provis—thank you, Pip. Perhaps it *is* Provis? Perhaps you know it's Provis?"

"Yes," said I.

"You know it's Provis. A letter, under date Portsmouth, from a colonist of the name of Provis, asking for the particulars of your address, on behalf of Magwitch. Wemmick sent him the particulars, I understand, by return of post. Probably it is through Provis that you have received the explanation of Magwitch—in New South Wales?"

"It came through Provis," I replied.

"Good day, Pip," said Mr. Jaggers, offering his hand; "glad to have seen you. In writing by post to Magwitch—in New South Wales—or in communicating with him through Provis, have the goodness to mention that the particulars and vouchers of our long account shall be sent to you, together with the balance; for there is still a balance remaining. Good day, Pip!"

We shook hands, and he looked hard at me as long as he could see me. Wemmick was out, and though he had been at his desk he could have done nothing for me. I went straight back to the Temple, where I found the terrible Provis.

Next day the clothes I had ordered all came home, and he put them on. Whatever he put on became him less (it dismally seemed to me) than what he had worn before. To my thinking there was something in him that made it hopeless to attempt to disguise him. The more I dressed him, and the better I dressed him, the more he looked like the slouching fugitive on the marshes.

Words cannot tell what a sense I had of the dreadful mystery that he was to me.

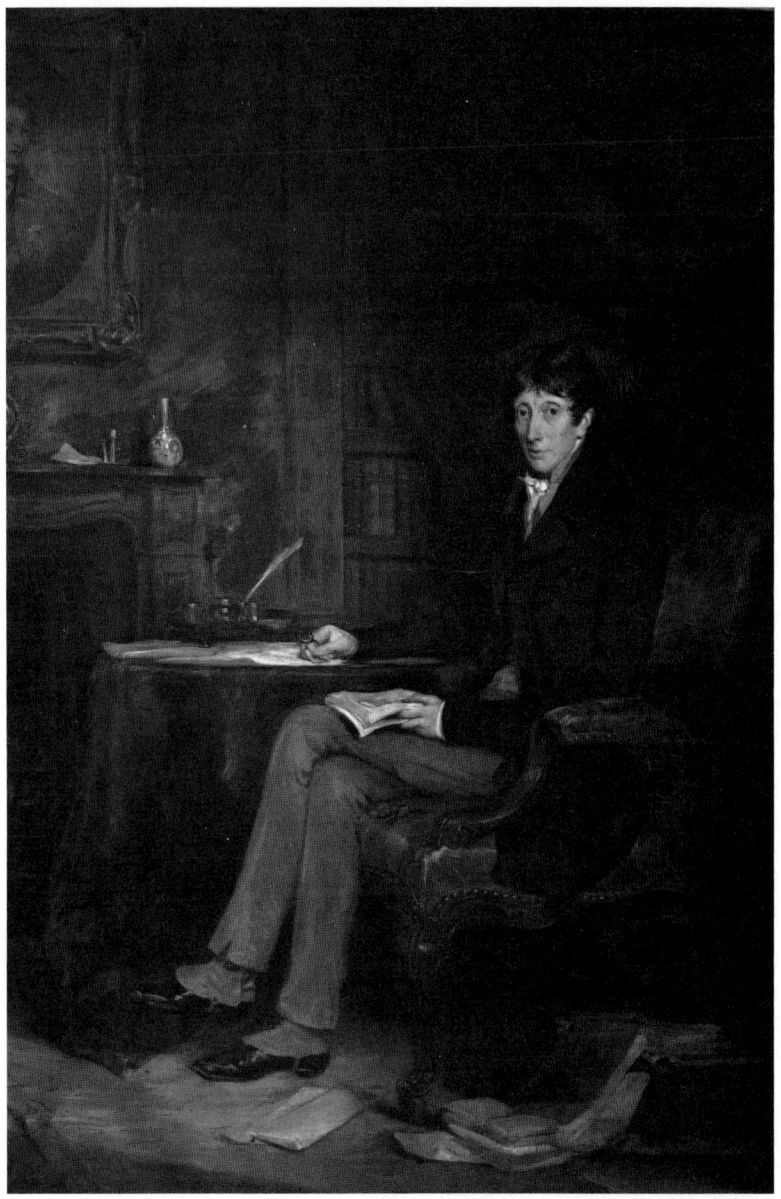

**HENRY, LORD MONTAGUE OF BROUGHTON**
*Sir Francis Grant*
National Galleries of Scotland

*Great Expectations* 883

## Humanities Note

Fine art, *Henry, Lord Montague of Broughton,* by Sir Francis Grant. The British painter Sir Frances Grant (1803–1878) was the fourth son of the Laird of Kilgraston. He took lessons from painter John Ferneley and exhibited his first picture at the age of thirty-six. Immediately successful, he was soon in demand as a fashionable portrait painter. He was named the President of the Royal Academy in 1866.

This portrait of *Henry, Lord Montague of Broughton* is painted with the style and naturalness that characterize Grant's work

You might want to have students consider the following questions:

1. What qualities do you see in young Lord Montague's face?
2. Do you think that Pip has come to resemble an upperclass gentleman like this one? Why or why not?

**56 Discussion** What nagging thought prevents Pip from trusting Provis?

**57 Discussion** How is Provis prepared to protect himself against intruders?

When he fell asleep of an evening, with his knotted hands clenching the sides of the easy chair, and his bald head tattooed with deep wrinkles falling forward on his breast, I would sit and look at him, wondering what he had done, and loading him with all the crimes in the calendar, until the impulse was powerful on me to start up and fly from him. Every hour so increased my abhorrence of him that I even think I might have yielded to this impulse in the first agonies of being so haunted, notwithstanding all he had done for me and the risk he ran, but for the knowledge that Herbert must soon come back.

One evening when dinner was over and I had dropped into a slumber quite worn out—for my nights had been agitated and my rest broken by fearful dreams—I was roused by the welcome footstep on the staircase. Provis, who had been asleep, too, staggered up at the noise I made, and in an instant I saw his jackknife shining in his hand.

"Quiet! It's Herbert!" I said, and Herbert came bursting in.

"Handel, my dear fellow, how are you, and again how are you, and again how are you? I seem to have been gone a twelvemonth! Why, so I must have been, for you have grown quite thin and pale! Handel, my—Halloa! I beg your pardon."

He was stopped in his running on and in his shaking hands with me, by seeing Provis. Provis, regarding him with a fixed attention, was slowly putting up his jackknife, and groping in another pocket for something else.

"Herbert, my dear friend," said I, shutting the double doors, while Herbert stood staring and wondering, "something very strange has happened. This is—a visitor of mine."

"It's all right, dear boy!" said Provis, coming forward, with his little clasped black book, and then addressing himself to Herbert. "Take it in your right hand. Lord strike you dead on the spot, if ever you split[3] in any way sumever. Kiss it!"

"Do so, as he wishes it," I said to Herbert. So Herbert, looking at me with a friendly uneasiness and amazement, complied, and Provis immediately shaking hands with him, said, "Now, you're on your oath, you know. And never believe me on mine, if Pip sha'n't make a gentleman on you!"

## Chapter 40

In vain should I attempt to describe the astonishment and disquiet of Herbert when he and I and Provis sat down before the fire, and I recounted the whole of the secret. Enough that I saw my own feelings reflected in Herbert's face, and, not least among them, my repugnance towards the man who had done so much for me.

"Look'ee here, Pip's comrade," Provis said to Herbert, after having discoursed for some time, "I know very well that once since I come back—for half a minute—I've been low. I said to Pip I knowed as how I had been low. But don't you fret yourself on that score. I ain't made Pip a gentleman, and Pip ain't a-goin to make you a gentleman, not fur me not to know what's due to ye both."

Herbert said, "Certainly," but looked as if there were no specific consolation in this, and remained perplexed and dismayed. We were anxious for the time when he would go to his lodging, and leave us together, but he was evidently jealous of leaving us together, and sat late. It was midnight before I took him round to Essex Street, and saw him

---

**3. split:** Slang for "tell."

safely in at his own dark door. When it closed upon him, I experienced the first moment of relief I had known since the night of his arrival.

Herbert received me with open arms, and I had never felt before so blessedly what it is to have a friend. When he had spoken some sound words of sympathy and encouragement, we sat down to consider the question, What was to be done?

"My poor dear Handel," said Herbert, "I am too stunned to think."

"So was I, Herbert, when the blow first fell. Still, something must be done. He is intent upon various new expenses—horses, and carriages, and lavish appearances of all kinds. He must be stopped somehow."

"You mean that you can't accept—"

"How can I?" I interposed, as Herbert paused. "Think of him! Look at him!"

An involuntary shudder passed over both of us.

"Then," said I, "after all, stopping short here, never taking another penny from him, think what I owe him already! Then again, I am heavily in debt—very heavily for me, who have now no expectations—and I have been bred to no calling, and I am fit for nothing."

"Well, well, well!" Herbert remonstrated. "Don't say fit for nothing."

"What am I fit for? I know only one thing that I am fit for, and that is to go for a soldier."

"My dear Handel," said he presently, "soldiering won't do. You would be infinitely better in Clarriker's house, small as it is. I am working up towards a partnership, you know."

Poor fellow! He little suspected with whose money.

I said to Herbert that even if Provis were recognized and taken, I should be wretched as the cause, however innocently. Yes; even though I was so wretched in having him at large and near me, and even though I would far rather have worked at the forge all the days of my life than I would ever have come to this!

But there was no staving off the question, What was to be done?

"The first and the main thing to be done," said Herbert, "is to get him out of England. You will have to go with him, and then he may be induced to go."

"But get him where I will, could I prevent his coming back?"

"My good Handel, is it not obvious that, with Newgate in the next street, there must be far greater hazard in your breaking your mind to him and making him reckless here than elsewhere. If a pretext to get him away could be made out of that other convict, or out of anything else in his life, now."

Herbert got up, and linked his arm in mine, and we slowly walked to and fro together, studying the carpet.

"Handel," said Herbert, stopping, "you feel convinced that you can take no further benefits from him, do you?"

"Fully. Surely you would, too, if you were in my place?"

"And you feel convinced that you must break with him?"

"Herbert, can you ask me?"

"Then you must get him out of England before you stir a finger to extricate yourself. That done, extricate yourself, in Heaven's name, and we'll see it out together, dear old boy."

It was a comfort to shake hands upon it, and walk up and down again, with only that done.

"Now Herbert," said I, "with reference to gaining some knowledge of his history. There is but one way that I know of. I must ask him point-blank."

58 **Discussion** How does Herbert assist Pip?

59 **Discussion** What does Pip plan to do about the riches Provis has offered him?

60 **Discussion** What plans do Pip and Herbert make to extricate Pip from his dilemma?

**61 Clarification** The phrase "coming out strong" means "spending lavishly."

**62 Discussion** As Provis starts his story, he keeps repeating a certain phrase. What is the phrase? What is the effect of this repetition?

**63 Clarification** "Epsom races" refers to a famous race track, Epsom Downs, in Surrey, England, where the Derby is held annually.

**64 Discussion** What kind of revenge would Provis take if he could get his hands on Compeyson?

"Yes. Ask him," said Herbert, "when we sit at breakfast in the morning." For, he had said, on taking leave of Herbert, that he would come to breakfast with us.

He came round at the appointed time, took out his jackknife, and sat down to his meal. He was full of plans "for his gentleman's coming out strong, and like a gentleman," and urged me to begin speedily upon the pocketbook, which he had left in my possession. When he had made an end of his breakfast, and was wiping his knife on his leg, I said to him, without a word of preface:

"After you were gone last night, I told my friend of the struggle that the soldiers found you engaged in on the marshes, when we came up. You remember?"

"Remember!" said he. "I think so!"

"We want to know something about that man—and about you. It is strange to know no more about either, and particularly you, than I was able to tell last night. Is not this as good a time as another for our knowing more?"

"Well!" he said, after consideration. "You're on your oath, you know, Pip's comrade?"

"Assuredly," replied Herbert.

"And look'ee here! Wotever I done is worked out and paid for," he insisted again.

"So be it."

He spread a hand on each knee, and, after turning an angry eye on the fire for a few silent moments, looked around at us and said what follows.

## Chapter 41

"Dear boy and Pip's comrade. I am not a-going fur to tell you my life, like a song or a storybook. But to give it you short and handy, I'll put it at once into a mouthful of English. In jail and out of jail, in jail and out of jail, in jail and out of jail. There, you've got it. That's *my* life pretty much, down to such times as I got shipped off, arter Pip stood my friend.

"When I was a ragged little creetur as much to be pitied as ever I see, I got the name of being hardened. 'This is a terrible hardened one,' they says to prison wisitors, picking out me. 'May be said to live in jails, this boy.' They always went on agen me about the devil. But what the devil was I to do? I must put something into my stomach, mustn't I?—Howsomever, I'm a-getting low, and I know what's due. Dear boy and Pip's comrade, don't you be afeerd of me being low.

"Tramping, begging, thieving, working sometimes when I could—though that warn't as often as you may think, till you put the question whether you would ha' been over-ready to give me work yourselves—a bit of a poacher,[1] a bit of a laborer, a bit of a waggoner, a bit of a haymaker, a bit of a hawker,[2] a bit of most things that don't pay and lead to trouble, I got to be a man. A deserting soldier in a traveler's rest, what lay hid up to the chin under a lot of taturs, learnt me to read; and a traveling giant what signed his name at a penny a time learnt me to write. I warn't locked up often now as formerly, but I wore out my good share of key metal still.

"At Epsom races, a matter of over twenty year ago, I got acquainted wi' a man whose skull I'd crack wi' this poker, like the claw of a lobster, if I'd got it on this hob. His right name was Compeyson; and that's the man, dear boy, what you see me a-pounding in the ditch.

"He set up fur a gentleman, this Compey-

---

**1. poacher** (pōch′ ər) *n*.: Person who hunts or fishes illegally on someone else's property.
**2. hawker** (hôk′ ər) *n*.: Peddler.

son, and he'd been to a public boarding school and had learning. He was a smooth one to talk, and was a dab at the ways of gentlefolks. He was good-looking, too.

"Compeyson took me on to be his man and pardner. And what was Compeyson's business in which we was to go pardners? Compeyson's business was the swindling, handwriting forging, stolen bank note passing, and such-like. All sorts of traps as Compeyson could set with his head, and keep his own legs out of and get the profits from and let another man in for, was Compeyson's business!

"There was another in with Compeyson, as was called Arthur—not as being so chrisen'd, but as a surname. Him and Compeyson had been in a bad thing with a rich lady some years afore, and they'd made a pot of money by it; but Compeyson betted and gamed, and he'd have run through the king's taxes. So Arthur was a-dying and a-dying poor and with the horrors on him, and Compeyson's wife (which Compeyson kicked mostly) was a-having pity on him when she could, and Compeyson was a-having pity on nothing and nobody.

"I mighta took warning by Arthur, but I didn't; and I won't pretend I was partick'ler—for where 'ud be the good on it, dear boy and comrade? So I begun wi' Compeyson, and a poor tool I was in his hands. Arthur lived at the top of Compeyson's house (over nigh Brentford, it was), and Compeyson kept a careful account agen him for board and lodging, in case he should ever get better to work it out. But Arthur soon settled the account. The second or third time as ever I see him, he come a-tearing down into Compeyson's parlor late at night, in only a flannel gown, with his hair all in a sweat, and he says to Compeyson's wife, 'Sally, she really is upstairs alonger me, now, and I can't get rid of her. She's all in white,' he says, 'wi' white flowers in her hair, and she's awful mad, and she's got a shroud hanging over her arm, and she says she'll put it on me at five in the morning.'

"Compeyson's wife and me took him up to bed agen, and he raved most dreadful. 'Why look at her!' he cries out. 'She a-shaking the shroud at me!'

"Compeyson's wife, being used to him, give him something to get the horrors off, and by-and-by he quieted. 'Oh, she's gone! Has her keeper been for her?' he says. 'Yes,' says Compeyson's wife.

"He rested pretty quiet till it might want a few minutes of five, and then he starts up with a scream, and screams out, 'Here she is! She's got the shroud again. Don't let her throw it over my shoulders. Don't let her lift me up to get it round me. She's lifting me up. Keep me down!' Then he lifted himself up hard, and was dead.

"Compeyson took it easy as a good riddance for both sides, and him and me was soon busy.

"Not to go into the things that Compeyson planned, and I done—which 'ud take a week—I'll simply say to you, dear boy, and Pip's comrade, that that man got me into such nets as made me his slave. I was always in debt to him, always under his thumb, always a-working, always a-getting into danger. He was younger than me, but he'd got craft, and he'd got learning, and he overmatched me five hundred times told and no mercy. My missis as I had the hard time wi'—Stop though! I ain't brought *her* in—

"There ain't no need to go into it," he said, looking round. "The time wi' Compeyson was a'most as hard a time as ever I had; that said, all's said. Did I tell you as I was tried, alone, for misdemeanor,[3] while with Compeyson?"

---

**3. misdemeanor** (mis' di mēn' ər) *n.*: Minor offense.

**65 Clarification** A "public boarding school" in England would be a private boarding school in America.

**66 Discussion** According to Provis, what kind of man is Compeyson?

**67 Discussion** How does Provis describe his relationship with Compeyson?

**Discussion** What strategy did Compeyson use to implicate Provis as the mastermind of the crime?

I answered, No.

"Well!" he said, "I *was*, and got convicted. As to took up[4] on suspicion, that was twice or three times in the four or five year that it lasted; but evidence was wanting. At last, me and Compeyson was both committed for felony—on a charge of putting stolen notes in circulation—and there was other charges behind. Compeyson says to me, 'Separate defenses, no communication,'[5] and that was all. And I was so miserable poor that I sold all the clothes I had, except what hung on my back, afore I could get Jaggers.

"When we was put in the dock,[6] I noticed first of all what a gentleman Compeyson looked, wi' his curly hair and his black clothes and his white pocket handkercher, and what a common sort of a wretch I looked. When the evidence was giv in the box,[7] I noticed how it was always me that had come for'ard, and could be swore to, how it was always me that the money had been paid to, how it was always me that had seemed to work the thing and get the profit. But, when the defense come on, then I see the plan plainer; for, says the counselor for Compeyson, 'My lord and gentlemen, here you has afore you, side by side, two persons as your eyes can separate wide; one, the younger, well brought up, who will be spoke to as such; one, the elder, ill brought up, who will be spoke to as such; one, the younger, seldom if ever seen in these here transactions, and only suspected; t'other, the elder, always seen in 'em and always wi' his guilt brought home.' And such-like. And warn't it me as had been tried afore, and as

---

4. **took up:** Arrested.
5. **separate . . . communication:** They would use different lawyers and not speak to each other about the trial.
6. **dock** *n.*: Place where the accused stands or sits in court.
7. **box** *n.*: Witness stand.

had been know'd up hill and down dale in Bridewells and Lockups? And when it come to speechmaking, warn't it Compeyson as could speak to 'em wi' his face dropping every now and then into his white pocket handkercher! and wi' verses in his speech, too—and warn't it me as could only say, 'Gentlemen, this man at my side is a most precious rascal'? And when the verdict come, warn't it Compeyson as was recommended to mercy on account of good character and bad company, and giving up all the information he could agen me, and warn't it me as got never a word but guilty? And when I says to Compeyson, 'Once out of this court, I'll smash that face of yourn!' ain't it Compeyson as prays the judge to be protected. And when we're sentenced, ain't it him as gets seven year, and me fourteen?

"I had said to Compeyson that I'd smash that face of his, and I swore Lord smash mine! to do it. We was in the same prison ship, but I couldn't get at him for long, though I tried. At last I come behind him and hit him on the cheek to turn him round and get a smashing one at him, when I was seen and seized. The black hole of that ship warn't a strong one, to a judge of black holes that could swim and dive. I escaped to the shore, and I was a-hiding among the graves there, envying them as was in 'em and all over, when I first see my boy!

"By my boy, I was giv to understand as Compeyson was out on them marshes, too. Upon my soul, I half-believe he escaped in his terror, to get quit of me, not knowing it was me as had got ashore. I hunted him down. I smashed his face. 'And now,' says I, 'as the worst thing I can do, caring nothing for myself, I'll drag you back.' And I'd have swum off, towing him by the hair, if it had come to that, and I'd a-got him aboard without the soldiers."

"Is he dead?" I asked after a silence.

## Grammar in Action

The term *dialect* refers to the speech of a particular group or class of people or of people from a particular region. Dialect differs from standard speech, the speech of the majority of educated people in a particular time or place. Read these examples from the novel. Which passage is written in dialect? How do you know?

"When I was a ragged little creetur as much to be pitied as ever I see, I got the name of being hardened. 'This is a terrible hardened one,' they says to prison wisitors, picking out me. 'May be said to live in jails, this boy.' They went on agen me about the devil."

"Then you must get him out of England before you stir a finger to extricate yourself. That done, then extricate yourself, in Heaven's name, and we'll see it out together, dear old boy."

Notice that in the first passage, which is written in dialect, the author makes use of a number of techniques to convey the speech of the character. Word choice, grammar, sentence structure, spelling, and pronunciation are all different from those

"Is who dead, dear boy?"

"Compeyson."

"He hopes *I* am, if he's alive, you may be sure," with a fierce look. "I never heard no more of him."

Herbert had been writing with his pencil in the cover of a book. He softly pushed the book over to me, and I read in it:

69 | Young Havisham's name was Arthur. Compeyson is the man who professed to be Miss Havisham's lover.

## Chapter 42

A new fear had been engendered in my mind by his narrative. If Compeyson were alive and should discover his return, I could hardly doubt the consequence. Compeyson stood in mortal fear of him and would release himself for good from a dreaded enemy by the safe means of becoming an informer.

Never had I breathed, and never would I breathe—or so I resolved—a word of Estella to Provis. But I said to Herbert that before I could go abroad, I must see both Estella and Miss Havisham. This was when we were left alone on the night of the day when Provis told us his story. I resolved to go out to Richmond next day, and I went.

On my presenting myself at Mrs. Brandley's, Estella's maid was called to tell me that Estella had gone into the country. Where? To Satis House, as usual. Not as usual, I said, for she had never yet gone there without me; when was she coming back? The answer was that her maid believed she was only coming back at all for a little while. I could make nothing of this, and I went home again in complete discomfiture.

Next day, I had the meanness to feign that I was under a binding promise to go down to Joe; but I was capable of almost any

meanness towards Joe or his name. Provis was to be strictly careful while I was gone, and Herbert was to take charge of him.

Having thus cleared the way for my expedition to Miss Havisham's, I set off by the early morning coach before it was yet light, and was out in the open country road when the day came creeping on, halting and whimpering and shivering, and wrapped in patches of cloud and rags of mist, like a beggar. When we drove up to the Blue Boar after a drizzly ride, whom should I see come out under the gateway, toothpick in hand, to look at the coach, but Bentley Drummle!

As he pretended not to see me, I pretended not to see him. It was a very lame pretense on both sides; the lamer because we both went into the coffee-room, where he had just finished his breakfast, and where I had ordered mine. It was poisonous to me to see him in the town, for I very well knew why he had come there.

I sat at my table while he stood before the fire. By degrees it became an enormous injury to me that he stood before the fire. And I got up, determined to have my share of it. I had to put my hands behind his legs for the poker when I went up to the fireplace to stir the fire, but still pretended not to know him.

"Is this a cut?"[1] said Mr. Drummle.

"Oh?" said I, poker in hand; "it's you, is it? How do you do? I was wondering who it was, who kept the fire off."

"You have just come down?" said Mr. Drummle.

"Yes," said I.

"Beastly place," said Drummle. "Your part of the country, I think?"

"Yes," I assented. "I am told it's very like your Shropshire."

"Not in the least like it," said Drummle.

"Do you stay here long?"

_____

**1. cut** *n*.: Act of snubbing someone.

70

69 **Discussion** What is the significance of this news?

70 **Critical Thinking and Reading** What metaphor does Dickens use to describe the dawn? Why do you think he chose to use such a figure of speech at this point in the story?

found in standard English. These are not mistakes, but rather part of a deliberate effort by the author to convey a particular type of speech.

Dialect adds realism, liveliness, color, and often humor to language. Try to imagine this novel without the dialect. What would be lost?

**Student Activity 1.** Find another passage of dialect in the novel and practice reading it aloud. Read your example aloud to a classmate and discuss ways to improve it.

**Student Activity 2.** Listen as volunteers read aloud their choices of passages written in dialect. After each reading discuss with your classmates and teacher what the passage contributes to characterization and plot.

71 **Discussion** Pip has an unexpected encounter with Drummle. How do they act toward each other?

72 **Reading Strategy** The plot becomes more and more entangled as characters reappear in different situations. As students read this chapter, have them predict what will happen.

73 **Discussion** Why does Pip believe that Estella has guessed his news before he has disclosed it?

71

"Can't say," answered Mr. Drummle. "Do you?"

"Can't say," said I.

"I am going out for a ride in the saddle," said Drummle. "I mean to explore those marshes for amusement. Out-of-the-way villages there, they tell me. Curious little public houses—and smithies—and that. Waiter!"

"Yes, sir."

"Is that horse of mine ready?"

"Brought round to the door, sir."

"I say. Look here, you sir. The lady won't ride today; the weather won't do."

"Very good, sir."

"And I don't dine, because I am going to dine at the lady's."

"Very good, sir."

Then Drummle glanced at me, with an insolent triumph on his great-jowled face that cut me to the heart.

After Drummle had left the room, I saw him through the window, seizing his horse's mane, and mounting in his blundering brutal manner, and sidling and backing away.

Too heavily out of sorts to touch the breakfast, I washed the weather and the journey from my face and hands, and went out to the memorable old house that it would have been so much the better for me never to have entered, never to have seen.

### Chapter 43

72

In the room where the dressing table stood, and where the wax candles burnt on the wall, I found Miss Havisham and Estella; Miss Havisham seated on a settee[1] near the fire, and Estella on a cushion at her feet. Estella was knitting, and Miss Havisham was looking on. They both raised their eyes as I went in, and both saw an alteration in me. I

---

1. **settee** (se tē') *n.*: Small or medium-sized sofa.

890   *The Novel*

derived that from the look they interchanged.

"And what wind," said Miss Havisham, "blows you here, Pip?"

73

Though she looked steadily at me, I saw that she was rather confused. Estella, pausing a moment in her knitting with her eyes upon me, and then going on, I fancied that I read in the action of her fingers, as plainly as if she had told me in the dumb alphabet, that she perceived I had discovered my real benefactor.

"Miss Havisham," said I, "I went to Richmond yesterday, to speak to Estella; and finding that some wind had blown *her* here, I followed.

"What I had to say to Estella, Miss Havisham, I will say before you, presently—in a few moments. It will not surprise you, it will not displease you. I am as unhappy as you can ever have meant me to be."

Miss Havisham continued to look steadily at me. I could see in the action of Estella's fingers as they worked that she attended to what I said—but she did not look up.

"I have found out who my patron is. It is not a fortunate discovery, and is not likely ever to enrich me in reputation, station, fortune, anything. There are reasons why I must say no more of that. It is not my secret, but another's."

As I was silent for a while, looking at Estella and considering how to go on, Miss Havisham repeated, "It is not your secret, but another's. Well?"

"When you first caused me to be brought here, Miss Havisham; when I belonged to the village over yonder, that I wish I had never left; I suppose I did really come here, as any other chance boy might have come—as a kind of servant, to gratify a want or a whim, and to be paid for it?"

"Aye, Pip," replied Miss Havisham, "you did."

"And that Mr. Jaggers—"

"Mr. Jaggers," said Miss Havisham, taking me up in a firm tone, "had nothing to do with it, and knew nothing of it. His being my lawyer, and his being the lawyer of your patron, is a coincidence. He holds the same relation towards numbers of people, and it might easily arise. Be that as it may, it did arise, and was not brought about by anyone."

Anyone might have seen in her haggard face that there was no suppression or evasion so far.

"But when I fell into the mistake I have so long remained in, at least you led me on?" said I.

"Yes," she returned, "I let you go on."

"Was that kind?"

"Who am I," cried Miss Havisham, striking her stick upon the floor, and flashing into wrath so suddenly that Estella glanced up at her in surprise, "who am I, for God's sake, that I should be kind?"

Waiting until she was quiet again, I went on.

"I have been thrown among one family of your relations, Miss Havisham, and have been constantly among them since I went to London. I know them to have been as honestly under my delusion as I myself. And I should be false and base if I did not tell you that you deeply wrong both Mr. Matthew Pocket and his son Herbert, if you suppose them to be otherwise than generous, upright, open, and incapable of anything designing or mean."

"They are your friends," said Miss Havisham.

"They made themselves my friends," said I, "when they supposed me to have superseded them; and when Sarah Pocket, Miss Georgiana, and Mistress Camilla were not my friends, I think."

This contrasting of them with the rest seemed, I was glad to see, to do them good with her. She looked at me keenly for a little while, and then said quietly:

"What do you want for them?"

"Miss Havisham, if you could spare the money to do my friend Herbert a lasting service in life, but which from the nature of the case must be done without his knowledge, I could show you how."

"Why must it be done without his knowledge?" she asked.

"Because," said I, "I began the service myself, more than two years ago, without his knowledge, and I don't want to be betrayed. Why I fail in my ability to finish it I cannot explain. It is a part of the secret which is another person's and not mine."

She gradually withdrew her eyes from me, and turned them on the fire.

"Estella," said I turning to her now, and trying to command my trembling voice, "you know I love you. You know that I have loved you long and dearly."

She raised her eyes to my face on being thus addressed, and her fingers plied their work, and she looked at me with an unmoved countenance. I saw that Miss Havisham glanced from me to her and from her to me.

"I should have said this sooner, but for my long mistake. It induced me to hope that Miss Havisham meant us for one another. While I thought you could not help yourself, as it were, I refrained from saying it. But I must say it now."

With her fingers still going, Estella shook her head.

"I know," said I, in answer to that action; "I know. I have no hope that I shall ever call you mine, Estella. I am ignorant what may become of me very soon, how poor I may be, or where I may go. Still, I love you. I have loved you ever since I first saw you in this house."

74 **Discussion** How does Miss Havisham react to Pip's outspoken support of the Matthew Pocket family and the suggestion that she help his friend Herbert financially?

75 **Discussion** What can you infer from Estella's silent response to Pip when he declares his love for her openly?

**76 Discussion** What symbolic action does Miss Havisham perform when Pip refers to her personal tragedy? What does the action signify?

**77 Discussion** Why has Estella encouraged Drummle? How will having a relationship with him accomplish two goals: harming herself (through the love of such a coarse person) and harming Pip? Of the two which goal is the more important to her? Why?

Looking at me perfectly unmoved and with her fingers busy, she shook her head again.

"It would have been cruel in Miss Havisham, horribly cruel, to practice on the susceptibility of a poor boy, and to torture me through all these years with a vain hope and an idle pursuit, if she had reflected on the gravity of what she did. But I think she did not. I think that in the endurance of her own trial, she forgot mine, Estella."

I saw Miss Havisham put her hand to her heart and hold it there, as she sat looking by turns at Estella and at me.

"It seems," said Estella very calmly, "that there are sentiments, fancies—I don't know how to call them—which I am not able to comprehend. When you say you love me, I know what you mean as a form of words, but nothing more. I don't care for what you say at all. I have tried to warn you of this, now, have I not?"

I said, in a miserable manner, "Yes."

"Yes. But you would not be warned, for you thought I did not mean it. Now, did you not think so?"

"I thought and hoped you could not mean it. You, so young, untried, and beautiful, Estella! Surely it is not in nature."

"It is in *my* nature," she returned.

"Is it not true," said I, "that Bentley Drummle is in town here, and pursuing you?"

"It is quite true," she replied, referring to him with the indifference of utter contempt.

"You cannot love him, Estella?"

Her fingers stopped for the first time, as she retorted rather angrily, "What have I told you? Do you still think, in spite of it, that I do not mean what I say?"

"You would never marry him, Estella?"

She looked towards Miss Havisham. Then she said, "Why not tell you the truth? I am going to be married to him."

I dropped my face into my hands, but was able to control myself better than I could have expected, considering what agony it gave me to hear her say those words. When I raised my face again, there was such a ghastly look upon Miss Havisham's that it impressed me, even in my passionate hurry and grief.

"Estella, dearest, dearest Estella, do not let Miss Havisham lead you into this fatal step. Put me aside for ever—you have done so, I well know—but bestow yourself on some worthier person than Drummle. Miss Havisham gives you to him as the greatest slight and injury that could be done to the many far better men who admire you, and to the few who truly love you."

My earnestness awoke a wonder in her that seemed as if it would have been touched with compassion, if she could have rendered me at all intelligible to her own mind.

"I am going," she said again, in a gentler voice, "to be married to him. The preparations for my marriage are making, and I shall be married soon."

"Such a mean brute, such a stupid brute!" I urged in despair.

"Don't be afraid of my being a blessing to him," said Estella; "I shall not be that. Come! Here is my hand. Do we part on this, you visionary boy—or man?"

"Oh, Estella," I answered, as my bitter tears fell fast on her hand, do what I would to restrain them; "even if I remained in England and could hold my head up with the rest, how could I see you Drummle's wife?"

"Nonsense," she returned, "nonsense. This will pass in no time."

"Never, Estella!"

"You will get me out of your thoughts in a week."

"Out of my thoughts! You are part of my existence, part of myself. You have been in every line I have ever read, since I first came here, the rough common boy whose poor heart you wounded even then. You have been in every prospect I have ever seen since—on the river, on the sails of the ships, on the marshes, in the clouds, in the light, in the darkness, in the wind, in the woods, in the sea, in the streets. You have been the embodiment of every graceful fancy that my mind has ever become acquainted with. Estella, to the last hour of my life, you cannot choose but remain part of my character, part of the little good in me, part of the evil. But, in this separation I associate you only with the good and I will faithfully hold you to that always, for you must have done me far more good than harm, let me feel now what sharp distress I may. O God bless you, God forgive you!"

I held her hand to my lips some lingering moments, and so I left her. But ever afterwards, I remembered—and soon afterwards with stronger reason—that while Estella looked at me merely with incredulous wonder, the spectral figure of Miss Havisham, her hand still covering her heart, seemed all resolved into a ghastly stare of pity and remorse.

All done, all gone! So much was done and gone that when I went out at the gate, the light of day seemed of a darker color than when I went in. For a while, I hid myself among some lanes and bypaths, and then struck off to walk all the way to London. For, I had by that time come to myself so far as to consider that I could not go back to the inn and see Drummle there; that I could not bear to sit upon the coach and be spoken to; that I could do nothing half so good for myself as tire myself out.

It was past midnight when I crossed London Bridge. I was not expected till tomorrow, but I had my keys, and, if Herbert were gone to bed, could get to bed myself without disturbing him.

I came in at that Whitefriars gate after the Temple was closed. The night-porter examined me with much attention as he held the gate a little way open for me to pass in. To help his memory I mentioned my name.

"I was not quite sure, sir, but I thought so. Here's a note, sir. The messenger that brought it said, Would you be so good as read it by my lantern?"

Much surprised by the request, I took the note. It was directed to Philip Pip, Esquire, and on the top of the superscription were the words, "PLEASE READ THIS HERE." I opened it, the watchman holding up his light, and read inside, in Wemmick's writing:

"DON'T GO HOME."

### Chapter 44

Turning from the Temple gate as soon as I had read the warning, I made the best of my way to Fleet Street, and there got a late hackney chariot[1] and drove to the Hummums in Covent Garden. In those times a bed was always to be got there at any hour of the night.

What a doleful night! How anxious, how dismal, how long! There was an inhospitable smell in the room of cold soot and hot dust.

I had left directions that I was to be called at seven, for it was plain that I must see Wemmick before seeing any one else, and equally plain that this was a case in which his Walworth sentiments only could be taken. It was a relief to get out of the room where the night had been so miserable, and I needed no second knocking at the door to startle me from my uneasy bed.

The castle battlements arose upon my view at eight o'clock. The little servant hap-

---

1. **hackney chariot:** Coach for hire.

78 **Discussion** When Pip hears the news that Estella is going to marry Drummle, how does his speech toward Estella change?

79 **Discussion** After his last impassioned speech to Estella, Pip realizes that he is left with two different impressions of Miss Havisham's and Estella's responses to his words. What are the two impressions that he has?

80 **Discussion** When Pip returns home, what new development takes his mind off his misery and turns it in another direction?

81 **Reading Strategy** A new twist in the plot increases the tension. Have students predict what will happen and follow the story carefully. What action does Pip take to clarify the message he received?

*Great Expectations* 893

**FEBRUARY FILL DYKE**
*Benjamin William Leader*
Published by permission of the Birmingham Museum and Art Gallery

pening to be entering the fortress with two hot rolls, I passed through the postern[2] and crossed the drawbridge in her company, and so came without announcement into the presence of Wemmick as he was making tea for himself and the Aged. An open door afforded a perspective view of the Aged in bed.

"Halloa, Mr. Pip!" said Wemmick. "You did come home, then?"

"Yes," I returned; "but I didn't go home."

"That's all right," said he, rubbing his hands. "I left a note for you at each of the

Temple gates, on the chance. Which gate did you come to?"

I told him.

"I'll go round to the others in the course of the day and destroy the notes," said Wemmick. "*Would* you mind toasting this sausage for the Aged P.?"

I said I should be delighted to do it.

"Then you can go about your work, Mary Anne," said Wemmick to the little servant, "which leaves us to ourselves, don't you see, Mr. Pip?" he added, winking, as she disappeared.

"I heard by chance, yesterday morning,"

---

**2. postern** (pōs′ tərn) *n.*: Back gate.

said Wemmick, "that a certain person not altogether of uncolonial pursuits, and not unpossessed of portable property—I don't know who it may really be had made some little stir in a certain part of the world by disappearing from such place, and being no more heard of thereabouts. From which conjectures had been raised and theories formed, I also heard that you at your chambers in Garden Court Temple, had been watched, and might be watched again."

"By whom?" said I.

"I wouldn't go into that," said Wemmick evasively; "it might clash with official responsibilities."

"You have heard of a man of bad character whose true name is Compeyson?" I asked.

He answered with a nod.

"Is he living?"

One other nod.

"Is he in London?"

He gave me one last nod, and went on with his breakfast.

"Now," said Wemmick, "questioning being over"—which he emphasized and repeated for my guidance—"I come to what I did, after hearing what I heard. I went to Garden Court to find you; not finding you, I went to Clarriker's to find Mr. Herbert."

"And him you found?" said I, with great anxiety.

"And him I found. Without mentioning any names or going into any details, I gave him to understand that if he was aware of anybody—Tom, Jack, or Richard—being about the chambers, or about the immediate neighborhood, he had better get Tom, Jack, or Richard out of the way while you were out of the way."

"Mr. Herbert, after being all of a heap for half an hour, struck out a plan. He mentioned to me as a secret that he is courting a young lady who has, as no doubt you are aware, a bedridden pa. Which pa lies a-bed in a bow window[3] where he can see the ships sail up and down the river. You are acquainted with the young lady, most probably?"

"Not personally," said I.

The truth was that she had objected to me as an expensive companion who did Herbert no good, and that, when Herbert had first proposed to present me to her, she had received the proposal with such very moderate warmth that Herbert had felt himself obliged to confide the state of the case to me, with a view to the lapse of a little time before I made her acquaintance.

"The house with the bow window," said Wemmick, "being by the riverside, down the Pool there between Limehouse and Greenwich; and being kept, it seems, by a very respectable widow, who has a furnished upper floor to let, Mr. Herbert put it to me, what did I think of that as a temporary tenement for Tom, Jack, or Richard. Now, I thought very well of it, for three reasons I'll give you. That is to say, firstly, it's altogether out of all your beats. Secondly, without going near it yourself, you could always hear of the safety of Tom, Jack, or Richard through Mr. Herbert. Thirdly, after a while, and when it might be prudent, if you should want to slip Tom, Jack, or Richard on board a foreign packet boat,[4] there he is—ready."

Much comforted by these considerations, I thanked Wemmick again and again, and begged him to proceed.

"Well, sir! Mr. Herbert threw himself into the business with a will, and by nine o'clock last night he housed Tom, Jack, or Richard—whichever it may be—you and I don't

---

3. **bow window:** Rounded window projecting out from a house.
4. **packet boat:** Boat that travels a regular route, carrying passengers, freight, and mail.

82 **Discussion** What news does Wemmick have for Pip?

83 **Discussion** "Tom, Jack, or Richard" is the equivalent of the familiar "Tom, Dick, and Harry," meaning everybody or nobody in particular. Why does Wemmick refer to Magwitch in such a roundabout way, as if his identity were not known?

84 **Discussion** How does Herbert plan to hide Magwitch until Herbert and Pip are ready for his escape out of London?

85 **Discussion** What objection does Herbert's fiancée, Clara, have regarding Pip's invitation to her house?

86 **Discussion** What are Wemmick's three reasons for approving of Herbert's plan?

87 **Discussion** What is Wemmick's final advice to Pip?

88 **Reading Strategy** Ask students to summarize the events of this section. Also ask them to evaluate Pip's behavior in this crisis.

**Reader's Response** In the struggle between the love of others and material wealth and success, which do you value more? Why?

want to know—quite successfully. At the old lodgings it was understood that he was summoned to Dover, and in fact he was taken down the Dover road and cornered out of it. Now, another great advantage of all this is that it was done without you, and when, if any one was concerning himself about your movements, you must be known to be ever so many miles off, and quite otherwise engaged.

"And now, Mr. Pip, I have probably done the most I can do; but if I can ever do more—from a Walworth point of view, and in a strictly private and personal capacity—I shall be glad to do it. Here's the address. There can be no harm in your going here tonight and seeing for yourself that all is well with Tom, Jack, or Richard before you go home. But after you have gone home, don't go back here. And let me finally impress one impor-

tant point upon you. Avail yourself of this evening to lay hold of his portable property. You don't know what may happen to him. Don't let anything happen to the portable property.

"I must be off. If you had nothing more pressing to do than to keep here till dark, that's what I should advise. You look very much worried, and it would do you good to have a perfectly quiet day with the Aged—he'll be up presently.

I soon fell asleep before Wemmick's fire, and the Aged and I enjoyed one another's society by falling asleep before it more or less all day. We had loin of pork for dinner, and greens grown on the estate, and I nodded at the Aged with a good intention whenever I failed to do it drowsily. When it was quite dark, I left the Aged preparing the fire for toast.

## Closure and Extension

### ANSWERS TO THINKING ABOUT THE SELECTION
*Recalling*

1. Mrs. Joe dies and Pip attends her funeral. He hears from Biddy that Orlick has been lurking around the house.
2. Pip receives five hundred pounds from his benefactor, but does not

learn that person's identity.
3. He consults Mr. Wemmick, who, through connections, finds a young shipping merchant needing capable help and capital for his business. The affair is managed so smoothly that Herbert does not know that a new job has been arranged for him with Pip's money and Mr. Wemmick's assistance.
4. The revelation shocks and repels him. Pip is also afraid of this ex-

convict, having seen the knife he carries and how ready he was to use it when they heard footsteps approaching their door. He is

## THINKING ABOUT THE SELECTION

### Recalling

1. What occurs in the subplot involving Orlick and Mrs. Joe?
2. Why is Pip's twenty-first birthday significant?
3. How does Pip secretly help Herbert?
4. Describe Pip's reaction when he discovers his benefactor.
5. Summarize the story that Provis tells Pip.
6. Why is Pip's visit to Miss Havisham so painful?
7. What fear leads him to plan Provis's escape from the country?

### Interpreting

8. What causes Pip to regret that he has ever "seen Miss Havisham's face"?
9. How has Miss Havisham's upbringing of Estella affected Estella, Pip, and Miss Havisham herself?
10. How are Provis and Joe similar? Explain the role each plays in Pip's life.
11. What is similar about the way that Pip relates to Provis and to Joe?

### Applying

12. Pip is disappointed by Provis's arrival. Why is a person's reaction to disappointment a good sign of his or her character?

## ANALYZING LITERATURE

### Understanding Theme

A **theme** is the central idea or insight into life revealed in a work of literature. When a writer does not state the theme directly, you can often discover it by considering the main conflict. In *Great Expectations,* Pip is divided between his love for himself and others and his longing for material success.

Keeping this conflict in mind, write a statement that you think expresses the theme of the novel.

## CRITICAL THINKING AND READING

### Paraphrasing Key Statements

**Paraphrasing** means expressing another person's statements in your own words. By paraphrasing key statements in a novel, you will gain a better insight into the main conflict and the theme. For example, reread Pip's statement beginning "It would have been cruel . . . ." (p. 892). Pip is saying that Miss Havisham would not have deceived him about his expectations if she had realized the seriousness of what she was doing. He says that her own sufferings kept her blind to his. This speech indicates that, in his willingness to forgive Miss Havisham, Pip is beginning to overcome his own conflict.

1. Paraphrase the speech beginning "Estella, dearest . . . ." (p. 892).
2. Explain how this speech relates to Pip's conflict and the book's theme.

## THINKING AND WRITING

### Responding to the Theme of a Novel

Suppose a friend of yours has argued that Dickens's theme is old-fashioned. Jot down some reasons why the theme is as relevant today as it was in Dickens's time. Try to imagine current situations to which this theme would apply. Use the ideas you have gathered to write a composition answering your friend's argument. In revising, make sure you have clearly stated Dickens's theme and shown how it applies to at least one modern situation. When you are finished, share your composition with your classmates.

*Great Expectations* 897

10. Suggested Response: Both men have been kind and generous toward Pip. They are also similar in that they come from the lower classes and are not educated.
11. Suggested Response: Pip experiences an inner conflict with regard to each of these men. He knows they deserve his devotion, but he also wants to reject them.

### Applying

12. Answers will differ, but most students will realize that dealing with disappointment in a constructive way is a sign of character.

**Challenge** How does Mr. Jaggers's manner reflect that of a lawyer cross-examining a witness?

### ANSWERS TO ANALYZING LITERATURE

Answers will differ, but students' responses should reflect the idea that love and devotion are worth more than material goods and status.

### ANSWERS TO CRITICAL THINKING AND READING

1. Suggested Response: Do not marry Drummle at the urging of Miss Havisham. Do not even consider my love for you. However, choose someone who is more worthy of you.
2. Suggested Response: Pip is beginning to overcome his inner conflict. He realizes that his dream of having wealth, status, and Estella is an illusion. Even at his own expense, he advises Estella to do something for her own good.

### THINKING AND WRITING

For help with this assignment, students can refer to Lesson 11, "Writing About Theme," in the Handbook of Writing About Literature.

### Publishing Student Writing

You might want to ask volunteers to read their compositions to the class.

897

afraid, too, that the money might have been obtained by some criminal act. Pip is too worried to sleep until he and Herbert can find another place for the man to stay.
5. Provis tells Pip how he fell under the spell of Compeyson, a master criminal, and was imprisoned in Compeyson's stead.
6. Pip learns that Estella is betrothed to Bentley Drummle.
7. Pip learns that Compeyson knows that Magwitch is in England, has been watching the Garden Court

apartment, and has been following him (Pip). The fear that Compeyson might learn the whereabouts of Magwitch and expose him to the police makes it imperative to get him out of the country.

### Interpreting

8. Suggested Response: Pip feels guilty about his treatment of Joe and Biddy.
9. Suggested Response: Estella has been used by Miss Havisham to seek revenge on all men for being

jilted by her lover. Her training toward this end has made Estella cold, haughty, and unable to love anyone. Pip has been deeply hurt, having misinterpreted Miss Havisham's motive in bringing Estella and him together and in encouraging Estella to bewitch him so that she could later break his heart. Miss Havisham herself has failed as a human being since her obsession with revenge blinded her to the damage she inflicted on Estella and Pip.

## Focus

**Literary Focus** Remind students that a traditional novel aims to represent reality. Its characters must seem real, its actions probable, its setting realistic. Consequently, the novel differs from a fairy tale or legend, where the writer may create a totally unreal world. The novelist's greatest gift is to actualize people and settings of other times and places and make them come alive for us, as Dickens does in *Great Expectations.*

**Look For** Discuss with students the concept of proper closure—that is the appropriate ending of a work. Explain the differences between denouement and catastrophe as endings in the drama, and extrapolate from these the idea of a correct closure in the novel. Although Dickens is sometimes accused of improbabilities in plots, his conclusions are always carefully foreshadowed.

**Writing/Prior Knowledge** Write the words "Happy Ending" on the board and have the class discuss such questions as: How realistic are happy endings? Why do we want them? What are some examples of stories with happy endings? Then have students proceed with the writing assignment.

**Vocabulary** Have all students work in groups to create a crossword puzzle or a word game using the vocabulary words from this and previous sections of the novel.

**Spelling Tip** Point out that the ending of *indelible* is spelled *ible,* not the more common *able.*

---

| | |
|---|---|
| **The Novel as a Whole** | ## Great Expectations, Chapters 45–58 |

**Great Expectations, Chapters 45–58**

You have learned how a novelist uses point of view, characterization, plot, setting, and theme to construct a narrative. While you have considered these elements separately, you have also seen some of the ways in which they work together. The first-person narrative in *Great Expectations,* for example, leads you to depend on Pip's view of events and characters. Similarly, the descriptions of settings often reveal important character traits. Also, your involvement in the events of the plot makes you more receptive to the theme of the story. You will better understand the novel as a whole by continuing to consider how its elements reinforce each other.

**Look For**

Elizabeth Bowen has written: "For people who live on expectations, to face up to their realizations is something of an ordeal." As you read the conclusion of *Great Expectations,* look for how Pip faces up to his ordeal.

**Writing**

You have been reading *Great Expectations* for some time now and probably have an idea about how it will end. Briefly summarize your version of the ending before you read the last chapters.

**Vocabulary**

Knowing the following words will help you as you read Chapters 45–58 of *Great Expectations.*

**truculent** (truk′ yōō lənt) *adj.*: savage; cruel (p. 899)

**averse** (ə vurs′) *adj.*: Opposed to (p. 901)

**tremulous** (trem′ yoo ləs) *adj.*: Shaking; unsteady (p. 905)

**vivacity** (vi vas′ ə tē) *n.*: Liveliness (p. 908)

**obdurate** (äb′ door ət) *adj.*: Stubborn; unbending (p. 911)

**proffered** (präf′ ərd) *adj.*: Offered (usually a verb) (p. 914)

**irresolute** (i rez′ ə lōōt) *adj.*: Unsure; indecisive (p. 915)

**tumult** (tōō′ mult) *n.*: Great noise or disturbance (p. 916)

**querulous** (kwer′ ə ləs) *adj.*: Complaining (p. 923)

**indelible** (in del′ ə b'l) *adj.*: Cannot be erased (p. 925)

**diffidence** (dif′ ə dəns) *n.*: Shyness; uncertainty (p. 930)

**assiduity** (as′ə dyōō′ ə tē) *n.*: Hard work and perseverance (p. 932)

**avarice** (av′ ə ris) *n.*: Greed (p. 935)

---

### Objectives

1 To understand a novel as a whole
2 To use criteria to evaluate a novel
3 To evaluate a novel

### Support Material

**Teaching Portfolio**
Teacher Backup, p. 995
Grammar in Action Worksheets, *Using Repetition,* p. 999; *Understanding Referent,* p. 1001
Usage and Mechanics Worksheet, p. 1003
Vocabulary Check, p. 1004
Critical Thinking and Reading Worksheet, *Using Criteria to Evaluate the Novel,* p. 1006

Language Worksheet, *Recognizing Dialect,* p. 1008
Selection Test, p. 1009

**Chapter 45**

Eight o'clock had struck before I got into the air that was scented, not disagreeably, by the chips and shavings of the longshore boat builders, and mast, oar, and block[1] makers. All that waterside region was unknown ground to me, and when I struck down by the river, I found that the spot I wanted was not where I had supposed it to be, and was anything but easy to find.

Selecting from the few queer houses upon Mill Pond Bank, a house with a wooden front and three stories of bow window, I looked at the plate upon the door, and read there Mrs. Whimple. That being the name I wanted, I knocked, and an elderly woman of a pleasant and thriving appearance responded. She was immediately deposed, however, by Herbert, who silently led me into the parlor and shut the door. It was an odd sensation to see his very familiar face established quite at home in that very unfamiliar room and region.

"All is well, Handel," said Herbert, "and he is quite satisfied, though eager to see you. My dear girl is with her father; and if you'll wait till she comes down, I'll make you known to her, and then we'll go upstairs. *That's* her father."

I had become aware of an alarming growling overhead, and had probably expressed the fact in my countenance.

"I am afraid he is a sad old rascal," said Herbert, smiling, "but I have never seen him."

While he thus spoke, the growling noise became a prolonged roar, and then died away.

"To have Provis for an upper lodger is quite a godsend to Mrs. Whimple," said Herbert, "for of course people in general won't

---

1. **block** (bläk) *n.*: Pulley.

---

stand that noise. A curious place, Handel, isn't it?"

It was a curious place, indeed, but remarkably well kept and clean.

"Mrs. Whimple," said Herbert, when I told him so, "is the best of housewives, and I really do not know what my Clara would do without her motherly help. For Clara has no mother of her own, Handel, and no relation in the world but old Gruffandgrim."

"Surely that's not his name, Herbert?"

"No, no," said Herbert, "that's my name for him. His name is Mr. Barley."

As we were thus conversing in a low tone while Old Barley's sustained growl vibrated in the beam that crossed the ceiling, the room door opened, and a very pretty, slight, dark-eyed girl of twenty or so came in with a basket in her hand: whom Herbert tenderly relieved of the basket, and presented blushing, as "Clara." She really was a most charming girl, and might have passed for a captive fairy whom the truculent ogre, Old Barley, had pressed into his service.

Clara returned soon afterwards, and Herbert accompanied me upstairs to see our charge. In his two cabin rooms at the top of the house, I found Provis comfortably settled. He expressed no alarm, and seemed to feel none that was worth mentioning, but it struck me that he was softened.

When Herbert and I sat down with him by his fire, I asked him first of all whether he relied on Wemmick's judgment and sources of information.

"Aye, aye, dear boy!" he answered, with a grave nod, "Jaggers knows."

"Then, I have talked with Wemmick," said I, "and have come to tell you what caution he gave me and what advice."

I told him how Wemmick had heard that he was under some suspicion, and that my chambers had been watched; how Wemmick had recommended his keeping close for a

*Great Expectations* 899

899

---

**Presentation**

**Motivation/Prior Knowledge**
Discuss with students what they believe influences change and growth. Tell them that in this last part of the novel, Pip comes to understand a new meaning of "great expectations." He changes and grows, and in doing so, he discovers an important new purpose in life.

**Master Teacher Note** *Great Expectations* ends with Pip's growth and enlightenment. The theme of the novel—that goodness comes from within a person, not from external sources like wealth—is articulated through the experiences of Pip. The novel conveys the importance of love and true friendship.

**Purpose-Setting Question**
What changes had to occur in Pip's character before he could recognize his new purpose?

**1 Discussion** What is the atmosphere of the Mill Pond Bank neighborhood?

**2 Discussion** What fanciful picture does Pip draw of the relationship between Clara and her father, based on his observation of both?

**3 Discussion** What plan does Herbert suggest for getting Provis safely out of London?

**4 Discussion** What uneasy thought occurs to Pip as he leaves the Mill Pond Bank area?

time, and my keeping away from him; and what Wemmick had said about getting him abroad. I added that, of course, when the time came, I should go with him, or should follow close upon him, as might be safest in Wemmick's judgment.

Herbert, who had been looking at the fire and pondering, here said that something had come into his thoughts arising out of Wemmick's suggestion, which it might be worthwhile to pursue. "We are both good watermen, Handel, and could take him down the river ourselves when the right time comes. No boat would then be hired for the purpose, and no boatmen; that would save at least a chance of suspicion, and any chance is worth saving. Never mind the season; don't you think it might be a good thing if you began at once to keep a boat at the Temple stairs and were in the habit of rowing up and down the river? You fall into that habit, and then who notices or minds? Do it twenty or fifty times, and there is nothing special in your doing it the twenty-first or fifty-first."

I liked this scheme, and Provis was quite elated by it. We agreed that it should be carried into execution, and that Provis should never recognize us if we came below Bridge and rowed past Mill Pond Bank. But we further agreed that he should pull down the blind in that part of his window which gave upon the east, whenever he saw us and all was right.

Our conference being now ended, and everything arranged, I rose to go, remarking to Herbert that he and I had better not go home together, and that I would take half an hour's start of him. "I don't like to leave you here," I said to Provis, "though I cannot doubt your being safer here than near me. Good-bye!"

"Dear boy," he answered, clasping my hands, "I don't know when we may meet again, and I don't like good-bye. Say good night!"

"Good night! Herbert will go regularly between us, and when the time comes you may be certain I shall be ready. Good night, good night!"

All things were as quiet in the Temple as ever I had seen them. The windows of the rooms of that side lately occupied by Provis were dark and still, and there was no lounger in Garden Court.

Next day, I set myself to get the boat. It was soon done, and the boat was brought round to the Temple stairs, and lay where I could reach her within a minute or two. Then, I began to go out as for training and practice—sometimes alone, sometimes with Herbert. At first, I kept above Blackfriars Bridge; but as the hours of the tide changed, I took towards London Bridge. The first time I passed Mill Pond Bank, Herbert and I were pulling a pair of oars; and, both in going and returning, we saw the blind towards the east come down. Herbert was rarely there less frequently than three times in a week, and he never brought me a single word of intelligence that was at all alarming. Still, I knew that there was cause for alarm, and I could not get rid of the notion of being watched. Once received, it is a haunting idea; how many undesigning persons I suspected of watching me it would be hard to calculate.

## Chapter 46

Some weeks passed without bringing any change. We waited for Wemmick, and he made no sign.

My wordly affairs began to wear a gloomy appearance, and I was pressed for money by more than one creditor. Even I myself began to know the want of money (I mean of ready money in my own pocket), and to relieve it by converting some easily spared articles of jewelry into cash. But I had quite determined that it would be a heartless fraud to take more money from my patron in the existing state of my uncertain thoughts and plans.

As the time wore on, an impression settled heavily upon me that Estella was married. Fearful of having it confirmed, though it was all but a conviction, I avoided the newspapers, and begged Herbert (to whom I had confided the circumstances of our last interview) never to speak of her to me.

It was an unhappy life that I lived. Condemned to inaction and a state of constant restlessness and suspense, I rowed about in my boat, and waited, waited, waited, as I best could.

There were states of the tide when, having been down the river, I could not get back through the eddy-chafed arches and starlings of Old London Bridge; then I left my boat at a wharf near the Custom House, to be brought up afterwards to the Temple stairs. I was not averse to doing this, as it served to make me and my boat a commoner incident among the waterside people there. From this slight occasion sprang two meetings that I have now to tell of.

One afternoon, late in the month of February, I came ashore at the wharf at dusk. Both in going and returning, I had seen the signal in his window, All well.

As it was a raw evening and I was cold, I

MOONLIGHT. A STUDY AT MILLBANK
*J. M. W. Turner*
*The Tate Gallery, London*

thought I would comfort myself with dinner at once; and as I had hours of dejection and solitude before me if I went home to the Temple, I thought I would afterwards go to the play. The theater where Mr. Wopsle was performing was in that waterside neighborhood, and to that theater I resolved to go.

When I came out of the theater after the play, I found Mr. Wopsle waiting for me near the door.

"How do you do?" said I, shaking hands with him as we turned down the street together. "I saw that you saw me."

"Saw you, Mr. Pip?" he returned. "Yes, of course I saw you. But who else was there?"

"Who else?"

"It is the strangest thing," said Mr. Wopsle, drifting into his lost look again, "and yet I could swear to him."

Becoming alarmed, I entreated Mr. Wopsle to explain his meaning.

"Whether I should have noticed him at first but for your being there," said Mr. Wopsle, "I can't be positive; yet I think I should."

Involuntarily I looked round me.

"Oh! He can't be in sight," said Mr. Wopsle. "He went out before I went off. I saw him go. I had a ridiculous fancy that he must be with you, Mr. Pip, till I saw that you were quite unconscious of him, sitting behind you there like a ghost."

"I dare say you wonder at me, Mr. Pip; indeed, I see you do. But it is so very strange! You'll hardly believe what I am going to tell you. I could hardly believe it myself, if you told me."

"Indeed?" said I.

"No, indeed. Mr. Pip, you remember in old times a certain Christmas Day, when you were quite a child, and I dined at Gargery's, and some soldiers came to the door to get a pair of handcuffs mended?"

"I remember it very well."

"And you remember that there was a chase after two convicts, and that we joined in it, and that Gargery took you on his back? And you remember that we came up with the two in a ditch, and that there was a scuffle between them, and that one of them had been severely handled and much mauled about the face by the other?"

"I see it all before me."

"And that the soldiers lighted torches, and put the two in the center, and that we went on to see the last of them, over the black marshes, with the torchlight shining on their faces—I am particular about that—with the torchlight shining on their faces, when there was an outer ring of dark night all about us?"

"Yes," said I. "I remember all that."

"Then, Mr. Pip, one of those two prisoners sat behind you tonight. I saw him over your shoulder."

"Steady!" I thought. I asked him then, "Which of the two do you suppose you saw?"

"The one who had been mauled," he answered readily, "and I'll swear I saw him! The more I think of him, the more certain I am of him."

"This is very curious!" said I, with the best assumption I could put on of its being nothing more to me. "Very curious indeed!"

I cannot exaggerate the enhanced disquiet into which this conversation threw me, or the special and peculiar terror I felt at Compeyson's having been behind me "like a ghost."

When Mr. Wopsle had imparted to me all that he could recall or I extract, and when I had treated him to a little appropriate refreshment after the fatigues of the evening, we parted. It was between twelve and one o'clock when I reached the Temple, and the gates were shut. No one was near me when I went in and went home.

Herbert had come in, and we held a very serious council by the fire. But there was

7

nothing to be done, saving to communicate to Wemmick what I had that night found out, and to remind him that we waited for his hint. As I thought that I might compromise him if I went too often to the castle, I made this communication by letter. I wrote it before I went to bed and went out and posted it; and again no one was near me. Herbert and I agreed that we could do nothing else but be very cautious.

## Chapter 47

The second of the two meetings referred to in the last chapter occurred about a week after the first. I had strolled up into Cheapside, and was strolling along it, surely the most unsettled person in all the busy concourse, when a large hand was laid upon my shoulder by some one overtaking me. It was Mr. Jaggers's hand, and he passed it through my arm.

"As we were going in the same direction, Pip, we may walk together. Where are you bound for?"

"For the Temple, I think," said I.

"Don't you know?" said Mr. Jaggers.

"Well," I returned, glad for once to get the better of him in cross-examination, "I do *not* know, for I have not made up my mind."

"You are going to dine?" said Mr. Jaggers. "You don't mind admitting that, I suppose?"

"No," I returned, "I don't mind admitting that."

"And are not engaged?"

"I don't mind admitting also that I am not engaged."

"Then," said Mr. Jaggers, "come and dine with me."

I was going to excuse myself, when he added, "Wemmick's coming." So I changed my excuse into an acceptance.

We went to Gerrard Street, all three together, in a hackney coach, and as soon as we got there, dinner was served.

"Did you send that note of Miss Havisham's to Mr. Pip, Wemmick?" Mr. Jaggers asked, soon after we began dinner.

"No, sir," returned Wemmick; "it was going by post, when you brought Mr. Pip into the office. Here it is." He handed it to his principal, instead of to me.

"It's a note of two lines, Pip," said Mr. Jaggers, handing it on, "sent up to me by Miss Havisham, on account of her not being sure of your address. She tells me that she wants to see you on a little matter of business you mentioned to her. You'll go down?"

"Yes," said I.

"When do you think of going down?"

"I have an impending engagement," said I, glancing at Wemmick, who was putting fish into the post office, "that renders me rather uncertain of my time. At once, I think."

"If Mr. Pip has the intention of going at once," said Wemmick to Mr. Jaggers, "he needn't write an answer, you know."

Receiving this as an intimation that it was best not to delay, I settled that I would go tomorrow, and said so.

"So, Pip! Our friend the Spider," said Mr. Jaggers, "has played his cards. He has won the pool."

It was as much as I could do to assent.

"So, here's to Mrs. Bentley Drummle," said Mr. Jaggers, "and may the question of supremacy be settled to the lady's satisfaction! To the satisfaction of the lady *and* the gentleman, it never will be. Now, Molly, Molly, Molly, Molly, how slow you are today!"

She was at his elbow when he addressed her, putting a dish upon the table. As she withdrew her hands from it, she fell back a step or two, nervously muttering some excuse. And a certain action of her fingers as she spoke arrested my attention.

*Great Expectations* 903

**9** Critical Thinking and Reading
As Molly serves Pip dinner, what
does he notice about her that
seems significant to him? What
conclusion can you draw about
his particular interest in this subject?

**10** Reading Strategy Pip makes an
important discovery about Molly
that prompts him to question Mr.
Jaggers and Wemmick about
Estella's history. Predict what the
outcome will be for Pip.

**11** Discussion What crime was
Molly charged with? How did Mr.
Jaggers get her acquitted?

**9**

The action of her fingers was like the action of knitting. She stood looking at her
master. Her look was very intent. Surely, I
had seen exactly such eyes and such hands
on a memorable occasion very lately!

He dismissed her, and she glided out of
the room. But she remained before me, as
plainly as if she were still there. I looked at
those hands, I looked at those eyes, I looked
at that flowing hair, and I compared them
with other hands, other eyes, other hair,
that I knew of, and with what those might be
after twenty years of a brutal husband and a
stormy life. I looked again at those hands
and eyes of the housekeeper, and thought of
the inexplicable feeling that had come over
me when I last walked—not alone—in the ruined garden, and through the deserted brewery. And I felt absolutely certain that this
woman was Estella's mother.

Wemmick and I took our leave early, and
left together. "Well!" said Wemmick, "that's
over!"

I asked him if he had ever seen Miss
Havisham's adopted daughter, Mrs. Bentley
Drummle? He said no.

"Wemmick," said I, "do you remember
telling me, before I first went to Mr. Jaggers's
private house, to notice that housekeeper?"

"Did I?" he replied. "Ah, I dare say I did."

"A wild beast tamed, you called her?"

"And what did *you* call her?"

"The same. How did Mr. Jaggers tame
her, Wemmick?"

"That's his secret. She has been with
him many a long year."

**10**

"I wish you would tell me her story. I feel
a particular interest in being acquainted
with it. You know that what is said between
you and me goes no further."

"Well!" Wemmick replied, "I don't know
her story—that is, I don't know all of it. But
what I do know, I'll tell you.

"A score or so of years ago, that woman
was tried at the Old Bailey[1] for murder and
was acquitted. She was a very handsome
young woman.

"Mr. Jaggers was for her and worked the
case in a way quite astonishing. It was a
desparate case, and it was comparatively
early days with him then, and he worked it
to general admiration; in fact, it may almost
be said to have made him. The murdered
person was a woman; a woman, a good ten
years older, very much larger, and very much
stronger. It was a case of jealousy. This
woman in Gerrard Street here had been married very young and was a perfect fury in
point of jealousy. The murdered woman—
more a match for the man, certainly, in
point of years—was found dead in a barn
near Hounslow Heath. There had been a violent struggle. She was bruised and scratched
and torn, and had been held by the throat at
last and choked. Now, there was no reasonable evidence to implicate any person but
this woman, and, on the improbabilities of
her having been able to do it, Mr. Jaggers
principally rested his case. You may be sure
that he never dwelt upon the strength of her
hands then, though he sometimes does
now."

**11**

I had told Wemmick of his showing us
her wrists that day of the dinner party.

"Well, sir!" Wemmick went on, "it happened—happened, don't you see?—that this
woman was so very artfully dressed from the
time of her apprehension that she looked
much slighter than she really was; in particular, her sleeves are always remembered to
have been so skillfully contrived that her
arms had quite a delicate look.

"It was attempted to be set up in proof of
her jealousy that she was under strong suspicion of having, at about the time of the

---

1. **Old Bailey:** Criminal court on Old Bailey Street in
London.

## Grammar in Action

The **repetition** of words and phrases is a device that is usually
associated with poetry. Great prose writers, however, often use
repetition to create a musical rhythm, emphasize certain words, or
imitate a circling, repetitive pattern of thought.

Read the following passage from *Great Expectations* and
notice the repeated words and phrases in italics:

He dismissed her, and she glided out of the room. But she
remained before me, as plainly as if she were still there. *I
looked at* those hands, *I looked at* those eyes, *I looked at*
that flowing hair, and I compared them with *other hands,
other eyes, other hair,* that I knew of, and with what those
might be after twenty years of a brutal husband and a stormy
life. *I looked again at* those *hands* and *eyes* of the housekeeper. . . .And I felt absolutely certain that this woman was
Estella's mother.

Pip is looking, again and again, at the hands and eyes of the
housekeeper, comparing them with Estella's hands and eyes.

murder, frantically destroyed her child by this man—some three years old—to revenge herself upon him. But Mr. Jaggers was altogether too many for the jury, and they gave in."

"Has she been in his service ever since?"

"Yes; but not only that," said Wemmick; "she went into his service immediately after her acquittal, tamed as she is now. She has since been taught one thing and another in the way of her duties, but she was tamed from the beginning."

"Do you remember the sex of the child?"

"Said to have been a girl."

"You have nothing more to say to me tonight?"

"Nothing. I got your letter and destroyed it. Nothing."

We exchanged a cordial good night, and I went home with new matter for my thoughts, though with no relief from the old.

## Chapter 48

Putting Miss Havisham's note in my pocket, that it might serve as my credentials for so soon reappearing at Satis House, in case her waywardness should lead her to express any surprise at seeing me, I went down again by the coach next day. But I alighted at the Halfway House, and breakfasted there, and walked the rest of the distance, for I sought to get into the town quietly by the unfrequented ways, and to leave it in the same manner.

The best light of the day was gone when I passed along the quiet echoing courts behind the High Street. An elderly woman, whom I had seen before as one of the servants who lived in the supplementary house across the back courtyard, opened the gate. The lighted candle stood in the dark passage within, as of old, and I took it up and ascended the staircase alone. Miss Havisham was not in her own room, but was in the larger room across the landing. Looking in at the door, after knocking in vain, I saw her sitting on the hearth in a ragged chair, close before, and lost in the contemplation of, the ashy fire.

Doing as I had often done, I went in, and stood, touching the old chimneypiece, where she could see me when she raised her eyes. There was an air of utter loneliness upon her that would have moved me to pity though she had willfully done me a deeper injury than I could charge her with.

"It is I, Pip. Mr. Jaggers gave me your note yesterday, and I have lost no time."

"Thank you. Thank you."

As I brought another of the ragged chairs to the hearth and sat down, I remarked a new expression on her face, as if she were afraid of me.

"I want," she said, "to pursue that subject you mentioned to me when you were last here, and to show you that I am not all stone. But perhaps you can never believe, now, that there is anything human in my heart?"

When I said some reassuring words, she stretched out her tremulous right hand, as though she was going to touch me.

"You said, speaking for your friend, that you could tell me how to do something useful and good. Something that you would like done, is it not?"

"Something that I would like done very very much."

"What is it?"

I began explaining to her that secret history of the partnership and told her how I had hoped to complete the transaction out of my means, but how in this I was disappointed. That part of the subject (I reminded her) involved matters which could form no

**12 Discussion** What further important information does Pip learn from Wemmick? What further insight into Mr. Jaggers's character does this story give?

**13 Reading Strategy** As students read this chapter, have them look for the dramatic changes in the relationship between Miss Havisham and Pip. When they have completed the chapter, have students summarize the changes.

**14 Discussion** What conflicting feelings does Pip have when he sees the changes in Miss Havisham?

**15 Discussion** What evidence indicates that Miss Havisham has had a change of heart?

Dickens captures the emotional intensity of this moment and the movement from one memory to another by repeating the phrase *I looked at.* He also repeats the traits that he observed—*hands, eyes,* and *hair.* Dickens uses repetition to imitate the searching of thought as it reaches for an idea.

**Student Activity.** Using this paragraph from *Great Expectations* as a model, write a paragraph of your own about a gradual discovery. Use repetition to create a distinctive rhythm, emphasize important words, and add to the drama of your description.

part of my explanation, for they were the weighty secrets of another.

"So!" said she, assenting with her head, but not looking at me. "And how much money is wanting to complete the purchase?"

I was rather afraid of stating it, for it sounded a large sum. "Nine hundred pounds."

"If I give you the money for this purpose, will you keep my secret as you have kept your own?"

"Quite as faithfully."

"And your mind will be more at rest?"

"Much more at rest."

"Are you very unhappy now?"

She asked this question, still without looking at me, but in an unwonted tone of sympathy. I could not reply at the moment, for my voice failed me. She put her left arm across the head of her stick, and softly laid her forehead on it.

"I am far from happy, Miss Havisham, but I have other causes of disquiet than any you know of. They are the secrets I have mentioned."

After a little while, she raised her head, and looked at the fire again.

" 'Tis noble in you to tell me that you have other causes of unhappiness. Is it true?"

"Too true."

"Can I only serve you, Pip, by serving your friend? Regarding that as done, is there nothing I can do for you yourself?"

"Nothing. I thank you for the question. I thank you even more for the tone of the question. But there is nothing."

She presently rose from her seat, and looked about the blighted room for the means of writing. There were none there, and she took from her pocket a yellow set of ivory tablets, mounted in tarnished gold, and wrote upon them with a pencil in a case

of tarnished gold that hung from her neck.

"You are still on friendly terms with Mr. Jaggers?"

"Quite. I dined with him yesterday."

"This is an authority to him to pay you that money, to lay out at your irresponsible discretion for your friend. I keep no money here; but if you would rather Mr. Jaggers knew nothing of the matter, I will send it to you."

"Thank you, Miss Havisham; I have not the least objection to receiving it from him."

She read me what she had written, and it was direct and clear, and evidently intended to absolve me from any suspicion of profiting by the receipt of the money. I took the tablets from her hand, and it trembled.

"My name is on the first leaf. If you can ever write under my name, 'I forgive her,' though ever so long after my broken heart is dust, pray do it!"

"Oh, Miss Havisham," said I, "I can do it now. There have been sore mistakes; and my life has been a blind and thankless one; and I want forgiveness and direction far too much to be bitter with you."

She turned her face to me for the first time since she had averted it, and to my amazement, I may even add to my terror, dropped on her knees at my feet.

To see her, with her white hair and her worn face, kneeling at my feet, gave me a shock through all my frame. I entreated her to rise, and got my arms about her to help her up, but she only pressed that hand of mine which was nearest to her grasp, and hung her head over it, and wept.

"Oh!" she cried, despairingly. "What have I done! What have I done!"

"If you mean, Miss Havisham, what have you done to injure me, let me answer. Very little. I should have loved her under any circumstances. Is she married?"

"Yes!"

16

It was a needless question, for a new desolation in the desolate house had told me so.

"What have I done! What have I done!" She wrung her hands, and crushed her white hair, and returned to this cry over and over again. "What have I done!"

Miss Havisham looked distractedly at me for a while, and then burst out again. What had she done!

"If you knew all my story," she pleaded, "you would have some compassion for me, and a better understanding of me."

"Miss Havisham," I answered, as delicately as I could, "I believe I may say that I do know your story. And I hope I understand it and its influences. Does what has passed between us give me any excuse for asking you a question relative to Estella?"

She looked full at me when I said this, and replied, "Go on."

"Whose child was Estella?"

She shook her head.

"But Mr. Jaggers brought her here, or sent her here?"

"Brought her here."

"Will you tell me how that came about?"

She answered in a low whisper and with caution: "I had been shut up in these rooms a long time when I told him that I wanted a little girl to rear and love, and save from my fate. He told me that he would look about him for such an orphan child. One night he brought her here asleep, and I called her Estella."

"Might I ask her age then?"

"Two or three. She herself knows nothing, but that she was left an orphan and I adopted her."

So convinced I was of that woman's being her mother that I wanted no evidence to establish the fact in my mind.

What more could I hope to do by prolonging the interview? I had succeeded on behalf of Herbert, Miss Havisham had told me all she knew of Estella, I had said and done what I could to ease her mind. No matter with what other words we parted; we parted.

Twilight was closing in when I went downstairs into the natural air. I called to the woman who had opened the gate when I entered that I would not trouble her just yet, but would walk round the place before leaving.

After I had finished my walk, I hesitated whether to call the woman to let me out at the locked gate, or first go upstairs and assure myself that Miss Havisham was as safe and well as I had left her. I took the latter course and went up.

I looked into the room where I had left her, and I saw her seated in the ragged chair upon the hearth close to the fire, with her back towards me. In the moment when I was withdrawing my head to go quietly away, I saw a great flaming light spring up. In the same moment I saw her running at me, shrieking, with a whirl of fire blazing all about her, and soaring at least as many feet above her head as she was high.

I had a double-caped greatcoat on, and over my arm another thick coat. That I got them off, closed with her, threw her down, and got them over her; that I dragged the great cloth from the table for the same purpose, and with it dragged down the heap of rottenness in the midst, and all the ugly things that sheltered there; that we were on the ground struggling like desperate enemies, and that the closer I covered her, the more wildly she shrieked and tried to free herself; that this occurred I knew through the result, but not through anything I felt, or thought, or knew I did. I knew nothing until I knew that we were on the floor by the great table, and that patches of tinder yet alight were floating in the smoky air, which a moment ago had been her faded bridal dress.

Then I looked round and saw the dis-

**17 Discussion** How does Pip describe the mood in Satis House?

**18 Discussion** What occurrence shocks Pip into action and changes the role he has played in this house?

19 **Discussion** What scene does Pip recall when he sees Miss Havisham lying on the large table in her room?

20 **Critical Thinking and Reading** What can you infer about Pip's motive for wanting to communicate only with Matthew Pocket?

21 **Literary Focus** How does the fire relate to the theme of the novel?

turbed beetles and spiders running away over the floor, and the servants coming in with breathless cries at the door.

She was insensible, and I was afraid to have her moved, or even touched. Assistance was sent for, and I held her until it came. When I got up, on the surgeon's coming to her with other aid, I was astonished to see that both my hands were burnt, for I had no knowledge of it through the sense of feeling.

On examination it was pronounced that she had received serious hurts, but that they of themselves were far from hopeless; the danger lay mainly in the nervous shock. By the surgeon's directions, her bed was carried into that room and laid upon the great table. When I saw her again, an hour afterwards, she lay indeed where I had seen her strike her stick, and had heard her say she would lie one day.

Though every vestige of her dress was burnt, she still had something of her old ghastly bridal appearance, for they had covered her to the throat with white cotton-wool, and as she lay with a white sheet loosely overlying that, the phantom air of something that had been and was changed was still upon her.

I found, on questioning the servants, that Estella was in Paris, and I got a promise from the surgeon that he would write by the next post. Miss Havisham's family I took upon myself, intending to communicate with Matthew Pocket only, and leave him to do as he liked about informing the rest.

There was a stage, that evening, when she spoke collectedly of what had happened, though with a certain terrible vivacity. Towards midnight she began to wander in her speech, and after that it gradually set in that she said innumerable times in a low solemn voice, "What have I done!" And then, "Take the pencil and write under my name, 'I forgive her!'"

## Chapter 49

My hands had been dressed twice or thrice in the night, and again in the morning. My left arm was a good deal burned to the elbow, and, less severely, as high as the shoulder; it was very painful, but the flames had set in that direction, and I felt thankful it was no worse.

Herbert was the kindest of nurses, and at stated times took off the bandages, and steeped them in the cooling liquid that was kept ready, and put them on again, with a patient tenderness that I was deeply grateful for.

Neither of us spoke of the boat, but we both thought of it. That was made apparent by our avoidance of the subject, and by our agreeing—without agreement—to make my recovery of the use of my hands a question of so many hours, not of so many weeks.

My first question when I saw Herbert had been, of course, whether all was well down the river. As he replied in the affirmative, with perfect confidence and cheerfulness, we did not resume the subject until the day was wearing away. But then, as Herbert changed the bandages, more by the light of the fire than by the outer light, he went back to it spontaneously.

"I sat with Provis last night, Handel, two good hours. He was very communicative, and told me more of his life. You remember his breaking off here about some woman that he had had great trouble with. The woman was a young woman, and a jealous woman, and a revengeful woman; revengeful, Handel, to the last degree."

"To what last degree?"

"Murder—does it strike too cold on that sensitive place?"

"I don't feel it. How did she murder? Whom did she murder?"

"Why, the deed may not have merited

quite so terrible a name," said Herbert, "but she was tried for it, and Mr. Jaggers defended her, and the reputation of that defense first made his name known to Provis. It was another and a stronger woman who was the victim, and there had been a struggle—in a barn."

"Was the woman brought in guilty?"

"No, she was acquitted."

"Yes? What else?"

"This acquitted young woman and Provis had a little child, a little child of whom Provis was exceedingly fond. On the evening of the very night when the object of her jealousy was strangled as I tell you, the young woman presented herself before Provis for one moment, and swore that she would destroy the child (which was in her possession), and he should never see it again; then she vanished. . . ."

"Did the woman keep her oath?"

"There comes the darkest part of Provis's life. She did."

"That is, he says she did."

22

"Why, of course, my dear boy," returned Herbert, in a tone of surprise, and bending forward to get a nearer look at me. "He says it all. I have no other information."

"No, to be sure."

"Now, whether," pursued Herbert, "he had used the child's mother ill, or whether he had used the child's mother well, Provis doesn't say; but she had shared some four or five years of the wretched life he described to us at this fireside, and he seems to have felt pity for her, and forbearance towards her. Therefore, fearing he should be called upon to depose[1] about this destroyed child, and so be the cause of her death, he hid himself, kept himself dark, as he says, out of the way and out of the trial, and was only vaguely talked of as a certain man called Abel, out of

---

1. **depose** (di pōz') *v.*: Testify.

whom the jealousy arose. After the acquittal she disappeared, and thus he lost the child and the child's mother."

"I want to know," said I, and "particularly, Herbert, whether he told you when this happened?"

"How old were you when you came upon him in the little churchyard?"

"I think in my seventh year."

"Aye. It had happened some three or four years, then, he said, and you brought into his mind the little girl so tragically lost, who would have been about your age."

23

"Herbert," said I, after a short silence, "the man we have in hiding down the river is Estella's father."

## Chapter 50

Early next morning we went out together, and at the corner of Giltspur Street by Smithfield, I left Herbert to go his way into the City, and took my way to Little Britain.

There were periodical occasions when Mr. Jaggers and Mr. Wemmick went over the office accounts, and checked off the vouchers, and put all things straight. On these occasions Wemmick took his books and papers into Mr. Jaggers's room, and one of the upstairs clerks came down into the outer office. Finding such clerk on Wemmick's post that morning, I knew what was going on; but I was not sorry to have Mr. Jaggers and Wemmick together, as Wemmick would then hear for himself that I said nothing to compromise him.

My appearance, with my arm bandaged and my coat loose over my shoulders, favored my object. Although I had sent Mr. Jaggers a brief account of the accident as soon as I had arrived in town, yet I had to give him all the details now. While I described the disaster, Mr. Jaggers stood before the fire. Wemmick

22 **Discussion** What does Pip know that Herbert does not?

23 **Reading Strategy** Have students summarize what clues point to the identity of Estella's father?

Fine Art, *Little London Model*, 1896, by James McNeill Whistler. The American-English artist James McNeill Whistler (1834-1903) did not confine his art to painting. He produced drawings, etchings, and lithographs as well.

*Little London Model* is a lithograph, an image produced by drawing on a smooth stone slab with a grease crayon, applying an oily ink that adheres only to the crayon, and then pressing paper onto the stone to transfer the drawing. This view of the Thames River demonstrates the same rhythm of line and simplicity of composition that characterizes Whistler's paintings.

You might want to use the following questions:

1. How does Whistler suggest a busy city without drawing in every detail?

2. Why is Whistler's lithograph an appropriate accompaniment to this section of the novel?

24 **Discussion** Does Pip share Wemmick's philosophy? Explain.

25 **Discussion** What is the "theme" that is so dear to Pip's heart? What connection does it have with the theme of the novel?

LITTLE LONDON MODEL
*James McNeill Whistler*
*Frank S. Benson Funds*
*The Brooklyn Museum*

leaned back in his chair, staring at me, with his hands in the pockets of his trousers.

My narrative finished, I then produced Miss Havisham's authority to receive the nine hundred pounds for Herbert. "I am sorry, Pip," said Mr. Jaggers, "that we do nothing for *you*."

"Miss Havisham was good enough to ask me," I returned, "whether she could do nothing for me, and I told her no."

"Everybody should know his own business," said Mr. Jaggers.

24 "Every man's business," said Wemmick, "is 'portable property.'"

25 As I thought the time was now come for pursuing the theme I had at heart, I said, turning on Mr. Jaggers:

"I did ask something of Miss Havisham, however, sir. I asked her to give me some information relative to her adopted daughter, and she gave me all she possessed."

"Did she?" said Mr. Jaggers.

"I know more of the history of Miss Havisham's adopted child than Miss Havisham herself does, sir. I know her mother."

Mr. Jaggers looked at me inquiringly, and repeated "Mother?"

"I have seen her mother within these three days."

"Yes?" said Mr. Jaggers.

910    The Novel

"And so have you sir. And you have seen her still more recently."

"Yes?" said Mr. Jaggers.

"Perhaps I know more of Estella's history than even you do," said I. "I know her father, too."

A certain stop that Mr. Jaggers came to in his manner assured me that he did not know who her father was.

"So! You know the young lady's father, Pip?" said Mr. Jaggers.

"Yes," I replied, "and his name is Provis—from New South Wales."

Even Mr. Jaggers started when I said those words.

"And on what evidence, Pip," asked Mr. Jaggers, "does Provis make this claim?"

"He does not make it," said I, "and has never made it, and has no knowledge or belief that his daughter is in existence."

Mr. Jaggers folded his arms and looked with stern attention at me, though with an immovable face.

Then I told him all I knew, and how I knew it, with the one reservation that I left him to infer that I knew from Miss Havisham what I in fact knew from Wemmick.

"Hah!" said Mr. Jaggers at last, as he moved towards the papers on the table. "—What item was it you were at, Wemmick, when Mr. Pip came in?"

But I could not submit to be thrown off in that way, and I made a passionate, almost an indignant appeal to him to be more frank and manly with me. And seeing that Mr. Jaggers stood quite still and silent, and apparently quite obdurate, under this appeal, I turned to Wemmick, and said, "Wemmick, I know you to be a man with a gentle heart. I have seen your pleasant home, and your old father, and all the innocent cheerful playful ways with which you refresh your business life. And I entreat you to say a word for me to Mr. Jaggers, and to represent to him that, all circumstances considered, he ought to be more open with me!"

I have never seen two men look more oddly at one another than Mr. Jaggers and Wemmick did after this apostrophe.

"What's all this?" said Mr. Jaggers. "You with an old father, and you with pleasant and playful ways?"

"Well!" returned Wemmick. "If I don't bring 'em here, what does it matter?"

Mr. Jaggers nodded his head retrospectively two or three times, and actually drew a sigh. "Pip," said he, "I'll put a case to you. Mind! I admit nothing."

He waited for me to declare that I quite understood that he expressly said that he admitted nothing.

"Now, Pip," said Mr. Jaggers, "put this case. Put the case that a woman, under such circumstances as you have mentioned, held her child concealed, and was obliged to communicate the fact to her legal adviser. Put the case that at the same time he held a trust to find a child for an eccentric rich lady to adopt and bring up."

"I follow you, sir."

"Put the case that he lived in an atmosphere of evil, and that he often saw children solemnly tried at a criminal bar,[1] where they were held up to be seen; put the case that he habitually knew of their being imprisoned, whipped, transported,[2] neglected, and cast out."

"I follow you, sir."

"Put the case, Pip, that here was one pretty little child out of the heap who could be saved; whom the father believed dead, and dared make no stir about; as to whom, over the mother, the legal adviser had this power: 'I know what you did, and how you

---

**1. bar** *n.*: Court.
**2. transported** (trans pôrt′ əd) *v.*: Sent out of the country to a colony for prisoners.

did it. Give the child into my hands, and I will do my best to bring you off. If you are saved, your child will be saved, too; if you are lost, your child is still saved.' Put the case that this was done, and that the woman was cleared."

"I understand you perfectly."

"But that I make no admissions?"

"That you make no admissions." And Wemmick repeated, "No admissions."

"Put the case, Pip, that passion and the terror of death had a little shaken the woman's intellects, and that when she was set at liberty, she was scared out of the ways of the world and went to him to be sheltered. Put the case that he took her in, and that he kept down the old wild violent nature, whenever he saw an inkling of its breaking out, by asserting his power over her in the old way. Do you comprehend the imaginary case?"

"Quite."

"Put the case that the child grew up, and was married for money. That the mother was still living. That the father was still living. That the mother and father, unknown to one another, were dwelling within so many miles, furlongs, yards if you like, of one another. That the secret was still a secret, except that you had got wind of it. Put that last case to yourself very carefully."

"I do."

"I ask Wemmick to put it to *himself* very carefully."

And Wemmick said, "I do."

"For whose sake would you reveal the secret? For the father's? I think he would not be much the better for the mother. For the mother's? I think if she had done such a deed, she would be safer where she was. For the daughter's? I think it would hardly serve her to establish her parentage for the information of her husband, and to drag her back to disgrace, after an escape of twenty years, pretty secure to last for life."

I looked at Wemmick, whose face was very grave. He gravely touched his lips with his forefinger. I did the same. Mr. Jaggers did the same. "Now, Wemmick," said the latter then, resuming his usual manner, "what item was it you were at when Mr. Pip came in?"

## Chapter 51

From Little Britain, I went, with my check in my pocket, to Miss Skiffins's brother, the accountant; and Miss Skiffins's brother, the accountant, going straight to Clarriker's and bringing Clarriker to me, I had the great satisfaction of concluding that arrangement.

Clarriker informing me on that occasion that the affairs of the house were steadily progressing, that he would now be able to establish a small branch-house in the East and that Herbert in his new partnership capacity would go out and take charge of it, I found that I must have prepared for a separation from my friend, even though my own affairs had been more settled. And now indeed I felt as if my last anchor were loosening its hold, and I should soon be driving with the winds and waves.

On a Monday morning, when Herbert and I were at breakfast, I received the following letter from Wemmick by the post.

> Walworth. Burn this as soon as read. Early in the week, or say Wednesday, you might do what you know of, if you felt disposed to try it. Now, burn.

When I had shown this to Herbert and had put it in the fire—but not before we had both got it by heart—we considered what to do. For, of course, my being disabled could now be no longer kept out of view.

"I have thought it over, again and

again," said Herbert, "and I think I know a better course than taking a Thames waterman. Take Startop. A good fellow, a skilled hand, fond of us, and enthusiastic and honorable."

"But how much would you tell him, Herbert?"

"It is necessary to tell him very little. Let him suppose it a mere freak, but a secret one, until the morning comes—then let him know that there is urgent reason for your getting Provis aboard and away. You go with him?"

"No doubt."

"Where?"

It had seemed to me, in the many anxious considerations I had given the point, almost indifferent what port we made for—the place signified little, so that he was out of England. Any foreign steamer that fell in our way and would take us up would do. As foreign steamers would leave London at about the time of high water, our plan would be to get down the river by a previous ebb tide,[1] and lie by in some quiet spot until we could pull off to one. The time when one would be due where we lay could be calculated pretty nearly, if we made inquiries beforehand.

Herbert assented to all this, and we went out immediately after breakfast to pursue our investigations. We found that a steamer for Hamburg[2] was likely to suit our purpose best, and we directed our thoughts chiefly to that vessel. We then separated for a few hours, and did what we had to do without any hindrance, and when we met again at one o'clock reported it done. I, for my part, was prepared with passports; Herbert had seen Startop, and he was more than ready to join.

Those two would pull a pair of oars, we settled, and I would steer: our charge would be sitter, and keep quiet; as speed was not our object, we should make way enough. We arranged that Herbert should not come home to dinner before going to Mill Pond Bank that evening; that he should not go there at all tomorrow evening, Tuesday; that he should prepare Provis to come down to some stairs hard by the house, on Wednesday, when he saw us approach, and not sooner; that all the arrangements with him should be concluded that Monday night; and that he should be communicated with no more in any way, until we took him on board.

These precautions well understood by both of us, I went home.

On opening the outer door of our chambers with my key, I found a letter in the box, directed to me; a very dirty letter, though not ill-written. It had been delivered by hand (of course since I left home), and its contents were these.

> If you are not afraid to come to the old marshes tonight or tomorrow night at nine, and to come to the little sluice house by the limekiln,[3] you had better come. If you want information regarding *your Uncle Provis*, you had much better come and tell no one and lose no time. *You must come alone.* Bring this with you.

I had had load enough upon my mind before the receipt of this strange letter. What to do now, I could not tell. And the worse was that I must decide quickly, or I should miss the afternoon coach, which would take me down in time for tonight. Tomorrow night I

---

**1. ebb tide:** The outgoing or falling tide.
**2. Hamburg** (ham′ bərg): Seaport in northwest Germany.

**3. limekiln** (lim′ kiln′) *n.:* Furnace in which limestone is burned to make lime, a substance used in mortar and cement.

*Great Expectations* 913

**33 Discussion** How do Pip and Herbert alter their plan as a result of Pip's injury?

**34 Clarification** Information about the tides would be necessary to Herbert and Pip's calculations. To row against an incoming tide would tire them and slow them down.

**35 Discussion** How do Pip and Herbert plan to make contact with an outgoing steamer so that Pip and Provis can escape safely?

36 **Discussion** When Pip receives a mysterious letter, why does he decide to comply with it?

37 **Literary Focus** Pip goes to the limekiln alone. What character traits are indicated by this action?

could not think of going, for it would be too close upon the time of the flight. And again, for anything I knew, the proffered information might have some important bearing on the flight itself.

Having hardly any time for consideration, I resolved to go. I should certainly not have gone but for the reference to my Uncle Provis. That, coming on Wemmick's letter and the morning's busy preparation, turned the scale.

The journey seemed long and dreary to me who could see little of it inside, and who could not go outside in my disabled state. Avoiding the Blue Boar, I put up at an inn of minor reputation down the town, and ordered some dinner. While it was preparing, I went to Satis House and inquired for Miss Havisham; she was still very ill, though considered something better.

My inn had once been a part of an ancient ecclesiastical[4] house, and I dined in a little octagonal common room, like a font.[5] As I was not able to cut my dinner, the old landlord with a shining bald head did it for me. This bringing us into conversation, he was so good as to entertain me with my own story—of course with the popular feature that Pumblechook was my earliest benefactor and the founder of my fortunes.

I had never been struck at so keenly for my thanklessness to Joe, as through the brazen impostor Pumblechook. The falser he, the truer Joe; the meaner he, the nobler Joe.

My heart was deeply and most deservedly humbled as I mused over the fire for an hour or more. The striking of the clock aroused me, but not from my dejection or remorse, and I got up and had my coat fastened round

---
4. **ecclesiastical** (i klē′ ze as′ ti k'l) *adj.*: Associated with the church.
5. **font** *n.*: Basin for holy water in a church.

my neck, and went out. I had previously sought in my pockets for the letter, that I might refer to it again, but I could not find it, and was uneasy to think that it must have been dropped in the coach. I knew very well, however, that the appointed place was the little sluice house by the limekiln on the marshes, and the hour nine. Towards the marshes I now went straight, having no time to spare.

## Chapter 52

It was a dark night, though the full moon rose as I left the enclosed lands, and passed out upon the marshes. Beyond their dark line there was a ribbon of clear sky, hardly broad enough to hold the red large moon.

The direction that I took was not that in which my old home lay, nor that in which we had pursued the convicts. My back was turned towards the distant Hulks as I walked on, and, though I could see the old lights away on the spits of sand, I saw them over my shoulder. I knew the limekiln as well as I knew the old battery, but they were miles apart, so that if a light had been burning at each point that night, there would have been a long strip of the blank horizon between two bright specks.

It was another half-hour before I drew near to the kiln. The lime was burning with a sluggish stifling smell, but the fires were made up and left, and no workmen were visible.

Coming up again to the marsh level out of this excavation, I saw a light in the old sluice house. I quickened my pace, and knocked at the door with my hand. There was no answer, and I knocked again. No answer still, and I tried the latch.

It rose under my hand, and the door yielded. Looking in, I saw a lighted candle on a table, a bench, and a mattress on a truckle bedstead.[1] As there was a loft above, I called, "Is there any one here?" but no voice answered. Then, I looked at my watch, and finding that it was past nine, called again, "Is there any one here?" There being still no answer, I went out at the door, irresolute what to do.

It was beginning to rain fast. Seeing nothing save what I had seen already, I turned back into the house, and stood just within the shelter of the doorway, looking out into the night. While I was considering that some one must have been there lately and must soon be coming back, or the candle would not be burning, it came into my head to look if the wick were long. I turned round to do so, and had taken up the candle in my hand, when it was extinguished by some violent shock, and the next thing I comprehended was that I had been caught in a strong running noose, thrown over my head from behind.

"Now," said a suppressed voice with an oath, "I've got you!"

"What is this?" I cried, struggling. "Who is it? Help, help, help!"

Not only were my arms pulled close to my sides, but the pressure on my bad arm caused me exquisite pain. I struggled ineffectually in the dark, while I was fastened tight to the wall. "And now," said the suppressed voice with another oath, "call out again, and I'll make short work of you!"

After groping about for a little, he found the flint and steel he wanted, and began to strike a light. Presently I saw his blue lips again, breathing on the tinder, and then a flare of light flashed up, and showed me Orlick.

He lighted the candle from the flaring match with great deliberation, and dropped the match, and trod it out. Then, he put the candle away from him on the table, so that he could see me, and sat with his arms folded on the table and looked at me. I made out that I was fastened to a stout perpendicular ladder a few inches from the wall.

"Now," said he, when we had surveyed one another for some time, "I've got you."

"Unbind me. Let me go!"

"Ah!" he returned, "I'll let you go. I'll let you go to the moon, I'll let you go to the stars. All in good time."

"Why have you lured me here?"

"Don't you know?" said he, with a deadly look.

"Why have you set upon me in the dark?"

"Because I mean to do it all myself. One keeps a secret better than two. Oh, you enemy, you enemy!"

As I watched him in silence, he put his hand into the corner at his side, and took up a gun with a brass-bound stock.

"Do you know this?" said he. "Do you know where you saw it afore?

'Yes," I answered.

"You cost me that place.[2] You did. Speak!"

"What else could I do?"

"You did that, and that would be enough, without more. It was you as always give Old Orlick a bad name.

"What are you going to do to me?"

"I'm a-going," said he, bringing his fist down upon the table with a heavy blow, and rising as the blow fell, to give it greater force, "I'm a-going to have your life!

"More than that, I won't have a rag of you, I won't have a bone of you, left on earth. I'll put your body in the kiln and let people

---

**1. truckle bedstead:** Low bed on wheels that can be rolled underneath another bed.

**2. that place:** His position as watchman for Miss Havisham.

38 **Discussion** Why does Orlick consider himself Pip's enemy?

39 **Clarification** Lime dissolves bone as well as flesh, so there would be no trace of Pip's body if it were put in the limekiln.

suppose what they may of you, they shall never know nothing."

My mind, with inconceivable rapidity, followed out all the consequences of such a death. Estella's father would believe I had deserted him, would be taken, would die accusing me; even Herbert would doubt me. Joe and Biddy would never know how sorry I had been that night, none would ever know what I had suffered, how true I had meant to be, what an agony I had passed through. The death close before me was terrible, but far more terrible than death was the dread of being misremembered after death. And so quick were my thoughts that I saw myself despised by unborn generations—Estella's children, and their children—while the wretch's words were yet on his lips.

"Wolf!" said he, folding his arms, "Old Orlick's a-going to tell you somethink. It was me as did for your shrew sister. I come upon her from behind, as I come upon you tonight. I giv' it her! I left her for dead, and if there had been a limekiln as nigh her as there is now nigh you, she shouldn't have come to life again.

"Wolf, I'll tell you something more," he continued. "It was Old Orlick as you tumbled over on your stairs that night."

I saw the staircase with its extinguished lamps. I saw the shadows of the heavy stair-rails, thrown by the watchman's lantern on the wall. I saw the rooms that I was never to see again, here a door half-open, there a door closed, all the articles of furniture around.

"And why was Old Orlick there? Old Orlick says to himself, 'Somehow or another I'll have him!' What! When I looks for you, I finds your Uncle Provis, eh? And when Old Orlick come for to hear that your Uncle Provis had mostlike wore the leg-iron wot Old Orlick had picked up, filed asunder, on these meshes ever so many year ago, and wot he

kep by him till he dropped your sister with it, like a bullock, as he means to drop you—hey?—when he come for to hear that—hey?—

"Old Orlick knowed you was a-smuggling your Uncle Provis away. Old Orlick's a match for you and know'd you'd come tonight! Now I'll tell you something more, wolf, and this ends it. There's them that's as good a match for your Uncle Provis as Old Orlick has been for you. There's them that can't and that won't have Magwitch—yes, *I* know the name!—alive in the same land with them, and that's had such sure information of him when he was alive in another land, as that he couldn't and shouldn't leave it unbeknown and put them in danger."

There was a clear space of a few feet between the table and the opposite wall. Within this space, he now slouched backwards and forwards. His great strength seemed to sit stronger upon him than ever before, as he did this with his hands hanging loose and heavy at his sides, with his eyes scowling at me. I had no grain of hope left.

I shouted out with all my might, and struggled with all my might. It was only my head and my legs that I could move, but to that extent I struggled with all the force, until then unknown, that was within me. In the same instant I heard responsive shouts, saw figures and a gleam of light dash in at the door, heard voices and tumult, and saw Orlick emerge from a struggle of men, as if it were tumbling water, clear the table at a leap, and fly out into the night!

After a blank, I found that I was lying unbound, on the floor, in the same place, with my head on some one's knee. Too indifferent at first even to look round and ascertain who supported me, I was lying looking at the ladder when there came between me and it, a face. The face of Trabb's boy!

916 *The Novel*

"I think he's all right!" said Trabb's boy, in a sober voice, "but ain't he just pale though!"

At these words, the face of him who supported me looked over into mind, and I saw my supporter to be—

"Herbert! Great Heaven!"

"Softly," said Herbert. "Gently, Handel. Don't be too eager."

"And our old comrade, Startop!" I cried, as he too bent over me.

"Remember what he is going to assist us in," said Herbert, "and be calm."

The allusion made me spring up, though I dropped again from the pain in my arm. "The time has not gone by, Herbert, has it? What night is tonight? How long have I been here?" For, I had a strange and strong misgiving that I had been lying there a long time—a day and a night—two days and nights—more.

"The time has not gone by. It is still Monday night."

"Thank God!"

"And you have all tomorrow, Tuesday, to rest in," said Herbert. "But you can't help groaning, my dear Handel. What hurt have you got? Can you stand?"

"Yes, yes," said I, "I can walk. I have no hurt but in this throbbing arm."

Entreating Herbert to tell me how he had come to my rescue, I learned that I had in my hurry dropped the letter, open, in our chambers, where he, coming home to bring with him Startop, whom he had met in the street on his way to me, found it very soon after I was gone. Its tone made him uneasy, so he set off for the coach office with Startop to make inquiry when the next coach went down. Finding that the afternoon coach was gone, and finding that his uneasiness grew into positive alarm, as obstacles came in his way, he resolved to follow in a post-chaise.

So he and Startop arrived at the Blue Boar, fully expecting there to find me, or tidings of me but finding neither. Among the loungers under the Boar's archway happened to be Trabb's boy, and Trabb's boy had seen me passing from Miss Havisham's in the direction of my dining place. Thus, Trabb's boy became their guide.

When I told Herbert what had passed within the house, he was for our immediately going before a magistrate in the town, late at night as it was, and getting out a warrant. But I had already considered that such a course, by detaining us there, or binding us to come back, might be fatal to Provis.

Wednesday being so close upon us, we determined to go back to London that night, three in the post-chaise. It was daylight when we reached the Temple, and I went at once to bed, and lay in bed all day.

They kept me very quiet all day, and kept my arm constantly dressed, and gave me cooling drinks. About midnight I got out of bed and went to Herbert, with the conviction that I had been asleep for four-and-twenty hours, and that Wednesday was past. It was the last self-exhausting effort of my fretfulness, for after that I slept soundly.

Wednesday morning was dawning when I looked out of window. The winking lights upon the bridges were already pale, the coming sun was like a marsh of fire on the horizon. The river, still dark and mysterious, was spanned by bridges that were turning coldly gray. As I looked along the clustered roofs, with church towers and spires shooting into the unusually clear air, the sun rose up, and a veil seemed to be drawn from the river, and millions of sparkles burst out upon its waters. From me, too, a veil seemed to be drawn, and I felt strong and well.

Herbert lay asleep in his bed, and our old fellow-student lay asleep on the sofa. I could

41

**41 Discussion** How do Pip's injury and exhaustion add to the suspense of the attempt to rescue Provis?

THE YORK-LONDON MAIL COACH
*Gilbert S. Wright*
© Three Lions

not dress myself without help, but I made up the fire which was still burning, and got some coffee ready for them. In good time they too started up strong and well, and we admitted the sharp morning air at the windows, and looked at the tide that was still flowing towards us.

"When it turns at nine o'clock," said Herbert cheerfully, "look out for us, and stand ready, you over there at Mill Pond Bank!"

## Chapter 53

It was one of those March days when the sun shines hot and the wind blows cold—when it is summer in the light, and winter in the shade. We had our peacoats[1] with us, and I took a bag. Of all my worldly posses-

---

**1. peacoats** (pē′ kōts′) *n.*: Heavy woolen jackets, often worn by sailors.

sions I took no more than the few necessaries that filled the bag. Where I might go, what I might do, or when I might return were questions utterly unknown to me.

We loitered down to the Temple stairs. Of course I had taken care that the boat should be ready, and everything in order. After a little show of indecision, we went on board and cast off. It was then about high water—half-past eight.

Our plan was this. The tide beginning to run down at nine, and being with us until three, we intended still to creep on after it had turned, and row against it until dark. We should then be well in those long reaches below Gravesend, where lone public houses are scattered here and there, of which we could choose one for a resting-place. There we meant to lie all night. The steamer for Hamburg, and the steamer for Rotterdam,² would start from London at about nine on Thursday morning. We should know at what time to expect them, according to where we were, and would hail the first, so that if by any accident we were not taken aboard, we should have another chance.

Old London Bridge was soon passed, and old Billingsgate market with its oyster boats and Dutchmen, and the White Tower and Traitor's Gate, and we were in among the tiers of shipping. And now, I, sitting in the stern,³ could see with a faster beating heart Mill Pond Bank and Mill Pond stairs.

"Is he there?" said Herbert.

"Not yet."

"Right! He was not to come down till he saw us. Can you see his signal?"

"Not well from here; but I think I see it. Now I see him! Pull both. Easy, Herbert. Oars!"

We touched the stairs lightly for a single moment, and he was on board and we were off again. He had a boat-cloak with him, and a black canvas bag, and he looked as like a river pilot⁴ as my heart could have wished.

"Dear boy!" he said, putting his arm on my shoulder, as he took his seat. "Faithful dear boy, well done. Thankye, thankye!"

The air felt cold upon the river, but it was a bright day, and the sunshine was very cheering. The tide ran strong, I took care to lose none of it, and our steady stroke carried us on thoroughly well. By imperceptible degrees, as the tide ran out, we lost more and more of the nearer woods and hills, and dropped lower and lower between the muddy banks, but the tide was yet with us when we were off Gravesend.

Our oarsmen were so fresh, by dint of having occasionally let her drive with the tide for a minute or two, that a quarter of an hour's rest proved full as much as they wanted. We got ashore among some slippery stones while we ate and drank what we had with us, and looked about. It was like my own marsh country, flat and monotonous, and with a dim horizon.

We pushed off again, and made what way we could. It was much harder work now, but Herbert and Startop persevered, and rowed, and rowed, and rowed, until the sun went down.

As the night was fast falling, and as the moon, being past the full, would not rise early, we held a little council—a short one, for clearly our course was to lie by at the first lonely tavern we could find. So they plied

---

**2. Rotterdam** (rät′ ər dam′): Seaport in the Netherlands.
**3. stern** n.: Rear end of the boat.

**4. river pilot:** Person who directs or steers ships on a river.

---

**42 Discussion** Have students discuss or list the items *they* would pack in a bag if they were going abroad for an indefinite stay.

**43 Discussion** Do you think their plan is a good one? Explain.

**44 Discussion** Why do you think Provis selected this particular costume?

**Discussion** What news do Pip, Herbert, Provis, and Startop hear that increases their uneasiness?

their oars once more, and I looked out for anything like a house. Thus we held on, speaking little, for four or five dull miles.

At this dismal time we were evidently all possessed by the idea that we were followed. As the tide made, it flapped heavily at irregular intervals against the shore; and whenever such a sound came, one or other of us was sure to start and look in that direction.

At length we descried a light and a roof, and presently afterwards ran alongside a little causeway[5] made of stones that had been picked up hard by. Leaving the rest in the boat, I stepped ashore, and found the light to be in the window of a public house. It was a dirty place enough, and I dare say not unknown to smuggling adventures, but there was a good fire in the kitchen, and there were eggs and bacon to eat. No other company was in the house than the landlord, his wife, and a grizzled male creature, the "jack"[6] of the little causeway.

With this assistant, I went down to the boat again, and we all came ashore, and brought out the oars, and rudder, and boathook, and all else, and hauled her up for the night.

While we were comforting ourselves by the fire after our meal, the jack asked me if we had seen a four-oared galley[7] going up with the tide. When I told him no, he said she must have gone down then, and yet she "took up too," when she left there.

"They must ha' thought better on't for some reason or another," said the Jack, "and gone down."

"A four-oared galley did you say?" said I.

"A four," said the Jack, "and two sitters."

"He thinks," said the landlord, "he thinks they was what they wasn't."

"*I* knows what I thinks," observed the jack.

"*You* thinks custom-'us,[8] Jack?" said the landlord.

"I do," said the Jack.

"Why, what do you make out that they done with their buttons, then, Jack?" asked the landlord.

"A custom-'us officer knows what to do with his buttons," said the jack. "A four and two sitters don't go hanging and hovering, up with one tide and down with another, and both with and against another, without there being custom-'us at the bottom of it."

This dialogue made us all uneasy, and me very uneasy. A four-oared galley hovering about in so unusual a way as to attract this notice was an ugly circumstance that I could not get rid of. When I had induced Provis to go up to bed, I went outside with my two companions (Startop by this time knew the state of the case), and held another council. We decided to lie where we were, until within an hour or so of the steamer's time, and then to get out in her track, and drift easily with the tide. Having settled to do this, we returned into the house and went to bed.

When I awoke, the wind had risen, and the sign of the house (the Ship) was creaking and banging about, with noises that startled me. Rising softly, for my charge lay fast asleep, I looked out of the window. It commanded the causeway where we had hauled up our boat, and, as my eyes adapted themselves to the light of the clouded moon, I saw two men looking into her. They passed by under the window, looking at nothing else, and struck across the marsh in the direction of the Nore.

---

**5. causeway** (kôz′ wā) *n.*: Raised path or road across wet ground.
**6. "jack":** Sailor.
**7. galley** (gal′ ē) *n.*: Large rowboat.

---

**8. custom-'us:** Customs officers, who inspect passengers and goods entering or leaving the country.

920    *The Novel*

My first impulse was to call up Herbert, and show him the two men going away. But, reflecting that he and Startop had had a harder day than I, and were fatigued, I forbore. Going back to my window, I could see the two men moving over the marsh. In that light, however, I soon lost them, and feeling very cold, lay down to think of the matter, and fell asleep again.

We were up early. As we walked to and fro, all four together, before breakfast, I deemed it right to recount what I had seen. I proposed that Provis and I should walk away together to a distant point we could see, and that the boat should take us aboard there.

We got aboard easily, and rowed out into the track of the steamer. By that time it wanted but ten minutes of one o'clock, and we began to look out for her smoke.

But it was half-past one before we saw her smoke, and soon after we saw behind it the smoke of another steamer. As they were coming on at full speed, we got the two bags ready, and took that opportunity of saying good-bye to Herbert and Startop. We had all shaken hands cordially, and neither Herbert's eyes nor mine were quite dry, when I saw a four-oared galley shoot out from under the bank but a little way ahead of us, and row out into the same track.

A stretch of shore had been as yet between us and the steamer's smoke, by reason of the bend and wind of the river; but now she was visible coming head on. I called to Herbert and Startop to keep before the tide, that she might see us lying by for her, and adjured Provis to sit quite still, wrapped in his cloak. He answered cheerily, "Trust to me, dear boy," and sat like a statue. Meantime the galley, which was skilfully handled, had crossed us, let us come up with her, and fallen alongside. Leaving just room enough for the play of the oars, she kept alongside, drifting when we drifted, and pulling a stroke or two when we pulled. Of the two sitters, one held the rudder lines, and looked at us attentively—as did all the rowers; the other sitter was wrapped up, much as Provis was, and seemed to shrink, and whisper some instruction to the steerer as he looked at us. Not a word was spoken in either boat.

Startop could make out, after a few minutes, which steamer was first, and gave me the word "Hamburg," in a low voice as we sat face to face. She was nearing us very fast, and the beating of her paddles grew louder and louder. I felt as if her shadow were absolutely upon us, when the galley hailed us. I answered.

"You have a returned transport there," said the man who held the lines. "That's the man, wrapped in the cloak. His name is Abel Magwitch, otherwise Provis. I apprehend that man, and call upon him to surrender, and you to assist."

At the same moment, without giving any audible direction to the crew, he ran the galley aboard of us. They had pulled one sudden stroke ahead, had got their oars in, had run athwart us, and were holding on to our gunwale,[9] before we knew what they were doing. This caused great confusion on board of the steamer, and I heard them calling to us, and heard the order given to stop the paddles, and heard them stop, but felt her driving down upon us irresistibly. In the same moment, I saw the steersman of the galley lay his hand on his prisoner's shoulder, and saw that both boats were swinging round with the force of the tide, and saw that all hands on board the steamer were running forward quite frantically. Still in the same moment, I saw the prisoner start up, lean across his captor, and pull the cloak from the neck of the shrinking sitter in the galley.

---

**9. gunwale** (gun′l) *n*.: Upper edge of the side of a boat.

46 **Discussion** How does Dickens heighten the suspense of this moment?

**47 Discussion** Why does Magwitch swim back to the boat when he might have escaped?

**48 Discussion** Do you believe this account of events? Explain.

Still in the same moment, I saw that the face disclosed was the face of the other convict of long ago. Still in the same moment, I saw the face tilt backward with a white terror on it that I shall never forget, and heard a great cry on board the steamer and a loud splash in the water, and felt the boat sink from under me.

It was but for an instant that I seemed to struggle with a thousand mill-weirs[10] and a thousand flashes of light; that instant passed, I was taken on board the galley. Herbert was there, and Startop was there, but our boat was gone, and the two convicts were gone.

What with the cries aboard the steamer, and the furious blowing off of her steam, and her driving on, and our driving on, I could not at first distinguish sky from water or shore from shore; but the crew of the galley righted her with great speed, and, pulling certain swift strong strokes ahead, lay upon their oars, every man looking silently and eagerly at the water astern. Presently a dark object was seen in it, bearing towards us on the tide. No man spoke, but the steersman held up his hand, and all softly backed water, and kept the boat straight and true before it. As it came nearer, I saw it to be Magwitch, swimming, but not swimming freely. He was taken on board, and instantly manacled at the wrists and ankles.

The galley was kept steady, and the silent eager look-out at the water was resumed. But the Rotterdam steamer now came up, and apparently not understanding what had happened, came on at speed. By the time she had been hailed and stopped, both steamers were drifting away from us, and we were rising and falling in a troubled wake of water. The look-out was kept, long after all

_____
10. **mill-weirs** (mil′ wirz′) *n.*: Low dams to back up or divert water for a mill.

was still again and the two steamers were gone, but everybody knew that it was hopeless now.

At length we gave it up, and pulled under the shore towards the tavern we had lately left, where we were received with no little surprise. Here I was able to get some comforts for Magwitch—Provis no longer—who had received some very severe injury in the chest and a deep cut in the head.

He told me that he believed himself to have gone under the keel of the steamer, and to have been struck on the head in rising. The injury to his chest (which rendered his breathing extremely painful) he thought he had received against the side of the galley. He added that he did not pretend to say what he might or might not have done to Compeyson, but, in that moment of his laying his hand on his cloak to identify him, that villain had staggered up and staggered back, and they had both gone overboard together; when the sudden wrenching of him (Magwitch) out of our boat, and the endeavor of his captor to keep him in it, had capsized us. He told me in a whisper that they had gone down, fiercely locked in each other's arms, and that there had been a struggle under water, and that he had disengaged himself, struck out, and swam away.

I never had any reason to doubt the exact truth of what he had told me. The officer who steered the galley gave the same account of their going overboard.

When I asked this officer's permission to change the prisoner's wet clothes, he gave it readily, merely observing that he must take charge of everything his prisoner had about him. So the pocketbook which had once been in my hands passed into the officer's. He further gave me leave to accompany the prisoner to London.

We remained at the public house until the tide turned, and then Magwitch was car-

## Primary Source

Dickens spent a great deal of his time helping to correct the social evils of London and of his time. In "Dickens: The Dark Pilgrimage," an essay in *Charles Dickens 1812–1870, a Centennial Volume* edited by E.W.F. Tomlin, Edgar Johnson states the following about Dickens, his work, and his humanitarianism:

It was true. Dickens's whole career, indeed, in its fusion of sympathy, high spirits, relish for the richness and variety of human nature, hatred of cruelty and injustice, his concrete awareness of actual human beings and their sufferings, and his insistence on weighing everything in terms of their living welfare, is singularly consistent. If in personal conflict he was sometimes bitter and unyielding, he could love with warm and generous love. And unlike those lovers of humanity who are so often unable to love real people but only an abstraction, it was men, women, and children whom he loved, with all their weaknesses and absurdities.

He laughed and wept and loved and hated: he could be desperately unhappy; he was never superior and indifferent. When he thought people evil it was hard for him ried down to the galley and put on board. Herbert and Startop were to get to London by land, as soon as they could. We had a doleful parting, and when I took my place by Magwitch's side, I felt that that was my place henceforth while he lived.

For now my repugnance to him had all melted away, and in the hunted wounded shackled creature who held my hand in his, I only saw a man who had meant to be my benefactor, and who had felt affectionately, gratefully, and generously towards me with great constancy through a series of years. I only saw in him a much better man than I had been to Joe.

His breathing became more difficult and painful as the night drew on, and often he could not repress a groan. I tried to rest him on the arm I could use, in any easy position, but it was dreadful to think that I could not be sorry at heart for his being badly hurt, since it was unquestionably best that he should die.

As we returned towards the setting sun we had yesterday left behind us, and as the stream of our hopes seemed all running back, I told him how grieved I was to think he had come home for my sake.

"Dear boy," he answered, "I'm quite content to take my chance. I've seen my boy, and he can be a gentleman without me."

No. I had thought about that while we had been there side by side. No. Apart from any inclinations of my own, I understand Wemmick's hint now. I foresaw that, being convicted, his possessions would be forfeited to the Crown.[11]

"Lookee here, dear boy," said he. "It's best as a gentleman should not be knowed to belong to me now. Only come to see me as if

_____
**11. forfeited to the Crown:** Seized by the government.

you come by chance alonger Wemmick. Sit where I can see you when I am swore to, for the last o' many times, and I don't ask no more."

"I will never stir from your side," said I, "when I am suffered to be near you."

I felt his hand tremble as it held mine, and he turned his face away as he lay in the bottom of the boat, and I heard that old sound in his throat—softened now, like all the rest of him. It was a good thing that he had touched this point, for it put into my mind what I might not otherwise have thought of until too late: that he need never know how his hopes of enriching me had perished.


**Chapter 54**

He was taken to the police court next day, and would have been immediately committed for trial but that it was necessary to send down for an old officer of the prison ship from which he had once escaped, to speak to his identity. Nobody doubted it; but Compeyson, who had meant to depose to it, was tumbling on the tides, dead, and it happened that there was not at that time any prison officer in London who could give the required evidence. I had gone direct to Mr. Jaggers at his private house, on my arrival over night, to retain his assistance, and Mr. Jaggers on the prisoner's behalf would admit nothing. It was the sole resource, for he told me that the case must be over in five minutes when the witness was there, and that no power on earth could prevent its going against us.

I imparted to Mr. Jaggers my design of keeping him in ignorance of the fate of his wealth. Mr. Jaggers was querulous and angry with me for having "let it slip through my fingers," and said we must memorialize

**49 Discussion** How has Pip's attitude toward Magwitch changed?

**50 Literary Focus** Why does Pip think it better that Magwitch not know that his dream has "perished"? How does Pip's attitude reflect the theme of the novel?

**51 Discussion** Why does Mr. Jaggers tell Pip that no power on earth can save Magwitch from a sentence of death?

to regard them as human; his heart could explain them only as monsters. The evil that they did he fought with unwavering hostility, attacking them with the weapons of caricature and burlesque, or melodrama and unabashed sentiment. His spontaneous sympathy with the fruitful and the creative enabled him to understand how human nature was crippled by exploitation and selfishness, and he fought his way steadily to an understanding of all those dark forces in society that blight men's health and happiness. The great roll call of Dickens's work on every page is a celebration of the true wealth of life.

by-and-by, and try at all events for some of it. But he did not conceal from me that although there might be many cases in which forfeiture would not be exacted, there were no circumstances in this case to make it one of them.

There appeared to be reason for supposing that the drowned informer had hoped for a reward out of this forfeiture, and had obtained some accurate knowledge of Magwitch's affairs. When his body was found, many miles from the scene of his death, and so horribly disfigured that he was only recognizable by the contents of his pockets, notes were still legible, folded in a case he carried. Among these were the name of a banking house in New South Wales where a sum of money was, and the designation of certain lands of considerable value. Both those heads of information were in a list that Magwitch, while in prison, gave to Mr. Jaggers, of the possessions he supposed I should inherit. His ignorance, poor fellow, at last served him; he never mistrusted but that my inheritance was quite safe, with Mr. Jaggers's aid.

After three days' delay, the witness came, and completed the easy case. He was committed to take his trial at the next session, which would come on in a month.

It was at this dark time of my life that Herbert returned home one evening, a good deal cast down, and said:

"My dear Handel, I fear I shall soon have to leave you."

His partner having prepared me for that, I was less surpised than he thought.

"We shall lose a fine opportunity if I put off going to Cairo,[1] and I am very much afraid I must go, Handel, when you most need me."

---

1. **Cairo** (kī′ rō): Capital of Egypt.

"Herbert, I shall always need you, because I shall always love you, but my need is no greater now than at another time."

"My dear fellow," said Herbert, "let the near prospect of our separation—for, it is very near—be my justification for troubling you about yourself. Have you thought of your future?"

"No, for I have been afraid to think of any future."

"But yours cannot be dismissed; indeed, my dear, dear Handel, it must not be dismissed. I wish you would enter on it now, as far as a few friendly words go, with me."

"I will," said I.

"In this branch-house of ours, Handel, we must have a—"

I saw that his delicacy was avoiding the right word, so I said, "A clerk."

"A clerk. And I hope it is not at all unlikely that he may expand (as a clerk of your acquaintance has expanded) into a partner. Now, Handel—in short, my dear boy, will you come to me?"

I thanked him heartily, but said I could not yet make sure of joining him as he so kindly offered.

"But if you thought, Herbert, that you could, without doing any injury to your business, leave the question open for a little while—"

"For any while," cried Herbert. "Six months, a year!"

"Not so long as that," said I. "Two or three months at most."

Herbert was highly delighted when we shook hands on this arrangement, and said he could now take courage to tell me that he believed he must go away at the end of the week.

On the Saturday in that same week, I took my leave of Herbert—full of bright hope, but sad and sorry to leave me—as he sat on one of the seaport mail coaches.

Back at the Temple, I encountered Wemmick, who was coming down, after an unsuccessful application of his knuckles to my door. I had not seen him alone since the disastrous issue of the attempted flight, and he had come, in his private and personal capacity, to say a few words of explanation in reference to that failure.

"The late Compeyson," said Wemmick, "had by little and little got at the bottom of half of the regular business now transacted, and it was from the talk of some of his people in trouble that I heard what I did. I kept my ears open, seeming to have them shut, until I heard that he was absent, and I thought that would be the best time for making the attempt. I can only suppose now that it was a part of his policy, as a very clever man, habitually to deceive his own instruments. You don't blame me, I hope, Mr. Pip? I'm sure I tried to serve you, with all my heart."

"I am as sure of that, Wemmick, as you can be, and I thank you most earnestly for all your interest and friendship."

"Thank you, thank you very much. It's a bad job," said Wemmick, scratching his head, "and I assure you I haven't been so cut up for a long time. What I look at is the sacrifice of so much portable property. Dear me!"

"What *I* think of, Wemmick, is the poor owner of the property."

"Yes, to be sure," said Wemmick. "Of course there can be no objection to your being sorry for him, and I'd put down a five-pound note myself to get him out of it. But what I look at is this. The late Compeyson having been beforehand with him in intelligence of his return, and being so determined to bring him to book, I do not think he could have been saved. Whereas the portable property certainly could have been saved. That's the difference between the property and the owner, don't you see?"

**Chapter 55**

He lay in prison very ill, during the whole interval between his committal for trial, and the coming round of the sessions. He had broken two ribs, they had wounded one of his lungs, and he breathed with great pain and difficulty, which increased daily.

Being far too ill to remain in the common prison, he was removed, after the first day or so, into the infirmary. This gave me opportunities of being with him that I could not otherwise have had.

The trial was very short and very clear. Such things as could be said for him were said—how he had taken to industrious habits, and had thriven lawfully and reputably. But nothing could unsay the fact that he had returned, and was there in presence of the judge and jury. It was impossible to try him for that, and do otherwise than find him guilty.

At that time it was the custom to devote a concluding day to the passing of sentences, and to make a finishing effect with the sentence of death. But for the indelible picture that my remembrance now holds before me, I could scarcely believe that I saw two-and-thirty men and women put before the judge to receive that sentence together.

Among the wretched creatures before the judge whom he must single out for special address was one who almost from his infancy had been an offender against the laws; who, after repeated imprisonments and punishments, had been at length sentenced to exile for a term of years; and who, under circumstances of great violence and daring, had made his escape and been resentenced to exile for life. That miserable man would seem for a time to have become convinced of his errors, when far removed from the scenes of his old offenses, and to have lived a peaceable and honest life. But in a fatal

54 **Discussion** How do Wemmick's thoughts contrast with Pip's?

55 **Discussion** What is the effect of summarizing Magwitch's life in terms that the judge uses? Compare and contrast this summary with your own knowledge of his life.

56 **Discussion** In his reply to the court, what character trait does Magwitch reveal?

57 **Discussion** Why does Pip pray that Magwitch will die?

moment, he had quitted his haven of rest and repentance, and had come back to the country where he was proscribed.[1] The appointed punishment for his return to the land that had cast him out being death, and his case being this aggravated case, he must prepare himself to die. Rising for a moment, a distinct speck of face in this way of light, the prisoner said, "My Lord, I have received my sentence of death from the Almighty, but I bow to yours," and sat down again.

I earnestly hoped and prayed that he might die before the recorder's report was made, but, in the dread of his lingering on, I began that night to write out a petition to the Home Secretary of State, setting forth my knowledge of him, and how it was that he had come back for my sake. I wrote it as fervently and pathetically as I could, and when I had finished it and sent it in, I wrote out other petitions to such men in authority as I hoped were the most merciful, and drew up one to the Crown itself. For several days and nights after he was sentenced I took no rest, except when I fell asleep in my chair, but was wholly absorbed in these appeals.

The daily visits I could make him were shortened now, and he was more strictly kept. The officer always gave me the assurance that he was worse, and some other sick prisoners in the room always joined in the same report.

As the days went on, I noticed more and more that he would lie placidly looking at the white ceiling, with an absence of light in his face, until some word of mine brightened it for an instant, and then it would subside again.

The number of the days had risen to ten, when I saw a greater change in him than I had seen yet. His eyes were turned towards the door, and lighted up as I entered.

---

**1. proscribed** (prō skrīb′ 'd) v.: Banished.

"Dear boy," he said, as I sat down by his bed; "I thought you was late. But I knowed you couldn't be that."

"It is just the time," said I. "I waited for it at the gate."

"You always waits at the gate, don't you, dear boy?"

"Yes. Not to lose a moment of the time."

"Thank'ee, dear boy, thank'ee. God bless you! You've never deserted me, dear boy."

I pressed his hand in silence, for I could not forget that I had once meant to desert him.

"Are you in much pain today?"

"I don't complain of none, dear boy."

"You never do complain."

He had spoken his last words. He smiled, and I understood his touch to mean that he wished to lift my hand, and lay it on his breast. I laid it there, and he smiled again, and put both his hands upon it.

The allotted time ran out, while we were thus; but, looking round, I found the governor of the prison standing near me, and he whispered, "You needn't go yet." I thanked him gratefully, and asked, "Might I speak to him, if he can hear me?"

The governor stepped aside, and beckoned the officer away. The change, though it was made without noise, drew back the film from the placid look at the white ceiling, and he looked most affectionately at me.

"Dear Magwitch, I must tell you, now at last. You understand what I say?"

A gentle pressure on my hand.

"You had a child once, whom you loved and lost."

A stronger pressure on my hand.

"She lived and found powerful friends. She is living now. She is a lady and very beautiful. And I love her!"

With a last faint effort, which would have been powerless but for my yielding to it, and assisting it, he raised my hand to his lips.

Then he gently let it sink upon his breast again, with his own hands lying on it. The placid look at the white ceiling came back, and passed away, and his head dropped quietly on his breast.

## Chapter 56

Now that I was left wholly to myself, I gave notice of my intention to quit the chambers in the Temple as soon as my tenancy could legally determine, and in the meanwhile to underlet them.[1] I was in debt, and had scarcely any money, and began to be seriously alarmed by the state of my affairs. I ought rather to write that I should have been alarmed if I had had energy and concentration enough to help me to the clear perception of any truth beyond the fact that I was falling very ill.

For a day or two, I lay on the sofa, or on the floor—anywhere, according as I happened to sink down—with a heavy head and aching limbs, and no purpose, and no power. Then there came one night which appeared of great duration, and which teemed with anxiety and horror; and when in the morning I tried to sit up in my bed and think of it, I found I could not do so.

Whether I really had been down in Garden Court in the dead of the night, groping about for the boat that I supposed to be there; whether I had two or three times come to myself on the staircase with great terror, not knowing how I had got out of bed; whether I had been inexpressibly harassed by the distracted talking, laughing, and groaning of some one, and had half-suspected those sounds to be of my own making; whether there had been a closed

iron furnace in a dark corner of the room, and a voice had called out over and over again that Miss Havisham was within it; these were things that I tried to settle with myself and get into some order, as I lay that morning on my bed. But the vapor of a lime-kiln would come between me and them, disordering them all, and it was through the vapor at last that I saw two men looking at me.

"What do you want?" I asked, starting; "I don't know you."

"Well, sir," returned one of them, "this is a matter that you'll soon arrange, I dare say, but you're arrested."

"What is the debt?"

"Hundred and twenty-three pound, fifteen, six. Jeweler's account, I think."

"What is to be done?"

"You had better come to my house," said the man. "I keep a very nice house."

I made some attempt to get up and dress myself. When I next attended to them, they were standing a little off from the bed, looking at me. I still lay there.

"You see my state," said I. "I would come with you if I could; but indeed I am quite unable. If you take me from here, I think I shall die by the way."

Perhaps they replied, or argued the point, or tried to encourage me to believe that I was better than I thought. Forasmuch as they hang in my memory by only this one slender thread, I don't know what they did, except that they forbore to remove me.

After I had turned the worse point of my illness, I began to notice that while all its other features changed, this one consistent feature did not change. Whoever came about me, settled down into Joe. I opened my eyes in the night, and I saw in the great chair at the bedside, Joe. I opened my eyes in the day, and, sitting on the window seat, still I saw Joe. I asked for cooling drink, and the

---

1. **gave . . . underlet them:** Gave notice that I would leave my apartment as soon as the lease could be terminated, and in the meantime, sublet my rooms.

*Great Expectations* 927

58 **Discussion** What is the relationship between Pip and Magwitch at the end of Magwitch's life?

59 **Discussion** What episodes from Pip's past are incorporated into his hallucinations?

**WAITING FOR THE VERDICT, 1857**
*Abraham Solomon*
From the collection of Barbara and Norman S. Namerow, Beverly Hills, California

dear hand that gave it me was Joe's. I sank back on my pillow after drinking, and the face that looked so hopefully and tenderly upon me was the face of Joe.

At last, one day, I took courage, and said, "*Is* it Joe?"

And the dear old home-voice answered, "Which it air, old chap."

"Oh, Joe, you break my heart! Look angry at me, Joe. Strike me, Joe. Tell me of my ingratitude. Don't be so good to me!"

For Joe had actually laid his head down on the pillow at my side, and put his arm round my neck, in his joy that I knew him.

"Which dear old Pip, old chap," said Joe, "you and me was ever friends. And when you're well enough to go out for a ride—what larks!"

After which, Joe withdrew to the window, and stood with his back towards me, wiping his eyes. And as my extreme weakness prevented me from getting up and going to him, I lay there, penitently whispering, "O God bless him! O God bless this gentle Christian man!"

Joe's eyes were red when I next found him beside me, but I was holding his hand and we both felt happy.

"How long, dear Joe?"

"Which you meantersay, Pip, how long have your illness lasted, dear old chap?"

"Yes, Joe."

"It's the end of May, Pip. Tomorrow is the first of June."

"And have you been here all the time, dear Joe?"

"Pretty nigh, old chap. For, as I says to Biddy when the news of your being ill were brought by letter, which it were brought by the post that how you might be amongst strangers, and that how you and me having been ever friends, a wisit at such a moment might not prove unacceptabobble. And Biddy, her word were, 'Go to him, without loss of time.' That," said Joe, summing up with his judicial air, "were the word of Biddy. 'Go to him,' Biddy say, 'without loss of time.' "

There Joe cut himself short, and informed me that I was to be talked to in great moderation, and that I was to take a little nourishment at stated frequent times, whether I felt inclined for it or not, and that I was to submit myself to all his orders. So I kissed his hand, and lay quiet, while he proceeded to indite a note to Biddy, with my love in it.

Evidently Biddy had taught Joe to write. As I lay in bed looking at him, it made me, in my weak state, cry again with pleasure to see the pride with which he set about his letter.

Not to make Joe uneasy by talking too much, even if I had been able to talk much, I deferred asking him about Miss Havisham until next day. He shook his head when I then asked him if she had recovered.

"Is she dead, Joe?"

"Why, you see, old chap," said Joe, "I wouldn't go so far as to say that, for that's a deal to say; but she ain't living."

"Dear Joe, have you heard what becomes of her property?"

"Well, old chap," said Joe, "it do appear that she had settled the most of it, which I meantersay tied it up, on Miss Estella. But she had wrote out a little coddleshell[2] in her own hand a day or two afore the accident, leaving a cool four thousand to Mr. Matthew Pocket. And why, do you suppose, above all things, Pip, she left that cool four thousand unto him? 'Because of Pip's account of him the said Matthew.' I am told by Biddy that air the writing," said Joe, repeating the legal turn as if it did him infinite good, " 'account of him the said Matthew.' And a cool four thousand, Pip!"

This account gave me great joy, as it perfected the only good thing I had done.

"And now," said Joe, "you ain't that strong yet, old chap, that you can take in more nor one additional shovel-full today. Old Orlick he's been a-bustin' open a dwelling'ouse."

"Whose?" said I.

"Not, I grant you, but what his manners is given to blusterous," said Joe apologetically; "still, a Englishman's 'ouse is his castle, and castles must not be busted 'cept when done in wartime. And wotsome'er the failings on his part, he were a corn and seedsman in his hart."

---

**2. coddleshell:** Joe means codicil (käd′ i s'l), an addition to a will.

*Great Expectations* 929

60 **Discussion** How does Joe help restore Pip to life after the worst of his illness has passed? In what way is Joe unchanged?

61 **Discussion** Why does Matthew Pocket's good fortune make Pip so happy?

**Discussion** How has Uncle Pumblechook met with misfortune?

**Discussion** What is significant about this particular memory?

**Discussion** As Pip's health improves and as he becomes stronger, what change does he notice in Joe's attitude toward him? How does the change affect Pip?

"Is it Pumblechook's house that has been broken into, then?"

"That's it, Pip," said Joe; "and they took his till, and they took his cashbox, and they slapped his face, and they pulled his nose, and they tied him up to his bed-post. But he knowed Orlick, and Orlick's in the county jail."

We looked forward to the day when I should go out for a ride, as we had once looked forward to the day of my apprenticeship. And when the day came, and an open carriage was got into the lane, Joe wrapped me up, took me in his arms, carried me down to it, and put me in, as if I were still the small helpless creature to whom he had so abundantly given of the wealth of his great nature.

And Joe got in beside me, and we drove away together into the country, where the rich summer growth was already on the trees and on the grass, and sweet summer scents filled all the air.

When we got back again and he lifted me out, and carried me—so easily!—across the court and up the stairs, I thought of that eventful Christmas Day when he had carried me over the marshes. We had not yet made any allusion to my change of fortune, nor did I know how much of my late history he was acquainted with. I was so doubtful of myself now, and put so much trust in him, that I could not satisfy myself whether I ought to refer to it when he did not.

"Have you heard, Joe," I asked him that evening, upon further consideration, "who my patron was?"

"I heerd," returned Joe, "as it were not Miss Havisham, old chap."

"Did you hear who it was, Joe?"

"Well! I heerd as it were a person what sent the person what giv' you the banknotes at the Jolly Bargemen, Pip."

"So it was."

"Astonishing!" said Joe, in the placidest way.

"Did you hear that he was dead, Joe?" I presently asked, with increasing diffidence.

"I think," said Joe, after meditating a long time, and looking rather evasively at the window-seat, "as I *did* hear tell that how he were something or another in a general way in that direction."

"Did you hear anything of his circumstances, Joe?"

"Not partickler, Pip."

"If you would like to hear, Joe—" I was beginning, when Joe got up and came to my sofa.

"Look'ee here, old chap," said Joe, bending over me. "Ever the best of friends; ain't us, Pip?"

I was ashamed to answer him.

"Werry good, then," said Joe, as if I *had* answered; "that's all right; that's agreed upon. Then why go into subjects, old chap, which as betwixt two sech must be for ever onnecessary?"

Another thing in Joe that I could not understand when it first began to develop itself, but which I soon arrived at a sorrowful comprehension of, was this: as I became stronger and better, Joe became a little less easy with me.

It was on the third or fourth occasion of my going out walking in the Temple gardens, leaning on Joe's arm, that I saw this change in him very plainly. We had been sitting in the bright warm sunlight, looking at the river, and I chanced to say as we got up:

"See, Joe! I can walk quite strongly. Now, you shall see me walk back by myself."

"Which do not overdo it, Pip," said Joe; "but I shall be happy fur to see you able, sir."

The last word grated on me, but how could I remonstrate! I walked no further

## Grammar in Action

Think of how awkward writing and speaking would be if we had to always refer to something by its name. To avoid that, writers will use pronouns that refer to the noun previously mentioned. A **referent** is the person, thing, idea, or condition to which a word refers. Referents must agree with the noun to which it refers in gender and number. Look at the lines from the novel:

"Is it Pumblechook's house that has been broken into, then?"

"That's it, Pip," said Joe, "and they took his till, and they took his cashbox, and they slapped his face, and they pulled his nose, and they tied him to his bed-post."

The referents of pronouns may be at times difficult to figure out. Context can help determine for what each pronoun stands. In this passage, *it* in the first sentence has its referent, *house,* in that sentence. When Joe uses *it* in the second sentence, he refers to the entire statement that Pip has just made. In Joe's statement, to whom do *they* refer? To whom does *he* refer?

than the gate of the gardens, and then pretended to be weaker than I was, and asked Joe for his arm. Joe gave it me, but was thoughtful.

It was a thoughtful evening with both of us. But before we went to bed, I had resolved that I would wait over tomorrow, tomorrow being Sunday, and would begin my new course with the new week. On Monday morning I would speak to Joe about this change, I would lay aside this last vestige of reserve, I would tell him what I had in my thoughts (that secondly, not yet arrived at), and why I had not decided to go out to Herbert, and then the change would be conquered for ever.

We had a quiet day on the Sunday, and we rode out into the country, and then walked in the fields.

"I feel thankful that I have been ill, Joe," I said.

"Dear old Pip, old chap, you're a'most come round, sir."

"It has been a memorable time for me, Joe."

"Likeways for myself, sir," Joe returned.

"We have had a time together, Joe, that I can never forget. There were days once, I know, that I did for a while forget; but I never shall forget these."

"Pip," said Joe, appearing a little hurried and troubled, "there has been larks. And, dear sir, what have been betwixt us—have been."

At night, when I had gone to bed, Joe came into my room, as he had done all through my recovery. He asked me if I felt sure that I was as well as in the morning.

"Yes, dear Joe, quite."

"And are always a-getting stronger, old chap?"

"Yes, dear Joe, steadily."

Joe patted the coverlet on my shoulder with his great good hand, and said, in what I thought a husky voice, "Good night!"

When I got up in the morning, refreshed and stronger yet, I was full of my resolution to tell Joe all, without delay. I hurried then to the breakfast-table, and on it found a letter. These were its brief contents.

Not wishful to intrude I have departured fur you are well again dear Pip and will do better without Jo. P.S. Ever the best of friends.

Enclosed in the letter was a receipt for the debt and costs on which I had been arrested. Down to that moment I had vainly supposed that my creditor had withdrawn or suspended proceedings until I should be quite recovered. I had never dreamed of Joe's having paid the money; but Joe had paid it, and the receipt was in his name.

What remained for me now, but to follow him to the dear old forge, and there to have out my disclosure to him, and my penitent remonstrance with him, and there to relieve my mind and heart of that reserved secondly, which had begun as a vague something lingering in my thoughts, and had formed into a settled purpose?

The purpose was that I would go to Biddy, that I would show her how humbled and repentant I came back, that I would tell her how I had lost all I once hoped for, that I would remind her of our old confidences in my first unhappy time. Then, I would say to her, "Biddy, I think you once liked me very well, when my errant heart, even while it strayed away from you, was quieter and better with you than it ever has been since. If you can like me only half as well once more, if you can take me with all my faults and disappointments on my head, if you can receive me like a forgiven child, I hope I am a little

65 **Discussion** What inspires Pip's new purpose?

65

**Student Activity 1.** Find another passage in the novel that contains at least four different pronouns. Read the passage aloud to a small group of classmates as they follow in their texts.

**Student Activity 2.** Explain the referent of each pronoun in the passage you just read, discussing each one with the group.

**Student Activity 3.** Write a brief summary of *Great Expectations* so far. In your description, be sure to use referents. Exchange papers with another classmate and underline the nouns and their referents.

worthier of you than I was—not much, but a little. And, Biddy, it shall rest with you to say whether I shall work at the forge with Joe, or whether I shall try for any different occupation down in this country, or whether we shall go away to a distant place where an opportunity awaits me which I set aside when it was offered, until I knew your answer. And now, dear Biddy, if you can tell me that you will go through the world with me, you will surely make it a better world for me, and me a better man for it, and I will try hard to make it a better world for you."

Such was my purpose. After three days more of recovery, I went down to the old place, to put it in execution.

## Chapter 57

The tidings of my high fortunes had a heavy fall, had got down to my native place and its neighborhood before I got there. I found the Blue Boar in possession of the intelligence, and I found that it made a great change in the Boar's demeanor. Whereas the Boar had cultivated my good opinion with warm assiduity when I was coming into property, the Boar was exceedingly cool on the subject now that I was going out of property.

It was evening when I arrived, much fatigued by the journey I had so often made so easily. The Boar could not put me into my usual bedroom, which was engaged (probably by some one who had expectations), and could only assign me a very indifferent chamber among the pigeons and postchaises up the yard. But I had as sound a sleep in that lodging as in the most superior accommodation the Boar could have given me, and the quality of my dreams was about the same as in the best bedroom.

Early in the morning while my breakfast was getting ready, I strolled round by Satis House. There were printed bills on the gate and on bits of carpet hanging out of the windows, announcing a sale by auction of the household furniture and effects, next week. The house itself was to be sold as old building materials, and pulled down.

The schoolhouse where Biddy was mistress, I had never seen, but the little roundabout lane by which I entered the village for quietness' sake, took me past it. I was disappointed to find that the day was a holiday; no children were there, and Biddy's house was closed. Some hopeful notion of seeing her, busily engaged in her daily duties, before she saw me, had been in my mind and was defeated.

But the forge was a very short distance off, and I went towards it under the sweet green limes, listening for the clink of Joe's hammer. Long after I ought to have heard it, and long after I had fancied I heard it and found it but a fancy, all was still. The limes were there, and the white thorns were there, and the chestnut trees were there, and their leaves rustled harmoniously when I stopped to listen, but the clink of Joe's hammer was not in the midsummer wind.

Almost fearing, without knowing why, to come in view of the forge, I saw it at last, and saw that it was closed. No gleam of fire, no glittering shower of sparks, no roar of bellows; all shut up, and still.

But the house was not deserted, and the best parlor seemed to be in use, for there were white curtains fluttering in its window, and the window was open and gay with flowers. I went softly towards it, meaning to peep over the flowers, when Joe and Biddy stood before me, arm in arm.

At first Biddy gave a cry, as if she thought it was my apparition, but in another moment she was in my embrace. I wept to see her, and she wept to see me; I because she looked so fresh and pleasant; she because I looked so worn and white.

"But, dear Biddy, how smart you are!"

"Yes, dear Pip."

"And Joe, how smart *you* are!"

"Yes, dear old Pip, old chap."

I looked at both of them, from one to the other, and then—

"It's my wedding-day," cried Biddy, in a burst of happiness, "and I am married to Joe!"

They had taken me into the kitchen, and I had laid my head down on the old deal table. Biddy held one of my hands to her lips, and Joe's restoring touch was on my shoulder. "Which he warn't strong enough, my dear, fur to be surprised," said Joe. And Biddy said, "I ought to have thought of it, dear Joe, but I was too happy." They were both so overjoyed to see me, so proud to see me, so touched by my coming to them, so delighted that I should have come by accident to make their day complete!

My first thought was one of great thankfulness that I had never breathed this last baffled hope to Joe. How often, while he was with me in my illness, had it risen to my lips. How irrevocable would have been his knowledge of it, if he had remained with me but another hour!

"Dear Biddy," said I, "you have the best husband in the whole world, and if you could have seen him by my bed you would have—But no, you couldn't love him better than you do."

"No, I couldn't indeed," said Biddy.

"And, dear Joe, you have the best wife in the whole world, and she will make you as happy as even you deserve to be, you dear, good, noble Joe!"

Joe looked at me with a quivering lip, and fairly put his sleeve before his eyes.

"And Joe and Biddy both, as you have been to church today and are in charity and love with all mankind, receive my humble thanks for all you have done for me, and all I have so ill-repaid! And when I say that I am going away within the hour, for I am soon going abroad, and that I shall never rest until I have worked for the money with which you have kept me out of prison, and have sent it to you, don't think, dear Joe and Biddy, that if I could repay it a thousand times over, I suppose I could cancel a farthing[1] of the debt I owe you, or that I would do so if I could!"

They were both melted by these words, and both entreated me to say no more.

"But I must say more. Dear Joe, I hope you will have children to love, and that some little fellow will sit in this chimney corner, of a winter night, who may remind you of another little fellow gone out of it for ever. Don't tell him, Joe, that I was thankless; don't tell him, Biddy, that I was ungenerous and unjust; only tell him that I honored you both, because you were both so good and true, and that, as your child, I said it would be natural to him to grow up a much better man than I did."

"I ain't a-going," said Joe, from behind his sleeve, "to tell him nothink o' that natur, Pip. Nor Biddy ain't. Nor yet no one ain't."

"And now, though I know you have already done it in your own kind hearts, pray tell me, both, that you forgive me! Pray let me hear you say the words, that I may carry the sound of them away with me, and then I shall be able to believe that you can trust me, and think better of me, in the time to come!"

"Oh, dear old Pip, old chap," said Joe. "God knows as I forgive you, if I have anything to forgive!"

---

**1. farthing** (fär′ thiŋ) *n.*: Small British coin equal to one fourth of a penny.

Great Expectations    933

69 **Discussion** Why is Pip thankful?

70 **Discussion** In what way does Pip hope Joe and Biddy will be reminded of him in time to come? What is Joe's attitude toward this idea?

71 **Literary Focus** How does this summary of later events relate to the theme of the novel?

72 **Discussion** What changes have eleven years of marriage made in the lives of Joe and Biddy?

"Amen! And God knows I do!" echoed Biddy.

"Now let me go up and look at my old little room, and rest there a few minutes by myself. And then when I have eaten and drunk with you, go with me as far as the finger post,[2] dear Joe and Biddy, before we say goodbye!"

I sold all I had, and put aside as much as I could, for a composition with my creditors—who gave me ample time to pay them in full—and I went out and joined Herbert. Within a month, I had quitted England, and within two months I was clerk to Clarriker & Co., and within four months I assumed my first undivided responsibility. For the beam across the parlor ceiling at Mill Pond Bank had then ceased to tremble under old Bill Barley's growls and was at peace, and Herbert had gone away to marry Clara, and I was left in sole charge of the Eastern branch until he brought her back.

Many a year went round, before I was a partner in the house; but I lived happily with Herbert and his wife, and lived frugally, and paid my debts, and maintained a constant correspondence with Biddy and Joe. It was not until I became third in the firm that Clarriker betrayed me to Herbert; but he then declared that the secret of Herbert's partnership had been long enough upon his conscience, and he must tell it. So, he told it, and Herbert was as much moved as amazed, and the dear fellow and I were not the worse friends for the long concealment. I must not leave it to be supposed that we were ever a great house, or that we made mints of money. We were not in a grand way of business, but we had a good name, and worked for our profits, and did very well.

---

2. **finger post:** Signpost.

**Chapter 58**

For eleven years I had not seen Joe nor Biddy with my bodily eyes—though they had both been often before my fancy in the East—when, upon an evening in December, an hour or two after dark, I laid my hand softly on the latch of the old kitchen door. I touched it so softly that I was not heard, and I looked in unseen. There, smoking his pipe in the old place by the kitchen firelight, as hale and as strong as ever, though a little gray, sat Joe; and there, fenced into the corner with Joe's leg, and sitting on my own little stool looking at the fire, was—I again!

"We giv' him the name of Pip for your sake, dear old chap," said Joe, delighted when I took another stool by the child's side (but I did *not* rumple his hair), "and we hoped he might grow a little bit like you, and we think he do."

I thought so, too, and I took him out for a walk next morning, and we talked immensely, understanding one another to perfection. And I took him down to the churchyard, and set him on a certain tombstone there, and he showed me from that elevation which stone was sacred to the memory of Philip Pirrip, Late of this Parish, and Also Georgiana Wife of the Above.

"Biddy," said I, when I talked with her after dinner, as her little girl lay sleeping in her lap, "you must give Pip to me, one of these days; or lend him, to all events."

"No, no," said Biddy gently. "You must marry."

"So Herbert and Clara say, but I don't think I shall, Biddy. I have so settled down in their home that it's not at all likely. I am already quite an old bachelor."

Biddy looked down at her child, and put its little hand to her lips, and then put the good matronly hand with which she had touched it into mine. There was something in the action and in the light pressure of Biddy's wedding ring that had a very pretty eloquence in it.

"Dear Pip," said Biddy, "you are sure you don't fret for her?"

"Oh, no—I think not, Biddy."

"Tell me as an old friend. Have you quite forgotten her?"

"My dear Biddy, I have forgotten nothing in my life that ever had a foremost place there, and little that ever had any place there. But that poor dream, as I once used to call it, has all gone by, Biddy, all gone by!"*

Nevertheless, I knew that while I said those words that I secretly intended to revisit the sight of the old house that evening alone, for her sake. Yes, even so. For Estella's sake.

I had heard of her as leading a most unhappy life, and as being separated from her husband, who had used her with great cruelty, and who had become quite renowned as a compound of pride, avarice, brutality, and meanness. And I had heard of the death of her husband from an accident consequent on his ill-treatment of a horse. This release had befallen her some two years before; for anything I knew, she was married again.

The early dinner-hour at Joe's left me abundance of time, without hurrying my talk with Biddy, to walk over to the old spot before dark. But what with loitering on the way to look at old objects and to think of old times, the day had quite declined when I came to the place.

There was no house now, no brewery, no building whatever left, but the wall of the old garden. The cleared space had been enclosed with a rough fence, and looking over it, I saw that some of the old ivy had struck root

_____
*The original ending of the book followed this paragraph. See the explanation on page 937.

anew, and was growing green on low quiet mounds of ruin. A gate in the fence standing ajar, I pushed it open, and went in.

A cold silvery mist had veiled the afternoon, and the moon was not yet up to scatter it. But the stars were shining beyond the mist, and the moon was coming, and the evening was not dark. I could trace out where every part of the old house had been, and where the brewery had been, and where the gates, and where the casks. I had done so, and was looking along the desolate garden-walk, when I beheld a solitary figure in it.

The figure showed itself aware of me as I advanced. It had been moving towards me, but it stood still. As I drew nearer, I saw it to be the figure of a woman. As I drew nearer yet, it was about to turn away, when it stopped, and let me come up with it. Then it faltered as if much surprised, and uttered my name, and I cried out:

"Estella!"

"I am greatly changed. I wonder you know me."

The freshness of her beauty was indeed gone, but its indescribable majesty and its indescribable charm remained. Those attractions in it I had seen before; what I had never seen before was the saddened, softened light of the once proud eyes; what I had never felt before was the friendly touch of the once insensible hand.

We sat down on a bench that was near, and I said, "After so many years, it is strange that we should thus meet again, Estella, here where our first meeting was! Do you often come back?"

"I have never been here since."

"Nor I."

The moon began to rise, and I thought of the placid look at the white ceiling, which had passed away. The moon began to rise,

73 **Discussion** What has changed Pip's attitude toward marriage?

74 **Discussion** What mood does this description create?

75 **Discussion** How has Estella changed in appearance?

Fine art, *The Proposal*, 1877, by William Powell Frith. The British painter William Powell Frith (1819-1909) vowed to devote his art to the description of scenes of ordinary life. Upon graduating from the Royal Academy school, Frith did just that and so became a favorite of the Victorians. He painted what the public wanted to see and received high prices for his works.

*The Proposal* is the second painting of this title and theme done by Frith. The story-telling skill of this artist allows the title and the scene itself to inform the viewer of the situation. The woman seems demure and the man shows a protective concern.

You might want to ask students the following questions:

1. Explain what is occurring in this picture.
2. Describe the different attitudes of the man and woman.
3. Is this picture an appropriate accompaniment to the final meeting of Pip and Estella? Explain.

**THE PROPOSAL, 1877**
*William Powell Frith*
Lady Scott, Boughton House, Kettering

936   *The Novel*

and I thought of the pressure on my hand when I had spoken the last words he had heard on earth.

Estella was the next to break the silence that ensued between us.

"I have very often hoped and intended to come back, but have been prevented by many circumstances. Poor, poor old place!"

The silvery mist was touched with the first rays of the moonlight, and the same rays touched the tears that dropped from her eyes. Not knowing that I saw them, and setting herself to get the better of them, she said quietly:

"Were you wondering, as you walked along, how it came to be left in this condition?"

"Yes, Estella."

"The ground belongs to me. It is the only possession I have not relinquished. Everything else has gone from me, little by little, but I have kept this. It was the subject of the only determined resistance I made in all the wretched years."

"Is it to be built on?"

"At last it is. I came here to take leave of it before its change. And you," she said, in a voice of touching interest to a wanderer, "you live abroad still."

"Still."

"And do well, I am sure?"

"I work pretty hard for a sufficient living, and therefore—Yes, I do well!"

"I have often thought of you," said Estella.

"Have you?"

"Of late, very often. There was a long hard time when I kept far from me the remembrance of what I had thrown away when I was quite ignorant of its worth. But since my duty has not been incompatible with the admission of that remembrance, I have given it a place in my heart."

"You have always held your place in *my* heart," I answered.

And we were silent again until she spoke.

"I little thought," said Estella, "that I should take leave of you in taking leave of this spot. I am very glad to do so."

"Glad to part again, Estella? To me, parting is a painful thing. To me, the remembrance of our last parting has been ever mournful and painful."

"But you said to me," returned Estella very earnestly, " 'God bless you, God forgive you!' And if you could say that to me then, you will not hesitate to say that to me now—now, when suffering has been stronger than all other teaching, and has taught me to understand what your heart used to be. I have been bent and broken, but—I hope—into a better shape. Be as considerate and good to me as you were, and tell me we are friends."

"We are friends," said I, rising and bending over her, as she rose from the bench.

"And will continue friends apart," said Estella.

I took her hand in mine, and we went out of the ruined place; and as the morning mists had risen long ago when I first left the forge, so the evening mists were rising now, and in all the broad expanse of tranquil light they showed to me, I saw no shadow of another parting from her.

*The passage below, which once followed the asterisk on page 935, made up the original ending of* Great Expectations. *Just before the book was published, however, Dickens substituted the ending you have already read.*

It was two years more before I saw herself. I had heard of her as leading a most unhappy life, and as being separated from

76 **Reading Strategy** Summarize the discussion between Estella and Pip. How has each of them changed?

77 **Discussion** Why does Estella say this?

78 **Critical Thinking and Reading** After students read the original ending, ask: Which ending do you prefer? Explain.

her husband, who had used her with great cruelty, and who had become quite renowned as a compound of pride, brutality, and meanness. I had heard of the death of her husband from an accident consequent on ill-treating a horse, and of her being married again to a Shropshire doctor who, against his interest, had once very manfully interposed on an occasion when he was in professional attendance upon Mr. Drummle, and had witnessed some outrageous treatment of her. I had heard that the Shropshire doctor was not rich, and that they lived on her own personal fortune. I was in England again—in London, and walking along Piccadilly with little Pip—when a servant came running after me to ask would I step back to a lady in a carriage who wished to speak to me. It was a little pony carriage which the lady was driving, and the lady and I looked sadly enough on one another.

"I am greatly changed, I know, but I thought you would like to shake hands with Estella, too, Pip. Lift up that pretty child and let me kiss it!" (She supposed the child, I think, to be my child.) I was very glad afterwards to have had the interview, for in her face and in her voice, and in her touch, she gave me the assurance that suffering had been stronger than Miss Havisham's teaching, and had given her a heart to understand what my heart used to be.

## Closure and Extension

### ANSWERS TO THINKING ABOUT THE SELECTION
*Recalling*

1. Pip realizes that she is Estella's mother.
2. Miss Havisham agrees to continue Pip's plan of assisting Herbert,

begs Pip's forgiveness, and gives him more information about Estella.
3. Pip struggles so hard to free himself from Orlick that he reinjures his arm severely.
4. Pip helps Magwitch by hiding him from his pursuers, and then he attempts an escape. After the attempt fails, Pip stays close to the dying man, comforting him until the end.
5. The key events include the following: Pip becomes ill and is nursed to health by Joe. Pip learns that

Miss Havisham has died and left her estate to Estella, with a small provision for Matthew Pocket. Orlick is jailed for robbing Pumblechook. Pip decides to return to the forge and marry Biddy, but arrives on her and Joe's wedding day. Pip works for Clarriker and eventually becomes a partner. He returns to England and finds another little Pip sitting by the chimney corner.
6. Pip and Estella are now middle-aged. He has long since given up

his dream of marrying her. Estella has lost her youthful beauty.

*Interpreting*

7. Suggested Response: Pip tells Miss Havisham about the suffering she has caused him, and she is shocked into looking at herself realistically.
8. Suggested Response: Pip is devoted to his benefactor even though he knows that such devotion will not bring him wealth or

## THINKING ABOUT THE SELECTION

### Recalling

1. What does Pip realize about Mr. Jaggers's housekeeper?
2. Explain the discussion between Pip and Miss Havisham before her accident and death.
3. How does Pip reinjure his arm before trying to row Magwitch to a steamer?
4. In what ways does Pip show loyalty to Magwitch before and after his capture?
5. What key events occur between Magwitch's death and Pip's meeting with Estella?
6. How are Pip and Estella changed when they meet again?

### Interpreting

7. What accounts for Miss Havisham's change of heart?
8. How does Pip's loyalty to Magwitch relate to the theme of the novel?
9. Why do you think Dickens altered the original ending of *Great Expectations*? Explain which ending you prefer.

### Applying

10. What would happen to Pip if the novel continued? Give reasons for your answer.

## ANALYZING LITERATURE

### Understanding the Novel as a Whole

By considering how the elements in *Great Expectations* work together, you will better appreciate the novel as a whole.

1. Find three examples of how the first-person narrative adds to the drama of the plot.
2. Show how the changes that Pip, Estella, and Miss Havisham experience relate to the theme of the novel.
3. Identify two passages where the setting creates a mood that enhances the action.

4. Why is the surprise return of Pip's benefactor valuable in pointing up the theme?
5. Choose a scene from the book and show how all the literary elements contribute to it.
6. Explain what this novel reveals about expectations and happiness.

## CRITICAL THINKING AND READING

### Using Criteria to Evaluate the Novel

**Criteria** are the standards by which a work is judged. You can develop criteria for evaluating a novel by answering the following questions about its elements. (You should think of additional questions as well.) Does the point of view involve you in the events of the story? Are the characters interesting and believable? Does the writer pace events so they do not move too quickly or too slowly? Does the writer describe the setting vividly? Is the central idea about life important? Does this idea flow naturally from the story?

Create a chart with the headings *Criteria, Opinions,* and *Evidence.* Under *Criteria,* list the above questions and some of your own. Briefly note your answers in the next column, *Opinions.* Then, under *Evidence,* list passages from the book that support your answers.

## THINKING AND WRITING

### Evaluating the Novel

Using your chart, write an evaluation of *Great Expectations.* Your chart should support your overall opinion of the book. If you liked the novel, for instance, most of the opinions on the chart should be positive. Begin your essay with an introduction briefly stating your general opinion of the novel. In the body of the essay, evaluate each of the elements based on your criteria. Conclude with a summary and restatement of your opinion. In revising, make sure you have discussed how the elements work together. Share your essay with your classmates when you have finished.

*Great Expectations* 939

---

(Answers begin on p. 938.)

men. Before she dies, Miss Havisham sees that her plans for revenge have hurt herself, Estella, and Pip. She is genuinely sorry for what she has done.

3. Suggested Response: At the start of the novel, the graveyard creates an atmosphere of mystery and fear. When Pip falls into Orlick's trap, the marshes create a similar atmosphere, adding to the suspense.

4. Suggested Response: The surprise return of Pip's benefactor shocks Pip out of his mistaken assumptions and brings him face-to-face with reality. This painful experience shows him that love is more important than wealth.

5. Answers will differ. Students should note how point of view, events, mood, setting, and characterization contribute to the scene.

6. Answers will differ. Students may respond that true happiness comes from devotion to others, not through a selfish pursuit of wealth or status.

### ANSWERS TO CRITICAL THINKING AND READING

Answers will differ. Make sure that students have created a chart with three headings and have filled in material under each of these categories.

### THINKING AND WRITING

For help with this assignment, students can consult Lesson 15, "Evaluating a Literary Work," in the Handbook of Writing About Literature.

### Publishing Student Writing

You might want to collect students' evaluations in a single folder or book.

### Writing Across the Curriculum

You might have students research and report on English criminal laws and courts in the middle of the nineteenth century. Consider informing the social studies department of this assignment, so that teachers can guide students to suitable resource materials.

---

status. He therefore affirms the value of love.

9. Answers will differ. Students may respond that Dickens believed his audience would prefer a happier ending and that Pip had earned happiness through his suffering.

### Applying

10. Answers will differ. Some students may feel that Pip will marry Estella, and they will then live near Joe, Biddy, and little Pip.

**Challenge** Do you think this novel could be easily turned into a play? Explain.

### ANSWERS TO ANALYZING LITERATURE

1. Suggested Response: The first-person narrative contributes to the intensity, suspense, and emotion of such scenes as Pip's first encounter with Magwitch, the convict's

encounter with Pip many years later, and Pip's last interview with Miss Havisham.

2. Suggested Response: The theme of the novel concerns the importance of love and devotion. Pip realizes that love is more important than wealth, advancement, or status. Estella is eventually able to sympathize with and respond to others' feelings. She is no longer the cruel beauty that Miss Havisham used to revenge herself on

# Making Generalizations

A **generalization** is a general statement or rule that is generally true for a variety of different cases or situations. After you have collected specific facts or cases from your reading, it is possible to make a generalization about the time, setting, or characters. By making generalizations as you read, you can increase your understanding and gain deeper insights into the material.

### Evaluating Generalizations

You can evaluate a generalization by determining if the specific facts support it. A generalization is valid if it applies to a number of situations in addition to the specific one you are considering. A valid generalization does not have to apply to all cases, but it does have to cover a significant number of cases.

### Activity

Review parts of *Great Expectations*. Then decide which of the following statements are sound generalizations and which are unsound ones.

1. All criminals who have been treated kindly will try to return the kindness.
2. People who strive to better themselves will always succeed.
3. All older sisters are cruel to their brothers.
4. Suffering teaches people life's real values.
5. Harboring grudges and bitter thoughts often does nothing but harm.

You should have selected sentences 4 and 5 as sound generalizations because the facts support them and they apply to a number of cases in the novel. Sentences 1, 2, and 3 are too broad. You cannot conclude that doing a kindness for a criminal will result in receiving a kindness from that criminal in the future. Many people who strive to improve themselves fail. And certainly, you cannot conclude that all older sisters are cruel to their brothers.

### Overgeneralizations

An overgeneralization is a generalization that is too broad. There are certain words that should signal overgeneralizations. Such words as *all, never, always, everyone, must,* and *no* make generalizations too broad to be valid. These words do not allow for exceptions to the general rule. And remember that even the most valid generalization applies to most, not all, cases. To avoid making overgeneralizations, use such qualifying words as *several, many, most, usually, often, and sometimes.*

## Hasty Generalizations

A hasty generalization is a generalization made too soon or before sufficient evidence has been gathered to support it. For example, after Pip returns from Miss Havisham's, he tells some tall tales about his experience. If at this point you make the generalization that Pip often tells tall tales, your generalization will be hasty, since it will be based on only one incident. Before generalizing, you should read on to see if Pip repeats this behavior.

## Guidelines

- Make sure you understand the main idea and supporting details of the material.
- Make sure the conclusions you draw are adequately supported by facts or evidence.
- Make sure the generalization you make applies to many different cases or situations.
- Make sure you do not use words such as *always* or *must,* which do not allow for any exceptions and which make the generalization too broad.

## Activity

Think about all the information you received about life in Victorian England from reading *Great Expectations.* Based on this information, make the following generalizations.
1. What generalization can you make about the life of convicts in Victorian England. What evidence supports your answer?
2. What generalization can you make about the life of the lower classes? (Think of Pip's family as lower class.) What evidence supports your answer?
3. What generalization can you make about the life of the middle classes? What evidence supports your answer?
4. What generalization can you make about the prospects of a young man who does not come from an upper-class family? What evidence supports your answer?
5. What generalization can you make about the role of women in Victorian England? What evidence supports your answer?

*Focus on Reading 941*

# YOU THE WRITER

## YOU THE WRITER
### Guidelines for Evaluating Assignment 1

1. Has the student written a character sketch that presents a vivid portrait of a character?
2. Has the student used vivid descriptive details to create the sketch?
3. Is the character sketch free from grammar, usage, and mechanics errors?

### Guidelines for Evaluating Assignment 2

1. Has the student retold an episode consistently from another character's point of view?
2. Has the student included information that only this character would know?
3. Has the student used dialogue?
4. Are the events related in chronological order?
5. Is the composition free from grammar, usage, and mechanics errors?

### Guidelines for Evaluating Assignment 3

1. Has the student, using Pip's voice, written a different ending for *Great Expectations*?
2. Does the student's ending include not only what happened in Pip's meeting with Estella but also the results of the meeting?
3. Is the new ending logical and believable?
4. Is the ending free from grammar, usage, and mechanics errors?

**Assignment**

**1.** Choose a character from *Great Expectations* and write a character sketch. Tell about the personality of the character. Cite evidence from the novel to support what you say about him or her.

**Prewriting.** Freewrite about the character you have chosen. Let your mind roam freely, exploring any aspect of his or her personality that comes to mind. Work for at least fifteen minutes. Then read over your freewriting. Underline any thoughts or ideas that can be supported with evidence from the novel.

**Writing.** Write the first draft of your character sketch. Be sure to add descriptive details that capture the essence of your character.

**Revising.** Revise your first draft. Check to see that you have created a vivid portrait of your character. If not, include additional details now. Proofread your character sketch and prepare a final draft.

**Assignment**

**2.** You learn about events in *Great Expectations* from Pip's point of view. Select an episode from this novel and retell it from another character's point of view.

**Prewriting.** First select your episode and your narrator. Draw two columns on a piece of paper. On one side, list details your narrator would know about the episode that Pip would not. On the other side, list details Pip included that your narrator could not know.

**Writing.** Retell the episode from your narrator's point of view. Make sure you include only information your narrator would know. Use dialogue in your retelling, and try to make the characters' voices distinctive. Relate events in chronological order.

**Revising.** When you revise your episode, make sure you have maintained a consistent point of view. Have you punctuated the dialogue correctly? Proofread your episode and prepare a final draft.

**Assignment**

**3.** Writers usually revise what they have written, sometimes even going so far as to change the ending of their novels. Dickens, in fact, wrote two endings for *Great Expectations*. Imagine that you (the author Charles Dickens) are still dissatisfied. Write a new ending.

**Prewriting.** Imagine you are Pip. Write in your journal about your meeting with Estella on that fateful night in December.

**Writing.** Use your freewriting as the basis for a new ending. Write the ending from Pip's point of view. Tell not only what happens on that fateful night but also the results of the meeting.

**Revising.** When you revise, make sure you have accurately captured Pip's voice. Does the new ending seem logical in relation to the rest of the novel? Proofread your ending and prepare a final draft.

# YOU THE CRITIC

**Assignment**

**1.** Novelists reveal their attitudes toward the subjects they write about and toward the characters they invent. Choose a character from *Great Expectations* and tell the author's attitude toward him or her.

    **Prewriting.** First select your character. For example, you might select Estella or Magwitch. Make an outline prior to writing your essay. In this way you will organize information according to main ideas, major details, and lesser details.

    **Writing.** Write your first draft following your outline. Does each paragraph have a main idea supported by major and lesser details?

    **Revising.** Make sure your opinion is adequately supported and your support is organized logically. Edit your sentences. Finally, proofread your final draft.

**Assignment**

**2.** Setting—the time and place of action—is often a key element in novels. Choose one of the episodes from *Great Expectations*. Referring to specific details in the episode, show how the author develops the setting. Then tell why the setting is important to the episode.

    **Prewriting.** List specific details from the episode that show how the author develops the setting.

    **Writing.** Write the first draft of your essay. Be sure you begin your essay with an introductory paragraph stating your thesis.

    **Revising.** Read your essay to a classmate. Ask whether the classmate thinks your reasoning is clear and logical. Allow the classmate to offer suggestions for improvements. Then revise and complete your final draft.

**Assignment**

**3.** The novelist Pearl Buck wrote of her debt to Charles Dickens as follows: "He taught me that beneath gruffness there may be kindness, and that kindness is the sweetest thing in the world, and goodness is the best thing in the world." Write an essay explaining how her comment relates to *Great Expectations*.

    **Prewriting.** Freewrite, exploring the meaning of Buck's comment. Think aloud on paper about how the comment relates to *Great Expectations*. Review your freewriting and underline the ideas you want to develop in a formal composition.

    **Writing.** Write the first draft of your essay. Begin by stating your thesis. Support your thesis with details from the novel.

    **Revising.** Make sure you have provided adequate support for your thesis. Do you want to add any quotations from the novel at this time? Proofread your essay and prepare a final draft.

*You the Critic*    943

---

**YOU THE CRITIC**

*Guidelines for Evaluating Assignment 1*

1. Has the student explained the author's attitude toward one of the characters?
2. Has the student supported his or her points with examples from the novel?
3. Is the essay organized logically?
4. Is the essay free from grammar, usage, and mechanics errors?

*Guidelines for Evaluating Assignment 2*

1. Has the student included a thesis statement about the setting?
2. Has the student referred to specific details in the novel?
3. Is the student's reasoning clear and logical?
4. Is the essay free from grammar, usage, and mechanics errors?

*Guidelines for Evaluating Assignment 3*

1. Has the student begun with a thesis statement explaining how Pearl Buck's comment relates to *Great Expectations*?
2. Has the student supported the thesis statement with details from the novel?
3. Has the student provided adequate support, including quotations from the novel?
4. Is the essay free from grammar, usage, and mechanics errors?

The lessons in the Handbook of Writing About Literature may be used for direct instruction in the writing process, specifically the process of writing about literature. In addition, students may use these lessons for reference and support when they are doing the Thinking and Writing assignments with the selections. References to appropriate lessons are suggested on the Annotated Teacher's Edition page with the assignment.

# HANDBOOK OF WRITING ABOUT LITERATURE

*Contents*  *945*

# SECTION 1: UNDERSTANDING THE WRITING PROCESS

## Lesson 1: Prewriting

Writing is a process that involves several stages:

1. *Prewriting:* planning the work to be done
2. *Drafting:* putting ideas down on paper
3. *Revising:* reworking the written draft
4. *Proofreading:* checking for errors in spelling, mechanics, and manuscript form
5. *Publishing* (or sharing): giving others the opportunity to experience the writing

This lesson will explain the steps to be taken during the prewriting stage.

### STEP 1: ANALYZE THE SITUATION

When you *analyze* something, you divide it into parts and then study these parts. When you have a piece of writing to do, begin by analyzing the writing situation into the following parts:

1. *Topic* (the subject you will be writing about): What, exactly, is this subject? Can you state it in a sentence? Is your subject too broad or too narrow?
2. *Purpose* (what you want the writing to accomplish): Is your purpose to explain? to describe? to persuade? to tell a story? What do you want the reader to take away from the writing?
3. *Audience* (the people who will be reading or listening to your work): What are the backgrounds of these people? Do they already know a great deal about your subject, or will you have to provide basic information?
4. *Voice* (the way the writing will sound to the reader): What impression do you want to make on your readers? What tone should the writing have? Should it be formal or informal? Should it be cool and reasoned or charged with emotion?

5. *Content* (the subject and all the information provided about the subject): How much do you already know about the subject? What will you have to find out? Will you have to do some research? What people, books, magazines, newspapers, or other sources can you consult?
6. *Form* (the shape that the writing will take, including its organization and its length): What will the final piece of writing look like? How long will it be? Will it be a single paragraph or several paragraphs? Will it take some special form such as verse or drama? In what order will the content be presented?

When you begin your prewriting, try to answer all these questions. Doing so will help you to clarify your goals. Some of the answers may already be provided for you. For example, a teacher might have given you a topic or a form to follow. However, many of the answers will be up to you. Writing always involves making decisions and choices.

### STEP 2: MAKE A PLAN

When you have analyzed the writing situation and examined your goals, you will usually find that some of your questions remain unanswered or that some of your answers are incomplete. Therefore, the next step is to make a plan for answering all your questions completely. For example, if you are unsure about your topic, you might want to do some general reading about the topic, perhaps in an encyclopedia. If you are unsure about what content you want to include, you will have to make a plan for gathering the information you need.

## STEP 3: GATHER INFORMATION

The content of a piece of writing—the ideas and information presented—can come from many different sources. Use the following methods to gather ideas and information.

1. *Freewriting:* Write out everything that comes to your mind when you think about the topic. Don't pause to punctuate or to think about spelling or proper form. Simply write, fast and furiously, for one to five minutes. Then study the freewriting for ideas that you can use.

2. *Clustering:* Write your topic in the middle of a piece of paper. Circle the topic. Then think about your topic and write down any other ideas that occur to you. Circle these ideas and draw lines connecting your ideas to the center circle. Continue in this manner until the page is full.

3. *Analyzing:* Break your subject down into parts. Study each part and describe it in your notes. Then look for relationships between the parts and between the parts and the whole.

4. *Questioning:* Make a list of questions about your topic. Begin the questions with *who, what, where, when, why,* and *how.* Then find the answers to your questions.

5. *Using outside sources:* Consult other people, books, and reference works.

6. *Making charts or lists:* Prepare charts or lists of information. For example, for a persuasive paragraph you might make a pros-and-cons chart. For a story you might make a time line or a list of events.

Note that all these techniques for gathering information can also be used to identify a topic in the first place.

## STEP 4: ORGANIZE YOUR NOTES

Once you have gathered enough information, you'll need to organize your information logically. Often people organize their notes in *chronological order,* in *spatial order,* by *degree* (less to more or more to less), or in *order of importance, value,* or *familiarity.* Sometimes the topic itself suggests a possible organization. After organizing your notes, make a rough outline.

## CASE STUDY: PREWRITING

George's English teacher asked the class to write a paragraph on some aspect of modern media. George decided to write about television. Here are some of his prewriting notes:

- Topic: television
- Purpose: to inform
- Audience: my English teacher and my classmates
- Voice: fairly formal, knowledgeable
- Content: not sure. Television is a pretty broad topic. I should be able to use a lot of my own knowledge about television.
- Form: single paragraph

George looked over his notes and decided that he would need a plan of action. First, his topic was definitely too broad. Therefore, he made the following clustering chart to narrow his topic:

1. Suggested Response: The fifth point needed fleshing out.
2. Suggested Response: He made a diagram to narrow his topic. He made a chart to organize his information and clarify his thinking.

George decided to use the subject "nondramatic television programs" as the main topic of his paragraph. His purpose would be to explain the types of nondramatic programs. To gather the information he needed, George looked at a weekly programming directory. There he found several types of nondramatic programs—newscasts, interview programs, talk shows, game shows, educational children's programs, and specials of various kinds. Next, George made a chart with the headings "Type of Program," "Description," and "Example." Finally, he used the programming directory and his own knowledge to complete the chart.

George looked over his chart and decided that in his paragraph he would first introduce his topic—nondramatic television programs. Then he would use topic organization, describing each type of program in turn.

## ACTIVITIES AND ASSIGNMENTS

A. Answer the following questions about the case study.

1. Find the section of George's notes in which he analyzed the writing situation. Which of his initial notes needed more fleshing out? Which were sufficient?
2. Why did George make a clustering diagram? Why did he make a chart? What purposes did these serve?

B. Choose one of the following topics or one of your own:

| Mexico | computers |
|---|---|
| wild animals | games |

Prepare to write a paragraph about your topic. Follow these steps:

1. Make notes about the topic, purpose, audience, voice, content, and form of your paragraph.
2. Look over your notes and decide what additional planning or research you need to do. Use prewriting techniques such as freewriting, clustering, analyzing, questioning, using outside sources, and making charts or lists to narrow your topic and to gather ideas.
3. Organize your notes and make a rough outline. Save your notes in a folder.

# Lesson 2: Drafting and Revising

## CHOOSING A METHOD FOR DRAFTING

After a writer has completed his or her pre-writing notes, the next step is to begin drafting, or putting ideas on paper in rough form. When you draft, keep the following points in mind:

1. Choose a drafting method that you are comfortable with. Some writers like to plan very carefully, make a thorough outline, and then write slowly, correcting and polishing the work as they go. Other writers like simply to get all their ideas down on paper quickly and then to go back and worry about details. Either method—the slow draft or the quick one—is fine. The choice is up to you.

2. Whichever method you choose, don't worry about getting everything perfect at the drafting stage. A rough draft is not meant to be perfect. It is simply another step toward the final product. Concentrate on getting your ideas down. At this stage in the writing process, you needn't be overly concerned about proper spelling, punctuation, capitalization, and the like. You can take care of these matters later.

3. As you write, work from your prewriting notes and keep your audience and purpose in mind.

4. Do not be afraid to change your original plans during drafting. Some of the best ideas are ones that were not planned ahead of time. Feel free to add, delete, or change ideas as you write.

5. Write as many drafts as you like. As the writer Neil Simon once observed, writing is not like baseball, in which you have only three chances and then you're out. The nice thing about writing is that you can do it over and over until you've got it the way you want it.

---

### CHECKLIST FOR REVISION

*Topic and Purpose*
- ☐ Is my topic clear?
- ☐ Does the writing have a specific purpose?
- ☐ Does the writing achieve its purpose?

*Audience*
- ☐ Will everything that I have written be clear to my audience?
- ☐ Will my audience find the writing interesting?
- ☐ Will my audience respond in the way I would like?

*Voice, Word Choice*
- ☐ Is the impression that my writing conveys the one that I intended it to convey?
- ☐ Is my language appropriately formal or informal?
- ☐ Have I avoided vague, undefined terms?
- ☐ Have I used vivid, specific nouns, verbs, and adjectives?
- ☐ Have I avoided jargon that my audience will not understand?
- ☐ Have I avoided clichés?
- ☐ Have I avoided slang, odd connotations, euphemisms, and gobbledygook (except for novelty or humor)?

*Content/Development*
- ☐ Have I avoided including unnecessary or unrelated ideas?
- ☐ Have I developed my topic completely?
- ☐ Have I supplied examples or details that support the statements that I have made?
- ☐ Are my sources of information unbiased, up-to-date, and authoritative?

*Form*
- ☐ Have I followed a logical method of organization?
- ☐ Have I used transitions, or connecting words, to make the organization clear?
- ☐ Does the writing have a clear introduction, body, and conclusion?

*Drafting and Revising*   949

---

**Motivation for Writing** Tell students that even the best writers revise their work many times. James Michener once said, for example, that he even rewrote his correspondence four or more times. The final result of the writing process—a nonfiction book, essay, poem, or short story—is deceptively clean-looking. Tell students that for each final product there may be several wastebaskets full of discarded versions.

To reinforce this point, you might want to bring in a variorum edition of a writer's work, or photographs of manuscripts indicating numerous revisions.

1. Suggested Response: This material was repetitive.
2. Suggested Response: He added new information to lines 6, 15, and 16.
3. Suggested Response: He added the words to create a parallel structure. The two phrases that are now parallel are "in the world and in the nation."
4. Suggested Response: *Viewers* is more specific and formal.
5. Suggested Response: The transitional word he added is "Finally."
6. Suggested Response: The new phrase is more specific and formal.
7. Suggested Response: This phrase is too vague.
8. Suggested Response: The new phrase is more specific and formal.
9. Suggested Response: One other change involves correcting the spelling of "Interview."
10. Suggested Response: One error is the misspelling of "controversial."

## REVISING YOUR DRAFT

Once you have finished drafting, you are ready to revise. Revising is the process of reworking what you have written to make it as good as it can be. When revising your draft, ask yourself the questions in the Checklist for Revision on the previous page.

## EDITORIAL SYMBOLS

When revising a rough draft, it is helpful to use the editorial symbols in the chart at the right.

## CASE STUDY: DRAFTING AND REVISING

George used his notes from the preceding lesson to begin writing a rough draft of his paragraph. Here is the beginning of his uncorrected rough draft:

There are many diferent types of nondramatic programs. There are non-dramatic programs that deal with current events. Including news reports, interview programs and specials of various kinds. There are also entertainment programs such as talk shows and game shows. And there are also educational programs and specials. First, about current events programs:

George stopped writing for a moment and looked at his draft. He observed that he had already written quite a bit and that he had a lot more to say. At this rate, George thought, my paragraph will be a hundred sentences long! He decided to narrow his topic and to include only current events programs. His topic would be "Nondramatic Television Programs Dealing with Current Affairs." He wrote a new rough draft based on this topic. Then he made revisions using the standard editorial symbols. George's rough draft with his corrections and revisions is shown on the next page.

## ACTIVITIES AND ASSIGNMENTS

A. Answer the following questions about the revised rough draft shown on the next page.

1. Why did George delete material from his first two sentences?
2. In what places did George add new information to his draft?
3. Why did George add the words "in the" before the word "nation"? What two phrases

| SYMBOL | MEANING | EXAMPLE |
|---|---|---|
| ⟲ | move text | Never! shall never forget. |
| ℓ or — | delete | for the ~~the~~ winter |
| ∧ | insert | too ^much^ money |
| ⊂ | close up; no space | space‿walk |
| ⊙ | insert period | few people⊙ She |
| ⌄ | insert comma | lions, tigers⌄ and bears |
| ⌄ | add apostrophe | dogs‵ tails |
| ⌄ ⌄ | add quotation marks | The Necklace |
| ∼ | transpose | to boldly go |
| ¶ | begin paragraph | him. ¶ When |
| / | make lower case | the new /Principal |
| ≡ | capitalize | principal Marion ≡Ohman |

in George's paragraph are parallel because of this change?

4. Why did George change the word "folks" to "viewers"?
5. What transitional word did George add to indicate that he was about to tell about the last of the types of programs?
6. Why did George change "are also good" to "serve a variety of purposes"?
7. Why did George delete "and things"?
8. Why did George change "things happening" to "situations of significance"?
9. What other revisions did George make? Why did he make them?
10. What errors still need to be corrected in George's paragraph?

B. Using your notes from the preceding lesson, draft a paragraph on your topic. Then revise your draft. Follow these steps in drafting and revising your paragraph:

1. If you haven't already done so, make a rough outline that shows how you will organize your paragraph. Your outline should include your main topic and two or three subtopics, or parts of the main topic. Under each subtopic, you should list the specific information, or details, that you will include in your paragraph.
2. Write an introductory sentence that presents your topic.
3. Based on your rough outline and your prewriting notes, quickly write out the body of your paragraph.
4. Write a conclusion of one or two sentences.

5. Use the checklist in this lesson to revise your draft. Make sure that you can answer "yes" to each of the questions. If your answer to a question is "no," use editorial symbols to make the necessary corrections.

Television keeps the American public informed by means of ~~special programs. These programs are~~ nondramatic programs that deal with current events. Including news reports, interview programs and specials of various kinds. News reports provide information about *such as the Macneil, Lerher News Hour* daily events in the world and *in the* nation. Interview programs such as the Barbara Walters Specials, give ~~folks~~ *viewers* a chance to ~~see~~ *observe close up* the people who make the news. *Finally* Specials about current events ~~are also good. They~~ *serve a variety of purposes. Some* bring political candidates together for debates ~~and things~~. *Others* ~~They~~ describe in depth political ~~things~~ *situations of significance* ~~happening~~ around the Globe. ~~They tell about~~ *Still others probe* controvershul issues facing ~~people~~ *voters and lawmakers*. Without programs such as these ~~where would we be?~~ *Americans would doubtless be less able to make informed, intelligent political decisions.*

952

You might also ask students if they understand the meaning of the term *proofreading.* Lead them to express the correct definition. Then lead them to see how errors in spelling and punctuation can prevent a piece of writing from being properly understood once it is published.

# Lesson 3:  Proofreading and Publishing

## PROOFREADING YOUR FINAL DRAFT

After you finish your final draft, the last step is to proofread the draft to make it ready for a reader. When you proofread the final draft, use the following checklist.

---

### CHECKLIST FOR PROOFREADING

*Grammar and Usage*
- ☐ Are all of my sentences complete? That is, have I avoided sentence fragments?
- ☐ Do all of my sentences express only one complete thought? That is, have I avoided run-on sentences?
- ☐ Do the verbs I have used agree with their subjects?
- ☐ Have all the words in my paper been used correctly? Am I sure about the meanings of all of these words?
- ☐ Is the thing being referred to by each pronoun (I, me, this, each, etc.) clear?
- ☐ Have I used adjectives and adverbs correctly?

*Punctuation*
- ☐ Does every sentence end with a punctuation mark?
- ☐ Have I used commas, semicolons, colons, hyphens, dashes, parentheses, quotation marks, and apostrophes correctly?

*Spelling*
- ☐ Am I absolutely sure that each word has been spelled correctly?

*Capitalization*
- ☐ Have I capitalized any words that should not be capitalized?
- ☐ Should I capitalize any words that I have not capitalized?

*Manuscript Form*
- ☐ Have I indented the first line(s) of my paragraph(s)?
- ☐ Have I written my name and the page number in the top right-hand corner of each page?
- ☐ Have I double-spaced the manuscript?

---

If your answer to any of these questions is "no," make the necessary corrections on your paper. Refer to a dictionary, writing textbook, or handbook of style as necessary.

## PUBLISHING, OR SHARING YOUR WORK

After you have proofread your final copy, it is ready to be shared with other people. Of course, much of the writing you do for school will be submitted to teachers. However, there are many other ways to share or publish your writing. The following are a few of these many ways:

1. Share your work in a small group.
2. Read your work aloud to the class.
3. Make copies for your parents, other relatives, or friends.
4. Have your work put on a class bulletin board.
5. Save your writing in a folder and, at the end of the year, bind the copies together into a booklet.
6. Submit your writing to the school literary magazine or start a literary magazine for your school or for your class.
7. Submit your writing to your school or community newspaper.
8. Enter your writing in literary contests for student writers.
9. Submit your writing to a magazine that publishes work by young people.

## CASE STUDY: PROOFREADING AND PUBLISHING

After revising his final draft, George made a fresh, clean copy. Then he read the Checklist for Proofreading and applied each question to his revised draft. While doing this, he found some errors he had overlooked when revising. Look at

Television keeps the American public informed by means of non-dramatic programs that deal with current events. Including news reports, interview programs, and specials of various kinds. News reports, such as the Macneil, Lerer News Hour, provide information about daily events in the world and in the nation. Interview programs, such as the Barbara Walters Specials, give viewers a chance to observe, close up, the people who make the news. Finally, specials about current events serve a variety of purposes. Some bring political candidates together for debates. Others describe, in depth, political situations of significance around the globe. Still others probe controversial issues facing voters and lawmakers. Without programs such as these, Americans would doubtless be less able to make informed, intelligent political decisions.

George's paragraph with the proofreading corrections that he made (in the left-hand column).

George made a clean final copy of his paragraph. Then he shared his paragraph with other students in a small group discussion.

## ACTIVITIES AND ASSIGNMENTS

A. Answer the following questions about the case study in this lesson.

1. What errors in spelling did George correct during proofreading?
2. What corrections on George's paper indicate the importance of checking the spellings of proper nouns such as names of people and places?
3. Which sentence fragment did he correct? How did he do this?
4. What punctuation errors did George correct?
5. What error in manuscript form did George correct?
6. Are there any changes that you think should still be made in George's paragraph? Explain.

B. Make a clean copy of your revised draft from the preceding lesson. Then use the Checklist for Proofreading to correct any errors that remain in your draft.

Share your proofread draft with your teacher and classmates.

1. Suggested Response: He corrected the spelling of "Lehrer" and "controversial."
2. Suggested Response: The correction of "Lehrer" indicates this.
3. Suggested Response: He corrected the sentence fragment beginning, "Including . . ." by adding a subject and making the verb agree with it.
4. Suggested Response: He added commas to lines 8, 10, and 17.
5. Suggested Response: He indented the paragraph.
6. Answers will differ; however, students should make reasonable suggestions.

# SECTION 2: UNDERSTANDING THE PARTS OF A LITERARY WORK: ANALYSIS AND INTERPRETATION

## Lesson 4: Writing About Images

### WHAT IS AN IMAGE?

An *image* is a word or group of words that stands for something that can be sensed. These lines, from Li Po's "Sitting Alone in Ching-t'ing Mountain," contain images of sight:

> Flocks of birds fly high and vanish;
> A single cloud, alone, drifts on.

These lines, from a traditional Native American song of the Nez Percé tribe, contain images of sound:

> Mad Coyote
> madly sings,
> then the west wind roars!

Literary works can also contain images of touch, taste, or smell.

### WHY WRITERS USE IMAGES

Writers use images for two purposes:
1. To create pictures, in words, of people, places, and things, and
2. To create feelings, or moods.

Consider the use of images in the following short poem:

A FARM PICTURE

Walt Whitman

> Through the ample open door of the peaceful
>   country barn,
> A sunlit pasture field with cattle and horses
>   feeding,
> And haze and vista, and the far horizon fading
>   away.

The images in this short poem
1. Create a picture of a simple country scene, and
2. Create a mood of contentment, or peacefulness.

### CASE STUDY: WRITING ABOUT IMAGES

#### Prewriting

Maria's English teacher asked the class to write an analysis of a favorite poem. Maria chose to write about the use of images in the following poem:

A DIRGE

Percy Bysshe Shelley

> Rough wind, that moanest loud
>   Grief too sad for song;
> Wild wind, when sullen cloud
>   Knells all the night long;
> Sad storm, whose tears are vain,
> Bare woods, whose branches strain,
> Deep caves and dreary main—
>   Wail, for the world's wrong!

Maria began by looking up all the words in the poem that she didn't know. Then she made a list of their definitions:

- dirge: a slow, sad song of grief or mourning; a funeral song
- sullen: gloomy, dismal, sad, depressing
- knell: to ring in a slow, solemn way
- main: the sea
- wail: cry out, as in grief

Then she reread the poem with these definitions in mind.

Next, Maria made a list of the images in the poem:

- Images of sight:
    "sullen cloud"
    "Sad storm . . . tears"
    "Bare woods . . . branches"
    "Deep caves"
    "dreary main"

- Images of sound:
    "A Dirge"
    the moaning wind
    the knelling cloud
    wailing

- Images of touch:
    rough, wild wind
    straining branches

- Images of taste:
    none

- Images of smell:
    none

Then Maria asked herself, "What picture is created by these images and what emotion is conveyed by them?" She wrote her answers in her prewriting notes, as follows:

- Picture created by images in the poem:
    stormy night near the sea
    raining (tears), the wind blowing hard
    bare trees, must be late fall or early winter
    outdoor scene, with woods and caves

- Mood created by the images:
    great sorrow, grief, despair

Maria decided to write a paragraph about how Shelley used images to create a mood of sorrow and despair. She made the following rough outline for her paragraph:

- Topic sentence:
    Tell what poem I'm writing about.
    State my purpose (to show that Shelley uses images to create a mood of sorrow).

- Body of paragraph:
    Describe the images of sight, sound, and touch in the poem.

- Conclusion of paragraph:
    Point out how the last line of the poem sums up the poem's mood.

## DRAFTING AND REVISING

Using her outline and her prewriting notes, Maria wrote a draft of her paragraph. Then she carefully revised and proofread the paragraph. The following is her rough draft with the handwritten corrections that she made:

In the poem "A Dirge" Percey Bysshe Shelly uses images to create a mood of great sorrow and despair. The images of sight in the poem reveal to the reader a outdoor scene at night during a storm. These images ~~of sight in the poem~~ include a "sullen cloud," "night," "bare woods," "deep caves," and a "dreary main." or sea In lines 3 and 4 a cloud "Knells all night long." In other words the cloud is like a bell, and its thunder is like a slow, solemn ringing ~~bell~~. The fierce power of the storm is conveyed by images of touch. The wind is described as "Rough," and the branches are straining. Through out the poem there are images of sound. The poem begins and ends with the moaning and wailing of the wind. The crying of the wind and the tolling of the thunder are, of course, appropriate to a dirge—a sad song about a world gone wrong.

1. Suggested Response: She corrected spelling and punctuation in lines 1, 8, 9, and 13.
2. Suggested Response: She deleted an awkward repetition in line 5.
3. Suggested Response: She added new details to lines 4, 7, and 9.
4. Suggested Response: She corrected a problem in organization by moving lines 7–9.

## PROOFREADING AND PUBLISHING

After making a clean final copy of her paragraph, Maria proofread it for errors in grammar, usage, spelling, punctuation, capitalization, and manuscript form. Then she shared it with her parents and with several of her classmates.

## ACTIVITIES AND ASSIGNMENTS

A. Study the corrections Maria made in her paragraph. Identify each of the following:
1. Places where Maria corrected errors in spelling and punctuation
2. A place where Maria deleted an awkward repetition
3. Places where Maria added new details
4. A place where Maria corrected a problem in organization

B. Choose one of the poems from the poetry unit of your anthology and write a paragraph about its images and the mood that the images create. Follow these steps:

1. Read the poem carefully. Look up any words you don't know and write out their definitions.
2. Make a chart listing the images of sight, sound, touch, taste, and smell used in the poem.
3. Make notes telling what picture is created by the images and what mood, or feeling, the images convey.
4. Write a topic sentence that gives the title and author of the poem and tells what mood is created by the images.
5. Write several body sentences explaining what images are used in the poem.
6. Write a concluding sentence that sums up the poem's mood.
7. Revise and proofread your paragraph carefully. Add any important details that you left out. Delete any unnecessary or repeated words. Check for errors in organization, grammar, spelling, usage, punctuation, and capitalization.
8. Make a clean final copy and share it with a friend.

# Lesson 5: Writing About Sound

## SOUND AND MEANING

Often writers use devices of sound to convey meaning. Consider the following line from John Steinbeck's short story, "The Leader of the People":

> The wind could be heard whishing in the brush on the ridge crests.

In this sentence, the repeated *sh* sounds in "whishing" and "brush" sound like the wind. In the best writing, the sounds of the words echo their meaning, or sense.

## TECHNIQUES INVOLVING SOUND

Writers use many special literary devices, or techniques, of sound. The chart below describes some of the most common.

Read the entries in the Handbook of Literary Terms and Techniques for the terms listed in the chart. Then read the following case study.

## CASE STUDY: WRITING ABOUT SOUND

Mark's English class was studying the use of sound in poetry. For a homework assignment, Mark decided to write about a poem by his classmate Sarah. Here is Sarah's poem, entitled "A Brief Vacation":

> Rrrrrrrrrrrrrrrrrrrrrrring!
> The books slam shut. Kaboom!
> Voices explode on the air:
>   WHATSTHEHOMEWORKKATIECALLMEWHATS
>   THEHEYYOUGUYSCOMEONWAITUPCOMEON
>   WAITUPCOMEONLETSGOLETS
>   GO!
> We pounce at the door, a pack,
> Squeeeeezing through, crowding and crushing,
> Chortling and chattering. Lockers clang.
> Hollering, hooting: YAHOO!
>   The aftershock rattles the walls.
>   Chalkdust
>     Slowly
>       Settles
>         Down.
> A broom swishes through the silent halls.

### Prewriting

First Mark read Sarah's poem aloud several times, listening carefully to its sounds. Then he marked up a copy of the poem (see next page).

---

### DEVICES OF SOUND

*Onomatopoeia:* the use of words that sound like what they refer to, as in "buzz" or "snap."

*Euphony:* the use of beautiful, pleasant sounds.

*Cacophony:* the use of harsh, jarring sounds.

*Alliteration:* the repetition of initial consonant sounds, as in "*l*ake water *l*apping."

*Rhyme:* the use of words that have identical end sounds, as in "rh*yme*" and "t*ime*" or "gr*ocer*" and "cl*oser*."

*Consonance:* partial rhyme in which consonant sounds are repeated but vowel sounds are not, as in "*m*o*ck*" and "*m*a*ke*."

*Assonance:* repetition of vowel sounds, as in "ab*ou*t the h*ou*se."

*Meter:* the use of words that have a regular rhythm, as in: "Is this the face that launch'd a thousand ships?"

*Parallelism:* the use of groups of words that have a similar grammatical structure, as in "In the house" and "on the corner." (two prepositional phrases)

*Repetition:* the use, again, of a sound, word, phrase, or sentence. Notice that alliteration, rhyme, consonance, and assonance are all forms of repetition.

---

Suggested Response: Most students should identify and correct errors such as the following: quotation marks around the poem's title; spelling of "Brief"; spelling of "onomatopoeia"; use of colon after that word; and so forth.

1. He underlined all the examples he could find of onomatopoeia:

Rrrrrrrrrrrrrrrrrrrrrrrrrriiing!

The books slam shut. Kaboom!

2. He circled the rhyming words:

. . . rattles the walls.

. . . the silent halls.

3. He underlined, twice, all the repeated sounds he could find:

crowding and crushing

Hollering, hooting

Next Mark made a list of the sound devices in the poem, with examples:

Onomatopoeia: "Ring"
"Slam shut"
"Kaboom!"

Rhyme: "walls"/"halls"

Alliteration: "pounce . . . pack"

Consonance: "Chortling and chattering"

Assonance: "hooting: YAHOO!"

Parallelism: "crowding and crushing"
"Chortling and chattering"

Cacophony: the sounds of the students all talking at once, the lockers clanging

Euphony: the repeated s sounds in the last line

(Mention in paper the contrast between the cacophony as the students are leaving and the euphony after they are gone)

Mark studied his prewriting notes. There seemed to be two ways of organizing them. He could use a chronological organization and discuss each line of the poem in turn, or he could use a topic organization and discuss each of the sound devices in turn. He decided to use the topic organization.

**Drafting and Revising.**

Mark used his prewriting notes to write a rough draft. The following is the first part of his draft:

In her poem A Breif Vacation, Sarah Bergman uses a number of literary devices to recreate the sound of kids leaving school at the end of the day. First, the poem contains many examples of onomatopoia. "Rrrrrrrrrrrrrrrrrrrrrrriing," in line 1; "slam shut" and "Kaboom," in line 2; "rattle," in line 12; and swish, in line 17. The words used to describe the students' talking and movements are also examples of onomatopoeia. Second, the poet makes use of lots of repeated sounds. Line 8, for example, contains an alliteration—the repeated p in "pounce" and "pack."

Mark finished his draft and then revised and proofread it carefully.

**Proofreading and Publishing**

After making clean final copies of his paper, Mark proofread them carefully. Then he gave one copy to his teacher and one to Sarah.

**ACTIVITIES AND ASSIGNMENTS**

A. Revise and proofread Mark's unfinished rough draft. Find and correct Mark's errors in spelling and punctuation. Also correct his one sentence fragment. Write out the corrected version on a separate sheet of paper.

B. Finish Mark's rough draft. Refer to his prewriting notes for information to use in the rest of the draft.

C. Write a two-paragraph composition on the use of sound in "Casey at the Bat," on page

551, or "The Raven," on page 563. Follow these steps:

1. Choose one of the two poems. Read the poem aloud several times and listen to its sounds.
2. Make a copy of the poem.
3. On the copy, make the following marks:
   a. Underline examples of onomatopoeia.
   b. Circle the rhyming words.
   c. Underline repeated sounds twice.
   d. In the margins, note examples of alliteration, consonance, assonance, parallelism, and repeated words.
4. Read the section on Meter in the Handbook of Literary Terms and Techniques. Then choose one stanza of your poem and mark its feet and strong stresses, as follows:

There was|a woman
Who lived|on a hill
If she's|not gone,
She lives|there still

5. Organize your notes and use them to write two paragraphs. In the first paragraph, tell what poem you are going to discuss, explain that you are going to write about techniques of sound in the poem, and then tell about the poem's meter and rhyme scheme. In the second paragraph, discuss other devices of sound used in the poem.
6. Revise and proofread your paper, make a clean final copy, and share it with your classmates.

**Motivation for Writing** You might call students' attention to figures of speech that they use in conversation; for example, a baseball announcer might say, "He tore the cover off the ball" (example of hyperbole). Lead students to see that such figures of speech make language more colorful.

You might also tell them that most writers do not set out to create figures of speech systematically. Usually, a new metaphor or simile will occur to a writer as he or she meditates on a subject.

Finally, it is worth pointing out that figures of speech are actually a means of learning something new about the world, because they cause us to see the world in unexpected ways.

# Lesson 6: Writing About Figures of Speech

## WHAT IS A FIGURE OF SPEECH?

A *figure of speech* is a group of words used to convey more than a literal meaning. The following are some of the most common figures of speech.

---

### FIGURES OF SPEECH

*Hyperbole:* exaggeration for emphasis: "I'm so hungry I could eat a horse."

*Personification:* speaking or writing about a nonhuman subject as though it were human: "The sea sang its ancient songs."

*Simile:* a comparison, using "like" or "as," that suggests one or more similarities between two very different subjects: "A human face is like a flower."

*Metaphor:* writing or speaking of one thing as though it were something very different. A metaphor, like a simile, suggests the similarities between things: "The hippo lay on the bank—a great, brown jug of lard."

---

## WHY WRITERS USE FIGURES OF SPEECH

Writers use figures of speech to make their descriptions vivid and interesting. Suppose, for example, that you wanted to describe a certain king as courageous. You could write:

King Richard was very courageous.

However, this sentence is dull and abstract. To make it more interesting, you could use a figure of speech:

King Richard had the heart of a lion.

## HOW WRITERS CREATE FIGURES OF SPEECH

Hyperbole is one of the simplest of all figures of speech. To create a hyperbole, a writer starts by choosing a subject and then some characteristic of the subject:

Subject:  myself
Characteristic:  hunger

Then the writer produces a sentence exaggerating the characteristic:

I'm so hungry I could eat a horse.

Personification, simile, and metaphor are a bit more complicated. As with hyperbole, the writer starts by choosing a subject and then a characteristic to be described. This subject is called the *tenor:*

Tenor:  the sea
Characteristic:  its rhythmical sound

Then the writer chooses a second subject, the vehicle, that has the same characteristic:

Vehicle:  a singer

Finally, the writer produces a sentence that compares the two subjects:

The sea sang its ancient songs.

## CASE STUDY: WRITING ABOUT FIGURES OF SPEECH

Gail's English teacher asked the class to choose a poem and to write a paragraph about the figures of speech used in that poem. Gail decided to write about the following poem:

TROUBLED WOMAN

Langston Hughes

She stands
In the quiet darkness,
This troubled woman
Bowed by
Weariness and pain
Like an
Autumn flower
In the frozen rain,
Like a
Wind-blown autumn flower
That never lifts its head
Again.

## Prewriting

Gail read the poem carefully several times. She decided that the central figure of speech used in "Troubled Woman" was a simile. For her prewriting notes, she made the following list:

- Tenor: woman
- Vehicle: flower
- Shared characteristics:
  bowed down
  in darkness
  weariness
  subject to external forces

Gail decided that the simile would be the focus of her paragraph.

## Drafting and Revising

Gail used her prewriting notes to write a rough draft of her paragraph. That draft, with her corrections and revisions, is in the right column.

## Proofreading and Publishing

Gail made a clean final copy of her paragraph for her teacher, who displayed it on the bulletin board.

In the poem "Troubled Woman," ~~author~~
Langston Hughes uses a simile to illustrate his
vision of a sad and ~~loanly~~ *lonely* woman. He says that
such a woman is "Like an/Autumn flower/In the
frozen rain" (lines 6-9). The image evoked
by Hughes's simile is one of desolation and
despair. *and the reader is moved to compassion for the woman* The visual image of the flower—with
its head bowed from the forces of the wind and
rain—is strikingly similer to the troubled woman
*The woman probably stands in a dark room.
The rain suggests a lack of sunshine in the flower's*
the author describes. Both are in darkness. *environ- ment*
Since the flower is subject to the external
forces of the natural elements, ~~therefore we~~ *the reader*
~~may~~ *can* conclude that the woman also suffers the
weight of external pressures. Finally, ~~both the~~
~~woman and~~ the flower ~~may be described as~~ *exemplifies the woman's weariness*
~~weary~~—the flower is at the end of its life, and
will " never [lift] its head/Again" (lines
11–12).

## ACTIVITIES AND ASSIGNMENTS

A. Answer the following questions about the draft in the case study.

1. Why do you think Gail moved the sentence that begins "The image evoked" to the end of her paragraph?
2. Why did Gail delete the word "therefore"?
3. Why did Gail change "we" to "the reader"?

1. Suggest Response: She moved it to the end because it makes a good summary.
2. Suggested Response: She already has a conjunction—"Since"—so she does not need "therefore."
3. Suggested Response: The new subject is more formal and appropriate.
4. Suggested Response: She reasons from the fact that the flower is subject to external forces. She therefore concludes that the woman must be subject to external forces as well. It is reasonable to conclude that the woman's "Weariness and pain" result at least partly from forces and situations external to her. However, it is also possible that the woman is responding to internal pressures.

4. Why does Gail think that "the woman also suffers the weight of external pressures"? Do you think it is safe to conclude that the poet meant to imply this? Why?

B. Choose a poem from the following list about which you would like to write a paragraph on figures of speech: "Casey at the Bat," on page 551; "The Seven Ages of Man," on page 579; "The Funeral," on page 595; "The Creation," on page 619; "The Eagle," on page 627; "I Wandered Lonely as a Cloud," on page 628; "A Dream Deferred" on page 630; "Dreams," on page 631; "The Sky Is Low," on page 632; or "Sea-Fever," on page 654. Follow these steps in writing your paragraph:

1. Read the poem several times. Then copy the poem by hand onto a separate sheet of paper. Writing out the poem in this way will familiarize you with the author's exact words.
2. On the copy, underline all the examples of figures of speech that you can find. List them on a separate sheet of paper under the following headings: Hyperbole, Personification, Simile, and Metaphor.
3. Decide which figure of speech you think is the most important to the meaning of the poem as a whole. Write a topic sentence stating that that figure of speech is the most prominent in the poem.
4. Write the rest of your paragraph, giving examples of the other figures of speech that you listed in your notes. Your concluding sentence should be a brief summary of the main idea of the paragraph.
5. Revise your rough draft using the Checklist for Revision on page 949.
6. Make a clean copy of your revised paragraph and proofread this copy using the Checklist for Proofreading on page 952. Share the proofread copy with your family and friends before turning it in to your teacher.

# Lesson 7: Writing About Setting

## WHAT IS SETTING?

The *setting* of a story, novel, poem, or play is the time and place in which the action occurs. To create a setting, a writer uses specific details, including images of sight, sound, touch, taste, and smell. A setting may be revealed by descriptions of scenery, weather, rooms, furniture, modes of transportation, clothing, customs, or dialects. In the opening lines of her story "The Big Wave," Pearl Buck creates a setting by using images of sight:

> Kino lived on a farm that lay on the side of a mountain in Japan. The mountain rose so steeply out of the ocean that there was only a strip of sandy shore at its foot. Upon this strip was a small fishing village where Kino's father sold his vegetables and rice and bought fish.
>
> Kino often looked down upon the thatched roofs of the village. The village houses faced one another, and those which stood by the sea did not have windows toward it. Since Kino enjoyed looking at the waves, he often wondered why the village people did not.

## THE FUNCTIONS OF A SETTING

A setting can serve many different functions, or purposes, as described in the chart at the top of the right column.

## CASE STUDY: WRITING ABOUT SETTING

Clinton read the Edgar Allan Poe short story, "The Cask of Amontillado," on page 139 of the text. He noticed that the writer made very interesting use of the setting of the story, and he decided to write a paragraph about this setting for his English class.

### Prewriting

Clinton reread "The Cask of Amontillado"

---

### USES OF SETTING

*To make the action of a narrative seem more realistic or believable:* Through setting a writer can give his or her readers the sense of actually being in some imaginary or exotic time and place.

*To teach readers about different ways of life:* Through setting a writer can reveal what life might be like in the future, what life was like in a past time and place such as ancient Rome, or what life is like in a contemporary society such as a fishing village in rural Japan.

*To create a mood:* An example of this would be when a writer of horror stories describes a scary abandoned house.

*To be the source of the central conflict, or struggle, in a literary work:* An example of this would be when a writer tells about characters in conflict with natural disasters such as blizzards or forest fires.

*To symbolize, or represent, some concept that the writer wishes to emphasize:* For example, a setting in the springtime can symbolize youth or renewal. A setting in winter can symbolize advanced age or death.

---

and noticed several points about Poe's use of setting that he had overlooked the first time. Then he made the following observations in his notebook:

- Setting:
  the underground vaults of the Montresor palace

- Important details about setting:
  dark (characters must carry torches)
  damp ("We . . . stood together upon the damp ground of the catacombs")
  moldy ("a bottle . . . that lay upon the mold")

**Motivation for Writing** Have students describe places that call up certain moods in them. Ask them to give concrete details in their descriptions, including tastes, sounds, smells, and sights. Then lead them to see how writers use descriptions of places to call up moods in readers.

Suggested Response: Make sure that students integrate the appropriate quotations into their paragraphs.

skeletons along walls ("long walls of piled skeletons")
water dripping ("The drops of moisture trickle among the bones")
bad air ("the foulness of the air caused our flambeaux rather to glow")

- Significance of setting:
  to provide backdrop for story
  to evoke mood of horror
  to symbolize narrator's state of mind as he plots revenge

Clinton decided that the setting's function as a backdrop was least important, and that the main idea of his paragraph would be Poe's symbolic use of the setting.

### Drafting and Revising

Clinton wrote a rough draft of his paragraph, as shown in the right column.

Clinton revised his paragraph to organize it more clearly. His changes are marked on the rough draft.

### Proofreading and Publishing

Clinton made a clean copy of his revised paragraph, proofread it, and handed it in to his English teacher. The teacher liked the paragraph so much that he asked Clinton to read it aloud to the class.

### ACTIVITIES AND ASSIGNMENTS

A. Clinton's paragraph includes no quotations from "The Cask of Amontillado." Rewrite the paragraph, adding some of the passages quoted in Clinton's prewriting notes and any other passages that you think might be helpful or interesting. Do not merely insert the quotations into the existing sentences. Instead, restructure the paragraph to include the quotes.

B. Choose one story from among the following in your text and write a one- or two-

The setting of Edgar Allan Poe's "Cask of Amontillado" does more than merely provide a backdrop for the action of the story. In addition, *of the story in the underground vaults of the Montresor palace* the setting also functions to evoke a spooky or gloomy mood. Most importantly, however, the setting is a symbol for the ~~mentality~~ *mental state* of the narrator, ~~of the story~~ who seeks vengeance for the offensive behavior of his ~~friend~~ *(o) acquaintance* Fortunato. Specific details about the setting that create the eerie mood include the darkness in the catacombs; the *flickering two* light of torches; the dampness and water dripping in the background; the human remains that surround the two characters; and the foul air and mold in the *damp, dark, twisting passages symbolize* ~~crypt.~~ The ~~setting is symbolic of~~ the twisted plot *mind of the narrator — a mind made ugly by its desire for revenge.* ~~for revenge lurking in the narrator's mind.~~ The setting of the story is as ~~ugly and~~ foul as human vengeance itself.

paragraph composition analyzing the writer's use of setting: "The Most Dangerous Game," on page 13; "The Lady or the Tiger?" on page 49; "Sonata for Harp and Bicycle," on page 33; "The Invalid's Story," on page 99; "The Man to Send Rain Clouds," on page 159; or "'If I Forget Thee, Oh Earth'," on page 165. Follow these steps:

1. Read the story you have chosen twice. The first time you read it, pay attention to the

action of the story. Then, in your second reading, pay close attention to the details of the setting.

2. Divide a paper into three columns and label them Setting, Details That Describe the Setting, and Significance of Setting. Then list elements from the story in these columns, including quotations from important passages.

3. Write a topic sentence that tells what story you are writing about and that suggests your purpose. Your purpose, of course, is to explain the significance of the setting.

4. Write the rest of your composition using information from your notes. If there are two main topics that you would like to cover, write two paragraphs. Otherwise, you may need only one paragraph.

5. Revise your composition, looking for ways to strengthen its content and overall organization. Delete unimportant details and add any that need to be added. Then make a clean copy of your revised composition and proofread it for errors in spelling and mechanics.

6. Share your final copy with your teacher, with your family, and with friends in your class.

# Lesson 8: Writing About Plot

## WHAT IS PLOT?

A literary work, such as a short story, novel, play, or narrative poem, usually presents a series of events. Such a series, or sequence, of events is called a *plot*. Understanding plot is central to interpreting any work that tells a story.

## THE PARTS OF A PLOT

The plot of a literary work can usually be divided into several sections, as follows:

1. *Introduction,* or *exposition:* In this part of the work, essential background information is given. Often the introduction describes the setting and presents the major characters.
2. *Inciting incident:* This is an event that creates the central conflict, or struggle, that the work is about.
3. *Development:* This part of the plot includes all the events that happen between the inciting incident and the climax.
4. *Climax:* This is the high point of interest and suspense in the work.
5. *Falling action:* This is the part in which the conflict begins to move to a resolution.
6. *Resolution:* This is the point at which the conflict in the work is ended, or resolved. The *denouement* is any action that occurs after the resolution.

In diagram form, a standard plot looks like this:

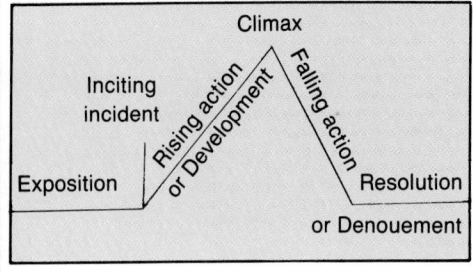

Of course, not all literary works follow this plot structure exactly. Some have no introduction or denouement. In some, the inciting incident happens before the actual beginning of the work. Finally, in some works, the climax and the resolution are the same event.

## SPECIAL TECHNIQUES OF PLOT

In creating a plot, writers make use of many special literary devices, or techniques. The following are some of the most common:

1. *Suspense:* This is a feeling of growing excitement or tension felt by the reader. Writers create suspense by raising questions in their readers' minds.
2. *Foreshadowing:* This is a hint, or clue, about something that will happen later in the work.
3. *Flashback:* This is a section of work that interrupts the action of the work to tell about an earlier event.
4. *Surprise ending:* This is an ending that catches the readers off guard—that presents an unexpected turn of events.

Read the sections on Plot and Conflict in the Handbook of Literary Terms and Techniques. Then read the following case study.

## CASE STUDY: WRITING ABOUT PLOT

Tamzin's English class learned about how plot is used in literary works. Then her teacher asked the class to choose a short story and to write a paragraph analyzing its plot. Tamzin selected Richard Connell's "The Most Dangerous Game," on page 13.

**Prewriting**

Tamzin read the short story twice to familiarize herself with all the techniques the author had

966 *Handbook of Writing About Literature*

used in constructing its plot. Then she made a list of events in the story. She studied this list, identified the central conflict, and then identified the parts of the plot. Finally, she made notes about each part, as follows:

- Introduction: long; sets up ominous mood; foreshadowing (Whitney's comment, "Even so, I rather think they understand one thing —fear"; pistol shots; General Zaroff's talk about hunting men)

- Inciting incident: Zaroff reveals his intention to hunt Rainsford; Rainsford is forced to accept the challenge.

- Development: Rainsford sets several traps for Zaroff. Zaroff allows Rainsford to escape several times so the hunt will continue. Suspense: who will win?

- Climax: Rainsford sees that his last trap has failed to kill Zaroff. Desperate, he jumps into the sea.

- False resolution: Zaroff sees that Rainsford has jumped off the cliff and is disappointed in the end of the hunt. He goes home for dinner at his palace.

- Real resolution: surprise ending; Rainsford, alive, appears in Zaroff's bedroom. Rainsford kills Zaroff.

### Drafting and Revising

Tamzin used her prewriting notes to write a rough draft of her paragraph. Then she revised what she had written to make her paragraph clearer and better organized.

### Proofreading and Publishing

Tamzin made a clean final copy of her paragraph and proofread the copy for errors in mechanics and spelling. She gave a copy to her English teacher, who displayed it on the bulletin board.

## ACTIVITIES AND ASSIGNMENTS

A. If you haven't already done so, read the short story "The Most Dangerous Game." Then use Tamzin's prewriting notes to write a paragraph about the story's plot. Follow these steps:

1. Write an introductory sentence that tells what your paragraph will be about. Do *not* begin your sentence with "This paragraph is about . . ." Instead, start with these words:

    The intriguing plot of Richard Connell's short story, "The Most Dangerous Game . . ."

2. In the body of your paragraph, explain the parts of the plot of the story in order of occurrence. Include direct quotations from the story, where possible, to make particular points. Otherwise, simply summarize events in your own words.
3. Write a concluding sentence that deals with Connell's use of a surprise ending.
4. Revise and proofread your paragraph and share it with your class.

    B. Choose one of the following stories for a paragraph on plot: "The Interlopers," on page 43; "The Lady or the Tiger?" on page 49; "The Cask of Amontillado," on page 139; "The Gift of the Magi," on page 183; or "The Necklace," on page 201.

Follow these steps when writing your paragraph:

1. Read the story twice.
2. Make a list of the events in the story. Then determine what the central conflict of the story is. Doing so will help you to identify the parts of the plot.
3. List the parts of the plot in your notes. First find the inciting incident—the point at which the conflict is introduced. Next find the resolution—the part of the story in which the conflict is resolved, or ended. Any material that appears before the inciting incident will be part of the introduction. The material after

*Writing About Plot* 967

the inciting incident and before the climax will be the development. The material after the resolution will be the denouement. Bear in mind that some stories will not have all these parts.

4. Use your prewriting notes to write a rough draft. In your topic sentence, identify your topic and purpose. In the body of your paragraph, present the parts of the plot in order of occurrence. Revise your rough draft, make a clean copy, and proofread it. Share your completed work with the rest of the class.

# Lesson 9: Writing About Character

## TYPES OF CHARACTER

Most short narratives center on the experiences of one main character, the *protagonist*. In addition to the main character, there may be one or more other characters. These other characters can be *major characters*—ones who play significant roles—or *minor characters*—ones who play less significant roles. In some narratives the main character is pitted against or is in conflict with a major character known as the *antagonist*.

## CHARACTERIZATION

*Characterization* is the process of developing, or revealing, the nature of a character. Writers use many techniques to reveal what their characters are like. Sometimes the narrator of a story or the speaker of a poem makes direct comments about characters. Thus a narrator might describe how a character looks or how the character is feeling. Sometimes the nature of a character is revealed by what other characters say about him or her. Finally, characters themselves often reveal what they are like by what they say and do. When reading a narrative, pay attention to how the writer uses these methods of characterization.

## ELEMENTS OF CHARACTER

No two characters are exactly alike. The following are some of the features that make characters distinct:

1. *Appearance:* What does the character look like? What kinds of clothes does the character wear? What do these aspects of appearance reveal about the character?
2. *Personality:* Does the character tend to be emotional or rational? inward or outgoing? competent or incompetent? controlled or uncontrolled? happy or depressed? radical or conservative? caring or cold? a leader or a follower? principled or unscrupulous?
3. *Background:* Where did the character grow up? What experiences has he or she had? Is the character experienced or naive? What is the character's social status? level of education? occupation? What are the character's hobbies or skills?
4. *Motivation:* What makes the character act as he or she does? What are the character's likes and dislikes? What are the character's wishes, goals, desires, dreams, and needs?
5. *Relationships:* How is the character related to other characters in the narrative? In what ways does he or she interact with these characters? What are the consequences of these interactions?
6. *Conflict:* Is the character involved in some conflict? If so, is this an internal conflict—one that takes place within the character—or an external conflict—a struggle between the character and some outside force? Is the conflict ever resolved? If so, how?
7. *Change:* Does the character change in the course of the narrative? Does he or she learn or grow? In other words, is the character static (unchanging) or dynamic (changing)?

When planning a piece of writing about a character, follow these steps:

1. Determine what type of character you are dealing with—the main character, another major character, or a minor character.
2. As you read the narrative, pay close attention to details of characterization. Note what the narrator says about the character, what other characters say about the character, and what the character says and does.

*Writing About Character* 969

**Motivation for Writing** Ask students to describe the types of characters they like to read about. Then have them describe the ways in which they learn about the traits of their favorite characters. Lead them to see that writers sometimes tell about a character's personality directly, but that often readers must make inferences about a character based on what he or she does or says.

Suggested Response: Students should follow all the specified steps in revising and proofreading the rough draft.

3. Answer the questions from this lesson about appearance, personality, background, motivation, relationships, conflict, and change. Find evidence in the narrative to support your answers.
4. Choose one aspect of the character to focus on in your paper. Write a topic sentence or thesis statement about this aspect of the character.
5. Find evidence from your prewriting notes to support your topic sentence or thesis statement.

## CASE STUDY: WRITING ABOUT CHARACTER

Victor's English class was asked to write a paragraph about character. Victor decided to write about the main character in Isabel Allende's "Uncle Marcos," on page 63.

### Prewriting

Victor read the short story twice to familiarize himself with Uncle Marcos, the story's main character. In his prewriting notes, Victor wrote out the answers to the questions in the lesson. Victor wrote notes about Uncle Marcos's appearance, personality, background, motivation, and relationships. He also thought about whether Uncle Marcos faced any conflicts and whether Uncle Marcos changed in the course of the story. In his notes Victor recorded many specific details of characterization taken from the story.

### Drafting and Revising

Victor used his prewriting notes to write a rough draft of his paragraph. Here is Victor's uncorrected rough draft:

> The main character of Isabel Allende's short story, "Uncle Marcos," a mysterious, adventuresome man named Uncle Marcos. He visits his sister, Nivea's home. It is somewhere in South America. In Clara's journal she characterizes Uncle Marcos, without having to consult a photograph, as "weather-beaten and thin" and a "strange, sharklike smile" that peers out at her from underneath his pirate's mustache. Who traveled to remote lands. One adventure was a flight on the skeleton of a prehistoric bird. The onlookers cheered Uncle Marcos as he headed into the clouds until he lost his way and did not return home and the crowd and his family thought Uncle Marcos was for dead. Clara loved Uncle Marcos stories and could repeat them all. All of the stories came back to her when her uncle arrived at her mother's home in a coffin. She wanted to keep his spirit alive.

Victor realized that his rough draft needed some major revision. As he revised, Victor added details, combined sentences, eliminated sentence fragments, and made several of his statements clearer.

### Proofreading and Publishing

After revising his draft, Victor made a clean final copy and proofread it carefully for errors in punctuation, spelling, capitalization, and manuscript form. Then Victor shared his paper with other students in his class discussion group.

### ACTIVITIES AND ASSIGNMENTS

A. Revise and proofread the rough draft from the preceding case study. Follow these steps:
1. Read through the rough draft, noting its overall organization. Does the draft have a topic sentence? Does it contain supporting evidence? Does it have a definite conclusion? If it doesn't, supply the missing part or parts. Do portions of his paper need to be rearranged?
2. Check to see whether any sentences can be improved by being combined.
3. Rewrite any parts that are unclear.
4. Check to make sure that transition words such as *however, although,* and *next* have been used to relate the sentences logically to one another.
5. Make sure that Victor's claims about the story are all supported by the text.

6. Correct any sentence fragments or run-ons in the draft.

7. Make any other changes that you feel are necessary. Use the Checklist for Revision on page 949 of this handbook.

8. Make a clean final copy of the revised paragraph and proofread it for errors in spelling, punctuation, capitalization, and manuscript form.

9. Share the proofread final draft with your classmates. Discuss the various ways in which your classmates revised the paragraph.

B. Choose a short story from the text and write a paragraph about one of its characters. Follow these steps:

1. Read once the story that you have selected. Decide which character you want to write about. Is the character the main character? a major character? a minor character? the protagonist? the antagonist? Make some preliminary notes about your impression of this character.

2. Read the story a second time and make notes about specific elements of the characterization. In your prewriting notes, write answers to the questions in the section on Elements of Character in this lesson.

3. Choose one aspect of the character that you want to focus on in a paragraph. Write a topic sentence that introduces this aspect of the character.

4. Use your prewriting notes to write the body of your paragraph. Support your claims about the character with evidence from the text.

5. Write a concluding sentence that summarizes the central point of your paragraph.

6. Revise and proofread your rough draft. Then share your draft with your classmates.

**Motivation for Writing** Ask students whether they have ever disagreed with a friend about what happened at a party or other gathering. Have students discuss why such disagreements arise. Lead them to see that different people have different perspectives on the same events. Then tell them that stories or novels may also be told from the vantage point of different characters, or even from the perspective of someone who does not participate in the story at all. Have them speculate as to how a change in point of view might affect a story.

# Lesson 10: Writing About Point of View

## WHAT IS NARRATION?

*Narration* is the act of telling a story. Literary works that tell stories are called *narratives.* Types of narratives include short stories, novels, and narrative poems. The speaker who tells the story is called the *narrator.*

## WHAT IS POINT OF VIEW?

*Point of view* is the perspective from which a narrative is told. In a work written from the *first-person point of view,* the narrator is a character in the work and uses pronouns such as *I, me,* and *we.* In a work written from the *third-person point of view,* the narrator is not a character in the work, and the narrator never uses the pronouns *I, me,* and *we.* In a third-person story, these pronouns are used only in dialogue.

Edgar Allan Poe's "The Cask of Amontillado," on page 139, is written from the first-person point of view. Notice the pronouns that the narrator uses to refer to himself:

> *We* had passed through long walls of piled skeletons, with casks and puncheons intermingling, into the inmost recesses of the catacombs. *I* paused again, and this time *I* made bold to seize Fortunato by an arm above the elbow.

Morley Callaghan's "All the Years of Her Life," on page 57, is written from the third-person point of view. The narrator stands outside the story and never uses *I, me,* or *we.*

Sometimes the narrator speaks from the point of view of one character, and everything is seen through this character's eyes. A narrator of this kind is said to have a *limited* point of view. At other times the narrator is all-knowing and relates events as seen through the eyes of more than one character. Such a narrator is said to have an *omniscient* point of view.

In most first-person narratives, the narrator is limited. However, in third-person narratives, the narrator may be either limited or omniscient. For example, both "The Lady or the Tiger?" on page 49, and "All the Years of Her Life," on page 57, are told from the third-person point of view. However, in the former story, the narrator can see inside the minds of all the characters and report what is going on there. Thus the narrator is omniscient, or all-knowing. In the latter story, the narrator sees into the mind of one character and one character only—Alfred Higgins. Thus the narrator is limited.

The point of view of a story therefore determines what information the narrator can provide. In a story written from the third-person omniscient point of view, the narrator can describe the thoughts of all the characters. In a story written from a first-person or third-person limited point of view, the narrator can describe all the characters' words and actions. However, such a limited narrator can report the thoughts of only one character.

## CHARACTERISTICS OF NARRATORS

You have seen that narrators differ significantly from one another. Some narrators are characters who take part in the action. Other narrators stand apart from the action and report it. Some narrators are limited to the point of view of one person. Others are all-knowing. The following are some additional characteristics of narrators:

1. *Reliability and unreliability:* Sometimes the narrator of a story is someone whom the reader can trust. In other words, the narrator

is reliable. At other times the narrator is un-
trustworthy, or unreliable.

2. *Subjectivity and objectivity:* If the narrator of
the story directly expresses opinions, beliefs,
or values, then the narrator is subjective. If the
narrator simply reports the facts of the story
and lets the reader draw his or her own opinions, then the narrator is objective.

## CASE STUDY: WRITING ABOUT NARRATION AND POINT OF VIEW

David's English class was given an assignment to write a paragraph about the narration
and point of view of a particular short story.
David decided to write about James Thurber's
"The Secret Life of Walter Mitty," on page 3.

### Prewriting

David read the story once quickly and decided that it was written from the third-person
limited point of view. Then he reread the story
carefully and made notes about the narration
and point of view. Here are David's prewriting
notes:

- Point of view: third-person limited; narrator
knows Mitty's thoughts only.

- Function of point of view: reveals the inner
life of the main character—Walter Mitty—
and causes the reader to identify with this
character.

- Narrator: reliable and objective—does not
appear to exaggerate or to present personal opinions. Details that the narrator
chooses to include from Mitty's life are
those that especially support the contrast
between Mitty's fantasies and reality.

### Drafting and Revising

David used his prewriting notes to write a
draft of his paragraph. Then he revised his draft
carefully, as shown in the right column.

### Proofreading and Publishing

David made a clean final copy of his paragraph. Then he proofread it for errors in grammar, usage, spelling, punctuation, capitalization,
and manuscript form. Finally, he shared the
paragraph with the class in an oral report.

*Writing About Point of View*   973

1. Suggested Response: He indented his paragraph.
2. Suggested Response: In line 7, he combined two sentences to eliminate unnecessary words.
3. Suggested Response: Some errors in punctuation, capitalization, and spelling are adding a comma in line 9, capitalizing the *i* of "in" in the same line, and corrected the spelling of "courageous" in line 10.
4. Suggested Response: He added clarifying details in line 5.
5. Suggested Response: He replaced "comes in" with "intrudes" (line 12); "stuff" with "thoughts" (line 14); and "really good" with "astonishing" (line 20).

## ACTIVITIES AND ASSIGNMENTS

A. Answer the following questions based on the case study.
1. What error in manuscript form did David correct at the beginning of his paragraph?
2. What sentences did David combine to eliminate unnecessary words?
3. What errors in punctuation, capitalization, and spelling did David correct?
4. To what sentence did David add clarifying details?
5. What informal words and phrases did David replace with words that are more formal?

B. If you haven't already done so, read Edgar Allan Poe's "The Cask of Amontillado," on page 139. Then write a one- or two-paragraph composition in which you discuss the narrator of the story and the point of view of that narrator.

Follow these steps when writing your composition:

1. Identify the point of view of the narrator. Is the point of view first-person or third-person? Is it limited or omniscient?
2. Decide whether you think the narrator is reliable or unreliable, subjective or objective.
3. Read the story again and make prewriting notes about the narrator and point of view.
4. Write a topic sentence that states the main idea of your composition. This sentence should make an assertion about the narrator that you will support in the body of your composition.
5. In the body of your composition, refer to specific parts of the story.
6. Revise your composition, proofread it, and share it with the rest of the class.

# Lesson 11: Writing About Theme

## WHAT IS THEME?

In popular usage a *theme* is simply a subject that is developed or expanded on. This is the meaning of the word that people have in mind when they speak of the theme of a variety show, an interior design, or a senior prom. However, the word also has a more technical meaning, one that is common in literary discussions. When used in such discussions, *theme* usually means the central idea or insight into life that a literary work conveys. In other words, the theme is the point or purpose of the work as a whole.

## IDENTIFYING THE THEME OF A LITERARY WORK

In some literary works the theme is a moral lesson learned by one of the characters. A fable or parable, for example, will have such a theme. However, the theme of a work is not always a moral lesson. Consider, for example, the following poem:

BEARS

Adrienne Rich

Wonderful bears that walked my room all night,
Where have you gone, your sleek and fairy fur,
Your eyes' veiled and imperious light?

Brown bears as rich as mocha or as musk,
White opalescent bears whose fur stood out
Electric in the deepening dusk,

And great black bears that seemed more blue
    than black,
More violet than blue against the dark—
Where are you now? Upon what track

Mutter your muffled paws that used to tread

So softly, surely, up the creakless stair
While I lay listening in bed?

When did I lose you? Whose have you
    become?
Why do I wait and wait and never hear
Your thick nocturnal pacing in my room?
My bears, who keeps you now, in pride and
    fear?

This poem deals with a universal experience. In childhood, people often imagine fantastic creatures stalking about in the darkness of their bedrooms. However, as they grow older, they stop having such fantastic imaginings. The central idea, or theme, of this poem is that such imaginative ability is wonderful and that its loss is something to be regretted.

In a simple traditional work, such as a fable or a parable, the theme is often explicitly stated. For example, the theme of Aesop's fable of "The Fox and the Crow" is the moral with which the fable ends: "Flattery will get you nowhere." However, in most literary works, the theme is not explicitly stated. Instead, it must be inferred from the work as a whole. The theme of Adrienne Rich's poem, for example, depends on all that occurs in the poem. It is not directly stated in any single line.

When attempting to identify the theme of a work, ask yourself, "What is the overall purpose or effect of the work?" Sometimes this purpose or effect will be suggested by the title of the work. Sometimes it will be suggested by the way in which the work ends. Often, however, the theme will be revealed throughout the entire work.

**Motivation for Writing** Write the following theme on the chalkboard: "Friendship is worth more than material goods." Then have students construct a plot that would communicate this theme. Lead them to see the difference between plot, as sequence of events, and theme—an insight into life. Tell them that, as readers, they will often have to infer the theme of a story by focusing on the central conflict or an important change that the main character experiences.

Suggested Response: Make sure that students have followed the specified steps.

## CASE STUDY: WRITING ABOUT THEME

Lila's English class was given an assignment to write a paragraph about the theme of a literary selection. Lila decided to write about the theme of Dorothy Canfield Fisher's essay "A Neighbor of Mine," on page 431.

### Prewriting

Lila read the story twice to make sure that she had not overlooked any clues to its theme. Then she took the following prewriting notes:

- Title: "A Neighbor of Mine"
- Author: Dorothy Canfield Fisher
- Theme: One shouldn't make broad generalizations about people.
- How theme is revealed:
  Selection opens with the narrator being "nettled" by her visitor's tendency to make broad generalizations.
  One of the narrator's neighbors, a "down-to-earth" man, stops by and discusses such topics as cows and forestry. The visitor describes the neighbor as being "natural" and "open" and asks, ironically, "Why can't authors be like that farmer?" In other words, the visitor is generalizing both about farmers and about authors. The visitor implies that authors are not open and natural.
  In a surprise ending, the "farmer" who lives nearby turns out to be Robert Frost, the famous poet. This ending proves that broad generalizations about groups of people, such as authors, can be wrong.

### Drafting and Revising

Lila wrote a rough draft based on her prewriting notes. She began with an opening sentence that stated the title of the essay, its author, and its theme. Then, in the body of her para-

graph, she showed how the theme was revealed in the work, using evidence taken from the essay. Finally, she ended with a concluding sentence about the evils of overgeneralizing about people. Once her draft was finished, Lila revised it carefully, making sure that all of her sentences supported her topic sentence.

### Proofreading and Publishing.

Lila proofed her revised paragraph for errors in grammar, usage, spelling, punctuation, capitalization, and manuscript form. Then she made two copies—one for her English teacher and one for her writing folder.

## ACTIVITIES AND ASSIGNMENTS

A. Using Lila's prewriting notes from the case study, write a paragraph about the theme of "A Neighbor of Mine." Follow these steps when writing your paragraph:

1. Read the essay once and look at Lila's prewriting notes. Then read the story a second time and add to these notes any important details that Lila omitted.
2. Write a topic sentence in which you state the theme of "A Neighbor of Mine."
3. Write the body of your paragraph, citing evidence to support the topic sentence.
4. Write a concluding sentence on the subject of overgeneralizing about people.
5. Revise your paragraph. Make a clean final copy. Then proofread for errors in spelling and mechanics. Share your paragraph with a classmate before turning it in to your English teacher.

B. Choose one of the following works and write a paragraph about its theme: "A Very Old Man with Enormous Wings," on page 173; "The Gift of the Magi," on page 183; "The Scarlet Ibis," on page 189; or "The Necklace," on page 201. Follow these steps when writing your paragraph:

1. Read the short story once. Write the theme of the work in a single sentence in your notes.
2. Read the work a second time, listing in your notes any details that support the theme you have stated. Look for these details, or evidence, in descriptions, figures of speech, quotations, the plot, and the title.
3. Write an introductory sentence that states the theme of your chosen work.
4. Write the body of your paragraph, providing evidence for the theme that you have stated in your opening sentence.
5. Write a concluding sentence that summarizes the central point of your paragraph.
6. Revise your paragraph.
7. Make a clean final copy. Proofread this copy. Then share it with a classmate and with your English teacher.

*Writing About Theme* 977

# SECTION 3: UNDERSTANDING THE WORK AS A WHOLE: INTERPRETATION AND SYNTHESIS

## Lesson 12: Writing About a Short Story

In this lesson you will learn how to write a multi-paragraph composition that presents an interpretation of a short story. Begin by reading the story carefully and answering the following questions about it:

1. *Author:* Who is the author of the story?
2. *Title:* What is the story's title? Does this title suggest the story's subject or theme?
3. *Setting:* What are the time and place of the story? What mood is created by the setting? Does the setting determine the action or conflict of the story?
4. *Point of view:* Is the story written from the first-person or third-person point of view? Is the narrator limited or omniscient?
5. *Central conflict:* What is the central conflict of the story? Is this conflict internal or external? If the conflict is external, is it between two people, between a person and nature, between a person and society, or between a person and a supernatural force?
6. *Plot:* What are the major events of the story? What happens in the introduction? What is the inciting incident? What happens during the development? What is the climax of the story? How is the central conflict resolved? What, if anything, happens after the resolution? That is, does the story have a denouement?

   What special plot devices are used in the story? Does the story make use of foreshadowing or flashbacks? Is the story suspenseful? If so, what expectations on the part of the reader create this suspense? Does the story have a surprise ending?
7. *Characterization:* Who is the main character, or protagonist? Who are the other major and minor characters? What is revealed in the story about each character's appearance, personality, background, motivations, and relationships? What conflicts do these characters face? Which of these characters change in the course of the story and in what ways? What roles do the minor characters play in advancing the action of the story?
8. *Devices of sound and figures of speech:* Does the story make use of special devices of sound such as onomatopoeia or parallelism? of figures of speech such as metaphor or hyperbole?
9. *Theme:* What is the theme, or central idea, of the story? How is this theme revealed?

   The point of your composition will be to support a general statement about the significance of the story. Begin with an introductory paragraph that names the author and title and states the story's main idea, or theme. In the first body paragraph of your composition, summarize the story's plot. In the other body paragraphs, discuss other elements of the story that are related to its theme. For example, you might devote one body paragraph to the story's setting and another to how the main character changes as a result of the central conflict. End with a concluding paragraph that relates the story's theme to everyday life.

*978    Handbook of Writing About Literature*

## CASE STUDY: WRITING ABOUT A SHORT STORY

Larry's English teacher asked the class to write a composition presenting an interpretation of the theme of a short story. Larry decided to write about Gabriel García Márquez's "A Very Old Man with Enormous Wings," on page 173.

### Prewriting

Larry read the short story once and then asked himself the following questions: What was the impact of the old man's appearance on the villagers? What were their reactions to the old man? How did their reactions relate to the theme of the story?

Larry decided that his composition would examine the theme of the story as suggested by the villagers' reactions to the old man. In the rough outline that Larry made for his composition, each major heading represents a paragraph:

- Introduction:
  Author
  Title
  Theme
  Magical realism

- Plot:
  Of story as a whole

- Theme
  Villagers' reactions to the old man's visit
  Interpretation of theme of the story as
    suggested by reactions

- Conclusion
  Significance of story for us all

Larry then reread the story and added to his notes details to be used as supporting evidence in each paragraph.

### Drafting and Revising

Larry wrote a rough draft of his four-paragraph composition, using information from his prewriting notes. Then he revised his draft by marking it with editorial symbols. Here is the first, or introductory, paragraph of Larry's composition with his corrections and revisions.

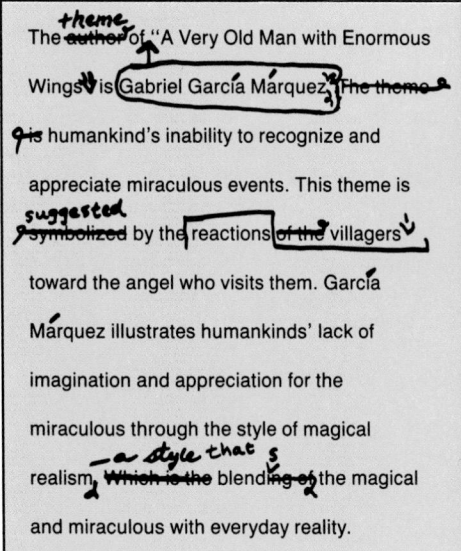

### Proofreading and Publishing

Larry made a clean final copy of his composition and proofread this copy carefully. Then he shared the copy with members of the class discussion group.

### ACTIVITIES AND ASSIGNMENTS

A. Answer the following questions based on the revised introductory paragraph from the case study.

1. What sentences in this paragraph did Larry combine?
2. What word did Larry replace with one that was more appropriate?
3. What sentence fragment did Larry correct?
4. What errors in punctuation and spelling did Larry catch? What errors did he miss?

B. If you haven't already done so, read "A Very Old Man with Enormous Wings," on page 173. Then make notes on the story and finish

1. Suggested Response: In lines 1 and 10, he combines two sentences.
2. Suggested Response: He replaced "symbolized" with "suggested."
3. Suggested Response: He corrected a sentence fragment in line 10.
4. Suggested Response: He added the accent marks in the author's name in lines 2 and 6 and 7; and he corrected the error in possession in villagers' in line 5. He has not yet corrected the repetition of some words.

Larry's composition. Feel free to change or replace Larry's introductory paragraph.

    C. Select a favorite short story to interpret in a three- to five-paragraph composition. As you plan and write your composition, follow these steps:

1. Read the short story carefully and answer the questions given at the beginning of this lesson.

2. Determine what the theme, purpose, or dominant effect of the story is. State this theme, purpose, or effect in a single sentence that you will use as the thesis statement of your composition.

3. Look over your answers from step 1 and find evidence to support your thesis statement.

4. Divide your evidence into groups and write a rough outline. Each group of evidence should be represented by a major heading in your outline.

5. Write a rough draft, based on your outline and your notes. Develop each major heading from your outline in a single paragraph. Before actually beginning your first draft, share your outline with a classmate or with your teacher and ask for comments and suggestions for improvement.

6. Revise and proofread your draft. Then share it with your teacher and with the rest of the class.

# Lesson 13: Writing About a Poem

Before writing about a poem, you must first understand the poem very well. Following these steps will help you to do so:

1. Read the poem through once, silently, and note any words that are unfamiliar. Look up these words in a dictionary and think about what they mean in the context of the poem.
2. Read the poem aloud and listen for any special devices of sound such as rhythm, rhyme, onomatopoeia, and alliteration.
3. Read the poem again, silently. This time pay close attention to the images and figures of speech in the poem.
4. Paraphrase the poem. That is, restate the poem in your own words. As you do so, think not only about what is stated directly in the poem but also about what is suggested or implied.

In your prewriting notes, answer the following questions about the poem:

1. *Author:* Who is the poem's author?
2. *Title:* What is the title of the poem? Does the title suggest the poem's subject or theme?
3. *Genre:* What is the poem's genre, or type? Is it a lyric poem—a highly musical work that expresses emotion? Is it a narrative poem—one that tells a story? Is it a dramatic poem—one that contains characters who speak dialogue? Is it a concrete poem—one with a shape that suggests its meaning?
4. *Stanza form:* Is the poem divided into stanzas? If so, how many lines does each stanza have? Is the poem written in some standard stanza form such as couplets, quatrains, sonnet form, haiku form, or limerick form? Does each stanza function as a separate unit of meaning, like a paragraph in a composition?
5. *Devices of sound:* Is the poem in free verse or in some regular meter? If the poem has some regular meter, how many feet are there in an average line? What kind of foot is most common in the poem?

   Does the poem have a regular rhyme scheme? If so, what is this rhyme scheme?

   Does the poem use onomatopoeia? alliteration? consonance? assonance? internal rhyme? euphony? cacophony? parallelism? repetition? Does it have a refrain? What examples can you find of these devices?
6. *Imagery:* What images of sight are used in the poem? of sound? of taste? of touch? of smell? What effects do these images have?
7. *Figures of speech:* Does the poem contain examples of metaphor? of simile? of personification? of hyperbole? of understatement? Does the poet make use of symbols? puns? allusions? paradoxes? irony?
8. *Other literary devices:* What is the poem's general mood? Does this mood change in the course of the poem?

   What is the poem's setting? How is the setting related to the poem's mood? to the action of the poem?

   What seems to be the poem's central message, or theme? What do you think the writer's purpose was?

   Is the poem written in complete sentences?

   Does the poem use punctuation, capitalization, or spacing in special ways?

   Does the poem invite the reader to contrast two or more things?
9. *Questions about lyric poems:* What can you infer about the poem's speaker? Does the poem give you any hints about the speaker's background, situation, personality, emotional state, or views?

*Writing About a Poem* 981

**Motivation for Writing** Tell students that poetry is the most concentrated and intense literary form. Poets usually try to make every word count. It is therefore advisable to read poems more than once and to read them aloud. It is also important to understand the meaning of every word that a poet uses.

Is the speaker of the poem addressing anyone in particular? If so, who? What can you infer about the relationship between the speaker and the speaker's audience?

10. *Questions about narrative and dramatic poems:* What can you infer about the main speaker of the poem? Is the poem told from the first-person or third-person point of view?

How many characters appear in the poem? What can you infer about these characters? about the relationships between or among them?

Does the poem tell a story? If so, does this story involve a conflict? What is the plot of the poem?

## A CASE STUDY: WRITING ABOUT A POEM

### Prewriting

Martha's English teacher asked the class to choose a poem and to write an interpretation of it. Martha chose Sara Teasdale's "There Will Come Soft Rains," on page 652.

Martha began by reading the poem several times, both silently and aloud. She then clarified terms that were unclear to her:

- "feathery fire": robins, with their red breast feathers

- "tremulous white": fragile white plum blossoms

Finally, Martha made notes about the elements of the poem. The following are some of her notes:

- Title: "There Will Come Soft Rains"

- Author: Sara Teasdale

- Stanza form:
  Couplets (rhyming, two-line stanzas)
  First three couplets deal with nature
  Last three couplets introduce ideas that war has occurred

- Alliteration:
  "swallows circling"
  "shimmering sound"
  "feathery fire"
  "whistling whims"
  "trees tremulous"

- Images of sight:
  Frogs in pools
  Circling swallows
  White trees
  Robins on wire

- Images of sound:
  Soft rains
  Singing frogs
  Whistling robins

- Images of touch:
  Softness of rain

- Images of smell:
  Smell of the ground

- Theme:
  If people were destroyed completely, nature would continue. People not that important. Also, perhaps, a warning about possibility of all-destructive war.

### Drafting and Revising

Martha used her prewriting notes to write a rough draft. She began by discussing, in the first paragraph, the fact that people tend to have a human-centered view of the universe. In the last sentence of her first paragraph, Martha stated her thesis:

Sara Teasdale, in her poem "There Will Come Soft Rains," challenges this human-centered view of the universe.

In her second paragraph Martha discussed the first three couplets of the poem. She explained how the poet uses literary devices to create a beautiful, peaceful scene from nature.

In her third paragraph Martha discussed the

last three couplets of the poem. She explained how the poet reveals, in these stanzas, that the scene being described is one after a war in which the people of earth have been destroyed.

Finally, in her concluding paragraph, Martha discussed the theme of the poem—that people are not all that important in the natural scheme of things and that nature will continue even if people are stupid enough to blow themselves up.

Martha wrote several drafts of her composition, revising it heavily each time.

### Proofreading and Publishing

After proofreading her final draft, Martha made a copy of it for her English teacher. She also read the poem and her composition to the class.

### ACTIVITIES AND ASSIGNMENTS

A. Using Martha's prewriting notes and the descriptions in the lesson, write a four-paragraph composition that offers an interpretation of "There Will Come Soft Rains," on page 652.

B. Choose a poem from the text and write an interpretation of it. Follow these steps:

1. Read the poem carefully several times. Follow the steps and answer the questions given in this lesson.
2. Come up with a one-sentence statement about the poem's overall theme, purpose, or effect. Use this sentence as the thesis statement of your composition.
3. Use the answers from your prewriting notes to develop your introduction, body paragraphs, and conclusion.
4. Revise and proofread your composition. Then prepare a dramatic reading and oral report. Read the poem to the class and then read your composition and discuss both.

*Writing About a Poem*  983

## ANSWERS TO ACTIVITIES AND ASSIGNMENTS, SECTION A

Make sure that students base their paragraphs on the prewriting notes provided.

**Motivation for Writing** Have students describe a television program or movie they have enjoyed. Then tell them that such shows can be classified as dramas. Ask students to distinguish between drama, fiction, and poetry. Lead them to see that dramas are different from other forms of literature because dramas are meant to be performed. Also lead them to see that dramas share many elements with other forms—plot, conflict, setting, and character.

### DRAMA AS LITERATURE

Drama shares much in common with other types of literature. Like all literary works, dramas express themes and make use of special devices of imagery, sound, and figurative language. Like short stories, novels, and narrative poems, dramas have plots, conflicts, settings, and characters. Therefore, when writing about dramas, you can make use of most of the techniques discussed in previous lessons in this handbook.

### DRAMA AS PERFORMANCE

In one major respect, drama differs from all other types of literature. Dramas, unlike most poems, stories, and novels, are written specifically to be performed before an audience. Therefore, when reading a drama, you should constantly imagine what it would be like to see the action on a stage and to hear the characters speak their lines.

The printed form of a drama reflects the fact that it is written to be performed. The printed page is made up of dialogue and stage directions. The *dialogue* is simply the lines to be spoken by the actors. The *stage directions* tell how the actors should speak and move; how the stage should look; what properties, or movable pieces, should be used by the actors; and what special effects of lighting or sound should be used during the production.

When writing about a drama, you can write about it purely as a work of literature or you can write about it as a performance. The following are some possible approaches to writing about drama.

*The drama as literature:*
1. Choose a character who intrigues you and write about how that character changes in the course of the drama.
2. Write an analysis of the plot of the drama. Explain the parts of the plot, including the introduction, the inciting incident, the development, the climax, the resolution, and the denouement.
3. Explain the theme of the drama and relate this theme to other elements of the work that reveal the theme.

*The drama as performance:*
1. Choose a character who intrigues you and write about how that character should be portrayed in an actual production.
2. Choose a scene from the drama and write a description of a stage setting for that scene as viewed from the audience.
3. Write a review of an actual performance of the drama. Comment on the quality of the acting, the set, the costumes, the lighting, and the sound.

### CASE STUDY: WRITING ABOUT DRAMA

Marvin's English class was asked to write a paragraph about drama. Marvin decided to write about Anton Chekhov's one-act play, *The Boor,* on page 227.

### Prewriting

Marvin read *The Boor* and thought about what aspect of the drama he would like to write about. He recalled that as he had read the play, he had formed a vivid picture in his mind of the character named Smirnov. He decided to write about how Smirnov should be portrayed in a performance of the play. Marvin charted his prewriting notes as shown on the next page.

984   *Handbook of Writing About Literature*

| CHARACTER: SMIRNOV | |
|---|---|
| *How to Portray* | *Evidence in Text* |
| 1. Appearance: dirty, as if he had been traveling for a long time without bathing | Smirnov says of himself, "All dusty, boots dirty, unwashed, uncombed, straw on my vest." |
| 2. Tone of voice: loud and rude | Luka says, "he curses and barges right in." Mme. Popova says, "I am not accustomed to such a tone." Mme. Popova complains about his shouting; stage directions describe him as shouting. |
| 3. Movements: quick and impulsive; overemphasized to match his raging temper | stage directions show him sitting down and jumping up again. he breaks chair in his hands. he seizes Mme. Popova's hand so hard that she cries out in pain. |

## Drafting and Revising

Marvin wanted to make sure that the topic sentence of his paragraph clearly introduced what he intended to write about in the body of the paragraph. He drafted this sentence:

> When I read Anton Chekhov's play *The Boor,* I knew that Smirnov had dirty clothes and a booming voice.

Marvin read his topic sentence and knew that it would need to be revised. First, he did not want to use the first-person pronoun "I" in his paragraph. Second, his sentence did not raise the subject of portraying Smirnov. Third, the sentence was too specific. The fact that Smirnov "had dirty clothes and a booming voice" should be saved for the body of the paragraph. Marvin rewrote his topic sentence as follows:

> Any faithful performance of Anton Chekhov's one-act play *The Boor* should portray the character of Smirnov as boisterous yet likable.

Marvin then wrote the body of his paragraph, providing evidence for his characterization of Smirnov as "boisterous yet likable." His concluding sentence summarized the main idea of his paragraph. After finishing his rough draft, Marvin revised it thoroughly, adding supporting evidence from the play.

## Proofreading and Publishing

Marvin made a clean copy of his revised paragraph and proofread it. Then he shared it with his English teacher and with the teacher of his drama class.

## ACTIVITIES AND ASSIGNMENTS

A. Starting with Marvin's topic sentence from the case study, write a paragraph about the character of Smirnov in the play *The Boor.* Follow these steps when writing your paragraph:

1. Read the play and then look over Marvin's prewriting notes. Add to your own notes any important details from the text that you think Marvin should have included.
2. Write Marvin's revised topic sentence at the top of your own paper. Then write the body of your paragraph, discussing the details of how you think Smirnov should be portrayed on stage. Support your statements with evidence from the dialogue and stage directions of the play.
3. Write a concluding sentence that summarizes the central idea of your paragraph.
4. Read over your rough draft, checking for errors in mechanics or style. Revise and proofread your paragraph carefully. Share it with a

*Writing About Drama* 985

Make sure that students have followed the prescribed steps in writing their paragraphs.

friend or relative before turning it in to your teacher.

B. Choose one of the dramas in the text and write a paragraph about it. Follow these steps:

1. Read the play you have chosen and decide which of the following aspects you would like to write about
   a. how a particular character changes during the course of the drama
   b. the plot of the drama
   c. the theme of the drama
   d. how a certain character should be portrayed in a performance
   e. how you would create the stage setting of a scene in the drama
2. In your prewriting notes, list evidence from the dialogue and stage directions to support the main idea of your paragraph.
3. Write a rough draft of your paragraph, including a topic sentence, a body of supporting evidence, and a concluding sentence.
4. Revise and proofread your rough draft. Then share it with the rest of the class.

# SECTION 4:  JUDGING A LITERARY WORK: EVALUATION

## Lesson 15:  Evaluating a Literary Work

### WHAT IS EVALUATION?

An *evaluation* of a literary work is a judgment about its value or quality. The following statement, for example, is an evaluation:

> The dismal setting of Edgar Allan Poe's "The Cask of Amontillado" is an excellent vehicle for his portrayal of the psychology of vengeance.

Notice that the statement expresses an opinion. An evaluation always represents someone's opinion about a work, not a fact about the work. However, the opinion expressed in an evaluation must be based on facts. In other words, it must be supported by evidence from the work being evaluated. Consider, for example, the following evaluation:

> The cheerful setting of Poe's "The Cask of Amontillado" is inappropriate to a story about vengeance and shows thoughtlessness on the part of the author.

The facts of the story contradict this opinion. The setting, in fact, is not cheerful. Because the evaluation is not based on facts, it is unsound.

### CRITERIA FOR EVALUATION

There are many different criteria, or standards, by which a literary work can be judged. The following are some of the most common criteria for evaluating literature:

1. *Originality* or *inventiveness:* One quality often found in great literature is originality. If an author explores a topic that has never been explored before or deals with a familiar topic in a new and imaginative way, the work is likely to be evaluated favorably. On the other hand, if the work is like a lot of other works and if the writer has nothing new or original to say, then the work is likely to be evaluated unfavorably. Such a work, one that lacks originality, is said to be trite or a cliché.

2. *Consistency* or *completeness of effect:* In a literary work, the author tries to achieve certain effects. For example, in "Casey at the Bat," the author tries to achieve the effect of humor. In "The Raven," the author tries to achieve an effect of growing horror. A work will be evaluated favorably if the effect is achieved. However, if something happens to spoil the effect, the work will be evaluated unfavorably. Consider, for example, the following limerick:

> There was an old man of Peru
> Who dreamed he was eating his shoe.
> He woke in the night
> In a terrible fright.
> You see, what happened was that when he
>   woke up he found that what he was dreaming
>   about was really happening.

The last three lines of this limerick break the rhythmical pattern and spoil the effect. The limerick should end with the line "And found it was perfectly true!"

3. *Importance:* Some literary works are judged to be better than others because they deal with matters of greater importance. For example, Sara Teasdale's poem "There Will Come Soft Rains" might be considered a greater work than the limerick quoted above because Teasdale's poem deals with a subject of greater

*Evaluating a Literary Work*   987

**Motivation for Writing** Write the word *Evaluation* on the chalkboard. Ask students what it means to evaluate a car, a piece of clothing, or a school. Have them list the factors, called criteria, that would enter into such evaluations. Then ask them what factors they would consider in evaluating a work of literature. Lead them to see that the elements they have learned—plot, setting, character, and so forth—would play a role in this evaluation. Elicit from them questions concerning these elements that they would want to answer. You might also have them decide which of these questions would be most important in deciding the value of a literary work.

significance—the possibility of war destroying the human race.

4. *Moral* or *ethical message:* Sometimes literary works are judged according to the moral or ethical messages they convey. A person who agrees with the message of the work will judge the work favorably. A person who disagrees will judge the work unfavorably. For example, a person who believes that people should be willing to make sacrifices for their loved ones might look favorably on O. Henry's short story "The Gift of the Magi," on page 183.

5. *Clarity:* Some works are more difficult to read than others. However, difficulty should not evoke a negative evaluation. If a work is difficult to read but is finally worth the effort, then the work will be judged favorably. However, if the work is simply unclear—if the author hasn't taken care to express well what he or she intends to express—then the work will be judged unfavorably.

### CASE STUDY: EVALUATING A LITERARY WORK

In Kevin's English class all the students save their writing in folders. From time to time they go back to pieces of writing that they've done in the past to revise them or to see how much their writing has changed or grown. When Kevin's English teacher asked the class to write a paragraph evaluating some aspect of a literary work, Kevin decided to write an evaluation of one of the pieces from his own writing folder. Looking through the folder, Kevin found this poem that he had written several months before, entitled "All Things Pass and Return Again."

> I walked along the lonely beach
> And saw the sets of footprints where each
> Of the last vacationers had tread.
> I heard a voice inside my head.

It said,
"Despair not, for soon
It will be June.
Again it will be June."

### Prewriting

When Kevin first wrote this poem, he thought it was pretty good. Now, however, it seemed clichéd and silly. Kevin decided to write about why he felt the poem didn't work. Its major problem, he thought, was lack of originality. He would write his paragraph about this lack of originality. The following are Kevin's prewriting notes:

- Topic: lack of originality in the poem "All Things Pass and Return Again"

- Audience: my classmates

- Purpose: to support the opinion that the poem lacks originality

- Evidence from the poem:
  Unoriginal theme, that things happen in cycles—has been dealt with before in countless literary works.
  Poem contains several clichés, including its title, the "lonely beach," the footprints on the sand, the voice inside the head.
  Unoriginal rhymes: "head" and "said," "soon" and "June"
- Conclusion: Poem should be rewritten or discarded.

### Drafting and Revising

Based on his prewriting notes, Kevin wrote a draft of his paragraph. However, after the draft was finished he realized that his readers wouldn't know the poem that he was writing about. Therefore, he added an introduction in which he quoted the entire poem.

### Proofreading and Publishing

After proofreading his paper carefully, Kevin shared it with the members of his discussion group. The other students were impressed that Kevin could be so objective about his own work.

## ACTIVITIES AND ASSIGNMENTS

A. Using Kevin's prewriting notes, write a paragraph evaluating his poem. Write the paragraph from your own point of view, not from Kevin's. Follow these steps:

1. Write a rough draft and then revise it carefully. Make sure that your quotations are verbatim, or word for word.
2. Proofread your revised draft and then share it with other students in a discussion group. Consider the similiarities and differences between the paragraphs written by the members of the group.

B. Choose a work from the text that you particularly like or dislike and write a paragraph evaluating some element of this work. Base your evaluation on the criteria discussed in the lesson; that is, deal with one of the following aspects of the work: its originality, its consistency or completeness of effect, its moral or ethical message, or its clarity. Follow these steps:

1. Choose the work you wish to evaluate and the aspect of the work you wish to focus on.
2. Write a topic sentence stating your opinion about that aspect of the work.
3. Gather evidence from the work to support your opinion.
4. Write a rough draft presenting your topic sentence and supporting evidence. Make sure that the draft has a concluding sentence.
5. Revise the draft. Proofread it carefully. Then share it with your teacher and with your classmates.

Make sure that students have followed Kevin's prewriting notes in making their evaluations.

# Lesson 16: Writing a Comparative Evaluation

## WHAT IS A COMPARATIVE EVALUATION?

As you learned in the preceding lesson, evaluating a literary work involves two major steps. First you state an opinion about the value or quality of the work. Then you support this opinion with evidence. When you write a *comparative evaluation,* you also follow this two-step procedure. First you state an opinion about which of the two works is better or worse in some respect. Then you support your opinion with evidence from the works. Suppose, for example, that you have read two stories set in the future. You might write a comparative evaluation explaining which author, in your opinion, did the better job of creating a vivid and believable future setting.

## STEPS IN WRITING A COMPARATIVE EVALUATION

Begin by choosing the works that you want to compare and the feature of the two works that you will be comparing. List these in your notes, as follows:

- Works to be compared: Arthur C. Clarke's novel *2001: A Space Odyssey* and Isaac Asimov's novel *I, Robot.*

- Feature to be compared: believability of the setting in the two novels

Then study each work and make notes about the feature that you are comparing. Decide which author has done the better job of handling the feature and list reasons why you think this is so.

When you write your composition, begin by explaining your topic and purpose in your introductory paragraph. Then write one paragraph about each of the works that you are comparing. Finally, conclude with a paragraph that summarizes your reasons for believing that one work is better than the other.

## CASE STUDY: WRITING A COMPARATIVE EVALUATION

### Prewriting

Jessica's English teacher asked the class to write a comparative evaluation of a character from Frank R. Stockton's story "The Lady or the Tiger?" on page 49, and Richard Connell's story "The Most Dangerous Game," on page 13. Jessica chose to compare the characterization of the king in Stockton's story to that of General Zaroff in Connell's story.

Jessica began by reading each story carefully, paying particular attention to details relating to the two characters. Based on her reading, Jessica decided that General Zaroff was a highly original, imaginative creation, whereas the king was unoriginal and stereotypical. This, Jessica decided, would be the opinion she would support in her composition. Jessica studied the stories for evidence to support her opinion and made the following prewriting notes:

- Introductory paragraph:
  Works to be compared: "The Lady or the Tiger?" by Frank R. Stockton, and "The Most Dangerous Game," by Richard Connell.
  Feature to be compared: Characterization (of the king and of General Zaroff).
  Opinion to be supported: General Zaroff is an original, imaginative character, whereas the king is an unoriginal stereotype.

- First body paragraph:
  The king a stock figure out of history and folklore.
  He is barbaric, all-powerful, bullying.
  Inflicts cruel punishments in an arena, like the ancient Roman emperors.
  Flat character, not described in any detail.
  Detail needed to make the king unique, memorable.

- Second body paragraph:
  General Zaroff has some stock or stereotypical elements about him:
    Wealthy person who indulges himself at other people's expense.
    Wealthy person who abuses his wealth and power.
  However, Zaroff is not a pure stereotype because of
    The many details used to describe him.
    His bizarre, twisted sense of humor.
    The unusual sport that he indulges in.

- Concluding paragraph:
  While both are very good stories, the characterization in Stockton's story is unoriginal, while the characterization in Connell's story is very original indeed.

### Drafting and Revising

Jessica used her prewriting notes to write a rough draft. Then she revised her draft several times. As she revised, she added specific details from the stories to support her argument.

### Proofreading and Publishing

Jessica proofread her final draft and shared it with the members of her class discussion group. The group had a heated debate about which of the two characters was, in fact, the more original.

## ACTIVITIES AND ASSIGNMENTS

A. If you haven't already done so, read "The Lady or the Tiger?" on page 49, and "The Most Dangerous Game," on page 13. Then use the prewriting notes from the case study to write a composition comparing the characterizations of the king and General Zaroff.

B. Choose two works from this textbook and write a comparative evaluation of them. The following works might be compared: "The Interlopers," by Saki, on page 43, and "The Scarlet Ibis," by James Hurst, on page 189; "The Invalid's Story," by Mark Twain, on page 99, and "The Good Deed," by Pearl S. Buck, on page 121; "The Cask of Amontillado," by Edgar Allan Poe, on page 139, and "Beware of the Dog," by Roald Dahl, on page 147. Follow these steps:

1. Choose one feature to compare—setting, plot, characterization, use of sound, use of figurative language, use of imagery, point of view, or theme.
2. State an opinion about the relative value or quality of the two works with respect to the feature you are comparing.
3. Gather evidence from the two works to support your opinion.
4. Write a four-paragraph composition. In the first paragraph, explain what works you are comparing, what feature you are comparing, and what opinion you have with regard to the two works. In the two body paragraphs, discuss the works—first one, then the other. Then, in your concluding paragraph, summarize the evidence you have presented to support your opinion.
5. Revise your paragraph using the Checklist for Revision on page 949. Then make a clean final copy; proofread this copy using the Checklist for Proofreading on page 952.
6. Share your composition with your teacher and with your classmates.

*Writing a Comparative Evaluation* 991

992

You might remind students that writing a composition involves a process with definite stages. Have them recall these stages. Then ask students how the same type of process might be helpful in writing a short story. Ask them, for instance, how they might find an idea for a story and what they might do during the prewriting stage. If students have trouble thinking of a story idea, have them focus on a conflict that might generate a good story. Then tell them that in this lesson they will learn about the process of writing a short story.

# SECTION 5: WRITING CREATIVELY
# Lesson 17: Writing a Short Story

## FINDING A STORY IDEA

As you have learned in preceding lessons, short stories contain many elements. The most important of these are setting, conflict, plot, character, point of view, and theme. An idea for a short story can begin with any of these. The following are some ways to go about coming up with a story idea:

1. Pick a time and place that interest you. The place might be a real one—a place that you have visited or would like to visit—or it might be an imaginary place, such as a schoolroom in the far future or a city on another planet.
2. Think of some conflict that interests you. This can be an external conflict, as in a football game or a war, or it can be an internal conflict, perhaps involving an important decision that someone has to make.
3. Think of an interesting person whom you know. Create a character based on this person.
4. Think of some belief that you hold and that you would like to communicate to others. Make this belief your theme and think of a situation in which this belief might be tested or shown to be true.

## DEVELOPING YOUR IDEA

Once you have an idea for one part of your story, develop the rest of the story by answering the following questions:

1. *Setting:* When does the action of the story occur? Where does the story take place? What images of sight, sound, touch, taste, and smell can I use to describe this place?
2. *Character:* Who is the main character in the story? What is this character's name? How does this character look, act, and talk? What personality traits does this character have? What is his or her background, social status, occupation, and level of education? What are his or her attitudes, beliefs, and values? What will be this character's relationship to other characters? What does this character love and hate? What changes will occur in this character in the course of the story? Will there be one major character with whom this character is in conflict? Will there be one or more minor characters? What will each of these characters be like? What roles will they play in the story? How will they be related to the main character?
3. *Conflict:* What will be the central conflict that the main character is involved in? Will this conflict be within the character's own mind? Will it be a conflict between the character and some outside force such as nature, another person, or society?
4. *Plot:* What events will occur in the story, and in what order?

> *Introduction:* What background information will you need to supply about the setting? about the characters?
> *Inciting incident:* What event will introduce the central conflict of the story?
> *Development:* What events will occur as a result of the central conflict? How will this conflict develop?
> *Climax:* What will be the high point of interest or suspense in the story?
> *Resolution:* What event will resolve, or end, the conflict?

*Denouement:* What, if anything, will happen after the conflict is resolved?

5. *Theme:* What will be the central idea of the story? How will this main idea be revealed?

6. *Point of view:* Will the story be told by one of the characters or by an outside narrator? In other words, will it be told from the first-person or the third-person point of view? Will the narrator be limited or omniscient?

It may help you to make charts for the various elements of your story. The plot, for example, can be charted on a time line.

## DRAFTING A STORY

As you write your story, use the material from the charts you prepared during prewriting. Begin with an introduction that grabs the attention of the reader. Present the events of the story in chronological order. Use lots of specific details to make the story vivid. Develop suspense by raising questions in the reader's mind. If you wish to do so, make use of such special literary techniques as foreshadowing, flashbacks, figurative language, onomatopoeia, and surprise ending.

## CASE STUDY: WRITING A SHORT STORY

Bill's favorite class in school was English. Bill's older brother, Mark, thought that Bill should concentrate less on English and more on classes in business and mathematics. However, Bill didn't agree. He felt that English classes were just as important as classes in those other subjects. Bill decided to write a short story about why English classes are important and valuable.

### Prewriting

Bill already had a theme—the importance of English classes—so he thought about how he might develop this theme. He sat down and made the following prewriting notes:

- Setting: a town in the year 2080

- Characters: Rob, a 9th-grade student; Rob's sister; members of the school board

- Plot: In this future time, no one reads literature anymore. Instead, people just watch television, and in school they spend all their time studying math and business and computer science. Rob finds some old books in his parents' attic and starts reading the stories in them. He is so excited that he goes to the local school board to try to get the members to start classes in this ancient subject called "Literature." To argue his case, Rob reads passages from an old literature text that he has found. The members of the school board are shocked by all of this fantasy and creativeness and recommend that Rob be sent for psychological counseling.

- Conflict: external, between Rob and members of the school board

### Drafting, Revising, and Publishing

Rob made several drafts of his short story. As he did so, he cut unnecessary scenes and added futuristic details. When he finished his story, he submitted it to his school literary magazine.

### ACTIVITIES AND ASSIGNMENTS

A. Using the prewriting notes from the case study, write a short story entitled "Who Needs to Study Literature Anyway?" Share your completed story with your classmates.

B. Write an original short story on a topic that interests you. Follow the steps outlined in the lesson and in the case study.

# Lesson 18: Writing a Poem

There are many kinds of poems and many ways to go about writing them. In this lesson you will learn about a few simple verse forms, then you will get a chance to produce verses of your own.

## THREE VERSE FORMS

1. *Haiku:* One of the simplest and most beautiful of verse forms is the haiku, a form that originated in Japan. A haiku is made up of three unrhymed lines. The first and third lines each have five syllables, and the second line has seven. Here is an example:

> The lightning flashes!
> And slashing through the darkness,
> A night-heron's screech.
> —Bashō

Notice that the poem conforms to the rules for haiku: It has five syllables in the first line, seven in the second, and five again in the third. Like most haiku, this poem is a portrayal, in words, of something that the speaker has seen, heard, touched, tasted, or smelled. The writer of haiku uses images—in this case images of lightning and of a heron's call—to capture a moment.

2. *Concrete poems:* A concrete poem is one in which words are arranged in particular shapes to form visual pictures. Consider the example shown in the next column . . .

The shape of the words on the page suggests what the poem is about. The words are arranged to form a picture that might be a flame, a bush, or even the mythical bird, the phoenix, with its wings outstretched. The large *O* in the center, with its exclamation marks, suggests both the moon and the word *oh!*

3. *Couplets:* A couplet is a pair of rhymed lines. The lines in a couplet usually have the same number of beats, or stresses, and usually

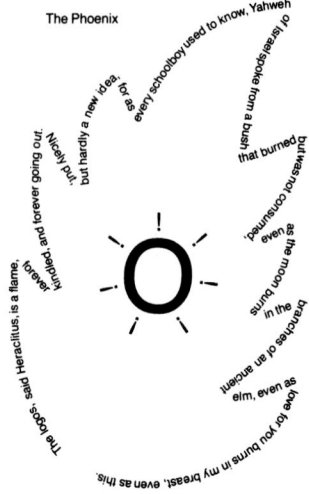

The Phoenix

have a similar rhythmical pattern. Often poems are made up of several couplets. The following short poem by Alexander Pope, "Engraved on the Collar of a Dog Which I Gave to His Royal Highness," is made up of one couplet:

> I am his Highness' dog at Kew;
> Pray tell me, sir, whose dog are you?

## CASE STUDY: WRITING A POEM

Christina read several haiku in her English class. She loved them because of their simplicity and power, and decided to write one herself.

### Prewriting

Christina first had to choose a subject for her haiku. She remembered one morning when she had gotten out of bed early and had seen a magnificent sunrise. She decided to write on this subject. In her prewriting notes she made a list of images from her memory of the sunrise:

gray clouds
pink glow, growing and expanding
jolt of brilliant light, rays of yellow
    bursting forth

As she thought about these images, Christina realized that the expanding pinkness of the clouds was like a pink rose budding. She therefore added this idea to her notes:

- Metaphor: a budding pink rose to describe the glow before the sun bursts through

## Drafting and Revising

Christina wrote several possible five- and seven-syllable lines for each line of her haiku. Here are the lines from Christina's rough draft:

Bud of a pink rose,
A budding pink rose,
Bud of pink rose-dawn.
The sun behind the gray clouds, and then
Sun hidden in growing clouds. Then—
Clouds around the sun. Then—
Clouds around the sun, and then—
Single brilliant ray.
Yellow brilliant ray.
Brilliant yellow rays.

Here is Christina's finished haiku:

Bud of pink rose-dawn,
Clouds around the sun, and then—
Brilliant yellow rays.

## Proofreading and Publishing

Christina checked her spelling and punctuation. Then she made several copies of her haiku and shared them with her family and with friends in her class.

## ACTIVITIES AND ASSIGNMENTS

A. Answer the following questions about the case study.
1. Why do you think Christina chose the line "Bud of pink rose-dawn" instead of the other two that she considered?

2. Why isn't the line "Clouds around the sun. Then—" appropriate for the second line of a haiku? Explain.
3. In what ways did Christina revise the third line of her haiku? What improvements did she make in each revision?

    B. Try your hand at writing a poem. Follow one of the sets of directions given below.

*Haiku:*
1. Choose a scene to portray in your haiku and make a list of images you can use.
2. Choose words that are vivid and precise. If you wish to do so, use a figure of speech—a simile, metaphor, personification, or hyperbole.
3. Write several versions of each line. Count the syllables in these lines carefully. Make sure that the syllable count is 5-7-5.

*Concrete Poem:*
1. Choose a subject that lends itself to visual representation.
2. Make a list of images to describe your subject.
3. Write a short description of your subject, using images from your list.
4. Arrange your words on a page to form a picture of your subject.

*Couplet:*
1. Choose an idea that you can convey in two short lines.
2. Write out the idea in sentence form.
3. Choose two rhyming words to use in your couplet.
4. Rewrite your sentences as necessary to make them end with your two rhyming words.
5. Rewrite your sentences as necessary so they will have the same number of beats, or stresses.

    When you finish drafting, revising, and proofreading your poem, share it with your classmates.

## ANSWERS TO ACTIVITIES AND ASSIGNMENTS, SECTION A

1. Suggested Response: This line has a more interesting rhythm and also combines the images of dawn and a flower in a suggestive way.
2. Suggested Response: This line only has six syllables.
3. Suggested Response: She emphasized the strong word "Brilliant" by making it first. She also made the image more vibrant by pluralizing "ray."

<br>

<br>

<br>

# Lesson 19: Writing a Dramatic Sketch

A *dramatic sketch* is a very short scene that makes a single point. The scene is written in the same form as a full-length drama and can be either serious or comic. Dramatic sketches are very common on television. You are probably familiar with the comic sketches on television variety shows.

## THE ELEMENTS OF A DRAMATIC SKETCH

A dramatic sketch begins with a title and a list of characters. The body of the sketch is made up of stage directions and of dialogue. The *stage directions* appear in square brackets or parentheses and are underlined or italicized. They tell what the setting for the sketch should look like, what special effects of lighting or music should be used, and how the characters should move or speak. Note the use of stage directions in the opening of *The Pen of My Aunt,* on page 239:

[*The scene is a French country house during the Occupation. The lady of the house is seated in her drawing room.*]

SIMONE. [*Approaching*] Madame! Oh, madame! Madame, have you—

These stage directions tell where the action takes place and describe how the first character, Simone, moves. Notice that the *dialogue* appears after the character's name and that the character's name appears in all capital letters.

## PLANNING A DRAMATIC SKETCH

When planning a dramatic sketch, you need to decide whether the sketch will be serious or comic, where the action will take place, what the setting will look like, what the characters will be involved in, and what events will occur.

When planning your setting, bear in mind that the set must be able to be reproduced on a stage. In your prewriting notes, list the time and place of the action and a few details describing important elements of the setting that the action of your sketch will require.

Next, briefly describe each of your characters. Think about how you want each character to look and to sound.

Finally, make a list of the events that will occur in the sketch. Make sure that the sketch has a definite beginning, middle, and end.

## WRITING THE SKETCH

Begin with a title and a list of characters. Following the list of characters, use stage directions to describe, briefly, the setting of the sketch. Then present the dialogue of the characters.

When appropriate, use stage directions to indicate how characters should move or speak. For example, you need to indicate when characters should enter and exit. It isn't necessary to describe all of a character's actions and ways of speaking. Describe only those that are essential to understanding what is happening.

As you write, speak the characters' lines aloud to make sure that they sound natural. Try to create a distinctive way of speaking for each of your characters.

## CASE STUDY: WRITING A DRAMATIC SKETCH

Kim's volleyball coach asked her to create a skit for the annual awards banquet. Kim thought about this assignment for a while and came up with an idea. She would write a sketch about a volleyball game attended by a visitor from another planet.

## Prewriting

Kim already had a subject for her dramatic sketch, so she began to think about a setting, characters, and a series of events. These she listed in her prewriting notes.

## Drafting and Revising

Using her prewriting notes, Kim wrote the following draft of her sketch:

*An Act of War*

Characters:

Mori Centauri: an extraterrestrial from the planet Llabyellov

The Android: chief of Llabyellov's Diplomatic Corps

[*The scene is an office of the Llabyellov Diplomatic Corps. The office is exotic and alien in appearance, but it is recognizable as an office. Seated at a desk is* THE ANDROID, *Commander of the Llabyellov Diplomatic Corps. He is an android and speaks in a monotonous, machinelike voice.*]

THE ANDROID [*Speaking into an intercom on his desk*] Send in Mori Centauri, please.

[*Enter* CENTAURI]

THE ANDROID. Ah, Attaché Centauri. Have you prepared the cultural report on the planet Earth? We must know the Earthlings' social customs soon so that we can prepare our advance cultural exchange unit.

CENTAURI. Well, actually, I've been kinda busy, what with all the starship launchings and Welcome Wagon efforts for newly encountered galactic species. I mean, I've got a datebook this thick [CENTAURI *makes a gesture indicating the height of the two antennae on top of his head*].

THE ANDROID. Are you saying that you haven't done anything as yet about planet Earth?

CENTAURI. Oh, no. Not at all. I mean, I have made a preliminary visit. You will have the report by next...

THE ANDROID. Give it to me orally. Now.

CENTAURI. Okay, your Perfectness, here goes. I visited one of their communities. It was located in the...let's see [CENTAURI *checks his notes*]...the Midwest Division of the United States Sector. I saw some sort of game. I believe it's called "valley ball" or "wally ball." At first it seemed kinda pointless—

THE ANDROID. [*Annoyance creeping into his monotone voice*] Do you mean to tell me that you traveled all the way to the planet Earth only to witness a pointless physical diversion and that you now intend to waste my time—

CENTAURI. Wait a minute...just lemme finish, your Magnificence. I said it *seemed* pointless, but then I realized that...well, you know how competitive they are...I realized that it was a very clever camouflage for [CENTAURI *glances around the office suspiciously, as if there might be someone eavesdropping, then leans forward and, lowering his voice, speaks in a confidential tone*] top-secret military training:

[CENTAURI *leans back with an air of importance*]

THE ANDROID. Well, don't just stand there. Finish your report!

CENTAURI. Okay, your Patience. It was like this. There were two groups of Earthlings— military trainees, that is—lined up on either side of an artificial obstacle set up between them. I think the obstacle was supposed to simulate one of those fences they have on Earth—what are they called? Oh, you know, they have little prickers on the top, so when you try to climb over, they get caught on your spacesuit, and then while you try to undo your spacesuit, they get tangled up in your antennae, and then when—

THE ANDROID. [*Thunders*] Continue!

CENTAURI. [*Hurt*] Well, anyway, the Earthlings had to jump high enough off the ground to hurl this ball at each other. Oh, I know it was only a ball, but it was supposed to simulate [CENTAURI *leans forward and agains uses his confidential tone*] a thermonuclear hand grenade!

THE ANDROID. Are you sure that the Earthlings have such devices?

1. Suggested Response: She uses stage directions at the beginning to set the scene. She also includes directions with some of the speeches. These directions tell characters how to move and how to speak their lines.
2. Suggested Response: The Android is impatient and businesslike. Centauri is more informal, almost clownlike. The extraterrestrial setting helps make these characters unique.

CENTAURI. Of course! How else can we explain this game? Anyway, the Earthlings—well, space age warriors, really—were very proficient at batting the device around without letting it touch the ground and explode. Now let me ask you this: suppose they respond to our friendly approaches by using their digging, setting, and spiking techniques?

THE ANDROID. Hmmm. Perhaps you are right. Perhaps we should not attempt to add such a planet to our social calendar as yet. Perhaps—

CENTAURI. Barbed wire! That's what it's called. A barbed wire net! Frightening. Perfectly frightening.

## Proofreading and Publishing

Kim proofread her revised draft and then made several clean final copies. Then she and her friend Lisa performed the sketch at the awards banquet.

## ACTIVITIES AND ASSIGNMENTS

A. Answer the following questions about the case study.
1. In what places did Kim use stage directions? What information did these directions convey?
2. What are the differences between the two characters in the skit? What makes them unique?
   B. Write a short dramatic sketch on a topic of your choice. Follow the steps outlined in the lesson and in the case study.

# Lesson 20: Writing a Personal Essay

The purpose of the *personal essay* is to share your thoughts, experiences, and perspectives with others. Writing a personal essay gives you the chance to speak in your own voice about something that is important to you.

Begin by choosing a topic for your essay. The topic should be one that you care about deeply and about which you have some personal knowledge. To come up with a topic, try doing some freewriting and clustering. See the explanations of these techniques on page 947.

Once you have a topic for your essay, decide on your purpose. Your purpose might be to tell a story, to describe something, to explain something, or to persuade people to believe or to act in some way. The writing strategies you use will depend on your purpose.

After deciding on your purpose, write a sentence that states the main point you want to communicate in your essay. This sentence will be your thesis statement. The following are examples of thesis statements for essays of various kinds:

1. *Narrative essay:* In the summer of 1982, something happened that taught me a lesson in humility.
2. *Descriptive essay:* Thanks to the efforts of conservationists, Boston Harbor is slowly regaining some of its former beauty.
3. *Expository essay:* Water skiing isn't easy, but with a little practice, almost anyone can learn to do it well.
4. *Persuasive essay:* Schools should place less emphasis on competition and grades and more emphasis on cooperation among students to achieve some shared goal.

Bear in mind that the topic, purpose, and thesis statement of a personal essay should have to do with your own experiences, opinions, thoughts, or values.

After writing your thesis statement, gather ideas and information for your essay. Draw on your own experiences. Use freewriting and clustering. Make lists and charts. If appropriate, conduct some interviews. The kind of information you gather will depend on your topic, purpose, and thesis. If you are writing a narrative essay (one that tells a story), draw a time line and mark on it the events you are going to tell about. If you are writing a descriptive essay, make a chart of the images of sight, sound, touch, taste, and smell that you will use. If you are writing an expository essay (one that explains), make a list of facts about your topic. Finally, if you are writing a persuasive essay, make a list of reasons for adopting the position that you want your audience to adopt.

Organize your notes into separate groups corresponding to the introduction, body, and conclusion of your essay. You may wish to have more than one paragraph in the body. Then use your notes to write a rough draft. As you write, keep your audience and purpose in mind. Finally, revise your essay, using the Checklist for Revision on page 949. Make a clean final copy; proofread this copy and share the proofread version with your classmates and teacher.

## CASE STUDY: WRITING A PERSONAL ESSAY

James was asked by his English teacher to write a personal essay on any topic that was of interest to him. He and his family had recently made a trip to New Hampshire, and he decided to write a descriptive essay about his experience there.

### Prewriting

In his essay James especially wanted to communicate to his readers the beauty of the

*Writing a Personal Essay* 999

1. Suggested Response: He improved his thesis statement by making it more general.
2. Suggested Response: The word *aghast* means "horrified." It would be more appropriate to the sight of a ghost that to the sight of a leaf!
3. Suggested Response: He corrected a run-on sentence in line 2.
4. Suggested Response: In line 9, he changed a sentence whose language was too informal.
5. Suggested Response: There is an example of alliteration in the last line: "a warm welcome to winter."

autumn leaves he had seen in the mountains of New England. He decided that this would be the purpose of his descriptive essay, and he made a list in his prewriting notes of the visual images he would use to accomplish this purpose.

### Drafting and Revising

James wrote the following sentence as a thesis statement for his essay:

> The oak leaves in the mountains of New Hampshire were especially beautiful: they turned to a brilliant red.

James thought about this sentence and realized that it was too narrow. It did not tell the reader what his entire essay was going to be about. He rewrote his thesis statement as follows:

> The mountains of northern New England are a spectacular sight in the autumn months, when they are washed in the brilliant colors of fall foliage.

Then he wrote and revised the rest of his essay, which is shown in the right-hand column.

### Proofreading and Publishing

James made a clean final copy of his essay and proofread it for errors in spelling and punctuation. He read it aloud to his family, and they all reminisced about their trip to New England. Then he shared the essay with his English teacher.

### ACTIVITIES AND ASSIGNMENTS

A. Answer the following questions about the preceding case study.
1. How did James improve his thesis statement?
2. What does *aghast* mean? Why did James change this word when he revised his essay?
3. What run-on sentence did James correct when he revised his essay? What sentence fragment?

*On a recent trip*
~~When I went~~ to New Hampshire with my family,
*amazed by*
I was ~~aghast at~~ the beautiful display ~~and~~

around every curve of the winding mountain
*encountered*
roads, we ~~were faced by~~ a new scene bursting
*Whose*
with color. I especially liked the oak trees. ~~Their~~
*There were*
leaves had turned a bright red. Also, yellows
*many shades of*
and oranges. From high atop Mount

Washington, we had a panoramic view of the
*as if*       *surrounded by*
entire area. It was ~~like~~ we stood on an island ~~in~~
*(a*
a ~~sea~~ of autumn color. The New England

foliage in October is a dazzling good-bye to
*a warm*
summer and welcome to winter.

4. Where did James change a sentence in which the language was too informal?
5. Find an example of alliteration in James's essay.
   B. In this exercise you will write a personal essay. It may be a single paragraph or multiple paragraphs, depending on the scope of your topic. Follow these steps when writing your essay:
1. Think of a topic that is of interest to you. It may help to review the definitions in this lesson of the different types of essays. This will also help you to decide on a structure and a plan for your essay.
2. Make a list in your prewriting notes of the information you will include. Organize the information in an outline that shows the order in which you plan to present this information.
3. Write a thesis statement that introduces the topic of your essay and arouses the reader's interest.

4. Write the body of your essay according to the outline you made in your notes. Conclude your essay by summarizing its central points.

5. Read your essay with this question in mind: Does my essay accomplish its purpose? Revise your essay accordingly. Also consult the Checklist for Revision on page 949.

6. Make a clean final copy of your essay. Then proofread this copy for errors in spelling and mechanics. When you are satisfied that there are no errors in spelling, capitalization, punctuation, or manuscript form, share your essay with a friend. Finally, turn in your essay to your English teacher.

**ACT**   See *Drama.*

**ALLITERATION**   *Alliteration* is the repetition of initial consonant sounds. Writers use alliteration to give emphasis to words, to imitate sounds, and to create musical effects. Notice, in the following lines from Walter de la Mare's "The Listeners," how the *s* sound imitates a whisper:

Never the least *stir* made the listeners,
   Though every word he *spake*
Fell echoing through the *shadowiness* of the
   *still* house
   From the one man left awake:
Ay, they heard his foot upon the *stirrup,*
   And the *sound* of iron on *stone,*
And how the *silence surged softly* backward,
   When the plunging hoofs were gone.

The title of Langston Hughes's poem "A Dream Deferred," on page 630, uses alliteration, as does E. E. Cummings's "*m*aggie and *m*illy and *m*olly and *m*ay," on page 653.

Prose writers use alliteration too, but not as frequently as poets do. Jane Austen used the technique for the titles of her novels *Pride and Prejudice* and *Sense and Sensibility.* Notice, too, that alliteration is the basis of tongue twisters: She *sells sea* shells by the *seashore.*
See *Repetition.*

**ALLUSION**   An *allusion* is a reference to a well-known person, place, event, literary work, or work of art. In "The Gift of the Magi," on page 183, O. Henry writes about a young couple and the Christmas gifts they give each other. At the end of the story, the narrator explains the Biblical allusion in the title: "The Magi, as you know, were wise men—wonderfully wise men—who brought gifts to the Babe in the manger. They invented the art of giving Christmas presents. Being wise, their gifts were no doubt wise ones...."

The broader your reading experiences, the easier it will be for you to spot and understand allusions. When you have read the *Odyssey,* on page 681, for example, you will have become familiar with a great many mythological characters, places, and events. Then poems like Margaret Atwood's "Siren Song," on page 744, will have more meaning for you.

**ANAPEST**   See *Meter.*

**ANECDOTE**   An *anecdote* is a brief story about an interesting, amusing, or strange event. Anecdotes are told to entertain or to make a point. In "A Lincoln Preface," on page 439, Carl Sandburg tells anecdotes about Abraham Lincoln.
See *Narrative.*

**ANTAGONIST**   An *antagonist* is a character or force in conflict with a main character, or protagonist. In James Thurber's "The Secret Life of Walter Mitty," on page 3, Mitty's wife is the antagonist.
See *Protagonist.*

**ASIDE**   An *aside* is a short speech delivered by an actor in a play, expressing the character's thoughts. Traditionally, the aside is directed to the audience and is presumed to be inaudible to the other actors.

In Anton Chekhov's *The Boor,* on page 227, the servant Luka is frightened by the shouting Smirnov. Before Luka exits, he says in an aside, "There's a demon in the house.... The Evil Spirit must have brought him." Smirnov does not react to the remark because, according to theatrical convention, he does not hear it.

**ASSONANCE**   *Assonance* is the repetition of vowel sounds followed by different consonants in two or more stressed syllables. Assonance is

found in the phrase "weak and weary" in Edgar Allan Poe's "The Raven," on page 563.
See *Consonance.*

**ATMOSPHERE**   See *Mood.*

**AUTOBIOGRAPHY**   An *autobiography* is a form of nonfiction in which a person tells his or her own life story. It may tell about the person's whole life or only a part of it. Both autobiographies and biographies are nonfiction. In most libraries, they are shelved in a special section, arranged alphabetically by subject.
See *Biography* and *Nonfiction.*

**BALLAD**   A *ballad* is a songlike poem that tells a story, often one dealing with adventure or romance. The earliest ballads, known as *folk ballads,* were meant to be sung and thus had regular rhythms and rhymes.

Early ballads were composed anonymously and then passed on orally from generation to generation. "Bonnie George Campbell" is an example of an early folk ballad:

High upon Highlands,
  And low upon Tay,
Bonnie George Campbell
  Rode out on a day;

Saddled and bridled,
  And gallant to see:
Home came his good horse,
  But home came not he.

The rest of the verses, which repeat variations of the last two lines, describe the feelings of Bonnie George's mother and bride.

A *literary ballad* is one written by a poet in conscious imitation of the folk ballad. Stephen Vincent Benét's "The Ballad of William Sycamore," on page 557, is an example.
See *Narrative Poem* and *Oral Tradition.*

**BIOGRAPHY**   A *biography* is a form of nonfiction in which a writer tells the life story of another person. Biographies have been written about many famous people, historical and contemporary, but they can also be written about "ordinary" people. Nicholas Gage's biography of his mother, *Eleni,* includes this passage in which he states the key idea he wants readers to understand about her:

> [She] was one of 600,000 Greeks who were killed during the years of war that ravaged the country from 1940 to 1949. Like many of the victims, she died because her home lay in the path of the opposing armies, but she would have survived if she hadn't defied the invaders of her village to save her children.

A *biographical essay* is shorter than a biography. In "Georgia O'Keeffe," on page 511, Joan Didion writes about the independent spirit of the famous painter.

Like autobiographies, biographies are usually shelved in a special section of the library, arranged alphabetically by subject.
See *Autobiography* and *Nonfiction.*

**BLANK VERSE**   *Blank verse* is poetry written in unrhymed iambic pentameter lines. This verse form was widely used by Elizabethan dramatists like William Shakespeare.
See *Meter.*

**CHARACTER**   A *character* is a person or animal who takes part in the action of a literary work. The *main character* is the most important character in a story. This character often changes in some important way as a result of the story's events. The princess is the main character in Frank R. Stockton's "The Lady or the Tiger?" on page 49. It is her heart the story explores. In the same story, other major characters are the king and the young man. They contribute to the events that lead to the princess's conflict. *Protagonist* is another word for the main character. The *antagonist* is a major character who opposes the protagonist. In Richard Connell's "The Most Dangerous Game," on page 13, Rainsford is the protagonist and General Zaroff is the antagonist.

Characters are sometimes classified as round or flat, dynamic or static. A *round character* shows many different traits—faults as well as virtues. Walter Mitty, in James Thurber's "The Secret Life of Walter Mitty," on page 3, is a round character. We know him not only as a mousy husband but also as a man who has a means of escape: his fantasies. His wife is a *flat character.* We see her only as a shrew. A *dynamic character* develops and grows during the course of the story, as does Doodle's brother in "The Scarlet Ibis," on page 189. A *static character* does not change. Walter Mitty, for example, is neither less mousy nor less inclined to fantasize at the end of the story than he was at the beginning.
See *Characterization, Hero/Heroine,* and *Motivation.*

**CHARACTERIZATION**   *Characterization* is the act of creating and developing a character. In *direct characterization,* the author directly states a character's traits. In "The Good Deed," for example, Pearl Buck says that old Mrs. Pan "was afraid of the children . . . it distressed her to hear her own language maltreated by their careless tongues."

In *indirect characterization,* an author tells what a character looks like, does, and says and how other characters react to him or her. It is up to the reader to draw conclusions about the character based on this indirect information. Toni Cade Bambara describes Granny Cain indirectly in the following passages from her story "Blues Ain't No Mockin Bird," on page 93:

'I don't know about the thing, the it, and the stuff,' said Grany, still talkin with her eyebrows. 'Just people here is what I tend to consider.'

Me and Cathy were waitin, too, cause Granny always got somethin to say. She teaches steady with no letup.

The most effective indirect characterizations usually result from showing characters acting or speaking. In Saki's "The Interlopers," on page 43, two enemies lie trapped under a fallen tree. When one of them, Ulrich, suddenly offers a drink of wine to the other, the reader knows that Ulrich is beginning to change his mind about the old feud.
See *Character.*

**CINQUAIN**   See *Stanza.*

**CLIMAX**   The *climax* of a story, novel, or play is the high point of interest or suspense. The events that make up the rising action lead up to the climax. The events that make up the falling action follow the climax.
See *Conflict* and *Plot.*

**COMEDY**   A *comedy* is a work of literature, especially a play, that has a happy ending. Comedies are usually humorous, but they vary considerably in the amount and kind of humor they employ. Anton Chekhov's *The Boor,* on page 227, is a comedy. The characters Mme. Popova and Smirnov doubtless consider their arguments serious indeed, but readers and viewers see their stubborn pride as humorous.
See *Drama, Farce,* and *Tragedy.*

**CONCRETE POEM**   A *concrete poem* is one with a shape that suggests its subject. William Burford's "A Christmas Tree" is a concrete poem:

Star,
If you are
A Love compassionate,
You will walk with us this year.
We face a glacial distance, who are here
Huddl'd
At your feet.

The lines of the poem appear on the page in the shape of a tree, and the words *star* and *at your feet* appear in appropriate positions, at the top and at the bottom.

**CONFLICT** A *conflict* is a struggle between opposing forces. Characters in conflict form the basis of stories, novels, and plays.

There are two kinds of conflict: external and internal. In an *external conflict,* the main character struggles against an outside force. This force may be another character, as in Richard Connell's "The Most Dangerous Game," on page 13, in which Rainsford struggles with General Zaroff. The outside force may be the standards or expectations of a group, such as the family prejudices that Romeo and Juliet struggle against. Their story, on page 321, shows them in conflict with society. The outside force may be nature itself, a person-against-nature conflict. The two men trapped by a fallen tree in Saki's "The Interlopers," on page 43, face such a conflict.

An *internal conflict* involves a character in conflict with himself or herself. An example is Frank R. Stockton's "The Lady or the Tiger?" on page 49, in which the princess struggles "beneath the combined fires of despair and jealousy." The story, as the author says, "involves a study of the human heart."

A story may have more than one conflict. In addition to the person-against-nature conflict of "The Interlopers," there is also a person-against-person conflict between the two men and an internal conflict for the main character, who must decide whether he should forgive his enemy.
See *Plot.*

**CONNOTATION** The *connotation* of a word is the set of associations that occur to people when they hear or read that word. Paul Laurence Dunbar, in his poem "Sympathy," on page 547, does not speak of a canary or of a parakeet, either of which suggests a pet and thus has positive connotations. Instead, he speaks of a "caged bird," which connotes a sad, trapped creature. The connotation of a word can be personal, based on individual experiences, but cultural connotations—those recognizable by most people in a group—most often determine a writer's word choices.
See *Denotation.*

**CONSONANCE** *Consonance* is the repetition in two or more words of final consonants in stressed syllables. These consonants are preceded by different vowel sounds. An example is the word pair a*dd*-rea*d*.
See *Assonance.*

**COUPLET** A *couplet* is a pair of rhyming lines, usually of the same length and meter. A couplet generally expresses a single idea. In the following couplet from a poem by William Shakespeare, the speaker comforts himself with the thought of his love:

> For thy sweet love rememb'red such wealth
> brings
> That then I scorn to change my state with
> kings.

See *Heroic Couplet* and *Stanza.*

**DACTYL** See *Meter.*

**DENOTATION** The *denotation* of a word is its dictionary meaning, independent of other associations that the word calls up. The denotation of the word *lake,* for example, is an inland body of water. "Vacation spot" and "place where the fishing is good" are connotations of the word lake.
See *Connotation.*

**DENOUEMENT** See *Plot.*

**DESCRIPTION** A *description* is a portrait in words of a person, place, or object. Descriptive writing uses sensory details, those that appeal to the senses: sight, hearing, taste, smell, and touch. Description can be found in all types of writing. Anne Morrow Lindbergh's essay

"'Sayonara,'" on page 483, is a descriptive essay, and John Masefield's poem "Sea-Fever," on page 654, is a description of those things that the speaker loves about the sailing life:

> And all I ask is a tall ship and a star to
>     steer her by,
> And the wheel's kick and the wind's song and
>     the white sail's shaking.
> And a gray mist on the sea's face and a gray
>     dawn breaking.

See *Image.*

**DEVELOPMENT**   See *Plot.*

**DIALECT**   *Dialect* is the form of a language spoken by people in a particular region or group. Pronunciation, vocabulary, and sentence structure are affected by dialect. In "A Red, Red Rose," on page 669, the poet Robert Burns uses a Scottish dialect:

> And I will love thee still, my dear,
>     Till a' the seas gang dry.

The word *a'* represents the Scottish pronunciation of *all,* and *gang* is the local word for *go.*

**DIALOGUE**   A *dialogue* is a conversation between characters. It is used to reveal character and to advance action. In a story or novel, quotation marks are generally used to indicate a speaker's exact words. A new paragraph usually indicates a change of speaker. Look at an example from Charles Dickens's *Great Expectations,* on page 758. The narrator is a young boy who is confronted by a fearful-looking man:

> "Oh! Don't cut my throat, sir," I pleaded in terror. "Pray don't do it, sir."
> "Tell us your name!" said the man. "Quick!"
> "Pip, sir."
> "Once more," said the man, staring at me. "Give it mouth!"
> "Pip. Pip, sir."

A drama, of course, depends entirely on dialogue and actions. Quotation marks are not used in the *script,* which is the printed version of a play. Instead, the dialogue follows the name of the speaker. Here is an example from Anton Chekov's *The Boor,* on page 229:

> **MME. POPOVA.** The day after tomorrow you will receive your money.
> **SMIRNOV.** I need the money today, not the day after tomorrow.
> **MME. POPOVA.** I am sorry, but I cannot pay you today.
> **SMIRNOV.** And I can't wait till the day after tomorrow.

**DICTION**   *Diction* is word choice. To discuss a writer's diction is to consider the vocabulary used, the appropriateness of the words, and the vividness of the language. Both the *denotation,* or literal meaning, and the *connotation,* or associations, of words contribute to the overall effect. Diction can be quite formal, as in this sentence from Charles Dickens's *Great Expectations,* which begins on page 757:

> I had heard of her as leading a most unhappy life, and as being separated from her husband, who had used her with great cruelty, and who had become quite renowned as a compound of pride, brutality, and meanness.

Diction can also be informal and conversational, as in these lines from Ernest Lawrence Thayer's "Casey at the Bat," on page 551:

> It looked extremely rocky for the Mudville nine
>     that day;
> The score stood two to four, with but an
>     inning left to play.
> So, when Cooney died at second, and Burrows
>     did the same,
> A pallor wreathed the features of the patrons
>     of the game.

See *Connotation* and *Denotation.*

**DIMETER**   See *Meter.*

**DIRECT CHARACTERIZATION**  See *Characterization.*

**DRAMA**  A *drama* is a story written to be performed by actors. The script of a drama is made up of dialogue, which is the words the actors say, and stage directions, which are comments on how and where action happens.

The drama's *setting* is the place where the action occurs. It is indicated by one or more sets that suggest interior or exterior scenes. *Props* are objects, such as a sword or a cup of tea, that are used onstage.

At the beginning of most plays, a brief exposition gives the audience some background information about the characters and the situation. Just as in a story or novel, the plot of a drama is built around characters in conflict.

Dramas are divided into large units called *acts* and into smaller units called *scenes.* A short one-act play, like Anton Chekhov's *The Boor,* usually has only one setting. A longer play may include many sets that change with the scenes, or it may indicate a change of scene with lighting. Look at these stage directions from William Gibson's *The Miracle Worker,* which begins on page 253:

*The room dims out quickly.*
*Time, in the form of a slow tune of distant belfry chimes which approaches in a crescendo and then fades, passes; the light comes up again on a day five years later, on three kneeling children and an old dog outside around the pump.*

See *Comedy, Farce, Genre, Stage Directions,* and *Tragedy.*

**DRAMATIC DIALOGUE**  See *Dramatic Poetry.*

**DRAMATIC IRONY**  See *Irony.*

**DRAMATIC MONOLOGUE**  See *Dramatic Poetry.*

**DRAMATIC POETRY**  *Dramatic poetry* is poetry that involves the techniques of drama. The dialogue used in Donald Justice's "Incident in a Rose Garden," on page 575, makes it a *dramatic dialogue.* A *dramatic monologue* is a poem spoken by one person. Sara Henderson Hay's "The Princess," on page 587, is an example.

**DYNAMIC CHARACTER**  See *Character.*

**END RHYME**  See *Rhyme.*

**EPIC**  An *epic* is a long narrative poem about the deeds of gods or heroes. Homer's the *Odyssey,* on page 681, is an example of epic poetry. It tells the story of the Greek hero Odysseus, the king of Ithaca.

An epic is elevated in style and usually follows certain patterns. The poet begins by announcing the subject and asking a Muse, one of the nine goddesses of the arts, literature, and sciences, to help. Early on, the poet asks an epic question. The epic itself is the answer. Odysseus asks,

Where shall a man find sweetness to surpass
his own home and his parents? In far lands
he shall not, though he find a house of gold.
What of my sailing, then, from Troy?
     What of those years
of rough adventure, weathered under Zeus?

See *Narrative Poem, Homeric Simile,* and *Epithet.*

**EPIC SIMILE**  See *Homeric Simile.*

**EPITHET**  An *epithet* is a word or phrase used to characterize or describe a person or thing. "Wrong-Way Corrigan" is an epithet that describes someone who flew in the wrong direction and ended up in Ireland instead of California. Oral poets, like Homer, tended to repeat the same epithets—such as "rosy-fingered Dawn" —as an aid to memory.

**ESSAY** An *essay* is a short, nonfiction work about a particular subject. While classification is difficult, four types of essays are sometimes identified. A *descriptive essay* seeks to convey an impression about a person, place, or object. In "'Sayonara,'" on page 483, Anne Morrow Lindbergh describes her good-bye after a journey to Japan.

A *narrative essay* tells a true story. In "Nameless, Tennessee," on page 477, William Least Heat Moon tells about his visit to a small town called "Nameless."

An *expository essay* gives information, discusses ideas, or explains a process. In "The Loch Ness Monster," page 489, John McPhee tells about an organization that gathers data on a forty-foot monster living in a Scottish lake.

A *persuasive essay* tries to convince readers to do something or to accept the writer's point of view. Martin Luther King's "'I Have a Dream'" speech, delivered during the days of the civil rights movement, makes an impassioned appeal for freedom and equality.

This classification of essays is loose at best. Most essays contain passages that could be classified differently from the essay as a whole. For example, a descriptive passage may be found in a narrative essay, or a factual, expository section may be used to support a persuasive argument.

See *Description, Exposition, Genre, Narration, Nonfiction,* and *Persuasion.*

**EXPOSITION** *Exposition* is writing or speech that explains, informs, or presents information. In the plot of a story or drama, the exposition is the part of the work that introduces the characters, the setting, and the basic situation. In William Gibson's *The Miracle Worker,* on page 253, the opening scene serves as an exposition, revealing that the infant Helen has had a serious fever that has left her blind and deaf.

See *Essay, Nonfiction,* and *Plot.*

**EXTENDED METAPHOR** In an *extended metaphor,* as in regular metaphor, a subject is spoken or written of as though it were something else. However, extended metaphor differs from regular metaphor in that several comparisons are made. An extended metaphor sustains the comparison for several lines or for an entire poem. The "caged bird" of Paul Laurence Dunbar's "Sympathy," on page 547, is an extended metaphor for a person who is not free. In the poem below, Robert Frost's "In a Glass of Cider," the speaker identifies himself as a "mite of sediment," or a speck of matter that settles in the bottom:

> It seemed I was a mite of sediment
> That waited for the bottom to ferment
> So I could catch a bubble in ascent.
> I rode up on one till the bubble burst,
> And when that left me to sink back reversed
> I was no worse off than I was at first.
> I'd catch another bubble if I waited.
> The thing was to get now and then elated.

The poet extends the metaphor to show the highs and lows of life. The last line expresses the theme of the poem.

See *Figurative Language* and *Metaphor.*

**FABLE** A *fable* is a brief story, usually with animal characters, that teaches a lesson, or moral. Fables are an ancient literary form found in many cultures. Among the most famous are Aesop's fables, written in Greece around the sixth century B.C., and the fables of La Fontaine, a seventeenth-century French poet.

**FALLING ACTION** See *Plot.*

**FANTASY** A *fantasy* is highly imaginative writing that contains elements not found in real life. Examples of fantasy include stories that deal with possible or supernatural elements, like Joan Aiken's "Sonata for Harp and Bicycle," on page 33; stories that resemble fairy tales, like Ursula K. Le Guin's "Gwilan's Harp," on page

209; and stories that deal with imaginary places and creatures, like J. R. R. Tolkien's *The Hobbit* and *The Lord of the Rings.*

Some writers consider science fiction a type of fantasy. Other writers make a distinction between the two kinds of writing.
See *Science Fiction.*

**FARCE**   A *farce* is an exaggerated comedy, one that relies on improbable situations, physical humor, and broad wit rather than on in-depth characters and believable plots. Anton Chekhov's *The Boor,* on page 227, can be classified as a farce because of the ridiculousness of the arguments between the two main characters. Contemporary television shows and movies are often farcical or include farcical elements.
See *Comedy* and *Drama.*

**FICTION**   *Fiction* is prose writing that tells about imaginary characters and events. The term is usually used for novels and short stories, but it also applies to dramas and narrative poetry. Some writers rely on their imaginations alone to create their works of fiction. Others base their fiction on actual events and people, to which they add invented characters, dialogue, and plot situations.
See *Genre, Narrative,* and *Nonfiction.*

**FIGURATIVE LANGUAGE**   *Figurative language* is writing or speech not meant to be interpreted literally.

Figurative language is often used to create vivid impressions by setting up comparisons between dissimilar things. Notice, for example, how vivid the image is in the excerpt from D. C. Berry's "On Reading Poems to a Senior Class at South High":

> Before
> I opened my mouth
> I noticed them sitting there
> as orderly as frozen fish
> in a package.

Though such figures of speech are especially important in poetry, they are used in prose as well. Look, for example, at this description from James Hurst's "The Scarlet Ibis," on page 189:

> ...the oriole nest in the elm was untenanted and rocked back and forth like an empty cradle. The last graveyard flowers were blooming, and their smell drifted across the cotton field and through every room of our house, speaking softly the names of our dead.

Some frequently used figures of speech are *metaphors, similes,* and *personifications.*
See *Literal Language.*

**FLASHBACK**   A *flashback* is a section of a literary work that interrupts the sequence of events to relate an event from an earlier time. Normally, events are told in chronological order, the order in which they happen in time. A flashback, however, interrupts chronological order to go back to an earlier time. A flashback may be a short part of the story, or the story may be built around a flashback. Mark Twain's "The Invalid's Story," on page 99, starts when the narrator is forty-one but feels sixty. Then the narrator jumps back in time to "One winter's night, two years ago," when the events happened that ruined his health.

**FLAT CHARACTER**   See *Character.*

**FOIL**   A *foil* is a character who is contrasted with another character. In Richard Connell's "The Most Dangerous Game," on page 13, General Zaroff surrounds himself with the trappings of civilization, but we see Rainsford as the more civilized man because of the contrast between the two men's views on hunting. Thus Rainsford serves as a foil for Zaroff, and Zaroff serves as a foil for Rainsford.

**FOLK TALE**   A *folk tale* is a story composed orally and then passed from person to person by word of mouth. Folk tales began as stories told aloud by primitive people. Eventually, scholars like Wilhelm and Jakob Grimm began collecting these tales. The Brothers Grimm published many European folk tales as *Grimm's Fairy Tales.*

See *Oral Tradition.*

**FOOT**   See *Meter.*

**FORESHADOWING**   *Foreshadowing* is the use in a literary work of clues that suggest events that have yet to occur. Use of this technique helps to create suspense, keeping readers wondering and speculating about what will happen next. Both the title of Grant Moss, Jr.'s "Before the End of Summer," on page 107, and this brief bit of dialogue from early in the story tell readers that something important will happen before the end of summer:

> "How long will it be?" he heard his grandmother say.
> "Before the end of summer."

See *Suspense.*

**FRAMEWORK STORY**   A *framework story* is one that contains a story within another story. A famous example of the framework story is Chaucer's *Canterbury Tales,* an account of a group of pilgrims who, on their way to Canterbury, take turns telling tales. In Toni Cade Bambara's "Blues Ain't No Mockin Bird," on page 91, the framing story is the main story about the Cain family's reactions to and attitude about the cameramen who want to film them for the county. The story within a story is the one Granny Cain tells the children about the filming of a man who attempts suicide.

**FREE VERSE**   *Free verse* is poetry not written in a regular rhythmical pattern, or meter. Free verse seeks to capture the rhythms of speech. It is the dominant form of contemporary poetry,

as in these lines from Leroy V. Quintana's "piñones":

> when i was young
> we would sit by
> an old firewood stove
> watching my grandmother make candy,
> listening to the stories
> my grandparents would tell
> about "the old days"
> and eat piñones

See *Meter.*

**GENRE**   A *genre* is a division or type of literature. Literature is commonly divided into three major genres: poetry, prose, and drama. Each major genre is in turn divided into smaller genres, as follows:
1. Poetry: Lyric Poetry, Concrete Poetry, Dramatic Poetry, Narrative Poetry, and Epic Poetry
2. Prose: Fiction (Novels and Short Stories) and Nonfiction (Biography, Autobiography, Letters, Essays, and Reports)
3. Drama: Serious Drama and Tragedy, Comic Drama, Melodrama, and Farce

See *Drama, Poetry,* and *Prose.*

**HAIKU**   *Haiku* is a three-line Japanese verse form. The first and third lines of a haiku have five syllables. The second line has seven syllables. A haiku seeks to convey a single vivid emotion by means of images from nature. The poems on page 664 are haiku. In the example below, the poet Shiki conveys loneliness through the image of wild geese in the fall:

> Railroad tracks; a flight
> of wild geese close above them
>   in the moonlit night.

Translators of Japanese haiku try to maintain the syllabic requirements. Western writers, however, sometimes use the form more loosely.

**HEPTAMETER**   See *Meter.*

**HEPTASTICH**   See *Stanza.*

**HERO/HEROINE**   A *hero* or *heroine* is a character whose actions are inspiring or noble. In ancient stories and myths the hero or heroine is usually morally, physically, and intellectually superior. In modern literature the main character is usually an ordinary human being.
See *Character.*

**HEROIC COUPLET**   A *heroic couplet* is a pair of rhymed lines in iambic pentameter. An *iamb* is a metrical foot made up of an unstressed and stressed syllable, respectively, and *pentameter* means that each line has five metrical feet. The stressed and unstressed syllables have been marked in the following iambic pentameter lines from Alexander Pope's *An Essay on Criticism:*

> "Tis with our judgements as our watches, none
> Go just alike, yet each believes his own.

See *Couplet, Meter,* and *Stanza.*

**HEXAMETER**   See *Meter.*

**HOMERIC SIMILE**   A *Homeric simile,* also called an *epic simile,* is an elaborate comparison of unlike subjects. In this example from the *Odyssey,* on page 681, Homer compares the bodies of men killed by Odysseus to a fisherman's catch heaped up on the shore:

> Think of a catch that fishermen haul in to a
>    half-moon bay
> in a fine-meshed net from the whitecaps of the
>    sea:
> how all are poured out on the sand, in throes
>    for the salt sea,
> twitching their cold lives away in Helios'
>    fiery air;
> so lay the suitors heaped on one another.

See *Figurative Language* and *Simile.*

**IAMB**   See *Heroic Couplet* and *Meter.*

**IMAGE**   An *image* is a word or phrase that appeals to one or more of the five senses—sight, hearing, touch, taste, or smell. Writers use images to re-create sensory experiences in words. See *Description.*

**INCITING INCIDENT**   See *Plot.*

**INDIRECT CHARACTERIZATION**   See *Characterization.*

**INTERNAL RHYME**   See *Rhyme.*

**IRONY**   *Irony* is the general name given to literary techniques that involve differences between appearance and reality, expectation and result, or meaning and intention. In *verbal irony* words are used to suggest the opposite of what is meant. In *dramatic irony* there is a contradiction between what a character thinks and what the reader or audience knows to be true. In *irony of situation* an event occurs that directly contradicts the expectations of the characters, the reader, or the audience. The humor in Ernest Lawrence Thayer's "Casey at the Bat," on page 551, derives in part from irony of situation. The speaker creates the expectation that Casey will save the day. However, at the end of the poem "there is no joy in Mudville" because "Mighty Casey has struck out."

**IRONY OF SITUATION**   See *Irony.*

**LEGEND**   A *legend* is a widely told story about the past, one that may or may not have a foundation in fact. Unlike a myth, a legend usually does have some basis in fact, though these facts are usually not provable. A legend may involve heroic deeds, but it does not have as many supernatural elements as a myth. The stories of Davey Crockett are American legends. A real Davey Crockett existed, but that "he killed him a b'ar when he was only three" is highly doubtful.
See *Myth* and *Oral Tradition.*

**LIMERICK**   A *limerick* is a humorous, rhyming, five-line poem with a specific meter and rhyme scheme. Most limericks have three strong stresses in lines 1, 2, and 5 and two strong stresses in lines 3 and 4. Most follow the rhyme scheme *aabba.* Here is an example, with the stressed syllables marked:

> There was a young lady named Bright
> Whose speed was far faster than light;
> She went out one day
> In a relative way,
> And returned on the previous night.

**LITERAL LANGUAGE**   *Literal language* uses words in their ordinary senses. It is the opposite of *figurative language.* If you tell someone standing on a diving board to jump in, you are speaking literally. If you tell someone standing on the street corner to go jump in the lake, you are speaking figuratively.
See *Figurative Language.*

**LYRIC POEM**   A *lyric poem* is a highly musical verse that expresses the observations and feelings of a single speaker. In ancient times lyric poems were sung to the accompaniment of the lyre, a type of stringed instrument. Modern lyric poems are not usually sung. However, they still have a musical quality that is achieved through rhythm and other devices such as alliteration and rhyme. Alfred, Lord Tennyson's "The Eagle," on page 627, is a lyric poem expressing the speaker's feeling of wonder as he watches an eagle dive from a cliff.

**MAIN CHARACTER**   See *Character.*

**METAPHOR**   A *metaphor* is a figure of speech in which one thing is spoken of as though it were something else. Unlike a simile, which compares two things using *like* or *as,* a metaphor states a comparison directly. In "Dreams," on page 631,

Langston Hughes uses a metaphor to show what happens to a life without dreams:

> Hold fast to dreams
> For if dreams die
> Life is a broken-winged bird
> That cannot fly.

Metaphors are especially important to poets, but prose writers use them as well. In *The Great Gatsby,* F. Scott Fitzgerald, a twentieth-century American novelist, described age thirty with a metaphor:

> Thirty—the promise of a decade of loneliness, a thinning list of single men to know, *a thinning briefcase of enthusiasm,* thinning hair.

Note that people often use metaphoric language in everyday speech, as in the expression "He's got an eagle eye."
See *Extended Metaphor* and *Figurative Language.*

**METER**   The *meter* of a poem is its rhythmical pattern. This pattern is determined by the number and types of stresses, or beats, in each line. To describe the meter of a poem, you must *scan* its lines. *Scanning* involves marking the stressed and unstressed syllables, as shown with the following two lines from "The Charge of the Light Brigade" by Alfred, Lord Tennyson, on page 569:

> Half a league, | half a league
> Half a league | onward

As you can see, each strong stress is marked with a slanted line ( ´ ) and each unstressed syllable with a horseshoe symbol ( ˘ ). The stressed and unstressed syllables are then divided by vertical lines (|) into groups called *feet.* The following types of feet are common in English poetry:

1. *Iamb:* a foot with one unstressed syllable followed by a stressed syllable, as in the word "again"

2. *Trochee:* a foot with a stressed syllable fol-

lowed by an unstressed syllable, as in the word "wonder"

3. *Anapest:* a foot with two unstressed syllables followed by one strong stress, as in the phrase "on the beach"

4. *Dactyl:* a foot with one strong stress followed by two unstressed syllables, as in the word "wonderful"

5. *Spondee:* a foot with two strong stresses, as in the word "spacewalk"

6. *Pyrrhic:* a foot with two unstressed syllables, as in the last foot of the line "and sud|denly"

7. *Amphibrach:* a foot with an unstressed syllable, followed by a stressed syllable, and another unstressed syllable, as in "that marvel|ous music"

8. *Amphimacer:* a foot with a stressed syllable, an unstressed syllable, and a stressed syllable, as in "here and gone"

Depending on the type of foot that is most common in them, lines of poetry are described as *iambic, trochaic, anapestic,* and so forth.

Lines are also described in terms of the number of feet that occur in them, as follows:

1. *Monometer:* verse written in one-foot lines

All things

Must pass

Away.

2. *Dimeter:* verse written in two-foot lines

Thomas | Jefferson

What do | you say

Under the | gravestone

Hidden | away?

—Rosemary and Stephen Vincent Benét, "Thomas Jefferson 1743–1826"

3. *Trimeter:* verse written in three-foot lines

I know | not whom | I meet

I know | not where | I go.

4. *Tetrameter:* verse written in four-foot lines
5. *Pentameter:* verse written in five-foot lines
6. *Hexameter:* verse written in six-foot lines
7. *Heptameter:* verse written in seven-foot lines

A complete description of the meter of a line tells both how many feet there are in the line and what kind of foot is most common. Thus the lines from the first poem quoted in this entry would be described as *iambic monometer. Blank verse* is poetry written in unrhymed iambic pentameter. Poetry that does not have a regular meter is called *free verse.*

**MONOLOGUE** A *monologue* is a speech by one character in a play, story, or poem. An example from Shakespeare's *Romeo and Juliet,* on page 321, is the speech in which the Prince of Verona commands the Capulets and the Montagues to cease their feuding (Act I, scene i, lines 62–84).
See *Dramatic Poetry* and *Soliloquy.*

**MONOMETER** See *Meter.*

**MOOD** *Mood,* or *atmosphere,* is the feeling created in the reader by a literary work or passage. The mood is often suggested by descriptive details. Often the mood can be described in a single word such as lighthearted, frightening, or despairing. The mood of Alfred, Lord Tennyson's "The Charge of the Light Brigade," on page 569, can be described as grand or heroic:

Half a league, half a league
Half a league onward,
All in the valley of Death
   Rode the six hundred.
"Forward the Light Brigade!
Charge for the guns!" he said.
Into the valley of Death
   Rode the six hundred.

See *Tone.*

**MORAL** A *moral* is a lesson taught by a literary work. A fable usually ends with a moral that is directly stated.

**MOTIVATION** *Motivation* is a reason that explains or partially explains a character's thoughts, feelings, actions, or behavior. Motivation results from a combination of the character's personality and the circumstances he or she must deal with. Mrs. Higgins, in Morley Callaghan's "All the Years of Her Life," on page 57, is motivated by fear for her son together with her own embarrassment at his being caught stealing.

When the motives of a main character are not clear and logical, neither that character nor the story seems believable. Adventure stories often do not concern themselves much with the characters' motivations. In contrast, serious fiction usually explores motivations in depth.
See *Character* and *Characterization.*

**MYTH** A *myth* is a fictional tale that explains the actions of gods or the causes of natural phenomena. Unlike legends, myths have little historical truth and involve supernatural elements. Every culture has its collections of myths. Among the most familiar are the myths of the ancient Greeks and Romans. The *Odyssey,* on page 681, is a mythical story, attributed to the ancient Greek poet Homer.
See *Legend* and *Oral Tradition.*

**NARRATION** *Narration* is writing that tells a story. The act of telling a story is also called *narration.* Novels and short stories are fictional narratives. Nonfiction works such as news stories, biographies, and autobiographies are also narratives. A narrative poem tells a story in verse.
See *Anecdote, Essay, Narrative Poem, Nonfiction, Novel,* and *Short Story.*

**NARRATIVE** A *narrative* is a story told in fiction, nonfiction, poetry, or drama.
See *Narration.*

**NARRATIVE POEM** A *narrative poem* is one that tells a story. "Casey at the Bat," on page 551, is a humorous narrative poem about the last inning of a baseball game. Edgar Allan Poe's "The Raven," on page 563, is a serious narrative poem about a man's grief over the loss of a loved one.
See *Ballad, Dramatic Poetry, Epic,* and *Narration.*

**NARRATOR** A *narrator* is a speaker or character who tells a story. The narrator may be either a character in the story or an outside observer. The writer's choice of narrator determines the story's *point of view,* which in turn determines the type and amount of information the writer can reveal.

When a character in the story tells the story, that character is a *first-person narrator.* This narrator may be a major character, a minor character, or just a witness. Readers see only what this character sees, hear only what he or she hears, and so on. The first-person narrator may or may not be reliable. We have reason, for example, to be suspicious of the first-person narrator of Edgar Allan Poe's "The Cask of Amontillado," on page 139.

When a voice outside the story narrates, the story has a *third-person narrator.* An *omniscient,* or all-knowing, third-person narrator can tell readers what any character thinks and feels. For example, in Guy de Maupassant's "The Necklace," on page 201, we know the feelings of both Monsieur and Madame Loisel. A *limited* third-person narrator, on the other hand, sees the world through one character's eyes and reveals only that character's thoughts, no one else's. For example, in Ursula K. Le Guin's "Gwilan's Harp," on page 209, readers share only Gwilan's experiences and feelings.
See *Speaker.*

**NONFICTION** *Nonfiction* is prose writing that presents and explains ideas or that tells about real people, places, objects, or events. Nonfiction narratives are about actual people, places, and events, unlike fictional narratives, which present imaginary characters and events. To be classed as nonfiction, a work must be true. Arthur C. Clarke's "If I Forget Thee, Oh Earth...," on page 165, presents a fictional account of the earth as viewed from space. "Single Room, Earth View," on page 517, presents a nonfictional account of the same subject.

Among nonfiction forms are essays, newspaper and magazine articles, journals, travelogues, biographies, and autobiographies. Historical, scientific, technical, political, and philosophical writings are also nonfiction.
See *Autobiography, Biography,* and *Essay.*

**NOVEL**   A *novel* is a long work of fiction. Like a short story, a novel has a plot that explores characters in conflict. However, a novel is much longer than a short story and may have one or more subplots, or minor stories, and several themes.

The novel has its roots in ancient storytelling traditions, but it became an especially important literary form in the late nineteenth and early twentieth centuries. The subject matter of a novel can range from the pure fantasy of J. R. R. Tolkien's *The Hobbit* to the realistic detail of Charles Dickens's *Great Expectations,* on page 757.
See *Fiction* and *Genre.*

**OCTAVE**   See *Stanza.*

**ONOMATOPOEIA**   *Onomatopoeia* is the use of words that imitate sounds. *Whirr, thud, sizzle,* and *hiss* are typical examples. Writers can deliberately choose words that contribute to a desired sound effect. In the following lines, from Edgar Allan Poe's "The Bells," on page 640, *clang, crash, roar,* and *twang* are onomatopoeic:

Oh, the bells, bells, bells!
What a tale their terror tells
Of Despair!

How they clang, and clash, and roar!
What a horror they outpour
On the bosom of the palpitating air!
Yet the ear it fully knows,
By the twanging
And the clanging,
How the danger ebbs and flows

**ORAL TRADITION**   The *oral tradition* is the passing of songs, stories, and poems from generation to generation by word of mouth. Many folk songs, ballads, fairy tales, legends, and myths originated in the oral tradition.
See *Ballad, Folk Tale, Legend,* and *Myth.*

**PARABLE**   A *parable* is a short narrative designed to convey a moral truth. The people and events in a parable represent abstract truths. The most famous parables are those told by Christ in the New Testament, but parables can be found in many cultures. In the following parable, Christ teaches that actions are more important than words:

"There was a man who had two sons. He went to the first and said, 'Son, go and work today in the vineyard.'
"'I will not,' he answered, but later he changed his mind and went.
"Then the father went to the other son and said the same thing. He answered, 'I will, sir,' but he did not go.
"Which of the two did what his father wanted?"
"The first," they answered.
—Matthew 21:28–31

**PARADOX**   A *paradox* is a statement that seems contradictory or absurd but that expresses a truth. Paradox also forms the basis of *epigrams,* which are short, witty sayings. Consider, for example, the following epigram from Oscar Wilde: "In this world there are only two tragedies. One is not getting what one wants, and the other is getting it." This statement seems absurd, but when one thinks about it, one can see how it might be true.

**PARODY**   A *parody* is a work done in imitation of another, usually in order to mock it, but sometimes just in fun. The following lines are Lewis Carroll's parody of the familiar children's rhyme, "Twinkle, Twinkle, Little Star":

> Twinkle, twinkle, little bat!
> How I wonder what you're at!
> Up above the world you fly,
> Like a teatray in the sky.

**PENTAMETER**   See *Meter*.

**PERSONIFICATION**   *Personification* is a type of figurative language in which a nonhuman subject is given human characteristics. When Edgar Lee Masters says on page 588 that "Sorrow knocked at my door, but I was afraid;/ Ambition called to me, but I dreaded the chances," he is personifying the abstract qualities of sorrow and ambition. In the short poem below, "Soft Snow," William Blake personifies both the snow and winter:

> I walked abroad in a snowy day;
> I asked the soft snow with me to play;
> She played and she melted in all her
>    prime,
> And the winter called it a dreadful crime.

See *Figurative Language*.

**PERSUASION**   *Persuasion* is writing or speech that attempts to convince the reader to adopt a particular opinion or course of action. A newspaper editorial that says a city council decision was wrong is an example of persuasive writing attempting to mold opinion. A television commercial showing the benefits of a new toothpaste is meant to move viewers to act, in this case to buy toothpaste.

**PLOT**   *Plot* is the sequence of events in a literary work. In most novels, dramas, short stories, and narrative poems, the plot involves both characters and a central conflict. The plot usually begins with an *exposition* that introduces the setting, the characters, and the basic situation. This is followed by the *inciting incident,* which introduces the central conflict. The conflict then increases during the *development* until it reaches a high point of interest or suspense, the *climax.* All the events leading up to the climax make up the rising action. The climax is followed by the falling action, which leads to the resolution, or end, of the central conflict. Any events that occur after the resolution make up the denouement.

**POETRY**   *Poetry* is one of the three major types of literature, the others being prose and drama. Most poems make use of highly concise, musical, and emotionally charged language. Many also make use of imagery, figurative language, and special devices of sound such as rhyme. Poems are often divided into lines and stanzas and often employ regular rhythmical patterns, or meters. However, some poems are written out just like prose, and some are written in free verse.
See *Genre*.

**POINT OF VIEW**   See *Narrator*.

**PROSE**   *Prose* is the ordinary form of written language. Most writing that is not poetry, drama, or song is considered prose. Prose is one of the major genres of literature and occurs in two forms: fiction and nonfiction.
See *Fiction, Genre,* and *Nonfiction*.

**PROTAGONIST**   The *protagonist* is the main character in a literary work. In "The Secret Life of Walter Mitty," on page 3, Walter Mitty is the protagonist.
See *Antagonist*.

**PUN**   A *pun* is a play on words based on different meanings of words that sound alike. Here is an example:

> Question: Define *wise*.
> Answer: It's what little kids are always asking, as in "Wise the sky blue?"

**PYRRHIC**   See *Meter.*

**QUATRAIN**   A *quatrain* is a stanza or poem made up of four lines, usually with a definite rhythm and rhyme scheme. The following quatrain is from Stephen Vincent Benét's "The Ballad of William Sycamore," on page 557:

> My father, he was a mountaineer,
> His fist was a knotty hammer;
> He was quick on his feet as a running deer,
> And he spoke with a Yankee stammer.

See *Stanza.*

**REFRAIN**   A *refrain* is a repeated line or group of lines in a poem or song. For example, in "The Charge of the Light Brigade," by Alfred, Lord Tennyson, on page 569, the line "Rode the six hundred" is repeated with variations at the ends of each stanza.
See *Repetition.*

**REPETITION**   *Repetition* is the use, more than once, of any element of language—a sound, a word, a phrase, a clause, or a sentence. In his famous civil rights speech, on page 499, Martin Luther King, Jr. repeats the words "I have a dream" eight times, each time in connection with a different image.

Poets use many kinds of repetition. Alliteration, assonance, rhyme, and rhythm are repetitions of certain sounds and sound patterns. A refrain is a repeated line or group of lines. In both prose and poetry, repetition is used for musical effects and for emphasis.
See *Alliteration, Assonance, Consonance, Refrain, Rhyme,* and *Rhythm.*

**RESOLUTION**   See *Plot.*

**RHYME**   *Rhyme* is the repetition of sounds at the ends of words. *End rhyme* occurs when the rhyming words come at the ends of lines, as in "The Desired Swan Song," by Samuel Taylor Coleridge:

> Swans sing before they die—'twere no bad thing
> Should certain persons die before they sing.

*Internal rhyme* occurs when the rhyming words appear in the same line, as in lines one and three of Edgar Allan Poe's "The Raven," on page 563:

> One upon a midnight dr*eary,* while I pondered, weak and w*eary,*
> Over many a quaint and curious volume of forgotten lore,
> While I nodded, nearly n*apping,* suddenly there came a t*apping,*

See *Repetition* and *Rhyme Scheme.*

**RHYME SCHEME**   A *rhyme scheme* is a regular pattern of rhyming words in a poem. The rhyme scheme of a poem is indicated by using different letters of the alphabet for each new rhyme. In an *aabb* stanza, for example, line one rhymes with line two and line three rhymes with line four. William Wordsworth's poem on page 628 uses an *ababcc* rhyme pattern:

> I wandered lonely as a cloud                     *a*
> That floats on high o'er vales and hills,         *b*
> When all at once I saw a crowd,                   *a*
> A host, of golden daffodils;                      *b*
> Beside the lake, beneath the trees,               *c*
> Fluttering and dancing in the breeze.             *c*

Many poems use the same pattern of rhymes, though not the same rhymes, in each stanza. The next stanza of Wordsworth's poem, for example, has this rhyme scheme: *dedeff.*
See *Rhyme.*

**RHYTHM**   *Rhythm* is the pattern of *beats,* or stresses, in spoken or written language. Some poems have a very specific pattern, or meter,

while prose and free verse use the natural rhythms of everyday speech.
See *Meter*.

**RISING ACTION**   See *Plot*.

**ROUND CHARACTER**   See *Character*.

**SATIRE**   *Satire* is a style of writing that uses humor—sometimes gentle and sometimes biting—to criticize people, ideas, or institutions in hopes of improving them. In "The Spreading '*You* Know,'" on page 523, James Thurber mocks people's tendency to use a careless phrase. Clearly, he would prefer they didn't.

**SCENE**   See *Drama*.

**SCIENCE FICTION**   *Science fiction* is writing that tells about imaginary events that involve science or technology. Many science-fiction stories are set in the future. The setting can be on Earth, in space, on other planets, or in a totally imaginary place. Arthur C. Clarke's "If I Forget Thee, Oh Earth...," on page 165, is a science-fiction story set on the moon after a nuclear disaster on earth.
See *Fantasy*.

**SENSORY LANGUAGE**   *Sensory language* is writing or speech that appeals to one or more of the senses.
See *Image*.

**SESTET**   See *Stanza*.

**SETTING**   The *setting* of a literary work is the time and place of the action. Time can include not only the historical period—past, present, or future—but also a specific year, season, or time of day. Place may involve not only the geographical place—a region, country, state, or town— but also the social, economic, or cultural environment.

In some stories, setting serves merely as a backdrop for action, a context in which the characters move and speak. In others, however, setting is a crucial element. Both the desert and Native American culture are important in Leslie Marmon Silko's "The Man to Send Rain Clouds," on page 159, and the lunar landscape and the future are important in Arthur C. Clarke's "If I Forget Thee, Oh Earth...," on page 165.

Description of the setting often helps establish the mood of a story. For example, in Edgar Allan Poe's "The Cask of Amontillado," on page 139, the setting contributes to the growing horror.
See *Mood*.

**SHORT STORY**   A *short story* is a brief work of fiction. A novel, by contrast, is a long work of fiction. In most short stories one main character faces a conflict that is worked out in the plot of the story. Great craftsmanship must go into the writing of a good story, for it has to accomplish its purpose in very few words.

The short story as a distinct literary form emerged in the nineteenth century. The American writers Edgar Allan Poe and Nathaniel Hawthorne were especially important in the development of the short story.
See *Fiction* and *Genre*.

**SIMILE**   A *simile* is a figure of speech in which *like* or *as* is used to make a comparison between two basically unlike subjects. "Claire is as flighty as Roger" is a comparison, not a simile. "Claire is as flighty as a sparrow" is a simile.

Poets often use similes. The following example is from Donald Justice's "Incident in a Rose Garden," on page 575:

> Sir, I encountered Death
> Just now among our roses.
> *Thin as a scythe* he stood there.

Prose writers also use similes. Hero is one

from Ursula K. Le Guin's "Gwilan's Harp," on page 216:

> The untuned strings of the harps hung on the wall wakened and answered softly, voice to voice, like eyes that shine among the leaves when the wind is blowing.

See *Figurative Language.*

**SOLILOQUY**  A *soliloquy* is a long speech expressing the thoughts of a character alone on stage. In William Shakespeare's *Romeo and Juliet,* on page 321, Romeo gives a soliloquy after the servant has fled and Paris has died (Act V, scene iii, lines 74–120).
See *Monologue.*

**SONNET**  A *sonnet* is a fourteen-line lyric poem, usually written in rhymed iambic pentameter. The *English,* or *Shakespearean, sonnet* consists of three quatrains (four-line stanzas) and a couplet (two lines), usually rhyming *abab cdcd efef gg.* The couplet usually comments on the ideas contained in the preceding twelve lines. The sonnet is usually not printed with the stanzas divided, but a reader can see distinct ideas in each. See the English sonnet by William Shakespeare on page 661.

The *Italian,* or *Petrarchan, sonnet* consists of an octave (eight-line stanza) and a sestet (six-line stanza). Often the octave rhymes *abbaabba* and the sestet rhymes *cdecde.* The octave states a theme or asks a question. The sestet comments on or answers the question. Henry Wadsworth Longfellow's "The Sound of the Sea," on page 660, is a Petrarchan sonnet.

The Petrarchan sonnet took its name from Petrarch, a fourteenth-century Italian poet. Once the form was introduced in England, it underwent change. The Shakespearean sonnet is, of course, named after William Shakespeare.
See *Lyric Poem, Meter,* and *Stanza.*

**SPEAKER**  The *speaker* is the imaginary voice assumed by the writer of a poem. In many poems the speaker is not identified by name. When reading a poem, remember that the speaker and the poet are not the same person, no more than an actor is the playwright. The speaker within the poem may be a person, an animal, a thing, or an abstraction. The speaker in the following stanza by Emily Dickinson is a person who has died:

> Because I could not stop for Death—
> He kindly stopped for me—
> The Carriage held but just Ourselves—
> And Immortality.

**SPONDEE**  See *Meter.*

**STAGE DIRECTIONS**  *Stage directions* are notes included in a drama to describe how the work is to be performed or staged. These instructions are printed in italics and are not spoken aloud. They are used to describe sets, lighting, sound effects, and the appearance, personalities, and movements of characters.
See *Drama.*

**STANZA**  A *stanza* is a group of lines in a poem, considered as a unit. Often the stanzas in a poem are separated by spaces.

Stanzas are sometimes named according to the number of lines found in them. A *couplet,* for example, is a two-line stanza. A *tercet* is a stanza with three lines. Other types of stanzas include the following:
1. *Quatrain:* a four-line stanza
2. *Cinquain:* a five-line stanza
3. *Sestet:* a six-line stanza
4. *Heptastich:* a seven-line stanza
5. *Octave:* an eight-line stanza

Sonnets, limericks, and haiku all have distinct stanza forms. A *sonnet* is a fourteen-line poem that is made up either of three quatrains and a couplet or of an octave followed by a sestet. A *limerick* consists of a single five-line stanza with a particular pattern of rhymes. A *haiku* is made up of a single three-line stanza. See *Haiku, Limerick,* and *Sonnet.*

**STATIC CHARACTER**   See *Character.*

**SURPRISE ENDING**   A *surprise ending* is a conclusion that violates the expectations of the reader but in a way that is both logical and believable. O. Henry's "The Gift of the Magi," on page 183, and Guy de Maupassant's "The Necklace," on page 201, have surprise endings. Both authors were masters of the form.

**SUSPENSE**   *Suspense* is a feeling of curiosity or uncertainty about the outcome of events in a literary work. Writers create suspense by raising questions in the minds of their readers. Suspense may stem from the physical danger faced by a character or from psychological tension, as in the battle of wills between Annie and Helen in William Gibson's *The Miracle Worker.*

**SYMBOL**   A *symbol* is anything that stands for or represents something else. An object that serves as a symbol has its own meaning, but it also represents abstract ideas. Marks on paper can symbolize spoken words. A flag symbolizes a country. A flashy car may symbolize wealth. Writers sometimes use such conventional symbols in their work, but they also sometimes create symbols of their own through emphasis or repetition.

In James Hurst's "The Scarlet Ibis," on page 189, the ibis symbolizes the character named Doodle. Doodle and the ibis have many traits in common. Both are beautiful and otherworldly. Both struggle against great odds. Both meet an unfortunate fate. Since a story says something about life or people in general, the ibis, in a larger sense, becomes a symbol for all those who struggle.

**TERCET**   See *Stanza.*

**TETRAMETER**   See *Meter.*

**THEME**   A *theme* is a central message or insight into life revealed through the literary work. The theme is not a condensed summary of the plot. Instead, it is a generalization about human beings or about life that the literary work communicates.

The theme of a literary work may be stated directly or implied. In James Hurst's "The Scarlet Ibis," on page 189, the narrator directly states one theme of the story: " . . . pride is a wonderful, terrible thing, a seed that bears two vines, life and death."

When the theme of a work is implied, readers think about what the work seems to say about the nature of people or about life. The story or poem can be viewed as a specific example of the generalization the writer is trying to communicate.

Note that there is usually no single correct statement of a work's theme, though there can be incorrect ones. Also, a long work, like a novel or a full-length play, may have several themes. Finally, not all literary works have themes. A work meant only to entertain may have no theme at all.

**TONE**   The *tone* of a literary work is the writer's attitude toward his or her audience and subject. The tone can often be described by a single adjective such as *formal* or *informal, serious* or *playful, bitter,* or *ironic.* When O. Henry discusses the young married couple in "The Gift of the Magi," on page 183, he uses a sympathetic tone. By contrast, Margaret Walker uses a grieving tone in her poem "Memory," on page 614. See *Mood.*

**TRAGEDY** A *tragedy* is a work of literature, especially a play, that results in a catastrophe for the main character. In ancient Greek drama the main character was always a significant person, a king or a hero, and the cause of the tragedy was a tragic flaw, or weakness, in his or her character. In modern drama the main character can be an ordinary person, and the cause of the tragedy can be some evil in society itself. The purpose of tragedy is not only to arouse fear and pity in the audience, but also, in some cases, to convey a sense of the grandeur and nobility of the human spirit.

Shakespeare's *Romeo and Juliet,* on page 321, is a tragedy. Romeo and Juliet both suffer from the tragic flaw of impulsiveness. This flaw ultimately leads to their deaths.
See *Comedy* and *Drama.*

**TRIMETER** See *Meter.*

**TROCHEE** See *Meter.*

**VERBAL IRONY** See *Irony.*

**VERISIMILITUDE** *Verisimilitude,* which literally means "similar to the truth," is the appearance of truth or reality in a work of fiction. A writer creates verisimilitude by giving characters realistic traits, mannerisms, speech, and so, and by describing realistic settings or situations. For example, in "Blues Ain't No Mockin Bird," beginning on page 91, Toni Cade Bambara creates characters who are believable and true to life.

**ABSTRACT** *adj.* Anything that is not concrete or definite is *abstract.* A photograph of a man or a woman is concrete because it contains many concrete details. A stick figure drawing, on the other hand, is abstract because many details are left out. Words, and the ideas that they stand for, can also be abstract. Examples of abstract words include *beauty, courage, truth, honor, thought, love,* and *freedom.*

When people write or think about abstract ideas, they can make their writing or thinking clear by using specific, concrete examples or illustrations. For instance, suppose that a writer wants to communicate the abstract idea that a character is angry. The writer can do this by describing a concrete action such as screaming or pounding a table with a fist. Another way to express abstract ideas clearly is to use figures of speech. For example, the simile "as gentle as a lamb" uses a concrete image—the lamb—to communicate an abstract idea—gentleness.

**ANALOGY** *n.* An *analogy* is a comparison that explains or describes one subject by pointing out its similarities to another subject. O. Henry ends his story "The Gift of the Magi," on page 183, by making an analogy between the three wise men, or Magi, of the Biblical tale and the two characters in his story. In the following passage, the writer makes an analogy between a vast desert and the sea:

> "This desert, like the sea, covers an enormous area. Like waves, its sands ripple off to the horizon and beyond. Here and there in this ocean of sameness, an island of green palms appears—an oasis."

Notice that an analogy can be expressed using a variety of literary techniques, such as simile, metaphor, and extended metaphor. See the definitions of these techniques in the Handbook of Literary Terms and Techniques.

**ANALYSIS** *n.* *Analysis* is the process of studying the parts of a whole. The process consists of three steps, as follows:
1. Divide the object you are studying into its parts.
2. Observe the characteristics of the parts.
3. Look for relationships among the parts and between the parts and the whole.

To analyze a tree, for example, you would first break it down into such parts as roots, trunk, branches, stems, and leaves. Then you would describe each part (for example, "The roots grow below ground and extend out in various directions"). Finally, you would tell how the parts are related to one another (for example, "Roots grow below the trunk; they gather water and nourishment for the rest of the tree").

When you analyze a literary work, you also break it into parts, observe the characteristics of these parts, and consider how the parts are related. For example, you might analyze an essay by studying the characteristics of and the relationships between three parts—the introduction, the body, and the conclusion. A drama, short story, or narrative poem might be analyzed into the parts of its plot—the introduction, the inciting incident, the development, the climax, the resolution, and the denouement.

**ARGUMENT** *n.* An *argument* is a set of statements consisting of a conclusion and one or more premises, or reasons for accepting the conclusion. The selection from Marchette Chute's *Shakespeare of London,* on page 527, begins with an argument. In her first paragraph, Chute offers a number of reasons for accepting the conclusion that acting on the Elizabethan stage was not easy.

When writing about literary works, people often present arguments. Their conclusions, which can be interpretations or evaluations, are supported by evidence drawn from the works. Thus someone might argue that Romeo is impulsive and offer the following reasons, or evidence, to support this conclusion: Romeo rushes into love and marriage. He kills Tybalt without stopping to think about the consequences. He kills himself without first making certain that Juliet is dead.

The term *argument* is also used to describe any brief account or summary of a literary work. Thus a paragraph describing the plot of *Romeo and Juliet* might be described as presenting "the argument of the play."
See *Conclusion, Deduction, Evidence, Induction,* and *Inference.*

**CATEGORIZATION** *n.* Categorization is the process of placing objects or ideas into groups, or classes. To categorize something, follow these steps:

1. Observe one of your subject's characteristics, or qualities.
2. Place the subject into a group with other things that have the same characteristic or quality.
3. Find or create a name for the group.

For example, Sally Ride's essay "Single Room, Earth View," on page 517, has the characteristic of being about a real-life, nonimaginary experience. Therefore, it can be placed in a category, or group, with other works about real-life experience. The name of this category is, of course, "nonfiction."

**CAUSE AND EFFECT** *n. phrase* When one event precedes and brings about another event,

the first is said to be a *cause* and the second an *effect.* For example, in "Casey at the Bat," on page 551, Casey's striking out causes the Mudville Nine to lose the game. Striking out is the cause and losing the game is the effect.

Cause and effect are extremely important in literary works. The plot of a story, for example, is a series of causes and effects. One event causes the next, which causes the next, and so on to the end of the story. Writers choose their language carefully to cause certain effects in their readers. A writer might use a pun, for example, to cause readers to laugh, or a dark and scary setting to cause readers to feel suspense and foreboding.

**COMPARISON** *n.* Comparison is the process of observing and pointing out similarities. A comparison of Anne Sullivan and Helen Keller, two characters in *The Miracle Worker,* on page 253, would point out the following similarities: Both are willful, determined, and independent; both overcome physical handicaps; and both learn, in the course of the play, to love other people.
See *Contrast.*

**CONCLUSION** *n.* A *conclusion* is anything that follows reasonably from something else. In an argument the conclusion is a statement that follows reasonably from the facts or evidence presented. In a literary work, such as an essay, the conclusion is the part of the work that comes last and that follows reasonably from everything that has preceded it.

**CONTRAST** *n.* Contrast is the process of observing or pointing out differences.
See *Comparison.*

**DEDUCTION** *n.* Deduction is a form of argument in which the conclusion has to be true if the premises are true. Consider, for example, the following argument:

Premise: Edgar Allan Poe died in 1849.
Premise: Word processors were invented in the twentieth century.
Conclusion: Edgar Allan Poe did not use a word processor.

If you accept the premises of this argument, then you must accept the conclusion. Therefore, the argument is a deduction.
See *Generalization* and *Inference.*

**DEFINITION** *n.* *Definition* is the process of explaining the meaning of a word or a phrase. There are many types of definitions.

The simplest, called *ostensive definition,* involves pointing out something and saying its name. Thus, if you point at an object and say, "chair," you are giving an ostensive definition of the word *chair.*

*Lexical definition,* the kind of definition found in dictionaries, involves using words to define other words. Types of lexical definition include definition by synonym, definition by antonym, definition by example, and genus and differentia definition.

In a *definition by synonym,* you use a word or phrase that has the same meaning: A *drama* is a "play."

In a *definition by antonym,* you use a word or phrase that has the opposite meaning: A *taciturn* person is one who is "not talkative."

In a *definition by example,* you list things to which the term being defined applies: *Conifers* include pines, spruces, firs, cedars, and yews.

In a *genus and differentia definition,* you first put the thing to be defined into a general category or group. Then you tell how it differs from other members of the group:

To be defined: *French horn*
Genus, or group: Brass instruments
Differentia: three valves
coiled tube
flaring bell
Definition: A *French horn* is "a brass instrument with three valves, a coiled tube, and a flaring bell."

Whenever you write about literature, make sure to define your key terms. Use the methods of lexical definition explained here.

**EVALUATION** *n.* *Evaluation* is the process of making judgments about the quality or value of something. When you evaluate a literary work, you must first analyze and interpret it. Once you understand the work, you are then in a position to make judgments about it. Note that it is extremely important that any judgments, or evaluations, that you make be specific and be supported by facts. For example, someone might say of a particular work, "The characters are unbelievable," and then give specific examples of unbelievable qualities or actions of the characters. The evaluation "I hated it" is not acceptable because it is too vague.
See *Opinion* and *Judgment.*

**EVIDENCE** *n.* *Evidence* is factual information presented to support an argument. In a criminal trial, lawyers present evidence, or facts, to prove or disprove the defendant's guilt or innocence. When you interpret or evaluate a literary work, you should present evidence to support the claims that you make about the work. For example, consider the statement, "The speaker in Gordon Parks's 'The Funeral' admires his father." You might support this claim by pointing out that the speaker describes his father as being a giant of a man.
See *Fact, Reason,* and *Support.*

**FACT** *n.* A *fact* is a statement that can be proved true or false by evidence. The following facts are true by definition:

$2 + 2 = 4$
*Alliteration* is "the repetition of initial consonant sounds."

The following facts can be proved by observation:

"The Secret Life of Walter Mitty" was written by James Thurber.

"The Raven" contains several examples of ono-matopoeia.

Facts are extremely important in literary works. To develop a setting, a writer presents facts about the time and place. To develop characters, a writer presents facts about those characters. Whenever you speak or write, you should present facts to support any opinions that you express.

See *Opinion.*

**GENERALIZATION** *n.*  A *generalization* is a statement that applies to more than one thing. The following statements are generalizations:

> The characters in Robert Frost's poems are usually simple country folk.
> A playwright creates both stage directions and dialogue.

The first statement applies to more than one character, and the second applies to more than one playwright.

*Deductive arguments* often begin with generalizations, as in the following:

> Premise: (generalization) Estella doesn't love anyone.
> Conclusion: Estella doesn't love Pip.

*Inductive arguments* often end with generalizations:

> Premise: The characters in "Mending Wall" are simple country folk.
> Premise: The characters in "Home Burial" are simple country folk.
> Premise: The characters in "The Death of the Hired Man" are simple country folk.
> Conclusion: (generalization) Many of Robert Frost's characters are simple country folk.

When making a generalization, be careful not to overgeneralize. For example, the statement "All poems rhyme" is an overgeneralization because some poems do not. To avoid overgeneralization, use qualifiers, or words that limit statements. Such words include *some, a few, many, often,* and *usually.*

See *Conclusion* and *Stereotype.*

**INDUCTION** *n.*  *Induction* is a form of argument in which the conclusion is probably but not necessarily true. The usual method for constructing an inductive argument is to observe several things and then make a generalization about them. For example, if you read several stories by Edgar Allan Poe and find that the first is a horror story, the second is a horror story, and so on, you might conclude, by induction, "All of Poe's stories are horror stories." However, notice that this conclusion is not absolutely certain because you have not read all of Poe's stories and because he may have written some stories that no one has read. For this reason, you would have to limit your conclusion to something like "Poe wrote many horror stories."

Note that most scientific laws are conclusions drawn by inductive reasoning. A scientist observes something several times—Mercury revolving around the sun, for example—and then draws a general conclusion: "Mercury revolves around the sun." However, this statement is not necessarily true for all time. At some time in the future, Mercury may cease to revolve around the sun, in which case the conclusion would become false. This possibility of falsification is what makes inductive conclusions only probably true.

See *Generalization* and *Inference.*

**INFERENCE** *n.*  An *inference* is any logical or reasonable conclusion. The conclusions of both inductive and deductive arguments are inferences. Interpreting and understanding written or spoken language involves making inferences again and again. To understand what the language really means, the reader or listener must play an active role. He or she must pay close attention to the language and draw reasonable conclusions from it.

For example, if you read the sentence "Melissa, a large Bengal tiger, lives at the San Diego Zoo," you can draw conclusions such as the following: Melissa lives in captivity; the tiger is female; it is probably not a good idea to try to pet Melissa; and Melissa is related to the wild tigers of Bengal.

The number of conclusions that you can draw is limited only by your thoughtfulness and by the information supplied in the sentence. Whenever you read or listen, think about the language and draw conclusions, or inferences, from it.
See *Conclusion, Deduction,* and *Induction.*

**INTERPRETATION** *n.* *Interpretation* is the process of determining the meaning or significance of speech, writing, art, music, or actions. Interpreting a literary work involves many different processes. These include the following:
1. Reading the work carefully and actively (questioning, predicting, clarifying, summarizing, and pulling it all together)
2. Analyzing the work into its parts and studying the characteristics of and relationships between these parts
3. Drawing conclusions about the meaning or significance of the work based on your analysis. In this final step, you relate your specific observations to your general conclusions

Often the aim of an interpretation is to state the work's central message, or theme. Facts drawn from careful reading and analysis of the work are then used to support this statement of theme. For example, your reading of "A Dream Deferred," on page 630, might lead you to this statement of theme:

> In "A Dream Deferred," Langston Hughes argues that delaying the fulfillment of a dream can have terrible consequences.

Then you would supply evidence from your analysis of the poem to support this general interpretation.
See *Analysis.*

**JUDGMENT** *n.* A *judgment* is a statement about the quality or value of something. Judgments are not facts. However, sound judgments are ones that are supported by facts.
See *Evaluation* and *Opinion.*

**MAIN IDEA** *n. phrase* The *main idea* is the central point that a speaker or writer wants to communicate. In an essay the main idea is often directly stated in a thesis statement or in the conclusion. In many literary works, the main idea is not directly stated but is implied by statements in the work or by the work as a whole.
See *Purpose.*

**OBJECTIVE** *adj.* Something is *objective* if it has to do with a reality that is independent of any particular person's mind, or personal, internal experiences. Statements of fact are objective because anyone can, at least in theory, determine whether they are true. The statement "James Weldon Johnson wrote 'The Creation'" is objective because it deals with an external reality. Anyone can determine whether the statement is true by checking an index of authors and titles or by looking up the poem in an anthology. The statement "Johnson's poem is powerful and moving" is subjective because it is a report of an individual's personal, internal experience of the poem.
See *Subjective.*

**OPINION** *n.* An *opinion* is a statement that can be supported by facts but that is not itself a fact. Types of opinions include judgments (statements about value or quality), predictions (statements about the future), and statements of obligation (moral or ethical statements). The following are examples of opinions:

Judgment: "I Hear America Singing" is a beautiful poem.
Prediction: In the future most writers will work on word processors.

Statement of Obligation: Walter Mitty should
be more assertive.

Whenever you express opinions, in speech or in writing, be ready to back up your opinion with facts. An opinion that can be supported with facts is sound. An opinion that cannot be supported with facts is unsound.
See *Fact, Judgment,* and *Prediction.*

**PARAPHRASE** *n.*   A *paraphrase* is a restatement in other words. In discussion or debate, you can make certain that you understand what someone else is saying by paraphrasing what has been said. When interpreting a literary work, you can paraphrase to clarify your understanding of the work. Simply put what the writer has said into your own words. When speaking or writing about a literary work, you can support the statements you make either by quoting from the work or by paraphrasing it.

**PREDICTION** *n.*   *Prediction* is the act of making statements about the future. Reading actively involves constantly predicting what will come next. Sometimes a reader's predictions are based on clues, or hints, provided by the writer. These clues are called *foreshadowing.* Often, however, a reader's predictions are based not on specific clues but on general knowledge of how people and characters act, what often happens in stories, and the like.

A prediction leads a reader to have certain expectations. These expectations can create suspense, as when a reader of a mystery story predicts that a character will come to trouble if she enters a certain house. Sometimes writers lead their readers to make certain predictions and then violate the expectations thus created. This happens, for example, in stories that have surprise endings.
See *Opinion.*

**PROBLEM SOLVING** *n. phrase*   *Problem solving* is the process by which a person comes up with a solution to some difficulty. Most problem solving involves the following steps:
1. State the problem as clearly as you can.
2. Identify your goal.
3. Examine the differences between the goal state (the situation that will exist when the problem is solved) and the initial state (the situation at the time when you begin working on the problem).
4. Take steps to reduce the differences between the initial state and the goal state.

The following are some *heuristics,* or rules of thumb, that are useful in solving many problems:
1. Break the problem down into parts and solve the parts separately.
2. Think of a simpler problem of the same type that you have solved before. Use part or all of your solution to solve the simpler problem.
3. Restate the problem in various ways.
4. Ask someone to help you with parts of the problem that are especially difficult.
5. Ask "What if" questions to come up with possible solutions. Test each of these solutions.
6. Define the key terms or concepts involved in the problem.
7. Use general thinking strategies such as diagramming, freewriting, clustering, or brainstorming.
8. Use means/ends analysis. That is, at each step in the solution, compare where you are to where you want to be.

**PURPOSE** *n.*   The *purpose* is the goal, or aim, of a literary work. When you speak or write, your purpose may be to tell a story, to describe, to explain or inform, to persuade, or to entertain. Of course, some literary works serve more than one purpose. For example, in "I Have a Dream," on page 499, Martin Luther King, Jr. both explains his vision of the future and attempts to persuade

others to share that vision.
See *Main Idea.*

**REALISTIC DETAILS/FANTASTIC DETAILS** *n. phrases* A *realistic detail* is one that is drawn from actual or possible experience; a *fantastic detail* is one that is not based on actual experience but is improbable or imaginary. Writers of fiction and poetry use realistic details to create the feeling that their creations might exist or happen in real life. Writers use fantastic details to heighten the reader's interest or to engage the reader's imagination. Edgar Allan Poe's "The Raven," on page 563, makes use both of realistic details, such as darkness and the rustling of curtains, and of fantastic details, such as a raven flying into a room and repeating the word "Nevermore" over and over. The realistic details help to create a believable and scary setting. The fantastic details help to heighten the ominous mood.

**REASON** *n.* A *reason* is a statement given in support of some conclusion. The term *reason* is also used to refer to the human ability to think logically and rationally.
See *Argument* and *Conclusion.*

**SOURCE** *n.* A *source* is anything from which ideas and information are taken. Writers draw on many sources, including their own experiences, other people, books, magazines, newspapers, movies, television, computerized information services, and reference works such as encyclopedias, dictionaries, almanacs, and atlases. Whenever you use a source in your own writing, you should credit the source by means of footnotes, endnotes, or in-text documentation.

Sources vary greatly in quality. The best sources are ones that are unbiased, authoritative, and up-to-date. Generally speaking, *firsthand sources,* such as eyewitness accounts or your own direct observations, are to be preferred to *secondhand sources,* such as statements

made about other people's firsthand experiences. Sally Ride's "Single Room, Earth View," on page 517, is a firsthand source of information about space travel. An article about Sally Ride's space travels, written by someone else, would be a secondhand source.

**STEREOTYPE** *n.* A *stereotype* is a fixed or conventional notion or characterization. The mad scientist, the macho football player, and the beautiful princess are all stereotypes. Most stereotypes, when applied to actual people, are misleading or false. For example, people often characterize teenagers as being careless drivers, loving rock and roll music, and so forth. However, these things are not true of all teenagers, and the stereotype thus leads to unfair or absurd conclusions. Generally speaking, stereotypes are to be avoided whenever possible.

Short story writers sometimes make use of stereotypes because they have very little space in which to develop their characters fully. However, even in works of fiction, stereotyping can be dangerous because it can lead to unwarranted conclusions—to overgeneralizations about groups of people.
See *Generalization.*

**SUBJECTIVE** *adj.* Something is *subjective* if it is based on personal experiences or feelings rather than on objective reality. The responses that a reader has when reading a literary work are subjective. Another reader will not necessarily have the same responses. Opinions that people express about literary works are also often subjective. Other people might agree or disagree with them. When a reader interprets or evaluates a literary work, one of his or her tasks is to find objective, or factual, evidence to support subjective responses. For example, a reader of William Wordsworth's "I Wandered Lonely as a Cloud," on page 628, might have a subjective experience of peacefulness and tranquility after reading the poem. If so, the reader should then try to identify the elements of the poem that caused this response.

Writers often try to re-create subjective experiences in their works. Sometimes they describe a character's subjective feelings directly, saying, for example, that a character is depressed or joyful or angry. At other times a character's subjective state will be implied by details such as what the character sees, says, or does.

See *Objective*.

**SUMMARIZE** *v.* To *summarize* something is to restate it briefly in other words. For example, a very brief summary of *Romeo and Juliet* might read as follows:

> Romeo and Juliet belong to families that are feuding with each other. Despite this feud, they meet, fall in love, and are married in secret.

However, their love is doomed because of the feud and because of their own impulsiveness. To avoid another marriage arranged by her family, Juliet takes a potion that makes her appear to be dead. Thinking that Juliet is dead, Romeo kills himself. Juliet, on discovering what Romeo has done, kills herself as well. Thus the play points out the dire consequences of traditional enmity, or hatred, between groups.

**SUPPORT** *v.* To *support* a statement is to provide evidence for it.

See *Evidence*.

**TIME ORDER** *n. phrase* *Time order* is organization by order of occurrence. In most novels, plays, short stories, and narrative poems, events are presented in time order. Time order is also used in some nonfiction works such as memoirs, biographies, and autobiographies. Another name for time order is *chronological order*.

# GLOSSARY

## READING THE GLOSSARY ENTRIES

The words in this glossary are from selections appearing in your textbook. Each entry in the glossary contains the following parts:

**1. Entry Word.** This word appears at the beginning of the entry, in boldface type.

**2. Pronunciation.** The symbols in parentheses tell how the entry word is pronounced. If a word has more than one possible pronunciation, the most common of these pronunciations is given first.

**3. Part of Speech.** Appearing after the pronunciation, in italics, is an abbreviation that tells the part of speech of the entry word. The following abbreviations have been used:

**n.** noun     **p.** pronoun   **v.** verb
**adj.** adjective  **adv.** adverb  **conj.** conjunction

**4. Definition.** This part of the entry follows the part-of-speech abbreviation and gives the meaning of the entry word as used in the selection in which it appears.

## KEY TO PRONUNCIATION SYMBOLS USED IN THE GLOSSARY

The following symbols are used in the pronunciations that follow the entry words:

| Symbol | Key Words | Symbol | Key Words |
|---|---|---|---|
| a | asp, fat, parrot | b | bed, fable, dub |
| ā | ape, date, play | d | dip, beadle, had |
| ä | ah, car, father | f | fall, after, off |
| | | g | get, haggle, dog |
| e | elf, ten, berry | h | he, ahead, hotel |
| ē | even, meet, money | j | joy, agile, badge |
| | | k | kill, tackle, bake |
| i | is, hit, mirror | l | let, yellow, ball |
| ī | ice, bite, high | m | met, camel, trim |
| | | n | not, flannel, ton |
| ō | open, tone, go | p | put, apple, tap |
| ô | all, horn, law | r | red, port, dear |
| o͞o | ooze, tool, crew | s | sell, castle, pass |
| o͝o | look, pull, moor | t | top, cattle, hat |
| yo͞o | use, cute, few | v | vat, hovel, have |
| yo͝o | united, cure, globule | w | will, always, swear |
| oi | oil, point, toy | y | yet, onion, yard |
| ou | out, crowd, plow | z | zebra, dazzle, haze |
| u | up, cut, color | ch | chin, catcher, arch |
| ur | urn, fur, deter | sh | she, cushion, dash |
| | | th | thin, nothing, truth |
| ə | a in ago | t͟h | then, father, lathe |
| | e in agent | zh | azure, leisure |
| | i in sanity | ŋ | ring, anger, drink |
| | o in comply | ' | [indicates that a |
| | u in focus | | following l or n is a |
| ər | perhaps, murder | | syllabic consonant, as in |
| | | | able (ā' b'l)] |

This pronunciation key is from *Webster's New World Dictionary*, Second College Edition. Copyright © 1986 by Simon & Schuster. Used by permission.

## A

**abashed** (ə basht') *adj.* Ill-at-ease; ashamed
**aberration** (ab' ər ā' shən) *n.* Mental derangement
**abhor** (əb hôr') *v.* Detest; intensely dislike
**abhorrence** (əb hôr' əns) *n.* Hatred and disgust
**abolitionist** (ab' ə lish' ən ist) *n.* Person in favor of doing away with slavery in the United States
**abstracted** (ab strak' tid) *adj.* Absent-minded
**adjure** (ə joor') *v.* To appeal to
**admonition** (ad' mə nish' ən) *n.* A warning
**advise** (əd vīz') *v.* To consult
**aesthetic** (es thet' ik) *adv.* Sensitive to art and beauty
**agile** (aj' əl) *adj.* Quick and easy of movement
**ague** (ā' gyo͞o) *n.* Chills and fever
**alleviate** (ə lē' vē āt) *v.* To lessen; relieve
**allude** (ə lo͞od') *n.* To refer to indirectly
**altimeter** (al tim' ə tər) *n.* An instrument for measuring the height of an aircraft above the surface of the earth or the sea
**amber** (am' bər) *n.* A yellowish resin used in jewelry
**ambiguity** (am' bə gyo͞o' ə tē) *n.* A statement or event whose meaning is unclear
**ambrosia** (am brō' zhə) *n.* Food of the gods
**ambrosial** (am brō' zhəl) *adj.* Like ambrosia, the delicious food of the Greek and Roman gods
**amphitheater** (am' fə thē' ə ter) *n.* An open space surrounded by rising rings of seats
**anathema** (ə nath' ə mə) *n.* Something greatly detested
**anguish** (an' gwish) *n.* Great suffering, as from worry or pain
**anomalous** (ə näm' ə ləs) *adj.* Departing from the usual situation
**aphorism** (af' ə rizm) *n.* A short, pointed sentence expressing a wise or clever observation or truth
**ardor** (är' dər) *n.* Emotional warmth; passion
**arpeggio** (är pej' ō) *n.* The notes of a chord played one after the other instead of together
**arrogant** (ar' ə gənt) *adj.* Proud; haughty
**arroyo** (ə roi' ō) *n.* A dry gully
**articulate** (är tik' yə lit) *adj.* Expressing oneself well
**asafetida** (as' ə fet' ə də) *n.* A bad-smelling substance from certain plants, used as medicine
**assiduity** (as' ə dyo͞o' ə tē) *n.* Hard work and perseverance
**asthma** (az' mə) *n.* A disease accompanied by difficulty in breathing
**astrakhan** (as' trə kan') *n.* Fur made from young lambs
**astuteness** (ə sto͞ot' nis) *n.* Shrewdness
**atoll** (a' tôl) *n.* A ring-shaped coral island
**audacious** (ô dā' shəs) *adv.* Brave; without fear
**augment** (ôg ment') *v.* To enlarge; increase
**avail** (ə vāl') *v.* To be of help
**avarice** (av' ə ris) *n.* Greed
**averse** (ə vurs') *adj.* Opposed to
**aversion** (ə vur' zhən) *n.* An intense dislike

**awe** (ô)   *n.* A mixed feeling of fear and wonder
**azure** (azh′ ər)   *adj.* Blue


## B

**balalaika** (bal′ ə līk′ ə)   *n.* A Russian stringed instrument somewhat like a guitar
**bamboozle** (bam bōō′ z′l)   *v.* To trick
**baritone** (bar′ ə tōn′)   *n.* A deep-toned male voice between a bass and a tenor
**barre** (bär)   *n.* A handrail held onto while doing ballet exercises
**bask** (bask)   *v.* To warm oneself pleasantly as in sunlight
**battery** (bat′ ə rē)   *n.* A mound of earth on which cannons are placed
**beached** (bē cht)   *adj.* Washed up and lying on a beach
**beguile** (bi gīl′)   *v.* To trick
**bellows** (bel′ ōz)   *n.* A device for blowing air on a fire
**bemuse** (bi myōōz′)   *v.* To stupefy or muddle
**benison** (ben′ ə z′n)   *n.* A blessing
**bereft** (bi reft′)   *adj.* Left in a sad and lonely state
**billet** (bil′ it)   *n.* A position, job
**bizarre** (bi zär′)   *adj.* Odd in appearance
**bland** (bland)   *adj.* 1. Pleasantly smooth; agreeable 2. In a mild and soothing manner
**blight** (blīt)   *n.* 1. Anything that destroys 2. Plant diseases that result in the death of leaves or whole plants
**bliss** (blis)   *n.* Great joy or happiness
**block** (bläk)   *n.* A pulley
**bluebottle** (bloō bät′ ′l)   *n.* A kind of fly
**bluster** (blus′ tər)   *v.* To speak in a noisy, swaggering manner
**bodice** (bäd′ is)   *n.* The upper part of a woman's dress
**bole** (bōl)   *n.* A tree trunk
**bonny** (bän′ ē)   *adj.* Pretty
**boor** (boōr)   *n.* A rude, unpleasant person
**bowler** (bōl′ ər)   *n.* A derby hat
**brace** (brās)   *n.* A pair
**bravado** (brə vä′ dō)   *n.* Pretended courage
**brazen** (brā′ z′n)   *adj.* Made of brass: having the sound of brass
**brewery** (broō′ ər ē)   *n.* An establishment where beer and similar beverages are made
**bristle** (bris′ ′l)   *v.* To become tense with fear or anger
**brood** (broōd)   *v.* To think about something in a troubled way
**brougham** (broōm)   *n.* A horse-drawn carriage
**brusquely** (brusk′ lē)   *adv.* In an abrupt and curt manner
**Byronic** (bī rän′ ik)   *adj.* Romantic, like the dashing British poet Lord Byron (1788–1824)


## C

**cairn** (kern)   *n.* A conical heap of stones built as a monument
**capon** (kā′ pän)   *n.* A roasted chicken
**carboy** (kär′ boi)   *n.* A large glass bottle enclosed in basketwork to prevent it from breaking
**cascade** (kas kād′)   *n.* A waterfall
**cashier** (kash ir′)   *v.* To dishonorably discharge

**catacomb** (kat′ ə kōm′)   *n.* Any of a series of vaults or passages in an underground burial place
**cataract** (kat′ ə rakt)   *n.* A large waterfall
**caul** (kôl)   *n.* The membrane enclosing a baby at birth
**causeway** (kôz′ wā)   *n.* A raised path or road across wet ground
**celestial** (sə les′ chəl)   *adj.* Of heaven; divine
**cellulose** (sel′ yoo lōs′)   *n.* The chief substance composing the cell walls or fibers of all plant tissue
**censer** (sen′ sər)   *n.* A container for burning incense
**censure** (sen′ shər)   *n.* Strong disapproval
**chagrin** (shə grin′)   *n.* Annoyance at a disappointment
**chalice** (chal′ is)   *n.* A cup or goblet
**challis** (shal′ ē)   *n.* A soft, lightweight fabric, usually printed with a design
**chaste** (chāst)   *adj.* Pure or clean in style; not ornate
**chattel** (chat′ ′l)   *n.* A movable item of personal property
**cherish** (cher′ ish)   *v.* To hold dear; feel love for
**chic** (shēk)   *n.* Fashionable
**chronic** (krän′ ik)   *adj.* Constant
**cipher** (sī′ fər)   *v.* To do arithmetic
**cirrus** (sir′ əs)   *adj.* Feathery
**cleave** (klēv)   *v.* Split
**clerk** (klurk)   *n.* An official who has minor duties in a church
**cloister** (klois′ tər)   *n.* A place devoted to religious seclusion
**coarse** (kôrs)   *adj.* Rough; crude; unrefined
**collaborate** (kə lab′ ə rāt′)   *v.* To work together
**collaborator** (kə lab′ ə rāt′ ər)   *n.* A person who helps an enemy invader of his or her country
**collation** (kä lā′ shən)   *n.* A light meal
**combatant** (käm′ bə tənt)   *adj.* Prepared for fighting
**compel** (kəm pel′)   *v.* To force
**compilation** (käm′ pə lā′ shən)   *n.* Making collections or anthologies
**complacent** (kəm plās′ ′nt)   *adj.* Self-satisfied
**comply** (kəm plī′)   *v.* To act as requested
**condescend** (kän′ də send′)   *v.* To lower oneself to another's level
**condescending** (kän′ də sen′ diŋ)   *adj.* Characterized by looking down on someone
**condolence** (kən dō′ ləns)   *n.* An expression of sympathy with a grieving person
**confidant** (kän′ fə dant′)   *n.* A close friend to whom one tells secrets
**conglomerate** (kən gläm′ ə rāt′)   *adj.* Whole made up of parts (usually a noun)
**conjecture** (kən jek′ chər)   *n.* A guess based on incomplete information
**connoisseurship** (kän′ ə sur′ ship)   *n.* Expert judgment
**conspire** (kən spīr′)   *v.* To plan and act together secretly, especially to commit a crime
**consternation** (kän stər nā′ shən)   *n.* Great fear or shock that confuses or bewilders
**contempt** (kən tempt′)   *n.* 1. The feeling or attitude toward a person one considers unworthy 2. Scorn; disrespect
**contrail** (kän′ trāl)   *n.* The white trail of condensed water vapor that sometimes form in the wake of aircraft
**conundrum** (kə nun′ drəm)   *n.* A puzzling question or problem

**cornice**  (kôr′ nis)  *n.* A horizontal projection along the top of a wall or building

**corroborate**  (kə räb′ ə rāt′)  *v.* To confirm

**cosmopolite**  (käz măp′ ə līt′)  *n.* A person at home in all parts of the world

**countenance**  (koun′ tə nəns)  *n.* Facial appearance

**countinghouse**  (koun′ tiŋ hous′)  *n.* An office where a firm keeps business records and handles correspondence

**cowling**  (kou′ liŋ)  *n.* A detachable metal cover for an airplane engine

**cravat**  (krə vat′)  *n.* A necktie

**craven**  (krā′ vən)  *n.* A coward (usually an adjective)

**credential**  (kri den′ shəl)  *n.* A paper that shows a person's credits and qualifications

**creditor**  (kred′ it ər)  *n.* A person to whom money is owed

**creed**  (krēd)  *n.* A statement of belief

**crepe**  (krāp)  *n.* A thin, black cloth worn to show mourning

**crepitation**  (krep′ ə tā′ shən)  *n.* A crackling sound

**crochet**  (krō shā′)  *n.* A kind of needlework

**cuirass**  (kwi ras′)  *n.* Armor for the upper body

**cunning**  (kun′ iŋ)  *n.* Cleverness; slyness

**cupidity**  (kyoo pid′ ə tē)  *n.* Greed

**D**

**dainty**  (dān′ tē)  *adj.* Delicately pretty

**dauntless**  (dônt′ lis)  *adj.* Unable to be intimidated

**deacon**  (dēk′ 'n)  *n.* A church officer who helps the minister

**debacle**  (di bäk′ 'l)  *n.* A bad defeat

**déclassé**  (dā′ klä sā′)  *adj.* Lowered in social status

**declivity**  (di kliv′ ə tē)  *n.* A downward slope

**deem**  (dēm)  *v.* To consider

**defer**  (di fur′)  *v.* To put off until a future time

**deferential**  (def ə ren′ sh'l)  *adj.* Very respectful

**defraud**  (di frôd)  *v.* To cheat

**dejection**  (di jek′ shən)  *n.* Lowness of spirits; depression

**deleterious**  (del′ ə tir′ ē əs)  *adj.* Injurious; harmful to health or well-being

**delicacy**  (del′ i kə sē)  *n.* A regard for what is proper

**delirious**  (di lir′ ē əs)  *adj.* In a state of temporary mental confusion, characterized by delusions and incoherence

**dell**  (del)  *n.* A small secluded valley

**deportment**  (di pôrt′ mənt)  *n.* A way of holding oneself or behaving

**depose**  (di pōz′)  *v.* To testify

**depot**  (dē′ pō)  *n.* A railroad or bus station

**depreciate**  (di prē′ shē āt′)  *v.* To reduce in value

**derisive**  (di rī′ siv)  *adj.* Scornful; mocking

**descant**  (des′ kant)  *n.* In two-part singing, the added melody sung above the main theme

**descry**  (di skrī′)  *v.* To catch sight of

**desiccate**  (des′ i kāt′)  *v.* To dry up

**desolate**  (des′ ə lit)  *adj.* Deserted, abandoned

**despotic**  (de spät′ ik)  *adj.* Absolute; unlimited

**desultory**  (des′'l tôr′ ē)  *adj.* Random

**determinate**  (di tur′ mi nit)  *adj.* Final

**dexterous**  (dek′ strəs)  *adj.* With skillful use of the hands

**diadem**  (dī′ ə dem)  *n.* A crown

**diffidence**  (dif′ ə dəns)  *n.* Shyness; uncertainty

**diffuse**  (di fyoos′)  *v.* To spread out

**diffuse**  (di fyooz′)  *adj.* Spread out; not concentrated

**dire**  (dīr)  *adv.* Dreadful; terrible

**discomfiture**  (dis kum′ fi chər)  *n.* Unease; confusion

**disconsolately**  (dis kän′ sə lit lē)  *adj.* Unhappily; sadly

**discreet**  (dis krēt′)  *adj.* Tactful; respectful

**disdain**  (dis dān′)  *v.* To reject with scorn

**disdainful**  (dis dān′ fəl)  *adj.* Scornful

**disheveled**  (di shev′ 'ld)  *adj.* Disarranged and untidy; tousled

**disillusionment**  (dis i loo′ zhən mənt)  *n.* Disappointment

**dismal**  (diz′ m'l)  *adj.* Gloomy; depressing

**dismay**  (dis mā′)  *v.* To discourage; make afraid

**disparity**  (dis par′ ə tē)  *n.* Condition of inequality

**dispatch**  (dis pach′)  *v.* To finish quickly

**dissemble**  (di sem′ b'l)  *v.* To conceal with false appearances; disguise

**dissolution**  (dis′ ə loo′ shən)  *n.* Disintegration; death

**ditty**  (dit′ ē)  *n.* A song

**divers**  (dī′ vərz)  *adj.* Several, various

**divining**  (də vīn′ iŋ)  *v.* Guessing

**docket**  (däk′ it)  *v.* To label

**doff**  (däf)  *v.* To lift

**doggerel**  (dôg′ ər əl)  *adj.* Dull verse that sounds like a jingle

**dowdy**  (dou′ dē)  *adj.* Shabby

**dowry**  (dou′ rē)  *n.* The property that a woman brings to her husband at marriage

**droll**  (drōl)  *adj.* Comic and amusing in an odd way

**dubious**  (doo′ bē əs)  *adj.* Uncertain; doubtful

**E**

**ebb**  (eb)  *v.* To lessen; weaken

**ebony**  (eb′ ə nē)  *n.* A hard dark wood used for furniture

**ecclesiastical**  (i klē′ zē as′ ti k'l)  *adj.* Associated with the church

**echo**  (e′ kō)  *n.* The repetition of a sound caused by reflection of sound waves

**ecstatic**  (ek stat′ ik)  *adj.* In a state of extreme emotion

**eddy**  (ed′ ē)  *n.* A circular current

**eerie**  (ir′ ē)  *adj.* Mysterious

**elation**  (i lā′ shən)  *n.* A feeling of great joy

**elegy**  (el′ ə jē)  *n.* A song of mourning

**eloquence**  (el′ ə kwəns)  *n.* Speech that is vivid, forceful, graceful and persuasive

**emanate**  (em′ ə nāt)  *v.* To come from a source, as fragrance

**eminence**  (em′ ə nəns)  *n.* A high or lofty place

**encroaching**  (in krōch′ iŋ)  *adj.* Intruding in a gradual or sneaking way

**enigmatic**  (en′ ig mat′ ik)  *adj.* Baffling; perplexing

**enjoin**  (in join′)  *v.* To order

**entrails**  (en′ trālz)  *n.* Internal organs, specifically intestines; guts

**enzyme**  (en′ zīm)  *n.* Any of various proteinlike substances, formed in plant and animal cells, that act to start or speed up specific chemical reactions

**euphony**  (yoo′ fə nē)  *n.* Pleasing sound

**evanesce**  (ev ə nes′)  *v.* To fade away

**ewer** (yo͞o′ ər)   *n.* A large water pitcher

**exacting** (ig zakt′ iŋ)   *adj.* Demanding

**exalt** (ig zôlt′)   *v.* To lift up

**exhilarated** (ig zil′ ə rāt′ əd)   *adj.* Lively

**exile** (eg′ zīl)   *n.* Enforced removal from one's native land

**exorbitant** (ig zôr′ bə tənt)   *adj.* Exceeding the appropriate limits

**expatriate** (eks pā′ trē āt)   *v.* To exile

**expectorate** (ik spek′ tə rāt)   *v.* To spit

**expediency** (ik spē′ dē ən sē)   *n.* Practicality

**expostulation** (ik späs ċ/ʰə lā′ sʰ'n)   *n.* Objection; complaint

**extract** (ik strakt′)   *v.* To draw out with special effort

**extrapolate** (ik strap′ ′ə lāt)   *v.* To arrive at a conclusion by making inferences based on known facts

**extricate** (eks′ trə kāt)   *v.* To free or disentangle

**exuberant** (ig zo͞o′ bər ənt)   *adj.* Very great; extreme


**F**

**fain** (fān)   *adj.* Gladly; eagerly

**fakir** (fə kir′)   *n.* A Moslem or Hindu beggar who claims to perform miracles

**fanatical** (fə nat′ ik'l)   *adj.* Unreasonably enthusiastic

**fandango** (fan daŋ′ gō)   *n.* A lively Spanish dance

**farthing** (fär′ tʰiŋ)   *n.* A small British coin equal to one fourth of a penny

**feign** (fān)   *v.* To pretend

**felicitous** (fə lis′ ə təs)   *adj.* Suitable to the occasion

**fervent** (fʉr′ vənt)   *adj.* Burning; passionate

**fester** (fes′ tər)   *v.* To form pus

**fetid** (fet′ id)   *adj.* Rancid; rank; smelly

**fetter** (fet′ ər)   *v.* To encircle with metal fasteners

**fickle** (fik′ əl)   *adj.* Changeable

**flag** (flag)   *v.* To grow weak or tired

**flagon** (flag′ ən)   *n.* A pitcher for water or wine

**flirt** (flʉrt)   *n.* A quick, uneven movement

**flout** (flout)   *v.* To show scorn or contempt for

**fond** (fänd)   *adj.* Tender and affectionate, with a possible meaning of foolish as well

**foreshadowing** (fôr sʰad′ ō iŋ)   *n.* A sign of something to come

**formality** (fôr mal′ ə tē)   *n.* Established rules or customs

**formidable** (fôr′ mə də b'l)   *adj.* 1. Awe-inspiring 2. Causing fear or dread

**forsaken** (far sāk′ ən)   *adj.* Abandoned; without hope

**fortnight** (fôrt′ nīt′)   *n.* Two weeks

**fountainhead** (foun′ t'n hed′)   *n.* Source

**fray** (frā)   *n.* A noisy fight

**fungus** (fuŋ′ gəs)   *n.* A parasite such as mold, mildew, and mushroom, which feeds on dead organic material and lacks chlorophyll

**furl** (fʉrl)   *v.* To roll up and tie

**furtive** (fʉr′ tiv)   *adv.* Preventing observation; sneaky

**futile** (fyo͞ot′'l)   *adj.* Useless; hopeless


**G**

**gallant** (gal′ ənt)   *adj.* Brave and noble

**galley** (gal′ ē)   *n.* A large rowboat

**galliard** (gal′ yərd)   *n.* A lively French dance

**garbling** (gär′ b'liŋ)   *n.* Confusion, mix-up

**gargoyle** (gär′ goil)   *n.* A strange and distorted animal form projecting from a building

**gaunt** (gônt)   *adj.* Looking grim, forbidding, or desolate; thin and bony

**gemmary** (jem′ ə rē′)   *n.* Knowledge of precious stones

**genesis** (jen′ ə sis)   *n.* Birth; origin; beginning

**genus** (jē′ nəs)   *n.* Main subdivision of a family of closely related species

**ghoul** (go͞ol)   *n.* An evil spirit that robs graves

**gilded** (gild′ əd)   *adj.* Overlaid with gold; made bright and attractive

**gingham** (giŋ′ əm)   *adj.* A cotton cloth, usually woven in stripes, checks, or plaids (most often, a noun)

**glee** (glē)   *n.* Lively joy; merriment

**glisten** (glis′ 'n)   *v.* To shine or sparkle with reflected light

**glower** (glou′ər)   *v.* To stare with sullen anger; scowl

**gorge** (gôrj)   *n.* A voracious, consuming mouth

**gossamer** (gäs′ ə mər)   *adj.* Light, thin, and delicate

**Gothic** (gät/ʰ ik)   *adj.* A style of architecture that makes use of pointed arches

**grievance** (grē′ vəns)   *n.* An injustice; complaint

**grotesque** (grō tesk′)   *adj.* Having a fantastic design

**guillotine** (gil′ lə tēn′)   *n.* An instrument that beheads a victim with a falling blade

**guinea** (gin′ ē)   *n.* A gold coin worth about one pound

**gunwale** (gun′'l)   *n.* The upper edge of the side of a boat

**guy** (gī)   *adj.* Used for steadying or guiding


**H**

**haggard** (hag′ ərd)   *adj.* Worn, as from lack of sleep; gaunt

**hamlet** (ham′ lit)   *n.* A very small village

**hapless** (hap′ lis)   *adj.* Unfortunate; luckless

**haughty** (hôt′ ē)   *adj.* Arrogant

**hawker** (hôk′ ər)   *n.* A peddler

**hecatomb** (hek′ ə tōm)   *n.* A large-scale sacrifice; often the slaughter of 100 cattle at one time

**heifer** (hef′ ər)   *n.* A young cow

**heliotrope** (hē′ lē ə trōp′)   *n.* A sweet-smelling plant

**hellions** (hel′ yənz)   *n.* Mischievous troublemakers

**herculean** (hər′ kyə lē′ ən)   *adj.* Of or relating to Hercules or his feats

**heretic** (her′ ə tik)   *n.* One who holds to a belief opposed to the established teachings of a church

**hermitage** (hʉr′ mit ij)   *n.* A secluded and solitary dwelling

**hieroglyph** (hī′ ər ə glif′)   *n.* A mark that looks like those used in the ancient Egyptian writing system

**hoax** (hōks)   *n.* A deceitful trick; fraud

**hose** (hōz)   *n.* Stockings

**host** (hōst)   *n.* A great number

**humility** (hyo͞o mil′ ə tē)   *n.* Humbleness; lack of pride

**hypothetical** (hī pə tʰet′ i k'l)   *adj.* Assumed; supposed

**hydroplane** (hī′ drə plān)   *n.* A seaplane


**I**

**idyll** (ī′ d'l)   *n.* A romantic scene, usually in the country

**idyllic** (ī dil′ ik)   *adj.* Pleasing and simple; peaceful

**imminent** (im′ ə nent)   *adj.* Likely to happen soon

**immolation**  (im' ə lā' sʰən)   n. Sacrifice
**immutable**  (i myo͞ot' ə b'l)   adj. Never changing
**impassively**  (im pas' iv lē)   adv. In an unfeeling or unemotional manner
**impediment**  (im ped' ə mənt)   n. An obstruction; hindrance
**imperious**  (im pir' ē əs)   adj. Overbearing; arrogant; domineering
**impertinence**  (im pʉrt''n əns)   n. Examples of insolence or lack of respect
**imprecation**  (im' prə kā' sʰən)   n. A curse
**impudence**  (im' pyo͞o dəns)   n. Disrespect
**impunity**  (im pyo͞o' nə tē)   n. Freedom from punishment
**inaccessible**  (in ək ses' ə b'l)   adj. Impossible to reach or enter
**inarticulate**  (in är tik' yə lit)   adj. Not able to speak well
**incantation**  (in' kan tā sʰən)   n. A spell
**incongruity**  (in' kən gro͞o' ə tē)   n. The quality of being out of place
**incredulity**  (in' krə do͞o' lə tē)   n. The inability to believe
**indelible**  (in del' ə b'l)   adj. Cannot be erased
**indenture**  (in den' chər)   n. A contract binding an apprentice to a master
**indignation**  (in' dig nā' sʰən)   n. Anger resulting from injustice
**indolently**  (in' də lənt lē)   adj. Lazily; idly
**indulge**  (in dulj')   v. To accept in a belittling way
**inexplicable**  (in eks' pli kə b'l)   adv. Unexplainable
**infallibility**  (in fal' ə bil' ə tē)   n. The condition of being unable to fail
**in lieu of**  (in lo͞o əv)   adj. Instead of
**insidious**  (in sid' ē əs)   adj. Characterized by treachery
**instigate**  (in' stə gāt')   v. To urge on; stir up
**integrity**  (in teg' rə tē)   n. The state of being of sound moral principle; uprightness; honesty; sincerity
**interment**  (in tʉr' mənt)   n. Burial
**interminable**  (in tʉr' mi nə b'l)   adj. Lasting or seeming to last forever
**intimate**  (in' tə māt)   v. To hint or imply
**intricate**  (in' tri kit)   adj. Complex
**introspective**  (in' trə spekt' iv)   adj. Causing one to look into one's own thoughts and feelings
**inviolable**  (in vī' ə lə b'l)   adj. Not to be changed
**ire**  (īr)   n. Anger
**iridescent**  (ir' ə des' 'nt)   adj. Having shifting, rainbowlike colors
**irresolute**  (i rez' ə lo͞ot)   adj. Unsure; indecisive


**J**

**jerkin**  (jʉr' kin)   n. A short, closefitting jacket
**jocund**  (jak' ənd)   adj. Cheerful
**journeyman**  (jʉr' nē mən)   n. A person who has learned a trade but still works for a master
**judicious**  (jo͞o dish' əs)   adj. Showing good judgment


**K**

**kimono**  (kə mō' nə)   n. A loose-fitting gown, part of the traditional costume of Japanese men and women
**kindling**  (kin' dliŋ)   n. Bits of dry wood for starting a fire

**kine**  (kīn)   n. cattle
**kinsman**  (kinz' mən)   n. A relative
**knouter**  (nout' ər)   n. Someone who beats criminals with a leather whip, or knout
**kvass**  (kväs)   n. A Russian drink made from rye or barley


**L**

**laconic**  (lə kän' ik)   adj. Not speaking much
**lagoon**  (lə go͞on')   n. Water enclosed by a circular coral reef
**lament**  (lə ment')   n. A song of mourning
**lamentable**  (lam' ən tə b'l)   adj. Distressing; sad
**lampetia**  (lam pē' sʰə)   n. A nymph
**languid**  (laŋ' gwid)   adj. Drooping; weak
**languor**  (laŋ' gər)   n. A lack of vigor; weakness; sluggishness
**lascar**  (läs' kər)   n. An Oriental sailor, especially a native of India
**lasso**  (las' ō)   v. Wrap around
**latent**  (lāt''nt)   adj. Hidden
**lateral**  (lat' ər əl)   adj. On the side
**lattice**  (lat' is)   n. A framework of wood or metal
**league**  (lēg)   n. Three miles
**lee**  (lē)   n. An area sheltered from the wind
**legion**  (lē' jən)   n. A group of soldiers
**lend**  (lend)   v. To pass along, as from parent to child
**lenticular**  (len tik' yoo lər)   adj. Shaped like a lentil bean
**lethargic**  (li tʰär' jik)   adj. Drowsy; without energy
**lethe**  (lē' tʰē)   n. Oblivion; forgetfulness
**levitation**  (lev' ə tā' sʰən)   n. Remaining in air with no physical support
**libation**  (lī bā' sʰən)   n. Wine or other liquids poured upon the ground as a sacrifice
**lift**  (lift)   n. British for "elevator"
**limekiln**  (līm' kiln')   n. A furnace in which limestone is burned to make lime, a substance used in mortar and cement
**lithe**  (lītʰ)   adj. Supple; limber
**livery**  (liv' ər ē)   n. Servants' uniforms
**loathsome**  (lōtʰ' səm)   adj. Disgusting
**lore**  (lôr)   n. Knowledge of a particular subject
**lozenge**  (läz''nj)   n. A diamond-shaped object
**lugger**  (lug' ər)   n. A ship equipped with a four-sided sail


**M**

**maelstrom**  (māl' strəm)   n. A large violent whirlpool
**magnanimous**  (mag nan' ə məs)   adj. Noble in mind; high-souled, especially in overlooking injury or insult
**malaria**  (mə ler' ē ə)   n. A disease associated with the tropics that causes chills and fever
**mammoth**  (mam' ətʰ)   adj. Enormous
**marauder**  (mə rôd' ər)   n. A raider; one who takes goods by force
**martial**  (mär' sʰəl)   adj. Military
**masochistic**  (mas' ə kiz' tik)   adj. Getting pleasure from pain
**maudlin**  (môd' lin)   adj. Tearfully sentimental from too much liquor
**maunder**  (môn' dər)   v. To talk in an unconnected way

**medley** (med′ lē)  *n.* A mixture of things not usually found together

**melancholy** (mel′ ən käl′ ē)  *adj.* Sad; gloomy

**melodramatically** (mel′ ə drə mat′ ik lē)  *adv.* In an extravagantly emotional manner

**meretricious** (mer′ ə trish′ əs)  *adj.* Attractive in a cheap, flashy way

**mewling** (myōōl′ iŋ)  *v.* Whimpering; crying like a baby

**milieu** (mēl yōō′)  *n.* Environment; setting

**mill-weir** (mil′ wir′)  *n.* A low dam to back up or divert water for a mill

**minuscule** (min′ nus kyōōl)  *adj.* Tiny; very small

**misdemeanor** (mis′ di mēn′ ər)  *n.* A minor offense

**molder** (mold′ ər)  *v.* To crumble into dust; decay

**monody** (män′ ə dē)  *n.* A poem of mourning; a steady sound; music in which one instrument or voice is dominant

**mooncalf** (mōōn′ kaf′)  *n.* A foolish young man

**Morgan** (môr′ gən)  *n.* A breed of saddle horse that originated in New England

**motley** (mät′ lē)  *n.* A clown's multicolored costume

**multitudinous** (mul′ tə tōōd′ ′n əs)  *adj.* Very numerous

**muster** (mus′ tər)  *n.* An assembly, especially of soldiers

**muted** (myōōt′ əd)  *adj.* Weaker; less intense

**N**

**naive** (nä ēv′)  *adj.* Unsophisticated

**narcissism** (när′ sə siz′m)  *n.* Egoism; overevaluation of one's own attributes or achievements or those of one's group

**nectar** (nek′ tər)  *n.* Drink of the gods

**newt** (nōōt)  *n.* A salamander

**niche** (nich)  *n.* A recess in a wall

**niter** (nīt′ ər)  *n.* A white or gray mineral

**nocturnal** (näk tur′ n′l)  *adj.* Happening in the night

**noncommissioned** (nän kə mish′ ənd)  *adj.* Referring to enlisted soldiers of a rank no higher than sergeant major

**novice** (näv′ is)  *adj.* A beginner

**O**

**oasis** (ō ā′sis)  *n.* A fertile place in the desert

**obdurate** (äb′dōōr ət)  *adj.* Stubborn; unbending

**obeisance** (ō bā′ s′ns)  *n.* A bow or another sign of respect

**oblation** (ä blā′ shən)  *n.* An offering to a god

**oblivion** (ə bliv′ ē ən)  *n.* Forgetfulness

**obsession** (əb sesh′ ən)  *n.* A compulsive preoccupation with an idea

**obstinate** (äb′ stə nit)  *adj.* Stubborn

**oculist** (äk′ yə list)  *n.* An old-fashioned term for an eye specialist

**offing** (ôf′ iŋ)  *n.* The distant part of the sea visible from the shore

**ominous** (äm′ ə nəs)  *adj.* Threatening; dangerous

**oppression** (ə presh′ ən)  *n.* Keeping others down by the unjust use of power

**oracle** (ôr′ ə k′l)  *n.* A source of wisdom

**ovipositor** (ō′ vi päz′ i tər)  *n.* A tubular structure of many female insects, usually at the end of the abdomen, for depositing eggs

**ozone** (ō′ zōn)  *n.* A form of oxygen with a sharp odor

**P**

**pacific** (pə sif′ ik)  *adj.* Peaceful

**paean** (pē′ ən)  *n.* A song of joy or triumph

**pagan** (pā′ gən)  *n.* One who is not a Christian, a Moslem, or a Jew

**painstakingly** (pānz′ tā′ kiŋ lē)  *adj.* Acting very carefully

**pallid** (pal′ id)  *adj.* Pale

**pallor** (pal′ ər)  *n.* Paleness

**palpable** (pal′ pə b′l)  *adj.* Able to be touched or felt

**palpitate** (pal′ pə tāt′)  *v.* To beat rapidly; throb

**panorama** (pan′ ə ram′ ə)  *n.* An unlimited view in all directions

**pantaloon** (pan′ t′l ōōn′)  *n.* A thin, foolish old man—originally a character in old comedies

**pantomime** (pan′ tə mīm′)  *n.* Wordless actions or gestures as a means of expression

**paradox** (par′ ə däks)  *n.* A contradiction

**paradoxically** (par′ ə däk′ si k′lē)  *adv.* In a way that seems opposite or contradictory

**paralytic** (par ə lit′ ik)  *n.* A paralyzed person

**pard** (pärd)  *n.* A leopard or panther

**parry** (par′ ē)  *v.* To ward off a sword-thrust

**patronage** (pā′ trən ij)  *n.* Encouragement shown to someone inferior

**peacoat** (pē′ kōt′)  *n.* A heavy woolen jacket, often worn by sailors

**pectoral** (pek′ tər əl)  *adj.* Located on the chest

**pensive** (pen′ siv)  *adj.* Thinking deeply

**penury** (pen′ yə rē)  *n.* Extreme poverty

**perennial** (pə ren′ ē əl)  *adj.* Lasting through the year or for a long time

**perfunctory** (pə fuŋk′ tər ē)  *adj.* Routine; superficial

**peridot** (per′ ə dät′)  *n.* A yellowish-green gem

**pernicious** (pər nish′ əs)  *adj.* Causing great injury or ruin

**perplexity** (pər plek′ sə tē)  *n.* State of being confused

**pertly** (purt′ lē)  *adv.* In a saucy manner

**peruse** (pə rōōz′)  *v.* To examine in detail

**perverse** (pər vurs′)  *adj.* Persisting in error

**petrel** (pet′ rəl)  *n.* A small, dark sea bird

**phosphorescence** (fäs′ fə res′ ′ns)  *n.* An emission of light resulting from exposure to radiation

**picturesque** (pik′ chə resk′)  *adj.* Like or suggesting a picture

**pilgrimage** (pil′ grəm ij)  *n.* A journey to a sacred place or shrine; a special trip to a place of personal significance

**pinion** (pin′ yən)  *v.* To confine or shackle

**pipe** (pīp)  *n.* A large barrel

**pirouette** (pir′ ōō wet)  *n.* A rapid turn on one foot or the point of the toe

**placidly** (plas′ id lē)  *adv.* Calmly; quietly

**plaintively** (plān′ tiv lē)  *adj.* Sadly

**plait** (plāt)  *n.* A braid

**plaiting** (plāt′ iŋ)  *n.* Braiding

**plunder** (plun′ dər)  *n.* Goods taken by force; loot

**poacher** (pōch′ ər)  *n.* A person who hunts or fishes illegally on someone else's property

**poise** (poiz)  *v.* To balance, suspend

**pollard** (päl′ ərd)  *n.* A tree with its top branches cut back to the trunk

**postern** (pōs′ tərn)  *n.* Back gate

**pottle** (pät′′l)  *n.* A pot that holds two quarts

**precariously** (pri′ ker′ ē əs lē)  *adj.* Insecurely

**precipitous** (pri sip′ ə təs)  *adj.* Steep; sheer

**preclude** (pri klōōd′)  *v.* To make impossible in advance

**premium** (prē′ mē əm)  *n.* A fee paid by an apprentice to a master

**presentiment** (pri zen′ tə mənt)  *n.* A feeling that something bad will occur

**procure** (prō kyōōr′)  *v.* To get; obtain

**prodigious** (prə dij′ əs)  *adj.* 1. Enormous 2. Wonderful; of great size

**proffered** (präf ərd)  *adj.* Offered (usually a verb)

**profoundly** (prə found′ lē)  *adv.* Deeply and intensely

**proliferate** (prō lif′ ər āt′)  *v.* Grow rapidly

**promissory** (präm′ i sôr′ ē) **notes**  *n.* Written promises to pay back borrowed money

**propriety** (prə prī′ ə tē)  *n.* Proper manner or behavior

**proscribe** (prō skrīb′)  *v.* To banish

**prostrate** (präs′ trāt)  *adj.* Lying face downward

**protozoa** (prōt′ ə zo′ ə)  *n.* Microscopic animals

**providential** (präv′ ə den′ shəl)  *adj.* As if decreed by God

**prow** (prou)  *n.* The forward part of a ship

**prudence** (prōōd′′ns)  *n.* Practical and sound judgment

**pugilist** (pyōō′ jə ləst)  *n.* A fighter; boxer

**pyre** (pīr)  *n.* A pile of wood on which a body is burned at a funeral

## Q

**quaff** (kwäf)  *v.* To drink

**quaint** (kwānt)  *adj.* Strange; unusual

**qualmish** (kwäm′ ish)  *adj.* Slightly ill

**querulous** (kwer′ ə lis)  *adj.* Complaining

## R

**raillery** (rāl′ ər ē)  *n.* Good-natured teasing

**rampage** (ram pāj′)  *v.* To rush about in wild anger

**rancor** (raŋ′ kər)  *n.* Hatred; spite

**rantipole** (ran′ tē pōl)  *n.* A wild and reckless person

**rapier** (rā′ pē ər)  *n.* A slender, two-edged sword with cuplike handle

**ravage** (rav′ ij)  *n.* Ruin; devastating damage

**raveled** (rav′′ld)  *adj.* Untwisted; unwoven

**rawboned** (rô′ bond′)  *adj.* Having little flesh or fat covering the bones; lean

**reciprocate** (ri sip′ rə kāt′)  *v.* Give or feel in return

**reel** (rēl)  *v.* To fall back; stagger

**reiteration** (rē it′ ə rā′ shən)  *n.* Repetition

**remnant** (rem′ nənt)  *n.* Remaining person or thing

**rend** (rend)  *v.* To tear

**repository** (ri päz′ ə tôr′ ē)  *n.* A place for safekeeping

**repress** (ri pres′)  *v.* To keep down; hold back

**resiliency** (ri zil′ yen sē)  *n.* The ability to bounce or spring back

**respite** (res′ pit)  *n.* Rest; relief

**resplendent** (ri splen′ dənt)  *adj.* Shining brightly; full of splendor

**retribution** (ret′ rə byōō′ shən)  *n.* Deserved punishment

**reverence** (rev′ ər əns)  *n.* A curtsy or bow

**rivalry** (rī′ v′l rē)  *n.* Competition

**roan** (rōn)  *n.* A horse of a solid color such as reddish brown or black with a thick sprinkling of white hair

**roebuck** (rō′ buk′)  *n.* A male deer

**rogue** (rōg)  *n.* A repulsive scoundrel

**row** (rou)  *n.* A noisy quarrel

**ruble** (rōō′ b′l)  *n.* A Russian coin

**rueful** (rōō′ fəl)  *adj.* Causing sorrow or pity

## S

**sallow** (sal′ ō)  *adj.* Of a sickly pale-yellowish complexion

**salve** (sav)  *n.* An ointment that soothes or heals skin irritations, burns, or wounds

**samurai** (sam′ ə rī′)  *n.* A member of a military class in feudal Japan who wore two swords

**sanitarium** (san′ ə ter′ ē əm)  *n.* A place where people go to rest and regain their health

**sans** (sanz)  *prep.* Without; lacking

**sash** (sash)  *n.* A sliding window-frame

**saturnalia** (sat′ ər nā′ lē ə)  *n.* An ancient Roman holiday marked by wild celebration

**scaffold** (skaf′ 'ld)  *n.* A raised platform on which criminals are executed

**scruple** (skrōō′ p'l)  *n.* A misgiving about something one feels is wrong

**scythe** (sīth)  *n.* A tool used for cutting down tall grass

**sedative** (sed′ ə tiv)  *n.* Something that soothes or quiets

**sentimental** (sen′ tə men′ t'l)  *adj.* Foolishly emotional

**sepulcher** (sep′ 'l kər)  *n.* A tomb

**serpentine** (sur′ pən tēn)  *n.* A coil of thin paper that unwinds as it is thrown

**settee** (se tē′)  *n.* A small sofa

**settle** (set′ 'l)  *n.* A bench

**shank** (shank)  *n.* A leg

**shrike** (shrīk)  *n.* A shrill-voiced bird that feeds on small animals

**singular** (siŋ′ gyə lər)  *adj.* Extraordinary; rare

**sinister** (sin′ is tər)  *adj.* Threatening harm or evil

**sleight** (slīt) **of hand**  *n.* Skill in deceiving onlookers

**slouching** (slouch′ iŋ)  *adj.* Drooping (usually a verb)

**smiter** (smīt′ ər)  *n.* One who hurts you

**solace** (säl′ is)  *v.* To comfort

**solicitor** (sə lis′ it ər)  *n.* A British lawyer who can assist clients but cannot plead cases in the higher courts

**speculation** (spek yə lā′ shən)  *n.* Consideration of some subject or idea

**speculatively** (spek′ yə lə tiv lē)  *adv.* In a meditative way

**spume** (spyōōm)  *n.* Foam; froth

**squall** (skwôl)  *n.* A brief, violent storm

**stay** (stā)  *n.* A heavy rope or cable used for support

**stateroom** (stāt′ rōōm)  *n.* A private cabin on a ship

**steep** (stēp)  *n.* A mountain slope

**steward** (stōō′ ərd)  *n.* The manager of an estate

**stifling** (stī′ fliŋ)  *adj.* Suffocating

**strenuous** (stren′ yoo wəs)  *adj.* Requiring great effort

**suavity**   (swa′ və tē)   *n.* Graceful politeness
**sublunary**   (sub′ loo ner′ ē)   *adj.* Earthly
**subterfuge**   (sub′ tər fyōōj′)   *n.* A deceptive action
**subtle**   (sut′ 'l)   *adj.* 1. Not obvious; delicately suggestive 2. Small
**succor**   (suk′ ər)   *n.* Aid; help; relief
**suffused**   (sə fyōōzd′)   *adj.* Filled with; spread throughout
**suitor**   (sōōt′ ər)   *n.* A man courting a woman
**sullen**   (sul′ ən)   *adj.* Showing resentment
**sunder**   (sun′ dər)   *v.* To break apart
**sundry**   (sun′ drē)   *adj.* Various; several
**superciliously**   (sōō′ pər sil′ ē əs lē)   *adv.* In a contemptuous or haughty manner
**supple**   (sup′ 'l)   *adj.* Flexible; adaptable
**surcease**   (sur′ sēs)   *n.* End
**surfeited**   (sur′ fit id)   *adj.* Supplied to excess
**surreal**   (sə rē′ əl)   *adj.* Strange
**surrey**   (sur′ ē)   *n.* A light, horse-drawn carriage
**susceptible**   (sə sep′ tə b'l)   *adj.* Receptive

**T**

**tambour**   (tam′ boor)   *n.* A drum
**tantalizingly**   (tan′ tə līz′ iŋ lē)   *adv.* In a teasing or tormenting way
**tartar**   (tär′ tər)   *n.* A ferocious, unmanageable person; stubborn; violent
**tedious**   (tē′ dē əs)   *adj.* Tiresome and boring
**tenor**   (ten′ ər)   *n.* A singer with voice ranging about an octave, or eight full notes, above and below middle C.
**tentative**   (ten′ tə tiv)   *adj.* Done with hesitation
**terrestrial**   (tə res′ trē əl)   *adj.* Of this world; earthly; mundane
**throng**   (throŋ)   *v.* To crowd into
**tintinnabulation**   (tin ti nab yōō lā′ sʰən)   *n.* The ringing of bells
**token**   (tō′ k'n)   *n.* A sign
**tonic**   (tän′ ik)   *adj.* Stimulating; invigorating
**trachoma**   (trə kō′ mə)   *n.* A disease of the eyelid and eyeball
**transgression**   (trans gresʰ′ ən)   *n.* Wrongdoing; sin
**transport**   (trans′ pôrt)   *n.* A strong emotion of joy or delight
**transport**   (trans port′)   *v.* To send out of the country to a colony for prisoners
**treble**   (treb′ 'l)   *n.* A high-pitched voice
**tremulous**   (trem′ yə ləs)   *adj.* Quivering; trembling; shaking; unsteady
**tribunal**   (trī byōō′ n'l)   *n.* Court
**trifle**   (trī′ fəl)   *n.* A small, unimportant thing
**trimmer**   (trim′ ər)   *n.* A person who changes his opinion to suit the circumstances
**truculent**   (truk′ yōō lənt)   *adj.* Savage; cruel
**tumult**   (tōō′ mult)   *n.* A great noise or disturbance; noisy commotion
**tycoon**   (tī kōōn′)   *n.* A wealthy and powerful person
**typhoon**   (tī fōōn′)   *n.* A violent tropical storm

**U**

**undulate**   (un′ joo lāt′)   *v.* To move in waves
**unredressed**   (un ri drest′)   *adj.* Not set right
**unrequited**   (un ri kwīt′ id)   *adj.* Not returned; unreciprocated
**unscrupulous**   (un skrōōp′ yə ləs)   *adj.* Without principles
**unwieldy**   (un wēl′ dē)   *adj.* Awkward; clumsy

**V**

**vanquish**   (vaŋ′ kwisʰ)   *v.* Defeat; conquer
**variable**   (ver′ ē ə b'l)   *adj.* Changeable; inconstant
**varmint**   (vär′ mənt)   *n.* An undesirable or troublesome person
**veery**   (vir′ ē)   *n.* A brown and cream-colored thrush
**venerable**   (ven′ ər ə b'l)   *adj.* Old and respected
**vex**   (veks)   *v.* To annoy
**vial**   (vī əl)   *n.* A small bottle containing medicine or other liquids
**vicarious**   (vī ker′ ē əs)   *adj.* Experiencing something by imagined participation in another's experience
**vigil**   (vij′ əl)   *n.* A watchful staying awake
**vile**   (vīl)   *adj.* Worthless; cheap; low
**visage**   (viz′ ij)   *n.* Face
**vivacious**   (vi vā′ sʰəs)   *adj.* Lively
**vivacity**   (vi vas′ ə tē)   *n.* Liveliness
**volley**   (väl′ ē)   *v.* To fire at the same time
**voluminously**   (və lōō′ mə nəs lē)   *adv.* Fully; in great volume
**vortex**   (vôr′ teks)   *n.* The center of a situation, which draws all that surrounds it
**votive**   (vōt′ iv)   *adj.* Done in fulfillment of a vow or pledge

**W**

**waverer**   (wā′ vər ər)   *n.* One who changes or is unsteady
**wayfarer**   (wā′ fər ər)   *n.* A traveler
**weird**   (wird)   *n.* Fate or destiny
**wheelwright**   (hwēl′ rīt′)   *n.* A person who makes and repairs wheels and wheeled vehicles
**wherry**   (hwer′ ē)   *n.* A light rowboat used on rivers
**whet**   (hwet)   *v.* To sharpen
**whey**   (hwā)   *n.* The thin, watery part of milk separated from the thicker curds
**whin**   (hwin)   *n.* A prickly, evergreen shrub
**whist**   (hwist)   *n.* A card game like bridge
**whitesmith**   (hwīt′ smitʰ′)   *n.* A tinsmith
**whittle**   (hwit′ 'l)   *v.* To reduce gradually, as if to cut away in slices by a knife
**withy**   (witʰ′ ē)   *adj.* Tough, flexible twigs
**woeful**   (wō′ fəl)   *adj.* Full of sorrow
**wrath**   (ratʰ)   *n.* Intense anger
**wreathe**   (rētʰ)   *v.* To curl around
**writhe**   (rītʰ)   *v.* To twist; turn

# INDEX OF FINE ART

*Index of Fine Art* 1039

# INDEX OF SKILLS

## ANALYZING LITERATURE

## CRITICAL THINKING AND READING

## READING IN THE ARTS AND SCIENCES

## SPEAKING AND LISTENING

## STUDY AND RESEARCH

## THINKING AND WRITING

## UNDERSTANDING LANGUAGE

# INDEX OF TITLES BY THEMES

# INDEX OF AUTHORS AND TITLES

*Page numbers in italics refer to biographical information.*

## ACKNOWLEDGMENTS (continued)

**Arte Público Press**
Lines from ''piñones'' by Leroy V. Quintana, originally published in *Revista Chicano-Riqueña* (now titled *The Americas Review*), Vol. 2, No. 2, 1974. Reprinted by permission.

**Atheneum Publishers, an imprint of Macmillan Publishing Co.**
William Gibson, *The Miracle Worker.* Copyright © 1956, 1957 William Gibson. Copyright © 1959, 1960 Tamarack Productions, Ltd., and George S. Klein and Leo Garel as trustees under three separate deeds of trust. Reprinted with the permission of Atheneum Publishers, an imprint of MacMillan Publishing Co.

**Margaret Atwood and Oxford University Press Canada**
''Siren Song'' from *You Are Happy* by Margaret Atwood. Copyright © 1974 by Margaret Atwood. Reprinted by permission of Margaret Atwood.

**D. C. Berry**
Lines from ''On Reading Poems to a Senior Class at South High'' by D. C. Berry. Reprinted by permission of the author, D. C. Berry, c/o The Center for Writers at the University of Southern Mississippi.

**Brandt & Brandt Literary Agents, Inc.**
''Sonata for Harp and Bicycle'' from *The Green Flash* by Joan Aiken. Copyright © 1957, 1958, 1959, 1960, 1965, 1968, 1969, 1971 by Joan Aiken. Lines from ''Thomas Jefferson 1743–1826'' from *A Book of Americans* by Rosemary & Stephen Vincent Benét. Copyright 1933 by Rosemary & Stephen Vincent Benét; copyright renewed © 1961 by Rosemary Carr Benét. ''The Most Dangerous Game'' by Richard Connell. Copyright 1924 by Richard Connell; copyright renewed 1952 by Louise Fox Connell. Reprinted by permission of Brandt & Brandt Literary Agents, Inc.

**Arthur C. Clarke and Scott Meredith Literary Agency, Inc.**
''If I Forget Thee, Oh Earth'' from *Expedition to Earth* by Arthur C. Clarke. Copyright © 1953, 1970 by Arthur C. Clarke; copyright 1951 by Columbia Publications, Inc. Reprinted by permission of the author and the author's agents, Scott Meredith Literary Agency, Inc., 845 Third Avenue, New York, NY 10022.

**Don Congdon Associates, Inc.**
''All the Years of Her Life'' by Morley Callaghan, published in *The New Yorker,* 1935. Copyright 1935 by Morley Callaghan; renewed © 1962 by Morley Callaghan. Reprinted by permission of Don Congdon Associates, Inc.

**Joan Daves**
''I Have a Dream'' by Martin Luther King, Jr. from *The Words of Martin Luther King, Jr.* Copyright © 1963 by Martin Luther King, Jr. ''Cradle Song'' from *Selected Poems of Gabriel* by Gabriela Mistral, translated by Langston Hughes. Copyright © 1957 by Indiana University Press. Reprinted by permission of Joan Daves.

**Dodd, Mead & Company, Inc.**
''Sympathy'' from *The Complete Poems of Paul Laurence Dunbar* by Paul Laurence Dunbar. ''The Death of a Tree'' from *Dune Boy* by Edwin Way Teale. Copyright © 1957 by Edwin Way Teale. Copyright renewed 1985 by Nellie Teale.

**Doubleday, a division of Bantam, Doubleday, Dell Publishing Group, Inc.**
''The New and the Old'' by Shiki, excerpts from *An Introduction to Haiku* by Harold G. Henderson. Copyright © 1958 by Harold G. Henderson. ''The Gift of the Magi'' by O. Henry from *The Complete Works of O. Henry.* Copyright 1905 by Press Publications Company. ''The Invalid's Story'' by Mark Twain from *The Comic Mark Twain Reader* edited by Charles Neider. Copyright © 1977 by Charles Neider. Lines from ''Sitting Alone in Ching-t'ing Mountain,'' from *Sunflower Splendor* by Wu-chi Liu and Irving Yucheng Lo. Copyright © 1975 by Wu-chi Liu and Irving Yucheng Lo. ''The Meadow Mouse'' by Theodore Roethke, copyright © 1963 by Beatrice Roethke, Administratrix of the Estate of Theodore Roethke, from *The Collected Poems of Theodore Roethke by Theodore Roethke.* Reprinted by permission of Doubleday, a division of Bantam, Doubleday, Dell Publishing Group, Inc.

**E. P. Dutton, a division of NAL Penguin Inc.**
From *Shakespeare of London* by Marchette Chute. Copyright 1949 by E. P. Dutton, renewed 1977 by Marchette Chute. Reprinted by permission of the publisher, E. P. Dutton, a division of NAL Penguin Inc.

**Estate of Dorothy Canfield Fisher**
''A Neighbor of Mine'' by Dorothy Canfield Fisher. Reproduced by permission of the Estate of Dorothy Canfield Fisher.

**Farrar, Straus and Giroux, Inc.**
Excerpt from ''Pieces of the Frame'' (titled, ''The Loch Ness Monster'') in *Pieces of the Frame* by John McPhee. Copyright © 1970, 1975 by John McPhee. Reprinted by permission of Farrar, Straus and Giroux, Inc.

**Penny Fitzgerald**
Excerpts from Homer's *The Odyssey* translated by Robert Fitzgerald. Copyright © 1961 by Robert Fitzgerald.

**Harcourt Brace Jovanovich, Inc.**
''Ithaca'' from *The Complete Poems of Cavafy* translated by Rae Dalven, copyright © 1948 and renewed 1976 by Rae Dalven. ''Sayonara'' from *North to the Orient,* copyright 1935, and renewed 1963 by Anne Morrow Lindbergh. ''A Lincoln Preface'' from *The Sandburg Range* by Carl Sandburg, copyright 1953 by Carl Sandburg; renewed 1985 by Margaret Sandburg, Janet Sandburg, and Helga Sandburg Crile. ''Splinter'' from *Good Morning, America,* copyright 1928, renewed 1956 by Carl Sandburg. Reprinted by permission of Harcourt Brace Jovanovich, Inc.

**Harcourt Brace Jovanovich, Inc. and Faber and Faber Ltd.**
''Macavity: The Mystery Cat'' from *Old Possum's Book of Practical Cats,* copyright 1939 by T. S. Eliot; renewed 1967 by Esme Valerie Eliot. Reprinted by permission.

**Harper & Row, Publishers, Inc.**
''A Very Old Man with Enormous Wings'' from *Leaf Storm and Other Stories* by Gabriel García Márquez. Copyright ©

1971 by Gabriel García Márquez. Reprinted by permission of Harper & Row, Publishers, Inc.

**Harvard University Press**
Lines from "Because I could not stop for Death" reprinted by permission of the publishers and the Trustees of Amherst College from *The Poems of Emily Dickinson* edited by Thomas H. Johnson, Cambridge, Mass.: The Belknap Press of Harvard University Press, copyright 1951, © 1955, 1979, 1983 by The President and Fellows of Harvard College.

**John Hawkins & Associates, Inc.**
"Make up your mind, snail!...," "In the falling snow...," and "Keep straight down this block..." "Whose town did you leave..." by Richard Wright. Reprinted by permission of John Hawkins & Associates, Inc.

**Sara Henderson Hay**
"The Princess" from *A Footing on this Earth* by Sara Henderson Hay. By permission of the author.

**David Higham Associates Limited**
"The Pen of My Aunt" from *Plays* by Gordon Daviot (Josephine Tey), William Heinemann Ltd, publishers.

**Henry Holt and Company, Inc.**
"The Ballad of William Sycamore" from *Ballads and Poems: 1915–1930* by Stephen Vincent Benét. Copyright 1931 by Stephen Vincent Benét. Copyright © 1959 by Rosemary Carr Benét. "The Runaway" and "In a Glass of Cider" from *The Poetry of Robert Frost* edited by Edward Connery Lathem. Copyright © 1969 by Holt, Rinehart and Winston, Inc. Copyright © 1962 by Robert Frost. Copyright © 1975 by Lesley Frost Ballantine. Reprinted by permission of Henry Holt and Company, Inc.

**Evelyn Tooley Hunt**
Lines from "Taught Me Purple" by Evelyn Tooley Hunt, from *Negro Digest,* February 1964. Used by permission of the author.

**James R. Hurst**
"The Scarlet Ibis" by James Hurst, published in *The Atlantic Monthly,* July 1960. Copyright *The Atlantic Monthly,* July 1960. Reprinted by permission of the author.

**Japan Publications, Inc.**
"Temple Bells die out" by Bashō; and "Dragonfly catcher" and "Bearing no flowers" by Chiyojo, reprinted from *One Hundred Famous Haiku* by Daniel C. Buchanan, with permission from Japan Publications, © 1973.

**Alfred A. Knopf, Inc.**
"Uncle Marcos" from *The House of the Spirits* by Isabel Allende, translated by Magda Bogin. Translation Copyright © 1985 by Alfred A. Knopf, Inc. Reprinted by permission of the publisher. "Dream Deferred" copyright 1951 by Langston Hughes. Reprinted from *The Panther and the Lash* by Langston Hughes. "Dreams" from *The Dream Keeper and Other Poems* by Langston Hughes. Copyright 1932 by Alfred A. Knopf, Inc. and renewed 1960 by Langston Hughes. "Troubled Woman" by Langston Hughes, from *Selected Poems of Langston Hughes,* copyright 1926 by Alfred A.

Knopf, Inc. and renewed 1954 by Langston Hughes. "Pendulum" copyright © 1958 by John Updike. Reprinted from *The Carpentered Hen and Other Stories* by John Updike. "To be of use" from *Circles on the Water* by Marge Piercy. Copyright © 1982 by Marge Piercy. Reprinted by permission of Alfred A. Knopf, Inc.

**Ursula K. Le Guin and Virginia Kidd**
"Gwilan's Harp" copyright © 1977 by Ursula K. Le Guin; reprinted by permission of the author and the author's agent, Virginia Kidd.

**The Literary Trustees of Walter de la Mare and The Society of Authors as their representative**
"The Listeners" from *The Complete Poems of Walter de la Mare* by Walter de la Mare. Reprinted by permission.

**Little, Brown and Company, in association with The Atlantic Monthly Press**
"Nameless, Tennessee" from *Blue Highways* by William Least Heat Moon. Copyright © 1982 by William Least Heat Moon. By permission of Little, Brown and Company, in association with the Atlantic Monthly Press.

**Liveright Publishing Corporation**
"maggie and milly and molly and may" is reprinted from *Complete Poems, 1913–1962,* by E.E. Cummings, by permission of Liveright Publishing Corporation. Copyright © 1923, 1925, 1931, 1935, 1938, 1939, 1940, 1944, 1945, 1946, 1947, 1948, 1949, 1950, 1951, 1952, 1953, 1954, 1955, 1956, 1957, 1958, 1959, 1960, 1961, 1962 by the Trustees for the E.E. Cummings Trust. Copyright © 1961, 1963, 1968 by Marion Morehouse Cummings.

**Macmillan Publishing Company**
"Jabberwocky" from *The Collected Verse of Lewis Carroll* (New York: Macmillan, 1933). "The Dark Hills" reprinted with permission of Macmillan Publishing Company from *Collected Poems* by Edwin Arlington Robinson. Copyright 1920 by Edwin Arlington Robinson, renewed 1948 by Ruth Nivison. "Uphill" from *The Poetical Works of Christina G. Rossetti* (New York: Macmillan, 1924). "There Will Come Soft Rains" reprinted with permission of Macmillan Publishing Company from *Collected Poems* by Sara Teasdale. Copyright 1920 by Macmillan Publishing Company, renewed 1948 by Mamie T. Wheless.

**Ellen C. Masters**
"George Gray" from *Spoon River Anthology* by Edgar Lee Masters, Macmillan Publishing Co. Reprinted by permission.

**NAL Penguin Inc.**
"The Necklace" from *Boule de Suif and Other Stories* by Guy de Maupassant, translated by Andrew R. MacAndrew. Copyright © 1964 by Andrew R. MacAndrew. From *Romeo and Juliet* by William Shakespeare, edited by J. A Bryant, Jr., copyright © 1964 by J. A. Bryant, Jr. Reprinted by arrangement with NAL Penguin Inc., New York, N.Y.

**The Nation Magazine**
"The Space" by Gary Soto from *The Nation Magazine,* August 18, 1976. Copyright 1976 by The Nation Company, Inc. Reprinted by permission.

**The New Yorker**
"Before the End of Summer" by Grant Moss, Jr., from *The New Yorker*, October 15, 1960; reprinted by permission, © 1960, The New Yorker Magazine, Inc. "Bears" from *The Diamond Cutters and Other Poems* (Harper & Row) by Adrienne Rich, © 1954, 1982 The New Yorker Magazine, Inc.

**Harold Ober Associates Inc.**
"The Good Deed" by Pearl S. Buck, (An excerpt from Kosloff School). Copyright 1953 by Pearl S. Buck; copyright renewed 1981. From *Dance to the Piper* by Agnes De Mille. Copyright 1951, 1952 by Agnes De Mille; copyright renewed 1979, 1980 by Agnes De Mille. Reprinted by permission of Harold Ober Associates Inc.

**Simon J. Ortiz**
"My Father's Song" by Simon J. Ortiz, from *New Worlds of Literature* by Jerome Beaty and J. Paul Hunter. Copyright 1989 by W. W. Norton & Company, Inc. Reprinted by permission of the author.

**Gordon Parks and Sterling Lord Literistic, Inc.**
"The Funeral" from *Whispers of Intimate Things* by Gordon Parks. Copyright © 1971, 1987 by Gordon Parks. Reprinted by permission.

**Rand McNally & Company and Unwin Hyman Ltd.**
Adapted from *Kon-Tiki: Across the Pacific by Raft* by Thor Heyerdahl, © 1984, 1978, 1950 by Thor Heyerdahl. Published in the U.S.A. by Rand McNally & Company.

**Random House, Inc.**
"Blues Ain't No Mockin Bird," copyright © 1971 by Toni Cade Bambara. Reprinted from *Gorilla, My Love*, by Toni Cade Bambara, by permission of Random House, Inc.

**Andrea Reynolds, attorney-in-fact for André Milos**
"The Red-Headed League" by Sir Arthur Conan Doyle. Reprinted by permission.

**Dr. Sally K. Ride**
"Single Room, Earth View" by Sally Ride, published in the April/May 1986 issue of *Air & Space/Smithsonian Magazine,* published by The Smithsonian Institution. Reprinted by permission of the author.

**Leslie Marmon Silko**
"The Man to Send Rain Clouds" from *Storyteller* by Leslie Marmon Silko. Reprinted by permission of the author.

**Simon & Schuster, Inc.**
"Georgia O'Keeffe" from *The White Album* by Joan Didion. Copyright © 1979 by Joan Didion. Reprinted by permission of Simon & Schuster, Inc. Pronunciation key from *Webster's New World Dictionary—Second College Edition.* Copyright © 1984 by Simon & Schuster, Inc. Reprinted by permission.

**Simon & Schuster, Inc.**
"Butch Cassidy" from *In Patagonia* by Bruce Chatwin. Copyright 1977 by Bruce Chatwin. Reprinted by permission of Summit Books, a division of Simon & Schuster, Inc.

**The Society of Authors as the Literary representative of the Estate of John Masefield**
"Sea-Fever" from *Salt-Water Poems and Ballads* by John Masefield. Reprinted by permission.

**Southern Methodist University Press**
"A Christmas Tree" by William Burford from *Man Now,* 1954, Southern Methodist University Press. Reprinted by permission of the publisher and WIlliam S. Burford.

**Sunstone Press**
Excerpt from "Three Songs of Mad Coyote" from Herbert J. Spinden, *Songs of the Tewa,* published by Sunstone Press, Santa Fe, NM. Reprinted by permission.

**Rosemary A. Thurber**
"The Secret Life of Walter Mitty" copyright 1942 James Thurber; copyright © 1970 Helen W. Thurber and Rosemary A. Thurber. From *My World—And Welcome To It,* published by Harcourt Brace Jovanovich, Inc. "The Spreading 'You Know'" copyright © 1961 James Thurber. From *Lanterns and Lances,* published by Harper & Row. Reprinted by permission.

**Yoshiko Uchida**
"Of Dry Goods and Black Bow Ties" by Yoshiko Uchida. Copyright 1979 by Yoshiko Uchida. Reprinted by permission of the author.

**Viking Penguin Inc.**
"The Boor" from *The Portable Chekhov* edited by Avrahm Yarmolinsky. Copyright 1947 by The Viking Press, Inc; copyright renewed © 1975 by Avrahm Yarmolinsky. "The Creation" from *God's Trombones* by James Weldon Johnson. Copyright 1927 by The Viking Press, Inc; copyright renewed 1955 by Grace Nail Johnson. "I Hear an Army" (Poem XXXVI) from *Collected Poems* by James Joyce. Copyright 1918 by B. W. Huebsch; copyright 1927, 1936 by James Joyce; copyright renewed 1946 by Nora Joyce. "Penelope" by Dorothy Parker from *The Portable Dorothy Parker.* Copyright 1928, renewed © 1956 by Dorothy Parker. "Solace" from *The Portable Dorothy Parker* edited by Brendan Gill. Copyright 1931, renewed © 1959 by Dorothy Parker. "The Interlopers" from *The Complete Short Stories of Saki* by Saki (H. H. Munro). Copyright 1930, renewed 1958 by The Viking Press, Inc. Reprinted by permission of Viking Penguin Inc.

**Watkins/Loomis Agency, Inc.**
"Beware of the Dog" from *Over to You* by Roald Dahl. Copyright 1946 by Roald Dahl. Copyright 1942, 1944, 1945 by Curtis Publishing Co. Copyright 1945 Hearst Magazines, Inc. Copyright 1944 Creative Age Press. Copyright 1944, 1945 Harper and Brothers. Reprinted by permission.

**Wesleyan University Press**
"Incident in a Rose Garden" copyright © 1967 by Donald Justice, reprinted from *The Orb Weaver: Night Light* by permission of Wesleyan University Press.

*Note:* Every effort has been made to locate the copyright owner of material reprinted in this book. Omissions brought to our attention will be corrected in subsequent editions.

## ART CREDITS

Cover and Title Page: Winslow Homer, *The New Novel,* Museum of Fine Arts, Springfield, Massachusetts, Horace P. Wright Collection; **p. 1:** Winslow Homer, *The Gulf Stream,* 1899, The Metropolitan Museum of Art, Wolfe Fund, 1906, Catherine Lorillard Wolfe Collection; **p. 11:** *Angst,* Edvard Munch, Three Lions; **p. 20:** *Hat, Knife, and Gun in Woods,* David Mann, Sal Barracca & Associates; **p. 23:** *Peering Through the Jungle,* Larry Noble, Sal Barracca & Associates; **p. 27:** *The Red Cedar,* Emily Carr, Vancouver Art Gallery; **p. 44:** *Winter in the Rockies,* Thomas Moran, Three Lions; **p. 48:** *Frank E. Stockton,* 1886 (detail), by J. W. Alexander, The Bettmann Archive; **p. 50:** *Tiger,* Samuel Marsden Brookes, The Oakland Museum, Kahn Collection; **p. 51:** Illustration from *The Arabian Knights,* Edmund Dulac; **p. 55:** E. Martin Hennings, *Passing By,* 1924, The Museum of Fine Arts, Houston, Gift of the Henry W. Ranger Fund, National Academy of Design; **p. 58:** *Self-Portrait,* 1944–45, Charley Toorop, Stedelijk Van Abbedmuseum, Eindhoven; **p. 70:** *Sir Arthur Conan Doyle,* 1927 (detail), H. L. Gates, By courtesy of the National Portrait Gallery, London; **p. 93:** *Sharecropper,* Elizabeth Catlett, Courtesy Evan Tibbs Collection; **p. 97:** *Open Doorway on the Beach,* K. Rodko, Three Lions; **p. 98:** *Samuel Longhorne Clemens,* 1935 (detail), Frank Edwin Larson, The National Portrait Gallery, Smithsonian Institution; **p. 109:** *Negro Boy,* Eastman Johnson, National Academy of Design; **p. 114:** *Anna Washington Derry,* 1927, Laura Wheeler Waring, National Museum of American Art, The Smithsonian Institution; **p. 120:** *Pearl S. Buck* (detail), Vita Petrosky Solomon, The National Portrait Gallery, Smithsonian Institution, Gift of the Pearl S. Buck Foundation; **p. 137:** *Summertime,* Mary Cassatt, Three Lions; **p. 161:** Henderson, William Penhallow, *Feast Day,* San Juan Pueblo, 1921, National Museum of American Art, Smithsonian Institution, Given in memory of Joshua C. Taylor; **p. 171:** *Summertime,* Raoul Dufy, Three Lions; **p. 188:** *Scarlet Ibis* (detail), John James Audubon, New York Historical Society; **p. 193:** *Boys in a Punt,* N. C. Wyeth, Courtesy of Dr. and Mrs. William A. Morton, Jr.; **p. 196:** *Scarlet Ibis,* John James Audubon, New York Historical Society; **p. 203:** *The New Necklace,* 1910, William McGregor Paxton, American, 1869–1941, oil on canvas; 35½ × 28½" (90.2 × 72.3 cm), Zoe Oliver Sherman Collection, Courtesy, Museum of Fine Arts, Boston; **pp. 222–23:** *The Sheridan Theatre,* 1937, Edward Hopper, Collection of the Newark Museum; **p. 319:** Johannes De Witt's drawing of the Swan Theatre, London, c. 1596, The Granger Collection; **p. 320:** *William Shakespeare* (detail), Unknown artist, By courtesy of the National Portrait Gallery, London; **pp. 428–29:** *Office in a Small City,* Edward Hopper, The Metropolitan Museum of Art, George A. Hearn Fund, 1953, © copyright 1979 by the Metropolitan Museum of Art; **p. 437:** *My Wife, Sackville River, Nova Scotia, 1918,* Arthur Lismer, Art Gallery of Ontario, Toronto, Gift of Arthur Lismer, 1951; **p. 438:** Carl Sandburg (detail) 1962, Miriam Svet, National Portrait Gallery, Smithsonian Institution; **p. 440:** *Lincoln Proclaiming Thanksgiving,* Dean Cornwell, Louis A. Warren Lincoln Library and Museum, Fort Wayne, Indiana; **p. 443:** *Peculiarsome Abe,* N. C. Wyeth, The Free Library of Philadelphia; **p. 457:** *Dancer in Pink,* Edgar Degas, Three Lions; **p. 475:** *Music and Literature, 1878,* William Harnett, Albright-Knox Art Gallery, Buffalo, New York, Gift of Seymour H. Knox, 1941; **p. 503:** *Woman with Violin,* Henri Matisse, Paris, Musée de l'Orangerie, Scala/Art Resource; **p. 511:** *The White Trumpet Flower, 1932,* Georgia O'Keeffe, San Diego Museum of Art, Gift of Inez Grant Parker in memory of Earle W. Grant; **p. 513:** *Cow's Skull: Red, White and Blue, 1931,* Georgia O'Keeffe, The Metropolitan Museum of Art, The Alfred Stieglitz Collection, 1952, © copyright 1984 by the Metropolitan Museum of Art, photograph by Malcolm Varon; **pp. 523, 524:** Copyright © 1961 James Thurber, from Lanterns and Lances, published by Harper & Row; **p. 528:** Reconstruction of the Second Globe Theatre at London; from a conjurer's circle on the floor cloth, Faustus is raising Mephistoceles through a trap, The Granger Collection; **pp. 544–45:** *Mist Fantasy, 1922,* J. E. H. MacDonald, Art Gallery of Ontario, Toronto, Gift of Mrs. S. J. Williams in memory of F. Elinor Williams, 1927; **p. 547:** The Granger Collection; **p. 549:** *Buffalo Chase,* George Catlin, National Museum of American Art, Smithsonian Institution; **p. 552:** *Baseball Players Practicing, 1875,* Thomas Eakins, Museum of Art, Rhode Island School of Design, Jesse Metcalf Fund and Walter H. Kimball Fund; **p. 558:** *I Got a Gal on Sourwood Mountain,* Thomas Hart Benton, Art Resource; **p. 565:** *The Raven,* Edouard Manet, Gift of W. G. Russel Allen, Courtesy, Museum of Fine Arts, Boston; **p. 568:** *Baron Alfred Tennyson* (detail) c. 1840, S. Laurence, By courtesy of the National Portrait Gallery, London; **pp. 570–71:** *Charge of the Light Brigade at the Battle of Balaklava, 1854,* Unknown artist, Three Lions; **p. 573:** *Portrait of Mme. Matisse,* Henri Matisse, The Hermitage, Leningrad, Bridgeman/Art Resource; **p. 575:** *The Race Track of Death on a Pale Horse,* Albert Pinkham Ryder, The Cleveland Museum of Art, Purchase from the J. H. Wade Fund; **p. 578:** *William Shakespeare* (detail), Unknown artist, By courtesy of the National Portrait Gallery, London; **p. 579:** The Seven Ages of Man, Milton Glaser, Signet Classic, New American Library; **p. 582:** *Edgar Lee Masters* (detail), *1946,* Francis J. Quirk, National Portrait Gallery, Smithsonian Institution; **p. 586:** *The Fairy Morgana,* Howard Pyle, Delaware Art Museum, Howard Pyle Collection; **p. 589:** *Quintet, 1961,* Samuel Reindorf, **p. 590:** *William Shakespeare* (detail), Unknown artist, By courtesy of the National Portrait Gallery, London; *Edwin Arlington Robinson* (detail) 1933, Thomas Richard Hood, National Portrait Gallery, Smithsonian Institution; *Christina Rossetti* (detail) *1877,* D. G. Rossetti, By courtesy of the National Portrait Gallery, London; **p. 591:** *James Joyce* (detail), Jaques-Emile Blanche, The Granger Collection; **p. 597:** *Horses of Neptune, 1892,* Walter Crane, Bayerische Staatgemäldesammlungen, Artothek; **p. 599:** *Orion in December, 1959,* Charles Burchfield, National Museum of American Art, Smithsonian Institution, Gift of S. C. Johnson & Sons, Inc.; **p. 600:** *Robert Browning,* The Granger Collection; *Lewis Carroll,* New York Public Library Picture Collection; **p. 602:** *Moonlit Cove, 1880–90,* Albert Pinkham Ryder, The Phillips Collection, Washington, D.C.; **p. 604:** *The Jabberwock, 1872,* John Tenniel, The Granger Collection; **pp. 606, 608:** From Old Possum's Book of Practical Cats, copyright 1939 by T. S. Eliot, renewed 1967 by Esme Valerie Eliot, reproduced by permission of Harcourt Brace Jovanovich, Inc., illustration by Edward Gorey; **p. 611:** *Pink Shell with Seaweed, c. 1938,* Georgia O'Keeffe, San Diego Museum of Art; **p. 612:** *James Weldon Johnson* (detail) c. 1925, Winold Reiss, National Portrait Gallery, Smithsonian Institution, Gift of Lawrence A. Fleischman and Howard Garfinkle with a matching Grant from the NEA; **p. 620:** *The Creation,* Aaron Douglas, Studio

Museum of Harlem, photo by John Lei/Omni; **p. 623:** *Eclipse, March 1970,* A. W. Thomas, National Museum of American Art, Smithsonian Institution; **p. 624:** *Baron Alfred Tennyson* (detail) *c. 1840,* S. Laurence, By courtesy of the National Portrait Gallery, London; *William Wordsworth,* The Granger Collection; *Langston Hughes* (detail) c. 1925, Winold Reiss, National Portrait Gallery, Smithsonian Institution, Gift of W. Tjark Reiss, in memory of his father Winold Reiss; Emily Dickinson, The Granger Collection; **p. 625:** *Carl Sandburg* (detail) *1962,* Miriam Svet, National Portrait Gallery, Smithsonian Institution; **p. 626:** *Eagle in a Snowstorm,* Hokusai, Reproduced from the Harari Collection of Japanese Paintings and Drawings, edited by J. Hillier, published by Lund Humphries, London; **pp. 632–33:** *Cap Bon Ami, 1961* (detail), Samuel Reindorf; **p. 635:** *Three Musicians, 1921,* Pablo Picasso, Collection, The Museum of Modern Art, New York, Mrs. Simon Guggenheim Fund; **p. 638:** *The House of Mystery, 1892* (also called *The Pink House, Blind House*), William Degouve de Nunques, State Museum, Kroller-Muller, Otterloo, The Netherlands; **p. 641:** *The Bells,* Edmund Dulac, New York Public Library, Astor, Lenox and Tilden Foundations; **p. 646:** *Coal (From America Today), 1920,* Thomas Hart Benton, Courtesy of The Equitable Life Assurance Society of the U.S.; **p. 649:** *Harmony in Red, 1908–09,* Henri Matisse, The Hermitage, Leningrad/Art Resource; **p. 650:** *Edward Estlin Cummings* (detail) 1958, Self-portrait, National Portrait Gallery, Smithsonian Institution; **pp. 654–55:** *The Much Resounding Sea, 1884,* Thomas Moran, National Gallery of Art, Washington, Gift of the Avalon Foundation; **p. 656:** *Año Siete,* Amato Peka, silkscreen, 21st Century Fox; **p. 658:** *Henry Wadsworth Longfellow* (detail), Thomas B. Read, National Portrait Gallery, Smithsonian Institution; *William Shakespeare,* Unknown artist, By courtesy of the National Portrait Gallery, London; **p. 662:** *Girl with Lantern on a Balcony at Night* (detail) *c. 1768,* Suzuki Harunobu, The Metropolitan Museum of Art, Fletcher Fund, 1929; *Richard Wright* (detail), *1949,* Miriam Troop, National Portrait Gallery, Smithsonian Institution; **p. 664:** *Girl with Lantern on a Balcony at Night, c. 1768,* Suzuki Harunobu, The Metropolitan Museum of Art, Fletcher Fund, 1929; **p. 670:** *Robert Burns* (detail), A. Nasmyth, By courtesy of the National Portrait Gallery, London; **pp. 676–77:** *Ulysses Deriding Polyphemus, 1829,* J. M. W. Turner; The National Gallery, London; **p. 680:** *Homer,* The New York Public Library Picture Collection; **p. 682:** *La Nef de Telemachus (The Ship of Telemachus),* The New York Public Library Picture Collection; **p. 687:** *The Cyclops* (detail), Odilon Redon, Rijksmuseum Kroller-Muller, Otterloo, Bridgeman/Art Resource; **p. 695:** *Polyphemus, the Cyclops,* N. C. Wyeth, Delaware Art Museum, photo by Jon MacDowell; **p. 700:** *The Raft of Odysseus,* N. C. Wyeth, Delaware Art Museum, photo by Jon MacDowell; **p. 704:** *Circe Meanwhile Had Gone Her Ways . . . , 1924,* Collection of the New York Public Library, Astor, Lenox and Tilden Foundations; **p. 718:** *Eumaeus, the Swineherd,* N. C. Wyeth, Delaware Art Museum, photo by Jon MacDowell; **p. 729:** *Penelope,* Henry Fuseli, Courtesy of Stirtung für Kunst, Kultur and Geshdchte, Küsnacht; **p. 731:** *The Trial of the Bow,* N. C. Wyeth, Delaware Art Museum, photo by Jon MacDowell; **p. 736:** *The Slaughter of the Suitors,* N. C. Wyeth, Delaware Art Museum, photo by Jon MacDowell; **p. 744:** *Ulysses and the Sirens,* Pablo Picasso, Musée Picasso; **pp. 752–53:** *Mid-Victorian Father Reading to Entire Family,* Three Lions; **p. 755:** *The Acquittal, 1859,* Abraham Solomon, From the collection of Barbara and Norman S. Namerow, Beverly Hills, California; **p. 756:** *Charles Dickens,* The Granger Collection; **p. 763:** *The Stone-breaker (1857–58),* Henry Wallis, Birmingham Museums and Art Gallery; **p. 773:** *Rustic Girl Seated,* John Constable, Victoria & Albert Museum Trustees, London; **p. 780:** *Miss Cicely Alexander, Harmony in Grey and Green,* James McNeill Whistler, The Tate Gallery, London; **p. 791:** *The Schoolmaster's Daughter,* James Sant, R.A., Royal Academy of Arts, London; **p. 795:** *John Randolph, 1805,* Gilbert Stuart, National Gallery of Art, Washington, Andrew W. Mellon Collection; **p. 804:** *Pat Lyon at the Forge 1826–27,* John Neagle, Henry H. and Zoë Oliver Sherman Fund 1975, Courtesy, Museum of Fine Arts, Boston; **p. 814:** *Mortlake Terrace,* J. M. W. Turner, National Gallery of Art, Washington, Scala/Art Resource; **p. 824:** *Ludgate Hill,* Gustav Doré, Reproduced by courtesy of the Trustees of The British Museum; **p. 827:** *Covent Garden, London,* John Wykeham Archer, British Library, London, Bridgeman/Art Resource; **p. 837:** *David Johnston, 1808,* Pierre-Paul Prud'hon, National Gallery of Art, Washington, Samuel H. Kress Collection; **p. 846:** *Omnibus Life in London, 1859,* William Maw Egley, The Tate Gallery, London; **p. 851:** *The White Girl 1862 (Symphony in White No. 1),* James McNeill Whistler, National Gallery of Art, Washington, Harry Whittemore Collection; **p. 859:** *The Seat of Major Norice, Maidstone, 1837,* George Sidney Shepherd, Maidstone Museums and Art Gallery; **p. 869:** *Only a Lock of Hair,* Sir John Everett Millais, City of Manchester Art Galleries; **p. 878:** *Adeline, Seventh Countess of Cardigan,* Richard Buckner, From the collection of Edmund Brudenell, Esq.; **p. 883:** *Henry, Lord Montague of Broughton,* Sir Francis Grant, National Galleries of Scotland, Tomm Scott of Edinburgh; **p. 894:** *February Fill Dyke,* Benjamin William Leader, Published by permission of the Birmingham Museum and Art Gallery; **p. 901:** *Moonlight, a Study at Millbank,* J. M. W. Turner, The Tate Gallery, London; **p. 910:** Little London Model, James Abbott McNeill Whistler, Frank S. Benson Funds, The Brooklyn Museum; **p. 918:** *The York-London Mail Coach,* Gilbert S. Wright, Three Lions; **p. 928:** *Waiting for the Verdict, 1857,* Abraham Solomon, From the collection of Barbara and Norman S. Namerow, Beverly Hills, California; **p. 936:** *The Proposal, 1877,* William Powell Frith, Lady Scott Boughton House, Kettering.

## PHOTOGRAPH CREDITS

**pp. 5, 9:** Culver Pictures; **p. 12:** The New York Times; **p. 35:** Alon Reininger/DPI; **p. 37:** Bill Binzen/Photo Researchers; **p. 42:** The Granger Collection; **p. 56:** AP/Wide World Photos; **p. 62:** Inge Morath/Magnum Photos; **p. 90:** Nikky Finney; **pp. 124–25:** Karl Dummels/Shoustal; **pp. 131, 135:** Ken Karp; **p. 138:** UPI/Bettmann Archive; **p. 147:** J. Allan Cash/Shostal; **p. 154:** Ken Karp; **p. 158:** Thomas Victor; **p. 164:** UPI/Bettmann Archives; **p. 166:** NASA; **p. 169:** NASA; **p. 172:** Reuters/Bettmann Newsphotos; **p. 182:** UPI/Bettmann News Photo; **p. 186:** Memory Shop; **p. 200:** The Bettmann Archives; **p. 216:** Thomas Victor; **p. 226:** The Bettmann Archive; **p. 238:** The New York Times; **p. 239:** Pierre Michaud/Bruce Coleman; **p. 245:** Ken Karp; **p. 249:** Study, House of Balzac, Paris, Giraudon/Art Resource; **p. 252:** AP/Wide World Photo; **pp. 256, 269, 281, 285, 304, 314, 315:** Culver Pictures; **pp. 322, 329:** Phototeque;

p. 335: Culver Pictures; p. 337: Phototeque; p. 341: Culver Pictures; p. 343: Phototeque; p. 350: Culver Pictures; p. 359, 366: Phototeque; p. 373: Memory Shop; p. 380: Culver Pictures; pp. 389, 401: Memory Shop; p. 413: Phototeque; p. 415: Memory Shop; p. 418: Phototeque; p. 433: Thomas Hollyman/Photo Researchers; p. 435: AP/Wide World Photo; p. 448: Nippon Kan Heritage Association; p. 450: Nippon Kan Heritage Association; p. 454: UPI/Bettmann Newsphoto; p. 457: Agnes De Mille in costume for "Stagefright," Performing Arts Research Center, The New York Public Library at Lincoln Center; p. 461: Agnes De Mille in "Rodeo," Performing Arts Research Center, The New York Public Library at Lincoln Center; p. 464: The Granger Collection; pp. 467, 471: © from *Kon-Tiki* by Thor Heyerdahl, published in the U.S. and Canada by Rand McNally and Co.; p. 476: AP/Wide World Photo; p. 478: from *Blue Highways: A Journey into America,* by William Least Heat Moon, copyright © 1982 by William Least Heat Moon, by permission of Little, Brown and Company in association with the Atlantic Monthly Press; p. 482: The Bettmann Archive; p. 483: Harvey Lloyd/The Stock Market; p. 484: Bob & Ira Spring/West Stock; p. 486: Topham/The Image Works; p. 488: Thomas Victor; p. 489: Academy of Applied Sciences, Boston/Photo trends; pp. 494–95: Everett C. Johnson/Folio; p. 498: UPI/Bettmann Newsphoto; pp. 500–01: Ernst Haas/Magnum; Flip & Debre Schulke/Black Star; Bettmann Newsphoto; Leonard Freed/Magnum Photos; p. 504: AP/Wide World Photo; p. 506: V. P. Weinland/Photo Research-ers; p. 510: Thomas Victor; pp. 516, 518, 520: NASA; p. 522: UPI/Bettmann Newsphoto; p. 526: The Bettmann Archive; p. 536: *Butch Cassidy,* Utah State Historical Society; p. 539: Jerry Bauer/Viking Penguin, Inc.; p. 556: AP/Wide World Photo; p. 562: UPI/Bettmann Newsphoto; p. 574: Thomas Victor; p. 582: Robert Frost, Dmitri Kessel/Life Magazine © Time Inc; p. 584: Stephanie Pfriender/The Stock Market; p. 590: AP/Wide World Photo; pp. 592–93: Harvey Lloyd/The Stock Market; p. 600: The Granger Collection; p. 612: Theodore Roethke, AP/Wide World Photo; Marge Piercy, Ben Barnhart, AP/World Wide Photo; Gary Soto, Dianne Trejo; pp. 628–29: Brian Seed/Click Chicago; p. 636: The Bettmann Archive; UPI/Bettmann Newsphoto; UPI/Bettmann Newsphoto; p. 650: The Bettmann Archive; The Bettmann Archive; Dmitri Kessel/Life Magazine © Time Inc.; UPI/Bettmann Newsphotos; p. 651: Marlene Foster; p. 652: Runk/Schoenberger/Grant Heilman; p. 662: Thomas Victor; p. 669: John Scheirer/The Stock Market; p. 742: Thomas Victor.

## ILLUSTRATION CREDITS

pp. 14–15: Chet Jezerski/Jeff Cavaty; p. 66: Manuel Garcia; pp. 72, 76, 81, 86, 100–01, 102–03, 140–41, 143: The Art Source; pp. 174–75, 178–79: Carlos Ochagavia/Frank and Jeff Lavaty & Associates; pp. 210, 212–13, 229, 236, 449, 450–51: The Art Source.